Freshfields Bruckhaus Deringer

on

Financial Services: Investigations and Enforcement

Butterworths™
A Member of the LexisNexis Group

Members of the LexisNexis Group worldwide

United Kingdom	Butterworths Tolley, a Division of Reed Elsevier (UK) Ltd, Halsbury House, 35 Chancery Lane, London, WC2A 1EL, and 4 Hill Street, Edinburgh EH2 3JZ
Argentina	Abeledo Perrot, Jurisprudencia Argentina and Depalma, Buenos Aires
Australia	Butterworths, a Division of Reed International Books Australia Pty Ltd, Chatswood, New South Wales
Austria	ARD Betriebsdienst and Verlag Orac, Vienna
Canada	Butterworths Canada Ltd, Markham, Ontario
Chile	Publitecsa and Conosur Ltda, Santiago de Chile
Czech Republic	Orac sro, Prague
France	Editions du Juris-Classeur SA, Paris
Hong Kong	Butterworths Asia (Hong Kong), Hong Kong
Hungary	Hvg Orac, Budapest
India	Butterworths India, New Delhi
Ireland	Butterworths (Ireland) Ltd, Dublin
Italy	Giuffré, Milan
Malaysia	Malayan Law Journal Sdn Bhd, Kuala Lumpur
New Zealand	Butterworths of New Zealand, Wellington
Poland	Wydawnictwa Prawnicze PWN, Warsaw
Singapore	Butterworths Asia, Singapore
South Africa	Butterworths Publishers (Pty) Ltd, Durban
Switzerland	Stämpfli Verlag AG, Berne
USA	LexisNexis, Dayton, Ohio

A CIP Catalogue record for this book is available from the British Library.

ISBN 0 406 91058 8

Typeset by Phoenix Photosetting, Chatham, Kent
Printed and bound in Great Britain by The Bath Press, Bath

Foreword by Lord Alexander of Weedon

The FSMA 2000 confers great powers and responsibilities on the Financial Services Authority. These will affect everyone in the financial services industry, individuals and companies alike. This excellent book will be an invaluable guide for all practitioners and lawyers.

My spell at the Takcover Panel introduced me to city regulation. It was a legal nirvana. There were a modest number of cases. The Takeover Code was rooted in simple principles – essentially fair play to shareholders – and the detailed rules were to be interpreted to meet the spirit of the Code. Parties were expected to take advice before they took action. There was a talented executive team available to give them prompt guidance. Formal Panel hearings were prompt, open and swift. The whole process was aimed to stop the train going off the rails rather than picking up the pieces after an accident. The best example of constructive dispute resolution I have ever come across.

I am glad that the Panel has survived the Financial Services Act largely intact. But sadly its healthy approach cannot be applied to the wider regulation of wholesale and retail markets. Pressures on wholesale traders are immense. Some, too, have by temperament a buccaneering streak in them. They need, and most of them welcome, clear guidance, rules monitoring and firm controls. The retail markets bring their own stresses. The pensions misselling scandal was a scar on the whole financial services industry. It involved many banks and insurance companies with good names who had traded on their reputation for integrity.

The retail markets have not yet served customers particularly well. The focus on customer welfare is diluted by the desire for corporate profitability, by individual targets, and the incentive of commission payments. Sometimes there is a rank lack of talent in sales and managerial positions. So regulation has, unwelcome as the cost is, to be comprehensive, thorough, technical and tough. It must, where appropriate, strike the right degree of fear.

The Financial Services and Markets Act reflects the vast nature of the task. It brings under one legal roof the old SIB and the self regulatory bodies. It builds and expands on the experience and failures of the past. Happily, the Act received pre-legislative scrutiny, which improved it a good deal, especially in securing protection of human rights. Lengthy and detailed work in Committee in the House of Lords, which fortunately in our parliament performs the vital task of revising legislation, improved it further. The range of the legislation is immense, varying from the task of authorisation to remedying market abuse. The Financial Services Authority has wide powers of delegated legislation normally only given to government ministers, and normally subject to parliamentary control. So it is immensely powerful. The FSMA will affect, and regularly affect, all involved in the financial services industry.

This very timely book aims to help them through the morass. It is written and edited by five specialist practitioners at Freshfields Bruckhaus Deringer, one of our finest law firms. It focuses especially on investigations and disciplinary enquiries. These can arise suddenly, often in areas where you least expect them, striking like lightning from an apparently clear blue sky. They are highly daunting, and sometimes career threatening, for the individuals directly involved. They are very demanding for controls departments, for those (often in-house lawyers) who have got to guide them through a protracted, costly and anxious process. This book will help practitioners and lawyers to navigate through the shoals. Its approach is logical, well ordered and full of practical common sense. The guiding principle of an open and co-operative relationship between firm and regulator is rightly seen as a constant thread. Clear, and down to earth, it will for many be a step-by-step map along the way in time of trouble.

This is an outstanding work in its field. Any book on the stodgy, indigestible diet of regulation can hardly carry the compulsion of a John Grisham novel. It is a book which once put down you may not want to pick up again. But you will need to, and you will be grateful.

Lord Alexander of Weedon QC is a past Chairman of the Takeover Panel, deputy Chairman of the Securities and Investments Board, and practices as an arbitrator, mediator and barrister.

Preface

As the new regime set up by the Financial Services and Markets Act 2000 has unfolded, it has become increasingly clear that those affected by it – which means nearly everyone involved in the financial services industry – will have to contend with a vast amount of law, regulation and guidance, much of it new or at least in a different and unfamiliar format. Reflecting on this, we concluded that it would be useful to cover those areas relating to investigations and disciplinary proceedings in a comprehensive, yet readable book. In particular, we wanted to cover the practical issues which our own experience has led us to believe were likely to arise.

We have tried to accomplish this by putting together in one place the relevant provisions of the Act, the FSA's stated policy and rules in the relevant area, and the practical issues which frequently arise, together with our suggestions on the practical ways as to how firms might address those issues. We have aimed to structure each chapter in a practical way with the lay user in mind, as much as his lawyer. We have not assumed knowledge of the basic concepts and principles underlying the regulations and the FSA's approach but have explained these, briefly, wherever possible.

In order to produce a book which will assist the user as soon as the new regime comes into force, we have been considering the various rules and regulations as they have gone through their formative process. For over a year we have therefore had a team of experienced practitioners following the progress of the new regime.

The editorial team has consisted of Ian Taylor, Guy Morton, Andrew Hart, David Scott and Simon Orton. Particular thanks are due to Simon, who bore much of the hard work of collating and reviewing the material and producing drafts of the text of the book. We also wish to thank all those at Freshfields Bruckhaus Deringer who have contributed their time and expertise, David Perry of 6 King's Bench Walk for his assistance on the criminal law aspects and Butterworths for all their hard work on the publication side.

Andrew Hart
October 2001

Contents

Foreword v
Preface vii
Glossary xvii
Table of statutes xxiii
Table of statutory instruments xxxiii
Table of cases xxxvii

Chapter 1 Introduction 1

The financial services regime 1
What does the regulatory regime comprise? 2
A single statutory regulator 2
Who is subject to the regime? 3
Enforcement under the regime 4
The main debates about the enforcement regime 4
The accountability of the FSA 5
The new market abuse regime 6
The FSA's internal decision-making procedures 6
Whether the disciplinary procedure is criminal for ECHR purposes 7
Discipline on the basis of general principles 7

Chapter 2 Some basic principles of the regime 11

Introduction 11
An overview of Chapter 2 11
An introduction to the regulatory regime 12
Firms to which the regime applies: authorisation and permission 12
Legal and policy framework of the FSA's regulatory functions 16
The fundamental requirements applicable to firms 22
The fundamental requirements applicable to individuals 31
Introducing the FSA Handbook 41
Conduct giving rise to enforcement 46
What types of conduct by firms give rise to enforcement? 46
What types of conduct by individuals give rise to enforcement? 59

Chapter 3 Steps to take when regulatory problems arise **63**
Introduction 63
What types of matters will concern the FSA? 64
How was the problem discovered? 65
Should the firm investigate? 66
Why investigate? 66
Who should investigate? 67
How should the investigation be carried out? 67
Should the firm report the problem? 75
The firm's obligation to report 75
The individual's obligation to report 85
Consequences of not reporting to the FSA 89
Obligations to report to other bodies 91
How should the firm deal with its customers? 92
What are the firm's obligations to act in the interests of customers? 92
What action should the firm consider taking? 96
What other internal action should the firm take? 96
Taking steps to ensure the problem will not recur 98
Dealing with employees 99
Does the problem potentially give rise to criminal proceedings? 101
Relevant types of criminal offences 101
Steps to take where criminal offences may be involved 102
Taking care about document destruction and creation 102
Document destruction 103
Document creation 104

Chapter 4 Information gathering and investigation **107**
Introduction 107
An overview of Chapter 4 107
Information gathering and investment powers 109
Introduction 109
Informal requests for information 114
Formal requests for information 122
Formal investigations 135
Practical guidance for the firm 154
Requesting information from particular types of person 169
Can the FSA compel information from a person who is suspected of a criminal offence? 172
Can the FSA investigate firms' unregulated business? 176
Objecting to the FSA's use of investigation powers 178
Introduction 178
What objection might you have? 178
How to object 183
The consequences of not complying with formal requests 184
Use of information obtained by the FSA 189
Can the FSA disclose information which it has obtained to others? 189
Use of information in criminal proceedings 195
Action which the FSA may take as a result of the investigation 195

Chapter 5 The disciplinary and enforcement process **199**

Introduction 199
An overview of Chapter 5 199
Outline of the procedure 201
Nature of the procedure 204
What is the regime designed to achieve? 204
The Regulatory Decisions Committee 207
The procedure in detail 211
Stage 1 – Conclusion of the investigation and referral to the RDC 211
Stage 2 – Issue of a warning notice 217
Stage 3 – Issue of a decision notice 244
Stage 4 – Issue of a final notice 251
Costs 253

Chapter 6 The Tribunal and appeals **255**

Introduction 255
Introduction to the Tribunal 255
Tribunal procedure 260
An overview of the process 260
Referring the case to the Tribunal 263
Procedure up to the hearing 266
The hearing 291
The Tribunal's decision 296
Reviews and appeals 302
Introduction 302
Review by the Tribunal 302
Appeals 304

Chapter 7 Disciplinary sanctions and other regulatory action against firms **307**

Introduction 307
An overview of Chapter 7 307
Disciplinary action 309
Introduction 309
What disciplinary powers does the FSA have? 309
When will the FSA take disciplinary action? 310
What disciplinary sanction will be imposed? 315
Restitution 320
Introduction 320
What is a restitution order? 321
When will the FSA make or apply for a restitution order? 326
How does the FSA make or apply for a restitution order? 329
How is restitution calculated and distributed? 333
How should the firm approach the question of a restitution order? 335
Injunctions 335
Introduction 335
What types of injunctions can be obtained? 336

In what circumstances will the FSA seek an injunction? 342
Procedure for seeking an injunction 343

Chapter 8 Disciplinary sanctions and other regulatory action against individuals 345

Introduction 345
An overview of Chapter 8 345
Action against approved persons 346
Disciplinary action 346
Withdrawal of approval 353
Prohibition orders 358
What is a prohibition order? 358
On what grounds can a prohibition order be made? 360
When will the FSA seek a prohibition order? 360
What is the procedure for imposing a prohibition order? 363
What is the effect of the prohibition order? 363
Will the making of an order be publicised? 364
Can the order be varied or revoked? 365
Injunctions and restitution orders against individuals 366
Injunctions and restitution orders 366

Chapter 9 'Own-initiative' powers 369

Introduction 369
An overview of Chapter 9 369
Variation of permission/intervention 371
On what grounds can the FSA exercise its own-initiative powers? 371
When in practice will the FSA exercise its powers? 386
What action can the FSA take? 390
The supervisory notice procedure 397
Introduction to the supervisory notice procedure 398
Stage 1: Recommendation from the FSA staff 401
Stage 2: The first supervisory notice 404
Stage 3: Representations from the firm 408
Stage 4: The second supervisory notice 412
Stage 5: Referring the matter to the Tribunal 415
Stage 6: Publication of the FSA's action 416
Urgent action 419
When in practice will the FSA take urgent action? 420
The procedure for taking urgent action 421
Practical guidance for firms taking urgent action 424
Alternative procedures in specific cases 427
Non-fundamental changes to permission 427
Action with the firm's agreement 430
Additional procedure for certain cases involving EEA firms 431
Cancellation of permission 432
Introduction 432

When will the FSA consider cancelling the firm's permission? 432
Procedure for cancelling a firm's permission 435
The consequences of cancelling permission 435

Chapter 10 Civil liability to third parties **437**

Introduction 437
Why might the firm incur civil liability? 438
Claims under the general law 439
Practical guidance for firms 439
Breach of contract 441
Negligence 442
Equitable claims 443
Misrepresentation 445
Breach of statutory duty 446
Contribution claims 447
Breach of statutory duty and other claims under the FSMA 2000 448
Actions for breach of statutory duty 448
Situations where there is expressly no right of action 454
Unenforceable agreements 455
Agreements that are expressly not unenforceable 458
Practical issues arising from the investigation and enforcement process 458
The overlap between civil claims and enforcement powers 459
The disclosure and use of material produced in the enforcement process 461
The impact of admissions or findings in the enforcement process 462

Chapter 11 Criminal prosecutions **465**

Introduction 465
What offences can the FSA prosecute? 466
When will the FSA pursue a criminal prosecution? 468
Which body will investigate and prosecute? 468
In what circumstances will the FSA prosecute? 470
Who can be prosecuted? 472
Criminal liability of the firm 472
Criminal liability of employees 473
Criminal liability of officers 474
What other options does the FSA have? 475
When will the FSA administer a caution? 475
Can the FSA use its other enforcement powers as well as prosecuting? 476
Practical guidance for firms 478
What approach should the firm take as against its employee? 478
Should the firm continue to co-operate with the FSA? 479
Are there any practical steps that the firm can take to protect its position? 480
Appendix: Criminal offences under the FSMA 2000 481

Chapter 12 The ombudsman scheme **483**

Introduction 483
An overview of the ombudsman scheme 484
Practical issues for firms 486
What approach will the firm take in relation to the process? 486
How should the firm deal with the ombudsman? 488
Risks of disclosing information to the ombudsman 488
Practical guidance for firms 491
Will the ombudsman investigate the complaint? 491
Complaints handling by firms 491
When can a complaint be made to the ombudsman? 493
What complaints can be referred to the scheme? 494
Is the ombudsman bound to investigate the complaint? 496
How does the ombudsman handle the complaint? 497
The ombudsman's general approach 498
Settlement of complaints 498
Determination of complaints 499
The ombudsman's powers to obtain information 500
What evidence will the ombudsman consider? 502
Is there an oral hearing? 502
The ombudsman's decision 503
How is the decision reached? 504
What remedies can the ombudsman grant? 505
Can the ombudsman award costs? 507
What is the effect of the ombudsman's decision? 507
Can the decision be appealed or challenged? 508
Is the decision made public? 509
How is the decision enforced? 510

Chapter 13 Market misconduct **511**

Introduction 511
An overview of the regime for combating market misconduct 512
The implications of the Human Rights Act 1998 515
Recognising market abuse 516
Introduction 516
What is market abuse? 516
Is there a market abuse problem? 533
Answering some common questions about market abuse 534
Investigations into market misconduct 539
Introduction 539
Practical steps to take when the problem arises 539
FSA investigations into market misconduct 544
Sanctions for market misconduct 555
Introduction 555
Criminal proceedings for market misconduct 556
Penalties and public censures for market abuse 558

Action where other regulatory authorities are involved 566
Other enforcement action available to the FSA 573
Civil liability arising from market abuse 583

Chapter 14 Regulated collective investment schemes **585**

Introduction 585
An overview of Chapter 14 585
Investigations into regulated collective investment schemes 587
Introduction 587
In what circumstances can an investigation be commenced? 589
What information can the investigator obtain? 593
How is an investigation commenced and controlled? 595
Enforcement action in relation to regulated collective investment schemes 596
Introduction 596
Enforcement in relation to unit trusts 598
Enforcement in relation to ICVCs 612
Enforcement in relation to recognised schemes 616

Chapter 15 Listed companies **625**

Introduction 625
The FSA's function as UK Listing Authority 626
The overlap with the FSA's wider regulatory functions 629
Who may be affected by the UKLA's enforcement powers? 630
UKLA information gathering and investigations 630
An overview of the UKLA investigation powers 630
The UKLA's powers of information gathering 635
Formal investigations under FSMA 2000, Pt VI 640
What use can be made of information obtained from the investigation? 651
Potential consequences of breaches of listing rules or Part VI 653
Introduction 653
Disciplinary action 656
Other regulatory action 662
The procedure for taking enforcement action 668
Civil liability to third parties 676

Chapter 16 Challenges and complaints **679**

Introduction 679
An overview of Chapter 16 679
Challenging the FSA 681
What options does the firm have? 681
Can the firm urgently prevent the FSA from taking action? 681
Bringing an application for judicial review 683
Bringing a civil action against the FSA 687

Complaining about the FSA 690
An overview of the complaints scheme 690
The complaints commissioner 692
When is the complaints scheme available? 694
What remedies are available? 699
How does the complaints scheme work? 702
Challenging the outcome of the complaints process 708

Index 711

Glossary of key terms

This section contains a simple glossary of certain key terms used in this book. For a detailed glossary of terms used in the Regulatory Processes manuals (the Authorisation, Supervision, Enforcement and Decision-Making manuals), see the FSA Handbook, Glossary of Definitions.

Appointed representative — A person who contracts with an authorised person to carry on certain activities set out in the Financial Services and Markets Act 2000 (Appointed Representatives) Regulations 2001, SI 2001/1217, for which the authorised person takes responsibility, and who is thereby an exempt person, under FSMA 2000, s 39.

Approved person — A person approved by the FSA under FSMA 2000, s 59 to carry out a function of a firm's which is specified by the FSA as a controlled function: see para 2.64 ff below.

Authorised person — A person authorised to carry on regulated activities under the FSMA 2000. In particular, this includes: (i) a person who has a Part IV permission; (ii) an incoming firm; (iii) a UCITS qualifier and (iv) an ICVC: see FSMA 2000, s 31 and para 2.6 ff below.

City Code — The City Code on Takeovers and Mergers issued by the Panel on Takeovers and Mergers: see para 13.224 ff below.

Code of market conduct — The Code which the FSA is required to issue under FSMA 2000, s 119 to give guidance to those determining whether or not behaviour amounts to market abuse: see para 13.20 ff below and the FSA Handbook at MAR 1.

Code of practice for approved persons — The code of practice which the FSA is required to issue under FSMA 2000, s 64 for the purpose of helping to determine whether an approved person's conduct complies with a Statement of Principle: see para 2.76 ff below and the FSA Handbook at APER.

Compensation Scheme The Financial Services Compensation Scheme established under FSMA 2000, s 213 for compensating persons in cases where authorised persons (and appointed representatives) are unable, or likely to be unable, to satisfy claims against them.

Competent authority The FSA in its capacity as UK Listing Authority in relation to the admission of securities to the official list (or the equivalent authority in another EEA state). The same phrase may also refer to a body acting as a competent authority as defined under one of the Single Market Directives.

Complaints commissioner The person appointed by the FSA to hear and determine complaints in accordance with the complaints scheme.

Complaints scheme The scheme for the determination of complaints made against the FSA under FSMA 2000, Sch 1, paras 7 and 8: see Chapter 16 below and the FSA Handbook at COAF.

Compulsory jurisdiction The jurisdiction of the Ombudsman to which firms are compulsorily subject: see para 12.4 below.

Controlled function Those functions relating to the carrying on of regulated activities by authorised persons that are specified by the FSA under FSMA 2000, s 59 and which are required to be carried out by an approved person: see para 2.64 ff below and, for a list of controlled functions, the FSA Handbook at SUP 10.4.5 R.

Controller A person who, in very broad terms, holds more than 10% of the shares of an undertaking or its parent, or is entitled to exercise or control the exercise of more than 10% of the voting power of the undertaking or its parent, or is able to exercise a significant influence over the management of the undertaking or its parent: for details, see FSMA 2000, s 422.

Decision notice A notice which the FSA is required under the FSMA 2000 to issue when deciding to take certain types of disciplinary or enforcement action

	(or certain decisions relating, broadly, to authorisation or approval under the FSMA 2000): see para 5.170 below and, for a list of decision notices, the FSA Handbook at DEC 2, Annex 1G.
Designated Professional Body	A professional body designated by HM Treasury in the Financial Services and Markets Act 2000 (Designated Professional Bodies) Order 2001, SI 2001/1226, under FSMA 2000, s 326. Members of a Designated Professional Body are exempt from the requirement to obtain a Part IV permission in relation to certain regulated activities.
Exempt person	A person who is exempt from the general prohibition in respect of particular regulated activities: see FSMA 2000, s 417(1).
Final notice	A notice which the FSA is required to issue under FSMA 2000, s 390 when taking certain types of disciplinary or enforcement action: see para 5.188 below.
Financial Services and Markets Tribunal	The Tribunal (defined below).
Firm	An authorised person.
Fit and proper	The fundamental test applicable to determine whether a firm or person is suitable to be involved in regulated activities: see para 2.43 ff below (the test of fit and proper applicable to firms) and para 2.69 ff below (the test of fit and proper applicable to approved persons).
FSA Register	The public register of authorised persons, authorised unit trusts, authorised OEICs, recognised schemes, recognised investment exchanges, recognised clearing houses, individuals subject to a prohibition order and approved persons (among others) which the FSA is required to maintain under FSMA 2000, s 347.
General prohibition	The prohibition under FSMA 2000, s 19 against a person carrying on a regulated activity unless he is an authorised person or an exempt person: see para 2.175 below.
Incoming firm	A firm primarily regulated in another EEA state that obtains automatic authorisation under FSMA 2000, Sch 3 or 4: see para 2.11 ff below.

ICVC	Investment Company with Variable Capital: see Chapter 14 below.
Intervention	The FSA's power to impose requirements upon an incoming firm under FSMA, Pt XIII: see para 9.4 below.
Market abuse	Behaviour which falls within FSMA 2000, s 118: see Chapter 13 below.
Notice of discontinuance	A notice which the FSA is required to issue if it decides not to take the action proposed in a warning notice or the action to which a decision notice relates: para 5.166 below and FSMA 2000, s 389.
OEIC	Open-Ended Investment Company: see Chapter 14 below.
Ombudsman	The Financial Ombudsman Service, and the ombudsmen appointed under it: see Chapter 12 below.
Part IV permission	Permission to carry on regulated activities given by the FSA under FSMA 2000, Pt IV: see para 2.6 ff below.
Principles for businesses	The 11 high-level FSA rules which prescribe the fundamental standards applicable to firms: see para 2.51 ff below and the FSA Handbook at PRIN.
Principles for good regulation	The principles to which the FSA is required to have regard when exercising its general functions, in accordance with FSMA 2000, s 2(3): see para 2.21 below.
Private warning	An informal warning given by the FSA as an alternative to taking formal disciplinary or enforcement action: see para 7.18 ff below.
Prohibition order	An order made by the FSA under FSMA 2000, s 56, prohibiting a person from performing specified functions: see para 8.44 ff below.
Recognised clearing house or RCH	A clearing house in relation to which the FSA has issued a recognition order under FSMA 2000, s 290 which remains in force.
Recognised investment exchange or RIE	An investment exchange in relation to which the FSA has issued a recognition order under FSMA 2000, s 290 which remains in force: see para 13.214 ff below.

Regulated activities — Those activities specified in accordance with FSMA 2000, s 22 in Pt II of the Financial Services and Markets Act 2000 (Regulated Activities) Order 2001, SI 2001/544 (the carrying on of which requires authorisation or exemption under the FSMA 2000).

Regulatory Decisions Committee or RDC — A Committee of the FSA Board responsible for taking certain enforcement decisions: see para 5.26 ff.

Regulatory objectives — The regulatory objectives of market confidence, public awareness, the protection of consumers and the reduction of financial crime, specified in FSMA 2000, ss 2(2) and 3 to 6: see para 2.20 below.

Restitution order — An order made by the FSA or the court under FSMA 2000, ss 382 to 386, requiring a person to pay compensation for losses and/or disgorge any gains it has made as a result of a regulatory breach or market abuse: see para 7.43 ff below.

Single Market Directives — The Banking Consolidation Directive, the Second Banking Coordination Directive, the Insurance Directives (the First, Second and Third Life Directives and the First, Second and Third Non-Life Directives) and the Investment Services Directive: see para 2.12 below.

Statements of principle for approved persons — The high-level principles made by the FSA under FSMA 2000, s 64, which prescribe the fundamental standards applicable to approved persons: see para 2.76 ff below and the FSA Handbook at APER.

Supervisory notice — A notice which the FSA is required to issue when it proposes or decides to take certain types of enforcement action: see para 9.104 ff below and, for a list of supervisory notices, FSMA 2000, s 395(13).

Threshold Conditions — The fundamental requirements for authorisation under the FSMA 2000, found in Sch 6: see para 2.38 ff below and the FSA Handbook at COND.

Top-up permission — An additional permission granted to an incoming firm or a UCITS qualifier to carry on a regulated activity not covered by its authorisation under FSMA 2000, Sch 3, 4 and/or 5: see para 2.14 below.

Tribunal The Financial Services and Markets Tribunal, constituted under FSMA 2000, s 132 (and Sch 13) and operated by the Lord Chancellor's Department: see Chapter 6 below.

UCITS qualifier A firm which is the operator, trustee or depositary of a scheme recognised under FSMA 2000, s 264 and authorised under FSMA 2000, Sch 5: see para 14.7 below.

UK Listing Authority or UKLA The FSA in its capacity as the UK's competent authority for listing: see Chapter 15 below.

UK regulated firm An authorised person that is primarily regulated in the UK: see para 2.15 below.

Variation of permission The FSA's powers to vary a firm's permission: see Chapter 9 below.

Voluntary jurisdiction The jurisdiction of the Ombudsman in which authorised or unauthorised persons participate voluntarily by contract: see para 12.4 below.

Warning notice A notice which the FSA is required under the FSMA 2000 to issue when it proposes to take certain types of disciplinary or enforcement action (or certain decisions relating, broadly, to authorisation or approval under the FSMA 2000): see para 5.70 below and, for a list of decision notices, the FSA Handbook at DEC 2, Annex 1G.

Withdrawal of approval The FSA's powers under FSMA 2000, s 63, to withdraw the approval of an approved person: see para 8.27 ff below.

Table of statutes

References in this Table to *Statutes* are to Halsbury's Statutes of England (Fourth Edition) showing the volume and page at which the annotated text of the Act may be found.

References in the right-hand column are to paragraph numbers.

PARA

Access to Justice Act 1999
  Sch 3 . . . . 13.207
Bank of England Act 1998 (4 *Statutes* 612) 1.8
Banking Act 1987 (4 *Statutes* 473) 7.53
  s 1(4) 16.29
  12, 19 . . . . 9.1
  39 . . . . 4.12, 4.72, 4.87, 4.239, 4.286
  41 . . . . 4.87, 4.109, 4.149
  82 . . . . 4.302
  93 . . . . 7.104
Broadcasting Act 1996 . . . . 4.274
Building Societies Act 1986 (5 *Statutes* 514) 4.12
  s 55 . . . . 4.149
Civil Liability (Contribution) Act 1978 (13 *Statutes* 649)
  s 1(1), (4) 10.26
  2(1) 10.26
Companies Act 1985 (8 *Statutes* 88) . . 4.15, 9.31, 9.64, 15.93
  s 310 . . . . 8.24
  434 . . . . 4.149, 14.34
Companies Act 1989 (30 *Statutes* 439) . . 2.53, 4.15, 4.267
Company Directors Disqualification Act 1986 (8 *Statutes* 837) . . . 4.312, 8.52, 15.99
Company Securities (Insider Dealing) Act 1985 . . . . 4.143, 4.286, 9.77
Competition Act 1980 (47 *Statutes* 397) . 4.15
Competition Act 1998 . . . . 4.15
Consumer Credit Act 1974 (11 *Statutes* 15) 9.10
Contempt of Court Act 1981 (11 *Statutes* 185)
  s 10 . . . . 4.286
Contracts (Rights of Third Parties) Act 1999 . . . . 4.83

PARA

Criminal Justice Act 1987 (12 *Statutes* 986) 4.15
  s 2(16) 3.153
Criminal Justice Act 1993 (8 *Statutes* 960)
  Pt IV (ss 36–51) 11.6
  Pt V (ss 52–64) 2.134, 4.144, 13.7, 13.40, 13.177, 15.14
  s 61 . . . . 13.177
Criminal Justice and Police Act 2001 . . 4.312
Criminal Procedure and Investigations Act 1996 (12 *Statutes* 1778) 4.248
  s 2(4) 5.85
  Pt II (ss 22–27) 5.85
Customs and Excise Management Act 1979 (13 *Statutes* 153) 2.186
Data Protection Act 1998 (7 *Statutes* 389): 3.25, 3.27
  s 51(3)(b) 3.32
Employment Relations Act 1999 . . . . 3.35
Employment Rights Act 1996 (16 *Statutes* 557)
  s 43B(1) 4.48
European Communities Act 1972 (10 *Statutes* 735) 4.152
Fair Trading Act 1973 (47 *Statutes* 75): 2.186, 4.15
Financial Services Act 1986 (30 *Statutes* 162) 4.267, 7.113, 8.58, 10.24, 10.54, 14.86, 15.107, 16.17, 16.20
  s 5 . . . . 10.52
  6 . . . . 7.55, 7.58
  (1) 7.104
  (2) 2.186, 7.110
  47 . . . . 11.5, 13.7, 13.45
  (2) 13.177
  47A 2.53, 13.227
  59 . . . . 8.44
  61 . . . . 2.186, 7.55, 7.58

PARA

Financial Services Act 1986—*contd*
s 61(1) 7.113
(a), (b) 7.104
(c) 7.110
62 . . . . 10.29
64–71 . . . . 9.1
Pt I, Ch VIII (ss 75–95) 14.46
s 79 . . . . 14.48
91 . . . . 14.66
93 . . . . 14.83
94 . . . . 14.17, 14.34
105 . . . . 4.12
(5A), (5B) 4.242
128C 9.31, 9.39
132 . . . . 10.52
Pt IV (ss 142–157) 15.6
s 150, 151 . . . . 10.51
177 . . . . 4.12, 4.139, 4.147, 4.149, 4.225, 13.150
(6A), (6B) 4.242
178 . . . . 4.286
179 . . . . 4.302, 10.24
187 . . . . 16.29, 16.32
200 . . . . 11.2
Financial Services and Markets Act 2000: 1.1–1.6, 1.8, 1.14, 1.19, 1.22, 1.26, 1.28, 2.3–2.5, 2.16–2.18, 2.22, 2.25, 2.36, 2.63, 2.82, 2.97, 2.106, 2.129, 2.132–2.138, 2.144, 2.145, 2.148, 2.156, 2.157, 2.176, 2.179, 2.182, 2.184, 2.186, 2.189, 3.42, 3.50, 3.110, 3.126, 4.3, 4.12, 4.17, 4.19, 4.30, 4.64, 4.68, 4.81, 4.82, 4.96, 4.113, 4.128, 4.129, 4.132, 4.151, 4.183, 4.210, 4.223, 4.242, 4.265, 4.275, 4.276, 4.278, 4.283, 4.291, 4.308, 5.5, 5.15, 5.17, 5.21, 5.22, 5.24, 5.32, 5.78, 5.89, 5.91, 5.109, 5.121, 5.170, 5.186, 6.1, 6.33, 6.67, 6.73, 6.77, 6.87, 6.95, 6.99, 6.105, 6.125, 6.162, 7.7, 7.8, 7.10, 7.48, 7.50, 7.56, 7.83, 7.97, 7.102, 7.109, 7.112, 7.118, 8.1, 8.5, 8.11, 8.13, 8.37, 8.48, 8.49, 8.52, 8.60, 8.76, 9.1, 9.4–9.7, 9.11, 9.18, 9.20, 9.23, 9.33, 9.38, 9.46, 9.48, 9.50, 9.52, 9.53, 9.67, 9.70, 9.76, 9.86, 9.104, 9.106–9.108, 9.153, 9.168, 9.214, 9.217, 9.218, 10.1, 10.23, 10.24, 10.27, 10.28, 10.33, 10.42, 10.50, 10.54, 10.58, 10.59, 10.61, 10.64, 10.65, 11.8, 11.10, 11.30, 11.36, 11.42, 12.1, 12.66, 13.9, 13.15, 13.32, 13.61, 13.73, 13.81, 13.91, 13.116, 13.140, 13.155,

PARA

Financial Services and Markets Act 2000—*contd*
13.160, 13.171, 13.215, 13.232, 13.244, 13.249, 13.276, 13.278, 14.1, 14.3, 14.16, 14.43, 14.56, 14.66, 14.102, 14.106, 14.120, 15.2, 15.3, 15.15, 15.33, 15.93, 15.141, 15.144, 15.145, 15.154, 15.158, 15.162, 15.171, 16.1, 16.7, 16.16, 16.18, 16.20, 16.29, 16.46, 16.48, 16.72, 16.79, 16.97
s 2(1) 2.19
(3) 2.19, 2.21, 15.10, 16.68, 16.70
3 . . . . 2.20, 9.235
4 . . . . 2.20
5 . . . . 2.20
(3) 9.26, 9.61
6 . . . . 2.20
8–11 . . . . 1.20
16 . . . . 4.14
19 . . . . 2.175, 4.144, 7.48, 9.252
20 . . . . 2.151, 2.177, 4.134
(1) 9.102, 9.103
(2) 9.102, 10.49, 10.52
(a) 11.7
(b) 10.52
(3) 9.102, 10.46, 10.49, 10.60
21 . . . . .4.144, 7.48
(1) 10.52
23 . . . . 4.144, 9.252, 11.29, 11.App
24 . . . . 11.App
(1) 4.144
25 . . . . 11.29, 11.App
26 . . . . 2.175, 10.52
(2) 10.55
(3) 10.53
27 . . . . 2.175, 10.52
(2) 10.55
(3) 10.53
28 . . . . 2.175
(2) 10.55
(3)–(6) 10.57
(7), (8) 10.56
(9) 10.55
29 . . . . 10.52
30(1) 10.52
(2), (3) 10.55
(4)–(7) 10.57
(10) 10.55
(11)–(13) 10.56
33 . . . . 9.251
38 . . . . 2.10
39 . . . . 2.10
Pt IV (ss 40–55) 2.7–2.9, 2.11, 2.12, 2.14, 2.15, 2.38, 2.40, 2.114, 4.14, 5.3, 9.21, 9.34, 9.42, 9.45, 9.81–9.83, 9.102, 9.103,

PARA

Financial Services and Markets Act 2000—*contd*
Pt IV (ss 40–55)—*contd* . . . 9.116, 9.117, 9.243, 10.36, 10.46, 13.228
s 40 . . . 9.81
41 . . . 2.39, 2.165
(2) . . . 2.38, 9.17, 9.243
42(7) . . . 9.81
(a) . . . 9.82
43 . . . 9.81–9.83
44(1) . . . 9.81, 9.82
45 . . . 2.139, 9.89
(1)(a) . . . 9.9, 9.14
(b) . . . 9.9, 9.21, 14.62
(c) . . . 9.9, 9.25, 14.65, 14.81
(2) . . . 9.81, 9.248
(3) . . . 9.240, 9.245, 9.248
(4) . . . 9.81
(5) . . . 9.248
46 . . . 9.9, 9.42
47 . . . 9.9, 9.64
(1) . . . 9.31
(2) . . . 9.32
(3) . . . 9.35
(4) . . . 9.35, 9.39
(5) . . . 9.39
48 . . . 9.84
(3) . . . 9.89, 9.118
(4) . . . 9.90
(5) . . . 9.90
(a), (b) . . . 9.89
(6) . . . 9.94, 11.App
(7), (8) . . . 9.94
(9) . . . 9.89, 9.94
49(1) . . . 9.45
(2), (3) . . . 9.49
50(2) . . . 9.47
51 . . . 4.14
(3) . . . 2.114
52 . . . 5.3
53(2) . . . 9.99, 9.136, 9.175, 9.194
(c) . . . 6.150
(3) . . . 9.101, 9.136, 9.196, 14.76
(4) . . . 9.129
(5) . . . 6.46, 9.129
(6) . . . 9.147
(7) . . . 9.165, 9.166
(8) . . . 9.164
(9) . . . 9.166
(10) . . . 9.129, 9.169
(11) . . . 9.166
54 . . . 5.3
55 . . . 6.10
(2) . . . 9.176, 9.248
56 . . . 2.68, 2.281, 8.44, 11.5, 11.App
(1) . . . 8.51
(2) . . . 8.50
(3) . . . 8.47, 8.50
(4) . . . 8.65
(6) . . . 2.153, 8.50, 8.66, 10.44
(7) . . . 8.71

PARA

Financial Services and Markets Act 2000—*contd*
s 56(8) . . . 8.47
57 . . . 5.3, 6.10, 8.62, 15.139, 15.145
(2), (4) . . . 8.63
58 . . . 5.3
(2)–(4) . . . 8.74
59 . . . 2.65, 2.146
(1), (2) . . . 2.64, 8.34, 10.44
61(1) . . . 2.66, 8.29
(2) . . . 8.33
63 . . . 2.66, 2.281, 5.3, 6.10, 8.38, 8.39
(1) . . . 8.29
(3), (4), (6) . . . 8.34
64 . . . 2.67, 2.76, 2.115, 2.116
(2) . . . 2.82
(7) . . . 2.84, 2.86
(8) . . . 2.78, 10.49
66 . . . 2.67, 8.8, 13.227, 14.12
(1)(b) . . . 2.180
(2)(a), (b) . . . 2.281
(3) . . . 8.24
(4) . . . 5.90, 5.154
(5) . . . 5.90, 13.169
(b) . . . 4.200
67 . . . 5.173, 8.25
(1) . . . 5.71
(2), (3) . . . 5.72
(4) . . . 5.163
69 . . . 2.126, 6.10, 7.36, 8.12
(1)(a) . . . 2.180
71 . . . 2.64, 3.59, 8.34, 8.67, 10.44
Pt VI (ss 72–103) . . . 9.64, 15.4, 15.6, 15.9, 15.10, 15.18, 15.42, 15.46, 15.47, 15.49, 15.50, 15.53, 15.55, 15.57, 15.69, 15.76, 15.88, 15.97, 15.99, 15.109, 15.155, 15.180
s 73(1) . . . 15.10, 16.68
(2) . . . 15.10
74(4) . . . 15.50
77 . . . 9.10, 15.135, 15.143, 15.168
78 . . . 15.168
(8)(b) . . . 15.170
(10) . . . 15.173
(11)(b) . . . 15.173
80 . . . 15.184
81 . . . 15.184, 15.185
83 . . . 11.5, 11.App, 15.47, 15.49, 15.54, 15.63, 15.69, 15.74, 15.155
(3) . . . 15.55
84 . . . 11.App
85 . . . 11.5, 11.29, 15.47, 15.49, 15.54, 15.63, 15.69, 15.74, 15.155
(2) . . . 15.55
(5) . . . 10.47, 15.182
88 . . . 15.147

PARA

Financial Services and Markets Act 2000—*contd*
s 89 . . . 15.119, 15.167
90 . . . 10.48, 15.183
(4) . . . 15.185
(6) . . . 15.186
91 . . . 15.166
(1) . . . 15.107
(2) . . . 15.114
(3) . . . 15.107, 15.114
(4) . . . 15.109
(6) . . . 15.111
(7)(a), (b) . . . 15.111
92 . . . 15.166
93 . . . 2.126
97 . . . 4.306, 15.47, 15.63, 15.67
(1)(a) . . . 15.50
(b) . . . 15.52
(c) . . . 15.52, 15.54
(2) . . . 15.42
(3) . . . 15.42
(a) . . . 15.59, 15.60, 15.73, 15.76, 15.79, 15.80, 15.88
(b) . . . 15.79, 15.80, 15.88
(c), (d) . . . 15.74
98 . . . 11.5, 11.App, 15.47, 15.49, 15.54, 15.63, 15.69, 15.74, 15.155
(2) . . . 15.55
(3) . . . 10.51
(4) . . . 15.187
100 . . . 15.128, 15.129
101 . . . 15.4
102 . . . 16.30
118 . . . 4.144, 13.19, 13.25, 13.89, 13.187
(1) . . . 13.28
(a) . . . 13.33
(c) . . . 13.50
(2)(a) . . . 13.38
(b) . . . 13.41
(c) . . . 13.46
(3) . . . 13.31
(5) . . . 13.96
(6) . . . 13.34
(8) . . . 13.64
(9) . . . 13.28
(10) . . . 13.27, 13.54
119 . . . 2.116, 13.20
120 . . . 13.22, 13.25, 13.63, 13.67, 13.225
122 . . . 2.118, 13.25
(1) . . . 13.22, 13.62, 13.99
(2) . . . 13.100
(3) . . . 13.22
123 . . . 13.25, 13.163, 13.166, 13.168, 13.170, 13.172, 13.189, 13.193, 13.225
(1)(b) . . . 13.82
(2) . . . 13.68, 13.79
(3) . . . 13.191
124 . . . 2.126, 13.199

PARA

Financial Services and Markets Act 2000—*contd*
s 124(1) . . . 13.193
(3) . . . 13.70, 13.76
(6) . . . 13.193
126 . . . 5.3, 13.208
127 . . . 6.10, 13.208
128 . . . 13.138
129 . . . 13.172, 13.209, 13.235, 13.251
130 . . . 13.180
131 . . . 10.60, 13.188
132 . . . 9.179
(3) . . . 6.4
133 . . . 14.114
(1) . . . 6.36, 9.140, 9.177
(2) . . . 9.177
(3) . . . 6.134
(4) . . . 6.7, 6.137, 9.180
(5) . . . 6.137, 6.148
(6) . . . 6.138, 7.35
(7) . . . 6.138
(8) . . . 6.9, 6.140, 6.151, 9.180
(9) . . . 5.175, 5.180, 6.104, 6.149
(10) . . . 6.149, 6.150
(11) . . . 6.152
134–136 . . . 13.207
137(1) . . . 6.169, 6.171
(4) . . . 6.169
138 . . . 2.20, 2.51, 2.111, 14.38
(1) . . . 2.174, 4.257
(7)–(9) . . . 9.26
139 . . . 2.114
142 . . . 4.137, 11.App
143(3), (5) . . . 13.227
144–146 . . . 2.114
148 . . . 2.113
149 . . . 2.119, 2.149
(1), (2) . . . 2.121
150 . . . 2.55, 2.143, 2.149, 3.59, 4.217, 4.312, 7.22, 10.4, 10.29, 13.276, 14.109
(2) . . . 10.31
(3) . . . 10.41
(4) . . . 10.31
(a) . . . 15.181
(5) . . . 10.35
151(1) . . . 11.7
(2) . . . 10.60
157 . . . 2.122, 2.149, 9.72
Pt X, Ch III (ss 159–164) . . . 6.140
s 159(1) . . . 6.140
161 . . . 4.14
Pt XI (ss 165–177) . . . 4.4, 4.93, 4.269, 4.287, 4.306, 14.38, 15.42, 15.76
s 165 . . . 4.13, 4.58, 4.59, 4.72, 4.74, 4.78, 4.111, 4.130, 4.150, 4.237, 4.245, 4.258, 4.293, 7.74, 13.131, 13.164, 15.19

PARA

Financial Services and Markets Act 2000—*contd*
s 165(1)–(3) 4.60, 4.107
(4) 4.60, 4.74
(5), (6) 4.61
(7) 14.12
(a) 4.63
(8) 4.63, 9.253
(9) 4.60
(11) 4.63
166 . . . . 4.13, 4.16, 4.58, 4.78, 4.178, 4.312, 7.74, 14.12, 15.19
(1) 4.72, 4.107
(2) 4.73
(d) 9.253
(3) 4.91
(4) 4.78
(5), (6) 4.87
167 . . . . 4.13, 4.108, 4.110, 4.130, 4.138, 4.140, 4.142, 4.148, 4.176, 4.234, 4.258, 4.312, 13.131, 13.152, 13.164, 14.12, 15.19
(1) 4.122, 15.59, 15.60, 15.78
(2), (3) 4.124
(4) 4.125, 9.253
(5) 4.123
168 . . . . 2.139, 4.138, 4.176, 4.312, 14.12, 15.19, 15.74
(1) 4.13, 4.108, 4.110, 4.134, 4.137, 4.140, 4.148, 4.156, 4.162, 4.234, 4.295, 13.152, 13.164
(2) 4.13, 4.108, 4.110, 4.144, 4.145, 4.147, 4.177, 4.234, 4.238, 13.131, 13.132, 13.141, 13.164, 14.34, 15.51
(c) 14.12
(3) 4.137, 4.144
(4) 4.13, 4.108, 4.110, 4.134, 4.140, 4.148, 4.162, 4.177, 4.234, 4.258, 4.295, 8.68, 13.131, 13.132, 13.152, 13.164, 15.51
(5) 4.134
169 . . . . 4.13, 4.108, 4.110, 4.159, 4.234
(1) 4.150
(a) 4.63
(2) 4.156
(3) 4.152
(4), (5) 4.153
(7), (8) 4.156
(9) 2.126, 4.156
(10)–(12) 4.156
170 . . . . 13.132
(2) 4.130, 4.135, 4.137, 4.159, 15.79

PARA

Financial Services and Markets Act 2000—*contd*
s 170(3) 4.175
(a) 4.162
(b) 4.160, 13.147
(4) 4.159, 14.40, 15.79
(5) 4.158, 5.58, 14.39
(6) 4.178, 5.58, 14.39, 15.88
(7), (8) 4.174, 14.39
(9) 4.175, 14.39, 14.40, 15.80
171 . . . . 4.69, 4.130, 4.243, 13.164
(3) 4.131, 13.152
(4) 15.59
172 . . . . 4.69, 4.243, 13.164
(1) 4.140
(2) 4.141
(3) 13.152
173 . . . . 4.69, 4.147, 4.243, 13.150, 13.164
(1) 14.34
174 . . . . . . 4.245, 4.246, 13.163, 15.69
(5) 4.243, 13.164
175 . . . . 13.164
(1) 4.116, 14.35
(2) 4.114
(3) 4.115, 14.35
(4) 4.118
(5) 4.70, 4.118, 4.267
(6) 4.117
(9) 4.114
176 . . . . 13.154, 14.38
(1) 4.292
(2) 4.293
(3) 4.294
(4) 4.295
(5) 4.296
(11) 4.293
177 . . . . 4.137, 4.285, 7.48, 11.App
(1), (2) 4.284, 13.154, 14.38
(3) 3.151, 11.5, 14.38, 15.76
(4) 4.106, 4.287, 9.56, 9.57, 11.2, 11.5, 14.38, 14.60, 15.76
(6) 4.297
Pt XII (ss 178–192) 9.43
s 191 . . . . 4.137, 11.App
Pt XIII (ss 193–204) . . 4.238, 10.46, 13.227
s 194 . . . . 2.139, 2.142
(1)(a) 9.9, 9.51
(b) 9.9, 9.56
(c) 9.9, 9.60
(3) 9.10
195 . . . . 9.9, 9.63
(4) 9.64
(5) 9.65
(6), (7) 9.39
196 . . . . 9.83
197 . . . . 6.10
(1) 9.99, 9.136, 9.175, 9.194
(2) 9.101, 9.136, 9.196
(3) 9.129
(4) 9.129, 9.176
(5) 9.147

PARA

Financial Services and Markets Act 2000—*contd*
s 197(6) . . . 9.165, 9.166
(7) . . . 9.164
(8) . . . 9.166, 9.176
(10) . . . 9.129, 9.166
198 . . . 7.99
199 . . . 9.235, 9.236
200 . . . 5.3
201 . . . 9.84, 9.89, 9.103
202 . . . 9.103
(1) . . . 10.52, 10.60, 11.7
(2) . . . 10.46, 10.49
203 . . . 9.10, 11.App
204 . . . 9.10
Pt XIV (ss 205–211) . . . 13.227
s 205 . . . 2.142, 7.9, 15.122
206 . . . 2.142, 15.122
(2) . . . 7.9, 9.246
207 . . . 5.71
(2), (3) . . . 5.72
208 . . . 5.163, 5.173, 6.10
210 . . . 2.126, 7.11, 7.13, 7.36
219, 220 . . . 4.14
Pt XVI (ss 225–234) . . . 12.8
s 225(1) . . . 12.5, 12.42
226(4) . . . 12.33
227(4) . . . 12.34
228(2) . . . 12.59
(3), (4) . . . 12.61
(5) . . . 10.67, 12.70, 12.71
(6) . . . 12.70, 12.71
(7) . . . 12.71
229(2)(a) . . . 12.63
(b) . . . 12.65
(3), (5) . . . 12.63
(8)(a) . . . 12.63
(9) . . . 12.79
230 . . . 12.68
231 . . . 4.14, 12.50
(4)–(6) . . . 12.52
232 . . . 12.53
Pt XVII (ss 235–284) . . . 6.10, 14.8, 14.57
s 235 . . . 14.7
(1), (2) . . . 14.22, 14.65
236 . . . 14.7
238 . . . 4.144, 14.6, 14.47
241 . . . 10.32
243 . . . 14.47
(1)(a), (b) . . . 14.52
(4)–(7) . . . 14.84
247 . . . 14.12, 14.52
248 . . . 14.12
254 . . . 14.48, 14.70
(1)(a) . . . 14.51
(b) . . . 14.55
(c) . . . 14.59
(d) . . . 14.61
(e) . . . 14.63
(2) . . . 14.64
255 . . . 5.3, 14.94, 14.95
257 . . . 9.105, 14.83, 14.86
(1) . . . 14.69

PARA

Financial Services and Markets Act 2000—*contd*
s 257(2) . . . 14.67
(5) . . . 10.32, 14.82
(6) . . . 14.79
258 . . . 14.83
(1) . . . 14.110
(2), (3) . . . 14.84
(4) . . . 14.85
(6) . . . 14.100
259 . . . 14.96
(1) . . . 14.74
(c) . . . 14.75
(2) . . . 14.75
(4) . . . 14.97
(5) . . . 14.77
(6) . . . 14.78
(12) . . . 14.97
260 . . . 5.3, 14.99
261(1), (2) . . . 14.99
262 . . . 5.3
264 . . . 14.7, 14.122
267 . . . 9.105
(1) . . . 14.123
(2) . . . 14.123, 14.126
(3)(c) . . . 14.126
(4) . . . 14.127
(5) . . . 14.127
(a) . . . 14.126
(6) . . . 14.126
268 . . . 14.131
(1) . . . 14.125
(3)(a) . . . 14.132
(b) . . . 14.133
(4) . . . 14.133
(7)(b) . . . 14.133
(12) . . . 14.132
269 . . . 5.3
(1), (2), (4)–(6) . . . 14.134
270 . . . 4.63, 14.7, 14.12, 14.41, 14.122, 14.135, 14.138, 14.143, 14.145, 14.146
272 . . . 4.63, 14.7, 14.12, 14.41, 14.122, 14.135, 14.136, 14.138, 14.143, 14.145, 14.146
279 . . . 9.105, 14.136, 14.138
280 . . . 5.3, 14.143
281 . . . 14.136, 14.139
282(3) . . . 14.146
(4) . . . 14.147
(6) . . . 14.146
(7)(b) . . . 14.149
(8) . . . 14.146
(10) . . . 14.147
(11) . . . 14.149
284 . . . 14.31, 14.35
(1) . . . 14.17
(2) . . . 14.18
(3) . . . 14.33
(4) . . . 14.39, 14.40
(5) . . . 14.36

PARA

Financial Services and Markets Act 2000—*contd*
s 284(6) 11.App, 14.35, 14.38
(7) 14.38
(8)–(10) 14.36
(11) 14.19
Pt XVIII (ss 285–313) 7.5
s 285 . . . . 2.10
286 . . . . 1.10, 13.215
289 . . . . 4.14
290 . . . . 13.215
291 . . . . 16.30
296 . . . . 9.10
300 . . . . 6.12
305 . . . . 4.14
Pt XIX (ss 314–324) 1.13, 6.10, 7.5
s 315 . . . . 1.10
320 . . . . 9.10, 9.105
321 . . . . 5.3
Pt XX (ss 325–333) 1.13, 6.10, 7.5, 8.47
s 327 . . . . 1.10
328 . . . . 9.10
331 . . . . 5.3
333 . . . . 11.App
Pt XXII (ss 340–346) 1.13
s 340 . . . . 2.147, 10.34
342(3) 3.68
343(3) 3.68
345 . . . . 5.3, 6.10, 7.5
346 . . . . 4.137, 11.5, 11.App
347 . . . . 2.26, 8.36
(2)(a)(i) 9.188
(f) 8.70
(4) 8.75
348 . . . . 4.90, 4.99, 4.101, 4.166, 4.169, 4.202, 4.211, 4.213, 4.216, 4.302, 5.51, 5.53, 5.76, 5.98, 6.76, 9.126, 10.71, 10.74, 12.17, 12.19, 13.157, 15.85, 15.86, 16.93
(1) 10.72
(2) 4.178
(3) 4.309
(4) 4.217, 10.73
(a) 5.54
(5)(a), (b), (f) 15.90
(6)(a) 15.90
349 . . . . 4.310
(1) 4.217, 6.76
(a) 4.312
(5) 4.312
351 . . . . 4.304, 11.5
352 . . . . 11.5, 11.App, 15.90
(1) 4.313
(3) 4.312
(6) 4.313
353 . . . . 4.82, 4.178
Pt XXIV (ss 355–379) 1.13
Pt XXV (ss 380–386) 13.227
s 380 . . . . 2.139, 2.150, 2.281, 8.77, 9.98, 12.15, 12.78, 13.246
(1) 7.104, 7.105, 8.78

PARA

Financial Services and Markets Act 2000—*contd*
s 380(2) 7.110, 7.111, 8.79
(3) 7.116, 7.117
(b) 8.80
(5) 7.113
(6)(b) 7.105, 7.111, 7.117
381 . . . . 2.142, 13.225, 13.235
(1) 13.237
(2) 13.240
(3) 13.243
(4) 13.243, 13.245
(6) 13.240
382 . . . . 2.139, 2.142, 2.150, 2.281, 7.48
(1) 8.82
(2) 7.48, 7.86
(3) 7.48, 7.90
(4), (5) 7.75
(7) 7.62, 10.67
(9)(b) 7.48
383 . . . . 13.81, 13.254, 13.255
(1)(b) 13.82
(3) 13.69, 13.225
(4) 13.255, 13.256
(9) 10.67
384 . . . . 2.139, 2.142, 2.150
(1) 7.46, 8.81
(2) 13.254, 13.255
(b) 13.82
(4) 13.69, 13.79
(5) 7.46, 7.86, 7.90, 13.256
(6), (7) 7.46
385 . . . . 5.3, 7.76
(2) 7.77
386 . . . . 6.10, 7.76
(2) 7.77
Pt XXVI (ss 387–396) 15.159
s 387 . . . . 5.72, 11.App, 14.114
(2) 5.100, 5.110, 9.131
(4) 5.159
388 . . . . 6.46, 14.114
(2) 5.164, 6.138, 7.35, 15.160
(3)–(5) 5.184
389 . . . . 13.169, 14.114
(1) 5.191
(2) 5.90, 5.165
(3) 4.200, 5.90, 5.166
390 . . . . 14.114
(1) 5.189, 5.193
(2) 5.189, 5.193, 6.149
(3)–(7) 5.192
(9), (10) 6.149
391 . . . . 14.114, 14.116
(1) 4.167, 4.169, 5.63, 5.76, 5.107, 5.182, 7.80, 9.156, 9.184, 13.210
(2), (3) 5.166, 5.167
(4) 4.170, 8.40
(5) 4.170, 9.184
(6), (7) 9.184
(8) 6.150, 8.70, 9.174
392 . . . . 5.81, 5.151

PARA

Financial Services and Markets Act 2000—*contd*
s 393 . . . . 5.150, 6.13, 6.33, 6.34, 8.64, 14.99, 14.114, 14.119
(2) 5.151
(3) 5.157
(4), (5) 5.176
(7) 5.156
(9) 5.178
(11) 5.179
(12), (13) 5.157, 5.177
(14) 5.157, 5.165
394 . . . . 5.81, 14.114, 14.119
(1) 5.82
(2)(a), (b) 5.83
(3) 5.83
(4) 5.83, 5.194
(a) 6.69
(5) 5.83
(6) 5.82, 5.194
(7) 5.194
(a)–(c) 5.83
(8) 8.70
395 . . . . 9.129, 14.114, 15.165
(1) 2.128
(2) 5.26, 9.108, 9.204, 9.227, 15.159
(3) 5.26, 9.108, 9.204
(5) 9.109
(9), (11) 2.128, 9.109, 16.20
(12) 9.109, 16.20
(13) 6.138, 9.165, 15.161
(b) 15.168
(d) 14.96
(e) 14.131
(f) 14.146, 14.149
397 . . . . 4.144, 11.5, 13.7, 13.45,13.177, 15.14
398 . . . . 9.57, 11.2, 11.5, 11.28, 11.App, 14.60, 15.42
(1) 3.106, 4.52, 4.106, 4.137, 4.287, 9.56
400 . . . . 3.145, 4.285, 4.288, 11.26
(2), (3), (5), (6) 11.31
401 . . . . 7.106, 11.1, 13.177
(2) 7.48
402 . . . . 13.177
(1) 11.1
(2) 11.6
403 . . . . 11.26
413 . . . . 3.36, 4.33, 4.70, 4.87, 4.89, 4.118, 4.207, 4.208, 4.235, 4.264, 4.266, 4.299, 5.83, 5.90, 6.70, 6.75, 12.44, 12.52, 14.36, 15.40, 15.71
(2) 6.68
417 . . . . 15.53, 15.117
(1) 4.112, 10.31
418 . . . . 2.60
420 . . . . 4.130, 9.49
421 . . . . 4.73, 4.124, 9.82

PARA

Financial Services and Markets Act 2000—*contd*
s 423 . . . . 11.31
(1) 4.285
425 . . . . 9.47, 9.49
Sch 1
para 1(2) 16.53
7 . . . . 16.38
(1) 16.43
(a) 16.52
(b) 16.44, 16.45
(4) 16.44, 16.86
8 . . . . 16.38
(1) 16.55
(2)(b)(iii) 16.92
(4) 16.60, 16.61
(7) 16.92
(9) 16.49
(10) 16.80
16(1) 4.75, 5.197, 7.39
(2) 7.41
19 . . . . 1.20, 5.77, 16.8
(2) 16.30
Sch 3 . . . . 2.8, 2.11, 2.12, 2.14, 2.15, 9.35, 9.49, 9.251
para 24 . . . . 9.34
Sch 4 . . . . 2.8, 2.11, 2.13–2.15, 4.137, 9.251
Sch 5 . . . . 2.8, 2.14, 14.7, 14.130
para 1(1), (3) 14.11
Sch 6 . . . . 2.38, 2.165
para 8 . . . . 2.38
Sch 7
para 1 . . . . 15.10, 15.42, 15.159
2 . . . . 15.10
Sch 13 . . . . 6.4
para 7(4) 6.100
9(d) 6.79
10 . . . . 6.6
11 . . . . 6.94, 6.96
12(1), (2) 6.142
(3)(b) 6.143
(4) 6.143
13 . . . . 5.198, 6.154, 6.155
(1), (2) 6.158
Sch 15
Pt I 4.63
Pt II 4.130, 4.234
Sch 17 . . . . 12.8
para 3 . . . . 12.2
10 . . . . 12.76, 16.30
14(2)(f) 12.5
16 . . . . 12.79

Friendly Societies Act 1992 (19 *Statutes* 184) 4.12

Human Rights Act 1998 (7 *Statutes* 497): 1.20, 1.21, 1.24–1.26, 1.26, 2.161, 3.25, 3.29, 4.155, 4.272, 4.316, 5.17, 5.20, 5.77, 12.17, 12.42, 12.74, 12.76, 13.182, 16.22, 16.25, 16.31, 16.65

PARA

Human Rights Act 1998—*contd*
s 3(2) 16.30
4(6) 16.30
6 . . . . 6.25
(1) 16.20
7(1)(a) 16.20
(3) 16.20
8(3) 16.34
(4) 16.35
Sch 1 (European Convention on Human Rights) 1.2, 1.22, 4.35, 4.242, 4.245, 4.246, 4.316, 5.17, 5.22, 5.23, 5.25, 6.5, 6.12, 6.19, 6.25, 6.108, 6.122, 6.128, 6.144, 12.42, 12.55, 12.74–12.77, 13.15, 13.16, 13.156, 13.162, 13.269, 13.271, 16.20, 16.25, 16.34, 16.36
Art 6 . . . . 13.182
(1) 1.24, 5.20, 6.24, 6.26, 6.88, 6.125, 6.142, 12.56, 12.57, 12.72, 12.77, 14.36, 16.17, 16.30
(2) 5.21, 6.24, 6.26, 11.8, 13.170
(3) 5.21, 6.24, 6.26, 11.8
7 . . . . 1.29, 2.161
8 . . . . 3.29, 4.274, 12.17, 14.36
(2) 3.30
14 . . . . 12.64, 12.72
41 . . . . 16.35
Protocol 1
Art 1 . . . . 7.42, 12.60, 12.64
Protocol 7 . . . . 6.24, 6.26
Art 4 . . . . 13.182

PARA

Insolvency Act 1986 (4 *Statutes* 721) . . . 4.15
s 221 . . . . 4.238
236 . . . . 4.286
Insurance Companies Act 1982 (22 *Statutes* 226) 4.12
s 37–45 . . . . 9.1
43A 4.149
Interpretation Act 1978 (41 *Statutes* 985) 11.26
Law Reform (Contributory Negligence) Act 1945 (31 *Statutes* 235) 10.15
Limitation Act 1980 (24 *Statutes* 698)
s 21 . . . . 10.17
Misrepresentation Act 1967 (29 *Statutes* 978)
s 2(2) 10.22
Pension Schemes Act 1993 (33 *Statutes* 580) 4.15, 12.65, 12.66
Pensions Act 1995 (33 *Statutes* 859) . . . 4.15
Police and Criminal Evidence Act 1984 (12 *Statutes* 801) 4.15, 4.248, 4.250
s 19(6) 4.299
Public Interest Disclosure Act 1998 . . 3.86, 4.47, 4.48, 4.208
Regulation of Investigatory Powers Act 2000
s 1(3) 3.25
17 . . . . 6.67
Supply of Goods and Services Act 1982 (39 *Statutes* 132) 10.15
Supreme Court Act 1981 (11 *Statutes* 966)
s 31(3) 16.19
Tribunals and Inquiries Act 1992 (10 *Statutes* 469) 6.5
Trustee Act 1925 (48 *Statutes* 257)
s 61 . . . . 10.17
Youth Justice and Criminal Evidence Act 1999 . . . . 4.242

Table of statutory instruments

References in the right-hand column are to paragraph numbers.

PARA

Civil Procedure Rules 1998 (SI 1998/3132 . . . . 4.189, 6.120, 10.1, 14.100, 14.120
- Pt 1 . . . . 6.21
- Pt 5
  - r 5.4 . . . . 7.81
- Pt 7 . . . . 7.78, 7.126
- Pt 25
  - r 25.1 . . . . 16.11
- Pt 29 . . . . 6.84, 6.86
- Pt 31
  - r 31.6, 31.12 . . . . 4.194
  - 31.17 . . . . 4.216
  - 31.22 . . . . 6.76
- Pt 32 . . . . 6.93
- Pt 34 . . . . 4.216
- Pt 39
  - r 39.2 . . . . 7.81
- Pt 40
  - r 40.12 . . . . 6.164
- Pt 52 . . . . 6.170
  - r 52.3(6) 6.173
  - 52.11(2) 6.163
- Pt 54 . . . . 16.9
  - r 54.1.22 . . . . 16.19
  - 54.3.7 . . . . 16.11
  - 54.3.9 . . . . 16.13
  - 54.3.12 . . . . 16.22
  - 54.4.7 . . . . 16.21
  - 54.5.4 . . . . 16.21
  - 54.10 . . . . 16.11
  - 54.10.4/5 . . . . 16.14
- Sch 1
  - Ord 45
    - r 5 . . . . 4.285

Financial Services and Markets Act 2000 (Collective Investment Schemes constituted in other EEA States) Regulations 2001, SI 2001/2383 . . . . 14.7

Financial Services and Markets Act 2000 (Collective Investment Schemes) Order 2001, SI 2001/1062 . . . . 14.7

Financial Services and Markets Act 2000 (Communications by Auditors) Regulations 2001, SI 2001/2587 . 3.68

Financial Services and Markets Act 2000 (Disclosure of Confidential Information) Regulations 2001, SI 2001/2188 . . . . 4.99, 4.310, 9.185, 13.133, 13.159, 13.162, 15.90
- reg 2 . . . . 4.312
  - 3(1) 4.166
    - (2) 15.92
    - (3) 4.312
  - 4 . . . . 4.312, 15.94
  - 5 . . . . 4.217, 4.312, 6.76
  - 6–8 . . . . 4.312
  - 9, 10 . . . . 4.312, 16.94
  - 11 . . . . 4.312
  - 12 . . . . 15.94, 16.94
    - (1) 15.92
      - (a), (b) 4.312
    - (2), (3) 4.312
- Sch 1 . . . . 4.312, 15.92, 15.94, 16.94
- Sch 2 . . . . 4.312, 15.94

Financial Services and Markets Act 2000 (Disclosure of Information by Prescribed Persons) Regulations 2001, SI 2001/1857 . . . . 4.82, 4.105, 4.178

Financial Services and Markets Act 2000 (EEA Passport Rights) Regulations 2001, SI 2001/1376 . . . . 2.12

Financial Services and Markets Act 2000 (Exemption) Order 2001, SI 2001/1201 . . . . 2.10
- art 6 . . . . 1.10

Financial Services and Markets Act 2000 (Own-initiative Power) (Overseas) Regulations 2001, SI 2001/2639: 9.31, 9.35

PARA

Financial Services and Markets Act 2000 (Prescribed Markets and Qualifying Investments) Order 2001, SI 2001/996 . . . . 13.31, 13.32
Financial Services and Markets Act 2000 (Promotion of Collective Investment Schemes) (Exemptions) Order 2001, SI 2001/1060 . . . . 14.47
Financial Services and Markets Act 2000 (Regulated Activities) Order 2001, SI 2001/544 . . . . 10.42
Pt III 13.32
art 72 . . . . 10.35
Financial Services and Markets Act 2000 (Rights of Action) Regulations 2001, SI 2001/2256
reg 1 . . . . 10.46
3(2) 10.35
4 . . . . 10.46
5(1), (3) 10.45
6(2) 10.42
(1) 10.35
7 . . . . 10.46
Financial Services and Markets Act 2000 (Service of Notices) Regulations 2001, SI 2001/1420 . . . 4.60, 4.107, 4.130, 4.159, 4.175, 5.74, 5.174, 5.190, 6.36, 9.152, 9.177
Financial Services and Markets Act 2000 (Variation of Threshold Conditions) Order 2001, SI 2001/250 . . . . . 2.38, 2.39
Financial Services and Markets Tribunal Rules 2001, SI 2001/2476 . . 6.4, 6.17, 6.46, 6.57, 6.58, 6.74, 6.99, 6.102, 6.105, 6.106, 6.109, 6.111, 6.113, 6.115, 6.120, 6.130, 6.131, 6.141, 6.156, 9.137, 9.177
r 2 . . . . 6.68, 6.81
(1) 6.32, 6.36, 6.40, 6.60
(2)(d) 6.135
4(1), (2) 6.36
(3), (5) 6.34
(6) 6.38
(7) 6.33
(8), (9) 6.40
5(1) 6.47
(2) 6.43
(3), (4) 6.60
6(1) 6.52
(2) 6.50
(3) 6.64
(4) 6.52, 6.64
7(1)–(3) 6.65
8(1)–(3) 6.67
(4) 6.71
(5), (6) 6.72
(7) 6.60, 6.64, 6.65
(8) 6.67, 6.68
9 . . . . 6.77
(1) 6.87, 6.93

PARA

Financial Services and Markets Tribunal Rules 2001—*contd*
r 9(2) 6.79, 6.80
(3) 6.81
(4) 6.81
(5) 6.81
(6), (7) 6.83
(8) 6.82
(9) 6.84
(10) 6.85
(11)(a), (b) 6.86
(12) 6.85
10(1) 6.89
(a) 6.119, 6.121
(c) 6.121
(d) 6.37, 6.47, 6.52, 6.166
(e) 6.104
(f) 6.54, 6.56
(g) 6.73
(k) 6.93
(l) 6.101
(m) 6.100
(q) 6.114
(2) 6.37, 6.47, 6.52
(3) 6.37, 6.47, 6.52
(4) 6.47, 6.52
(5) 6.48, 6.53
(8) 6.73
(9) 6.39
11(1) 6.162
12(2) 6.95
(3)–(5) 6.97
(6) 6.94
13 . . . . 6.107
(1) 6.89
(2), (3) 6.108
14 . . . . 6.33
(1) 6.110
(2) 6.112
(3) 6.48, 6.53, 6.123
(a) 6.112
(4) 6.110, 6.112
15 . . . . 6.33
(3) 6.34
16 . . . . 6.89
(1) 6.123
(b) 6.81
(2)–(4) 6.83
17(1) 6.32, 6.81, 6.85, 6.108, 6.124
(2) 6.81, 6.124
(3)–(5) 6.124
(6), (7) 6.129
(10) 6.121
(11) 6.129
18 . . . . 6.85
(2) 6.135
(3) 6.108
19(1) 6.122
(2) 6.92, 6.132
(a) 6.101
(3) 6.133, 6.134
(4) 6.135

PARA

Financial Services and Markets Tribunal Rules 2001—*contd*
r 20(1) 6.144
(2), (4) 6.146
(5) 6.144
(6) 6.143
21(2), (3) 6.155
22 . . . . 6.167
(1)–(4) 6.166
(5), (6) 6.168
23(2), (3) 6.172
24(1), (2) 6.173
(3)–(5) 6.174
25(1) 6.163
26(2) 6.77, 6.87
(3) 6.89
27(1) 6.48, 6.53, 6.89
28 . . . . 6.164
29 . . . . 6.79
31 . . . . 6.36, 6.52
Insolvency Rules 1986, SI 1986/1925 . 4.286
Money Laundering Regulations 1993, SI 1993/1933 . . . . 11.6
Open-Ended Investment Companies Regulations 2001, SI 2001/1228: 5.3, 6.10, 14.8, 14.16
reg 3 . . . . 14.103
8, 9 . . . . 14.114, 14.116
10, 11 . . . . 14.114
23 . . . . 14.114
(1), (2) 14.102
(3) 14.103
24(3) 14.114, 14.119
25 . . . . 9.105, 14.110
(1) 14.106
(2) 14.105

PARA

Open-Ended Investment Companies Regulations 2001—*contd*
reg 25(5) 14.106
(6) 10.32, 14.109
(7) 14.108
26(1), (2) 14.110
(3), (4) 14.111
(5) 14.110, 14.111
(7) 14.121
27(1) 14.107
(4) 14.117
(5), (6) 14.108
(12) 14.117
(15) 14.116
28 . . . . 14.114, 14.119
29(1), (2) 14.119
30(1) 14.27, 14.28, 14.30
(2)(a)–(g) 14.29
(3) 14.33
(4) 14.39, 14.40
(5) 14.36
(6) 14.35, 14.38
(7) 14.38
(8) 14.36
80 . . . . 14.38
81, 82 . . . . 14.36
Public Interest Disclosure (Prescribed Persons) Order 1999, SI 1999/1549 . . . . 4.48
Telecommunications (Lawful Business Practice) (Interception of Communications) Regulations 2000, SI 2000/2699 . . . . 3.25
Unfair Terms in Consumer Contracts Regulations 1999, SI 1999/2083 . 7.99

Table of cases

References in the right-hand column are to paragraph numbers.

PARA

A

A v B Bank (Bank of England intervening) [1993] QB 311, [1992] 1 All ER 778, [1992] 3 WLR 705, 135 Sol Jo 11 . . . . . 4.239, 4.277, 4.286
AB & Co, Re [1900] 1 QB 541, CA 4.238
Agip (Africa) Ltd v Jackson [1990] Ch 265, [1992] 4 All ER 385, [1989] 3 WLR 1367, 134 Sol Jo 198, [1990] 2 LS Gaz R 34; affd [1991] Ch 547, [1992] 4 All ER 451, [1991] 3 WLR 116, 135 Sol Jo 117, CA 10.19
Albert and Le Compte v Belgium (1982) 5 EHRR 533 . . . . . 5.20, 6.24
Ali (Saif) v Sydney Mitchell & Co (a firm) [1980] AC 198, [1978] 3 All ER 1033, [1978] 3 WLR 849, 122 Sol Jo 761, HL 2.155, 10.15
Allen v Gulf Oil Refining Ltd [1981] AC 1001, [1981] 1 All ER 353, [1981] 2 WLR 188, 125 Sol Jo 101, [1981] RVR 70, HL 6.107
American Cyanamid Co v Ethicon Ltd [1975] AC 396, [1975] 1 All ER 504, [1975] 2 WLR 316, [1975] FSR 101, [1975] RPC 513, 119 Sol Jo 136, HL 7.103, 16.13
Arrows Ltd, Re [1992] Ch 545, [1992] 2 WLR 923, [1992] BCLC 126, [1992] BCC 125, [1992] 8 LS Gaz R 27 . . . . . 4.286
Associated Provincial Picture Houses Ltd v Wednesbury Corpn [1948] 1 KB 223, [1947] 2 All ER 680, 45 LGR 635, 112 JP 55, [1948] LJR 190, 92 Sol Jo 26, 177 LT 641, 63 TLR 623, CA 16.20
A-G v Observer Ltd [1990] 1 AC 109, [1988] 3 WLR 776, [1988] NLJR 296, sub nom A-G v Guardian Newspapers Ltd (No 2) [1988] 3 All ER 545, HL 12.17, 12.19
A-G for Alberta v Huggard Assets Ltd [1953] AC 420, [1953] 2 All ER 951, [1953] 2 WLR 768, 97 Sol Jo 260, PC 4.238
A-G for Gibraltar v May [1999] 1 WLR 998, CA 4.244
A-G for Tuvalu v Philatelic Distribution Corpn Ltd [1990] 2 All ER 216, [1990] 1 WLR 926, [1990] BCLC 245, 134 Sol Jo 832, [1990] 25 LS Gaz R 36, CA 4.285
A-G's Reference (No 7 of 2001) (29 March 2001, unreported), CA 4.244

B

Baden v Société Générale pour Favoriser le Développement du Commerce et de l'Industrie en France SA [1992] 4 All ER 161, [1983] BCLC 325, [1993] 1 WLR 509n; affd [1992] 4 All ER 279n, [1985] BCLC 258n, CA 10.19
Balabel v Air India [1988] Ch 317, [1988] 2 All ER 246, [1988] 2 WLR 1036, 132 Sol Jo 699, [1988] NLJR 85, CA 4.207
Balini v Spain 1994) A 303-B 6.142
Baltic Shipping Co v Translink Shipping Ltd and Translink Pacific Shipping Ltd [1995] 1 Lloyd's Rep 673 . . . . . 4.239

PARA

Bank of Credit and Commerce International (Overseas) Ltd v Akindele [2001] Ch 437, [2000] 4 All ER 221, [2000] All ER (D) 798, [2000] 3 WLR 1423, [2000] 26 LS Gaz R 36, [2000] NLJR 950, CA 10.20
Bank of Credit and Commerce International (Overseas) Ltd (in liquidation) v Price Waterhouse (a firm) (Abu Dhabi (Emirate) (third parties) (Governor and Co of the Bank of England intervening) [1998] Ch 84, [1997] 4 All ER 781, [1997] 3 WLR 849, [1998] BCC 511; revsd [1998] BCC 617, [1998] 15 LS Gaz R 32, 142 Sol Jo LB 86, [1998] PNLR 564, CA 4.216, 4.308, 4.310, 4.311, 10.72
Bank of England v Riley [1992] Ch 475, [1992] 1 All ER 769, [1992] 2 WLR 840, CA 4.275
Barclays Bank plc v Quincecare Ltd [1992] 4 All ER 363, 1988 FLR 166, [1988] 1 FTLR 507: 10.15
Barings plc (in liquidation) v Coopers & Lybrand [2000] 3 All ER 910, [2000] 1 WLR 2353, [2000] NLJR 681, CA 4.216, 4.308
Bedford Insurance Co Ltd v Instituto de Resseguros do Brasil [1985] QB 966, [1984] 3 All ER 766, [1984] 3 WLR 726, [1984] 1 Lloyd's Rep 210, 218n, [1985] FLR 49, 128 Sol Jo 701, [1985] LS Gaz R 37, 134 NLJ 34 . . . . 10.52
Belmont Finance Corpn Ltd v Williams Furniture Ltd [1979] Ch 250, [1979] 1 All ER 118, [1978] 3 WLR 712, 122 Sol Jo 743, CA 10.19
Belmont Finance Corpn v Williams Furniture Ltd (No 2) [1980] 1 All ER 393, CA 10.20
Benthem v Netherlands (1985) 8 EHRR 1, ECtHR 5.20
Bishopsgate Investment Management Ltd (in liquidation) v Maxwell (No 2) [1994] 1 All ER 261, [1993] BCLC 1282, [1993] BCC 120, CA 10.16
Blyth v Birmingham Waterworks Co (1856) 20 JP 247, 25 LJ Ex 212, 11 Exch 781, 2 Jur NS 333, 4 WR 294, 156 ER 1047, [1843-60] All ER Rep 478, 26 LTOS 261 . . . . 10.15
Boardman v Phipps [1967] 2 AC 46, [1966] 3 All ER 721, [1966] 3 WLR 1009, 110 Sol Jo 853, HL 10.18
Bolam v Friern Hospital Management Committee [1957] 2 All ER 118, [1957] 1 WLR 582, 101 Sol Jo 357, 1 BMLR 1 . . . . 2.155, 10.15
Bolkiah v KPMG (a firm) [1999] 2 AC 222, [1999] 1 All ER 517, [1999] 2 WLR 215, [1999] 1 BCLC 1, [1999] PNLR 220, [1999] NLJR 16, 143 Sol Jo LB 35, HL 4.80
Bolton (HL) (Engineering) Co Ltd v TJ Graham & Sons Ltd [1957] 1 QB 159, [1956] 3 All ER 624, [1956] 3 WLR 804, 100 Sol Jo 816, 168 Estates Gazette 424, CA 11.27
Bray v Ford [1896] AC 44, 65 LJQB 213, 73 LT 609, 12 TLR 119, HL 10.18
Bristol and West Building Society v Mothew (t/a Stapley & Co) [1998] Ch 1, [1996] 4 All ER 698, [1997] 2 WLR 436, [1996] NLJR 1273, 140 Sol Jo LB 206, [1997] PNLR 11, sub nom Mothew v Bristol & West Building Society 75 P & CR 241, CA 4.80, 10.18
British and Commonwealth Holdings plc (in administration) v Barclays de Zoete Wedd Ltd [1998] All ER (D) 491, [1999] 1 BCLC 86, 143 Sol Jo LB 14 . . . . 4.213
British Coal Corpn v Dennis Rye Ltd (No 2) [1988] 3 All ER 816, [1988] 1 WLR 1113, 132 Sol Jo 1430, CA 4.202
British Telecommunications Ltd v Sheridan [1990] IRLR 27, CA 6.171
Buckinghamshire County Council v Moran [1990] Ch 623, [1989] 2 All ER 225, [1989] 3 WLR 152, 88 LGR 145, 58 P & CR 236, [1989] NLJR 257, CA 4.210, 5.121
Burton v Bevan [1908] 2 Ch 240, 77 LJ Ch 591, 15 Mans 272, 99 LT 342 . . . . 2.186

C

Caparo Industries plc v Dickman [1990] 2 AC 605, [1990] 1 All ER 568, [1990] 2 WLR 358, [1990] BCLC 273, [1990] BCC 164, 134 Sol Jo 494, [1990] 12 LS Gaz R 42, [1990] NLJR 248, HL 10.15
Castellain v Preston (1883) 11 QBD 380, 52 LJQB 366, 31 WR 557, [1881-5] All ER Rep 493, 49 LT 29, CA 10.68
Cayne v Global Natural Resources [1984] 1 All ER 225, CA 7.103
Chantrey Martin (a firm) v Martin [1953] 2 QB 286, [1953] 2 All ER 691, [1953] 3 WLR 459, 46 R & IT 516, 97 Sol Jo 539, 97 Sol Jo 572, CA 4.88, 4.235
Clark Boyce v Mouat [1994] 1 AC 428, [1993] 4 All ER 268, [1993] 3 WLR 1021, [1993] 40 LS Gaz R 42, [1993] 3 NZLR 641, 137 Sol Jo LB 231, PC 10.18
Coco v AN Clark (Engineers) Ltd [1968] FSR 415, [1969] RPC 41 . . . . 12.17, 12.19
Company Securities (Insider Dealing) Act 1985, Inquiry under the, Re [1988] AC 660, [1988] 1 All ER 203, [1988] 2 WLR 33, [1988] BCLC 153, 4 BCC 35, 132 Sol Jo 21, [1988] 4 LS Gaz R 33, [1987] NLJ Rep 1181, HL 4.143, 4.286, 6.125, 9.77, 12.51
Company's Application, a, Re [1989] Ch 477, [1989] 2 All ER 248, [1989] 3 WLR 265, [1989] ICR 449, [1989] IRLR 477, [1989] BCLC 462, 133 Sol Jo 917 . . . . 4.54, 4.208

PARA

Council of Civil Service Unions v Minister for the Civil Service [1985] AC 374, [1984] 3 All ER 935, [1984] 3 WLR 1174, [1985] ICR 14, 128 Sol Jo 837, [1985] LS Gaz R 437, [1985] LRC (Const) 948, sub nom R v Secretary of State for Foreign and Commonwealth Affairs, ex p Council of Civil Service Unions [1985] IRLR 28, HL 16.20
Credit Lyonnais Bank v Kaufmann. See Kaufmann v Credit Lyonnais Bank
Crown Estate Comrs v Dorset County Council [1990] Ch 297, [1990] 1 All ER 19, [1990] 2 WLR 89, 88 LGR 132, 60 P & CR 1 . . . . 10.76

D

DR Insurance Co v Seguros America Banamex [1993] 1 Lloyd's Rep 120 . . . . 10.52
Dada v Metal Box Co Ltd [1974] ICR 559, [1974] IRLR 251, 9 ITR 390, NIRC 6.94
De Cubber v Belgium (1984) 7 EHRR 236, ECtHR 6.24
Derry v Peek (1889) 14 App Cas 337, 54 JP 148, 58 LJ Ch 864, 1 Meg 292, 38 WR 33, [1886–90] All ER Rep 1, 61 LT 265, 5 TLR 625, HL 10.22
Devis (W) & Sons Ltd v Atkins [1977] AC 931, [1977] 3 All ER 40, [1977] 3 WLR 214, [1977] ICR 662, [1977] IRLR 314, 13 ITR 71, 121 Sol Jo 512, 8 BLR 57, HL 12.60
Director General of Fair Trading v Buckland [1990] 1 All ER 545, [1990] 1 WLR 920, [1990] BCLC 162, 5 BCC 817, [1990] 26 LS Gaz R 37 . . . . 4.285
Douglas v Hello! Ltd [2001] 2 All ER 289, [2001] All ER (D) 2435, [2001] 2 WLR 992, [2001] 1 FLR 982, CA 3.29

E

Eagle Trust plc v SBC Securities Ltd [1992] 4 All ER 488, [1993] 1 WLR 484, [1991] BCLC 438 . . . . 10.16
Engel v Netherlands (1976) 1 EHRR 647, ECtHR 5.21
Esso Petroleum Co Ltd v Hall Russell & Co Ltd and Shetland Islands Council, The Esso Bernicia [1989] AC 643, [1989] 1 All ER 37, [1988] 3 WLR 730, [1989] 1 Lloyd's Rep 8, 132 Sol Jo 1459, HL 10.68

F

Fayed v United Kingdom (1994) 18 EHRR 393, ECtHR 16.30
Feldbrugge v Netherlands (1986) 8 EHRR 425, ECtHR 6.26, 12.55

G

Galileo Group Ltd, Re, Elles v Hambros Bank Ltd (Bank of England intervening) [1999] Ch 100, [1998] 1 All ER 545, [1998] 2 WLR 364, [1998] 1 BCLC 318, [1998] BCC 228, [1997] 46 LS Gaz R 30, 142 Sol Jo LB 21 . . . . 4.213, 4.216, 4.310
Garvin v Domus Publishing Ltd [1989] Ch 335, [1989] 2 All ER 344, [1988] 3 WLR 344, 132 Sol Jo 1091, [1988] 33 LS Gaz R 44 . . . . 4.247
Goddard v Nationwide Building Society [1987] QB 670, [1986] 3 All ER 264, [1986] 3 WLR 734, 130 Sol Jo 803, [1986] LS Gaz R 3592, [1986] NLJ Rep 775, CA 4.266
Gomba Holdings UK Ltd v Minories Finance Ltd [1989] 1 All ER 261, [1988] 1 WLR 1231, [1989] BCLC 115, 5 BCC 27, 132 Sol Jo 1323, CA 4.88
Gorham v British Telecommunications plc [2000] 4 All ER 867, [2000] 1 WLR 2129, 144 Sol Jo LB 251, CA 10.15, 10.30, 10.36
Gorris v Scott (1874) LR 9 Exch 125, 43 LJ Ex 92, 2 Asp MLC 282, 22 WR 575, 30 LT 431 . 10.37
Gotha City v Sotheby's [1998] 1 WLR 114, [1997] 30 LS Gaz R 28, 141 Sol Jo LB 152, CA . 4.202
Grant v Borg [1982] 2 All ER 257, [1982] 1 WLR 638, 126 Sol Jo 311, HL 11.34
Gray v Barr [1971] 2 QB 554, [1971] 2 All ER 949, [1971] 2 WLR 1334, [1971] 2 Lloyd's Rep 1, 115 Sol Jo 364, CA 8.24
Green v Hampshire County Council [1979] ICR 861 . . . . 10.76
Group Josi Re (formerly known as Group Josi Reassurance SA) v Walbrook Insurance Co Ltd [1996] 1 All ER 791, [1996] 1 WLR 1152, [1996] 1 Lloyd's Rep 345, CA 10.55
Grupo Torras SA v Al Sabah [2000] All ER (D) 1643 . . . . 10.19
Guinness plc v Saunders [1990] 2 AC 663, [1990] 1 All ER 652, [1990] 2 WLR 324, [1990] BCLC 402, 134 Sol Jo 457, [1990] 9 LS Gaz R 42, HL 10.16, 10.18

PARA

H

Hadjianastassiou v Greece (1992) EHRR 219, ECtHR 6.142
Hadley v Baxendale (1854) 23 LJ Ex 179, 9 Exch 341, 18 Jur 358, 2 WR 302, 156 ER 145, [1843-60] All ER Rep 461, 2 CLR 517, 23 LTOS 69 . . . . 10.14
Hakansson and Sturesson v Sweden (1990) 13 EHRR 1, ECtHR 6.126
Halford v United Kingdom (1997) 24 EHRR 523, [1997] IRLR 471, [1998] Crim LR 753, 94 LS Gaz R 24, ECtHR 3.30, 3.31
Hearts of Oak Assurance Co Ltd v A-G [1932] AC 392, 101 LJ Ch 177, [1932] All ER Rep 732, 76 Sol Jo 217, 147 LT 41, 48 TLR 296, HL 4.109, 4.273
Hedley Byrne & Co Ltd v Heller & Partners Ltd [1964] AC 465, [1963] 2 All ER 575, [1963] 3 WLR 101, [1963] 1 Lloyd's Rep 485, 107 Sol Jo 454, HL 10.15
Henderson v Merrett Syndicates Ltd [1995] 2 AC 145, [1994] 3 All ER 506, [1994] 3 WLR 761, [1994] NLJR 1204, HL 10.15
Heron II, The. See Koufos v C Czarnikow Ltd, The Heron II
Herring v Templeman [1973] 3 All ER 569, 72 LGR 162, 117 Sol Jo 793, CA 4.273, 16.20
Highfield Commodities Ltd, Re [1984] 3 All ER 884, [1985] 1 WLR 149, [1984] BCLC 623, 128 Sol Jo 870 . . . . 7.103
Hoffmann-La Roche & Co AG v Secretary of State for Trade and Industry [1975] AC 295, [1974] 2 All ER 1128, [1974] 3 WLR 104, 118 Sol Jo 500, HL 7.103
Huckerby v Elliott [1970] 1 All ER 189, 134 JP 175, 113 Sol Jo 1001 . . . . 11.34, 11.35
Hunt v Severs [1994] 2 AC 350, [1994] 2 All ER 385, [1994] 2 WLR 602, [1994] 2 Lloyd's Rep 129, [1994] 32 LS Gaz R 41, [1994] NLJR 603, 138 Sol Jo LB 104, HL 10.66
Hussain v New Taplow Paper Mills Ltd [1988] AC 514, [1988] 1 All ER 541, [1988] 2 WLR 266, [1988] ICR 259, [1988] IRLR 167, 132 Sol Jo 226, [1988] 10 LS Gaz R 45, [1988] NLJR 45, HL 10.66

I

IJL, GMR and AKP v United Kingdom (2000) 9 BHRC 222 . . . . 4.242
Infabrics Ltd v Jaytex [1985] FSR 75; affd [1987] FSR 529, CA 3.154
Initial Services Ltd v Putterill [1968] 1 QB 396, [1967] 3 All ER 145, [1967] 3 WLR 1032, 2 KIR 863, 111 Sol Jo 541, CA 4.54
Investors Compensation Scheme Ltd v West Bromwich Building Society [1998] 1 All ER 98, [1998] 1 WLR 896, [1998] 1 BCLC 531, [1997] NLJR 989, [1997] PNLR 541, [1997] CLC 1243, HL 10.13

J

Jefferson Ltd v Bhetcha [1979] 2 All ER 1108, [1979] 1 WLR 898, 144 JP 125, 123 Sol Jo 389, CA 11.45

K

Kaufmann v Credit Lyonnais Bank (1995) 7 Admin LR 669, sub nom Credit Lyonnais Bank v Kaufmann [1995] CLC 300 . . . . 4.195
Keech v Sandford (1726) 2 Eq Cas Abr 741, Sel Cas Ch 61, Cas temp King 61, 25 ER 223, [1558-1774] All ER Rep 230 . . . . 10.18
Kingsley v United Kingdom (2001) Times, 9 January, ECtHR 16.17
Kirklees Metropolitan Borough Council v Wickes Building Supplies Ltd [1993] AC 227, [1992] 3 All ER 717, [1992] 3 WLR 170, [1992] 2 CMLR 765, 90 LGR 391, [1992] NLJR 967, HL 7.103
Kokkinakis v Greece (1993) 17 EHRR 397, ECtHR 2.161
König v Germany (1978) 2 EHRR 170, ECtHR 5.20
Koufos v C Czarnikow Ltd, The Heron II [1969] 1 AC 350, [1967] 3 All ER 686, [1967] 3 WLR 1491, [1967] 2 Lloyd's Rep 457, 111 Sol Jo 848, HL 10.14

L

L (minors) (police investigation: privilege), Re [1997] AC 16, [1996] 2 All ER 78, [1996] 2 WLR 395, 160 LG Rev 417, [1996] 2 FCR 145, [1996] 1 FLR 731, [1996] Fam Law 400, [1996] 15 LS Gaz R 30, [1996] NLJR 441, 140 Sol Jo LB 116, HL 4.199
Ladd v Marshall [1954] 3 All ER 745, [1954] 1 WLR 1489, 98 Sol Jo 870, CA 6.163

PARA

Lancashire County Council v Municipal Mutual Insurance Ltd [1997] QB 897, [1996] 3 All ER 545, [1996] 3 WLR 493, 95 LGR 234, [1996] 21 LS Gaz R 27, 140 Sol Jo LB 108, CA . 3.130
Law Society v KPMG Peat Marwick (sued as KPMG Peat Marwick McLintock) [2000] 4 All ER 540, [2000] 1 WLR 1921, [2000] NLJR 1017, 144 Sol Jo LB 227, CA 4.86
Le Compte, Van Leuven and De Meyere v Belgium (1981) 4 EHRR 1, ECtHR 5.20
Legal and General Assurance Society Ltd v Pensions Ombudsman [2000] 2 All ER 577, [2000] 1 WLR 1524, [1999] 46 LS Gaz R 40, [1999] NLJR 1733, 144 Sol Jo LB 8 . . . . 12.29
Lehman Bros Inc v Phillips [1998] 1 All ER 577, [1998] 1 BCLC 240, [1998] BCC 726, CA . 4.238
L'Estrange v F Graucob Ltd [1934] 2 KB 394, 103 LJKB 730, [1934] All ER Rep 16, 152 LT 164, DC 10.13
Lewin v Bland [1985] RTR 171, 148 JP 69 . . . . 11.35
Leyland Cars v Vyas [1980] AC 1028, [1979] 3 WLR 762, [1979] ICR 921, 123 Sol Jo 768, sub nom BL Cars Ltd (formerly Leyland Cars) v Vyas [1979] 3 All ER 673, HL 6.60
Lithgow v United Kingdom (1986) 8 EHRR 329, ECtHR 7.42
London United Investments plc, Re [1992] Ch 578, [1992] 2 All ER 842, [1992] 2 WLR 850, [1992] BCLC 285, [1992] BCC 202, [1992] 8 LS Gaz R 27, [1992] NLJR 87, 136 Sol Jo LB 32, CA 4.275, 4.286
Lyell v Kennedy (No 3) (1884) 27 Ch D 1, 53 LJ Ch 937, [1881-5] All ER Rep 814, 50 LT 730, CA 5.96

M

MGN Pensions Trustees v Invesco Asset Management Ltd (14 October 1993, unreported) . . 4.195
MacKinnon v Donaldson Lufkin and Jenrette Securities Corpn [1986] Ch 482, [1986] 1 All ER 653, [1986] 2 WLR 453, 130 Sol Jo 224 . . . . 4.238
Mahon v Air New Zealand Ltd [1984] AC 808, [1984] 3 All ER 201, [1984] 3 WLR 884, [1984] LS Gaz R 3336, 128 Sol Jo 752, CA, PC 3.154
Mahon v Rahn (No 2) [2000] 4 All ER 41, [2000] 2 All ER (Comm) 1, [2000] 1 WLR 2150, [2000] 26 LS Gaz R 38, [2000] NLJR 899, [2000] EMLR 873, CA 4.105, 4.214
Mantovanelli v France (1996) 24 EHRR 370, ECtHR 6.26
Marsh & McLennan Companies UK Ltd v Pensions Ombudsman [2001] IRLR 505 . . . . . 12.29
Meek v City of Birmingham District Council [1987] IRLR 250, CA 6.142
Melton Medes Ltd v Securities and Investments Board [1995] Ch 137, [1995] 3 All ER 880, [1995] 2 WLR 247 . . . . 4.312c, 4.314, 10.24, 16.32, 16.33
Meridian Global Funds Management Asia Ltd v Securities Commission [1995] 2 Ac 500, [1995] 3 All ER 918, [1995] 3 WLR 413, [1995] 2 BCLC 116, [1995] BCC 942, [1995] 28 LS Gaz R 39, PC 11.27
Messier-Dowty Ltd v Sabena SA [2001] 1 All ER 275, [2000] 1 All ER (Comm) 833, [2000] 1 WLR 2040, [2000] 1 Lloyd's Rep 428, [2000] 10 LS Gaz R 36, 144 Sol Jo LB 124, CA . 12.13
Mid East Trading Ltd, Re [1998] 1 All ER 577, [1998] 1 BCLC 240, [1998] BCC 726, [1998] 03 LS Gaz R 24, 142 Sol Jo LB 45, CA 4.238
Minter v Priest [1930] AC 558, 99 LJKB 391, [1930] All ER Rep 431, 74 Sol Jo 200, 143 LT 57, 46 TLR 301, HL 4.207
Mirror Group Newspapers plc (inquiry), Re [2000] Ch 194, [1999] 2 All ER 641, [1999] All ER (D) 255, [1999] 3 WLR 583, [1999] 1 BCLC 690 . . . . 4.149, 4.229, 4.286, 13.153
Moran v Lloyd's [1981] 1 Lloyd's Rep 423, [1981] Com LR 46, 124 Sol Jo 615, CA . . 4.273, 16.20
Morgan Crucible Co plc v Hill Samuel & Co Ltd [1991] Ch 295, [1991] 2 WLR 655, [1990] BCC 686, [1990] NLJR 1271, sub nom Morgan Crucible Co plc v Hill Samuel Bank Ltd [1990] 3 All ER 330, [1991] BCLC 18; revsd sub nom Morgan Crucible Co plc v Hill Samuel & Co Ltd [1991] Ch 295, [1991] 2 WLR 655, [1991] BCC 82, [1990] NLJR 1605, sub nom Morgan Crucible Co plc v Hill Samuel Bank Ltd [1991] 1 All ER 148, [1991] BCLC 178, CA 10.15
Muller v Linsley & Mortimer (a firm) [1995] 03 LS Gaz R 38, 139 Sol Jo LB 43, [1996] PNLR 74, CA 4.210, 5.121

N

Neale v Hereford and Worcester County Council [1986] ICR 471, sub nom Hereford and Worcester County Council v Neale [1986] IRLR 168, CA} 6.171
Noorani v Merseyside TEC Ltd [1999] IRLR 184, CA 6.94
Norman v Mathews [1916] WN 78, 85 LJKB 857, 114 LT 1043, 32 TLR 303; affd 32 TLR 369, CA 6.154

PARA

Norwest Holst Ltd v Secretary of State for Trade [1978] 1 Ch 201, [1978] 3 All ER 280, [1978] 3 WLR 73, 122 Sol Jo 109, CA 4.273

O

O'Reilly v Mackman [1983] 2 AC 237, [1982] 3 All ER 1124, [1982] 3 WLR 1096, 126 Sol Jo 820, HL 16.28

Osman v United Kingdom (1998) 29 EHRR 245, [1999] 1 FLR 193, [1999] Fam Law 86, [1999] Crim LR 82, 5 BHRC 293, ECtHR 16.30

P

Parry v Cleaver [1970] AC 1, [1969] 1 All ER 555, [1969] 2 WLR 821, [1969] 1 Lloyd's Rep 183, 113 Sol Jo 147, HL 10.66

Parry-Jones v Law Society [1969] 1 Ch 1, [1968] 1 All ER 177, [1968] 2 WLR 397, 111 Sol Jo 910, CA 4.199

Pauger v Austria (1997) 25 EHRR 105, ECtHR 6.126

Pergamon Press Ltd, Re [1971] Ch 388, [1970] 3 All ER 535, [1970] 3 WLR 792, 114 Sol Jo 569, CA 4.109, 4.149, 4.229, 4.273

Peyman v Lanjani [1985] Ch 457, [1984] 3 All ER 703, [1985] 2 WLR 154, 48 P & CR 398, 128 Sol Jo 853, CA 10.22

Price Waterhouse (a firm) v BCCI Holdings (Luxembourg) SA [1992] BCLC 583 . . 4.54, 4.197, 4.206

R

R v Boal [1992] QB 591, [1992] 3 All ER 177, [1992] 2 WLR 890, 95 Cr App Rep 272, [1992] ICR 495, [1992] IRLR 420, 156 JP 617, [1992] BCLC 872, [1992] 21 LS Gaz R 26, 136 Sol Jo LB 100, CA 11.31

R v BBC, ex p Lavelle [1983] 1 All ER 241, [1983] 1 WLR 23, [1983] ICR 99, [1982] IRLR 404, 126 Sol Jo 836 . . . . 11.45

R v Broadcasting Standards Commission, ex p BBC [2000] 3 All ER 989, [2000] 3 WLR 1327, [2001] 1 BCLC 244, [2000] 17 LS Gaz R 32, 144 Sol Jo LB 204, [2000] EMLR 587, CA 4.274

R v Chesterfield Justices, ex p Bramley [2000] QB 576, [2000] 1 All ER 411, [2000] 2 WLR 409, [2000] 1 Cr App Rep 486, [2000] Crim LR 385 . . . . 4.299

R v Director of Serious Fraud Office, ex p Smith [1993] AC 1, [1992] 3 WLR 66, 95 Cr App Rep 191, [1992] 27 LS Gaz R 34, [1992] NLJR 895, 136 Sol Jo LB 182, sub nom Smith v Director of Serious Fraud Office [1992] 3 All ER 456, [1992] BCLC 879, HL 4.249

R v Financial Intermediaries, Managers and Brokers Regulatory Association, ex p Cochrane [1991] BCLC 106, [1990] COD 33 . . . . 16.20

R v Gayle [1999] Crim LR 502, CA 4.249

R v HM Inspectorate of Pollution, ex p Greenpeace Ltd [1994] 4 All ER 321, [1994] 1 WLR 570, CA 16.14

R v Hertfordshire County Council, ex p Green Environmental Industries Ltd [2000] 2 AC 412, [2000] 1 All ER 773, [2000] 2 WLR 373, [2000] 09 LS Gaz R 42, [2000] NLJR 277, [2000] EGCS 27, HL 4.242, 4.275

R v Immigration Appeal Tribunal, ex p Khan [1983] QB 790, [1983] 2 All ER 420, [1983] 2 WLR 759, [1982] Imm AR 134, 127 Sol Jo 287, CA 6.142

R v Institute of Chartered Accountants in England and Wales, ex p Brindle [1993] BCC 736; revsd [1994] BCC 297, CA 11.45

R v Insurance Ombudsman Bureau, ex p Aegon Life Assurance Ltd [1994] COD 426, [1994] CLC 88, [1993] LRLR 100 . . . . 12.75

R v International Stock Exchange of the United Kingdom and the Republic of Ireland Ltd, ex p Else (1982) Ltd [1993] QB 534, [1993] 1 All ER 420, [1993] 2 WLR 70, [1993] 2 CMLR 677, [1993] BCLC 834, [1993] BCC 11, CA 16.20

R v Investors Compensation Scheme Ltd, ex p Bowden [1996] AC 261, [1995] 3 All ER 605, [1995] 2 BCLC 342, [1995] 30 LS Gaz R 32, 139 Sol Jo LB 188, sub nom R v Investors Compensation Board, ex p Bowden [1995] 3 WLR 289, HL 12.64

R v Johal [1973] QB 475, [1972] 2 All ER 449, [1972] 3 WLR 210, 56 Cr App Rep 348, 136 JP 519, 116 Sol Jo 195, CA 6.57

R v Life Assurance Unit Trust Regulatory Organisation Ltd, ex p Ross [1993] QB 17, [1993] 1 All ER 545, [1992] 3 WLR 549, [1992] BCLC 509, CA 16.20

R v Odeyemi [1999] Crim LR 828, CA 4.249

R v Osieh [1996] 1 WLR 1260, [1996] 2 Cr App Rep 145, [1997] Crim LR 133, CA 6.57

PARA

R v Panel on Take-overs and Mergers, ex p Fayed [1992] BCLC 938, [1992] BCC 524, CA . 11.45
R v Panel on Take-overs and Mergers, ex p Guinness plc [1990] 1 QB 146, [1989] 1 All ER 509, [1989] 2 WLR 863, [1989] BCLC 255, 4 BCC 714, 133 Sol Jo 660, [1988] NLJR 244, CA: 11.45
R v Pointer [1997] Crim LR 676, CA 4.249
R v Personal Investment Authority Ombudsman Bureau Ltd, ex p Johannes Mooyer (5 April 2001, unreported) 12.75
R v Ram [1973] QB 475, [1972] 2 All ER 449, [1972] 3 WLR 210, 56 Cr App Rep 348, 136 JP 519, 116 Sol Jo 195, CA 6.57
R v Secretary of State for Education and Science, ex p Avon County Council [1991] 1 QB 558, [1991] 1 All ER 282, [1991] 2 WLR 702, 89 LGR 121, [1990] NLJR 781, CA 16.11
R (on the appliction of Alconbury Developments Ltd) v Secretary of State for the Environment, Transport and the Regions [2001] UKHL 23 [2001] 2 All ER 929, [2001] 2 WLR 1389, 145 Sol Jo LB 140 . . . . 16.17
R v Secretary of State for Transport, ex p Factortame Ltd (No 2) [1991] 1 AC 603, [1990] 3 WLR 818, [1990] 3 CMLR 375, [1990] 2 Lloyd's Rep 365n, [1991] 1 Lloyd's Rep 10, 134 Sol Jo 1189, [1990] 41 LS Gaz R 36, [1990] NLJR 1457, sub nom Factortame Ltd v Secretary of State for Transport (No 2) [1991] 1 All ER 70, HL 16.13
R (on the application of Fleurose) v Securities and Futures Authority Ltd [2001] All ER (D) 189 . . . . 1.27, 1.29, 2.161, 5.20, 5.22
R v Securities and Futures Authority, ex p Panton (1995) CA LTL 6/3/95, CA 16.17
R v Securities and Investments Board, ex p Independent Financial Advisers Association [1995] 2 BCLC 76 . . . . 16.20
R v Securities and Investments Board, ex p Sun Life Assurance Society plc [1996] 2 BCLC 150: 16.20
R v Sheffield Hallam University (Board of Governors), ex p R [1995] ELR 267, [1994] COD 470 . . . . 16.20
R v Shivpuri [1987] AC 1, [1986] 2 All ER 334, [1986] 2 WLR 988, 83 Cr App Rep 178, 150 JP 353, [1986] Crim LR 536, 130 Sol Jo 392, [1986] LS Gaz R 1896, [1986] NLJ Rep 488, [1986] LRC (Crim) 702, HL 2.186
R v Sunderland City Council, ex p Redezeus Ltd (1994) 94 LGR 105, 27 HLR 477 . . . . . . 2.127
Ridehalgh v Horsefield [1994] Ch 205, [1994] 3 All ER 848, [1994] 3 WLR 462, [1994] 2 FLR 194, [1994] Fam Law 560, [1994] BCC 390, CA 6.154
Rio Tinto Zinc Corpn v Westinghouse Electric Corpn [1978] AC 547, [1978] 1 All ER 434, [1978] 2 WLR 81, 122 Sol Jo 23, HL 4.246
Rowell v Pratt [1938] AC 101, [1937] 3 All ER 660, 106 LJKB 790, 81 Sol Jo 765, 157 LT 369, 52 TLR 982, HL 4.216
Royal Brunei Airlines Sdn Bhd v Tan [1995] 2 AC 378, [1995] 3 All ER 97, [1995] 3 WLR 64, [1995] BCC 899, [1995] 27 LS Gaz R 33, [1995] NLJR 888, PC 10.19
Rush & Tompkins Ltd v Greater London Council [1989] AC 1280, [1988] 1 All ER 549, [1988] 2 WLR 533, 132 Sol Jo 265, [1988] 6 LS Gaz R 37, [1988] NLJR 22, 40 BLR 53, CA; revsd [1989] AC 1280, [1988] 3 All ER 737, [1988] 3 WLR 939, 22 Con LR 114, 132 Sol Jo 1592, [1988] NLJR 315, 43 BLR 1, HL 4.210, 5.121, 12.44

S

Saunders v United Kingdom (1996) 23 EHRR 313, [1998] 1 BCLC 362, [1997] BCC 872, [1997] 2 BHRC 354, ECtHR 4.242
Science Research Council v Nassé [1980] AC 1028, [1979] 3 All ER 673, [1979] 3 WLR 762, [1979] ICR 921, [1979] IRLR 465, 123 Sol Jo 768, HL 6.60
Secretary of State for Defence v Guardian Newspapers Ltd [1985] AC 339, [1984] 3 All ER 601, [1984] 3 WLR 986, 128 Sol Jo 751, [1984] LS Gaz R 3426, HL 4.143
Securities and Investment Board v Vandersteen Associates NV [1991] BCLC 206 . . . . 7.53, 7.108
Securities and Investments Board v Financial Intermediaries Managers and Brokers Regulatory Association Ltd [1992] Ch 268, [1991] 4 All ER 398, [1991] 3 WLR 889, [1991] BCLC 815, [1991] NLJR 1035 . . . . 16.28
Securities and Investments Board v Lloyd-Wright [1993] 4 All ER 210 . . . . 7.103
Securities and Investments Board v Pantell SA [1990] Ch 426, [1989] 2 All ER 673, [1989] 3 WLR 698, [1989] BCLC 590 . . . . 7.53, 7.116, 7.121
Securities and Investments Board v Pantell SA (No 2) [1993] Ch 256, [1991] 4 All ER 883, [1991] 3 WLR 857, [1992] BCLC 58; affd [1993] Ch 256, [1992] 1 All ER 134, [1992] 3 WLR 896, [1993] BCLC 146, [1992] 31 LS Gaz R 40, [1992] NLJR 931, 136 Sol Jo LB 198, CA 2.186, 7.53, 7.54, 7.113, 7.115, 10.54, 10.56
Securities and Investments Board v Scandex Capital Management A/S [1998] 1 All ER 514, [1998] 1 WLR 712, [1998] 06 LS Gaz R 24, [1998] NLJR 85, CA 2.186, 7.53, 7.113

PARA

Smith v Eric S Bush [1990] 1 AC 831, [1989] 2 All ER 514, [1989] 2 WLR 790, 87 LGR 685, 21 HLR 424, 17 Con LR 1, 133 Sol Jo 597, [1989] 1 EGLR 169, [1989] NLJR 576, [1989] 17 EG 68, 18 EG 99, HL 10.15
Smith New Court Securities Ltd v Citibank NA [1997] AC 254, [1996] 3 WLR 1051, [1997] 1 BCLC 350, [1996] 46 LS Gaz R 28, [1996] NLJR 1722, 141 Sol Jo LB 5, sub nom Smith New Court Securities Ltd v Scrimgeour Vickers (Asset Management) Ltd [1996] 4 All ER 769, HL 10.22
Smith (Wallace) Trust Co Ltd (in liquidation) v Deloitte Haskins & Sells (a firm) [1996] 4 All ER 403, [1997] 1 WLR 257, [1997] BCC 29, CA 4.213
Sociedade Nacional de Combustiveis de Angola UEE v Lundqvist [1991] 2 QB 310, [1990] 3 All ER 283, [1991] 2 WLR 280, CA 4.246
South Shropshire District Council v Amos [1987] 1 All ER 340, [1986] 1 WLR 1271, 130 Sol Jo 803, [1986] 2 EGLR 194, [1986] LS Gaz R 3513, [1986] NLJ Rep 800, [1986] RVR 235, 280 Estates Gazette 635, CA 4.210, 5.121
Spring v Guardian Assurance plc [1995] 2 AC 296, [1994] 3 All ER 129, [1994] 3 WLR 354, [1994] ICR 596, [1994] IRLR 460, [1994] 40 LS Gaz R 36, [1994] NLJR 971, 138 Sol Jo LB 183, HL 10.15
Swansea City and County v Johnson [1999] Ch 189, [1999] 1 All ER 863, [1999] 2 WLR 683 12.29

T

Target Holdings Ltd v Redferns (a firm) [1996] AC 421, [1995] 3 All ER 785, [1995] 3 WLR 352, [1995] 31 LS Gaz R 36, [1995] NLJR 1164, 139 Sol Jo LB 195, HL 10.16, 10.17
Tate Access Floors Inc v Boswell [1991] Ch 512, [1990] 3 All ER 303, [1991] 2 WLR 304, 134 Sol Jo 1227, [1990] 42 LS Gaz R 35, [1990] NLJR 963 . . . . . 4.247
Taylor v Director of the Serious Fraud Office [1999] 2 AC 177, [1998] 4 All ER 801, [1998] 3 WLR 1040, [1999] EMLR 1, HL 5.98
Terrapin Ltd v Builders' Supply Co (Hayes) Ltd [1967] RPC 375 . . . . . 12.19
Tesco Stores Ltd v Secretary of State for the Environment [1995] 2 All ER 636, [1995] 1 WLR 759, 70 P & CR 184, [1995] 2 EGLR 147, [1995] 24 LS Gaz R 39, [1995] NLJR 724, [1995] 27 EG 154, HL 2.127, 12.60, 16.20, 16.71
Tesco Supermarkets Ltd v Nattrass [1972] AC 153, [1971] 2 All ER 127, [1971] 2 WLR 1166, 69 LGR 403, 135 JP 289, 115 Sol Jo 285, HL 11.27, 11.28
Three Rivers District Council v Bank of England (No 3) [2000] 3 All ER 1, [2000] All ER (D) 690, [2000] 2 WLR 1220, [2000] 3 CMLR 205, [2000] NLJR 769, HL 16.33
Tournier v National Provincial and Union Bank of England [1924] 1 KB 461, 93 LJKB 449, 29 Com Cas 129, [1923] All ER Rep 550, 68 Sol Jo 441, 130 LT 682, 40 TLR 214, CA: 4.54, 4.268

U

Unilever plc v Procter & Gamble Co [2001] 1 All ER 783, [2000] 1 WLR 2436, [2000] FSR 433, [1999] 44 LS Gaz R 40, 143 Sol Jo LB 268, CA 4.210, 5.121
United Pan-Europe Communications NV v Deutsche Bank AG [2000] 2 BCLC 461; revsd [2000] 2 BCLC 461, CA 10.16, 10.18

W

W v Egdell [1990] Ch 359, [1990] 1 All ER 835, [1990] 2 WLR 471, 134 Sol Jo 286, 4 BMLR 96, [1990] 12 LS Gaz R 41, CA 4.199
Waugh v British Railways Board [1980] AC 521, [1979] 2 All ER 1169, [1979] 3 WLR 150, [1979] IRLR 364, 123 Sol Jo 506, HL 4.205, 4.206
Westdeutsche Landesbank Girozentrale v Islington London Borough Council [1996] AC 669, [1996] 2 All ER 961, [1996] 2 WLR 802, 95 LGR 1, [1996] NLJR 877, 140 Sol Jo LB 136, HL 10.16
Westminster City Council v Croyalgrange Ltd [1986] 2 All ER 353, [1986] 1 WLR 674, 84 LGR 801, 83 Cr App Rep 155, 150 JP 449, [1986] Crim LR 693, 130 Sol Jo 409, [1986] LS Gaz R 2089, [1986] NLJ Rep 491, HL 2.186
Westminster City Council v Haywood [1996] 2 All ER 467, [1996] 3 WLR 563; revsd [1998] Ch 377, [1997] 2 All ER 84, [1997] 3 WLR 641, [1998] ICR 920, CA 12.65, 12.75
Williams (JD) & Co Ltd v Michael Hyde & Associates Ltd [2000] All ER (D) 930, [2001] BLR 99, CA 2.155, 10.15

PARA

Woolgar v Chief Constable of Sussex Police [1999] 3 All ER 604, [2000] 1 WLR 25, 50 BMLR 296, [1999] 23 LS Gaz R 33, [1999] NLJR 857, CA 4.312a

X

X v Bedfordshire County Council [1995] 2 AC 633, [1995] 3 All ER 353, [1995] 3 WLR 152, 160 LG Rev 103, [1995] 3 FCR 337, [1995] 2 FLR 276, [1995] Fam Law 537, [1995] ELR 404, 26 BMLR 15, [1995] NLJR 993, HL 10.24

Y

Young v Robson Rhodes [1999] 3 All ER 524

Z

Z v United Kingdom [2001] 2 FCR 246, [2001] Fam Law 583, ECtHR 16.30
Z Ltd v A-Z and AA-LL [1982] QB 558, [1982] 1 All ER 556, [1982] 2 WLR 288, [1982] 1 Lloyd's Rep 240, 126 Sol Jo 100, CA 9.92

1 Introduction

CONTENTS

The financial services regime 1

The main debates about the enforcement regime 4

THE FINANCIAL SERVICES REGIME

1.1 The Financial Services and Markets Act 2000 ('FSMA 2000') came fully into effect on 1 December 2001, bringing to a close a process of consultation and debate which had continued since May 1997, when the Government announced that it would be introducing legislation to reform the regulation of the financial services industry.

1.2 The process itself has been unprecedented. The Bill was subjected to pre-legislative scrutiny by a Joint Committee of both Houses of Parliament. It was the first ever Bill to be carried over from one session of Parliament to the next under new parliamentary procedures. It was also among the first pieces of legislation required to be certified as compliant with the European Convention on Human Rights ('ECHR').

1.3 But the most important aspect of the process was the very extensive consultation, undertaken by HM Treasury, by Parliament through the Joint Committee and by the Financial Services Authority ('the FSA') itself. Although the FSMA 2000 received Royal Assent in June 2000 and, to a large extent, the scope of the regime and its framework were fixed at that stage, the debates continued, but the subject matter moved on to the FSA's detailed rules, which were still the subject of consultation.

What does the regulatory regime comprise?

1.4 The regime comprises:

- one main piece of primary legislation, the FSMA 2000 (replacing arrangements previously found in at least six pieces of primary legislation);
- ultimately, in excess of 60 pieces of secondary legislation, primarily made by HM Treasury; and
- several volumes of detailed rules in the FSA Handbook.

1.5 The FSMA 2000 is in many respects no more than a framework for regulation, notwithstanding its length. It creates the basic regulatory structure, imposes certain obligations on the regulated community and others, and gives the FSA a raft of functions and powers, subject to certain safeguards. What the FSMA 2000 does not do is to provide the detailed rules, nor does it explain in what situations the FSA will in practice use its extensive powers. Rather, the FSA is empowered to make detailed rules and is required to publish its policy on the use of particular powers. HM Treasury is also authorised to make certain regulations by statutory instrument.

1.6 This structure allows the details of the regulatory regime to be changed over time without the need to undergo the unwieldy and slow political and parliamentary processes which further primary legislation would entail. This should allow the FSMA 2000 to be an enduring piece of legislation, capable of adapting with the dynamic financial services world over a period of time.

1.7 In the enforcement context, the question of how and when the FSA will in practice use its powers is one of the most important questions. It is to the FSA's Handbook, where its detailed rules and policy are contained, and potentially in due course to the published enforcement decisions of the FSA and the jurisprudence of the new Financial Services and Markets Tribunal (the 'Tribunal'), that the regulated community must turn for an answer.

A single statutory regulator

1.8 The main effect of the FSMA 2000 is to bring together in one body the functions of a series of different regulators, each of which regulated aspects of what can be described as financial services business, often with a different regulatory philosophy and approach, as well as a different set of functions and powers[1]. It was this piecemeal approach to regulation which the FSMA 2000 was intended to cure. In addition, the FSMA 2000 puts into place a detailed enforcement regime for listed companies and covers some areas of business which previously were wholly unregulated.

1 Many of these functions were in fact carried out by the FSA before the FSMA 2000 came into effect. For example, the Bank of England's former role as banking supervisor was formally transferred to the FSA in 1998 by means of the Bank of England Act 1998 and the FSA carried out

the work of the Insurance Directorate of HM Treasury and the work of the SROs (see para 1.9 below) under service level agreements.

1.9 The result is a single body, the FSA, which may appear to be significantly more powerful than the sum of its individual parts. However, although the legal structure is different and the powers in some respects more draconian, there are many similarities in practical terms to the powers of the former self-regulatory organisations (or SROs)[1] which previously regulated investment business, and some of the previous statutory powers, for example those of the Department of Trade and Industry, which investigated insider dealing. For some firms, or parts of firms, which either were unregulated or were regulated by bodies operating in a rather different environment, the new enforcement regime will mark a fundamental change in approach.

1 The Securities and Futures Authority ('SFA'); the Investment Management Regulatory Organisation ('IMRO') and the Personal Investment Authority ('PIA').

Who is subject to the regime?

1.10 The regulated community now includes:

- investment businesses (previously regulated by the SROs) including certain types of business which were previously unregulated;
- banks (previously regulated by the Bank of England);
- building societies (previously regulated by the Building Societies Commission);
- insurance companies (previously regulated by the Insurance Directorate of HM Treasury);
- recognised investment exchanges and clearing houses (previously regulated by the FSA and in certain respects HM Treasury[1]);
- Lloyd's (which was previously regulated for solvency purposes by HM Treasury, but otherwise regulated itself under Lloyd's Acts[2]);
- professional firms (for example, solicitors or accountants) offering certain types of services[3];
- friendly societies;
- credit unions[4] (previously regulated by the Registry of Friendly Societies); and
- mortgage lenders (previously unregulated[5]).

1 HM Treasury retains a role, setting recognition requirements: FSMA 2000, s 286 and see para 13.213 ff below.
2 Lloyd's agents are regulated both by the FSA and by Lloyd's.
3 Professional firms are regulated primarily by their designated professional body, but the FSA can choose to directly regulate them.
4 Under art 6 of the Financial Services and Markets Act 2000 (Exemption) Order 2001, SI 2001/1201, credit unions are exempt from the activity of accepting deposits until July 2002.
5 Mortgage lending is a regulated activity under the Regulated Activities Order but the mortgage regime will not come into effect until 'N3' which HM Treasury has said will be 31 August 2002.

1.11 In addition, the FSA has taken on the former responsibilities of the London Stock Exchange as the UK's competent authority for admitting securities to the official list ('UK Listing Authority'). Companies whose shares are admitted to the list, and their directors, are therefore now, to that extent, regulated by the FSA.

Enforcement under the regime

1.12 Notwithstanding the breadth of the regulated community, the policing of the industry generally operates on a 'one size fits all' basis. Irrespective of the type of firm or business involved, the legal framework and the general policy and approach of the FSA are broadly the same, though the implementation of policy in any case will depend upon the particular circumstances and this may include the nature of the business involved. The discussion in this book of the treatment by the FSA of misconduct or regulatory breaches therefore applies to a large extent equally to all the business sectors outlined in para 1.10 above.

1.13 There are, however, some specific enforcement rules applicable to different types of businesses. Some of these, for example the FSA's powers as UK Listing Authority in relation to companies admitted to listing and its powers in relation to regulated collective investment schemes, are covered in this book. Certain others (for example, its powers in relation to Lloyd's[1], in relation to professional firms[2], and in relation to auditors and actuaries[3], and its insolvency powers[4]) are not.

1 FSMA 2000, Pt XIX.
2 FSMA 2000, Pt XX.
3 FSMA 2000, Pt XXII.
4 FSMA 2000, Pt XXIV, and see the FSA Handbook at ENF Chapter 10.

THE MAIN DEBATES ABOUT THE ENFORCEMENT REGIME

1.14 The proposals for the new regulator and its processes sparked considerable debate, which continued through the pre-legislative and Bill stages of the FSMA 2000 and through the subsequent consultation on the FSA's detailed rules. The FSA's enforcement function was one of the main areas of concern, particularly because of the magnifying effect of putting together in one place powers previously dispersed across a number of different bodies and pieces of legislation and the introduction or enhancement of a number of statutory powers. Even Sir Howard Davies, Chairman of the FSA, acknowledged that the FSA's powers 'look intimidating brought together in one place'[1].

1 Quoted in the Financial Times, 13 November 1998.

1.15 What is particularly striking about the regime, and something of a recurring theme here, is the range of different enforcement powers available to the FSA when a regulatory problem arises. These include not only the disciplinary powers, which are aimed primarily at punishing and deterring, but also powers enabling the FSA to prevent breaches, compensate those who have suffered losses, place restrictions on firms in order to protect consumers and for other purposes, and prosecute criminal offences. Since the different powers are aimed at addressing different consequences of regulatory breaches, firms can face regulatory action on a multitude of fronts arising from the same problem. Since it is the same body, the FSA, which has all these powers, the regime allows a single fact finding investigation to take place, with the FSA considering only afterwards what regulatory action or combination of action it is appropriate to take.

1.16 Again, although this may look intimidating, and the range of powers is more extensive, in broad terms the position is not significantly different from that already familiar to firms previously regulated by the SROs. If anything, the risk of multiple investigations by different regulators involved in different aspects should be reduced.

1.17 The debates which took place during the consultation process, particularly the debates before the Joint Committee, did have a significant effect on the shape of the regime. Although the details of the debates are now primarily of historical interest, it may be helpful to outline some of the main issues which arose in the enforcement context because this should assist in understanding the regime as it is now and also because some of the issues have not been resolved and may yet come to be tested in individual cases. Most of these issues are discussed in more detail later on in this book.

1.18 Five of the main issues are particularly worthy of note.

The accountability of the FSA

1.19 First, as the Joint Committee noted[1], the FSA was to become one of the most powerful financial regulators in the world in terms of scope, powers and discretion. Given this, and the concerns that existed within the industry as to whether the FSA's culture and approach would be significantly different from that of the then existing regulators, it was perhaps inevitable that the question of the FSA's accountability was a focus for debate. As a result of that debate, the FSMA 2000 contains various mechanisms, structures and safeguards to ensure that the FSA is properly accountable for its actions.

1 See the First Report of the Joint Committee, para 103.

1.20 A number of points are of particular relevance in the present context. First, the FSA is required to maintain a Practitioner Panel and a Consumer Panel and to have regard to any representations made to it by them[1]. This gives a voice to both consumers and the industry, who will often be pulling in different directions, and allows them to air any issues of concern to them and to make representations in relation to specific issues[2]. Second, whilst the FSA has a statutory immunity from civil claims for damages, this is qualified in some important respects. The FSA can still be liable to damages claims under the Human Rights Act 1998 or where it acts in bad faith[3]. Perhaps as importantly, though, there is a procedure for making complaints about the FSA to an independent complaints commissioner who can report that a complaint is well-founded, criticise the FSA and recommend that the FSA pay compensation or take remedial action. A robust complaints procedure was viewed as an essential counterbalance to the statutory immunity. The complaints procedure and, more generally, the ability of firms to challenge or bring legal actions against the FSA, is discussed in Chapter 16 below.

1 FSMA 2000, ss 8 to 11.
2 For more detailed information on the Practitioner Panel, see the Financial Services Practitioner Forum Annual Report 2000.
3 FSMA 2000, Sch 1, para 19. This is discussed further in Chapter 16 below.

The new market abuse regime

1.21 Second, the new market abuse regime was a major topic of debate. The main concern was uncertainty – that the offence was insufficiently well defined to allow people to assess whether their actions would amount to market abuse. There were also concerns about whether the regime was fair, particularly given the lack of any need for intent, and whether it offered the safeguards required under the Human Rights Act 1998.

1.22 As a result of concerns expressed by the Joint Committee, the Government recognised that there was a real possibility of the market abuse regime being classified as criminal for ECHR purposes[1] and it therefore included in the FSMA 2000 certain safeguards necessary for those accused of committing market abuse. These are discussed in more detail in the introduction to Chapter 13.

1 See the Memorandum from HM Treasury to the Joint Committee, 14 May 1999, para 13.

1.23 Much of the debate, though, has been less about the process than about clarifying the precise scope of the conduct that will constitute market abuse. The statutory definition of market abuse is complex and in some respects unclear and it is likely to be the subject of judicial authority in due course. In addition, within the boundaries of the statutory definition, the FSA can affect the scope of the regime on an ongoing basis by making amendments to the Code of Market Conduct. Consultation and debate about the details of the regime will no doubt continue.

The FSA's internal decision-making procedures

1.24 Third, an issue which was much aired is the nature of the FSA's internal process before reaching decisions on enforcement issues. Most enforcement issues have historically been resolved without recourse to a full tribunal process and this has generally been viewed as a positive element of the former regime. If that was to continue, it was important that there were appropriate procedures within the FSA to ensure that cases would be fairly handled before the FSA reached its decision as to what enforcement action was appropriate. There was also a need to ensure that the process met the fair trial guarantees of the Human Rights Act 1998[1]. The concerns about the process were perhaps heightened by the terminology adopted in the Bill as it was originally introduced, which described the Tribunal as an 'Appeal Tribunal', giving the impression that, in cases where the matter could not be resolved without recourse to a tribunal procedure, the industry would have recourse only to a tribunal exercising the limited role of an appellate body.

1 ECHR, art 6(1): this is discussed further at paras 5.20 and 6.23 below.

1.25 Attention was therefore focused on the FSA's internal decision-making process. Various types of internal structures were proposed, in order to resolve the tensions involved. These are outlined in Chapter 5 below, together with a detailed analysis of the final structure which has been adopted. The question remains as to whether the process adopted satisfies the requirements of the Human Rights Act 1998 and whether it addresses the concerns that were expressed. The answer can only be assessed on a case-by-case basis.

Whether the disciplinary procedure is criminal for ECHR purposes

1.26 Fourth, an important question is whether the FSA's disciplinary powers are criminal or civil in nature for human rights purposes. The approach taken by the Government is that disciplinary proceedings will be classified as civil for ECHR purposes[1]. Hence, the FSMA 2000 makes no provision, at least in the context of disciplinary proceedings, for the safeguards which the Human Rights Act 1998 requires to be provided where a person is subjected to a criminal charge.

1 See the Second Report of the Joint Committee, para 9, HM Treasury's Response to the Second Report, at Part X and the Memorandum from HM Treasury dated 14 May 1999, para 10.

1.27 The question whether a particular proceeding is criminal falls to be tested on a case-by-case basis and there are certainly arguments[1] that the disciplinary process may be criminal in serious cases, depending upon the punishment that is proposed. This is discussed in more detail at para 5.22 below.

1 Notwithstanding the decision in *R (on the application of Fleurose) v Securities and Futures Authority Ltd* [2001] All ER (D) 189, discussed at para 5.22 below.

Discipline on the basis of general principles

1.28 Finally, a point which has historically been the subject of much discussion, and which continued to be debated through the Bill stages of the FSMA 2000, is whether the FSA should be able to use its general principles as a basis for taking disciplinary action. As with the previous regime for investment business, the FSA prescribes various high-level general principles with which it expects the regulated community to comply[1]. The principles sit above the specific rules. Among other things, they indicate how the FSA approaches situations where there are no detailed rules, which would include new products and businesses. The importance of the principles is thus in allowing regulation to be flexible and not stifle innovation. For this reason, the principles are deliberately drafted in very general terms.

1 The Principles for Businesses: these are discussed in more detail at para 2.51 below.

1.29 The FSA's position is that it can and may use the principles as the basis for disciplinary and enforcement action. The issue remains live, however, because of the lack of clarity as to what is prohibited by rules drafted in such a general way. The Human Rights Act 1998[1] requires a criminal offence to be clearly defined so that an individual can foresee to a reasonable degree what acts and omissions will make him liable. If disciplinary proceedings based on a breach of general principles are, in a particular case, held to be criminal in nature then they may also be too uncertain to fulfil the requirement of the human rights legislation. Moreover, this may, in any event, be a basic rule of natural justice[2]. This issue is discussed in more detail at para 2.156 ff below.

1 ECHR, art 7: see para 2.161 below.
2 See *R (on the application of Fleurose) v Securities and Futures Authority Ltd* [2001] All ER (D) 189.

1.30 The flowchart opposite provides a diagrammatic description of the scope of each chapter of the book and should be a useful reference guide for the reader.

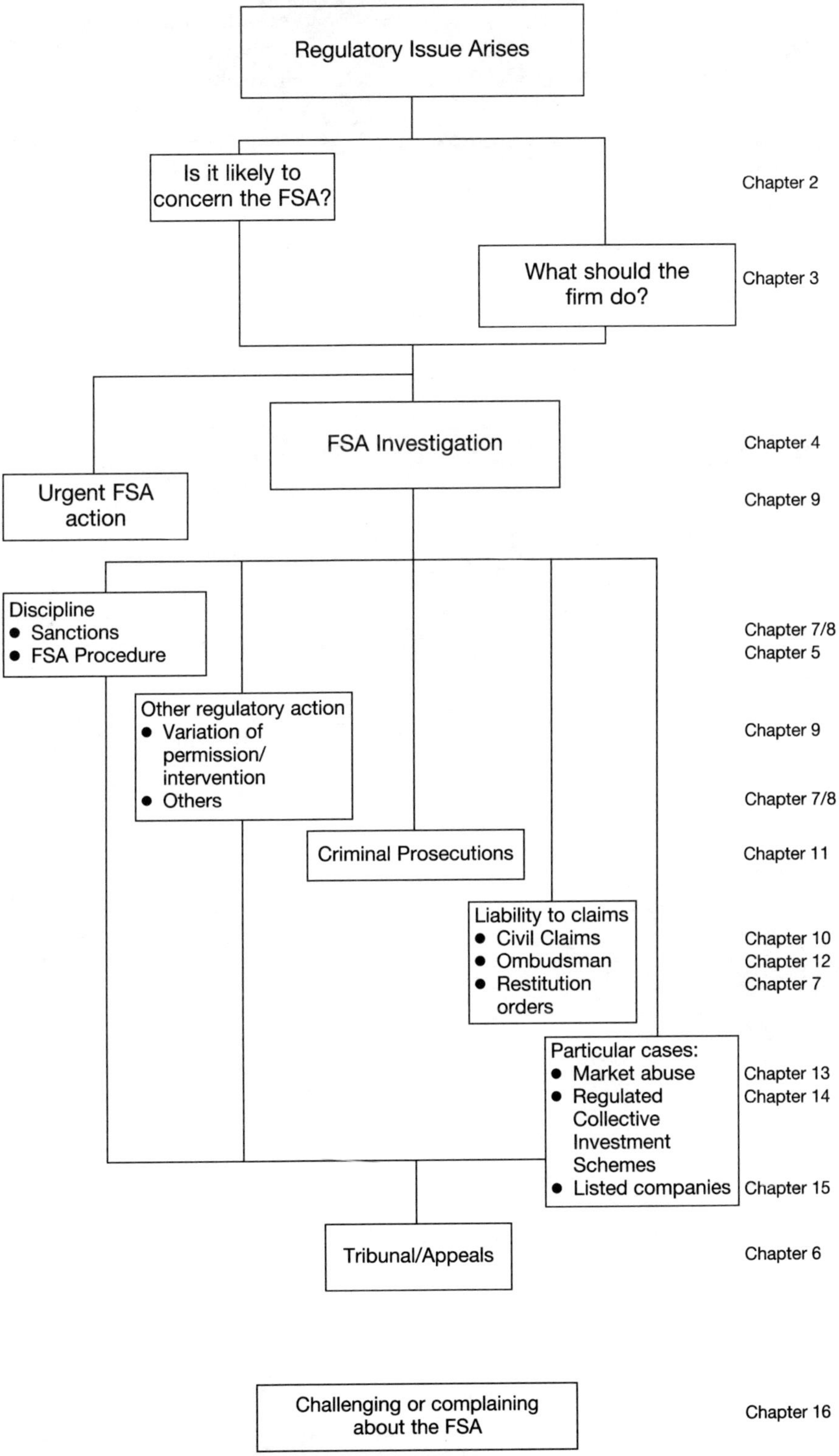
Regulatory Issue Arises
Is it likely to concern the FSA?
Chapter 2
What should the firm do?
Chapter 3
FSA Investigation
Chapter 4
Urgent FSA action
Chapter 9
Discipline
● Sanctions
● FSA Procedure
Chapter 7/8
Chapter 5
Other regulatory action
● Variation of permission/ intervention
● Others
Chapter 9
Chapter 7/8
Criminal Prosecutions
Chapter 11
Liability to claims
● Civil Claims
● Ombudsman
● Restitution orders
Chapter 10
Chapter 12
Chapter 7
Particular cases:
● Market abuse
● Regulated Collective Investment Schemes
● Listed companies
Chapter 13
Chapter 14
Chapter 15
Tribunal/Appeals
Chapter 6
Challenging or complaining about the FSA
Chapter 16

2 Some basic principles of the regime

CONTENTS

Introduction	**11**
An introduction to the regulatory regime	**12**
Conduct giving rise to enforcement	**46**

INTRODUCTION

An overview of Chapter 2

2.1 In this chapter, we provide an introduction to the basic principles and scope of the regime, to set in context the discussion in this book of the FSA's investigation, enforcement and disciplinary powers and the practical issues for firms to consider where possible regulatory breaches come to light.

2.2 A number of issues relating to the scope of the regime are addressed:

- in para 2.3 ff, we provide a brief introduction to the relevant aspects of the regulatory regime, including the basic framework of the regime, the fundamental principles which apply and the FSA's general approach to enforcement issues. This helps to explain the FSA's policy and approach on a particular regulatory issue. Also included (at para 2.106 ff) is an explanation of the FSA Handbook, how it is structured and, particularly, the different types of provision contained in it;
- in para 2.131 ff, we look at the different types of conduct which could amount to a 'regulatory breach' and thus give rise to the enforcement issues

discussed in this book, both conduct by firms (para 2.131 ff) and by individuals (para 2.178 ff).

AN INTRODUCTION TO THE REGULATORY REGIME

Firms to which the regime applies: authorisation and permission

2.3 At the most basic level, there are two types of firms: those that are within the regime and those that are outside it. Firms within the regime are allowed to carry on particular regulated activities and are in principle subject to the range of powers of the FSA under the FSMA 2000 and to the FSA's rules as set out in its Handbook. Firms outside the regime are not allowed to carry on regulated activities (it is a criminal offence for them to do so[1]) and although there are a number of provisions under the FSMA 2000 applicable to such unregulated firms, these are primarily prohibitions with criminal penalties for breach. Such firms are not generally subject to the FSA's rules or to its regulatory powers[2].

1 Note that it is not a criminal offence for an authorised firm to carry on additional activities outside the scope of its regulatory 'permission', although it may be liable to regulatory enforcement action for doing so: see para 2.175 ff below.

2 There are various exceptions where the FSA can exercise its regulatory powers in relation to those who are unregulated. For example, the market abuse regime (see Chapter 13 below) applies to all persons whether or not regulated under the FSMA 2000 and the FSA's powers as UK Listing Authority (see Chapter 15 below) apply to listed companies whether or not they are regulated. Firms which are unregulated can also in some instances become involved in an investigation relating to a regulated firm (see Chapter 4 below). Note also that where the FSMA 2000 contains criminal prohibitions, an unregulated firm could be subject to the FSA's actions as a criminal prosecuting authority (see Chapter 11 below).

2.4 So far as those within the regime are concerned, the FSMA 2000 differentiates in a number of respects between different classes of firms authorised to carry on regulated activities. The key distinction is between those whose authorisation is derived from a permission granted by the FSA under the FSMA 2000[1] and those whose authorisation is derived from the EU Treaties and/or Directives for inwardly passporting firms, as outlined in more detail below. The nature of the authorisation is important because some of the FSA's enforcement powers derive their logic from the authorisation process[2]. In addition, though, some of the substantive FSA rules apply to a lesser extent, and in some cases do not apply at all, to inwardly passporting firms, including some of the rules that relate to enforcement.

1 Or, in some instances, an exemption from authorisation granted by or under the FSMA 2000.

2 Most notably, 'intervention' takes the form of a variation of the firm's permission, so that different provisions are required for inwardly passporting firms that do not have a 'permission': see para 2.7 below and Chapter 9.

2.5 The following section provides a brief introduction to the permission system and the different classifications of firms authorised under the FSMA 2000 are also introduced.

An introduction to the permission system

2.6 The way that firms are brought within the regime is, for most firms, via the permission system. Whilst a detailed analysis of the system for obtaining permissions is beyond the scope of this book[1], a very brief introduction is worthwhile.

1 For a more detailed discussion, see the FSA Handbook at AUTH. For a general explanation, see *Blackstone's Guide to the Financial Services and Markets Act 2000*, Blair, Minghella, Taylor, Threipland & Walker, 2001, Chapters 5 & 6.

2.7 The permission system is found at FSMA 2000, Pt IV. The regime marks a significant change from the old system of obtaining authorisation under the various pieces of legislation applicable to the different types of regulated business. Instead, now that there is a single statute and a single regulator, firms have a single permission covering all of the regulated activities which the firm is permitted to carry on. The permission is tailored specifically to the firm, by means of the FSA's ability to assess specifically what is required for that firm and, first, to give permission for more or less regulated activities than the firm has applied for, second, to describe each regulated activity in the way appropriate to that particular firm and, third, to impose limitations or requirements on the firm's permission. The FSA's primary concern in doing so is to ensure that the firm satisfies, and will continue to satisfy, certain basic criteria known as the threshold conditions[1]. The firm emerges from this process with a single 'Part IV permission' and, as a result, is automatically authorised under the FSMA 2000.

1 The threshold conditions are described in more detail at para 2.38 ff below.

2.8 A Part IV permission is the route for obtaining authorisation for firms incorporated in the UK or in non-EEA overseas jurisdictions. A firm incorporated in another EEA state has the choice of incorporating a UK subsidiary which will obtain a separate authorisation through a Part IV permission or obtaining authorisation through the mechanisms set up in the EU Single Market Directives[1]. There are three EEA bases of obtaining authorisation under the FSMA 2000:

- Schedule 3 allows EEA firms to obtain authorisation to exercise EEA passport rights in the UK;
- Schedule 4 allows EEA firms to obtain authorisation to carry on certain additional types of regulated activities under Treaty Rights; and
- Schedule 5 provides an automatic permission for so-called 'UCITS Qualifiers' which means operators, trustees and depositaries of EEA collective investment schemes which are recognised by the FSA under the FSMA 2000[2], to the extent that, broadly, they carry on activities relating to the scheme.

1 It is not possible for a firm established in another EEA state to apply for authorisation through a Part IV permission, because of the fundamental principle of EU financial services legislation that a firm must have its primary EU regulation in the place where it has its head office: see, for example, the Investment Services Directive, art 3(2) and the Banking Consolidation Directive, art 6(1) and see also threshold condition 2 at para 2.39 below. The Single Market Directives are listed at footnote 1 to para 2.12 below.

2 The recognition of collective investment schemes is described briefly in Chapter 14 below.

2.9 There are further, specific provisions regarding the authorisation of certain specific types of bodies, for example Lloyd's.

2.10 In addition, certain persons are exempt from authorisation under the FSMA 2000. This includes in particular:

- appointed representatives[1] – persons who contract with a firm to carry out certain types of business and for whom the firm takes full responsibility;
- recognised investment exchanges and clearing houses[2];
- members of Lloyd's[3];
- members of professions to the extent that they are regulated by a designated professional body[4]; and
- persons specified in an order made by HM Treasury[5], including various international organisations such as the World Bank, the European Bank for Reconstruction and Development and the European Investment Bank.

1 FSMA 2000, s 39.
2 FSMA 2000, s 285.
3 FSMA 2000, s 316.
4 FSMA 2000, s 327.
5 FSMA 2000, s 38 and see the Financial Services and Markets Act 2000 (Exemption) Order 2001, SI 2001/1201.

Firms primarily regulated outside the UK

2.11 The fact that a firm has its authorisation under Schs 3 or 4, rather than under a Part IV permission, has wider repercussions in terms of how it is treated under the FSMA 2000, including how it is treated in the enforcement context. It is therefore important to understand the reasons why there are these different bases of authorisation.

Passport rights

2.12 Under the various Single Market Directives[1], a firm which is authorised in one EEA state has a 'passport' which allows it to carry on certain regulated activities prescribed in the Directives anywhere in the EEA, to the extent that it is authorised to carry on those activities in its home state. Such a firm authorised outside the UK has the right under EU law either to establish a branch in the UK to carry on in the UK the business covered by its passport or to carry on that business cross-border into the UK. To the extent that it wants to do this the firm does not need to apply for a Part IV permission under the FSMA 2000. The policy reason for this is that the firm has undergone a process of authorisation in its home state, based on the fulfilment of certain basic prudential requirements, the minimum standards for which are laid down in the Directives, and which are the responsibility of the firm's home state regulator, not the FSA, to police. Instead, it obtains authorisation under the much simpler procedure set out in FSMA 2000, Sch 3[2], which essentially involves a series of notifications. To the extent that the firm carries on regulated activities under a Schedule 3 authorisation, the firm is referred to in the FSMA 2000 as an 'EEA firm'.

1 The Banking Consolidation Directive (2000/12/EC), the Insurance Directives (79/267/EEC, 90/619/EEC, 92/96/EEC (life) and 73/240/EEC, 88/357/EEC and 92/49/EEC (non-life)) and the Investment Services Directive (93/22/EEC).

2 See also the Financial Services and Markets Act 2000 (EEA Passport Rights) Regulations 2001, SI 2001/1376.

Treaty rights

2.13 The Single Market Directives only, however, give firms passport rights in relation to certain types of regulated activities. The firm may want to carry on in the UK different or additional activities for which it is also authorised in its home state. Although it has no automatic right to carry on those activities under its passport, provided that the relevant provisions of the firm's home state satisfy certain criteria[1], the firm can obtain authorisation to carry on those activities under FSMA 2000, Sch 4. Again, this is a much simpler process than applying for a Part IV permission. To the extent that the firm carries on regulated activities under a Schedule 4 authorisation, the firm is referred to in the FSMA 2000 as a 'Treaty firm'.

1 They must either satisfy specific conditions applied at EEA level or be recognised by the UK as affording at least equivalent protection to consumers as that afforded to consumers under the FSMA 2000 in relation to the same activity: see FSMA 2000, Sch 4.

Top-up permissions

2.14 Finally, the firm may wish to carry on in the UK further regulated activities in relation to which neither Sch 3 nor Sch 4 apply[1]. This could be because the activities are outside the EEA passporting regime but within the scope of the regulated activities which require authorisation in the UK. An example would be trading commodity derivatives in the UK. To that extent, the firm must obtain a Part IV permission and fulfil the normal criteria[2]. This is known as an 'additional permission' or a 'top up permission'.

1 This could also apply in relation to a firm with a Schedule 5 permission: see para 2.8 above.

2 These are described briefly at para 2.38 below.

Terminology

2.15 Against that background, the following terminology is adopted in this book:

- ***Firms*** refers to all firms whatever the nature of their permission;
- ***UK regulated firms*** refers to firms with a Part IV permission and includes EEA and Treaty firms to the extent that the relevant activity is one the subject of a top-up permission; and
- ***Incoming firms*** refers collectively to both EEA firms and Treaty firms, to the extent that the relevant activity is one covered by their Sch 3 or Sch 4 authorisation.

Individuals working for firms

2.16 In addition to the authorisation regime applicable to firms carrying on regulated activities, the FSMA 2000 introduces, for the first time, a statutory regime for the approval of individuals working for authorised firms[1]. The system of individual approval is backed by its own enforcement and disciplinary powers and a separate body of requirements applicable to approved individuals. This is discussed in detail at para 2.63 ff below.

1 Previously, certain individuals were registered with the SROs and were subject to the regulatory regime.

Legal and policy framework of the FSA's regulatory functions

2.17 The fundamental objectives and principles governing the FSA's discharge of its functions are found in the FSMA 2000 itself. These are explained and amplified by policy objectives and the explanations set out in the FSA Handbook. Since these fundamental objectives and principles are key to understanding the FSA's approach, they are briefly described here.

2.18 This involves looking at three issues:

- the 'regulatory objectives' and 'principles of good regulation' which the FSMA 2000 requires the FSA to apply;
- the range of tools available to the FSA to fulfil those objectives and comply with those principles; and
- the FSA's general approach to enforcement.

The FSA's regulatory objectives and principles of good regulation

2.19 The FSMA 2000 prescribes a set of 'regulatory objectives' and a set of 'principles of good regulation'[1] and requires the FSA in, among other things, determining its policy, making rules and issuing guidance, to act so far as reasonably possible in a way which is compatible with, and which the FSA considers most appropriate for the purpose of meeting, the regulatory objectives[2], and to have regard to the principles of good regulation[3].

1 This is what the FSA calls the second set of obligations, but there is no label given to them in the FSMA 2000.
2 FSMA 2000, s 2(1).
3 FSMA 2000, s 2(3).

The regulatory objectives

2.20 The four regulatory objectives[1] are:

- maintaining confidence in the UK financial system[2]. The FSA regards this as including preserving both stability and the expectation that the financial system will remain stable. This does not preclude firms from failing but requires the FSA to seek to minimise the impact of failures upon market confidence;

- promoting public understanding of the financial system[3], including promoting awareness of the benefits and risks associated with different kinds of investment or other financial dealing and the provision of appropriate information or advice[4];
- securing appropriate protection for consumers[5]. This does not mean protecting consumers from the volatility inherent in investing on financial markets (the FSMA 2000 says there is a general principle that consumers should take responsibility for their decisions), but means protecting them from risks such as the collapse of a firm, fraud, bad faith or mis-selling and of buying products or services which are too complex or unsuitable; and
- reducing the extent to which it is possible for financial services to be used for a purpose connected with financial crime[6], for example, money laundering, fraud or dishonesty or criminal market misconduct. This includes making the regulated community aware of the risk of their business being used for these purposes, as well as ensuring they take appropriate measures and devote adequate resources to the prevention, detection and monitoring of financial crime.

1 For a detailed explanation of how the FSA interprets these objectives, see 'A new regulator for the new millennium', January 2000 and 'Building the new regulator: progress report 1', December 2000. The following is a summary of the relevant provisions of the FSMA 2000 and those policy papers.
2 This is amplified by FSMA 2000, s 3.
3 This is amplified by FSMA 2000, s 4.
4 The implementation of this objective can be seen in the increasing number of press releases from the FSA warning of the risks of particular practices. Examples include 'Be wary of exotic ISAs warns Watchdog' (March 2001), 'The FSA launches new "shop around" website for consumers' (December 2000), 'Take care of your money and avoid the cowboys – with these top tips from the FSA' (July 2000).
5 This is amplified by the FSMA 2000, s 5. 'Consumers' has a broad definition under the FSMA 2000, s 138.
6 This is amplified by the FSMA 2000, s 6. 'Financial crime' includes fraud or dishonesty, misconduct or misuse of information relating to a financial market or handling the proceeds of crime.

The principles of good regulation

2.21 The seven principles of good regulation can be summarised as follows[1]:

- efficiency and economy in the allocation and deployment of resources;
- the responsibilities of those who manage the affairs of firms;
- proportionality – that a burden or restriction imposed on firms and markets should be proportionate to the benefits expected to result;
- facilitating innovation;
- the international character of financial services and markets and desirability of maintaining the competitive position of the UK;

- the need to minimise impeding or distorting competition; and
- the desirability of facilitating competition between firms.

1 FSMA 2000, s 2(3), and see 'A new regulator for the new millennium', January 2000.

Applying the regulatory objectives and principles of good regulation

2.22 The regulatory objectives and principles of good regulation are relevant considerations when the FSA formulates, broadly, rules, codes, policy and guidance. The FSMA 2000 does not specifically require the FSA to take such factors into account every time it exercises one of its powers. They are, on the face of it, thus relevant indirectly, rather than directly, to the FSA's decision on how to act in a particular situation.

2.23 Nonetheless, the requirements of proportionality and efficiency/economy may be viewed by firms as a useful tool in dealing with what are perceived to be unreasonable or disproportionate actions by the FSA. The question whether they can be used as a basis for challenging the exercise of a particular power in a particular case is therefore likely to be tested in the Tribunal and the courts. In a number of instances[1], the FSA Handbook contemplates efficiency/economy and proportionality being relevant to the FSA's decision on how to act in a particular case. It may be that this is because, in making its policy on how it acts in particular cases, the FSA has to have regard to the need for proportionality; hence, proportionality becomes applicable to particular cases through the side door.

1 See, for example, the FSA Handbook at ENF 3.5.2, 3.5.13(9) and 6.6.2(6). In addition, proportionality falls within the three basic principles underlying the FSA's approach to its enforcement powers: see para 2.36 below.

2.24 In any event, the principles for good regulation are recurrent themes in FSA policy and understanding them helps to explain the FSA's approach to enforcement and discipline.

The FSA's regulatory toolkit

2.25 Enforcement and discipline are not the FSA's only means of achieving its regulatory objectives. The FSMA 2000 and the FSA Handbook give the FSA a broad range of powers and functions to enable it to do so. The FSA refers to these as its 'regulatory toolkit'[1]. Understanding briefly what these are helps to place the enforcement and discipline regime into perspective. As part of this, it is helpful to look briefly at the FSA's general approach to supervision.

1 For a more detailed discussion of the tools available and the way in which the FSA uses them, see 'A new regulator for the new millennium', January 2000 and 'Building the new regulator: progress report 1', December 2000.

2.26 The FSA's tools are wide-ranging in their nature and effect. Some allow the FSA to influence the industry as a whole[1]; others are designed to influence the behaviour of consumers in general[2]. The protection of consumers is a recurrent theme as well as one of the FSA's prescribed regulatory objectives. Five of the eleven Principles for Businesses[3] relate specifically to how firms deal with their non-market counterparty customers[4]. Another important part of the regime is the public register which the FSA is required to keep[5], of those who are, broadly, authorised or recognised under the FSMA 2000, approved persons[6] and those against whom a prohibition order has been made[7]. Consumers and others should therefore readily be able to ascertain whether they are dealing with someone who is entitled to carry on regulated activities.

1 For example, the training and competence regime, the ability to make rules, market monitoring, sector wide projects (for example the pensions review, the Y2K work and the work carried out on particular 'themes', such as e-commerce, money laundering, the treatment of retail customers after the point of sale and the implications of a low inflation environment) and the FSA's liaison with overseas regulators.
2 For example, consumer education, ensuring proper disclosure to consumers, complaints handling mechanisms, the ombudsman service, the compensation scheme, the issuing of public statements by the FSA to try to influence the behaviour of consumers and firms, and product approval processes.
3 The Principles for Businesses are described at para 2.51 below.
4 The practical importance for firms of keeping consumers in mind when dealing with a particular regulatory issue is discussed at para 3.110 ff below.
5 FSMA 2000, s 347.
6 Approved persons are those individuals who are approved by the FSA: see para 2.16 above and para 2.63 ff below.
7 For a discussion of prohibition orders, see Chapter 8 below.

2.27 The FSA does have a group of regulatory tools designed to influence the behaviour of individual firms. These include authorisation, the policing of the perimeter, the supervision of firms and the ability to impose conditions and restrictions on a firm's permission[1], as well as investigation, enforcement and discipline. The ability to vet firms and individuals at entry is seen as a particularly important tool, broadly on the basis that 'prevention is better than cure'. In practice, the FSA also addresses compliance issues without resort to enforcement by making its concerns clear to firms and issuing private warnings[2].

1 This refers to the 'own initiative' power (replacing what was formerly known as intervention), described more fully in Chapter 9 below.
2 See para 7.18 ff below.

2.28 Investigation, enforcement and discipline is therefore only a part, albeit an important part, of the overall armoury available to the FSA for ensuring regulatory compliance and, more broadly, the fulfilment of its regulatory objectives. This broader context is relevant when considering how the FSA is likely to react in a particular situation.

The FSA's approach to supervision

2.29 Supervision has traditionally been one of the most important planks of the regulatory system and, on a day-to-day basis, it is the FSA's supervisory role which is most visible to firms. The regime involves a new approach to supervision and one which is tailored to the firm and, as will be seen, is potentially sensitive to disciplinary and enforcement issues arising in relation to the firm. In addition, the FSA's approach to supervision has an impact on its policy on enforcement.

For these reasons, a brief explanation of the policy on supervision needs to be given[1].

1 For a detailed explanation, see the FSA Handbook at SUP 1 and see also 'A new regulator for the new millennium', January 2000 and 'Building the new regulator: progress report 1', December 2000.

2.30 The FSA adopts a risk based approach to supervision. This involves every firm being given an individual risk assessment, based on two main criteria[1]. The first is the likely impact if a regulatory risk[2] materialised[3]. The second is the probability of a regulatory risk occurring. In assessing this latter criterion, the FSA looks at factors such as the firm's strategy, the risks inherent in its business (for example, credit, market and operational risks), its financial soundness, the nature of its customers and the products and services it offers, its internal systems and controls and compliance culture and its internal organisation[4].

1 This is a development of the so-called 'RATE' (Risk Assessment Tools of Supervision and Evaluation) approach developed by the Bank of England in the period leading up to the transfer of its regulatory functions to the FSA. See also Pillar II (Supervisory Review Process) of the Basle Capital Accord.
2 This means a risk to the FSA's statutory objectives. The FSA has identified 15 such risks: see 'Building the new regulator: progress report 1', December 2000, Chapter 1.
3 As to factors which the FSA says will be relevant, see the FSA Handbook at SUP 1.3.3. Only around 1% of firms fall with the 'high' impact category, but they have a combined market share of 64%: 'Building the new regulator: progress report 1', December 2000.
4 See the FSA Handbook at SUP 1.3.4.

2.31 Based on this analysis, the FSA classifies the firm, giving an overall judgement as to the firm's priority for the FSA and the nature of the relationship which the FSA will seek to have with the firm[1]. The intensity of its supervisory effort thus depends on the classification[2]. At one end of the range are low impact firms, which the FSA supervises less closely. Routine monitoring visits will largely be replaced by sample visits to monitor general compliance standards in a sector, visits as part of sectoral reviews or cross-FSA thematic work, as well as visits to deal with specific issues. At the other end of the range are high impact firms. The FSA takes a rather different approach to high impact firms. It expects to maintain a close and continuous relationship with them in order to develop and sustain a detailed knowledge of current and potential risk areas in the firm.

1 See the FSA Handbook at SUP 1.3.5.
2 See 'Building the new regulator: progress report 1', December 2000, paras 56 and 62.

2.32 It should be immediately apparent from this that if a serious problem does arise which is not handled properly by the firm, or which exposes significant issues relating to its internal organisation, its systems and controls or its compliance culture, or which leads to serious enforcement action being taken against it, this could affect the FSA's assessment of the risk profile of the firm and therefore affect how it is supervised[1].

1 'Where significant problems arise in an institution, this is likely to lead to a more intensive relationship with the FSA until the issue is resolved to the FSA's satisfaction': 'Building the new regulator: progress report 1', December 2000, para 58.

2.33 A further point to note is that the FSA's approach to supervision relies partly upon its expectations as to how firms will address problems which arise. The principles of good regulation[1] require the FSA to have regard to the role of management in firms and to the need for the FSA to use its resources efficiently and economically. As a result, there is an increased emphasis on the role of management and the FSA expects management, first, to ensure that the firm acts in compliance with the regulatory requirements and, second, if a problem does arise, to take appropriate steps to remedy the problem and deal fairly with any consumers who have been disadvantaged as a result[2]. It would be reasonable to assume that the corollary will be an increased use of enforcement and disciplinary action where the firm or its management are not seen to respond appropriately[3].

1 See para 2.21 above.
2 The issue of how firms should respond when problems arise is discussed in more detail in Chapter 3.
3 'We will aim to give institutions a greater incentive to behave in ways which reduce their regulatory burden. For example, an institution which takes prompt and effective remedial action as necessary following a discussion with the FSA of its risk assessment will – all other things being equal – see a reduction in the intensity of its regulatory relationship': 'Building the new regulator: progress report 1', December 2000, para 62.

The FSA's general approach to enforcement[1]

2.34 As has been outlined above, enforcement is only one of a range of tools available to the FSA. In many instances it may be possible to address regulatory non-compliance without recourse to disciplinary or other enforcement action[2]. Thus, it may be appropriate, particularly where the contravention is minor or the firm has immediately and fully remedied it, for the FSA to issue a private warning[3] or, in some situations, not to take even that step. The FSA will also need to consider whether the situation requires the exercise of any of its investigative powers and, again, this will depend upon the circumstances and, particularly, whether the firm is fully investigating the problem itself and providing the appropriate information voluntarily to the FSA[4]. It is therefore important that the firm responds, and is seen to respond, appropriately when an actual or possible regulatory breach arises[5].

1 See the FSA Handbook at ENF chapters 1.3 and 11.
2 See the FSA Handbook at ENF 11.2.1.
3 See the FSA Handbook at ENF 11.3 and para 7.18 ff below. Of the approximately 260 enforcement cases concluded in the year to 31 March 2001 in relation to investment business firms regulated by the FSA's predecessors, approximately 60% resulted in no action or in an informal warning: see the FSA's Annual Report 2000/2001. A very similar pattern can also be seen in the previous year.
4 A detailed discussion of FSA policy in exercising its investigative powers appears in Chapter 4 and its policy in deciding whether the imposition of disciplinary sanctions or other enforcement action is appropriate in Chapter 7.
5 As to what this involves, see Chapter 3 below.

2.35 Clearly, some situations are so serious that a full regulatory investigation must take place, followed by, if appropriate, disciplinary and perhaps other enforcement action. Even short of this, though, firms should expect the imposition of enforcement and discipline to be a regular feature of the regime. The FSA views this as an important aspect of its toolkit. Apart from punishing the firm, the imposition of sanctions, which will normally be made public, sends important messages to the market more widely. As well as the obvious deterrent effect, there are considerations of maintaining market confidence, promoting public awareness of regulatory standards, showing that regulatory standards are being upheld, protecting consumers and deterring financial crime[1].

1 See the FSA Handbook at ENF 1.2.1 and 11.2.1.

2.36 Three principles underlie the FSA's approach to its enforcement powers[1]:

- that the effectiveness of the regulatory regime depends to a significant extent on maintaining an open and co-operative relationship between the FSA and firms. This is reflected in Principle 11[2] and reinforces the need for firms to deal properly with the FSA when regulatory problems arise, as discussed in more detail in Chapter 3;
- that the FSA will seek to exercise its enforcement powers in a manner that is transparent, proportionate and consistent with its publicly stated policies[3]. The FSA has wide powers of action and its policy often says little about how those powers will be exercised in practice. This general statement of policy is thus of real importance;
- that the FSA will seek to ensure fair treatment when exercising its enforcement powers. This reflects the FSA's legal duties, but is nonetheless important as a general statement of policy, particularly in areas where there are no prescribed procedures or obvious safeguards, for example the use of the FSA's investigation powers[4].

1 See the FSA Handbook at ENF 1.3.1.
2 Principle 11 of the Principles for Businesses: see para 2.51 below.
3 Proportionality in this context is a separate issue from the requirement under the FSMA 2000 for the FSA to have regard to the principle of proportionality when making its rules and policies: see para 2.21 above.
4 See Chapter 4.

The fundamental requirements applicable to firms

2.37 The regulatory regime involves certain fundamental conditions and broad principles applicable to firms on an ongoing basis[1]. These conditions and principles underlie and permeate every aspect of the regulatory structure. They are directly relevant to some of the enforcement and discipline issues discussed and, more generally, are important in understanding how the enforcement regime works.

1 As set out in more detail below, some of these requirements do not apply to incoming firms that do not have a top-up permission.

The threshold conditions

2.38 The conditions referred to above are the 'threshold conditions' prescribed in FSMA 2000, Sch 6[1]. The FSA is required, when giving or varying a firm's Part IV permission (or imposing or varying conditions or requirements applied to its permission[2]), to ensure that the firm will satisfy, and continue to satisfy, the threshold conditions in relation to all of the regulated activities for which the firm has, or will have, permission[3]. The FSA thus has to ensure that the firm not only complies with these conditions at the outset but that it will continue to comply with them.

1 See also the Financial Services and Markets Act 2000 (Variation of Threshold Conditions) Order 2001, SI 2001/2507.
2 See further in Chapter 9.
3 FSMA 2000, s 41(2).

2.39 The threshold conditions can be summarised as follows[1]:

- ***Threshold condition 1 – Legal status:*** where a firm is carrying on insurance or deposit-taking, it is required to have a specified legal status;
- ***Threshold condition 2 – Location of offices:*** a UK incorporated firm must have both its head office and its registered office in the UK or, if it is not incorporated but has its head office in the UK, must carry on business here[2];
- ***Threshold condition 3 – Close links:*** if the firm has 'close links' (as defined) with another person, then the FSA must be satisfied that those links are not likely to prevent the FSA's effective supervision of the firm and that, if the firm is subject to the laws and regulations of a non-EEA state, neither those overseas provisions nor any deficiency in their enforcement would prevent the FSA's effective supervision of the firm[3];
- ***Threshold condition 4 – Adequate resources:*** the resources of the firm must be adequate in relation to the regulated activities it seeks to carry on;
- ***Threshold condition 5 – Suitability:*** the firm must satisfy the FSA that it is a fit and proper person having regard to all the circumstances, including its connection with any person, the nature of any regulated activity it seeks to carry on and the need to ensure its affairs are conducted soundly and prudently. This is the most important threshold condition for the purposes of this book and is discussed in more detail below[4].

1 What follows is a brief summary of the threshold conditions and the FSA's guidance on their meaning and how they will be applied. For a more detailed explanation, see FSMA 2000, s 41 and Sch 6, and the FSA Handbook at COND. Note also that HM Treasury may specify additional threshold conditions for non-EEA based insurance businesses: FSMA 2000, Sch 6, para 8. See also the Financial Services and Markets Act 2000 (Variation of Threshold Conditions) Order 2001, SI 2001/2507.
2 See para 2.9 above.
3 In broad terms, the FSA is concerned to ensure it will receive the information it needs to supervise the firm, to determine whether the firm is compliant and to identify and assess the risks it poses.
4 See para 2.41 ff below.

To whom and what do the threshold conditions apply?

2.40 The threshold conditions relate to all firms that apply for and have a Part IV permission. They apply to all of such a firm's regulated activities wherever they are conducted[1]. So far as incoming firms are concerned, only threshold conditions 1, 3, 4 and 5 apply and they only apply to the extent that the firm applies for, or has, a top-up permission[2].

1 See the FSA Handbook at COND 1.1.3.
2 See the FSA Handbook at COND 1.1.1. For a more detailed explanation of the inclusion of EEA and Treaty firms within the UK regulatory regime, and of top-up permissions, see para 2.11 ff above.

How are the threshold conditions relevant to enforcement?

2.41 The threshold conditions are, in the enforcement context, directly relevant to the FSA's variation of permission or intervention powers[1]. They may also be relevant to the FSA's other enforcement powers[2].

1 See Chapter 9 below.
2 See Chapter 7 below.

2.42 As to which threshold conditions are likely to be relevant, threshold condition 3 could be relevant if, for example, a particular regulatory issue which arises, or the manner in which the firm deals with one, suggests that its close links are impeding the FSA's effective supervision of it. Threshold condition 4 could also be relevant, for example if the losses sustained by the firm, or its customers, arising from a particular regulatory issue cast doubt on the adequacy of its financial resources. These will, however, be comparatively rare situations. It is threshold condition 5 – suitability: the question whether a firm is fit and proper to be carrying on its regulated activities – that is most relevant to enforcement. The question whether the firm is fit and proper can arise in many situations, for example one that highlights issues about the firm's systems and controls, the supervision or training of staff, or about the firm's response to a regulatory problem. We therefore review this in detail below.

How does the FSA assess whether a firm is fit and proper?

2.43 What does 'fit and proper' mean? The first point to bear in mind is that we are dealing here only with the question whether the *firm* is fit and proper. The question whether particular individuals working for the firm are fit and proper is considered according to a different set of criteria[1].

1 See para 2.69 ff below.

2.44 Considering whether a firm is fit and proper is an assessment personal to the firm, done on a case-by-case basis, and involves looking at all relevant matters, whether arising in the UK or elsewhere[1]. Three broad considerations are highlighted:

- whether the firm conducts, or will conduct, its business with integrity and in compliance with proper standards;

- whether the firm has, or will have, a competent and prudent management; and
- whether the firm can demonstrate that it conducts, or will conduct, its affairs with the exercise of due skill, care and diligence.

1 See the FSA Handbook at COND 2.5.3 to 2.5.5 generally.

2.45 The meaning of each is outlined below. There is a substantial overlap with the FSA's Principles for Businesses[1], which are said to comprise the main dimensions of the 'fit and proper' test and therefore also need to be borne in mind.

1 These are discussed at para 2.51 below.

2.46 ***Conducting business with integrity in compliance with proper standards*** The question whether a firm conducts its business with integrity does not require a great deal of explanation. The FSA has identified various matters that may be relevant to integrity and proper standards, which can be summarised very broadly as follows[1]:

- being open and co-operative with the FSA and other applicable regulators and ready, willing and organised to be compliant;
- convictions for offences involving fraud or other dishonesty or financial offences such as money laundering, market abuse or insider dealing;
- previous regulatory breaches, or previous investigations or enforcement proceedings by the FSA or other regulators;
- refusals to grant, or the revocation of, relevant authorisations or licences;
- the establishment and maintenance of proper systems and controls;
- procedures to ensure employees are aware of and compliant with applicable regulatory requirements and standards and to determine they are acting properly; and
- dismissals from employments or positions of trust and disqualifications as a director.

1 For the full list, see the FSA Handbook at COND 2.5.6.

2.47 ***Competent and prudent management and exercising due skill, care and diligence*** The FSA has identified various matters that may be relevant under these heads. These include[1]:

- a governing body composed of individuals with an appropriate range of skills and experience and organised appropriately;
- approved persons acting with due skill, care and diligence in performing their 'controlled functions'[2] or managing the business for which they are responsible;

2.47 Some basic principles of the regime

- adequate systems of internal control;
- prudent control of financial and other risks;
- human resources policies and procedures to ensure the firm employs only persons who are honest and committed to high standards of integrity;
- that the firm has conducted enquiries to give it reasonable assurance that it will not pose unacceptable risks to consumers or the financial systems;
- appropriate money laundering prevention systems and training; and
- appropriate auditors and actuaries with sufficient experience.

1 For a full list, see the FSA Handbook at COND 2.5.7.
2 For a brief explanation of the approval of individuals who perform controlled functions, see para 2.64 below.

2.48 ***What does this mean in practice?*** Various points are evident from these lists of relevant matters. First, the issue of suitability is a broad one, taking into account not only the firm's standards of organisation, but also its compliance culture and its standards of integrity and those of the people it employs. The FSA will take into consideration anything that could influence a firm's continued ability to satisfy the suitability threshold condition[1]. Therefore, in considering whether a particular problem gives rise to issues about whether the firm is fit and proper, the firm needs not only to consider the specific matters outlined, but also to keep in mind the broad test.

1 See the FSA Handbook at COND 2.5.2(2).

2.49 Second, once systems and controls, and even human resources procedures, are taken into account, unless the particular breach is minor or perhaps a specific breach of a technical requirement which the firm's systems were able to, and did, pick up, most regulatory problems could in some way be framed or viewed as bearing on whether the firm is fit and proper. That is not, of course, to say that the particular concerns would be sufficient to lead to a finding that the firm is not fit and proper: that is rare. However, these lists of relevant factors give an indication of those matters which are potentially of interest to the FSA generally. Many of the same matters may, for example, be relevant to whether there has been any breach of the Principles for Businesses[1]. For this reason, the factors outlined above should be treated as sign-posts to the issues which are likely to concern the FSA. They recur as a theme throughout the enforcement regime.

1 See para 2.51 ff below.

2.50 Third, in general terms, if there is a concern that a particular issue impacts on whether the firm is fit and proper then the problem may well be one that the FSA would regard as serious. It needs to be properly handled and the firm's response may well come under scrutiny. Indeed, how the firm responds is itself relevant to whether it is fit and proper[1].

1 As to how the firm should respond, see Chapter 3 below. If the FSA is not already aware of the matter then the firm may be obliged to report it: see para 3.41 ff below.

The Principles for Businesses[1]

2.51 The second set of fundamental requirements applicable to firms are the so-called Principles for Businesses. They differ from the threshold conditions in that instead of being conditions laid down by the FSMA 2000 they are high-level rules made by the FSA[2]. The FSA describes the Principles as a general statement of the fundamental obligations of authorised firms under the regulatory system[3]. Although not linked to the threshold conditions in legal terms, the FSA regards the Principles as expressing, among other things, the main dimensions of the 'fit and proper' standard of threshold condition 5[4] and they clearly also overlap with threshold condition 4[5]. Being able and willing to abide by the Principles is therefore a critical factor in applications for authorisation and breaking them may call into question whether a firm already authorised is still fit and proper[6].

1 Generally, see the FSA Handbook at PRIN.
2 Primarily under FSMA 2000, s 138: see the FSA Handbook at PRIN, Schedule 4.
3 See the FSA Handbook at PRIN 1.1.2.
4 See the FSA Handbook at PRIN 1.1.4.
5 For a discussion of the threshold conditions, see para 2.38 above.
6 See the FSA Handbook at PRIN 1.1.4.

The Principles

2.52 With that brief introduction, the Principles are as follows:

- Principle 1: A firm must conduct its business with integrity.
- Principle 2: A firm must conduct its business with due skill, care and diligence.
- Principle 3: A firm must take reasonable care to organise and control its affairs responsibly and effectively, with adequate risk management systems.
- Principle 4: A firm must maintain adequate financial resources.
- Principle 5: A firm must observe proper standards of market conduct.
- Principle 6: A firm must pay due regard to the interests of its customers and treat them fairly.
- Principle 7: A firm must pay due regard to the information needs of its clients, and communicate information to them in a way which is clear, fair and not misleading.
- Principle 8: A firm must manage conflicts of interest fairly, both between itself and its customers and between a customer and another client.
- Principle 9: A firm must take reasonable care to ensure the suitability of its advice and discretionary decisions for any customer who is entitled to rely upon its judgment.
- Principle 10: A firm must arrange adequate protection for clients' assets when it is responsible for them.
- Principle 11: A firm must deal with its regulators in an open and co-operative way, and must disclose to the FSA appropriately anything relating to the firm of which the FSA would reasonably expect notice[1].

1 Principle 11 is directly relevant to how a firm must respond when a regulatory problem arises. There are two components: notification of matters to the FSA (discussed in detail at para 3.41 ff below) and co-operation with the FSA (discussed in detail at para 4.27 ff below).

How are the Principles applied?

2.53 The Principles are binding rules made by the FSA and firms must comply with them. They are, however, expressed in very broad terms and no detailed explanation of what each involves accompanies them. This is deliberate. Although the regulatory regime involves a large volume of detailed rules and guidance applicable to particular aspects of firms' businesses, complying with all the specific requirements is not necessarily sufficient. The Principles sit above the detailed rules[1]. Because of their generality, they also cover new or unforeseen situations and those where there is no need for guidance. This is seen as an important aspect of regulation. It recognises that the market moves more quickly than the regulator and allows the FSA to let firms develop new products and markets, knowing that the regulatory regime is sufficiently adaptable to apply to them. It also means that the rulebook does not have to address every issue in every area of business[2].

1 They are, however, often interrelated with the detailed rules. Many of the FSA's Conduct of Business rules are expressly linked to one or more of the Principles: see, for example, the FSA Handbook at COB 2.5.2, 6.1.3 and 7.8.2. In addition, for example, there is an overlap between Principle 3 and the FSA Handbook at SYSC (Senior management systems and controls), between Principle 4 and the FSA Handbook at IPRU (the Interim Prudential Sourcebook) and between Principle 5 and the Code of Market Conduct (see Chapter 13 below).

2 The Principles for Businesses are the successors of the Principles made by the Securities and Investments Board under the Financial Services Act 1986, s 47A. Section 47A was introduced by the Companies Act 1989 in response to widespread industry complaint that the rule-making policy adopted under the 1986 Act had resulted in an excessively lengthy and detailed rule book. The Principles made under s 47A formed a new category of rules, breach of which, though giving rise to disciplinary sanctions, did not in itself give rise to civil liability under the Act. That distinction continues to apply: see para 10.31 below.

2.54 For these reasons, the Principles are commonly used as the basis for investigating firms or taking enforcement action against them. This became an unpopular aspect of the former regime[1] because in some situations it meant that a firm could be disciplined even where it could show that it had technically complied with a particular rule or where there was no particular rule prohibiting its conduct. Breach of the Principles was also sometimes used as an additional basis for enforcement action even where there was a clear breach of a particular rule, sometimes worsening the appearance of the firm's conduct.

1 This point was frequently made during the passage of the Financial Services and Markets Bill through Parliament.

2.55 The FSA has stated[1] that in determining whether a Principle has been breached it is necessary to look at the standard of conduct required by the Principle in question, and that under each of the Principles the onus will be on the FSA to show that the firm was at fault in some way. For example, Principles 3 and 9 require the taking of reasonable care, Principles 6 and 7 refer to paying due regard: hence, the FSA would have to show that the firm had failed to take reasonable care, pay due regard, and so on. It is certainly the case that each of the Principles contains a standard which connotes that regard must be had to the particular circumstances. However, firms will recognise that many of the concepts are so broadly drawn that there is a risk of compliance being more easily judged with the benefit of hindsight[2].

1 See the FSA Handbook at PRIN 1.1.7.
2 The use of the Principles as the basis for enforcement action under the new regime is discussed in more detail at para 2.156 below. Note that breach of the Principles does not give rise to a right of action for private individuals under FSMA 2000, s 150: see the FSA Handbook at PRIN 3.4.4.

2.56 Firms need to have the Principles squarely in mind in considering how to act when a regulatory problem arises. For example:

- the firm's obligations under Principles 6, 7 and 8 may require it to consider its customers[1];
- the firm may be required, under Principle 11, to notify the FSA[2];
- the firm must, under Principle 11, co-operate with the FSA[3]; and
- the firm's obligations under Principle 3 may require it to consider the position of any employees involved and the implications for its systems and controls[4].

1 This is discussed in more detail at para 3.110 ff below.
2 This is discussed in more detail at para 3.41 ff below.
3 This is discussed in more detail at para 4.27 ff below.
4 This is discussed in more detail at para 3.128 ff below.

Obligations to clients and customers

2.57 Principles 6–10 impose requirements on firms in relation to their clients or customers. The extent of the obligation varies according to the particular circumstances including the nature of the client concerned. There are two reasons for this. First, what constitutes, for example, 'due regard' or 'fairly', depends upon the precise situation in the particular case, including the nature of the client[1]. One example which the FSA has given is that the information needs of a general insurance broker will be different from those of a retail general insurance policyholder. Second, Principles 6, 8 and 9[2] refer to customers, rather than clients. Customers, in this context, means clients who are not market counterparties[3].

1 See the FSA Handbook at PRIN 1.2.1.
2 The same point is to some extent true of Principle 7. The only requirement of Principle 7 relating to market counterparties is that a firm must communicate information in a way that is not misleading: see the FSA Handbook at PRIN 3.4.1.
3 See the FSA Handbook at PRIN 1.2.2. For an explanation of the classification of customers, see the FSA Handbook at COB 4.1.

2.58 The FSA thus makes a clear distinction between different types of clients and imposes lesser obligations on firms when dealing with market counterparties. This is a general feature of the regulatory system[1].

1 See, for example, the Conduct of Business Sourcebook and the Inter-Professionals Code.

To whom and to what types of business do the Principles apply?

2.59 The Principles apply to a different extent to UK regulated firms, other group members of UK regulated firms and incoming firms[1].

1 For an explanation of UK-regulated firms and incoming firms, see paras 2.8 to 2.15 above.

2.60 ***UK regulated firms*** UK regulated firms are subject to the Principles in relation to the conduct of their regulated activities[1] in the UK and, in certain respects, beyond the UK[2]. In addition:

- Principles 3 and 4 also apply to the firm's unregulated activities[3];
- Principle 11 applies with respect to activities wherever they are carried on[4] and, in addition, it applies, so far as it relates to informing the FSA, with respect to the firm's unregulated activities[5]. Therefore, it seems that the firm's obligation to the FSA to deal with regulators in an open and co-operative way includes other regulators with recognised jurisdiction whether in the UK or not and the firm's obligation to report applies equally to its unregulated activities.

1 Also, ancillary activities in relation to designated business activities that constitute dealing in investments as principal, and in certain respects with regard to the communication and approval of financial promotions: see the FSA Handbook at PRIN 3.2.1 and 3.2.2.
2 For the detailed rules on territorial application, see the FSA Handbook at PRIN 3.3.1 and see also the explanation at PRIN 1.1.6. Broadly, Principles 4 and 11 apply with respect to activities wherever they are carried on; Principles 1, 2 and 3 apply in a prudential context (see para 2.168 ff below) with respect to activities wherever they are carried on but more generally with respect to activities carried on from a UK establishment; Principle 5 applies to activities everywhere if they have, broadly, a negative impact on confidence in the UK financial system or were carried on from a UK establishment, and Principles 6 to 10 apply, generally speaking, to activities carried on from a UK establishment.
3 In the case of Principle 3, only in a prudential context: see the FSA Handbook at PRIN 3.2.3.
4 See the FSA Handbook at PRIN 3.3.1.
5 See the FSA Handbook at PRIN 3.2.3.

2.61 ***Other group members of a UK regulated firm*** Other group members of a UK regulated firm are relevant to Principle 3 (organisation and control, but only in a prudential context), Principle 4 (assessing the adequacy of the firm's financial resources) and Principle 11 (but only in so far as relates to informing the FSA)[1].

1 See the FSA Handbook at PRIN 3.2.3.

2.62 ***Incoming firms*** Incoming firms are, generally speaking, subject to the Principles in relation to the same activities as UK regulated firms but only in so far as responsibility for the matter in question is not reserved by a European Community instrument to the firm's home state regulator[1].

1 See the FSA Handbook at PRIN 3.1.1 for the more detailed rules. See also the FSA Handbook at SYSC, Appendix 1 for guidance on the reservation of responsibility to a home state regulator.

The fundamental requirements applicable to individuals

2.63 It is not only firms that are regulated by the FSA. As outlined briefly above, the FSMA 2000 introduces for the first time a statutory regime for the approval of individuals working for authorised firms. Since some degree of personal responsibility is involved in virtually every regulatory problem, it is relevant to understand the fundamental requirements applicable to individuals and briefly to review the way in which individuals are regulated by the FSA.

Brief introduction to approved persons

2.64 Under the FSMA 2000, persons performing certain functions (known as 'controlled functions') for regulated firms in relation to their regulated activities are, broadly, required to be approved by the FSA for the performance of the particular function[1]. It is for the FSA to specify what the controlled functions are, within the parameters set by the FSMA 2000.

1 Firms are obliged, broadly, to take reasonable care to ensure that no person performs a controlled function in relation to a regulated activity of the firm unless the FSA approves the performance by the person of the particular controlled function: see FSMA 2000, s 59(1) and (2). Breach by the firm can lead to a damages claim by a private person who suffers loss as a result: FSMA 2000, s 71 and see Chapter 10 below. It could also lead to disciplinary and/or enforcement proceedings against the firm and/or the persons concerned.

2.65 Controlled functions fall into three broad categories[1]:

- those involving the exercise of a significant influence on the conduct of the firm's affairs;
- those involving dealing with the firm's customers; and
- those involving dealing with the property of customers.

1 FSMA 2000, s 59. A full list of controlled functions can be found in the FSA Handbook at SUP 10.4.

2.66 The basic criterion for the approval of a particular person to perform a particular controlled function is that the FSA is satisfied he is a fit and proper person to perform the function to which the application relates[1]. A test of 'fit and proper' is thus critical not only for the authorisation of firms but also for the approval of individuals. As with firms, the obligation to be fit and proper is a continuing one: if the FSA considers that an approved person is not fit and proper, then it may withdraw his approval[2]. However, as will be seen, the test is interpreted differently for individuals than it is for firms.

1 FSMA 2000, s 61(1).
2 FSMA 2000, s 63 and see para 8.27 below.

2.67 As a result of being an approved person, an individual is subject to the FSA's Statements of Principle and Code of Practice for approved persons[1] and is also amenable to regulatory disciplinary proceedings for misconduct[2].

1 FSMA 2000, s 64 and see para 2.76 ff below.
2 FSMA 2000, s 66 and see para 2.182 below and Chapter 8.

2.68 In addition to being able, through the granting and withdrawal of approvals, to ensure that only appropriate people exercise 'controlled functions' in relation to a firm's regulated activities, the FSA has the rather broader power to prohibit any person, whether an approved person or not, from performing particular functions[1]. At its most extreme, it seems that the FSA can prohibit a person from being involved in any aspect of the business of any regulated firm[2]. The basis for imposing a prohibition order is, again, that the person is not fit and proper to perform functions in relation to a regulated activity carried on by an authorised person.

1 FSMA 2000, s 56 and see para 8.44 ff below.
2 There is a question as to the precise scope: see para 8.50 below.

The test of fit and proper

2.69 As outlined above, approval is subject to a test of whether a person is fit and proper. The FSA has given guidance on the considerations that it will take into account[1]. The three primary considerations (said to be the most important considerations and presumably, therefore, not the only ones) are:

- honesty, integrity and reputation;
- competency and capability; and
- financial soundness.

1 See, generally, the FSA Handbook at FIT.

2.70 Each is the subject of detailed guidance which will be applied in general terms but is expressly not exhaustive of the matters that could lead to a person being declared not fit and proper to perform a particular function in a particular firm[1].

1 See the FSA Handbook at FIT 1.3.3.

2.71 A person does not fail to be fit and proper simply because his conduct falls within one or more of the matters listed in the guidance. If a matter comes to the FSA's attention which suggests that the person might not be fit and proper, the FSA will take into account how relevant and how important that matter is[1].

1 See the FSA Handbook at FIT 1.3.4.

2.72 It may be helpful to give some examples of the matters listed in the guidance. First, in assessing honesty, integrity and reputation the FSA takes into account, among others, factors which can be summarised as follows[1]:

- criminal offences, particularly for dishonesty, fraud or financial crime[2];

- adverse findings or settlements in relevant civil proceedings;
- involvement in investigations or disciplinary proceedings by the FSA or other bodies and any suspension, criticism or censure, public or private[3];
- contraventions of FSA rules or other applicable regulatory standards or rules;
- justified complaints relating to regulated activities;
- dismissals, including resigning when asked; and
- whether the person has been candid and truthful in his dealings with regulators[4], and whether he demonstrates a readiness and willingness to comply with the requirements and standards of the regulatory system and other legal, regulatory and professional requirements and standards.

1 For a full list, see the FSA Handbook at FIT 2.1.
2 Convictions for drug or alcohol or other abusive acts are relevant to competence and capability: see para 2.74 below.
3 Note the inclusion of private censures. Whilst it may be tempting to accept a private censure without further argument given the lack of any formal consequences (and indeed there may in practice be no other option) it would clearly count against the individual on his record: see further the discussion at para 7.18 ff below.
4 This is an important aspect of the regime and a constant theme: see further Chapter 3 below.

2.73 The breadth of the guidance requires comment. The FSA is clearly trying to cast its net widely so as to ensure that issues which could potentially impact upon an individual's integrity cannot be hidden from it, or be prevented from being taken into account, by using a convenient legal label or process. An example would be settling legal proceedings on a without prejudice basis[1] or asking the employee to resign rather than dismissing him. Whilst there may therefore be good reasons for the FSA to take this approach, the effect of it doing so is potentially far-reaching and there is a risk of unfairness and of people being, in effect, guilty until proven innocent. For example, it may be going too far to take into account that a person was merely interviewed in the course of an investigation, or was notified of potential disciplinary or criminal proceedings that never materialised, or that a complaint was made against him that was never substantiated. Each of these is, however, included within the guidance. In simple terms, however, any matter which impacts on the honesty, integrity or reputation of a person is relevant to whether he is fit and proper.

1 Correspondence that is 'without prejudice' may not fall within the statutory protection that protects legally privileged material from disclosure: see para 4.264 ff below.

2.74 Second, competence and capability[1] involves considering whether the person satisfies the requirements of the FSA's Training and Competence Sourcebook[2] and whether he has demonstrated by experience and training that he is able, or will be able if approved, to perform the particular controlled function. Drug or alcohol abuse or other 'abusive acts' are relevant to capability, in terms of the person's continuing ability to perform the particular function.

1 See the FSA Handbook at FIT 2.2.
2 See the FSA Handbook at TC.

2.75 Third, in assessing financial soundness[1], the FSA will have regard to any factors including (but not limited to) whether the person has:

- been the subject of a judgment debt or award that remains outstanding or was not satisfied within a reasonable period of time; or
- made an arrangement with creditors, been made bankrupt or had assets sequestered;
- in both cases, whether in the UK or elsewhere.

The fact that a person is of limited financial means will not, in itself, affect his suitability.

1 See the FSA Handbook at FIT 2.3.

Statements of Principle and Code of Practice for approved persons[1]

2.76 The FSMA 2000[2] empowers the FSA to issue Statements of Principle with respect to the conduct expected of approved persons and requires the FSA, if it does issue a Statement of Principle, also to issue a Code of Practice for the purpose of helping to determine whether or not a person's conduct complies with the Statement of Principle.

1 Generally, see the FSA Handbook at APER.
2 FSMA 2000, s 64.

2.77 The FSA has issued seven Statements of Principle, four of which apply to all approved persons and three of which apply only to persons approved to perform significant influence functions (which, broadly, means senior management)[1], together with a corresponding Code of Practice. These are outlined below.

1 The issuance of three Statements of Principle applicable solely to 'persons approved to perform significant influence functions' highlights the increasing importance of the role of senior management within the regulatory system: see para 2.97 below.

What are the Statements of Principle?

2.78 The Statements of Principle are the fundamental, high-level principles applicable to approved persons from day to day in the performance of their 'controlled functions', breach of which can give rise to disciplinary or other enforcement consequences for the individual[1].

1 See para 2.182 ff below. Note that breach does not of itself give rise to any right of action by persons affected or affect the validity of any transaction: FSMA 2000, s 64(8).

What conduct is subject to the Statements of Principle?

2.79 The Statements of Principle do not apply to all conduct by all employees working for authorised firms. They apply to approved persons in relation to the performance of the controlled functions for which that person is approved.

2.80 This gives rise to two points. First, the fact that a person is approved for one function does not bring all of his functions within 'controlled functions'. To the extent he performs other functions for the firm, he is not subject to the Statements of Principle[1]. This is, however, subject to the caveat that issues arising in relation to his other functions may impact on whether he is a fit and proper person to be performing a controlled function.

1 See the FSA Handbook at APER 1.2.6, 1.2.7 and 1.2.9.

2.81 Second, the basic premise is that any person carrying out a controlled function needs to be an approved person, and is therefore subject to the Statements of Principle, but there are complex rules on the territorial scope of the approved person's regime, depending on the nature of the firm concerned. These are not reviewed here[1].

1 For details, see the FSA Handbook at SUP 10.1.

What is the Code of Practice?

2.82 The Code of Practice is the Code which the FSA is required to issue for the purpose of helping to determine whether a person's conduct complies with a Statement of Principle[1]. Under the FSMA 2000, the Code of Practice may specify:

- conduct which, in the FSA's opinion, complies with a Statement of Principle;
- conduct which, in the FSA's opinion, does not comply; and
- factors which, in the FSA's opinion, are to be taken into account in determining whether or not a person's conduct complies.

1 FSMA 2000, s 64(2).

2.83 In fact, the current Code of Practice describes conduct which is non-compliant and factors to be taken into account in determining whether or not conduct complies, but the FSA has not specified any conduct which does comply with the Statements of Principle[1]. In addition, included with the Code of Practice are various pieces of 'guidance' which are expressly not part of the Code and do not have binding force.

1 The closest is at APER 4.3.4, which relates to Statement of Principle 3 (see para 2.93 below). It was thought that examples of compliant behaviour would be too obvious to be worthwhile and, in addition, it would be difficult to find examples that would be helpful in the context of all the business sectors covered by the regime.

2.84 The Code is only an aid to interpreting the Statements of Principle. It has evidential effect: it may be relied upon so far as it tends to establish whether or not conduct complies with a Statement of Principle[1]. The fact that an approved person's conduct was of a type specified in the Code as not complying with a particular Statement of Principle is not therefore of itself determinative that the conduct breached the relevant Statement of Principle. It will, however, be strong evidence that the conduct did not comply. Equally, if the Code did specify conduct which in the FSA's view complied with the Statements of Principle, that would not provide an absolute safe harbour for approved persons who conducted themselves in that way, although, again, it would be strong evidence that they had complied and indeed it would be difficult for the FSA to take action against them in that situation.

1 FSMA 2000, s 64(7) and see the FSA Handbook at APER 3.1.5.

2.85 The Code is not exhaustive of the conduct that may contravene the Statements of Principle. The fact that a person's conduct is not proscribed by or mentioned in the Code does not necessarily mean it complies with the Statements of Principle. Conduct needs to be measured against the Statements themselves, using the Code as an indication of the types of conduct which the FSA regards as unacceptable.

2.86 Three additional points are relevant in applying the Code. First, the FSA has the power to supplement or amend the Code and has said that it may do so if there is a risk that unacceptable practice may become prevalent, so as to make clear what conduct falls below the standards expected. However, it is the Code of Practice in issue at the time when the conduct occurred that is relevant to assessing whether the person complied with the Statement of Principle[1]. Having said that, since the Code is not exhaustive, it seems that the Statements of Principle could be breached even if the conduct concerned was not expressly prohibited under the Code at the relevant time.

1 FSMA 2000, s 64(7) and see the FSA Handbook at APER 3.1.2.

2.87 Second, as to whether there has been any breach of a Statement of Principle, to the extent that the Statements impose particular standards, for example to take reasonable care or exercise due skill, care and diligence, then it may be necessary to look beyond the Code in order to understand what the applicable standard of behaviour was and whether the person's conduct fell below that standard. How the FSA approaches such issues is discussed at para 2.153 ff below. In addition, the significance of conduct that is specified in the Code as tending to show compliance or to show a breach is assessed in the light of all the circumstances, including the circumstances of the particular case, the characteristics of the particular controlled function and the behaviour to be expected in that function[1].

1 See the FSA Handbook at APER 3.1.3.

2.88 Third, as to the consequence of any breach, a breach of a Statement of Principle is capable of leading to disciplinary action, but not every breach will do so. An important question is the circumstances when in practice individuals will be disciplined for breaches. The FSA can only take action where it appears to it appropriate in all the circumstances to do so. In addition, as may be clear from the way in which the Code is framed, an element of personal culpability is required. What, precisely, this means is discussed at para 2.182 and Chapter 8 below.

The Statements and Code

2.89 It is important to have a broad understanding of the Statements of Principle and Code of Practice generally, as well as a more detailed understanding of those Statements of Principle particularly likely to be relevant when a regulatory problem arises, most notably Statement of Principle 4[1]. The Statements of Principle are set out below together with an outline of the Code applicable to each to give a flavour of the areas intended to be covered[2]. Some general provisions of the Code applicable to all Statements of Principle are also set out below.

1 Disclosure and dealings with regulators: see para 2.95 ff below.
2 For the full Code of Practice, see the FSA Handbook at APER.

2.90 There are seven Statements of Principle. The first four apply to all approved persons and the final three only to those performing a significant influence function.

2.91 ***Statement of Principle 1 – integrity*** An approved person must act with integrity in carrying out his controlled function. Conduct outlawed under the Code[1] includes deliberately misleading clients, the firm or the FSA, deliberately recommending unsuitable investments, deliberately failing to correct misunderstandings of the customer, the firm or the FSA, deliberately preparing inaccurate or inappropriate records, deliberately misusing assets or confidential information of a client or the firm, deliberately designing transactions so as to disguise regulatory breaches or deliberately failing to disclose conflicts of interest in connection with dealings with clients. The use of the word 'deliberately' in each reflects the fact that this Statement of Principle is directed at integrity.

1 See the FSA Handbook at APER 4.1.

2.92 ***Statement of Principle 2 – acting with due skill, care and diligence*** An approved person must act with due skill, care and diligence in carrying out his controlled function. Some of the instances of non-compliant conduct specified by the Code[1] are similar to those applicable to Statement of Principle 1, save that in each case the emphasis is on doing something without reasonable grounds or failing to do something which ought to have been done. This reflects the difference between a lack of integrity (which it seems from the above involves proof of deliberate misconduct) and a failure to take reasonable care. Additional areas covered include undertaking, recommending or providing advice on transactions without a reasonable understanding of the risk exposure to a customer or the firm or continuing to undertake a controlled function despite having failed to meet the training and competence standards.

1 See the FSA Handbook at APER 4.2.

2.93 ***Statement of Principle 3 – proper standards of market conduct*** An approved person must observe proper standards of market conduct in carrying out his controlled function. The Code[1] makes clear that a factor to be taken into account is whether the person, or his firm, has complied with the Inter-Professional Code[2], the Code of Market Conduct[3] or other relevant market codes and exchange rules. Compliance with those codes or rules will tend to show compliance with this Statement of Principle.

1 See the FSA Handbook at APER 4.3.
2 The FSA Handbook at MAR Chapter 3.
3 The FSA Handbook at MAR Chapter 1, and see Chapter 13 below.

2.94 This leaves open two questions. First, whether the Statement of Principle is capable of being breached in a situation where there is no code or set of rules applicable to the particular market. It is thought that, in principle, the answer is that it is, particularly given the wide wording of the Statement of Principle. Second, whether the Statement of Principle is capable of being breached where the conduct falls within the scope of a market code or rule but does not amount to a breach of that code or rule. The answer to this is that it cannot be ruled out that a breach of the Statement of Principle would still have been committed, particularly if the reason why the applicable market code or rule had not been breached was technical or unmeritorious. The Code provides that compliance with applicable market codes or rules will tend to show compliance with the Statement of Principle, but this falls short of providing a safe harbour[1].

1 A similar issue arises in the context of market abuse and is discussed at para 13.265 ff below.

2.95 ***Statement of Principle 4 – dealings with regulators*** An approved person must deal with the FSA and with other regulators in an open and co-operative way and must disclose appropriately any information of which the FSA would reasonably expect notice.

2.96 The requirements of this Statement of Principle and the Code of Practice[1] are considered in more detail at para 3.85 ff below (so far as relates to reporting) and para 4.42 ff below (so far as relates to co-operating). It should be apparent that this Statement of Principle broadly parallels the firm's obligation under Principle 11, taking into account that in many situations the individual's disclosure obligation should be limited to making the appropriate report internally, rather than reporting direct to the FSA.

1 See the FSA Handbook at APER 4.4.

2.97 ***Statements of Principle 5–7 for those exercising significant influence functions*** The last three Statements of Principle are a key element in the FSA's measures for ensuring proper accountability of senior management for compliance with the attainment of the key regulatory objectives laid down by the FSMA 2000[1]. The text of the Statements of Principle, in particular Statement of Principle 5, is closely linked to the requirements imposed on firms by the FSA Handbook to ensure proper apportionment of responsibilities[2]. These not only require firms to assign specific responsibilities to particular individuals but also require them to assign to a particular person the function of apportioning responsibility[3]. The result should be to ensure there is always an individual in the firm capable of taking responsibility for a particular matter.

1 This is the subject of a long and somewhat troubled history. For the measures applicable under the pre-existing regime, see SFA Board Notice 473 and Appendix 38 to the SFA rules.

2 See the FSA Handbook at SYSC.
3 The 'apportionment and oversight' function: see the FSA Handbook at SYSC 2.1.

2.98 ***Statement of Principle 5 – organising the business*** An approved person performing a significant influence function must take reasonable steps to ensure that the business of the firm for which he is responsible in his controlled function is organised so that it can be controlled effectively. Conduct which the Code indicates the FSA regards as non-compliant[1] includes failing to take reasonable steps to (a) apportion responsibilities for all areas of the business within his control, (b) apportion responsibilities clearly (including implementing confusing or uncertain reporting lines, authorisation levels or job descriptions), or (c) ensure that suitable people are responsible for those aspects of the business under the person's control (including failing properly to review staff, giving undue weight to financial performance when considering suitability or allowing managerial vacancies to remain without arranging suitable cover). The business strategy in the relevant area is also relevant: if the strategy is to enter high-risk areas, then the degree of control and strength of monitoring reasonably required will be that much higher.

1 See the FSA Handbook at APER 4.5. Note also the guidance accompanying the Code of Practice: see the FSA Handbook at APER 4.5.10 to 4.5.15.

2.99 ***Statement of Principle 6 – managing the business*** An approved person performing a significant influence function must exercise due skill, care and diligence in managing the business of the firm for which he is responsible in his controlled function. The Code of Practice[1] refers to an individual failing to take reasonable steps adequately to inform himself about the affairs of the business for which he is responsible, delegating authority without reasonable grounds for believing the person delegated to have the necessary capacity, competence, knowledge, seniority or skill, failing to take reasonable steps to maintain an appropriate understanding of the matters delegated and failing to supervise and monitor adequately the persons delegated to. Relevant factors to be taken into account include the competence, knowledge, seniority and past performance of the delegate[2].

1 See the FSA Handbook at APER 4.6.
2 Note also the guidance accompanying the Code of Practice: see the FSA Handbook at APER 4.6.11 to 4.6.14.

2.100 ***Statement of Principle 7 – compliance with regulatory requirements*** An approved person performing a significant influence function must take reasonable steps to ensure that the business of the firm for which he is responsible in his controlled function complies with the relevant requirements and standards of the regulatory system. Non-compliant conduct includes[1] failing to take reasonable steps to (a) implement adequate and appropriate systems of control, (b) monitor compliance with the relevant requirements and standards, (c) obtain information about the reason why actual or suspected significant breaches may have arisen, or (d) review and, if appropriate, improve systems following the identification of significant breaches.

1 See the FSA Handbook at APER 4.7. Note also the guidance accompanying the Code of Practice: see the FSA Handbook at APER 4.7.11 to 4.7.14.

2.101 ***Provisions of the Code applicable to all Statements of Principle*** The Code contains some factors relevant in determining whether or not conduct complies with each of the Statements of Principle and, in addition, some further factors relating solely to Statements of Principle 5–7.

2.102 The factors to be taken into account in relation to all of the Statements of Principle are whether[1]:

- the person's conduct relates to activities that are subject to other provisions of the FSA Handbook; and
- his conduct is consistent with the requirements and standards of the regulatory system relevant to his firm.

1 See the FSA Handbook at APER 3.2.1.

2.103 These are, however, only factors to be taken into account. The fact that an individual complied with, or did not breach, the relevant part of the FSA Handbook, or did not cause the firm to breach any of its own obligations, would not preclude a finding that a Statement of Principle had been breached.

2.104 As to the factors to be taken into account in relation to Statements of Principle 5 to 7, which apply only to those exercising a significant influence function, these are[1]:

- whether the person exercised reasonable care when considering the information available to him;
- whether he reached a reasonable conclusion which he acted on;
- the nature, scale and complexity of the firm's business;
- the role and responsibility of the particular person as an approved person performing a significant influence function; and
- the knowledge he had, or should have had, of regulatory concerns arising in the business under his control.

1 See the FSA Handbook at APER 3.3.

2.105 In addition, the provisions of the FSA's rules relating to senior management arrangements, systems and controls[1] need to borne particularly in mind when considering whether Principles 5 to 7 may have been breached.

1 See the FSA Handbook at SYSC.

Introducing the FSA Handbook

2.106 It should already be clear that the FSMA 2000, notwithstanding its length, provides little more than a framework for the regulatory regime. The detailed rules are to be found in the FSA Handbook[1], to which reference is frequently made throughout this book. However, not everything contained in the FSA Handbook is in any sense binding on firms. A substantial proportion of the content is no more than non-binding guidance. Other provisions are said to be of evidential value. Yet further provisions comprise the FSA's policy on how it will act. The precise nature of the provision in question therefore requires some thought.

1 Some of the detailed provisions are also to be found in secondary legislation made under the FSMA 2000. The secondary legislation is generally less relevant in the enforcement context, but certain Statutory Instruments are relevant and reference to them is made where appropriate.

2.107 Why is this relevant in a book about enforcement? When a problem arises, firms need to understand the precise nature and effect of the rules concerned, not only the specific rules which may have been breached in the particular situation, but also those rules which prescribe how the firm and the FSA should act in the context of the ensuing regulatory investigation and enforcement proceedings. Is the rule binding? If not, does it matter that the firm has not complied? Does the FSA have to act in the way stated in its policy? It can readily be seen that an understanding of how the FSA Handbook works underlies an understanding of the regime.

2.108 Outlined below are the main powers that the FSA has to make the rules and other provisions contained in the FSA Handbook, how the FSA has signified in the FSA Handbook the nature of each rule or provision and the effect in legal terms of rules made under the various statutory rule-making provisions.

2.109 The FSA has the following main statutory powers and duties under the FSMA 2000 to make the provisions of the FSA Handbook:

- the power to make general rules;
- the power to make specific types of rules;
- the duty to issue codes;
- the power to make evidential or other non-binding provisions;
- the power to give guidance; and
- the duty to publish policy and procedures.

2.110 Each of these is considered in turn. Further information can be found in the Reader's Guide to the FSA Handbook and in the FSA Handbook at GEN[1].

1 Note that the provisions of the FSA Handbook are to be given a purposive interpretation: see the FSA Handbook at GEN 2.2.1. The purpose of any provision is to be gathered first and foremost from the text of the provision in question and its context among other relevant provisions: GEN 2.2.2.

General rules

2.111 The FSA has a general rule-making power under FSMA 2000, s 138, allowing it to make such rules applying to authorised persons, in respect of both their regulated and their unregulated activities, as appear to the FSA to be necessary or expedient for the purpose of protecting the interests of consumers.

2.112 This provision forms the basis of a significant proportion of the FSA Handbook, including (largely) the Principles for Businesses[1].

1 See para 2.51 ff above.

2.113 Unless the rule specifies otherwise, these rules normally have binding effect[1] and breach can give rise to the regulatory consequences discussed in this book[2]. These rules are denoted by 'R' in the FSA Handbook.

1 See the FSA Handbook, Reader's Guide, para 19. Precisely what effect the rule has will depend upon the language that is used. For example, is it expressed in mandatory language?
2 The FSA can also waive or modify rules as they apply to specific firms: see FSMA 2000, s 148 and the FSA Handbook at SUP Chapter 8.

Specific types of rules

2.114 The FSA is also empowered to make specific types of rules applicable to certain areas. Examples include client money rules[1], price stabilising rules[2], money laundering rules[3] and financial promotion rules[4]. Again, unless the rule specifies otherwise, these rules normally have binding effect[5] and breach can give rise to the regulatory consequences discussed in this book. These rules are also denoted by 'R' in the FSA Handbook[6].

1 FSMA 2000, s 139.
2 FSMA 2000, s 144.
3 FSMA 2000, s 146.
4 FSMA 2000, s 145.
5 See footnote 1 to para 2.113 above.
6 In addition, various provisions of the FSMA 2000 empower the FSA to give directions or impose other requirements (for example, as to the manner in which applications for Part IV permission are to be made: FSMA 2000, s 51(3)). Such directions or other requirements are denoted by 'D' in the FSA Handbook. They are binding. See further the FSA Handbook, Reader's Guide, para 21.

2.115 The FSA's Statements of Principle for approved persons[1] also constitute binding rules. These are denoted by 'P' in the FSA Handbook.

1 FSMA 2000, s 64: see para 2.76 above.

Codes

2.116 In two instances, the FSA is required to issue codes of conduct and the FSMA 2000 prescribes the effect that those codes have. The two codes are:

- the Code of Practice for approved persons[1]; and
- the Code of Market Conduct[1].

1 FSMA 2000, s 64: see para 2.76 above.
2 FSMA 2000, s 119: see Chapter 13 below.

2.117 The Code of Practice for approved persons is discussed in detail above. Provisions of the Code are denoted by 'E' in the FSA Handbook, indicating that they are of evidential effect.

2.118 The Code of Market Conduct is discussed in detail at para 13.20 ff below. The effect of the Code is twofold[1]:

- in so far as it provides that behaviour does not amount to market abuse, that behaviour is taken as not amounting to market abuse. To that extent, the Code is binding, and such provisions are denoted in the FSA Handbook by the letter 'C'[2];
- otherwise, the Code may be relied upon in so far as it indicates whether or not behaviour amounts to market abuse. To that extent, it is not binding but is only of evidential effect, and such provisions are denoted in the FSA Handbook by the letter 'E'[3].

1 FSMA 2000, s 122 and see the more detailed discussion at para 13.20 ff below.
2 See the FSA Handbook, Reader's Guide, para 23.
3 See the FSA Handbook, Reader's Guide, para 26/27.

Evidential or other non-binding provisions

2.119 In addition to giving evidential effect to the Codes, at least to a large extent, the FSMA 2000[1] allows the FSA to prescribe rules which have evidential effect. The rule does not stand on its own, but relates to some other binding rule and indicates in what circumstances that other rule will have been complied with or contravened.

1 FSMA 2000, s 149.

2.120 These rules have a non-binding effect. In other words, contravention of the rule does not of itself give rise to regulatory consequences. However, contravention of the rule may indicate that some other rule has been contravened, and that contravention may give rise to regulatory consequences. The FSA says[1] that compliance with or contravention of these rules creates a rebuttable presumption that the other rule has been complied with or contravened.

1 See the FSA Handbook, Reader's Guide, para 24.

2.121 Where the FSA provides for a rule of this type:

- it does so by stating in the rule that contravention does not give rise to the consequences specified under the FSMA 2000[1];
- the rule must also state either that contravention of the rule may be relied on as tending to establish contravention of some other, specified rule or that

compliance with the rule may be relied on as tending to establish compliance with some other, specified rule[2]; and

- it denotes this type of rule in the FSA Handbook by using the letter 'E'.

1 FSMA 2000, s 149(1).
2 FSMA 2000, s 149(2).

Guidance

2.122 The FSA may also give guidance[1] consisting of information and advice relating to the operation of the FSMA 2000 and the FSA's rules, any matters relating to the FSA's functions, for the purpose of meeting its regulatory objectives, or in relation to other matters where the FSA considers it desirable to give information or advice. The FSA has made extensive use of this power in the FSA Handbook, with the relevant provisions being denoted by the letter 'G'[2].

1 FSMA 2000, s 157.
2 Guidance may also be given to firms individually under FSMA 2000, s 157: see the discussion in the FSA Handbook at SUP Chapter 9.

2.123 The FSA has made clear[1] that such guidance is entirely non-binding, and has no evidential effect, in the sense that following it or failing to follow it does not of itself have any disciplinary consequences, nor is there any presumption that departing from guidance is indicative of a breach of the relevant rule. Having said that, the FSA has conceded that if a person acts in accordance with guidance in the circumstances contemplated by that guidance, then the FSA will proceed on the footing that the person has complied with the aspects of the rule or other requirement to which the guidance relates. Guidance cannot, however, affect any rights that any third parties might have.

1 See the FSA Handbook, Reader's Guide, paras 28 to 30.

2.124 On the face of it, therefore, it would seem that, in the context of enforcement, guidance can only be used by the firm in its defence and not by the FSA against it. However, this is probably too hasty an assumption. First, even if guidance cannot be expressly cited by the FSA in support of enforcement action, it is clearly an aid to the FSA's views about the proper application of a rule and therefore the way in which the FSA will approach a particular set of facts. Second, the fact that a particular standard or practice is referred to in guidance makes it at least more likely that that standard will generally be followed. Since good industry practice is undoubtedly likely to be relevant to the interpretation of some principles and rules, guidance will therefore, at least at one remove, be relevant to the application of those principles and rules and to the firm's exposure to enforcement action. Guidance cannot therefore be ignored. The practical result seems to be that the firms should normally follow guidance unless there is some good reason to the contrary.

Policy and procedures

2.125 The provisions of the FSA Handbook outlined thus far primarily concern the behaviour of firms. Various provisions relate to the FSA's behaviour, particularly in the context of enforcement. To what extent do these bind the FSA?

2.126 The FSA is required, under the FSMA 2000, to publish a statement of its policy on the exercise of various of its powers, including (in the enforcement context):

- its policy on the imposition, and amount, of penalties against approved persons for misconduct[1] and against firms for contraventions of the FSMA 2000 or the FSA's rules[2];
- in its capacity as UK Listing Authority, its policy on the imposition, and amount, of penalties against issuers or applicants and their directors[3];
- its policy on the imposition, and amount, of penalties for market abuse[4]; and
- its policy on the conduct of interviews where it directs that an overseas regulator may attend and take part[5].

1 FSMA 2000, s 69 and see Chapter 8 below.
2 FSMA 2000, s 210 and see Chapter 7 below.
3 FSMA 2000, s 93 and see Chapter 15 below.
4 FSMA 2000, s 124 and see Chapter 13 below.
5 FSMA 2000, s 169(9) and see Chapter 4 below.

2.127 In each of the first three cases, the FSA is required to have regard to its policy when exercising or deciding whether to exercise the relevant power. The policy is thus binding on the FSA[1]. However, each policy statement tends to be worded very broadly, generally making clear that the FSA will have regard to all the relevant circumstances of the case including a non-exhaustive list of factors[2]. As a result, it is in practice likely to be difficult for a firm to complain that the FSA did not follow its policy in the particular case. Statements of policy are denoted in the FSA Handbook by the letter 'G'.

1 It is not clear whether the policy is the only factor to which the FSA is allowed to 'have regard': this is a matter of statutory interpretation. If it is, then the policy is strictly binding: see for example *R v Sunderland City Council, ex p Redezeus Ltd* (1994) 27 HLR 477. If it is not, then whilst the FSA must 'have regard to' it, that could include considering it and deciding to afford it no weight as a relevant factor in its decision how to act: see *Tesco Stores Ltd v Secretary of State for the Environment* [1995] 1 WLR 759, HL.
2 See, for example, the FSA Handbook at ENF 11.4.1 (criteria for determining whether to take disciplinary action) and 13.3.1 (factors relevant to the amount of fines).

2.128 The FSMA 2000 also requires the FSA to determine and publish its procedure in one respect, namely in relation to the giving of supervisory notices and warning/decision notices[1]. This procedure is expressly binding. The FSA must follow its stated procedure[2] and it could in principle be challenged if it failed to do so. The statement of procedure is denoted in the FSA's Handbook by the letter 'G'.

1 FSMA 2000, s 395 (1).
2 FSMA 2000, s 395(9). Note, however, that a failure to do so does not affect the validity of the FSA's action: FSMA 2000, s 395(11).

2.129 Beyond complying with these specific requirements imposed on it under the FSMA 2000, the FSA has in the Handbook provided a great deal of information as to how it will exercise its other powers, for example the circumstances when injunctions or restitution orders will be appropriate or the giving of private warnings. This transparency is of great benefit to the regulatory regime. But is this guidance in any sense binding on the FSA?

2.130 In strict terms, this material is only guidance and not binding. However, if the FSA chooses publicly to state its policy and then acts otherwise than in accordance with that policy, it is possible that judicial remedies may be available to the firm[1], depending upon the circumstances. There may also be grounds for making a complaint about the FSA. These issues are considered in Chapter 16. In practice, the FSA's policy statements tend to be very broadly drawn, generally making it difficult for the firm to challenge the implementation of the policy in any particular case[2]. Such guidance is also denoted in the FSA Handbook by the letter 'G'.

1 There are limited grounds upon which the FSA's actions could be judicially reviewed: see para 16.20 below. Relevant factors in this particular context include: (i) a failure by the FSA to follow its policy may help to indicate that the decision was irrational and/or procedurally unfair (depending, among other things, upon the nature of the policy) and (ii) the publication of the policy may give rise to a legitimate expectation on the part of firms that it will be followed and/or constitute an estoppel by representation upon the FSA. For a more detailed discussion, see *Judicial Review*, Supperstone and Goudie, 1997, Chapters 5 and 7.

2 One particular area of policy which may be relevant to firms wishing to challenge the FSA's actions in the particular case is the general approach which the FSA has indicated it will adopt to its enforcement function, namely transparency, proportionality and consistency and fair treatment to those subject to its powers: see para 2.36 above and Chapter 16.

CONDUCT GIVING RISE TO ENFORCEMENT

What types of conduct by firms give rise to enforcement?

2.131 The processes and consequences discussed in this book all arise from a regulatory breach of some description having been committed. The purpose of the following paragraphs is to outline the different types of conduct which may give rise to these consequences.

2.132 Types of conduct fall broadly into four categories:

- breaches of the FSMA 2000;
- breaches of specific rules or regulations made by the FSA or HM Treasury under their powers granted under the FSMA 2000;
- breaches of the Principles for Businesses; and
- conduct giving rise to concerns of failure to be fit and/or proper;

and there are an additional three particular types of misconduct falling into those categories which are worth highlighting separately, namely:

- issues arising abroad with implications in the UK;
- issues arising in a firm's unregulated business; and
- breach of the perimeter.

Breaches of the FSMA 2000

2.133 The top level of regulation is the FSMA 2000 itself. It contains a number of prohibitions, breach of which may have regulatory consequences. The prohibitions can be divided into three types:

- those which have criminal law consequences;
- those which have the specific consequences provided for in the FSMA 2000; and
- those which have no specified consequences.

Breaches with criminal law consequences

2.134 As to those provisions breach of which is a criminal offence[1], whilst the consequences may seem to be primarily in the criminal sphere (where the FSA will often act as the prosecuting authority[2]), the FSA will have the power to investigate first and then decide what action to take. That action may not be limited to, or may not even include, a criminal prosecution. The breach may also give rise to regulatory enforcement action where the person concerned is an authorised firm or approved person, because the breach would not only be a potential criminal offence but would also probably amount to a contravention of a requirement imposed by or under the FSMA 2000. As will be seen[3], this is one of the key phrases which may trigger disciplinary or other enforcement action. The breach may also cast doubt on whether the firm or person concerned is fit and proper, again with potential enforcement consequences. Precisely what action is appropriate depends upon the nature of the regulatory concerns to which the matter gives rise.

1 For example, the general prohibition, unlawful financial promotion, making misleading statements and insider dealing (under the Criminal Justice Act 1993, Pt V). Criminal prosecutions under the FSMA 2000 are discussed more generally in Chapter 11 below.
2 This is discussed in Chapter 11 below.
3 See para 2.142 below.

Breaches with specified consequences

2.135 As to those provisions in the FSMA 2000 which give rise to consequences specified in the FSMA 2000, examples include:

- failing without reasonable excuse to comply with an information gathering requirement, which is punishable as contempt of court[1]; and
- breach of the market abuse provisions, which gives rise to liability to a civil penalty[2].

1 See Chapter 4 below.
2 See Chapter 13 below.

2.136 Again, the specified consequences are only part of the picture, particularly for those within the regulated community. The breach is likely also to amount to the contravention of a requirement imposed by or under the FSMA 2000[1], and could also cast doubt on whether the firm or a person concerned is fit and proper, in each case potentially giving rise to regulatory concerns and disciplinary or other action appropriate to address those concerns.

1 See para 2.142 below.

Breaches with no specified consequences

2.137 Finally, as to those breaches for which no consequences are specified, the breach is likely to amount to the contravention of a requirement by or under the FSMA 2000[1], and could also cast doubt on whether the firm or a person concerned is fit and proper. As a result, it could give rise to disciplinary or other enforcement action as described below for breaches of specific rules.

1 See para 2.142 below.

Breaches of specific rules

2.138 At the level below the FSMA 2000, there are a large number of specific rule-making powers allowing the FSA, or in some instances HM Treasury, to make specific rules or regulations applicable to firms generally or specific types of firms or specific parts of firms' businesses.

2.139 Although the relevant rule is not imposed directly by the FSMA 2000, its breach could give rise to regulatory consequences under the FSMA 2000. This is because the FSMA 2000 prescribes various criteria for the exercise of the FSA's enforcement powers and these criteria are, generally speaking, capable of being fulfilled by a breach of a rule or regulation imposed indirectly, by the FSA or HM Treasury under their statutory powers, rather than directly by the FSMA 2000. They include in particular the following:

- circumstances suggesting the breach of specific rules, which may allow the FSA to invoke its formal investigative powers[1];
- the breach of a requirement imposed by or under the FSMA 2000: the key phrase, discussed in detail below;
- the breach of a requirement imposed by or under any other Act whose contravention constitutes an offence which the FSA has the power to prosecute under the FSMA 2000, which may allow the FSA to impose or apply for a restitution order or to apply for a civil injunction[2];
- failure to satisfy the threshold conditions, including in particular failing to be fit and proper, which may allow the FSA to vary or cancel the firm's permission[3];

- it being desirable to act in order to protect the interests of consumers or potential consumers, which may enable the FSA to vary or cancel the firm's permission or impose similar action in relation to an incoming firm[4].

1 FSMA 2000, s 168 and, for a detailed discussion, see para 4.108 ff below.
2 FSMA 2000, ss 380, 382 and 384: see Chapter 7 below. For a list of those offences under the FSMA 2000 and others Acts which the FSA has the power to prosecute under the FSMA 2000, see para 11.5 ff below. The Secretary of State also has, under the same provisions, the power to apply for a restitution order or civil injunction in relation to contraventions which he has the power to prosecute under the FSMA 2000.
3 FSMA 2000, s 45 and see paras 9.14 ff and 9.239 ff below. For a discussion of the threshold conditions, and the test of fit and proper, see para 2.38 above.
4 FSMA 2000, ss 45 and 194 and see paras 9.25 ff and 9.60 ff below.

2.140 The FSA will in certain types of emergency situations excuse conduct that would otherwise amount to a breach of its rules[1].

1 For details, see the FSA Handbook at GEN 1.3.

2.141 Certain specific types of breaches may have additional or alternative types of consequences. For example, there are specific powers relating to listed companies[1], market abuse[2] and regulated collective investment schemes[3].

1 See Chapter 15 below.
2 See Chapter 13 below.
3 See Chapter 14 below.

Contravention of a requirement imposed by or under the FSMA 2000

2.142 This is the phrase which appears most often in the enforcement provisions of the FSMA 2000. Where a firm contravenes a requirement imposed on it by or under the FSMA 2000, it could be susceptible to[1]:

- disciplinary action[2];
- a restitution order[3];
- a civil injunction[4]; and
- the imposition of intervention action on an incoming firm[5].

1 The same test is also found in the provisions relating to enforcement action against regulated collective investment schemes: see Chapter 14 below.
2 FSMA 2000, ss 205 and 206 and see para 7.8 ff below.
3 FSMA 2000, ss 382 and 384 and see para 7.50 below.
4 FSMA 2000, s 381 and see para 7.100 ff below.
5 FSMA 2000, s 194 and see para 2.51 ff below.

2.143 A similar test is applied to determine whether a firm incurs civil liability to private persons for, broadly, breach of statutory duty[1]. The test is whether the firm has contravened an FSA rule. This is a less complicated test and precisely what it means is discussed at para 10.31 ff below.

1 FSMA 2000, s 150.

2.144 In considering whether the firm has contravened a requirement imposed on it by or under the FSMA 2000, there are two main questions. First, what constitutes a 'requirement by or under the FSMA 2000' and, second, when will such a requirement have been contravened.

2.145 ***Meaning of requirement by or under the FSMA 2000*** The FSMA 2000 does not provide any definition of the phrase, leaving some scope for uncertainty. Certain propositions can however be made.

2.146 First, it certainly includes breaches of requirements imposed directly by the FSMA 2000. In principle, this should include any provision of the FSMA 2000 which imposes a requirement on an authorised person to do something or not to do something. An example would be the requirement that authorised firms must take reasonable care not to allow a person to perform a controlled function unless the person was approved by the FSA to carry out that function[1]. The use of the word 'must' indicates that the provision is mandatory. This may be important in determining whether the particular provision amounts to a 'requirement' for these purposes.

1 FSMA 2000, s 59 and see para 2.64 above.

2.147 Second, the phrase extends to requirements imposed by the FSA where the FSMA 2000 not only empowers the FSA to make the relevant rules but also specifically imposes a requirement on a person to comply with them. An example would be the rules relating to auditors and actuaries[1]. In that case, the requirement is probably one imposed directly under the FSMA 2000, namely the statutory requirement to comply with those rules made by the FSA.

1 FSMA 2000, s 340.

2.148 Third, the phrase certainly includes to some extent rules and regulations derived indirectly from the FSMA 2000, in other words the rules of the FSA[1] and the regulations of any other body, such as HM Treasury, made under powers granted under the FSMA 2000. To the extent that those rules or regulations impose requirements on firms, those requirements will amount to requirements imposed under the FSMA 2000.

1 Or the UKLA's Listing Rules: see para 15.154 below.

2.149 In relation to such provisions, the more difficult question may be whether the particular provision amounts to a 'requirement'. The different wording of s 150[1] suggests that there is a distinction between a 'rule' and a 'requirement'. As has already been seen[2], the FSA has the power to make various types of rules and other provisions, and the effect of any particular provision depends upon its type and the nature of the wording used. Thus:

- it can make rules which are only of evidential effect[3], breach of which should not of itself amount to contravention of a requirement;

- it can and does give guidance[4], which is non-binding and should not therefore amount to a requirement the contravention of which would attract enforcement consequences;
- the most difficult area concerns those rules which do not amount to evidential provisions or guidance but which are not expressed in such a way as to indicate that they amount to a requirement. The FSA recognises[5] that some rules are not expressed in mandatory language and, as indicated above, the FSMA 2000 seems to distinguish between rules and requirements. There does therefore seem to be scope for FSA rules which do not amount to a requirement for these purposes. Whether a particular rule falls within this category will depend primarily upon the precise wording used; and
- the Principles for Businesses are rules made by the FSA under the FSMA 2000 and the above therefore applies equally to them.

1 Contravention of a 'rule' may give rise to a damages claim for breach of statutory duty, for private persons only: see para 10.27 ff below.
2 See the discussion of the FSA Handbook at para 2.106 ff above.
3 FSMA 2000, s 149 and see para 2.119 above.
4 FSMA 2000, s 157 and see para 2.122 above.
5 See the FSA Handbook, Reader's Guide, para 19.

2.150 Fourth, it seems that prohibitions in the FSMA 2000 which attract criminal law consequences also fall within the phrase 'requirement imposed by or under the FSMA 2000'. The word 'requirement' is a broad one and does not differentiate between any particular types of prohibition, for example criminal, civil or regulatory. Furthermore, the FSMA 2000 seems to contemplate, in the provisions relating to injunctions and restitution orders[1], that such requirements are included.

1 FSMA 2000, ss 380, 382 and 384: see Chapter 7 below. The definition of 'relevant requirement' in relation to the FSA distinguishes between (i) requirements imposed by or under the FSMA 2000 and (ii) requirements imposed by or under any other Act which the FSA has the power to prosecute under the FSMA 2000. It must have been intended that criminal prohibitions under the FSMA 2000 would be included in the former; otherwise, they would be excluded from the definition of 'relevant requirement' (which cannot have been intended).

2.151 Finally, the FSMA 2000 specifically provides[1] that, where a firm carries on a regulated activity otherwise than in accordance with its permission, it is taken to have contravened a requirement imposed on it by the FSA under the FSMA 2000. This is discussed in more detail at para 2.175 below.

1 FSMA 2000, s 20.

2.152 ***When will such a requirement have been contravened?*** Many FSA rules or other applicable requirements impose strict obligations, which will be contravened simply when there is a failure to comply. Take, for example, an obligation on a firm to make a periodic report to the FSA on a particular matter. If the firm fails to make the relevant report by the time prescribed, it will clearly have contravened the requirement.

2.153 Some other types of rules do not impose strict obligations, but instead require the firm or an approved person to, for example, 'take reasonable care' or 'pay due regard'. Examples include the Principles for Businesses[1], the Statements of Principle for approved persons[2] and the firm's obligation not to employ a prohibited person[3]. In those cases, assessing whether the firm has contravened the requirement is more complicated and requires the FSA to consider whether the firm (or approved person) has met the standard required of it.

1 See the discussion at para 2.55 above.
2 See para 2.76 ff above.
3 FSMA 2000, s 56(6).

2.154 In considering whether a firm (or an approved person) has taken reasonable care, the FSA regards the following factors as particularly relevant[1]:

- what information the firm or approved person knew at the relevant time and what information it ought to have known in all the circumstances;
- what steps the firm or approved person took to comply with the rule and what steps it ought to have taken in all the circumstances; and
- the standards of the regulatory system that applied at the time of the behaviour.

1 See the FSA Handbook at ENF 11.7.

2.155 Where the rules apply a standard such as taking reasonable care, the issue of what the applicable standard was and whether the firm's behaviour met that standard may be one of the key points at issue between the firm and the FSA. It is important to appreciate that the standard required to be observed is only to take *reasonable* care. What the FSA has not made clear in this guidance is that there is not necessarily only one view of what a reasonable firm would have done in the particular situation. In the context of claims under the civil law, it may be sufficient for the firm to show that a responsible body of firms would accept the firm's practice as proper, even if the FSA identifies another body of opinion which would regard a different practice as proper[1].

1 See *Bolam v Friern Hospital Management Committee* [1957] 1 WLR 582 and *Saif Ali Sydney Mitchell and Co* [1980] AC 198 (per Lord Diplock) but note the limitations of this doctrine: see *JD Williams & Co Ltd v Michael Hyde & Associates Ltd* [2001] BLR 99, CA.

Breaches of the Principles for Businesses

2.156 On a more general level, as we have seen, firms are subject to the Principles for Businesses, which are deliberately drafted at a high level of generality[1]. The Principles are rules made by the FSA under the FSMA 2000. Breach will therefore amount to the breach of a requirement imposed on the firm under the FSMA 2000 and is in principle no different from breach of any other FSA rule[2]. Serious breaches of the Principles may carry wider consequences than other rule breaches because the Principles are said to embody the main elements of the 'fit and proper' standard. Hence, breach of the Principles may indicate that the firm is not suitable to be carrying on particular regulated activities and thus lead to the variation or cancellation of its permission[3].

1 There are also regulatory general principles applicable to approved persons, namely the Statements of Principle. The extent to which breach has enforcement consequences is outlined at para 2.178 ff below.
2 Breaching a Principle makes a firm liable to disciplinary sanctions: see the FSA Handbook at PRIN 1.1.7.
3 See Chapter 9 below.

The issues

2.157 A question which has been the subject of much debate, as already noted, is whether breach of the Principles should in itself give rise to regulatory consequences, particularly disciplinary consequences[1]. The practice of the FSA's predecessor regulators for investment business[2] was to discipline firms for breach of the regulatory general principles which preceded the Principles for Businesses[3] and the FSA made clear throughout the consultation process which preceded the FSMA 2000 that it intended to continue to do so[4].

1 See, for example, the First Report of the Joint Committee at paragraphs 230 to 248 and the discussion in Standing Committee on 25 November 1999.
2 The SROs: SFA, IMRO and the PIA.
3 In a large proportion of successful IMRO or SFA enforcement cases, breach of one or more of the previous principles was one of the charges cited. By way of illustration, the following are some of the many examples of regulatory action in 2000 based wholly or substantially on breaches of principles: IMRO's action against *Coutts & Co* (13 July 2000); *Yorkshire Bank plc* (1 November 2000); and *National Westminster Bank plc* (24 November 2000) and the SFA's action against *Messrs Butler, Felton, Katsis and Wales* (Board Notice 541) and *PH Pope & Son* (Board Notice 555).
4 See, for example, Consultation Page 17 ('Enforcing the new Regime'), December 1998, paras 91–95, and the FSA's Response to Consultation Paper 17, July 1999, paras 54–58.

2.158 This gives rise to two main issues. First, whether it is appropriate for the FSA to subject firms to an additional 'charge' of breach of the Principles where there is already a clear charge of a breach of a particular rule. Principle 2 is a good example: failing to act with due skill, care and diligence could be added to almost any charge sheet, giving the appearance that the firm had committed a further breach in addition to the breach of one or more specific rules. For example, if a firm is accused of producing inaccurate or misleading marketing material in relation to a particular product, should it also face a charge of breach of Principle 2, that it failed to act with due skill, care and diligence?

2.159 This example can also be used to demonstrate the second issue. If the firm shows that it did not, technically, breach the relevant rules regarding marketing material, or even that those rules did not apply in the specific circumstances, can it still be charged with a breach of Principle 2? In other words, should the Principles be used by the regulator to subject a firm to regulatory consequences in circumstances where no particular regulatory breach could otherwise be identified or where there were no applicable regulations?

2.160 Two important considerations need to be borne in mind in discussing these issues. First, as has already been outlined[1], the original rationale for introducing high-level principles was to reduce the need for detailed rules covering every aspect of regulated activity. If the Principles for Businesses are to have this benefit then clearly the FSA need the ability to take enforcement action based on them.

1 See para 2.53 above.

2.161 Second, the Human Rights Act 1998 may affect the FSA's ability to rely upon the Principles as the basis for disciplinary action. There is an issue whether FSA disciplinary proceedings will be criminal for ECHR purposes and it may in some circumstances be arguable that they are[1]. If a particular disciplinary process is 'criminal' for ECHR purposes, then it will have to fulfil various additional requirements, one of which is the need for certainty in the activities which are prohibited[2]. This requires offences to be sufficiently clearly defined that people can reasonably foresee what actions will make them liable. It is very questionable whether a regulatory 'charge' which consists of a breach of Principles arising from behaviour which does not breach the applicable FSA guidance, or where there is no or insufficient guidance, will pass this hurdle[3]. In any event, it may be arguable that the same principle applies under English law, irrespective of how the proceedings are classified for ECHR purposes[4].

1 This is discussed in more detail at para 5.20 ff below.
2 ECHR, art 7. See, for example, *Kokkinakis v Greece* (1993) 17 EHRR 397.
3 See the views of Lord Lester of Herne Hill, QC and Monica Carrs-Frisk at Annex D to the First Report of the Joint Committee of Parliament.
4 'I am prepared to accept as a basic principle of fairness in a disciplinary context that the person should know what charge or case he has to meet; and that he should only be found guilty of misconduct if at the time he committed the alleged offence he knew or ought reasonably to have known that what he did was an offence. For this purpose, the convention adds nothing to what must be a basic understanding of natural justice': Morrison J in *R v Securities and Futures Authority Ltd, ex p Fleurose* [2001] All ER (D) 189.

The FSA's policy

2.162 The FSA's policy[1] is that there may be cases where it is appropriate to discipline on the basis of breach of the Principles alone. Examples include where there is no detailed rule which prohibits the behaviour but it clearly contravenes a Principle, or where a firm has committed a number of breaches of detailed rules which, individually, may not merit disciplinary action but the cumulative effect of which indicates the breach of a Principle. In any case, it will be for the FSA to show that the firm has been at fault in some way, as indicated by the terms of each Principle[2].

1 See the FSA Handbook at ENF 11.6. Note that in certain contexts (accepting deposits, general insurance business and certain types of long-term insurance business) the FSA will apply the Principles only in the prudential context, meaning that it would not expect to exercise its powers brought into play by contravention of a Principle unless the contravention amounted to a serious

or persistent violation which had implications for confidence in the financial system, or for the fitness and propriety of the firm, or for the adequacy of the firm's financial resources: see the FSA Handbook at PRIN 1.1.3.

2 For example, some of the Principles require firms to 'take reasonable care'; others require them to 'pay due regard', etc. See the discussion at para 2.55 above.

2.163 Some further indication of the FSA's likely policy can be found in the Consultation Papers which preceded the Handbook, where the FSA indicated[1] that it will invoke the Principles as a basis for disciplinary or enforcement action where:

- it is clear that the conduct in question violates the Principles, regardless of whether any detailed rule has strictly been breached; or
- the behaviour in question is closely analogous to behaviour which would constitute a breach of a detailed rule; or
- there is evidence of systematic and repeated breach of detailed rules.

This is wide-ranging and clearly envisages the use of Principles in the two areas identified above.

1 See Consultation Page 17 ('Enforcing the new Regime'), December 1998, paras 91–95, and the FSA's Response to Consultation Paper 17, July 1999, paras 54–58.

2.164 The FSA does, however, recognise that the application of the Principles should be reasonably predictable. It has said that it will use them fairly and not in an arbitrary or unpredictable fashion[1]. Thus, the FSA has, in its Conduct of Business Sourcebook, linked many of its conduct of business rules to specific Principles for Businesses[2]. This may suggest that breach of the rule would be likely also to amount to a breach of the relevant Principle. The linkage between Principles and specific rules[3] seems to be intended to improve the certainty and predictability of use of each Principle. The use of the Principles for discipline and enforcement is likely to be a common feature of the regime.

1 See Consultation Paper 17 and the Response (footnote 1 to para 2.163 above). The Principles are therefore elaborated on by means of rules, evidential provisions and guidance. They do not 'operate in a vacuum but in harmony with the other materials making up the framework within which firms must operate. However...the Principles may be particularly relevant in situations for which no rule or guidance exists. In these circumstances it will be necessary for firms and supervisors alike to make judgments based on the values embodied in the principles': Response to Consultation Paper 13, October 1999.

2 Many examples could be given. To take only three, see the FSA Handbook at COB 2.5.2, 6.1.3 and 7.8.2.

3 Other rules that interrelate with the Principles include SYSC (senior management arrangements, systems and controls), MAR 1 (Code of Market Conduct) and IPRU (Interim Prudential Sourcebook).

Failure to be fit and proper

2.165 The concept of fitness and propriety – that is, that authorised firms are fit and proper to carry on regulated business – is the bedrock of the regulatory system and the foundation for the suitability criterion that is one of the threshold criteria underlying the firm's authorisation[1].

1 FSMA 2000, s 41 and Sch 6 and see the detailed discussion at para 2.43 above. Fitness and propriety is relevant also to individuals, although its meaning is different in that context: see para 2.69 above.

2.166 With one exception, a failure to be fit and proper does not of itself give rise to regulatory enforcement consequences, but:

- the circumstances which give rise to the failure to be fit and proper may amount to a breach of a specific rule for which the usual disciplinary and other enforcement consequences would be applicable, and in particular could well amount to the breach of one or more of the Principles[1]; and
- the situation could certainly be investigated by the FSA[2].

The one exception is that it could lead to the FSA imposing conditions or restrictions on the firm by the variation of its permission or the cancellation of its permission[3].

1 See para 2.156 above.
2 Either as circumstances suggesting the breach of a specific rule (see para 4.134 below) or on the basis there was 'good reason' to investigate the firm's business (see para 4.122 below).
3 See Chapter 9.

Issues arising abroad with implications in the UK

2.167 Issues arising in the non-UK business of a firm (either a UK regulated firm or an incoming firm) could have regulatory implications in the UK. For example, there may be reporting lines into or out of the UK or some degree of control or compliance function may be exercised from or to the UK. If so, a matter occurring abroad may give rise to regulatory concerns in the UK. To what extent can the FSA take action as a result of such matters?

UK regulated firms

2.168 So far as UK regulated firms are concerned, the Principles for Businesses have a wide territorial application, as outlined at para 2.60 above. Some of the Principles apply to the firm's activities wherever they are conducted; others apply to its activities everywhere to the extent they are carried on from the firm's UK establishment; and Principles 1 to 3 apply 'in a prudential context' to the firm's activities wherever they are conducted (and in some respects outside that context as well). By 'prudential context', the FSA means[1] the context in which the activities have, or might reasonably be regarded as likely to have, a negative effect on:

- confidence in the financial system; or
- the ability of the firm to meet either the 'fit and proper' test in the threshold conditions or the requirements and standards relating to financial resources.

1 See the FSA Handbook at PRIN, Glossary of Definitions.

2.169 In practice, this involves drawing a distinction between enforcement action that is disciplinary and that which is essentially protective or preventative in nature. Disciplinary action will rarely be relevant to prudential supervision. However, the cancellation of a firm's permission is essentially prudential in nature. Enforcement action in the prudential context thus covers action like variation and cancellation of permission and withdrawal of approval, but not, generally, fines and public censures.

2.170 The firm may also have an obligation to report to the FSA some matters occurring overseas, which are likely to be of interest to the FSA[1]. Furthermore, the firm owes the FSA a duty to deal in an open and co-operative manner with all of its regulators, including its overseas regulators. In principle, a breach of either of these obligations would also be a UK regulatory breach giving rise to the various potential enforcement actions outlined in this book.

1 For a further discussion of the notification obligation under Principle 11 and the specific FSA rules on reporting, see para 3.41 ff below.

2.171 Finally, whilst it is, mostly, unlikely that a person based overseas will need to be an approved person, it is still possible for his activities to have UK regulatory consequences. For example, if it impacted on whether he was 'fit and proper', it could lead to the FSA refusing to approve him if he returned to the UK or, in an extreme case, making a prohibition order or, perhaps more likely, indicating to the firm that its links with that person gave the FSA cause for concern about the firm.

Incoming firms

2.172 A matter occurring in the overseas business of an incoming firm may be relevant in so far as it impacts on issues which it is the FSA's responsibility to enforce. In particular, as has been seen, the Principles for Businesses apply to incoming firms in the same way as they apply to UK regulated firms except, broadly speaking, in so far as responsibility for the matter in question is reserved to the firm's home state regulator. Incoming firms are also required to comply with various specific FSA rules, such as most of the Conduct of Business rules. The FSA may also be concerned about the activities of those approved persons who work for incoming firms, wherever their activities are conducted. Further, where an incoming firm has a top-up permission, the FSA has an increased regulatory responsibility for it. Finally, in certain limited circumstances, the incoming firm's authorisation can be withdrawn.

2.173 Overall, there is substantial scope for the FSA to take an interest in what happens in relation to an incoming firm overseas. The precise extent and nature of that interest, and the nature of the enforcement action that could result, will depend on the circumstances.

Issues arising in a firm's unregulated business

2.174 Issues arising in the firm's unregulated business may have regulatory implications, broadly because:

- the issue may amount to the breach of a rule notwithstanding the fact that it occurred in the firm's unregulated business. The FSMA 2000[1] allows the FSA to make rules in relation to the carrying on by firms of not only regulated activities but also unregulated activities. This applies only where the rule concerned indicates that it applies to unregulated activities[2];
- more generally, the conduct may give rise to concerns about whether the firm is fit and proper or whether it complies with the Principles for Businesses in relation to its regulated business or may be relevant to the adequacy of the firm's resources or other prudential matters.

The possible regulatory consequences would depend upon the circumstances but in principle any of those outlined in this book could be relevant.

1 FSMA 2000, s 138(1).
2 See the FSA Handbook at GEN 2.2.17.

Breach of the perimeter

2.175 Breach of the perimeter (also referred to as 'breach of the general prohibition') refers to the carrying on of a regulated activity without authorisation[1]. The FSA has broad powers of investigating and dealing with breaches of the perimeter, including the power to bring civil proceedings to prevent the breach and prosecutions for the criminal offence committed. In addition, any transactions entered into are unenforceable against the other party, who is entitled to recover any money or other property transferred under the agreement and compensation for any loss[2]. A detailed discussion of these powers is outside the scope of this book, since it is not on the whole an issue for the regulated community.

1 For which there is a 'general prohibition' under FSMA 2000, s 19. There is an exception for 'exempt persons' who do not require authorisation.
2 FSMA 2000, ss 26 and 28. In certain circumstances, agreements made by regulated firms through unregulated third parties can also be unenforceable: FSMA 2000, s 27. These provisions are briefly discussed in Chapter 10 below.

2.176 One question for firms is whether they commit the criminal offence of breaching the general prohibition if they carry on an activity for which they do not have permission. This question arises from the nature of the authorisation process. Firms apply for, and receive, permission to carry on particular regulated activities. Once they receive permission, they are 'authorised persons' for the purposes of the FSMA 2000. However, they are not permitted to carry on other regulated activities outside their permission. Thus, for example, a firm with permission to carry on particular types of investment business (only) is not permitted also to carry on insurance business.

2.177 The answer is that since the firm is an 'authorised person' for the purposes of the FSMA 2000, it would not commit a criminal breach of the general prohibition. The FSMA 2000 makes clear[1] that in this situation the firm has contravened a requirement by or under the FSMA 2000[2], but has not committed an offence, is not liable to transactions being void or unenforceable and is not subject to civil damages claims for breach of statutory duty[3]. However, the firm has clearly committed a regulatory breach, with the same potential consequences as any other breach of specific rules or regulations, and may also have breached the Principles for Businesses and caused the FSA to have doubts about whether it is fit and proper.

1 FSMA 2000, s 20.
2 See para 2.142 ff above.
3 Save in cases specified by HM Treasury. In practice, under the regulations that have been made, a private person will normally have a right of action: see para 10.46 below.

What types of conduct by individuals give rise to enforcement?

2.178 There will be frequent examples where the same incident constitutes both a breach by a firm and misconduct by an individual. Regulatory problems do not arise in a vacuum. If 'the firm' has done or omitted to do something, and so committed a breach, at some level this is almost bound to have been caused by the acts or omissions of particular individuals. Those in the frame might include, for example, not only the particular salesman who missold the investment to a consumer, but also the back office staff who failed to notice the consumer had not returned the relevant form, the internal audit staff who did not pick up the same problem on their periodic review the following week, the training department whose courses had not been sufficient to make the salesman aware of his responsibilities, the line manager who took three months to refer the consumer's complaint to the relevant department and the compliance officer who investigated the matter and identified only that there had been a problem with the sale of the investment but not the other matters outlined above and decided that the specific issue could be resolved without needing to tell the FSA.

2.179 Not all of these individuals will have done anything wrong. Indeed, some of them may not even be amenable to FSA discipline[1]. But the example illustrates the number of people who may in some way be culpable and the complexities involved in assigning blame.

1 Some of them may not be approved persons – ie personally authorised under the FSMA 2000: see para 2.64 above.

2.180 The FSMA 2000 leaves the question when individuals are to be subjected personally to enforcement action largely in the hands of the FSA. As has already been seen, it is left to the FSA to determine, subject to broad statutory criteria, which functions are to be 'controlled functions' which may be performed only by people approved by the FSA and to issue Statements of Principle and a Code of Practice as to the conduct to be expected of such persons[1]. It is also left to the FSA to determine its policy on the imposition of penalties against approved persons[2], in other words the circumstances when it will seek to discipline individuals, and to decide in each case whether it is appropriate to do so[3]. These aspects are considered in more detail in Chapter 8 below. We outline here the types of acts which could give rise to enforcement action against individuals, both approved persons and others.

1 For an outline of these, see para 2.76 above.
2 FSMA 2000, s 69(1)(a).
3 FSMA 2000, s 66(1)(b).

2.181 There are four general bases upon which the FSA can take enforcement action against individuals:

- failure to comply with a Statement of Principle, which could give rise to disciplinary action for misconduct[1] or to the FSA applying to the court for an injunction or restitution order[2];
- being knowingly concerned in a contravention by an authorised person, which could give rise to disciplinary action for misconduct[3] or allow the FSA to apply to the court for an injunction or restitution order against the person[4];
- not being a fit and proper person to perform functions in relation to a firm's regulated activities, which could lead to the FSA withdrawing the person's approval[5] or imposing a prohibition order[6]; or
- breaching or being reasonably likely to breach a requirement imposed on him by or under the FSMA 2000, which could allow the FSA to apply for an injunction or a restitution order[7].

Each of these is considered in turn below[8].

1 FSMA 2000, s 66(2)(a) and see Chapter 8 below.
2 FSMA 2000, ss 380 or 382 and see Chapter 8 below.
3 FSMA 2000, s 66(2)(b) and see Chapter 8 below.
4 FSMA 2000, ss 380 and 382 and see Chapter 8 below.
5 FSMA 2000, s 63 and see Chapter 8 below.
6 FSMA 2000, s 56 and see Chapter 8 below.
7 FSMA 2000, ss 380 or 382 and see Chapter 8 below.
8 In addition, there are other bases for taking specific types of enforcement action, such as market abuse (see Chapter 13 below), criminal prosecutions for offences under the FSMA 2000 (see Chapter 11 below) and action against directors of listed companies (see Chapter 15 below).

Failure to comply with a Statement of Principle

2.182 A failure by an approved person to comply with a Statement of Principle can in some circumstances give rise to disciplinary action for misconduct by the FSA against the individual[1] and could also lead to an injunction or restitution order being imposed[2]. In addition, it could be relevant to demonstrating that the person was not a fit and proper person to be carrying out a controlled function, in which case it could lead to his approval being withdrawn or to a prohibition order being made against him[3].

1 For a more detailed discussion, see para 8.7 ff below.
2 The basis for this would be that the failure to comply constituted the contravention of a requirement by or under the FSMA 2000; see paras 2.189 and 8.76 ff below.
3 For a discussion of withdrawal of approval and prohibition orders, see paras 8.27 ff and 8.44 ff below.

2.183 The Statements of Principle for approved persons are discussed in detail at para 2.76 above. Each requires in some form that the person's conduct fell below the relevant applicable standard. The Statements are drawn in very general terms and whilst some assistance on their meaning is provided by the Code of Practice, the Code is not exhaustive and is only of evidential effect. This means that it will often not be clear whether the individual's conduct did amount to a breach.

Knowingly concerned in a contravention by the relevant authorised person

2.184 In many instances, an individual approved person may be susceptible to disciplinary or other enforcement action because of his involvement in a regulatory breach committed by the firm. The test used is whether he was knowingly concerned in a contravention by the relevant authorised person of a requirement imposed on that authorised person by or under the FSMA 2000. The meaning of 'requirement imposed by or under the FSMA 2000' has been considered at para 2.142 above. We consider here when a person's actions will amount to being knowingly concerned in such a contravention.

2.185 On the face of it, the phrase is unclear. For example, is it enough that the individual knows about the relevant actions or omissions which amounted to a breach? Or does he also have to know that those actions did or could constitute a breach? And is it sufficient that, for example, he had line responsibility for what happened, and perhaps knew that it was happening? Or should have known that it was happening? Or does he need to be actively involved?

2.186 Some of these issues have been addressed in the context of similar wording[1] in the Financial Services Act 1986[2]. A number of points can be made[3]:

- first, ignorance of the law is no defence. Hence, it is irrelevant whether the person had any knowledge that the matters amounted to a breach. The person is to be judged on the facts as he believed them to be, but on the law as it is[4];
- second, it seems that actual knowledge of the facts is required[5], although in the criminal law context wilful blindness has been capable of being sufficient[6]. It is not therefore clear whether the fact that a person should have known, but did not know, about the relevant matters, in a situation where he had deliberately shut his eyes to the obvious, would make him liable to disciplinary action under this limb (although his lack of knowledge may of course amount to a breach of a Statement of Principle, for which he could be disciplined if he should have had knowledge);
- third, it seems that mere knowledge will not be sufficient; some sort of actual involvement in the contravention must be established[7];
- fourth, it appears from criminal law authority that the person must be aware of the true nature of the conduct in which he was involved, although he need not be aware of the precise details[8].

1 'Knowingly concerned in the contravention': Financial Services Act 1986, ss 6(2) and 61.
2 The concept of 'knowingly concerned' is also well known in criminal law, for example in the Customs & Excise Management Act 1979, the Fair Trading Act 1973 and various Finance Acts. The criminal law cases demonstrate that a fairly broad test has been applied, at least in the criminal law context. See further, footnote 8 below.
3 Note that (1) the second and third points below are obiter dicta and therefore not strictly binding, albeit they are strongly persuasive given the seniority of the judge concerned; and (2) it may be that the courts will take a different approach in the context of the FSMA 2000.
4 See *Burton v Bevan* [1908] 2 Ch 240 and *Securities and Investments Board v Scandex Capital Management A/S* [1998] 1 All ER 514, per Millett LJ at 521. This point was also made by the Economic Secretary in Standing Committee on 28 October 1999.
5 *Securities and Investments Board v Pantell SA (No 2)* [1992] 1 All ER 134, per Steyn LJ at 147.
6 See *Westminster County Council v Croyalgrange Ltd* [1986] 2 All ER 353, HL: '. . . it is always open to a tribunal of fact, when knowledge on the part of a defendant is required to be proved, to base a finding of knowledge on evidence that the defendant had deliberately shut his eyes to the obvious or refrained from enquiry because he suspected the truth but did not want to have his suspicion confirmed': per Lord Bridge, 359. In the civil law context, issues about wilfully shutting one's eyes to the obvious have been considered in detail in relation to knowing assistance and knowing receipt claims (see paras 10.19 and 10.20 below).
7 *Securities and Investments Board v Pantell SA* [1992] 1 All ER 134, per Steyn LJ at 147.
8 This principle emerges from the criminal law cases: see *R v Hussain* [1969] 2 QB 567, CA, approved in *R v Shivpuri* [1987] AC 1, HL. The government's view is that the principle applies: see the Economic Secretary to the Treasury, House of Commons Standing Committee, 28 October 1999.

2.187 This phrase is therefore a reasonably broad one, although its precise meaning is unclear. The third of the above points may give some indication that those with managerial responsibility but who were not directly or actively involved in the matter would not be regarded as having been 'knowingly concerned' in it, but caution should be exercised until the approach of the FSA and the courts to this question becomes clearer. In addition though, whether the person's conduct would amount to a breach of a Statement of Principle, for which he could instead be disciplined, is a separate question.

Failure to be a fit and proper person

2.188 The need for an individual to be fit and proper is central to his being granted approval by the FSA to carry on controlled functions[1]. Equally, where the FSA considers that a person lacks fitness or propriety, it may take action to withdraw his approval or make a prohibition order against him. The test of fit and proper in the context of individuals has been considered in detail at para 2.69 above.

1 See para 2.64 above.

Breach of a requirement imposed by or under the FSMA

2.189 The meaning of this phrase has been considered at para 2.142 above. In addition, the Statements of Principle for approved persons[1] probably constitute requirements imposed by or under the FSMA 2000[2].

1 See para 2.76 ff above.
2 The consequences of failing to comply with the Statement of Principle are outlined at para 2.182 above.

3 Steps to take when regulatory problems arise

CONTENTS

Introduction **63**

Should the firm investigate? **66**

Should the firm report the problem? **75**

How should the firm deal with its customers? **92**

What other internal action should the firm take? **96**

Does the problem potentially give rise to criminal proceedings? **101**

Taking care about document destruction and creation **102**

INTRODUCTION

3.1 The purpose of this chapter is to review some of the legal and practical points that arise at the outset, when a matter comes to the firm's attention raising issues that may be of concern to the regulator. As will be seen, the firm is likely to be under a duty to the FSA to take certain immediate steps, such as notifying the FSA. Beyond this, though, it may be prudent for the firm to act in a particular way to protect its own interests as well as the interests of, among others, its employees and its customers.

3.2 Whether the firm needs to take any action and, if so, what action it should take, depends upon the nature and seriousness of the particular problem. But a number of points should at least be considered in most cases. The primary issues that immediately arise include:

- whether the firm should investigate;
- whether the firm should report the problem;
- how the firm should deal with its customers;
- whether the firm should be taking any action internally (for example, to remedy any defects in procedures and to deal with any employees);
- whether the problem potentially gives rise to criminal proceedings; and
- taking care over document creation and retention.

These are addressed in turn below, after considering two initial points, namely, first, the scope of those matters that are likely to be of concern to the FSA and, second, the question of how the problem was discovered.

3.3 The guiding principle of an open and co-operative relationship between firm and regulator[1] drives much of the discussion below. This approach is fundamental to the UK regulatory regime and needs to be borne in mind throughout. Moreover, the firm's response to the regulatory problem is of itself a part of the firm's systems and controls. Handling the problem properly is an important part of demonstrating that the firm takes reasonable care to organise and control its affairs responsibly and effectively[2].

1 Principle 11, Principles for Businesses: see para 2.52 above and paras 3.39, 4.27 and 4.180 below.
2 Principle 3, Principles for Businesses: see para 2.52 above.

What types of matters will concern the FSA?

3.4 The first issue is to identify those types of problems that potentially raise regulatory concerns. The scope of matters that may be relevant will become evident from, among other things, the discussion of the firm's reporting obligation that follows below but, briefly, the FSA's approach is to cast its net wide and firms therefore need to do the same. The matters that may be of regulatory concern are not limited to possible breaches of specific rules. They include breaches of the applicable general principles[1], which are drafted at a high level of generality and thus cover a wide range of matters. Examples of conduct likely to concern the FSA include conduct giving rise to concerns about:

- whether particular persons are fit and proper to be involved in the firm's regulated activities[2];
- the firm's integrity or standards of market conduct or those of its employees[3];
- the firm's internal supervision or controls[4]; or
- how the firm has dealt with its customers, particularly consumers[5].

1 Breach of the Principles for Businesses or, for approved persons, the Statements of Principle, can give rise to disciplinary or other enforcement consequences: see paras 2.156 ff and 2.182 above. For a detailed discussion of the Principles for Businesses see para 2.51 ff above and, of the Statements of Principle, para 2.76 ff above.

2 As to the meaning of fit and proper in relation to individuals, see para 2.69 ff above. This would include anything relevant to their integrity, their training or competence to carry out the job and their financial soundness.
3 See Principles 1 and 5, Principles for Businesses and Statements of Principle 1 and 3 for approved persons, and the FSA Handbook at MAR.
4 See Principle 3, Principles for Businesses, Statements of Principle 5–7 for approved persons, and the FSA Handbook at SYSC.
5 See Principles 6–9, Principles for Businesses and Statements of Principle 1 and 2 for approved persons, and the FSA Handbook at COB. See also the discussion at para 3.110 ff below.

3.5 These examples are little more than illustrative. In assessing whether the matter is potentially of interest to the regulator, firms need to have in mind all of their obligations and the standards expected of them in the light of the Principles for Businesses and the Statements of Principle for approved persons, as well as those matters that the FSA has indicated need to be reported to it[1].

1 See para 3.41 ff below.

How was the problem discovered?

3.6 How the firm reacts initially will depend to some extent upon the circumstances in which the problem was discovered, and in particular whether it was the firm or the FSA which became aware of the problem first.

3.7 There are many ways that a regulatory issue can come to light. The firm might become aware of it, among other things, when a specific 'incident' occurs, from the confessions or reports of an employee, through regular or specific internal audit or compliance checks, from customer complaints or even from market activity or rumour. The FSA, for its part, could also pick up the issue in a variety of ways[1]. Examples include from information obtained on a regular monitoring visit to the firm, in the course of reviewing an issue relating to another firm, or on receiving a report from another regulator. The FSA could also pick up a story in the press or receive a customer complaint.

1 Sources for complex perimeter enforcement cases in the year to 31 March 2000 include the industry, other regulators, the public, the police, accountants and solicitors, DTI/trading standards and other prosecutors, the press and anonymous reports: see the FSA's 1999/2000 Annual Report.

3.8 As will be seen[1], if it is the firm that discovers the problem, it will need quickly to consider notifying the FSA. Obviously, if it was the FSA that discovered the problem first, then this will not be an issue, but there will instead be other issues to confront, not least how to explain why the problem went unnoticed by the firm. Even where the firm discovers the problem first, the FSA will want to know how it discovered the problem and this may be relevant to what enforcement action it is appropriate to take[2]. The best position, from the firm's point of view, is for its systems or controls to have identified the problem.

1 See para 3.41 ff below.
2 See, for example, the FSA Handbook at ENF 3.5.13(8) (policy on variation of permission: see para 9.199 below). The answer may also give rise to questions about the firm's systems and controls.

SHOULD THE FIRM INVESTIGATE?

3.9 The firm will normally be faced at the outset with a limited amount of information about the problem and the obvious question is whether it should carry out further investigations and, if it should, what ought to be the procedure for those investigations. We review:

- the reasons why the firm should investigate;
- who should investigate; and
- how the investigation should be carried out.

Each is considered in turn below.

Why investigate?

3.10 It is difficult to assess the seriousness of the problem, and therefore what action, if any, needs to be taken, before the firm has a proper understanding of what the problem involves. Equally, if it is necessary to contact the FSA, or indeed any other regulators, then the firm will want to ensure that it understands the problem and can demonstrate to the regulator that it has the matter properly in hand. However, problems which may seem at first to be minor or one-dimensional can turn out to have wider consequences, or be part of a wider problem, and may therefore need to be treated more seriously than it appeared initially. Action may be required across a broad front, including not only in relation to the regulator, but also potentially involving customers, staff, systems, market counterparties, the firm's insurers, sometimes the police and even the press. It is therefore imperative for the firm to get to the root of the problem as quickly as possible and to make some kind of assessment as to its implications. Moreover, taking proper steps to investigate when a problem arises may of itself be viewed as relevant to whether the firm's systems and controls are adequate. A failure to take proper steps to investigate may, particularly, impact on the FSA's view of the firm's compliance department[1].

1 The importance of reviewing the reasons for significant breaches and assessing the implications for the firm's systems is also reflected in the Code of Practice applicable to Statement of Principle 7: see the FSA Handbook at APER 4.7 and see para 2.100 above.

3.11 Carrying out a proper review of the problem and its implications can, however, be time consuming. Even where the firm needs or wishes to carry out an exhaustive internal review, this does not mean that it can delay taking any action whatsoever until that process has been completed. Some action may need to be taken promptly and there is clearly a trade off between, on the one hand, understanding the problem fully and thus being in a position to assess properly what action is appropriate, and, on the other hand, reacting, and being seen to react, with the proper expedition.

Who should investigate?

3.12 The first question is how the investigation should be structured and, particularly, who should carry it out. Whilst there are attractions in allowing internal audit or compliance to carry out an internal review, and this is often part of their normal role, it is important to recognise the potential risks that may occur unless the internal investigation is properly structured. Primarily, any report produced by internal audit or compliance, and their notes (even handwritten notes) of any discussions they have with the staff involved, could be at risk of being liable to disclosure not only to the FSA but also to other parties, for example if legal proceedings arose from the matter[1]. Equally, if management, understandably, take steps to interview the staff involved as soon as the problem comes to light, and do so without consulting the legal department, they may create documents which could be liable to be disclosed. Documents of this nature, particularly those created at an early stage when there is not yet a full understanding of the problem, can often cause problems later, however anodyne they may seem at the time they are written.

1 Issues relating to the disclosure of documents are considered in more detail at paras 3.155 ff and 4.189 ff below.

3.13 In addition, it is important to recognise that reporting lines and compliance structures can sometimes be viewed by the FSA as having played some part in the problem. Any implications which the problem may have for internal supervision and controls are likely to be of particular interest to the FSA[1]. The firm would be well advised to ensure that the review, whoever conducts it, is able to cast an objective eye over the possibility of such issues arising.

1 See, for example, the FSA Handbook at ENF 11.4.1(1) and 13.3.3(1). Examples of cases where failures in systems and controls have been cited as an important part of the charges include *Lloyds TSB Bank plc* (IMRO, 23 November 2000); *Yorkshire Bank plc* (1 November 2000); and *Natwest Capital Markets Ltd* (SFA Board Notice 545, 18 May 2000).

3.14 There are, therefore, often strong reasons for involving internal or external legal counsel at an early stage, to seek to ensure that documents created are protected from disclosure by legal professional privilege[1], and to help provide an objective view on the problem so that the action to be taken can be properly assessed from the outset.

1 See further para 3.155 below.

How should the investigation be carried out?

3.15 We consider here four issues, namely:

- the scope of the investigation;
- gathering together and reviewing the documents;
- investigating employees; and
- interviewing employees.

3.16 As a preliminary point, the firm should keep careful track of what steps it has taken and, if appropriate, the reasons why it decided not to take particular steps, so that it can explain the extent of its investigation to the FSA if it is asked to do so.

The scope of the investigation

3.17 One of the first points is to decide upon the scope of the investigation. This will depend upon the nature and seriousness of the matter concerned: not every minor breach requires an exhaustive investigation aimed at identifying any underlying systemic causes. Equally, though, the FSA will expect the firm to have considered whether there are any wider implications, particularly since, among other things, this is relevant to whether the firm needs to notify the FSA[1]. It also allows the firm to consider how the problem can be prevented from recurring[2].

1 See para 3.42 below. The need to identify any wider implications is reinforced by the FSA's requirements in respect of firms' internal complaints handling procedures: see the FSA Handbook at DISP and see Chapter 12 below.
2 This is a relevant issue for the FSA: see para 3.131 ff below.

Gathering together and reviewing the documents

3.18 The firm should consider gathering together, at an early stage, all the potentially relevant documents. These will include:

- the working files of any members of staff or department involved, including back office files, compliance or internal audit files and the files of any person to whom any relevant person reported;
- material stored electronically, including e-mails and documents on the hard drives of the people concerned; and
- tapes of telephone conversations on the lines of those people involved.

To the extent that any of this material relates to specific employees, there may be additional points to consider, discussed at para 3.22 ff below.

3.19 Gathering the material together allows the firm to ensure that none of the evidence is destroyed or tampered with[1]. It also allows the firm to react promptly to requests by the FSA for documents or information and thus to be seen to have the matter under control. Also it assists the firm in carrying out its own review, and ensuring that the scope of its review is appropriate.

1 This may be a criminal offence: see para 3.151 below.

3.20 There are a number of practical points to consider. In particular:

- it is important to preserve files intact, as the order of the file may be relevant and this will also assist in demonstrating that it has not been tampered with and that documents have not been removed;

- careful consideration needs to be given as to whether electronic documents have been deleted;
- a record should be kept of where each file was found; and
- a record should be kept of the chain of custody of each file, again to allow the firm to address any questions about whether it has been tampered with.

3.21 Once the documents have been gathered together, the firm will want to review them as part of its internal review. Among other things, this allows the firm to identify those documents that could or should be withheld from the FSA if there is an investigation[1], so that the firm is ready and able to respond swiftly to any requests from the FSA.

1 Primarily, this means legally privileged material but may also include documents that are covered by a duty of banking confidence: see paras 4.264 ff and 4.267 ff below.

Investigating employees

3.22 In reality, any question about what the firm has done involves reviewing the activities of one or more employees, not only those who were directly involved, but also others who may have been involved less directly or may have relevant evidence, for example back office staff or a person to whom an employee under suspicion reported. The firm may wish to ensure at an early stage that it has identified all the relevant people, so that it is in a position to assess whether or not their conduct should be reviewed and whether or not they are likely to have relevant documents or other evidence. Steps can also then be taken, for example to obtain evidence or secure their future co-operation, if any of those people is likely to be unavailable to the firm in the future for any reason.

3.23 In some cases, it may be appropriate, whilst the firm reviews the activities of the relevant employees, to take immediate action to suspend suspect employees or remove them from sensitive positions[1]. This is a matter of common sense, particularly where the circumstances suggest that the breach may result from some deliberate action by an employee. But it may also be viewed by the FSA as a positive step taken by the firm in response to the breach, in order to protect its customers, ensure that the breach is not repeated in the short term and protect the evidence.

1 In so far as it takes any disciplinary action, the firm should ensure that it complies with the terms of any disciplinary procedure (or where there is no such procedure in place, the ACAS Code of Practice on disciplinary proceedings). This should reduce the risk of an employee successfully claiming that he has been treated unfairly.

3.24 Three issues are worth further consideration:

- first, to ensure that material relating to employees recorded in the ordinary course of the firm's business has been lawfully recorded;
- second, to ensure that adequate arrangements are in place that allow the firm to review that material once a problem comes to light; and

- third, the extent to which a more intrusive investigation can be made into a particular individual after a problem comes to light.

We discuss the first two questions together, and provide some practical guidance, and then consider the third. The same English legal issues[1] arise in relation to all three questions, but the importance of the legal issue differs according to the question.

1 There may also be applicable overseas legal considerations, for example data protection legislation applies throughout the EU and in some other countries and many other states have their own privacy laws. These could be relevant if, for example, a telephone call was taped at an overseas branch of the firm. How the firm acts where it is required under the UK legislation to provide information to the FSA when asked to do so, but is constrained by applicable overseas law from doing so, is a particularly difficult problem in practice. See further para 4.277 below.

Material recorded in the ordinary course of business

3.25 Firms regularly monitor and store e-mails and tapes of telephone conversations and indeed often do so under a regulatory obligation. But the interception and recording of communications, including both e-mails and telephone calls, by the firm, even within its own private telecommunications system, may have other legal implications. In particular, firms need to have in mind the Data Protection Act 1998[1], the Regulation of Investigatory Powers Act 2000[2] and the employee's possible right under the Human Rights Act 1998 to respect for privacy in connection with family life and correspondence[3]. The firm's ability not only to record the material but also to review the material recorded may be restricted[4].

1 Recording, reviewing and using tapes of telephone calls, CCTV and e-mails relating to employees, among other things, may amount to the processing of personal data about a data subject (ie the employee) under the Data Protection Act 1998, in which case the firm, as a data controller, must comply with the eight Data Protection Principles and the other provisions of the Data Protection Act 1998. In the current context, the firm will be concerned to ensure data is acquired and stored fairly and lawfully. It will also be necessary to consider whether the data subject must be informed about the firm's activities, or whether exemptions under the Act may be relied upon. Failure to comply with the Act may give rise to enforcement action by the Information Commissioner or a claim for damages by the employee. For a more detailed discussion, see *Data Protection*, Jay and Hamilton (1st edn, 1999).

2 The Regulation of Investigatory Powers Act 2000, s 1(3) prohibits the interception of communications on a private telecommunications system and makes it actionable at the suit of the sender or recipient. But interceptions are permitted if they fall within the Telecommunications (Lawful Business Practice) (Interception of Communications) Regulations 2000, SI 2000/2699: see footnote 2 to para 3.26 below.

3 The right to respect for privacy, and the question whether the employee has such a right against the firm, is discussed at para 3.29 ff below.

4 Most of these hurdles can be overcome if the employee has consented to the monitoring operation. 'Consent' is defined for these purposes in the Data Protection Directive (95/46/EC).

3.26 The firm therefore needs to have appropriate arrangements in place to ensure that the recording and review of material does not contravene the applicable requirements. In broad terms, those arrangements need to include:

- an understanding on the part of employees that their e-mails and telephone calls are monitored, stored and reviewed for various purposes, including to ascertain regulatory compliance, and, preferably, their consent to this;

- a policy on the use of e-mails, the telephone[1] and computers for private purposes, to ensure, among other things, that there is no expectation on the part of employees that they have any right to privacy;
- the waiver by employees of any rights to privacy in respect of material recorded, including any private conversations, e-mails or electronic documents created or held;
- if practical, employees' consent more generally to their conduct being investigated in other ways by the firm, for example by reviewing the contents of their desks, offices and hard drives, and monitoring them by CCTV, without prior notice; and
- ensuring e-mails and telephone calls are monitored and recorded for the sole purpose of[2]:
  - — establishing the existence of facts; and/or
  - — ascertaining compliance with applicable regulatory practices or procedures; and/or
  - — preventing or detecting crime.

1 It may be appropriate to make a telephone line available specifically for private calls which will not be monitored or recorded.
2 These are the relevant purposes permitted under the Lawful Business Practice Regulations: see footnote 2 to para 3.25 above.

3.27 In reviewing the material subsequently once the problem comes to light, the firm should ensure that the information is used and disclosed only to the extent[1]:

- covered by the employee's consent; or
- that it is necessary to do so in order to comply with a legal obligation; or
- that it is necessary to do so for the firm's own legitimate interests[2].

The firm also needs to take care if it wishes to use for some other purpose information which it has come across during an investigation carried out for a particular purpose.

1 These are the relevant conditions of the First Data Protection Principle and are provided in order to give some indication of the parameters of permitted processing. For a more detailed discussion of this and the other requirements of the Data Protection Act 1998, see *Data Protection*, Jay and Hamilton (1st edn, 1999).
2 This last condition may only be relied upon where no unwarranted prejudice to the data subject's privacy is caused. Since the issues of 'prejudice' and whether that prejudice is 'unwarranted' will depend upon the circumstances, it will be preferable to seek consent where it is practical to do so.

Investigations into employees

3.28 The firm may wish to go further than simply reviewing the material that it already has relating to the particular employee. It may wish to conduct a more intrusive investigation, for example by checking the contents of the employee's office or desk, including locked cupboards or drawers, reviewing the hard drive on his computer, or monitoring his telephone. Some of these steps may need to be taken late at night. To what extent is the firm limited in its ability to take this kind of action?

3.29 The main limitation is the employee's possible ECHR right to respect for privacy[1]. Whilst the ECHR rights apply primarily as between, broadly, public authorities and private individuals or companies, it cannot be ruled out that courts will start to apply those rights horizontally, for example to create a direct right of respect for privacy as between employer and employee[2]. There have been ECHR inspired developments towards an English law concept of privacy in any event[3]. Moreover, whether or not an employee has a directly enforceable right to privacy as against his employer, the employee may seek to raise ECHR based arguments (for example relating to the way evidence was collected) before a court or tribunal subsequently considering, for example, whether he was fairly dismissed or whether it is appropriate for the FSA to take action against him. A court or tribunal is required under the Human Rights Act 1998 to act in a way that is compatible with the ECHR and this may well involve it considering such arguments if they are raised. In this way, the ECHR rights may effectively be enforceable horizontally.

1 ECHR, art 8.
2 For a discussion, see *Human Rights Law and Practice*, edited by Lester and Pannick, 1st edn, 1999 at 2.6.3.
3 See *Douglas v Hello! Ltd* [2001] 2 All ER 289.

3.30 Assuming the employee has a right to privacy as against the employer, this includes a right to privacy at work and could be infringed by, for example, the tapping of a telephone at work[1]. But the right is not an absolute one. It can be interfered with provided this is done in accordance with the law, for a legitimate aim and is necessary in a democratic society for specified purposes[2]. The test of necessity requires there to be a pressing social need for the interference and for the means employed to be proportionate to the legitimate aim pursued[3]. The key for the firm is thus to ensure that the investigation is carried out in a way that is proportionate to the legitimate aim sought to be achieved[4].

1 See, for example, the high profile case of *Halford v United Kingdom* (1997) 24 EHRR 523.
2 These are the interests of national security, public safety or the economic well-being of the country, the prevention of disorder or crime, the protection of health or morals or the protection of the rights and freedoms of others: art 8(2).
3 See *Human Rights Law and Practice*, edited by Lester and Pannick, 1st edn, 1999, at 4.8.43.
4 The firm also needs to ensure that the consents discussed at para 3.26 above are in place.

3.31 Precisely what this means will depend upon the situation. Difficult questions include whether the firm can listen to ostensibly private telephone calls, and read private e-mails, and whether it can undertake in secret other particularly intrusive forms of investigation, such as going through someone's desk, locked cupboards and hard drive late at night. Answers to these questions cannot be given in the abstract, since the relevant issues such as legitimate aim, pressing social need and proportionality depend to such a large extent on the particular situation. In general terms, the firm will probably not be entitled to obtain and review material from a source which the employee would reasonably expect to be private[1], at least not without consent.

1 For example, a telephone which was specifically designated for private calls: see *Halford v United Kingdom* (1997) 24 EHRR 523.

3.32 An additional limitation is found in the statutory restrictions outlined at para 3.25 above, which limit the purposes for which the firm can obtain material about its employees and impose requirements on the way in which it uses and handles that material. The points discussed at paras 3.26 and 3.27 above therefore apply equally in this context[1].

1 The firm may also wish to have regard to the guidance on the monitoring of employees contained in s 6, draft Code of Practice issued by the Information Commissioner ('the use of personal data in employer/employee relationships'). The draft Code is indicative of the Commissioner's approach to the Data Protection Principles in this context. The final Code, once issued, constitutes guidance as to good practice, under the Data Protection Act 1998, s 51(3)(b).

Interviewing employees

3.33 There are a number of issues to consider when the firm comes to interview an employee. We consider:

- whether the employee should be invited to take independent legal advice;
- who should carry out the interview; and
- the conduct of the interview.

3.34 We consider here an interview held as part of the firm's investigation into the matter, not a disciplinary hearing held to decide what action to take in relation to the particular employee. Different considerations may be relevant to the latter[1].

1 For a discussion of disciplinary interviews, see *Harvey on Industrial Relations and Employment Law* at [471] et seq.

Independent legal advice

3.35 Should the employee be independently represented at the interview? It is difficult to provide any absolute rule. If the individual asks to bring a lawyer to the interview, it is usually imprudent as well as counter-productive to refuse[1]. Beyond this, if there is a real, rather than purely technical, risk of the employee facing a criminal prosecution, or a real risk that his interests and those of the firm will conflict, the firm should make clear to the individual that he may wish to take his own legal advice. It is then a matter for the employee whether or not he wishes to do so.

1 Whilst it will rarely be appropriate to do so in practice, it is worth noting that if the firm combines the interview with a disciplinary hearing, the employee is entitled in the disciplinary context to be accompanied (but not represented) by a fellow worker or trade union official under the Employment Relations Act 1999.

Who should carry out the interview?

3.36 The interview should normally be carried out by a lawyer. The main reason is to seek to ensure that the interview, and any notes (including manuscript notes) of it, are legally privileged and therefore protected from disclosure to third parties[1] and the FSA[2]. Legally qualified staff or outside counsel thus need to be involved[3] and proper consideration needs to be given as to what steps are required in order to accomplish this in the particular circumstances.

1 Third parties who may have an interest in obtaining such material would include not only customers but also any other parties who may in any way have been involved in or affected by the transaction and who might seek to claim from the firm any losses or expenses they have incurred as a result: see generally Chapter 10.

2 The FSA is (see Chapter 4 below) normally entitled to interview the employee itself. The FSA cannot require the firm to produce or disclose legally privileged material: FSMA 2000, s 413 and see para 4.264 below. Note that the FSMA 2000 contains its own definition of legal privilege for these purposes which may not cover, among others, without prejudice material.

3 In some circumstances, it may be possible to claim privilege over notes of an interview conducted by a non-lawyer, if the dominant purpose of the interview related to legal proceedings or the interview was held to obtain information to pass to a lawyer. However, this is likely to raise some difficult issues: see further para 4.193 ff below.

3.37 It is normally good practice for an interview to be conducted by two people, to split the tasks of asking questions and taking notes, to help ensure that all the relevant points are properly covered, and to ensure that the process is witnessed so that any allegations subsequently made by the employee as to what transpired can properly be rebutted.

The conduct of the interview

3.38 How the interview is conducted will depend very much upon the circumstances, but it is possible to make some general points:

- the person conducting the interview should ensure he understands in advance what questions he will ask and what documents he will put to the person being interviewed;
- in the employment law context, it is good practice to tell the employee in advance why he is being interviewed, so that he has a chance to prepare. In the context of an investigation, whether this will be appropriate and/or practicable will depend upon the circumstances;
- at the outset, the purpose of the interview may need to be explained[1];
- if appropriate, it should be made clear to the employee that he has no right to control the use that is made of the information disclosed at the interview, which is a matter purely for the firm[2];
- a detailed note of the interview should be taken[3]; and
- it will rarely be productive to conduct an interview in a heated manner (indeed, given the need for objectivity it will normally be sensible for the interviewer not to have been involved in the events in issue).

1 Among other things, it may be sensible to make clear that the interview is not a disciplinary hearing but that information obtained in it may be used for the purpose of disciplinary proceedings, if they should result.
2 If the interview is legally privileged, it is the firm's privilege and not that of the employee. For a further discussion, see para 4.208 below.
3 In some circumstances, it may be appropriate to agree the note of the interview with the employee.

SHOULD THE FIRM REPORT THE PROBLEM?

3.39 If the problem is not already known to the FSA, or if their understanding is partial or mistaken, the firm needs to think quickly about reporting it to them. Both regulated firms and their employees who are approved persons owe extensive duties of disclosure to the FSA[1], breach of which is treated extremely seriously[2].

1 These rules will be familiar to firms formerly regulated by one of the SROs, which had similar notification rules and also required firms to comply with the former General Principle 10, which is similar to Principle 11 of the FSA Principles for Businesses.
2 See, for example, *First Atlantic Equities Ltd Powell, Yaras, Marceau and Martin* (SFA Board Notice 462) (Mr Marceau admitted that he failed to deal with the SFA in an open and co-operative manner and as a result ceased to be fit and proper); *Jardine Fleming Asset Management Ltd* (IMRO Public Register, 28 August 1996) (failure to keep IMRO informed was one of the four charges leading to an agreed settlement involving a fine of £400,000 and termination of authorisation) and the *Morgan Grenfell/Peter Young* affair (IMRO Public Register, 17 April 1997, 26 February 1998, 20 May 1998 and 6 January 1999) (breach of the predecessor to Principle 11 featured among the charges against those involved).

3.40 In the following paragraphs, we consider:

- the scope of the firm's obligations to report to the FSA;
- the obligation of individual employees to do so;
- the potential consequences of not complying with these obligations; and
- the obligations which there may, in some circumstances, be to report to other bodies.

The firm's obligation to report

3.41 The firm's basic reporting obligation, contained in Principle 11, is to disclose to the FSA appropriately anything relating to the firm of which the FSA would reasonably expect notice[1].

1 Principle 11, Principles for Businesses; see para 2.52 above. In addition to the obligation to report, Principle 11 also contains an obligation to be open and co-operative, which is considered at paras 4.27 ff and 4.180 below.

3.42 This is self-evidently a wide obligation and has to some extent been fleshed out by four detailed rules in the FSA Handbook[1]. The detailed rules are set out below to the extent they are relevant in the enforcement context, together with a summary of the accompanying guidance. They are outlined below under four headings as follows[2]:

- Rule 1: matters having a serious regulatory impact;
- Rule 2: breaches of rules and other requirements under the FSMA 2000;
- Rule 3: civil, criminal or disciplinary proceedings against a firm; and
- Rule 4: fraud, errors and other irregularities.

1 See the FSA Handbook at SUP Chapter 15. For the application of these rules in relation to incoming firms, see the FSA Handbook at SUP 15, Annex 1R. In addition to the notification rules outlined here, SUP Chapter 15 contains other reporting rules not so directly relevant in the enforcement context. The FSA Handbook also contains various detailed notification requirements, the details of which are beyond the scope of this book as they are not generally relevant for enforcement purposes.

2 An additional rule requires firms to notify the FSA immediately if information they have provided to the FSA may be false, misleading or inaccurate or may have changed: see footnote 2 to para 3.84 below.

3.43 The broad, basic principle found in Principle 11 is, though, paramount and needs to be kept in mind, particularly where there is doubt on whether the specific rules require a particular matter to be reported. The detailed rules are not exhaustive of Principle 11. The FSA has provided guidance on the application of Principle 11, which is explained below following the discussion of the four specific rules.

Rule 1: Matters having a serious regulatory impact

3.44 A firm must notify the FSA[1] immediately it becomes aware, or has information which reasonably suggests, that any of the following has or may have occurred or may occur in the foreseeable future:

- the firm failing to satisfy one or more of the threshold conditions[2];
- any matter which could have a significant adverse impact on the firm's reputation;
- any matter which could affect the firm's ability to continue to provide adequate services to its customers and which could result in serious detriment to a customer of the firm; or
- any matter in respect of the firm which could result in serious financial consequences to the financial system or to other firms.

1 See the FSA Handbook at SUP 15.3.1.

2 For a discussion of the threshold conditions, see para 2.38 ff above.

3.45 The FSA acknowledges that the circumstances which could give rise to these consequences are wide-ranging and the probability of any matters resulting in such an outcome, and the severity of the outcome, difficult to predict[1]. However, it expects firms to consider properly all the potential consequences of events, including the probability of the event happening and the severity of the outcome, and to make a judgment on whether the matter needs to be reported in the light of that.

1 See the FSA Handbook at SUP 15.3.2/3.

3.46 Applying this requirement may not, however, be straightforward. Three points may in particular be made. First, the test has both subjective and objective elements but is mostly an objective one. The subjective part is that the firm must become aware of the matter, but there is an objective alternative that the firm 'has information which reasonably suggests' the problem. This means that, in assessing whether the firm properly complied with its reporting obligation, the question can be asked 'should the firm have appreciated?' (rather than 'did the firm know?').

3.47 Second, the rule places a heavy onus on firms to try to predict what the future consequences of a particular event may be. Whilst, in theory, the firm should be judged by reference to what consequences of a particular matter were foreseeable at the relevant time, there may in practice be a temptation to judge what consequences were foreseeable by reference to what actually happened and it may be difficult for firms to show otherwise.

3.48 Third, this is exacerbated by the broad terms of each of the four categories of consequences. The FSA has not provided any guidance on the second, third or fourth categories. There is plenty of room for disagreement over whether something had a significant adverse impact on the firm's reputation or affected its ability to continue to provide adequate services to its customers, let alone whether it was foreseeable that one of these consequences might occur.

3.49 The obligation is to make immediate notification[1]. As to the form and manner of the notification, see para 3.74 ff below.

1 See the discussion at para 3.80 below.

Rule 2: Breaches of rules and other requirements under the FSMA 2000

3.50 A firm must notify the FSA[1] of:

- a significant breach of a rule (including one of the Principles for Businesses[2]) or a Statement of Principle[3];
- a breach of any requirement imposed by the FSMA 2000 or by regulations or orders made under the FSMA 2000 by HM Treasury (except if the breach is a criminal offence, in which case the next point applies);
- the bringing of a prosecution for, or a conviction of, any offence under the FSMA 2000;

by (or against) the firm, or any of its directors, officers, employees, approved persons or appointed representatives.

1 See the FSA Handbook at SUP 15.3.11.
2 For an explanation, see para 2.52 above.
3 See para 2.90 ff above.

3.51 The notification must be made immediately the firm becomes aware, or has information which reasonably suggests, that any of the above has occurred, may have occurred or may occur in the foreseeable future[1].

1 See the FSA Handbook at SUP 15.3.11. In assessing what may occur in the foreseeable future, firms should consider both the probability of it happening and the severity of the outcome should it do so: see the FSA Handbook at SUP 15.3.12.

3.52 A notification under this rule is required to include[1]:

- information about any circumstances relevant to the breach or offence;
- identification of the rule or requirement or offence; and
- information about any steps which the firm or any other person has taken or intends to take to rectify or remedy the breach or prevent any future occurrence.

1 See the FSA Handbook at SUP 15.3.14.

3.53 As to the manner and form of the notification to the FSA, see para 3.74 ff below.

3.54 This is another extremely broad provision, requiring the firm to blow the whistle on itself, its employees and a limited range of others, in a variety of situations. A number of points can be made in considering how it applies.

3.55 First, it requires the firm to report breaches of the FSA's rules, but only those which are 'significant'. Significance is to be determined by reference to the potential financial losses to customers or the firm, the frequency of the breach, implications for the firm's systems and controls and if there were delays in identifying or rectifying the breach[1]. It is important to recognise that the FSA's views on the significance of a particular breach may not always be the same as the views of the firm and in practice the question for the firm will be whether the FSA is likely to view the breach as significant.

1 See the FSA Handbook at SUP 15.3.12.

3.56 Second, the obligation is to make notification immediately the firm becomes aware, or has information which reasonably suggests, that a breach has occurred or may occur. Thus, whilst there may be scope for the firm to make further enquiries, and in the meantime not to notify the FSA, where it only has a 'suspicion' that there may have been a breach, as soon as the information available to it reaches the state of 'reasonably suggesting' there may have been a breach, it must immediately notify. In that situation, it is not entitled first to take further steps to investigate the matter to decide whether or not there has been a breach. If it did so, decided that a breach had occurred, and then notified the FSA, it could be in breach of this rule[1]. Technically, it would be in breach of the rule even if it investigated and, after investigating the matter, decided there had been no breach or offence and there was therefore nothing to report to the FSA, but the likelihood of this coming to the FSA's attention, or of the FSA taking action, must be rather lower.

1 See also the discussion at para 3.80 below.

3.57 Third, the FSA requires relatively specific information to be provided to it on the notification, which may not always sit easily with the obligation to notify immediately the information reasonably suggests a breach may have occurred. It may be difficult in practice for firms to provide the information which the FSA is asking for when making the first notification to the FSA, given the early stage at which the notification has to be made.

3.58 Fourth, the rule is sufficiently wide to enable the FSA to charge the firm with breach of this rule where a problem arises which the firm did not know about but in the FSA's view should have known about and prevented. In that type of situation, the FSA may be more concerned with management, systems and controls issues, but it may be that a breach of this rule will also be alleged. Whether the firm had breached the rule would depend upon the nature of the information available to it at the time and whether it reasonably suggested that the particular breach might occur (even if at the time it did not in fact consider that a breach might occur).

Rule 3: Civil, criminal or disciplinary proceedings against the firm

3.59 The firm must notify the FSA[1] immediately if:

- civil proceedings are brought against the firm and the amount of the claim is significant in relation to the firm's financial resources or its reputation;
- any action is brought against the firm under FSMA 2000, ss 71 or 150[2];
- disciplinary measures or sanctions have been imposed on the firm by any statutory or regulatory authority, professional organisation or trade body (other than the FSA) or the firm becomes aware that one of those bodies has started an investigation into its affairs;
- the firm is prosecuted for, or convicted of, any offence involving fraud or dishonesty or any penalties are imposed on it for tax evasion; or
- it is a trustee of an occupational pension scheme and is removed as trustee by a court order.

1 See the FSA Handbook at SUP 15.3.15.
2 Actions for damages which the FSMA 2000 allows investors to bring arising from the breach by the firm of certain requirements under the FSMA 2000 or the FSA rules: see Chapter 10.

3.60 A notification under this rule must be made immediately[1] and should include details of the matter and an estimate of any likely financial consequences[2]. As to the manner and form of the notification, see para 3.74 ff below.

1 See the discussion at para 3.80 below.
2 See the FSA Handbook at SUP 15.3.16.

3.61 The FSA has provided no further guidance on the application of this rule. The firm is required to report to the FSA the fact that another regulator (for example, an overseas regulator) has started an investigation into the firm's affairs. There is nothing in the rule to confine it to those situations where the investigation could involve or impact on matters occurring in the firm's UK operations. Nor is the firm entitled to wait until the enquiry concludes.

Rule 4: Fraud, errors and other irregularities

3.62 A firm must notify the FSA[1] immediately if one of the following events arises and the event is significant:

- it becomes aware that an employee may have committed a fraud against one of its customers;
- it becomes aware that a person, whether or not employed by it, may have committed a fraud against it;
- it considers that any person, whether or not employed by it, is acting with intent to commit a fraud against it;
- it identifies irregularities in its accounting or other records, whether or not there is evidence of fraud; or
- it suspects that one of its employees may be guilty of serious misconduct concerning his honesty or integrity and which is connected with the firm's regulated activities or ancillary activities[2].

1 See the FSA Handbook at SUP 15.3.17.
2 This corresponds to the types of situations where the FSA may need to consider withdrawing the approval of an approved person or making a prohibition order against any person: see Chapter 8 below.

3.63 The manner and form of the notification are explained at para 3.74 ff below.

3.64 The FSA has provided guidance on the meaning of significant (in the phrase 'and the event is significant'[1]). In determining whether a matter is significant, the firm should have regard to[2]:

- the size of any monetary loss or potential monetary loss to itself or customers (either in terms of a single incident or a group of similar or related incidents);
- the risk of reputational loss to the firm; and
- whether the incident or a pattern of incidents reflects weaknesses in the firm's internal controls.

1 See para 3.62 above.
2 See the FSA Handbook at SUP 15.3.18.

3.65 The FSA has given three reasons for this rule. First, it needs to be aware of fraudulent or irregular activity in order to act, if necessary, to prevent effects on consumers or other firms. Second, it may wish to assess the effect on the firm of any losses or reputational damage. Finally, it may lead the FSA to assess whether the incident suggests weaknesses in the firm's internal controls[1]. This gives some indication of the FSA's likely approach in considering what action to take when such a matter is notified to it and thus of the potential implications of the matter.

1 See the FSA Handbook at SUP 15.3.19/20.

Notifications under Principle 11

3.66 The specific rules outlined above do not replace the firm's general obligation under Principle 11 to disclose to the FSA appropriately anything relating to the firm of which the FSA would reasonably expect notice. This means that even where a particular matter does not fall within the above rules, the firm must still consider whether it should notify the FSA pursuant to its general obligation.

The general obligation

3.67 The general obligation is, though, wide and unspecific. The FSA has therefore given guidance[1] on the type of information which it regards as being included. Among other things, this makes clear that matters relating to the firm's non-regulated activities or affecting other group companies may well be notifiable to the FSA[2]. Incoming firms are also generally required to comply with Principle 11 in the same way as UK regulated firms, in so far as responsibility for the matter in question is not reserved to the firm's home state regulator[3].

1 See the FSA Handbook at SUP 15.3.7–15.3.10.
2 The potential relevance of issues arising in a firm's unregulated business to the FSA's enforcement role is discussed at para 2.174 above.
3 See para 2.62 above and, in relation to the guidance on Principle 11 to incoming firms, see the FSA Handbook at SUP 15, Annex 1R.

3.68 Among the type of information listed by the FSA as being encompassed within Principle 11, particularly relevant in the enforcement context is the requirement to notify any significant failure in the firm's systems or controls (including those reported to the firm by its auditors[1]).

1 See also the FSA Handbook at SUP Chapter 3, and in particular 3.7.2. Note that auditors (and actuaries) have a statutory obligation to report to the FSA certain matters specified in regulations made by HM Treasury: see FSMA 2000, ss 342 and 343 and The Financial Services and Markets Act 2000 (Communications by Auditors) Regulations 2001, SI 2001/2587. See also the FSA Handbook at SUP 3.8.10. The Regulations require auditors to report a wide range of matters, including significant regulatory breaches (or suspected breaches) and matters relevant to whether the firm continues to satisfy the threshold conditions. The FSMA 2000 protects the auditor (or actuary) by providing that he does not contravene any duty to which he is subject (eg a duty of confidence) by giving information or his opinion to the FSA if he is acting in good faith and reasonably believes the information or opinion is relevant to any functions of the FSA: FSMA 2000, ss 342(3) and 343(3).

3.69 The scope of the matters covered in the FSA's guidance on Principle 11 is limited, because of the breadth of the matters covered by the detailed rules. Whilst this, when combined with the specific rules outlined above, provides guidance to firms as to when they should report a particular matter to the FSA, it expressly does not exhaust the implications of Principle 11[1]. Firms therefore need to keep the general principle firmly in mind and not to focus solely on the detailed rules.

1 See the FSA Handbook at SUP 15.2.2(1) and 15.3.8.

Does the firm have to report to the FSA known misconduct of others?

3.70 There is no clear general whistleblowing obligation or other general obligation to report known misconduct relating to others. The formulation of Principle 11 removes any doubt there may have been under the old regime[1]. Firms are required under the FSA's rules outlined above to report certain types of breaches or conduct by their employees, directors, officers and appointed representatives[2]. In addition, under Rule 4 a firm must notify the FSA about a significant fraud committed against it by any person, whether or not its employee. Beyond this, there are certain, very limited whistleblowing obligations mentioned at para 3.107 ff below.

1 Principle 11 refers specifically to reporting matters 'relating to the firm' (whereas the previous SIB General Principle 10 did not contain the same wording and the practice was wider in certain respects: see SFA Board Notice 141).
2 See, for example, Rule 2 at para 3.50 ff above and Rule 4 at para 3.62 ff above.

Reports to other regulators

3.71 Principle 11 extends to require the firm to co-operate with its other regulators, for example, exchanges or overseas regulators, and it could be treated by the FSA as having committed a UK regulatory breach if it failed to do so. A failure to comply with its obligations to other regulators could also be relevant to whether the firm was a fit and proper person[1]. The extent of the obligation to report to other regulators depends on the situation and the obligations that the firm has to the other regulator. But the lack of formal reporting obligations to the other regulator may not of itself be determinative. Situations can be envisaged which the FSA would regard as being so serious that any responsible firm would report them to its regulator, whatever its formal obligations.

1 For an explanation of fitness and propriety in relation to firms, see para 2.43 ff above and see in particular the criteria at para 2.46 ff above.

Timing of the notification

3.72 Principle 11 does not expressly require the notification to be made 'promptly'[1], but instead uses the word 'appropriately'. The FSA has indicated that the timing of the notification will depend on the event that has occurred[2], but that it expects firms to discuss relevant matters with it at an early stage, before making any internal or external commitments. The latter part of that sentence is particularly significant. Although, as will be seen, the FSA expects firms to take action to address issues which arise, and not to wait for the FSA to do so, it is clear that it expects to be notified in appropriate circumstances before the firm takes any action, whether that action is internal (for example, disciplining employees or remedying systems) or external (for example, compensating customers).

1 Compare the previous SIB Principle 10.
2 See the FSA Handbook at SUP 15.3.9.

3.73 As to the manner and form of the firm's notification to the FSA, see para 3.76 below.

How to notify the FSA

Making notifications under specific rules

3.74 Notifications to the FSA are required[1] to be in writing, in English, and to give the firm's FSA Firm Reference Number, unless the notification rule states otherwise or the notification relates solely to Principle 11 and not to one of the specific rules. Details of how to make the notification are found in the FSA's Handbook at SUP 15.7.4 to 15.7.9. Notifications can be made by post, hand-delivery, fax or e-mail. A notification not made in compliance with the rules is considered invalid and the firm may therefore be in breach of the notification requirement[2].

1 See the FSA Handbook at SUP 15.7.1.
2 See the FSA Handbook at SUP 15.7.15.

3.75 In some urgent cases, though, it seems that written notification may not be enough[1]. Firms are required to have regard to the urgency and significance of a matter and, if appropriate, to notify their usual supervisory contact by telephone or other prompt means before submitting a written notification. Oral notifications must be given direct to a member of the firm's usual supervisory contact. It is not sufficient to leave a message with another person or on a voice-mail system.

1 See the FSA Handbook at SUP 15.7.2.

Making notifications under Principle 11

3.76 Notifications under Principle 11[1], rather than under one of the specific rules, may be made to the FSA orally or in writing, although the FSA may request written confirmation of a matter. The FSA regards it as the firm's responsibility to ensure that matters are properly and clearly communicated to it[2] and suggests that a firm provide a written notification if the matter is complex or if it may require the FSA to take action. The point made above about notifications in urgent cases applies equally.

1 See the FSA Handbook at SUP 15.3.10.
2 See, further, at para 3.81 ff below.

Who makes the notification?

3.77 From the FSA's point of view, it is entitled to rely on any information it receives from a firm and to consider any notification as having been made by a person authorised to do so[1]. The firm therefore needs to consider having in place procedures to ensure that only appropriate employees make notifications to the FSA.

1 See the FSA Handbook at SUP 15.7.3.

When was the notification made?

3.78 Whilst not expressly stated in this context[1], it would be prudent for the firm to assume that it is the firm's responsibility to ensure delivery of the notification to the FSA within the requisite time. It may therefore be sensible to keep a proof of delivery, for example, a proof of posting, a fax transmission report, a recorded delivery receipt or record of a courier service.

1 This point is expressly made in the FSA's reporting rules: see the FSA Handbook at SUP 16.3.16.

3.79 If the notification is made by e-mail, it is unclear whether it would be sufficient that the firm dispatched the e-mail and did not receive a report indicating any difficulty with its transmission. It is thought that firms should take steps to ensure that an e-mail was properly received, for example by requesting an automatic or manual receipt and, if none is received, checking by telephone that the e-mail has been received.

3.80 With regard to the timing of the notification, the FSA has specified that if the rule requires notification to be made within a specified period, the firm must give the notification so as to be received by the FSA no later than the end of that period[1]. The FSA has also given guidance that if the rule does not require notification to be made within a specified period, the firm should act reasonably in deciding when to notify[2].

1 See the FSA Handbook at SUP 15.7.10. If the end of the period falls on a day which is not a business day, the notification must be given so as to be received by the FSA no later than the first business day after the end of that period.
2 See the FSA Handbook at SUP 15.7.11.

The contents of the report to the FSA

3.81 Where the firm is under an obligation to report, what should be the content of its report? It is difficult to do more than state a few general propositions.

3.82 First, in some instances where the firm is notifying in accordance with a specific rule, the FSA's guidance indicates what information the FSA expects to be notified to it (see for example Rules 2 and 3 above). In such cases, the firm should comply with this as far as possible.

3.83 Second, it will generally be better to provide the FSA promptly with an indication that there is a potential problem which the firm is investigating, and some information about the nature of the problem, than to present it with the results of a report which has taken some time to produce relating to a problem of which the FSA was not until then aware. One of the FSA's first questions will be when this first came to the firm's notice and why it was not brought to its attention. The FSA will expect the firm to investigate internally and, if satisfied that it is doing so in a responsible manner and keeping it informed, may, depending upon the circumstances, be content not to intervene and carry out its own investigation until the firm's investigation is complete.

3.84 Third, the firm must avoid providing the FSA with incomplete information which might be false or misleading. At its most extreme, this could constitute a criminal offence[1]. In addition, the FSA has made a rule requiring firms to take reasonable steps to ensure that all information they give to the FSA is both factually accurate (or, in the case of estimates and judgments, fairly and properly based after appropriate enquires) and complete (in that it should include anything of which the FSA would reasonably expect notice[2]). There is precedent (albeit under the previous regime) for a compliance officer being disciplined for providing information in the course of an interview with the regulator which was false, misleading or inaccurate in a material particular. It was held that it was his duty, as compliance officer, to ensure the correctness of the answers which he gave in the course of his interviews. Instead, by casting himself to some extent in the role of 'fencing advocate', he had provided information which was patently wrong in certain material particulars[3]. There is no particular reason to expect any different approach to be adopted.

1 See paras 3.106 and 4.287 below.
2 See the FSA Handbook at SUP 15.6.1. Any limitations on the scope of the information should therefore be made clear: see the FSA Handbook at SUP 15.6.3. In addition, firms are required to notify the FSA immediately if they become aware, or have information which reasonably suggests, that they have or may have provided the FSA with information which was or may have been false, misleading or inaccurate or may have changed in a material particular: see the FSA Handbook at SUP 15.6.4.
3 *Capel-Cure Myers Management Ltd, Pattison and Nead*: SFA Board Notice 446, 10/97. The report stresses that no aspect of the proceedings reflected on his integrity.

The individual's obligation to report

3.85 The individual's obligation to report is the duty to deal with the FSA and other relevant regulators in an open and co-operative way and to disclose appropriately any information of which the FSA would reasonably expect notice[1].

1 Statement of Principle 4: see the FSA Handbook at APER 2.1.2. For a discussion of the nature and effect of the Statements of Principle and Code of Practice for approved persons, see para 2.76 ff above.

3.86 The Code of Practice[1] applicable to Statement of Principle 4 provides some assistance in determining whether or not conduct complies with this principle[2]. It describes three types of conduct which, in the FSA's opinion, do not comply with Statement of Principle 4 and sets out factors to be taken into account in determining whether or not a person's conduct complies. One of these three types of conduct relates to approved persons generally, one relates to those who are responsible within the firm for reporting to the FSA, and the third relates to co-operation with the regulator, rather than the obligation to report, and is not therefore relevant here[3]. We therefore consider, first, the obligation so far as relates to approved persons generally and, second, so far as relates to those responsible for reporting to the FSA. Finally, we look at whether individuals have obligations to report to other regulators. Whether or not an individual has an obligation to report a matter to the FSA, if he does so that report may well be protected under the Public Interest Disclosure Act 1998, so that the firm must not discipline him or subject him to any detriment as a result[4].

1 See the FSA Handbook at APER 4.4.
2 The Code of Practice is only evidential guidance: see para 2.84 above.
3 This is discussed at para 4.42 ff below.
4 See the discussion at para 4.48 below. The FSA believes that firms should ordinarily be the first port of call for disclosures by employees and therefore encourages firms to adopt and publicise appropriate internal procedures (although there is currently no requirement to do so). The FSA has a dedicated telephone line and e-mail address for disclosures. Note that the FSA has indicated it will regard as a serious matter any evidence that a firm had acted to the detriment of a worker who made a protected disclosure: this could call into question the fitness and propriety of the firm or relevant members of its staff. For further discussion see Consultation Paper 101, 'Whistleblowing, the FSA and the financial services industry', July 2001.

The obligation on approved persons generally

3.87 An approved person's conduct does not, in the FSA's opinion, comply with the Statement of Principle if he fails to report promptly in accordance with the firm's internal procedures or, if none exist, direct to the FSA, information which it would be reasonable to assume would be of material significance to the FSA, whether in response to questions or otherwise[1].

1 See the FSA Handbook at APER 4.4.4.

3.88 Matters to be taken into account in determining the person's compliance or otherwise with the Statement of Principle are[1]:

- the likely significance to the FSA of the information which it was reasonable for the individual to assume;
- whether the information related to the individual himself or to his firm; and
- whether any decision not to report the matter internally was taken after reasonable enquiry and analysis of the situation.

Each is considered briefly below.

1 See the FSA Handbook at APER 4.4.6.

3.89 The emphasis is therefore on reporting internally within the firm and the Code seems to indicate that the person is, in the normal course, only expected to report direct to the FSA if there are no relevant internal procedures. Having said that, the provision is a negative one; it explains when a person's conduct fails to comply. It does not positively indicate that a person's conduct will comply if he reports internally and there may therefore be circumstances when he will not be absolved from responsibility by virtue of having done so[1]. As ever, the focus needs to be on the broad Statement of Principle and not purely on the detailed provisions of the Code. Moreover, there may be situations where the FSA will treat a person as though he was responsible for reporting the matter to the FSA, and therefore measure his conduct against the matters set out at para 3.94 ff below, even though he did not have that responsibility within the firm. In particular, the FSA has indicated that if a person takes steps to influence the decision so as not to report to the FSA or acts in a way that is intended to obstruct the reporting of the information to the FSA, the FSA will, in respect of that information, view him as one of those who has taken on responsibility for deciding whether to report that matter to the FSA[2]. It is unclear how this will be applied in practice. Particularly, senior management who are involved in a matter may often have the risk of being held accountable for the decision whether to report to the regulator.

1 Such circumstances ought to be relatively rare, particularly given the three factors to be taken into account.
2 See the FSA Handbook at APER 4.4.5.

3.90 The obligation is to report whether in answer to questions or otherwise. In other words, the individual cannot wait until he is asked about the matter but must take steps to volunteer information where appropriate.

Likely significance of the information

3.91 The first of the three factors to be taken into account in determining whether or not the person's conduct complied with Statement of Principle 4 is the likely significance to the FSA of the information which it was reasonable for the person to assume. This may be a difficult test to apply in practice. It requires the FSA to assess what it was reasonable for the person to assume at the time about how the FSA would judge the significance of the information. The test is primarily an objective one. It is necessary to look at what it was reasonable for the person to assume, not at what he did assume. Equally, though, it would be wrong for the FSA to judge the person's behaviour by reference to what the FSA regards as the significance of the information. There may also be room for a more subjective element. It could be argued that the question of what it was reasonable for the person to assume about what the FSA would regard as significant requires regard to be had to the circumstances of the particular person concerned. In other words, the level of knowledge about the FSA's practices which it is reasonable for some approved persons to have may be different from that of others: compare, for example, a compliance officer with a sales person. It seems that the test is, in this way, tailored to some extent to the particular person.

Whether the information related to the person or the firm

3.92 The second factor is self-explanatory. The implication is that it may be more egregious for a person to withhold information relating to his own personal position.

Whether any decision not to report was taken after reasonable enquiry and analysis

3.93 The third factor provides some protection for individuals. If the person makes a reasonable decision having undertaken reasonable enquiries then this will be a factor in his favour even if the decision was, on the FSA's view, the wrong one. But if he does not undertake reasonable enquiries and analysis or does not make a reasonable decision then this may be a factor against him.

Approved persons responsible for reporting to the FSA

3.94 Different considerations apply to those approved persons who are one of those responsible within the firm for reporting matters to the FSA[1]. Such a person's conduct fails, in the FSA's opinion, to comply with the Statement of Principle if he fails promptly to inform the FSA of information of which he is aware and which it would be reasonable to assume would be of material significance to the FSA, whether in response to questions or otherwise[2].

1 This may include those who take steps to influence that decision or obstruct the reporting: see para 3.89 above.
2 See the FSA Handbook at APER 4.4.7.

3.95 Matters to be taken into account in determining the person's compliance or otherwise with the Statement of Principle are[1]:

- the likely significance of the information to the FSA which it was reasonable for the person to assume[2]; and
- whether any decision not to inform the FSA was taken after reasonable enquiry and analysis of the situation[3].

1 See the FSA Handbook at APER 4.4.8.
2 This is discussed at para 3.91 above.
3 This is discussed at para 3.93 above.

3.96 The key here is that those responsible within the firm for reporting matters to the FSA (or who assume such responsibility: see para 3.89 above) are personally responsible to the FSA if they do not do so. There are two points to note regarding this.

3.97 First, if several people have responsibility within the firm for making reports to the FSA, no express distinction is drawn between the person responsible for reporting the particular matter, or deciding not to do so, and those who were not involved in the decision at all. In principle, if any of them has committed a breach of the Statement of Principle, it should be only the former that has done so. The FSA's general policy[1], that personal culpability is a key element in deciding whether an individual should be held responsible, should help to ensure that this is the case.

1 See para 8.13 ff below.

3.98 Second, and most important, those responsible for making reports to the FSA need to have this personal obligation constantly in mind, particularly where there is pressure from within the firm not to report a particular matter for some reason.

Disclosure to other regulators

3.99 The duty on individuals extends to openness and co-operation with other regulators, for example exchanges or overseas regulators. The FSA regards individuals as having breached their duties to it if they fail to co-operate or be open with other relevant bodies. The extent of the duty to be open and co-operate with other regulators, and what this requires to be reported to the relevant regulator, will depend upon the situation and the individual's obligations to the relevant regulator. The lack of any formal obligations to another regulator may not in itself be determinative. Some issues may be sufficiently serious that the FSA would expect any responsible regulated person to report them, whatever his formal obligations.

3.100 Failure to be open and co-operative with other regulators could give rise to disciplinary consequences[1], could impact on the FSA's view of whether the person remained fit and proper[2], and potentially gives rise to additional enforcement consequences[3].

1 For misconduct arising from the breach of Statement of Principle 4: see Chapter 8.
2 The question whether a person demonstrates a readiness and willingness to comply with the applicable legal, regulatory and professional requirements and standards is a factor to be taken into account: see para 2.72 above.
3 The withdrawal of his approval or a prohibition order: see Chapter 8.

Consequences of not reporting to the FSA

3.101 To understand the importance for firms and individuals of complying with these obligations, it is worth briefly reviewing the potential consequences of failing to do so. If the firm or individual fails to report a matter to the FSA (or internally when obliged to do so) then this may have a number of consequences:

- it may have an effect on the FSA's approach to the investigation;
- it may be more likely that the FSA will bring disciplinary proceedings for the original breach;
- it will be relevant to the size of the disciplinary penalty and to what other regulatory response is appropriate for the original breach;
- the firm and/or the approved person may be liable to disciplinary or other regulatory action for the failure to report;
- there may in some situations be a risk of criminal liability for misleading the FSA.

Each of these is considered in turn.

Effect on the FSA's approach to the investigation

3.102 In the short term, a failure fully to co-operate with the FSA, including a failure to report the problem to it, is almost bound to compound the original problem and affect the way the FSA chooses to handle the case. It may make the FSA suspicious of the firm, as a result not trusting the firm to investigate matters itself, and may increase the likelihood that the FSA will decide to exercise its compulsory powers of investigation, rather than allow the firm to co-operate voluntarily[1]. The potential practical effect from the firm's perspective is to lessen the firm's ability to maintain any control over the process, at risk of increasing the burden caused by the investigation[2].

1 See para 4.26 ff below.
2 For a discussion of the reasons for and benefits of co-operating with the FSA in the context of its investigation, see para 4.50 ff below.

More likely the FSA will bring disciplinary proceedings

3.103 One of the factors to be taken into account by the FSA in deciding whether to bring disciplinary proceedings for a particular breach is whether the breach was brought to its attention and, if so, how quickly, effectively and completely[1]. Failure to report the matter properly may therefore make it more likely that the firm will face disciplinary action in relation to the original problem.

1 See the FSA Handbook at ENF 11.4.1(2)(a) and see para 7.28 ff below.

May affect the sanction imposed for the original breach

3.104 Similarly, whether the firm brought the misconduct to the FSA's attention is one of the factors to be taken into account by the FSA in determining the proper disciplinary or other regulatory response to any breach[1]. Failure to do so could therefore result in an increased penalty or in a more severe regulatory response than might otherwise have been the case.

1 See, for example, the FSA Handbook at ENF 13.3.3(5) (relevant to the size of the fine to be imposed) and ENF 3.5.13(8) (relevant to whether it is appropriate to use the own-initiative power as a matter of urgency).

The failure to report may have its own disciplinary consequences

3.105 Furthermore, the failure to report is in itself a regulatory breach[1], which could result in disciplinary action or to an additional disciplinary charge being brought. It could also impact on the FSA's view of whether the firm or individual was fit and proper, potentially exposing them to other types of regulatory enforcement action[2].

1 Namely, as appropriate, breach of Principle 11 of the Principles for Businesses, Statement of Principle 4 of the Statements of Principle for approved persons, or the specific rules outlined at paras 3.44 to 3.65 above in relation to firms. For an example of a firm being fined for taken internal disciplinary action but failing to report the matter to the FSA, see *Holt, Carr and Nicholson Barber* (24 July 2000, SFA Board Notice 550).
2 In relation to the firm, the variation or cancellation of its permission (see Chapter 9); in relation to the individual, the withdrawal of his approval or the making of a prohibition order (see Chapter 8). In reality these are unlikely to be under consideration save in a very serious case.

Potential criminal liability

3.106 The FSMA 2000 prescribes various criminal offences which relate to the provision of information to the FSA including the offence of knowingly or recklessly providing false or misleading information to the FSA in purported compliance with a requirement imposed by or under the FSMA 2000[1]. A failure to provide information to the FSA is not of itself a criminal offence, but, for example, deliberately or recklessly misleading the FSA by providing one piece of information whilst withholding another could be a criminal offence[2].

1 FSMA 2000, s 398(1) and see para 4.287 below.
2 This would also probably be a breach of the FSA's rules: see para 3.84 above.

Obligations to report to other bodies

3.107 In some situations, the firm may be under an obligation to report a matter to bodies other than the FSA. This could arise either in relation to the firm's own conduct or in relation to the conduct of others (for example, its employees) of which it is aware.

Reporting the firm's conduct to other bodies

3.108 As outlined above, the FSA regards both firms and approved persons as under an obligation to be open and co-operative with any other applicable regulators, for example stock exchanges or overseas regulators. Moreover, it is obviously possible for conduct which gives rise to a regulatory issue in the UK also to raise regulatory concerns in other jurisdictions in which the firm does business. There may indeed be reporting obligations in those other jurisdictions in those circumstances. From a practical perspective, if the firm concludes that it has obligations to report to a regulator, it needs to bear in mind that regulators communicate with one another. It needs to take care to avoid a situation where something it should have reported to one regulator is reported to that regulator by another regulator. It also, obviously, may need to provide the same information to each regulator.

Reporting the conduct of others

3.109 There is no general whistleblowing obligation under English law, although there are certain well-known exceptions, for example in relation to money laundering and terrorism. The firm may, however, owe obligations to other regulators in the UK or other jurisdictions, or indeed more general obligations in other jurisdictions, to report known misconduct by its employees or even by other firms. The firm must not focus solely on its obligations to the FSA and lose sight of any obligations it may have to others.

HOW SHOULD THE FIRM DEAL WITH ITS CUSTOMERS?

3.110 The protection of consumers is one of the FSA's key regulatory objectives under the FSMA 2000[1] and an important factor in many of the decisions the FSA takes in the enforcement context. Firms also owe duties to the FSA under the Principles for Businesses as regards their actions in dealing with their customers, both consumers and others[2]. We consider, first, the FSA's requirements on how a firm should deal with its customers when a regulatory problem arises and, second, what in practice this requires the firm to do.

1 For a discussion of the FSA's regulatory objectives, see para 2.19 ff above.
2 Principles 6–10 of the Principles for Businesses: see para 2.52 above.

What are the firm's obligations to act in the interests of customers?

3.111 Firms owe their customers certain general regulatory obligations outlined below. In addition, the way that the firm treats its customers may have specific regulatory and legal implications. Each of these is considered in turn below.

3.112 As a practical matter, particularly in less serious cases, if the firm is seen to be taking all the appropriate steps to address the problem that has arisen, which would include dealing properly with its customers, then the FSA may be prepared to deal with the matter solely within the supervisory relationship and without the need for the enforcement division to become involved, for example by issuing a private warning[1].

1 For a discussion of private warnings, see para 7.18 ff below.

The firm's general obligations to its customers

3.113 The Principles for Businesses require firms to[1]:

- pay due regard to the interests of customers and treat them fairly[2];
- pay due regard to the information needs of clients and communicate information to them in a way which is clear, fair and not misleading[3];
- manage conflicts of interest fairly, both between itself and its customers and between a customer and another client[4].

Customers means, in this context, clients which are not market counterparties[5]. These duties do not, therefore, apply to all of the firm's customers (since they do not apply to market counterparties), but they are not confined to, for example, consumers.

1 See para 2.52 above.
2 Principle 6.
3 Principle 7.

4 Principle 8.
5 See the FSA Handbook at PRIN 1.2.2 and, in relation to Principle 7, see the FSA Handbook at PRIN 3.4.1. For the rules on classifying customers, see the FSA Handbook at COB Chapter 4.

3.114 In addition, the FSA requires firms to have in place arrangements for dealing with certain types of customer complaints and those arrangements are required to satisfy certain basic criteria[1]. Where a complaint is made by a customer, the firm has positive obligations to deal with the complaint fairly[2].

1 See the FSA Handbook at DISP and see Chapter 12.
2 See the FSA Handbook at DISP 1.3.5(3) and (5).

3.115 Failure to comply with these obligations, including Principles 6, 7 and 8, would in itself constitute a regulatory offence capable of leading to disciplinary proceedings and sanctions[1]. In addition, in a serious case it could give rise to sufficient concerns about the firm to cause the FSA to exercise its power to vary or cancel the firm's permission[2].

1 The use of the Principles as the basis for disciplinary action is discussed at para 2.156 ff above. The former SIB Principles 5 and 6 (broadly similar to Principles for Businesses 6 to 8) were on occasions used as the basis for disciplinary action under the previous regime. For illustrative examples, see *David Coakley Ltd* (SFA Board Notice 189, June 1994); *Duncan and Allied Provincial Securities* (SFA Board Notice 276, August 1995); *Swiss Bank Corporation* (SFA Board Notice 438, August 1997) and a number of IMRO pensions cases, for example, *Adams and Neville Asset Management Ltd* (23 May 1996) and *Willis Coroon Financial Planning Ltd* (14 October 1996).
2 See generally Chapter 9.

How far do the obligations extend?

3.116 It is difficult to give any definitive guidance on the extent of the firm's duties to its customer, but some general comments can be made. First, the extent of the duty may depend in part upon the nature of the customer concerned because, for example, what is involved in paying 'due regard' will depend upon the circumstances.

3.117 Second, a firm would be likely to be in breach if it unfairly put its own interests ahead of those of its customers. An example would be using the client's money in a high-risk investment trading strategy to try to recover losses already made for which the firm may have been liable, when the client had stipulated for his money to be used only for investments without any speculative risk[1].

1 See *First European Investment Corporation, Hamilton, Kaidbey and Abou-Hamdan*, SFA Board Notice 463.

3.118 Third, it is not clear that the Principles require a firm to give its customers treatment preferential to their legal rights, for example by offering them compensation or some other remedy to which they would have no legal entitlement. The customer's legal entitlement for this purpose needs to be assessed against the powers of the ombudsman and the powers of the FSA or a court to order restitution, which could result in the customer recovering in circumstances where a court would not award damages[1]. If the customer made a complaint, the firm would obviously also have to operate its complaints procedures.

1 See the discussion at, respectively, Chapter 12 below and para 7.43 ff below.

3.119 Fourth, a difficult question is whether the firm can use the same sort of defensive strategy which it might want to adopt if it were a defendant to possible civil proceedings, such as not volunteering information and facts which are unhelpful to it unless and until necessary in the legal process. In principle, such action could be regarded as inappropriate to the extent of breaching the Principles, although this would depend upon the circumstances of the case and the nature of the customer concerned. For example, action which may be appropriate in dealing with a customer of equal commercial strength may be viewed rather differently as against a consumer.

Other regulatory implications of how the firm treats customers

3.120 How the firm has dealt with its customers may have other regulatory implications. It will be a relevant factor for the FSA in deciding what regulatory action is appropriate and, particularly, whether it should exercise its powers:

- to take disciplinary action against the firm[1];
- to vary or cancel the firm's permission on its own-initiative[2];
- to apply for a civil injunction against the firm[3]; or
- to impose or apply for a restitution order against the firm[4];

and, if so, in each case what action it should take. Each is considered in turn below.

1 See generally Chapter 7 below.
2 Or to impose intervention action against an incoming firm. This is the power for the FSA to impose restrictions or limitations on the firm's business: see generally Chapter 9 below.
3 To restrain further breaches, require the firm to take remedial steps or secure its assets: see para 7.97 ff below.
4 An order requiring the firm to compensate investors for their losses or to disgorge profits arising from a regulatory breach: see para 7.43 ff below.

Disciplinary action

3.121 The question of what remedial steps the firm took since the breach was identified, including identifying whether consumers have suffered loss and compensating them, is a relevant factor for the FSA in deciding whether to take disciplinary action[1] and the same question is relevant to the FSA's decision about the appropriate level of the fine to be imposed on the firm[2]. Failure to take appropriate steps to investigate whether customers have suffered loss, and to compensate them, therefore increases the risk that the firm will encounter disciplinary proceedings for the original breach and potentially increases the likely level of the punishment.

1 See the FSA Handbook at ENF 11.4.1(2)(c) and see para 7.28 ff below.
2 See the FSA Handbook at ENF 13.3.3(5) and see para 7.37 ff below.

Varying or cancelling the firm's permission

3.122 The firm's conduct in failing to protect properly the interests of its customers may provide the FSA with grounds, and good reason, to exercise its own-initiative or intervention powers. A serious breach of Principles 6, 7 or 8 could in itself lead to own-initiative or intervention action[1]. Moreover, if the FSA perceives serious potential risks to consumers, or their assets, then it may wish to take such action as a matter of urgency[2].

1 See the FSA Handbook at ENF 3.5.8(2).
2 See the FSA Handbook at ENF 3.5.13(1) & (2) and see para 9.194 ff below.

Applying for a civil injunction

3.123 The firm's failure properly to protect the interests of its customers may give rise to concerns which would most effectively be addressed by the FSA applying for an injunction to require the firm to remedy the breach or to secure its assets. The factors specified as relevant to such applications, and which give some idea of the concerns that would potentially give rise to such an application being made, include the risk of loss or other adverse effects to consumers and whether the interests of consumers are adequately protected[1]. If the firm fails to take appropriate steps to protect the interests of consumers, particularly, it may increase the likelihood of the FSA taking action to safeguard their interests.

1 See the FSA Handbook at ENF 6.6.2 and see para 7.97 ff below.

Imposing or applying for a restitution order

3.124 The FSA will generally consider, when it decides whether to make or apply for a restitution order, what other means are available for those affected to obtain redress and whether it would be a more efficient or cost-effective route to use a restitution order instead[1]. The precise factors to be taken into account are discussed in more detail in Chapter 7. However, given the purpose of restitution orders, it should be apparent that the firm's response to customers who have suffered losses, particularly where large numbers of customers are affected, will impact on the FSA's consideration whether to make or apply for a restitution order. If the FSA does make or apply for a restitution order, particularly if it takes this step other than with the co-operation and assistance of the firm, then the firm will, to a significant extent, lose control over how much compensation should be paid to customers.

1 See the FSA Handbook at ENF 9.3.1 and see para 7.64 ff below.

Other legal implications of how the firm treats customers

3.125 Outside the regulatory arena, the firm may have legal obligations to its customers as a result of the legal relationship which underlies the activities which the firm is undertaking – for example, an investment management contract (if the firm is a fund manager). Such a contract, or the underlying legal relationship itself, may require the firm to take certain types of action to protect the interests of its customers. If so, failure to take the necessary steps could expose the firm to additional liability[1].

1 The firm's potential civil liability is discussed in more detail in Chapter 10 below.

3.126 Moreover, if the firm fails to pay compensation, or adequate compensation, or the FSA decides that it is not an appropriate case to exercise its powers to secure redress on behalf of customers, then the customer still has a number of options available to secure redress from the firm. These include complaining to the ombudsman (who has the power to order the payment of compensation)[1] or bringing a legal action based on the FSMA 2000[2] or on some other basis.

1 See generally Chapter 12 below.
2 See generally Chapter 10 below.

What action should the firm consider taking?

3.127 In general terms, therefore, when a problem arises which affects customers, the firm needs to take, and to be seen to be taking, steps to look after the interests of those customers, particularly but not solely where consumers are involved. Precisely what steps need to be taken will depend upon the circumstances, but these will generally include:

- keeping customers informed;
- safeguarding customers' interests, for example, by taking steps to secure assets, to remedy the problem or to ensure that no further losses are suffered; and
- identifying or taking steps to identify what losses have been suffered and either paying compensation or at least reassuring customers that compensation will be paid in due course.

WHAT OTHER INTERNAL ACTION SHOULD THE FIRM TAKE?

3.128 Firms are primarily responsible for managing themselves. It is for the firm to take the steps which it needs to take to deal with all of the issues to which a particular regulatory breach gives rise, and not for the regulator to have to tell the firm what to do. The FSA will thus want to see not only that the firm has investigated the matter, and that it is dealing appropriately both with its regulator and with any customers affected, but also that it has taken all the appropriate internal steps to address the consequences of the issue[1].

1 The Code of Practice for approved persons suggests that these matters are relevant to compliance with the Statements of Principle by those exercising 'significant influence functions' (see para 2.76 ff above). In particular: (a) failing to review the competence, knowledge, skills and performance of staff to assess their suitability to fulfil their duties despite evidence that their performance is unacceptable may indicate a breach of Statement of Principle 5 (see the FSA Handbook at APER 4.5.9 and 4.5.14), and (b) failing to take reasonable steps to ensure that procedures and systems of control are reviewed and, if appropriate, improved following the identification of significant breaches may indicate a breach of Statement of Principle 7 (see the FSA Handbook at APER 4.7.7 and 4.7.13).

3.129 Taking the appropriate internal steps may require the firm to consider a number of issues, including particularly the following:

- what steps should the firm take to ensure the problem will not recur?
- how should the firm deal with any employees who were involved?
- should the firm be taking any legal action (against employees or third parties)?
- should the firm notify its insurers?

3.130 It is the first two of these issues that are of primary interest to the FSA and these are discussed in detail below. The third, taking legal action, could in some circumstances be of relevance to the FSA, for example if financial fraud was involved, if customers would be entitled to money which the firm has the right to recover on their behalf, or if legal claims are contemplated which might affect the solvency of the firm. The fourth point, notifying the firm's insurers, particularly its professional indemnity insurers, is an important practical consideration which should not be overlooked[1]. It may also be relevant to the FSA, particularly if a failure to notify resulted in the firm being unable, because it then had no insurance coverage, to pay compensation to customers[2]. The failure to notify could potentially amount to a failure by the firm to conduct its business with due skill, care and diligence in breach of Principle 2, for which there could be regulatory consequences not only against the firm[3] but also against any individuals involved who were approved persons[4].

1 Particularly if there is a risk of civil claims which may be covered by the firm's indemnity insurance, for example claims for breach of statutory duty, negligence or breach of contract or trust (see Chapter 10). It is possible that the firm's insurance may also cover its liability to a regulatory penalty or a restitution (and the costs of dealing with a regulatory enquiry): whilst it is established that it is contrary to public policy to insure against liability consequent on the commission of a criminal offence (see *Lancashire County Council v Municipal Mutual Insurance Ltd* [1996] 3 All ER 545, CA), it is not clear whether public policy prevents insurance against non-criminal regulatory liability.
2 This could result in claims being made against the compensation scheme: see the FSA Handbook at COMP. The financial resources of the firm, taking into account any insurance cover, is a relevant factor for the FSA in considering whether to take urgent action: see the FSA Handbook at ENF 3.5.13(5) and see para 9.194 ff below.
3 The consequences of breaching the Principles are discussed at para 2.156 ff above.
4 The individual would be likely to be 'knowingly concerned' in the firm's breach or may have breached a Statement of Principle: see para 2.182 ff above.

Taking steps to ensure the problem will not recur

3.131 The FSA is likely to be interested not just in the particular breach that occurred but also more generally in the reasons why it occurred. It will want to see that the firm has considered, and addressed, any specific weaknesses in its systems or controls which allowed the problem to arise and also any more general issues that the problem highlights, such as systems and controls more generally, compliance culture or the need for further employee training on compliance issues. The firm therefore needs to ensure that it thinks about these wider issues and does not focus purely on the specific breach.

Why does this matter?

3.132 The firm's response to the regulatory issue may itself be relevant in assessing whether it has appropriate systems and controls in place[1]. On a practical level, if the firm can show, at the time when it reports the problem to the FSA or shortly thereafter, that it has put a stop to the conduct in question, has assessed whether there are any wider implications and has taken, or is in the process of taking, the necessary steps to address those implications, then this should help to lessen the risk that the problem is elevated from the supervisory relationship to the FSA's enforcement division and thus allow the matter to be addressed informally, for example, by a private warning[2]. The key point here is for the firm to show that it is in control, that it is investigating properly and keeping the FSA fully informed, and that it intends to take whatever action needs to be taken to address the implications of the problem.

1 As noted at footnote 1 to para 3.128 above, this is also relevant to compliance with Statement of Principle 7 by those exercising 'significant influence functions'.
2 See para 7.18 ff below.

3.133 Where the problem is referred to the FSA's enforcement division, the firm's conduct generally following discovery of the problem will be relevant to the FSA's enforcement decisions, such as whether or not to take formal disciplinary action against the firm for the breach[1] and, if so, the extent of the relevant punishment and whether to exercise as a matter of urgency its own-initiative power to vary the firm's permission[2]. The firm does, however, also need to bear in mind that the existence of wider, systemic issues increases the nature and seriousness of the problem in the FSA's eyes[3] and makes it more likely that the FSA will exercise its formal disciplinary or other enforcement powers and that any disciplinary sanction it imposes will be greater.

1 See the FSA Handbook at ENF 11.4.1(2) and 13.3.3(5) and see para 7.27 ff below.
2 Or to intervene in an incoming firm. See the FSA Handbook at ENF 3.5.13(8) and para 9.196 ff below.
3 See, for example, the FSA Handbook at ENF 11.4.1(1).

What steps should the firm take?

3.134 What steps are required to be taken by the firm will depend upon the circumstances. They include:

- preventing the conduct from continuing;
- assessing whether any deficiencies in systems or controls gave rise to or contributed to the problem (or failed to pick up that the problem had occurred), and then remedying those deficiencies;
- considering the position of any employees involved, not only from a disciplinary perspective but also from the perspective of whether they had been properly trained or require further training; and
- considering whether the problem highlights any issues regarding the level of supervision being provided by management, and addressing those issues.

Dealing with employees

3.135 It is rare that a regulatory breach occurs without an individual being involved who has taken or failed to take some kind of action, whether inadvertently or deliberately. Most cases therefore potentially give rise to questions about the conduct of particular individuals. Whilst it may in some cases be clear that the individual has deliberately flouted the rules, and in other cases it may be equally clear that the error was inadvertent, it may in many cases not be so simple. The issue of whether the firm should support the individual concerned can make dealing with the personnel implications of possible regulatory breaches something of a minefield. Although it is not the purpose of this book to address the employment law issues[1], there are some important issues to consider in the regulatory context. How will the FSA expect the firm to be approaching these issues? Can the firm wait for the FSA to investigate and decide on the position of the individual? Or does it need to take some kind of action itself?

1 For a detailed discussion, see Harvey on *Industrial Relations and Employment Law*.

3.136 In answering these questions, we consider:

- why this is important to the FSA; and
- what the firm is required to do.

Why is this important to the FSA?

3.137 The FSA expects firms, under Principle 3[1], to take reasonable care to organise and control their affairs responsibly. It expects management to take responsibility for what happens in firms[2]. Also, it expects firms to review the suitability of those who act for them if something happens to make a fresh look appropriate[3]. Each of these points is illustrative of a general regulatory concern to see that firms take appropriate internal steps to review the activities of their employees and, if appropriate, take disciplinary or other action against them and do not simply wait for the FSA to take steps or to require the firm to do so. The FSA may, however, in some circumstances expect to be consulted before the firm takes action[4].

1 Principle 3 of the Principles for Businesses: see para 2.52 above.

2 This is one of the principles of good regulation: see para 2.21 above. It is also reflected directly in the Code of Practice for approved persons: see footnote 1 to para 3.128 above.
3 See the FSA Handbook at SYSC 3.2.14.
4 See para 3.72 above. In any event, the FSA will often need to be notified of the matter under Principle 11: for a case where a firm was fined for not doing so, see *Holt, Carr and Nicholson Barber* (24 July 2000, SFA Board Notice 550).

What is the firm required to do?

3.138 Where there is a particular employee involved, one of the FSA's first questions to the firm is often to ask what the firm intends to do about him or her. This can be a difficult area in practice.

3.139 The starting point is that the firm needs to have taken, or be in the course of taking, appropriate steps to investigate the problem, including, where necessary, the role of particular individuals. This is discussed at para 3.9 ff above, together with various points to consider in investigating and interviewing employees. The firm may initially be able to satisfy the FSA's enquiries by reassuring the FSA that such investigations are still underway. Depending upon the situation, it may also be appropriate for the firm to suspend the particular employee or at least remove him from any sensitive positions, pending the outcome of the investigation. The firm plainly needs to have in place terms and conditions of employment that allow it to take appropriate action against its employees[1].

1 Such as an express power of suspension, or appointment to an alternative position, pending the outcome of an investigation where breach of any regulatory obligation is alleged or suspected; and an express power to dismiss summarily where the employee breaches a regulatory obligation. Other provisions which will help protect the firm include appropriate restrictive covenants (including, for example, the protection of confidential information) and clear provisions regarding the treatment of bonuses and share options in respect of employees who are dismissed.

3.140 Eventually, though, the firm needs to decide what, if any, disciplinary action to take. This can present difficulties. The firm needs to consider very carefully the nature and seriousness of the disciplinary charges which are merited against the individual. The FSA may have its own view of the seriousness of the matter. If the firm's action against its employee is too lenient, then it may indicate to the FSA that the firm does not take the matter sufficiently seriously. If it is too strong, then it may indicate to the FSA that the firm regards the matter as more serious than the FSA had anticipated. This could also potentially be used by the FSA in any regulatory proceedings against the firm in which the seriousness of the matter is a relevant factor[1]. But it may be difficult for the firm to control the outcome of its disciplinary process in the way that this may suggest. If the firm is to have, and be seen to have, a fair and reasonable disciplinary process, then that process will need to be based on a judgment of the merits of the charges against the individual, and not on what the firm wishes to achieve vis-à-vis its regulator.

1 The seriousness of the matter is relevant to most of the FSA's enforcement decisions. Examples include deciding whether or not to take disciplinary action (see the FSA Handbook at ENF 11.4.1), whether to impose a fine or a public statement (ENF 12.3.3), the amount of any fine (ENF 13.3.3) and whether to apply for an injunction (ENF 6.6.2).

3.141 Another difficult question is at what point in time the firm must consider whether disciplinary action is merited against its employee. There may in practice be pressure from the FSA for the firm to undertake its internal disciplinary process before the FSA concludes its own investigation[1]. As already indicated, there can be a tendency for the regulator to make reference in its disciplinary charges to action already taken by the employer and this may cause a concern that action taken by the employer will worsen the employee's position before the regulator. In some situations, there may be merit in the firm waiting until the regulatory investigation is complete because the FSA will have access to sources of information external to the firm and additional information may emerge which casts further light on the matter.

1 In principle, the timing ought to be irrelevant to the FSA, provided that, in appropriate cases, steps have been taken to remove the employee from any sensitive positions. The FSA should be able to decide whether to bring regulatory disciplinary charges against the employee based on the evidence and then to seek to prove those charges based on that evidence.

DOES THE PROBLEM POTENTIALLY GIVE RISE TO CRIMINAL PROCEEDINGS?

3.142 If, in the circumstances, there is a risk that the breach may have involved the commission of criminal offences by the firm or its employees, then the firm's dealings with the FSA may be more complicated and, in addition, the firm needs to be particularly aware of the potential for conflict between its interests and those of the relevant members of staff.

3.143 We outline here some of the main areas of potential criminal conduct in this context and then briefly consider what steps the firm might consider taking in those circumstances[1].

1 A more detailed discussion of criminal prosecutions, including the practical issues that arise, can be found at Chapter 11 below.

Relevant types of criminal offences

3.144 Areas which potentially give rise to issues about criminal liability include:

- breach of the perimeter;
- unlawful financial promotion;
- money laundering;
- insider dealing;
- misleading statements and practices;
- provision of false or misleading information to the FSA, an investigator appointed by the FSA, or the firm's auditor or actuary;
- deliberate destruction of documents; or
- acting in breach of a prohibition order.

3.145 Under FSMA 2000, s 400, if an offence committed by the firm was committed with the consent or connivance of an officer of the firm, or is attributable to neglect on that officer's part, then the officer (as well as the firm) is guilty of the offence and may be prosecuted and punished accordingly[1].

1 This is discussed in detail at para 11.31 ff below.

Steps to take where criminal offences may be involved

3.146 If the firm suspects that it or one of its employees may have committed a criminal offence, then it will need to consider whether to report that to the FSA. Under the FSA's specific notification rules[1], the obligation to report in respect of criminal offences arises only where the firm becomes aware, or has information which reasonably suggests, that a criminal prosecution or conviction may occur. The simple fact that certain actions had occurred which may constitute a criminal offence should not, without more, fall within this. However, the specific notification rules do not supplant the firm's general duties to the FSA[2] to report to it matters of which it would expect notice and it cannot therefore be ruled out that the FSA would expect to be notified, depending upon the circumstances, for example if the matter also had other regulatory implications. The firm must also be open and co-operative with the FSA in its investigation of the matter[3].

1 See para 3.50 ff above.
2 Principle 11, Principles for Businesses: see para 3.66 ff above.
3 Principle 11: see para 4.27 ff below.

3.147 The firm is not entitled to withhold information from the FSA on the ground of the privilege against self-incrimination. The privilege applies only to restrict in certain respects the use of information once obtained[1]. It does not prevent the information from being obtained, nor does it allow the firm to refuse to provide it.

1 It prevents the use of self-incriminating statements in criminal proceedings or proceedings for market abuse. This is discussed at para 4.242 ff below.

3.148 If there is a real risk that an employee will be prosecuted for a criminal offence, then the firm should probably advise the employee that he should consider obtaining independent legal advice[1].

1 This is discussed in more detail at para 3.35 above.

TAKING CARE ABOUT DOCUMENT DESTRUCTION AND CREATION

3.149 As with any other situation which may potentially be contentious, from the time when the firm discovers a potential problem it needs to bear in mind the need to take particular care about the documents it creates and destroys.

Document destruction

3.150 Normal document destruction processes, including the erasion of e-mails and the destruction of tapes of relevant telephone lines, should be stopped immediately. It is important that an appropriately worded notice is disseminated and preserved, so that the firm can later demonstrate that it took appropriate steps to inform the relevant people.

3.151 Why does this matter? It is a criminal offence[1] for any person who knows or suspects that an investigation is being or is likely to be conducted by the FSA or the Secretary of State under the FSMA 2000 to:

- falsify, conceal, destroy or otherwise dispose of a document which he knows or suspects is or would be relevant to such an investigation; or
- cause or permit the falsification, concealment, destruction or disposal of such a document,

unless he shows that he had no intention of concealing facts disclosed by the documents from the investigator.

1 FSMA 2000, s 177(3).

3.152 The offence is potentially very broad. It applies to a person who no more than suspects that an investigation is likely to be conducted, and to documents which the person suspects would be relevant to that investigation. It applies not only to the person who takes the action, but also to any person who causes or permits someone else to do so.

3.153 In addition, if the criminal offence is investigated by another authority, then there are other, parallel offences that may be applicable[1].

1 For example, a similar offence applies in relation to investigations by the Serious Fraud Office: Criminal Justice Act 1987, s 2(16). Some of the different criminal investigation bodies that may have jurisdiction are briefly outlined at Chapter 11 below.

3.154 Moreover, on a practical level, if it subsequently appeared that documents had been destroyed after the matter came to the firm's attention, this could cause embarrassment, and suspicion, with the FSA and the Tribunal, as well as with the court if any legal proceedings were to result. A court could draw negative inferences and, in some cases, may refuse to give the firm the benefit of any doubt or to draw any inference in its favour[1].

1 See *Mahon v Air New Zealand Ltd* [1984] AC 808 and *Infabrics v Jaytex* [1985] FSR 75, discussed at Documentary Evidence, Hollander & Adam, 7th edition, 2000, from 8-08.

Document creation

3.155 The firm also needs to take care not to create, so far as possible, additional documents which might be prejudicial to it. There are broadly two concerns, namely that:

- such material might be disclosable to the FSA, or indeed to other regulators, in the context of any regulatory investigation which ensues[1]; and
- the material, either in the FSA's hands or in the firm's hands, might be disclosable to third parties who might bring legal proceedings against the firm arising from the problem[2].

1 The extent of the information that the FSA, or an investigator appointed by it, can require to be produced is discussed in Chapter 4 below.
2 The risks of disclosure of material are discussed in detail at para 4.189 ff below.

3.156 In order to illustrate this, it may be helpful to explain what sorts of documents are likely to cause concern. The firm will of course have created documents in the course of its business which relate to the problem, for example records of transactions, records of checks carried out, and internal memos and e-mails created during the ordinary course of business. Those documents will contain the primary facts relating to the problem. They will form the basis for the FSA's investigation and any enforcement action, and may also form the basis for any legal claim brought by any third party. In general, there is no question of withholding them[1].

1 There are certain categories of documents which the FSA cannot require to be disclosed to it, namely documents protected by legal professional privilege and, in some circumstances, documents in relation to which the firm owes a banker's duty of confidence: see para 4.262 ff below.

3.157 The concern therefore primarily arises in relation to documents that the firm creates after the problem has arisen. Examples include:

- material produced in order to assist the FSA, for example explanations of the firm's procedures, schedules of likely investor losses, and so on. There may be some difficult tensions between seeking to assist the FSA in this way and trying to ensure that the firm does not produce material that would expose it to claims from third parties;
- reports containing opinions or conclusions, even provisional ones, as to the reasons for problems, responsibility for those problems and how to rectify the problems;
- notes of early meetings with potential witnesses, particularly where the full scope of the problem was still unknown and/or people had not yet had the opportunity to refresh their memories from the documents.

3.158 However, as indicated, certain types of documents may be protected from disclosure, particularly those which are legally privileged. If it is necessary to produce any material, then consideration should be given as to whether it should be structured in such a way as to try to ensure that the material is protected. Simply copying a document to a lawyer is unlikely to be sufficient[1].

1 For a more detailed discussion, see para 4.189 ff below.

3.159 To whatever extent a document is perceived as harmless at the time it is written, it is impossible to predict all the situations in which it could come to be scrutinised and with hindsight it may be better for the firm had it not been produced. Whilst in some situations it may be necessary to produce material of this nature, in many situations it is not.

3.160 Documents which may need to be disclosed can be produced in many ways. They include not only physical documents but also e-mails which, on many systems, are stored even when deleted and thus capable of retrieval, and telephone calls on taped lines. All methods of document creation should be avoided, even to the extent of staff being warned not unnecessarily to discuss the problem on taped lines.

3.161 Finally, firms need to bear in mind that the risk of being required to disclose material should not be assessed purely in the UK context. If overseas regulators, customers or market counter-parties are involved, then there may be similar considerations in other jurisdictions and the types of material that can be disclosed may be different in those other jurisdictions.

4 Information gathering and investigation

CONTENTS

Introduction	**107**
Information gathering and investigation powers	**109**
Objecting to the FSA's use of investigation powers	**178**
Use of information obtained by the FSA	**189**

INTRODUCTION

An overview of Chapter 4

4.1 In this chapter, we outline the action that may be taken by the FSA to investigate a problem. This considers the regulatory process from the time when a potential regulatory issue is discovered, through the investigation stage, up to the point where the FSA considers what action to take in the light of the information it has obtained, and also how the firm might respond to that process.

4.2 We therefore deal with three main issues:

- the FSA's powers to obtain information from firms, including its formal and its informal powers and its ability to initiate a formal investigation (para 4.10 ff below);
- the grounds which a firm might have to object to the FSA's use of formal powers, the steps to take if it wishes to do so and the consequences of not complying with formal requests (para 4.260 ff below); and
- the use the FSA can make of the information (para 4.300 ff below).

In addressing each issue, we look at the practical steps that a firm subjected to the process can take, for example to minimise the disruption caused by the process and to protect its own legitimate interests.

4.3 The FSA's power to investigate and address breaches of the perimeter (the criminal offence of carrying on regulated activities without authorisation or exemption under the FSMA 2000[1]) is outside the scope of this book. However, if a regulated firm acts beyond the scope of its permission then that could give rise to regulatory consequences[2] and this is encompassed in the discussion that follows.

1 For a brief explanation, see para 2.175 above.
2 See further the discussion at para 2.176 above.

4.4 The FSMA 2000[1] provides, in this area, a reasonably detailed framework for the FSA's extensive investigation powers. The FSA's policy in relation to the use of those powers is found in the FSA Handbook at ENF Chapter 2 and at other parts of the Handbook as specified below. In addition, Consultation Paper 17 ('Enforcing the new regime'), December 1998 and the FSA's Response to Consultation Paper 17, July 1999, provide some further clarification of the FSA's approach to the use of these powers.

1 FSMA 2000, Pt XI.

A brief overview

4.5 Potential problems can come to the FSA's attention in a variety of ways. These include reporting by firms, enquiries from other regulators, complaints or enquiries from customers, reports or issues relating to other firms, whistleblowing by actuaries or auditors or from the FSA's own monitoring visits to the firm. As we have seen in Chapter 3 above, if the FSA is not already aware of a potential problem which comes to light, then the firm may have to report the matter to it.

4.6 If the FSA wishes to understand more about the problem, then it has a variety of powers which it can use to obtain information, each power being exercisable in specific situations, allowing certain categories of material to be obtained from a particular range of people. The scope of the FSA's investigation thus depends upon precisely which power is being invoked. There are broadly, though, three types of powers. First, the FSA has the ability to require firms to provide information without exercising its formal statutory powers. Second, in some circumstances the FSA can investigate directly itself by exercising statutory powers to require information to be provided to it. Third, there are statutory powers to initiate formal investigations, conducted by appointing a formal investigator who reports to the FSA.

4.7 The FSA regards all these powers as fact-finding in nature. In other words, the FSA first needs to obtain the facts relating to a problem so that it can then decide how to act in the light of those facts. The powers of investigation are therefore central to all of the FSA's enforcement functions[1].

1 'Information is the key to effective regulation. The FSA must have access to detailed, up-to-date and relevant information in order to make good regulatory decisions': the Financial Secretary to HM Treasury in Standing Committee, 23 November 1999.

4.8 The FSA has made clear that three principles underpin its approach[1]. First, it expects to maintain an open and co-operative relationship with firms. Second, it will exercise its powers in a manner that is proportionate, transparent and consistent with its policy. Third, the FSA will seek to ensure the fair treatment of those involved in any particular case. We discuss at para 4.260 ff below whether a firm can object if the FSA fails to act in accordance with these policies and, at para 4.300 ff below, the use that can be made of the information that the FSA obtains.

1 See the FSA Handbook at ENF 1.3.1 and see the more detailed discussion at para 2.34 ff above.

4.9 The guiding principle of an open and co-operative relationship between firm and regulator[1] drives much of the discussion on how a firm should deal with the FSA once a regulatory problem arises. This approach is fundamental to the UK regulatory regime, has some advantages for the firm as well as the FSA, and needs to be borne in mind throughout.

1 Principle 11, Principles for Businesses: see paras 2.52 above and 4.27, 4.50 and 4.180 below.

INFORMATION GATHERING AND INVESTIGATION POWERS

Introduction

The range of powers available

4.10 In the following paragraphs, we outline the statutory and other powers available to the FSA, and in some circumstances also the Secretary of State, to require the provision of information. There are broadly three types of powers, which we review separately, namely:

- the power to obtain information informally from firms by requesting co-operation and assistance from them (para 4.26 ff);
- the statutory powers to make formal requests for information from firms (para 4.57 ff); and
- the statutory powers to initiate a formal investigation (para 4.108 ff).

4.11 The statutory scheme is complicated. It allows both for the FSA to gather information itself and for it, or the Secretary of State, to commence formal investigations and appoint investigators in a variety of circumstances. There are a number of different grounds for commencing a formal investigation, which overlap to a large extent, and precisely what information can be demanded, and from whom, differs depending upon the ground for the formal investigation.

4.12 Whilst the investigation powers under the FSMA 2000 seem very wide in scope, particularly when brought together in the way that they are in the FSMA 2000, they are comparable with various pre-existing statutory powers, for example, the powers of inspectors appointed by the Department of Trade and Industry to investigate insider dealing[1], the powers of the Secretary of State under the Financial Services Act 1986[2] and of the Bank of England (and latterly the FSA) under the Banking Act 1987[3], as well as the non-statutory powers of the SROs.

1 Financial Services Act 1986, s 177.
2 Financial Services Act 1986, s 105.
3 Banking Act 1987, s 39. These provisions also replace provisions in legislation such as the Insurance Companies Act 1982, the Building Societies Act 1986 and the Friendly Societies Act 1992. This Part of the FSMA 2000 'represents a synthesis – put together with some care – of the rather confusing array of investigative powers exercised by the existing regulators . . . [It] provides the FSA with a single, coherent set of powers, appropriate for a modern regulator dealing with developing markets, bounded by appropriate safeguards, and drawing on the best of what exists at present': the Financial Secretary to HM Treasury in Standing Committee, 23 November 1999.

4.13 The range of information gathering and investigation powers outlined in this chapter is as follows:

FSA's informal powers:	
Principle 11	to require firms to co-operate under Principle 11, without resorting to statutory powers;
Statement of Principle 4	to require approved persons to co-operate;
The FSA's rules	powers under the FSA rules to require specific types of co-operation and assistance from firms.
The FSA's formal information gathering powers:	
Section 165	to require firms, and certain others, to provide information in relation to any matter relevant to the exercise of the FSA's statutory functions;
Section 166	to require firms, and certain others, to obtain a report from a skilled person on any matter relevant to the exercise of the FSA's statutory functions.
The FSA's investigation powers, mostly shared with the Secretary of State:	
Section 167	to investigate the business, ownership or control of an authorised person;
Section 168(1) & (4)	to investigate various criminal or regulatory offences;
Section 168(2)	to investigate certain serious criminal or regulatory offences, namely insider dealing, market abuse, breach of the general prohibition, unlawful financial promotion or misleading statements and practices;
Section 169	to investigate at the request of an overseas regulator.

4.14 In addition, the FSA has various other investigation powers exercisable in specific circumstances, namely to:

- investigate the affairs of collective investment schemes or open ended investment companies, discussed at para 14.10 ff below;
- investigate market abuse, discussed in this chapter at para 4.144 ff below and also discussed more specifically at para 13.141 ff below; and
- investigate listed companies and applicants for listing, discussed at para 15.46 ff below; or
- require the provision of information in connection with various applications made to it[1].

Also, certain other bodies have investigation powers under the FSMA 2000, including HM Treasury[2], the Director General of Fair Trading[3], the ombudsman[4] and the manager of the Compensation Scheme[5].

1 See, for example, FSMA 2000, ss 51 (relating to applications for Part IV permissions) and 289 (relating to applications for recognition by exchanges or clearing houses). These powers are not reviewed because they do not arise in the enforcement context.
2 FSMA 2000, s 16.
3 FSMA 2000, ss 161 and 305.
4 FSMA 2000, s 231 and see para 12.50 ff below.
5 FSMA 2000, ss 219 and 220.

4.15 This list, notwithstanding its length, is not exhaustive of the various investigation regimes to which firms could be subjected. Firms can be required to produce documents and information to a range of different bodies exercising different, often overlapping, jurisdictions for different purposes[1]. The FSA has agreed guidelines on co-operation with certain criminal investigating or prosecuting bodies with overlapping jurisdiction. These can be found in the FSA Handbook at ENF Chapter 2, Annex 1G and are briefly discussed at para 11.10 ff below.

1 Examples include the DTI under the Companies Acts 1985 and 1989, the SFO under the Criminal Justice Act 1987, OPRA under the Pension Schemes Act 1993 and Pension Act 1995, the Police under the Police and Criminal Evidence Act 1984, liquidators under the Insolvency Act 1986, the Take-over Panel, the Recognised Investment Exchanges (see para 13.213 ff below), the Office of Fair Trading under the Fair Trading Act 1973 and the Competition Act 1980 (among others) and the Competition Commission under the Fair Trading Act 1973 and Competition Act 1998.

When will the FSA use its formal powers?

4.16 In the normal course, most issues relating to firms which come to the FSA's attention are, to start with, addressed within the supervisory relationship between the FSA and the firm and enquiries will be made of the firm in that context. Indeed, many day-to-day issues are resolved within the supervisory relationship without the involvement of any enforcement personnel[1]. As will be seen, the firm has an obligation to co-operate with and assist the FSA under Principle 11[2], to which the FSA gives a broad interpretation, and the FSA rules that amplify it[3]. This will be sufficient in many instances to enable the FSA to obtain the information it needs. The FSA will look to obtain information in this way unless it appears that this will not achieve the necessary results, in which case it will use its statutory powers[4].

1 Thus, whilst there were, in the year to 31 March 2001, more than 7500 investment business firms regulated by the FSA's predecessors, around 760 'preliminary enquiries' were opened and, of these, only 226 cases were referred for formal investigation: see the FSA's Annual Report 2000/2001.
2 Principle 11, Principles for Businesses. For a detailed discussion of the obligation to co-operate under Principle 11, see para 4.27 ff below.
3 See para 4.39 ff below.
4 See the FSA Handbook at SUP 2.1.6.

4.17 Enforcement staff therefore usually need to become involved only where the supervisory relationship breaks down, or where the nature and seriousness of the matter is such that it should not be handled within the supervisory context, or where there are other particular circumstances requiring enforcement action (such as a need for immediate action or action to protect or secure compensation for consumers). Thus, although the FSA has a wide range of investigation powers available to it under the FSMA 2000, it will often be able to address any issues without resort to those powers.

The FSA's general policy on the use of its formal powers

4.18 The FSA Handbook contains limited guidance on the use of the FSA's formal powers[1]. The FSA's starting point is that if information received by it raises a regulatory concern, then it may need to make further enquiries. The nature of those enquiries depends upon its views as to the nature and seriousness of its concerns and upon the attitude of the firm or individual concerned.

1 See the FSA Handbook at ENF 2.5.4 to 2.5.11.

4.19 The types of matters which could give rise to a need for further enquiries could include any matter which concerns a firm's business and relates to the FSA's performance of its statutory functions. Broadly[1], such matters will include circumstances which suggest that:

- a firm or approved person may have acted in a way which prejudiced the interests of consumers;
- a firm or approved person may have acted in breach of the requirements of the FSMA 2000 or the FSA's rules;
- a firm may no longer meet the threshold conditions[2] or an approved person may no longer be a fit and proper person to perform a controlled function[3];
- a firm may have been used or may be being used for the purposes of financial crime or money laundering;
- the FSA should be concerned about the ownership or control of a firm or about a person who has acquired influence over a firm; or
- the conduct of certain types of regulated activities in which a firm is involved are a cause of serious public concern.

1 See the FSA Handbook at ENF 2.5.5.
2 See para 2.38 ff above.
3 See para 2.69 ff above.

4.20 However, this guidance simply summarises the main elements of the FSA's statutory functions, and thus tells firms little about how the FSA will go about implementing those functions in practice. Some threads can however be drawn together.

4.21 First, the FSA has made clear that it may be appropriate to address many issues without the need for formal disciplinary or other enforcement action, but within the relationship between firms and their supervisors. Where this happens, there is unlikely to be any need for any formal investigation powers to be used. Some cases, on the other hand, are sufficiently serious as to require an effective and thorough investigation using statutory powers[1].

1 See the FSA Handbook at ENF 2.5.8. If the FSA does decide to use its statutory powers, it will have to decide which powers to use, having regard to the objectives of its enquiries and the relative effectiveness of its available powers to achieve those objectives: see the FSA Handbook at ENF 2.5.6.

4.22 Second, it is the FSA's general policy to use its enforcement powers in a manner that is transparent, proportionate and consistent with its publicly stated policies and to seek to ensure fair treatment of those who are subject to the exercise of its enforcement powers[1]. The policy of proportionality, in other words that the use of enforcement powers should be proportionate to the concerns to which the issue gives rise, is important for firms and, as discussed at para 4.272 below, if the FSA seeks to use its powers in a disproportionate way then it may be possible for the firm to challenge its actions. The need for fair treatment is also important. But it is unclear that this would, for example, require the FSA to accept assistance tendered voluntarily without resorting to its formal powers.

1 See the FSA Handbook at ENF 1.3.3 and see para 2.36 above.

4.23 Thirdly, the FSA is required by the principles of good regulation[1] to have regard to the need to use its resources in the most efficient and economic way when, among other things, deciding its policy. Whilst this probably does not give firms the right to complain about how the FSA chooses to act in a particular case[2], there should in general terms be pressure on the FSA to ensure that it acts in a cost-effective manner.

1 These are discussed at para 2.21 above.
2 See the discussion at para 2.22 ff above.

4.24 Fourth, in the policy papers which preceded the FSA Handbook, the FSA recognised specifically that these are compulsory powers giving rise to serious potential liability for failure to comply. However, the statutory tests for the exercise of the compulsory powers present fairly low hurdles for the FSA to overcome. In response to concerns that it might use its investigation powers to mount fishing expeditions where there was slim, or no, evidence of wrongdoing, the FSA confirmed that it did not intend to use the powers on a speculative basis[1].

1 See the FSA's Response to Consultation Paper 17, para 92.

Practical guidance for firms

4.25 Notwithstanding the lack of guidance in the FSA Handbook, it is possible to provide some general guidance on the types of considerations likely to be relevant to the FSA in deciding whether to exercise its formal powers in a particular case. They are likely to include the following:

- whether the firm is assisting and co-operating fully with the FSA;
- whether the firm needs the FSA to impose a formal requirement, for example because of the firm's duties of confidentiality to third parties;
- whether the FSA is likely to need to obtain information or documents from third parties who cannot be compelled to provide them under Principle 11 or the FSA's rules;
- whether a specific 'incident' has occurred, particularly one which has given rise to public concern;
- whether the FSA is simply obtaining further information following a report from the firm on a particular issue;
- whether the issue gives rise to any consumer protection concerns; and
- the nature and seriousness of the concerns and, particularly, whether there is the need for an effective and thorough investigation.

Informal requests for information

4.26 Once an issue which raises regulatory concerns comes to the FSA's attention, the FSA is likely, often without using any of its formal powers, to ask the firm to provide information about the problem. How should the firm respond to this request? There are likely to be three main considerations. First, the scope of the firm's obligations to co-operate with the FSA, second, the obligations of the firm's employees to co-operate with the FSA and, third, the practical consequences of assisting or not assisting the FSA. These are considered in turn below.

The firm's obligation to co-operate with the FSA

4.27 The firm has a general obligation under Principle 11[1] to co-operate with the FSA, the scope of which is the subject of guidance in the FSA Handbook, and two specific obligations under the FSA's rules[2]. As will be seen, these obligations are sufficiently broad in scope to allow the FSA to conduct an intrusive investigation into the firm, with the firm having limited ability to object to or challenge the process. In reality, there will often be little option but to co-operate and maintaining a close mutual relationship with the FSA may be the most effective way for the firm to have some sort of control over the process.

1 Principle 11 of the Principles for Businesses: see para 2.52 above.
2 See the FSA Handbook at SUP 2.

4.28 Under Principle 11, a firm is required to deal with its regulators in an open and co-operative manner and must disclose to the FSA appropriately anything relating to the firm of which the FSA would reasonably expect notice.

4.29 There are two limbs to this. First, the need to deal with the FSA in an open and co-operative way and, second, the requirement to give the FSA notice of matters that arise. The first of these limbs is considered here. The scope of the firm's obligations under the second is discussed at para 3.41 ff above.

4.30 In addition, a firm has two specific obligations under the FSA's rules, namely to:

- permit the FSA or its representatives to have access, with or without notice, during reasonable business hours to any of the firm's business premises and to take reasonable steps to ensure that its agents, suppliers under material outsourcing arrangements[1] and appointed representatives give that permission in relation to their premises[2]; and
- take reasonable steps to ensure that each of its suppliers under material outsourcing arrangements deals in an open and co-operative way with the FSA in the discharge of its functions under the FSMA 2000 in relation to the firm[3].

These are considered further below.

1 'Material outsourcing' means outsourcing services of such importance that weakness, or failure, of the services would cast doubt on the firm's continuing satisfaction of the threshold conditions or compliance with the Principles for Businesses: see the FSA Handbook, Glossary of Definitions.
2 See the FSA Handbook at SUP 2.3.5.
3 See the FSA Handbook at SUP 2.3.7.

The obligation under Principle 11

4.31 The FSA has provided detailed guidance on the co-operation that it expects from firms under Principle 11. Although this guidance appears in the FSA's Supervision Manual[1], and is phrased primarily in the language of supervision, as we have seen, many regulatory issues may be dealt with in that context and, in addition, it applies in the enforcement context as well[2]. Broadly, the FSA expects to be able to rely upon Principle 11 to obtain the information it needs from firms in many situations.

1 See the FSA Handbook at SUP 2.3.
2 See the FSA Handbook at ENF 2.5.1 and SUP 2.1.8.

4.32 ***What information and co-operation can the firm be required to provide?*** The FSA has given guidance that the firm should[1]:

- make itself readily available for meetings with the FSA;
- give the FSA reasonable access to any records, files, tapes or computer systems which are within the firm's possession or control and provide any facilities which the FSA may reasonably request;

- produce to the FSA specified documents, files, tapes, computer data or other material in the firm's possession or control as reasonably requested;
- print information in the firm's possession or control which is held on computer or on microfilm or otherwise convert it into a readily legible document or other record which the FSA may reasonably request;
- permit the FSA to copy documents or other material on the premises of the firm at the firm's reasonable expense and remove copies and hold them elsewhere or provide any copies as reasonably requested; and
- answer truthfully, fully and promptly all questions which are reasonably put to it by the FSA.

It should also take reasonable steps to ensure its employees, agents and appointed representatives, and other members of its group, and their employees and agents, provide the same assistance[2].

1 See the FSA Handbook at SUP 2.3.3. Note that the FSA may make these requests in order to assist other regulators and may pass on information to such other regulators without notifying the firm: see the FSA Handbook at SUP 2.3.11.
2 See the FSA Handbook at SUP 2.3.4.

4.33 This is subject to the statutory limitations on the documents the FSA can require firms to produce, in particular documents falling within the statutory test for legal privilege[1]. The FSA has also indicated that it would not normally seek information protected by the (rather limited) statutory protection for banking confidentiality[2].

1 FSMA 2000, s 413 and see the discussion at para 4.264 ff below.
2 See the FSA Handbook at SUP 2.2.3 and see para 4.267 ff below.

4.34 The FSA may also conduct 'mystery shopping' on a firm, or its agents or appointed representatives, approaching them in the role of a potential retail customer and will record any telephone calls or meetings held. It can do this to establish a firm's normal practices in a way which would not be possible by other means[1].

1 See the FSA Handbook at SUP 2.4.

4.35 ***Can the FSA require information or co-operation on demand?*** The FSA has stated that it can seek access to premises without notice, although it has said that this will be 'on rare occasions'[1]. No guidance is given on when this is likely to be appropriate or on what information or documents the FSA might seek such a visit. The FSA has also made a specific rule[2] requiring firms to permit access to their premises with or without notice. Whether the FSA can legitimately demand immediate assistance will depend upon the circumstances, in particular in the light of the ECHR right to privacy[3]. This is discussed further at para 4.274 below.

1 See the FSA Handbook at SUP 2.3.2.
2 See para 4.30 above and the discussion at para 4.39 ff below.
3 If the firm has such a right: see para 4.274 below.

4.36 ***How will the firm be asked to provide information or co-operation?*** The FSA may seek assistance by a variety of means. It may do so by making a visit to the firm whether on a regular basis, on a sample basis, for special purposes or when the FSA has a particular reason for visiting a firm. It may seek meetings at the FSA's office or elsewhere. Or it may seek information or documents over the telephone, at meetings, or in writing[1] (including by e-mail).

1 See the FSA Handbook at SUP 2.3.1.

4.37 ***What does this mean for the firm?*** This guidance confirms that there is little that the FSA cannot ask of a firm, even without exercising its statutory powers. Whilst the policy outlined above is only guidance, is not expressed in mandatory language (the word 'should' is used, not 'must'), and therefore seems strictly not to be binding[1], it does show the level of co-operation which the FSA expects from firms and if firms do not comply then they are at risk of breaching Principle 11, with the potential consequences outlined at para 4.52 below. Whether the lack of co-operation is sufficient to amount to a breach of Principle 11 will depend on the circumstances of the particular case.

1 See the discussion at para 2.122 ff above.

4.38 The scope of the co-operation which the FSA expects, the ability to require access to premises without notice (without the FSA providing any proper policy guidance on when that is likely to be appropriate or what it may seek during such a visit), and the obligation to take reasonable steps to ensure that any company within the same group, or employees or agents, comply, all add up to a set of powers which could be very intrusive. The firm has limited ability to challenge the use of Principle 11 in this way[1].

1 For a discussion of how it might challenge the use of the FSA's powers, see para 4.260 ff below.

Specific obligations under the FSA rules

4.39 The two specific obligations under the FSA's rules (outlined at para 4.30 above) are different in nature from the guidance on Principle 11 set out above because they have the status of FSA rules. Hence, a failure to comply would, on the face of it, amount to a regulatory contravention.

4.40 The scope of these rules requires comment. First, the FSA has given no guidance on the circumstances when it will exercise what is potentially a very intrusive right to demand immediate access to the firm's premises (although it has said that it normally expects to give reasonable notice[1]) and the rule itself contains no limitations or conditions. Nonetheless, the FSA's duties as a public body may impose some limitations and, as a result, there may be a means for the person concerned to object if the FSA behaves unreasonably. This is discussed further at para 4.272 ff below.

1 See the FSA Handbook at SUP 2.3.6.

4.41 Second, the FSA has said[1] that the obligation relating to material outsourcing arrangements requires the firm, when it appoints or renews the appointment of a supplier under a material outsourcing arrangement, to satisfy itself that the terms of its contract require the supplier to give the FSA access to premises and co-operate with it in the same way as the firm (save that the co-operation the firm is expected to procure from the supplier does not extend to matters outside the scope of the FSA's functions in relation to the firm). The firm must therefore ensure that there are appropriate terms in the relevant outsourcing agreements. But which outsourcing arrangements will be material outsourcing arrangements? The answer may not always be clear. The FSA has said that a supplier under a material outsourcing arrangement is one that supplies services of such importance that weakness, or failure, of the function would cast doubt on the firm's continuing satisfaction of the threshold conditions or compliance with the Principles for Businesses[2]. This is not an easy test to apply and there may be a risk of the question whether a particular contractor was such a supplier being judged with hindsight.

1 See the FSA Handbook at SUP 2.3.8/9.
2 See the FSA Handbook, Glossary of Definitions.

Obligations of the firm's employees to co-operate with the FSA

4.42 The nature and scope of the duties of the firm's employees to co-operate with the FSA depend upon whether the particular employee is an approved person[1] or not.

1 For an explanation of 'approved persons', see para 2.64 ff above.

Duties of approved persons

4.43 Approved persons owe a general duty to the FSA under Statement of Principle 4[1] in similar terms to the firm's duty under Principle 11. An approved person must deal with the FSA and other regulators in an open and co-operative way and must disclose appropriately any information of which the FSA would reasonably expect notice. As with Principle 11, there are two limbs to this. First, notifying the FSA or others of relevant matters that come to light. Second, co-operating with the FSA. The first, the obligation on approved persons to report matters to the FSA and others, is discussed at para 3.85 ff above.

1 For an explanation of the Statements of Principle for approved persons and the Code of Practice, see para 2.76 ff above.

4.44 So far as co-operating with the FSA is concerned, the Code of Practice provides[1] that, in the FSA's view, conduct which does not comply with Statement of Principle 4 includes failing without good reason:

- to inform a regulator of information of which the approved person was aware in response to questions from that regulator;
- to attend an interview or answer questions put by a regulator, despite a request or demand having been made; or

- to supply a regulator with appropriate documents or information when requested or required to do so and within the time limits attaching to such a request or requirement.

1 See the FSA Handbook at APER 4.4.9.

4.45 This differs from the firm's obligation in that it specifically envisages the individual being able to claim there was good reason for not co-operating with the FSA. No indication as to what might constitute good reason is given. In particular, it is not clear to what extent the individual can claim he was simply obeying orders from more senior employees. Beyond this, the obligation is a wide one, with the lack of specificity serving to highlight this.

4.46 It is important to recognise the effect of this provision of the Code. The Code is of evidential effect only. In other words, failure to comply with this provision tends to indicate that the person's conduct failed to comply with the Statement of Principle but it is not determinative of that. The failure to comply with the provision of the Code does not of itself constitute a regulatory breach. In addition, the Code is not exhaustive of the implications of Statement of Principle 4. Approved persons therefore need to have in mind the broad Statement of Principle, and not focus purely on the specific guidance in the Code. These issues are discussed in more detail at para 2.82 ff above.

4.47 There is in this area scope for divergent interests as between the firm and its employees[1]. When the regulator asks the firm to provide documents or information or to attend a meeting, it will in practice be addressing those requests at particular individuals from the firm, many of whom will be approved persons. If the firm fails to comply, or even instructs the individual not to comply because, for example, it wishes to take a tough stance against its regulator for its own reasons, it could be argued by the FSA that the individual was personally in breach of the Statement of Principle. Whether the individual committed a breach may depend upon whether the FSA regards him as having had 'good reason' for not complying in view of the instructions he received from the firm[2]. There is also a separate question whether, if he did commit a breach, he would be disciplined for that breach. This depends upon the application of the FSA's policy on when it will discipline individuals personally, which broadly is based on personal culpability, and for it to be appropriate in the circumstances for the FSA to take action against the individual[3].

1 In a serious case, this could result in the employee needing to obtain his own legal advice.
2 The effect of the Public Interest Disclosure Act 1998 (discussed at para 4.48 below) may, in certain circumstances, provide an argument that such instructions would not constitute 'good reason' for not reporting to the FSA.
3 This is discussed in detail at para 8.4 ff below.

4.48 If an individual disobeys his instructions and does assist the FSA, then the firm needs to be careful not to discipline him or subject him to any detriment as a result. It is likely that his disclosure to the FSA will be protected under the Public Interest Disclosure Act 1998[1].

1 The FSA is a 'prescribed person' to whom employees may make disclosure of certain types of information under the protection of the Act: see the Public Interest Disclosure (Prescribed Persons) Order 1999, SI 1999/1549. Those types of information include (i) that a criminal offence has been committed, and (ii) a failure to comply with a legal obligation: Employment Rights Act 1996, s 43B(1). It is not clear whether 'legal obligation' would include an FSA rule, but it is possible that it would. See the discussion of administrative law requirements in *Whistleblowing: the New Law*, Bowers, Lewis and Mitchell, 1st edn, 1999, at 3-03. See also the discussion at para 3.86 above.

Duties of other employees

4.49 Whilst other employees who are not approved persons are not under any personal obligation to co-operate with the regulator, their actions are not entirely clear of regulatory consequences. First, as has been seen, the firm's own obligation extends to taking reasonable steps to ensure that its employees comply[1]. The firm may therefore be at risk of committing a regulatory breach if the employee does not co-operate with the FSA. At least, the firm may need to consider, and be seen to consider, taking disciplinary action against the individual or requiring him to submit to further training. Second, the individual's conduct could in a serious case have regulatory consequences against him personally because it could impact on the FSA's view if it later came to consider whether he was a fit and proper person[2].

1 See para 4.32 above.
2 One of the relevant considerations is whether the person has been candid and truthful in all his dealings with regulators and demonstrates a readiness and willingness to comply with the requirements and standards of the regulatory system: see para 2.72 above.

Practical issues in assisting the FSA

4.50 For a variety of reasons outlined below, it will normally be in the firm's interests 'voluntarily' to provide the co-operation and assistance that the FSA seeks, although in some situations the firm may want the FSA to impose a formal requirement on it.

4.51 First, as will be seen, the FSA has wide-ranging formal powers to obtain information from the firm and can reach the decision to exercise those powers without great difficulty. Those powers include interviewing employees, requesting documents, e-mails, electronic records and tapes of telephone lines, requiring the firm to procure auditors' reports, and even approaching the firm's bankers or solicitors for information. But a wide-ranging or unfocused regulatory investigation is likely to require a significant amount of the firm's management's time and to cause a corresponding disruption to its business. The firm will often prefer to provide information informally and to maintain a close and co-operative relationship with the FSA in order to assist it in focusing its enquiries, thereby minimising unnecessary cost and disruption. This is attractive also from the FSA's point of view, since it enables it to use its resources more effectively.

4.52 Second, if the firm does not provide the FSA with the necessary co-operation and assistance, it risks committing a regulatory breach, with broadly the same consequences as are discussed at para 3.101 ff above in relation to failing to notify the FSA of a matter which ought to be reported to the FSA. In addition, if the firm or any person knowingly or recklessly provides false or misleading information to the FSA in purported compliance with a requirement imposed by or under the FSMA 2000, they may commit a criminal offence[1]. This should cover the provision of information under Principle 11. Principle 11 is a rule made by the FSA under its statutory powers, so the provision of information under Principle 11 is in compliance with a requirement imposed under the FSMA 2000.

1 FSMA 2000, s 398(1).

4.53 Third, in some situations there may be reasons why the firm would want to be the subject of a formal investigation or be required formally to provide information, rather than providing information to the FSA solely under Principle 11. For example, the firm may be concerned about its obligations of confidentiality to other parties. Or there may come a stage when, from the firm's perspective, the (limited) protections that it has in the context of a formal investigation, for example being notified of its scope, greater legal certainty as to the extent of the powers being exercised against it, and a statutory protection against self-incrimination[1], make it preferable to be subjected to a formal investigation.

1 There is no express statutory protection against self-incrimination in relation to statements tendered voluntarily, or pursuant to a request under Principle 11 or Statement of Principle 4. See the FSA Handbook at SUP 2.2.5 and ENF 2.10.5 and the discussion at 4.242 ff below.

4.54 The first of these, the question whether Principle 11 overrides the firm's obligations of confidentiality, requires further comment. The firm is likely to owe duties of confidence to its clients, the precise scope of which will depend on its terms of business or, to the extent they are silent, the terms that the law will imply in the particular circumstances of the relationship. Sometimes, it will be clear from the language used in the firm's terms of business that the firm can provide confidential information to the regulator without any formal requirement being imposed on it. In many cases, however, this will not be clear and the question will then arise whether the duty is such as to allow the disclosure to be made. A disclosure made under a legal obligation will normally be permitted[1]. It is less clear that a voluntary disclosure to a regulator would be permitted. It is likely that it would[2], although this would depend upon the circumstances.

1 To the extent that the duty of confidence is the banker's duty of confidence (discussed at para 4.268 below), that duty does not preclude disclosure of confidential information under compulsion of law: see *Tournier v National Provincial and Union Bank of England* [1924] 1 KB 461. So far as other duties of confidence are concerned it is likely, although by no means certain, that the scope of the duty would be interpreted so as to permit disclosures required by law (in the present context, although relating to employees rather than customers, see *Re A Company's Application* [1989] Ch 477) or, if not, and therefore the disclosure was potentially in breach, there may be a sufficient public interest to justify the disclosure (see Denning MR in *Initial Services Ltd v Putterill* [1968] 1 QB 396). For a discussion of the balance of public interest in the context of banking supervision, see *Price Waterhouse v BCCI Holdings (Luxembourg) SA* [1992] BCLC 583 (Millet LJ). The precise answer in any case will depend upon the circumstances.

2 Given the statutory scheme of regulation, and the existence of Principle 11 (see para 2.52 above), most disclosures said to be voluntary could be classed as made under compulsion of law. Even where this does not apply, the points made at footnote 1 above about the need to interpret the scope of the duty of confidence in the particular case and in relation to the public interest are relevant.

4.55 One concern would be that taking such a stance could be regarded by the FSA as a failure to co-operate and therefore a breach of Principle 11. However, it ought to be possible to make clear to the FSA that the firm would prefer a formal investigation, together with the firm's wish to co-operate within the context of that formal investigation, without unduly risking breaching Principle 11.

4.56 Finally, there will be a number of practical and mechanical issues to consider when providing material to the FSA. These are discussed in the context of a formal investigation at para 4.179 ff below. They are relevant also in this context.

Formal requests for information

4.57 In the following paragraphs, we look at the two formal information gathering powers, which allow the FSA to obtain information itself in certain situations without initiating a formal investigation and appointing an investigator. Indeed, as will be seen, the FSA does not even have to suspect that any regulatory breach has been committed in order to exercise these powers. They are simply information gathering powers.

4.58 The two powers are:

- to obtain information or documents by notice in writing[1]; and
- to require a firm to commission a report from a skilled person[2].

Each is considered in turn below, including the circumstances when the power can be exercised, the FSA's policy on when it will be exercised, what information can be sought, the relevant procedure and practical issues for firms.

1 FSMA 2000, s 165.
2 FSMA 2000, s 166.

Obtaining information by notice in writing

4.59 The FSA has a general information gathering power under FSMA 2000, s 165, applicable whether or not there is any formal investigation ongoing. It allows the FSA to obtain information or documents on any matter subject to very broad limitations.

4.60 The FSA may, to the extent reasonably required in connection with the exercise of its functions under the FSMA 2000[1], either:

- by notice in writing given to an authorised person[2], require him to provide or produce specified information or documents, or information or documents of a specified description, before the end of such reasonable period as may be specified and at such place as may be specified[3]; or
- through an officer, or member of staff or agent, of the FSA who has written authorisation to do so, require the person to provide or produce information or documents without delay[4] (in which case there is no requirement for any notice in writing to be given)[5].

1 FSMA 2000, s 165(4).
2 Or one of the other persons in relation to whom the power can be exercised: see para 4.63 below. As to the manner in which such written notice must be given, see The Financial Services and Markets Act 2000 (Service of Notices) Regulations 2001, SI 2001/1420.
3 FSMA 2000, s 165(1) and (2).
4 The Government's view is that this means without unjustified or unreasonable delay: see Financial Secretary to HM Treasury in Standing Committee, 23 November 1999.
5 FSMA 2000, s 165(3) and (9).

4.61 The FSA may require information to be provided in such form as it may reasonably require[1]. It may also require the documents or information to be verified or authenticated in such manner as it may reasonably require[2]. This might include requiring information to be verified on oath in appropriate circumstances.

1 FSMA 2000, s 165(5).
2 FSMA 200, s 165(6).

4.62 Various ancillary provisions applicable more generally are discussed at para 4.111 ff below.

4.63 The power applies primarily in relation to authorised firms but also extends to:

- a person who was at any time, but has ceased to be, an authorised person[1];
- a person 'connected with' an authorised person – that is, broadly, a member of the same group or partnership, a controller of an authorised person or the various types of connected persons listed in FSMA 2000, Sch 15, Pt I[2];
- a recognised investment exchange or recognised clearing house; and
- an operator, trustee or depositary of a collective investment scheme recognised under FSMA 2000, ss 270 or 272[3], who is not an authorised person.

The power may also be exercised at the request of an overseas regulator[4].

1 FSMA 2000, s 165(8).
2 FSMA 2000, s 165(7)(a) and (11). This covers, broadly, officers, managers, employees and agents. It specifies different types of persons depending upon the precise legal nature of the authorised person.
3 See para 14.7 below.

4 FSMA 2000, s 169(1)(a). Note that it is not clear that this would always fulfil the criterion of being reasonably required in connection with the exercise of the FSA's functions under the FSMA 2000.

The scope of the power

4.64 The power is a general one, although mainly confined to firms and those connected with firms. The only criterion for its use is that the information is reasonably required in connection with the FSA's functions under the FSMA 2000. There is no need for any link between the regulatory concern which leads the FSA to seek the information and the firm asked to provide the information. A firm could therefore be asked to provide information where the FSA was concerned about an issue relating to another firm, or even where there was no regulatory concern in an enforcement sense, but rather the information was needed by the FSA in connection with another of its statutory functions.

4.65 As indicated above, the power overlaps substantially with Principle 11, but it does have wider repercussions in terms of connected persons and also allows the FSA to require that, for example, information is verified or authenticated; it may be beyond the firm's duty under Principle 11 to do so.

When will the power be exercised?

4.66 The FSA has given little guidance on when in practice it will seek to obtain information under this power. It has made clear[1] that the power can be used in a range of circumstances, including for routine supervisory purposes[2] or even its consumer education function. In practice, if the FSA seeks information from an authorised firm, it can probably obtain it pursuant to the firm's general obligations under Principle 11[3]. If the firm is for some reason unwilling to co-operate, then the FSA may need to make a formal requirement under this provision in order to use the sanctions which are available for non-compliance[4]. Indeed, in some situations the firm may prefer to be subjected to a formal request under this provision[5].

1 See the FSA Handbook at ENF 2.5.3.
2 The Government's view was that this power is intended primarily for supervisory purposes: see the Financial Secretary to HM Treasury in Standing Committee, 23 November 1999.
3 Principle 11 extends to requiring firms to take reasonable steps to ensure that certain types of connected people provide information to the FSA: see para 4.32 above.
4 In particular, the possibility of having the firm punished for contempt of court or of obtaining a warrant allowing the police to enter the firm's premises and obtain the information: see para 4.283 ff below.
5 See the discussion at para 4.53 above.

4.67 To the extent that the FSA seeks information from a person who is not an authorised firm, for example a connected person or a firm that used to be authorised, it may find that the information will not be provided voluntarily, perhaps because the relevant firm is not able legally to provide it, and that the formal power needs to be used.

What information can the FSA require the firm to provide?

4.68 Given the wide meaning of information and documents[1], and the (rather broad) sole criterion that the information or documents be reasonably required by the FSA in connection with its exercise of its functions under the FSMA 2000, there is little that the FSA could not request within the scope of this section[2]. A request could cover any type of document or other record containing information, as well as requiring people to provide information which is not recorded, for example their recollections or knowledge[3].

1 See para 4.112 ff below.
2 But see the exceptions outlined at para 4.70 below.
3 A difficult question is whether this would include a person's opinions: for example, could the FSA ask for a compliance report to be produced on a particular issue? It seems doubtful that such a request would fall within this provision, but it may be something that the FSA could request under Principle 11: see para 4.32 above.

4.69 The FSA could also call meetings, by requiring information to be provided in a particular form (orally) at a particular time and place. Whether they could interview a person under this provision is less clear[1]. Generally, the difference between a meeting and an interview may be one that is more of emphasis than of substance, although one distinction is that it is not clear whether the FSA could insist upon tape recording a meeting held under this provision.

1 On the face of it, the provision is broad enough to include an interview. However, (i) the FSMA 2000 tends to refer specifically to 'attending and answering questions' where interviews are envisaged: see, for example, ss 171 to 173, and (ii) the statutory privilege against self-incrimination does not apply to requests under this section: see para 4.245 below.

4.70 There are two types of information which firms cannot be required to produce, namely legally privileged material[1] and, with various exceptions, information which is subject to a banker's duty of confidentiality[2]. In addition, there may be particular grounds for objecting to complying with a particular request. Whether the firm can object and how it might do so, are discussed at para 4.260 ff below, and the consequences of failing to comply are discussed at para 4.283 ff below.

1 FSMA 2000, s 413 and see para 4.264 ff below. Note that the FSMA 2000 effectively contains its own definition of legal privilege for these purposes.
2 FSMA 2000, s 175(5) and see para 4.267 ff below.

What should the firm do if faced with a formal request?

4.71 There are various practical issues which a firm might wish to consider before providing material to the FSA. These are discussed at para 4.179 ff below.

Requiring the commission of reports

4.72 The FSA may[1] require a person to provide it with a report on any matter about which the FSA has required or could require the provision of information or production of documents under s 165[2].

1 FSMA 2000, s 166(1).

2 This power will be familiar to banks as it replaces, and is broadly similar to the Banking Act 1987, s 39, and will be familiar to perhaps a lesser extent to investment business firms, for whom the FSA's predecessor regulators did in practice in some enforcement cases appoint their own reporting accountants (under a variety of different investigation rules). Notwithstanding its use for some time, the scope of s 39 has not been explored by the courts.

4.73 The power can be exercised in relation to[1]:

- an authorised person;
- any member of an authorised person's group[2] or a partnership of which he is a member; or
- any person who has at any relevant time fallen within one of these categories;

in each case who is or was at the relevant time carrying on a business.

1 FSMA 2000, s 166(2).
2 'Group' is defined in FSMA 2000, s 421.

The scope of the power

4.74 The only limitation is that the report must be on a matter about which the FSA has exercised or could exercise its powers under s 165. This means that it must be reasonably required in connection with the exercise by the FSA of functions conferred on it by or under the FSMA 2000[1]. As has been seen in the discussion of the s 165 power[2], this is a broad test which allows the FSA to use the power outside the enforcement or even the supervisory context.

1 FSMA 2000, s 165(4) and see para 4.60 above.
2 See para 4.64 above.

When will the power be exercised?

4.75 The FSA's policy on when in practice it will use this power is found in the FSA Handbook at SUP 5.3[1]. This has been the focus of much debate. As indicated above, there is very little statutory control over when the FSA may require a report to be produced, provided it is reasonably required in connection with the FSA's functions. Beyond this, there is no particular hurdle that must be passed, such as that the FSA reasonably suspects a contravention of a rule. Requiring firms to produce these reports has an obvious attraction from the FSA's perspective in that the cost falls on the firm[2]. But the converse is the potential cost to the regulated community of having to commission such reports as a matter of routine.

1 As at the date of writing, SUP Chapter 5 (the FSA's rules on reports by skilled persons) had not been finalised and, in particular, the FSA was still consulting on its policy on the use of skilled persons (SUP 5.3) and the appointment and reporting process (SUP 5.4). The discussion of the FSA's detailed rules that follows is therefore based on the draft SUP Chapter 5, published in Consultation Paper 91 ('Reports by skilled persons'), May 2001. The discussion of the statutory framework and the practical issues that arise should not, though, be affected by any changes.
2 This is an exception to the general rule that the costs of investigation are not imposed on the firm or person that is being investigated: FSMA 2000, Sch 1, para 16(1).

4.76 The FSA has indicated that reports may be used for a variety of purposes[1], namely for diagnostic purposes (to identify and measure risks), for monitoring purposes (to track the development of identified risks, where these arise), in the context of preventative action (to limit or reduce identified risks and so prevent them from crystallising or increasing) and for remedial action (to respond to risks when they have crystallised). The latter two purposes, preventative action and remedial action, are those most likely to be relevant in the enforcement context. For example, the FSA may consider that a report is required in order to assess consumer losses arising from the firm's breaches and therefore the compensation which the firm should pay or to assess the systems and controls implications of a particular issue that has arisen. These two situations correspond to what has been common practice in many instances under the previous regime for those firms conducting investment business.

1 See the draft rules at SUP 5.3.1.

4.77 The FSA Handbook[1] provides detailed guidance on the factors which the FSA will take into account when making the decision whether to require a skilled person's report in any particular case. In the enforcement context specifically[2], where the FSA has decided to use its statutory powers to make further enquiries into the particular matter, the FSA will need to consider which of its statutory powers to use, having regard to the objectives of the enquiries and the relative effectiveness of its available powers to achieve those objectives. In particular, it has indicated that if its objectives are limited to gathering historic information or evidence for determining whether enforcement action may be appropriate, its information gathering and investigation powers are likely to be more effective and appropriate than its power to require a report from a skilled person. However, if its objectives include obtaining expert analysis or recommendations for remedial action, the power to require a report may be an appropriate power to use instead of, or in conjunction with, its other powers. This policy addresses one potential concern, namely that the power to require a firm to commission a skilled person's report might be used to place on a firm the cost of the investigation itself.

1 See the draft rules at SUP 5.3.
2 See the FSA Handbook at ENF 2.5.6.

Who is appointed to produce the report?

4.78 The person appointed to produce the report must be nominated or approved by the FSA and appear to the FSA to have the skills necessary to make a report on the matter concerned[1]. Depending upon the precise nature of the report required, the person appointed could be, for example, an accountant, actuary, lawyer[2] or other professional, such as a person with relevant business, technical or technological skills.

1 FSMA 2000, s 166(4). There is nothing in s 166 to prevent the FSA from nominating the firm's own (for example) internal audit or compliance staff to produce the report. Equally, though, there is nothing in the section or in the draft rules to suggest that the provision was intended to be used in that way, and it is thought that Principle 11 or s 165 would provide a more appropriate means to achieve such a result. If a member of the firm's staff were appointed, there would be some difficult conflict of interest issues.

2 The report of a lawyer commissioned by the firm to advise it would normally be legally privileged: see para 4.196 ff below. Whilst the firm clearly could not assert privilege against the FSA in relation to a report commissioned from a lawyer in response to a requirement imposed by the FSA under FSMA 2000, s 166, the firm may wish to take steps to try to ensure that the report retains the protection of legal privilege as against other parties: see para 4.202 below.

4.79 The FSA will notify the firm if it decides to nominate the skilled person itself. Even when the FSA is content to approve an appointment by the firm, the firm will need to consult with the FSA to ensure that the appointment will be approved.

4.80 The FSA may, in some circumstances, seek the appointment of a skilled person who has previously acted for the firm, for example its auditor or actuary. Whilst this may be viewed as cost-effective, and may enable a report to be produced more quickly than by a skilled person who was unfamiliar with the firm, it could raise difficult conflict of interest issues[1]. It is unclear whether the FSA would seek the appointment of such a person in a serious enforcement context.

1 There may be an issue whether the FSA should be entitled to nominate a skilled person who owes fiduciary duties to the firm or has confidential information from the firm in circumstances which would prevent him from acting for another party as a matter of general law: see, for example, *Prince Jefri Bolkiah v KPMG* [1999] 2 WLR 215, HL, *Bristol and West BS v Mothew* [1998] Ch 1, CA and *Young v Robson Rhodes* [1999] 3 All ER 524. But, against this, see s 165(5) (discussed at para 4.87 below). If the firm did appoint such a skilled person, it seems likely that it would be consenting to the skilled person acting notwithstanding any duties he may otherwise have to the firm. Therefore, the issue would need to be taken up with the FSA beforehand. Alternatively, the question of Chinese walls may need to be addressed.

The terms of appointment of the skilled person

4.81 The draft rules contain various requirements regarding the terms of the skilled person's contract. First, under the FSMA 2000, although approved or nominated by the FSA, the person is actually appointed by the firm and it is the firm that must bear the cost[1].

1 As noted above, this is an exception to the general rule that the cost of enforcement is borne by the regulated community generally and not by the firm which is the subject of the enforcement proceedings.

4.82 Second, the firm must, in its contract with the skilled person, require and permit the skilled person during and after the course of his appointment[1]:

- to co-operate with the FSA in the discharge of its functions under the FSMA 2000 in relation to the firm[2];
- to report to the FSA various specified categories of matters which the skilled person reasonably believes to be relevant to the FSA[3].

The contract must also require the skilled person to prepare the report and must waive any duty of confidentiality the skilled person may have to the firm which might limit the provision of information or opinion by the skilled person to the FSA in accordance with the above requirements[4].

1 See the draft rules at SUP 5.5.1.
2 The draft rules contain guidance as to what this should include: see SUP 5.5.2. Note, in particular, that this may involve direct communication between the FSA and the skilled person: see the draft rules at SUP 5.5.4, 5.4.10 and 5.4.12.
3 For details, see the draft rules at SUP 5.5.1.
4 See the draft rules at SUP 5.5.1(3). See also FSMA 2000, s 353 and the Financial Services and Markets Act 2000 (Disclosure of Information by Prescribed Persons) Regulations 2001, SI 2001/1857: see footnote 1 to para 4.178 below.

4.83 In addition, the contract must[1]:

- be governed by the laws of a part of the UK; and
- include an express right for the FSA to enforce the above requirements directly against the skilled person[2].

1 See the draft rules at SUP 5.5.5.
2 This should be possible under the Contracts (Rights of Third Parties) Act 1999.

4.84 These rules apply equally to reports commissioned in the supervisory context. Thus, in any instance where a skilled person is appointed, he must be required to report to the FSA relevant issues which he comes across, apparently whether or not within the scope of the matters upon which he was asked to report.

4.85 Whether the particular matter is required to be reported will depend upon the skilled person's assessment of its significance to the FSA. This may be rather a difficult imposition on the skilled person, who may be chosen for his technical skills and experience in the particular area, not his knowledge or understanding of the regulatory regime. For example, it is one thing to ask someone to assess particular aspects of the firm's IT systems, but another to expect him to assess the significance of what he sees for consumers or the firm's fitness or propriety.

4.86 The draft rules contain further guidance on the same issues but do not otherwise prescribe the contents of the contract between the firm and the skilled person[1]. Thus, for example, there is nothing expressly to prevent the firm from agreeing budgeting provisions and costs limits with the skilled person, provided that this does not impact on the skilled person's ability to fulfil the terms of his appointment[2].

1 The FSA may ask to see a copy of the draft contract and may indicate that it considers particular matters require further clarification or discussion before the contract is finalised: see the draft rules at SUP 5.5.9.
2 The skilled person may also seek to limit his liability to the firm. Note that the skilled person may owe a duty of care to the FSA as well as to the firm: see *Law Society v KPMG Peat Marwick* [2000] 4 All ER 540, CA.

Assistance from the firm's normal auditor, actuary or other person

4.87 Any person who provides, or has provided, similar services to the firm is under a duty to provide the person appointed with all such assistance as he may reasonably require, and this is enforceable by injunction[1]. In other words, the firm's normal auditor, actuary or other relevant person must, or can be forced to, assist the person appointed by the FSA[2]. Neither the FSMA 2000 nor the FSA's rules explain who bears the cost of this assistance, but, often, it will in practice be the firm that does so.

1 FSMA 2000, s 166(5) and (6). Under the previous regime, there was no similar express duty in relation to a report commissioned under the Banking Act 1987, s 39 although the firm's banker, solicitor and auditor had a duty to co-operate in a formal investigation commenced under s 41.

2 If it is a report from a lawyer that is being obtained, the firm's normal lawyer could not be required to disclose material that is protected under FSMA 2000, s 413 as being, broadly, legally privileged: see para 4.264 below.

4.88 The assistance is limited to that reasonably required but is otherwise undefined. Precisely what assistance it is reasonable for the person appointed to require is likely to be the subject of some debate. Whilst there may be little resistance to, say, spending a relatively small amount of time explaining the firm's systems, the way in which particular funds have been valued or the rationale for particular controls, auditors or actuaries may take a different view if the person appointed wants access to their own files and working papers, which may be the property of the auditor or actuary, not of his client, and which he may therefore properly withhold from his client[1]. The FSA has not provided any guidance on this point, although its views on the meaning of reasonable assistance as between the firm and the person undertaking the report are instructive in this regard and are discussed at para 4.89 below.

1 See *Chantrey Martin & Co v Martin* [1953] 2 All ER 691, CA and *Gomba Holdings UK Ltd v Minories Finance Ltd* [1989] 1 All ER 261, CA.

How should the firm deal with the skilled person?

4.89 The FSA requires the firm to provide all reasonable assistance to any skilled person appointed[1]. The FSA has indicated[2] that reasonable assistance includes giving access at all reasonable business hours to the firm's accounting and other records, in whatever form, providing such information and explanation as the skilled person reasonably considers necessary or desirable for the performance of his duties and permitting a skilled person to obtain directly from the firm's auditors such information as he reasonably considers necessary or desirable for the proper performance of his duties[3]. Failing to co-operate with the skilled person would be a breach of the FSA's rules and probably also a breach of Principle 11[4]. Practical guidance for firms on dealing with the skilled person is outlined at para 4.94 below.

1 See the draft rules at SUP 5.5.11. The firm would not, though, need to provide information or documents protected under FSMA 2000, s 413 as being, broadly, legally privileged (see para 4.264 ff below) and, in certain circumstances, it may be possible to withhold information or documents protected by a duty of banking confidentiality (see FSMA 2000, s 175(5) and para 4.267 ff below): note that the application of that provision to s 166 is not entirely clear.

2 See the draft rules at SUP 5.5.13.

3 The firm must also take reasonable steps to ensure that, when reasonably required by the skilled person, its appointed representatives waive any duty of confidentiality and provide the same reasonable assistance to the skilled person: see the draft rules at SUP 5.5.12.

4 Principle 11, Principles for Businesses. For the obligation to co-operate and consequences of breach, see para 4.27 ff above.

4.90 Confidential information which the skilled person obtains relating to a person's business or affairs will be covered by the statutory confidentiality restrictions, applying both to the skilled person and to the FSA[1].

1 FSMA 2000, s 348 and see the draft rules at SUP 5.6.1. The skilled person is a 'primary recipient' and therefore commits a criminal offence if he discloses improperly confidential information which he has obtained relating to the firm's business or affairs. For a detailed explanation, see para 4.304 ff below.

The skilled person's report

4.91 The skilled person will normally report to the FSA through the firm and the FSA has indicated that in the normal course the firm will be given the opportunity to provide written comments on the report prior to its submission to the FSA[1]. The report may be required by the FSA to be in such form as is specified in the notice requiring the firm to commission it[2].

1 See the draft rules at SUP 5.4.9.
2 FSMA 2000, s 166(3). See also the draft rules at SUP 5.4.1 to 5.4.4. The scope of the report will not necessarily be static, though. The FSA expects in substantial or complex cases to receive a perodic update from the skilled person to allow for a re-focusing of the report if necessary.

4.92 The firm is expected to take reasonable steps to ensure that the skilled person delivers a report in accordance with the terms of his appointment. It is unclear what additional steps this might require a firm to take.

4.93 The requirement imposed by the FSA on the firm to provide a skilled person's report is not an 'information requirement' under FSMA 2000, Pt XI and a failure to provide it could not therefore be punished as a contempt of court in the same way as other failures to provide information[1].

1 See para 4.284 ff below.

Practical issues for firms

4.94 The appointment of a skilled person raises a number of practical questions for the firm. Issues which the firm may need to consider include:

- whether the firm can control the scope of the report sought by the FSA;
- whether there are any staffing issues, to ensure that the skilled person is provided with the assistance he needs from the firm to prepare his report;
- whether there is a risk of prejudicial material being produced as a result of the skilled person's work which might need to be disclosed to third parties;
- whether the firm should and could obtain a 'private' dual report from another skilled person; and
- the firm's relationship with the skilled person.

Each of these is considered in turn below.

4.95 ***Can the firm control the scope of the report?*** It is for the FSA to determine the matter upon which it requires the firm to commission a report and thereby to determine the scope of the report; it can also determine the issues to be covered[1]. The scope of the work carried out by the skilled person is important to the firm, as it impacts not only on the cost of having the skilled person produce the report, which it is for the firm to bear, but also on the amount of management time involved and other disruption to the firm's business. If faced with a request by the FSA for a report which seems unfocused in its objectives or unrealistically wide in its scope, the first step for the firm may be to seek to have the scope of the report narrowed. How can it accomplish this?

1 See the draft rules at SUP 5.4.3.

4.96 The FSMA 2000 does not provide any right of recourse to a firm faced with what it believes is an inappropriately broad request for a report. However, the breadth of the request may stem from a lack of understanding of the firm's business by the FSA and it may be possible to reach agreement with the FSA on the nature of the report that is really required. If this is unsuccessful, the firm may be able to have the FSA's decision to require the report judicially reviewed by a court or may be able to make a complaint to the independent complaints commissioner[1].

1 These options are discussed in Chapter 16 below. Note that the complaints regime may provide a means of recourse after the event, but is unlikely to provide a mechanism for preventing the FSA from proceeding.

4.97 ***Are there any staffing issues?*** The firm's obligation to assist the skilled person has been outlined at para 4.89 above. Providing the necessary assistance may entail a significant amount of time of the firm's employees and relevant management. Among other things, the skilled person may need someone to work with him, to help him access the firm's computer systems or understand the firm's documents and processes. There will therefore be staffing issues to consider when the firm is planning for the skilled person. If there are likely to be staffing difficulties, it may be worth raising this with the FSA, particularly if it may impact on the timing of producing the report or if it may provide a reason for seeking to limit the scope of the report.

4.98 ***Is there a risk of prejudicial, discloseable material being produced?*** The skilled person's report, and any discussions the firm has with the skilled person and documents it provides to him, will clearly be discloseable to the FSA[1]. But such material could also be discloseable to third parties who might bring civil claims against the firm arising from the same matter. The potential disclosure implications of the investigation process are considered more generally at para 4.189 ff below. There are three primary points to note for present purposes.

1 This is subject to any issues about legal privilege where the skilled person is a lawyer: see footnote 2 to para 4.78 above.

4.99 First, relevant documents will exist not only in the firm's hands but also in the hands of the skilled person and the FSA. Documents which the firm has are unlikely to be protected from disclosure to third parties, unless they are legally privileged[1] or, in some circumstances, were received by the firm from the skilled person or the FSA. Documents held by the skilled person or the FSA are, however, likely to be protected from disclosure under the FSMA 2000, at least unless or until made publicly available, for example in Tribunal proceedings in public[2].

1 The meaning of legal privilege is considered at para 4.196 ff below.
2 The skilled person is a 'primary recipient' under FSMA 2000, s 348 and confidential information which he obtains in the discharge of his functions is therefore strictly protected under the FSMA 2000, subject to the Gateway Regulations: see para 4.304 ff below.

4.100 Second, if the firm is to protect its position then it will need to take care in the documents that it creates for the skilled person and the discussions that it has with him. If the firm is to co-operate fully with the skilled person then it may be difficult in practice to do much to lessen this risk. But it may, for example, be possible to avoid creating particularly damaging material and instead provide the skilled person with an oral briefing on the relevant subject.

4.101 Third, as should be apparent from the above, if the firm is provided with a copy of the skilled person's report, it could potentially be required to disclose this in litigation[1]. Moreover, the skilled person could potentially be summonsed and required to give evidence about what was said to him[2].

1 Provided the information was not protected under FSMA 2000, s 348: see para 4.304 ff below.
2 Subject to the same proviso.

4.102 ***Should the firm obtain a dual report?*** Whilst the firm will have little control over the skilled person, his report can have a significant impact on it, not only in terms of its liability to regulatory action but also in relation to its potential civil liability. Such reports have in the past been used to help the FSA, or its predecessors, assess the extent of losses suffered by customers for which a restitution order might be made. Equally, a report into the firm's systems and controls could lead the FSA to take action which would have a significant impact on the firm's business.

4.103 In many instances, the conclusions reached by the report will be a matter for judgement, on which more than one view may be tenable, and it will be critical for the firm to ensure the most favourable conclusion is, at least, strongly put forward. If the firm is to have the knowledge and ability to raise questions on the critical areas, then it may want to consider engaging a second expert to conduct a parallel investigation. The second expert would act purely for the firm and it may be possible for his work to be structured so as to be legally privileged, and thus protected from disclosure both to the FSA and to third parties. His role would be to assist the firm in its dealings with the FSA and the skilled person, particularly in technical areas where experts might disagree. There is a clear cost involved, in that the firm must pay for two skilled persons carrying out much of the same work, but this may be outweighed by the benefits in large or complex cases.

4.104 ***The firm's relationship with the skilled person*** It should be apparent that there may be some tensions in the firm's relationship with the skilled person. It is the firm that commissions the report, contracts with the skilled person and pays him. The firm is also required to provide him with all reasonable assistance, which may involve it bearing a significant cost in terms of management time. On the other hand, the skilled person will have to be scrupulously independent from the firm in terms of the contents of his report and will have to refer to the FSA any material concerns he sees, whether or not related to the matters upon which he was instructed to report.

4.105 If the skilled person reports to the FSA, as he is required to do, on any matter of concern regarding the firm, is he exposed to liability to the firm? Provided the skilled person reasonably believed that the information was relevant to the FSA's discharge of its public functions and made the disclosure in good faith, he will be protected[1]. It is not, though, difficult to imagine a situation where the firm might believe there was a real issue. An example might be where the skilled person reported on some matter he had noticed which was outside the scope of its original report, the firm was as a result subjected to the significant cost and time of a regulatory investigation into that new matter and, at the end of the process, the FSA concluded that there was no cause for any concern. If the skilled person acted without the requisite belief, then he may be liable for breach of confidence or possibly libel[2]. Whether the skilled person reasonably believed is partly an objective test but it is not a particularly high test and in practice it may be difficult for the firm to overcome this hurdle.

1 See the Financial Services and Markets Act 2000 (Disclosure of Information by Prescribed Persons) Regulations 2001, SI 2001/1857 and see the discussion at para 4.178 below.

2 His report to the FSA may attract absolute privilege against use in libel proceedings: see *Mahon v Rahn (No 2)* [2000] 4 All ER 41, CA but note that the Court left open the question whether this applies to information proferred spontaneously (and perhaps maliciously) to a financial regulator. It is therefore possible that different considerations would apply if the report to the FSA falls outside the skilled person's reporting obligation and is thus effectively proferred voluntarily.

4.106 However, both the skilled person and the firm need to be wary of concealing from the FSA any issues which arise in the course of preparing the report and which might give the FSA cause for concern. As well as the potential for the firm thereby to commit a regulatory breach, it is possible that criminal offences may be committed. In particular:

- the firm (on whom the requirement to produce the report is placed under s 166) would be guilty of a criminal offence if, in purported compliance with that requirement, it knowingly or recklessly provided information which was false or misleading in a material particular[1]; and
- the skilled person would be guilty of an offence if, in purported compliance with a requirement imposed by or under the FSMA 2000, he knowingly or recklessly gave the FSA information which was false or misleading in a material particular[2].

1 FSMA 2000, s 177(4).

2 FSMA 2000, s 398(1).

Procedure for making formal requests

4.107 The procedure for making formal requests under ss 165 or 166 is a simple one[1]. The FSMA 2000 allows the FSA to impose its requirement by notice in writing. All that the FSA need do, therefore, is to notify the firm or other person in writing[2] of, as appropriate:

- the information or documents that they are required to produce and the time and place of production[3]; or
- the matter on which a report is required to be produced by a skilled person[4].

The FSA can also require information or documents to be provided under s 165 without delay and without giving any written notice in certain circumstances[5].

1 There is no prescribed procedure for the FSA to reach a decision internally on whether to make a formal request under these provisions and neither is that decision capable of being referred to the Tribunal.
2 As to the manner in which written notices must be given, see The Financial Services and Markets Act 2000 (Service of Notices) Regulations 2001, SI 2001/1420 and see the FSA Handbook at DEC 5.3.
3 FSMA 2000, s 165(1) and (2).
4 FSMA 2000, s 166(1).
5 FSMA 2000, s 165(3) and see para 4.60 above.

Formal investigations

4.108 In the following paragraphs, we outline the FSA's formal investigation powers. There are four general investigation powers, namely:

- section 167 investigations – into the business, ownership or control of an authorised person;
- section 168(1) and (4) investigations – into various regulatory or criminal offences;
- section 168(2) investigations – into certain serious criminal or regulatory offences, namely insider dealing, market abuse, breach of the perimeter, unlawful financial promotion or misleading statements and practices; and
- section 169 investigations – at the request of an overseas regulator.

4.109 Each type of investigation carries with it a different set of powers to require particular categories of persons, including those who are not the subject of the investigation, to provide certain types of information. Whilst the detailed scope differs according to which power is being used, in broad terms the FSA can ask the firm to disclose almost any relevant information it has, however it is recorded. This includes documents and records, e-mails, material on its computer system and tapes of telephone calls. It can also interview people and ask for explanations of documents to be given. The mechanism used is the appointment of an investigator to conduct a factual enquiry[1]. As will already be apparent, the investigators have wide powers. But they are, as a matter of law, required to act fairly in conducting their investigations[2].

1 This is not new: see, for example, the Banking Act 1987, s 41.
2 See *Hearts of Oak Assurance Co Ltd v A-G* [1932] AC 392 and *In re Pergamon Press Ltd* [1971] 1 Ch 388. See also para 4.272 ff below.

4.110 In the following paragraphs, we review:

- certain general points applicable to all formal requests;
- each of the formal investigation powers in turn, namely:
  - section 167 investigations,
  - section 168(1) or (4) investigations,
  - section 168(2) investigations, and
  - section 169 investigations;
- the procedure for a formal investigation; and
- practical guidance for firms in dealing with formal investigations.

As outlined at para 4.14 above, the FSA has various other formal investigation powers which are not reviewed here.

General points applicable to all formal requests

4.111 The FSMA 2000 and the FSA Handbook contain various ancillary provisions applicable to all of the formal information gathering and investigation powers considered here, including the FSA's formal information gathering power under s 165[1]. The ancillary provisions are as follows:

- the meaning of 'documents' and 'information';
- requiring copies or explanations of documents;
- requiring an explanation of where a document is located;
- documents in the possession of third parties;
- the effect on liens;
- documents that need not be provided; and
- the warning about the need to comply.

Each of these is considered in turn below, followed by a brief discussion of FSA interviews. The detailed analysis of the scope of each power needs to be read against these ancillary provisions.

1 See para 4.59 ff above.

Meaning of documents and information

4.112 The FSMA 2000 contains many references to 'documents' and 'information'. 'Document' includes information recorded in any form and in relation to information recorded otherwise than in legible form, references to its production include references to producing a copy of the information in legible form[1]. In other words, 'document' includes information held electronically, including e-mails or other electronic material, information stored on microfiche and tapes, for example, of telephone calls. If asked to produce information which is stored electronically or, for example, stored on microfiche, the firm must produce the information in legible form.

1 FSMA 2000, s 417(1).

4.113 The FSMA 2000 provides no definition of 'information'. It ought to follow from the definition of 'documents' that 'information' means information not recorded in any form. In other words, it would include a person's knowledge.

Copies or explanations of documents

4.114 Where a document is produced in response to a requirement, the person to whom it is produced may take copies or extracts or require the person producing it, or any relevant person, to provide an explanation of it[1]. Notably, this is not confined to the person producing the document but allows the investigator to ask a different person[2] for an explanation of it.

1 FSMA 2000, s 175(2).
2 The categories of 'relevant person' who can be required to provide an explanation are, broadly, employees, directors, controllers, auditors, accountants, actuaries and lawyers: see FSMA 2000, s 175(7).

Location of documents not produced

4.115 If a person who is required to produce a document fails to do so, he may be required to state to the best of his knowledge and belief where the document is[1].

1 FSMA 2000, s 175(3).

Documents in the possession of third parties

4.116 If the FSA or an investigator has power to require a person to produce a document, but it appears that the document is in the possession of a third person, that power may be exercised in relation to the third person[1]. Third parties holding documents but who are not otherwise within the scope of the investigation power used may therefore nonetheless be required to produce documents.

1 FSMA 2000, s 175(1).

Effect on liens

4.117 If a person claims a lien on a document, its production pursuant to one of these formal powers does not affect the lien[1].

1 FSMA 2000, s 175(6).

Exceptions to the requirements to produce information or documents

4.118 There are two statutory exceptions to the requirement to produce documents and information. First, a firm cannot be required to produce, disclose or permit the inspection of a 'protected item' which broadly means a legally privileged communication[1]. However, a lawyer can be required to furnish the name and address of his client[2]. Second, there is a restriction on the disclosure of documents in relation to which the person owes a banker's obligation of confidence[3], with certain, fairly wide exceptions.

1 FSMA 2000, s 413. For a detailed discussion, see para 4.264 below. Note that the FSMA 2000 effectively contains its own definition of legal privilege for these purposes.
2 FSMA 2000, s 175(4). This could, for example, be relevant in a money laundering enquiry.
3 FSMA 2000, s 175(5). For a detailed discussion, see para 4.267 below.

4.119 In addition, there may be specific reasons for objecting to the production of information or documents in the circumstances of the particular case. This is discussed at para 4.260 ff below.

Warning of the need to comply

4.120 The investigators appointed by the FSA will make clear to those to whom their enquiries are addressed when they are using statutory powers, and will inform them of the statutory requirements and the possible penalties for failure to comply[1].

1 See the FSA Handbook at ENF 2.11.2. The consequences of failing to comply are discussed at para 4.283 ff below.

Interviews

4.121 As will be seen, the FSA has various powers to require people to submit to interview. The FSA will not always use its statutory powers to interview but, if appropriate, its investigators will seek to conduct the interview on a voluntary basis[1]. The FSA has not, however, given any indication of when it is likely to be appropriate to seek to interview a person voluntarily first. Where criminal proceedings against the person are in prospect, there are some additional considerations, discussed at para 4.242 ff below. Various practical issues to consider in relation to interviews are outlined at para 4.221 ff below, together with the FSA's policy on how it will conduct interviews.

1 See the FSA Handbook at ENF 2.14.1.

Section 167 investigations – into the business of an authorised person

When can an investigation be commenced?

4.122 If it appears to it that there is good reason for doing so, the FSA may appoint an investigator to conduct an investigation on its behalf into[1]:

- the nature, conduct or state of business of an authorised person (or appointed representative); or

- a particular aspect of that business; or
- the ownership or control of an authorised person.

The power is also exercisable by the Secretary of State[2].

1 FSMA 2000, s 167(1).
2 See footnote 8 to para 4.144 below.

4.123 Business includes any part of a business even if it does not consist of carrying out regulated activities[1]. The investigation could therefore be carried out wholly, or partly, into the firm's unregulated business or its overseas business.

1 FSMA 2000, s 167(5).

4.124 Although the power is aimed primarily at authorised persons, it is widened in two respects. First[1], the investigator may, if he thinks it necessary for the purposes of his investigation, also investigate the business of a person who is or has at any relevant time been either a member of the same group[2] as the person under investigation or a partnership of which that person was a member[3], in which case the investigator must give that other person written notice of his decision.

1 FSMA 2000, s 167(2) and (3).
2 'Group' is defined in FSMA 2000, s 421.
3 This does not, therefore, extend to a member of the same partnership.

4.125 Second, the power may be exercised in relation to a former authorised person (or former appointed representative), but only in relation either to business carried on at any time when he was an authorised person (or appointed representative) or to the ownership or control of the former authorised person during the same period[1].

1 FSMA 2000, s 167(4).

4.126 ***When will the power be exercised?*** The FSA has indicated only that it will rely on this power where it has general concerns about a firm or an appointed representative, but the circumstances do not at that stage suggest any specific breach or contravention[1].

1 See the FSA Handbook at ENF 2.5.9.

4.127 ***The scope of the power*** The breadth of the activities that can be investigated is notable. At its widest, the investigation can probably extend to the non-regulated businesses of a company in the same group as a company that used to be an authorised person.

4.128 Why does the FSA need such a wide general investigation power? The FSA's statutory duties are fairly broad and they include, among other things, the duty for the FSA to satisfy itself that firms are, and will continue to be, fit and proper to be carrying on their regulated activities and a duty to protect consumers[1]. The FSA needs to have regard not only to how the firm conducts its regulated activities, but also to other factors which impact upon its business, including its financial state and the financial risks of its business generally, the way in which it is controlled, and so on. Many of these other factors relate to matters outside its regulated activities. They may relate to non-regulated activities, activities abroad or to the way in which other group companies control the firm or conduct their own businesses. The circumstances in which the FSA may seek to investigate the firm's unregulated business or its overseas business are discussed in more detail below[2].

1 For a general discussion of the FSA's role under the FSMA 2000, see para 2.19 ff above.
2 Respectively, at paras 4.252 and 4.236 below.

4.129 Against that background, it is unsurprising that the hurdle for the use of this power is a low one. It only has to 'appear to the FSA' that there is 'good reason' for investigating. No guidance is given in the FSMA 2000 as to what might constitute good reason and the FSA's policy refers only to 'general concerns' about the firm, which suggests a fairly low test will in practice be applied. Whether or not it appeared to the FSA that there were good reasons is a subjective test[1]. However, it is thought that 'good reason' cannot be wholly without limits and that it should be judged objectively by reference to the FSA's regulatory objectives under the FSMA 2000[2] and its stated policy on the use of its formal investigation powers generally[3].

1 Economic Secretary to HM Treasury in Standing Committee, 23 November 1999.
2 The regulatory objectives are outlined at para 2.20 above. 'The FSA must exercise its powers in a way that is connected to its functions under the [Act] and the good reason test will be set in context': Economic Secretary to HM Treasury in Standing Committee, 23 November 1999.
3 As to which, see para 4.18 ff above.

What information can the firm be asked to provide?

4.130 An investigator appointed under s 167 may require[1]:

- the person who is the subject of the investigation, or a connected person[2], to attend before him at a specified time and place and answer questions or otherwise to provide such information as the investigator may require[3]; or
- any person to produce at a specified time and place any specified documents or documents of a specified description.

The investigator must give the person written notice of the requirement[4].

1 FSMA 2000, s 171.
2 This has a wider meaning than in s 165 (see para 4.63 above) as it also includes persons listed in FSMA 2000, Sch 15, Pt II, namely a person who is, or was at the relevant time, the partner, manager, employee, agent, appointed representative, banker, auditor, actuary or solicitor of any of the person under investigation, its parent or subsidiary undertaking (as defined in FSMA 2000, s 420) a subsidiary undertaking of its parent undertaking or a parent undertaking of its subsidiary undertaking.
3 For a discussion of the meaning of 'information', see para 4.113 above.
4 FSMA 2000, s 170(2) and see para 4.159 ff below. As to the manner in which written notices are to be given, see The Financial Services and Markets Act 2000 (Service of Notices) Regulations 2001, SI 2001/1420 and see the FSA Handbook at DEC 5.3.

4.131 These requirements can only be imposed so far as the investigator reasonably considers the question, provision of information or production of the document to be relevant to the purposes of the investigation[1].

1 FSMA 2000, s 171(3).

4.132 The power is therefore wide ranging as against the person under investigation and a wide variety of connected third parties but more limited as against unconnected third parties, who can only be required to produce documents. 'Documents' has a wide definition under the FSMA 2000[1]. It includes information recorded in any form. Hence, this would include, for example, e-mails or tapes of telephone conversations. The main practical effect is that such third parties cannot be compelled to an interview or be required to answer questions (other than in some circumstances to explain documents[2]).

1 See para 4.112 above.
2 See para 4.114 above.

4.133 In determining whether particular material is to be required, the investigator applies an objective test, albeit a fairly low test. The investigator must reasonably consider it to be relevant to the purposes of the investigation. If the firm believes that the information is wholly irrelevant, then there is scope for making that clear to the investigator, to seek to undermine the basis upon which he reasonably considers it relevant, or even for objecting to producing the material on that basis. As to how that objection might be made, see para 4.260 ff below.

Section 168(1) and (4) investigations – into certain criminal or regulatory offences

When can an investigation be commenced?

4.134 The FSA may appoint an investigator to conduct an investigation on its behalf if it appears to it that there are circumstances suggesting that the various regulatory offences outlined below may have been committed[1]. The regulatory offences covered are as follows:

- breaches of FSMA 2000, s 20: carrying on a regulated activity other than in accordance with the firm's permission[2];
- offences under the money laundering regulations;
- contraventions by firms of FSA rules, including the Principles for Businesses[3];
- lack of fitness and propriety for individuals, including approved persons[4];
- breaches by individuals or firms in relation to prohibition orders[5];
- breaches by firms in relation to the performance of controlled functions by individuals who are not approved persons[6]; and
- misconduct by approved persons[7].

1 FSMA 2000, s 168(4) and (5).
2 This is the equivalent for authorised firms of breaching the general prohibition (although it does not give rise to a criminal offence): see para 2.175 ff above.
3 The Principles for Businesses are outlined and discussed at para 2.51 ff above.
4 The requirement for individuals to be fit and proper is discussed at para 2.69 ff above.
5 See para 8.44 ff below.
6 For a brief explanation of controlled functions and approved persons, see para 2.64 ff above. As to the requirement upon firms to take reasonable care to ensure their controlled functions are carried on by approved persons, see para 8.34 below.
7 See para 8.8 ff below.

4.135 Subject to certain exceptions covered by the other investigation powers, this covers most of the regulatory requirements and standards normally applicable to the regulated community. This is therefore the most likely type of investigation to be commenced where a problem arises in relation to the firm involving some kind of rule breach. Notice of the investigation is normally required to be given to the person under investigation[1].

1 FSMA 2000, s 170(2) and see para 4.159 ff below.

4.136 Breach of these requirements is a matter purely for the FSA. The Secretary of State does not have any parallel power to investigate.

4.137 The FSA may also appoint an investigator to conduct an investigation on its behalf if it appears to it that there are circumstances suggesting that the various criminal or regulatory offences outlined below may have been committed[1]. The breaches covered are as follows:

- contravention of insurance business regulations made under FSMA 2000, s 142;
- the criminal offences of providing false or misleading information to the FSA[2] or to the firm's auditors or actuaries[3];
- criminal offences in relation to notification of changes in control over authorised persons[4];
- in relation to Treaty firms, the criminal offences under FSMA 2000, Sch 4.

The Secretary of State also has power to commence such an investigation[5]. Again, notice of the investigation is normally required to be given to the person under investigation[6].

1 FSMA 2000, s 168(1) and (3).
2 FSMA 2000, ss 177 (which includes the offence of destroying, etc documents relevant to an investigation: see para 3.151 above) and 398(1).
3 FSMA 2000, s 346.
4 FSMA 2000, s 191.
5 See footnote 8 to para 4.144 below.
6 FSMA 2000, s 170(2) and see para 4.159 ff below.

4.138 ***When will the power be exercised?*** The FSA has given very little guidance on the circumstances when it will seek to exercise this power[1], other than to say that it will do so when it appears to it that circumstances suggest that one of these breaches may have been committed. It may extend an investigation started under s 167 to cover additional matters under s 168, given that, as will be seen, investigators appointed under these provisions have wider powers of investigation.

1 See the FSA Handbook at ENF 2.5.10/11.

4.139 ***The scope of the power*** Again, the hurdle for the use of this power is a low one: it need only 'appear to the FSA' that there are 'circumstances suggesting' that one of these offences 'may have been' committed. Contrast, for example, a requirement for the FSA to have reasonable grounds to suspect the offence has been committed. This means that it will be difficult for a firm to challenge the appointment of an investigator on the ground that the statutory test had not been met[1]. Whether the firm would be able to challenge the investigator's use of its powers subsequently is of course a different question[2].

1 This test was the subject of considerable debate in Standing Committee, 23 November 1999. It reflects the test formerly found in the Financial Services Act 1986, s 177 in relation to insider dealing investigations, but is otherwise lower than the statutory tests previously used. 'Reasonable suspicion' was seen by the Government as being too high a test, akin to that of the police making an arrest, and unsuitable for the FSA when deciding simply whether or not to investigate.
2 This is considered at para 4.260 ff below.

What information can the firm be required to provide?

4.140 An investigator appointed under s 168(1) or (4) has the same powers as one appointed under s 167[1].

1 FSMA 2000, s 172(1). For the powers applicable to section 167 investigations, see para 4.130 above.

4.141 In addition[1], the investigator may require a person who is neither the subject of the investigation nor a person connected with that person to attend and answer questions at a specified time and place, or otherwise to provide such information[2] as the investigator may require for the purposes of the investigation, provided in both cases that the investigator is satisfied that the requirement is necessary or expedient for the purposes of the investigation.

1 FSMA 2000, s 172(2).
2 As to the meaning of 'information', see para 4.113 above.

4.142 The main difference in practice between this and the powers of the investigator carrying out a section 167 investigation is that the limitations on the requirements that can be made of unconnected third parties, discussed at para 4.132 above, do not apply here.

4.143 The test applied by the investigator when considering imposing a requirement on an unconnected third party is different in nature from that applied when considering imposing a requirement on the firm or a connected person. Rather than focusing on the relevance or otherwise of the material to the investigation, the test seems to look at the reasons for obtaining the information from the third party, rather than some other source like the firm itself[1]. Although neither 'necessary' nor 'expedient' expressly requires the investigator to consider whether the material is relevant to the investigation, it is thought that this is implicit, because it cannot be necessary or expedient for the purposes of the investigation to obtain information which is irrelevant.

1 'Necessary or expedient' gives a margin of discretion to the investigator: see Lord Diplock in *Secretary of State for Defence v Guardian Newspapers Ltd* [1985] AC 339, 350. Precisely what 'necessary' means depends upon the circumstances. It 'lies somewhere between "indispensable" on the one hand and "useful" or "expedient" on the other': Lord Griffiths in *In re an Inquiry under the Company Securities (Insider Dealing) Act 1985* [1988] 2 WLR 33, 65. 'By including the words "or expedient", we were ensuring that that option could be used where it was not absolutely necessary to obtain the information, but where the alternatives might be unduly cumbersome or problematic.... The term "expedient" does not allow for fishing. There must be a link between the requirement and the purposes of the investigation': Economic Secretary to HM Treasury in Standing Committee, 23 November 1999.

Section 168(2) investigations – into certain serious criminal or regulatory offences

When can an investigation be commenced?

4.144 The FSA may appoint an investigator to conduct an investigation on its behalf if it appears to it that there are circumstances suggesting that[1]:

- the criminal offences of insider dealing[2], misleading statements or practices[3] or falsely claiming to be authorised or exempt[4] may have been committed;
- there may have been a breach of the general prohibition[5];
- there may have been a contravention of the restrictions on financial promotion[6]; or
- market abuse may have taken place[7].

The Secretary of State has parallel powers of investigation[8].

1 FSMA 2000, s 168(2) and (3).
2 Under the Criminal Justice Act 1993, Pt V.
3 FSMA 2000, s 397.
4 FSMA 2000, s 24(1).
5 The criminal offence of breaching the general prohibition against carrying on regulated activities without being authorised or exempt, under FSMA 2000, ss 19 and 23 (and see para 2.175 above).
6 FSMA 2000, ss 21 and 238.
7 FSMA 2000, s 118 and see Chapter 13 below.
8 This will normally mean the Secretary of State for Trade and Industry, but could mean any Secretary of State. The Secretary of State's power to investigate is a reserve power that is not generally exercised. Primarily, it reflects the potential overlap between financial services investigations and the Secretary of State's wider responsibilities for company law, but it could also allow the DTI, rather than the FSA, to conduct the investigation in a particular case if there were particular reasons, such as a conflict of interest in the FSA: the Economic Secretary to HM Treasury in Standing Committee, 23 November 1999.

4.145 This is the most serious of the investigation procedures. As will be seen, in contrast with the other investigation powers, the appointment of an investigator under s 168(2) will not generally be notified to the person under investigation, at least in the first instance[1]. Furthermore, such an investigator has the widest powers to obtain information from the widest range of people.

1 See para 4.159 ff below.

4.146 ***When will the power be exercised?*** Leaving aside market abuse and insider dealing, which are discussed separately in Chapter 13 below, these investigations are aimed primarily at situations where people are carrying out unauthorised business in some way. The FSA's primary aim in exercising these powers in those circumstances will be to protect the interests of consumers[1]. It may therefore need to consider at an early stage whether it should take urgent enforcement action[2], as well as continuing its fact-finding investigation. There is also the potential for the powers to overlap with those of other investigating or prosecuting bodies, such as the Serious Fraud Office and Department of Trade and Industry. How such issues are resolved is discussed at para 11.10 ff below.

1 See the FSA Handbook at ENF 2.7.2. For a further discussion of the FSA's policy in this area, see the FSA Handbook at ENF 2.7.
2 See the FSA Handbook at ENF 2.7.4.

What information can the firm be required to provide?

4.147 An investigator appointed under s 168(2) may require any person whom he considers is or may be able to give information which is or may be relevant to the investigation[1] to:

- attend at a specified time and place and answer questions or otherwise provide such information as he may require for the purposes of the investigation; or
- produce at a specified time and place any specified documents or documents of a specified description which appear to the investigator to relate to any matter relevant to the investigation; or
- otherwise give him all assistance in connection with the investigation which he is reasonably able to give.

This provision is similar to the powers of inspectors appointed by the Department of Trade and Industry to investigate insider dealing under the pre-existing legislation[2].

1 FSMA 2000, s 173.
2 Financial Services Act 1986, s 177.

4.148 The provision is different from those applicable to s 167 investigations and s 168(1) and (4) investigations, primarily because the power is expressed not by reference to the person under investigation but instead by reference to those who may hold relevant information. The rationale is that in an investigation of this nature it may not be clear to the FSA, at least at the outset, who is under investigation. Rather, they may be investigating a situation.

4.149 The provision is particularly notable for its breadth, in terms of the types of information that can be required and the persons from whom it can be obtained. At its widest, a person whom the investigator considers *may be able* to give information which *may be relevant* to the investigation can be required to give *all assistance which he is reasonably able to give*[1]. This presents a low hurdle to the investigator and gives him a broad discretion as to the assistance he requires. There are, however, some limitations. He must act fairly[2]. He can only require reasonable assistance, which means he cannot place demands on people that are unreasonable, whether as to the time they must expend or the expense they must incur in preparation for the questions or in any other respect[3]. Also if, for whatever reason, the person concerned does not have legal representation, then that is a factor to be taken into account in determining what is reasonable[4].

1 This is a common statutory provision: see, for example, the Financial Services Act 1986, s 177; the Banking Act 1987, s 41; the Companies Act 1985, s 434; the Insurance Companies Act 1982, s 43A and the Building Societies Act 1986, s 55.
2 See, for example, *In re Pergamon Press* [1971] Ch 388 and see para 4.272 ff below.
3 See *In re Mirror Group plc* [1999] 3 WLR 583 at 601.
4 See *In re Mirror Group plc* [1999] 3 WLR 583 at 604.

Section 169 investigations - at the request of an overseas regulator

When can an investigation be commenced?

4.150 The FSA may, at the request of an overseas regulator, exercise its s 165 information gathering power[1] or appoint an investigator to investigate any matter[2].

1 Its power under FSMA 2000, s 165 to require information to be provided to it: see para 4.60 above.
2 FSMA 2000, s 169(1).

4.151 The decision whether to commence an investigation at the request of an overseas regulator is different from that regarding any other type of investigation. The FSMA 2000 does not require any particular evidential hurdle to have been passed (for example, that it appears to the FSA there are circumstances suggesting an offence has been committed). Rather, the FSA has a general discretion whether or not to accede to the request and commence an investigation.

4.152 If the FSA receives the request from a competent authority pursuant to a Community obligation, for example under one of the single market directives[1], it must consider whether the exercise of its investigation power is necessary to comply with its Community obligations[2]. The FSMA 2000 does not require the FSA to commence an investigation in that situation, but that must be the expectation.

1 Those EU Directives listed at para 2.12 above.
2 FSMA 2000, s 169(3). 'Community obligations' refers to EU legal requirements and is a phrase derived from the European Communities Act 1972: the Economic Secretary to HM Treasury in Standing Committee, 23 November 1999.

4.153 In any other case, in deciding whether or not to accede to the request by exercising its investigative power, the FSA may take into account in particular[1]:

- whether a UK regulatory authority would receive corresponding assistance in the relevant overseas country;
- whether the case concerns the breach of a law, or other requirement, which has no close parallel in the UK or involves the assertion of a jurisdiction not recognised by the UK;
- the seriousness of the case and its importance to persons in the UK;
- whether it is otherwise appropriate in the public interest to give the assistance sought; and
- the FSA may decide not to assist unless the overseas regulator makes an appropriate contribution to the cost[2].

1 FSMA 2000, s 169(4).
2 FSMA 2000, s 169(5).

4.154 ***When will the power be exercised?*** The FSA has provided little guidance on its policy as to when it will accede to such requests from overseas regulators. It has said[1] that it will first consider whether it is able to assist without using its formal powers, for example by obtaining the information voluntarily. Where that is not possible, it will take account of the various factors listed above but may give particular weight to the seriousness of the case and its importance to persons in the UK, and to the public interest.

1 See the FSA Handbook at ENF 2.8.7.

4.155 Given the increasing importance of co-operation between regulators, and the ever more international nature of financial services business, firms should expect that the FSA will actively use this power in order to obtain information for the purposes of investigations overseas[1]. As the factors above indicate, the extent to which the FSA will be willing to assist the overseas regulators may in practice depend largely on its relationship with the regulator concerned. Crucially, this is not something that the firm is likely to be able to influence, except by showing a willingness to provide the information voluntarily, or unless there are particular reasons why the overseas investigation should not be carried on here which will be convincing to the FSA[2].

1 'The FSA is keen to promote co-operation with overseas regulators. It views assistance to overseas regulators as an essential part of [the principles for good regulation]': see the FSA Handbook at ENF 2, Annex 2G, para 4.
2 Note, for example, that if the safeguards of the Human Rights Act 1998, for example the privilege against self-incrimination, were not available in the overseas jurisdiction, that might be grounds for the firm to seek to prevent certain information from being passed to the overseas body: see further at para 4.316 below.

What information can the firm be required to provide?

4.156 An investigator appointed under s 169 has identical powers to one appointed under s 168(1)[1]. A representative of the overseas regulator may be allowed to attend and take part in any interviews. This is also within the FSA's discretion (exercised by giving a direction to the investigator) and is subject to the FSA publishing its policy with respect to the conduct of such interviews and to the FSA being satisfied that any information obtained by the overseas regulator as a result of the interview will be subject to the same safeguards against disclosure as apply under the FSMA 2000[2].

1 FSMA 2000, s 169(2). As to the powers of an investigator appointed under s 168(1), see para 4.140 ff above.
2 FSMA 2000, s 169(7) to (12). As to the safeguards which apply under the FSMA 2000, see para 4.304 ff below. The FSA has indicated that in deciding whether to direct that the overseas regulator may attend the interview, it may take into account factors including the complexity of the case, the nature and sensitivity of the information sought, the FSA's own interest in the case, costs and the availability of resources, and the availability of similar assistance to UK authorities in similar circumstances: see the FSA Handbook at ENF 2.11.8. The FSA has published a detailed policy with respect to the conduct of such interviews (which the FSMA 2000 requires it to do); this can be found at ENF 2, Annex 2G.

Procedure for investigations

4.157 A firm that is subjected to a formal investigation may want to understand not only what information it can be asked to provide but also the procedure for starting and carrying out the investigation. We review the investigation process, and in particular:

- how an investigation is started;
- whether the person under investigation will be notified of it;
- whether the investigation will be made public;
- how the investigation is conducted and controlled; and
- how the investigation concludes.

How is the investigation started?

4.158 The investigation is commenced by the appointment of an investigator under one of the statutory powers outlined above[1]. The FSMA 2000 allows the FSA, or the Secretary of State, to appoint as investigator one of its own staff[2] and the FSA has indicated that it will normally do so[3].

1 The FSMA 2000 does not prescribe any particular procedure which the FSA must follow in reaching the decision to commence an investigation, nor has the FSA given any indication how that decision is taken. It is thought that the decision is taken by the FSA enforcement staff involved.
2 FSMA 2000, s 170(5).
3 See the FSA Handbook at ENF 2.11.3.

Is the person under investigation notified of the investigation?

4.159 The FSA is required to give written notice of the appointment of an investigator to the person who is the subject of the investigation[1], subject to the two exceptions outlined below[2]. Where notice is given, it must specify the provisions under which, and as a result of which, the investigator was appointed and state the reason for his appointment[3]. The person who is the subject of the investigation will therefore normally be informed at the outset of the nature of, and reasons for, the investigation. There is, however, no specific requirement for him to be informed of the scope of the investigation, although that information may be encompassed within the above.

1 FSMA 2000, s 170(2). As to the manner in which written notices are to be given, see The Financial Services and Markets Act 2000 (Service of Notices) Regulations 2001, SI 2001/1420 and see the FSA Handbook at DEC 5.3.
2 In addition, it is not clear that any notice is required in respect of an investigation under s 169 at the request of an overseas regulator. However, the FSA has indicated in its policy on the conduct of interviews in the presence of the overseas regulator (see para 4.156 above) that it will in general provide written notice of such an investigation to the person under investigation: see the FSA Handbook at ENF 2, Annex 2G, para 15.
3 FSMA 2000, s 170(4).

4.160 The first exception[1] is where the investigation is commenced under s 168(2)[2], in which case there is no requirement for any notification. The rationale is that, in many cases, the FSA or the Secretary of State, will, at least in the first instance, be investigating a situation (for example a suspicious movement in the price of a particular share), rather than a person, or may not know the identity of the perpetrator. The FSA has said that once it becomes clear who the persons under investigation are, the FSA will consider notifying them[3]. It has also said that it will normally notify them when it proceeds to exercise its statutory powers to require information from them, but will not do so if this would prejudice the FSA's ability to conduct the investigation effectively. In the meantime, it will provide an indication of the nature and subject matter of its investigation to those who are required to provide information[4].

1 FSMA 2000, s 170(3)(b).
2 An investigation on circumstances suggesting market abuse, insider dealing, breach of the perimeter, unlawful financial promotion: see para 4.144 above.
3 See the FSA Handbook at ENF 2.12.4.
4 See the FSA Handbook at ENF 2.12.5/6.

4.161 Because of the seriousness of such investigations and the proceedings to which they could give rise, and the potential disadvantage that a person could suffer by not being aware that he was being investigated, this policy requires closer analysis. In practice the firm may become aware of the nature of the investigation when first asked to provide information to the investigator. But this is not the same as giving proper notice to the person under investigation. Moreover, the policy outlined above does not preclude the FSA from choosing to obtain information from others, knowing exactly who is the subject of its investigation but deciding not to approach or notify that person until later. It is difficult to see why this would be justified, or why the FSA should not give the person notice at the time when his identity becomes apparent, save where there are reasons to believe that giving notice might prejudice the investigation.

4.162 The second exception[1] is that, in an s 168(1) or (4) investigation[2], the FSA or the Secretary of State does not need to notify the person under investigation if it believes that the notice would be likely to result in the investigation being frustrated. The FSA has not provided any indication of what it would regard as frustrating or likely to frustrate an investigation. This could, however, include situations where there are issues about document destruction, about misleading information being provided to the FSA, or concerns that serious fraud or criminal misconduct have been committed. There only has to be a belief by the FSA (not a 'reasonable belief' or 'reasonable grounds for believing'), but it has to be a belief that the notice 'would be likely' to result in the investigation being frustrated.

1 FSMA 2000, s 170(3)(a).
2 Investigations into regulatory breaches or certain criminal offences: see para 4.134 ff above.

4.163 An individual or firm who is aggrieved about the decision not to notify him, does not have any particular means of challenging the decision, and in any case is likely only to know about it after the event. It may be possible to make a formal complaint[1], although this is unlikely to be of real benefit in relation to the substantive action arising from the investigation, or the point could be made before the Tribunal if the final enforcement decision is referred to the Tribunal[2].

1 See Chapter 16 below.
2 See Chapter 6 below.

Is the investigation made public?

4.164 The FSA does not normally make public the fact that it is or is not investigating a particular matter, or any of the findings or conclusions of an investigation, but it may make a public announcement in certain exceptional circumstances[1]. The norm, and the expectation, is therefore that the investigation will not be made public. However, there are various ways that information regarding an investigation, or its results, could come into the public domain, and these are outlined below.

1 See the FSA Handbook at ENF 2.13.1.

4.165 First, the FSA will, in exceptional circumstances, make a public announcement that it is or is not investigating a particular matter[1] if it considers such an announcement is desirable to maintain public confidence in the financial system, protect consumers, prevent widespread malpractice or help the investigation itself, for example by bringing forward witnesses. Particular examples given by the FSA are where the matters under investigation have become the subject of such public concern, speculation or rumour that it is desirable for the FSA to make public the fact of its investigation in order to allay the concern or contain the rumour or speculation[2].

1 See the FSA Handbook at ENF 2.13.2 and 2.13.4.
2 See the FSA Handbook at ENF 2.13.5. In addition, in the context of a takeover bid, the FSA has indicated that it may make a public announcement that it is *not* going to investigate a matter where the FSA considers (following discussion with the Takeover Panel) that this is appropriate in the interests of preventing or eliminating public uncertainty, speculation or rumour: see the FSA Handbook at ENF 2.13.3. Generally, where the matter relates to a takeover bid, the FSA will discuss any announcement beforehand with the Takeover Panel: see ENF 2.13.5.

4.166 The FSA's ability to make a public announcement in these situations is subject to the general statutory prohibition preventing the disclosure of confidential information relating to the business or affairs of any person obtained by the FSA in the discharge of its functions under the FSMA 2000[1]. The FSA may be able to announce the fact that it is investigating a firm in relation to a particular matter of public knowledge, but the announcement would probably need to be in bland terms in order to avoid disclosing any confidential information relating to the business or affairs of the firm prohibited from disclosure under FSMA 2000, s 348[2].

1 FSMA 2000, s 348. This is discussed in more detail at para 4.304 below.
2 It may, though, be arguable that publication would be a permitted disclosure under paragraph 3(1), Financial Services and Markets Act 2000 (Disclosure of Confidential Information) Regulations 2001, SI 2001/2188 (the 'Gateway Regulations'), as having been made by the FSA for the purpose of enabling or assisting it to discharge its public functions. For a discussion of the Gateway Regulations, see para 4.312 below.

4.167 Where disclosure is permitted under the FSMA 2000, the FSA's policy is to make the announcement where 'desirable' for one of the reasons outlined above. 'Desirable' is a fairly low test (it does not, for example, have to be 'necessary' for the FSA to make the public announcement). However, given the overall policy set out above, public announcements ought to be rare in practice[1].

1 Contrast also the FSA's ability (according to the FSA Handbook) to publicly announce an investigation with the statutory prohibition against publishing details of a warning notice, which is a later part of the process: see FSMA 2000, s 391(1) and para 5.76 ff below.

4.168 Second, publicity may in some cases be unavoidable, for example where the FSA makes enquiries among the general public which attract local publicity[1].

1 See the FSA Handbook at ENF 2.13.6.

4.169 Third, the FSA will not normally publish details of the information found by the investigation or conclusions reached (this will normally be precluded by a statutory prohibition[1]). However, it may do so in exceptional circumstances. The example given by the FSA[2] is where the fact that it was investigating was made public and the FSA subsequently concludes that the concerns that prompted the investigation were unwarranted. The FSA anticipates that the firm may in that situation want it to clarify the matter.

1 The prohibition against publishing a warning or decision notice or any details concerning them (FSMA 2000, s 391(1)) and/or the statutory confidentiality restriction (FSMA 2000, s 348): see, respectively, paras 5.76 ff and 4.304 ff below. For an explanation of warning and decision notices, see Chapter 5 below.
2 See the FSA Handbook at ENF 2.13.7.

4.170 Fourth, the FSA may have taken some other action whilst the investigation was continuing, for example used its own-initiative powers or applied to the court for an injunction or for a restitution order, and may wish to make some sort of public statement in connection with that other action. Indeed, it may be under a duty to do so[1]. The FSA's general policy on publication in relation to the various enforcement action it can take is set out at para 5.194 below and its specific policy in relation to each type of enforcement action is discussed where the power concerned is considered. The FSA's starting point is that it is generally appropriate to publish details of successful court applications or administrative enforcement action.

1 The use of such powers may involve the issue of a final or supervisory notice, and thus give rise to a duty to publish such information as the FSA considers appropriate, when the final notice is issued or the supervisory notice takes effect: FSMA 2000, s 391(4) and (5). See also the FSA Handbook at ENF 2.13.10/11.

4.171 Fifth, where the matter arises in the context of a takeover bid, the FSA will consult the Takeover Panel and give due weight to its views[1].

1 See the FSA Handbook at ENF 2.13 generally.

4.172 Finally, it is important to appreciate that if or when any enforcement action results from the matters investigated, it is likely that publicity will arise either in the Tribunal, if the matter is referred to the Tribunal, or in any event when the enforcement action is finally taken[1].

1 See further paras 5.194 and 6.32 below.

How is the investigation conducted and controlled?

4.173 Once a formal investigation has been commenced, the person appointed as investigator has broad statutory powers for gathering information not only from the person under investigation but also from various third parties. The precise extent of the powers available in any case depends upon the statutory provision under which the investigation was commenced. The particular powers applicable to each type of investigation have been outlined above.

4.174 The FSA (or, as appropriate, the Secretary of State) controls the investigation by giving directions to the investigator, which may control its scope, the period during which it is to be conducted, its conduct and its reporting[1]. In particular, directions may confine the investigation to particular matters, extend it to particular matters, require the investigator to discontinue the investigation or to take only such steps as are specified or require the investigator to make specified interim reports[2]. The FSA has not given any guidance on the way in which it will use its ability to give these directions.

1 FSMA 2000, s 170(7).
2 FSMA 2000, s 170(8).

4.175 ***Changes to the scope or conduct of the investigation*** If the FSA or the Secretary of State issues a direction changing the scope or conduct of the investigation and, in the opinion of the FSA (or, as appropriate, the Secretary of State), the person subject to investigation is likely to be significantly prejudiced by not being made aware of it, the person must be given written notice of the change[1]. This is subject to the same two exceptions as the requirement to notify the commencement of the investigation[2]. The FSA has given limited guidance on how it will apply this in practice, indicating that examples of being significantly prejudiced might include being subjected to unnecessary costs of dealing with an aspect of the investigation which the FSA no longer intends to pursue or where a person may inadvertently incriminate himself by not knowing of the change in scope[3]. The statutory test gives the FSA a substantial amount of discretion as to whether a particular change needs to be notified. The FSA's views on what is likely significantly to prejudice the person under investigation may be rather different from the views of the person under investigation. But it is clear from the provision that it is the FSA's views that count and it may be difficult to challenge a decision by the FSA not to notify a change in a particular case[4].

1 FSMA 2000, s 170(9). As to the manner in which written notices are to be given, see The Financial Services and Markets Act 2000 (Service of Notices) Regulations 2001, SI 2001/1420 and see the FSA Handbook at DEC 5.3.
2 FSMA 2000, s 170(3). See para 4.159 above.
3 See the FSA Handbook at ENF 2.12.2.
4 There is no right to refer such a matter to the Tribunal and, in any event, the firm is unlikely to be aware of it until afterwards. As to the firm's potential options, see Chapter 16 below.

4.176 The FSA contemplates[1] that there may be circumstances where it has appointed an investigator under s 167 but circumstances subsequently come to light to suggest that one of the specific regulatory or criminal offences may have been committed, in which case it may decide to extend the appointment to cover one of the s 168 powers. In that case there could be a desire on the FSA's part to extend the investigation because an investigator appointed under one of the section 168 powers can obtain a greater scope of information from a wider class of people[2].

1 See the FSA Handbook at ENF 2.5.11.
2 See para 4.140 above.

4.177 However, the FSA has not said what it will do where the opposite is true. What if there were originally circumstances to suggest, say, market abuse, but on a closer examination it becomes apparent that what might have been committed is a more limited breach of one of the FSA's rules or a breach of the Principles for Businesses? In that situation, will the FSA terminate the investigation under s 168(2) and appoint the same investigators under s 168(4)? Although this would seem fair on the face of it, particularly given that it would also trigger a statutory requirement for notice to be given to the person under investigation[1], there is nothing in the FSMA 2000 to require the FSA to do so and the clear disadvantage for the FSA would be that any further information could then be obtained only from a more limited class of people.

1 See para 4.159 above.

The conclusion of the investigation

4.178 Ultimately, the investigator must make a report to the FSA or, as appropriate, the Secretary of State[1]. Where the FSA has given a person written notice of the appointment of an investigator and it decides to discontinue the investigation without any present intention to take further action, it will confirm this to the person concerned as soon as it considers it appropriate to do so having regard to the circumstances of the case[2].

1 FSMA 2000, s 170(6). Under FSMA 2000, s 353 and the Financial Services and Markets Act 2000 (Disclosure of Information by Prescribed Persons) Regulations 2001, SI 2001/1857, the investigator will not, generally speaking, breach any duties (eg duties of confidence) by disclosing information: (a) to any person (eg a witness) for the purpose of enabling or assisting the investigator to discharge his functions, or (b) to the FSA provided that (in the case of (b) only) the disclosure is made in good faith and the person reasonably believes the information to be relevant to the discharge of a public function by the FSA. This does not apply to information which is protected as confidential information under FSMA 2000, s 348(2): see para 4.304 ff below. The Regulations apply also to a skilled person appointed under FSMA 2000, s 166 (see para 4.82 above) but do not appear to apply to an investigator appointed under FSMA 2000, Pt VI (see para 15.46 ff below).

2 See the FSA Handbook at ENF 2.12.7.

Practical guidance for the firm

4.179 If the firm is faced with a formal investigation, or asked to provide information in the context of an investigation into another firm, what general approach should it take in its dealings with the FSA? Are there any steps it can take to ease the process of providing documents to the FSA or the investigator? Are there any risks in preparing additional documents for the FSA or the investigator? What steps should be taken before individuals are interviewed? How are interviews conducted? We outline here some of the practical issues that arise and how the firm might address them, namely:

- the general approach of being open and co-operative with the FSA;
- practical steps to take when providing documents;
- the risks of producing material for, or in, an investigation; and
- practical steps to take in relation to interviews.

The general approach: being open and co-operative with the FSA

4.180 The importance of maintaining an open and co-operative relationship with the FSA, and what this may require of the firm, has been discussed at para 4.50 ff above. The commencement of a formal investigation does not excuse the firm its obligations under Principle 11 to co-operate with the FSA[1], nor does it necessarily prevent an open and co-operative relationship from continuing. The firm can still co-operate with the FSA within the context of the formal investigation and, as demonstrated by much of the discussion that follows, in most situations it will probably be in the firm's interests to do so[2]. The FSA envisages that information will be provided to it on a voluntary basis even within the more formal context. Equally, where there is a formal investigation, the firm may wish to maintain a good relationship with the investigator appointed by the FSA, as well as with the FSA itself. The discussion that follows thus also applies in relation to investigators.

1 The consequences of non-compliance with Principle 11 are outlined at para 4.52 above.
2 The same practical factors as are discussed at para 4.50 above apply equally in the context of a formal investigation.

Practical steps to take when providing documents

What documents does the FSA really want?

4.181 When faced with a wide-ranging or unspecific request for documents from the FSA or an investigator, the first question will often be to ask what documents are really sought. Often, a wide, formal request is issued to ensure that all of the primary documents are captured. It may be that the width of the request is intended as a safety net, that some or much of the documentation it covers is immaterial and that it imposes an unnecessary burden both on the firm and on the FSA. By maintaining a dialogue with the FSA or the investigator, the firm may be able to agree sensible limits on the categories of documents that are to be provided or, for example, to provide material on a rolling basis in order to lessen the burden on resources.

Reviewing documents to remove those that need not be provided

4.182 Firms will often want to review the material that falls within the FSA's or investigator's request before providing it. Why would the firm do this? There are three main considerations.

4.183 First, legally privileged material is generally protected from disclosure to the FSA[1] as well as to third parties in the context of any legal proceedings. But if privileged material is disclosed to the FSA, there is a risk of that material losing the protection as a result and being susceptible to disclosure to a third party who brings legal proceedings against the firm[2]. If the particular document disclosed is part of a chain of documents, then the risk may extend to the whole chain. This is quite apart from the more direct prejudice that the firm could suffer by making available to the FSA sensitive material which it did not need to disclose.

1 The firm cannot be required by the FSA to disclose legally privileged material: see para 4.264 below. Note that the FSMA 2000 effectively contains its own definition of legal privilege for this purpose.
2 The issue is whether the firm has, by providing it to the FSA, waived its legal privilege in the particular material, so that it is no longer protected from disclosure. This is considered in more detail at para 4.201 ff below.

4.184 Second, the firm may owe duties of confidentiality to third parties which are overridden only if the firm is required to provide the relevant information to the regulator[1]. If the firm provides the FSA with information confidential to customers or others which it is not obliged to provide to the FSA, either because the material is outside the strict terms of the FSA's request or because it can properly be withheld, for example because it is covered by an obligation of banking confidence[2], then the firm may expose itself to claims if the third party suffers loss as a result.

1 The nature and extent of the firm's obligations of confidentiality will depend upon the particular circumstances. For example, some confidentiality undertakings would allow the disclosure of information voluntarily to the regulator, whereas others would allow the disclosure of information only when 'required' by the regulator. This is discussed in more detail at paras 4.54 above and 4.267 below.

2 In some situations, the firm may not be required to produce documents which are subject to an obligation of banking confidence: see para 4.267 ff below.

4.185 Third, there is a more practical consideration, namely that the firm may want to know what documents and information it is providing to the FSA or the investigator. Among other things, this enables the firm to anticipate and therefore deal more effectively with any questions that arise from the material. It also allows witnesses to prepare themselves to answer questions at any interviews[1].

1 This is discussed further at para 4.221 ff below.

4.186 Whether the FSA or the investigator will allow the firm a timetable for providing the material that will enable it to review the documents may be another matter. Certainly, the first two of the considerations outlined above should be good reason for the firm to ask for sufficient time. There may, however, be other issues putting pressure on the timetable. The firm's best option will normally be to discuss the matter with the FSA or the investigator.

Keeping track of what has been provided

4.187 A practical consideration that is easy to overlook is the need for the firm to keep track of what material it has provided to the FSA or the investigator. This can be done by indexing and numbering the material and taking copies. This enables the firm to deal more effectively with requests that it receives for explanations or for further material arising from documents that have been provided, and enables witnesses to prepare themselves to answer questions at any interview. It also enables the firm to deal with any dispute that may arise over what material has been provided to the FSA.

Providing tapes of telephone calls, copies of e-mails etc

4.188 Difficult logistical issues may arise when the firm needs to identify the relevant material from a large source, for example locating relevant e-mails and other documents held on a computer system or identifying the relevant telephone calls on tapes. Where material produced over a substantial period needs to be reviewed, significant resources can be required to identify the relevant material, copy it and, so far as telephone calls are concerned, prepare transcripts. The practical considerations outlined above in favour of reviewing material, where possible, before providing it to the FSA, apply equally to the provision of such material. Again, it is often important for the firm to maintain a constructive dialogue with the FSA to ensure that unnecessarily wide requests are minimised and to manage their expectations on timing.

The risks of producing material for or in an investigation

4.189 As has been highlighted at para 3.155 above, firms need to be careful not to produce additional documentary material during the investigation and enforcement process which could be discloseable to third parties in any legal proceedings which might be brought against the firm, or indeed which the firm might wish to bring. The primary concern is to ensure that the firm does not unnecessarily increase its potential exposure to civil claims by third parties by producing material which, if any third party does bring a claim against the firm, will need to be disclosed under the Civil Procedure Rules[1] and is likely to assist the third party in establishing that claim and/or otherwise to be prejudicial to the firm. Equally, it would not wish to produce material which would assist a third party in defeating a claim brought by the firm.

1 Or the rules of any other jurisdiction in which such claims might be brought.

4.190 These concerns relate not so much to the records which the firm creates in the normal course of its business, which will mostly be discloseable in any event, but to any further material produced after the problem came to light, which for example:

- takes a position inconsistent with that which the firm adduces in the legal proceedings;
- indicates how the firm interprets the facts and whether it believes it acted wrongly; or
- assesses what losses were suffered as a result of the firm's errors.

4.191 Why does this matter? If legal proceedings are brought against the firm, it will be for the claimant to prove that the firm's actions amounted to a breach of its duties and that he suffered loss as a result. Documents of this nature can make that task considerably easier or can harm the firm's defence, for example by reducing the credibility of its evidence. Often, a firm will not know the full facts at the outset of the investigation and could therefore interpret wrongly the information available to it. Material which may seem relatively harmless, particularly at a time when the firm is focusing on the regulatory aspects of the problem, could thus prejudice the firm's defence to any civil claims subsequently made against it. Equally, if the firm takes proceedings against a third party, they could assist the third party in resisting the claims brought by the firm.

4.192 Since the firm is likely to need to produce material in order to co-operate with its regulator and to respond properly to the investigation process, it is important to understand what material can be required to be disclosed to third parties and whether documents can be produced in a way that will reduce the risk of disclosure. Of course, a copy of the relevant material may be not only in the firm's hands, but also in the FSA's hands and it may be that the third party will try to obtain a copy from the FSA. What are the risks? And what are the firm's options? In the following paragraphs[1]:

- first, we outline the basic rules on the disclosure of documents;
- second, we consider four types of material that can cause particular difficulty, namely:
  - — communications with or from compliance officers;
  - — communications with the firm's employees;
  - — without prejudice communications; and
  - — information provided to the FSA or the investigator;
- third, we review whether the same material can be obtained by the third party from the FSA; and
- finally, we outline some practical steps the firm can take to reduce the risks.

1 The discussion that follows relates to English legal proceedings. Documents may also need to be produced in proceedings in other jurisdictions, in which case different rules may apply.

The basic rules on the disclosure of documents

4.193 Material that is relevant to a civil legal claim made against or by the firm could be discloseable to the third party, unless in the circumstances the material is protected by the doctrine of legal professional privilege. Precisely what this means requires further explanation.

4.194 The question whether material is discloseable in the context of a particular civil claim depends upon the relevance of the material to the claim. If the firm relies on the document, if the document adversely affects its case, or if it supports or adversely affects the third party's case then, in principle, and subject to the discussion that follows, it falls within the firm's disclosure obligations[1]. In addition, the court can order the disclosure of particular documents or classes of documents that may be relevant[2].

1 See Civil Procedure Rules, Part 31, Rule 31.6.
2 See Civil Procedure Rules, Part 31, Rule 31.12.

4.195 Assuming the material is relevant to the claim being made, one question is whether the fact that it was produced in the context of the regulatory enforcement process precludes a court from requiring the firm to disclose it. Until 1995, it was thought that such documents might be protected from disclosure to third parties by the doctrine of public interest immunity, broadly on the basis that there is a public interest in promoting the candid provision of information between regulator and regulated. However, it was held in *Kaufmann v Credit Lyonnais Bank*[1] that there is no general class of public interest immunity applicable to such documents. There is therefore no general rule that protects material produced for or by the regulator as a class from being disclosed. In other words, the mere fact that the material was produced in this context does not of itself prevent a court from requiring it to be disclosed. Having said that, *Kaufmann* was only a first instance decision[2], judicial trends may change, and there may be scope for arguing that different considerations apply under the new regime. The decision also does not preclude a claim of public interest immunity based on the contents of a particular document.

1 [1995] CLC 300. The case related to documents provided to the Bank of England and The Securities Association, the predecessor to the SFA, under the previous regime. They included a report by Credit Lyonnais' lawyers, a report by their accountants and correspondence with TSA. Compare *MGN Pension Trustees v Invesco Asset Management Ltd* (14 October 1993, unreported, Evans-Lombe J).

2 The reasoning seems to apply equally in the context of the new regime. Factors which were relevant to the court's decision included (i) that there was no expectation that the information would be wholly confidential because the TSA was able to disclose it to other regulators, (ii) that the provision of the information could probably have been required under the TSA's rules, and where there is a requirement to provide information the public interest in promoting candour is rather less compelling, and (iii) given that the TSA's primary responsibility was to protect investors, the need for a class-based immunity allowing information to be withheld from investors needed to be clearly demonstrated. These factors in particular would seem to be equally relevant now.

4.196 Since there is no general immunity for such material, the question whether a particular document is discloseable depends primarily[1] upon whether it is protected from disclosure by the doctrine of legal professional privilege. Whether material is legally privileged depends upon who produced it and for what purpose. Very broadly[2], material can only be legally privileged if it is a communication with a legal advisor sent or received for the purposes of legal advice ('legal advice privilege') or was produced for the purposes of existing or contemplated legal proceedings ('litigation privilege'). In addition, documents that are properly 'without prejudice' are generally speaking protected in the same way[3]. The application of legal privilege in four common situations is considered below. Five general points may, however, first be usefully made[4].

1 As indicated above, there may still be scope for public interest immunity to apply to particular documents.

2 For a more detailed analysis of legal privilege, see *Privilege*, Passmore; *Disclosure*, Matthews and Malek and *Documentary Evidence*, Hollander and Adam.

3 See para 4.210 below.

4 The discussion here is limited to various points that may be particularly relevant. For a more detailed analysis of legal privilege, see the works referred to at footnote 2 above.

4.197 First, communications between the firm or its lawyers and third parties, for example in which information is sought from third parties, are unlikely to be legally privileged unless they are produced for the purposes of existing or contemplated legal proceedings[1]. This is an important limitation in practice.

1 A report prepared by accountants for legal advisors is therefore unlikely to be privileged unless litigation is contemplated: see *Price Waterhouse v BCCI Holdings (Luxembourg) SA* [1992] BCLC 583, CA. Communications with third parties who act purely as the agent of the client or solicitor for the purpose of providing the information may, however, be covered by legal advice privilege and therefore be privileged irrespective of whether any proceedings are in contemplation. The prime example would be the firm's employees: see *Disclosure*, Matthews and Malek, at 9.014 and see the discussion at para 4.207 below.

4.198 Second, the purpose for which the document was produced is critical. Material produced internally to enable the firm to take legal advice may well be privileged[1]. Material produced in the context of the firm's defence to regulatory enforcement proceedings may also be privileged, although this is less clear for reasons discussed below. But it may be difficult to produce information requested by the FSA during its investigation in a way that is legally privileged, if producing it for the FSA is the main purpose behind the document. Again, this is likely in practice to be a significant limitation on the firm's ability to rely on the doctrine of legal privilege in this context. Material produced for commercial purposes will generally not be legally privileged.

1 Legal advice is interpreted fairly widely, to include all communications within the continuum aimed at keeping solicitor and client informed, but it may not include the solicitor's advice on purely commercial issues: for further discussion, see *Disclosure*, Matthews and Malek, at 9.009/10. Note, however, that it may be questionable whether internal communications within the firm not involving a lawyer but, for example, collecting together information for submission to a lawyer, would fall within the statutory protection for legal privilege (whatever their status under the general law): see para 4.265 below.

4.199 Third, a difficult question yet to be decided by the courts is whether 'litigation privilege' covers material produced for regulatory proceedings in the same way as material produced for legal proceedings in court. To the extent that there is any authority on the answer, it is that proceedings before a tribunal exercising judicial or quasi-judicial functions which are adversarial in nature are 'legal proceedings' for these purposes, but that a purely administrative fact-finding process is not[1].

1 See *In re L (a minor)* [1997] AC 16, HL. See also *Parry-Jones v Law Society* [1968] 1 All ER 177 and *W v Edgell* [1990] 1 All ER 835.

4.200 If this is the correct test, it seems clear that the FSA's investigation is not a legal proceeding, and firms should therefore treat with care the production of documents in that context, particularly documents involving third parties. Proceedings before the Tribunal[1] are almost certainly legal proceedings and material produced for the purposes of those proceedings should therefore be privileged, provided it fulfils the other requirements for legal privilege. Whether proceedings before the Regulatory Decisions Committee[2] are legal proceedings, is more difficult[3] and produces uncertainty in practice. It should, though, be possible to minimise the risks caused by this uncertainty by ensuring that many documents are protected either by legal advice privilege or by litigation privilege (if they are produced with possible Tribunal proceedings primarily in mind), and other documents may properly be without prejudice and therefore gain similar protection[4].

1 For a discussion of the Tribunal, and when matters can be referred to it, see Chapter 6 below.
2 For an explanation, see para 5.26 ff below.
3 The FSMA 2000 indicates that, for some purposes, the issue of a warning notice constitutes 'proceedings' (see, for example, ss 66(5)(b) and 389(3)) and the consideration of a case by the Regulatory Decisions Committee could perhaps be viewed as quasi-judicial.
4 See the discussion at para 4.210 below.

4.201 Fourth, a document that is legally privileged will not necessarily remain privileged forever[1]. The privilege in a document can in principle be waived by the firm and once this has been done it no longer attracts the same protection. The concern is that the provision of a document to one third party, for example the FSA, could cause privilege to be waived generally, thus entirely destroying the protection.

1 Although the basic legal principle is that a document that is privileged remains privileged.

4.202 Where privileged material is produced by one party to another within a confidential relationship then, provided there was no intention to waive privilege, the privilege should be maintained against other third parties[1]. There is a good argument that, depending upon the precise situation and the terms on which the material is disclosed, this would apply to ensure that privileged material provided to the FSA remains privileged as against any other party, including third parties who might bring civil claims against the firm. This is because the disclosure to the FSA is made within the confines of the confidentiality obligation imposed by the FSMA 2000[2].

1 *City of Gotha v Sothebys* [1998] 1 WLR 114. See also *British Coal Corpn v Dennis Rye Ltd (No 2)* [1988] 1 WLR 1113.

2 FSMA 2000, s 348: see para 4.304 ff below. This seems also to have been the Government's view: the Economic Secretary to HM Treasury in Standing Committee, 23 November 1999. However, whilst this is thought to be the better argument, it is not clear that it would succeed because the FSMA 2000 does allow the FSA to disseminate the information in certain situations, for example to other regulators, and envisages that it will do so. It is possible that a court would take the view that the provision of the information to the FSA sufficiently impacted on its confidentiality to destroy the privilege. Indeed, the expectation that information would be disclosed by a regulator was one of the points against public interest immunity made by Arden J in *Kaufmann*.

4.203 Fifth, even if the material remained privileged as against third parties notwithstanding its disclosure to the FSA, the FSA will generally speaking (see para 4.304 ff below) be able to use it in Tribunal proceedings or in certain court proceedings[1]. If the Tribunal or court hearing is in public, then the information is likely no longer to be confidential and, as a result, no longer privileged and will not then be protected from disclosure.

1 The ability to refer in Tribunal or court proceedings to documents that are otherwise protected may in effect also allow the FSA to bypass the statutory confidentiality restrictions outlined at para 4.304 ff below.

Communications with or from compliance officers

4.204 Compliance staff are often involved when regulatory problems arise and indeed this is frequently part of their normal role. However, the production of documents by compliance officers causes a number of problems. First, it is important to understand from the outset that documents created by compliance staff, even those who are legally qualified, in the course of their routine compliance function will not be legally privileged[1].

1 But if a legally qualified compliance officer produces a document the purpose of which is to give legal advice to the firm, then that may be legally privileged.

4.205 Second, if the compliance department investigates the matter once the problem comes to light, with one possible exception it is likely that neither the documents which they produce in the context of their investigation, for example notes of interviews with other staff, nor their report, will be legally privileged. Such reports and documents can in practice be particularly damaging[1]. If the reason, or one of the reasons[2], for having the compliance department investigate and produce a report is to enable the firm to address the compliance issues arising from the problem, then the investigation is very unlikely to be privileged and, as a result, it is very unlikely that any material produced will be protected from disclosure. This applies even more so if the purpose of the investigation is to assess the commercial implications of the matter.

1 See the discussion at para 4.190 above.
2 See *Waugh v British Railways Board* [1980] AC 521, HL: an accident report was held to have been produced not only in anticipation of litigation but also, at least equally, for the purpose of railway operation and safety. This was insufficient for a claim to privilege.

4.206 In order to be privileged, the document must be produced either in response to a request from a legal advisor to enable him to provide legal advice[1] or in relation to existing or contemplated litigation. In either case, there will be issues as to whether the particular document does fall within the scope of, as applicable, legal advice privilege or litigation privilege and the answer will depend very much upon the circumstances. As a practical matter it may assist if it was demonstrable on the face of the report that it was produced for the requisite purpose[2]. Generally, it may assist that a lawyer was instructed before the report was prepared and was involved in determining its parameters and that the report is addressed to him and not to the firm.

1 Such legal advice could be from an external or internal lawyer. It could also include legal advice from a compliance officer who is legally qualified provided that is the main purpose for which he has been asked to investigate, but in practice it may be difficult to demonstrate that the purpose for the investigation was to enable him to provide legal advice to the firm. Generally, care must be exercised in relying upon legal advice privilege: see *Price Waterhouse v BCCI Holdings (Luxembourg) SA* [1992] BCLC 583.
2 This will not, though, be conclusive: see *Waugh v British Railways Board* [1980] AC 521, HL. Nonetheless, it may be helpful to mark documents 'legally privileged – created to obtain legal advice and for legal proceedings', where appropriate.

Communications between the firm and its employees

4.207 The firm's communications with its employees can also cause difficulties. Communications with employees to obtain information for transmission to the firm's lawyer to enable him to advise will normally be covered by legal advice privilege[1]. Thus, the firm can seek information internally for transmission to the lawyer or the lawyer can seek that information from the firm's employees directly, provided this is done in each case for the dominant purpose of obtaining legal advice or for the dominant purpose of litigation. In many instances, it will be preferable for the lawyer to collect the information directly, to reduce the risk of any difficulty arising based on the information having been obtained for commercial as well as legal purposes[2].

1 The key is to ensure that the documents are produced as part of the continuum aimed at keeping solicitor and client informed, so that advice may be sought and given: see *Minter v Priest* [1930] AC 558 and *Balabel v Air India* [1988] 2 All ER 246. It will not, therefore, normally be necessary for the communication to be made for the purposes of existing or contemplated litigation.
2 This should also help to reduce the risk of information being discloseable to the FSA because of the difficulties in interpreting the statutory protection under the FSMA 2000, s 413: see para 4.265 below.

4.208 Where the communications are privileged, the privilege is that of the firm, not the employee[1], so that it is a matter solely for the firm whether it wishes to waive the privilege and disclose the communication, for example to the FSA.

Even if the information is damaging to the employee, the employee has no general right to prevent the disclosure[2]. The employee, for his part, is likely to be bound by a duty of confidentiality that prevents him disclosing the privileged communication[3] and he could also not be required to disclose it under the FSMA 2000[4].

1 For a further discussion, see *Disclosure*, Matthews and Malek at 10.02.
2 This is subject to any specific confidentiality restriction existing in the particular circumstances. From an employment law perspective, the firm might consider specifically advising the employee that the firm may disclose information provided and may rely on it in disciplinary proceedings: see the discussion at para 3.38 above.
3 Note that this is limited in scope. The facts which the employee reported to the firm are unlikely of themselves to be legally privileged, although the employee may owe a duty of confidence which prevents him from disclosing them to any other party (other than the regulator: see *In re a Company's Application* [1989] Ch 477). It is only the communication for the privileged purpose that is protected. Note also that the firm's ability to prevent or redress an unauthorised disclosure to the FSA may be limited by the Public Interest Disclosure Act 1998: see para 4.48 above.
4 FSMA 2000, s 413 and see the discussion at para 4.264 ff below.

4.209 But some communications between firm and employee are not made for a privileged purpose and will not be protected from disclosure. It is difficult to provide any definitive guidance as to precisely where the line is drawn. Broadly, in so far as the firm communicates with its employee as its agent, there ought to be no difficulty. But where the firm and the employee are in a hostile stance as against one another, communications between them are unlikely to be privileged. A prime example is where the firm interviews an employee for disciplinary purposes, rather than for the purposes of obtaining legal advice on the matter, in which case that interview is unlikely to be privileged. The firm could be required to disclose what was said and any notes of the interview could also be required to be disclosed.

Without prejudice communications

4.210 The enforcement process may involve settlement discussions between the firm and the FSA[1] and, separately, the matter may give rise to disputes between the firm and other parties which the firm wishes to settle. In order to reach settlements, the firm may wish to provide information to the FSA or, if relevant, to a third party and/or to make admissions about its conduct. To what extent can any such material generated be used against the firm subsequently if a third party seeks to bring civil claims against it[2]? Generally speaking, discussions that are genuinely[3] aimed at settlement are protected as though they were legally privileged, subject to various limitations[4].

1 For details, see para 5.116 ff below.
2 A separate question arises as to whether that material can be used against the firm in any Tribunal proceedings (if a settlement is not, ultimately, reached with the FSA). This is considered at para 6.68 below. Note that without prejudice communications are not protected under the FSMA 2000 in the same way as legally privileged material: see para 4.264 ff below. Hence, there is nothing, on the face of it, to prevent the FSA, the Tribunal or the ombudsman from requiring the firm to disclose such material.
3 The fact that a document is marked 'without prejudice' does not conclusively or automatically render it privileged. A court may seek to ascertain for itself whether the document concerned was genuinely a negotiating document: see *Buckinghamshire County Council v Moran* [1989] 2 All ER 225, CA and *South Shropshire District Council v Amos* [1987] 1 All ER 340, CA. But the rule does not apply solely to admissions: 'At a meeting of that sort the discussions between the parties' representatives

may contain a mixture of admissions and half-admissions against a party's interest, more or less confident assertions of a party's case, offers, counter-offers, and statements . . . about future plans and possibilities' – per Robert Walker LJ in *Unilever plc v Proctor and Gamble Co* [2001] 1 All ER 783.

4 See *Rush & Tompkins Ltd v Greater London Council* [1989] 1 AC 1280 and, for the limitations, *Muller v Linsley & Mortimer* [1996] PNLR 74, CA and *Unilever plc v Proctor and Gamble Co* [2001] 1 All ER 783, CA. For a more general discussion, see *Documentary Evidence*, Hollander & Adam.

Information provided to the FSA or the investigator

4.211 Communications between the firm and the FSA or an investigator are not generally legally privileged and, as already discussed[1], are not protected from disclosure by any general class of public interest immunity. In principle, therefore, any material that the firm produces for submission, and actually provides, to the FSA or an investigator may be capable of being required to be disclosed to third parties[2]. There are two additional points to note.

1 See para 4.195 above.

2 This is by no means an absolute rule and there may be circumstances when the document would be protected. For example, the document may contain confidential information which the firm had received from the FSA and which is protected under FSMA 2000, s 348 (see para 4.304 ff below). Alternatively, it may, in some circumstances, be possible for the document to be legally privileged.

4.212 First, the firm is likely to have a copy not only of the final document provided to the FSA but also of any drafts that were produced[1]. Those drafts would in principle also be disclosable documents. It may, however, be possible to produce them in a way that makes them legally privileged, for example if they were produced for the purpose of obtaining legal advice on the information that should be provided to the FSA. Care therefore needs to be taken.

1 Indeed, many computer systems store each version of a document automatically.

4.213 Second, the firm may have provided information to the FSA in interviews between the FSA and the firm's employees and the firm will often have copies of transcripts of the interviews[1]. Such transcripts could potentially be required to be disclosed to a third party, even if the interview was held compulsorily[2], save to the extent that they contain information which is protected under the FSMA 2000[3].

1 See para 4.230 below.

2 See *Wallace Smith Trust Co Ltd v Deloitte Haskins & Sells* [1996] 4 All ER 403 (Simon Brown LJ at 419), applied in *British & Commonwealth Holdings plc v Barclays de Zoete Wedd* [1998] All ER (D) 491.

3 FSMA 2000, s 348: see para 4.304 ff below. Note that this is limited in its effect in this context: the mere fact that the firm provides information to the FSA does not confer on that information a protection against disclosure from the firm to third parties. Note also that it may be possible for a court to order the transcripts to be disclosed with the relevant parts excised: see *Re Galileo Group Ltd, Elles v Hambros Bank Ltd* [1998] 1 All ER 545.

4.214 In some situations, the firm will produce information to the FSA in relation to the FSA's enquiries into another firm or person. Where the firm does so, there is a different concern, namely whether that can give rise to libel proceedings against the firm. A communication with the FSA where the FSA seeks evidence for its enforcement functions is probably protected by an absolute privilege against use in libel proceedings, but it is not clear whether information spontaneously (and perhaps maliciously) proferred to the regulator would do so[1].

1 See *Mahon v Rahn (No 2)* [2000] 4 All ER 41, CA.

Can the third party obtain material from the FSA?

4.215 The FSA's files could potentially contain a great deal of information that may assist a third party seeking to bring a claim against the firm. The FSA may have a report from its investigator, possibly transcripts of interviews, and the various documents which the firm and any other parties involved have produced for it or for the investigator. It will also have other material produced in the enforcement process which followed the investigation, such as a preliminary findings letter, the recommendation to the Regulatory Decisions Committee of what action to take, and the underlying material on which the recommendation is based[1]. Each of these documents could help the third party show that breaches were committed by the firm. The FSA may also have produced other material, such as schedules of investor losses, which could be of use to the third party in proving its losses. Is there a risk of the third party being able to obtain access to the FSA's documents in order to sue the firm?

1 The process which leads to the production of these documents is considered in Chapter 5 below.

4.216 The answer is that there is a risk, but generally speaking it is a lower risk. The court does have the power to order a person that is not party to the legal proceedings, like the FSA, to give disclosure of documents in certain situations[1]. However, material of this nature is likely to be protected under the FSMA 2000 as confidential information obtained by the FSA in the discharge of its functions which relates to the business or affairs of any person[2]. Where this is the case, since the FSMA 2000 does not expressly give the court any ability to override this confidentiality restriction, and since it would therefore be a criminal offence for a person to disclose such information[3], it is very unlikely that a court could order the FSA to give disclosure[4].

1 If one of the parties to the proceedings can demonstrate to the court that the FSA has documents which are likely to support his case or adversely affect the firm's case and that the disclosure is necessary in order to dispose fairly of the claim and save costs: see Civil Procedure Rules, Part 31, Rule 31.17. It is also possible that the court may summons FSA staff members to appear before it: see Civil Procedure Rules, Part 34.
2 FSMA 2000, s 348: see para 4.304 ff below.
3 See para 4.313 below.
4 See *BCCI v Price Waterhouse (Bank of England intervening)* [1997] 4 All ER 781 (Laddie J); *Re Galileo Group Ltd; Elles v Hambro Bank Ltd* [1998] 1 All ER 545 (Lightman J); *Barings plc v Coopers & Lybrand* [2000] 3 All ER 910, CA; and *Rowell v Pratt* [1938] AC 101.

4.217 There are some important caveats. First, if the material has been used in open court, for example in Tribunal proceedings in public relating to enforcement action that the FSA has taken, then it is unlikely to be confidential any more and will not therefore be protected from disclosure[1]. This may be an important caveat in practice, because civil legal proceedings may follow the conclusion of the regulatory enforcement process. Second, it is likely that the statutory protection does not preclude a court from ordering disclosure of the material by a person where that disclosure would be permitted under the Gateway Regulations[2].

1 FSMA 2000, s 348(4): see para 4.308 below.

2 The Financial Services and Markets Act 2000 (Disclosure of Confidential Information) Regulations 2001 (the 'Gateway Regulations'), SI 2001/2188: see para 4.312 below. This is the implication of the authorities cited at footnote 4 to para 4.216 above, particularly *Rowell v Pratt*, although the point has not been directly decided. Note that the Gateway Regulations (para 5) allow the disclosure of information for the purposes of civil proceedings arising by or under the FSMA 2000. On its own, this might seem to encompass breach of statutory duty claims under s 150, but s 349(1) makes clear that the disclosure is only permitted when made for the purpose of facilitating the carrying out of a public function; it is unclear whether claims by investors under s 150 would fulfil this criterion. For a further discussion of the Gateway Regulations, see para 4.312 below (and see in particular footnote 8).

What can the firm do to reduce the risk of disclosure?

4.218 There are three main steps that the firm can take to reduce the risk of disclosure. First, whilst the firm cannot influence the nature of the material that the FSA produces which might be discloseable, it has control over the nature and scope of the material that it produces. The risk of producing damaging material which might need to be disclosed to third parties needs to be borne in mind and weighed against the need to provide material to the FSA and the terms in which the material should be produced and provided.

4.219 Second, the firm needs to consider structuring the production of material in such a way as to ensure it is legally privileged. This will not always be possible but should at least be considered.

4.220 Third, if a privileged document is to be provided to the FSA, then it may assist the firm in maintaining the claim to privilege over that material to try to agree in advance with the FSA the terms on which the document is provided. If it is possible in the particular circumstances to agree restrictions on its use, then that should assist.

Practical steps to take in relation to interviews

4.221 From the perspective of the individuals within the firm, being interviewed by the FSA is often one of the most difficult parts of the process. We outline here some practical guidance relating to interviews, both voluntary interviews and compulsory ones[1], and, in particular, we address the following points:

- preparing for the interview;
- who should attend the interview?
- how will the interview be conducted?
- will there be a record of the interview?

1 As noted at para 4.121 above, the FSA has indicated that it will, if appropriate, first seek to conduct interviews on a voluntary basis. It should be noted that statements made in voluntary interviews do not attract the (limited) statutory protection against self-incrimination: see paras 4.53 above and 4.242 ff below.

Preparing for the interview

4.222 It is important that the individuals who are to be interviewed prepare themselves thoroughly for the interview. This should include reviewing the relevant documents, refreshing their memories and familiarising themselves fully with the main issues and areas on which they are likely to be questioned.

Who should attend the interview?

4.223 Although the FSMA 2000 does not require it, the FSA has indicated[1] that the individual may, if he wishes, be accompanied by a legal advisor. This gives rise to two questions. First, whether a legal advisor should attend the interview and, second, if so, then which legal advisor.

1 See the FSA Handbook at ENF 2.14.2 and 2.14.3(1).

4.224 If the individual is concerned about his own personal position, for example because he may have committed a criminal offence or is likely to be charged with misconduct, then he potentially increases his exposure by not having a legal advisor present. Where the individual is less likely to be viewed by the FSA as personally culpable, and is being interviewed more as a witness who has relevant information, then it is less clear that a legal advisor needs to be present. Nonetheless, this can often be helpful, to provide general support and to give an objective view of the interview afterwards.

4.225 As to who should attend, the difficult question is whether the firm's lawyers, whether members of the legal or compliance[1] department or outside counsel, can or should attend or whether the individual should be personally represented. The FSA's view is not clear from its guidance, but it has been the practice of investigators appointed by the Department of Trade and Industry to question the basis upon which the lawyer is present, to ask whether he also represents any others in relation to the enquiry and to consider whether there are any conflict of interest issues that might prejudice the investigation. Situations where the lawyer advises both the witness and his employer are identified as requiring particular care[2].

1 In some circumstances, it may be possible for this role to be fulfilled by the firm's compliance officer, if he is legally qualified or if the FSA is willing to allow a non-legal advisor to be present. This will not, though, always be appropriate, particularly if the compliance officer is also a potential witness.
2 See DTI Investigations Handbook, HMSO, Appendix C 'Notes for the guidance of inspectors appointed under Section 177 of the Financial Services Act 1986', paras 24, 31 and 32.

4.226 Why is this distinction relevant? Even if there has until this point been no conflict between the interests of the firm and those of the individual, there may be a possibility of a conflict arising in the future, for example if the firm wishes to take disciplinary action against the individual. Information may emerge at the interview which suggests that such action is appropriate. This would place in a difficult position a lawyer who attends the interview on behalf of both. Unless it was made clear that he was acting only for the firm, he may also be disqualified from acting for either[1]. The formal interview may therefore be the stage at which an individual needs to obtain separate legal advice, particularly if that individual is likely to be viewed by the FSA or the investigator as a suspect as much as a witness.

1 See the Guide to the Professional Conduct of Solicitors, 8th edition, 1999 at 15.03. The adviser therefore needs to be clear as to who he is advising. As indicated above, it is unclear whether the FSA would allow a lawyer who was representing only the firm to attend the interview.

How will the interview be conducted?

4.227 The FSA has indicated[1] that the individual will, in a compulsory interview, be given an appropriate warning. Although not made clear, this presumably relates to the consequences of providing false or misleading information or of not complying with the FSA's or the investigator's requests[2]. The FSA will also, in a compulsory interview, explain the limited use that can be made of the answers in criminal proceedings or proceedings for market abuse against the person[3].

1 See the FSA Handbook at ENF 2.14.3(2).
2 The consequences of non-compliance with formal requests are discussed at para 4.283 ff below.
3 This is discussed in more detail at para 4.242 ff below. This does not apply in a voluntary interview: see footnote 1 to para 4.221 above.

4.228 The FSA has given very little guidance on the conduct of the interview. How it is conducted will depend very much upon the circumstances[1]. Some general points can be made about how the individual might respond to questions, namely:

- that he should answer only within his own knowledge;
- that he should not speculate;
- that he should ask for time to consider the answer, where needed; and
- that he should generally not answer questions about documents that he has not seen until he has properly considered them.

The individual does not, however, have the right to refuse to answer a question on the ground that to do so might incriminate himself[2].

1 Additional considerations, outlined at para 4.248 ff below, arise when a person is interviewed under caution for the purpose of obtaining evidence for use in criminal proceedings.
2 This is discussed in more detail at para 4.242 ff below.

4.229 Generally, the FSA must act fairly[1]. This can only be judged properly based on the circumstances of each case. Nonetheless, it may be possible for lengthy questioning, particularly revisiting areas already covered by compulsory questioning, to be unfair and oppressive[2].

1 See *In re Pergamon Press Ltd* [1971] Ch 388. This was in a slightly different context, but it is thought that the same principles apply.
2 See for example *In re an Inquiry into Mirror Group Newspapers plc* [2000] Ch 194. Again, this was in a slightly different context, but it is thought that the same principles apply.

Will there be a record of the interview?

4.230 A record is kept of a compulsory interview, and the individual will be given a copy of it. This will normally be a tape-recording[1]. As regards voluntary interviews, the investigator will always make a record if the interviewee is the subject of the investigation and in other cases may make a record. If a record is made, it will give a copy to the person interviewed[2].

1 See the FSA Handbook at ENF 2.14.3.
2 See the FSA Handbook at ENF 2.14.2.

Requesting information from particular types of person

4.231 The breadth of the information gathering armoury available to the FSA, either directly or through investigators appointed by it, and the array of people against whom it can be deployed, should be apparent from the discussion above. The purpose of the following paragraphs is to discuss some of the particular issues which are raised by the imposition of these powers on three particular categories of person, namely:

- third parties unconnected to the firm;
- the firm's solicitors, bankers, auditors and actuaries; and
- other members of the same group as the firm, particularly overseas members.

Third parties unconnected to the firm

4.232 The principal point to have in mind is the breadth of possible involvement of unconnected third parties, whether or not they carry on any regulated business. Third parties can be involved to a varying extent in each of the four types of formal investigation outlined at para 4.108 ff above, including being required in some instances not only to produce documents or information, but also to answer questions, potentially even on oath. If they produce a document, then they can be required to provide an explanation of it. If they fail to comply with a requirement, they could be subject to proceedings for contempt of court or to a warrant to search their premises[1].

1 See para 4.283 ff below.

4.233 In addition, although on the face of it the FSA's general information gathering power can only be exercised against authorised persons and those connected with them, if it appears that a document is in the possession of a third person then that power may be exercised in relation to that third person. An unregulated third party, unconnected with any authorised person but for some reason holding documents for an authorised person, could therefore be required by the FSA to produce the relevant documents.

The firm's solicitors, bankers, auditors and actuaries

4.234 The firm's solicitors, bankers, auditors and actuaries (and those of other group members) can be required to provide documents or information, in exactly the same way as the firm, in any of the section 167, 168 or 169 investigations outlined above[1].

1 They are included as 'connected persons' in relation to s 167, 168(1), 168(4) or 169 investigations (see footnote 2 to para 4.130 above and FSMA 2000, Sch 15, Pt II), in relation to s 168(1) or (4) investigations, could be involved as a person who is neither the subject of the investigation nor a person connected with such a person, and, in relation to s 168(2) investigations, could be involved as a person who may be able to give relevant information.

4.235 There are, however, some limitations:

- many of the records of, or correspondence with, solicitors, but by no means necessarily all, will be covered by the doctrine of legal professional privilege and will be 'protected items' under the FSMA 2000, which a person cannot be required to produce, disclose or permit the inspection of[1];
- the doctrine of legal professional privilege[2] may also protect work carried out by other professionals (for example, accountants or actuaries) in circumstances where the main purpose of their work was to assist the lawyers to advise or for actual or contemplated legal proceedings, and in some situations may also protect communications with other third parties; and
- there is a limited protection for banking secrecy[3].

There is nothing to prevent the FSA from requiring, for example, auditors or solicitors (subject to legal privilege) to produce their working papers, even though some of these documents would not normally be discloseable to their own client[4].

1 Section 413 and see the discussion at para 4.264 below. Note (i) a lawyer can nonetheless be required to furnish the name of his client, and (ii) legal privilege effectively has its own definition under the FSMA 2000 for this purpose.
2 See para 4.189 ff above.
3 See para 4.267 ff below.
4 See *Chantrey Martin & Co v Martin* [1953] 2 All ER 691, CA.

Other members of the firm's group

Why might other group members be relevant?

4.236 The requirements that can be imposed on firms to provide information and documents either to the FSA or to an investigator can be imposed equally on a wide range of connected persons, including other companies within the same group as the firm. Indeed, the FSA regards the obligation on firms under Principle 11 to co-operate with it as extending to taking reasonable steps to ensure that other group companies co-operate with it[1]. Many of these other group companies may, however, be based overseas and therefore hold any relevant documents overseas.

1 See para 4.32 above.

Can the FSA require overseas companies to provide information to it?

4.237 As has been seen, the provisions are extremely wide. Why should an overseas company which may have little to do with the group's UK regulated business (or may even be an entirely unconnected third party) be subjected to the application of UK extra-territorial regulatory jurisdiction purely because, for example, the FSA believes the information to be reasonably required in connection with its functions in the UK, and even though the FSA is not alleging that the UK firm has been involved in any regulatory contravention[1]?

1 This would be a possible application of s 165.

4.238 There is a general principle of English law that legislation is not intended to have effect overseas unless Parliament has made clear in the legislation that it intended it to do so[1]. The FSMA 2000 does not expressly authorise or prevent the FSA, or an investigator appointed by it, from exercising its powers in order to require the provision of information held overseas, whether by a group company or by an unconnected third party. The FSMA 2000 does envisage the investigation powers applying to overseas bodies that are authorised persons, for example incoming firms[2], and to other bodies that commit specific contraventions such as breach of the perimeter[3]. But there is nothing to suggest that the investigation powers apply in respect of documents held overseas, or that they apply against connected overseas companies or wholly unconnected third parties based overseas. It is, thus, unclear what approach a court would take.

1 See, for example, *Re A B & Co* [1900] 1 QB 541 (Lindley MR at 544) and *A-G for Alberta v Huggard Assets Ltd* [1953] AC 420 (Privy Counsel). Similarly, save in exceptional circumstances, a court will not require a foreign bank which is not a party to an action to produce documents outside the jurisdiction concerning business transacted outside the jurisdiction: see *McKinnon v Donaldson, Lufkin and Jenrette Securities Corpn* [1986] Ch 482.
2 See, for example, the intervention powers in Pt XIII (discussed in Chapter 9 below). This is perhaps comparable with the position under the Insolvency Act 1986, s 221 which allows overseas companies to be wound up; hence Parliament was taken to have intended that the court's powers under s 236 could be used to require the production of documents held overseas: see *Re Mid East Trading Ltd, Lehman Bros Inc v Phillips* [1998] 1 All ER 577.
3 FSMA 2000, s 168(2).

Is the firm able to provide the information?

4.239 Providing information from connected companies overseas may cause problems. For example, the non-UK firm may owe obligations of confidentiality to customers or as a matter of law in its home jurisdiction, which under the relevant applicable law may or may not be overridden by the imposition of requirements extra-territorially from the UK. There may therefore be an important legal or practical bar to it providing the information. By way of example, this can be a particular issue for a firm that is connected with a bank in a jurisdiction which has strict banking secrecy laws. It may not be open to the overseas bank to release information to the UK institution or to the FSA. Indeed, to do so could be a criminal offence. But it is quite possible for the overseas bank to have information relevant to a regulatory enquiry in the UK, for example if funds used in a trade suspected of constituting market abuse were sourced from an account at the bank, or if that account was the destination of the proceeds of a particular investment which was the subject of an investigation. Similarly, data protection laws in some jurisdictions might be breached by the disclosure of the information, and in some cases this would be a criminal offence. The firm's exposure to breaches of the law overseas does not, though, necessarily give it grounds under English law for refusing to comply with the requirements imposed on it[1].

1 See *A v B Bank (Bank of England intervening)* [1992] 1 All ER 778: an injunction restraining the bank in New York was not 'reasonable excuse' for non-compliance with a notice under the Banking Act 1987, s 39 requiring the production of documents. A similar issue arises in the context of freezing orders: see *Baltic Shipping Co v Translink Shipping Ltd* [1995] 1 Lloyd's Rep 673 and see *Mareva Injunctions and Anton Piller Relief*, Gee, 4th edition from page 289.

How might the firm address these issues?

4.240 In practice, the firm is likely to want to assist the FSA to the extent that it can do so because:

- the FSA has made clear in its guidance on the obligation of co-operation under Principle 11[1] that it expects firms to take reasonable steps to ensure that group companies co-operate with it (although it has not specified that this includes overseas companies); and
- if the FSA does have difficulty obtaining information about a firm's business because of its group structure, this could, in a serious case, cast doubt on whether the firm continues to satisfy the threshold conditions, because of its close links with others[2], and could amount to grounds for the FSA to vary the firm's permission or even, in a particularly serious case, to cancel it.

1 See para 4.32 above.
2 The close links threshold condition: see para 2.39 above.

4.241 As ever, the answer will often be a practical one of maintaining a close and open relationship with the FSA and the investigator, which may enable such problems to be resolved by discussion. For example, the FSA may be able to obtain the information that it seeks through mutual assistance with the regulator or other authority in the relevant overseas jurisdiction.

Can the FSA compel information from a person who is suspected of a criminal offence?

4.242 The FSA can compel information to be provided by a person suspected of a criminal offence. In accordance with the decision of the European Court of Human Rights in the case of *Ernest Saunders*[1], the FSMA 2000[2] draws a distinction between the requirement that can be imposed upon a person to provide information and the use to which the information obtained in that way can be put. There is no right under the FSMA 2000 or the ECHR[3] to refuse to provide information or to answer a question required under compulsion in the investigation stage of the process on the ground of self-incrimination, but there are limitations on the uses which can be made of the answer.

1 *Saunders v United Kingdom* (1996) 23 EHRR 313.
2 This reflects the Financial Services Act 1986, s 105(5A) and (5B) and 177(6A) and (6B) introduced in the wake of *Saunders* by the Youth Justice and Criminal Evidence Act 1992.
3 This was recently reaffirmed by the House of Lords in *R v Hertfordshire County Council ex p Green Environmental Industries Ltd* [2000] 1 All ER 773 and by the European Court of Human Rights in the so-called Guinness 3 case: *IJL, GMR and AKP v UK* (2000) 9 BHRC 222 and [2001] Crim LR 133.

4.243 Generally, a statement made by a person to an investigator in compliance with an information requirement[1] is admissible in evidence in any proceedings (whether criminal or civil, and subject to any procedural rules relating to the admissibility of evidence). However, it is not admissible in criminal proceedings or proceedings for market abuse[2] against the person who made the statement, in that:

- no evidence relating to the statement may be adduced; and
- no question relating to it may be asked;

by or on behalf of the prosecution or the FSA, unless evidence relating to it is adduced or a question relating to it is asked in the proceedings by or on behalf of the person who gave it[3]. This is subject to the exception that the statement can be used in relation to criminal proceedings for perjury or for the criminal offences under the FSMA 2000 of providing false or misleading information to the FSA.

1 That is, a requirement to provide information imposed by an investigator under FSMA 2000, ss 171, 172, 173 or 175: see s 174(5). This provision does not, therefore, cover all statements made to the FSA: see para 4.245 below.
2 The application of this provision in the context of market abuse is considered at para 13.162 ff below.
3 FSMA 2000, s 174.

4.244 The protection is limited. If the FSA cannot use the statement in the criminal proceedings, then it can still use it in order to obtain evidence by other means which it can use in those proceedings. Indeed, the FSA has made clear that it will use what it regards as its fact-finding powers in this way[1]. In addition, the privilege relates only to statements; it does not prevent the use of any documents[2].

1 See Consultation Paper 17 ('Enforcing the New Regime'), December 1998, para 68. Contrast the implied undertaking against the collateral use of information obtained on disclosure or through a freezing order: see *A-G for Gibraltar v May* [1999] 1 WLR 998. In addition, an express undertaking against collateral use is normally required in respect of a freezing order. For further discussion, see *Mareva Injunctions and Anton Pillar Relief*, Gee, 1998, Chapter 19.
2 See *A-G's Reference (No 7) of 2001* (29 March 2001, unreported, CA).

4.245 It is possible for individuals to be required to provide, or voluntarily to provide, a statement in circumstances where this statutory protection against use would not apply. For example, an employee or officer of an authorised person could be required to provide information orally to the FSA under s 165[1], and that requirement would have statutory force, but any statement provided would not attract the protection of s 174 as it would not be made in compliance with an 'information requirement' for this purpose[2]. Equally, an approved person could be asked to attend a meeting with the FSA or provide a statement without the FSA using its statutory powers and would need to comply because of his obligations under Statement of Principle 4[3]. Again, this would not attract the protection of s 174. The same point could be made in relation to other employees of an authorised person, who could effectively be compelled to attend an interview because of the firm's obligations under Principle 11 and the regulatory expectation that those who work for authorised firms should be willing to co-operate with the regulator. Similarly, a statement provided entirely voluntarily would not fall within s 174. Nonetheless, the statutory protection reflects the position under the ECHR in accordance with the decision in *Saunders*. If the FSA tried to adduce in evidence a statement made under compulsion, to which s 174 did not apply, the ECHR may provide a means for the individual to try to have it excluded. It would, though, be difficult to argue that a statement provided entirely voluntarily (for example, by a person who had no obligation to co-operate with the FSA) should be excluded.

1 See para 4.59 ff above.
2 See footnote 1 to para 4.243 above.
3 See para 4.42 above.

4.246 It is not only individuals who may attract criminal liability under the FSMA 2000. The firm itself may have committed a criminal offence. But it is difficult to see how a firm could be protected by s 174 because it is difficult to see how it could be the firm, as distinct from particular individual employees or officers, that makes a statement to the FSA. Can a statement made by an employee or officer of the firm be used in evidence in criminal proceedings against the firm? There is no English or ECHR authority on this point, although its logic has been recognised by at least one member of the House of Lords[1]. It may be that the introduction of the ECHR will militate in favour of recognising such a right. In principle, companies have human rights in the same way as individuals and the *Saunders* protection should therefore apply to a company, whatever the limitations on the wording of s 174. Equally, companies can only act through individuals. Therefore, if the right is to have any value in the corporate context, the company ought to be able to claim the privilege against self-incrimination in relation to statements made by its officers or employees. It is not clear whether the FSA will accept this.

1 *Rio Tinto Zinc Corpn v Westinghouse Corpn* [1978] AC 547, per Lord Fraser (652) and see also Lord Wilberforce (617) and Viscount Dilhorne (632). It was unnecessary to decide the point in that case and the House of Lords declined to do so, although there were some indications that upholding such a claim would be stretching English Law. See also the Court of Appeal in *Sociedade Nacional de Combustiveis de Angola UEE v Lundqvist* [1990] 3 All ER 283.

4.247 Individual employees or officers being prosecuted for a criminal offence cannot claim to exclude statements from the company or other officers or employees on the grounds of privilege against self-incrimination[1].

1 See *Gavin v Domus Publishing Ltd* [1989] 2 All ER 344; *Tate Access Floors Inc v Boswell* [1990] 3 All ER 303.

The FSA's procedure in obtaining information where a criminal offence is suspected

4.248 The FSA has indicated[1] that, when its inquiries lead it to consider the institution of criminal proceedings against a person who has been required to answer questions under compulsion, fairness to the person concerned requires that he should be given an opportunity voluntarily to answer the FSA's questions so that his answers can be put to the criminal court in any subsequent prosecution. The FSA therefore will ordinarily afford a potential defendant an opportunity to submit voluntarily to an interview under caution conducted in accordance with the requirements of the Criminal Procedure and Investigations Act 1996 and the Police and Criminal Evidence Act 1984[2].

1 See Consultation Paper 17 ('Enforcing the new regime'), para 69, and the FSA's Response to Consultation Paper 17, para 99.
2 See the FSA Handbook at ENF 2.14.4.

4.249 It is important to note that this interview is voluntary on the part of the individual. This is consistent with the Police Code of Conduct, which makes clear that an interview under caution cannot take place once a police officer reaches the conclusion that there is sufficient evidence for a successful prosecution. The reason for this is that it is wrong for adverse inferences to be drawn from a person choosing to remain silent once that point has been passed[1]. The FSA could, however, probably still use its statutory powers to compel an interview[2], for example as part of the continuing regulatory investigation.

1 See *R v Pointer* [1997] Crim LR 676, *R v Gayle* [1999] Crim LR 502 and *R v Odeyimi* [1999] Crim LR 828.
2 See *R v Director of Serious Fraud Office, ex p Smith* [1993] AC 1, HL.

4.250 If the person does agree to be interviewed[1], he will be warned of his right to remain silent and the consequences of doing so and will be informed that he is entitled to have a legal adviser present. If already interviewed by the FSA under compulsory powers, he will be provided with the transcript or other record of the compulsory interview and an explanation of the difference between the two types of interviews. He will also be told of the limited use that can be made of his previous answers, as outlined above. The interview will be subject to the safeguards of PACE Code C[2].

1 See the FSA Handbook at ENF 2.14.4/5.
2 For details, see Archbold 2001, at 15–265 (and in particular from 15–294).

What are the consequences of refusing to answer questions?

4.251 It is always possible for a person to refuse to answer a question, whatever the consequences, so it is worth briefly examining the consequences of doing so. If a person refuses to answer questions in response to a compulsory requirement by the FSA, the primary consequence is that a court, if it decides he has done so without reasonable excuse, may treat him as though he had committed a contempt of court. It could therefore fine him or even imprison him. There may, in some situations, be reason for refusing to answer questions, for example if, contrary to the policy outlined above, a person against whom the FSA intended to bring a criminal prosecution was required to submit to a further compulsory interview. In those circumstances, the person would need to argue that he had a 'reasonable excuse' for not complying. These and some other possible consequences of failing to provide information to the FSA are outlined at para 4.283 ff below.

Can the FSA investigate firms' unregulated business?

4.252 Although, for the most part, the FSA is likely to be interested chiefly in a firm's regulated business, there is nothing to prevent the FSA from asking the firm questions about its unregulated business, or non UK business, or even from exercising its compulsory powers to require the firm to provide such information, if this information is relevant to the discharge of the FSA's functions.

Why is unregulated business relevant to the FSA?

4.253 Information relating to unregulated business could be relevant to the FSA in a number of respects, particularly regarding UK regulated firms. A number of examples follow.

4.254 First, the conduct of the firm's unregulated activities may be relevant to whether it continues to fulfil the threshold conditions[1]. The threshold conditions which are likely to be particularly relevant are, first, the need for adequate resources and, second, suitability (that the firm is a fit and proper person to be carrying on regulated business). The considerations relevant to suitability are set out at para 2.43 ff above. As will be seen, those are very general considerations, not in any way confined to the firm's regulated business or indeed its UK business.

1 For an explanation of the threshold conditions, see para 2.39 above. They do not apply to incoming firms that do not have a top-up permission.

4.255 Second, the conduct of the firm's unregulated activities may be relevant to whether it has failed to comply with any of the Principles for Businesses. As discussed at para 2.59 ff above, the scope of application of the Principles varies depending upon the Principle concerned and whether the firm is a UK firm or an incoming firm. However, it can be seen that the firm's activities overseas and/or its unregulated business may be relevant to whether it complies with the Principles.

4.256 More generally, issues which occur in the firm's unregulated, or non-UK, business may cause the FSA to ask questions about the firm's conduct of its regulated business. For example, issues might arise which raise questions about the firm's internal organisation, its controls and risk management systems and the training which it gives to its staff. These may lead naturally to the FSA wanting to know whether there are similar issues in its regulated activities.

4.257 Finally, the FSA has power under the FSMA 2000 to make rules applying to the carrying on by authorised persons of unregulated activities if this appears to it necessary or expedient for the purpose of protecting the interests of consumers[1].

1 FSMA 2000, s 138(1). Rules are to be interpreted as not applying to a firm with respect to the carrying on of unregulated activities unless and then only to the extent that a contrary intention appears: see the FSA Handbook at GEN 2.2.17.

How could the FSA investigate non-regulated business?

4.258 The FSA could invoke various powers in order to investigate such matters. For example it could use:

- the general information gathering power under s 165[1], on the basis that the information was reasonably required in connection with the exercise of its functions under the FSMA 2000;
- the power to commence an investigation under s 167[2], on the basis it appeared to the FSA there was 'good reason to do so', which expressly applies to investigating a part of the business of an authorised person which does not consist of carrying out regulated activities;
- the power to commence an investigation under s 168(4)[3], among other things on the basis that there were circumstances suggesting that an authorised person had contravened one of the Principles for Businesses or that an approved person was not a fit and proper person to be carrying on a controlled function.

1 See para 4.59 above.
2 See para 4.122 above.
3 See para 4.134 above.

Should the firm volunteer information regarding its non-regulated business?

4.259 A difficult question for the firm is whether it should volunteer information to the FSA regarding problems it is having with an unregulated activity, on the basis that this is information of which the FSA would reasonably expect notice under Principle 11[1]. The FSA has made clear that Principle 11, in so far as it relates to informing the FSA, applies equally to unregulated activity[2]. Indeed, the rules the FSA has made on the circumstances that need to be notified to it are not confined to regulated business, nor do they contain any particular territorial limits[3]. The answer is, therefore that the firm may need to notify the FSA of something that has happened that relates to its non-regulated activities. Whether a notification is required, and if so the extent of the notification, will depend upon the precise circumstances in the case.

1 Principle 11, Principles for Businesses: see para 3.41 ff above.
2 See para 2.60 above.
3 For a detailed discussion of what information needs to be notified to the FSA, see the FSA Handbook at SUP 2 and para 3.41 ff above.

OBJECTING TO THE FSA'S USE OF INVESTIGATION POWERS

Introduction

4.260 The breadth of the investigation powers available to the FSA, or investigators appointed by the FSA (or in certain circumstances the Secretary of State), should by now be apparent. The purpose of the following paragraphs is to outline the options available to a firm faced with an apparently unreasonable request for information or documents, or one with which, for particular reasons, it does not wish to comply.

4.261 We consider, first, what objection a firm might have to a particular request for documents or information, second, how it might go about making good that objection and, third, the potential consequences of not complying with a formal request.

What objection might you have?

4.262 Firms or individuals could have many reasons for objecting to providing information and it is impossible, and would not be useful, to try to produce an exhaustive list. We outline here some of the more common reasons for objecting and discuss briefly whether each is likely to be a legitimate reason for declining to provide the information.

4.263 Some of the more likely objections include the following:

- the material requested is protected by legal privilege;
- the material is the subject of a duty of banking confidentiality;
- the firm wishes to co-operate and should not be subjected to the exercise of a formal power;
- the request is contrary to the FSA's stated policy, unreasonable, oppressive or disproportionate;
- providing the information might incriminate an individual;
- providing the information might incriminate the firm;
- providing the information would give rise to difficulties for the firm in another jurisdiction.

Each is considered in turn, below.

The material is protected by legal privilege

4.264 The FSMA 2000 provides that a person may not be required to produce, disclose or permit the inspection of 'protected items'[1]. 'Protected items' means:

- communications between a professional legal adviser and his client (or a person representing his client) made (i) in connection with the giving of legal advice to the client, or (ii) in connection with, or in contemplation of, legal proceedings and for the purposes of those proceedings; or
- communications between any of the above persons and any other person made in connection with, or in contemplation of, legal proceedings and for the purposes of those proceedings; or
- items (i) enclosed with or referred to in any of the above communications, and (ii) made in connection with the giving of legal advice to the client or in connection with, or in contemplation of, legal proceedings and for the purposes of those proceedings, and (iii) in the possession of a person entitled to possession of them[2].

Communications or items are not 'protected items' if held with the intention of furthering a criminal purpose.

1 FSMA 2000, s 413.
2 It is not wholly clear what this is intended to cover, but it may be intended to address the principle that a non-privileged document does not become a privileged document simply because it is enclosed with a privileged document.

4.265 This complex provision broadly mirrors the doctrine of legal professional privilege and allows firms to decline to provide or disclose documents which are protected under it. However, because the FSMA 2000 effectively contains its own definition of what is legally privileged, rather than just incorporating the common law definition wholesale, firms need to take care in relying upon this provision. In particular, the definition is unclear in some respects and will need to be clarified by the courts. It is not clear that it does mirror precisely the current common law position regarding the extent of legal professional privilege[1]. For example, reference is made to communications between a lawyer and his client, whereas the common law protects a much wider category of documents. Importantly, the provision is static whereas the law develops constantly. Accordingly, in considering whether a particular document created, or to be created, will be protected from disclosure under the FSMA 2000 it must be measured as against this provision and not against the common law doctrine.

1 In some respects it seems to be wider than the common law position. In others, it may be narrower (for example, it probably does not protect 'without prejudice' communications, which the law normally treats as though privileged (see paras 4.210 above and 6.68 below), it is not clear whether internal communications within the firm for the purposes of obtaining legal advice would be protected, and it is not clear whether it would protect common interest privilege).

4.266 An additional difference between the statutory provision and the common law is the level of protection that it provides. Section 413 simply prevents the FSA from requiring the firm to produce, disclose or permit the inspection of the document. It is not clear whether it prevents the FSA from obtaining either the document or information regarding its contents from some other source[1]. Significantly, it does not prevent the FSA from asking a person (for example, a third party) if he is willing to provide a copy of it voluntarily. If the FSA does obtain the information from another source, then the provision does not prevent the FSA from making use of the information and does not give the firm any right to restrain its use. The firm may nonetheless be able to obtain an injunction to prevent the misuse of its privileged documents[2]. Additionally, if the material is to be used by the FSA in the Tribunal, then it may be possible to persuade the Tribunal not to consider it[3].

1 It refers to communications between 'a' professional legal adviser and 'his client', and does not therefore seem to be confined to situations where the firm holding the document is the client to whom the advice was given. However, this is far from clear.
2 *Goddard v Nationwide Building Society* [1987] QB 670, CA. The court will restrain a litigant from making use of privileged material. Whether it would restrain the FSA in circumstances where the FSMA 2000 contains provisions for the protection of privilege but does not include this protection may be open to question.
3 The Tribunal has a discretion to regulate its own procedure: see para 6.122 ff below.

The material is the subject of a duty of banking confidentiality

4.267 Confidentiality does not generally provide a basis for declining to produce material to the FSA. However, the FSMA 2000 does contain[1] a limited protection for one specific type of confidentiality, namely the banker's duty of confidence[2]. A brief explanation of the duty of confidence is given, before explaining the statutory protection it receives.

1 FSMA 2000, s 175(5).
2 Legislative respect for the banker's duty of confidence is not new. For example, similar protection was introduced into the Financial Services Act 1986 by the Companies Act 1989.

4.268 A bank owes its customer a qualified duty of confidence[1]. What amounts to a 'bank' for these purposes is unclear. It seems not to be limited to those institutions that are authorised to carry on a banking business, but quite how far it extends is a moot point[2]. Where a banker's duty exists, it extends to all information obtained in the course of acting as banker for the customer[3]. The qualifications[4] are that the duty does not preclude the disclosure of information:

- under compulsion of law;
- where there is a duty to the public to disclose;
- where the interests of the bank require disclosure; or
- where the disclosure is made with the express or implied consent of the customer.

1 See *Tournier v National Provincial and Union Bank of England* [1924] 1 KB 461.
2 One difficult question is whether a custodian would amount to a bank for these purposes. Whilst they did not address this question directly, the view of the Financial Law Panel is that the substance, rather than form, of the relationship is key and, citing Clerk & Lindsell, that the categories of confidence will evolve and expand in line with new commercial relationships and methods of conducting business: see Legal Uncertainties in the Secondary Debt Market, January 1997. Thus, for example, in the Panel's view, a syndicate lender that is not a bank is probably bound by a *Tournier*-style duty. Professor Jack's Committee on Banking Services: Law and Practice also reviewed in some detail the operation of *Tournier*, but did not address the question of what constituted a 'bank': see the report by the Review Committee, presented to Parliament in February 1989.

3 In this respect, it is wider than the normal duty of confidentiality which might apply to information which one person receives *from* another. It could include information which the bank receives about his customer from a third party because he is the customer's banker. It may not, though, be entirely clear whether information was obtained in the course of acting 'as a banker'. For example, the bank may obtain the information when carrying out foreign exchange transactions or executing share sales for its customer.

4 See *Tournier v National Provincial and Union Bank of England* [1924] 1 KB 461. For a more detailed discussion, see *Confidentiality*, Toulson and Phipps, 1996, Chapter XIV.

4.269 The FSMA 2000 provides that no person may be required under Pt XI to disclose information or produce a document in respect of which he owes an obligation of confidence by virtue of carrying on the business of banking, unless:

- he is the person under investigation or a member of that person's group;
- the person to whom the obligation of confidence is owed is the person under investigation or a member of that person's group;
- the person to whom the obligation of confidence is owed consents to the disclosure or production; or
- the imposing of the requirement with respect to such information or document has been specifically authorised by the FSA (or, if appropriate, the Secretary of State).

4.270 The protection is therefore extremely limited. It does not apply in favour of the person under investigation or members of its group, but only for unconnected third parties and it does not prevent the FSA obtaining the information from some other source. Moreover, the fourth exception demonstrates that it can be readily overcome.

The firm wishes to co-operate and should not be subjected to the exercise of a formal power

4.271 Whilst this may be an important practical objection, it is one which may best be made to the FSA itself in the context of a good working relationship. It is difficult to see any legal basis for making an objection on this ground, particularly since the FSA's policy[1] makes clear that, in some instances, for example due to the seriousness of the matter, the FSA will want to use its compulsory powers irrespective of whether the firm is willing to provide information voluntarily.

1 See para 4.16 ff above.

The request is contrary to the FSA's policy, unreasonable, oppressive or disproportionate

4.272 Objections such as these may be legitimate objections to the use of the FSA's powers in the particular case, remediable through the mechanism of judicial review or under the Human Rights Act 1998. This is a complex area and a detailed discussion is beyond the scope of this book[1]. It may, however, be helpful to give a flavour of how it might potentially apply. It can readily be seen from the discussion that follows that whether any objection or challenge is available, and on what basis, will depend very much upon the circumstances of the particular case.

1 Further discussion can be found in Chapter 16 below.

4.273 First, public law bodies owe duties to those affected by their decisions, the scope of which may encompass these sorts of objections. If, for example, the FSA decided to take a particular course of action based on irrelevant considerations, or perhaps different considerations from those set out in the FSA Handbook, or acted in a way that was objectively wholly unreasonable, then the decision may be susceptible to challenge. More generally, the FSA has to act fairly[1]. In addition, the FSA has indicated in relation to various of its powers, as well as in its general policy on the use of its enforcement powers, that it will seek to act in a way that is proportionate to the concerns giving rise to the use of the particular power[2]. If, to take an extreme example, it demanded an interview at 4 a.m. where there was no good reason for this, then the firm or individual may be able to object.

1 See *Hearts of Oak Assurance Co Ltd v A-G* [1932] AC 392 and *In re Pergamon Press Ltd* [1971] Ch 388 and see the cases at footnote 1 to para 4.286 below. But note that all the rules of natural justice probably do not apply to investigations: see *Herring v Templeman* [1973] 3 All ER 569, *Norwest Holst v Secretary of State for Trade* [1978] 1 Ch 201 and *Moran v Lloyd's* [1981] 1 Lloyd's Rep 423.

2 Proportionality is also one of the principles for good regulation: see para 2.21 above.

4.274 Second, the FSA has to act in a way that is ECHR compatible. Article 8 of the Convention contains a right to respect for privacy, which applies to individuals, even within the workplace, but it is not yet clear whether it applies to companies[1]. As discussed in more detail at para 3.30 above[2], the right is not an absolute one but can be overridden provided this is done in accordance with the law, for a legitimate aim and is necessary in a democratic society for various specified reasons. The test of necessity requires the FSA to consider whether there is in the particular case a pressing social need for the interference and whether the means employed are proportionate to the aim pursued. The test may be higher where the interference is particularly intrusive. This will normally enable the FSA or an investigator to carry out its investigation, but it requires the FSA or the investigator to consider the extent of the intrusion that is merited in the particular case and may therefore provide some parameters for the conduct of investigations. The need for proportionality in particular is likely to form the basis for individuals, and perhaps firms, to challenge or object to the use of the investigation powers on human rights grounds.

1 In *R v Broadcasting Standards Commission, ex p BBC* [2000] 3 All ER 989, the Court of Appeal held that a company had the right to complain under the Broadcasting Act 1996 that its privacy had been infringed, albeit whilst expressly not commenting on the application of ECHR, art 8.

2 For a more general discussion of the right, see *Law of the European Convention on Human Rights*, Harris O'Boyle and Warbrick, 1995, at Chapter 9.

Providing the information might incriminate an individual

4.275 Self-incrimination is not a basis for refusing to provide information under the FSMA 2000[1]. However, there are limitations on the use that can be made of self-incriminating statements that are obtained using compulsory powers. These are discussed at para 4.242 ff above.

1 This follows from, among others, *Bank of England v Riley* [1992] Ch 475, *Re London United Investments plc* [1992] 2 All ER 842, CA, and *R v Hertfordshire County Council, ex p Green Environmental Industries Ltd* [2000] 1 All ER 773.

Providing the information might incriminate the firm

4.276 As with para 4.275 above, self-incrimination does not provide a basis for refusing to provide information under the FSMA 2000. In addition, it is not yet clear whether a statement by an individual employee attracts the privilege against self-incrimination in the context of potential criminal proceedings against the company for whom he works[1].

1 For a more detailed discussion, see para 4.246 above.

Providing the information would give rise to difficulties for the firm in another jurisdiction

4.277 A problem which can arise in practice is that the provision of information to a UK regulator would potentially expose the firm to civil or criminal sanctions for breach of applicable overseas requirements, for example banking secrecy laws or data protection legislation. To what extent does this enable the firm to refuse to comply? Whilst the answer will always depend upon the circumstances, the courts have not always been sympathetic to such concerns[1] and the firm will often therefore need to find a pragmatic solution, usually in discussion with the FSA.

1 See for example *A v B Bank Ltd (Bank of England intervening)* [1992] 1 All ER 778, discussed at para 4.239 above.

How to object

4.278 In the first instance, it may be worth raising the objection with the FSA since an overly wide request for documents or information may arise from a lack of understanding of the situation on their part. Failing this, trying to make good the objection presents a number of difficulties, not least because the FSMA 2000 contains no procedure for appealing against the exercise of these investigation powers. The firm has no right of recourse to the Financial Services and Markets Tribunal in this regard.

4.279 There are, however, three possible options:

- the firm could simply refuse to comply with the request;

- the firm could make a complaint under the statutory complaints procedure; or
- the firm could bring a legal challenge to the FSA's, or the investigator's, decision to impose the requirement.

Refusal to comply with the request

4.280 The consequences of failing to provide information in response to a compulsory requirement are discussed at para 4.283 ff below. The firm would effectively be waiting for the FSA to take action against it for the failure to comply and then seeking to defend that action on the basis that the FSA's requirement was unlawful or unreasonable. This may in some circumstances be appropriate but, unless carefully handled, would be a relatively high-risk strategy, first because of the range of action the FSA could take as a result of the breach and, second, because of the serious consequences if the firm failed to establish that it was right for it to refuse to provide the information[1].

1 For examples of cases where this course of action has been taken, see footnote 1 to para 4.286 below.

Making a complaint

4.281 The complaints procedure, and the potential remedies which it provides, is considered at para 16.37 ff below. In practice, it is unlikely to provide a means for avoiding responding to a request for information. It is much more likely to be used as a means for making a complaint about the FSA's behaviour, and perhaps seeking some compensation, after the event.

Challenging the FSA in court

4.282 The procedure for bringing legal proceedings against the FSA in order to challenge its decisions is outlined at para 16.6 ff below. If the firm or individual wishes to take action which could prevent the FSA from pursuing its request, then this is likely to be the applicable route.

The consequences of not complying with formal requests

4.283 If the firm, or indeed any person, is subjected to a formal request for information from the FSA, or an investigator appointed by it (or where applicable by the Secretary of State), in the exercise of powers under the FSMA 2000, failure to comply could have a number of consequences as outlined below.

Contempt of court

4.284 The primary consequence is that the person on whom the requirement was imposed could be punished by a court as though he were in contempt of court[1]. This means he could be fined or, in a serious case, even committed to prison. The procedure is that the person imposing the requirement (the FSA or the person appointed to investigate) certifies to the court that the person has not complied and the court, if satisfied that he failed without reasonable excuse to do so, may deal with him as if he were in contempt of court.

1 FSMA 2000, s 177(1) and (2). This provision does not apply in relation to the provision of information under Principle 11.

4.285 One important question will be who, precisely, is the person on whom the requirement was imposed[1]. It may not be the firm, or solely the firm, but as will be seen these requirements can be imposed on a range of 'connected persons' which includes employees, officers and directors. Even if the requirement was imposed on the firm, rather than the individual, the individual may not be absolved from responsibility. The FSMA 2000 allows the court, where dealing with a body corporate, to treat not only the company but also any director or officer as being in contempt[2]. The meaning of the word 'officer' is not entirely clear, but it may include to some extent those who exercise managerial functions or are responsible for maintaining accounts or other records[3]. There is therefore scope for personal liability for certain of those involved in the firm's default.

1 For example, where an investigator writes to the firm's Compliance Director requesting information, is that a request imposed on him or on the firm? In most situations, unless the FSA specifies otherwise, it would be natural to expect that it had been imposed on the firm, not on the individual.
2 This reflects the position under RSC Order 45, rule 5 (incorporated into the Civil Procedure Rules by Schedule 1). In that context, it has been held that a director or officer who is aware of the requirement is under a duty to take reasonable steps to ensure it is obeyed and if he wilfully failed to take those steps then, unless he reasonably believed some other director or officer was taking them, could be punished for contempt: *A-G for Tuvalu v Philatelic Distribution Corpn Ltd* [1990] 2 All ER 216 (Woolf LJ). It seems that the mere fact that the person is a director is not in itself sufficient: see *Director General of Fair Trading v Buckland* [1990] 1 All ER 545.
3 There is no definition of the phrase 'officer' in the context of the FSMA 2000, s 177. It is not therefore clear whether it includes those (for example, the compliance officer) who exercise management over different parts of the firm but who are not normally counted as an 'officer' for company law purposes. However, FSMA 2000, s 400 defines 'officer' (for the purposes of that section) as meaning a director, member of the committee of management, chief executive, manager, secretary or other similar officer, or a person purporting to act in any such capacity, and an individual who is a controller. The inclusion of 'manager' is notable. This is defined in FSMA 2000, s 423 to include, very broadly, those who exercise managerial functions or are responsible for maintaining accounts or other records.

4.286 It is the ability to be excused by the court if it is not satisfied that the person acted 'without reasonable excuse' that allows firms not to comply in exceptional circumstances. However, the point is only relevant when the application for contempt is being considered and it would therefore be unsafe to rely on it save in fairly exceptional circumstances[1].

1 Cases in which a similar exception has been considered include the following: a journalist had a 'reasonable excuse' under the Financial Services Act 1986, s 178 for refusing to disclose his sources relying by analogy on the Contempt of Court Act 1981, s 10: *In re an Inquiry under the Company Securities (Insider Dealing) Act 1985* [1988] AC 660, HL. An overseas injunction restraining compliance was not a 'reasonable excuse' under the Banking Act 1987, s 39: *A v B Bank Ltd (Bank of England intervening)* [1992] 1 All ER 778. But a direction under the Insolvency Rules that a

section 236 interview should not be made available to the SFO could amount to a 'reasonable excuse': *In re Arrows Ltd* [1992] Ch 545. Unfair questioning may amount to a 'reasonable excuse': *In re Mirror Group Newspapers plc* [2000] Ch 194. See also *Re London United Investments plc* [1992] 2 All ER 842, CA.

Criminal offences

4.287 Second, there may be a possibility of a criminal offence having been committed. If a person were knowingly or recklessly to provide information which was false or misleading in a material particular in purported compliance with a requirement imposed under the FSMA 2000, Pt XI[1] or otherwise by or under the FSMA 2000[2], then that would be a criminal offence. Whilst it may in some circumstances be clear that a person has knowingly or recklessly provided false or misleading information, the precise scope of the offence is not entirely clear. It is likely that the deliberate provision of partial information which was true but misleading could be sufficient. An example would be to provide one piece of information which was true but, on its own, misleading, whilst withholding another piece of information that would provide the full picture. It is difficult to see that a simple failure to comply with a requirement to provide information could, without more, amount to a criminal offence[3].

1 FSMA 2000, s 177(4).

2 FSMA 2000, s 398(1). This would include providing false or misleading information in compliance with the firm's obligations under Principle 11: see para 4.27 above.

3 Among other things, the firm is unlikely to have provided any information. Against this, since firms are under a duty to be open with the FSA, it could perhaps be argued, depending upon the circumstances, that a failure to provide information amounts to providing information to the FSA that there is no relevant information, and that the offence could therefore be committed by omission.

4.288 To the extent that a firm commits any criminal offence, then any officer who consented to or connived in that conduct, or to whose neglect it is attributable, could personally be prosecuted for a criminal offence[1].

1 FSMA 2000, s 400 and see the discussion of this provision at para 11.31 ff below.

Other regulatory consequences

4.289 Third, the firm's failure to provide information could also have regulatory consequences, either because it amounted to a breach of Principle 11 for which the FSA could discipline the firm and/or any approved persons who were involved or because it demonstrated that the firm, or individuals who are approved persons, were not fit and proper, in which case it could lead to wider regulatory repercussions, for example the use of own-initiative powers[1] or the withdrawal of the individual's approval[2]. Under the old regime, a compliance officer who passed on to the FSA information which he had received from the business unit, was held personally liable to disciplinary action when that information was incorrect[3].

1 See Chapter 9 below.

2 See para 8.27 ff below.

3 See para 3.84 above.

Warrants

4.290 Finally, the FSA may be able to obtain a warrant to enter the relevant premises and seize the material. It needs to be borne in mind that the power to obtain a warrant is not available solely to remedy the situation where information has not been provided but is, in certain situations, available pre-emptively where there are grounds for believing that information would not be provided if it were requested. It is therefore a useful tool for the FSA, or an investigator, to obtain information or documents which it has the power to obtain under its compulsory powers.

4.291 The FSA does not expect to need to obtain a warrant to enter the premises of authorised firms. It expects authorised persons to grant access voluntarily as part of their duty to co-operate under Principle 11 and has also made a specific rule to require them to do so[1]. This rule exists notwithstanding that, in the course of the legislative history of the FSMA 2000, a proposed power to allow the FSA to obtain access to the premises of authorised persons without a warrant was dropped and the FSMA 2000 only therefore allows forced access to premises if a warrant is first obtained from a magistrate.

1 See paras 4.30 and 4.40 above.

When can a warrant be obtained?

4.292 A magistrate may issue a warrant if satisfied on information given on oath by or on behalf of the Secretary of State, the FSA or an investigator that there are reasonable grounds for believing that one of the following three sets of conditions is satisfied[1].

1 FSMA 2000, s 176(1).

4.293 The first set of conditions[1] is that:

- a person on whom an information requirement[2] has been imposed has failed (wholly or in part) to comply with it; and
- there are on the premises documents or information which have been required.

1 FSMA 2000, s 176(2).
2 A requirement to produce documents or other information in accordance with the FSA's powers under FSMA 2000, s 165 or in one of the formal statutory investigations listed at para 4.110 above: FSMA 2000, s 176(11).

4.294 The second set of conditions[1] is that:

- the premises are of an authorised person or appointed representative;
- there are on the premises documents or information in relation to which an information requirement could be imposed; and

- if such a requirement were to be imposed (i) it would not be complied with, or (ii) the documents or information to which it related would be removed, tampered with or destroyed.

1 FSMA 2000, s 176(3).

4.295 The third set of conditions[1] is that:

- one of the criminal offences which gives rise to an investigation under s 168(1) or (4)[2] for which there is a maximum sentence on conviction on indictment of two years or more has been or is being committed by any person;
- there are on the premises documents or information relevant to whether that offence has been or is being committed;
- an information requirement could be imposed in relation to those documents or information; and
- if such a requirement were to be imposed (i) it would not be complied with, or (ii) the documents or information to which it related would be removed, tampered with or destroyed.

1 FSMA 2000, s 176(4).
2 These are the criminal offences included among the contraventions listed at, respectively, paras 4.134 and 4.137 above.

What does a warrant do?

4.296 If the magistrate decides to issue a warrant, it authorises the police to[1]:

- enter the premises;
- search the premises and take possession of any documents or information appearing to be documents or information of a kind in respect of which the warrant was issued or to take, in relation to any such documents or information, any other steps which may appear to be necessary for preserving or preventing interference with them;
- take copies of or extracts from any documents or information appearing to be of the relevant kind;
- require any person on the premises to provide an explanation of any document or information appearing to be of the relevant kind or state where it may be found; and
- use such force as may be reasonably necessary.

1 FSMA 2000, s 176(5).

4.297 It is a criminal offence intentionally to obstruct the exercise of any rights conferred by a warrant[1].

1 FSMA 2000, s 177(6).

When will the FSA apply for a warrant?

4.298 The FSA has given very little guidance on when in practice it will apply for a warrant. It will consider using these powers when it has concerns about whether information requirements will be complied with and it believes that the statutory grounds are made out[1]. It will usually seek to ensure that the investigator is named on the warrant and entitled to accompany the police on the search.

1 See the FSA Handbook at ENF 2.15.2 and 2.15.4.

Practical guidance for firms

4.299 If the firm finds itself subject to a warrant to search its premises, it must obviously comply and not obstruct the exercise of the warrant. The firm does, however, have a legitimate interest in protecting any legally privileged material[1]. Therefore, whilst it is unlikely to have had the opportunity to review its files to identify any specific privileged documents before the warrant is executed, it may wish to assert a claim to privilege in relation to files which it believes may contain privileged material. This will place the authorities on notice of the issue and a mechanism will need to be found for ascertaining whether privileged material that can be withheld exists.

1 Legally privileged material is clearly protected, but the extent and basis of that protection is not entirely clear. In particular, compare the FSMA, s 413 and the Police and Criminal Evidence Act 1984, s 19(6). The former precludes the firm from being required to produce, disclose or permit the inspection of certain classes of privileged material: see para 4.264 ff above. The latter applies a test of whether a constable has 'reasonable grounds for believing' material to be legally privileged and may involve a different test of legal privilege. See also *R v Chesterfield Justices, ex p Bramley* [2000] QB 576.

USE OF INFORMATION OBTAINED BY THE FSA

4.300 In the following paragraphs we consider various issues relating to the use that the FSA may make of information which it obtains about firms and others and in particular:

- can the FSA disclose information which it has obtained to others?
- can the information be used in criminal proceedings?
- the action which the FSA may take as a result of its investigation.

Can the FSA disclose information which it has obtained to others?

4.301 In an atmosphere of increasing co-operation between regulators, particularly, but by no means exclusively, around Europe, it is quite possible that the FSA would regard information which it obtains about the firm or particular employees of the firm as needing to be disclosed to another regulator[1]. Examples include other UK regulators such as the exchanges or the home state regulator of an incoming firm. Even in relation to a UK regulated firm, the FSA may come across something relating to the firm's overseas operations of which it believes the relevant overseas regulator should be aware. Information could also be relevant to other prosecuting authorities such as the Serious Fraud Office.

1 'We have to recognise the increasingly international nature of much of the financial services business conducted in the UK. So an important part of supervision involves co-ordinated relationships with key foreign supervisors, including information sharing, regular meetings and joint visits': speech by Howard Davies, FSA Chairman, to the Swiss Bankers Association, 1 September 2000.

4.302 The FSA may therefore want to pass on to others information which it has obtained about the firm. To what extent is it allowed to do so? The FSMA 2000 contains a general prohibition on the disclosure of confidential information obtained under the FSMA 2000[1], breach of which is a criminal offence. This is, however, subject to various exceptions outlined below which, in very general terms, do allow the FSA to disclose information in the sorts of situations outlined above. We consider the prohibition and its exceptions in detail before looking at whether the firm has any ability to object to information being passed on in this way.

1 FSMA 2000, s 348. This is similar to the pre-existing position under, among others, the Financial Services Act 1986, s 179 and the Banking Act 1987, s 82 although there are some differences in the drafting of the section.

4.303 The question whether the FSA can be forced to disclose to third parties, for example those who wish to bring legal claims against the firm, information which it has regarding the firm is considered at para 4.215 ff above.

The prohibition on the disclosure of confidential information

4.304 Discussion of the prohibition can, for simplicity, be broken down as follows:

- to whom does the prohibition apply?
- what does it prevent?
- what information does it apply to?
- what are the exceptions?
- what are the penalties for breach?

There is an additional prohibition under the FSMA 2000, s 351 in relation to information obtained under the competition provisions of the FSMA 2000.

To whom does the prohibition apply?

4.305 The prohibition applies to a 'primary recipient' or any person obtaining the information directly or indirectly from a primary recipient.

4.306 Primary recipient means the FSA, the UK Listing Authority[1], the Secretary of State, any person who is or has been employed by any of the foregoing, a skilled person appointed to provide a report under s 166[2], or any auditor or expert instructed by any of the foregoing. Expert includes a person appointed to carry out an investigation by the FSA or Secretary of State under the FSMA 2000, Pt XI or appointed by the UK Listing Authority under the FSMA 2000, s 97. This would include an investigator appointed under any of the powers discussed at para 4.110 ff above or for an investigation in relation to a listed company under Chapter 15 below but it is not clear whether an investigator appointed to carry out an investigation into a collective investment scheme as discussed at Chapter 14 below would be a primary recipient unless he was also an FSA employee.

1 This is also the FSA: see para 15.6 ff below.
2 See para 4.72 above.

4.307 There is no express need for the person obtaining the information directly or indirectly from the primary recipient to have any knowledge that the information was covered by these provisions. The lack of knowledge, and suspicion, will, however, be relevant to whether that person commits any criminal offence in breaching the prohibition[1].

1 See para 4.313 below and see also footnote 2 to para 4.308 below.

What information does it apply to?

4.308 The prohibition applies to 'confidential information', which is defined as information which:

- relates to the business or other affairs of any person[1]; and
- was received by the primary recipient for the purposes of, or in the discharge of, any functions of the FSA, the UK Listing Authority, or the Secretary of State under any provision made by or under the FSMA 2000[2]; and
- is not prevented from being confidential information, either:
  - because it has been made available to the public by disclosure or use not prohibited under the prohibition[3], or
  - because it is in the form of a summary or collection of information so framed that it is not possible to ascertain from it information relating to any particular person.

1 This is sufficiently wide to include the business or affairs of a person other than the person under investigation: see *BCCI v Price Waterhouse (Bank of England intervening)* [1997] 4 All ER 781, 791 (Laddie J).
2 It was thought that whether the information was received for this purpose depends upon the intention of the primary recipient: see *BCCI v Price Waterhouse (Bank of England intervening)* [1997] 4 All ER 781, 791 (Laddie J). But this was disapproved by the Court of Appeal in *Barings plc v Coopers & Lybrand* [2000] 3 All ER 910, Lord Woolf MR indicating that the offence was only committed if the person concerned had knowledge of the circumstances which meant that the prohibition applied to the information.
3 This exception is important in practice, because documents are no longer confidential once they have been referred to in Tribunal proceedings in public: Tribunal proceedings are normally held in public (see para 6.32 below). Alternatively, documents may be referred to in a public hearing

in a civil court, for example on an application for an injunction or restitution order and, again, could lose their confidentiality as a result. When documents are put before a court to be read in evidence, the onus is on the person contesting that they did not enter the public domain: see *Barings plc v Coopers & Lybrand* [2000] 3 All ER 910, CA, Woolf MR.

4.309 It is immaterial whether or not the information was received by virtue of a requirement to provide it imposed by or under the FSMA 2000[1], and whether it was received for other purposes as well as the purposes outlined above[2].

1 Information provided 'voluntarily' or under Principle 11 would therefore be covered.
2 FSMA 2000, s 348(3).

What does it prevent?

4.310 The prohibition prevents the disclosure of the confidential information. Disclosure means providing it to someone who did not already have it. Hence, there is no disclosure of information when it is transmitted to a person who already had knowledge of it[1]. In addition, the so-called Gateway Regulations outlined below place restrictions on the purposes for which information may be disclosed and allows restrictions to be placed on the purposes for which information disclosed may be used[2]. Finally, where the disclosure of information is prohibited, it seems that a court could not order the relevant person to disclose the information[3].

1 See *BCCI v Price Waterhouse (Bank of England intervening)* [1997] 4 All ER 781, 796 (Laddie J) and *In re Gallileo Group Ltd* [1999] Ch 100 (Lightman J).
2 This is permitted by the FSMA 2000, s 349.
3 See the discussion at para 4.216 above.

What are the exceptions?

4.311 Confidential information may be disclosed with the consent of the person from whom the primary recipient obtained it and, if different, the person to whom it relates[1].

1 This is widely construed and would include, for example, customers of the firm to whose affairs the information relates: see *BCCI v Price Waterhouse (Bank of England intervening)* [1997] 4 All ER 781, 796 (Laddie J).

4.312 In addition, the FSMA 2000[1] allows the disclosure of information which is made for the purpose of facilitating the carrying out of a public function[2] and is permitted by regulations (known as 'Gateway Regulations') made by HM Treasury. Both of these conditions need to be complied with before confidential information can be disclosed[3]. The Gateway Regulations[4] are complex and in very broad terms the disclosures that they permit include the following:

- by the FSA, the Secretary of State or HM Treasury, or an employee of or auditor or expert instructed by the FSA or the Secretary of State, to any person, or by any person[5] to the FSA, the Secretary of State or HM Treasury, for the purpose of assisting or enabling them to discharge any of their public functions[6];

- by any person for the purposes of criminal investigations or proceedings, whether in the UK or elsewhere[7];
- broadly, by any person[8] for the purposes of, among other things, civil proceedings arising under or by virtue of the FSMA 2000 (and certain other legislation)[9], proceedings before the Tribunal, any other civil proceedings to which the FSA is (or is proposed to be) party, proceedings under the Company Directors Disqualification Act 1986 and certain proceedings under the Insolvency legislation[10];
- to comply with an EEA obligation[11];
- in relation to so-called 'single market directive information'[12], disclosures to certain limited bodies, in some circumstances subject to further conditions, and disclosures by the same categories of bodies for certain purposes[13];
- in relation to information not subject to restrictions under the Directives, disclosures by any person to a range of bodies for the purposes of enabling or assisting them to discharge specified functions[14] or by any of those bodies to any person for the purpose of discharging the same functions[15], or to various disciplinary bodies for the purposes, broadly, of disciplinary proceedings initiated or which may be initiated by them[16] and by each disciplinary body to any person for the same purposes[17].

The Gateway Regulations allow information to be disclosed subject to conditions on its use[18]. Where such a condition is imposed, the relevant person commits a criminal offence if he discloses the information in breach of the condition without the consent of the person who disclosed it to him[19].

1 FSMA 2000, s 349.
2 For a definition, see the FSMA 2000, s 349(5).
3 There is no requirement to inform the person to whom the information relates of the disclosure. Contrast the position where the police wish to disclose confidential information: 'In order to safeguard the interests of the individual, it is, in my judgment, desirable that where the police are minded to disclose, they should, as in this case, inform the person affected of what they propose to do in such time as to enable that person, if so advised, to seek assistance from the court. In some cases, that may not be practicable or desirable, but in most cases that seems to me to be the course that should be followed': Kennedy LJ in *Woolgar v Chief Constable of the Sussex Police* [1999] 3 All ER 604, CA.
4 The Financial Services and Markets Act 2000 (Disclosure of Confidential Information) Regulations 2001, SI 2001/2188.
5 The phrase 'by any person' is used as shorthand. The Regulations refer to a primary recipient or a person obtaining confidential information directly or indirectly from a primary recipient. As indicated above, this is the test for those who are bound by the statutory confidentiality restriction.
6 Gateway Regulations, reg 3. This is subject to any applicable 'directive restrictions' – ie under the Investment Services Directive, art 25, the Banking Consolidation Directive, art 30, the Third Life Insurance Directive, art 15, the Third Non-Life Insurance Directive, art 16 the UCITS Directive, art 50, and the Listing Particulars Directive, art 25: see reg 3(3).
7 Gateway Regulations, reg 4. 'Criminal investigation' means an investigation of any crime, including an alleged or suspected crime, and an investigation of whether a crime has been committed: reg 2.
8 The rules relating to those to whom such information can be disclosed are complex: see Gateway Regulations, reg 5.

9 This appears to be a broad phrase, capable of encompassing not only proceedings brought by the FSA (for example, for an injunction or a restitution order: see para 7.43 ff below), but potentially also proceedings for breach of statutory duty under FSMA 2000, s 150 (see para 10.27 ff below). Note that in order for the gateway to apply, the disclosure must be made for the purpose of facilitating the carrying out of a public function: FSMA 2000, s 349(1)(a). It is not clear whether this would always exclude the use of the gateway in relation to private civil law claims: in *Melton Medes v Securities and Investments Board* [1995] 3 All ER 880, it seems to have been accepted by Lightman J that this may be relevant to the SIB's responsibilities for the protection of investors and for the maintenance of proper standards of integrity and fair dealing. The same argument could be made in relation to the FSA (depending upon the circumstances).

10 Gateway Regulations, reg 5.

11 Gateway Regulations, reg 6.

12 That is, confidential information received by the FSA in the course of discharging its functions as competent authority under any of the single market directives (these are listed at para 2.12 above). The gateway also encompasses information received under the UCITS Directive.

13 Gateway Regulations, regs 8 to 10.

14 Gateway Regulations, reg 12(1)(a). The bodies concerned include (among others) recognised investment exchanges and clearing houses, the Takeover Panel, the Society of Lloyd's, a designated professional body, a skilled person appointed under FSMA 2000, s 166 (see para 4.72 ff above), a person appointed to conduct a statutory investigation (see para 4.110 ff above), an auditor or actuary, the Occupational Pensions Regulatory Authority, overseas regulators, the ombudsman (see Chapter 12 below), and the Pensions Ombudsman. The functions specified in relation to each are widely drawn. For a full list, see Schedules 1 and 2 to the Regulations. Note the limitations on the confidential information to which reg 12 applies: see reg 11.

15 Gateway Regulations, reg 12(2).

16 Gateway Regulations, reg 12(1)(b). The disciplinary proceedings concerned include those relating to (among others) (i) the exercise of professional duties by barristers, solicitors, auditors, accountants, valuers or actuaries, and (ii) the discharge of duties by officers or servants of the Crown, the FSA, the Takeover Panel and various other bodies.

17 Gateway Regulations, regs 12(3).

18 Gateway Regulations, reg 7. Note that such conditions cannot be placed on the FSA, the Secretary of State HM Treasury or the Bank of England.

19 FSMA 2000, s 352(3) and Gateway Regulations, reg 7.

What are the penalties for breach?

4.313 Breach of the prohibition against disclosure, or of any restrictions on use imposed under the gateway regulations, constitutes a criminal offence[1] unless the person proves that[2]:

- he did not know and had no reason to suspect that the information was confidential information; and
- he took all reasonable precautions and exercised all due diligence to avoid committing the offence.

It is not clear from the FSMA 2000 whether the above two defences are alternative or whether the defendant has to prove both. Logically, they ought to be alternatives, since they are dealing with different situations.

1 FSMA 2000, s 352(1).

2 FSMA 2000, s 352(6).

4.314 Breach of the prohibition does not confer a personal cause of action in favour of those whose consent to the disclosure was required[1].

1 See *Melton Medes Ltd v Securities and Investments Board* [1995] 3 All ER 880.

Can the firm object to the FSA providing information to others?

4.315 The FSA's decision to provide information to another regulator is not one in which the firm has any right to become involved. Indeed, the firm will not normally know about any contact there may be between the FSA and any other regulators or prosecuting authorities. It is therefore very rare that the firm can object.

4.316 In one situation, the Human Rights Act 1998 may provide grounds for the firm to object to the FSA providing particular information to a particular overseas regulator. That is if the relevant overseas regulator does not provide equivalent ECHR protections for the firm or individual employees. In that situation, it may be objectionable on ECHR grounds for the FSA to provide the particular information to the overseas regulator, but this will depend very much on the precise circumstances. For example, if the overseas jurisdiction does not recognise any privilege against self-incrimination, then it may arguably be wrong for the FSA to provide a regulator in that jurisdiction with a record of an interview with an individual who may have committed a criminal offence there.

Use of information in criminal proceedings

4.317 Generally speaking, a statement made by a person to the FSA in response to the exercise of compulsory investigation powers[1] cannot be used in criminal proceedings against that person, except proceedings for perjury or for providing false or misleading statements to the FSA. The statement can, however, be used as a means for obtaining evidence from other parties which can be used in the proceedings[2].

1 The statutory protection does not, however, encompass all of the compulsory investigation powers and does not apply to statements tendered voluntarily: see para 4.245 above. It also does not prevent other evidence (for example, documentary evidence) compulsorily obtained from the person from being used against him.

2 For a more detailed discussion see para 4.242 ff above.

4.318 Since the FSA regards its investigation powers as fact-finding powers, it is likely in practice that the approach which the FSA will take will be to obtain the strongest possible evidence by whatever means and then to consider what action it is appropriate for it to take and what evidence is admissible for the purpose of taking such action.

Action which the FSA may take as a result of the investigation

4.319 The main purpose of the investigation is for the FSA to gather the facts relating to the problem[1], so that it can decide what regulatory action should be taken. It is important to realise that the investigation does not necessarily lead to disciplinary charges being brought, nor is it confined to that. Rather, there is a whole range of options for enforcement action open to the FSA.

1 See the FSA Handbook at ENF 2.11.1.

4.320 The various options available generally are as follows:

- in relation to firms, the FSA could decide to:
  - — institute disciplinary proceedings (see para 7.7 ff below),
  - — vary the firm's permission (see para 9.7 ff below),
  - — cancel the firm's permission (see para 9.239 ff below),
  - — issue, or apply for, a restitution order (see para 7.43 ff below),
  - — apply for a civil injunction (see para 7.97 ff below),
  - — start insolvency proceedings in relation to the firm (see the FSA Handbook at ENF 10),
- in relation to individuals who are approved persons, the FSA could decide to:
  - — institute disciplinary proceedings (see para 8.4 ff below),
  - — withdraw the person's approval (see para 8.27 ff below),
  - — make a prohibition order (see para 8.44 ff below),
  - — make, or apply for, a restitution order (see para 8.81 ff below),
  - — apply for a civil injunction (see para 8.77 ff below),
- in relation to individuals who are not approved persons, the FSA could decide to:
  - — make a prohibition order (see para 8.44 ff below),
  - — make, or apply for, a restitution order (see para 8.81 ff below),
  - — apply for a civil injunction (see para 8.77 ff below),
- in relation to any firm or person, whether or not regulated, the FSA could decide to:
  - — prosecute various offences (see para 11.5 ff below),
  - — provide information to another regulatory or prosecuting authority whether in the UK or overseas (see para 4.312 above), or
  - — commence proceedings for market abuse (see Chapter 15 below).

4.321 The FSA has additional powers applicable in specific situations, such as those enabling it to address market abuse (see Chapter 13 below), to deal with issues relating to regulated collective investment schemes (see Chapter 14 below) and relating to its enforcement function in relation to listed companies (see Chapter 15 below).

4.322 The basis for deciding whether to pursue each of these options is considered in the Chapter where the particular course of action is discussed and the procedure for the FSA to do so is also outlined[1].

1 There are two main procedures which are discussed in detail in, respectively, Chapters 5 and 9 below. Which applies is specified in the discussion of each type of enforcement action. Note that in relation to some types of enforcement action, there is no specified procedure (and, again, where this is the case it is specified).

5 The disciplinary and enforcement process

CONTENTS

Introduction	**199**
Nature of the procedure	**204**
The procedure in detail	**211**

INTRODUCTION

An overview of Chapter 5

5.1 In this chapter, we review the FSA's procedure where it wishes to impose disciplinary sanctions or take certain other enforcement measures. We review the process from the conclusion of the FSA's investigation until the question of disciplining the firm or individual or imposing the relevant sanction is resolved by mutual agreement, finally determined by the FSA or referred for decision by the Tribunal. The procedures of the Tribunal are reviewed in Chapter 6 below.

5.2 The question whether the FSA will impose disciplinary sanctions must not be viewed in isolation. As has been seen[1], a regulatory breach can give rise to a range of potential consequences, only some of which are disciplinary in nature. The possible enforcement action which the FSA can take, and the circumstances when the FSA is likely to consider taking each, including its policy on disciplinary action, are considered mainly in Chapters 7, 8 and 9 below. We concentrate here on the process.

1 A list of various potential enforcement consequences can be found at para 4.320 above.

Other situations where the same procedures apply

5.3 The procedure outlined in this chapter, known as the warning/decision notice procedure, applies not only where the FSA wishes to impose disciplinary sanctions against firms and approved persons, but also where the FSA seeks to take any of the following enforcement measures[1]:

- impose a restitution order[2];
- cancel a firm's permission otherwise than at its request[3];
- impose a prohibition order against an individual[4];
- withdraw the approval of an approved person[5];
- impose a sanction for market abuse[6];
- revoke the authorisation or, as appropriate, recognition of a unit trust scheme[7], an open-ended investment company[8], or a recognised collective investment scheme[9];
- disqualify an auditor or actuary[10];
- make a disapplication order in respect of a professional firm[11]; and
- decline applications to revoke or vary certain requirements, directions or orders already imposed[12].

1 Warning and decision notices are also required to be issued in certain non-enforcement situations, such as when the FSA proposes to refuse an application for a Part IV permission (see FSMA 2000 , s 52).
2 FSMA 2000, s 385 and see para 7.43 ff below.
3 FSMA 2000, s 54 and see para 9.239 ff below.
4 FSMA 2000, s 57 and see para 8.44 ff below.
5 FSMA 2000, s 63 and see para 8.27 ff below.
6 FSMA 2000, s 126, and see para 13.187 ff below.
7 FSMA 2000, s 255 and see para 14.47 ff below.
8 FSMA 2000, s 262 and the Open-Ended Investment Companies Regulations 2001, SI 2001/1228 and see para 14.102 ff below.
9 FSMA 2000, s 280 and see para 14.135 ff below.
10 FSMA 2000, s 345.
11 FSMA 2000, s 331.
12 FSMA 2000, ss 58, 200, 260, 269, 321 or 331.

5.4 Most of the above are outlined in detail elsewhere in this book. Where appropriate, reference is made to the warning notice and decision notice procedure outlined here and any specific points (for example in relation to the contents of the notices or the identity of those upon whom they must be served) are highlighted.

5.5 This list is not however exhaustive of all the enforcement action which the FSA can take. An alternative procedure, known as the supervisory notice procedure, applies to various other courses of action which the FSMA 2000 allows the FSA to take. The supervisory notice procedure is discussed in detail in

Chapter 9 below in the context of variations of permission, but is also applicable to certain other types of action[1]. Again, where the supervisory notice procedure applies to a particular course of action, this is made clear in the discussion of the relevant action.

1 For a full list, see para 9.105 below.

5.6 There are separate procedures, outlined in Chapter 15 below, for the exercise of the FSA's powers in relation to listed companies. In that context, the FSA acts in its capacity as the UK Listing Authority and separate, self-standing procedures apply[1].

1 In practice, as is outlined in Chapter 15 below, those procedures are very similar to those discussed here.

5.7 The procedures outlined here do not apply to, among others, the FSA's decisions to exercise its information gathering and investigation powers[1], to prosecute criminal offences[2], and to apply to the courts for injunctions or restitution orders[3] or insolvency orders[4]. The procedure applicable to each of these decisions is discussed where the action itself is considered. In addition, there is a modified procedure in relation to fines for the late submission of reports to the FSA[5].

1 These are discussed in Chapter 4 above.
2 This is outlined in Chapter 11 below.
3 See Chapter 7 below.
4 Insolvency orders are not reviewed in this book. The FSA's powers in respect of insolvency are discussed in the FSA Handbook at ENF, Chapter 10.
5 For details, see the FSA Handbook at DEC 4.5.2.

Outline of the procedure

5.8 Before looking at the procedure in detail, it may be helpful to have an overview of how it works. The procedure is summarised in the chart which appears at figure 5.1 overleaf. There are six parts to the process, four of which are covered in this chapter.

5.9 The initial stage, discussed in Chapter 4, is the fact-finding investigation undertaken by the FSA, or on its behalf by an investigator, when it becomes aware of the regulatory issue that has arisen. The primary purpose is to give the FSA a command of the facts, so that it is in a position to assess properly what regulatory action it should take.

5.10 The first stage covered in this chapter[1] arises where the FSA's investigation is nearing its conclusion. At that stage, the FSA normally issues a preliminary findings letter, giving the firm the opportunity to agree with, dispute or correct the facts as the FSA then sees them. Having done so, and having considered the response, the FSA staff concerned decide whether or not to make a recommendation to the decision-making body to set the enforcement process in motion. In some circumstances, no preliminary findings letter is issued.

1 See para 5.40 ff below.

5.10 The disciplinary and enforcement process

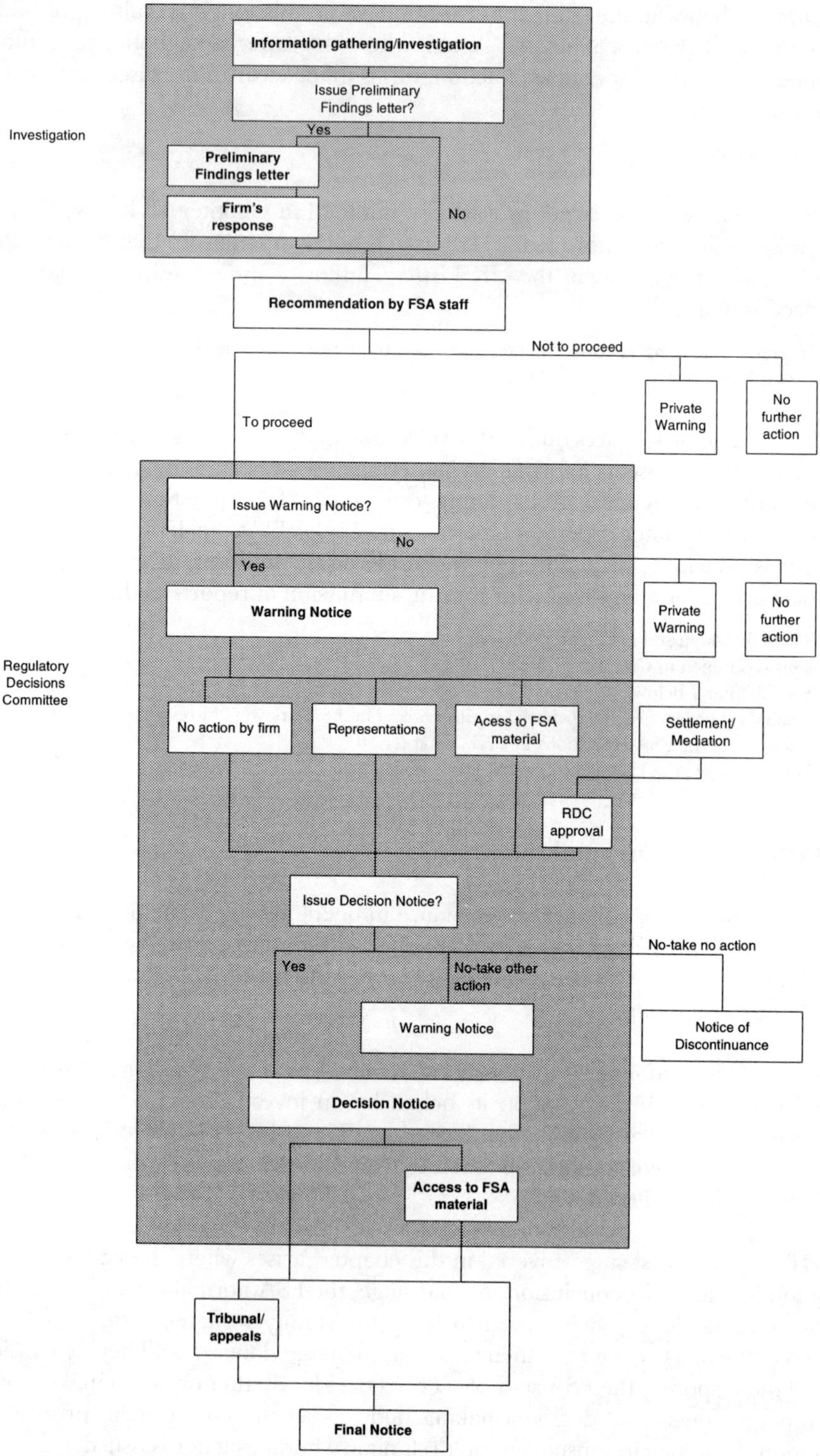

Figure 5.1

5.11 The second stage[1] is the consideration of the recommendation and, if appropriate, the issue of a so-called 'warning notice' by the FSA, a decision which in most instances is made by a body called the Regulatory Decisions Committee (or 'RDC'). As will be seen, the RDC is to some extent independent of the FSA and entirely separate from the enforcement staff who have investigated the matter. It is the RDC that decides whether to institute the enforcement process by issuing a warning notice, informing the firm that the FSA proposes to take a particular course of action against it and giving it the opportunity to review the FSA's file, make representations and enter into settlement discussions, and possibly a mediation, with a view to disposing of the matter.

1 See para 5.66 ff below.

5.12 The third stage[1] is where, following the process of representations and settlement discussions, the RDC reaches a decision on the appropriate action to take and if it decides that it should continue with the action it had proposed, it issues a 'decision notice'. If it now proposes a different course of action, then it may need to issue another warning notice. Once a decision notice has been issued, although the matter has been decided so far as the FSA is concerned, it has still not been finally determined as against the firm, which has the right to refer the matter to the Financial Services and Markets Tribunal.

1 See para 5.162 ff below.

5.13 The next stage is therefore the reference to the Tribunal, which is an independent body run by the Lord Chancellor's department, which also runs the Court Service. The nature and procedures of the Tribunal are reviewed in Chapter 6 below. It is important to appreciate that the Tribunal is not an appeal body, but a tribunal of first instance, able to consider all of the evidence, whether or not available to the FSA, and to reach its own decision on what action it is appropriate for the FSA to take. In some cases, there may be a right of appeal from the Tribunal, but only on points of law.

5.14 The final stage[1], and the fourth stage covered in this chapter, is when the action taken by the FSA takes effect, either because the firm or individual has not elected to refer the matter to the Tribunal or because the Tribunal has reached a decision and any further appeals have also been disposed of. At this stage, the FSA issues a 'final notice'. The action then takes effect.

1 See para 5.188 ff below.

5.15 Very little of this process can be found in the FSMA 2000. For example, there is no mention of the RDC. The FSMA 2000 contains just the framework, requiring warning notices, decision notices and final notices to be issued in certain circumstances and requiring decisions to be taken with a degree of separation of functions within the FSA. It also provides some protections for the individual or firm subjected to the process. The details of the procedure are to be found in the FSA's rules and, in particular, the Decision-making Manual.

5.16 Although the procedure has a number of stages, and in complex cases is likely to take a long time to complete, it need not always be implemented in a way that is lengthy and complicated. The procedure has to fit a range of different scenarios across the entire regulated community, from single person firms to international investment banks, and from single issue problems to complex disputes involving several firms and/or individuals and large numbers of consumers. The process therefore needs to have the flexibility to deal with a diverse range of situations.

NATURE OF THE PROCEDURE

What is the regime designed to achieve?

5.17 The shape of the disciplinary process was the subject of a great deal of debate within the consultation process which preceded the FSMA 2000. There were two main concerns to be addressed. First, there is a tension between the need for an efficient and effective process from the FSA's point of view and the need for the process to be fair from the point of view of those who are subjected to it. Second, it needs to comply with the ECHR fair trial guarantees implemented in the UK under the Human Rights Act 1998.

Efficient yet fair?

5.18 One of the important features of the previous regime for investment business, which both the FSA and, largely, the regulated community wanted to preserve, was that the majority of disciplinary issues were resolved by agreement between regulator and regulated, rather than by being pursued to a final conclusion in the appropriate tribunal. From the FSA's point of view, settlement is an effective means of enforcing the regime without the need to devote the resources which would be required if every disciplinary case were disputed. It also relieves the FSA of the uncertainty inherent in the outcome of a tribunal process and therefore the prospect of losing enforcement cases. From the firm's point of view, settlement allows the firm to put the issue behind it and move on, and to avoid incurring the substantial cost and significant amount of management time which would be involved in taking a case to its conclusion. In principle, therefore, the use of settlement was, and is, seen by all concerned as an important part of the regulatory process.

5.19 However, the settlement process under the old regime had tended to leave firms with a sense that they had been unfairly treated. This arose particularly from the fact that any discussions were held with those who had investigated the firm. This process tended to leave firms feeling that the regulator had already reached a decision and that there was no real opportunity to have anyone listen to their case, at least short of taking the matter to a formal tribunal (which the firm might not want to do for a number of reasons). The risk of enacting a new regime which perpetuated this was that the process would be perceived as unfair, with the result either that firms would be increasingly willing to take cases to a conclusion before the Tribunal, resulting in a less efficient and more costly system of enforcement, or that firms would remain unwilling to take cases to the Tribunal but their sense of grievance would remain and over the longer term would be damaging to the relationship between regulator and regulated. Faced with these tensions, the challenge was to devise a system which would preserve the efficient and effective disposal of enforcement cases, whilst at the same time enabling firms to feel they had been treated fairly.

Impact of the Human Rights Act 1988

5.20 An additional complication was provided by the Human Rights Act 1998, which requires the FSA, as a public body, to act in a way that is ECHR compatible. That includes, among other things, the right under art 6(1), where a person's civil rights and obligations or any criminal charge against him are being determined, to a fair trial within a reasonable time by an independent and impartial tribunal established by law[1]. It is likely that the FSA's enforcement proceedings involve the determination of the firm's civil rights and obligations, attracting this protection[2].

1 For an outline of the safeguards that this involves, see para 6.26 ff below.

2 See, for example, *König v Germany* (1978) 2 EHRR 170, *Le Compte, Van Leuven and De Meyere v Belgium* (1981) 4 EHRR 1, *Albert and Le Compte v Belgium* (1982) 5 EHRR 533 and *Benthem v Netherlands* (1985) 8 EHRR 1. In *R v Securities and Futures Authority, ex p Fleurose* [2001] All ER (D) 189, it was common ground that art 6(1) applied to the disciplinary proceedings in question.

5.21 Moreover, certain enforcement proceedings may constitute the determination of a 'criminal charge' for ECHR purposes, requiring the various additional safeguards under arts 6(2) and 6(3)[1]. Whether a particular matter amounts to the determination of a 'criminal charge' depends not upon whether the FSMA 2000 describes it as a criminal offence but upon a separate set of principles developed by the European Court of Human Rights[2]. There are three main factors taken into account in determining whether proceedings are civil or criminal for this purpose namely:

- the characterisation of the matter in English law (if described as 'criminal' in English law, that will normally be determinative; if described as 'civil', this is only a factor to be taken into account);
- the nature of the offence, including whether it overlaps with criminal law and, significantly in this context, whether the offence is of general application or applies only to a particular group of people; and
- the nature and level of the penalty.

1 For a brief outline of some of the main safeguards involved, see para 13.15 below.

2 See, in particular, *Engel v Netherlands* (1976) 1 EHRR 647 and, for a further discussion, see *Human Rights Practice*, edited by Simor and Emmerson, June 2000, from 6.046.

5.22 The Government maintains[1] that FSA disciplinary proceedings will be classed as civil for ECHR purposes, primarily because they affect only a defined set of persons who are part of a regulated community which they have chosen to join. For this reason, the disciplinary process under the FSMA 2000 does not contain the criminal fair trial guarantees[2]. In *R v Securities and Futures Authority, ex p Fleurose*[3], it was held that disciplinary proceedings under the old regime were not criminal for ECHR purposes. The main reasons for reaching that conclusion apply equally under the FSMA 2000[4], although there are some potentially significant differences[5]. Also, the issue is assessed on a case-by-case basis and, as was recognised in *Fleurose*, there may be some disciplinary proceedings whose characteristics are so akin to criminal proceedings that the concept of fairness requires more or less the same protections in both. There therefore remains a possibility that a court would regard the FSA's disciplinary proceedings in a particular case as the determination of a criminal charge, particularly where the penalty proposed was severe in its nature and effect or, for example, akin to a criminal offence, or at least would conclude that similar protections should be applied. If a particular case were held to constitute the determination of a criminal charge, there is nothing in the FSMA 2000 to prevent the FSA from affording the person concerned the criminal fair trial safeguards, so it is not thought that this would invalidate the FSMA 2000 in any way. But it would impact on the procedures outlined below[6]. For example, the person may be entitled to free legal advice and assistance and self-incriminating statements made under compulsion could not be used in evidence.

1 See Memorandum from HM Treasury to the Joint Committee, 14 May 1999.
2 The Government did, however, accept there was a risk that the market abuse provisions could be criminal in nature and therefore included appropriate provisions within the FSMA 2000: see para 13.15 below. The same safeguards apply to those matters which clearly constitute criminal offences under the FSMA 2000.
3 [2001] All ER (D) 189.
4 Primarily, that the fines imposed are recoverable as a civil debt, and that the regime applies not to society as a whole but only to those who have 'volunteered' to be subject to it.
5 The principal one is that the regime now has a statutory basis, with the result that there is more 'state' involvement and that fines have a statutory, rather than contractual, basis.
6 For a discussion of the Human Rights issues arising from the FSMA 2000, see the Second Report of the Joint Committee, 27 May 1999.

Resolving these tensions

5.23 There were various ways that the regime could have been designed in order to resolve these competing factors. At one end of the spectrum, the FSA could undergo a full tribunal process internally before reaching a decision, by a separate body segregated from the investigation and enforcement staff and fulfilling the need for independence and impartiality. Whilst this would be ECHR compliant, and be likely to be perceived as fair, it would be an expensive and unwieldy process and therefore likely to be unwelcome both to the FSA and, on the whole, to the regulated community as well. At the other end of the spectrum, the FSA could become little more than a prosecuting authority, able to reach a decision only that there was a case to answer, with an independent body then to reach its own decision on whether that case was made out. Whilst this would have been an efficient process, it would have deprived the FSA of the ability to make its own enforcement decisions, and therefore of some of its authority.

5.24 The system devised attempts to bridge the gap between these two extremes. It is achieved through a combination of the FSMA 2000, which provides the framework, and the FSA's rules, which fill in the details. Whilst the two were developed in tandem, there is nothing in principle to prevent the FSA from amending its rules in the future to provide for a different structure, subject to complying with the statutory framework.

5.25 What the system does is to give the FSA the ability, and authority, to make enforcement decisions, but with four important safeguards. First, the decisions themselves are taken away from the FSA staff responsible for investigation and enforcement and are instead placed in the hands of a separate committee, the RDC, which, although answerable to the FSA Board, is to a large extent independent from the FSA[1]. Second, it places a heavy emphasis on the settlement of cases and includes various mechanisms intended to achieve a more transparent and fairer settlement and/or representations process. Third, it allows the decision to be reviewed in its entirety by a wholly independent tribunal, the Financial Services and Markets Tribunal (or 'Tribunal'), which has a wide scope of enquiry, whose primary task is to decide what action it is appropriate for the FSA to take in the particular case, and which can also make recommendations about the FSA's procedures[2]. Fourth, the decision does not take effect until the Tribunal process (and any appeal) is complete or the firm has foregone the opportunity to take advantage of it. The ability to have the case reviewed in its entirety by the Tribunal should also enable the process to fulfil the ECHR fair trial guarantees[3].

1 For a detailed discussion of the RDC, see para 5.26 ff below.
2 For a detailed discussion of the Tribunal process, see Chapter 6 below.
3 These are outlined at para 6.26 ff below.

The Regulatory Decisions Committee

5.26 The FSA's procedure in relation to the giving of warning notices and decision notices is required to be designed to secure, among other things, that the decision which gives rise to the obligation to give the notice is taken by a person not directly involved in establishing the evidence on which that decision is based[1].

1 FSMA 2000, s 395(2). Where the FSMA 2000 requires the supervisory notice procedure to be followed (see para 5.5 above), rather than the warning/decision notice procedure, an exception to this rule may be available: see paras 9.108 and 9.204 below and FSMA 2000, s 395(3).

5.27 The FSA's procedures therefore need to ensure that there is a separation of functions within the FSA between those who investigate and those who take the enforcement decisions. This not only allows the FSA to comply with its statutory obligations, but also is important in enabling the procedure to be seen by the regulated community to be fair and therefore in increasing the prospect of settlement[1]. The FSA's answer to this is the Regulatory Decisions Committee (or 'RDC'), which has been formed to take most of the decisions which involve the giving of warning notices and decision notices (as well as certain other notices known as supervisory notices, discussed in more detail in Chapter 9 below)[2].

1 See the discussion at para 5.17 ff above.
2 For a full list of those decisions for which the RDC is responsible, see the FSA Handbook at DEC 4.1.4.

What is the RDC?

5.28 The RDC is a committee appointed by the FSA Board to exercise certain regulatory powers on its behalf. It is accountable to the FSA Board for the decisions it takes[1]. It is not involved in establishing the evidence on which its decisions are based.

1 See the FSA Handbook at DEC 4.2.1.

5.29 The RDC comprises a Chairman, one or more Deputy Chairmen, and a panel of other members[1]. The FSA has not indicated how many other members there will be. The RDC is outside the FSA's management structure[2]. It is supported by its own staff, the RDC Secretariat, which is separate from the FSA staff involved in making recommendations to the RDC[3].

1 See the FSA Handbook at DEC 4.2.2.
2 See the FSA Handbook at DEC 4.2.3.
3 See the FSA Handbook at DEC 4.2.4.

Who are the RDC members and how are they appointed?

5.30 The RDC comprises current and recently retired practitioners with financial services industry skills and knowledge and other suitable individuals representing the public interest[1]. It consists of[2]:

- a Chairman, who is employed by the FSA[3] and appointed by the FSA Board on the recommendation of an independent group established for the purpose[4]; and
- one or more Deputy Chairmen and a panel of other members, appointed by the FSA Board on the recommendation of the Chairman. They are not employees of the FSA.

All members are appointed for fixed periods. They may be removed by the FSA Board but only in the event of misconduct or incapacity[5].

1 See the FSA Handbook at DEC 4.2.3.
2 See the FSA Handbook at DEC 4.2.3.
3 See the FSA Handbook at DEC 4.2.5. Christopher FitzGerald, former General Counsel at Natwest Group, was appointed the first Chairman of the RDC on 19 July 2001.
4 A non-executive member of the FSA Board chairs the independent group but beyond that, the FSA has provided no information regarding it. It appears that it is constituted purely for the purpose of appointing a Chairman as or when this is required.
5 See the FSA Handbook at DEC 4.2.6/7.

To whom does the RDC report?

5.31 The FSA Handbook states[1] that the RDC is accountable to the FSA Board for its decisions but gives no further details about the manner in which it will be accountable.

1 See the FSA Handbook at DEC 4.2.1.

Is the RDC independent?

5.32 The RDC fulfils the statutory requirement for the separation of functions within the FSA, in that it is not directly involved in obtaining the evidence upon which its decisions are based. This is all that is required by the FSMA 2000.

The procedure of the RDC

5.33 The FSA has provided various details about the RDC's procedure, which are set out below[1]. First[2], the RDC will meet as a full committee or in panels. Each meeting must include the Chairman or a Deputy Chairman, who will chair the meeting, and at least two other members. The composition and size of the panels, and the pattern of their meetings, may vary depending on the nature of the particular matter under consideration. The implication, although it is not made clear, is that the same panel will deal with all the various stages on one particular matter. If this is correct, the panel that considers the warning notice also hears the firm's representations on it and decides whether to issue a decision notice. The relevant RDC members will need to be vigilant to approach the firm's representations in a fair minded way.

1 In addition, the FSA Handbook contains provisions relating to meetings where the person concerned makes representations to the RDC. These are outlined at para 5.107 below.
2 See the FSA Handbook at DEC 4.2.8.

5.34 Second[1], members of the RDC are required to declare potential conflicts of interest to the Chairman, and to the RDC Secretariat and, where the Chairman considers it reasonable and appropriate, will be required to stand down from consideration of the particular matter. The Chairman must also declare any conflicts of interest. It is notable that conflicts are not declared to the firm concerned, but are only addressed within the RDC, although disclosures of, and steps taken to manage, potential conflicts are recorded by the RDC Secretariat[2].

1 See the FSA Handbook at DEC 4.2.10.
2 See the FSA Handbook at DEC 4.2.11.

5.35 Third[1], meetings of the RDC are held in private, and are conducted in the manner the RDC considers suitable in order to enable it to determine fairly the matters which it is required to consider. There is, therefore, flexibility in the procedure adopted in RDC meetings, subject to an overriding consideration of fairness. As noted below, a record is kept of the meetings, although it is not clear that the firm has any means of gaining access to this record.

1 See the FSA Handbook at DEC 4.2.12.

5.36 Fourth[1], the RDC may require appropriate FSA staff to attend its meetings. The staff are entitled to put to it the previous disciplinary record of the firm or individual and may also draw to its attention the general compliance history of the firm or individual, including that under the previous regime. The RDC may not, however, consider any of these matters for the purpose of proving a later breach, although they may be considered when determining whether to take action and the amount of any penalty. Plainly, the firm's compliance history may be relevant to what sanction should be imposed in a disciplinary case[2], and that is clearly the purpose of it being drawn to the RDC's attention. But it would be preferable from a firm's perspective for this information to be withheld from the RDC, when considering whether to issue a warning notice, until the RDC has reached a view on whether or not the alleged breaches took place. There is otherwise a risk that it will improperly tend to influence the RDC or, at least, undermine the perceived fairness of the process. That risk may be unavoidable when it comes to issuing a decision notice, if the same panel of the RDC is involved, because evidence on compliance history will have been provided to the panel at the earlier, warning notice stage.

1 See the FSA Handbook at DEC 4.2.14 to 4.2.16.
2 This is clear from the above and seems correct as a matter of principle. See, for example, the list of matters relevant to the FSA's decision whether or not to take disciplinary action, in the FSA Handbook at ENF 11.4.1(3), and the list of matters relevant to the amount of a fine against a firm, at ENF 13.3.3(6), discussed further in Chapter 7 below.

5.37 Fifth, the basis upon which the RDC takes its decisions has not been specified in the FSA Handbook. However, it ought to be the case that the RDC applies the FSA's policies, including those set out in the FSA Handbook. Thus, for example, where the FSA Handbook sets out the FSA's policy on a particular matter, such as taking disciplinary action against individuals, or the amounts of fines, the assumption should be that the RDC applies the same policy.

5.38 Sixth[1], each member of the RDC present is entitled to vote on the matter under consideration, and the Chairman of the meeting has a casting vote if required.

1 See the FSA Handbook at DEC 4.2.13.

5.39 Finally[1], the RDC Secretariat will keep a record in relation to each decision of who took the decision, the representations made to the RDC, the material considered by it, the nature of the decision, the reasons for the decision and the dates on which the decision was taken and communicated to the person concerned. The Secretariat is also required to record and fully document all disclosures of potential conflicts of interest and the steps taken to manage them[2]. This is intended to improve the accountability of the RDC and the record may also be valuable to firms seeking to challenge the FSA's decisions and/or refer them to the Tribunal. However, it is not clear that firms will be able to gain access to this record[3].

1 See the FSA Handbook at DEC 4.2.19.
2 See para 5.34 above.
3 See the discussion at para 5.85 below.

THE PROCEDURE IN DETAIL

Stage 1 – Conclusion of the investigation and referral to the RDC

5.40 Before any question arises of the RDC making a decision as to what action it is appropriate for the FSA to take, the fact-finding investigation has to conclude and lead to the matters being referred to the RDC for decision[1]. This is effectively the first stage of the decision-making process. As will be seen, the firm or individual who is subject to the process has the opportunity to have some input at this stage and thus to try to prevent the matter from being taken any further. There are three parts to this process, namely:

- the issue by the FSA staff involved of a preliminary findings letter, and the person's opportunity to respond;
- the FSA's decision whether or not to recommend to the RDC that action be taken; and
- the contents of the recommendation that is made to the RDC.

These are considered in turn below.

1 Where the FSA seeks to impose only a financial penalty for the late submission of reports, the matter is not referred to the RDC but is handled by FSA staff and a modified procedure applies. The modified procedure is outlined in the FSA Handbook at DEC 4.5.2.

Preliminary findings letter

What is the preliminary findings letter?

5.41 A preliminary findings letter is a letter sent by the FSA staff, or the investigator appointed by the FSA, carrying out the fact-finding investigation. It sets out the facts which they consider relevant to the matters under investigation and invites the person concerned to confirm that those facts are complete and accurate[1]. Although, it would seem from this that the preliminary findings letter is intended to be purely factual, there is always a risk that conclusions can, however inadvertently, be introduced under the guise of 'facts'. A document of that kind would require a great deal of time and care on the part of the firm to correct it. This is discussed further below[2].

1 See the FSA Handbook at ENF 2.5.12/13.
2 See para 5.44 ff below.

When is a preliminary findings letter issued?

5.42 The preliminary findings letter is issued before the FSA staff consider whether to recommend that enforcement action be initiated[1].

1 See the FSA Handbook at ENF 2.5.12.

Will the firm receive a preliminary findings letter in every case?

5.43 There is no statutory requirement for a preliminary findings letter; it is purely a creation of the FSA's procedure. The FSA Handbook states that the FSA staff, or the investigator, will generally send a preliminary findings letter unless it is not practicable to do so. Whilst this anticipates it will not always be practicable, no further clarification is given. However, since the focus of the preliminary findings letter is on confirming the facts found by the investigation, presumably in order to ensure so far as possible that the FSA does not proceed on an incorrect factual basis, it would be sensible to expect one to be issued in most cases likely to be referred to the RDC.

What should the firm do when it receives a preliminary findings letter?

5.44 The person concerned will be invited to confirm that the facts set out in the letter are complete and accurate and will be given a reasonable period, normally 28 days, for a response[1]. The person therefore has an opportunity to respond. It would be well advised to make use of that opportunity and, at the very least, to consider the preliminary findings letter very carefully. For a variety of reasons, the person concerned needs to take particular care over precisely what is said in the preliminary findings letter and what it accepts to be correct. It may later regret having agreed to facts which seemed innocuous at the time.

1 See the FSA Handbook at ENF 2.5.13. If the person wishes to respond, it must do so within that period (unless an extension is agreed). The FSA is expressly not obliged to take into account any response received outside the period: see the FSA Handbook at ENF 2.5.14.

5.45 The preliminary findings letter may seem to be innocuous because, on the face of it, its purpose is simply to recite the facts. However, it would be wrong to assume that it is necessarily purely factual[1] and it can in practice be drafted in terms that, on closer analysis, are too broad or ambiguous[2].

1 For example, there may be a difference between 'failing' to do something and 'not doing' the same thing. The first may imply that there was some kind of duty or obligation, and therefore introduces a conclusion, whereas the second does not.

2 For example, it might be said that someone was 'fully aware' without it being clear precisely what this meant.

5.46 The letter, and the person's response, will form the basis of whatever regulatory action the FSA decides to take. As a starting point, therefore, it is important that it is correct. Moreover, the question whether the person has committed any regulatory breaches will often depend upon the interpretation of the facts and precisely how those facts are put. If the person fails properly to rebut points made in the preliminary findings letter, whilst it may nonetheless later seek to argue those points were wrong, there will always be a suspicion that the person initially rightly accepted the point but later thought better of it as he appreciated the consequences and tried to recover lost ground.

5.47 In addition, the person needs to be alert to the potential for claims by other parties who were involved or affected. Among other things, a breach of the

FSA's rules can give rise to a claim for breach of statutory duty on the part of private investors who suffer loss[1] and may also allow the FSA to make a restitution order[2]. The firm may also, as a result, incur civil liability to others, for example corporate clients or market counterparties[3]. There may be factual areas which are less significant for the FSA's disciplinary purposes, but which could have a substantial impact on the person's liability to civil claims or to a restitution order. An example is whether there was a sufficient connection for legal purposes between the breaches and any investor losses that may have been suffered. It is also important to bear in mind in this context that the preliminary findings letter could be a discloseable document in any civil proceedings[4]. If the person is seen, in its response or lack of response, to have accepted the facts as alleged by the FSA, it may make it difficult to argue in subsequent legal proceedings that those facts were wrong. Equally, misguided comments in the person's response could increase its exposure to third parties. It is difficult to predict, or control, the circumstances when the preliminary findings letter, and the response, could reappear.

1 FSMA 2000, s 150 (among others). Such claims are discussed at para 10.27 ff below.
2 See para 7.43 ff below.
3 Generally, see Chapter 10 below.
4 This is discussed in more detail at para 4.189 ff above.

5.48 The response gives the person probably the first opportunity to comment on the facts, refute any misconceptions, and also to begin to develop the themes of its defence. Its principal aim in responding may be to try to ensure that the matter is taken no further. When it receives a Preliminary Findings Letter it should be apparent to the firm that there is a prospect of the FSA bringing regulatory proceedings against it. As will be seen, once those proceedings are initiated by the issue of a Warning Notice, the firm will have a great deal to do within a fairly limited time, and it may therefore be prudent for the firm to begin carrying out the work that will be needed in order to respond to the FSA's proceedings, if it has not already done so.

To whom does the firm respond?

5.49 The response is sent to the FSA staff, or the investigator, who issued the preliminary findings letter. The RDC is not involved at this stage.

What happens to the firm's response?

5.50 The FSA staff take into account any response they receive within the required period, in considering whether to recommend that enforcement action be initiated[1].

1 See the FSA Handbook at ENF 2.5.14.

Are the preliminary findings letter and response confidential?

5.51 The contents of the preliminary findings letter, and the firm's response to it, will in general be protected by the confidentiality restrictions under the

FSMA 2000[1] and should not therefore in general be disclosed outside the FSA. However, there are some exceptions.

1 FSMA 2000, s 348: this is discussed in detail at para 4.304 ff above.

5.52 First, the FSA may pass information to other regulators, for example exchanges or overseas regulators, particularly, but by no means only, where the FSA is carrying out its investigation in order to assist those other regulators. The FSA is permitted to disclose information to other parties under the Gateway Regulations which permit the disclosure of information which is otherwise subject to the statutory confidentiality restrictions[1]. Thus, the preliminary findings letter, and the response to it, might be able to be disclosed.

1 For an explanation of the Gateway Regulations, see para 4.312 above.

5.53 Second, there is a possibility of third parties obtaining disclosure of the preliminary findings letter, and the firm's response to it, from the firm in the context of civil proceedings brought by a third party against the firm[1]. These documents could potentially be of relevance and value to the third party.

1 This is subject to the application of FSMA 2000, s 348: see para 4.304 ff above.

5.54 Third, if the information in the preliminary findings letter, and the response, come into the public domain, for example as a result of Tribunal proceedings in public[1], then it ceases to be confidential and the statutory protection falls away[2]. The result is that the documents could be disclosable in the context of any civil proceedings. If, therefore, the regulatory proceedings are concluded in the Tribunal, the statutory protection for the preliminary findings letter may be only temporary.

1 Most Tribunal proceedings are held in public: see para 6.32 below.
2 The protection of FSMA 2000, s 348 applies only to 'confidential information'. Information is not confidential information if it has been made available to the public by virtue of being disclosed in any circumstances in which, or for any purposes for which, disclosure is not precluded by s 348: FSMA 2000, s 348 (4)(a).

Is there a risk of any publicity at this stage?

5.55 As a result of the statutory confidentiality restrictions outlined above, there will not normally be any publicity attaching to the process at this stage. However, the FSA may, in tandem with conducting its investigation, have taken some other regulatory action which it may have made public, depending upon the circumstances in which that action was taken and the FSA's policy in publicising such action. Examples include the urgent use of the FSA's own-initiative or intervention powers[1] or an application for a civil injunction or a restitution order[2]. In broad terms, the FSA will generally publicise successful enforcement action[3].

1 See para 9.194 ff below.
2 See, respectively, paras 7.97 ff and 7.43 ff below.
3 For a discussion of the FSA's policy on publicity relating to different types of enforcement action, see the discussion of the relevant enforcement action and see para 5.194 below.

Whether to refer the matter to the RDC

5.56 Once the FSA staff, or the investigator, have concluded their investigation and, if appropriate, have issued a preliminary findings letter, and waited for a response, the next question will be whether the matter should be referred to the RDC[1] for a decision on what, if any, regulatory action should be taken. The FSA staff can also decide at this stage to take no further action.

1 For a list of those decisions for which the RDC is responsible, see the FSA Handbook at DEC 4.1.4. This includes all of those decisions listed at para 5.3 above, save for certain types of decision under the final bullet point. Where the RDC is not responsible for a decision, the same procedure applies, generally speaking, except that the decision is taken by a different body under FSA 'executive procedures': see the FSA Handbook at DEC 4.3. For simplicity, and because all the relevant enforcement powers involve the RDC, we refer here only to the RDC.

Who takes the decision to refer the matter to the RDC?

5.57 The FSA Handbook[1] says only that the FSA staff will, if they consider the action is appropriate, recommend that a warning notice be given. Presumably, this decision is taken by those enforcement staff who were responsible for the investigation, together with those to whom they report, where appropriate.

1 See the FSA Handbook at DEC 2.2.1.

5.58 An investigator may, however, have been appointed to conduct the investigation, in which case he will have submitted a report to the FSA[1]. Often, the investigator will be a member of the FSA's staff[2], in which case he may be in a position to decide whether the matter should be referred to the RDC. It is not clear whether a staff member who was the appointed investigator will make this recommendation, or whether his role is confined purely to gathering facts. In cases where the investigator is not a member of the FSA's staff, the interaction between him and the FSA staff considering whether to recommend enforcement action is again not clear.

1 FSMA 2000, s 170(6).
2 FSMA 2000, s 170(5) and see para 4.158 above.

How is the decision taken?

5.59 The FSA Handbook says very little about how the FSA staff take the decision whether to recommend that enforcement action be initiated. Clearly, they have to consider the facts found by the investigation and the response to any preliminary findings letter, and decide what action is appropriate in the light of those facts, presumably applying the FSA's policy.

5.60 In many instances, however, there will be room for disagreement whether or not a particular situation merits enforcement action. The FSA Handbook suggests[1] that, in order to make a recommendation, the FSA staff have to positively consider enforcement action to be appropriate. If they cannot positively recommend action, then it seems that no action should be taken.

1 See the FSA Handbook at DEC 2.2.1.

Does the FSA have any options other than to recommend enforcement action?

5.61 The FSA staff may decide, as a result of the investigation, to take no further action, for example if it appeared that no breaches had been committed. Alternatively, they may have concerns about the behaviour of a firm but consider that it is not appropriate in all the circumstances to bring formal disciplinary action. Examples given by the FSA[1] are where the breach was minor in nature or degree or the person concerned took immediate and full remedial action. In those circumstances, whilst there is no clear discussion in the FSA Handbook, it seems that the FSA staff may decide not to recommend enforcement action but may nonetheless issue a private warning in order to let the person know that it came close to formal enforcement action being taken. It seems that a private warning may thus be issued without any formal process being undergone and without the matter being reviewed by the RDC[2].

1 See the FSA Handbook at ENF 11.3.1.
2 For a more detailed discussion of private warnings, and the potential difficulties they may pose, see para 7.18 ff below.

Is the firm informed about the recommendation?

5.62 The FSA Handbook does not explain whether the firm is informed about the recommendation. Where the FSA's decision is to make a recommendation the firm will in due course hear about the RDC's decision if it is to issue a warning notice and it would therefore seem that there is little reason for it to be notified at this stage. Where the FSA's decision is against making a recommendation, it is thought that the decision may in practice be communicated where the person was aware that investigations had been undertaken by the FSA[1].

1 See the discussion at para 4.178 above.

Will there be any publicity?

5.63 The decision whether to refer the matter to the RDC will not normally be made public. The same issues and exceptions arise as are discussed at para 5.55 above in the context of preliminary findings letters. In addition, since there is a statutory prohibition on publishing a warning notice[1], it would seem wrong for any publicity to arise from the recommendation on which the warning notice was based.

1 FSMA 2000, s 391(1) and see para 5.76 below.

The recommendation by the FSA staff to the RDC

What is contained in the recommendation?

5.64 The FSA has given no indication what will be contained in the recommendations made by its staff. The recommendations will, though, need to address both whether there has been a breach and what action is thought to be appropriate. The RDC may therefore be aware, from the outset, of matters relevant to the issue of sanction, such as the person's previous compliance history[1].

1 This may give rise to certain issues, as discussed at para 5.36 above.

Does the firm receive a copy of the recommendation?

5.65 There is no provision for the FSA to provide a copy of the recommendation to the firm at the time it is made. However, it should in most cases come to be disclosed in due course when the person has the right of access to the FSA's material[1].

1 See para 5.81 ff below.

Stage 2 – Issue of a warning notice

5.66 Once the FSA staff decide to make a recommendation for enforcement action, the RDC has to decide whether or not to accept that recommendation and issue a warning notice. We review the process from that point to the next formal stage, which is when the RDC decides whether to issue a decision notice. We consider in particular:

- the options open to the RDC considering the FSA staff recommendation and how it reaches its decision;
- if the RDC does decide to proceed, the nature of the warning notice it is required to issue;
- the firm's rights following issue of the warning notice and, in particular:
  - the right of access to the FSA's material,
  - the right to make representations,
  - settlement discussions with the FSA, and
  - the mediation procedure where settlement discussions break down;
- rights which third parties may have on issue of the warning notice;
- whether the FSA can make further investigations following the representations and settlement process; and
- the likely length of time between the warning notice and decision notice.

The RDC considers the FSA staff recommendation

5.67 As indicated above, the first step taken by the RDC is to consider whether to accept the recommendation of the FSA staff that enforcement action should be initiated. The RDC may decide:

- to take no further action, with or without a private warning[1]; or
- to send a warning notice to the firm or individual.

1 See the FSA Handbook at DEC 2.2.2. A private warning may, alternatively, be issued by the FSA without review by the RDC : see para 5.61 above. For a discussion of private warnings, see para 7.18 ff below.

How does the RDC decide whether to take the action proposed?

5.68 Although the point has not been made clear, it should be assumed that the RDC applies the FSA's policy on the circumstances when particular types of enforcement action are appropriate. The FSA's policy in relation to taking disciplinary action is outlined at para 7.27 ff below. The FSA's policy on taking other types of enforcement action is outlined in the discussion of the relevant action.

Can the firm make submissions on the recommendation?

5.69 Conclusion of the investigation, recommendation by the FSA staff and consideration by the RDC as to whether to issue a warning notice are internal processes within the FSA, in which the firm has no right to be involved. Accordingly, there is no provision allowing the person who is the subject of the process to make submissions on the substance of the FSA's recommendation, either at the point when the FSA consider whether to make a recommendation or when the RDC decide what to do as a result of that recommendation. There is, of course, nothing to prevent the person from writing either to the FSA or to the RDC if it has reason to do so.

When will the firm find out the RDC's decision?

5.70 If the RDC decides not to take any further action then, in cases where the FSA had previously informed the person that it intended to recommend action, the FSA will communicate that decision promptly to the person concerned[1]. It is not clear whether in practice the decision will be communicated to the person concerned in other cases where the person was aware that its conduct was under investigation[2]. If the RDC accepts the FSA staff's recommendation, the person concerned will be informed when it receives the warning notice.

1 See the FSA Handbook at DEC 2.2.6.
2 See also para 4.178 above.

The issue of a warning notice

What is a warning notice?

5.71 A warning notice is a notice which the FSMA 2000 requires to be issued where the FSA proposes to take various types of enforcement action, including the disciplinary measures of fining or making a public statement in respect of a firm or approved person[1]. This is an important part of the process from the perspective of the person concerned and, as will be seen, that person then has various rights to obtain information and to try to influence the FSA's decision whether to take the action that it proposes.

1 FSMA 2000, ss 67(1) (for approved persons) or 207 (for firms). Various other types of enforcement action to which this process applies are listed at para 5.3 above, together with the statutory provision from which each is derived.

What must a warning notice contain?

5.72 A warning notice must[1]:

- be in writing;
- state the action which the FSA proposes to take;
- give reasons for the proposed action;
- explain whether the person has a right of access to the FSA's material[2] and if so what material and whether any secondary material exists to which it must be allowed access;
- state that the person is entitled to make representations to the FSA[3], and specify a reasonable period for making those representations; and
- where appropriate, state that the mediation scheme is available[4].

In addition, the FSMA 2000 imposes specific requirements with regard to warning notices relating to specific types of regulatory action[5].

1 See the FSA Handbook at DEC 2.2.5, 2.2.7 and 2.2.9 and FSMA 2000, s 387. The final two bullet points are found in the FSA Handbook, rather than the statutory provision (save for the need to specify the period for making representations).
2 This is discussed in more detail at para 5.81 ff below.
3 This is discussed in more detail at para 5.99 ff below.
4 This is discussed in more detail at para 5.129 ff below.
5 See, for example, FSMA 2000, ss 67(2) (fines against approved persons), 67(3) (public statements relating to approved persons), 207(3) (fines against firms), and 207(2) (public statements about firms).

5.73 The warning notice should be of real assistance to the person concerned, who will know at the outset precisely what action the FSA proposes to take against it, for example the amount of any fine or the terms of a public statement the FSA proposes to make. It should therefore be in a position to assess the significance or otherwise of the matter to its business and to take any decisions going forward accordingly.

When does the firm receive the warning notice?

5.74 The FSA Handbook does not specify when a warning notice will be sent to the person who is the subject of it but this is likely to be done soon after the RDC has decided to give it. There are detailed rules on the service and receipt of notices[1].

1 See the Financial Services and Markets Act 2000 (Service of Notices Regulations) 2001, SI 2001/1420. Among other things, these prescribe the date when a notice is treated as having been received, as outlined in the FSA Handbook at DEC 5.3.

Can the firm challenge the warning notice?

5.75 The person in relation to whom the warning notice was issued has no opportunity or right to challenge the decision to issue it. However, the notice does not of itself have any effect. Rather, the person has the right to make representations to the RDC after the notice has been issued, with a view to influencing the RDC's decision whether to proceed with the enforcement action by issuing a decision notice[1] and ultimately it also has the right to challenge in the Tribunal the enforcement action set out in the decision notice. It is therefore unlikely the person will want to use time and resources challenging the issue of the warning notice. Different considerations may, however, apply if the notice is defective, for example because in the firm's view it does not give adequate reasons. It may be possible, in a particular case, to seek a judicial review of the notice if requests to the RDC for better reasons are not met. Mechanisms for challenging, or complaining about, the FSA's decisions are discussed in Chapter 16 below.

1 For a discussion of decision notices, see para 5.162 ff below.

Is there any risk of publicity?

5.76 No publicity ought to arise from the issue of a warning notice. First, there is a statutory prohibition which, generally speaking, prevents the FSA from disclosing confidential information which it obtains relating to people's affairs, breach of which constitutes a criminal offence[1]. Second, the issue is addressed directly by a specific statutory prohibition preventing either the FSA or the person to whom a warning notice is issued (or copied) publishing the warning notice or any details concerning it[2].

1 FSMA 2000, s 348 and see para 4.304 ff above.
2 FSMA 2000, s 391(1).

5.77 Whereas a breach of the former would be a criminal offence, the FSMA 2000 does not specify any particular penalty or consequence for breach of the latter. If the person who is the subject of the process publishes information about the warning notice in breach of the prohibition, it is likely to have contravened a requirement imposed by or under the FSMA 2000 and as a result would be exposed to regulatory enforcement action[1]. If the FSA breaches the prohibition, on the other hand, there are no clear consequences. The FSA would probably have acted unlawfully, but this is unlikely to be of much assistance to the person concerned, since the publication cannot be undone. A damages claim against the FSA or its staff would not be an option, because of their statutory immunity to liability for damages[2], at least in the absence of bad faith or a right to damages under the Human Rights Act 1998. It may be possible to obtain an injunction to prevent further publications being made by the FSA or perhaps to obtain some sort of remedy through the complaints procedure[3], but it is quite possible that no adequate remedy would be available.

1 For a discussion of this test, and the possible consequences, see para 2.142 ff above.
2 FSMA 2000, Sch 1, para 19. This is discussed in more detail at para 16.29 below.
3 See para 16.37 ff below.

What is the effect of receiving a warning notice?

5.78 The warning notice has no effect of itself as against the person who is the subject of the enforcement action. It is the first stage in the process of enforcement and, because it is a pre-requisite under the FSMA 2000, unless it is issued the FSA cannot take the enforcement action[1].

1 Certain types of enforcement action do not require the issue of a warning notice: see paras 5.5 to 5.7 above.

5.79 The issue of the notice does, however, give the person to whom it is issued a number of options and rights, in particular:

- to have access to certain of the FSA's documents;
- to make representations to the RDC;
- to enter into settlement discussions with the FSA; and
- in some situations to try to resolve the matter through a mediation.

Each of these is considered in turn below.

5.80 In some circumstances, third parties may have the right to be notified of the warning notice and, if so, may also have a right of access to the FSA's documents. Rights of third parties are discussed at para 5.150 below.

The right of access to the FSA's material

When is the firm entitled to access to the FSA's documents?

5.81 A person issued with a warning notice[1] usually has a right of access to certain of the FSA's documents[2]. The right is triggered by the issue of the warning notice. It does not arise in relation to all warning notices prescribed under the FSMA 2000, but does arise in the vast majority of cases[3].

1 A similar right arises on the issue of a decision notice: see para 5.174 below.
2 FSMA 2000, s 394.
3 Those excluded include those required to be issued where the firm has applied to vary or revoke action already taken by the FSA. For a list of those that are included, see FSMA 2000, s 392.

What documents is the firm entitled to review?

5.82 The FSA is required to allow the person access to certain types of material, in particular[1]:

- the material on which the FSA relied in taking the decision which gave rise to the obligation to give the warning notice (in other words, the decision of the RDC to propose that enforcement action be taken). This might be termed 'primary material'; and
- any secondary material which, in the FSA's opinion, might undermine that decision. Secondary material means[2] other material not included within the above 'primary material', which was considered by the FSA in reaching the decision or was obtained by it in connection with the matter but not considered by it in reaching that decision.

1 FSMA 2000, s 394(1).
2 FSMA 2000, s 394(6).

5.83 This is subject to various exceptions allowing the FSA to refuse to allow access to certain categories of material, in particular:

- material which was intercepted under a warrant issued under the interception of communications legislation or which indicates that such a warrant was issued or that material has been intercepted in such a way[1];
- material which is covered by the statutory protection for legal privilege[2], in which case the FSA must give the person written notice of the existence of the item and its decision not to allow him access to it[3];
- material which relates to a case involving a different person and was taken into account by the FSA in this case only for the purposes of comparison with other cases[4]; or
- if, in the FSA's opinion, allowing the person access to the material[5]:
  - — would not be in the public interest, or
  - — would not be fair having regard to (i) the likely significance of the material to the person in relation to the matter in respect of which he has been given the warning notice, and (ii) the potential prejudice to the commercial interests of another person which would be caused by the material's disclosure.

1 FSMA 2000, s 394(2) and (7)(a) and (b).
2 FSMA 2000, ss 394(2) and (7)(c) and 413. For a detailed discussion see para 4.264 above. Note that the FSMA 2000 effectively contains its own definition of legal privilege for this purpose, which may not equate in all respects with the common law definition.
3 FSMA 2000, s 394(2), (4) and (7)(c).
4 FSMA 2000, s 394(2)(a) and (b). Such material ought to be taken into account only for the purposes of assessing the appropriate sanction or punishment, and not in order to ascertain whether the person committed the breach.
5 FSMA 2000, s 394(3). If the FSA refuses to allow access to material on this basis, it must give the person written notice of the refusal and the reasons for it: FSMA 2000, s 394(5).

5.84 These access provisions are complex and the scope of the obligation to provide access, and precisely what material the person concerned can expect to see, thus requires closer analysis. Firms need to be aware that the statutory provisions giving access to the FSA's documents are not all-embracing. Material may be taken into account by the RDC without the firm having any right to see or comment upon it. It is only in the Tribunal that the firm may have a wider right of access to documents[1].

1 This may depend on what applications are made to the Tribunal with regard to disclosure, and the Tribunal's views in the particular case: see further para 6.58 ff below.

5.85 ***Primary material*** The obligation to provide access to the material on which the FSA relied is relatively straightforward. The reference to the FSA (in the phrase 'material on which the FSA relied') needs to be read as referring to the RDC, since it is the RDC that makes, on the FSA's behalf, the decision to issue the warning notice. One point that is unclear is the meaning of the word 'material', and in particular whether it includes any oral representations made to the RDC in its meeting and any knowledge held by members of the RDC (for example, from their prior experience of the firm) revealed at the RDC meeting. The word 'material' is not defined in the FSMA 2000 (the words 'information' and 'documents' are more usually used). It seems to have been derived from the

Criminal Procedure and Investigations Act 1996[1], in which context it is defined as referring to material of all kinds and in particular including references to information and objects[2]. Material does not, therefore, appear to be limited to documentary material[3]. It may thus be arguable that a note of any oral representations made at the meeting and of any discussions in which RDC members revealed their own personal knowledge should be made[4] and provided, at least to the extent that the RDC relied upon such material (or if it falls within the definition of secondary material, as discussed below). Finally, any legal advice upon which the RDC relied is not required to be disclosed[5].

1 'In broad terms we are persuaded that a case may be made for aligning the requirement [to provide access] more closely to the rules on disclosure that apply in criminal cases': Economic Secretary to HM Treasury in Standing Committee, 9 December 1999.
2 Criminal Procedure and Investigations Act 1996, s 2(4). The same issue, of whether non-documentary material should be provided, should not arise in the context of a criminal prosecution, because there is a duty on the prosecutor to record material which consists of information not recorded in any form: see para 4.1, Code of Practice issued under Part II, Criminal Procedure and Investigations Act 1996. For a discussion more generally, see Archbold 2001, at Chapter 12 below.
3 This appears to be supported by para 4.1 of the Code of Practice, which refers to 'material which . . . consists of information which is not recorded in any form'.
4 A record of the meeting ought in any case to have been made by the RDC Secretariat: see para 5.39 above.
5 This is discussed further at para 5.90 below.

5.86 ***Secondary material*** A limited amount of secondary material must be provided. The test is set out above. It is fairly complicated and, notably, it is not simply a test of 'relevance'[1]. It also gives the FSA a degree of discretion on what material should be provided[2]. There is therefore scope for material to exist which, although relevant to the decision, was not relied upon by the RDC in taking that decision, and in the FSA's view does not undermine that decision. That material could be of interest and relevance to the firm but falls outside the access provisions.

1 This is deliberate. There were concerns that a test of 'relevance' would result in a 'bureaucratic and unhelpful' disclosure process, given the large amount of information which the FSA has about firms, for example from its supervisory relationship: see Economic Secretary to HM Treasury in Standing Committee, 9 December 1999.
2 At least at this stage: the person concerned may be able to obtain access to the material in the Tribunal – see paras 5.94 and 6.58 ff below.

5.87 One document to which the firm may wish to have access is the record of the RDC meeting that led to the issue of the warning notice. This record should have been kept by the RDC Secretariat[1]. It may contain a record of certain primary or secondary material, in which case access should be given to that primary or secondary material[2]. But the person concerned may wish to have information about the conduct of the meeting, as distinct from the material relied upon the RDC in reaching its decision at the meeting, for example:

- whether any conflicts of interest were declared and how they were dealt with;
- the basis upon which the decision was made, and by whom; and

- whether any member of the FSA staff was present at the meeting (and, as already identified, what oral representations were made to the RDC).

1 See para 5.39 above and the FSA Handbook at DEC 4.2.19.
2 Particularly if it contains a note of any oral representations made and subject to the points discussed at para 5.85 above.

5.88 It is unlikely that any of the information in para 5.87 above would fall within the definition of secondary material (unless perhaps it records reasoned objections of a member of the RDC to the proposed course of action) and thus within the access provisions. There is therefore a potential lack of transparency which could impact on the perceived fairness of the process, with the possible consequences already outlined[1]. This may encourage people to take cases to the Tribunal, in the perhaps mistaken belief that irrelevant considerations taken into account by the RDC, or divisions within the RDC about what action it was appropriate to take, would come to light to the person's benefit at that stage.

1 See para 5.19 above.

5.89 ***The exceptions*** The four exceptions to the access provisions are outlined above. Whilst the FSA must notify the person where material exists which is being withheld within two of the exceptions[1], the FSMA does not require it to do so in relation to material falling within the other two exceptions[2]. The fact that some of this material exists may not therefore be known to the person, at least pending a possible application for further disclosure in any Tribunal proceedings[3]. It is difficult to see why the mere existence of some of this material[4] should be kept from the person.

1 Namely, legally privileged material and material withheld on the basis access would not be in the public interest or would be unfair: see para 5.83 above.
2 Namely, material intercepted under a warrant, and material relating to others and used for purposes of comparison: see para 5.83 above.
3 See para 6.73 below.
4 Particularly, material relating to others and used for purposes of comparison: see para 5.83 above.

5.90 One point is particularly worth highlighting. Any legal advice which the RDC or the FSA may have obtained need not be disclosed. Importantly, the statutory definition for the legally privileged material that may be withheld[1] is drawn widely, to include not only legal advice privilege but also what is known as litigation privilege. This would include, very broadly, correspondence with third parties for the purposes of legal proceedings. The FSMA 2000 does not define legal proceedings and from the perspective of the person against whom enforcement action is being taken it is clearly important that it encompasses not only civil claims but also the regulatory proceedings[2]. However, certain of the material which the FSA obtains could potentially be classified as having been obtained for the purposes of regulatory enforcement proceedings and therefore could arguably be withheld by the FSA (if structured appropriately by the FSA). This could include witness statements and any expert reports which the FSA commissions to assist it in determining whether there has been a regulatory breach. If the FSA were to take the approach that witness statements could be withheld, then the whole rationale for the provision of access to the FSA's material would be undermined.

1 FSMA 2000, s 413 and see the discussion at para 4.264 ff above.

2 In some specific respects, the FSMA 2000 clearly anticipates that there are 'proceedings' when a warning notice is issued: see for example FSMA 2000, ss 66(4) and (5) and 389(2) and (3). For a more detailed discussion of legal privilege, see para 4.193 ff above and, for the meaning of 'proceedings' in this context, see para 4.199 above.

5.91 So far as expert reports are concerned, such reports may often be at the hub of the FSA's case. Where the rule concerned requires firms to comply with a particular standard, for example to 'take reasonable care' or 'pay due regard', an important issue will be what the requisite standard was and whether the person's actions fell below that standard. In a market abuse case, a key question will be whether the person's behaviour fell below the standard of the 'regular user' and identifying the views of the regular user will therefore be critical. In considering the answer to these types of questions, the RDC may well rely upon the report of an expert. It appears to have been envisaged in the parliamentary debates that such reports would be disclosed and indeed one of the issues debated was what amendments were required to ensure that any reports detrimental to the FSA's case would also be disclosed[1]. Nonetheless, it may be arguable, depending upon how the production of such reports was structured by the FSA, that such reports would be 'protected items' under the FSMA 2000 and as a result would not need to be disclosed.

1 See Economic Secretary to HM Treasury in Standing Committee, 9 December 1999.

Who decides what material to give the firm?

5.92 The FSA Handbook provides that it is the RDC, rather than the FSA's enforcement staff, that is responsible for any decision (in connection with warning or decision notices issued by the RDC) to refuse access to FSA material[1]. In other words, it is for the RDC to decide whether particular material falls within one of the exceptions and whether it should therefore be withheld. It is not, though, clear who takes the more general decision on what material falls within the scope of the primary and secondary material to which the FSA is obliged to provide access. It may be the FSA enforcement staff who are responsible for doing so, since they have the requisite resources and knowledge.

1 See the FSA Handbook at DEC 4.1.2 and 4.1.4.

How does the firm obtain access to the material?

5.93 Where the FSA receives a request for access to material[1], it will within a reasonable period after the request was made provide facilities for the inspection and copying of the material that it considers it is required to disclose or a photocopy of the material. The FSA provides the first copy of the relevant material free of charge, but will charge in respect of subsequent copies provided to the same person. Whilst the FSA has stated that it will provide these facilities within a reasonable period, given the very limited time available for the person to respond to the warning notice, as discussed below[2], that period will need to be fairly short, perhaps no more than a few days.

1 See the FSA Handbook at DEC 2.4.6. The FSA Handbook states only that the FSA 'may' provide these facilities, but the practice ought to be that it will do so. Otherwise, it is difficult to see how it will be providing access, as it is required to do. Similarly, it is unclear whether the option of allowing access or providing a photocopy is intended to be at the request of the FSA or of the person concerned.
2 See para 5.110 below.

What action can the firm take if it believes it is entitled to additional material?

5.94 The right of access is not supported by any express right to challenge the material provided, or not provided, the unwritten assumption being that the FSA will comply with its statutory obligations. This potentially emasculates the right which the firm has to be told of the existence of certain categories of material which the FSA is withholding from it and the reasons why it is withholding them[1].

1 See para 5.89 above.

5.95 So, what can the person do if it suspects there is additional material which for some reason has not been disclosed? There are a number of options:

- it can discuss the matter with the FSA, to see whether the issue can be clarified or resolved informally;
- it can try to raise the issue directly with the RDC;
- if it cannot be resolved, it could bring proceedings for a judicial review of the FSA's decision not to provide the relevant material[1], make a complaint against the FSA[2], or take no action for the time being, with the intention of raising the non-provision of material if or when the matter as a whole comes to be heard before the Tribunal[3].

The person does not have any right to refer to the Tribunal the question whether the FSA should disclose the additional material, at least outside the context of referring the enforcement action as a whole to the Tribunal following the issue of a decision notice[4].

1 For a further discussion of judicial review, see para 16.16 ff below.
2 The complaints procedure is discussed at para 16.37 ff below.
3 See Chapter 6 below.
4 See para 5.175 below.

Should the firm request access to the FSA's material?

5.96 There will rarely be good reason for not asking for access to the FSA's material, at least to inspect the documents and obtain a better understanding of the FSA's case. Whether the person should ask for copies of the documents may be a more difficult question, particularly where some of the documents are potentially harmful. There is a risk of the firm being required, in the context of any civil proceedings that may be brought against it by third parties arising from the same matter, to disclose to third parties documents which it has obtained from the FSA[1]. This needs to be borne in mind if there are real concerns about the possibility of significant claims from third parties. The answer may therefore depend upon balancing, in the particular case, the importance of defending the regulatory enforcement proceedings against the likelihood of substantial claims being made by third parties[2]. These problems only arise in so far as the firm actually takes copies of the FSA's material. If there are serious risks, it may be possible to inspect the FSA's files without taking copies to avoid giving rise to these issues, or for the firm's lawyers to take copies of a selection of the documents[3], or just make notes about the material, which in either case should be protected from disclosure to third parties by the doctrine of legal professional privilege.

1 For a further discussion, see para 4.189 ff above. This is subject to any applicable statutory restrictions on the disclosure of confidential information: see paras 4.304 ff above and 5.98 below.
2 If the person decides not to obtain copies of the documents at the warning notice stage, it will have another opportunity to do so at the decision notice stage and again when the matter is referred to the Tribunal, although the same issues about the risk of disclosure to others will arise each time.
3 See *Lyell v Kennedy (No 3)* (1884) 27 Ch D 1.

5.97 The primary disadvantage of not exercising the right of access is likely to be that the person will not be in a position to engage as fully as it might in the process of making representations to the FSA, which takes place between the warning and decision notices. This might impede settlement of the dispute or make it more likely that a decision notice is issued with a higher or more punitive sanction than the person might otherwise have been able to obtain. Ultimately, it may not be in as strong a position as it would otherwise have been before the Tribunal.

What use can the firm make of the FSA's material?

5.98 The primary use of the FSA material disclosed is, from the perspective of the person concerned, to assist the person in making representations to the RDC and more generally to prepare its defence to the regulatory proceedings. To the extent that the material contains confidential information which the FSA has obtained from another person, or which relates to the business or affairs of another person, it may be covered by the statutory prohibition against disclosure and, as a person receiving the information directly or indirectly from the FSA, the firm or individual may commit a criminal offence if it discloses the information in breach[1]. Beyond this, there is no express limitation on the uses that the person may make of the material, although it is possible that a court would imply a restriction that it could not be used for any purpose other than preparing the defence to the regulatory proceedings[2].

1 FSMA 2000, s 348. For a more detailed explanation, see para 4.304 ff above.
2 Unused prosecution material disclosed in criminal proceedings is subject to an implied undertaking not to use the material for any purpose other than the conduct of the defence: *Taylor v Serious Fraud Office* [1999] 2 AC 177, HL.

The right to make representations

Why should the firm make representations?

5.99 The warning notice will contain a statement that the person concerned has a certain amount of time in which to make representations[1]. Why should the person put itself to the time and effort of doing so, particularly when the RDC has already apparently decided to propose enforcement action against it, and the person will in any event have the opportunity to refer the matter to an independent body, the Tribunal, at the end of the process? Whilst there may be cases where the person will prefer not to make representations at this stage, these are likely to be exceptional. The ability to make representations is the firm's opportunity to influence the process at an early stage and, particularly, to see if the matter can be disposed of on acceptable terms.

1 See the FSA Handbook at DEC 2.2.7.

Does the firm have to make representations?

5.100 There is no express requirement on the firm or individual to make representations[1]. Therefore, the person may choose to keep its arguments to itself pending the hearing before the Tribunal, although it is difficult to see why in practice it would do so. Failure to make representations to the RDC ought not to prejudice the person's position before the Tribunal[2]. The firm may, though, wish to respond at least by reserving its position.

1 Among other things, this would be inconsistent with the FSMA 2000: the warning notice must specify a reasonable period within which the person 'may make' representations: FSMA 2000, s 387(2).
2 See also the default provision discussed at para 5.102 below.

5.101 If the person decides not to make any contact at all with the FSA following receipt of the warning notice, then two additional provisions of the FSA Handbook are relevant.

5.102 First[1], where the FSA has received no response or representations by the time a decision is to be made about giving a decision notice, the RDC may regard the allegations or matters in the warning notice as undisputed and give a decision notice accordingly. This does not, however, affect the firm's right to refer the decision notice to the Tribunal[2].

1 See the FSA Handbook at DEC 4.4.13.
2 It is thought that the fact the RDC was entitled by virtue of this provision of the FSA's rules to regard the matter as undisputed should not of itself affect the Tribunal in determining what action it is appropriate for the FSA to take.

5.103 Second[1], in exceptional cases where the person, having received the decision notice, can show on reasonable grounds that it did not receive the warning notice or that it had reasonable grounds for not responding within the specified period, the RDC may permit it to make representations before deciding to give a notice of discontinuance[2] or a further decision notice[3].

1 See the FSA Handbook at DEC 4.4.14.
2 Such a notice would be issued if the RDC, having heard the representations, decided that the action should not be taken: see para 5.166 below.
3 That decision notice would probably be issued under the rules discussed at para 5.184 below.

How are representations made?

5.104 Representations can be made orally or in writing, or probably both[1]. Written representations are likely to be the norm, although there may be situations where the person prefers to meet the RDC and put its case in person.

1 The FSA Handbook is silent on whether both types of representations can be made, but it is likely that both are permissible.

5.105 Written representations must be sent to the FSA at the address stated on the warning notice[1].

1 See the FSA Handbook at DEC 4.4.6.

5.106 If the person wishes to make oral representations, it should notify the FSA of this in writing at the address stated in the warning notice, specifying the matters on which it wishes to make oral representations, an estimate of how much time the representations will take, and the names of any legal representatives appointed to attend[1]. This notification is required to be made at least five business days before the end of the period for representations specified in the warning notice.

1 See the FSA Handbook at DEC 4.4.8. As to the firm's ability to appoint a legal representative, see para 5.107 below.

5.107 As regards the procedure for making oral representations[1]:

- the RDC may specify the place where the representations will be received;
- the RDC may specify that the representations will be received in private. Whilst not expressly stated, this may indicate that in some circumstances they may be received in public, but no indication has been given of when this might be appropriate and in general this process ought to be private[2];
- the firm may appoint a representative (who can be a lawyer) to attend the meeting and make, or assist it in making, the representations[3];
- the RDC may limit the type, length and content of any representations;
- the RDC may ask the person or his representative to clarify any issue arising out of the representations;
- the RDC may require the person (and any representative) to leave the meeting after they have made their representations[4].

1 See the FSA Handbook at DEC 4.4.9/10.
2 Note that there are restrictions on publication regarding warning notice (see FSMA 2000, s 391(1) and the discussion at para 5.76 above).
3 See the FSA Handbook at DEC 4.4.9.
4 The use of the word 'and' does not seem to contemplate the RDC requiring the representative alone to leave the meeting.

5.108 The precise procedure used is thus determined on a case by case basis.

What should the representations contain?

5.109 The content of the representations will depend entirely upon the situation and it is impossible to give much guidance in the abstract. Neither the FSMA 2000 nor the FSA's rules prescribe any limitations on the nature or content of the representations that can be made, although, as already noted[1], the RDC may limit the type, length and content of oral representations. The overriding consideration is that the representations are the person's main opportunity to have an input into the process, short of undergoing a full Tribunal procedure. The person will therefore want to stress as much as possible the main points of its defence, with a view to influencing the RDC's decision. The areas which it might want to consider covering include:

- the key factual points which the person made in its response to the preliminary findings letter, assuming the preliminary findings letter was not agreed;
- reasons why the person did not breach the relevant rules or regulations and in particular, where appropriate, the firm's case on the standard that was appropriate in the market at the time and why its conduct did not fall below that standard;
- reasons why the proposed sanction or other action is inappropriate;
- points in the person's favour, such as the steps it has taken since the problem arose in dealing with its customers, and with the FSA, and addressing any issues internally; and
- any particular complaints or issues that the person may have about the FSA's procedures and how they were implemented in the case.

1 See para 5.107 above.

Within what period must the firm make its representations?

5.110 When deciding to issue the warning notice, the RDC will have decided on a reasonable period for the person concerned to make representations. The period, which may not be less than 28 days, will be stated in the warning notice[1]. The FSA has stated[2] that in deciding upon the period for making representations, the RDC will have regard to the circumstances of each case, including the nature of the action proposed and its likely effect on the person concerned. However, it has also made clear that the period will normally be 28 days from the date when the person receives the warning notice, subject to the right to seek an extension of time. Firms should therefore expect to have 28 days to respond.

1 FSMA 2000, s 387(2).
2 See the FSA Handbook at DEC 4.4.3.

Can the firm ask for an extension of time?

5.111 The person concerned may ask for an extension of time, within 14 days of receiving the warning notice, if it considers the period specified in the warning notice is too short[1]. The FSA has indicated[2], by way of example, that this may be appropriate where a person has entered into or wishes to enter into settlement discussions with the FSA. Clearly, though, the circumstances where an extension of time may be needed are not limited to this. For example, the matter may be particularly complicated, the firm may have had little idea of what was going to be alleged against it until it received the warning notice, and it may need to review the FSA's material before it can prepare its representations. The firm may also have had no control, and no warning, over the timing of the warning notice. It may have been received at a particularly busy time of year, or at a time when key people were away.

1 See the FSA Handbook at DEC 4.4.4.
2 See the FSA Handbook at DEC 4.4.4.

5.112 The need for a request to be made within 14 days of receiving the warning notice needs to be borne in mind. This may cause difficulty in practice as it may often not be apparent until the process of preparing the representations is well under way that additional time is required. The FSA's rules do not expressly allow firms to apply for an extension outside the 14-day period.

5.113 Requests for extensions of time are considered by the RDC and the person concerned will be promptly notified of the decision[1]. It is not clear that the RDC would grant any further extensions of time if, for example settlement discussions were still in progress at the end of the extended period[2].

1 See the FSA Handbook at DEC 4.4.5.
2 See the FSA Handbook at DEC Appendix 1.

5.114 No guidance has been given on the factors the RDC will take into account in deciding whether to accede to a request for an extension of time. The warning notice will not explain the basis upon which the FSA came to its original decision on the period to be permitted for representations[1]. The person concerned will not therefore be able to address whatever concerns gave rise to the original decision on the period considered reasonable. The reasons for requesting an extension of time are likely therefore to relate primarily to the firm, such as the availability of relevant people, the amount of preparatory work that needs to be done and the need to review the FSA's material.

1 Contrast a supervisory notice: see para 9.129 below.

Will the firm's written representations be disclosable to third parties?

5.115 The question whether material produced by the person concerned and given to the FSA may be disclosable to third parties in legal proceedings brought in relation to the same matter is considered at para 4.211 ff above.

The right to enter into settlement discussions

5.116 The settlement of disciplinary and other regulatory enforcement issues has in the past been an important part of the regulatory regime[1]. This remains the case and in some respects the regime facilitates this process.

1 For a more general discussion, see para 5.18 above.

When will settlement discussions take place?

5.117 Whilst there is no bar on settlement discussions taking place before a warning notice has been issued, the FSA believes such discussions are likely to be less productive until then[1] and therefore anticipates that settlement discussions will normally happen only afterwards. It is usually only after the warning notice has been issued that the person knows what is alleged against it and what sanction the FSA proposes. It is only then that any meaningful discussions can normally take place.

1 See the FSA Handbook at DEC Appendix 1, para 1.2.1.

Does the firm have to take part in settlement discussions?

5.118 There is no requirement upon the person to undertake settlement discussions with the FSA; such a requirement would not sit easily with the consensual nature of a settlement process. Having said that, there are, generally speaking, strong reasons militating in favour of at least exploring settlement with the FSA, as outlined at para 5.18 above. There may be less imperative for individuals to reach a settlement with the FSA, than for firms, particularly where the individual feels he needs to be fully vindicated in order to restore his reputation.

With whom are the discussions held?

5.119 The discussions are held with the FSA staff[1], rather than with the RDC. The FSA Handbook does not specify who within the FSA is involved in those discussions, but it is to be anticipated that it will be the same enforcement staff who investigated the firm. The position under the former regime[2], so far as the settlement discussions themselves are concerned, is therefore only improved to the extent that the RDC are involved in overseeing the process[3] and that there is also a mediation scheme[4]. It is impossible to give guidance in the abstract on the nature of the settlement discussions and how the firm should approach them. This will depend very much upon the nature of the breach alleged, the action that the FSA is seeking to take, the significance and potential implications of the matter for the firm and what it seeks to achieve through the settlement discussions, and the existing relationship with the regulator, particularly the enforcement staff involved.

1 See the FSA Handbook at DEC Appendix 1, para 1.2.1.
2 See the discussion at para 5.18 above.
3 See para 5.123 below. This is, however, similar to the former position where any settlement was subject to ratification by an Enforcement Committee.
4 See para 5.129 below.

Can the firm be candid with the FSA in its settlement discussions?

5.120 The FSA Handbook suggests that the FSA and the person should agree that any discussions take place on a without prejudice basis and that neither party may subsequently rely on admissions or statements made in the context of the discussions or documents recording the discussions[1].

1 See the FSA Handbook at DEC Appendix 1, para 1.2.1.

5.121 Where the FSA and the person agree that the discussions are without prejudice, this gives a certain amount of protection to those discussions. The doctrine of 'without prejudice' protects the firm in two ways. First, it means that admissions it makes in its discussions with the FSA cannot subsequently be used against it in the regulatory proceedings. Second, it gives those discussions a protection similar to that which applies to legal privilege, which means, in broad terms, that they cannot be required to be disclosed to any third party[1]. This is significant because, as has been highlighted already[2], the risk of creating unattractive documents which could be useful to third parties who may wish to bring legal proceedings against the firm arising from the same matter is one to which the firm should have regard at all times. Documents which are genuinely without prejudice should mostly be protected[3]. A court will, however, want to see that documents described as 'without prejudice' are properly so-called[4]. That ought not to be a problem in the disciplinary context[5].

1 This would be the general position in a civil court. If the question of whether a document should be disclosed was considered in a regulatory context, though, note that without prejudice communications are not specifically protected under the FSMA 2000: see para 4.265 above.
2 See para 4.189 ff above.
3 See *Rush & Tomkins Ltd v Greater London Council* [1989] AC 1280, HL, *Unilever plc v Proctor & Gamble Co* [2001] 1 All ER 783, CA and *Muller v Linsley & Mortimer* [1996] PNLR 74, CA and see the discussion at para 4.210 above.
4 See, for example, *Buckinghamshire County Council v Moran* [1989] 2 All ER 225, CA and *South Shropshire District Council v Amos* [1987] 1 All ER 340, CA.
5 In the context of a restitution order, there could be a difficult issue whether discussions between the firm and the FSA should be protected from disclosure to those investors for whose benefit the restitution order was made, if those investors later seek to bring civil claims against the firm.

5.122 There are various caveats to this. First, there is the potential for admissions made in this context to affect the approach of the RDC in deciding whether to issue a decision notice, if for any reason no settlement takes place[1]. Second, matters disclosed to the regulator in the context of without prejudice discussions will inevitably remain in the regulator's mind and if they give rise to any additional points that need to be addressed, then the FSA may well, subsequently, seek to deal with those points[2]. Finally, the firm's admissions may come to be embodied in the agreed terms finally reached and therefore in the decision notice and final notice issued by the FSA, in which case they will become publicly known and any admissions of breaches could form the basis for civil claims by third parties[3].

1 See the discussion at para 5.126 below.
2 It is not clear whether the FSA would be entitled so to use matters disclosed in that context as a matter of law; this may depend upon construing the extent of the privilege agreed between the parties in the particular case: see the authorities referred to in footnote 3 to para 5.121 above and *Documentary Evidence*, Hollander & Adam, 7th edn, 2000 at page 171.
3 See para 5.47 above and, generally, Chapter 10 below.

What happens if a settlement is reached?

5.123 If the FSA staff and the person subjected to enforcement action reach terms of settlement, that is not the end of the matter; it is for the RDC to decide whether or not to approve the settlement. The process is as follows. Once the

FSA staff and the person reach terms, those terms are put in writing and agreed. They must include a statement of the facts, any breaches admitted by the person and the action proposed to be taken[1]. The terms are then considered by the RDC, which may[2]:

- ask to meet the relevant FSA staff or the person in order to assist in its consideration of the proposed settlement; and/or
- accept the proposed settlement; or
- decline the proposed settlement.

1 See the FSA Handbook at DEC Appendix 1, para 1.2.2.
2 See the FSA Handbook at DEC Appendix 1, para 1.2.3.

5.124 Where the RDC declines the proposed settlement, it may invite the FSA staff and the person to enter into further discussions to try to achieve a settlement[1]. It may also extend the period for representations to allow those discussions to take place (if it has not already done so). In that situation, it will be important that the RDC indicates to both parties, at the same time, why it declined the proposed settlement, so that the process is transparent and fair and so that the RDC's reasons can provide a framework for further discussion.

1 See the FSA Handbook at DEC Appendix 1, para 1.2.4.

5.125 Where the RDC accepts the settlement, it issues either a decision notice or a notice of discontinuance, as appropriate, based on the terms of the settlement[1].

1 See the FSA Handbook at DEC Appendix 1, para 1.2.3(1). As to a decision notice or notice of discontinuance, see, respectively, paras 5.170 and 5.166 below.

5.126 The RDC may therefore see the admissions made by the person and yet reject the settlement and instead move to the decision notice stage. This gives rise to the risk that without prejudice admissions made by the person are known to the RDC when it decides whether to issue a decision notice. It is difficult to see how the risk can be avoided unless a member of the RDC assesses the settlement and then drops out of the panel for the purposes of considering whether a decision notice should be issued. Currently, the FSA Handbook does not contain any mechanism to address this.

5.127 In reaching a settlement with the FSA, the firm must keep in mind the other potential regulatory consequences of the same matter. If it admits a breach in order to settle a disciplinary case, will it find that being used as the basis for imposing a restitution order? It is important, so far as possible, to bring an end to all of the regulatory consequences at the same time.

What happens if a settlement cannot be reached?

5.128 If the FSA staff and the person cannot reach settlement, then in some circumstances the matter may move on to a mediation[1]. Alternatively, or where the mediation has failed, it will proceed to the decision notice stage[2] after the person has made representations to the RDC (if this has not already been done).

1 See para 5.129 below.
2 See para 5.162 ff below.

The right to mediate

5.129 Mediation is a non-binding dispute resolution process, frequently used in commercial litigation situations to aid parties to reach settlement. It involves a neutral third party, who acts as a mediator and engages in shuttle diplomacy between the parties. The mediator does not try to determine the rights and wrongs of the dispute. He is there purely to help the parties to reach an agreed settlement. Mediation can be particularly useful to break down barriers where the parties' views are entrenched on particular points and this is impeding settlement. The FSA has introduced a mediation process for use in certain types of enforcement cases as an aid to settlement[1]. The use of mediation in the regulatory context is novel and the FSA will operate it on a pilot basis for one year and monitor and review its operation at the end of that period[2].

1 The rules of the mediation scheme can be found in the FSA Handbook at DEC Appendix 1.
2 See the FSA Handbook at DEC Appendix 1, para 1.12.1.

When will mediation take place?

5.130 Mediation may be available to supplement the informal settlement discussions between the person concerned and the FSA staff where the parties consider that the involvement of a neutral mediator is required to facilitate further progress[1]. It therefore arises at some time after the issue of the warning notice, following settlement discussions which break down, but before issue of the final notice[2].

1 See the FSA Handbook at DEC Appendix 1, para 1.3.3.
2 See the FSA Handbook at DEC Appendix 1, para 1.4.3.

Does the firm always have a right to mediate?

5.131 The first point to note is that the person cannot be obliged to submit the case for mediation[1], since mediation is a consensual process.

1 See the FSA Handbook at DEC Appendix 1, para 1.4.4.

5.132 But if the firm wishes to mediate, is the FSA obliged to do so? There are certain categories of cases, outlined below, where the FSA does not offer the option of mediation. Aside from those categories, it is not clear whether a person automatically has the right to refer a case to mediation, or whether this is subject to the FSA agreeing to do so at the time in the particular case. The FSA Handbook seems to suggest that this is an option available to the person concerned[1] but there are also indications that it requires the agreement of both parties[2].

1 '... the mediation scheme will be available to the person ...': see the FSA Handbook at DEC Appendix 1, para 1.4.5; 'if the person agrees to submit the case to mediation': see the FSA Handbook at DEC Appendix 1, para 1.6.1.

2 '. . . where the parties consider that the involvement of a neutral mediator is required . . .': see the FSA Handbook at DEC Appendix 1, para 1.3.3.

5.133 The warning notice will, where appropriate, state that the mediation scheme is available[1]. The three categories of case where mediation is not available are those involving[2]:

- allegations of a criminal offence;
- allegations of unfitness or impropriety based on judgments about dishonesty or lack of integrity; or
- the exercise of the FSA's own initiative power on a variation of permission.

1 See the FSA Handbook at DEC 2.2.9.
2 See the FSA Handbook at DEC Appendix 1, para 1.4.2.

5.134 These appear intended to prevent firms or the FSA from compromising certain serious regulatory matters. However, the categories are widely drawn and the scope of the exceptions is therefore currently unclear.

Who will be the mediator?

5.135 The mediation scheme is administered by an independent body[1], which provides a panel of experienced mediators and which has suitable expertise and experience in the administration of mediation schemes. The mediators on the panel are all experienced commercial mediators accredited by or registered with the mediation provider[2]. Experience and expertise of the financial services sector is not compulsory but is desirable.

1 See the FSA Handbook at DEC Appendix 1, para 1.5.1. It was announced, on 25 June 2001, that CEDR Solve had been appointed the mediation provider.
2 See the FSA Handbook at DEC Appendix 1, para 1.7.2.

5.136 The mediation provider recommends a mediator to the parties, who are free to accept or decline the recommendation[1]. If either party declines the recommendation, the mediation provider will seek to obtain agreement on another mediator from the panel. If the parties cannot agree a mediator within seven days of a mediation notice[2] being received by the mediation provider, the mediation provider appoints a mediator.

1 See the FSA Handbook at DEC Appendix 1, para 1.7.2.
2 For an explanation of a mediation notice, see para 5.138 below.

5.137 In accepting appointments, mediators are required to confirm to the parties that they have no conflicts of interest[1].

1 See the FSA Handbook at DEC Appendix 1, para 1.7.2.

How is the mediation initiated?

5.138 Where the parties agree to submit the case to mediation, they send a joint mediation notice in an agreed form to the mediation provider and the RDC

Secretary. The mediation notice will commit each party to use best endeavours to progress the mediation process in a timely manner[1].

1 See the FSA Handbook at DEC Appendix 1, para 1.6.1/2.

5.139 Once the parties have agreed to mediate, and the mediation notice has been sent, there are various initial matters to be addressed which the mediation provider will liaise with the parties in order to deal with, namely[1]:

- the appointment of the mediator[2];
- a suitable date and timetable for the mediation process;
- the duration of the mediation, normally not longer than one full day, although more time may be required in complex cases;
- the mediation timetable including any further extensions of time required from the RDC[3]. If the mediation has not started within the allotted timetable, the FSA may decline to mediate and the matter will be referred to the decision notice stage;
- the venue (any venue acceptable to the parties and the mediator);
- the terms of the mediation agreement. This sets out the terms on which the mediation takes place and in particular is required to provide that:
  - the mediation will be without prejudice and confidential[4],
  - the parties who attend have authority to agree proposed settlement terms[5],
  - either party may withdraw from and terminate the mediation at any stage before or during the mediation. Either party or the mediator may withdraw if the mediation has not taken place within the agreed timetable, and the mediator may withdraw from and terminate the mediation if a criminal offence by or involving a party is disclosed to him[6], and
  - the costs of the mediator and the mediation provider (which are agreed at the outset) will be borne half each by the firm or individual and the FSA. Each party bears its own legal costs in relation to the mediation.

1 See the FSA Handbook at DEC Appendix 1, para 1.7.
2 See para 5.136 above.
3 See para 5.140 below.
4 This is discussed at para 5.143 below.
5 This is discussed at para 5.146 below.
6 See the FSA Handbook at DEC Appendix 1, para 1.9.3.

What effect does this have on the timetable?

5.140 If the firm or individual has not yet made its representations to the RDC, then it may want to await the outcome of the settlement discussions and mediation before doing so. Recognising the tight timetable involved, the FSA allows[1] the firm or individual to request in the mediation notice that the 28-day time period for making representations to the RDC be extended by a maximum of 14 days to allow time for the mediation to be completed. On receiving the mediation notice, the RDC notifies the parties and the mediation provider of its agreement to the requested extension, or any other extension it sees fit. If required, the person may apply to the RDC for a subsequent extension in order to complete the mediation. The FSA's rules limit the total extension to 28 days other than in exceptional circumstances[2].

1 See the FSA Handbook at DEC Appendix 1, para 1.6.3/4.
2 It is not clear whether this will be realistic.

What is the procedure for the mediation?

5.141 The procedure for the mediation is as follows[1]:

- once appointed, the mediator may call a preliminary meeting with parties and any advisers to ensure, among other things, that the parties are properly prepared, that they agree the issues for discussion and that they understand how the process will operate[2];
- at least one week before the mediation, each party submits a short case summary setting out the issues in dispute and any documents referred to in it[3];
- the mediation takes place at the agreed time and place[4];
- the parties may bring legal or other advisors of their choice with them to the mediation[5].

1 For a more general discussion of mediation procedure, see *Mediation: principles process practice*, Boulle and Nesic, 2001.
2 See the FSA Handbook at DEC Appendix 1, para 1.8.1.
3 See the FSA Handbook at DEC Appendix 1, para 1.7.10.
4 See the FSA Handbook at DEC Appendix 1, para 1.9.1.
5 See the FSA Handbook at DEC Appendix 1, para 1.11.1.

What are the possible outcomes?

5.142 The mediation will have one of two outcomes, either a proposal for settlement agreed between the parties, or no agreed proposal[1].

- if no agreed proposal is reached, the mediation will be terminated and the case will proceed to the decision notice stage (once the person has had the chance to make representations to the RDC, if he has not already done so and is within the time for doing so);
- if a settlement proposal is agreed, it will be considered by the RDC, which will decide whether to approve it. There are three options:
  - — if it is approved, a decision notice, and subsequently a final notice, is issued reflecting the terms of the agreement reached,
  - — if it is not approved, the parties may return to the mediation provided the RDC consents, in which case the RDC will ensure its views are clearly stated as to why the previous terms were not acceptable[2],

— if the RDC does not consent to a further mediation, the case will continue towards the decision notice stage (once the person has had the chance to make representations to the RDC if he has not already done so and is within the time frame for doing so).

1 See the FSA Handbook at DEC Appendix 1, para 1.10.
2 See the FSA Handbook at DEC Appendix 1, para 1.7.9(4).

Confidentiality in the mediation process

5.143 The FSA recognises[1] that confidentiality is a key element of the mediation process. Further, the process is conducted on a 'without prejudice' basis[2]. Matters disclosed in, and documents created for the purposes of, the mediation cannot therefore be referred to in the public domain and matters disclosed by one party to the mediator in confidence will not be disclosed to the other party without consent. After the mediation, such matters retain the confidential status they had in the mediation itself[3].

1 See the FSA Handbook at DEC Appendix 1, para 1.7.8(1).
2 See the FSA Handbook at DEC Appendix 1, para 1.7.7(1)(a). As to the consequences of this, and the risks, see the discussion at para 5.120 above.
3 See the FSA Handbook at DEC Appendix 1, para 1.7.8(3).

5.144 There are, however, three exceptions[1]:

- if any information indicating potentially criminal conduct is disclosed to the mediator, the mediator is not required to keep that matter confidential (and may choose to terminate the mediation);
- the terms of any settlement reached will, if approved by the RDC, be incorporated in a decision notice and subsequent final notice (or a notice of discontinuance), which may be made public; and
- the FSA may publish information regarding the operation of the mediation scheme on an anonymous basis in its annual report.

1 See the FSA Handbook at DEC Appendix 1, para 1.7.8(3).

5.145 It is not thought that any of these exceptions gives rise to any particular issues. The same general issue discussed in the context of settlement negotiations[1] arises here, namely the difficulty of isolating from the RDC, if it subsequently has to decide whether or not to issue a decision notice, information, particularly admissions made by the firm or individual, which came to its attention from the mediation process.

1 See para 5.126 above.

Who attends the mediation?

5.146 The FSA recognises[1] that a key feature of mediation is that those who attend on behalf of each party must have full authority to agree the settlement terms. Having said that, the FSA will generally be represented by its enforcement staff during the mediation, even though it is the RDC that ultimately must agree to the settlement. The FSA has stated that it will endeavour to ensure the relevant members of the RDC are available for consultation by telephone, to enable a clear indication to be given to the parties and the mediator of whether the RDC will find the proposed terms acceptable. However, this expressly does not compromise the ability of the RDC subsequently to decline to approve the settlement terms.

1 See the FSA Handbook at DEC Appendix 1, para 1.7.9(1).

5.147 This may be an unsatisfactory element of the mediation scheme for two reasons. First, the FSA staff will plainly not have the authority to settle cases, making the outcome of the mediation uncertain. One of the benefits of a mediation is to enable the views of the decision-maker to be influenced by the process of mediation. This could well be lost in the scheme proposed, where the parties could undergo a mediation only for the RDC to remain aloof and entrenched in its views. Second, it gives the FSA staff a potential tactical advantage in the mediation, because they can always argue that, whilst they understand the logic of a particular position, the RDC will not settle for lower than, say, a particular level of fine. The FSA Handbook does however state that if the RDC declines to approve the settlement terms, it may consent to the parties returning to the mediation process to explore further settlement options and, if so, will ensure its views are clearly stated as to why the terms previously agreed were not acceptable.

When should the firm consider mediation?

5.148 Mediation is worth considering in any case where the person wishes to achieve a settlement but there are significant barriers to reaching agreement at a level or in a manner that it can accept. It will be important for the person to have an idea of what it wants to achieve through the mediation process, not just in terms of the settlement that it is trying to reach but also in terms of the barriers which it thinks need to be broken down. For example, it may be that the settlement discussions have become too heated and the introduction of an independent third party could help to restore some balance. Or the main issue could be one of interpretation of the FSA's rules or one of expert evidence, where there is room for reasonable disagreement but neither side is giving any credit to the other side's views. The mediator may be able to help each side in seeing the matter a little more from the other's perspective. Or the firm may be trying to achieve something in the settlement that is important to it commercially but makes little difference to the FSA, for example by not exposing it to potential civil liability to other market counterparties. Again, a mediator may help the FSA to understand the firm's concerns.

5.149 There is rarely much to be lost from the firm's perspective, even if the mediation does not result in a settlement. There may even be something to be gained. For example, a better understanding of the FSA's case may help the firm prepare for the Tribunal, or the FSA may better understand the firm's case and as a result lower its own views of what sanction is appropriate. In an appropriate case, the firm may even wish to suggest to the mediator that he sets out his views at the end of the process. Mediation is unlikely to delay the case by more than a couple of weeks and the cost is unlikely to be high relative to the overall cost of defending the regulatory proceedings.

What rights do other parties have?

5.150 The FSA must in certain circumstances give a copy of a warning notice to a third party[1] and that third party then has various statutory rights. The relevant provisions are outlined below.

1 FSMA 2000, s 393.

Right to receive a copy of a warning notice

5.151 An obligation to provide a copy of the warning notice to a third party may arise in relation to most, but not all, warning notices[1]. In relation to such warning notices, a copy of the notice must be given to a third party if any of the reasons contained in the warning notice:

- identifies the third party (being a person other than the person to whom the notice was given); and
- in the opinion of the FSA is prejudicial to that person.

There is no requirement to give the person a copy of the notice if the FSA has given him a separate warning notice in relation to the same matter or gives him such a notice at the same time[2].

1 It applies in relation to those listed at FSMA 2000, s 392. These are the same warning notices as give rise to a right of access to the FSA's documents: see para 5.81 above.
2 FSMA 2000, s 393(2).

5.152 The FSA has not given any indication of when in practice it expects to serve a copy of a warning notice. The decision in any case is made by the RDC[1]. A flavour of the underlying intention is provided by the parliamentary debates which preceded the FSMA 2000, where the Government talked about 'third parties implicated in a warning notice'[2]. This would include a situation where the particular regulatory problem related not only to one firm but also to other firms or particular individuals in the firm. In that situation, a warning notice relating to one person may need to address matters that implicate another.

1 See the FSA Handbook at DEC 4.1.2.
2 Economic Secretary to HM Treasury in Standing Committee, 9 December 1999.

5.153 This may be illustrated with an example. Assume a firm, 'X Co', breached a regulatory rule by mispricing an investment belonging to a customer and selling it to another firm, 'Y Co'. In fact, it was one of X Co's traders, T, who carried out the pricing and the trading. In that situation, questions could clearly arise about not only X Co (why did this happen? who authorised it? were its systems and controls adequate?) but also T (did he do it deliberately? was he aware of the rules? was there some personal benefit involved?) and even Y Co (why was it involved? what did it know?). A warning notice relating to proposed disciplinary action against X Co alleging, say, that its controls had been inadequate, is likely to identify T and perhaps also Y Co on the reasons for taking that action. It may also be prejudicial to them in that the resolution of the matter between X Co and the FSA may involve findings or admissions which adversely affect them, for example, that there was a breach by T of which Y Co (or one of its employees) was aware. Whilst such findings or admissions are unlikely strictly to bind Y Co and T[1], they could in practice expose them to regulatory proceedings and civil claims from third parties, as well as affecting their reputation.

1 See para 10.74 ff below.

5.154 The FSA would in that situation be obliged to serve a copy of the notice on Y Co and T unless it was also issuing them with a warning notice at the same time, or had already done so. This may give rise to complications because the FSA may have disciplinary proceedings pending against Y Co and T. If it serves a notice on X Co which must be copied to Y Co and T then, as will be seen, Y Co and T have some rights to become involved immediately. This may become particularly difficult at the decision notice stage[1]. The FSA may therefore need to wait until its investigations are complete as against all three and then to proceed against all of them at the same time. There may, however, be situations where it cannot do this, particularly given the statutory two-year limitation period in relation to proceedings for misconduct against individuals, but not firms[2].

1 See the discussion at para 5.170 below.
2 FSMA 2000, s 66(4) and see para 8.8 below.

5.155 What is also notable from this example is that the test of what is prejudicial to a person is potentially a wide one. It is difficult to see why it should be limited to matters that have a regulatory impact on the person, or even to matters that have a financial impact. A matter likely to affect a person's reputation adversely could be prejudicial to him. It is the RDC's view of whether a matter is prejudicial to a person that matters for these purposes[1].

1 However, the same test is used in relation to whether a decision notice should be copied to a third party, and a decision by the FSA not to provide a copy of a decision notice may be challenged in the Tribunal: see para 5.179 below.

5.156 The notice need not be given to the third party if the FSA considers it impracticable to do so[1]. No indication has been provided by the FSA as to what it regards this as meaning. This ought to relate to the practicability of giving the notice, not the practicability of dealing with the consequences.

1 FSMA 2000, s 393(7).

Rights to become involved in the process

5.157 A third party provided with a copy of a warning notice has three rights:

- the right to make representations to the FSA within the reasonable period specified on the notice, which must be not less than 28 days[1];

- a right of access to the FSA's material on the same basis as the person to whom the warning notice was given[2], but only in so far as the material which the FSA is required to disclose relates to the matter which identifies the third party[3] (and the notice must explain the effect of this provision[4]); and
- the right to be given a notice of discontinuance where that is served on the person on whom the warning notice was served[5].

As will be seen, the third party has further rights at the decision notice stage.

1 FSMA 2000, s 393(3). For a discussion of the process of making representations, see para 5.99 ff above. The same provisions of the FSA Handbook apply to the third party: see the FSA Handbook at DEC 4.4.12. There is no express statutory limitation as to the issues on which the third party may make representations, but in practice this is likely to be limited to the matter which identifies or affects him and indeed the FSA Handbook seems to suggests that the right to make representations is limited to those matters that affect him: see the FSA Handbook at DEC 4.4.12.
2 See para 5.81 above.
3 FSMA 2000, s 393 (12).
4 FSMA 2000, s 393 (13).
5 FSMA 2000, s 393 (14). Notices of discontinuance are discussed at para 5.166 below.

Further investigations or further action by the FSA

5.158 If the process of making representations gives rise to new issues which the FSA wishes to investigate, or which lead it to believe that other action is required, to what extent can it take additional steps? There are two separate questions. The first is whether the FSA, having heard the firm's representations, can take a different kind of action against the firm from that which was originally proposed in the warning notice or further action in addition to that proposed in the warning notice. The answer to this is that it can, but that it may need to issue another warning notice[1]. It may, however, first need to obtain further information, particularly if information was supplied to it by the firm on a without prejudice basis with the result that it cannot be relied by the FSA upon against the firm[2].

1 This is considered at para 5.164 below.
2 See the discussion at para 5.122 above.

5.159 The second question is therefore whether, in the light of the representations made, the FSA can make further investigations into the matter. There is nothing to prevent the FSA from doing so. It is the FSA which controls the timetable and, provided the RDC was content to allow it, the FSA could make further investigations and put further material before the RDC for use at the decision notice stage. This is subject to the statutory requirement[1] for the FSA to consider 'within a reasonable period' whether to issue a decision notice. It is not clear whether this refers to a reasonable period after issue of the warning notice or after the representations. Nonetheless, the period for further investigations could not extend indefinitely or even unreasonably. In undertaking further investigations, the FSA would also need to be careful not to misuse information provided in confidence or on a without prejudice basis by the person in the representations process[2].

1 FSMA 2000, s 387(4).
2 See the discussion at para 5.120 ff above.

5.160 Will the FSA in practice do this? The FSA Handbook seems to anticipate that the RDC will consider the written and any oral representations at the same meeting at which it decides whether to issue a decision notice[1] and the expectation must be that there will not normally be room for further investigations by the FSA between the warning notice and decision notice stages. However, as indicated above, there is nothing to prevent this from happening in an appropriate case.

1 See the FSA Handbook at DEC 2.3.1.

How long does this process take?

5.161 The FSA Handbook anticipates that between one and three months will elapse between issuing a warning notice and a decision notice. This comprises:

- 28 days for making representations in the normal course;
- potential extensions of time for making representations;
- between 14 and 28 days for a mediation, if this is required; and
- a possible further extension of time if the mediation has to be reconvened and then an additional period to allow the RDC to convene a meeting and decide whether to issue a decision notice.

Stage 3 – Issue of a decision notice

Considering the representations made by the firm

5.162 Assuming that no settlement could be reached, even with assistance from the mediation process, the next step is for the RDC to consider the written representations and any oral representations made by the person and to decide whether it should take:

- the action it proposed in its warning notice; or
- some other action; or
- no action.

It is thought that the RDC considers the question of what action the FSA should take by reference to the FSA's policy on taking the relevant action, in the same way as the decision to issue a warning notice[1].

1 See para 5.68 above.

5.163 If the RDC decides to take the action specified in the warning notice, it must issue a decision notice[1]. The process for doing so, and the effect of the notice, is discussed in detail below.

1 So far as disciplinary action is concerned, see FSMA 2000, ss 208 (for firms) and 67(4) (for approved persons). Equivalent provisions exist in relation to the other enforcement action which involve the warning/decision notice procedure: for the relevant references, see para 5.3 above.

5.164 If the RDC wishes to take some other action, there are two possibilities depending upon what action it wishes to take:

- if the action which it wishes to take is under the same Part of the FSMA 2000 as the action proposed in the warning notice, then the FSA may simply issue a decision notice[1]. This would allow the FSA, having proposed, say, a fine, to decide to issue a greater or smaller fine, or a public censure, but not to decide to cancel or vary the firm's permission or require it to pay restitution;
- otherwise, it seems that the FSA must discontinue the action to which the original warning notice applied, by issuing a notice of discontinuance[2], and then issue a new warning notice in relation to the action now proposed.

1 FSMA 2000, s 388(2).
2 See para 5.166 below.

5.165 If the RDC decides to take no action, it must give a notice of discontinuance to the person to whom the warning notice was given[1] and to any third party to whom a copy of the warning notice was given[2].

1 FSMA 2000, s 389. It does not need to do so if the discontinuance of the proceedings results in the granting of an application made by the person to whom the warning or decision notice was issued: see FSMA 2000, s 389(2). This could apply, for example, if the FSA had originally decided not to accede to the person's request to vary or revoke action which it had already taken, and therefore issued a warning notice, but subsequently decided to accede to that request.
2 FSMA 2000, s 393(14).

The notice of discontinuance

5.166 A notice of discontinuance is simply required to identify the proceedings which are being discontinued[1] and to state that the FSA may publish such information about the matter as it considers appropriate if the person to whom it was given consent (and a similar statement must appear where the notice is copied to a third party[2]). The FSA sends the notice of discontinuance to the person concerned (and any third party who was provided with a copy of the warning or decision notice).

1 FSMA 2000, ss 389(3) and 391(2) and (3).
2 See para 5.167 below.

Will the notice of discontinuance be published?

5.167 Information relating to a notice of discontinuance can be published by the FSA with the consent of the person concerned and, in so far as relevant to the third party, the consent of any third party to whom the notice was copied[1]. With such consent, the FSA may publish such information as it considers appropriate about the matter to which the discontinued proceedings related.

1 FSMA 2000, s 391(2) and (3). Note that the FSMA 2000 does not as such prohibit the publication of information about the notice of discontinuance without the consent of the person concerned (or the third party). It says that the notice of discontinuance must state that information may be published if the person consents.

5.168 The FSA has not given any guidance on the circumstances when it will seek the person's consent to publish information, and what information it will then publish[1]. It is thought that this is most likely to be appropriate in those situations where the FSA may have considered making public the fact that it was investigating the matter, namely where it is the subject of public concern, speculation or rumour, and it is appropriate for the FSA, perhaps having made public that it was investigating, to make clear that no regulatory proceedings will result[2]. Indeed, in that situation the firm may want the FSA to make some sort of public announcement.

1 See the FSA Handbook at DEC 5.2.2.
2 See further the discussion at para 4.165 above.

5.169 As with other instances where third parties have rights to become involved, it is not clear, and the FSA have not provided their views, how the third party's rights interact with those of the firm. Can the third party veto a publication to which the FSA and the firm have both consented? The answer appears to be that it can, unless the information can be published in such a way that it is not relevant to the third party.

The decision notice

What is a decision notice?

5.170 A decision notice is the notice which the FSMA 2000 requires the FSA to issue when it decides to take any of various courses of action[1] following issue of a warning notice. Normally, this will arise because the FSA has decided that the action it proposed in a warning notice is appropriate, but it may alternatively decide to take a limited range of action other than that proposed in the warning notice[2]. In some circumstances, and with the person's consent, a decision notice may be issued without any related warning notice being issued[3].

1 See the list at para 5.3 above.
2 See para 5.164 above.
3 See para 5.184 below.

5.171 Although the issue of a decision notice signifies that the FSA, through the RDC, has reached a decision that the sanction or action it proposed is appropriate, it does not of itself give rise to any obligation on the part of the firm or individual subject to the enforcement process. Instead, as we will see, they have the right to refer the matter to the Tribunal, which can look at the entire case afresh.

What must a decision notice contain?

5.172 A decision notice must[1]:

- be in writing;
- give the FSA's reasons for the decision to take the action to which the notice relates;
- explain whether the person concerned has a right of access to the FSA's material and if so what this means and whether there is any secondary material to which the person must be allowed access[2]; and
- give an indication of any right the person has to have the matter referred to the Tribunal and the procedure on such a reference[3].

1 FSMA 2000, s 388(1) and the FSA Handbook at DEC 2.3.2.
2 For a discussion of the right of access to the FSA's material, and of the meaning of secondary material, see para 5.81 ff above. The discussion there applies equally in the context of a decision notice. As to whether the person would wish to exercise the right at the decision notice stage, see para 5.174 below.
3 See para 5.175 below. As to whether the firm should refer the matter to the Tribunal, see para 5.183 below.

When does the firm receive a decision notice?

5.173 The person concerned receives a decision notice when the RDC decides to take action which gives rise to an obligation under the FSMA 2000 to issue a decision notice[1]. There are detailed rules on the service and receipt of statutory notices[2].

1 The FSMA 2000 contains varying requirements on the timing for provision of a decision notice. For example, s 208 requires one to be provided without delay, whereas s 67 is silent on the point.
2 See the Financial Services and Markets Act 2000 (Service of Notices) Regulations 2001, SI 2001/1420. Among other things, the regulations make provision for when a notice is treated as having been received. See also the FSA Handbook at DEC 5.3.

What is the effect of receiving a decision notice?

5.174 Although termed a 'decision notice', the notice does not of itself have any effect. It gives the person two rights. First, the person has a right of access to the FSA's material, on the same basis as the right which arose on issue of the warning notice[1]. The decision notice need not necessarily have been based solely on the material available to the RDC at the warning notice stage together with the person's representations. The FSA may in the meantime have continued to obtain or create further material, for example obtaining further evidence which refutes points made by the firm in its representations. There is, though, no continuing disclosure obligation requiring the FSA to provide such material to the person on an ongoing basis. The additional material may be relevant to the person's assessment of whether to refer the case to the Tribunal and it may therefore wish to exercise its right of access before making that decision.

1 For a detailed discussion, see para 5.81 ff above.

5.175 Second, and most importantly, the person has a right to refer the case to the Tribunal, so that the case can be heard and determined in an independent forum. A detailed discussion of the nature of the Tribunal, and the procedure for

Tribunal proceedings, is found in Chapter 6 below. It is only if the person decides not to take this step, which it normally has 28 days to do[1], or for some reason does not do so within the requisite period, that the FSA issues a further notice, the final notice[2], and the action set out in the decision notice takes effect. In the meantime, the FSA cannot take the relevant action[3].

1 For the detailed rules, see para 6.36 below.
2 See para 5.188 ff below.
3 FSMA 2000, s 133(9).

What rights do third parties have?

5.176 In the same way as for a warning notice[1], a decision notice must be copied to a third party if one of the reasons set out in the notice relates to a matter which identifies a person other than the person to whom the notice is given and in the opinion of the FSA is prejudicial to that third party[2]. In addition, if the decision notice was preceded by a warning notice, a copy must be given to each person to whom the warning notice was copied[3]. This is subject to the same exceptions as for warning notices[4] and applies to the same types of notices[5].

1 See para 5.151 above.
2 FSMA 2000, s 393(4).
3 FSMA 2000, s 393(5).
4 See paras 5.151 and 5.156 above.
5 See footnote 1 to para 5.151 above.

5.177 A third party to whom a copy of a decision notice is given has a right of access to the FSA's material in the same way as the person to whom the decision notice was given, but only in so far as the material which the FSA must disclose relates to the matter which identifies the third party[1]. The copy of the notice must be accompanied by a description of the right of access[2].

1 FSMA 2000, s 393(12). For a discussion of the right of access to FSA material, see para 5.81 ff above.
2 FSMA 2000, s 393(13).

5.178 The third party also has the right to refer the matter to the Tribunal, but limited to[1]:

- the decision in question, so far as it is based on the reason which identifies him and is prejudicial to him; or
- any opinion expressed by the FSA in relation to him.

1 FSMA 2000, s 393(9).

5.179 A person who alleges that a copy of the decision notice should have been given to him but was not may also refer that alleged failure to the Tribunal as well as either of the two matters outlined above[1].

1 FSMA 2000, s 393(11).

5.180 Whilst introducing an element of fairness to third parties, these provisions potentially introduce an element of uncertainty so far as the person primarily subject to the enforcement proceeding is concerned. In particular, the FSA Handbook does not explain, and it is not clear, how the third party's ability to challenge the decision notice interrelates with the right of the person who is the subject of the enforcement proceeding to agree the decision notice and elect not to refer the matter to the Tribunal, possibly for predominantly commercial reasons as discussed below. Equally, it is not clear how it interrelates with the ability of the firm and the FSA to reach an agreed settlement of the matter, the terms of which need to be embodied in a decision notice. It would seem that the third party can in this way prevent the matter from being disposed of[1].

1 Once the decision notice is referred to the Tribunal, it does not take effect until the reference, and any appeal, has been finally disposed of: FSMA 2000, s 133(9). There is, on the face of it, nothing in the FSMA 2000 to restrict the effect of this in cases where it is a third party who refers the matter to the Tribunal.

5.181 Does this matter in practice? Provided the FSA brings regulatory proceedings against all of those involved in a matter at the same time, then there should rarely in practice be any difficulty. There could, however, still be cases where an individual or firm was concerned that findings in a decision notice relating to another firm might make it more likely that third parties may bring civil claims and might therefore seek to challenge that finding even though it was innocuous in regulatory terms. If, on the other hand, the FSA is unable or unwilling to run all of its cases relating to a particular matter concurrently, then real difficulties could be foreseen.

Publicity

5.182 No publicity ought to arise from the issue of a decision notice. The statutory prohibition against publication which applies to warning notices applies equally to decision notices. Hence, neither the FSA nor the person to whom the decision notice is given or copied may publish the notice or any details concerning it[1]. However, if the firm does not challenge the decision notice, then publicity will normally arise shortly afterwards[2].

1 FSMA 2000, s 391(1) and see the discussion at para 5.76 above.
2 See para 5.194 below.

Should the firm accept the decision notice?

5.183 Whether or not the person concerned should accept the decision notice depends very much upon the particular circumstances. There, are however, various recurrent themes which fall for consideration in many situations. From the point of view of firms there may well be pressure to put the issue behind them and focus on future business. The process thus far is likely to have caused significant cost, disruption, and use of management time and other resources, and the prospect of running the case before the Tribunal may be an unwelcome one. The firm may also in practice be concerned about preserving its relationship with the FSA and being able to move forward positively in that context as well. Added to this, whilst the matter will to date have been primarily kept confidential, although the final notice would be published shortly if the firm did not refer the matter to the Tribunal[1], there may be a likelihood of rather greater publicity in a case in the Tribunal[2]. Against this will weigh factors such as reputational issues arising from the nature of the sanction proposed, the public relations consequences of being seen to admit liability, rather than to continue fighting to the end, and the potential effect of making admissions in terms of the firm's potential civil liability to third parties arising from the breaches[3]. There are therefore likely to be difficult, and conflicting, considerations in each case.

1 See para 5.194 below.
2 Tribunal proceedings are normally held in public: see para 6.32 below. In practice, if the case is of general interest, ongoing proceedings and a lengthy 'trial' may allow the story to be continuously run in the Press for some time.
3 For a discussion of the relevance of admissions made in this context, see para 10.74 ff below.

Issuing a further decision notice

5.184 The FSA may[1], with the consent of the person concerned, give the person a further decision notice relating to different action in respect of the same matter, after giving the original decision notice but before the FSA takes the action to which the decision notice relates. The person has the same right to refer the matter to the Tribunal as he had in relation to the original decision notice and may also have a right of access to the FSA's material[2].

1 FSMA 2000, s 388(3) to (5).
2 It is not clear whether the original decision notice falls away; this may depend upon the circumstances when the further decision notice is issued: see further para 5.186 below.

5.185 In that situation, the FSA has prescribed the following procedure[1]:

- the FSA staff will recommend to the RDC that the further decision notice is given, either before or after obtaining the person's consent[2];
- the RDC will consider whether the action proposed is appropriate in the circumstances;
- if it considers that the action proposed is not appropriate, it will decide not to give the further decision notice, the original decision notice will stand and the person's rights in relation to that notice will not be affected;
- if the RDC considers that the action proposed is appropriate, it will issue the further decision notice, subject to the person's consent being, or having been, obtained.

1 See the FSA Handbook at DEC 2.3.6.
2 The FSA will normally require consent to be in writing, in the form either of a letter or a signed memorandum from the individual or on behalf of the body corporate or partnership: see the FSA Handbook at DEC 2.3.7.

5.186 The FSA has not given any indication of when in practice it will make use of this procedure. However, it could be appropriate in a number of situations. For example, it could be used to allow discussions between the FSA and the person to continue after a decision notice has been issued and for the case to be settled before a decision is made by the Tribunal (or, if the matter has not been referred to the Tribunal, before the FSA issues a final notice and takes the action which it decided to take in the original decision notice). It could also be used where the FSA decides to take some other action which would require the issue of a further warning notice[1], and neither the firm nor the FSA want to waste further time going through a second warning notice procedure and waiting a further 28 days for the period for representations to expire. In that situation, the firm may consent to cutting short the procedure, but without prejudice to its right to refer the second decision notice to the Tribunal. The FSMA 2000 here provides a certain amount of flexibility which may be useful in practice.

1 For the limitations on the action which can be taken in a decision notice, in the light of the warning notice given, see para 5.164 above.

5.187 Third parties identified in, and who may be prejudiced by, the decision notice may be entitled to receive a copy and would then have additional rights[1].

1 See para 5.176 above.

Stage 4 – Issue of a final notice

5.188 The final stage is for the FSA to issue a final notice giving effect to the regulatory action which is being imposed.

When is a final notice issued?

5.189 A final notice is issued in two situations[1]:

- where the RDC has issued a decision notice and the matter was not referred to the Tribunal within the requisite period, in which case the FSA must, on taking the action to which the decision notice relates, give the person concerned, and any person to whom the decision notice was copied, a final notice; or
- where the FSA has given a person a decision notice and the matter was referred to the Tribunal, in which case the FSA must give the person, and any person to whom the decision notice was copied, a final notice on taking action in accordance with any directions given by the Tribunal, or the court on an appeal from the Tribunal.

1 FSMA 2000, s 390(1) and (2).

5.190 The final notice is therefore issued when the FSA makes the public statement or issues the fine or restitution order, and so on. This can only be done once the Tribunal process has been exhausted or the person concerned has not availed itself of the opportunity to refer the matter to the Tribunal[1].

1 As to how the FSA is required to issue statutory notices, and the date when a notice is treated as having been received, see the Financial Services and Markets Act 2000 (Service of Notices) Regulations 2001, SI 2001/1420 and see the FSA Handbook at DEC 5.3.

5.191 If the FSA decides for some reason not to take the action referred to in a decision notice, then it must issue a notice of discontinuance[1]. For a discussion of notices of discontinuance, see para 5.166 above.

1 FSMA 2000, s 389(1).

What must a final notice contain?

5.192 The final notice must[1] set out the terms of, as appropriate, the statement, order, financial penalty or other action together with details of the date on which the action takes effect. In relation to a financial penalty, it must state how and the period within which it is to be paid (which must not be less than 14 days beginning with the date on which the final notice is given), and how it will be recovered if not paid. In relation to a public statement, it must set out the terms of the statement and give details of the manner in which, and date on which, it will be published.

1 For the detailed requirements, see FSMA 2000, s 390(3) to (7).

To whom must a final notice be given?

5.193 The final notice must be given to the person to whom the FSA gave the decision notice and also to any person to whom the decision notice was copied[1].

1 FSMA 2000, s 390(1) and (2).

Publicity

5.194 Once a final notice has been issued, the FSA is under a duty[1] to publish such information about the matter to which the final notice relates as it considers appropriate. It may not, however, publish information if publication would, in its opinion, be unfair to the person with respect to whom the action was taken or prejudicial to the interests of consumers[2]. Information may be published in such manner as the FSA considers appropriate[3]. It is the RDC, not the FSA enforcement staff, that decides what information it is appropriate to publish about the matter[4]. The FSA Handbook says very little about the policy behind publication of enforcement action as a general matter[5]. However, there is a statutory duty to publish and therefore an expectation that the FSA will publish information about regulatory action at the conclusion of the regulatory process. This reflects that, generally speaking, the publication of successful enforcement action is seen as an important aspect of the FSA's regulatory objectives, highlighting the regulatory requirements and standards, demonstrating that they are being effectively enforced, and thereby helping to maintain confidence in the financial system, promoting public awareness and contributing towards consumer protection[6].

1 FSMA 2000, s 391(4).
2 FSMA 2000, s 391(6).
3 FSMA 2000, s 391(7).
4 See the FSA Handbook at DEC 4.1.2.

5 Publication is addressed specifically in relation to various types of enforcement action: see the FSA Handbook at, for example, ENF 6.11.1 (injunctions), 9.10.1 (restitution orders), 7.8.1 (withdrawal of approval) and 8.12 (prohibition orders).
6 See, for example, the FSA Handbook at ENF 12.2.2.

5.195 There is no prohibition on the firm publishing material relating to the matter at this stage, although there are often practical reasons for not doing so.

Costs

5.196 The question of who should bear the costs of the FSA's investigation and the disciplinary process was the subject of a great deal of debate in the consultation which preceded the FSMA 2000[1]. It was a feature of the previous regime that the regulators normally imposed those costs on the person who was the subject of the investigation, the rationale being that the cost of non-compliance should be borne by the person concerned, rather than by the industry as a whole.

1 See the First Report of the Joint Committee at para 206.

5.197 The position is however different under the new regime. The FSMA 2000 provides[1] that the FSA, in determining its policy with respect to the amount of penalties to be imposed by it under the FSMA 2000, must take no account of the expenses which it incurs, or expects to incur, in discharging its functions. In other words, the cost of enforcement is borne by the regulated community as a whole, by means of the annual fees payable to the FSA, and not by individual firms.

1 FSMA 2000, Sch 1, para 16(1).

5.198 In certain circumstances, costs orders may be made by the Tribunal in relation to the costs incurred in the specific case before the Tribunal, although the normal rule is that there is no order for costs in the Tribunal. This issue is discussed in more detail at para 6.153 ff below[1].

1 See also FSMA 2000, Sch 13, para 13.

5.199 In some situations, firms will agree to pay the legal costs of an employee who is the subject of an investigation or enforcement process. It is not thought that there is any objection to this, and indeed it is a relatively usual practice[1].

1 Different considerations may apply if the firm offered to pay a fine levied by the FSA against the employee personally, since this would remove much of the deterrent effect of imposing the fine.

6 The Tribunal and appeals

CONTENTS

Introduction	**255**
Tribunal procedure	**260**
Reviews and appeals	**302**

INTRODUCTION

Introduction to the Tribunal

6.1 One of the primary protections for firms subject to FSA enforcement action is the ability to require the FSA to prove its case before the Financial Services and Markets Tribunal (known as 'the Tribunal'). The Tribunal has an important role in the regulatory structure in providing a possible means of recourse for a firm aggrieved by a particular decision which the FSA has taken in its case. In addition, as Tribunal decisions are published, a body of precedent will build up which should help to define the parameters within which the FSA can operate and thereby effect the FSA's approach in cases more generally. The Tribunal therefore forms a key part of the checks and balances on the FSA's actions under the FSMA 2000.

6.2 In this chapter, we review, at para 6.17 ff below, the procedure for referring cases to the Tribunal, the Tribunal process that follows the reference and the practical issues that arise and, at para 6.161 ff below, the limited options open to the firm, or indeed the FSA, where it disagrees with the Tribunal's decision, namely to obtain a review of the decision by the Tribunal or to appeal on a point of law.

6.3 Before turning to the detailed procedures, there are four initial points to consider, namely:

6.3 The Tribunal and appeals

- what is the Tribunal?
- what can the Tribunal do in determining cases referred to it?
- what matters can be referred to the Tribunal? and
- when in practice should firms consider referring a case to the Tribunal?

What is the Tribunal?

6.4 The Tribunal is the Financial Services and Markets Tribunal constituted under the FSMA 2000[1], and operating under rules made by the Lord Chancellor under powers granted to him in the FSMA 2000[2]. The Tribunal appointed to hear any particular case is drawn from two panels, whose members are appointed by the Lord Chancellor and may be removed by him on the ground of incapacity or misbehaviour. The first panel is a panel of chairmen, all of whom must be legally qualified, and one of whom will be chosen in each case to chair the particular Tribunal appointed to hear that case. The second panel is a panel of lay persons who have appropriate experience to deal with matters of the kind that may be referred to the Tribunal. It is likely that the key members chosen to hear each particular case will be those with experience in the relevant area.

1 FSMA 2000, s 132 and Sch 13.
2 The Financial Services and Markets Tribunal Rules 2001, SI 2001/2476, made under FSMA 2000, s 132(3).

6.5 The Tribunal is thus entirely independent from the FSA. It is set up and run by the Lord Chancellor's department, operates under rules set by that department[1] and is funded by that department. It has no regulatory agenda of its own. The Rules of the Tribunal aim to be fair and even handed to all parties, as well as to be ECHR compatible[2].

1 Subject to the supervising role of the Council on Tribunals, under the Tribunals and Inquiries Act 1992. The Tribunal system as a whole has recently been reviewed by Sir Andrew Leggatt, on appointment from the Lord Chancellor. As at the date of this book, Sir Andrew Leggatt's report has been published, proposing various changes to the Tribunal system as a whole, and the Lord Chancellor's Department has commenced a consultation process on its recommendations ('Tribunals for Users, Consultation Paper about the Report of the Review of Tribunals by Sir Andrew Leggatt', Lord Chancellor's Department, August 2001).
2 The need for ECHR compatibility is discussed in more detail at para 6.23 ff below.

6.6 One of the members of the panel of chairmen is appointed by the Lord Chancellor to preside over the discharge of the Tribunal's functions, and is known as the President of the Tribunal[1]. The Lord Chancellor may also appoint one or more Deputy Presidents. The functions of the President include giving practice directions on the practice and procedure to be followed by the Tribunal in relation to references to it[2].

1 On 30 July 2001, the Lord Chancellor's Department announced that Stephen Oliver QC had been appointed to this position.
2 FSMA 2000, Sch 13, para 10.

What can the Tribunal do?

6.7 The basic function of the Tribunal, prescribed under the FSMA 2000[1], is, on determining a reference made to it, to determine what, if any, is the appropriate action for the FSA to take in relation to the matter referred to it.

1 FSMA 2000, s 133(4).

6.8 The purpose and effect of this is that the Tribunal is a first instance tribunal, able to consider all of the evidence and to reach its own decision. The person concerned is 'innocent' until the FSA proves its case before the Tribunal. This process is not fettered by the FSA internal decision-making process that preceded it. The Tribunal is not therefore an appellate body nor is it conducting a review of the FSA's decision. It decides, simply, what action it is appropriate for the FSA to take in the particular case. But it is limited to taking the same kind of action as that decided upon by the FSA, as explained at para 6.138 ff below.

6.9 The Tribunal also has the ability, when determining a reference, to make recommendations as to the FSA's regulating provisions or its procedures[1]. The FSMA 2000 does not limit the sorts of recommendations that the Tribunal can make in this regard, for example to cases where it regards those rules or procedures as unfair or as incompatible with the FSMA 2000 or on some other basis. It is an important aspect of the accountability regime that this wholly independent body has an unfettered ability to make recommendations about the FSA's rules and procedures.

1 FSMA 2000, s 133(8). The meaning of 'regulating provisions' is discussed at para 6.140 below.

What matters are referred to the Tribunal?

6.10 Not every decision taken by the FSA in relation to a person is capable of being referred to the Tribunal. Recourse to the Tribunal only exists where the FSMA 2000 specifically so provides. Broadly, this coincides with those types of decisions which involve the giving of warning/decision notices (see Chapter 5 above) or supervisory notices (see para 9.104 ff below). In the enforcement context, this includes cases where the FSA wishes to:

- formally discipline a firm[1] or an approved person[2];
- vary a firm's permission[3] or take equivalent action in relation to an incoming firm[4];
- cancel a firm's permission[5];
- make a restitution order against a person[6];
- withdraw approval from an approved person[7];
- issue a prohibition order against any person[8];
- impose a penalty for market abuse[9];
- exercise its enforcement powers in relation to a unit trust or other regulated collective investment scheme[10] or OEIC[11];

- exercise its enforcement powers as UK Listing Authority in relation to listed companies, applicants for listing directors and/or sponsors[12];
- exercise certain powers in relation to Lloyd's[13], auditors and/or actuaries[14] or in relation to members of the professions[15].

Details of the procedure applicable in relation to each of the above, including the right of reference to the Tribunal, are outlined in the relevant chapter indicated in the footnotes below.

1 FSMA 2000, s 208 and see Chapter 7 below.
2 FSMA 2000, s 67 and see Chapter 8 below.
3 FSMA 2000, s 55 and see Chapter 9 below.
4 FSMA 2000, s 197 and see Chapter 9 below.
5 FSMA 2000, s 55 and see Chapter 9 below.
6 FSMA 2000, s 386 and see Chapters 7 (firms), 8 (individuals) and 13 (market abuse).
7 FSMA 2000, s 63 and see Chapter 8 below.
8 FSMA 2000, s 57 and see Chapter 8 below.
9 FSMA 2000, s 127 and see Chapter 13 below.
10 FSMA 2000, Pt XVII and see Chapter 14 below.
11 The Open-Ended Investment Companies Regulations 2001, SI 2001/1228 and see Chapter 14 below.
12 FSMA 2000, Pt VI and see Chapter 15 below.
13 FSMA 2000, Pt XIX.
14 FSMA 2000, s 345.
15 FSMA 2000, s 331.

6.11 But the FSA can also take many decisions which affect firms or others where there is no right of reference to the Tribunal. Examples include deciding to:

- issue a private warning[1];
- investigate a firm[2];
- not notify a firm that an investigation has been commenced into it[3];
- require a firm to provide particular information either itself or by an investigator in connection with an investigation[4];
- apply to a court for an injunction or restitution order[5];
- vary a firm's permission by 'executive procedures' and without the matter being considered by the Regulatory Decisions Committee[6];
- publish information about enforcement action it has taken[7].

1 See para 7.18 ff below.
2 See Chapter 4 above.
3 See para 4.162 ff above.
4 See paras 4.59 ff and 4.108 ff above.
5 See Chapters 7 (firms) and 8 (individuals).
6 See para 9.115 ff below.
7 See para 5.194 above.

6.12 HM Treasury has the power[1] to extend the scope of the Tribunal's functions to allow those who are the subject of disciplinary proceedings for market abuse by recognised investment exchanges or clearing houses to refer the relevant decision to the Tribunal. HM Treasury can exercise this power either to ensure consistency as between the market abuse decisions of the different bodies or to ensure the relevant processes are ECHR compatible.

1 FSMA 2000, s 300.

When should the firm refer a case to the Tribunal?

6.13 If a firm or individual is the subject of a decision by the FSA with which it disagrees[1], and which is capable of referral to the Tribunal, then the immediate question is whether it should refer that decision to the Tribunal. Whether the matter is referred to the Tribunal is entirely within the firm's control: the FSA enforcement staff have no right to do so if, for example, they disagree with the decision made by the Regulatory Decisions Committee. Answering this question may involve weighing up a number of conflicting factors. We outline briefly here some of the main considerations[2].

1 Or is provided with a copy of a decision notice by the FSA as a third party identified in it to whom, in the FSA's view, it is prejudicial: FSMA 2000, s 393 and see para 5.176 ff above.
2 See also para 5.183 above.

6.14 On the positive side, the person has the opportunity to make the FSA prove its case before the Tribunal. The person may believe that the FSA's decision was unwarranted or excessive or there may be mitigating factors that it believes were not properly taken into account by the FSA or aspects of the FSA's procedure which it believes will seem unattractive to the Tribunal. In short, there may be the prospect of the Tribunal coming to the conclusion that no action should be taken or that less serious action is warranted. In addition, the case may highlight aspects of the FSA's rules or procedures which the Tribunal may wish to comment upon[1].

1 Also, if the person believes that the FSA has acted unreasonably, then there may be a prospect of the FSA being required to contribute to or pay the person's costs of the Tribunal proceedings.

6.15 On the negative side, there is the cost, disruption and management time likely to be involved in prolonging the process, as well as the risk of the Tribunal deciding that a stronger sanction should be imposed or of awarding costs against the person if it decides that it has acted vexatiously or frivolously. Also, it may result in the person's actions coming under public scrutiny and the matter attracting greater publicity than it otherwise would.

6.16 Thus, whether or not to refer a decision to the Tribunal will depend very much upon the particular case[1]. The most important factors overall are likely to be the importance of the matter, what the person seeks or hopes to achieve and the merits of the FSA's case.

1 The Government estimated that between 30 and 50 cases a year may come before the Tribunal: Economic Secretary to HM Treasury in Standing Committee, 4 November 1999.

TRIBUNAL PROCEDURE

An overview of the process

6.17 In the following paragraphs we review the Tribunal's rules[1], which contain the details of its procedures. We look, first, at how cases are referred to the Tribunal (para 6.33 ff below), secondly, at the procedure involved in taking the case from the referral up to the hearing (para 6.41 ff below), thirdly, at the hearing (para 6.118 ff below) and, fourthly, at the Tribunal's decision (para 6.136 ff below). In each case, we outline some of the practical issues that arise.

1 The Financial Services and Market Tribunal Rules 2001, SI 2001/ 2476 (the 'Tribunal Rules').

6.18 Before looking at the detailed rules, it may be helpful briefly to review what the rules are designed to achieve, and to provide a short overview of the process. Some initial points are then made about the publicity likely to arise from the Tribunal process.

What are the Tribunal rules designed to achieve?

6.19 The Tribunal Rules aim, among other things, to be flexible and to be ECHR compatible. Understanding these two factors assists in understanding the nature of the rules and the Tribunal's approach to each particular case. They are discussed briefly below.

Flexibility in the process

6.20 The importance of the Tribunal, not only as a means of recourse for those subjected to decisions by the FSA but also as an aspect of the accountability regime of the FSA, has already been discussed. If the Tribunal is to have these benefits then firms and individuals must have confidence in its ability to reach a just result in each case. But, as Lord Woolf's reforms to civil litigation procedure have highlighted, reaching the right result is not the only consideration. If that can be achieved only slowly and at great cost, then people are likely to be deterred from using the process. Effective access to justice thus requires expedition and cost also to be taken into account.

6.21 These considerations are equally important in the context of the Tribunal, which considers cases ranging from complex multi-issue disputes which may involve large firms and substantial numbers of consumers, to single issues relating to individuals or sole traders. In some cases, cost and expedition assume real significance, particularly if the person concerned would otherwise effectively have no access to the Tribunal. In other cases, the person may be primarily concerned that the Tribunal reaches the right result, with the cost of the process being of rather less importance. In those cases, whilst it is important that the procedure is not unduly lengthy, costly or complex, if there is to be confidence in the Tribunal then justice must not be seen to be overly subordinated to expedition and cost. In the civil litigation context[1], the concept of proportionality – that cases should be dealt with in a way that is proportionate to the amount of money involved, the importance of the case, the complexity of the issues and the financial position of each party – is the key that allows the court to balance these different factors. How is this same balance to be achieved in the Tribunal?

1 See the Civil Procedure Rules, Pt 1.

6.22 As will be seen, the Tribunal Rules say comparatively little about how the procedure works in practice, giving the Tribunal appointed to hear each case a great deal of flexibility on the procedure to be adopted in that case and requiring it to use that flexibility to ensure the just, expeditious and economical determination of the reference. Whilst there is no mention of proportionality, these three factors should enable the Tribunal to adopt a similar approach and to perform the exercise of balancing these factors appropriately in the particular circumstances of each case.

ECHR compatibility

6.23 The Lord Chancellor's Department has indicated[1] that the Tribunal's rules aim to be compatible with the European Convention on Human Rights. We briefly review here why they need to be compatible and what this involves[2].

1 See Explanatory Note to the Draft Rules, January 2001, 'Procedure Rules – Main Features'.
2 For a more detailed discussion, see *Law of the European Convention on Human Rights*, Harris, O'Boyle and Warbrick 1995, *Human Rights Law and Practice*, edited by Lester and Pannick, 1999 and *Human Rights Practice*, edited by Simor and Emmerson, June 2000.

6.24 ***Why must the Tribunal process be ECHR compatible?*** There are two main reasons why the Tribunal procedure needs to comply with the ECHR. First, the enforcement process as a whole is likely to involve the determination of a person's civil rights and therefore needs to comply with the fair trial guarantees of art 6(1) of the ECHR[1]. Whilst there are various safeguards built into the enforcement process before the matter reaches the Tribunal, for example the involvement of the Regulatory Decisions Committee, it is in the Tribunal procedures that any defects in the process, from the ECHR perspective, must be cured. The Tribunal therefore has an important role of ensuring that the process as a whole fulfils the ECHR requirements[2].

1 See para 5.20 above. In some situations, including in particular proceedings for market abuse, the proceedings may involve the determination of a 'criminal charge' for ECHR purposes: see the discussion at para 5.21 ff above. In those cases, the process must also fulfil the additional requirements for criminal proceedings found in art 6(2) and (3) and (once ratified and incorporated into UK law) Protocol 7. Proceedings in relation to market abuse involve the additional criminal protections of: (a) the privilege against self-incrimination and (b) legal aid (see para 13.15 below).
2 See, for example, *Albert and Le Compte v Belgium* (1983) 5 EHRR 533. There may be limits on the extent to which earlier defects are capable of being 'cured': see *De Cubber v Belgium* (1984) 7 EHRR 236. It is only art 6 defects that may be cured in the Tribunal; any unlawful invasions of privacy in breach of art 8, for example, would not be cured.

6.25 Second, the Tribunal is itself a public body and it would be unlawful for it to act in a way that was incompatible with an ECHR right[1].

1 Human Rights Act 1998, s 6.

6.26 ***What does ECHR compatibility involve?*** The basic fair trial guarantee is the right to a fair and public trial within a reasonable time by an independent and impartial tribunal established by law and for judgment to be pronounced publicly[1]. This includes the right[2]:

- to a public hearing, normally an oral hearing, subject to certain exceptions[3];
- for the hearing to take place within a reasonable time;
- to the disclosure of documents[4];
- to a reasonable opportunity to present the case to the court under conditions that do not substantially disadvantage the person as against the FSA (known as 'equality of arms');
- to adduce evidence and to comment on the other side's evidence and submissions[5];
- to a judgment containing reasons; and
- for judgment to be pronounced publicly, subject to certain exceptions[6].

Additional safeguards for criminal proceedings can be found in art 6(2) and (3) and Protocol 7[7].

1 ECHR, art 6(1).
2 This is not intended to be a comprehensive list of the art 6(1) rights. For a more detailed discussion, see *Law of the European Convention on Human Rights*, Harris, Boyle and Warbick, 1995, *Human Rights Law and Practice,* edited by Lester and Pannick, 1999, and *Human Rights Practice*, edited by Simor and Emmerson, June 2000.
3 The right to a public hearing is discussed at para 6.124 below.
4 See, for example, *Feldbrugge v Netherlands* (1986) 8 EHRR 425.
5 *Mantovanelli v France* (1996) 24 EHRR 370.
6 The public pronouncement of judgment is discussed further at para 6.144 ff below.
7 For a more detailed discussion see *Law of the European Convention on Human Rights*, Harris, O'Boyle and Warbick, 1995, *Human Rights Law and Practice*, edited by Lester and Pannick, 1999 and *Human Rights Practice*, edited by Simor and Emmerson, June 2000.

An outline of the procedure

6.27 Before turning to the detailed rules, it may be helpful to have a brief overview of how the process works. The first step is for the person to whom the decision notice or supervisory notice was given (referred to as 'the applicant') to refer the matter to the Tribunal. This is done by issuing a reference notice, which must be done within 28 days subject to obtaining an extension of time. Once a reference notice has been issued, the matter has been placed before the Tribunal and its procedural rules become applicable. At that stage, certain information about the case is normally entered on a register, which is publicly available.

6.28 The FSA, and then the applicant, each set out in a document their case on why the action taken or proposed to be taken by the FSA is (or in the case of the applicant, is not) appropriate. The parties also disclose relevant documents to each other, and the Tribunal can order further documents to be disclosed.

6.29 After this, there is no defined process. Rather, the Tribunal decides upon the procedure required to take the particular matter to a hearing, by making directions on the basis of ensuring the just, expeditious and economical determination of the reference. This might include, for example, appointing an expert, giving permission for the parties to call expert evidence or requiring witness statements or other documents to be filed. The Tribunal also has the power to determine particular issues as preliminary issues and to strike out any document or even the reference as a whole.

6.30 The case is heard by the Tribunal at an oral hearing, normally in public although the Tribunal can order that the hearing (or a part of it) be held in private in certain circumstances. It is for the Tribunal to decide on the procedure adopted for the hearing. The applicant is entitled to be legally represented at the hearing, and indeed throughout the process.

6.31 Finally, the Tribunal makes its decision. This is also normally made public, again subject to the Tribunal's ability to decide otherwise in certain cases. In certain situations the Tribunal may be prepared to review that decision on particular grounds set out in the rules. The applicant and the FSA also have the right to apply for permission to appeal to the Court of Appeal on matters of law only.

Publicity in the Tribunal process

6.32 The Tribunal has been designed as an essentially public process, partly with the ECHR requirements in mind and partly because transparency is of itself viewed as beneficial. It is important to appreciate this at the outset because, whilst there are opportunities for applicants to request that the process be kept private, the general expectation is that publicity will arise. In particular, in the absence of any specific directions to the contrary from the Tribunal:

- on the commencement of Tribunal proceedings, particulars of the case are put in the Tribunal's register[1], which is open to public inspection[2];
- any hearings as the case proceeds, including any pre-hearing review and any preliminary issues hearing, are likely to take place in public[3];
- the final hearing itself will be in public[4]; and
- judgment will be pronounced publicly[5].

1 See para 6.40 below.
2 Tribunal Rules, r 2(1) (definition of 'register').
3 Tribunal Rules, r 17(1) and see, for example, paras 6.85 and 6.108 below.
4 See para 6.124 ff below.
5 See para 6.144 ff below.

Referring a case to the Tribunal

6.33 In those cases where the FSMA 2000 allows it, a firm or person to whom a decision notice or supervisory notice[1] is given may refer the matter to the

Tribunal[2]. This is done by filing a 'reference notice' with the Tribunal, and at the same time sending a copy to the FSA[3].

1 Note that if it is the first supervisory notice that is referred to the Tribunal, it is possible that the FSA would go on to give the second supervisory notice notwithstanding the reference to the Tribunal. In that case, the FSA must file a copy of the subsequent notice: Tribunal Rules, r 11.
2 The Tribunal Rules apply also to a third party who makes a reference to the Tribunal under FSMA 2000, s 393 (see para 5.176 ff above), subject to certain modifications found at Tribunal Rules, r 15.
3 Tribunal Rules, r 4(7).

What is a reference notice?

6.34 A reference notice is the notice issued by a person who wishes to refer a matter to the Tribunal. The notice is required to state[1]:

- the name and address of the applicant;
- the name and address of the applicant's representative (if any);
- the applicant's UK address for service, if different from that above and no representative is named; and
- that the notice is a reference notice; and
- the issues concerning the decision or supervisory notice that the applicant wishes the Tribunal to consider.

A copy of the relevant decision or supervisory notice must be filed as well[2].

1 Tribunal Rules, r 4(3).
2 Tribunal Rules, r 4(5). Where the applicant is a third party on whom a copy of the decision notice was served under FSMA 2000, s 393 (see para 5.176 ff above), this is not required: Tribunal Rules, r 15(3).

6.35 The reference notice is a relatively straightforward document, the only potential complexity being the requirement to state in it the issues concerning the decision notice or supervisory notice that the applicant wishes the Tribunal to consider. Therefore, whilst the burden of proof in the Tribunal is on the FSA to substantiate the action that it wishes to take, and not on the applicant to challenge that action, and whilst it is for the FSA to take the first step in explaining what the case is about[1], the applicant needs at least to have given some thought to the grounds for referring the matter to the Tribunal before he files the reference notice. The Tribunal Rules do not, however, prescribe what information must be provided in this regard and in principle it ought to be permissible for the reference notice to say little more than that the applicant wishes the Tribunal to consider whether it is appropriate for the FSA to take the relevant action.

1 See para 6.42 below.

When can the reference notice be filed?

6.36 A reference notice cannot be filed until the relevant supervisory notice or decision notice which gives rise to the right to refer the case to the Tribunal has been issued. Once that notice has been issued, the reference must be made before the end of the period of 28 days beginning with the date on which the relevant decision notice or supervisory notice was given[1]. Time therefore starts running on the date when the decision notice or supervisory notice is given (not the date it is received)[2]. Time stops running when the reference is made. It is unclear when this occurs, but it appears that the reference is made when the reference notice is sent to the Tribunal[3].

1 FSMA 2000, s 133(1) and the Tribunal Rules, r 4(2).
2 For the detailed rules on the service of statutory notices, see The Financial Services and Markets Act 2000 (Services of Notices) Regulations 2001, SI 2001/1420 and see the FSA Handbook at DEC 5.3.
3 It seems that the reference is made when the reference notice is filed: Tribunal Rules, r 4(1). 'Filed' means sent to the Tribunal: Tribunal Rules, r 2(1). For the rules regarding the sending and receipt of Tribunal notices, including the reference notice, see Tribunal Rules, r 31.

6.37 If the time for serving the notice is likely to expire, or has expired, then it may be possible to have the time extended[1]. The Tribunal is empowered to grant an application for an extension of time[2] if satisfied that to do so would be in the interests of justice. The Tribunal must also consider whether the decision notice or supervisory notice was such as to notify the applicant properly and effectively of the action proposed by the FSA and whether the applicant had been notified of the right to refer the matter to the Tribunal and the time limit for doing so.

1 A time limit which has been extended can be further extended by the Tribunal, upon an application (see para 6.39 below), provided the Tribunal is satisfied that the further extension would be in the interests of justice: Tribunal Rules, r 10(3).
2 Tribunal Rules, r 10(1)(d) and (2). As to how such an application is made, see para 6.79 ff below.

Does the applicant have any other options at the same time?

6.38 At the same time as filing and serving the reference notice, the applicant may want to consider applying for directions from the Tribunal on particular procedural issues. The Tribunal will consider what directions are required in due course, but there may be certain issues which the applicant considers necessary to be addressed at the outset. The Tribunal Rules expressly allow the applicant to make an application for directions when filing the reference notice[1].

1 Tribunal Rules, r 4(6).

6.39 Whether any directions are required, and if so, what directions, depends entirely on the circumstances. Examples of directions which may be relevant at this stage are:

- to extend the time limit for making the reference[1];
- to keep the matter confidential, by the Tribunal directing that no particulars about the reference should be entered in the Tribunal's register[2];
- to suspend the action which the FSA is taking with immediate effect or on a specified date[3]; or
- to obtain early disclosure of documents from the FSA[4].

The procedure for the making and determination of applications for directions is considered at para 6.79 ff below.

1 See para 6.37 above.
2 The Tribunal may make such a direction if satisfied that this is necessary, having regard to (a) the interests of morals, public order, national security or the protection of the private lives of the parties or (b) any unfairness to the applicant or prejudice to the interests of consumers that might result: Tribunal Rules, r 10(9). This is similar to the criteria for deciding to hold a hearing in private (discussed at para 6.124 ff below) save that there is, in this context, no (express) additional requirement for the Tribunal to be satisfied that such a direction would not prejudice the interests of justice. It is not clear when in practice the Tribunal will make such a direction. For a brief explanation of the register, see para 6.40 below.
3 This relates only to supervisory notices issued by the FSA on an urgent basis: see para 9.194 ff below. The Tribunal may only suspend the relevant action where satisfied that this would not prejudice the interests of any persons intended to be protected by the action or the smooth operation or integrity of the relevant market. This may make it difficult in practice to obtain a suspension: see para 6.104 ff below.
4 The applicant might, for example, wish to seek the FSA's documents relating to the procedure which led to the decision notice or supervisory notice being issued. This material may not otherwise be disclosable: see further the discussion at para 6.63 below. Moreover, a person issued with a supervisory notice will not yet have had any right of access to the FSA's material and may therefore need to seek a direction for early disclosure to enable it to begin preparing its case: see para 6.61 ff below.

What does the Tribunal do when it receives the reference notice?

6.40 On receiving the reference notice[1], if no application for directions has been made at the same time (and subject to any directions given by the Tribunal), the secretary of the Tribunal enters particulars of the reference on the Tribunal's register[2] and informs the parties in writing of:

- the fact that the reference has been received;
- the date when the Tribunal received the reference notice;
- the Tribunal's decision on any application for directions; and
- the date on which this information is being sent to the parties[3].

If an application for directions was included with the reference notice, the secretary simply refers the application for directions to the Tribunal and takes no further action until that application has been determined[4]. The matter should not, therefore, appear on the register in the meantime.

1 Tribunal Rules, r 4(9).
2 The register is a register of references and decisions, which is open to public inspection: Tribunal Rules, r 2(1). It is not clear what information about a reference will be included on it.
3 As will be seen, the date of receipt of this information sets the timing for the next stage, which is the FSA filing its statement of case.
4 Tribunal Rules, r 4(8).

Procedure up to the hearing

6.41 Having issued and served a reference notice, the person has referred the matter to the Tribunal and the Tribunal's procedures apply. We consider here the procedure involved in taking the case from the reference notice to the hearing, and in particular:

- the procedure for each party to explain its case by filing, in the case of the FSA, a statement of case and, in the case of the applicant, a reply;
- the disclosure of documents by each party to the other;
- applications for directions, including the pre-hearing review;
- the treatment of witnesses, including experts;
- the Tribunal's power to suspend the FSA's action pending determination of the reference;
- the power to hold a preliminary hearing of one or more issues; and
- the Tribunal's various powers to consolidate and dispose of cases.

The statement of case and reply

The FSA's statement of case

6.42 Since the burden of proof in the Tribunal is on the FSA, once the applicant files a reference notice, the first stage is for the FSA to file a written statement of case with the Tribunal, which it must also serve on the applicant.

6.43 ***What does the statement of case contain?*** The statement of case is required to[1] set out all the matters and facts upon which the FSA relies to support the referred action, and to specify the statutory provisions under which the action was taken, the reasons for taking the action and the date on which the statement of case is filed. The statement of case is required to be accompanied by the FSA's initial disclosure of documents, as discussed at para 6.58 ff.

1 Tribunal Rules, r 5(2).

6.44 The statement of case is an important document. It provides the main explanation of the FSA's reasons for seeking to take the action which has been referred to the Tribunal and is therefore likely to form the focus of the case and the applicant's arguments in response. It is not clear who within the FSA will be responsible for it, and for the conduct of the Tribunal proceedings more generally, but it is likely to be the same enforcement staff who recommended to the Regulatory Decisions Committee that the relevant action should be taken[1].

1 Note that the FSA has made an appointment of a FSA Leading Advocate for high profile Tribunal cases, High Court actions and criminal cases. As regards the process of making recommendations to the Regulatory Decisions Committee, see para 5.56 ff above.

6.45 The statement of case will explain the penalty (or other action) that the FSA seeks to impose on the applicant and will address matters relevant to the question of what action should be taken, such as the person's previous compliance history. Prejudicial evidence of this nature, which is not relevant to the question of whether the applicant committed the relevant breach, is therefore likely to be before the Tribunal from the outset.

6.46 An issue which the Tribunal Rules do not address is to what extent the FSA can depart in its statement of case from the reasons which it gave in its decision notice or supervisory notice for taking the relevant action[1]. Can it entirely abandon its original grounds and instead rely on new grounds for taking the same action, for example based on an entirely different rule breach? If not, to what extent can it move away from its original reasons, while maintaining the same basic grounds[2]? The answer is not clear. The Tribunal Rules require the FSA to set out the facts and matters upon which it 'relies' to support the referred action. It thus focuses on the present, rather than on the matters which were relied upon at the time when the decision to issue the decision notice or supervisory notice was taken. The FSMA 2000 allows the Tribunal to determine 'the matter referred to it', but that phrase is not defined. On a narrow construction, the matter referred to it is the particular sanction or action which the FSA seeks to take. On a wider construction, which would seem the better construction, it encompasses the reasons for taking that action which the FSA is required to give in its decision notice or supervisory notice. But whether that limits the FSA to the precise reasons it gave, or only to the broad grounds, is more difficult to assess. Much will depend on the extent to which the FSA seeks to depart from its original reasons or grounds in any particular case. This ought to be apparent because the statement of case is required to specify the reasons, and these can be compared with those specified in the decision notice or supervisory notice. There is a separate question whether the applicant should object if the FSA did attempt to rely on different grounds or reasons. This will be a tactical question for the applicant, depending upon, among other things, its views on the merits of the additional grounds, the prospect of using the change to embarrass the FSA in the Tribunal proceedings and the risk that, if the applicant objected, the FSA would commence the process again by issuing a warning or supervisory notice on the different basis.

1 Both decision notices (FSMA 2000, s 388) and, generally, supervisory notices (see, for example, FSMA 2000, s 53(5)) are required to give reasons.
2 There may be a risk of this in practice, for example if the enforcement staff who have conduct of the Tribunal case for the FSA disagree with the way that the Regulatory Decisions Committee decided to put the case in the warning/decision notices or supervisory notices.

6.47 ***When must the FSA file the statement of case?*** The FSA must file its statement of case no later than 28 days after the day on which it received the information about the reference sent by the secretary of the Tribunal, as discussed at para 6.40 above[1]. The FSA may apply for an extension of the time for filing its statement of case[2], which the Tribunal may grant if satisfied that to do so would be in the interests of justice[3]. A time limit extended may be further extended by the Tribunal[4].

1 Tribunal Rules, r 5(1).
2 Or will be treated as having made such an application if it files its statement of case out of time without applying for a direction extending time: Tribunal Rules, r 10(4).
3 Tribunal Rules, r 10(1)(d) and (2). The procedure for making applications for directions is considered at para 6.79 ff below.
4 Tribunal Rules, r 10(3).

6.48 If the FSA does not file a statement of case within the applicable time limit, then the Tribunal may direct of its own initiative that the FSA file a statement of case by a specified date[1]. It also has the power to, if appropriate, determine the reference without an oral hearing, make a costs order, strike out the statement of case, or part of it, or debar the FSA from contesting the reference[2].

1 Tribunal Rules, r 10(5).
2 Tribunal Rules, rr 14(3) and 27(1).

The applicant's reply

6.49 Once the FSA files its statement of case, the applicant must file a written reply.

6.50 ***What should the reply contain?*** The reply is required to[1]:

- state the grounds on which the applicant relies in the reference;
- identify all matters in the statement of case which are disputed by the applicant;
- state the applicant's reasons for disputing them; and
- specify the date on which it is filed.

1 Tribunal Rules, r 6(2).

6.51 The applicant will clearly wish to explain those points in the statement of case which it disputes, and the reasons why. But its reasons for requiring the FSA to prove its case in the Tribunal, or for disagreeing with the action the FSA wishes to take, may go beyond this. The person may have positive points to make, for example about action it took once the regulatory breach arose[1], it may have points to make in mitigation[2], or it may wish to raise issues about the FSA's procedures[3]. To the extent it wishes to rely on them, the applicant needs to make all of these points in its reply[4]. The reply will (together with the statement of case) form the basis on which the Tribunal will decide what the issues are and what procedure is required to have those issues determined[5].

1 Relevant points include how the breach came to the applicant's attention, how quickly and completely the applicant notified the FSA of it, the level of co-operation with the FSA, and the steps taken by the applicant to identify and address any customer losses, employee issues and implications for systems and controls: see generally Chapter 3 above.
2 For example, that the breach was not particularly serious, that no customers were affected or their interests were protected by the applicant, or that the breach was an isolated incident with no systemic implications.
3 For example, about whether the applicant has been treated fairly in the investigation and enforcement process. This would be unlikely to be relevant to the merits of the case but the applicant may wish to seek a recommendation from the Tribunal about the FSA's procedures or rules: see para 6.140 below.
4 It is thought that this is what is encompassed by the phrase 'the grounds on which the applicant relies in the reference'.
5 This is subject to the applicant or the FSA being allowed to supplement or amend their documents: see, respectively, paras 6.54 and 6.56 below.

6.52 ***When must the reply be filed?*** The reply must be filed so as to be received by the Tribunal no later than 28 days after the date on which the applicant received a copy of the FSA's statement of case[1]. A copy must be served on the FSA at the same time[2]. The applicant can apply for an extension of time[3], which the Tribunal may grant if satisfied that to do so would be in the interests of justice[4]. A time limit extended may be further extended[5].

1 Or, if the FSA was permitted to serve an amended statement of case, 28 days after the applicant receives a copy: Tribunal Rules, r 6(1). Rules relating to the giving and sending of notices are found at Tribunal Rules, r 31.
2 Tribunal Rules, r 6(4).
3 Or will be treated as having made such an application if it files its reply out of time without applying for a direction extending time: Tribunal Rules, r 10(4).
4 Tribunal Rules, r 10(1)(d) and (2). The procedure for making applications for directions is considered at para 6.79 ff below.
5 Tribunal Rules, r 10(3).

6.53 If a reply is not filed in accordance with the applicable time limit, then the Tribunal may of its own initiative direct that the applicant file a reply by a specified date[1]. It also has the power to, if appropriate, determine the reference without an oral hearing (but it cannot dismiss the reference without notifying the applicant and giving it an opportunity to make representations), make a costs order or dismiss all or part of the reference[2].

1 Tribunal Rules, r 10(5).
2 Tribunal Rules, rr 14(3) and 27(1).

Supplementary statements

6.54 There is no provision for the automatic exchange of additional statements by the parties. In practice, the applicant may have raised in its reply various positive points to which the FSA may wish to respond and, equally, the applicant and the Tribunal may want to know what the FSA's case is on these points. Whilst there is no mechanism automatically requiring the FSA to serve a further response, the Rules[1] do allow the Tribunal (on an application by a party or of its own initiative) to permit or require a party to provide further information or a supplementary statement (or to amend a statement). If a supplementary statement is likely to assist the just, economical and expeditious determination of the reference[2], for example by clarifying what the issues are so that the witness, expert and documentary evidence is directed to those issues, then this may well be attractive to the Tribunal.

1 Tribunal Rules, r 10(1)(f). The procedure for making applications for directions is considered in para 6.79 ff below.
2 These are the criteria applied in giving directions: see para 6.87 below.

6.55 When should applicants be considering applying for a direction to require a response from the FSA to the person's reply document? In practice, this should at least be under consideration in any case where points are raised in the reply that were not addressed by the FSA in its statement of case. By requiring the FSA to explain at the outset its case on those new points, the applicant allows itself to prepare to address the FSA's case on those points at the hearing. There is otherwise a risk of being caught by surprise at the hearing and being unable to deal properly with the FSA's points. There is, however, a potential disadvantage, which is that the FSA may use the supplementary statement as an opportunity to improve upon its case in the light of the applicant's reply. The applicant will therefore need to consider where the balance lies in the particular case.

Can the parties amend their statements of case?

6.56 A party may apply at any time for a direction permitting or requiring the amendment of the statement of case or reply[1]. The Tribunal may also make a direction of its own initiative. The procedure for making applications for directions is considered at para 6.79 ff below.

1 Tribunal Rules, r 10(1)(f).

6.57 The Tribunal Rules do not address the extent to which the FSA will be permitted to amend its case. For example, if in its statement of case the FSA gave two reasons for taking the relevant action, can it amend its case to abandon those two reasons and rely instead upon two entirely different reasons? There are three, separate questions, namely, first, whether the Tribunal would be entitled to consider the new reasons given by the FSA, second if so, whether it should as a matter of discretion allow the FSA to make the amendments and, third, whether the applicant should consent or object to the amendments being made. The first and third questions arise equally in relation to the FSA's statement of case and are considered at para 6.46 above. The additional question which arises when considering amendments to the statement of case is how the Tribunal should exercise its discretion whether to allow the FSA to make the amendments. The answer will depend very much upon the circumstances[1], including factors such as the reasons why the amendments are now being sought and why the case was not put in this way from the outset, the extent of the amendments, any prejudice that would be caused to the person concerned and, possibly, whether the FSA could commence a new enforcement procedure based on the amended 'charges'[2].

1 By way of analogy, it is notable that a criminal court has a broad discretion, albeit statutory, to amend an indictment: see *R v Osieh* [1996] 2 Cr App Rep 145 and *R v Johal and Ram* (1972) 56 Cr App Rep 348 and see the discussion at Archbold 2001, 1–149.
2 If the reasons the FSA now proposed to give for taking the action were fundamentally different from those given in the decision notice or supervisory notice, then the applicant may also have grounds to apply for the FSA to pay its costs of the Tribunal process on the basis that it had acted unreasonably: see para 6.153 ff below.

Disclosure of documents

6.58 The Tribunal Rules contain provision for the disclosure of documents by the parties. Unusually, this happens sequentially rather than by mutual exchange and the extent of the disclosure obligation is different for the FSA and for the applicant. Nonetheless, the reality is likely to be that the FSA has already, in the course of its investigation, had access to whatever documents and information it or its investigator believed to be relevant. The disclosure process is unlikely therefore to reveal much to the regulator.

6.59 We consider here:

- the FSA's obligation to provide initial disclosure;
- the applicant's obligation to provide disclosure;
- the FSA's obligation to provide secondary disclosure;
- the documents that are not required to be disclosed by either party;
- the Tribunal's power to give directions relating to disclosure; and
- the use that the applicant can make of documents disclosed.

The FSA's obligation to provide initial disclosure

6.60 At the same time as filing its statement of case, the FSA must file with the Tribunal and send the applicant a list of[1]:

- the documents on which it relies in support of the referred action[2]; and
- the further documents considered by the FSA in reaching (or maintaining[3]) the decision to issue the warning notice or supervisory notice, or obtained by it in connection with the matter to which the notice relates (whether before or after giving the notice) but not considered by it in reaching (or maintaining) that decision[4], which in the opinion of the FSA might undermine the decision to take the referred action.

Certain categories of documents need not be included on the list[5] and, in addition, the FSA may apply (without giving notice to the applicant) for a direction authorising it not to include particular documents on its list[6]. Once it has served its list, the FSA must, upon request, provide the applicant with a copy of any document specified in it or make such a document available for inspection or copying[7].

1 Tribunal Rules, r 5(3) and (4).
2 This test looks at the present, rather than the past – ie what are the documents upon which the FSA now relies in support of the referred action? So far as the meaning of 'referred action' is concerned, whilst not entirely clear, it seems that this encompasses both the decision to (for example) impose a penalty and the penalty itself: see Tribunal Rules, r 2(1).
3 This is the wording of the Tribunal Rules (r 2(1), definition of 'further material') but it is not entirely clear what it is intended to mean.
4 See the definition of 'further material' at Tribunal Rules, r 2(1).
5 This is discussed further at para 6.67 ff below.
6 This is discussed further at para 6.71 ff below.
7 Tribunal Rules, r 8(7).

6.61 A number of points should be noted regarding the timing and nature of the FSA's disclosure. First, if the action to which the reference relates was one that required the supervisory notice procedure, rather than the warning/decision notice procedure, to be followed, then this will be the first opportunity the applicant will have had to have access to any of the FSA's material. It may therefore wish to consider applying to the Tribunal at the time it issues the reference notice for a direction for the FSA to give immediate disclosure so that it can start preparing its case at that stage rather than having to wait 28 days for the FSA to serve its statement of case[1].

1 See para 6.39 above.

6.62 Second, where the warning/decision notice procedure was used, the material which the FSA has to disclose at the Tribunal stage corresponds broadly with the material to which the FSA was required to provide access when it gave the relevant warning and/or decision notice[1], although there are some differences (for example, the material upon which the FSA now relies may not equate entirely with the material upon which it relied at the time when it took the relevant decision). Broadly, therefore, the applicant may already have had access to much of this material. Further disclosure by the FSA may occur in due course, after the applicant serves its reply[2].

1 The FSA's obligation to give access to its material is discussed in detail at para 5.81 ff above.
2 See para 6.65 below.

6.63 Third, one omission from the categories of material which the FSA is required to disclose is material relating to the decision itself, and in particular the record kept by the Regulatory Decisions Committee of, for example, who was present at the RDC meeting at which the decision to take the relevant action was made and what representations and material were put before the RDC, including what oral evidence from the FSA staff[1]. The Tribunal is able to require the disclosure of additional documents and, as will be seen, the Tribunal Rules prescribe a low test, leaving the question whether to order disclosure in the discretion of the Tribunal dealing with the particular case[2]. However, save perhaps for oral evidence given by FSA staff to the RDC, the Tribunal may perhaps take the view that this material is irrelevant, as the Tribunal is considering the matter de novo and so is not concerned with the FSA's decision-making process. There may, however, be some prospect of obtaining disclosure, for example if the applicant is seeking a recommendation from the Tribunal about the FSA's procedures. It will be a matter for the Tribunal to decide in each case.

1 Such a record is kept as a matter of course, so that there is a clear record in relation to each decision: see the FSA Handbook at DEC 4.2.19 and see para 5.39 above.
2 This is discussed further at para 6.73 below.

The applicant's obligation to provide disclosure

6.64 At the same time as filing its reply, the applicant must send the Tribunal and the FSA a list of all the documents on which it relies in support of its case[1]. The applicant does not have to provide the FSA with certain types of documents, discussed below, but will in practical terms need to disclose them if it is to rely on them in support of its case[2]. Similarly, to the extent that the applicant relies on documents that are confidential in support of its case, it must disclose such documents; confidentiality is not a ground for withholding disclosure[3]. The obligation of disclosure is thus limited to those documents on which the applicant relies in support of its case. The likelihood is that the FSA will already have had access to the applicant's records during the course of its investigation. Once it has served its list, the applicant must, upon request, provide the FSA with a copy of, or make available for inspection or copying, any document specified in the list[4].

1 Tribunal Rules, r 6(3) and (4).
2 See the discussion at para 6.70 below.
3 In the context of employment tribunals, the House of Lords has suggested that the tribunal should inspect the confidential document and consider whether justice can be done by adopting special measures such as covering up, substituting anonymous references for specific names or, in rare cases, hearing the matter in private: see the consolidated *Nassé* and *Vyas* appeals [1979] 3 All ER 673. Whilst the employment tribunal is applying a different test, it may be appropriate to seek a direction from the Tribunal in this context to treat in a similar way the disclosure of particularly sensitive material (particularly to avoid it being disclosed in a public hearing).
4 Tribunal Rules, r 8(7).

The FSA's obligation to provide secondary disclosure

6.65 The Tribunal Rules may require the FSA to give further disclosure following the filing by the applicant of its reply. In particular, the FSA must file a list of any further material which might be reasonably expected to assist the applicant's case as disclosed by its reply and which is not mentioned in the list already provided by the FSA[1]. The list must be filed (and a copy sent to the applicant at the same time) so that it is received no later than 14 days after the day on which the FSA received the reply[2]. Certain categories of documents need not be included on the list[3] and, in addition, the FSA may apply (without giving notice to the applicant) for a direction authorising it not to include particular documents on its list[4]. Once it has served its list, the FSA must, upon request, provide the applicant with a copy of any document specified in it or make such a document available for inspection or copying[5].

1 Tribunal Rules, r 7(1).
2 Tribunal Rules, r 7(2) and (3).
3 See para 6.67 ff below.
4 See para 6.71 ff below
5 Tribunal Rules, r 8(7).

6.66 This broadens the FSA's duty of disclosure, requiring the FSA to disclose a wider category of adverse documents, encompassing not only those that might undermine its case but also those that might assist the applicant's case as the applicant has put that case in its reply. Whether material might reasonably be expected to assist the applicant's case is an objective test. It is for the FSA to reach this assessment in the first instance, although if the applicant believes that there may be further material which should be disclosed, an application could be made to the Tribunal for a direction accordingly, as discussed further below[1].

1 See para 6.73 ff below.

What documents do not need to be provided?

6.67 In parallel with the provisions of the FSMA 2000, certain types of documents do not need to be disclosed. The relevant types of documents are as follows[1]:

- documents which are, broadly, protected under the FSMA 2000 because they are legally privileged[2];

- documents which relate to a case involving a different person and were taken into account by the FSA in the applicant's case only for purposes of comparison with other cases[3];
- documents the disclosure of which is prohibited by the Regulation of Investigatory Powers Act 2000, s 17[4];
- any document in respect of which an application has been or is being made for a direction authorising a party not to include the document in the list[5].

1 Tribunal Rules, r 8(1) to (3) and (8).
2 Such documents must be included in the list but need not be disclosed: Tribunal Rules, r 8(8). Various issues which arise are considered at para 6.68 below.
3 Such documents need not be included in the list: Tribunal Rules, r 8(1). The same category of documents is excluded from the access provisions of the FSMA 2000 as discussed in more detail at para 5.82 ff above.
4 Broadly, the effect of this is to ensure that the Tribunal is bound by the provisions of the Regulation of Investigatory Powers Act 2000 which exclude from legal proceedings (subject to certain exceptions) matters which disclose that communications have been or will be intercepted. Such documents need not be included in the list: Tribunal Rules, r 8(2).
5 Applications for such directions are discussed at para 6.71 ff below. Such documents need not be included in the list: Tribunal Rules, r 8(3).

6.68 ***Legally privileged material*** Both the FSA and the applicant could have legally privileged documents which they will want to withhold from disclosure[1]. Among other things, the disclosure of the material in this context may constitute a waiver of the privilege or may result in the document being disclosed in a public forum (the Tribunal hearing), and in either case destroy the protection of legal privilege so that it could be discloseable in other proceedings, for example proceedings brought by third parties who may have claims against the applicant. As noted above, although the Tribunal Rules allow such documents not to be disclosed, they do require them to be identified in the list of documents. In practice, this can often be done generically, without identifying individual documents that are legally privileged.

1 Note that the meaning of legal privilege applicable in this context is that under FSMA 2000, s 413(2): see Tribunal Rules, r 8(8) and the definition of 'protected item' in r 2. That is not the same in all respects as the common law meaning and, in particular, it does not appear to encompass 'without prejudice' material and it may not include certain internal communications that would normally be legally privileged: see para 4.264 ff above. For a brief discussion of the common law meaning of legal privilege and the documents that are likely to be covered, see para 4.196 ff above.

6.69 The requirement to list privileged material should be unobjectionable from the FSA's perspective, since the parallel provisions in the FSMA 2000 require the FSA to give the applicant notice of the existence of such items[1]. In some instances, though, material which may be privileged will be an important part of the FSA's case, for example an expert report. The question whether that material should be disclosed has been discussed at para 5.91 above. In the context of the Tribunal that issue is less likely to cause difficulty because the FSA will need either to disclose the report, if it is to rely upon it, or to obtain a new report for disclosure and use in the Tribunal proceedings.

1 FSMA 2000, s 394(4)(a) and see para 5.83 above.

6.70 The position is different so far as relates to the applicant. The FSMA 2000 provides that a person may not be required under the FSMA 2000 to produce, disclose or permit the inspection of a privileged document[1]. However, the question whether the document is to be disclosed is within the applicant's control, as it need only list those documents on which it relies in support of its case. That could include privileged material such as legal advice, for example if one of its arguments in its defence is that it took and complied with legal advice on the matter in question. But if it wishes to rely on that legal advice before the Tribunal, then in practical terms it will need to disclose that advice at some stage[2]. The question, therefore, is whether the applicant wishes to rely on the legally privileged material in support of its case.

1 This is broadly the effect of FSMA 2000, s 413. See also footnote 1 to para 6.68 above.
2 It may be possible to seek ancillary directions to protect the applicant's position, for example to have the hearing in private either wholly or so far as relates to the disclosure of the legally privileged information.

The Tribunal's power to give directions relating to disclosure

6.71 ***Authorising a party not to disclose documents*** The Tribunal can make a direction authorising a party not to include a document in its list. The grounds for making such a direction are[1] that disclosure of the document:

- would not be in the public interest[2]; or
- would not be fair, having regard to:
  - — the likely significance of the document to the applicant in relation to the matter referred to the Tribunal, and
  - — the potential prejudice to the commercial interests of a person other than the applicant which would be caused by disclosure of the document.

Such a direction may be made on an application by either party (although in practice it is most likely to be the FSA that seeks to make use of this provision). The application is made without giving notice to the other party[3].

1 Tribunal Rules, r 8(4).
2 It is thought that this would include a document protected by the doctrine of public interest immunity.
3 Tribunal Rules, r 8(4).

6.72 Whether the Tribunal will be prepared to make such a direction will depend largely upon the situation. Whilst the grounds for making the direction mirror one of the exceptions to the statutory right of access to the FSA's material[1], there is an important difference that in this context it is for the Tribunal, not the FSA, to decide whether or not the document should be disclosed[2]. In order to do so, the Tribunal may require that the document be produced to it together with a statement of the reasons why its inclusion in the list would, as applicable, not be in the public interest or not be fair, and it may also invite the other party to make representations[3].

1 This is discussed at para 5.83 above.
2 If the Tribunal refuses an application for such a direction, it will direct the relevant party to revise its list so as to include the document and to file a copy of that list as revised and send a copy to the other party: Tribunal Rules, r 8(6).
3 Tribunal Rules, r 8(5).

6.73 ***Directing further disclosure*** In contrast with the statutory provision allowing access to the FSA's documents in the course of the FSA's decision-making process[1], the Tribunal Rules on disclosure are only the starting point. The Tribunal's powers to give directions expressly include a direction requiring any party to file and, if appropriate, copy to the other party (or make available for copying and inspection), any document that is in its custody or under its control which the Tribunal considers is or may be relevant to the determination of the reference and which has not already been disclosed or made the subject of a direction that it need not be disclosed[2]. The only exceptions are that the Tribunal may not give a direction if satisfied that[3]:

- a document is protected under the FSMA 2000 because it is, broadly, legally privileged[4]; or
- the document should not be disclosed on one of the grounds on which the Tribunal could authorise it not to be disclosed[5].

For the purpose of determining whether to direct that a document is disclosed, the Tribunal may require the document to be produced to the Tribunal, hear the application in the absence of any party and invite any party to make representations[6].

1 See para 5.81 ff above.
2 Tribunal Rules, r 10(1)(g).
3 Tribunal Rules, r 10(8)).
4 See para 6.68 above.
5 These are outlined at para 6.71 above.
6 Tribunal Rules, r 10(8).

6.74 The Tribunal can therefore override the FSA's objections to producing a document on the ground that it relates to some other person and was used for the purposes of comparison. It also allows the applicant to apply for a direction requiring the FSA to produce any other classes of documents which do not fall within the categories of document normally included within the list, for example, those relating to the FSA's internal decision-making process in reaching the decision to issue the warning or decision notice or the supervisory notice in the case[1]. Equally, the Tribunal could require the applicant to disclose additional material. Whether or not to direct the disclosure of a particular document is within the discretion of the Tribunal in the particular case, provided only that the document is within a party's custody or control and that it is or may be relevant to the determination of the reference (and subject to the exception for privileged material). The test of 'is or may be relevant to the determination of the reference' is a low one. For example, there is on the face of it no need for the party concerned to show that the document concerned is directly relevant to the issues as they are pleaded. The key question is therefore how the Tribunal will exercise its discretion in the particular case. It is likely the Tribunal will apply the test of ensuring the just, expeditious and economical determination of the matter[2]. The breadth of the discretion means that a party may be able to persuade the Tribunal to order the disclosure of material notwithstanding that its relevance cannot at that time be specified, or even notwithstanding that the documents to be disclosed cannot be identified with precision by the person making the application. But the wider and less specific the request, the less likely that the Tribunal will grant it[3].

1 This is discussed at para 6.63 above.
2 This is the test applicable to the giving of directions generally: see para 6.77 below.
3 Particularly, an application that is no more than a 'fishing expedition' is likely to have a low prospect of success.

6.75 When in practice should the applicant consider making an application for specific disclosure? How should it act if it wishes to do so? The starting point for the applicant will often be the FSA's lists of documents, which will list the material that the FSA is declining to disclose on the basis of the statutory protection for legal privilege. If the applicant believes that any of this material is not truly a 'protected item' within FSMA 2000, s 413, then it can apply to the Tribunal for a direction that the FSA disclose it. Beyond this, the applicant may suspect that the FSA holds additional relevant material that may be of assistance to it, or that material from comparable cases should be disclosed (for example, because the FSA staff referred to other cases in the settlement discussions that took place earlier) or the applicant may wish to see documents relating to the internal decision-making process followed by the FSA in the case. Initially, it may be sensible to seek disclosure of the material through correspondence with the FSA. Among other things, this may help to establish whether the material exists and the FSA's views on its relevance and may therefore assist the applicant in formulating an application to the Tribunal for a direction that the material be disclosed. As has already been discussed, the more speculative the application, the less likely the Tribunal will be prepared to make the direction.

What use can the applicant make of documents disclosed to it?

6.76 Applicants must take care not to disclose or use for purposes other than the Tribunal proceedings documents disclosed to them by the FSA in Tribunal proceedings. Such documents may contain confidential information which the FSMA 2000 protects from disclosure[1] and, as a person receiving such information directly or indirectly from the FSA, the firm or individual could commit a criminal offence if it disclosed that information to third parties for other purposes[2]. This may not prevent the applicant from disclosing or using information relating solely to itself which was obtained by the FSA from it alone. But caution needs to be exercised. The FSA's investigations may have involved it obtaining information from third parties or the information may relate to some other person, and in either case there would be a risk of committing the criminal offence. In addition, there may be a possibility of the applicant, having received the relevant documents in the course of the Tribunal proceedings, being restricted as a matter of law to using those documents only for the purposes of those proceedings[3].

1 Note that the protection would fall away if the document were disclosed in public, for example at the Tribunal hearing (unless the Tribunal orders the hearing (or part of it) to be held in private): see footnote 3 to para 4.308 above.
2 FSMA 2000, s 348. For an explanation, see para 4.304 ff above. Note that certain types of disclosure are permitted under the so-called Gateway Regulations: see para 4.312 ff above. Among other things, the Gateway Regulations (reg 5) allow the FSA (and the firm or individual) to disclose information to any person for the purposes of proceedings before the Tribunal which have been initiated or for the purpose of bringing an end to such proceedings or of facilitating a determination of whether they should be brought to an end. But the disclosure must be made for the purpose of facilitating the carrying out of a public function: FSMA 2000, s 349(1)).
3 It is possible that the law would imply a confidentiality restriction equivalent to the implied undertakings given on disclosure in court proceedings (see Civil Procedure Rules, Part 31, r 31.22). For a discussion of the implied undertaking, see *Disclosure*, Matthews & Malek, 2000, Chapter 13.

Applications for directions

6.77 After the parties have provided disclosure, the Tribunal Rules do not prescribe any particular procedure to prepare the case for the hearing. It is for the Tribunal to decide what steps are appropriate in the particular case, which it does by giving directions to the parties to take particular procedural steps. The Tribunal has a general power to regulate its own procedure, subject to the provisions of the FSMA 2000 and the Tribunal Rules[1]. More specifically, the Tribunal Rules[2] allow the Tribunal to give directions at any time to:

- enable the parties to prepare for the hearing;
- assist the Tribunal to determine the issues; and
- generally ensure the just, expeditious and economical determination of the reference.

1 Tribunal Rules, r 26(2).
2 Tribunal Rules, r 9.

6.78 Such directions may be given either on the application of one or more parties, or by the Tribunal on its own initiative. Or they may be given at a pre-hearing review. We consider, first, the rules on applying for or giving directions generally, secondly, the pre-hearing review, thirdly, the question of what directions can be made and, fourthly, practical guidance for applicants on applying for directions.

Rules relating to directions generally

6.79 Directions may be made by the Tribunal either on its own initiative or on an application by a party or all the parties[1]. Directions are likely to be determined by the chairman alone, rather than by the full Tribunal[2].

1 Tribunal Rules, r 9(2).
2 Tribunal Rules, r 29 and see FSMA 2000, Sch 13, para 9(d). There is no provision for appealing to the full Tribunal interlocutory decisions made by the chairman.

6.80 Where the Tribunal gives a direction of its own initiative, it may give prior notice to the parties of its intention to do so, but it need not do so[1].

1 Tribunal Rules, r 9(2).

6.81 Where a party makes an application for a direction, the application must include the reasons for making it[1]. It must be filed at the Tribunal[2] and a copy must normally be sent at the same time to the other party[3]. If any party objects to the directions applied for, the Tribunal considers the objection and, if it considers it necessary for the determination of the application, gives the parties an opportunity to make representations[4]. Applications are normally considered on paper, without an oral hearing[5], and even where the Tribunal decides to hear representations, those representations are likely to be in writing[6].

1 Tribunal Rules, r 9(3).
2 Unless the application is made at the hearing of the reference or at the pre-hearing review: Tribunal Rules, r 9(3).
3 This is not required if the application is made with the consent of all parties or an application without notice is permitted under the Tribunal Rules: r 9(4). The latter encompasses, in particular, applications for a direction authorising a party not to include a particular document in its list (see para 6.71 above).
4 Tribunal Rules, r 9(5).
5 Tribunal Rules, r 16(1)(b). If the Tribunal decides to hold an oral hearing, that will normally be in public: Tribunal Rules, r 17(1) and (2) and see para 6.124 below.
6 See, for example, the definition of 'representations': Tribunal Rules, r 2.

6.82 The Tribunal Rules allow a party to object to directions even once they have been made. This clearly applies to directions made on the Tribunal's own initiative, but it is not confined to such directions. The party seeking to object is allowed to apply to the Tribunal showing good cause why the direction should be varied or set aside[1]. The Tribunal may not vary or set aside the direction without first notifying any person who applied for the direction and giving it an opportunity to make representations.

1 Tribunal Rules, r 9(8).

6.83 As to how directions are made[1]:

- they may be given orally or in writing;
- notice of any written direction (or refusal to give a direction) is given to the parties unless the Tribunal decides otherwise in any particular case[2];
- directions containing a requirement may specify a time limit for complying and must include a statement of the possible consequences of failing to comply with the requirement; and
- the Tribunal will also consider whether the decision should be pronounced publicly[3].

1 Tribunal Rules, r 9(6) and (7).
2 An example might be where the Tribunal makes a direction authorising a party not to disclose certain documents in its list.
3 In particular, the Tribunal is required to consider whether there are circumstances making it undesirable to make a public pronouncement of the whole or any part of its decision and may, in consequence, take any steps (including making the decision anonymous, editing the text or declining to publish the whole or part of the decision) with a view to ensuring the minimum restriction on public pronouncement that is consistent with the need for the restriction: Tribunal Rules, r 16(2) to (4).

The pre-hearing review

6.84 In appropriate cases, the Tribunal may decide to hold a pre-hearing review, which is an oral hearing where the Tribunal considers what further procedural steps are required to take the case to the final hearing. The chairman of the Tribunal decides whether to direct that a pre-hearing review should be held[1]. No indication has been given as to the sorts of cases where a review is likely to be ordered, but this should include the more complex cases and those which are scheduled for a hearing over several days[2].

1 Tribunal Rules, r 9(9).
2 This is broadly the practice in the civil litigation context: see, for example, the Civil Procedure Rules, Pt 29.

6.85 The pre-hearing review is held on not less than 14 days' notice[1] at any time before the main hearing of the reference[2]. It is held before the chairman of the Tribunal, normally in public[3], and the parties may appear and may be represented, whether or not by a lawyer[4].

1 Tribunal Rules, r 9(10).
2 Tribunal Rules, r 9(12).
3 The Rules discussed at para 6.124 below apply: see Tribunal Rules, r 17 (1).
4 Tribunal Rules, r 18.

6.86 The purpose of the hearing is twofold. The chairman is required to:

- give all directions appearing necessary or desirable for securing the just, expeditious and economical conduct of the reference[1]; and
- endeavour to secure that the parties make all admissions and agreements as they ought reasonably to have made in relation to the proceedings[2].

1 Tribunal Rules, r 9(11)(a). It may be instructive to have in mind the issues that would be considered by a civil court at a case management conference: see Civil Procedures Rules, Pt 29, 29PD-005.
2 Tribunal Rules, r 9(11)(b). Again, this reflects the approach of the civil courts in considering what directions to make at a case management conference: see Civil Procedure Rules, Pt 29, 29PD-005.

What directions can the Tribunal make?

6.87 The Tribunal has a general power to regulate its own procedure, subject to the FSMA 2000 and the Tribunal Rules[1] and it may, therefore, generally speaking, make any directions it thinks appropriate to enable the parties to prepare for the hearing, to assist the Tribunal to determine the issues and generally to ensure the just, expeditious and economical determination of the dispute[2]. The difficulty in balancing the three relevant factors of justice, expedition and economy has already been outlined[3] and the weight of each of these factors is likely to differ from case to case. The Tribunal exercises its discretion to ensure that the procedure adopted is that appropriate to the particular case.

1 Tribunal Rules, r 26(2).
2 These are the factors relevant to the exercise of its discretion: Tribunal Rules, r 9(1).
3 See the discussion at para 6.20 ff above.

6.88 Additionally, the Tribunal's discretion must be exercised in a way that allows the procedure to be ECHR compatible and, in particular, it must comply with the fair trial guarantees of Art 6(1)[1]. This may restrict its freedom of action in certain respects, for example by requiring it to hold an oral hearing, to hold the hearing in public and to allow each party the same opportunity to test the other party's evidence and put forward its own case[2]. But provided the minimum ECHR standards are fulfilled, this does not prevent the Tribunal from requiring a more complex procedure to be undertaken in more serious cases.

1 These are briefly outlined at para 6.26 above.
2 These are given only as examples. They would not necessarily apply in every case.

6.89 Subject to these points, precisely what is required will vary from case to case, but the Tribunal Rules do give some examples of particular directions which the Tribunal may make, including[1]:

- fixing, and altering, the time and place of the hearing[2], providing for an oral hearing[3], and adjourning any oral hearing;
- extending or varying any time limit;
- suspending the effect of a statutory notice, or preventing it from taking effect, pending the outcome of the reference[4];
- permitting or requiring a party to provide further information or supplementary statements[5] or to amend a statement;
- requiring a party to provide additional disclosure[6];
- requiring any party to provide a statement of relevant issues and facts, identifying those that are and are not agreed;
- requiring a party to file documents for a hearing;
- requiring a party to file a list of witnesses whom it wishes to call to give evidence at the hearing and statements of the evidence which those witnesses intend to give if called[7];
- making provision as to any expert witnesses to be called including the number of witnesses and the evidence to be given by them; or providing for the appointment of an expert by the Tribunal and for the expert to send the parties copies of any reports he produces[8];
- providing for the manner in which any evidence may be given[9];
- requiring that the register includes no particulars about the reference[10];
- consolidating references[11], directing that a preliminary hearing be held[12], ordering a document to be struck out on the basis it is scandalous, frivolous or vexatious, or ordering a reference to be struck out for want of prosecution[13]; and
- taking steps for non-compliance with directions or the Tribunal Rules[14].

1 Tribunal Rules, r 10(1).
2 See para 6.119 ff below.

3 The rules on oral hearings are at Tribunal Rules, r 16. See also paras 6.81 above and 6.123 below.
4 This is discussed further at para 6.104 ff below.
5 The use of supplementary statements is discussed at para 6.54 above.
6 This is discussed in detail at para 6.73 ff below.
7 The use of witness evidence is discussed at para 6.92 below.
8 The involvement of expert witnesses is discussed at para 6.98 ff below.
9 The provisions relating to evidence at the hearing are discussed at para 6.130 ff below.
10 This may be done in order to keep the matter confidential: see para 6.39 above. The register is explained briefly at para 6.40 above.
11 This is discussed further at para 6.109 ff below.
12 Tribunal Rules, r 13(1) and see para 6.107 ff below.
13 Tribunal Rules, r 26(3).
14 In particular, the Tribunal may make a costs order, dismiss the whole or part of the reference (if the applicant is in default), or strike out the whole or part of the FSA's statement of case and/or debar the FSA from contesting the reference (if the FSA is in default): Tribunal rules, r 27(1).

Practical guidance for applicants

6.90 The applicant's approach to the question of directions depends very much upon its strategy more generally. For example, does it wish to have the matter resolved swiftly, or is it preferable to spin out the process? Is it looking primarily to achieve a cost-effective Tribunal process, or a particularly thorough investigation of the matter? Is its case focused on disputing certain key conclusions or facts, or is it more wide-ranging? Does it need the FSA's co-operation on other procedural matters, that would militate against behaving aggressively? These and other factors will dictate the applicant's approach to the procedure and will determine whether it actively seeks directions or waits to react to events.

6.91 Against this background, the issues that the applicant might consider include:

- whether the applicant should take the lead in suggesting appropriate directions and the timetable more generally;
- whether the applicant should seek to agree those directions with the FSA first, or simply make an application to the Tribunal;
- whether the applicant should be making any substantial interlocutory applications, for example for a preliminary issues hearing or an application to strike out part or all of the FSA's case;
- whether there are any areas of the FSA's case that are unclear to the applicant and, if so, what directions are required to enable those areas to be clarified;
- whether there is any additional documentary material that the applicant wishes to see;
- what evidence the applicant will be seeking to rely upon at trial (including expert evidence) and what directions are required to ensure that it can do so;
- whether the evidence should be limited in any way; and

- whether the applicant has any particular views on how the trial should be conducted.

Precisely what directions the applicant should seek, and what strategic approach it should take, will depend very much upon the situation.

Witnesses

6.92 The Tribunal Rules[1] allow the parties to call witnesses at the hearing including, with the consent of the Tribunal, expert witnesses. We consider here the procedural aspects of preparing witnesses for the hearing, and, in particular, whether:

- the parties are required to produce witness statements;
- the Tribunal can compel witnesses to attend; and
- expert evidence can be used.

1 Tribunal Rules, r 19(2).

Are the parties required to produce witness statements?

6.93 There is no provision in the Tribunal Rules automatically requiring witness statements to be produced or for them to be filed by any particular date although the Tribunal clearly has the power to make appropriate directions in each case[1]. Whether it is appropriate to require the production of witness statements will therefore fall for determination in each case, based upon what is required to, among other things, ensure the just, expeditious and economical determination of the reference in that case[2]. Nonetheless, it is thought that the provision of witness statements is likely to be the norm. Since the parties have the right to call and question witnesses at the hearing, it will normally be more efficient, as well as assisting the parties and the Tribunal to prepare for the hearing, for statements of those witnesses' evidence to have been exchanged in advance. It is, however, possible that the Tribunal would try to limit the extent of the witness statements, to prevent their production becoming over-elaborate and costly and to keep the ambit of the case within appropriate bounds[3].

1 Tribunal Rules, r 10(1)(k).
2 Tribunal Rules, r 9(1) and see para 6.87 above.
3 The civil courts have similar powers under Civil Procedure Rules, Pt 32.

Can the Tribunal compel witnesses to attend?

6.94 The Tribunal can compel the attendance of witnesses, by issuing a witness summons[1] requiring a person to attend before it to give evidence as a witness and/or to produce a document in his custody or under his control which the Tribunal considers it necessary to examine[2]. The Tribunal also has the power to set aside or vary a witness summons on application by the person to whom it is addressed[3].

1 Tribunal Rules, r 12 and FSMA 2000, Sch 13, para 11.

2 The scope of the similar power which can be exercised by an employment tribunal has been considered in *Dada v Metal Box Co Ltd* [1974] IRLR 251 (Sir John Donaldson) and *Noorani v Merseyside Tec Ltd* [1999] IRLR 184, CA. Broadly, to make the order, the Tribunal must be satisfied, first, that the witness can give evidence relevant to the issues in dispute and, second, that it is necessary to issue a witness summons. This assessment is a matter in the discretion of the Tribunal.
3 Tribunal Rules, r 12(6).

6.95 The Tribunal cannot require a person to file a document which is protected under the FSMA 2000 because it is, broadly, legally privileged or which should not be disclosed on one of the grounds listed at para 6.71 above[1]. These are the same exceptions as apply to the Tribunal's ability to require a party to produce a document, considered at para 6.73 above.

1 Tribunal Rules, r 12(2). The Tribunal has additional powers for the purpose of satisfying itself that any document should not be filed: see para 6.73 above.

6.96 Non-compliance with a witness summons issued by the Tribunal carries serious consequences. It is a criminal offence[1] for a person to:

- refuse or fail, without reasonable excuse[2], to attend following the issue of a summons by the Tribunal or to give evidence[3] or
- alter, suppress, conceal or destroy, or refuse to produce, a document which he may be required to produce for the purposes of proceedings before the Tribunal[4].

1 FSMA 2000, Sch 13, para 11.
2 'Reasonable excuse' is interpreted fairly narrowly in the context of witness summonses issued by the High Court: see the discussion in *Contempt*, Arlidge, Eady & Smith, at 11-102.
3 This broadly reflects the common law of contempt for failing to attend court following the issue of a subpoena or witness summons: see *Contempt*, Arlidge, Eady & Smith, 1999 at 11-87 to 11-103.
4 Conduct of this nature in relation to criminal proceedings would be likely to amount to the common law offence of perverting the course of justice: see Archbold 2001 at 28-1 and see *Contempt*, Arlidge, Eady & Smith, at 11-84.

6.97 A witness summons must be sent so as to be received by the person to whom it is addressed not less than seven days before the time specified in the summons[1]. In some circumstances, the expenses of the witness in attending must be paid or tendered to him in advance by the party at whose request the summons was issued[2]. The summons must contain a statement warning of the criminal offences outlined above[3].

1 Tribunal Rules, r 12(3).
2 Tribunal Rules, r 12(5).
3 Tribunal Rules, r 12(4).

Can expert evidence be called?

6.98 Expert evidence will often be a key part of the case or the person's defence to it. For example, where the regulatory breach alleged involves establishing that the person's conduct fell below a particular standard, evidence may well be required as to what the applicable standard was and as to whether the person's conduct fell below that standard. In market abuse cases, for example, the test of the regular user is likely frequently to require expert evidence[1]. In cases where such issues arise, they often represent the critical point of disagreement between the FSA and the person concerned. In that situation, it is important for the person to have a credible, independent expert whose view is that its conduct did not fall below the requisite standard. Notwithstanding their potential importance, the Tribunal Rules say little about the use of experts. We consider below whether the Tribunal can hear expert evidence and in what circumstances it will do so.

1 For a further discussion, see para 13.50 ff.

Can the Tribunal hear expert evidence?

6.99 The Tribunal Rules and the FSMA 2000 envisage that either of two types of experts could be relevant in appropriate cases, namely experts appointed by the parties and experts appointed by the Tribunal.

6.100 As to experts appointed by the Tribunal, the FSMA 2000[1] allows the Tribunal to appoint one or more experts to assist it if it appears to it that a matter before it involves a question of fact of special difficulty. The Tribunal Rules[2] indicate that where the Tribunal directs the appointment of an expert, it is likely to direct him to send copies of his report to the parties.

1 FSMA 2000, Sch 13, para 7(4).
2 Tribunal Rules, r 10(1)(m).

6.101 As to experts appointed by the parties, the Tribunal Rules indicate that the Tribunal may grant directions making provision as to any expert witnesses to be called, including the number of such witnesses and the evidence to be given by them[1] and they also make clear[2] that the parties may not call their own expert evidence without the consent of the Tribunal. Before applying for such a direction, there are a number of practical issues to consider, including precisely what are the issues that need to be addressed by an expert and what type of expertise is required. In addition, ancillary directions may be appropriate, such as requiring experts to meet, after filing their reports, with a view to identifying those issues that are in dispute between them.

1 Tribunal Rules, r 10(1)(l).
2 Tribunal Rules, r 10(2)(a).

When in practice will the Tribunal allow expert evidence to be used?

6.102 The Tribunal Rules give no indication as to when in practice expert evidence will be permitted, either in the form of a single expert appointed by the Tribunal or in the form of party appointed experts. The question for the Tribunal in deciding whether or not to make a direction permitting the use of experts is the same as in relation to any other application for a direction, namely whether it is appropriate to enable the parties to prepare for the hearing, to assist the Tribunal to determine the issues and generally to ensure the just, expeditious and economical determination of the dispute[1]. The answer will depend upon the circumstances of the case. In appropriate cases, strong arguments in favour of experts could be made. Cases before the Tribunal may involve complex issues about the standards to be expected of those involved in the market[2] and, because they will be reported, may have an impact on the behaviour of others in the market. It is important that the Tribunal is properly informed when reaching its decisions in such cases and that the interests of expedition and economy do not outweigh the interests of justice. On the other hand, it should be recognised that the use of multiple experts is often perceived as tending to increase the cost and time of litigation and it may be that this will be reflected in the approach of the Tribunal to the question of experts in particular cases.

1 See para 6.87 above.
2 This will be particularly important in market abuse cases, in relation to the 'regular user' test: see para 13.50 ff below.

6.103 An additional factor that may in practice be relevant is the presence of lay persons with relevant experience on the Tribunal. There may be a temptation for the Tribunal to take the lay person's views on issues which should be the subject of expert evidence. The lay member can certainly assist the Tribunal in reaching a decision based on conflicting evidence before it[1], but it is difficult to see how the Tribunal can properly reach a decision on questions of expert opinion without giving the parties the opportunity to adduce evidence on those issues.

1 In the employment tribunal context, it is established that the lay member should, if he intends to use his specialist knowledge to disagree with evidence that has been given, disclose his specialist knowledge and bring to the relevant party's attention the facts that cause him to disagree with the evidence, and give the party an opportunity to address the point: see *Harvey on Industrial Relations and Employment Law* at T [888].

Suspending the FSA's action

6.104 In most cases, particularly those which involve the warning/decision notice procedure, the action which the FSA wishes to take will not take effect until the Tribunal process has been completed[1]. But in some cases, most notably where the FSA takes urgent action to vary a firm's permission[2], the action can take effect immediately, or on a particular date, with the Tribunal then considering afterwards whether to revoke, or vary, the action which the FSA has already taken. In those cases, the applicant may apply to the Tribunal for a direction suspending the effect of the FSA's action or, as the case may be, preventing that action from taking effect, until the reference to the Tribunal (and any appeal) has been determined[3]. But the Tribunal may only give such a direction if it is satisfied that to do so would not prejudice:

- the interests of any persons, whether consumers, investors or otherwise, intended to be protected by the supervisory notice that was issued; or
- the smooth operation or integrity of any market intended to be protected by that notice.

1 FSMA 2000, s 133(9) and see para 5.174 above.

2 See para 9.194 below. This applies in relation to all those powers which involve the supervisory notice procedure: see para 9.105 below. In addition to varying a firm's permission, examples include suspending a listing of the shares of a listed company (see para 15.168 ff below) and taking various action in relation to collective investment schemes (see Chapter 14 below).
3 Tribunal Rules, r 10(1)(e).

6.105 Urgent action taken with immediate effect by the FSA, or with effect on a particular date, and only tested later in the Tribunal, can have a serious effect on a firm's reputation and its business. Whilst the FSMA 2000 normally[1] enables the FSA to take such action only where it reasonably considers this necessary, it does not provide firms with any means to ensure this is not abused[2]. Such action can in some circumstances be taken by the FSA's staff without reference to the Regulatory Decisions Committee[3]. This provision in the Tribunal's Rules allows the firm to require the FSA to justify the need for urgent action in the Tribunal at an early stage and allows the Tribunal to provide immediate redress where the urgent action was clearly improper.

1 For an exception, see para 15.139 below.
2 See the discussion at para 9.214 ff below.
3 See para 9.201 ff below.

6.106 But it will be only in rare cases that this provides an effective remedy. First, however quickly the Tribunal can be set up and hear the application and the FSA's response to it, time will have elapsed since the action took effect and immediate damage will have been done. Second, there is likely to be a heavy burden on the applicant in practice to show that the FSA's urgent action should be suspended. The Tribunal Rules make clear that the need to protect investors, particularly consumers, and markets remains the primary concern. The application will be determined based on the limited evidence available to the Tribunal at the relevant time, not based on a detailed consideration of the entire case, which will only take place at the final hearing[1]. All of this is likely to militate in favour of the Tribunal intervening only where it is clear that the action was inappropriate.

1 No indication is given in the Tribunal Rules as to how the evidence in support of such an application should be presented.

Preliminary hearings

6.107 The Tribunal may direct that particular questions of fact or law which appear to be in issue be determined at a preliminary hearing[1]. Whether or not to hold a preliminary hearing is entirely within the Tribunal's discretion. The Tribunal Rules do not prescribe any particular criteria that are relevant, nor is a preliminary hearing confined to issues which would potentially be decisive of the case[2]. It is therefore difficult to give any guidance as to when in practice one is likely to be held[3].

1 Tribunal Rules, r 13.
2 The question whether the preliminary issue could potentially be decisive of the case, either legally or because it is likely to encourage settlement, is the test normally applied in the Chancery division of the High Court: see the Chancery Guide at 3.10.
3 In the context of employment tribunals, tribunals have been urged to hold preliminary hearings

only sparingly, because of the scope for appeals against decisions and thus for further hearings: see the discussion in *Harvey on Industrial Relations and Employment Law* at T [732]. Employment tribunals have therefore been encouraged to apply the (former) practice of the High Court that: (i) preliminary issues on points of law should be decided only exceptionally in clear and simple cases, (ii) the question of law should be carefully defined so there can be no confusion over what is being decided, and (iii) they should not normally be tried without first determining the facts: see *Allen v Gulf Oil Refining Ltd* [1981] AC 1001 and see the discussion in *Harvey on Industrial Relations and Employment Law* at T [736].

6.108 Where a preliminary issue hearing is held, there is an oral hearing unless the parties agree otherwise in writing[1]. It is normally held in public and the parties have the right to be represented in the same way as a final hearing[2]. If, in the Tribunal's opinion, the determination of the issue substantially disposes of the reference, it may treat the preliminary hearing as the hearing of the reference and make the appropriate order disposing of the reference[3]. However, it may not dispose of the reference without an oral hearing unless the parties have agreed in writing that it may do so[4].

1 This is required by the ECHR fair trial guarantees: see para 6.26 above.
2 Tribunal Rules, r 17(1) and 18(3) and see paras 6.124 and 6.135 below.
3 Tribunal Rules, r 13(2). As to the orders that the Tribunal can make, see para 6.137 ff below.
4 Tribunal Rules, r 13(3).

Withdrawal or consolidation of cases

6.109 The Tribunal Rules contain a number of provisions regarding the withdrawal or consolidation of cases. These are outlined below.

Withdrawal by applicants

6.110 The applicant may withdraw the reference to the Tribunal:

- at any time before the hearing by filing a notice to that effect; or
- at the hearing, with the Tribunal's permission;

and the Tribunal may determine any reference that is withdrawn[1] and may make a costs order[2].

1 Tribunal Rules, r 14(1).
2 Tribunal Rules, r 14(4) and see 6.153 ff below.

6.111 It is not clear from this what determination the Tribunal will make. It ought, in the normal course, simply to determine that the action which the FSA sought to take in the decision notice or supervisory notice is appropriate. However, the Tribunal Rules do not limit the Tribunal in this way, leaving open the possibility that the Tribunal might make some other determination. This flexibility may be to allow the Tribunal to give effect to a settlement between the FSA and the applicant by making a determination in accordance with the agreed terms. In theory, there is a risk of it making some other determination of its own accord, but in practice that ought not to happen and, if it did, then remedies may be available to the firm[1].

1 The decision should be susceptible to judicial review: see Chapter 16.

Withdrawal by the FSA

6.112 The Tribunal Rules[1] allow the FSA to state that it does not oppose the reference or is withdrawing its opposition to it:

- at any time before the hearing by filing a notice to that effect; or
- at the hearing, with the Tribunal's permission;

in which case the Tribunal may determine the reference without an oral hearing[2] and may make a costs order[3].

1 Tribunal Rules, r 14(2).
2 Tribunal Rules, r 14(3)(a).
3 Tribunal Rules, r 14(4) and see para 6.153 ff below.

6.113 As with withdrawals by applicants[1], it is not made clear what determination the Tribunal will make in such a case. It ought simply to determine that it is inappropriate for the FSA to take any action, but the Tribunal Rules do not limit it in this way and this may allow some flexibility to enable the Tribunal to give effect to a settlement between the FSA and the applicant by making a determination in accordance with the agreed terms.

1 See para 6.110 ff above.

Consolidation of references

6.114 The Tribunal Rules[1] permit the Tribunal to make a direction, where two or more references have been filed:

- in respect of the same matter; or
- in respect of separate interests in the same subject in dispute; or
- which involve the same issues;

to provide that the references or any particular issue or matter raised in them be consolidated or heard together.

1 Tribunal Rules, r 10(1)(q). The procedure for making applications for directions, and for directions by the Tribunal on its own initiative, is outlined at para 6.79 ff above.

6.115 The Tribunal Rules do not provide any criteria on which the Tribunal will decide whether or not cases should be consolidated. The Tribunal is therefore likely to apply the normal criteria of seeking to ensure the just, expeditious and economical determination of the dispute[1].

1 See para 6.87 above.

6.116 Why might cases need to be consolidated? This could be appropriate in a number of different scenarios. For example, the FSA may have issued several decision notices or supervisory notices against the same firm arising out of the same matter if it wanted to take a series of different actions against that firm (for example, to discipline it, vary its permission and order it to pay restitution). Another example is where two closely connected firms, or a firm and an approved person working for it, are both disciplined in relation to the same matter. A further example is where a decision notice is required to be given to more than one person (for example, an approved person and the firm that employed him or some other person prejudicially affected by the decision notice) and both of those persons elect to refer the same decision notice to the Tribunal. In each of those situations, the determination of the issues may involve many of the same questions of fact or law, and require the same witnesses and experts to attend, and it may therefore be appropriate for all the issues to be determined at one hearing. Whether it is appropriate will nonetheless depend on the circumstances. For example, there may be good reasons why issues relating to the firm and its employee should not be heard at the same time.

6.117 A more difficult scenario is where several unconnected firms are being disciplined in relation to different aspects of the same regulatory problem. For example, the trustee, fund manager and custodian of a unit trust fund in which problems arose, and various of their employees. In that case a single consolidated reference may be too unwieldy, and the interests of the various participants too diverse, for the matter usefully to be consolidated. Some of the parties may wish the matter to be heard in private, others not. The firms involved may be concerned at the potential for sensitive commercial information being made available to other firms within the Tribunal process, and so on. In addition, there may come a point at which the involvement of multiple parties with different interests will tend to make the process less, not more, efficient, and increase the attraction of separate processes. Another relevant factor may be the risk of different Tribunals reaching inconsistent decisions. As this should illustrate, a number of different factors may be relevant and what approach the firm will wish to take to the consolidation of cases will therefore depend very much upon the particular circumstances.

The hearing

6.118 Finally, the matter comes before the Tribunal for a hearing. We consider here the procedural questions of when the hearing will take place and how the hearing is conducted. Before looking at these, though, it is worth recalling that the Tribunal is a first instance tribunal before which the FSA must prove its case, and which can make a range of decisions based, primarily, on the question of what action it is appropriate for the FSA to take in relation to the matter referred to it[1]. Understanding the role of the Tribunal assists in understanding the procedural rules that govern its hearings.

1 As the Economic Secretary to HM Treasury put it in Standing Committee (4 November 1999): 'The Tribunal will be required to consider the facts of the case and arrive at its own view on the rights and wrongs. In doing so, it is not constrained by what the FSA did or did not do, or did or did not consider relevant' . See also the discussion at para 6.8 above.

When will the hearing take place?

6.119 The time, place and estimated length of the hearing will have been fixed by the Tribunal[1].

1 Tribunal Rules, r 10(1)(a).

6.120 It will be important to ensure, particularly in cases of any complexity, that all the witnesses, experts and counsel, among others, are available. In such cases, the applicant may wish to press the Tribunal to fix the hearing date as early as possible, and the procedure can then be determined by reference to that date[1].

1 This is the approach taken by the civil courts under the Civil Procedure Rules. There is nothing in the Tribunal Rules to prevent a similar approach from being taken. It will be a matter for the Tribunal in each case to fix the timetable for that case.

6.121 The Tribunal can alter the time and place of the hearing, and can adjourn the hearing[1]. A daily list of all hearings which are to be held, together with information about the time and place fixed for the hearings, is available for public inspection, subject to any direction in any case regarding privacy[2].

1 Tribunal Rules, r 10(1)(a) and (c).
2 Tribunal Rules, r 17(10).

How is the hearing conducted?

6.122 The procedure adopted for the hearing itself is left largely within the discretion of the Tribunal according to what is appropriate in the particular case, subject to certain basic rules. The Tribunal is required[1] to conduct the hearing in such manner as it considers most suitable to the clarification to the issues before it and generally to the just, expeditious and economical determination of the proceedings. The need to balance these three factors thus permeates the entire process[2]. The Tribunal also needs to ensure that the procedure is ECHR compatible[3].

1 Tribunal Rules, r 19(1).
2 For a discussion of these factors, see para 6.20 ff above.
3 This is discussed at para 6.23 ff above.

Is there an oral hearing?

6.123 There will normally be an oral hearing, although the Tribunal may determine a reference without one if the parties agree in writing[1].

1 Tribunal Rules, r 16(1). The case may also be disposed of without an oral hearing if the FSA withdraws its opposition or the FSA or the applicant fail to file, as applicable, their statement of case or reply: see r 14(3).

Is the hearing in public?

6.124 The general rule is that hearings of the Tribunal, including oral hearings on procedural matters, are held in public[1]. The Tribunal does have the power to direct that all or part of a hearing is in private, but it may only do so if[2]:

- all of the parties apply for it to be held in private; or
- one of the parties applies and the Tribunal[3] is satisfied that a hearing in private is necessary having regard to:
  - — the interests of morals, public order, national security or the protection of the private lives of the parties, or
  - — any unfairness to the applicant or prejudice to the interests of consumers that might result from a hearing in public,

and, in any event, the Tribunal must be satisfied that this would not prejudice the interests of justice.

Further, before directing that the entire hearing should be in private, the Tribunal is required to consider whether only part of the hearing should be heard in private[4].

1 Tribunal Rules, r 17(1) and (2).
2 Tribunal Rules, r 17(3).
3 Having given the other party an opportunity to make representations: Tribunal Rules, r 17(4).
4 Tribunal Rules, r 19(5).

6.125 Applicants may be concerned to avoid confidential information about their internal workings being aired in public in a situation where, the applicant believes, there is no call for any regulatory action. To what extent does it have the right to opt for a private hearing? Significantly, these provisions do not give the applicant the unequivocal right to opt for a private hearing and, indeed, there are substantial hurdles in the way if it applies for the hearing to be in private[1]. First, unless the FSA agrees that the hearing should be in private, the Tribunal has to go on to consider whether a private hearing is 'necessary' having regard to the various factors outlined above and also whether it should order part only of the hearing to be in private. This is a high hurdle[2].

1 This has been the subject of a great deal of controversy, not least because it represents a very significant change from the position under the former regime and also because it appears to run contrary to various Ministerial statements made in Parliament during the bill stages of the FSMA 2000. However, the presumption of a public hearing is consistent with the general policy of the Council on Tribunals and the Lord Chancellor's Department, and with the rules and practice of other tribunals. There are also relevant ECHR issues, although art 6(1) would not of itself prevent the Tribunal from allowing a private hearing purely at the option of the applicant (but not of the FSA).
2 There is room for argument that 'necessary' should not be interpreted as imposing a particularly high test in this context. The meaning of 'necessary' depends upon the circumstances. It 'lies somewhere between "indispensable" on the one hand and "useful" or "expedient" on the other': Lord Griffiths in *In re an Inquiry under the Company Securities (Insider Dealing) Act 1985* [1988] 2 WLR 33, 65.

6.126 Second, the rules outlined above also require the Tribunal to be satisfied that a private hearing would not prejudice the interests of justice. This may reflect the broader public interest in maintaining a transparent system in which the public is aware of the outcome of Tribunal cases and of the developing Tribunal jurisprudence. In other words, there may be wider considerations for the Tribunal to take into account than purely the applicant's interests in having a private hearing[1].

1 This reflects the position under the ECHR, which is, broadly, that a person can waive his right to a public hearing unless there is a public interest consideration otherwise: see *Hakansson and Sturesson v Sweden* (1990) 13 EHRR 1 and *Pauger v Austria* (1997) 25 EHRR 105.

6.127 There is therefore clearly a significant risk of the Tribunal proceedings being in public and indeed applicants need to approach the Tribunal process in the expectation that the proceedings will be in public in most cases, at least unless the FSA has agreed otherwise. Having said that, there is nothing to prevent the firm from applying for the hearing to be in private in the particular case. There will be many reasons to justify such an application. Common reasons are likely to include the following:

- the confidentiality of the information which will be referred to in the proceedings;
- the potential prejudice to existing customers which the reporting of the case may cause; and
- the potential impact of publicity on other related proceedings, such as an ongoing fraud investigation or pending criminal proceedings.

Alternatively, the applicant could apply for directions that would allow the hearing to be in public but, equally, would protect the most sensitive confidential information. Measures that the Tribunal could take could include hearing certain evidence in private or anonymising certain references in documents[1].

1 See further footnote 3 to para 6.64 above.

6.128 If the proceedings relate not to the firm but to one of its employees, then the firm may be placed in a difficult position. The employee has an ECHR right to a public hearing, which the firm's objections cannot override[1] notwithstanding it is the firm's confidential information that is at risk of being aired in the public forum. In that situation, the firm has no ability to ensure the hearing as a whole is held in private but may nonetheless be able to control the risk of its confidential information being made public by persuading the Tribunal to make other directions, such as those outlined at para 6.127 above.

1 Even if the firm has the right to object. The firm may, of course, be party to the Tribunal proceedings, either because proceedings against the employee were consolidated with those against the firm (see para 6.114 ff above) or because the firm was provided with a copy of the decision notice relating to the employee and exercised its own right to refer the decision to the Tribunal (see para 5.176 ff below).

6.129 Where the hearing, or part of the hearing, is heard in private, only certain people are entitled to attend, namely:

- the parties and their representatives;

- various members and staff of the Tribunal (whether or not involved in the particular matter)[1]; and
- any other person whom the Tribunal permits to attend[2].

The Tribunal may also direct that information about the whole or part of the proceedings (including information that might help to identify any person) is not to be made public[3].

1 For details, see Tribunal Rules, r 17(6).
2 Tribunal Rules, r 17(7).
3 Tribunal Rules, r 17(11). This direction may extend to the information entered in the register.

What submissions and evidence will the Tribunal hear?

6.130 As already discussed[1], the procedure for the hearing is left largely for the Tribunal to determine on the basis of what is suitable to the clarification of the issues before it and to the just, expeditious and economical determination of the reference. The Tribunal Rules do not therefore prescribe what submissions must be made and precisely how evidence will be taken. They do, however, make certain provisions with regard to the submissions and evidence that are put before it.

1 See para 6.122 above.

6.131 First, the Tribunal Rules make no provision about the order in which the Tribunal hears the parties. It is thought that it will normally hear the FSA first. Following this, the usual process would be for the applicant to respond and for the FSA to have the opportunity to reply to that response.

6.132 Second, the parties are entitled to give evidence (including, with consent of the Tribunal, expert evidence), call witnesses, question any witnesses and address the Tribunal on the evidence and generally on the subject matter of the reference[1]. This suggests that the process will involve the examination and cross-examination of witnesses and the making of submissions, broadly in a similar way to a court procedure. Quite how the evidence is given will depend upon the circumstances, but it may be that minor witnesses offering evidence that is not contentious will not need to be called in person, whereas the Tribunal is likely to want to hear personally from the key witnesses, and to see them responding to questions from the other side.

1 Tribunal Rules, r 19(2).

6.133 Third, evidence may be admitted by the Tribunal whether or not admissible in a court of law[1]. The strict rules of evidence do not therefore apply, but instead the question of admissibility is within the Tribunal's discretion.

1 Tribunal Rules, r 19(3).

6.134 Finally, the Tribunal can admit evidence whether or not it was available to the FSA when taking the referred action[1]. This important provision reflects the position of the Tribunal as a de novo finder of fact, not an appellate body[2].

1 Tribunal Rules, r 19(3) and FSMA 2000, s 133(3).
2 This is discussed at para 6.8 above.

Can the applicant be represented?

6.135 The Tribunal Rules[1] allow the applicant to appear and be represented by any person, whether or not legally qualified[2]. The Tribunal does retain a discretion to refuse to permit a person to assist or represent a party at the hearing if there are good and sufficient reasons for doing so[3]. This is likely to be used only in relatively extreme circumstances. Where a party fails to attend or be represented at the hearing, certain default provisions apply[4].

1 Tribunal Rules, r 18.
2 Moreover, a party's representative may do anything permitted or required by the Tribunal Rules to be done by that party: Tribunal Rules, r 2(2)(d).
3 Tribunal Rules, r 18(2).
4 Tribunal Rules, r 19(4).

The Tribunal's decision

6.136 We consider in the following paragraphs the question of what decisions the Tribunal can make and the procedure for doing so. In particular, we review:

- what decisions the Tribunal can make;
- how the Tribunal makes its decision;
- whether the decision is made public; and
- what is the effect of the decision.

Each is considered in turn, below.

What decisions can the Tribunal make?

6.137 The basic question for the Tribunal is what (if any) is the appropriate action for the FSA to take in relation to the matter referred to it[1]. Having determined that question, the Tribunal must remit the matter to the FSA with such directions (if any) as the Tribunal considers appropriate for giving effect to its determination[2].

1 FSMA 2000, s 133(4).
2 FSMA 2000, s 133(5).

6.138 There are limitations on the determinations that the Tribunal can make. In particular:

- in determining a matter resulting from a decision notice, it may not direct the FSA to take action which the FSA would not have had the power to take when giving the decision notice[1]. This refers to the requirement that a decision notice which was preceded by a warning notice must relate to action under the same Part of the FSMA 2000 as the action proposed in the warning notice[2]. For example, if the FSA proposed to fine a firm for its regulatory breaches, the Tribunal could direct that the FSA impose a different fine or a public censure, but not a restitution order or a variation of the firm's permission;

- in determining a reference made as a result of a supervisory notice, the Tribunal may not direct the FSA to take action which would have otherwise required the giving of a decision notice[3]. Thus, if the FSA proposed to vary a firm's permission, the Tribunal could direct that the FSA vary the permission in a different way to that proposed, but not that it fine the firm for a rule breach or impose a restitution order.

1 FSMA 2000, s 133(6).
2 FSMA 2000, s 388(2). See also para 5.164 above.
3 FSMA 2000, s 133(7). For a list of supervisory notices, see FSMA 2000, s 395(13) and see also para 9.105 below.

6.139 Aside from these limitations, the Tribunal has scope to direct any action that it thinks appropriate. It is particularly worth bearing in mind that it can increase as well as decrease the punishment or other action taken.

6.140 A secondary question for the Tribunal may be whether to make recommendations as to the FSA's procedures or regulating provisions[1]. It is not entirely clear what is meant by 'regulating provisions', as this is not a term used generally in the FSMA 2000[2]. It seems, broadly, to be open to the Tribunal to recommend that the FSA changes its rules or procedures in particular respects. The Tribunal should be in a better position than anyone else, at least outside the FSA, to see how in practice the FSA is using the extensive powers granted to it. It is clearly not the Tribunal's role to be a watchdog; its role is primarily to determine specific issues between regulator and regulated. However, the FSMA 2000 does give it a more general role within the accountability regime, by giving it the power to make such recommendations.

1 FSMA 2000, s 133(8).
2 The term is defined for the purposes of Part X, Chapter III to mean: (i) rules, (ii) general guidance, (iii) the Statements of Principle and Code of Practice for approved persons and (iv) the Code of Market Conduct: FSMA 2000, s 159(1). It is thought likely that the same meaning applies here.

6.141 The Tribunal Rules do not give any guidance as to the types of situations when the Tribunal might consider making recommendations or as to what recommendations it might make. Recommendations could perhaps relate to legal issues, for example if the Tribunal disagrees with the way that the FSA is interpreting particular provisions or powers in its rules or procedures, but there is nothing to confine them to such issues. From the applicant's perspective, it may be worth considering asking the Tribunal to make a recommendation if for example, in the applicant's view, the FSA's approach to its statutory powers was unfair, its procedures were implemented in a way that was inappropriate, or the FSA's legal interpretation of its powers was open to question.

How does the Tribunal make its decision

6.142 The Tribunal takes its decision by a majority of the Tribunal members[1]. The decision is recorded in writing, signed and dated by the chairman. It must give reasons[2] and state whether it was taken unanimously or by majority[3].

1 FSMA 2000, Sch 13, para 12(1).

2 In the context of employment tribunals, this has been interpreted to require an outline of the story, the tribunal's factual conclusions, the reasons why it reached its overall conclusions on those facts and, where appropriate, guidance on appropriate practices: see *Meek v City of Birmingham District Council* [1987] IRLR 250 (Bingham LJ). In the context of immigration tribunals, see *R v Immigration Appeal Tribunal, ex p Khan* [1983] 2 All ER 420, CA. ECHR, art 6(1) requires the decision to 'indicate with sufficient clarity the grounds on which [the Tribunal] based their decision. It is this, inter alia, which makes it possible for [the applicant] to exercise usefully the right of appeal available to him': *Hadjianastassiou v Greece* (1992) EHRR 219. See also *Hiro Balani v Spain* A 303-B (1994).

3 FSMA 2000, Sch 13, para 12(2).

6.143 The Tribunal will inform the parties of its decision and, as soon as reasonably practicable, send them a copy of the decision[1]. It will also notify them of any applicable provision regarding appeals and the time and place for making any appeal or application for permission to appeal[2]. The decision must also be sent to any authorised person concerned who was not party to the proceedings[3], for example whose employee or appointed representative was the subject of the proceedings, and to HM Treasury[4].

1 FSMA 2000, Sch 13, para 12(3).

2 Tribunal Rules, r 20(6).

3 FSMA 2000, Sch 13, para 12(3)(b).

4 FSMA 2000, Sch 13, para 12(4).

Is the decision made public?

6.144 The Tribunal will normally pronounce its decisions in public[1]. It may for example give the decision in open court or publish it in writing and it will also normally enter the decision in its register, which is publicly available[2]. There are three main reasons for this. First, the aim is to have so far as is possible an open and transparent system. Second, for reasons already discussed[3], there is a general interest in making the Tribunal's jurisprudence available to the public. Finally, it is an ECHR requirement that judgment be pronounced publicly[4]. Moreover, it is the FSA's normal policy to make public its successful enforcement action, for a variety of reasons discussed in Chapter 5 above. The outcome, if the applicant is unsuccessful, will therefore almost inevitably be publicity.

1 Tribunal Rules, r 20(1).

2 Tribunal Rules, r 20(5).

3 See para 6.126 above.

4 See para 6.26 above.

6.145 But what about cases where the applicant is successful in vindicating itself? So far as the rest of the regulated community are concerned, those may be among the most valuable cases in terms of Tribunal jurisprudence. But from the perspective of the applicant involved, there may be a strong wish not to attract further publicity and not to have the judgment, perhaps containing confidential or otherwise sensitive information[1], made publicly available.

1 It is not clear how much detail will normally appear in the Tribunal's decisions.

6.146 The Tribunal is, however, required[1], where the hearing or any part of it was in private, to consider whether, having regard to the reason for the hearing (or any part of it) being in private and the outcome of the hearing, it would be undesirable to make a public pronouncement of the whole or part of its decision and may, in consequence, take any step (including anonymising the decision, editing the text or declining to publish the whole or part of the decision) but any such step is required to be taken with a view to ensuring the minimum restriction on public pronouncement that is consistent with the need for the restriction.

1 Tribunal Rules, r 20(2). Before reaching a decision, the Tribunal is required to invite the parties to make representations on the matter: Tribunal Rules, r 20(4).

6.147 The focus is therefore on minimising the extent to which decisions are kept from the public. It has, in particular, been suggested that the power to amend the text of a decision, for example to anonymise details of the parties, will be sufficient to protect the parties in sensitive cases without the Tribunal ever needing to resort to making no public pronouncement. It is unclear whether this will be realistic in a market which relies to a large extent on trading in information. Applicants may wish to press the Tribunal to decide not to make the decision public in cases which have not attracted publicity and where the applicant has been successful in vindicating itself.

What is the effect of the Tribunal's decision?

6.148 The Tribunal's decision on the reference is binding on the FSA and, through the FSA, on the applicant. The mechanism is complex. When the Tribunal makes its determination, it remits the matter to the FSA with such directions as the Tribunal considers appropriate to give effect to the determination[1]. What follows depends upon whether the matter arose from a decision notice or a supervisory notice.

1 FSMA 2000, s 133(5).

6.149 Assuming it arose from a decision notice, once the reference has been determined, and there is no appeal or any appeal has been disposed of[1], the statutory prohibition against the FSA taking the action specified in the decision notice comes to an end[2]. The FSA is, however, obliged to act in accordance with the Tribunal's determination and its directions[3]. It must therefore take whatever action the Tribunal determined to be appropriate and, on taking the action, is required to issue a final notice[4]. The applicant must comply with the final notice and if it does not do so then the obligation can be enforced against it[5].

1 For the provisions relating to appeals, see para 6.169 ff below.
2 FSMA 2000, s 133(9).
3 FSMA 2000, s 133(10).
4 FSMA 2000, s 390(2).
5 FSMA 2000, s 390(9) and (10).

6.150 Assuming the matter arose from a supervisory notice, the FSA is again obliged to act in accordance with the Tribunal's determination and its directions[1]. In many cases the decision will already have taken effect[2], in which case either no action is required or the FSA must revoke or vary its action depending upon the nature of, and in accordance with, the Tribunal's determination. If the action has not already taken effect, then it takes effect when it is no longer open to review[3], which means, broadly, once it has been determined in the Tribunal and has not been appealed or any appeal has been determined[4]. The decision then takes effect but, again, the FSA must act in accordance with the Tribunal's determination and directions. A supervisory notice is unlikely of itself to require any positive action from the firm. Consequently, no question of enforcing the Tribunal's determination against the firm arises, although the applicant may, plainly, have to take action in order to comply with the notice – for example, ensuring its business complies with its permission as amended.

1 FSMA 2000, s 133(10).
2 Because it took effect either immediately or on a specified date that has passed: see para 9.99 below.
3 See, for example, FSMA 2000, s 53(2)(c).
4 For a more detailed explanation, see FSMA 2000, Section 391(8) and para 9.174 below.

6.151 If the Tribunal makes a recommendation regarding the FSA's rules or procedures[1], this is not binding and does not have any formal effect.

1 FSMA, Section 133(8) and see para 6.140 above.

6.152 If the Tribunal makes an order, for example a costs order[1], then that may be enforced as if it were an order of the county court[2].

1 See para 6.153 ff below.
2 Or, in Scotland, an order of the Court of Session: FSMA 2000, s 133(11).

Costs

6.153 Costs in Tribunal cases do not generally 'follow the event'. In other words, the Tribunal will not as a matter of course award costs against the losing party or indeed against any party.

6.154 However, the Tribunal, does have the power to make costs awards in certain exceptional cases[1], namely if it considers that:

- a party has acted vexatiously, frivolously[2] or unreasonably[3]; or
- the FSA decision which was the subject of the reference was unreasonable[4].

1 FSMA 2000, Sch 13, para 13.
2 A claim is frivolous and vexatious if it 'is one which on the face of it is clearly one which no reasonable person could properly treat as bona fide, and contend that he had a grievance which he was entitled to bring before the Court': see *Norman v Matthews* (1916) 85 LJKB 857, 859 (Lush J).

3 As to the meaning of 'unreasonable', in the context of wasted costs orders in civil litigation, it 'aptly describes conduct which is vexatious, designed to harass the other side rather than advance the resolution of the case, and it makes no difference that the conduct is the product of improper zeal and not improper motive': see *Ridehalgh v Horsefield* [1994] Ch 205232 (Bingham MR).

4 It is not clear what 'unreasonable' means in this context and in particular whether it is used in the *Wednesbury* sense or whether a softer test is to be applied.

6.155 In either case, the Tribunal can order the relevant party to pay to another party to the proceedings the whole or part of the costs or expenses incurred by the other party in connection with the proceedings[1]. It may do so either by ordering an amount fixed by the Tribunal to be paid or by ordering costs and/or expenses to be assessed on such basis as it may specify[2]. Before making a costs order, the Tribunal must give the paying party an opportunity to make representations against the making of the costs order[3].

1 FSMA 2000, Sch 13, para 13.

2 Tribunal Rules, r 21(3). The assessment is made by, as applicable, a costs official (in England or Wales), the Auditor of the Court of Session or the Taxing Master of the Supreme Court of Northern Ireland.

3 Tribunal Rules, r 21(2).

6.156 The Tribunal Rules do not provide any guidance on when in practice the Tribunal is likely to exercise its discretion to make costs awards. It ought, though, to be used only in exceptional cases.

6.157 The amount of costs ordered to be paid is within the Tribunal's discretion. It can order the whole of the costs and expenses incurred in the proceedings or a particular portion of them, for example the cost of a particular application which one party has made or resisted frivolously or unreasonably.

6.158 In those, probably rare, cases where it orders the cost of the whole proceeding to be paid, the question arises whether 'proceedings' refers only to the Tribunal proceedings or whether it includes the FSA enforcement proceedings which led to the Tribunal proceedings. It is most likely that this refers to the cost of the Tribunal proceedings[1], although this is not entirely free from doubt[2].

1 The phrase 'the proceedings' seems to refer back to 'the proceedings on a reference': see FSMA 2000, Sch 13, para 13(1) and (2).

2 The FSMA 2000 refers elsewhere (see para 4.200 above) to 'the proceedings' as meaning the FSA enforcement process from issue of the warning notice.

6.159 The ability for costs to be awarded against the regulator did not exist in the previous regime. It is plainly important to redress the unnecessary cost to which the applicant has been put in the particular case. But it has a significant potential role more generally to deter the FSA from abusing its powers.

6.160 Applicants must not, however, lose sight of their own potential exposure to costs orders. The use of costs orders also has a role to play in deterring applicants from taking hopeless cases to the Tribunal.

REVIEWS AND APPEALS

Introduction

6.161 In most cases the outcome of the Tribunal will be the end of the matter. However, both the FSA and the applicant do have limited additional options available for a short period of time on specified grounds. The main option is to seek permission to appeal to the Court of Appeal but there may also be an option of asking the Tribunal to review its own decision. We consider the latter option first.

Review by the Tribunal

6.162 The Tribunal Rules allow the Tribunal to set aside or vary its own decision in certain very limited circumstances. The FSMA 2000 does not require the Tribunal Rules to contain this procedure, the extent to which it is intended to be used is not clear[1] and in any event, as will be seen, there is only a brief opportunity for the parties to seek to use it.

1 A similar provision appears in the rules of the Employment Tribunal: r 11(1) and see the discussion in *Harvey on Industrial Relations and Employment Law* at T [1111]. It is not known whether the Tribunal will take a similar approach.

The grounds for varying or setting aside a decision

6.163 The Tribunal[1] may review and, if appropriate, set aside[2] the relevant decision if satisfied that[3]:

- its decision determining a reference was wrongly made as a result of an error on the part of the Tribunal staff[4]; or
- new evidence has become available since the conclusion of the hearing to which the decision relates, the existence of which could not have been reasonably known or foreseen[5].

1 This may be the same or a different Tribunal: see para 6.167 below.
2 Although it may appear that there is no power to vary the decision, the Tribunal's powers, if it sets a decision aside, allow it to substitute it with a different decision: see para 6.168 below.
3 Tribunal Rules, r 25(1).
4 Compare the 'slip rule': see para 6.164 below.
5 The existence of new evidence may be relevant to both civil and criminal law appeals. In those contexts, it may be relevant: (i) why the evidence was not used before; (ii) whether it is significant and (iii) whether it is credible: see Civil Procedure Rules, Pt 52, r 52.11(2), *Ladd v Marshall* [1954] 3 All ER 745 and the Criminal Appeal Act 1968, s 23. These factors may also be relevant to the Tribunal when considering a review of its decision.

6.164 These grounds are fairly narrowly drawn[1]. The extent to which the Tribunal will be willing to use the review procedure in practice is not clear. It is plainly available in wider circumstances than the normal 'slip rule' which allows a tribunal to correct accidental slips or omissions in judgments or orders. Such a rule is found, separately, at r 28(3)[2]. There would need to be something akin to a manifest administrative error within the Tribunal, or some important piece of new evidence. Even a serious procedural defect is unlikely to fall within the grounds for review. In any event, as will be seen, the error or new evidence must have come to light within a very short period after the Tribunal's decision was made.

1 There is not, for example, a general ground that the interests of justice require a review (such as is available to employment tribunals, for example).
2 This provision broadly mirrors Civil Procedure Rules, Pt 40, r 40.12.

6.165 These rules apply equally to the FSA as they do to the applicant. This means that the applicant could be successful before the Tribunal, only to be confronted with a review of the decision based on a piece of new evidence.

The procedure for a review

6.166 The Tribunal may consider granting a review either of its own initiative or on an application by a party to the case[1]:

- if the Tribunal proposes to review its decision of its own initiative, it will notify the parties of that proposal not later than 14 days after the date on which the decision was sent to the parties[2];
- if a party wishes to apply for the Tribunal to review its decision, it must do so either immediately following the decision at the hearing or file its application not later than 14 days after the date on which the decision was sent to the parties[3]. The application is required to be in writing stating the grounds in full[4].

The parties have an opportunity to make representations on any application or proposal for review[5].

1 Tribunal Rules, r 22(1).
2 Tribunal Rules, r 22(3).
3 This is subject to the Tribunal's ability to extend any time limit under the Rules: Tribunal Rules, r 10(1)(d).
4 Tribunal Rules, r 22(2).
5 Tribunal Rules, r 22(4).

6.167 The review may be determined either by the same members of the Tribunal who decided the case or a differently constituted Tribunal[1].

1 Tribunal Rules, r 22(4).

The outcome of a review

6.168 Where it decides to set aside the decision the reviewing Tribunal must either substitute such decision as it thinks fit or order a re-hearing before either the same or a differently constituted Tribunal[1]. Therefore, there is, in effect, a power to vary a decision as well as to set it aside.

1 Tribunal Rules, r 22(5). Where it does so, the Chairman of the Tribunal certifies to the secretary that the decision has been varied or set aside. The secretary is required immediately to make the necessary correction in the register and to send a copy of the corrected entry to each party: r 22(6).

Appeals

6.169 The FSMA 2000 allows a party to a Tribunal reference, which would include the FSA as well as the applicant, to appeal to the Court of Appeal[2] in certain circumstances set out below[1]. The appeal can only be made with the permission of the Tribunal or the Court of Appeal. There is a possible right of further appeal to the House of Lords, subject to obtaining the leave of the Court of Appeal or House of Lords[3].

1 FSMA 2000, s 137(1).
2 Or, in Scotland, to the Court of Session. For simplicity, the discussion below refers only to the Court of Appeal.
3 FSMA 2000, s 137(4).

6.170 It is beyond the scope of this book to review the procedure of the Court of Appeal and House of Lords in considering applications for permission to appeal and the procedure for such appeals[1]. We briefly consider:

- the statutory basis upon which an appeal can be made; and
- the procedure for applying to the Tribunal for permission to appeal.

1 These can be found in, respectively, the Civil Procedure Rules, Pt 52 (and see 52.PD-069) and the House of Lords Practice Direction and Standing Orders applicable to Civil Appeals.

On what basis can the firm appeal?

6.171 An appeal to the Court of Appeal is available only on a point of law arising from a decision of the Tribunal disposing of the reference[1]. An appeal is not therefore available on a preliminary issue, unless it was determinative of the reference[2]. Nor is it available on a point of procedure or on a point of law arising from a procedural hearing.

1 FSMA 2000, s 137(1). As to the meaning of a 'point of law', the Court of Appeal has held (in the context of appeals to the Employment Appeals Tribunal) that the appellate body 'can .. interfere if it is satisfied that the Tribunal has misdirected itself as to the applicable law, or if there is no evidence to support a particular finding of fact, since the absence of evidence to support a finding of fact has always been regarded as a pure question of law. It can also interfere if the decision is perverse, in the sense explained by May LJ in *Neale v Hereford and Worcester and County Council* [1986] ICR 471 at 483': Donaldson MR in *British Telecommunications Ltd v Sheridan* [1990] IRLR 27. For a more detailed discussion, see *Harvey on Industrial Relations and Employment Law* at T [1630].
2 In some circumstances, a preliminary hearing may substantially determine the reference, although it need not do so: see para 6.107 ff above.

Applying to the Tribunal for permission to appeal

6.172 An application for permission to appeal can be made[1] either:

- orally at the hearing after the decision is announced by the Tribunal; or
- in a written application filed not later than 14 days after the decision is sent to the party making the application.

1 Tribunal Rules, r 23(2). As to the contents of the application, see r 23(3).

6.173 The application is considered by the Chairman of the Tribunal without an oral hearing in most cases where it is not made immediately at the hearing[1]. No guidance is given in the Tribunal Rules as to the basis upon which the Tribunal will decide whether or not to grant permission. The test applied in the context of civil claims is that either the appeal has a real prospect of success or there is some other compelling reason why it should be heard[2]. It is unclear whether the Tribunal, or the Court of Appeal if an application for permission to appeal is made to it, will apply this or some other test.

1 Tribunal Rules, r 24(1) and (2).
2 Civil Procedure Rules, Pt 52, r 52.3(6) and see the commentary for a discussion of this test.

6.174 The Tribunal's decision whether or not to grant permission to appeal is either given immediately following an oral application or notified to the parties by the secretary, together with the reasons[1]. The decision is, in any event, recorded in writing together with the reasons[2]. Where the Tribunal refuses the application, it directs the appellant to seek permission from the Court of Appeal, if he wishes to do so, within 14 days of the Tribunal's refusal[3].

1 Tribunal Rules, r 24(4).
2 Tribunal Rules, r 24(3).
3 Tribunal Rules, r 24(5).

7 Disciplinary sanctions and other regulatory action against firms

CONTENTS

Introduction 307

Disciplinary action 309

Restitution 320

Injunctions 335

INTRODUCTION

An overview of Chapter 7

7.1 The FSA's investigations into a particular matter could reveal not only a breach of regulatory requirements for which the firm and perhaps also its employees could or should be held culpable, but also, perhaps, that losses have been caused to a number of investors, that there are continuing breaches and in some cases that there are other matters of more general regulatory concern such as systemic failures within the firm or matters impacting on market confidence or consumer protection. Whilst these may be interrelated as the various consequences of the same problem, each gives rise to concerns of a different nature and may need to be addressed separately and in a different way. The FSA has the ability to take a range of enforcement actions, aimed at meeting different types of concerns, and a particular course of action can generally either be taken alone or in combination with other action, depending upon what is appropriate in the circumstances of the case. For example, it may be appropriate both to fine the firm and to require it to pay restitution to customers. Also, the FSA may impose each type of action separately, or at different times, so that the conclusion of the process relating to one type of enforcement action does not necessarily represent the conclusion of the entire enforcement process arising from the matter.

7.2 In this chapter we discuss the different types of regulatory action which the FSA can take against authorised persons. We focus here on the substance of each type of enforcement action: what it is and when it can be imposed. The procedure for taking action has been considered generally in Chapter 5 above, although we highlight any particular points to note regarding the process in respect of each power.

7.3 In particular, we review the FSA's powers:

- to take disciplinary action against firms (para 7.7 ff);
- to order restitution to be made to investors or to apply to the court for such an order (para 7.43 ff); and
- to make applications to the court for civil injunctions (para 7.97 ff).

7.4 The FSA has three additional general powers not covered in this chapter, namely:

- to discipline approved persons and/or exercise other enforcement powers against approved persons and others who work for firms, considered in Chapter 8 below;
- to vary or cancel a firm's permission or intervene in an incoming firm, considered in Chapter 9 below; and
- to prosecute various criminal offences, considered in Chapter 11 below.

7.5 The FSA also has various specific powers, for example:

- to deal with cases of market misconduct, considered in Chapter 13 below;
- in relation to regulated collective investment schemes, considered in Chapter 14 below;
- in its capacity as UK Listing Authority in relation to listed companies or applicants for listing, considered in Chapter 15 below;
- to disqualify auditors and actuaries[1];
- in relation to the Lloyd's insurance market[2];
- in relation to recognised investment exchanges and recognised clearing houses[3]; and
- in relation to professionals and designated professional bodies[4].

1 FSMA 2000, s 345.
2 FSMA 2000, Part XIX.

3 FSMA 2000, Part XVIII and see the FSA Handbook at REC Chapter 4. The enforcement powers of the recognised investment exchanges in relation to their members are briefly considered in Chapter 15 below.
4 FSMA 2000, Part XX and see the FSA Handbook at PROF Chapter 3.

7.6 It is notable at the outset that disciplinary action is, generally speaking, available only against authorised firms and approved persons. The FSA has no general ability to take disciplinary action against those who are not part of the regulated community. However, certain other enforcement powers may be available against such persons in certain circumstances, for example applications for injunctions and restitution orders, criminal prosecutions, and fines and restitution orders for market abuse.

DISCIPLINARY ACTION

Introduction

7.7 In the following paragraphs, we review the FSA's powers to take disciplinary action against authorised persons and its policy on when and how it uses those powers in practice. In common with many other aspects of the regime, the FSMA 2000 provides only the basic framework for the FSA's powers, allowing the FSA to take action in certain situations but leaving it to the FSA to determine when in practice it will be appropriate to do so. The FSA has made plain that it may be possible to address many instances of non-compliance without recourse to disciplinary action[1]. In many respects, therefore, it is the FSA's policy on when it will take formal action and what action it will take that will be of primary interest. The relevant policy is found in the FSA Handbook at ENF Chapters 11 to 13 and is discussed below. The procedure for taking disciplinary action is considered separately in Chapter 5 above. The question of publicity arising from disciplinary action is also considered in Chapter 5.

1 See the FSA Handbook at ENF 11.2.1 and see para 7.13 below.

What disciplinary powers does the FSA have?

7.8 The FSMA 2000 allows the FSA to impose a fine and/or publicly censure an authorised person. In addition, the FSA may, in some circumstances, issue informal private warnings to firms rather than taking any formal disciplinary action. As will be seen, these warnings do carry potential regulatory consequences. The circumstances when the FSA will issue a private warning, and the potential consequences, are discussed at para 7.18 ff below.

7.9 If the FSA considers that an authorised person has contravened a requirement imposed on it by or under the FSMA 2000, it may:

- publish a statement to that effect[1]; and/or

- impose on it a penalty, in respect of the contravention, of such amount as it considers appropriate[2].

1 FSMA 2000, s 205.
2 FSMA 2000, s 206(1). Note that the FSA cannot both impose a penalty and withdraw the firm's authorisation: FSMA 2000, s 206(2) and see the discussion at para 9.248 ff below.

7.10 The primary question is thus whether the firm has contravened a requirement imposed by or under the FSMA 2000[1], in other words, broadly, breached one of the FSA's rules or a requirement imposed under regulations made under the FSMA 2000 or directly by the legislation. It is important to appreciate that this includes not only breaches of specific rules but also breaches of the Principles for Businesses, which are wide-ranging in their potential application[2].

1 For a detailed discussion of what is encompassed within this phrase, see para 2.142 ff above.
2 The Principles for Businesses are discussed at para 2.52 above. The question of when they will be used as the basis for disciplinary action is considered at para 2.156 ff above.

7.11 The provisions outlined here form the framework for the imposition of disciplinary sanctions against firms. A key question is when in practice the FSA will take such action and how it will determine the amount of any penalty. The FSMA 2000[1] requires the FSA to prepare and issue a statement of its policy with respect to the imposition and amount of penalties and in the case of any particular contravention to have regard to the policy in force at the time the contravention occurred. The FSA's policy in this regard is discussed at paras 7.12 ff and 7.27 ff below.

1 FSMA 2000, s 210.

When will the FSA take disciplinary action?

7.12 Discipline, indeed enforcement action more generally, is only one of a number of actions available to the FSA to address a particular regulatory issue[1]. Not every rule breach will lead to the FSA taking disciplinary action against the relevant firm[2]. In this section, we consider the FSA's policy in two key respects, namely:

- when will formal disciplinary action be appropriate? and
- when will the FSA give an informal private warning?

The FSA's policy on what disciplinary action to take, in those cases where formal action is appropriate, is considered separately at para 7.27 ff below.

1 See the FSA Handbook at ENF 11.2.1.
2 Of the 262 enforcement cases concluded by the FSA relating to investment business firms in the year to March 2001, 12% were concluded with an informal warning (and a further 45% were concluded with the FSA taking no further action): see the FSA's 2000/2001 Annual Report. The figures during the previous year were 23% and 37% respectively: see the FSA's 1999/2000 Annual Report.

When will formal disciplinary action be appropriate?

7.13 In deciding whether or not to take formal disciplinary action in respect of conduct appearing to the FSA to be a breach, the FSA considers the full circumstances of the case[1], including in particular the following potentially relevant factors:

- the nature and seriousness of the breach, including whether it was deliberate or reckless, its duration and frequency, the amount of any benefit gained or loss avoided as a result, whether it reveals serious or systemic weaknesses, the impact on financial markets and public confidence, the loss or risk of loss caused to consumers or other market users, the nature and extent of any financial crime and whether there are a number of smaller issues which indvidually may not justify disciplinary action but which do so when taken collectively;
- the conduct of the firm or approved person after the breach, including how quickly, effectively and completely they brought the breach to the attention of the FSA (or another relevant regulator), the degree of co-operation shown during the investigation, and any remedial steps taken since the breach was identified[2];
- the previous regulatory record of the firm or approved person, including previous disciplinary action, any undertakings given to the FSA not to act or engage in particular behaviour, whether the FSA has previously had to intervene in the firm's business or request the firm to take remedial action, and the extent to which such action has been taken, and the general compliance history of the firm or person[3];
- whether the FSA has given any guidance on the conduct in question and the extent to which the firm or approved person has sought to follow it[4];
- action taken by the FSA in previous similar cases; and
- action which any other regulatory authority has taken or proposes to take in respect of the same matter[5].

The FSA thus undertakes a reasonably broad analysis of the situation to decide whether in all the circumstances formal disciplinary action is appropriate. Some instances may be able to be addressed by the firm's supervisors without the need for formal action and, in others, a private warning may be given[6].

1 See the FSA Handbook at ENF 11.4.1. FSMA 2000, s 210 requires the FSA to prepare and issue a statement of its policy with regard to the imposition and amount of penalties and to have regard to that policy in exercising or deciding whether to exercise its power to impose a penalty.

2 This is discussed in more detail at para 7.14 below.

3 Note that it will be relevant whether any informal private warnings have been given in the past: see para 7.18 ff below. Correspondence between the FSA and the firm regarding concerns about aspects of the firm's business will also form part of the firm's compliance history: see the FSA Handbook at ENF 11.3.9.

4 If a person acts in accordance with guidance in the circumstances contemplated by that guidance, the FSA will proceed on the footing that the person has complied with the aspects of the rule or other requirement to which the guidance relates: see the FSA Handbook, Readers' Guide at para 2.9 and see para 2.122 ff above.

5 See further, para 7.15 below.
6 See the FSA Handbook at ENF 12.3.1. For discussion of private warnings, see para 7.18 ff below.

7.14 Two points in particular require further comment. First, the list of factors highlights, among other things, the relevance of the firm's conduct after the breach came to light. Factors specifically said to be relevant[1] are whether the firm brought the matter to the attention of the FSA or another relevant regulator, what level of co-operation it gave, and what action the firm took to identify and compensate consumer losses, to discipline staff involved, to address any systemic failures, and to ensure that similar problems do not arise in the future. Firms need to have each of these points in mind when deciding what action to take when a matter of potential regulatory concern arises. Each of these issues is considered in detail in Chapter 3 above.

1 See the FSA Handbook at ENF 11.4.1(2).

7.15 Second, it is relevant whether any other regulatory authority is taking action in relation to the same matter. It is important to appreciate that the FSA will not decline to take any action simply because some other regulatory authority, such as a recognised investment exchange or an overseas regulator, claims jurisdiction. The FSA may want to consider taking its own enforcement action for a number of reasons. The FSA may have tougher enforcement powers than the other regulator, for example allowing it to impose a larger fine. It may have powers which allow it to address issues which the other regulator cannot address, for example to restrict the firm's future activities by varying its permission. Or it may have different concerns from those of the other regulator, for example the protection of UK consumers and the integrity of the UK financial markets, which require it to act. It can readily be seen that the fact that another regulator is considering, say, disciplinary action in relation to the matter, may be largely irrelevant to the FSA's concerns.

7.16 The FSA will examine all the circumstances of the case and consider whether, in the light of the relevant investigation, disciplinary and enforcement powers, the other regulator's action would be adequate to address the FSA's concerns or whether it would be appropriate for the FSA to take its own action[1]. It recognises[2] that it may be appropriate for both authorities to be involved and to take action. Where overseas regulators are involved, both the FSA and the overseas regulator may have an interest in taking action to protect their regulatory standards[3].

1 See the FSA Handbook at ENF 11.4.1(6) and 11.8.4(1).
2 See the FSA Handbook at ENF 11.8.4(2) and (3).
3 See the FSA Handbook at ENF 11.8.5.

7.17 The implication for firms is that they may be involved in multiple investigations and enforcement proceedings arising from the same problem. The FSA is developing operating arrangements with other UK regulatory authorities, with a view to ensuring that cases are approached in a co-ordinated, effective and efficient manner and that those who are the subject of investigations or potential disciplinary action are treated fairly[1]. It is also involved in various international initiatives.

1 See the FSA Handbook at ENF 11.8.3. Other UK regulatory authorities with whom the FSA may have to deal include the recognised investment exchanges and clearing houses, the Society of Lloyd's, the designated professional bodies, the Department of Trade and Industry, the Serious Fraud Office and the police, to name but a few.

When will the FSA give an informal private warning?

7.18 In some situations, despite having concerns about the behaviour of a firm (or approved person), the FSA may decide that it is not appropriate in all the circumstances to bring formal disciplinary action[1]. Examples given by the FSA of where this may be appropriate are where the matter giving cause for concern is only minor in nature or degree or where full and immediate remedial action was taken by the firm. In those situations, the FSA may give the firm a private warning, to make it aware that it came close to being subject to formal disciplinary action[2].

1 See the FSA Handbook at ENF 11.3.1. According to the FSA's figures, around one quarter of cases in the year to 31 March 2000 were concluded with an informal warning and around half that number in the following year: see footnote 2 to para 7.12 above.
2 See the FSA Handbook at ENF 11.3.1. A private warning may also be given to an individual whom the FSA is considering disciplining (see para 8.7 below). A private warning may be issued by the FSA staff or by the RDC (see paras 5.61 and 5.67 above).

What is a private warning?

7.19 A private warning is a warning to the firm that it came close to being subjected to formal action. It will[1]:

- state that the FSA has had cause for concern arising from the firm's conduct, although no determination has been made by the FSA that a firm has contravened a requirement;
- state that the FSA does not presently intend to take formal disciplinary action having regard to all the circumstances of the case;
- explain that the private warning will form part of its compliance history and may be taken into account by the FSA in deciding whether to bring disciplinary action against it in the future; and
- require the firm to acknowledge receipt and invite it to comment if it wishes to do so.

1 See the FSA Handbook at ENF 11.3.4.

What benefits does a private warning have?

7.20 There are clear benefits in the FSA being able to give these private warnings. Primarily, the system has a flexibility which allows the FSA to deal informally with more minor or inconsequential breaches which do not merit formal action but which do require some sort of acknowledgement that there has been wrongdoing. Usually, this benefits both the FSA, who are spared the cost of taking formal enforcement action for minor breaches, and the firm, which is not subjected to formal action.

What is the effect of the private warning?

7.21 The private warning does not have any formal effect. It says that the FSA had cause for concern but that no determination has been made[1]. It is, however, important to recognise that the private warning is not wholly free from regulatory consequences. As the FSA makes clear, it forms part of the firm's compliance history. As such it may influence the FSA's decision whether to commence disciplinary action in the future, although it will not be relied upon in determining whether a breach has taken place or in determining the level of sanction, if any, to be imposed[2]. In other words, it is relevant in deciding whether or not a future breach merits disciplinary action, but not in proving that the breach had occurred or in deciding what disciplinary action should be taken for the future breach. When considering the future breach, the FSA will have to assess the significance of the private warning. The FSA has indicated that the age of the private warning will be taken into account (although a long-standing warning may still be relevant) and several private warnings may be relevant cumulatively even though they relate to separate areas of the firm's business or different subsidiaries of the same parent, for example if they show concerns about compliance culture or the common management team[3].

1 The use of the word 'determination' is deliberate. It is a determination that triggers the ECHR fair trial guarantees.
2 See the FSA Handbook at ENF 11.3.6.
3 See the FSA Handbook at ENF 11.3.7/8.

7.22 The private warning may also have other less tangible effects. The fact that it recites the FSA's view that there has been cause for concern may raise difficult questions about whether it must be disclosed to others, for example the firm's other regulators or its insurers. The practical effect may be that such other parties will take the view that a breach has been committed. For the same reason, there may be a risk of civil claims being brought against the firm[1].

1 FSMA 2000, s 150 and more generally: see Chapter 10 below.

7.23 This can be particularly problematic for approved persons, who will have an unsubstantiated stain on their regulatory record. If they are dual registered, then they may need to disclose it to their other regulator. It could also potentially affect their future employment prospects.

What practical steps can the firm take?

7.24 When issuing a private warning, the FSA will invite the person to comment on the warning if he wishes to do so[1]. That response will also form a part of the compliance history[2]. If the person feels that there are good reasons why the private warning was not merited, or may be misinterpreted in the future, then it is important to respond appropriately at least to try to ensure that the compliance history reflects a more balanced view.

1 See the FSA Handbook at ENF 11.3.4.
2 See the FSA Handbook at ENF 11.3.6.

Can the firm challenge a private warning?

7.25 The person to whom the private warning is issued does not have any right to intervene in the process or to refer the matter to the Tribunal. One option might be to press the FSA into taking formal action, so that the person can vindicate himself before the Tribunal, but this will usually involve rather greater risk than accepting the warning. Other means of challenging the warning, if the firm wishes to do so, may be available. Despite the wording, it may be possible to claim that the warning amounted in reality to a 'determination' by the FSA without the ECHR fair trial guarantees[1] (although this would be difficult). It may also be possible to challenge the decision to issue the private warning by judicial review, or to bring a complaint before the independent complaints commissioner. Each of these is outlined in Chapter 16 below. In practice, it is the ability to comment on the warning that provides the best means of mitigating its potential effect.

1 These are outlined in Chapter 6 above.

How long does an informal warning last?

7.26 The FSA Handbook is silent on when an informal warning will cease to form part of the compliance history, although it does indicate that warnings may be 'long-standing'[1]. Equally, there is no specific provision allowing the firm to apply to the FSA to have the warning revoked or varied, and no provision enabling the FSA to do so. The implication is that the warning will remain permanently on the FSA's database[2]. There may, though, be scope in practice for seeking to agree with the FSA at the time the warning is given that it will only remain on the database for a particular period of time or for asking for it to be removed after a particular period has elapsed. Certainly, as the FSA has indicated, the relevance of the warning ought normally to diminish over time.

1 See the FSA Handbook at para 11.3.7.
2 Contrast the rules of two of the FSA's predecessors, SFA and IMRO, which specifically provided for warnings to be varied or revoked on application.

What disciplinary sanction will be imposed?

7.27 We review here three key issues regarding the disciplinary sanction to be imposed, namely:

- how the FSA chooses between a fine and a public censure;
- how the FSA determines the contents of the public censure; and
- how it determines the amount of the fine.

Each is considered in turn below.

Choosing which sanction to impose

7.28 As we have seen, the FSA can impose a fine or a public censure. Before looking at how the FSA chooses which to impose, it is worth briefly reviewing the purpose of each.

7.29 The FSA regards the publication of a censure or statement of misconduct as a serious sanction[1]. Such statements can have a serious effect on the person's business or reputation. They also allow the FSA to highlight the standards of conduct expected and demonstrate that those standards are being effectively enforced. This helps maintain confidence in the financial system and promote public awareness of the standards expected.

1 See the FSA Handbook at ENF 12.2.2.

7.30 Financial penalties are seen as having similar aims, but they also deter firms from committing contraventions, help to deter others and demonstrate generally the benefits of compliant behaviour[1].

1 See the FSA Handbook at ENF 13.1.2.

7.31 Against that background, how does the FSA decide which to impose? Since the imposition of a fine will normally be made public in any event, in reality the decision is not whether to impose one or the other but whether to impose a public censure or both a fine and a public censure. In reaching that decision, the FSA will consider all the circumstances of the case and the following factors in particular may be relevant[1]:

- if the firm has made a profit or avoided a loss as a result of the breach, this may be a factor in favour of a fine, since it should not be permitted to benefit from the breach;
- the more serious the breach, the more likely the FSA is to impose a fine;
- if the firm admitted the breach, provided full and immediate co-operation to the FSA and took steps to ensure consumers were fully compensated, this may be a factor in favour of a public censure, depending on the nature and seriousness of the breach[2];
- a poor disciplinary record or compliance history may be a factor in favour of a fine, in order to deter future cases;
- the FSA will seek to achieve a consistent approach to similar cases;
- inadequate means to pay the appropriate level of fine may be a factor in favour of a lower level of fine or a public censure. However, it would only be in an exceptional case that the FSA would agree to a public censure instead of a fine if a fine would otherwise be appropriate. The FSA has given two examples of exceptional cases, namely verifiable evidence that an approved person would suffer serious financial hardship if the FSA imposed a fine, or verifiable evidence that the firm would be unable to meet other regulatory requirements, particular financial resources requirements[3].

It is however important to recognise that public censures without additional sanctions, such as a fine, were rarely used in the previous regime[4].

1 See the FSA Handbook at ENF 12.3.3. This list is expressly non-exhaustive.
2 For an example of a case where these factors were relevant (and where there were no losses to customers), see *WH Ireland Limited*: SFA Board Notice 547.
3 See for example the PIA cases of *Premiere Financial Services Limited* and *Burgess Wreford & Unsworth*: PIA/D0015/99 and PIA/D0016/99.
4 In the calendar year 2000, neither PIA nor IMRO issued any formal public reprimands without further sanctions; SFA issued only one such reprimand.

The contents of the public censure

7.32 The precise contents of the censure, whether given by the FSA alone or together with a fine, may be important for the firm. Even statements which seem innocuous from the FSA's point of view could potentially have a serious impact on the firm. For example:

- they may impact on the firm's reputation;
- they could amount to a finding against the firm which could lead to claims by third parties, make the firm liable to a restitution order[1], increase the firm's susceptibility to adverse findings by the ombudsman[2], and potentially prejudice any claim the firm may have against its insurers[3];
- they could cause the firm difficulties with overseas regulators.

1 See para 7.43 ff below.
2 See Chapter 12 below.
3 See also the discussion at para 3.130 above.

7.33 The firm may want to try, to the extent it can do so, to ensure that the censure does not contain statements which are unnecessary from the FSA's perspective but have a significant collateral impact on the firm. To what extent does the firm have any input in the contents of the censure?

7.34 The FSA has given little or no indication as to how it will determine the contents of a public censure and as to what, in general terms, it expects to say[1]. It has indicated in the context of fines, that it will issue a press release, giving details of the behaviour and the penalty imposed[2]. The procedure for imposing a public censure, set out in detail in Chapter 5 above, does contain certain elements which may be of assistance to the firm. In particular:

- the FSA is required to notify the firm or individual of the contents of the statement when it issues its warning notice[3]. The firm or individual will therefore know at the outset precisely what is proposed;
- there is an opportunity to try to agree the statement with the FSA and possibly, where there is deadlock, to refer the matter to an independent mediator[4];
- if the firm is still unable to accept the statement proposed, then there is the option of referring the matter for determination by the Tribunal[5].

1 Practice under the previous regime differed as between the various regulators. The SFA tended to provide a reasonably full explanation, IMRO less so and the PIA relatively little explanation.
2 See the FSA Handbook at ENF 13.4.2.
3 For an explanation of the warning notice, see para 5.71 above.
4 This is discussed at para 5.129 above.
5 This is discussed at para 5.175 and Chapter 6 above.

7.35 It may, however, be imprudent to press this too far in practice. If the FSA has issued a warning notice proposing only a public censure, and not also a fine, it is certainly able, after hearing any representations, to issue a decision notice imposing a fine[1]. Also, if the firm referred the decision to impose a public censure to the Tribunal based on objections to the wording of the proposed statement, there may be a risk of the Tribunal deciding that a fine would be more appropriate[2]. Similarly, if the FSA proposed a fine, it may be unlikely that the firm would refer the entire matter to the Tribunal based purely on objections to the wording of the public statement which was to accompany the fine.

1 FSMA 2000, s 388(2) and see para 5.164 above.
2 FSMA 2000, s 133(6) and see para 6.138 above.

The amount of the fine

7.36 The FSA is required[1] to issue a statement of its policy with respect to the imposition and amount of fines imposed on firms[2] and to have regard to[3] that statement in exercising or deciding whether to exercise its powers.

1 FSMA 2000, s 210.
2 And approved persons: FSMA 2000, s 69.
3 The meaning of 'have regard to' has been considered at footnote 1 to para 2.127 above.

How does the FSA determine the amount of the fine?

7.37 In accordance with these obligations, the FSA has given a reasonably detailed account of the factors relevant to determining the appropriate level of a fine. Generally[1], the FSA does not adopt a tariff of penalties for different kinds of contravention because there will be few cases in which all the circumstances will be the same[2]. However, the FSA does aim to ensure consistency in its treatment of enforcement cases, specifically in relation to the amount of fines in similar cases.

1 There is an exception for contraventions involving the submission of returns no more than 28 days late. These are not covered here but the FSA's policy can be found in the FSA Handbook at ENF 13.5.
2 See the FSA Handbook at ENF 13.3.1.

7.38 The FSA will consider all the relevant circumstances of a case to determine the level of fine that is appropriate and in proportion to the contravention in question[1]. Certain particular factors have been identified that may be relevant. They can be summarised as follows[2]:

- the seriousness of the misconduct or breach;
- the extent to which the breach was deliberate or reckless, in which case the FSA may be more likely to impose a higher fine;

- whether the person is an individual and the size, financial resources and other circumstances of the firm or individual. The size and resources of the firm may also be relevant to the seriousness of the breach and to mitigation issues such as the steps which it was reasonable to expect the firm to take after the problem arose;
- the amount of profits accrued or loss avoided as a result of the contravention, consistent with the principle that a person should not benefit from his contravention and to act as an incentive to firms to be compliant;
- the conduct of the firm or approved person following the contravention[3];
- the previous disciplinary record and general compliance history[4];
- what action the FSA has taken previously in relation to similar behaviour. The FSA will seek to ensure consistency, but does not adopt a tariff system and there may be other factors relevant in the particular case; and
- action taken by other regulatory authorities. This may be relevant either because action is being taken relating to the same matter or because action taken by the FSA's predecessor regulators on similar matters is relevant to the level of fine[5].

1 See the FSA Handbook at ENF 13.3.1.
2 For a full list, see the FSA Handbook at ENF 13.3.3.
3 The detailed factors are similar to those outlined at para 7.14 above.
4 Private warnings will specifically not be taken into account: see the FSA Handbook at ENF 13.3.3(6) and see para 7.21 above.
5 Fines by the FSA's predecessors have ranged from £1,000 to £2m, with the majority being less than £100,000. Major fines in high profile cases have included £2m against *Morgan Grenfell* in relation to the Peter Young affair (IMRO, 14 April 1997), £270,000 against *Hambros Bank* for the receipt and use of information relating to the Co-operation Wholesale Society (SFA Board Notice 522, 16 September 1999) and £375,000 against *Rudolf Wolff & Co Ltd* in relation to the Sumitomo metal trading affair (SFA Board Notice 540, 1 March 2000).

7.39 The FSA is prohibited from taking into account, in its policy on the amounts of fines, the expenses which it has incurred or expects to incur in discharging its functions[1]. This represents a marked departure from the position under the previous regime, where firms tended to be charged the cost of the investigation into their conduct.

1 FSMA 2000, Sch 1, para 16(1).

7.40 Different policy factors are taken into account by the FSA in determining the amount of a fine for market abuse. These are outlined at para 13.200 below.

What happens to the money paid as fines?

7.41 An issue which attracted much debate during the Bill stages of the FSMA 2000 was whether the FSA should be entitled to retain the proceeds of fines which it levies. The concern, which the Government accepted, was that the FSA should not be seen to have any incentive, real or apparent, to maximise fine income for its own benefit[1]. The FSMA 2000[2] therefore requires the FSA to prepare and operate a scheme for ensuring that fines paid to the FSA are applied for the benefit of authorised persons. The scheme which the FSA will operate correlates with its arrangements for raising fees, which involve firms being grouped into fee-blocks of those offering broadly similar products and services. Penalties paid will be allocated to the appropriate fee-block within which the relevant activities fall, so ensuring that the penalty reduces the cost of regulation for the relevant business sector[3].

1 See the First Report of the Joint Committee, from para 222, and the Response by HM Treasury of 17 June 1999, section V, para F.
2 FSMA 2000, Sch 1, para 16(2).
3 See Consultation Paper 59 ('The FSA's post-N2 fee raising arrangements'), June 2000, and Consultation Paper 79 ('Feedback statement to CP56 and second Consultation paper on the FSA's post-N2 fee raising arrangements'), December 2000. Penalties for market abuse against those who are neither authorised nor approved persons will be applied for the benefit of all authorised persons.

Practical guidance for firms

7.42 If the firm is to have any real ability to discuss with the FSA the amount of the fine that is appropriate, it will need to put together reasons why a lower fine should be imposed and evidence to support those reasons. Precisely what those reasons are will depend upon the circumstances of the particular case. But the FSA will be considering the criteria outlined at para 7.38 above, so they will normally form the focus of the firm's response. In addition to the factors relating to the firm, it may be useful to compile evidence about previous fines levied in similar situations and evidence, sometimes including expert evidence, on the seriousness or otherwise of the firm's breaches. Finally, in the light of the express policy to use fines for deterrent purposes, there may be scope for challenging the imposition of a fine that was wholly disproportionate to the breach but justified primarily by the need to make an example out of the firm[1].

1 The basis for the challenge would be the ECHR right to property in art 1 of the First Protocol to the Convention. This requires a fair balance to be struck between the demands of the general interest of the community and the requirements of the protection of the individual's fundamental rights. The requisite balance will not be found if the person concerned has had to bear an 'individual and excessive burden': see *Lithgow v United Kingdom* (1986) 8 EHRR 329.

RESTITUTION

Introduction

7.43 The FSA can, in certain circumstances, secure compensation for investors who have suffered losses arising from a regulatory breach by a firm or sometimes by others. The FSA does this either by making a restitution order itself or by applying to the court for a restitution order to be made. But one of the principles of good regulation to which the FSA must have regard is to make effective use of resources and it will not always be an effective use of the FSA's resources to be seeking compensation on behalf of customers. Compensation is primarily a private matter between customers and the firm. Why should the FSA become involved in such disputes? From the FSA's perspective, whether this is appropriate in the particular case will depend upon a number of considerations. From the firm's perspective as well, there can be advantages as well as disadvantages in being subject to a restitution order. For example, in some situations the firm may want to be able to compensate large numbers of disgruntled customers in an efficient way, rather than handling individual claims, and it may want to be seen to be dealing fairly with its customers.

7.44 In the following paragraphs we review the FSA's powers to make and apply for restitution orders, and consider, in particular:

- what is a restitution order?
- when will the FSA make or apply for a restitution order?
- how does the FSA make or apply for a restitution order?
- how is restitution calculated and distributed? and
- how should the firm approach the question of a restitution order?

In certain circumstances, a restitution order can be made against a person who works for a firm, including an approved person. The availability of restitution orders against individuals is considered at para 8.81 ff below. Restitution orders can also be made in the context of market abuse. To the extent that there are differences in the rules or policy, these are considered at para 13.254 ff below.

What is a restitution order?

7.45 A restitution order can be summarised as an order made either by the FSA or by the court requiring a person either to compensate those who have suffered loss from a regulatory breach or to disgorge profits that should not have been made. A restitution order can most simply be explained by reviewing the statutory provisions.

Restitution orders made by the FSA

7.46 The FSA may make a restitution order if satisfied that[1]:

- an authorised person has contravened, or been knowingly concerned in the contravention of:
  - a requirement imposed by or under the FSMA 2000[2], or
  - a criminal offence under any other Act which the FSA has the power to prosecute[3], and
- profits have accrued to the person as a result of the contravention, and/or
- one or more persons have suffered loss or been otherwise adversely affected as a result of the contravention,
- in which case the FSA may require the person concerned, in accordance with such arrangements as the FSA considers appropriate, to pay to the

appropriate person[4] or distribute among the appropriate persons such amount as appears to the FSA to be just having regard to:

— the profits appearing to the FSA to have accrued, and/or

— the extent of the loss or other adverse effect.

The FSA can therefore only make a restitution order against an authorised firm[5].

1 FSMA 2000, s 384(1), (5), (6) and (7).
2 The meaning of this phrase is discussed at para 2.142 ff above.
3 For a list of the relevant offences, see para 11.6 below.
4 In other words, the person or persons to whom the profits are attributable or who have suffered the loss or other adverse effects.
5 The FSA has wider powers in market abuse cases: see para 13.254 ff below.

7.47 The meaning of this test, and the scope of restitution orders that can be made, is discussed at para 7.49 below. How the amount of a restitution order, and the distribution of any payment, are determined, is considered at 7.85 ff below.

Restitution orders made by the court

7.48 The court's power to make a restitution order[1] is very similar to the FSA's power as set out at para 7.46 above. The differences are as follows:

- there must first be an application made to the court either by the FSA or by the Secretary of State[2];
- the court can make a restitution order against any person, not only an authorised person. It could therefore order restitution to be paid by:
  - — an approved person,
  - — an exempt person,
  - — any other person, whether authorised or approved or not, who is knowingly concerned in a contravention by an authorised person[3], or
  - — any other person[4] who contravenes a requirement by or under the FSMA 2000 or a requirement which the FSA or the Secretary of State has the power to prosecute;
- the court orders the person concerned to pay the FSA such sum as appears to the court to be just (having regard to the same matters as are set out at para 7.46 above) and directs the FSA how to pay or distribute the money, which the FSA must then do[5].

The meaning of this test, and the scope of restitution orders that can be made, is discussed at para 7.49 below. How the amount of a restitution order, and the distribution of any payment, are determined, is considered at 7.85 ff below. As to when the FSA will make an application to the court, rather than using its powers to make the restitution order itself, see para 7.69 ff below.

1 FSMA 2000, s 382.

2 The Secretary of State can make an application in relation to the contravention of a requirement imposed by or under the FSMA 2000 whose contravention constitutes a criminal offence which the Secretary of State has the power to prosecute under the FSMA 2000: s 382 (9)(b). The Secretary of State has parallel powers to prosecute offences under the FSMA 2000: see s 401(2).
3 For the meaning of the phrase 'knowingly concerned', see the discussion at para 7.51 below.
4 Examples of contraventions which could be committed by unregulated persons include breach of the general prohibition (FSMA 2000, s 19), unlawful financial promotion (FSMA 2000, s 21), or failing to provide information or documents when required to do so (FSMA, s 177).
5 FSMA 2000, s 382(2) and (3).

The test for making a restitution order

7.49 Certain elements of the test for making a restitution order, common to restitution orders made by the court and the FSA, require further explanation.

Requirement for a regulatory breach

7.50 The starting point is that there must have been a regulatory breach, either a breach of a requirement imposed by or under the FSMA 2000 or a criminal breach which, as appropriate, the FSA or the Secretary of State has the power to prosecute. The meaning of these phrases has already been outlined[1]. An admission by the firm that it committed a breach, made for example in order to settle the FSA's disciplinary proceedings against it, or an adverse finding against it, could thus form the basis for making a restitution order against it. This highlights the need for the firm always to have in mind the range of potential consequences of its actions and not to focus purely on the issue before it at any time.

1 See footnotes 2 and 3 to para 7.46 above and footnote 2 to para 7.48 above.

Persons knowingly concerned in the breach

7.51 A restitution order may be made not only against the firm or person who committed the breach but also (or alternatively) against any other person[1] who was knowingly concerned in the contravention.

1 Whether or not an authorised person – if the restitution order is made by the court. A restitution order made by the FSA may be made (see para 7.46 above) only against an authorised person (save in cases of market abuse: see para 13.254 ff below).

7.52 This is an important provision. It means that if the firm that committed the breach does not have sufficient resources to compensate investors, then another firm with greater resources that was involved, albeit less directly, may be required to do so or the order could be made against both. Two issues are critical and, as we will see, the answer to both is unclear.

7.53 First, the third party must have been 'knowingly concerned' in the contravention by the firm. Whilst there is some authority on the meaning of that phrase, considered at para 2.184 ff above[1], and it seems to be a reasonably broad test, precisely what it encompasses is not clear. Examples of third parties whom courts have held to be, or indicated were, knowingly concerned include the relevant firm's solicitors[2], an associated firm that knowingly received funds from the relevant transactions[3], the firm's managing director[4], and the firm's servants and agents[5]. But the implications of the test are not limited to these examples. For example, it might, in appropriate circumstances, include the trustee of a fund where it was the manager that committed the regulatory breach. Whether the person is knowingly concerned will depend to a large extent upon his knowledge of the facts that constitute the breach.

1 The cases cited arise from the Banking Act 1987, which contains the predecessors to the current provisions and uses the same language in relation to injunctions. For a discussion of injunctions, see para 7.97 ff below.
2 See *SIB v Pantell (No 2)* [1993] 1 All ER 134.
3 See *SIB v Pantell* [1989] 2 All ER 673.
4 See *SIB v Scandex Capital Management A/S* [1998] 1 Al ER 514.
5 See *SIB v Vandersteen Associates NV* [1991] BCLC 206.

7.54 Second, a restitution order will not be made in every case where the statutory test is satisfied. It is a matter within the discretion of, as appropriate, the FSA or the court. A key issue is therefore whether it is appropriate to make the third party pay restitution. No guidance has been given on how the discretion to make orders against those knowingly concerned will be exercised but courts have suggested that they may make less stringent orders against third parties than against the firm that committed the breach and they have suggested that it might be appropriate to link the two so that, for example, the third party is required to pay if the firm does not do so[1].

1 See *SIB v Pantell (No 2)* [1993] 1 All ER 134.

Disgorging gains

7.55 Restitution orders can be made not only to compensate investors for their losses but also to require the firm to disgorge gains that it should not have made[1]. The purpose of this is to discourage non-compliant behaviour by ensuring that firms do not benefit from it.

1 Whilst compensation for investor losses was a regular feature of the previous regulatory regime, the SROs did not have the ability to require firms to repay profits. The Financial Services Act 1986, ss 6 and 61 did allow profits to be required to be repaid, but the statutory provisions were rarely used in practice.

7.56 The FSMA 2000 envisages such profits being repaid to those to whom those profits are attributable. This can cause difficulty in practice. In some situations, it will be clear that a profit that has made is attributable to a particular identifiable person, for example if a commission is wrongly taken on the sale of a particular financial product and, in those cases, there is no particular complexity in requiring the firm to repay the profit to that person. In other cases, it may be clear that the profit is attributable to a particular person, but less clear that that person should benefit by receiving the profit because it would constitute a windfall gain. Of most difficulty are those cases where the profit cannot sensibly be attributed to any particular person. The prime example would be profits made from insider dealing or market abuse[1].

1 The powers of the FSA and the court to make a restitution order in cases of market abuse are considered separately at para 13.254 ff below.

7.57 The FSA Handbook does not contain any indication as to how these issues are addressed. Where there are real difficulties in assessing to whom profits should be paid, or it is otherwise inappropriate for a restitution order to be made, the firm can be deprived of its profits by an alternative means, namely by a fine being levied of sufficient amount to cancel out the profits[1]. The income from the fine would go to reduce the cost of regulation of the relevant section of the authorised community[2].

1 The amount of any profits made is a relevant factor in determining the amount of any fine: see para 7.38 above.
2 See para 7.41 above.

Other adverse effects

7.58 Restitution orders can be made to address not only losses suffered but also 'other adverse effects' from the contravention. It is not entirely clear what this envisages[1]. The effects which may have been suffered from the contravention could include non-financial effects, such as damage to reputation or, bearing in mind that this relates primarily to consumers, stress. Losses may also have been suffered that are indirect or impossible to quantify precisely. For example, at what price would the customer have bought and then sold the investment if it had been properly managed and priced? What alternative investment would he have made had this investment not been missold to him? The main effect of the phrase seems to be to make clear that the discretion of the FSA and the court to order restitution extends beyond those cases where investors can demonstrate that they have suffered what a court would regard as loss for which it could award damages. In other words, the FSA and the court can bypass technical arguments about whether loss can be proved, and focus instead on how it is appropriate for them to exercise their discretion in the particular case.

1 Although the same words appear in the Financial Services Act 1986, ss 6 and 61 there is no authority on their meaning.

Repayment of money only

7.59 Although the phrase 'restitution' may suggest otherwise, a restitution order can only require the repayment of money. It cannot, for example, be used to secure the return of securities or other investments wrongly transferred. An injunction may, however, be available for such purposes[1].

1 See para 7.97 ff below.

Restitution order is discretionary

7.60 Finally, as the above discussion highlights, the making of a restitution order is within the discretion of the FSA or the court, as applicable. An order will not automatically be made just because the statutory test is satisfied. The question of how the FSA exercises this discretion is discussed at para 7.64 ff below. The principles on which the court exercises its discretion are not yet clear[1].

1 There is no discussion of the relevant principles in any of the reported cases under the previous regime.

The effect of a restitution order

7.61 So far as the firm is concerned, the effect of a restitution order, once finally made, is to bind the firm to make the payment for distribution by the FSA. The question of how this obligation can be enforced is considered at para 7.82 ff below.

7.62 The effect so far as customers are concerned is rather different. From their perspective, the payment is effectively ex gratia. It does not prevent them from bringing their own legal proceedings to recover losses they have suffered in respect of the same matter[1], although it is likely that the ombudsman or a court, in assessing what damages were recoverable, would take into account the payments already made to them[2]. In practice, customers are unlikely to bring proceedings unless in their view the compensation they have received significantly fails to address their recoverable losses.

1 Where the restitution order is made by the court, the FSMA 2000 specifically provides that nothing in the statutory provision affects the right of any person other than the FSA or the Secretary of State to bring proceedings in respect of the same matter: FSMA 2000, s 382(7) and (in respect of market abuse) s 383(9). There is no similar express provision in relation to restitution orders made by the FSA. The meaning and effect of this provision is considered in more detail at para 10.64 ff below.
2 This is discussed in more detail at para 10.64 ff below.

7.63 Can the firm insist upon finality as the price for agreeing with the FSA to pay restitution? There is nothing in the FSA Handbook enabling the firm to require customers to settle all their claims when they receive restitution. But, equally, there is nothing expressly to preclude it and it may be worth considering and raising with the FSA in an appropriate case.

When will the FSA make or apply for a restitution order?

7.64 A restitution order is a useful means for enabling customers (and others) to be compensated in a cost-effective and fair manner, and the FSA regards its purpose as essentially restorative[1]. However, it is clearly not the FSA's role, or an appropriate use of its resources, to secure compensation in every case where there has been a regulatory breach. In many cases, the effects of the breach will be confined to market counterparties or other large customers of the firm, who will have the sophistication and resources to pursue legal remedies for themselves. In other cases, the effect will be limited to a small number of consumers, who are likely to be able either to agree compensation with the firm or to use the ombudsman scheme[2]. The proportion of cases where it will be appropriate for the FSA to devote its resources to seeking restitution orders is likely therefore to be reasonably limited but, as we will see, encompasses the most serious cases in terms of their systemic effect.

1 See the FSA Handbook at ENF 9.9.2.
2 The ombudsman scheme is discussed in Chapter 12 below.

7.65 We consider here two separate issues, namely:

- the FSA's policy on when it will consider a restitution order; and
- the FSA's policy on choosing between making an order and applying to court for an order.

In what circumstances will the FSA consider a restitution order?

7.66 The FSA has given detailed guidance[1] on the factors which it will consider when deciding whether to exercise its powers to seek or obtain restitution. In making that decision, it will consider all the relevant circumstances of the case but, in particular, may take into account a non-exhaustive list of factors that may be summarised as follows:

- whether quantifiable profits have been made that are owed to identifiable persons and/or whether there are identifiable persons who have suffered quantifiable losses or other adverse effects. If not, this may militate against making a restitution order;
- the number of persons who have suffered loss or other adverse effects and the extent of those losses or adverse effects. Individual losses may be more efficiently and effectively redressed by pursuing claims directly with the firm or through the ombudsman scheme. However, if a large number of people were affected or the losses are substantial, individually or collectively, it may be more appropriate for the FSA to pursue a restitution order (possibly in combination with disciplinary action or a criminal prosecution);
- the costs that would be incurred by the FSA in securing redress and whether these costs are justified by the benefit that would result from such action;
- the availability of redress through the ombudsman scheme or the compensation scheme[2]. Neither such scheme, however, addresses losses suffered from breaches of the general prohibition;
- the availability of redress through another regulatory body, such as the Takeover Panel, and whether the firm concerned has complied with the requirement of that other body to make redress;
- whether persons who have suffered losses are in a position to bring civil proceedings on their own behalf. The FSA considers the cost to the person of bringing the claim and the likelihood of success in relation to the size of any sums that may be recovered;
- the solvency of the firm, and the availability of the FSA's other powers, such as to apply for an administration order, winding-up order, bankruptcy order or compulsory insolvency order or for the appointment of a receiver against a firm or a person conducting regulated activities in breach of the general prohibition[3];

- the conduct of the persons who have suffered loss, including the extent to which they have contributed to their own loss or failed to take reasonable steps to protect their own interests;
- the context, including the statutory tests for making a restitution order and, in addition, if the matter arises during the context of a takeover bid the FSA will consult the Takeover Panel and give due weight to its views.

1 See the FSA Handbook at ENF 9.6.

2 The compensation scheme applies where the firm concerned is unable to pay claims against it, for example because it has been put into insolvency proceedings. For further information, see the FSA Handbook at COMP.

3 The FSA's powers in relation to insolvency can be found in the FSA Handbook at ENF Chapter 10.

7.67 A restitution order is likely, therefore, to be in contemplation in those cases where large numbers of consumers have suffered significant losses, or perhaps more so where the losses suffered are significant overall but relatively small individually[1]. If the breach primarily affects market professionals, then the FSA is likely to regard them as able to pursue their own remedies. If it affects a relatively small number of consumers, then the FSA may take the view that the matter can be more effectively handled by each customer individually with the firm or through the ombudsman.

1 By way of example, in calendar years 1999 and 2000, compensation was paid in 12 IMRO enforcement cases, the compensation, ranging from, in total, £20,000 to £210m. In five of these cases, more than 1,000 customers were involved.

7.68 In some situations, the firm may want to encourage the FSA to make a restitution order, or may want to agree a restitution order with the FSA. The question of how the firm might approach these issues is considered at para 7.94 below.

When will the FSA apply to court for an order?

7.69 The FSA's power to make a restitution order and its power to apply to the court for a restitution order overlap to a large extent where an authorised firm is involved (or in a case of market abuse[1]). In those cases where the FSA does have concurrent powers, how does it choose which course of action to take?

1 See para 13.254 ff below.

7.70 The FSA expects authorised firms to comply with requirements which it imposes and therefore that the additional force of a court order will not be required in relation to such firms. Its policy is therefore that in cases where it is appropriate to exercise its powers to obtain restitution from such firms, it will generally first consider using its administrative powers before considering taking court action[1]. However, there may be situations where the FSA will choose to apply to court for a restitution order. Examples which the FSA have identified[2] are:

- where the FSA wishes to combine the application with some other application, for example for an injunction to prevent the firm from committing further breaches or to freeze its assets[3];
- where the FSA wishes to bring related court proceedings against an unauthorised person and the factual basis of those proceedings is likely to be the same as for the restitution claim against the firm; or
- where the FSA suspects that the firm may not comply with an administrative order and therefore wants the additional force of a court order.

1 See the FSA Handbook at ENF 9.7.2.
2 See the FSA Handbook at ENF 9.7.3.
3 See para 7.97 ff below.

7.71 In practice, it is likely that these situations will arise relatively rarely. For example, the FSA is likely to want to make any application for an injunction against a firm on an urgent basis and, in any event, at an early stage following discovery of the problem and may not be in a position to substantiate a claim for restitution at the same time. Equally, it should be rare that the FSA has such concerns about an authorised firm as to believe that the potential sanction of contempt of court is required before the firm will comply. In that situation, the FSA would also have to be seriously considering cancelling the firm's permission[1].

1 See Chapter 9 below.

How does the FSA make or apply for a restitution order?

7.72 In the following paragraphs we consider five procedural issues relating to restitution orders, namely:

- how does the FSA or the court obtain the information it needs to consider whether an order should be made?
- how does the FSA make a restitution order?
- how does the FSA apply to the court for a restitution order?
- is there a risk of publicity arising from a restitution order?
- how is a restitution order enforced?

How does the FSA or the court obtain the information required?

7.73 In order to consider whether to make a restitution order and, if so, the terms and amount of the order, the FSA and, if appropriate, the court, will need evidence not only as to the regulatory breach but also as to the amount of the losses suffered by customers (or others) as a result of the breach, the profits the firm made from the breach and the identity of those who suffered loss and those to whom any profits are attributable. This may go substantially beyond the evidence required, for example, for any disciplinary proceedings. How does the FSA or the court obtain this additional information?

7.74 The FSA has a wide range of information gathering and investigation powers exercisable where authorised firms, among others, commit regulatory breaches[1]. Precisely which power would be available in the particular case depends upon the nature of the contravention in issue. In addition to the specific investigation powers:

- firms have extensive duties of co-operation with the FSA which enable the FSA to obtain much of the information it needs without using any formal powers[2];
- the FSA has a general power to require firms to provide information to it[3];
- the FSA's power to require a firm to obtain a report from a skilled person such as an auditor or actuary[4] is likely to be particularly important in this context, not only to assist in determining the amount of any profits or losses but also in determining how any amounts payable should be distributed.

These should enable the FSA to obtain the relevant information, both from the firm and from others who were involved.

1 These are considered in Chapter 4 above. For a list, see paras 4.13 and 4.14 above.
2 Principle 11, Principles for Businesses: see para 4.27 ff above.
3 FSMA 2000, s 165: see para 4.59 above.
4 FSMA 2000, s 166: see para 4.72 above. See also the FSA Handbook at ENF 9.8.6.

7.75 If an application for a restitution order is made to the court, to a large extent the court will decide whether to act upon the evidence which the FSA puts before it and any evidence which the firm provides in response. The court does however also have its own fact-finding powers[1] in connection with an application for a restitution order. It may require the person concerned to supply it with such accounts or other information as it may require for any one or more of the following purposes, namely:

- to establish what, if any, profits have accrued to the person as a result of the contravention;
- to establish whether any person or persons have suffered any loss or adverse effect as a result of the contravention and, if so, the extent of that loss or adverse effect; and
- to determine how any amounts are to be paid or distributed;

and it may require any accounts or other information supplied to be verified in such manner as it may direct.

1 FSMA 2000, s 382(4) and (5).

How does the FSA make a restitution order?

7.76 Where the FSA seeks to impose a restitution order against a firm, it must follow the warning/decision notice procedure[1]. This is considered in Chapter 5 above. Among other things, the firm will have the right to discuss the proposed restitution order with the FSA and ultimately can refer the matter to the Tribunal for determination.

1 FSMA 2000, ss 385 and 386.

7.77 Specific points to note in this context are as follows:

- the warning notice must specify the amount which the FSA proposes to require the firm to pay or distribute[1];
- the decision notice must[2]:
  - state the amount that the firm is to pay or distribute,
  - identify the person or persons to whom that amount is to be paid or among whom it is to be distributed, and
  - state the arrangements in accordance with which the payment or distribution is to be made.

1 FSMA 2000, s 385(2).
2 FSMA 2000, s 386(2).

How does the FSA apply to the court for an order?

7.78 An application for a restitution order[1] is made by the FSA issuing a claim form in the High Court under the Civil Procedure Rules[2]. It will, of course, be possible for the firm to oppose the application.

1 Before the FSA makes an application, it must reach the internal decision that such an application is appropriate. The FSA has indicated that the decision to bring such proceedings will be taken by the Chairman of the RDC (see the FSA Handbook at DEC 4.6), although it may be made by others in urgent cases (for details, see footnote 1 to para 7.126 below).
2 For a more detailed explanation of the procedure, see the Civil Procedure Rules, Part 7.

Is there a risk of publicity?

7.79 There is a risk of publicity arising from a restitution order. The nature of that risk depends upon the process used and requires some explanation.

7.80 If the FSA decides to make a restitution order itself, as distinct from applying to the court for an order, then the warning and decision notice procedure will normally be confidential[1]. But once the restitution order is finally made[2], the FSA is likely to publish it, in line with its general policy to publish details of successful enforcement action[3]. The FSA may, however, decide not to publish details of the restitution order, for example where this could damage market confidence or undermine market integrity in a way that could be damaging to the interests of consumers[4]. If the matter is referred to the Tribunal, then publicity could arise at that stage because the presumption is that Tribunal proceedings will be held in public[5].

1 There are statutory restrictions on publishing a warning or decision notice or any details concerning one: see FSMA 2000, s 391(1) and see more generally the discussion at para 5.76 above.
2 Upon the issue of the final notice either because the firm does not contest the decision notice or following Tribunal proceedings and any appeal: see para 5.188 above.
3 See the FSA Handbook at ENF 9.10.1. For a more detailed explanation of the general policy, see para 5.194 above.
4 See the FSA Handbook at ENF 9.10.1. In addition, where the behaviour that gave rise to restitution occurred in the context of a takeover bid, in deciding whether or not to publish the matter the FSA will consult the Takeover Panel and, if it believes that publication may affect the timetable or outcome of the bid, will give due weight to its views.
5 See the discussion at para 6.32 above.

7.81 If the FSA applies to the court for a restitution order, then the claim form will be a public document once it has been served[1]. Publicity could therefore arise at an early stage[2]. Any hearing before the court is also likely to be in public, although there is scope for persuading the court to hold it in private, for example because it involves confidential information or it is necessary to do so in the interests of justice[3]. If the hearing is in public, then a transcript of the judgment or order is also publicly available[4]. If the court makes a restitution order, then the FSA's normal policy on the publication of successful enforcement action applies, as outlined at para 7.80 above.

1 See the Civil Procedure Rules, Pt 5, r 5.4.
2 Contrast this with the statutory prohibition against publishing details of a warning or decision notice: see para 7.80 above.
3 For further explanation, see the Civil Procedure Rules, Pt 39, r 39.2 and the accompanying Practice Direction, 39 PD-001.
4 See Civil Procedure Rules, Practice Direction 39 PD-001, para 1.11.

How is a restitution order enforced?

7.82 In most cases, firms will comply with a restitution order, whether made by the FSA or the court. However, there may be cases where the firm is not willing or able to do so, and in those cases how is the order enforced?

7.83 The FSMA 2000 does not contain any specific provision for the enforcement of restitution orders. Enforcement is therefore a matter of general principle. As a result, if a person fails to comply with an order made by the FSA:

- this is likely to constitute the contravention of a requirement imposed by or under the FSMA 2000, potentially giving rise to disciplinary and other regulatory enforcement proceedings[1];
- the FSA could apply to the court for an injunction to require the firm to remedy the contravention and to prevent it from dissipating its assets[2];
- it may cause the FSA to doubt whether the firm remains fit and proper to perform regulated activities, which could lead to its permission being varied, or equivalent intervention action being imposed on an incoming firm, or even to its permission being cancelled[3];

- it could give rise to concerns about the firm's solvency, which might lead the FSA to consider exercising its insolvency powers[4].

1 For a discussion of this phrase and its potential consequences, see para 2.142 ff above.
2 Applications to court for injunctions are discussed in para 7.97 ff below.
3 These issues are discussed in Chapter 9 below.
4 See the FSA Handbook at ENF Chapter 10.

7.84 If an authorised firm fails to comply with an order made by the court, each of the above could apply. In addition, whether or not the person concerned is an authorised firm, the court could enforce the restitution order in the same way as any other court order.

How is restitution calculated and distributed?

7.85 One of the primary questions for a firm faced with the prospect of a restitution order is how much it will be ordered to pay and to whom that money will be distributed. The answer depends to a large extent upon the circumstances and it is difficult to give any general guidance. Indeed, the FSA has provided very little guidance on this in the FSA Handbook.

How is restitution calculated?

7.86 The starting point is the statutory provisions[1] which enable the FSA or the court to order the payment of such sum as appears to be just, having regard to, as appropriate, the amount of the profits which have accrued to the firm and/or the amount of the losses or other adverse effects that have been suffered.

1 FSMA 2000, ss 382(2) and 384(5).

7.87 Three points are notable. First, the amount awarded is within the discretion of, as appropriate, the FSA or the court applying the test set out above. The amount need not correlate directly with the amount of the profits and losses, although in most cases the two are likely to correlate. Thus, in cases where the precise amounts of profits or losses are incapable of being determined sensibly, the focus may be on obtaining a consistent and fair result, sometimes through the use of mathematical models adopting various assumptions[1]. Or the restitution order may seek to compensate non-financial adverse effects in monetary terms[2].

1 The report of a skilled person may be important here: see para 7.74 above.
2 This is discussed at para 7.58 above.

7.88 Second, it will clearly be relevant whether any payments have already been made[1].

1 See the FSA Handbook at ENF 9.8.3 and 9.8.4 and the discussion at para 10.64 ff below.

7.89 Third, the amount of the restitution order is in practice likely to be linked with the method of distribution, because in many cases the overall figure will simply amount to the sum of the restitution payable to individual investors. The position may be different where profits are being disgorged, since the amount of the profit may be a defined figure and the main issue is how that amount should be distributed.

How is restitution distributed?

7.90 It is for the FSA or, as applicable, the court to determine how the restitution payments are distributed[1]. The payment can only be distributed among those to whom the profits which the firm wrongfully made are attributable or who suffered the loss or other adverse affect.

1 FSMA 2000, ss 382(3) and 384(5): see paras 7.46 to 7.48 above.

7.91 The FSA has given no guidance on how it expects this to work in practice. The expectation must be that the payment will be distributed in such a way as to compensate each person for their losses or repay to them the profits that are attributable to them. The practical issues discussed at para 7.87 ff above also arise here[1].

1 See also para 7.56 above.

Can the person compensated object?

7.92 It should by now be clear that both the amount of compensation and its distribution may be determined to achieve a fair and reasonable result, rather than the result that most closely parallels the legal claims of each customer (or other person) against the firm. There is, therefore, a real risk of a particular customer not receiving the amount to which he believes he is entitled, either because of the calculation of the amount or because the payment has been distributed in a way that favours others over him. What can the person do in that situation?

7.93 There is no express right for any customer to become involved in the process of making a restitution order, either before the FSA or before the court and, in any event, he is unlikely to want to object until after the order has been made and the terms are made known to him. At that stage, there are two options. First, if the restitution order was made by the FSA, the customer may be able to apply to have it judicially reviewed[1]. Second, he can accept the payment and then take legal action for the remainder of his claim[2].

1 Judicial review is briefly outlined in Chapter 16 below.
2 See para 7.62 above. He may also be able to bring a claim for the remainder before the ombudsman: see Chapter 12 below.

How should the firm approach the question of a restitution order?

7.94 From the firm's perspective, the prospect of being subjected to a restitution order may seem to be worrying, particularly where overall very significant losses were suffered by large numbers of people. Indeed, in some cases, the figures may be so significant, or the firm may feel sufficiently strongly about the issue as a matter of principle, that the firm will want to resist the restitution order and try to avoid incurring liability for any losses. In addition, the firm may be concerned about the risk of customers (or others) making further claims, or trying to obtain a double recovery.

7.95 In many cases, however, there may be good practical reasons for the firm to agree to a restitution order, particularly if a full and final settlement of claims can be achieved at the same time. A restitution order may in the long run prove rather cheaper for the firm than dealing with, and defending itself against, large numbers of individual claims, brought either in the courts or through the ombudsman. Being seen to pay restitution quickly and fairly may allow the firm to reclaim some moral high ground and repair any damage to its reputation. It also allows the firm to be seen to be co-operating with the FSA and taking appropriate steps to protect the interests of customers. This may assist the firm in any disciplinary proceedings arising from the same matter[1] and generally in minimising the regulatory fall-out from the problem which has arisen. Indeed, the firm's agreement to a restitution order may be part of a package of measures to bring the regulatory side of the matter to a close.

1 The payment of restitution may be relevant to the amount of any fine imposed: see para 7.38 above.

7.96 The aim will often therefore be to work with the FSA to agree a basis upon which restitution can be paid and distributed to customers and others. It will be important to find a practical solution to the real difficulties which, as outlined above, the calculation of restitution can pose. Also, in some instances, the firm may want to be seen to be offering restitution at an early stage and taking the lead in assessing what payments should be made.

INJUNCTIONS

Introduction

7.97 In some situations, the FSA may need to prevent a firm from continuing to carry on an activity in breach of the regulatory requirements or may want to freeze its assets in order, for example, to protect the interests of consumers. Whilst the FSA has various powers to intervene in the business of regulated firms[1], it cannot exercise those powers against those who are outside the regulated community. Alternatively, it may consider that its own powers against those who are regulated carry insufficient weight, because the penalties for non-compliance are inadequate. In those types of situations, the FSA may wish to seek a civil injunction from the court and the FSMA 2000 allows it to do so.

1 It does this by varying a firm's permission (or imposing an equivalent restriction on an incoming firm): see Chapter 9 below.

7.98 In the following paragraphs we consider the FSA's power to apply for an injunction from the court, and in particular:

- the types of injunctions that can be obtained and the grounds on which they can be granted (para 7.100 ff);
- the circumstances when the FSA will seek an injunction (para 7.122 ff); and
- the procedure involved, including any attendant publicity (para 7.125 ff).

There is a separate provision enabling the FSA to apply for an injunction in cases of market abuse. This is considered at para 13.235 ff below.

7.99 The FSA has additional powers to apply for injunctions under the Unfair Terms in Consumer Contracts Regulations 1999 or, in the context of insurance, an injunction in relation to an incoming firm at the request of an overseas regulator in certain specified circumstances relating to the EU First Life and First Non-life Insurance Directives[1]. These powers are not reviewed here. The FSA's policy can be found in the FSA Handbook at ENF 6.8 to 6.10.

1 FSMA 2000, s 198.

What types of injunctions can be obtained?

7.100 There are broadly three different types of injunctions, namely:

- to restrain contraventions of regulations;
- to require breaches to be remedied; and
- to secure assets.

The grounds upon which each can be obtained are outlined in turn below. The FSA's policy on when it will be appropriate to apply for an injunction is considered at para 7.122 ff below.

Injunctions generally

7.101 Whilst a detailed discussion of injunctive relief as a general matter would be inappropriate in this context, two points are worth highlighting at the outset because they underlie much of the discussion that follows.

7.102 First, injunctive relief is discretionary. The court is not obliged to grant an injunction simply because the FSA establishes that the statutory grounds outlined below have been fulfilled. Outside of the regulatory context, complex rules have developed as to the factors to be taken into account by the court in exercising its discretion to grant an injunction[1]. Thus, for example, the claimant is required to show that damages would not be an adequate remedy for the breach, the claimant must not have unreasonably delayed bringing the action for an injunction, and the court will consider whether the injunction would cause undue hardship or otherwise would be unjust. The extent to which the same factors are relevant in the context of statutory injunctions under the FSMA 2000 is not clear[2]. It is certainly open to those seeking to resist an injunction to argue any points relevant to the court's discretion. Whilst the court clearly has a discretion whether to grant an injunction in each particular case, its general approach is likely to be receptive towards granting an injunction where the FSA considers that one is required, assuming the application is supported by appropriate evidence from someone of appropriate seniority.

1 For a detailed discussion of injunctive relief, see *Equitable Remedies*, Spry, 5th edn, 1997 at Chapter 4.

2 Which factors apply is a matter of statutory interpretation: see *Equitable Remedies*, Spry, 4th edn, 1990 at 435 to 436.

7.103 Second, in many cases an injunction is applied for initially on an interim basis. An interim injunction can be obtained relatively swiftly and without a full trial. Whilst the purpose of an interim injunction is theoretically only to preserve the position pending a full trial on whether or not an injunction should be granted, in practice the matter may never proceed to a full trial, so that the granting of an interim injunction will tend to dispose of the matter. It is thus the interim application which is often likely to be most relevant. Different factors are normally taken into account by courts when considering whether to grant an interim injunction. The court is here involved in a balancing exercise[1], taking into account, among other things, the prospects of the claimant ultimately being successful[2] and the consequences of granting or refusing interim relief. The court will make the order that appears to it to be the most just in all the circumstances. It is likely that the court will take a similar approach when considering making an interim injunction under the FSMA 2000 but it should be noted that it is likely in practice to be reasonably receptive to the FSA's views on the need for an interim injunction, particularly if the purpose of seeking the injunction is to protect consumers or markets[3].

1 See *Equitable Remedies*, Spry, 5th edn, 1997 at 470 to 475.

2 The claimant need only show that there is a serious issue to be tried in favour of a final injunction: see *American Cyanamid Co v Ethicon Ltd* [1975] AC 396. But a higher or different test may be required to be satisfied in cases of mandatory injunctions and freezing orders: see paras 7.114 and 7.120 below. Note that in cases where the grant or refusal of an interim injunction will have the practical effect of putting an end to the action, the court may be more willing to give detailed consideration to the evidence and the prospects of the claim: see *Cayne v Global Natural Resources plc* [1984] 1 All ER 225.

3 Note that the court has a discretion not to require a cross-undertaking in damages from the FSA and is likely not to do so: Sec *SIB v Lloyd-Wright* [1993] 4 All ER 210, applying *Kirkless Metropolitan Borough Council v Wickes Building Supplies Ltd* [1992] 3 All ER 717, *Re Highfield Commodities Ltd* [1984] 3 All ER 884 and *F Hoffmann- La Roche & Co AG v Secretary of State for Trade and Industry* [1974] 2 All ER 1128, HL.

Restraining contraventions

7.104 If, on the application of the FSA, the court is satisfied that[1]:

- there is a reasonable likelihood that any person will contravene:
  - — a requirement imposed by or under the FSMA 2000, or
  - — a requirement imposed by or under some other Act contravention of which constitutes an offence which the FSA has the power to prosecute under the FSMA 2000, or
- that any person has contravened any such requirement and there is a reasonable likelihood that the contravention will continue or be repeated;

then the court may make an order restraining the contravention[2].

1 FSMA 2000, s 380(1).
2 This is similar to the previous powers under the Financial Services Act 1986, ss 6(1) and 61(1)(a) and (b) and the Banking Act 1987, s 93.

7.105 An injunction may also be granted upon application by the Secretary of State, relating to the contravention of requirements by or under the FSMA 2000 which constitute a criminal offence which the Secretary of State has the power to prosecute under the FSMA 2000[1].

1 FSMA 2000, s 380(1) and (6)(b).

7.106 The meaning of a requirement imposed by or under the FSMA 2000 has been considered at para 2.142 ff above. For a list of those requirements which the FSA has the power to prosecute, see para 11.5 ff below[1].

1 The Secretary of State has parallel powers to prosecute, in England & Wales and Northern Ireland, any offence under the FSMA 2000 or subordinate legislation made under the FSMA 2000: s 401.

7.107 There are several points to note. First, the test of 'reasonable likelihood' of a contravention is not a high one. There may be arguments both about whether a particular action would amount to a regulatory contravention and whether the firm was reasonably likely to take that course of action. So far as the latter is concerned, the FSA will need evidence to substantiate the existence of the reasonable likelihood. Quite what the court will require will depend upon the circumstances[1]. It may be sufficient that the firm had refused to respond positively to a request by the FSA for an undertaking not to take a particular action. Conversely, it is difficult to see that an injunction would be granted where the firm had given such an undertaking, at least absent any evidence that it intended not to comply with it.

1 See, for example, *SIB v Vandersteen Associates NV* [1991] BCLC 206, where Harman J accepted that there was a reasonable likelihood of future contraventions without discussion of the test. Vandersteen was a Belgian company that had been cold-calling UK investors.

7.108 Second, as already indicated[1], the court may be asked to grant an injunction on an interim basis in the first instance and, in such cases, the court conducts a balancing exercise. In cases where there is a real issue whether a particular activity is legitimate or not, it may, depending upon the circumstances, be that the court will prefer to order an expedited trial rather than to prevent someone from carrying on what may turn out to be a lawful business.

1 See para 7.103 above.

7.109 Third, the FSMA 2000 provides that the injunction is to restrain the contravention. It does not specify against whom it can be made. In the normal course, an injunction is likely only to be needed against the wrongdoer, the person who commits or is intending to commit the relevant breach. But, it is possible to envisage situations where injunctions may be appropriate against others including persons who are not members of the regulated community.

Requiring breaches to be remedied

7.110 If, on the application of the FSA, the court is satisfied that[1]:

- any person has contravened:
  - a requirement imposed by or under the FSMA 2000, or
  - a requirement imposed by or under some other Act contravention of which constitutes an offence which the FSA has the power to prosecute under the FSMA 2000, and
- there are steps which could be taken for remedying the contravention, including mitigating its effect;

then the court may make an order requiring that person, and any other person who appears to have been knowingly concerned in the contravention, to take such steps as the court may direct to remedy it, including mitigating its effect[2].

1 FSMA 2000, s 380(2).
2 This is similar to the previous power under the Financial Services act 1986, s 61(1)(c) although there was previously no reference to 'mitigating [the] effect' of the contravention. See also the Financial Services Act 1986, s 6(2).

7.111 An injunction may also be granted upon application by the Secretary of State, relating to the contravention of requirements by or under the FSMA 2000 constituting a criminal offence which the Secretary of State has the power to prosecute[1].

1 FSMA 2000, s 380(2) and (6)(b).

7.112 The meaning of a requirement imposed by or under the FSMA 2000 is considered at para 2.142 ff above. For a list of those contraventions which the FSA has the power to prosecute, see para 11.5 ff below[1].

1 As to the Secretary of State's powers of prosecution under the FSMA 2000, see footnote 1 to para 7.106 above.

7.113 Three points require further comment. First, such an injunction could be used in a variety of situations, ranging from providing a remedy to particular customers in respect of transactions which breach the regulatory rules to requiring firms to take particular steps in relation to, for example, their systems and controls (in much the same way as a variation of permission). So far as the former is concerned, the injunction may require more than simply the payment of money, as that could often be accomplished by a restitution order[1]. It could, for example, be used to order securities to be transferred[2] or other steps to be taken[3]. The FMSA 2000 further ensures that the injunction is a flexible tool, by providing[4] that references to remedying a contravention include references to mitigating its effect. This allows the court flexibility to address situations where, strictly speaking, the rule breach is incapable of being remedied and the steps which it wishes to order to be taken would be better described as mitigating the effect of the breach[5]. An example would be publishing a correction to a misleading advertisement, which arguably could not remedy the breach, as it had already occurred and any damage had already been caused, but might better be classed as mitigating its effect.

1 In the context of the Financial Services Act 1986, it was held that an injunction should be directed to individual transactions, rather than to secure compensation for investors as a class (for which a restitution order would now be the appropriate remedy): see *SIB v Pantell (No 2)* [1993] 1 All ER 134, CA.
2 For this reason, it is likely to be a particularly important tool in the context of market misconduct. For the FSA to obtain such an order, the investor concerned would need to consent to it and, for example, would need to return the shares or money which he had obtained; it therefore operates as a form of 'statutory recession': see *SIB v Pantell (No 2)* [1993] 1 All ER 134, CA.
3 It may be possible for the FSA to use this to obtain an interim payment for investors, on the basis that an interim payment is a step to mitigate the effect of the contravention: see *Securities and Investment Board v Scandex Capital Management A/S* [1998] 1 All ER 514.
4 FSMA 2000, s 380(5).
5 This addresses doubts expressed by Scott LJ in *SIB v Pantell (No 2)* [1993] 1 All ER 134 based on the wording of the Financial Services Act 1986, s 61(1).

7.114 Second, in some circumstances it may be possible for an injunction to be granted on an interim basis in the first instance[1]. Whether this is appropriate will depend very much upon the situation. An interim injunction requiring the firm to take steps in relation to a particular transaction (for example, to pay money or transfer securities to a third party) would, even more so than in the case of other types of injunctions, effectively dispose of the matter, because the relevant steps would have been taken before the case came to a full trial. The courts recognise that this may be the effect of interim injunctions requiring positive steps to be taken, known as mandatory injunctions[2], and this may be an important factor in deciding whether an interim injunction is appropriate. For example, it may be more appropriate to grant an injunction securing the person's assets pending a full trial (see para 7.116 ff below). However, an interim injunction may be more likely to be appropriate where the matter is one between the firm and the FSA, for example requiring the firm to take particular steps with regard to its controls or its conduct of business. Again, whether it was appropriate would depend upon the circumstances.

1 See para 7.103 above.
2 For further discussion, see *Equitable Remedies*, Spry, 5th edn at page 546.

7.115 Third, an injunction may be granted not only against the person who committed the breach but also against any person who was knowingly concerned in it. This would allow the court to make an order against individual employees who had some involvement as well as against other firms. The same issue arises in the context of restitution orders and is considered at para 7.51 ff above. It is irrelevant whether the third party received or gained anything from the contravention, although this may be relevant to the court's exercise of its discretion[1].

1 See Scott LJ in *SIB v Pantell (No 2)* [1993] 1 All ER 134 at 144; see also Steyn LJ at 148.

Securing assets

7.116 If, on the application of the FSA, the court is satisfied that any person may have[1]:

- contravened:
  - a requirement imposed by or under the FSMA 2000, or
  - a requirement imposed by or under some other Act contravention of which constitutes an offence which the FSA has the power to prosecute under the FSMA 2000, or
- been knowingly concerned in such a contravention;

then the court may make an order restraining the person from disposing of, or otherwise dealing with, any assets of his which it is satisfied he is reasonably likely to dispose of or otherwise deal with[2].

1 FSMA 2000, s 380(3).
2 There was no equivalent provision under the previous regime, although the courts were prepared to use their inherent jurisdiction to make a freezing order on the application of the FSA in support of likely proceedings for a restitution order or a remedial injunction: see *SIB v Pantell SA* [1989] 2 All ER 673.

7.117 An injunction may also be granted upon application by the Secretary of State, relating to the contravention of requirements by or under the FSMA 2000 which constitute a criminal offence which the Secretary of State has the power to prosecute[1].

1 FSMA 2000, s 380(3) and (6)(b).

7.118 The meaning of a requirement imposed by or under the FSMA 2000 is considered at para 2.142 ff above. For a list of those contraventions which the FSA has the power to prosecute, see para 11.5 ff below[1].

1 As to the Secretary of State's powers of prosecution under the FSMA 2000, see footnote 1 to para 7.106 above.

7.119 A number of points should be made. First, this order is a freezing order. It does not in itself grant any substantive remedy, but will normally be made ancillary to, or in support of, some other proceedings. The purpose is to secure the person's assets to ensure that he is not able to dissipate them and thereby defeat potential claims arising from the breach[1]. Typically, this may be made in support of an application for an injunction to require remedial steps to be taken[2]. It could, for example, also be used to protect the assets from which restitution might be made to investors[3].

1 The provision enables an injunction to be made only in relation to a contravention which has already taken place. However, the FSA has said that it may ask the court to grant an injunction in the exercise of its inherent jurisdiction where it has evidence showing that there is a reasonable likelihood that a person will commit a breach and that this will result in the dissipation of assets belonging to investors: see the FSA Handbook at ENF 6.5.2.

2 See para 7.110 ff above.

3 See the FSA Handbook at ENF 6.6.2(5). The FSA also suggests that it could be used to safeguard funds containing client assets, but whether that is right would depend upon whether the assets were the firm's assets or the client's assets, because the provision refers to 'assets of his' (ie the firm's). A freezing order may nonetheless be available under the court's inherent jurisdiction: see footnote 2 to para 7.116 above.

7.120 Second, the injunction will normally be sought on an interim basis, often urgently. The test normally applied by the courts in considering whether to grant a freezing order is whether there is a good arguable case that the firm will incur liability, a real risk that its assets might otherwise be dissipated such that any award or judgment would go unsatisfied and that it is just and convenient to grant the injunction[1]. It is unclear given the language whether the same test will be applied in relation to statutory injunctions under this provision. In most cases, the interim injunction will stay in place until the trial of the substantive matter in support of which it has been granted.

1 For further discussion, see *Mareva Injunctions and Anton Piller Relief*, Gee, 4th edn, 1998.

7.121 Third, the injunction can be granted not only against the person who committed the breach but also against a person who was knowingly concerned in it[1].

1 This is discussed further at paras 7.51 ff and 7.115 above. It is notable that in *SIB v Pantell SA* [1989] 2 All ER 673 the injunction was granted also against a third party who was arguably knowingly concerned.

In what circumstances will the FSA seek an injunction?

7.122 In deciding whether to seek an injunction, the FSA applies a broad test of whether that would be the most effective means of dealing with the FSA's concerns[1]. The FSA will consider all relevant circumstances and take into account a wide range of factors. Some of those which may be relevant include the following[2]:

- the nature and seriousness of the contravention, including the loss or other adverse effects on consumers and risk to client assets;
- whether the conduct has ceased and consumers are adequately protected;
- whether there are steps that could be taken to remedy the contravention, for example by withdrawing a misleading financial promotion or publishing a correction, writing to clients or investors to notify them of FSA action, providing financial redress, and repatriating funds from an overseas jurisdiction;

- the costs that the FSA would incur in applying for and enforcing an injunction and the benefits that would result;
- the disciplinary record and general compliance history of the person;
- whether the conduct can be adequately addressed by other disciplinary powers;
- the extent to which another regulator can adequately address the matter; and
- whether there is information to suggest that the person who is the subject of the possible application is involved in financial crime.

In any case where in the FSA's view any potential exercise of its power may affect the timetable or outcome of a takeover bid, the FSA will consult the Takeover Panel before taking any steps and give due weight to its views[3].

1 See the FSA Handbook at ENF 6.6.2.
2 For a full list, see the FSA Handbook at 6.6.2.
3 See the FSA Handbook at EMF 6.6.2(11).

7.123 The power to apply for an injunction, particularly against an authorised person, overlaps in various respects with the FSA's own powers and, where this is the case, the FSA will consider the relative effectiveness of the other powers available to it compared with injunctive relief. Breach of an injunction would amount to a contempt of court and could be punished accordingly. The FSA may feel that this additional weight is needed, for example because the firm has not complied with requirements imposed by the FSA or is unlikely to do so.

7.124 In practice, it is likely that firms will see injunctions being used most commonly:

- to prevent and address perimeter breaches by unauthorised firms[1];
- to provide a remedy to those affected by market misconduct[2];
- in support of proceedings for restitution orders or other significant civil claims from investors[3]; and
- to protect client assets which the firm holds.

1 For a brief explanation of perimeter breaches, see para 2.175 above.
2 This is addressed in more detail in Chapter 13 below.
3 For a discussion of restitution orders, see para 7.43 ff above.

Procedure for seeking an injunction

7.125 We consider:

- the procedure for the FSA to make an application to the court for an injunction; and
- whether the making of an injunction will be made public.

Procedure for making an application to the court

7.126 An application for an injunction[1] is made by issuing a claim form in the High Court under the Civil Procedure Rules. It will, of course, be possible for the firm to oppose the application[2].

1 Before the FSA makes an application to the court, it must reach a decision that such an application is appropriate in the particular case. The FSA has indicated that a decision to begin (or discontinue) such proceedings will be made by the RDC Chairman (see Chapter 5 above) or, in an urgent case and if the Chairman is not available, a Deputy Chairman and where possible, but subject to the need to act swiftly, one other RDC member. In an exceptionally urgent case, the decision could be taken by a senior FSA staff member. For details, see the FSA Handbook at DEC 4.6.

2 For a more detailed analysis of the procedure, see the Civil Procedure Rules, Part 7.

7.127 The FSA may, in appropriate cases, be able to obtain an urgent interim injunction without any notice being given to the firm. This is particularly likely to be relevant where the injunction sought is to restrain further market abuse or to restrain the disposal of assets. In those cases, there will be a further hearing shortly afterwards at which the firm will have the opportunity to be heard.

Publication of an injunction

7.128 There is no specific prohibition against the FSA making public the fact that it is applying for, or has obtained, an injunction. Indeed, the FSA's claim form, issued to commence the civil action against the firm in which the application is sought, will normally be a public document. Moreover, the FSA has indicated that, in line with its general policy, it will normally publish details of successful applications to the court for injunctions[1]. In some circumstances, the FSA may regard it as particularly important to publicise the injunction to ensure that consumers are aware of the position, for example where the injunction prevents further illegal activity. However, there may be situations where the FSA decides not to publicise the injunction, or not to do so immediately[2], for example where this might damage market confidence or undermine market integrity in a way which would be prejudicial to the interests of consumers.

1 See the FSA Handbook at ENF 6.11.1. For a discussion of the general policy, see para 5.194 above.

2 Where the matter arises in the context of a takeover bid, and in the FSA's view publication may affect the timetable or outcome of the bid, it will consult the Takeover Panel over the timing of publication and give due weight to its views: see the FSA Handbook at ENF 6.11.1.

7.129 This policy does not distinguish between interim injunctions and final injunctions, but it does suggest that (as was the practice under the previous regime) the interim injunction, for which the test is not particularly high, will usually be made public. Where this would be unfair or inappropriate, or there is no good reason for publication, it may be possible for the firm to seek restrictions on publication from the court at the time when it grants the injunction. At the very least, the FSA could be pressed to justify the need for publication in the case.

7.130 The hearing of the application for an injunction may itself be held in public.

8 Disciplinary sanctions and other regulatory action against individuals

CONTENTS

Introduction 345

Action against approved persons 346

Prohibition orders 358

Injunctions and restitution orders against individuals 366

INTRODUCTION

An overview of Chapter 8

8.1 The FSMA 2000 introduces, for the first time, a statutory regime for the regulation of those who work for firms. Thus, whilst the regulatory regime operates primarily at the level of firms, it is not confined to firms. The mechanism for bringing those who work for firms personally within the regime is the approved persons regime, described briefly at para 2.64 ff above. Approved persons are in general terms regulated by the FSA and they can be disciplined by the FSA for misconduct or, in more serious cases, their approval for one or more functions could be withdrawn. Not all employees are, however, required to be approved persons. Those who are not cannot be disciplined by the FSA, but they can be prohibited from being involved with regulated firms if their conduct demonstrates that they are not fit and proper. And in some instances, restitution orders and injunctions can be made against individuals, both approved persons and others, either instead of, or as well as, the relevant firm. Finally, individuals are also subject to the regime in so far as they commit market abuse or one of the criminal offences under the FSMA 2000.

8.2 Since the various enforcement powers available against those who work for firms are aimed at addressing different concerns, they are not mutually exclusive and may be used separately or in combination. By way of illustration, if an approved person caused the firm to commit a serious regulatory breach and then tried to conceal assets and destroy incriminating evidence, his conduct could potentially give rise to disciplinary action, the withdrawal of his approval, the making of a prohibition order, a civil injunction and prosecution for criminal offences. The purpose of and basis for the exercise of each power would be different. The various enforcement powers outlined in this chapter therefore need to be viewed not in isolation but as part of an overall scheme to allow the FSA to take appropriate enforcement action in relation to the activities of those who work for firms.

8.3 In this chapter, we review:

- at para 8.4 ff below, the enforcement action that can be taken against approved persons, namely disciplinary action and the withdrawal of approval;
- at para 8.44 ff below, prohibition orders; and
- at para 8.76 ff below, the application of injunctions and restitution orders to individuals.

ACTION AGAINST APPROVED PERSONS

Disciplinary action

8.4 We review, in the following paragraphs, the FSA's power to take disciplinary action against approved persons and its policy on when and how it uses those powers in practice. In particular, we consider:

- what disciplinary powers does the FSA have?
- when will the FSA seek to discipline an approved person?
- what disciplinary sanction will be imposed?
- what is the procedure? and
- what publicity will there be?

8.5 In common with many other aspects of the regime, the FSMA 2000 provides only the basic framework for the FSA's powers, allowing the FSA to take action in certain situations but leaving it to the FSA to determine when in practice it will be appropriate for it to do so. The FSA has made plain that it may be possible to address many instances of non-compliance without recourse to disciplinary action[1]. In many respects, therefore, it is the FSA's policy on when it will take formal action and what action it will take that will be of primary interest. The ability of the regulator to discipline personally those working for a firm who were involved in the firm's breach will be familiar to firms formerly regulated by one of the self-regulatory organisations but is new for many other types of authorised persons.

1 See the FSA Handbook at ENF 11.2.1 and see paras 7.7 and 7.13 above.

8.6 The FSA's policy on taking disciplinary action against approved persons overlaps in some respects with its policy on taking disciplinary action against firms, outlined in Chapter 7 above. Reference is made to Chapter 7 where appropriate below.

What disciplinary powers does the FSA have?

8.7 The FSA can impose a fine and/or publicly censure an approved person. In addition, it will in some circumstances issue informal private warnings to approved persons. Whilst these warnings do not amount to formal disciplinary action, they are not free from regulatory consequences. The circumstances when the FSA will issue a private warning, the nature of a private warning and the consequences, are discussed at para 7.18 ff above. We focus here on formal disciplinary action.

8.8 The FSA may take disciplinary action against a person if[1]:

- it appears to the FSA he is guilty of 'misconduct', that is, while an approved person, he:
  - has failed to comply with a Statement of Principle; or
  - has been knowingly concerned in a contravention by the relevant authorised person of a requirement imposed on the authorised person by or under the FSMA 2000; and
- the FSA is satisfied that it is appropriate in all the circumstances to take action against him.

Each element of this test is considered in turn below. The FSMA 2000 imposes an additional requirement that the FSA may not take such action after the end of the period of two years beginning with the first day on which the FSA knew of the misconduct, unless proceedings in respect of it against the person concerned were begun before the end of that period[2]. There is therefore a two year limitation period for bringing proceedings for misconduct. Time starts to run when the FSA knows of the misconduct, which includes having information from which the misconduct can reasonably be inferred[3]. The proceedings are begun when a warning notice is issued under FSMA 2000, s 67(1)[4].

1 FSMA 2000, s 66.

2 FSMA 2000, s 166(4).
3 FSMA 2000, s 166(5)(a).
4 FSMA 2000, s 166(5)(b).

Misconduct while an approved person

8.9 The FSA can only take such action against a person in relation to his conduct while he was an approved person. This includes both current and former approved persons. Thus, a person who is not and has not been an approved person, because he does not carry out a 'controlled function' for which he requires FSA approval, is not within the scope of the FSA's disciplinary powers. Equally, an approved person is only subject to discipline for his actions in relation to a controlled function, in other words the functions for which he is approved by the FSA. To the extent he carries on activities for which approval is not required, the FSA's disciplinary jurisdiction does not apply[1]. If, therefore, a person exercises five functions, four of which are controlled functions, it is fairly clear that he cannot be disciplined in relation to the fifth, although his conduct in relation to the fifth may call into question whether he is fit and proper to be approved for the other four.

1 Although the FSA would be able to exercise other enforcement powers against him, for example to make a prohibition order: see para 8.44 ff below.

Failure to comply with a Statement of Principle

8.10 The Statements of Principle are outlined at para 2.76 ff above, together with an explanation of the Code of Practice which the FSA is required to issue to help determine whether or not a person's conduct has complied with a Statement of Principle. An important point to keep in mind is that it is the Statements of Principle, not the Code of Practice, that are paramount. The Code of Practice only has evidential effect[1].

1 The effect of the Code of Conduct is discussed in more detail at para 2.82 ff above.

Knowingly concerned in a contravention

8.11 The meaning of 'knowingly concerned in a contravention' is discussed at para 2.184 ff above. The question whether a person has been knowingly concerned in a contravention depends in part upon his knowledge at the relevant time. The meaning of 'contravention of a requirement imposed by or under the FSMA 2000' is considered at para 2.142 ff above.

Appropriate in all the circumstances to take action

8.12 As with the provisions relating to discipline against firms, the FSMA 2000 provides only the framework for the imposition of disciplinary sanctions, leaving to the FSA the key question of when in practice it will take such action and how it will determine the amount of any penalty. Again, the FSA is required[1] to prepare and issue a statement of its policy with respect to the imposition and amount of penalties and, in the case of any particular contravention, to have regard to the policy in force at the time the contravention occurred when exercising, or deciding whether to exercise, its powers. The FSA's policy in this regard is discussed below. However, the FSMA 2000 imposes the additional requirement that the FSA must be satisfied that it is appropriate in all the circumstances to take action against the person. This makes clear that the mere fact of a breach does not of itself mean that disciplinary action against an approved person will result. This reflects what is one of the more difficult questions in this context, namely in what circumstances the FSA should look to punish the approved person instead of, or in addition to, the firm.

1 FSMA 2000, s 69.

When will the FSA seek to discipline an approved person?

8.13 It is rare that the firm commits a breach without one or more persons working for the firm having had some sort of involvement in that breach[1]. As we have seen, the FSMA 2000 gives the FSA a broad discretion to decide when such persons should be disciplined, provided they were approved persons at the relevant time, by requiring the FSA to be satisfied that it is appropriate in all the circumstances to take disciplinary action. In broad terms, the FSA's policy is to discipline approved persons only where there is evidence of personal culpability. Quite what this means requires more careful analysis.

1 See the example given at para 2.178 above.

The FSA's policy

8.14 The primary responsibility for ensuring compliance with the firm's regulatory obligations rests on the firm itself[1]. Normally, therefore, the firm will be the FSA's main focus. However, in some cases, it will not be appropriate to hold the firm responsible for the actions of those who work for it, for example where the firm can show it took all reasonable steps to prevent the breach. In other cases, it may be appropriate to take action against both the firm and the approved person, for example where the firm failed to take reasonable care to maintain proper systems and controls and the person took advantage of this.

1 See the FSA Handbook at ENF 11.5.1/2.

8.15 The FSA has given the following broad guidance as to when it will be appropriate to take such disciplinary action:

- the FSA will only take disciplinary action against an approved person where there is evidence of personal culpability, which means either that the behaviour was deliberate or that it was below the standard which would be reasonable in all the circumstances[1];
- in determining whether it is appropriate to take disciplinary action the FSA may consider, among other factors[2]:
  - — whether action against the firm, rather than the approved person, would be a more appropriate regulatory response; and

— whether disciplinary action would be a proportionate response to the nature and seriousness of the breach by the approved person;

- the FSA will not discipline approved persons on the basis of holding them responsible for the acts of others. In particular, it will not take action against an approved person exercising a 'significant influence function'[3] simply because a regulatory failure has occurred in an area of business for which he is responsible. The FSA will only consider that such a person may have breached Statements of Principle 5 to 7[4] if his conduct was below the standard it was reasonable to expect in all the circumstances. An approved person will not be in breach if he has exercised due and reasonable care when assessing information, has reached a reasonable conclusion and has acted on it[5];
- in assessing whether a person has breached a Statement of Principle, the FSA will take into account the context in which the conduct occurred, including the precise circumstances of the individual case, the characteristics of the particular controlled function and the behaviour to be expected in that function[6].

1 See the FSA Handbook at ENF 11.5.3.
2 See the FSA Handbook at ENF 11.5.11.
3 Broadly, equivalent to senior management.
4 The Statements of Principle applicable to those exercising significant influence functions: see para 2.97 ff above.
5 See the FSA Handbook at ENF 11.5.6.
6 See the FSA Handbook at APER 3.1.3. See also para 2.101 ff above.

What does the FSA's policy mean?

8.16 In considering what this means, it may be helpful to consider the position of all approved persons before looking at some additional factors relevant to those approved persons who exercise 'significant influence' functions.

8.17 ***Approved persons generally*** The question whether the particular person who caused or was involved in the problem should be disciplined revolves around the existence or otherwise of personal culpability. Whilst this may seem to be a subjective test, taking into account the person's state of mind, the FSA has made plain that an objective test may be used. As has already been outlined, by personal culpability, the FSA means either that the behaviour was deliberate or that the person's conduct was below the standard of behaviour which the FSA would reasonably expect from a person carrying out his particular functions. Whether behaviour was deliberate is clearly subjective, since it depends on the intentions of the person. It may be difficult to argue that deliberate misconduct (in the sense of acting deliberately and in the knowledge that the actions constituted, or would cause, a breach[1]) should not be punished. Among other things, it may cast doubt on the integrity of the person and whether he is fit and proper to be an approved person at all.

1 It is not, though, clear that this is what the FSA means by 'behaviour [that] was deliberate'. An alternative interpretation would be that the test is whether the actions were deliberate, irrespective of whether the person had any knowledge that the consequences might constitute a breach.

8.18 The alternative question is whether the person's conduct fell below the applicable standard. This is an objective test, and it would be quite possible for a person to fail that test without any reference being made to his state of mind at the relevant time. Indeed, a person could fall below the applicable standard whilst acting with the best of intentions. Thus, for example, if a person made an error and unwittingly caused a breach, he may be 'personally culpable' within this policy if his conduct fell below the standard reasonably to be expected of him.

8.19 ***Those exercising significant influence functions*** The discussion above applies equally to those exercising significant influence functions, but there are some additional factors. The person exercising a significant influence is less likely to have been directly involved. Rather, the question is often whether the breach was allowed to happen because of failures in the systems and controls, or failures in supervision, in the area for which that person was responsible. In considering whether such a person should be disciplined personally, it is necessary to consider, first, whether he has been knowingly concerned in a rule breach by the firm, or has breached a Statement of Principle and, second, whether it is appropriate for the FSA to take action against him.

8.20 As to the first question, whether there has been a breach, unless the person had some active involvement in the breach, it is less likely he will have been knowingly concerned in it[1]. The question is therefore likely to be whether he committed a breach of any of the Statements of Principle. Statements of Principle 5 to 7, which are those additional Principles applicable to persons exercising significant influence functions, each contain an objective standard ('reasonable steps', 'due skill, care and diligence', 'reasonable care') and in considering whether a person complied with that standard the FSA takes into account factors such as the nature, scale and complexity of the business, the role and responsibility of the person concerned and the knowledge that he had or should have had of the regulatory concerns in the business under his control[2].

1 For a discussion of 'knowingly concerned', see para 2.184 ff above.
2 See para 2.104 above.

8.21 Again, therefore, an objective test is applied. The difficulty lies in predicting how this works in practice. Most regulatory issues which were not caused deliberately, as well as many that were, are capable at some level of being attributed to a systemic failure of some description, for example a failure of controls, a lack of training or an unclear compliance manual. It is then but a short step to an arguable case that a person exercising a significant influence function fell below the applicable standard in allowing that failure to occur.

8.22 The second question, whether it is appropriate to take disciplinary action, thus remains important. The FSA will not discipline such persons simply because a breach of the regulatory requirements has occurred in an area for which they are responsible[1]. The question is again one of personal culpability, whether it would be more appropriate to take action only against the firm and whether it is proportionate to take disciplinary action against the person.

1 See the FSA Handbook at ENF 11.5.6 and see para 8.15 above.

8.23 The culpability of senior managers also needs to be viewed against the general policy[1] of devolving regulatory responsibility from the FSA to those who manage firms. This is more efficient from the FSA's point of view, and may allow it to intervene less in firms' businesses. But the corollary is that the FSA is likely to want senior management to take, and be seen to take, responsibility for the firm.

1 The principle of responsibility of those who manage firms: outlined at para 2.21 above.

What disciplinary sanction will be imposed?

8.24 Where formal disciplinary action is appropriate, the FSA can impose a fine of such amount as it considers appropriate or publish a statement of the person's misconduct[1]. Since the imposition of a fine is normally made public, the choice is in reality simply whether or not to fine the person. The purpose of each sanction, how the FSA chooses which sanction to impose, and the amount of the fine[2] and the contents of the statement, are discussed in the context of firms in Chapter 7 above. That discussion applies equally to approved persons.

1 FSMA 2000, s 66(3).
2 A common question is whether the firm can indemnify its employees in respect of any liability they incur for regulatory fines. Subject to anything to the contrary in the FSA's rules, there is nothing as a matter of general law prohibiting the firm from reimbursing the employee on an ex gratia basis. Whether the firm can enter into an agreement to indemnify its employees is less clear. First, an indemnity against the consequences of a criminal offence is likely to be contrary to public policy (see, for example, *Gray v Barr* [1971] 2 All ER 949). There is currently no authority on whether an indemnity against a (non-criminal) regulatory offence would also be unenforceable. Second, a provision indemnifying a director or officer could be void under the Companies Act 1985, s 310. This would not prevent the firm from obtaining Directors & Officers Insurance covering such liability, but in practice such policies tend to exclude penalties and fines. See also footnote 1 to para 3.130 above.

What is the procedure?

8.25 Where the FSA seeks to impose a fine or make a public statement, the warning/decision notice procedure applies[1]. The procedure is considered in detail in Chapter 5 above. Among other things, the person has the right to refer the matter to the Tribunal.

1 FSMA 2000, s 67.

What publicity will there be?

8.26 The question of publicity is discussed in Chapter 5 above. That discussion applies to approved persons as it does to firms. Generally, it is the FSA's policy to publish successful enforcement action[1].

1 See, in particular, para 5.194 above.

Withdrawal of approval

8.27 The process of granting approval to persons to carry out certain specified functions for firms, known as 'controlled functions', has been outlined at para 2.64 ff above. The need for a person carrying out certain functions to be specifically approved in this way is driven primarily by consumer protection considerations. Thus, the FSA's power to withdraw a person's approval in certain circumstances, which is considered here, is also aimed primarily at protecting consumers[1]. In the following paragraphs, we consider:

- on what grounds can the FSA withdraw a person's approval?
- when will the FSA in practice seek to do so?
- what is the effect of the FSA withdrawing approval?
- what is the procedure for the FSA to do so? and
- practical issues for firms.

1 A similar power existed under the previous regime for investment business, in that each of the SROs could expel from their register or terminate the registration of any registered person. This was from time to time used in practice. See, for example, the IMRO cases of *Yates* (9 March 2000, falsification of records) and *Drage* (23 March 2000, theft of money) and the SFA cases of *Holt* (Board Notice 550, allowing customers to be overcharged) and *Patel* (Board Notice 565, carrying out and concealing unauthorised trades).

8.28 The withdrawal of approval must not be viewed in isolation from the FSA's other powers. Precisely what action or combination of action is required will depend upon what has happened and what the FSA seeks to achieve. For example, it may be appropriate to discipline an approved person in order to punish him for his act of misconduct and also to withdraw his approval in order to ensure that he cannot continue to perform his controlled function. He may also carry out other controlled functions, approval for which may also need to be withdrawn. But even this does not prevent him from carrying out other, non-controlled functions for the same or another firm. If the FSA wishes to prevent him from doing so, then it will need to make a prohibition order against him. The FSA has expressly indicated that it may need to consider using these other powers as well as withdrawing approval[1].

1 See the FSA Handbook at ENF 7.6.

On what grounds can the FSA withdraw a person's approval?

8.29 The criterion for withdrawing approval mirrors that for granting approval, namely whether or not the person is a fit and proper person to perform the relevant function[1]. The sole ground for withdrawing approval is thus that the FSA considers that the person in respect of whom the approval was given is not a fit and proper person to perform the function to which the approval relates[2].

1 FSMA 2000, s 61(1) and see para 2.66 above.
2 FSM 2000, s 63(1).

8.30 'Fit and proper' is a broad test[1]. The withdrawal of approval is thus aimed at addressing broad concerns about a person's suitability to be involved in the relevant activities on the firm's behalf. Withdrawal of approval is different in nature and purpose to the disciplinary powers available to punish particular breaches. The concerns that lead to a finding that a person is not fit and proper may arise from a particular rule breach and, as will be seen, the seriousness of the breach will in that situation be a relevant factor, but they need not do so[2].

1 The meaning of fit and proper in the context of individuals is outlined at para 2.69 ff above.
2 'Withdrawal of approval does not imply criticism of the individual and is not intended as a punishment': the Financial Secretary to HM Treasury in Standing Committee, 26 October 1999.

When will the FSA seek to withdraw approval?

8.31 The statutory ground for withdrawing approval provides no more than a framework. It does not expressly oblige the FSA to withdraw approval in every case where lack of fitness and propriety is made out (although, as discussed below, this is likely to be the result), but leaves to the FSA's discretion when the power should be exercised.

8.32 The question whether a person is fit and proper is assessed against a wide range of factors and, in contrast with the question whether a person has committed a particular rule breach, is largely a matter of judgement for the FSA. Fitness and propriety is, though, fundamental to the regulatory regime. As a result, as indicated above, it is perhaps unlikely that the FSA would reach a finding of lack of fitness and propriety and yet take no action. It may be more likely for the FSA to address lesser concerns in an informal way[1], for example by making clear that the person requires further training or should be supervised more closely[2], reserving to the more serious cases the sanction of withdrawal of approval, which may have a substantial impact on the relevant person's employment prospects.

1 The FSA does not have any power to take formal intervention-type action against an approved person, for example by imposing restrictions or requirements on his approval: see the discussion at para 9.95 ff below.
2 Alternatively, the firm may submit a fresh application for approval, modifying the nature of the tasks performed so that a new approval can be given for that modified function.

8.33 In considering whether to withdraw approval, the FSA will take account of all relevant factors[1]. The following factors may particularly be relevant:

- whether the person has the qualifications, training and competence prescribed in the FSA's rules in relation to the particular function in question[2];
- the criteria for assessing fitness and proprietary outlined at para 2.69 ff above. These broadly fall under three heads, namely: (i) honesty, integrity and reputation; (ii) competence and capability and (iii) financial soundness;
- whether and to what extent the person has failed to comply with the Statements of Principle for approved persons or has been knowingly concerned in a contravention by the relevant firm[3];

- the relevance, materiality and length of time since the occurrence of any matters indicating unfitness;
- the severity of the risk which the person poses to consumers and confidence in the financial system;
- the person's disciplinary record and compliance history;
- the nature of the particular controlled function which the person performs, the nature and activities of the firm concerned and the markets within which it operates[4].

There may be other relevant matters, for example abuse of drugs or other substances or serious convictions[5]. Where there are such other matters, the FSA will consider whether the conduct or matter is relevant to the question whether the person is fit and proper for the particular controlled function. The FSA may also have regard to the cumulative effect of a number of factors each of which may not be sufficient considered in isolation[6].

1 See the FSA Handbook at ENF 7.5.2. For a few practical examples of similar regulatory action under the previous regime, see footnote 1 to para 8.27 above.
2 The FSMA 2000 singles this out by prescribing as a potentially relevant factor the matters set out in FSMA 2000, s 61(2). Qualifications, training and competence are specified in that provision. See also the FSA Handbook at TC.
3 This equates with misconduct by approved persons for which the FSMA 2000 allows the FSA to discipline them, as discussed at para 8.8 ff above.
4 See the FSA Handbook at ENF 7.5.4.
5 See the FSA Handbook at ENF 7.5.5.
6 See the FSA Handbook at ENF 7.5.3.

What is the effect of the FSA withdrawing approval?

8.34 The practical effect of withdrawal of approval is to prevent the person from carrying out the particular controlled function or functions to which the approval related. However, the FSMA 2000 does not place any specific prohibition on the person from carrying out that function nor can this give rise to disciplinary sanctions by the FSA against him[1]. The effect is achieved in two ways. First, an obligation is imposed on firms[2] to take reasonable care to ensure that no person performs a controlled function in relation to its regulated activities, either when employed by the firm or when working for it under contracting arrangements[3]. If the firm fails to take reasonable care, then the FSA may take enforcement action against it[4]. Second, if the person continues to carry out a controlled function notwithstanding the withdrawal of his approval for that function, then the FSA may consider making a prohibition order against him[5].

1 His conduct would no longer be 'while an approved person' and he could not therefore be disciplined by the FSA: see para 8.4 ff above.
2 FSMA 2000, s 59(1) and (2). The firm concerned will be notified of the withdrawal of approval: FSMA 2000, s 63(3), (4) and (6).
3 This might include freelancers or outsourcing.
4 The firm may also be exposed to civil actions for damages, primarily by private persons: FSMA 2000, s 71 and see para 10.44 below.
5 See the FSA Handbook at ENF 8.5.6 and para 8.44 ff below.

8.35 The withdrawal of approval does not, though, prevent the person from continuing to work for the firm, in relation to any controlled functions for which his approval has not been withdrawn[1] or any other functions not prescribed by the FSA as controlled functions.

1 This is similar to the position under the previous regime, where an individual might be expelled from one register (for example, compliance officers) but not another (for example, directors). See for example SFA Board Notice 521.

8.36 A further likely consequence is that the withdrawal of approval will be publicised. The FSA has indicated that it will generally publicise a decision to withdraw approval once a final notice has been issued, unless this would prejudice the interests of consumers[1]. The publication of FSA enforcement action generally is considered at para 5.194 above.

1 See the FSA Handbook at ENF 7.8.1. In addition, the FSA's public register includes information about approved persons: see FSMA 2000, s 347.

8.37 Once approval has been withdrawn, the person concerned cannot perform the relevant controlled function until a new approval is obtained. If the firm believes that the person has remedied the matters that caused concern and should be regarded as fit and proper to carry out one or more controlled functions, then a new application for approval could be made on his behalf. This is likely to be difficult where the matter of concern related to his honesty or integrity, but perhaps less so where it was a matter of qualifications, training or competence. The FSA has given no indication of any specific considerations or factors that it will take into account in relation to such an application. The application would therefore be considered in the same way as any other application for approval[1]. It may be that the FSA would have in mind similar factors as are applicable to applications to remove a prohibition order[2].

1 See para 2.64 ff above and the FSA Handbook at SUP 10.
2 See the FSA Handbook at ENF 8.9.2 and para 8.71 below.

What is the procedure for withdrawing approval?

8.38 The procedure where the FSA wishes to withdraw a person's approval is the warning/decision notice procedure discussed in detail in Chapter 5 above[1]. Among other things, there will be a right to refer the matter to the Tribunal for determination.

1 FSMA 2000, s 63.

8.39 There are two particular points to note. First, warning notices, decision notices and final notices relating to withdrawals of approval must be given by the FSA not only to the person concerned but also to the person on whose application the approval was given and the person by whom the person's services are retained, if not the same person[1]. In other words, the firm for whom the person performs one or more controlled functions must be notified and if the person is employed by another body which contracts with the firm, then that body must also be notified. Each of those parties has the right to refer the matter to the Tribunal.

1 FSMA 2000, s 63.

8.40 Second, the decision to withdraw approval takes effect on the date specified in the final notice[1].

1 See the FSA Handbook at ENF 7.7.1. A final notice in respect of an order is required to state the date from which the order has effect: FSMA 2000, s 391(4). For a discussion of final notices, see para 5.188 ff above.

Practical issues for firms

8.41 How should the firm deal with an employee against whom the FSA has brought proceedings for the withdrawal of approval? This can cause real tensions because the firm, on the one hand, may wish to be seen to take proactive steps to remove from any sensitive positions those employees whose conduct is questionable but, on the other hand, will not wish to expose itself to claims by its employees, for example for breach of contract. This will be an ongoing issue because the regulatory process could take several months, perhaps longer.

8.42 The firm has a number of options, including:

- standing by the employee and supporting him in the regulatory process;
- taking no view on the merits of the action being taken by the FSA against the employee but suspending him pending the outcome of the regulatory process, provided the firm's terms and conditions of employment allow it to do so;
- moving the employee out of a sensitive position and providing him with other work, provided he consents or the terms and conditions of employment allow the firm to do so[1];
- taking its own disciplinary action against the employee without awaiting the outcome of the FSA's regulatory process.

Which option is appropriate will depend upon the precise circumstances. In many situations the FSA will expect to see the firm taking its own decision on what disciplinary action is merited and not awaiting the outcome of the regulatory process. It may not therefore be appropriate for the firm to take an entirely neutral stance[2].

1 If the employee does not consent, this could constitute a serious breach of contract entitling the employee to treat himself as having been constructively dismissed.
2 This is discussed in more detail at para 3.135 ff above.

8.43 Depending on what course of action the firm takes, there may be a risk of Employment Tribunal proceedings being commenced by the employee against the firm whilst the regulatory proceedings are still pending. The interaction of the two can cause difficulty in practice. For example, the employee may not wish to provoke the firm into taking an overtly hostile stance against him which could reflect on its involvement in the regulatory proceedings. Also, from the firm's perspective, it needs to consider whether any of the evidence which it would want to use to defend itself against the employee would impact negatively on the FSA's view of the firm[1].

1 For example, if the evidence will be that the employee was well known to be questionable, or was largely left to his own devices, then this may cause questions to be raised about management or about the firm's systems or controls.

PROHIBITION ORDERS

8.44 The FSA has the power to make a prohibition order against a person[1], preventing him from being involved in either regulated activities generally or certain specific types of activities. This power is, broadly speaking, aimed at protecting consumers and markets. In the following paragraphs, we consider:

- what is a prohibition order?
- on what grounds can a prohibition order be made?
- when will the FSA seek a prohibition order?
- what is the procedure for doing so?
- what is the effect of the prohibition order?
- is the making of an order publicised? and
- can an order be varied or revoked?

1 FSMA 2000, s 56. A similar power existed under the Financial Services Act 1986, s 59 but was rarely used in practice.

8.45 As with the FSA's other enforcement powers, prohibition orders should not be considered in isolation, but may be used by the FSA concurrently with taking other action, such as disciplining or withdrawing the approval of an approved person or prosecuting any person for a criminal offence[1].

1 See the FSA Handbook at ENF 8.10.

What is a prohibition order?

8.46 A prohibition order is an order prohibiting an individual from performing:

- a specified function;
- any function falling within a specified description; or
- any function.

8.47 The order may relate to[1]:

- a specified regulated activity, any regulated activity falling within a specified description, or all regulated activities; and/or
- authorised persons generally or any person within a specified class of authorised persons;

and can be made in relation to regulated activities carried on by an exempt person or a professional firm under FSMA 2000, Pt XX[2].

1 FSMA 2000, s 56(3).
2 FSMA 2000, s 56(8).

8.48 The FSMA 2000 therefore gives the FSA a significant degree of flexibility to prescribe the extent to which the person is prohibited. A prohibition order can be used either as a rather blunt tool, to prevent a person from working in regulated financial services business generally, or as a more sophisticated instrument, to prevent him from working in particular areas or for particular types of firms. For example, it could prohibit the person from working in a particular type of business (for example, insurance), or on particular types of products (for example, derivatives), or in particular types of roles (for example, those that involve handling client money or, to take another example, as managing director or chief executive). Thus, the FSA can make a prohibition order as narrow or almost as broad as circumstances require[1].

1 See the Financial Secretary to HM Treasury in Standing Committee, 26 October 1999.

8.49 The power is clearly a fairly draconian one. Not only does it allow the FSA to impose requirements relating to persons who would not otherwise be directly accountable to the FSA, it potentially impacts seriously on the livelihood of the person concerned. At its widest, it seems that a person could be prohibited from carrying out any activity, whether regulated or not, in relation to any organisation which is authorised under the FSMA 2000. This is not, therefore, a power to be exercised lightly or routinely[1]. The FSA seems to recognise this in its policy on when it will exercise the power, as outlined at para 8.53 ff below.

1 See the Financial Secretary to HM Treasury in Standing Committee, 26 October 1999.

8.50 As the above may indicate, it is not entirely clear whether a prohibition order can extend to prohibiting the person from carrying out any activities whatsoever for authorised firms, whether or not those activities relate to the firm's regulated business. In other words, whether a person can be prohibited from working for a firm in its unregulated business. The FSMA 2000 is ambiguous[1]. HM Treasury now seems to take the narrower view[2]; the FSA seems to take the wider view[3].

1 Compare 'any function' (s 56(2)) and the list of functions at s 56(3). It is not clear whether s 56(3) qualifies s 56(2) or is merely illustrative of the orders that can be made. See also the extent of the firm's duty to take reasonable care not to engage a prohibited person: s 56(6). Note also the test for making a prohibition order (see para 8.51 below).
2 'Functions in relation to any regulated activities': Explanatory Notes to the FSMA 2000, para

134. But compare the statement by the Financial Secretary to HM Treasury in Standing Committee, 26 October 1999: 'it may make an order prohibiting someone from working in the financial services industry at all'.

3 An order may prevent the person 'from being employed' by any authorised firm: see the FSA Handbook at ENF 8.1.2 and 8.4.2(2).

On what grounds can a prohibition order be made?

8.51 There is only one ground for making a prohibition order, namely that it appears to the FSA that a person is not a fit and proper person to perform functions in relation to a regulated activity carried on by an authorised person[1].

1 FSMA 2000, s 56(1).

8.52 As will be seen, the meaning of fit and proper in this context is that outlined in relation to approved persons at para 2.69 ff above. It is notable that, apart from this provision, those persons who are not approved persons are not required under the FSMA 2000 to be fit and proper[1]. Nonetheless, it is clearly relevant to the question as to whether the firm is fit and proper that it has honest employees who adhere to proper standards[2].

1 There are, however, obligations on certain employees to be competent and properly trained (see the FSA Handbook at TC), which is one aspect of fitness and propriety. Note also that the concept of 'fitness' may be relevant in other contexts, for example under the Company Directors (Disqualification) Act 1986.

2 See para 2.47 above.

When will the FSA seek a prohibition order?

8.53 The FSA may exercise the power to make a prohibition order[1] where it considers that an individual presents such a risk to consumers or to confidence in the market generally that it is necessary either to prevent him from carrying out any function in relation to regulated activities or from being employed by any firm, or to restrict the functions which he may carry out or the type of firm by which he may be employed. The stress is thus on addressing a risk to consumers or to market confidence and the power is one which is envisaged to be used only in serious situations.

1 See the FSA Handbook at ENF 8.1.2.

8.54 In deciding whether to make a prohibition order, the FSA will consider[1] all the relevant circumstances, including whether any other enforcement action should be taken or has been taken against the individual, whether by the FSA or by other regulators. The factors which the FSA will take into account differ to some extent dependent upon the nature of the person against whom it is considering making the order. They are outlined below.

1 See the FSA Handbook at ENF 8.4.3.

8.55 Where the FSA considers making a prohibition order, but decides not to do so, it may consider issuing a private warning to the person concerned, to let him know that this was under active consideration[1]. For a discussion of the nature and effect of private warnings, see para 7.18 ff above.

1 See the FSA Handbook at ENF 11.3.3.

Prohibition orders against approved persons

8.56 The FSA's power to withdraw approval from an approved person whom it considers is no longer fit and proper to be carrying on the particular function to which the approval relates has already been reviewed[1]. That power is exercisable on a very similar ground to the power to issue a prohibition order, namely a failure to be fit and proper. A prohibition order does, however, have more serious consequences for the person concerned, because of its wider scope and the more serious consequences of breach. It may therefore be appropriate to make a prohibition order as well as withdrawing approval. This will only be done[2] where the approved person is an individual and presents a degree of risk to consumers or confidence in the financial system that cannot be sufficiently addressed by the withdrawal of his approval or other disciplinary sanction.

1 See para 8.27 ff above.
2 See the FSA Handbook at ENF 8.5.1.

8.57 In deciding whether to exercise the power against an approved person, the FSA will consider the following factors[1]:

- whether the person is fit and proper to perform functions in relation to regulated activities[2];
- whether and to what extent the approved person has committed misconduct[3];
- the relevance, materiality and length of time since the occurrence of any matters indicating that he is unfit;
- the particular controlled function that the person is performing, the nature and activities of the firm concerned and the markets in which he operates;
- the severity of the risk which the person poses to consumers and to confidence in the financial system; and
- the person's previous disciplinary record and general compliance history.

The FSA may have regard to the cumulative effect of a number of factors each of which may, in isolation, be insufficient[4]. The FSA may also consider making a prohibition order where the person has continued to act notwithstanding the withdrawal of his approval[5].

1 See the FSA Handbook at ENF 8.5.2. This is a non-exhaustive list: see the FSA Handbook at ENF 8.5.4.
2 The criteria for fitness and propriety can be found in the FSA Handbook at FIT and are outlined at para 2.69 ff above. They broadly fall into three categories namely: (i) honesty, integrity and reputation, (ii) competence and capability and (iii) financial soundness.

3 In other words, failed to comply with a Statement of Principle for approved persons or been knowingly concerned in a contravention by the relevant firm: see para 8.8 ff above.
4 See the FSA Handbook at ENF 8.5.3.
5 See the FSA Handbook at ENF 8.5.5. So far as the individual is concerned, breach of a prohibition order carries more serious consequences than carrying on a controlled function without approval: see para 8.65 ff below and compare para 8.34 ff above.

8.58 In practice, as should be apparent, prohibition orders are likely to be used against approved persons in two types of situation[1]. First, where necessary to enforce compliance with the withdrawal of the person's approval. Second, where the person's conduct is such that a wider scope of prohibition is required than could be accomplished solely by the withdrawal of approval.

1 As noted at para 8.44 above, similar powers existed under the Financial Services Act 1986 but in practice were rarely used.

Prohibition orders against others

8.59 The FSA's power to make a prohibition order extends beyond approved persons[1]. It includes both those working for regulated firms but not carrying out controlled functions and those not working for regulated firms. It also includes individuals who are exempt persons.

1 See the FSA Handbook at ENF 8.6 to 8.8.

8.60 Broadly, the FSA will consider making a prohibition order against such persons where the relevant person has shown himself to be unfit to perform functions in relation to regulated activities[1]. The FSA has given three examples of where it will consider the fitness and propriety of a person who is neither an approved person nor employed by a firm, namely[2]:

- where the person has been involved in conducting regulated activities in breach of the general prohibition[3];
- where the person has been involved in other misconduct or offences under the FSMA 2000 which call into question his honesty, integrity or competence; or
- where he appears likely to pose a risk to consumers or confidence in the financial system in the future.

1 See the FSA Handbook at ENF 8.6.1 and 8.8.1.
2 See the FSA Handbook at ENF 8.8.2.
3 For an explanation of the general prohibition, see para 2.175 above.

8.61 In determining whether a person other than an approved person is fit and proper, the FSA will take into account the criteria set out at para 8.57 above to the extent they are relevant[1].

1 For details, see the FSA Handbook at ENF 8.6.2, 8.7.2 and 8.8.3.

What is the procedure for imposing a prohibition order?

8.62 Where the FSA wishes to make a prohibition order, the warning/decision notice procedure applies and there is a right to refer the matter to the Tribunal[1]. The procedure for issuing warning and decision notices is discussed in detail in Chapter 5 above and the procedure for references to the Tribunal in Chapter 6 above.

1 FSMA 2000, s 57.

8.63 Specific points to note in this context are as follows:

- the warning notice must set out the terms of the proposed prohibition[1];
- the decision notice must[2]:
  - name the individual to whom the prohibition applies;
  - set out the terms of the order; and
  - be given to the individual named in the order.

1 FSMA 2000, s 57(2).
2 FSMA 2000, s 57(4).

8.64 There is no specific requirement for the firm to be provided with a copy of the warning and decision notice[1], although it is likely it will be provided with a copy as a third party named in the notice to whom it is prejudicial[2]. Where the FSA seeks both to withdraw an approved person's approval and to prohibit him, it is likely that the two will be run in tandem, although there is nothing to require this.

1 Contrast the position in relation to withdrawal of approval: see para 8.39 above. The Government considered it unnecessary to include such a requirement (see Standing Committee, 26 October 1999) and the issue is therefore considered on a case by case basis.
2 FSMA 2000, s 393 and see para 5.151 ff above.

What is the effect of the prohibition order?

8.65 A prohibition order has two primary effects. First, it is a criminal offence for a person to perform or agree to perform a function in breach of a prohibition order[1] subject to the defence of showing that the person took all reasonable precautions and exercised all due diligence to avoid committing the offence.

1 FSMA 2000, s 56(4). Contrast this with the effect of withdrawing a person's approval: see para 8.34 ff above.

8.66 Second, firms are obliged to take reasonable care to ensure that no function of theirs in relation to the carrying on of a related activity is performed by a person who is prohibited from performing that function by a prohibition order[1]. The FSA may consider taking disciplinary action against a firm that breaches this provision[2]. It regards a search of the FSA register as an essential part of the firm's statutory duty of taking reasonable care. Where the search does not reveal a record of the prohibition order, it will only consider taking action where the firm had access to additional information indicating that a prohibition order had been made[3].

1 FSMA 2000, s 56(6). Note that this applies only to regulated activities. If a prohibition order can cover unregulated activities (see para 8.50 above), then this obligation may not cover the full extent of the prohibition order, although the firm would still need to take reasonable care because of its more general regulatory duties such as the Principles for Businesses (see para 2.52 above).
2 See the FSA Handbook at ENF 8.11.2.
3 See the FSA Handbook at ENF 8.11.3.

8.67 In addition, to the extent that the firm breaches its statutory duty, a private person who suffers loss as a result may have a civil claim against it[1].

1 FSMA 2000, s 71. Such civil claims are considered at para 10.44 below.

8.68 Finally, if it appears to the FSA that there are circumstances suggesting that an individual may have performed or agreed to perform a function in breach of a prohibition order, then the FSA can initiate a formal investigation under FSMA 2000, s 168(4)[1].

1 This is discussed in detail in Chapter 4 above.

Will the making of an order be publicised?

8.69 The FSA will generally publicise a decision to make a prohibition order once a final notice has been issued[1]. The question of publication following successful enforcement action is discussed generally at para 5.194 above.

1 See the FSA Handbook at ENF 8.12.1.

8.70 In this context, there is an additional consideration. The FSA is required to maintain on its public register in relation to each prohibition order that has been made at least the name of the individual against whom it has been made and details of the effect of the prohibition order[1]. The FSA has clarified that it will not enter details of a prohibition order onto the register until a final notice has been issued[2]. But once the decision is no longer open to review[3], the FSA will consider what additional information about the circumstances of the prohibition order it is appropriate to include. The FSA will balance any possible prejudice to the person concerned against the interests of consumer protection. The FSA will maintain the entry on the FSA register while the prohibition order remains in effect and for some time afterwards once it is revoked[4].

1 FSMA 2000, s 347(2)(f).
2 See the FSA Handbook at ENF 8.12.2. For an explanation of a final notice, see para 5.189 above.
3 This ought to refer to 'once a final notice has been issued'. The phrase 'no longer open to review' normally applies in the context of supervisory notices. As to its meaning, see para 9.174 below (and see FSMA 2000, s 391(8)).
4 See para 8.75 below.

Can an order be varied or revoked?

8.71 A prohibition order, once made, remains effective without time limit. It is therefore important that the FSMA 2000 allows the FSA[1], on the application of the individual named in a prohibition order, to vary or revoke an order. The FSA allows such applications to be made at any time after the prohibition order has been made[2]. When considering whether to grant or refuse such an application, the FSA takes into account all the relevant circumstances, including various factors outlined in the FSA Handbook[3].

1 FSMA 2000, s 56(7).
2 See the FSA Handbook at ENF 8.9.1.
3 See the FSA Handbook at ENF 8.9.2.

8.72 If the person wishes to perform a controlled function, then the relevant firm will also need to apply for him to be approved to act in that capacity[1].

1 The process of approval is discussed briefly at para 2.64 ff above. Details can be found in the FSA Handbook at SUP 10.

8.73 An important question is when in practice the FSA will consider varying or revoking a prohibition order. The FSA will not generally grant an application to vary a prohibition order unless it is satisfied that the proposed variation will not result in a recurrence of the risk to consumers or to confidence in the financial system that resulted in the order being made[1]. The FSA has also indicated that it will not revoke a prohibition order unless it is satisfied that the person is fit to carry out functions in relation to regulated activities generally or those specific activities which were prohibited. In either case, therefore, the concerns that gave rise to the making of the order must have been dispelled or, in the case of a variation, must not be prejudiced.

1 See the FSA Handbook at ENF 8.9.4.

8.74 As to the procedure for assessing the application:

- if the FSA decides to grant the application, it gives the applicant a written notice[1], which is neither a warning or decision notice nor a supervisory notice;
- if it proposes to refuse the application, then the warning notice/decision notice procedure applies[2].

1 FSMA 2000, s 58(2).
2 FSMA 2000, s 58(3) and (4). For a detailed explanation, see Chapter 5 above.

8.75 If a successful application is made to vary the order, then a note of the variation will be made on the FSA's register. If a successful application to revoke the order is made, then a note will be made on the register to the effect that the order has been revoked and the reasons for the revocation of the order[1]. The FSA maintains an annotated record of revoked prohibition orders for a period of six years from the date of the revocation, after which period the record will be removed from the register. The effect of this is potentially to prolong the stigma of a prohibition order for some years after the order has been revoked.

1 See the FSA Handbook at ENF 8.12.5. The FSA is entitled under the FSMA 2000 to remove the entry but has indicated that it will not immediately do so. If it does not remove the entry, this information is required to be placed on the register by FSMA 2000, s 347(4).

INJUNCTIONS AND RESTITUTION ORDERS AGAINST INDIVIDUALS

Injunctions and restitution orders

8.76 The availability of injunctions and restitution orders is considered in detail in Chapter 7 above. The purpose of the following paragraphs is to outline briefly their applicability to individuals personally. As will be seen, whilst the FSMA 2000 does allow injunctions and restitution orders to be made against individuals, this is likely in practice to be appropriate comparatively rarely, at least other than in perimeter enforcement cases or where the person has made some personal gain. We first consider injunctions before turning to restitution orders.

Injunctions

8.77 The FSMA 2000 allows the court, on application by the FSA, to make three types of injunctions[1], namely:

- to restrain a contravention;
- to remedy a contravention; and
- to secure assets.

We consider each of these in turn.

1 FSMA 2000, s 380 and see para 7.97 ff above.

Restraining contraventions

8.78 The FSMA 2000 does not specify against whom an injunction to restrain a contravention can be made[1]. In principle, it could be made not only against the firm that would commit the contravention but also, where appropriate, against any individual, for example an employee or officer, who needs to be restrained in order to ensure that the contravention does not take place. Indeed, where the FSA is dealing with perimeter breaches by corporate bodies, it may often seek an injunction not only against the corporate body but also against those individuals who are involved. Save for perimeter breaches, though, the expectation is that it will ordinarily be sufficient to restrain the firm. Employees or officers are likely to be personally restrained only where there is some good reason for doing so. An injunction could in principle also be sought against an approved person who would otherwise fail to comply with a Statement of Principle[2].

1 FSMA 2000, s 380(1).
2 The failure to comply would probably amount to the contravention of a 'relevant requirement' – ie a requirement imposed by or under the FSMA 2000: see paras 2.189 and 7.104 ff above.

Remedying contraventions

8.79 An injunction to require a person to take steps to remedy or mitigate the effect of a contravention can be made against the person who committed the contravention (which could include a firm that committed a regulatory breach but also an approved person who failed to comply with a Statement of Principle[1]) and also against any person who appears to have been knowingly concerned in the firm's contravention[2]. The use of the phrase 'knowingly concerned' allows an injunction to be made against an employee or officer who, in broad terms, was knowingly involved in the breach[3]. But, again, it will be comparatively rare that it is appropriate for the court to make an injunction against the employee or officer personally. An example of when it might be appropriate would be where a particular step that needs to be taken is required to be taken by the individual personally, for example because he has transferred to himself or a body controlled by him assets which are to be returned to the customer.

1 See footnote 2 to para 8.78 above.
2 FSMA 2000, s 380(2).
3 The meaning of 'knowingly concerned' is considered at para 2.184 ff above.

Securing assets

8.80 An injunction to secure assets can be made against the person that committed the contravention[1] and also against any person knowingly concerned in the firm's contravention[2]. Again, the use of the phrase 'knowingly concerned' allows, in broad terms, an injunction to be made against an employee or officer who was knowingly involved in the breach[3]. The purpose of an injunction of this nature is to secure assets in support of some other proceedings, to ensure that the relevant person does not dissipate his assets in order to defeat any judgment that might be made against him[4].

1 In theory, this could include not only a firm that committed a regulatory breach but also an approved person who failed to comply with a Statement of Principle: see footnote 2 to para 8.78 above.
2 FSMA 2000, s 380(3)(b).
3 The meaning of 'knowingly concerned' is considered at para 2.184 ff above.
4 This is discussed in more detail at para 7.119 above.

Restitution orders

8.81 Restitution orders can be made either by the FSA or by the court. Save in cases of market abuse[1], the FSA can only make a restitution order against an authorised person[2].

1 Considered separately in Chapter 13 below.
2 FSMA 2000, s 384(1).

8.82 The court can, however, make a restitution order against any person who commits a contravention, whether or not an authorised person (this could, for example, include an approved person who fails to comply with a Statement of Principle[1]). It can also make a restitution order against any person who was knowingly concerned in the contravention[2]. In theory, therefore, a restitution order could be made against an individual employee or officer who was, in broad terms, knowingly involved in the breach. But an order against an individual is unlikely to be a more efficient or effective means for securing compensation for consumers, save perhaps for certain perimeter enforcement cases, and is therefore unlikely normally to be in prospect.

1 See footnote 2 to para 8.78 above.
2 FSMA 2000, s 382(1). The meaning of 'knowingly concerned' is considered at para 2.184 ff above. See also, more generally, the discussion of restitution orders at para 7.43 ff above.

9 'Own-initiative' powers

CONTENTS

Introduction	**369**
Variation of permission/intervention	**371**
The supervisory notice procedure	**397**
Urgent action	**419**
Alternative procedures in specific cases	**427**
Cancellation of permission	**432**

INTRODUCTION

An overview of Chapter 9

9.1 In this chapter, we review the provisions of the FSMA 2000 and the FSA Handbook which in certain situations allow the FSA to intervene directly in the business of firms in the interests of its wider regulatory objectives. The 'own-initiative' powers replace what was formerly known as intervention[1], encompassing different concepts, with different terminologies and procedures.

1 Intervention will be familiar to many firms: see Financial Services Act 1986, s 64 to 71, Banking Act 1987, ss 12 and 19 and Insurance Companies Act 1982, ss 37 to 45, as well as the rules of the SROs. The concept is rather different under the FSMA 2000, although it is not yet clear whether there will be a significant difference in practice.

9.2 Before looking in detail at the various provisions, procedures and practice, we provide a brief overview of the regime as a whole. We then review:

- at para 9.7 ff, the FSA's power to vary a firm's permission or intervene in an incoming firm; and
- at para 9.239 ff, the FSA's power to cancel a firm's permission.

9.3 The own-initiative powers cover those occasions when the regulator needs to take a direct involvement in the commercial affairs of the firm. It is not normally the FSA's role to intervene in the management of a firm's business. Primarily, the FSA's role is to vet firms at entry before they are granted permission and authorisation and then to ensure that the firms themselves comply with the applicable standards and do not imperil consumers or the financial system. However, the FSA occasionally needs to intervene directly in a firm's business, for example by imposing restrictions on the types of business it can do or the customers it can deal with or by imposing requirements on it, such as requiring it to maintain particular assets. At its most extreme, this can involve the cancellation of the firm's permission and its authorisation.

9.4 The purpose of the own-initiative powers is to protect consumers and ensure that the firm continues to fulfil the threshold conditions as demonstrated by the primary situations when the powers can be exercised[1]. The mechanism by which this is achieved involves, for most firms, the permission regime. As already outlined[2], each firm has a bespoke permission tailored to its particular circumstances and requirements. The own-initiative power enables the FSA, in certain circumstances, to vary the terms of, or apply limitations or restrictions to, a firm's permission, thereby directly affecting the way it can conduct its business. Under the FSMA 2000, this is categorised as the FSA varying the firm's permission on its own initiative; hence, the terminology used. The term 'intervention' is still applicable in relation to incoming firms which do not have a permission[3]. Although different conceptually, the power in respect of such firms is similar in practice[4]. For simplicity, except for when the two are being distinguished specifically, we refer in this chapter to both of these powers as the 'own-initiative' powers.

1 Summarised at para 9.9 below. For details, see para 9.14 ff below. Or, in relation to incoming firms, the purpose may be to secure that the firm does not contravene the regulatory requirements and standards (see para 9.51 ff below).
2 See para 2.6 ff above.
3 In relation to incoming firms with top-up permission (see para 2.14 above), the own-initiative power may be exercised: see also para 9.47 below.
4 Although it is more restricted: see para 9.83 below.

9.5 The own-initiative powers are exercisable in a range of different situations, provided that one of the applicable tests prescribed under the FSMA 2000 is met[1]. Meeting the test is, however, only a small piece of the picture. An important factor is the FSA's policy on when in practice it will seek to exercise these powers; this is found in the FSA Handbook[2]. In many instances, particularly where the concerns arise in the supervisory, rather than enforcement, context, the FSA expects firms to comply voluntarily with its reasonable requirements and therefore expects that it will not normally need to exercise its formal powers. There may, however, be occasions when the use of formal powers is required, for example where the problem is particularly serious or where the use of formal powers is needed to excuse the firm from its legal obligations to other parties which might otherwise prevent it from complying. The FSA Handbook also provides guidance on what action it is appropriate for the FSA to take when the use of the power is appropriate[3].

1 The tests are outlined at para 9.7 ff below.

2 The FSA's policy is discussed at para 9.67 ff below.
3 See para 9.80 ff below.

9.6 The procedures for the use of the own-initiative powers, and the firm's ability to oppose the process, are set out in framework in the FSMA 2000 and detailed in the FSA Handbook. The procedure is different in various respects[1] from the warning/decision notice procedure considered in Chapter 5 above, but the firm still has the right of recourse to the Tribunal[2]. In urgent situations, the FSA can implement its powers with immediate effect, with the matter to be considered fully only afterwards[3].

1 See para 9.113 below.
2 The procedure, known as the supervisory notice procedure, is considered at para 9.104 ff below. Variants of the procedure applicable in specific situations are outlined at paras 9.194 ff and 9.219 ff below.
3 The use of the powers as a matter of urgency is considered at para 9.194 ff below.

VARIATION OF PERMISSION/INTERVENTION

On what grounds can the FSA exercise its own-initiative powers?

9.7 In considering whether a particular situation gives rise to the risk of the FSA exercising its own initiative powers, the first question is whether the situation falls within any of the circumstances when the FSMA 2000 allows those powers to be exercised. If it does, then the next question is whether the FSA will, in accordance with its stated policy, exercise those powers in the particular situation. That first question is considered in the following paragraphs. The FSA's policy is considered at para 9.67 ff below. The flowchart overleaf illustrates the different questions which arise, outlined in this chapter.

9.8 We review here nine separate statutory tests for the exercise of the own-initiative powers, comprising five circumstances when a firm's permission can be varied (for UK regulated firms and incoming firms with top-up permissions[1]), and four circumstances where the intervention power (applicable only to incoming firms) can be exercised. Two of the sets of circumstances apply similarly to both.

1 In other words, a permission allowing the firm to carry on additional regulated activities not covered by its passport or Treaty rights. See para 2.14 above.

9.9 The circumstances are as follows:

- Variations of permission:
  - Case A: actual or likely failure to satisfy the threshold conditions[1];
  - Case B: failure to carry on during a 12-month period a regulated activity for which the firm has permission[2];
  - Case C: desirable to exercise the power to protect the interests of consumers[3];

9.9 'Own-initiative' powers

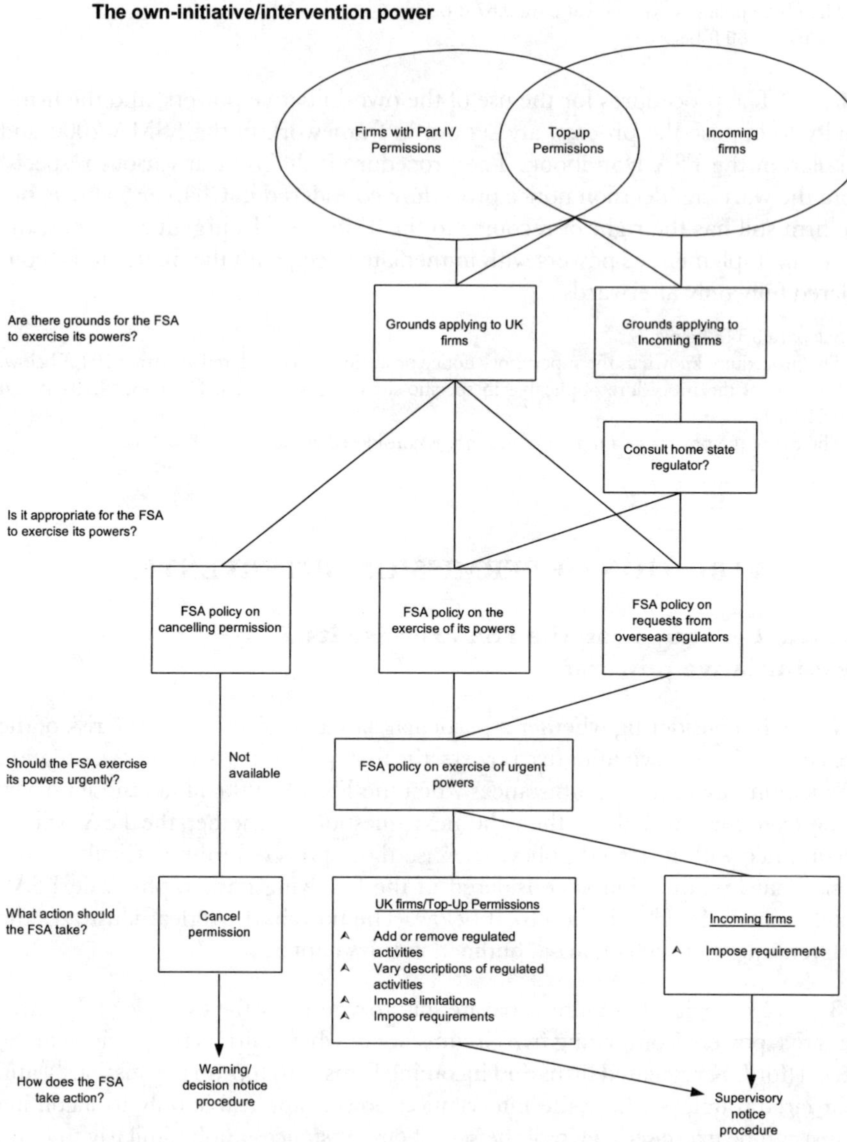

Figure 9.1

- — Case D: at the request of or for the purpose of assisting an overseas regulator[4];
- — Case E: on the acquisition of control over a UK regulated firm[5];

- Intervention:
  - — Case 1: actual or likely contravention of a requirement imposed by or under the FSMA 2000[6];
  - — Case 2: provision of false or misleading information knowingly or recklessly to the FSA[7];

— Case 3: desirable to exercise the power to protect the interests of consumers[8];

— Case 4: at the request of, or for the purpose of assisting, an overseas regulator[9].

Each of these is considered in turn below[10].

1 FSMA 2000, s 45(1)(a) and see para 9.14 below.
2 FSMA 2000, s 45(1)(b) and see para 9.21 below.
3 FSMA 2000, s 45(1)(c) and see para 9.25 below.
4 FSMA 2000, s 47 and see para 9.31 below.
5 FSMA 2000, s 46 and see para 9.42 below.
6 FSMA 2000, s 194(1)(a) and see para 9.51 below.
7 FSMA 2000, s 194(1)(b) and see para 9.56 below.
8 FSMA 2000, s 194(1)(c) and see para 9.60 below.
9 FSMA 2000, s 195 and see para 9.63 below.
10 Whilst there are some differences (for example, a breach of the FSA rules is not of itself a ground for intervention action against a UK regulated firm, and Case C represents a new ground), many of these grounds are similar to those previously applied by the SROs.

9.10 There are a number of similar powers which may be applicable in particular circumstances and which are not set out here. Those include:

- the FSA's power to give directions in relation to regulated collective investment schemes, including OEICs[1];
- the FSA's power to give directions in relation to a recognised investment exchange or recognised clearing house[2];
- the FSA's power, as UK Listing Authority, to discontinue or suspend the listing of securities[3];
- the FSA's power to give a disapplication direction in relation to a member of a designated professional body[4];
- the FSA's power to impose requirements on a former underwriting member of Lloyd's[5];
- the FSA's power to intervene in an incoming firm if the Director General of Fair Trading informs it that the firm (or certain persons connected with it) has done certain things relevant to its fitness to be granted a licence under the Consumer Credit Act 1974[6]; and
- the power of the Director General of Fair Trading to impose a prohibition or restriction on an incoming firm in relation to consumer credit business[7].

1 See Chapter 14 below.
2 FSMA 2000, s 296. The FSA's role with respect to recognised investment exchanges is briefly discussed at para 13.213 ff below.
3 FSMA 2000, s 77 and see Chapter 15 below.
4 FSMA 2000, s 328 and see the FSA Handbook at ENF Chapter 18.
5 FSMA 2000, s 320.
6 FSMA 2000, s 194(3).
7 FSMA 2000, ss 203 and 204.

9.11 The nine tests have been drafted fairly widely, and the FSA has a significant amount of discretion to decide whether the power can be exercised in the circumstances[1]. As a result, it will often be difficult for firms to argue that the test for taking action had not been met and it is likely that the real issue will be whether the action the FSA proposes is appropriate given the concerns which have arisen. A secondary issue may be whether that action can be directed to address not only the concerns which gave rise to the test being met but also any other concerns (irrelevant for that purpose) which the FSA has in relation to the firm.

1 Of the circumstances when the own-initiative powers can be exercised, the most powerful in practice, in terms of the breadth of discretion which they give to the FSA, are failure to satisfy the threshold conditions, contravention of requirements under the FSMA 2000 and where it is desirable to act in order to protect consumers. As will be seen, these are capable of application in a wide range of situations.

9.12 The powers overlap with the FSA's power to apply to the court for a civil injunction in certain circumstances. The circumstances when a civil injunction may be appropriate are considered at para 7.122 ff above.

UK regulated firms: variation of permission

9.13 The five circumstances when the own-initiative power may be exercised are outlined below, together with an explanation of the FSA's policy as to the circumstances when each may be applicable. This needs to be read together with the FSA's general approach on the use of its own-initiative powers, which is discussed at para 9.67 ff below. There are three additional considerations which may be relevant in particular cases[1] and these are set out at para 9.44 below.

1 Namely: (i) in any case, the FSA's ability to have regard to a person in a 'relevant relationship' with the firm; (ii) when the FSA is considering the variation or cancellation of a top-up permission and (iii) when the FSA is dealing with a firm which is connected with an EEA firm. For details, see para 9.44 ff below.

Case A: Failing or being likely to fail to satisfy the threshold conditions

9.14 The FSA may exercise its own-initiative power in relation to an authorised person if it appears to the FSA that the authorised person is failing or is likely to fail to satisfy the threshold conditions[1].

1 FSMA 2000, s 45(1)(a).

9.15 ***Which threshold conditions are likely to be relevant?*** The threshold conditions are outlined at para 2.39 above. Those most likely to be relevant in this context are:

- adequate resources;
- suitability (the need for the firm to be a fit and proper person having regard to all the circumstances[1]); and
- close links, for example if the firm's connection with another person causes the FSA concern about its ability to supervise the firm properly.

1 The suitability threshold condition is outlined in some detail at para 2.43 ff above.

9.16 In practice, serious non-compliance with the Principles for Businesses[1] may tend to show that the firm is failing to meet the threshold conditions, because the Principles express the main elements of the suitability threshold condition and overlap with others, such as the requirement for adequate resources.

1 These are explained in more detail at para 2.52 above.

9.17 ***When will the test be satisfied?*** The test for the exercise of the own-initiative power under this head appears on the face of it to be a low one. It only has to 'appear to the FSA' that the firm 'is likely to fail to satisfy' the threshold conditions. The firm need not yet have failed to meet any of the regulatory requirements. Indeed, the likelihood of it failing to do so need be apparent only to the FSA. The test is thus primarily within the FSA's discretion. This approach is perhaps understandable given the purpose of the provision, which is to enable the FSA to protect consumers and ensure confidence in the UK financial markets, by ensuring not only that firms are compliant with the threshold conditions but also that they will continue to be compliant[1]. The question whether a firm complies with the threshold conditions is primarily a matter of judgement; even more so, predicting whether it will continue to comply.

1 See, for example, FSMA 2000, s 41(2).

9.18 However, failure to satisfy the threshold conditions is a very serious matter (generally, significantly more serious than, say, a breach of the FSA's rules) as a firm's continued ability to meet the threshold conditions is fundamental to its continuing to have permission under the FSMA 2000. It is therefore thought that the FSA should not lightly reach the view that a firm is likely to fail to do so. The matter would need to be sufficiently serious that the FSA is concerned the firm should no longer be carrying on regulated activities.

9.19 Nonetheless, because of the subjective nature of the statutory test, firms are to a large extent reliant upon the FSA taking a reasonable approach, at least unless or until the matter comes to be considered by the Tribunal[1]. In practice, it may be difficult for firms to challenge the imposition of the own-initiative power on the ground that the statutory test was not met.

1 The firm has the right to refer the exercise of this power to the Tribunal: see para 9.104 ff below.

9.20 ***When will the FSA consider using this power?*** The FSA has provided guidance[1] on the circumstances when it will consider using its own-initiative power under this provision, namely:

- where the firm's material and financial resources appear inadequate for the scale or type of regulated activity it is carrying on; or
- where the firm appears not to be a fit and proper person to carry on regulated activity because:
  - it has not conducted its business in compliance with high standards, including being at risk of, or involved in, financial crime,
  - it has not been managed competently and prudently and has not exercised due skill, care and diligence in carrying on one or more or all of its regulated activities, or

— it has breached requirements imposed on it by or under the FSMA 2000 (including the Principles for Businesses) and the breaches are material in number or in individual seriousness.

This illustrates the breadth of the circumstances when the FSA may seek to use its own-initiative power under Case A.

1 See the FSA Handbook at ENF 3.5.8(1).

Case B: Failing to carry on a regulated activity for 12 months

9.21 The FSA may exercise its own-initiative power in relation to an authorised person if it appears to it that the authorised person has failed, during a period of at least 12 months, to carry on a regulated activity for which it has a Part IV permission[1].

1 FSMA 2000, s 45(1)(b).

9.22 ***When will the test be satisfied?*** Again, the test is on the face of it a low one: it only has to appear to the FSA that the firm has not carried on the regulated activity during a period of at least 12 months. However, the question whether the firm has done so should be capable of objective determination. If, as a matter of fact, the FSA is mistaken and the firm has in fact carried on that activity during that period, the FSA ought not to exercise the power.

9.23 ***When will the FSA consider using this power?*** As has been seen[1], each firm has a unitary permission tailored to its particular circumstances, permitting it to carry out specific regulated activities. The FSMA 2000, and the FSA's rules, allow that permission to be varied where circumstances change, for example if the firm wishes to carry on additional regulated activities which its permission does not allow. Because of this, it is seen as inappropriate for firms to have permission to do something which they do not require, held on a precautionary basis in case the firm decides to carry on that activity. This provision allows the FSA to vary, on its own initiative, the firm's permission so as to remove from its scope any regulated activities that the firm is not carrying on.

1 See para 2.6 ff above.

9.24 The FSA has not provided any guidance on the circumstances when it will exercise this power. Normally, any regulatory issues relating to the firm ceasing to carry on a regulated activity are discussed between the firm and its FSA supervisor and addressed within that context[1].

1 See the FSA Handbook at SUP 6.2.7, 6.3.7 and 6.3.41.

Case C: Desirable to exercise the power to protect the interests of consumers

9.25 The FSA may exercise its own-initiative power in relation to an authorised person if it appears to the FSA that it is desirable to do so in order to protect the interests of consumers or potential consumers[1].

1 FSMA 2000, s 45(1)(c).

9.26 No definition of 'consumers' is provided in this provision nor is any indication given of what interests of consumers might require protection. In order to understand the purpose of the power, and what is meant by the interests of consumers, it needs to be read with the 'protection of consumers' regulatory objective[1], in which context, 'consumers' has a wide statutory definition[2].

1 For an explanation, see para 2.20 above.
2 FSMA 2000, s 5(3) and see s 138(7) to (9). Very broadly, 'consumers' encompasses existing, past and potential customers, as well as those who have had a less direct involvement with the firm.

9.27 ***When will the test be satisfied?*** This is arguably the widest of the own-initiative power provisions, allowing the FSA to act in a very broad range of circumstances. Again, the test is a relatively low one. It only has to 'appear to the FSA' that it is 'desirable' to exercise the power for the purposes specified. This is a subjective test, based on the FSA's judgment, and it will be difficult for firms to argue that it had not been met.

9.28 ***When will the FSA consider using this power?*** The example provided by the FSA of when it may be appropriate to act on this basis is where it appears that the interests of consumers are at risk because the firm appears to have breached any of Principles 6 to 10 to such an extent that it is desirable that limitations, restrictions or prohibitions are placed on the firm's regulated activity[1].

1 See the FSA Handbook at ENF 3.5.8(2).

9.29 Whilst this is uncontroversial, particularly as Principles 6 to 10 are those which most directly relate to the firm's dealings with its customers[1], this policy gives little real guidance. In addition, although the FSA singles out Principles 6 to 10 for specific mention, the test could be met by breaches of other Principles for Businesses. In particular, it is possible to envisage situations where there were concerns relating to the inadequacy of financial resources[2] or lack of internal systems and controls[3] which made it desirable in the interests of consumers for restrictions to be placed on the firm.

1 The Principles for Businesses are outlined at para 2.52 above. It may be possible for such concerns about risks to consumers to arise as a result of how the firm acts after the problem arises. As regards the application of these Principles when a regulatory problem arises, see para 3.110 ff above.
2 Principle 4: see para 2.52 above.
3 Principle 3: see para 2.52 above.

9.30 The focus in this context is not so much on the breach of the relevant Principle, as on the potential effect of the situation on consumers. Serious breaches of Principles not giving rise to concerns about consumers may also be addressed under Case A. There is clearly, though, an overlap between the two.

Case D: At the request of an overseas regulator

9.31 The FSA's own-initiative power may be exercised[1] in respect of an authorised person at the request of, or for the purpose of assisting, a regulator who is (a) outside the UK and (b) of a kind prescribed in regulations to be made by HM Treasury[2].

1 FSMA 2000, s 47(1). These provisions are broadly similar to those found in the Financial Services Act 1986, s 128C introduced to implement various EU single market directives.
2 HM Treasury has prescribed, broadly, authorities exercising functions corresponding to: (i) the FSA's functions under the FSMA 2000; (ii) the functions of the UK Listing Authority under the FSMA 2000, Pt VI; (iii) the Secretary of State under the Companies Act 1985 and (iv) the investigation and enforcement of insider dealing: see the Financial Services and Markets Act 2000 (Own-initiative Power) (Overseas Regulators) Regulations 2001, SI 2001/2639.

9.32 This power is exercisable both in relation to UK regulated firms and in relation to incoming firms that have a top-up permission[1]. It is exercisable irrespective of whether the FSA also has powers of intervention exercisable under Cases A, B, C or E[2].

1 There is a similar power in relation to incoming firms more generally: see para 9.63 below.
2 FSMA 2000, s 47(2).

9.33 This is different in nature from the other bases for exercising the own-initiative power. Specifically, there is no particular hurdle or test which has to be overcome (for example, that the firm has contravened UK, or overseas, regulations or poses a potential risk to UK, or overseas, consumers). There simply has to be a request from an overseas regulator[1]. The FSA then has a discretion whether or not to exercise its power in response to that request. Various factors outlined below are or may be relevant to the exercise of that discretion. Which factors apply depends upon the FSA's EEA obligations.

1 On one view, it could be that there does not even have to be a request, just a reason to assist the overseas regulator because the FSMA 2000 uses the words 'at the request of, or for the purpose of assisting'. However, on an alternative view, there does have to be a request: the purpose of the additional words 'for the purpose of assisting' the overseas regulator being simply to ensure that the FSA is able to take whatever action it thinks appropriate and is not limited to the specific action requested by the overseas regulator. In practical terms, it seems unlikely the FSA would take action unless requested to do so.

9.34 The FSA has an additional power in FSMA 2000, Sch 3[1], exercisable at the request of a host state regulator in an EEA state, to impose on a UK firm, which does not have a Part IV permission but which is doing business in that host state under the Directives, the same requirements that it could impose on a variation of permission if the UK firm had a Part IV permission in relation to the business it was carrying on[2].

1 FSMA 2000, Sch 3, para 24.
2 This is similar to the FSA's power to intervene in an incoming firm: see para 9.83 below.

9.35 ***Relevant factors where the FSA has relevant EEA obligations***
In certain circumstances[1], the FSA must consider whether it is necessary to exercise its own-initiative powers in order to comply with a Community obligation[2]. Where the FSA does judge it necessary to take action in order to comply with a Community obligation, the FSMA 2000 expressly disapplies the factors normally applicable to the exercise of the FSA's discretion[3] but does not say how the FSA should act or what factors it should take into account.

1 Where the request is made by a host state regulator (within the meaning in the FSMA 2000, Sch 3) or the Swiss supervisory authority, acting in pursuance of a provision of Community legislation (or the agreement between the EC and Switzerland) or any rule of law in force in an EEA state (or Switzerland) the purposes connected with the implementation of such provision: see FSMA 2000, s 47(3) and the Financial Services and Markets Act 2000 (Own-initiative Power) (Overseas Regulators) Regulations 2001, SI 2001/2639.
2 'Community obligation' is not expressly defined in the FSMA 2000. It means obligations under EC law and includes, in particular, the obligations of co-operation and collaboration with other EEA authorities under the Banking Consolidation Directive, the Insurance Directives and the Investment Services Directive: see the FSA Handbook at ENF 3.5.19 and the Explanatory Notes to the FSMA 2000 (para 112) and see footnote 1 to para 2.12 above.
3 FSMA 2000, s 47(4). As to the factors applicable in other cases, see para 9.39 below.

9.36 How will the FSA exercise its discretion in that situation? The FSA views co-operation and collaboration under the various EEA directives as essential to the effective regulation of the international market in financial services[1]. Its policy is therefore that it will exercise its own-initiative power wherever:

- an EEA competent authority requests it do so; and
- it is satisfied that the use of the power is appropriate (having regard to the considerations relevant to its general approach to the use of its powers discussed at para 9.67 ff below) to enforce effectively the regulatory requirements imposed pursuant to the Single Market Directives or other Community obligations.

1 See the FSA Handbook at ENF 3.5.21.

9.37 As to what this policy means in practice, whilst the FSA says that it will have regard to the same factors as are relevant to the use of its own-initiative power domestically, it is not clear how these factors can be applied for the purpose of ensuring the effective enforcement of the Directives. For example, will it be realistic, on a request from an overseas regulator, to give the firm the opportunity to agree voluntarily to take the steps required to address any concerns? How, particularly in the context of a request relating to an incoming firm from that firm's home state regulator, will it apply the principle that the firm's own management should be primarily responsible for ensuring it conducts its business in accordance with the regulatory requirements? Also, is it appropriate, in that context, for the FSA to take formal action 'only if' necessary to secure compliance with the regulatory requirements or to address the consequences of non-compliance[1]? These factors may or may not be relevant in the context of a request from the particular overseas regulator given the particular EC provision under which the request is made.

1 See the FSA Handbook at ENF 3.5.3 and see para 9.67 ff below.

9.38 Although the FSMA 2000 does not specifically require the FSA to use its own-initiative powers where it finds that this is necessary in order to comply with a Community obligation, the strong implication is that it will normally use its powers in this situation.

9.39 ***Relevant factors in other situations*** In any other situation[1], the FSMA 2000 prescribes a number of factors which the FSA may take into account in deciding whether or not to exercise its power[2]:

- whether, in the country or territory of the regulator concerned, corresponding assistance would be given to a UK regulatory authority;
- whether the case involves the breach of a law, or other requirement, which has no close parallel in the UK or involves the assertion of a jurisdiction not recognised by the UK;
- the seriousness of the case and its importance to persons in the UK;
- whether it is otherwise appropriate in the public interest to give the assistance sought; and
- the FSA may decide not to exercise its power unless the regulator concerned undertakes to make such contribution towards the cost of its exercise as the FSA considers appropriate.

1 In other words, in any situation where the FSA does not consider the exercise of its own-initiative power to be necessary in order to comply with a Community obligation: FSMA 2000, s 47(4).
2 FSMA 2000, s 47(4) & (5) and (in relation to an incoming firm) s 195(6) & (7). These are the same factors as were formally contained in the Financial Services Act 1986, s 128C.

9.40 The FSA will actively consider any requests from relevant overseas regulators[1]. In doing so:

- it may take account of all of the above factors but may give particular weight to the seriousness of the case and its importance to persons in the UK and also to any specific request made by the overseas regulator to vary, rather than cancel, the firm's permission;
- it will carefully consider whether the relevant authority's concerns would provide grounds for the FSA to exercise its own-initiative power if they related to a UK firm[2];
- it will wish to be confident that the authorities in the jurisdiction concerned would have powers available to them to provide broadly similar assistance in aid of UK authorities and would be willing properly to consider doing so.

1 See the FSA Handbook at ENF 3.5.22 to 3.5.25.
2 It is not necessary for the overseas provisions to mirror precisely those which apply to UK firms. However, the FSA will not assist in the enforcement of regulatory requirements or other provisions that appear to extend significantly beyond the purposes of UK regulatory provisions: see the FSA Handbook at ENF 3.5.24.

9.41 The FSA will thus undertake a reasonably broad analysis of the appropriateness in the particular case of exercising its discretion in favour of using its own-initiative power. Particular stress is placed on the seriousness of the case and its importance to people in the UK (which is notable as a peculiarly domestic factor in this context). Beyond that, an important consideration in practice may well be the relationship between the FSA and the relevant overseas regulator, particularly given the weight placed increasingly by the FSA on the need for co-operation among regulators internationally[1].

1 'We have to recognise the increasingly international nature of much of the financial services business conducted in the UK. So an important part of our supervision includes co-ordinated relationships with key foreign supervisors, including information sharing, regular meetings and joint visits': Howard Davies to the Swiss Bankers Association, 1 September 2000.

Case E: On the acquisition of control over a UK regulated firm

9.42 If it appears to the FSA that a person has acquired control over a UK authorised person that has a Part IV permission but there are otherwise no grounds for the FSA to exercise its own-initiative power, then the FSA may nonetheless vary the firm's permission by imposing or varying a requirement[1] if it appears to it that the likely effect of the acquisition of control on the authorised person or any of its activities is uncertain[2].

1 The imposition of a requirement is one of the actions available to the FSA when it varies a firm's permission: see para 9.81 below.
2 FSMA 2000, s 46.

9.43 Whilst this provision is noted for completeness, it is unlikely to be relevant in the enforcement context[1]. It is ancillary to the FSA's powers in the FSMA 2000, Pt XII to vet changes in control of authorised persons and to approve, object to or impose conditions in respect of a proposed change in control.

1 The example given by the Economic Secretary to HM Treasury in Standing Committee (21 October 1999) of when this might apply was of a takeover of an insurance company that had in the past deliberately over-reserved for its liabilities. It was said that the FSA would want to ensure that the business did not make any sudden changes to its business plan (for example to put those assets to other uses), or that if it did the impact would not work to the material detriment of existing customers.

Additional considerations which may be relevant

9.44 As outlined briefly at para 9.13 above, three additional considerations may be relevant depending upon the circumstances.

9.45 ***Having regard to those in a relevant relationship*** First, in considering whether to vary or cancel a Part IV permission, the FSA may have regard to any person appearing to it to be, or likely to be, in a relationship with the person which is relevant[1].

1 FSMA 2000, s 49(1).

9.46 What constitutes a relevant relationship is not defined but is left to the FSA to interpret in the particular circumstances of the case[1]. The FSA Handbook[2] is, however, silent on the meaning of this phrase and the circumstances when the FSA will seek to make use of this provision. It is thought that this ties in particularly with the 'suitability' and 'close links' threshold conditions[3] but it does not seem to be limited to these. A firm's employees, directors, controllers or perhaps even others could therefore be viewed by the FSA as being relevant.

1 See the Explanatory Notes to the FSMA 2000, para 119. Note that it appears to have been common ground in Standing Committee (although it is not entirely clear) that 'relevant' relates to continued satisfaction of the threshold conditions (see Financial Secretary to HM Treasury, 21 October 1999).
2 See the FSA Handbook at ENF 3.5.27.
3 See para 2.39 above.

9.47 ***Varying top-up permissions*** Second, if the FSA is considering varying or cancelling a 'top-up' permission of an incoming firm[1], then it must take into account[2]:

- the home state authorisation[3] of the firm;
- any relevant directive; and
- relevant provisions of the EC Treaty.

1 For an explanation, see para 2.14 above.
2 FSMA 2000, s 50(2).
3 For a definition, see FSMA 2000, s 425.

9.48 The purpose of this provision[1] is to enable the above three matters to inform the FSA's view on whether the firm is fit and proper to continue to hold the additional permission and whether the cancellation or variation it proposes is appropriate in the light of the wider assessment of the firm which the home state regulator is responsible for making. Again, the FSA has provided no indication of how in practice it will apply this[2].

1 See Explanatory Notes to the FSMA 2000, para 121.
2 See the FSA Handbook at ENF 3.5.28.

9.49 ***Firms connected with EEA firms*** Third, before cancelling or varying a permission of a firm which is connected with an EEA firm[1], the FSA must consult with the firm's home state regulator[2]. This covers, for example, the situation where the firm is part of a group of companies which is primarily regulated elsewhere in the EEA. In that situation, the FSA clearly needs to consult with the home state regulator.

1 For a definition of 'EEA firm', see FSMA 2000, s 425 and Sch 3 and see the discussion at para 2.12 above. 'Connected with' means a subsidiary undertaking or a subsidiary undertaking of a parent undertaking of the EEA firm: FSMA 2000, s 49(3). As to the meaning of 'parent undertaking' and 'subsidiary undertaking' see FSMA 2000, s 420.
2 FSMA 2000, s 49(2).

Incoming firms: intervention

9.50 The four grounds on which the FSMA 2000 allows the FSA to exercise its intervention power in relation to incoming firms are set out in turn below. Where the FSA is considering exercising its power of intervention in relation to an EEA firm, there is an additional procedure which needs to be followed in certain situations, resulting from the requirements of the various single market directives. Broadly, the FSA is required to give the firm's home state regulator the opportunity to take appropriate action against the firm before the FSA does so[1].

1 The procedure, and the circumstances when it must be followed, is set out at para 9.236 ff below.

Case 1: Contravention of a requirement imposed by or under the FSMA

9.51 The FSA may exercise its power of intervention in respect of an incoming firm if it appears to the FSA that the firm has contravened, or is likely to contravene, a requirement imposed on it by or under the FSMA 2000 (in a case where the FSA is responsible for enforcing compliance in the UK)[1].

1 FSMA 2000, s 194(1)(a).

9.52 ***When will the test be satisfied?*** The meaning of contravention of a requirement imposed by or under the FSMA 2000 has been considered at para 2.142 ff above. Broadly, this covers breaches not only of specific rules and regulations but also of applicable general principles and breaches of prohibitions imposed directly under the FSMA 2000, for example those with criminal law consequences.

9.53 This provision is, in very broad terms, the equivalent for incoming firms of the provision allowing the FSA to use its own-initiative power in respect of UK regulated firms that are failing or likely to fail the threshold conditions[1]. However, contravention of a requirement imposed by or under the FSMA 2000 may be a lower hurdle than failure to satisfy the threshold conditions. In theory, any single contravention, or likely contravention, of any of the FSA's rules could lead to intervention action against an incoming firm (whereas, in contrast, a single rule breach by a UK regulated firm would generally be unlikely to mean that the firm was failing to meet the threshold conditions). The provision only applies, however, to those rules for which the FSA is responsible for ensuring compliance.

1 Case A: see para 9.14 above. The threshold conditions do not generally apply to incoming firms, from a UK regulatory perspective: see para 2.40 above.

9.54 The test is, again, a relatively low one. At its lowest, it need only 'appear to the FSA' that the firm is 'likely to contravene' a regulatory requirement in order for the intervention power to be exercisable. Whether the firm has committed a breach should be capable of objective ascertainment, although there may be room for argument (and where there is it is the FSA's views that matter in this context). Whether the firm is likely to commit a breach, where it has not yet done so, is more a matter of judgment and it may be difficult to challenge the FSA's view unless, for example, it is plainly unreasonable. It may therefore be difficult for firms to argue that the test had not been met.

9.55 ***When will the FSA consider using this power?*** The FSA has not provided any policy guidance on the use of this power specifically. The general policy outlined at para 9.67 ff below applies[1]. In addition, the FSA will seek, and take account of, the views of the firm's home state regulator[2].

1 See para 9.71 below.
2 See the FSA Handbook at ENF 4.4.3.

Case 2: Provision of false or misleading information

9.56 The FSA may exercise its power of intervention in respect of an incoming firm if it appears to the FSA that the firm has, in purported compliance with any requirement imposed by or under the FSMA 2000, knowingly or recklessly given the FSA information which is false or misleading in a material particular[1].

1 FSMA 2000, s 194(1)(b). The wording mirrors that of the criminal offence under FSMA 2000, s 177(4) or, particularly, s 398 (1), discussed at para 4.287 above.

9.57 The provision of prompt and accurate information to the FSA is one of the central tenets of the regulatory regime. For UK regulated firms, the obligation is embodied in Principle 11 of the Principles for Businesses[1]. Furthermore, knowingly or recklessly to provide false or misleading information to the FSA is, in many instances, a criminal offence[2]. If the FSA seeks to exercise its intervention power under this head then the firm needs to be aware that there could be a serious potential problem, possibly with criminal law consequences.

1 The requirement on a firm to deal with its regulators in an open and co-operative way and to disclose to the FSA appropriately anything relating to the firm of which the FSA would reasonably expect notice: see para 2.52 above.
2 See, for example, FSMA 2000, ss 177(4) and 398.

9.58 ***When will the test be satisfied?*** Again, the test is a relatively low one. It need only 'appear to the FSA' that the firm has knowingly or recklessly provided false or misleading information. Again, whether or not the firm has done so ought to be capable of determination objectively, but there may be room for argument, and where there is it is the FSA's views that count. It may therefore be difficult to show that the statutory test for the exercise of the intervention power had not been met.

9.59 ***When will the FSA consider using this power?*** The FSA has not provided any policy guidance on the use of this power specifically. The general policy outlined at para 9.67 ff applies[1]. In addition, the FSA will seek, and take account of, the views of the firm's home state regulator[2].

1 See para 9.71 below.
2 See the FSA Handbook at ENF 4.4.3.

Case 3: Desirable to exercise the power to protect the interests of customers

9.60 The FSA may exercise its power of intervention in respect of an incoming firm if it appears to the FSA that it is desirable to exercise the power in order to protect the interests of actual or potential customers[1].

1 FSMA 2000, s 194(1)(c).

9.61 This power appears to be similar to Case C, discussed at para 9.25 above in relation to UK regulated firms. However, there is one difference, namely that the FSMA 2000 uses here the term 'customers' whereas in that context it refers to 'consumers'. The reason for this distinction is not clear. Whilst the

FSA has a statutory objective of protecting consumers, the term 'customers' is not generally used in the FSMA 2000. 'Customers' is not therefore defined[1], but probably refers to a narrower category than 'consumers'[2].

1 'Consumers' is also not defined within the context of Case C, although, as noted at para 9.26 above, it probably refers to the wide definition in FSMA 2000, s 5(3).
2 'Customers' may refer to those consumers who actually deal with the firm. In the context of the FSA Handbook, 'customer' has a technical meaning of, broadly, a 'client who is not a market counterparty' (arising from the classification of clients under the Conduct of Business Sourcebook); 'client' also has a technical meaning: see the FSA Handbook, Glossary of Definitions.

9.62 The FSA has not issued any policy guidance on the use of this power specifically. The general policy outlined at para 9.67 ff applies[1]. In addition, the FSA will seek, and take account of, the views of the firm's home state regulator[2].

1 See para 9.71 below.
2 See the FSA Handbook at ENF 4.4.3.

Case 4: At the request of an overseas regulator

9.63 The FSA may exercise its power of intervention in respect of an incoming firm at the request of, or for the purpose of assisting, an overseas regulator[1]. The power of intervention may be exercised under this head irrespective of whether it is also exercisable under Cases 1, 2 or 3.

1 FSMA 2000, s 195.

9.64 An 'overseas regulator' means in this context either a home state regulator or a regulator outside the UK which exercises any of the following functions[1]:

- a function corresponding to any function of the FSA under the FSMA 2000;
- a function corresponding to one exercised by the competent authority under Part VI of the FSMA 2000 in relation to the listing of shares[2];
- a function corresponding to any functions of the Secretary of State under the Companies Act 1985;
- a function in connection with investigating or enforcing insider dealing; and
- any other types of function prescribed in HM Treasury regulations.

1 FSMA 2000, s 195(4). This broadly corresponds with the types of overseas regulators prescribed by HM Treasury for the purposes of s 47: see para 9.31 above.
2 See Chapter 15 below.

9.65 If the firm's home state regulator asks the FSA to exercise its power of intervention or notifies the FSA that the firm's EEA authorisation has been withdrawn, then the FSA must consider whether exercising its intervention power is necessary in order to comply with a Community obligation[1]. The meaning of 'Community obligation', and the considerations applied by the FSA in deciding whether to act pursuant to one, are discussed at para 9.35 above.

1 FSMA 2000, s 195(5).

9.66 Subject to the two points outlined above, this power is the same as Case D in relation to UK regulated firms[1]. The discussion of that power, and the considerations applicable to the decision whether to exercise it, therefore apply equally. An additional consideration is that the FSA will seek, and take account of, the views of the firm's home state regulator[2].

1 See para 9.31 above.
2 See the FSA Handbook at ENF 4.4.3.

When in practice will the FSA exercise its powers?

9.67 The FSA has set out in some detail its general approach on the use of the own-initiative powers. It is important to bear this general approach in mind when looking at the specific provisions of the FSMA 2000 which allow the FSA to exercise these powers. As has been seen, the FSMA 2000 contains a series of hurdles, the passing of any one of which gives the FSA the right to exercise its powers. The hurdles are relatively low and give the FSA a significant amount of discretion. In addition, there is no specific requirement for the exercise of the power in the particular case to be commensurate with, or even directed at, the mischief which has given rise to the hurdle being met (although the FSA owes certain general duties like any other public body which restrict its freedom of action to some extent[1]). The FSA's policy on when it will exercise these powers is therefore important.

1 See further Chapter 16 below.

9.68 We consider here the FSA's general approach to using its own initiative powers. Its approach to the exercise of its powers as a matter of urgency is discussed separately at para 9.194 ff below and its policy on the cancellation of a firm's permission is considered at para 9.243 ff below.

The FSA's general approach[1]

Setting the use of the own-initiative power in context

9.69 When an issue of concern arises in relation to a firm, the use of its own-initiative powers is only one of a range of tools available to the FSA to deal with the situation. Precisely what action it is appropriate for the FSA to take in the particular case will depend upon what the FSA needs to achieve having regard to its regulatory objectives. For example, if the issue relates to an isolated breach for which there is no doubt the firm will be able to compensate investors, and which does not give rise to ongoing regulatory concerns, then the variation of the firm's permission is unlikely to be under consideration, whereas disciplinary action might. Equally, if the regulatory issue was relatively minor and was spotted by the firm's normal controls before it led to any particular incident involving harm to investors, then, again, it may be unlikely that the use of these powers would be appropriate, but it may be appropriate to increase the supervision and monitoring of the firm, perhaps together with giving it a private warning.

1 See the FSA Handbook at ENF 3.5.2 to 3.5.8. It may be of interest to compare the former IMRO Statement of Intervention Policy, which set out four fundamental principles: (i) that the regulator must act promptly to prevent investor loss from occurring or to halt existing investor loss, wherever such loss may result from rule breaches; (ii) interventions must aim to ensure that failures to comply with the rules are corrected and do not recur; (iii) the regulator must intervene only to the extent necessary to protect investors and enforce compliance with the rules and (iv) interventions must be applied fairly and consistently, having regard to the seriousness of the issue and the circumstances of the firm or individual.

9.70 In the context of considering whether the own-initiative power should be used, the FSA has stated[1] that, in considering how to deal with a concern about a firm, it will have regard to the responsibilities of the firm's management to deal with the concerns[2] and to the principle that a restriction imposed on a business should be proportionate to the objectives which the FSA seeks to achieve[3]. The FSA will proceed on the basis that it is the firm (together with its directors and senior management) that is primarily responsible for ensuring it conducts its business in compliance with the regulatory requirements[4]. There seems therefore to be something approaching a presumption against taking action save in relatively serious circumstances.

1 See the FSA Handbook at ENF 3.5.2.
2 This is one of the principles for good regulation (see para 2.21 above). It is not made clear whether having regard to the responsibilities of management will tend towards, or against, regulatory action. This may depend upon whether or not management are perceived to be properly addressing the situation.
3 This is also one of the principles of good regulation (see para 2.21 above). Under the FSMA 2000, it is not clear that the FSA is required to have regard to these principles in deciding what action to take in a particular case (as opposed to when determining its general policy), but these two principles, and most notably proportionality, are expressly said to be relevant to the consideration of what action is appropriate in each case in this context. See further the discussion at para 2.23 above.
4 See the FSA Handbook at ENF 3.5.3.

Applying this general approach to incoming firms

9.71 In relation to the imposition of intervention action against incoming firms, the FSA has provided only a general policy statement that it will adopt broadly the same approach as it does to its power in relation to UK regulated firms, but with suitable modification for the differences in the statutory grounds[1]. It will also seek, and take account of, the views of the firm's home state regulator[2]. The potential difficulty is that it is not clear how some of the factors discussed below could apply to incoming firms.

1 See the FSA Handbook at ENF 4.4.2.
2 See the FSA Handbook at ENF 4.4.3.

The own-initiative power in the context of supervision

9.72 Many issues which arise may be able to be addressed in the context of the FSA's day-to-day supervision and monitoring of the firm, without any enforcement action being taken[1]. The FSA may make clear to the firm that it expects it to take certain steps to ensure it continues to meet the regulatory requirements. This could include asking it to improve particular weaknesses that the FSA sees, for example in its finances, conduct of business or controls. In the vast majority of cases, the FSA will seek to agree with the firm the steps to be taken to address its concerns. The FSA envisages that firms will take such steps, without the need for any formal action on the FSA's part[2].

1 See the FSA Handbook at ENF 3.5.4 to 3.5.5.
2 The FSA's power to give firms individual guidance under FSMA 2000, s 157 may also be relevant and may overlap to some extent with the power to vary permission. See the FSA Handbook at SUP Chapters 7 and 9.

9.73 There may, however, be occasions where the FSA needs to exercise its formal powers, notwithstanding that the matter has arisen in the supervisory context, particularly where the FSA believes it cannot rely on the firm taking effective action or if the firm fails to comply with the FSA's reasonable request to take remedial steps[1]. Examples given[2] include where the FSA is concerned that the consequences of the firm not taking the step may be serious and the firm appears unwilling or unable to take adequate and timely steps to address the FSA's concerns or where the imposition of formal action may assist the firm to take steps which would otherwise be difficult because of legal obligations owed to third parties.

1 See the FSA Handbook at ENF 3.5.6. There is no discussion in the FSA Handbook of whether the FSA will exercise its formal powers if the firm disputes that the action the FSA is requesting is reasonable. It is to be presumed that a 'reasonable request' is, for these purposes, one which the FSA believes to be reasonable and that if the firm disagrees the FSA will take the formal action and the firm may challenge that action in the Tribunal (see para 9.104 ff below). In some circumstances, the firm could also potentially be exposed to disciplinary action for failing to co-operate with the FSA, which may be a breach of Principle 11 (see paras 2.52 and 2.156 ff above).
2 See the FSA Handbook at ENF 3.5.6 and SUP 7.3.1.

9.74 The latter point is an important one in practice. If the steps which are required impact on the firm's contractual obligations to others[1], or could otherwise expose it to liability to third parties[2], then it is unlikely that, as a matter of law, it will be protected by having taken such steps voluntarily in order, for example, to protect the interests of consumers. It may assist the firm to have been required to take those steps by the FSA pursuant to the FSA's formal statutory powers. Whether this will, in fact, be sufficient to protect the firm from liability in the particular case will depend upon the firm's legal obligations in that case and the precise circumstances which led to the need for the intervention action. The firm may not be absolved from liability.

1 An example would be undertaking not to carry on business in a particular area where the firm had ongoing contractual obligations to third parties.
2 An example would be suspending a particular product of the firm's, which could potentially expose the firm to liability to the holders of the product.

9.75 The FSA has identified various examples of circumstances where it may need to use its formal powers in the context of its supervision activities[1]. These include where:

- the firm's management, business or internal controls give rise to risks that are not fully captured by the FSA's rules;

- the firm becomes or is to become involved in new products or selling practices which present risks not captured by existing requirements; or
- a change in a firm's structure, controllers, activities or strategy generates uncertainty or creates unusual or exceptional risks.

1 See the FSA Handbook at SUP 7.3.2 and ENF 3.5.3. Similar circumstances may, alternatively, lead to the FSA issuing individual guidance to the firm under FSMA 2000, s 157: see the FSA Handbook at SUP 9.3.

The own-initiative power in the context of enforcement

9.76 As regards the use of the own-initiative power in the context of the FSA's enforcement function, the FSA will consider taking such action only if[1]:

- the firm's business is being conducted in such a way that the FSA judges it necessary to act in order to:
  - secure compliance with the FSMA 2000, the Principles for Businesses and the FSA's rules, and/or
  - address the consequences of non-compliance.

1 See the FSA Handbook at 3.5.3.

9.77 The use of the words 'only if' and 'necessary to act' may seem to indicate that the FSA applies a high test. The test is phrased subjectively, so that it is the FSA's view of whether it is necessary to act that matters for these purposes. Nonetheless, it may be open to the firm to argue that action was not necessary[1] because, for example, the firm was taking other steps that would address the FSA's concerns.

1 Precisely what 'necessary' means depends upon the circumstances. It 'lies somewhere between "indispensable" on the one hand and "useful" or "expedient" on the other': Lord Griffiths in *In re an Inquiry under the Company Securities (Insider Dealing) Act 1985* [1988] 2 WLR 33, 65.

9.78 Circumstances where the FSA will consider taking action[1] include where the FSA has serious concerns about a firm, or about the way its business is being or has been conducted, but the concerns are not such as to suggest it should cancel the firm's permission[2]. The particular concerns which are said to be relevant to the exercise of the FSA's powers under each of Cases A to E and 1 to 4 are discussed in relation to each case at para 9.7 ff above.

1 See the FSA Handbook at ENF 3.5.8.
2 The cancellation of permission is considered at para 9.239 ff below. It is included within this chapter as it is the most serious form of action which the FSA can take using its own-initiative power.

9.79 The process (outlined above in the supervisory context) of requesting the firm to take steps voluntarily before considering formal action, is not specifically said to apply in the enforcement context. However, whether the firm was co-operating and addressing the issues itself ought to be relevant to the FSA when considering whether it is 'necessary to act' by using its formal powers in the enforcement context[1]. Hence, it will be important how the firm responds in the particular case[2].

1 This is reinforced by the need for the FSA to act proportionately and the policy of proceeding on the basis that it is primarily for the firm to ensure regulatory compliance (see para 9.70 above).
2 For a discussion of how firms might respond when a regulatory issue arises, see Chapter 3 above.

What action can the FSA take?

9.80 In the following paragraphs, we consider the action which the FSA can take against firms by using its own-initiative powers. This involves reviewing:

- the types of action that the FSA can take;
- some particular points relating to restrictions imposed on the firm's assets;
- whether the FSA can impose restrictions on the firm's employees;
- the question of when the FSA's action takes effect; and
- the effect of the action which the FSA takes.

In relation to UK regulated firms (and incoming firms to the extent they have a top-up permission[1]), the FSA also has the power to cancel the firm's permission. This is considered separately at para 9.239 ff below.

1 For a brief explanation of top-up permissions, see para 2.14 above.

What action can the FSA take?

9.81 So far as UK regulated firms are concerned, the own-initiative power is:

- the power to vary a firm's Part IV permission in any of the ways mentioned in FSMA 2000, s 44(1) or to cancel it[1]; and
- it extends to including any provision in the permission as varied that could be included if a fresh permission were being given in response to an application for a new permission under FSMA 2000, s 40[2]. This covers limitations which can be imposed under s 42(7) and requirements which can be imposed under s 43.

This applies equally to incoming firms to the extent they have a top-up permission.

1 FSMA 2000, s 45(2). The cancellation of permission (and certain ancillary provisions) is discussed at para 9.239 ff below.
2 FSMA 2000, s 45(4).

9.82 This allows the FSA to do any of the following:

- vary a Part IV permission in any of the ways mentioned in FSMA 2000, s 44(1), namely add or remove a regulated activity to or from those for which it gives permission, vary the description of a regulated activity, or cancel or vary a requirement already imposed under FSMA 2000, s 43;

- impose limitations on the firm, which means incorporating in the description of a regulated activity such limitations (for example as to circumstances in which the activity may, or may not, be carried on) as it considers appropriate[1]; and/or
- include in the firm's permission such requirements as it considers appropriate[2], including requirements:
  - — requiring the firm to take, or refrain from taking, specified action,
  - — extending to the firm's unregulated activities,
  - — imposed by reference to the firm's relationship with its group[3] or other members of the group, and/or
  - — expiring at such date as the FSA may specify.

1 FSMA 2000, s 42(7)(a).
2 FSMA 2000, s 43.
3 For the meaning of 'group' see FSMA 2000, s 421.

9.83 So far as incoming firms are concerned (at least beyond any top-up permission), the 'intervention' power is the power to impose any requirement in relation to the firm which the FSA could impose if the firm's permission was a Part IV permission and the FSA was entitled to exercise its power under Part IV to vary its permission[1]. In other words, of the powers outlined above, only the imposition of requirements under FSMA 2000, s 43 is relevant. Since the firm does not have a Part IV permission into which any such requirement can be included, this is achieved by imposing the requirement on the firm.

1 FSMA 2000, s 196.

What does this mean in practice?

9.84 This plainly can encompass a wide range of action. In the enforcement context, the FSA has indicated[1] that:

- the limitations it may impose include limitations on the number, or category, of customers that a firm can deal with, the number of specified investments that a firm can deal in, and the activities of the firm so that they fall within specific regulatory regimes; and
- examples of the requirements it may impose include requirements not to take on new business, not to hold or control client money, or not to trade in certain categories of investments, or an 'assets requirement' (one that prohibits or restricts the disposal of or dealing with any of the firm's assets or requires assets to be transferred to a trustee[2]).

1 See the FSA Handbook at ENF 3.2.2 to 3.2.10 and, as regards incoming firms, ENF 4.2.
2 There are specific provisions applicable to assets requirements: see FSMA 2000, ss 48 and 201 and see para 9.112 below.

9.85 Notably, neither the statutory examples of 'limitations' and 'requirements' nor the FSA's policy are expressed to be exhaustive of the action the FSA can take[1]. The basic position is therefore that the FSA can incorporate such limitations as it considers appropriate, impose such requirements as it considers appropriate and/or add, remove or vary the regulated activities for which the firm has permission. These are very broad and mostly, subjective tests and they give the FSA a very wide discretion in the sort of action it may seek to take in the particular case.

1 For further examples of the way in which variation of permission may be used (albeit in the context of applications by firms), see the FSA Handbook at SUP Chapter 6.

How will this be applied?

9.86 The breadth of the range of action which the FSA can take is thus reasonably clear. What is not clear is what sorts of limitations or restrictions are likely to be applicable in particular types of situations[1]. There is little indication in the FSA Handbook. Two of the FSA's policy statements may, however, assist. First, the FSA will have regard to the principle that a restriction imposed on a firm should be proportionate to the objectives which the FSA is seeking to achieve[2] and, second, it will only take formal action against a firm affecting the conduct of the firm's commercial business if it is being conducted in such a way that the FSA judges it necessary to act in order to secure compliance with the FSMA 2000, the Principles for Businesses and the FSA's rules and/or address the consequences of non-compliance[3]. The second appears to be directed primarily at the circumstances when the FSA will take formal action, rather than at what action it will take in those circumstances. The first point, proportionality, may be more relevant in practice and may, particularly, be the focus of challenges by firms to FSA action which they consider to be unwarranted.

1 It is notable that although the SROs which formerly regulated investment business had the ability to impose intervention orders tailored to the particular case (albeit their powers were not quite as flexible as the FSA's powers under the FSMA 2000), in practice intervention was largely used as a blunt instrument to prevent a firm from carrying on any further investment business. For an example of the SFA taking a more refined approach, see the case of *Sobhag Stockbroking Ltd* (SFA Board Notice 325, 23 May 1996).
2 See the FSA Handbook at ENF 3.5.2 and see para 9.70 above.
3 See the FSA Handbook at ENF 3.5.3 and see para 9.76 above.

Taking action in relation to incoming firms

9.87 As regards the imposition of requirements upon incoming firms, the FSA will adopt broadly the same approach as it does in relation to UK regulated firms but with suitable modification for the differences in the statutory grounds for exercising the powers[1]. It will also seek, and take account of, the view of the firm's home state regulator. As has been highlighted[2], it is not clear how this will work in practice.

1 See the FSA Handbook at ENF 4.4.2.
2 See para 9.71 above.

Taking action in the supervisory context

9.88 The FSA's own-initiative and intervention powers apply not only in the enforcement context but also in the context of supervision. The FSA's policy in seeking to exercise its powers in that context is outlined in the FSA Handbook at SUP Chapter 7.

Restrictions on the firm's assets

9.89 The FSMA 2000 contains additional provisions where the FSA imposes an 'assets requirement' on a firm. An assets requirement is a requirement[1]:

- prohibiting the disposal of, or other dealing with, any of the firm's assets (whether in the UK or elsewhere) or restricting such disposals or dealings; or
- that all or any of the firm's assets, or all or any assets belonging to consumers but held by the firm or to its order, must be transferred to and held by a trustee approved by the FSA.

This gives rise to two particular issues addressed in the FSMA 2000. The application of these when the FSA imposes an assets requirement on an incoming firm is not entirely clear[2].

1 FSMA 2000, s 48(3).

2 FSMA 2000, s 201 provides that the requirement imposed on an incoming firm 'has the same effect in relation to the firm as it would have in relation to an authorised person if it had been imposed on the authorised person by the FSA acting under s 45'. It seems to have been the intention (see the marginal note in the FSMA 2000 ('Effect of certain requirements on other persons') and see the Explanatory Notes to the FSMA 2000, para 406) that the effect of this provision would be to apply s 48 equally where an assets requirement was imposed on an incoming firm. It is not, though, clear that it does have this effect. Section 201 provides only that the requirement has the same effect 'in relation to the firm'. This would seem to mean, for example, that the firm could not, because of s 48(5)(a), bring a claim against a bank which refused to make payment based on a reasonably held belief that the payment instruction was incompatible with the assets requirement (see para 9.90 below). However, since it only provides that it has effect 'in relation to the firm', it is not clear that a bank that made payment would incur any liability under s 48(5)(b) (see para 9.90 below) or that a trustee would incur criminal liability if it released assets without the FSA's consent (s 48(9) and see para 9.94 below). Even if this is correct, third parties must still take care. If they are knowingly concerned in a contravention of an assets requirement by a firm, they may be liable to a restitution order (see Chapter 7 above). Also, if they are themselves authorised then other regulatory enforcement consequences may arise.

How does the requirement affect banks with whom the firm holds accounts?

9.90 An assets requirement prohibiting the firm from disposing of or dealing with its assets may affect third-party institutions with whom the firm keeps an account. The FSMA 2000 allows the assets requirements to bind the bank directly, by providing that if the FSA gives notice of the requirement to the third party institution, then[1]:

- the institution does not breach its contract with the firm if, having been instructed by or on behalf of the firm to transfer any sum or otherwise make any payment out of the firm's account, it refuses to do so in the reasonably held belief that complying with the instruction would be incompatible with the requirement; and

- if it does comply with such an instruction, it is liable to pay the FSA an amount equal to the amount transferred from, or otherwise paid out of, the firm's account in contravention of the requirement.

1 FSMA 2000, s 48(4) & (5).

9.91 This is an important provision both protecting and, if relevant, punishing institutions. The first limb gives the institution protection on the basis of its 'reasonably held belief' that to comply with the instruction would be incompatible with the requirement the FSA has imposed on the firm. It will be of comfort to institutions that, even if that belief is wrong, the institution should not be liable provided it held that belief reasonably[1].

1 The provision may, though, leave open the question whether the institution could be liable to the firm on a non-contractual basis. This issue was raised in the Parliamentary debates in Standing Committee (21 October 1999). The response of the Economic Secretary to HM Treasury was that they found it difficult to envisage circumstances in which an institution such as a bank would owe other non-contractual duties. It is not, though, clear that the provision would necessarily exclude liability for a concurrent duty in negligence, or that other duties would not exist in certain situations (for example, the duties of a trustee).

9.92 The second limb is the corollary of this. The institution will be liable to the FSA if it makes a payment in compliance with such an instruction and that payment contravenes the requirement the FSA has imposed[1]. What is notable is that, in contrast with the first limb, liability is strict[2]. It arises if the payment contravenes the FSA's requirement. It is not open to the institution to argue that it reasonably believed that the payment was not incompatible with the requirement.

1 One difficult issue will be whether a third-party bank based outside the jurisdiction, perhaps with a UK branch on which the assets requirement was served, could be held liable to the FSA under this provision in respect of a payment from an account held abroad. See also the discussion at 4.237 ff above.

2 Compare the position of a third party, such as a bank, served with notice of a freezing order granted by a court. If the bank assists in a breach of the order, it may be liable in contempt of court, but only if it does so knowingly. 'It is necessary to show that the person to whom notice was given authorised the disposal of an asset, or knowing that a payment was likely to be made under an authority derived from him, deliberately refrained from taking steps to prevent it, before the corporation can be guilty of contempt of court': see *Z Ltd v A-Z and AA-LL* [1982] QB 558, CA and see the discussion in *Mareva Injunctions and Anton Piller Relief*, Gee, at page 286.

9.93 The message from this is clear. Institutions should err on the side of caution and, if in doubt, refuse to comply with the firm's instruction. If they refuse to make a payment based on a reasonable belief which they hold then they should be excused liability to their customer even if that belief was wrong[1]. If however they make a payment which in fact contravenes the requirement then they expose themselves to liability to the FSA.

1 Subject to the point made at footnote 1 to para 9.91 above.

What is the effect of vesting assets in a trustee?

9.94 The FSMA 2000 contains ancillary provisions applicable where an assets requirement is imposed requiring assets to be transferred to and held by a trustee approved by the FSA[1]. Once the firm has given the trustee written notice that the assets are held on this basis[2]:

- it is a criminal offence to release or deal with those assets while the requirement is in force except with the consent of the FSA[3];
- if, while the requirement is in force, the firm creates any charge over those assets, then that charge is (to the extent it confers security over those assets) void against the liquidator and any of the firm's creditors[4];
- but neither (i) the restriction on releasing or dealing with the assets, nor (ii) the statutory restrictions on when assets are taken to be held in accordance with the FSA's requirement that they be transferred to a trustee[5] affects any equitable interest or remedy of a person who is a beneficiary of a trust as a result of the FSA imposing the requirement[6]. In other words, the trust law position is preserved for the beneficiary (which will normally be either the firm or its customer, if it held the assets on its behalf), so that a court could potentially grant trust law remedies in relation to any breaches of trust.

1 Assets held by a trustee are taken to be held in accordance with the FSA's requirement only if (a) the firm has given the trustee written notice that they are to be held by him in accordance with the requirement, or (b) they are assets into which assets to which (a) applies have been transposed by the trustee on the firm's instructions: FSMA 2000, s 48(8).
2 See footnote 1 above. Note that, in contrast with the provisions relating to banks, it is for the firm, rather than the FSA, to give notice to the trustee.
3 FSMA 2000, s 48(6) & (9).
4 FSMA 2000, s 48(7).
5 See footnote 1 above.
6 FSMA 2000, s 48(11).

Can the FSA impose restrictions on the firm's employees?

9.95 One question which arises is whether the FSA can impose on a particular employee of a firm restrictions or requirements on the nature or scope of the activities that employee can undertake, in the same way as it can vary a firm's permission. Can it, for example, take action as a matter of urgency to prevent the firm's employees from further involvement in a particular area of business?

9.96 There is no equivalent power in relation to employees[1]. To the extent that the employee carries out a function which is specified as a 'controlled function', the FSA has a discretion whether or not to approve him for that function[2], and if he is approved then in certain circumstances it can withdraw that approval[3]. It cannot, however, attach conditions or limitations to the grant of the approval and it cannot withdraw approval as a matter of urgency. To the extent that the employee carries out other functions which are not controlled functions, the FSA has little direct control over the employee short of making a prohibition order against him[4]. A prohibition order may be capable of being used as a fairly flexible tool, but it is likely to be appropriate only in particularly serious cases and, again, it cannot be put into effect as a matter of urgency.

1 Contrast the former position under the rules of the SROs, which could take intervention action against registered individuals.
2 For a brief discussion of approved persons, see para 2.64 ff above.
3 This is discussed in more detail at para 8.27 ff above.
4 For further details, see para 8.44 ff above.

9.97 The FSA may, though, be able to accomplish its objectives through other means. First, there is on the face of it nothing to prevent the FSA from using its own-initiative powers against the firm to vary the firm's permission to impose a requirement upon it relating to a particular employee. For example, it could require the firm to suspend a particular employee or not to involve a particular employee in a particular area of business. Such a requirement could, as will be seen, be imposed in appropriate cases as a matter of urgency. It could be enforced directly against the firm and, if the employee is an approved person, possibly against the employee as well[1].

1 If the firm breached the requirement, the individual may be liable to disciplinary consequences as an approved person knowingly concerned in a contravention by the firm: see para 8.8 above.

9.98 Second, the FSA may be able to take action to prevent a particular employee from committing regulatory breaches, if there were evidence he was likely to do so. In that situation, the FSA may be able to obtain an injunction against him[1]. This could be obtained on an urgent basis in an appropriate case. The basis upon which an injunction could be obtained in this context is, however, limited to cases where regulatory breaches are likely and the scope of the injunction would similarly be limited to restraining the likely breach.

1 FSMA 2000, s 380 and see para 8.77 ff above.

When does the FSA's action take effect?

9.99 The FSA may impose its action with effect[1]:

- immediately; or
- on a specified date; or
- when the matter is no longer open to review.

1 FSMA 2000, ss 53(2) and 197(1).

9.100 Broadly, this allows the FSA to take the action either as a matter of urgency[1] or so that it takes effect in the normal way once the full decision-making process, including any Tribunal proceedings, has been completed[2].

1 By taking it immediately or on a specified date. It is of course possible that action may need to be taken on a specified date for some reason other than urgency, for example if the matter causing concern to the FSA will only become a live issue on a particular date. The FSA has not provided any guidance as to the circumstances when it will seek to take action on a specified date.
2 As to the meaning of 'no longer open to review', see para 9.174 below.

9.101 The FSA may impose action immediately or on a specified date only if, having regard to the ground on which it is exercising its own-initiative power, it reasonably considers that it is necessary for the action to take effect immediately or on a specified date[1]. It must state this in its first supervisory notice. Urgent action is discussed in more detail at para 9.194 ff below.

1 FSMA 2000, ss 53(3) and 197(2) (although the latter omits the word 'reasonably': see the discussion at para 9.196 below).

What is the effect of the FSA's action?

9.102 The effect of a variation of permission, so far as concerns a firm which has a Part IV permission, is to vary the permission from the date when the action takes effect. If the firm carries on a regulated activity otherwise than in accordance with the permission as varied (in other words, if it breaches the permission or the restrictions or limitations that have been imposed on it) then:

- the firm is taken to have contravened a requirement imposed on it by the FSA under the FSMA 2000[1], which could lead to further enforcement action, for example disciplinary action or to the FSA applying to the court for a civil injunction[2];
- in certain cases, this could give rise to an action for breach of statutory duty by a person who suffers loss as a result[3];
- but it does not amount to a criminal offence and does not make any transaction void or unenforceable[4].

If an assets requirement is breached, then there may be further specific consequences, including, in some circumstances, criminal law consequences[5].

1 FSMA 2000, s 20(1).
2 For the meaning of contravention of a requirement by or under the FSMA 2000 and a brief discussion of the possible consequences, see para 2.142 ff above.
3 FSMA 2000, s 20(3) and see para 10.46 below.
4 FSMA 2000, s 20(2).
5 See para 9.89 ff above.

9.103 The effect so far as an incoming firm that does not have a Part IV permission is concerned is to impose the requirement on the firm from the date when the intervention takes effect. The requirement has the same effect in relation to the firm as a variation of permission and the three bullet points in para 9.102 above apply equally[1].

1 FSMA 2000, ss 201 and 202. In relation to the first bullet point, the requirement is, simply, a requirement imposed upon the firm by or under the FSMA 2000 (and there is therefore no need for an express provision equivalent to s 20(1)).

THE SUPERVISORY NOTICE PROCEDURE

9.104 The own-initiative powers are different in their purpose and nature from the FSA's disciplinary powers and the exercise of these powers by the FSA involves a different procedure under the FSMA 2000[1], known as the 'supervisory notice' procedure. Among other things, this allows action to be taken urgently by the FSA.

1 For the process applicable to the FSA's disciplinary and many other enforcement powers, known as the 'warning/decision notice' procedure, see Chapter 5 above.

Introduction to the supervisory notice procedure

Other powers involving the supervisory notice procedure

9.105 The supervisory notice procedure also applies to a number of the FSA's other powers, namely:

- giving directions in relation to certain types of collective investment schemes[1], or an OEIC[2], considered in Chapter 14 below;
- imposing certain requirements on former underwriting members of Lloyd's[3]; and
- a similar procedure applies where the FSA, acting as the UK Listing Authority, seeks to discontinue or suspend a listing of securities, as discussed in Chapter 15 below.

Reference is therefore made to para 9.104 ff when discussing such other powers elsewhere in this book.

1 FSMA 2000, ss 257, 267 and 279.
2 The Open-Ended Investment Companies Regulations 2001, SI 2001/1228, reg 25.
3 FSMA 2000, s 320.

The basic framework

9.106 The flowchart opposite provides a useful guide to the supervisory notice procedure. The FSMA 2000 provides only a framework for the FSA's procedures; the detailed procedures are contained in the FSA Handbook[1]. The FSMA 2000 does contain some basic requirements, as follows[2].

1 See the FSA Handbook at DEC Chapter 3.
2 The same, or similar, requirements apply in relation to warning/decision notices and are discussed in more detail in Chapter 5 above.

9.107 First, the FSMA 2000 requires the FSA to issue notices termed 'supervisory notices' when it proposes or decides to use its own-initiative powers[1] (hence, the 'supervisory notice procedure').

1 For a further discussion, see paras 9.129 and 9.165 below.

9.108 Second, in the same way as for warning/decision notices[1], the FSMA 2000 requires that the FSA's procedures for the giving of supervisory notices are designed to secure that the decision which gives rise to the obligation to give the notice is taken by a person not directly involved in establishing the evidence on which that decision is based[2]. In short, the FSA staff that investigate the firm cannot generally be the people who decide to impose the variation of permission.

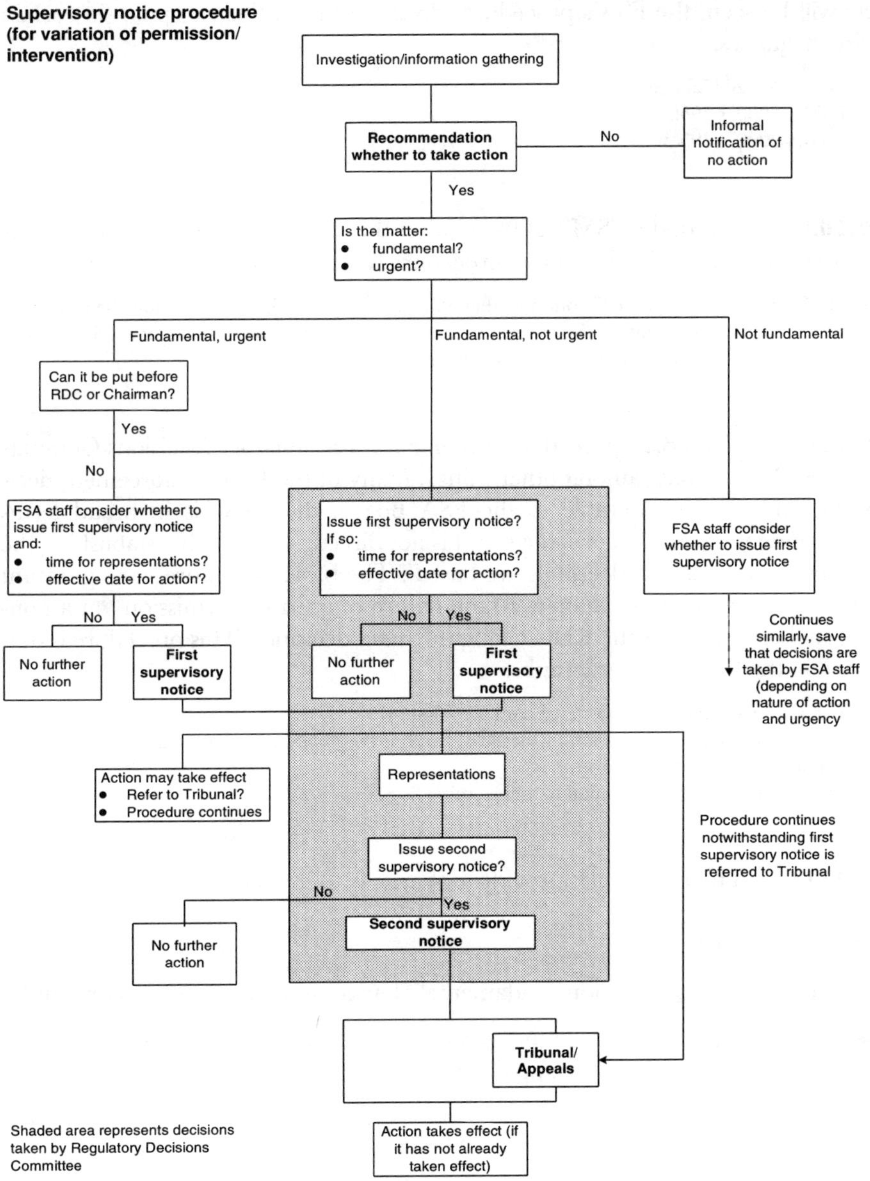

Figure 9.2

There is an exception, allowing the FSA's procedures to permit a decision to be taken without the separation of functions[3] if:

- the FSA considers that in the particular case it is necessary in order to protect the interests of consumers; and
- the person taking the decision is of a level of seniority laid down by the FSA's procedures.

As will be seen, the FSA's procedures do make use of this exception in certain circumstances.

1 See para 5.26 ff above.
2 FSMA 2000, s 395(2).
3 FSMA 2000, s 395(3).

9.109 Third, the FSMA 2000 requires the FSA to publish a statement of its procedure and to follow its stated procedure when giving a supervisory notice[1].

1 FSMA 2000, s 395(5) and (9). But note that a failure in a particular case to follow the procedure does not affect the validity of the supervisory notice given in that case, although the Tribunal may take the failure into account: see FSMA 2000, s 395(11) and (12).

9.110 The FSA's procedures provide for a Regulatory Decisions Committee[1] ('RDC') to take, among other things, many of the FSA's enforcement decisions. Although answerable to the FSA Board, the RDC is in broad terms independent of the FSA executive and is not directly involved in establishing the evidence on which its decisions are based[2]. The basic procedure, for significant (termed 'fundamental') changes to the nature of a firm's permission[3] on a non-urgent basis, involves the RDC taking the main decisions. This procedure is outlined in the following paragraphs.

1 For a more detailed discussion, see para 5.26 ff above.
2 For a more detailed discussion of the RDC, and of the policy which has led to the procedure adopted, see Chapter 5 above.
3 Or equivalent action in relation to an incoming firm.

9.111 The FSA's rules provide for variants to the basic procedure for[1]:

- urgent decisions[2];
- decisions regarding non-fundamental changes to a firm's permission[3]; and
- decisions in cases where there is no dispute between the FSA and the firm as to the need for the action proposed[4].

These are outlined at paras 9.194 ff and 9.219 ff below.

1 As to who decides which procedure is applicable, see para 9.115 below.
2 Urgent decisions are initially taken either by the RDC or by FSA staff, depending on the circumstances. The urgent use of the FSA's own-initiative powers is discussed in detail at para 9.194 ff below.
3 Or equivalent action in relation to an incoming firm. Such decisions are not taken by the RDC but by senior FSA staff, subject to safeguards designed to secure the separation of functions save in certain exceptional situations. The distinction between fundamental and non-fundamental variations of permission is considered at para 9.118 below and the procedure for non-fundamental variations of permission is considered at para 9.220 ff below.
4 This is discussed in more detail at para 9.232 ff below.

9.112 There are a number of possible stages in the supervisory notice procedure, as follows:

- Stage 1: a recommendation from the FSA staff;
- Stage 2: the issue of a first supervisory notice;
- Stage 3: representations from the firm;
- Stage 4: the issue of a second supervisory notice;
- Stage 5: a reference to the Tribunal and, possibly, further appeals; and
- Stage 6: publication of the action.

Each is described in turn below.

Comparing the warning/decision notice procedure

9.113 The supervisory notice procedure differs significantly from the warning/decision notice procedure applicable to many of the FSA's enforcement powers and considered in detail at Chapter 5 above. In particular, the supervisory notice procedure may not involve a preliminary findings letter, the firm has no right of access to the FSA's material, third parties have no right to become involved, and there are no formal settlement or mediation provisions. The provisions on when and how the enforcement action takes effect are also different, and there is a right to refer the matter to the Tribunal at an earlier stage. In many other respects, though, the procedure is similar and the firm will be asking itself many of the questions that are addressed in Chapter 5 above.

9.114 There is also an overlap between the two procedures. In particular, in relation to most of the powers which involve the supervisory notice procedure, if once the enforcement action has been imposed the firm applies for it to be revoked or varied and the FSA wishes to decline that application, then it will be the warning/decision notice procedure that applies.

Stage 1: Recommendation from the FSA staff

9.115 The first stage is when the FSA supervision or enforcement staff who investigated the matter consider whether, in the light of their investigations[1], any formal action is appropriate. In doing so, they must also consider[2]:

- whether the matter is urgent; and
- which body is the appropriate decision-maker to consider the recommendation.

1 In many cases, the firm will have received a preliminary findings letter towards the end of the FSA's investigation, in which case it will have had an opportunity to respond: see the FSA Handbook at ENF 2.5.12 to 2.5.15 and the discussion at para 5.41 ff above. A preliminary findings letter will not be issued if it is not practicable to do so, particularly in urgent cases: see the FSA Handbook at ENF 2.5.12.
2 See the FSA Handbook at DEC 3.1.3.

9.116 These two questions are interlinked and the answer determines who considers the FSA staff recommendation and how the FSA takes the decision whether to accept the recommendation and issue the first supervisory notice. In particular:

- the RDC is responsible only for decisions relating to variations of permission (or equivalent action in relation to an incoming firm) which would make a fundamental change to the nature of the Part IV permission (whether indefinitely or for a limited period)[1];
- decisions with respect to other 'non-fundamental' variations of permission (or equivalent action in relation to an incoming firm) are taken instead by senior FSA staff members under so-called 'executive procedures'[2]; and
- even if the matter is within the responsibility of the RDC, because it would make a fundamental change, the relevant decisions may in certain circumstances be taken not by the RDC but by others under powers delegated by the RDC, namely:
  — in certain urgent cases[3]; or
  — in cases where the firm consents to the action to be taken, before the supervisory notice procedure is commenced[4].

1 See the FSA Handbook at DEC 4.1.4(2) (firms with a Part IV permission) or (7) (incoming firms).
2 These are discussed at para 2.220 ff above.
3 See para 9.194 ff below.
4 These modified procedures are discussed at para 9.232 ff below.

9.117 The question of when action can be imposed urgently is considered at para 9.135 ff below and the procedure in urgent cases (and the practical issues that arise) at para 9.194 ff below. The application of the modified procedures where the firm consents to the action is considered at para 9.232 ff below. We outline here the procedure where it is the RDC that is the decision-making body[1]. The first issue is therefore what is meant by a fundamental change to the nature of a firm's permission.

1 The discussion below therefore refers to the RDC as the decision-making body. As indicated above, in many cases it will not be the RDC that takes the relevant decisions and in those cases references to the RDC should be read as referring to the relevant decision-making body.

What is a 'fundamental change' to a permission?

9.118 Making a fundamental change to the nature of a firm's permission means (in the context of the own-initiative powers)[1]:

- removing a type of activity or investment from the firm's permission;
- restricting a firm from taking on new business, dealing with a particular category of client or handling client money; or
- imposing or varying an assets requirement[2].

1 See the FSA Handbook at DEC 4.1.5.
2 For the definition of 'assets requirement', see FSMA 2000, s 48(3) and see also para 9.89 ff above.

9.119 This also encompasses imposing a requirement on an incoming firm with effect equivalent to making a fundamental change to the nature of a permission[1].

1 See the FSA Handbook at DEC 4.1.4(7).

9.120 It should be apparent that a wide range of action, which a firm might regard as serious, would not amount to a fundamental change for this purpose. For example, a requirement imposed on the firm regarding its systems and controls, its employees, its financial position or (subject to the second bullet point at para 9.118 above) the conduct of its business is unlikely to fall within this[1]. As already indicated, the decision to take such action is not taken by the RDC, but by service FSA staff members[2].

1 Some examples are given in the FSA Handbook at DEC 4.1.8.
2 For further details, see para 9.220 ff below.

What can the firm do to influence the decision whether to make a recommendation?

9.121 The firm has no input into the process at this stage and, indeed, in some cases will not even know that a decision whether to recommend the use of the own-initiative powers is being taken.

What factors are taken into account?

9.122 No specific guidance has been given as to the factors taken into account by the FSA staff in deciding whether to recommend that action is taken and when that action should be imposed. In principle, the FSA staff should apply the FSA's policy in relation to the use of the own-initiative powers[1] and make a recommendation based on that policy.

1 This would include the FSA's general policy (see para 9.67 ff above), its policy as to when each Case for the use of own-initiative or intervention powers is met (see para 9.7 ff above) and, where appropriate, its policy on the use of powers as a matter of urgency (see para 9.196 ff below).

Does the FSA have any options other than to recommend a variation of permission?

9.123 The use of the own-initiative powers should not be viewed in isolation. In many cases, the FSA will be considering generally what action it should take in the light of the matters that have occurred. This may include not only varying permission, but also discipline, restitution orders and injunctions[1], action against approved persons[2] and/or criminal prosecutions[3]. The use of the own-initiative powers may be just one of a number of options available, aimed at addressing the various consequences of the same problem. In other cases, the use of the own-initiative powers may be considered on its own by the FSA, perhaps because it is taking action as a matter of urgency and will later conclude its investigations and consider whether any other action is warranted. Again, therefore, the firm needs to have in mind the other regulatory action that may result from the same matter.

1 See Chapter 7 above.
2 See Chapter 8 above.
3 See Chapter 11 below.

9.124 Even where it is appropriate to exercise its own-initiative powers, the FSA may consider not taking formal action to vary the firm's permission, but instead making clear to the firm what steps are required and giving it the opportunity to comply voluntarily. This may be more likely where the problem has arisen and been handled within the supervisory relationship[1].

1 See further paras 9.72 and 9.79 above.

Is the firm informed about the recommendation?

9.125 There is no formal requirement upon the FSA to inform the firm about the recommendation. However, the FSA Handbook indicates[1] that, in practice, the FSA may sometimes inform the firm that it is intending to recommend that action be taken. Often, though, the firm will only become aware of the FSA's intentions at the next stage, after consideration by the RDC.

1 See the FSA Handbook at DEC 3.1.6.

Is there any risk of publicity?

9.126 The decision whether to make a recommendation of action is in practice very unlikely to be made public. In addition, if the FSA disclosed any confidential information about the firm, that could constitute a criminal offence[1].

1 FSMA 2000, s 348 and see para 4.304 ff above.

Stage 2: The first supervisory notice

9.127 The recommendation by the FSA staff is considered by the RDC, which normally means a panel comprising the Chairman or Deputy Chairman and at least two other members[1]. The RDC may decide either[2]:

- to take no action; or
- to give a first supervisory notice to the firm.

1 This need not apply in urgent cases: see para 9.194 ff below. The size and composition of the Panel may vary depending upon the nature of the particular matter under consideration: see the FSA Handbook at DEC 4.2.8/9. For a detailed discussion of the procedure of the RDC, see the FSA Handbook at DEC 4.2 and see also para 5.33 ff above.
2 See the FSA Handbook at ENF 3.7.5.

A decision to take no action

9.128 If the RDC decides to take no action, then no further action is taken. If the FSA had previously informed the firm that it intended to recommend action, the FSA will communicate the decision promptly to the firm[1]. In other cases, the firm may in practice be told informally that no action is being taken.

1 See the FSA Handbook at DEC 3.1.6.

What is a first supervisory notice?

9.129 The first supervisory notice is the written notice which the FSMA 2000 requires the FSA to issue if it proposes to take certain courses of action (or takes the action with immediate effect)[1], including to vary a firm's permission[2] or to impose a similar requirement on an incoming firm[3].

1 The term 'supervisory notice' only appears in s 395 of the FSMA 2000, where the various types of notice to which the term applies are listed. The specific statutory provisions relating to each type of supervisory notice do not use the term 'supervisory notice', but just require a 'written notice' to be given.
2 FSMA 2000, s 53(4).
3 FSMA 2000, s 197(3).

9.130 Such a first supervisory notice must[1]:

- give details of the action proposed;
- inform the firm of when the action takes effect[2];
- state the FSA's reasons for the action and for its determination as to when the action takes effect;
- inform the firm that it may make representations to the FSA within such period as may be specified in the notice[3], whether or not the firm has referred the matter to the Tribunal; and
- inform the firm of its right to refer the matter to the Tribunal[4], and provide an indication of the procedure on such a reference[5].

1 FSMA 2000, s 53(5) and, for incoming firms, s 197(4) and see the FSA Handbook at ENF 3.1.5. For the contents of the other types of supervisory notice, reference needs to be made to the relevant statutory provision under which the supervisory notice is issued.
2 The statutory provisions only require this to be specified if the action takes effect immediately or on a specified date, but the FSA Handbook indicates that this may always be stated: see DEC 3.1.5. As to when the action takes effect, see para 9.135 ff below.
3 See para 9.143 ff below.
4 See para 9.140 below.
5 FSMA 2000, ss 53(10) and 197(10).

What is the period for the firm to make any representations?

9.131 When issuing the notice, the RDC must decide on the period for the firm to make any representations. This is left wholly within the FSA's discretion. No minimum period is prescribed under the FSMA 2000, nor is the period required to be a 'reasonable' one[1].

1 Contrast the 'warning/decision notice procedure' for disciplinary action, where the period must be reasonable and is subject to a minimum period of 28 days: see FSMA 2000, s 387(2) and para 5.110 above.

9.132 This is an important decision from the firm's perspective, because, first, it may have known little or nothing about the proposed action before receiving the first supervisory notice, second, the process of making representations is an important one if the firm wishes to find a mutually acceptable compromise with the FSA and to avoid having to fight the matter in the Tribunal and, finally, in any event the firm will need time to prepare for making its representations. Reasons why the firm might want to make representations are discussed at para 9.148 ff below.

9.133 In making its decision on the period for representations, the RDC has regard to the circumstances of the case, including the nature of the action proposed and its likely effect on the person concerned, and it also has particular regard to the risk to the FSA's regulatory objectives of any delay in imposing the proposed action[1]. This highlights the difficult balance between ensuring that the firm is treated fairly and ensuring that the FSA's regulatory concerns are addressed in a timely manner. It also suggests that, in practice, it is the latter that is likely to prevail. The FSA has indicated that in practice the period for making representations will normally be 28 days from the date when the person receives the notice, subject to the right to seek an extension of time[2].

1 See the FSA Handbook at DEC 4.4.3. For an explanation of the regulatory objectives, see para 2.20 above.
2 See the FSA Handbook at DEC 4.4.3.

9.134 The procedure for making representations is discussed at para 9.143 ff below.

When should the action proposed by the FSA take effect?

9.135 When the proposed action takes effect depends upon what is specified in the notice. Again, this is a matter for the RDC when deciding to issue the first supervisory notice. It is plainly an important decision from the firm's perspective because the RDC may decide to take action immediately, on a summary basis, giving the firm little or no opportunity to be heard until afterwards and the action taken may be given, or may attract, immediate publicity[1].

1 For a more detailed discussion, see para 9.194 below.

9.136 The FSMA 2000 allows own-initiative action to take effect either[1] immediately, if the first supervisory notice states that this is the case, or on such date as may be specified in the notice, or, if no date is specified in the notice, when the matter to which the notice relates is no longer open to review[2]. Action may be imposed immediately or on a specified date only if the FSA, having regard to the ground on which it is exercising its own-initiative power, reasonably considers it necessary for the action to take effect immediately or on the specified date[3]. Broadly, this equates with urgent action, although there may be other reasons for specifying a particular date. The factors relevant to the decision of whether urgent action should be taken are considered at para 9.196 ff below.

1 FSMA 2000, s 53(2) or, for incoming firms, s 197(1).
2 As to the meaning of 'no longer open to review', see para 9.174 below.
3 FSMA 2000, s 53(3) or, for incoming firms, s 197(2) and see further the discussion at para 9.196 below.

9.137 Given the potential consequences for the firm of action being imposed immediately on a summary basis, and the statutory requirements for the FSA reasonably[1] to consider that urgent action is necessary and to specify in its first supervisory notice its reasons for determining that such action is warranted, there is clearly scope for firms to challenge the imposition of action on a short timeframe[2].

1 Or, in the case of urgent action against an incoming firm, the word 'reasonably' is omitted: see para 9.196 below.
2 This is contemplated in the Tribunal's Rules, which in certain circumstances allow the Tribunal to suspend the FSA's action: see para 6.104 ff above. See also the discussion at para 9.214 below.

What is the effect of the first supervisory notice?

9.138 The first supervisory notice is the first formal step in the enforcement process and it gives the firm various rights. However, because of the FSA's ability to take immediate action, it may also have more serious immediate consequences[1].

1 Contrast a warning notice: see para 5.78 above.

9.139 The effect of a first supervisory notice is as follows:

- it gives the firm the right to refer the matter to the Tribunal[1];
- it gives the firm the right to make representations to the FSA within the period specified in the notice[2];
- it may have a more substantive effect, depending upon what is stated in the notice:
  - if it specifies that the proposed action takes effect immediately, then the action takes effect immediately;
  - if it specifies that the proposed action takes effect on a particular date, then the action will take effect on that date without any further notice being issued by the FSA, unless the firm can, in the meantime, either persuade the FSA not to take the action or persuade the Tribunal to suspend the action;
  - if it does not specify any date when the action takes effect, then the action will not take effect until, broadly, the enforcement process is completed[3].

1 See para 9.140 below.
2 See para 9.143 below.
3 That is, when the matter is 'no longer open to review': for the meaning of this phrase, see para 9.174 below.

The firm's right to refer the matter to the Tribunal

9.140 The firm has an immediate right to refer the matter to the Tribunal[1]. It need not wait to make representations to the FSA or for the issue of a second supervisory notice[2]. Any reference must be made within 28 days of the date on which the first supervisory notice was given[3].

1 The FSMA 2000 omits specifically to provide any such right in relation to incoming firms, but seems to imply that there is such a right: see the discussion at para 9.176 below.

2 Contrast the position where the warning/decision procedure is prescribed: see Chapter 5 above.
3 FSMA 2000, s 133(1) and see para 6.36 above. This is subject to the Tribunal allowing references to be made out of time in certain circumstances: see para 6.37 above. For a further discussion of referring the FSA's own-initiative action to the Tribunal, see para 9.176 below. As to the procedure for making a reference to the Tribunal, see para 6.33 ff above.

9.141 The right to refer the matter to the Tribunal at this early stage is a necessary safeguard because the action proposed may take effect as a matter of urgency, before the remainder of the process is undergone. The firm's right to do so is not, however, limited to urgent cases although, in practice, firms may be unlikely to exercise the right in other cases.

9.142 The 28-day time limit needs to be kept in mind, particularly if the firm wishes first to make representations to the FSA. Losing the ability to refer the first supervisory notice to the Tribunal should not, however, affect the firm's ability subsequently to refer the second supervisory notice to the Tribunal.

Stage 3: Representations from the firm

9.143 Following the issue of the first supervisory notice, the firm has the right to make representations to the FSA within the period specified in the notice. We consider here, first, whether the firm can obtain further time to make its representations, second, why it should consider making representations and, finally, various points relating to how those representations should be made.

Can the firm request additional time?

9.144 The period within which the firm must make any representations will have been determined by the FSA without reference to the firm (although the FSA has indicated that it will normally be 28 days[1]). This may be insufficient, the firm may have had little idea that it would receive a supervisory notice and key people may be unavailable. There could be many reasons why the firm needs extra time. Can it obtain extra time?

1 See para 9.133 above.

9.145 The FSA Handbook allows the firm to request additional time for making representations, by making a written request to the FSA within 14 days of receiving the first supervisory notice, if it considers that the period stated in the notice is too short[1]. The request will be considered by the RDC and the decision will be notified promptly to the firm[2].

1 See the FSA Handbook at DEC 4.4.4.
2 See the FSA Handbook at DEC 4.4.5.

9.146 No guidance is given on what factors the FSA will take into account in deciding whether to accede to such a request. It seems likely that the same factors will be taken into account as were relevant to the original decision on the period for representations[1]. How the FSA applied these factors in its original decision should be apparent from the first supervisory notice and the reasons given in that notice as to why the FSA reached that original decision should therefore be in the firm's mind in deciding how to frame its request. In practice, if it is apparent that the FSA's decision was influenced largely by a perceived risk to the FSA's regulatory objectives of any delay in imposing the proposed action, then it may be unlikely that the firm will be able to obtain any significant extension of time, at least without persuading the FSA that the risk can be safeguarded in the meantime.

1 These are discussed at para 9.133 above.

9.147 The need for any requests for additional time to be made within 14 days of receiving the first supervisory notice must be borne in mind. This may cause difficulty in practice as it may not be apparent until further on in the process of preparing for representations that additional time is required. No indication has been given as to whether the RDC will consider a request outside that period[1].

1 The FSMA 2000 (ss 53(6) and 197(5)) provides only that the FSA 'may' extend the period allowed under the notice for making representations. It does not specifically require the FSA to consider any such request in every case.

Why should the firm make representations?

9.148 Given that the firm has the option of referring the matter to the Tribunal at this stage, that it is under no obligation to make any representations, and that there are no formal settlement or mediation provisions, firms may ask why they should make any representations at all. It is not clear whether representations will, in this context, be a one-way process, without the engaging of views which would take place in a settlement process[1]. Also, the firm will not have had the benefit of the FSA's material[2], so may not fully understand the case it has to meet. Nonetheless, whilst there may be occasions when the firm would rather await the Tribunal, these will be relatively rare, particularly given the publicity likely to arise from the Tribunal process[3]. Thus, this is the firm's main opportunity to influence the decision, with a view to avoiding incurring the time, cost, publicity and aggravation of Tribunal proceedings. There is not a great deal to be lost and there could be much to be gained. At best, it may be possible to dissuade the FSA from taking the action. Perhaps more realistically, it may be possible to persuade the FSA to soften its stance in certain respects important to the firm. There may therefore be a variety of different reasons for wanting to engage in the representations process and in most (non-urgent) cases, it is likely that firms will want to do so.

1 Contrast the warning/decision notice procedure: see para 5.116 ff above.
2 Again, contrast the warning/decision notice procedure: see para 5.81 ff above.
3 Tribunal proceedings are, generally speaking, held in public: see para 6.32 above.

9.149 One consideration that may be important, particularly if the matter could give rise to civil proceedings by or against the firm, is the risk of producing or receiving from the FSA written material which could carry disclosure implications in the context of any civil legal proceedings. This issue is discussed at para 4.189 ff above.

Does the firm have to make representations?

9.150 The firm is not under any obligation to make representations to the RDC.

How are representations made?

9.151 If the firm does wish to make representations, then they can be made either in writing or orally or, probably, both[1].

1 See the FSA Handbook at DEC 4.4.6 to 4.4.11.

9.152 ***Making written representations*** The firm's primary response will normally be a written one. Any written representations are required to be sent to the FSA, at the address stated in the first supervisory notice[1].

1 See the FSA Handbook at DEC 4.4.6.

9.153 Precisely what points the firm makes in its written representations will plainly depend upon the particular circumstances. Neither the FSMA 2000 nor the FSA's rules prescribes any limitations on the nature or content of the written representations the firm can make[1]. This is an important opportunity for the firm to have an input into the process. The sorts of areas which it might want to consider covering include:

- any reasons why the statutory test for applying the own-initiative power was not passed (for example, the reasons why the firm is not likely to fail to fulfil the threshold conditions or does not pose a risk to consumers);
- any reasons why the FSA's concerns are misconceived, or should not concern the FSA to the extent that they do or should not result in any action being taken;
- any reasons why the action proposed is inappropriate to address the concerns;
- any steps the firm has taken to address the concerns (and why in light of this no further action is required from the FSA);
- any particular reputational or other issues relevant to the decision; and
- any mitigating factors.

1 As noted below, the RDC can limit oral representations.

9.154 ***Making oral representations*** If the firm wishes to make oral representations[1], it will need to notify this request in writing to the FSA at the address stated in the first supervisory notice, at least five business days before the end of the period for representations specified in the notice. The notification is required to specify the matters on which the person wishes to make oral representations, include an estimate of how much time the representations will take and provide the names of any legal representatives appointed to attend[2].

1 See the FSA Handbook at DEC 4.4.7 to 4.4.11.

2 The firm is entitled to appoint a representative (who may be a lawyer) to attend the meeting and who makes, or assists, in making, the representations: see the FSA Handbook at DEC 4.4.9.

9.155 Whilst oral representations will normally be secondary to written ones, there are a number of reasons why the firm might want to make oral representations. It might want the opportunity to highlight to the RDC particular aspects of its written points or, for example, air grievances which it has with the procedure. For some firms, it may be particularly important to have the opportunity to meet the decision maker.

9.156 Oral representations are made at a time and place specified by the RDC, as soon as is reasonably possible after receiving the notification. The FSA Handbook contains various provisions relating to such meetings[1]:

- the RDC may specify that the representations will be received in private. Whilst not expressly stated, this may indicate that in some circumstances they may be received in public, but no indication has been given of when this might be appropriate and in general this process ought to be private[2];
- the firm may appoint a representative (who can be a lawyer) to attend the meeting and make, or assist it in making, the representations[3];
- the RDC may limit the type, length and content of any representations;
- the RDC may ask the person or his representative to clarify any issue arising out of the representations;
- the RDC may require the person (and any representative[4]) to leave the meeting after they have made their representations.

1 See the FSA Handbook at DEC 4.4.10.
2 Note that there are restrictions on publication regarding warning and decision notices (see FSMA 2000, s 391(1) and the discussion at para 5.76 above) but these do not apply to supervisory notices.
3 See the FSA Handbook at DEC 4.4.9.
4 The use of the word 'and' does not appear to contemplate the RDC requiring the representative alone to leave the meeting.

9.157 It will be important in practice, particularly to avoid unnecessary references to the Tribunal, that the procedure adopted is one which allows the firm to come away feeling it has been fairly heard and properly treated. With this in mind, the provision allowing firms to be assisted by legal or other representatives is clearly important.

Making no representations

9.158 It is open to the firm not to respond to the first supervisory notice or make any representations, and if it takes this approach then three additional provisions of the FSA Handbook are relevant.

9.159 First, if the firm notifies the FSA that it wishes to make oral representations, but then chooses not do so so, the RDC will nevertheless decide the matter[1].

1 See the FSA Handbook at DEC 4.4.8.

9.160 Second[1], if the FSA receives no response or representations by the time a decision is to be made about the issuing of the second supervisory notice, the RDC may regard the allegations or matters in the first supervisory notice as undisputed and give a second supervisory notice accordingly. This does not, however, preclude the firm from referring the matter to the Tribunal[2].

1 See the FSA Handbook at DEC 4.4.13.
2 It is thought that the fact that the RDC was entitled, by virtue of this provision of the FSA's rules, to regard the matter as undisputed should not of itself affect the Tribunal's view of what action it is appropriate for the FSA to take.

9.161 Third[1], there is a provision allowing firms to make late representations after receiving the second supervisory notice where they can show in exceptional cases on reasonable grounds that they did not receive the first supervisory notice or had reasonable grounds for not responding within the specified period. Whilst this seeks to provide additional flexibility, the provision envisages the issue of a further supervisory notice the status of which is unclear[2].

1 See the FSA Handbook at DEC 4.4.14.
2 It is not clear on what basis a further notice could be issued, at least unless the FSA revokes the second supervisory notice and issues a new, first supervisory notice. Contrast the warning/decision notice procedure, where there is specific provision allowing a further decision notice to be issued: see para 5.184 above.

Stage 4: The second supervisory notice

9.162 The next stage is for the RDC to consider the oral and written representations that have been made, if any, and to decide, in the light of those representations, what action, if any, to take.

What decision does the RDC make?

9.163 The RDC considers any representations and decides[1]:

- whether or not to take the action proposed;
- if the action has already been taken[2], whether or not to rescind the action; and
- whether to take the action in a different way to that proposed in the first supervisory notice.

1 See the FSA Handbook at DEC 3.1.8/9.
2 For example, because it was specified in the first supervisory notice to take immediate effect or to take effect on a specified date which has now passed: see para 9.139 above.

What happens if the RDC decides to take no action?

9.164 If the RDC decides not to take any action, or to rescind the action which has already been taken, then it must give the firm a written notice[1]. This is not a supervisory notice, nor is it a notice of discontinuance[2]. It is simply a notice informing the firm of the FSA's decision.

1 FSMA 2000, s 53(8) and, for incoming firms, s 197(7) and see the FSA Handbook at ENF 3.7.16.
2 See para 5.165 above.

What happens if the RDC decides to take the action?

9.165 If the RDC decides to take the proposed action, or not to rescind action that has already been taken, then it must give the firm a second supervisory notice[1].

1 FSMA 2000, ss 53(7), 197(6) and 395(13) and see the FSA Handbook at DEC 3.1.9.

9.166 The second supervisory notice will[1] inform the firm of its right to refer the matter to the Tribunal (and provide an indication of the procedure on such a reference).

1 FSMA 2000, s 53(7), (9) and (11) and, for incoming firms, s 197(6), (8) and (10) and see the FSA Handbook at ENF 3.1.10(1).

9.167 References to the Tribunal are considered at para 9.176 ff below.

9.168 There is no requirement either under the FSMA 2000 or in the FSA Handbook for the second supervisory notice to give any reasons why the RDC decided to take the action. The firm may not therefore have any idea why its representations were rejected. There is, however, nothing to prevent the firm asking the FSA or the RDC voluntarily to provide details of their reasons, or to disclose the record of the RDC meeting at which the decision was made (which should include the reasons for the decision[1]). It may be helpful for firms to understand why their representations were rejected in order to preclude unnecessary references to the Tribunal[2].

1 For further details, see para 5.39 above.
2 If the matter is referred to the Tribunal, it may be possible to obtain disclosure of any documents recording the reasons for this decision, for example a record of the relevant RDC meeting: see para 6.73 above.

What happens if the RDC decides to take different action?

9.169 If the RDC decides to vary the firm's permission in a different way to that proposed in the first supervisory notice, then the provisions to which reference is made at para 9.166 above do not apply. Instead, the second supervisory notice must contain the same information as a first supervisory notice[1]. The consequences of this are not made clear either in the FSMA 2000 or in the FSA Handbook, but logically the result should be to put the process back to the first supervisory notice stage[2]. There will therefore be another opportunity for the firm to make representations, which the RDC will consider and following which it will decide whether to issue a second supervisory notice. The firm also has the normal rights to refer the matter to the Tribunal either immediately[3] or on issue of the subsequent 'second' supervisory notice[4]. As should be apparent, in non-urgent cases this could involve a fairly cumbersome process.

1 FSMA 2000, s 53(10) and, for incoming firms, s 197(9) and see the FSA Handbook at DEC 3.1.10(2). As regards the contents of a first supervisory notice, see para 9.129 above.
2 Among other things, it otherwise makes no sense for the notice to give the firm an opportunity to make representations. Contrast the warning/decision notice procedure, where there is, first, some latitude in the decision that can be taken in a decision notice as compared with the warning notice that preceded it (see para 5.164 above) and, second, specific provision allowing the issue of a further decision notice without a warning notice (with the firm's consent: see para 5.184 ff above).
3 See para 9.140 above.
4 See para 9.166 above.

What are the consequences of the FSA issuing a second supervisory notice?

9.170 The second supervisory notice represents the conclusion of the enforcement process from the FSA's internal point of view. It means that the FSA has decided that the action it proposed in its first supervisory notice is appropriate. It is not, however, necessarily determinative of that question because the matter could come to be heard by the Tribunal.

9.171 There are, therefore, two interlinked consequences of the FSA issuing a second supervisory notice:

- the firm has the right to refer the FSA's decision to the Tribunal; and
- the decision may take effect.

9.172 The firm's right to refer the matter to the Tribunal is considered at para 9.176 below. As to when the decision takes effect, as has been seen, own-initiative action can take effect either immediately on the issue of the first supervisory notice, or on a specified date or when the matter is no longer open to review[1]. Thus, in many instances, the decision will already have taken effect by the time the second supervisory notice is issued, because it took effect immediately on the issue of the first supervisory notice or on a specified date which has already passed. In those cases, the decision to which the second supervisory notice relates is the decision not to rescind the action already taken. In such cases, the second supervisory notice does not have any effect on the action which the FSA has taken.

1 For a more detailed discussion, see para 9.135 ff above.

9.173 In other cases, the action may not yet have taken effect, either because the specified date has not yet occurred (although this may be unlikely by this stage) or because the matter is not yet 'no longer open to review'. In those cases, the decision to which the second supervisory notice relates is the FSA's decision to impose that action.

9.174 A matter to which a supervisory notice relates is still open to review if[1]:

- the period during which any person may refer it to the Tribunal is still running;

- the matter has been referred to the Tribunal but has not been dealt with;
- the matter has been referred to the Tribunal and dealt with but the period during which an appeal may be brought against the Tribunal's decision is still running; or
- such an appeal has been brought but not yet determined.

1 FSMA 2000, s 391(8).

9.175 Once the matter is no longer open to review, own-initiative action for which no effective date was specified in the first supervisory notice takes effect[1].

1 FSMA 2000, s 53(2) and, for incoming firms, s 197(1).

Stage 5: Referring the matter to the Tribunal

9.176 The Tribunal[1] has an important role in relation to the exercise of the FSA's own-initiative powers. So far as variations of permission are concerned, the FSMA 2000 provides[2] that an authorised person who is aggrieved by the exercise of the FSA's own initiative power may refer the matter to the Tribunal. There is no equivalent provision relating to the imposition of intervention on incoming firms. However, the FSMA 2000 clearly envisages that there is a right to refer that decision to the Tribunal[3] and it is therefore not thought that this omission is significant.

1 The Financial Services and Markets Tribunal: see para 6.4 above.
2 FSMA 2000, s 55(2).
3 For example, it requires the supervisory notice to make this clear: FSMA 2000, s 197(4) and (8).

When can a reference be made to the Tribunal?

9.177 The firm has the right to refer the matter to the Tribunal on the issue of either the first or second supervisory notice. In either case, it must do so before the end of the period of 28 days beginning with the date on which the supervisory notice was given[1], subject to the Tribunal deciding to allow the reference to be made out of time[2].

1 As to when notice was given, for the detailed rules on the service of notices, see the Financial Services and Markets Act 2000 (Service of Notices) Regulations 2001, SI 2001/1420.
2 FSMA 2000, s 133(1) and (2). For a more detailed discussion of this provision, and the Tribunal rules on making references out of time, see para 6.36 ff above.

9.178 The nature and rules of the Tribunal, and the procedure on a reference to it, are considered in detail in Chapter 6 above. For present purposes, it may be worth underlining some key points.

What is the Tribunal?

9.179 The Tribunal is a statutory tribunal[1] operated by the Lord Chancellor's Department under rules made by that Department. It is entirely independent from the FSA. The Tribunal is not an appeal body. It is a first instance tribunal. Among other things[2], it has the power to consider any relevant evidence whether or not available to the FSA at the time it made its decision and it is the FSA, not the firm, that bears the burden of proof.

1 FSMA 2000, s 132.
2 See para 6.4 ff above.

What does the Tribunal do?

9.180 The purpose of the Tribunal in considering a matter referred to it is to determine what (if any) is the appropriate action for the FSA to take in relation to the matter referred to it[1]. It therefore considers what action is appropriate in the particular case, unfettered by the decision-making process that went before. The Tribunal may also, on determining a reference, make recommendations as to the FSA's rules or procedures[2].

1 FSMA 2000, s 133(4), and see para 6.137 ff above.
2 FSMA 2000, s 133(8), and see para 6.140 ff above.

9.181 The firm aggrieved by the FSA's decision therefore has the opportunity to argue before the Tribunal any points whatsoever that are relevant to that decision. This could include, for example, whether the statutory test for imposing the own-initiative power was passed, whether the action proposed or taken is appropriate and in some cases it may be relevant also to raise any issues the firm may have about the FSA's procedures or the way that they were implemented in the particular case.

When should the firm consider making a reference to the Tribunal?

9.182 Whether the firm should refer a particular case to the Tribunal will depend very much upon the circumstances. In deciding whether or not to do so, relevant factors are likely to include the nature and seriousness of the action which the FSA has taken or wishes to take, the potential publicity which could arise from Tribunal proceedings[1] and the time and cost of the process. For example, if the FSA's action has a significant impact on the firm's business or reputation, it may well be appropriate to refer the matter to the Tribunal. Alternatively, in some cases the firm may regard the matter as giving rise to issues of principle. In other cases, the firm may not regard a reference to the Tribunal as worthwhile, particularly if the action which the FSA proposes would not materially affect its business and, perhaps, would not otherwise attract significant adverse publicity. There will therefore be a range of factors to balance in each case.

1 Tribunal proceedings are generally speaking held in public: see para 6.32 above.

Stage 6: Publication of the FSA's action

9.183 Generally speaking, transparency, deterrence, consumer education and market confidence provide strong policy reasons militating in favour of the

FSA publishing its successful enforcement action. As we will see, this general policy applies equally to the own-initiative powers.

Is the FSA entitled to publish its own-initiative action?

9.184 In contrast with the issue of warning and decision notices[1], there is no statutory prohibition on the publication of information relating to a supervisory notice. Rather:

- the FSMA 2000 is silent on publication until the supervisory notice takes effect;
- once the supervisory notice takes effect, the FSA is under a duty to publish such information about the matter to which the supervisory notice relates as it considers appropriate[2];
- this is subject to the proviso that it may not publish information if publication would, in its opinion, be unfair to the person with respect to whom the action was taken or prejudicial to the interests of consumers[3];
- if the FSA does decide to publish information, then it may do so in such manner as it considers appropriate[4].

1 FSMA 2000, s 391(1) and see para 5.76 above.
2 FSMA 2000, s 391(5).
3 FSMA 2000, s 391(6).
4 FSMA 2000, s 391(7).

9.185 Several points should be noted. First, there is nothing to prohibit the FSA from publishing information about a supervisory notice before the notice takes effect, provided it does not breach the statutory prohibition against the disclosure of confidential information[1].

1 For a discussion of the prohibition, and the Gateway Regulations which allow certain types of disclosure, see para 4.304 ff above.

9.186 Second, it is not entirely clear when a supervisory notice 'takes effect'. It is likely that this is intended to refer to the time when the action to which the supervisory notice relates takes effect[1].

1 As to when this occurs, see para 9.136 above. On an alternative, rather literal, reading, a supervisory notice 'takes effect' when the notice is issued by the FSA, at which time, for example, it gives the firm the right to make representations or refer the matter to the Tribunal. It is unlikely that this is what the provision was intended to mean since the FSA would then be under an obligation to publish information notwithstanding that no action may have yet been taken, or indeed be likely to be taken for some time.

9.187 Third, given that the action can take effect, and be published, immediately on issue of the first supervisory notice, before the firm has had any opportunity to be involved, the provision requiring the FSA not to publish if publication would, in its opinion, be unfair to the firm (or prejudicial to consumers) is clearly important. However, whether there is any 'unfairness to the firm' is a judgement to be made by the FSA. Is it likely in practice that the FSA would reach a view that it would be unfair to the firm to publish its action in a situation where it is also sufficiently concerned about the position to regard urgent action as being necessary[1]?

1 This, and various other practical issues that arise when firms are confronted with urgent action, is considered further at para 9.211 below.

9.188 Finally, in order to understand the FSA's policy, discussed below, on when it will publish information about a supervisory notice, and what information it will publish, it should be noted that the FSA is required to maintain a public record of information about firms[1]. Among other things, the record must include information about the services which the firm holds itself out to provide[2]. Apart from certain minimum requirements, though, the FSA is required to record only such information as it considers appropriate[3].

1 FSMA 2000, s 347.
2 FSMA 2000, s 347(2)(a)(i).
3 FSMA 2000, s 347(2).

In what circumstances will the FSA publish its own-initiative action?

9.189 The FSA approaches the question of publicity on a case-by-case basis depending upon the nature of the action taken and the circumstances of the case[1].

1 See the FSA Handbook at ENF 3.7.3.

9.190 The FSA will not normally publish a supervisory notice issued in support of its supervisory (as distinct from enforcement) function, which does not bring about a fundamental change to the firm's permission, where this would disclose confidential information about the firm or would prejudice consumers' interests[1].

1 See the FSA Handbook at ENF 3.7.4.

9.191 However, where the matter is a serious one which arises in the context of the FSA's enforcement function, different considerations apply[1]. The FSA regards the publication of fundamental variations of permission (and similar intervention action in relation to incoming firms), and the maintenance of an accurate public record, as important elements of its approach to consumer protection. It will aim to balance the interests of consumers and the possibility of unfairness to the firm. Therefore, the FSA will publish, and include in the public record, relevant details of fundamental variations of permission (and equivalent intervention action), but will use its discretion not to do so if it considers this would best serve the interests of the firm's existing customers.

1 See the FSA Handbook at ENF 3.7.5.

9.192 This leaves a range of 'non-fundamental' action arising from the FSA's enforcement function, in relation to which the FSA has provided no indication of how it will normally approach the question of publication. Overall, firms' expectations should be that the FSA's action will be published in most serious cases. This gives rise to difficult practical issues from the firm's perspective where the FSA takes urgent action. These are discussed at para 9.211 ff below.

Can the firm object to publication?

9.193 Since the FSA recognises that publication may be unfair to the firm, or not in the interests of consumers, there may be scope for the firm to discuss with the FSA the nature and extent of any publicity relating to its action, and to try to stress any particular factors militating against publication, or certain types of publication, in the particular case[1]. However, ultimately, the FSA has a significant amount of discretion in what action it takes to publicise the matter and it will be difficult for the firm to challenge, or prevent the FSA from taking, action which the FSA regards as appropriate, at least unless the FSA acts wholly unreasonably. There is, for example, no right to refer the issue of publication to the Tribunal. As to other possible methods and grounds of challenge, see Chapter 16 below.

1 It may be possible to press the FSA to explain why publication is needed in the particular case, given the risks to consumers, the nature of the business, and so on.

URGENT ACTION

9.194 The FSMA 2000 allows the FSA to take own-initiative action against firms as a matter of urgency. This is achieved by the FSA specifying, when issuing the first supervisory notice[1], that the proposed action takes effect immediately or on a specified date[2]. The scope and flexibility of the own-initiative powers has already been highlighted[3] and it is important to appreciate at the outset that there are no limitations on the type of action that can be taken on an urgent basis.

1 FSMA 2000, s 53(2) and, for incoming firms, s 197(1).
2 Taking action on a specified date can equate with taking urgent action (for example, it could be used to give the firm a limited opportunity to challenge the action or dissuade the FSA before the action takes effect). However, it need not always do so; there may be reasons other than urgency for specifying a particular date.
3 See para 9.85 above.

9.195 From the firm's perspective, the prospect of immediate action being taken against it by its regulator raises a number of serious issues. What immediate steps should it take? Does it have any opportunity or ability to object to the process? What publicity will arise? How can it protect its business? In the following paragraphs, we review the provisions relating to urgent action, and in particular:

- when in practice will the FSA take urgent action?
- the procedure for FSA decision making in urgent cases; and
- practical guidance for firms facing urgent action.

When in practice will the FSA take urgent action?

9.196 The FSA may take urgent action only if it reasonably considers this necessary having regard to the ground on which it is exercising its own-initiative power[1]. Perhaps in recognition of the serious potential consequences of the summary powers conferred, this involves a higher hurdle for the FSA than many of the statutory tests found in the FSMA[2]. The use of the word 'necessary'[3] and the express need for reasonableness add a certain amount of objectivity[4]. However, the question whether urgent action should be taken is nonetheless largely within the FSA's discretion and it will be difficult for firms to challenge the imposition of urgent action on the basis that the test was not met. The key question for firms is therefore how the FSA exercises that discretion.

1 FSMA 2000, s 53(3) and, for incoming firms, s 197(2) (although this omits the word 'reasonably': see footnote 4 below).
2 Compare, for example, the tests for the imposition of own-initiative powers (see para 9.7 ff above) or the tests for the use of the FSA's investigation powers (see Chapter 4 above).
3 See footnote 1 to para 9.77 ff above.
4 The word 'reasonably' is only found in s 53(3). It is not, though, clear whether the word 'reasonable' adds anything to the FSA's general public law duties. The FSA is, in any event, not entitled to act 'unreasonably' in the *Wednesbury* sense of acting so unreasonably that no reasonable body could have acted in that way. Whether the test here raises this threshold depends upon the meaning of 'reasonable' in this context and in particular whether it connotes a higher standard than *Wednesbury* reasonableness.

9.197 The FSA will consider exercising its powers as a matter of urgency where[1]:

- the information available to it indicates serious concerns about the firm or its business that need to be addressed immediately; and
- circumstances indicate that it is appropriate to use statutory powers immediately to require and/or prohibit certain actions by the firm in order to ensure the firm addresses these concerns.

1 See the FSA Handbook at ENF 3.5.11.

9.198 Such situations are likely to include one or more of the following characteristics[1]:

- information indicating significant loss, risk of loss or other adverse effects for consumers, where action is necessary to protect their interests;
- information indicating that a firm's conduct has put it at risk of being used for the purposes of financial crime, or of being otherwise involved in crime;
- evidence that the firm has submitted to the FSA inaccurate or misleading information so that the FSA becomes seriously concerned about the firm's ability to meet its regulatory obligations; and/or
- circumstances suggesting a serious problem within the firm or with the firm's controllers[2] that calls into question the firm's ability to continue to meet the threshold conditions[3].

1 See the FSA Handbook at ENF 3.5.12.
2 Broadly, this refers to a person who exercises control over the firm: see the FSA Handbook at ENF Glossary of Definitions.
3 The threshold conditions are outlined at para 2.39 above.

9.199 The FSA also needs to consider whether the urgent exercise of its powers is an appropriate response to such concerns. The FSA has indicated that in doing so it will consider the full circumstances of the case, but has identified a number of factors that may be relevant including the following[1]:

- the extent of any loss or risk of loss or other adverse effect on consumers;
- the extent to which customer assets appear to be at risk;
- the nature or extent of any false or inaccurate information provided by the firm;
- the seriousness of any suspected breaches and the steps that need to be taken to correct them;
- the financial resources of the firm, particularly where the firm may be required to pay significant compensation to consumers;
- the risk of the firm's business being used to facilitate crime;
- the risk that a firm's conduct or business presents to the financial system;
- the firm's compliance history and its conduct since the issue arose; and
- the impact that the use of the powers will have on the firm's business and its customers, including the effect on the firm's reputation and on market confidence[2].

1 For a full list, see the FSA Handbook at ENF 3.5.13.
2 The FSA recognises the need to be satisfied that the impact of any own-initiative action is proportionate to the concerns being addressed, in the context of the overall aim of achieving its statutory objectives.

9.200 Urgent own-initiative action is different from other types of enforcement action in one significant respect. It is normally taken by the FSA on a summary basis, without the firm having any opportunity to be heard, any review of the decision, or challenge, taking place only afterwards. This is reflected in the use of words such as 'information indicating', 'circumstances suggesting' and 'suspected breach'. The FSA will be considering whether to take action not following an exhaustive enquiry but on a summary basis because of particularly serious concerns and based on the information available to it at the time. The serious potential effect of taking action on this basis should mean that the power is used only where justified by the seriousness and immediacy of the concerns.

The procedure for taking urgent action

9.201 As we have seen, own-initiative action falls generally into two different categories: action which would make a fundamental change to the nature of the firm's permission, and action which would not[1]. In principle, the need for urgent action could arise in either category. Normally, decisions relating to fundamental action are taken by the Regulatory Decisions Committee[2], and decisions relating to non-fundamental action are taken by the FSA's executive procedures[3]. In urgent cases, however, there are slightly different decision-making procedures.

1 As to what constitutes a fundamental change to the firm's permission, see para 9.118 above.
2 See para 9.110 above.
3 See para 9.220 below.

Urgent fundamental variations of permission

9.202 When the FSA staff make a recommendation in relation to an urgent, fundamental matter, the following procedure applies[1]:

- in general, but subject to the need to act swiftly, the recommendation will be put before a panel of the RDC;
- in an urgent case where, in the opinion of the FSA staff, the action proposed should occur before it is practicable to convene an RDC panel, the recommendation will be put before the Chairman or a Deputy Chairman of the RDC and where possible (but subject to the need to act swiftly) one other RDC member;
- in an exceptionally urgent case, where, in the FSA's opinion:
  - — the action should take effect before it is possible to make a recommendation to the Chairman of the RDC, and
  - — an urgent decision on the proposed action is necessary to protect the interests of consumers,

the recommendation will be put before a member of the FSA's executive of at least director of division level[2]. In these circumstances, the FSA will ensure so far as possible that the person making the decision has not been involved in establishing the evidence on which the decision is based, but there may be exceptional cases where this does not occur, as discussed below.

1 See the FSA Handbook at DEC 4.5.7.
2 This is a senior level of management within the FSA.

9.203 A number of points should be noted. First, the decision to issue the first supervisory notice could, as a result, be taken, not by a full panel of the RDC, but by the RDC Chairman or a Deputy Chairman alone or even in some cases by senior staff within the FSA.

9.204 Second, where the recommendation is put before a member of the FSA's staff, the FSA Handbook makes clear that there may be cases where that person was involved in investigating the matter. In that situation, the statutory requirement for the separation of functions[1] may not be complied with. This is permitted[2] provided the FSA considers this necessary in the particular case in order to protect the interests of consumers and provided the decision is taken by a person of the seniority laid down by the FSA's procedures. The FSA has indicated that this may happen in cases where the FSA believes action is needed to protect the interests of consumers in the face of a material threat to those interests but where the requirements for the separation of functions cannot be met[3]. In such a case the decision will be made by a person of at least director of division level or a member of a committee which reports directly to the FSA Chairman's Committee[4]. This ought to occur only in the most critical and urgent cases, where it is impracticable to ensure the separation of functions because of the urgency of the matter.

1 FSMA 2000, s 395(2): see para 9.108 above.
2 FSMA 2000, s 395(3).
3 See the FSA Handbook at DEC 4.3.18.
4 See the FSA Handbook at DEC 4.3.19.

9.205 Third, the question of how urgent the matter is and therefore which route it is appropriate to take is a question for the FSA staff dealing with the matter, subject obviously to the ability of the person before whom the recommendation is put to question whether he is the appropriate person to consider the recommendation.

9.206 Fourth, the person before whom the recommendation is placed also takes the various associated decisions required to be taken at the same time[1], such as deciding on the period for the firm to make representations and when the action should take effect (which, in this situation, will normally be immediately).

1 For a more detailed discussion, see para 9.127 ff above.

9.207 Finally, any subsequent decisions (such as the consideration of any representations made by the firm and the decision whether to issue a second supervisory notice) are considered by the RDC in the normal way. Subject to the above, therefore, the procedure outlined at para 9.104 ff above applies.

9.208 It should be apparent that, taken overall, this procedure gives the FSA staff some latitude in dealing with the matter. Most notably, a decision to impose with immediate effect measures that could significantly affect the firm's business could in some circumstances be taken by the FSA's enforcement staff and those to whom they report. As has been seen[1], the Tribunal potentially has the ability to remedy any obvious mistakes or abuses but, first, it is not clear quite how that process will work or whether it will provide an effective remedy in practice and, second, the risk is perhaps less that there will be obvious mistakes or abuses than that judgements may be made by those whose approach is not perceived as sufficiently independent. This clearly gives rise to practical issues for firms, as discussed below.

1 See para 6.104 ff above. Similarly, under the former regime, there was express provision in the rules of the SFA and IMRO allowing firms to apply for a stay of an intervention order, pending appeal.

Urgent non-fundamental variations of permission

9.209 In principle there is nothing to preclude urgent action being required in relation to a non-fundamental variation to the nature of a firm's permission (or equivalent action for incoming firms), although given the nature of the variations which ought to be encompassed within non-fundamental variations this may be less likely in practice.

9.210 The decision to take non-fundamental action can be taken either by an individual FSA staff member or by the FSA's 'senior staff committee'[1]. Where the decision is to be taken by an individual staff member, there is no prescribed procedure in urgent cases (and probably no need for such a procedure). However, where the decision is to be taken by the senior staff committee, the FSA Handbook prescribes that[2]:

- in general, but subject to the need to act swiftly in urgent cases, the FSA staff's recommendation will go before the senior staff committee (or a sub-committee)[3];
- in an urgent case, if, in the FSA staff's opinion, the action proposed should occur before it is practicable to convene a meeting of the senior staff committee (or sub-committee), the FSA staff's recommendation may be considered by the senior staff committee's chairman or a deputy chairman and, where possible, but subject to the need to act swiftly, one other member of the senior staff committee;
- in an exceptionally urgent case, if, in the FSA staff's opinion, the action should be taken before a recommendation to the chairman or a deputy chairman can be made, and an urgent decision about the proposed action is necessary to protect the interest of consumers, the FSA staff's recommendation will be considered and the decision made by a member of the FSA's executive of at least director of division level.

This is very similar to the procedure applicable in urgent fundamental cases, considered at para 9.202 ff above (save that references to the RDC are instead to the senior staff committee).

1 See para 9.225 ff below.
2 See the FSA Handbook at DEC 4.3.12.
3 See para 9.226 below.

Practical guidance for firms facing urgent action

9.211 From the firm's perspective, the first that it may know about the action against it may be when it receives a first supervisory notice setting out the variation decided upon and when it takes effect, the FSA having by then already decided that urgent action is necessary. That action may substantially affect the firm's business and it will not only take effect immediately, before the firm has had any opportunity to have any input into the process, but is also likely to be publicised immediately. How should the firm react in that situation?

9.212 The answer will depend largely upon the particular situation. In deciding what to do, the firm will need to consider its position quickly and the following may be some of the questions it will need to ask itself:

- What, precisely, is the action the FSA is taking or requiring the firm to take? How does that action impact upon the firm's business? As has been seen[1], the own-initiative power is a flexible instrument. The FSA's action could range from preventing the firm from carrying out certain types of business, or indeed any further business, to requiring it to vest assets in a trustee, to requiring it to take certain steps with regard to its systems and controls or (possibly) prohibiting it from involving particular individuals in a particular area of business. Some action will have a greater effect on the firm's business than others.
- What are the reputational issues? The fact that urgent enforcement action has been taken is likely to be publicised and may have a serious reputational impact. But if the action arises in the context of an already well publicised regulatory matter, then the reputational impact may be rather less.
- If the firm has a large consumer clientele, how is the action likely to be perceived by them and what are the implications for consumer confidence?
- Are there any potential issues about damaging market confidence? Might the FSA's action itself have a negative impact upon market confidence?
- Might the FSA's action expose the firm to claims from third parties, for example market counterparties in areas of business in which the firm can no longer trade[2]?
- What knowledge does the firm currently have about the problems or concerns that underlie the FSA's actions? The firm may have had some involvement in the problem prior to receiving the FSA's first supervisory notice. Has it already investigated sufficiently thoroughly to take a strong position? If not, how secure can the firm be about what it now says to the FSA? To what extent is it possible to carry out urgent investigations?
- What are the firm's views of the underlying merits of the FSA's actions? Are the reasons given in the first supervisory notice for taking the action accurate, or at least within reasonable bounds and, in the firm's view, do they merit the action taken? Given those reasons, does the firm accept that there is a need for the FSA to take the action as a matter of urgency?

1 See para 9.80 ff above.
2 This issue has been highlighted and briefly discussed at paras 9.73 and 9.74 above.

9.213 Ultimately, if the firm wishes to challenge the FSA's action, it can refer the matter to the Tribunal and require the FSA to prove in that independent forum that its action was appropriate. However, that is likely to take some time and in the meantime there are likely to be two main issues of concern:

- can the firm prevent the FSA's action from taking effect?
- can it prevent the action from being publicised?

Can the firm prevent the FSA's urgent action from taking effect?

9.214 Where action is specified in the first supervisory notice to take immediate effect, the FSMA 2000 and the FSA Handbook do not give the firm any right to object to the action or to have the decision to take it reviewed by the FSA before it takes effect. However, if there are compelling reasons why the action should not be taken urgently, then it may be worth trying to contact the person who made the decision, to see if they are willing to consider those points and to alter their view. It may also be worth trying to contact the Chairman of the RDC, particularly if the decision was made by a member of the FSA's staff.

9.215 Assuming this is unsuccessful, the firm does have the right to refer the matter to the Tribunal and the Tribunal Rules permit the Tribunal to suspend the FSA's action pending the full hearing of the matter. This is discussed in more detail at para 6.104 above. In practice, given that the Tribunal will be considering the request for a suspension on an urgent basis, probably with minimal factual information, and with an assessment by the FSA that it is necessary to take action urgently, an application to suspend the FSA's action is likely to be successful only in cases of obvious mistake or abuse. Nonetheless, there may be little to be lost by making the application. It is not, though, clear from the Tribunal Rules whether and if so how it will be possible to convene the Tribunal on an urgent basis.

9.216 Alternatively, particularly if it is not possible to convene the Tribunal urgently[1], the firm may be able to apply for the FSA's action to be judicially reviewed by a court, and for the action to be stayed in the meantime. If there are ECHR grounds for objecting to the FSA's action, the firm may seek to commence normal court proceedings and to apply for a stay of the FSA's action in support of those proceedings. These options are outlined in more detail in Chapter 16 below.

1 The firm will, generally, need to show that there are no alternative remedies available: see further the discussion at para 16.18 below.

Can the firm prevent the FSA's action from being publicised?

9.217 Again, the FSMA 2000 and the FSA Handbook do not give the firm any right to object to the publication of urgent own-initiative action and publication is not, of itself, an issue that the firm can refer to the Tribunal. However, it may be that the action will not yet have been publicised by the time the firm receives the first supervisory notice so, in practice, there may be a window of opportunity to influence the decision on whether the matter should be publicised and, if so, what will be said.

9.218 The provisions of the FSMA 2000 and the FSA's policy regarding the publication of own-initiative action are outlined at para 9.183 ff above. As has been seen, the FSA may not publish information if, in its opinion, publication would be unfair to the person with respect to whom the action was taken or prejudicial to the interests of consumers. The firm may therefore wish to stress any unfairness to the firm or likely prejudice to consumers. The potential impact on market confidence may also be relevant.

ALTERNATIVE PROCEDURES IN SPECIFIC CASES

9.219 In the following paragraphs, we review two variants of the procedure, applicable in specific cases, namely:

- where the action proposed would involve a non-fundamental change to the nature of the firm's permission (or equivalent intervention action for an incoming firm) (para 9.220 ff below); and
- where the firm and the FSA agree on the need for the relevant action (para 9.232 ff below);

and, finally, a separate procedure applicable in certain cases involving EEA firms (para 9.236 ff below).

Non-fundamental changes to permission

9.220 If the variations which the FSA proposes to make to the firm's permission (or equivalent intervention action in relation to an incoming firm) would not make a fundamental change to the nature of the firm's permission then slightly different procedures apply[1]. In many cases, the exercise of the own-initiative power to make non-fundamental changes to permission will arise in the supervisory, rather than enforcement, context. However, it is plainly not limited to the supervisory context[2].

1 The meaning of 'fundamental change' is considered at para 9.118 above.
2 See, for example, the FSA Handbook at ENF 4.7.1.

9.221 The primary difference between this and the procedure for fundamental changes is that the FSA's decisions are in this case taken by what is known as 'executive procedures'. In other words, the RDC does not have responsibility for taking the FSA's decisions in the case, but they are instead taken by senior members of the FSA's staff. How this works is outlined below.

9.222 The procedure for non-fundamental changes is based on the same statutory framework as that for fundamental changes and, apart from the question of who takes the FSA's decisions, is the same as that outlined at para 9.104 ff above. At each stage of the process, the same rules and considerations apply, with the difference that references to the RDC need to be read as references to the FSA decision maker under the FSA's executive procedures.

9.223 In practice, from the firm's perspective, the considerations of how to deal with the FSA may be different in this context. If the variation which the FSA is seeking would have only limited effect on the firm's business and, for example, would not in any way damage the firm's reputation[1], then there may be less need to oppose the process. The firm may be equally concerned to safeguard its relationship with the FSA as to protect its own perceived interests and position.

1 For instance, minor variations may well not be published by the FSA: see para 9.190 above.

The FSA's executive procedures

9.224 Under the executive procedures, the FSA's decisions are made either:

- by an individual staff member; or
- by a 'senior staff committee'.

The FSA Handbook indicates that the FSA Chairman's Committee may from time to time determine that particular categories of decision will be made by a senior staff committee[1], but no indication has been given of what categories of decision this currently comprises. Otherwise, the decisions are made by an individual staff member.

1 See the FSA Handbook at DEC 4.3.1.

9.225 Where an individual staff member is to make the decision, the decision will be made by an executive director of the FSA Board (or his delegate, who must be at least the level of 'associate'), on the recommendation of an FSA staff member of at least the level of 'associate'[1] and with the benefit of legal advice from an FSA staff member of at least the same level[2]. The person concerned may consult with colleagues and may refer the matter to a more senior level if he considers it appropriate[3]. If he considers that the matter warrants collective consideration, he may either consult colleagues and then take the decision himself or may refer it to a senior staff committee for the decision to be taken by the committee.

1 Note that this will not necessarily involve anyone of any seniority in the FSA.
2 See the FSA Handbook at DEC 4.3.4. The person taking the decision is accountable to the FSA Board: see the FSA Handbook at DEC 4.3.5.
3 See the FSA Handbook at DEC 4.3.6.

9.226 Where a senior staff committee is to make the decision, the decision is made at a meeting of the committee or a sub-committee[1], including at least an individual with authority to act as chairman and two other members. The committee operates on the basis of a recommendation from an FSA staff member of at least the level of associate, and with the benefit of legal advice from an FSA staff member of at least the same level[2]. Generally, the recommendation will go before the committee or a sub-committee[3]. In urgent cases, a slightly different procedure may apply[4].

1 The 'senior staff committee' is a committee consisting of such FSA staff members as the FSA Chairman's Committee may from time to time determine. It is accountable for its decisions to the FSA Chairman's Committee and, through it, to the FSA Board. The committee may operate through standing or sub-committees to consider particular decisions or classes of decision, for which accountability lies through the committee: see the FSA Handbook at DEC 4.3.8 to 4.3.10.

2 See the FSA Handbook at DEC 4.3.11.
3 See the FSA Handbook at DEC 4.3.12.
4 See para 9.210 above.

9.227 ***Is there a separation of functions?*** In general[1], the decision-making process will comply with the statutory requirement for the separation of functions[2], so that the decision to give a supervisory notice will not be taken by a person directly involved in establishing the evidence on which that decision is based. However, there may be situations where it would be permissible under the FSMA 2000 for the FSA to make a decision without the separation of functions. The FSA's guidance on when it considers this may be appropriate, and the procedure in cases where it is, is considered at para 9.204 above[3].

1 See the FSA Handbook at DEC 4.3.3 and 4.3.17 to 4.3.19.
2 FSMA 2000, s 395(2) and see para 9.108 above.
3 The FSA indicated during the consultation process that this might be appropriate, for example when a director of division or managing director needs to talk directly to the senior management of the firm about the factual position in order to be able to make a decision. This guidance has not been repeated in the FSA Handbook.

9.228 ***Other safeguards for firms*** There are certain procedural safeguards for firms. The supervisory notice will identify the decision-maker[1]. The FSA has internal procedures requiring staff to disclose conflicts of interest, for consideration of whether the conflict precludes the staff member from being involved in taking the relevant decision[2]. In addition, the decision-maker is required to maintain a record equivalent to that maintained by the RDC[3].

1 See the FSA Handbook at DEC 4.3.13.
2 See the FSA Handbook at DEC 4.3.16.
3 See the FSA Handbook at DEC 4.3.15 and para 5.39 above.

9.229 ***Issues relating to the procedure*** Whilst it may be possible for the FSA to satisfy, in technical terms, the statutory requirement for the separation of functions by taking decisions in this way, the practical question for firms is whether this procedure is sufficient to ensure that a fair decision will be taken.

9.230 The FSA staff who investigated the firm decide whether the matter is suitable for this procedure, based on their view of whether or not the action proposed would amount to a fundamental change to the nature of the firm's permission. Many requirements which could be classified as 'non-fundamental' could be capable of causing a significant costs burden or disruption to the firm or impacting on its business or reputation. The same FSA staff members decide whether to propose that the action takes effect immediately. In many cases, the decision-maker will be one or more FSA staff members and they may decide that urgent action is necessary, and then publish that action, potentially with immediate financial and reputational effects on the firm but without the RDC, let alone the Tribunal, having considered the matter.

9.231 The importance of these procedures being used only where manifestly appropriate, and of decisions being taken appropriately where they are used, should be apparent. Whilst ultimately the fairness of the outcome can be tested in the Tribunal, for a variety of reasons firms may not wish to refer cases to the Tribunal and there are, generally, strong policy reasons for the FSA to seek to ensure that firms have confidence in its decision-making processes[1].

1 These general policy considerations are discussed at para 5.18 ff above.

Action with the firm's agreement

9.232 In some cases, the FSA will be in a position to inform the firm of its concerns and the action it is considering before it starts to exercise the statutory processes outlined at para 9.104 ff above. Where the firm consents to the action at that stage, the FSA may decide to use a simplified decision-making process.

9.233 The modified process is as follows[1]:

- the FSA staff make their recommendation of action to at least one other member of staff who is at an appropriate level of seniority and not directly involved in supervising the firm concerned or in establishing the evidence on which the decision is based;
- the senior staff consider the recommendation and, if they are satisfied that the firm agrees to the recommended action, consider whether the FSA should give a first supervisory notice[2];
- if they decide to give a first supervisory notice and, as expected, the firm accepts its terms, they consider whether to give a second supervisory notice confirming the decision[3];
- they only give the second supervisory notice if satisfied that the firm accepts the terms of the first supervisory notice and the circumstances of the case have not changed materially since the giving of that notice;
- if the FSA staff are not satisfied, or the circumstances of the case have changed, they refer consideration of whether to give a second supervisory notice to the RDC, which follows the normal procedures for the giving of second supervisory notices[4].

1 See the FSA Handbook at DEC 4.5.10 to 4.5.13.
2 For an explanation of a first supervisory notice, see para 9.127 ff above.
3 For an explanation of a second supervisory notice, see para 9.162 ff above.
4 See para 9.162 ff above.

9.234 From the firm's perspective, it is difficult to see that the process could cause any significant detriment. If the firm for some reason objects to the first supervisory notice when it is issued, it is able to make representations or refer the matter to the Tribunal in the normal way.

9.235 The primary downside to the firm would be that the first decision had been taken at the wrong level and, second, that the period for representations may be too short (but this can be addressed by asking for an extension of time).

Additional procedure for certain cases involving EEA firms

9.236 Where the FSA exercises its power of intervention in relation to an EEA firm exercising EEA rights in the UK[1], an additional procedure may apply. It applies if it appears to the FSA that its power of intervention is exercisable in relation to such a firm in respect of[2]:

- a contravention of a requirement imposed by the FSA under the FSMA 2000; and
- for the contravention of which any of the single market directives[3] provides that a procedure of the kind that follows shall apply[4].

1 This is a reference to its rights under FSMA 2000, s 3: see para 2.11 ff above.
2 FSMA 2000, s 199.
3 See footnote 1 to para 2.12 above.
4 The requirements to which the directives apply such procedures include the FSA's Conduct of Business sourcebook (which apply to incoming firms, with the exception of COB 9). See the FSA Handbook at ENF 4.5.6. For an example, see the Investment Services Directive, art 18.

9.237 The additional procedure is as follows[1]:

- the FSA must, in writing, require the firm to remedy the situation;
- if the firm fails to comply within a reasonable time, the FSA must give a notice to that effect to the firm's home state regulator, requesting it to:
  - — take all appropriate measures for the purpose of ensuring that the firm remedies the situation which has given rise to the notice, and
  - — inform the FSA of the measures it proposes to take or has taken or the reasons for not taking such measures,
- the FSA may not exercise its power of intervention unless satisfied that the firm's home state regulator has failed or refused to take measures for the purpose outlined above or that the measures taken have proved inadequate for that purpose;
- however, the FSA may nonetheless take urgent action in order to protect the interests of consumers before doing or being satisfied as to any of the above and, in such a case, must, at the earliest opportunity, inform the firm's home state regulator and the EU Commission (which has the power to require the FSA to rescind or vary the requirements it has imposed).

1 FSMA 2000, s 199 and see the FSA Handbook at ENF 4.5.5 and 4.5.7.

9.238 This means that where, in any situation, any of the criteria outlined above is fulfilled and the FSA wishes to exercise its power of intervention in relation to an incoming firm, it will first need to consider whether the additional procedure applies and then to comply with that procedure.

CANCELLATION OF PERMISSION

Introduction

9.239 The question of cancelling a firm's permission can arise either from an application by the firm or from the FSA's use of its own-initiative powers. In either case, the FSA has a right to cancel the firm's permission and, in certain circumstances, it may have a duty to do so[1]. An explanation of the cancellation of permission on the application of the firm, can be found in the FSA's Handbook at SUP Chapter 6.4.

1 The duty can also arise where the firm applies for a variation (rather than cancellation) of its permission.

9.240 Cancellation of permission does not arise in relation to incoming firms, save to the extent they have a 'top-up permission'[1].

1 For a brief explanation of top-up permissions, see para 2.14 above.

9.241 The cancellation of permission by the FSA on its own-initiative is the most serious application of its own-initiative power. The FSA has:

- the right, in relation to Cases A to D[1], not only to vary a firm's permission but to cancel it; and
- in any case, a duty to cancel the firm's permission if, as a result of the variation of permission, there are no longer any regulated activities for which the firm has permission and once the FSA is satisfied that it is no longer necessary to keep the permission in force[2].

1 These are four of the tests for the imposition of the FSA's own-initiative power and are discussed at para 9.7 ff above.
2 FSMA 2000, s 45(3).

9.242 We consider here, first, when the FSA will consider cancelling the firm's permission on its own initiative and, second, the consequences of it doing so.

When will the FSA consider cancelling the firm's permission?

9.243 The FSA will consider cancelling a firm's permission in three main circumstances[1], namely:

- where it has very serious concerns about a firm, or the way its business is or has been conducted; or
- where the firm's regulated activities have come to an end and it has not applied for cancellation of its permission; or
- when requested to do so by an overseas regulator.

1 See the FSA Handbook at ENF 5.5.1.

9.244 The first of these is the main, general criterion. The underlying concern is the FSA's obligation to ensure that the firm satisfies, and will continue to satisfy, the threshold conditions[1].

1 FSMA 2000, s 41(2).

9.245 The FSA has provided little guidance on when in practice it will exercise these powers[1]. It is thought that this may occur in similar circumstances to a variation of permission, but where the concerns relate to the whole or most of the firm's activities.

1 So far as concerns requests from overseas regulators, the FSA will consider whether or not it is required to cancel the permission in order to comply with a Community obligation. It will also consider the factors outlined at paras 9.35 ff and 9.39 ff above in relation to the exercise of its own-initiative powers generally in response to a request from an overseas regulator, as well as any specific request by the overseas regulator to cancel the firm's permission: see the FSA Handbook at ENF 5.5.7. In some situations, the FSA may be required to cancel the permission in order to comply with an obligation under one of the single market directives, in which case the expectation should be that it will do so.

Can the FSA choose not to cancel the firm's permission?

9.246 Even where the matter is extremely serious, it may be appropriate for the FSA to vary the firm's permission first, before seeking to cancel it. The reason is that, as will be seen, variation of permission can be accomplished as a matter of urgency, whereas cancellation cannot. In practice, a firm's permission can be varied in such a way as to have the same effect as cancellation, for example by removing all of the firm's regulated activities. In urgent and serious cases, this is how the FSA may deal with the issue[1].

1 See the FSA Handbook at ENF 5.5.4/5.

9.247 If the FSA does remove all the firm's regulated activities, it will be under an obligation to cancel the firm's permission once it is satisfied that it is no longer necessary to keep the permission in force[1]. On the wording of the provision, therefore, the obligation to cancel seems to arise only if the FSA is satisfied it is no longer necessary to keep the permission in force[2]. In other words, it is largely within the FSA's discretion.

1 FSMA 2000, s 45(3).
2 The alternative would have been an obligation to cancel unless the FSA was satisfied that it was necessary to keep the permission in force.

9.248 The FSA may prefer the firm to remain within the regulatory system for a period, and therefore not to cancel its permission, and it clearly believes that the FSMA 2000 enables it to do so. Examples of reasons given by the FSA in the enforcement context include to enable the FSA to[1]:

- continue to monitor the firm;
- use its administrative enforcement powers against the firm[2];
- supervise an orderly winding down of the firm's regulated business[3]; or

- impose a financial penalty on the firm[4].

1 See the FSA Handbook at ENF 5.5.6.
2 This refers to the powers which the FSA has generally in relation to the regulated community (such as, for example, investigation, discipline, making restitution orders, and so on). To a large extent, these could not be exercised against a formerly authorised person after its permission had been cancelled. The FSA may therefore want to preserve the person's status as an authorised person until it has taken the appropriate action: see also the FSA Handbook at SUP 6.4.24/25.
3 For further details, see the FSA Handbook at SUP 6.4. The FSA will not normally cancel a firm's permission on application from the firm until the firm can demonstrate that it has, in relation to business carried on under that permission, as appropriate: (i) ceased to carry on all regulated activities or fully run off or transferred all insurance liabilities: (ii) repaid all client money and client deposits: (iii) discharged custody assets and any other property belonging to clients: and (iv) discharged, satisfied or resolved complaints against the firm: see the FSA Handbook at SUP 6.4.19 to 6.4.22.
4 FSMA 2000, s 206. It is not, though, clear that the FSA could prevent a firm from carrying out any regulated activities but keep its permission in place in order to fine it, given the express statutory prohibition against both fining a firm and cancelling its permission: FSMA 2000, s 206(2).

9.249 The problem with this is that it is difficult to see where the line is drawn in practice between varying a firm's permission and cancelling it. The FSA can, through varying the firm's permission, effectively achieve the same as cancelling it, but without the firm having the same procedural safeguards. In some situations there may be reasons for doing so, for example the need to supervise the orderly winding down of the business (in the same way as the FSA would do if the firm had applied to cancel its permission[1]). As the above indicates, though, the FSA may choose not to cancel the firm's permission for purely enforcement related reasons. By the time it does seek to cancel permission, the additional procedural safeguards applicable to cancellations of permission may be of much less benefit to the firm[2]. In the meantime, the FSA would also retain its regulatory powers over the firm.

1 See footnote 3 to para 9.248 above.
2 If the FSA had decided to cancel the firm's permission at the outset when seeking to vary its permission, the cancellation of permission would have proceeded using the warning/decision notice procedure and as a result the firm would (among other things) have had a right to review the FSA's material at an early stage and without prejudice discussions may have taken place between the firm and the FSA which may have affected the outcome (see Chapter 5 above). The ultimate safeguard is, though, the right of referral to the Tribunal, which is available in any event.

9.250 If the firm does not wish to remain authorised once its permissions have been removed, can it challenge the FSA's decision not to cancel its permission? It is thought that a decision not to cancel permission would fall within the matters that could be referred to the Tribunal, although this is not entirely clear[1]. If so, the FSA would have the burden of proof and the Tribunal would have a broad discretion to decide what action it was appropriate for the FSA to take[2]. This may avoid the difficulties which an application for judicial review would present given the very low statutory test applicable in this context.

1 The question is whether the firm is 'aggrieved by the exercise of the FSA's own-initiative power': FSMA 2000, s 55(2). The power to cancel is found in FSMA 2000, s 45(2) and (3), which is part of what is defined as the own-initiative power (see FSMA 2000, s 45(5)).
2 See, generally, Chapter 6 above.

Procedure for cancelling a firm's permission

9.251 The procedure for cancelling permission is different from the procedures outlined above for varying the firm's permission. In particular, instead of issuing first and second supervisory notices, the procedure involves the issue of warning and decision notices[1] and contains additional safeguards for the firms. It is the same procedure as is used in relation to the imposition of disciplinary sanctions on firms and individuals and is described in detail in Chapter 5 above.

1 FSMA 2000, s 54.

9.252 One important difference is that such action cannot be imposed as a matter of urgency. However, if the FSA wishes as a matter of urgency to prevent the firm from carrying on any regulated activities, it can achieve the same by varying the firm's permission to impose restrictions or remove all its regulated activities. As has already been discussed[1], the distinction between varying and cancelling permission may therefore be somewhat artificial in many respects.

1 See para 9.249 above.

The consequences of cancelling permission

9.253 If the firm's permission is cancelled and, as a result, there is no regulated activity for which it has permission, the FSA must give a direction withdrawing its authorisation[1]. If, however, the top-up permission of an incoming firm is cancelled, the firm may still have permission to carry on other regulated activities under FSMA 2000, Sch 3 and/or 4[2] and, in that case, its authorisation would not be withdrawn.

1 FSMA 2000, s 33.
2 See para 2.11 ff above.

9.254 Once a firm has no authorisation, it is outside the regulatory system and, therefore, commits the criminal offence of breaching the general prohibition if it carries on a regulated activity[1].

1 FSMA 2000, ss 19 and 23 and see para 2.175 above.

9.255 It is, generally speaking, then outside the scope of the FSA's administrative powers, although certain powers may still be exercised against it, including[1]:

- certain information gathering and investigation powers[2];
- the FSA's power to apply to the court for an injunction and/or restitution order[3];
- its powers in respect of market abuse[4];
- certain insolvency powers[5]; and
- its power to prosecute certain criminal offences[6].

1 See the FSA Handbook at SUP 6.4.23.
2 See, for example, FSMA 2000 ss 165(8) and 166(2)(d) and 167(4) (applying the investigation powers to a former authorised person) and see Chapter 4 above.
3 See, respectively, paras 7.43 and 7.97 above.
4 See Chapter 13 below.
5 See the FSA Handbook at ENF Chapter 10.
6 See Chapter 11 below.

10 Civil liability to third parties

CONTENTS

Introduction **437**

Claims under the general law **439**

Breach of statutory duty and other claims under the FSMA 2000 **448**

Practical issues arising from the investigation and enforcement process **458**

INTRODUCTION

10.1 The primary focus of discussion thus far has been on the potential regulatory implications of a problem. But it is important not to lose sight of the possible civil law implications, in particular the firm's potential exposure to claims from customers or other third parties. To some extent, those potential claims arise from the FSMA 2000, but they also arise more generally. In this chapter, we outline some of the main issues[1] and, in particular, we consider:

- the firm's potential liability as a matter of general law (para 10.6 ff below);
- its potential civil liability under the FSMA 2000 (para 10.27 ff below); and
- certain practical issues arising from the impact that the regulatory process may have on the firm's potential civil liability (para 10.62 ff below).

1 The procedure for bringing or defending civil claims is not discussed here. For a discussion, see the Civil Procedure Rules.

Why might the firm incur civil liability?

10.2 In many situations where a problem arises, in addition to possible breaches of the applicable regulatory requirements, the firm may also have breached a legal obligation which it owed to customers or other third parties and caused them to suffer financial loss or other loss for which it could be required to compensate them[1]. As we will see, the firm's exposure to civil liability may arise directly from a finding that regulatory breaches have been committed, or it could arise entirely independently from the regulatory breaches, or it could arise in a situation where there are no regulatory issues.

1 Major problems which have both had regulatory implications and caused widely reported civil litigation include the collapse of BCCI, the collapse of Barings, the Maxwell/MGN pension fund problems and the Sumitomo copper-trading affair.

10.3 Moreover, whilst the focus of this chapter is on possible claims for damages, it is important to recognise that other remedies could be sought. For example, a party might seek an injunction requiring the firm to take a particular step[1], for example to transfer assets belonging to another party or, where it acts as a trustee[2], to bring claims against other parties on behalf of the beneficiaries, or an injunction requiring it to refrain from taking some step[3], for example committing further or threatened[4] breaches of its legal obligations.

1 For a general discussion of mandatory injunctions, see *Equitable Remedies*, Spry, 5th edn, 1997 from page 534.
2 For example, of a pension fund or unit trust.
3 For a general discussion of injunctions, see *Equitable Remedies*, Spry, 5th edn, 1997 from page 446.
4 In some circumstances, an injunction may be available on a quia timet basis, to restrain a threatened breach: see *Equitable Remedies*, Spry, 5th edn, 1997 from page 468.

10.4 The person who has suffered loss may be able to establish that the firm is liable to him under general legal principles. However, in various situations, he need not do so; the FSMA 2000 itself provides, in certain circumstances, a means for obtaining redress by giving those who suffer loss an action similar to an action for breach of statutory duty[1]. The FSMA 2000 also impacts in other ways upon the firm's potential liability[2].

1 The primary provision is FSMA 2000, s 150. The relevant provisions are discussed at para 10.27 ff below.
2 See paras 10.49 ff, 10.52 ff and 10.60 ff below.

10.5 This discussion must, however, be placed in context. In some cases, particularly those involving losses to significant numbers of consumers, the FSA will largely address the issue of compensation by seeking to impose a restitution order[1]. A similar result might be achieved by the FSA applying to the court for an injunction to require the firm to remedy its breach[2]. Also, individual customers could seek compensation themselves through the ombudsman scheme[3]. The firm may also need to consider voluntarily compensating customers, particularly consumers, as part of its own response to the regulatory issue[4]. Overall, therefore, there should be a lesser likelihood in practice of individual customers pursuing claims through the legal process. The greater risk is of civil claims from other market counterparties who were involved or from large corporate clients who suffered loss. Nonetheless, understanding the firm's potential exposure to a civil law claim is an important part of assessing what compensation to offer or the amount of a restitution order. The principles outlined here may therefore be relevant even where the firm anticipates being able to address the issue of compensation without recourse being made to the civil courts.

1 See para 7.43 ff above.
2 See para 7.97 ff above.
3 See Chapter 12 below.
4 See the discussion at paras 3.110 ff above and 10.64 ff below.

CLAIMS UNDER THE GENERAL LAW

10.6 The question whether the firm is liable and on what basis depends upon the circumstances of the particular case and, particularly, the nature of the relationship between the firm and the person claiming to have suffered loss from its actions. We briefly outline some of the main bases for claims that may be made, as follows:

- breach of contract;
- negligence;
- equitable claims;
- misrepresentation;
- breach of statutory duty; and
- contribution claims.

We first consider some practical guidance for firms and then briefly review each of these potential claims[1].

1 The discussion that follows is intended as a brief overview, to give a flavour of the nature of each type of claim. It is not intended as a comprehensive statement of the law in each area. Where appropriate, cross-references are provided to other texts where a more detailed analysis can be found.

Practical guidance for firms

10.7 Whilst the nature and extent of the risk of claims being made against the firm depends entirely upon the particular situation, there are some general practical points that can be made. First, it is prudent for firms to be alert, throughout the regulatory process, to the potential for claims to be made against them, not only by their customers, but also by any market counterparties who were involved in the relevant transaction and any other parties who may have suffered financial loss from the firm's actions. In practical terms, the starting point for a firm is to consider, first, who may have suffered loss as a result of its actions and, second, whether there is likely to be any legal basis for each of those persons to recover their losses, or alleged losses, from the firm[1].

1 The limitation rules also need to be borne in mind. In some circumstances, it may be possible for the relevant claims to be statute barred by the time the issue comes to light so far as the firm is concerned. The rules are complex: for a detailed discussion, see *Butterworths Law of Limitation.*

10.8 Second, the question of what loss was suffered will be an important issue. Compensatable loss not only includes direct losses but may also include to some extent the relevant person's indirect losses, such as his exposure to others arising from the firm's actions[1]. The need to prove loss, and to show that it was caused in legal terms by the firm's actions, is not too remote, and is of a type for which a court will award compensation, will in many situations be one of the primary difficulties for third parties seeking to recover from the firm[2]. There may also be issues about whether the person concerned took appropriate steps to mitigate his loss, which can give rise to important tactical options for the firm after the problem has arisen.

1 The rules on the losses that can be recovered are complex. For a detailed discussion, see *McGregor on Damages*, 16th edn, 1997.

2 See further the discussion at para 10.38 below.

10.9 Third, whether there is any legal basis for the firm to be liable for a person's losses will depend upon the situation. In some cases, it will be fairly clear on what basis the third party will formulate its claim, but in others it will be less clear. The capacity of third parties to be inventive in situations where no obvious claim exists should not be underestimated. Nonetheless, in considering whether a third party is likely to have a claim, there are a number of questions which the firm could ask itself, for example:

- does the firm owe any duties to those who have suffered loss under the terms of any relevant contracts, both express terms and any terms which might be implied?
- does the firm owe any non-contractual duties to anyone who may have suffered loss, which might form the basis of a claim in negligence?
- is the firm acting as trustee or otherwise in a fiduciary capacity or has it received any property from or otherwise been involved in assisting a person acting in such a capacity?
- did the firm provide any incorrect or misleading information to the person, on the basis of which they may have contracted with the firm? and
- if another firm had the more direct interface with the customers who suffered loss, but the firm was at least partly responsible for causing that loss, then the firm may have an exposure to a contribution claim.

10.10 Finally, the firm need not necessarily only be the recipient of a legal claim. It may wish to bring proceedings against one or more parties, for example to recover assets or to bring actions against employees. Indeed, in some situations the firm may be under a duty to bring legal proceedings on behalf of customers or others.

Breach of contract

10.11 A breach of contract claim against the firm will require the relevant person to show, very broadly, that, first, there was a contract between him and the firm, second, the firm has breached one of the terms, and third, he has suffered loss referable in legal terms to the firm's breach and of a kind which a court will compensate with an award of damages. In addition, there are a number of defences to an action for breach of contract that may be available to the firm.

10.12 Whether the firm has a contract with the relevant person is not always clear. Whilst in many instances there will be a written contract, it is quite possible for a contract to exist even though the agreement between the parties was not reduced to writing[1]. Breach of contract could therefore be alleged against the firm notwithstanding there was no written contract.

1 For a discussion of the elements of a contract, see *Chitty on Contracts*, 28th edn, 1999, Chapter 2. As to the lack of any formal requirements, generally speaking, see *Chitty on Contracts* at 4-001.

10.13 Assuming there is a written agreement, the contract will contain express terms[1], which the court may need to construe in order to assess whether there has been any breach[2]. The contract may also contain other terms not expressly written into it, but which the court would imply[3]. If there is no written agreement, then the court will need to ascertain the terms[4].

1 Where there is a written contract, signed by the parties, the parties are bound by the terms whether or not they have read them and/or appreciated their effect: *L'Estrange v F Graucob Ltd* [1934] 2 KB 394.
2 The basic task is to ascertain the meaning which the document would convey to a reasonable person having all the background knowledge which would reasonably have been available to the parties in the situation in which they were at the time of the contract: *Investors Compensation Scheme Ltd v West Bromwich Building Society* [1998] 1 WLR 896 (per Lord Hoffmann at 912).
3 Terms will be implied by law in two primary situations: first, where necessary to give business efficacy to the contract, and second, where the term represents the obvious, but unexpressed, intention of the parties: see the discussion in *Chitty on Contracts*, 28th edn, 1999, at 13-004.
4 As to how it does so, see *Chitty on Contracts*, 28th edn, 1999, at Chapter 12.

10.14 In principle, an award of damages should be available to compensate a party for loss that they have suffered from a breach of contract[1]. Hence, the requirement to have suffered loss is at the heart of any claim. The question of what losses are referable, in legal terms, to the firm's breach is the subject of complex legal rules of, first, causation[2] and, second, remoteness of damage[3] and, in addition, there are limitations on the types of losses that can be compensated by an award of damages[4]. As well as the legal complexities, proof of loss can cause practical difficulties as discussed at para 10.38 below.

1 For a discussion of damages for breach of contract, see *Chitty on Contracts*, 28th edn, 1999, at Chapter 27. Other remedies may be available for the breach of contract, including an injunction or, in exceptional circumstances, specific performance: see *Chitty on Contracts*, at Chapter 28.
2 Whether the breach has 'caused' the loss: see *Chitty on Contracts*, from 27-024.
3 Whether loss of the kind in question was reasonably foreseeable at the time the contract was made – either because it arises naturally from the breach or because it was specifically in the contemplation of the parties at that time as being the probable result of a breach: *Hadley v Baxendale* (1854) 9 Exch 341 and *Koufos v C Czarnikow Ltd (The Heron II)* [1969] 1 AC 350 and see the discussion at Chitty on Contracts, 28th edn, 1999, 27-039.
4 The basic rule is that damages should place the innocent party in the position in which he would have been had the contract been properly performed. For a more detailed discussion, see *McGregor on Damages*, 16th edn, 1997.

Negligence

10.15 The starting point for a claim in negligence is the existence of a relationship which gives rise to a duty on the firm to take reasonable care[1]. Firms will be under such a duty in many situations[2], often, but by no means only, where a contract also exists[3]. Where there is such a duty, then if the firm's actions fall short of the standard of care required[4] and it thereby causes loss[5], it may be liable subject to any applicable defences[6]. Claims for negligence may arise, among other things, from a negligent misstatement[7] or from the negligent performance of services causing financial loss.

1 The categories of such relationships constantly expand. There are three classic formulations for determining whether such a duty exists: (i) that a test of foreseeability, proximity and fairness is applied, (ii) that it depends upon an assumption of responsibility, and (iii) that categories of negligence are developed incrementally and by analogy with established categories: see *Caparo Industries plc v Dickman* [1990] 2 AC 605, *Smith v Bush* [1990] 1 AC 831 and *Spring v Guardian Assurance plc* [1995] 2 AC 296, among others. For further discussion of the principles, see *Clerk & Lindsell on Torts*, 18th edn, 2000 at Chapter 7.
2 By way of illustration, recent cases have decided that: (i) an insurance company may owe a duty of care, in relation to pensions misselling, not only to its customer but also to his dependents: *Gorham v British Telecommunications plc* [2000] 4 All ER 867, CA; (ii) a bank owes a duty to exercise reasonable care in and about executing a customer's order to transfer money: *Barclays Bank plc v Quincecare Ltd* [1992] 4 All ER 363; (iii) financial advisers who issue a defence document in the course of a contested takeover may owe a duty of care to the successful bidder: *Morgan Crucible Co plc v Hill Samuel & Co Ltd* [1991] Ch 295 and (iv) Lloyd's managing agents owe a duty of care to names: *Henderson v Merrett Syndicates Ltd* [1995] 2 AC 145. At the time of writing, a claim by Unilever plc against Mercury Asset Management in relation to the investment of pension fund assets is being closely watched by the industry.
3 There will often be an express term in a contract requiring the relevant party to use reasonable care and skill or, where there is no express term, this may be an implied term, in some instances implied under the Supply of Goods and Services Act 1982. Breach of such a term may give rise to tortious liability, as well as liability for breach of contract. Where liability arises both contractually and in tort, the claimant can choose on what basis to sue: see *Henderson v Merrett Syndicates Ltd* [1995] 2 AC 145. For a discussion of the overlap between tort and contract claims, and the differences between them, see *Chitty on Contracts*, 28th edn, 1999, at 1-059.
4 Precisely what standard is required and whether the firm's action fell below that standard are likely to be two of the main issues. The concept of reasonableness is important: 'negligence is the omission to do something which a reasonable man, guided upon those considerations which ordinarily regulate the conduct of human affairs, would do; or doing something which a prudent and reasonable man would not do': Alderson B in *Blyth v Birmingham Waterworks Co* (1856) 11 Ex 781 and see the discussion in *Clerk & Lindsell on Torts*, 18th edn, 2000, at 7-189. There may be room

for disagreement among reasonable men as to what practice is proper, in which case it may be sufficient for the firm to show that a responsible body of opinion would accept the firm's practice as proper, even if the claimant can identify another body of opinion which would regard a different practice as proper: see *Bolam v Friern Hospital Management Committee* [1957] 1 WLR 582 and *Saif Ali v Sydney Mitchell and Co* [1980] AC 198 (Lord Diplock) but note that this doctrine may not apply to situations concerned with neglect through oversight: see *JD Williams & Co Ltd v Michael Hyde & Associates Ltd* [2000] All ER (D) 930, CA.

5 The same issues of (i) causation, (ii) remoteness of damage and (iii) the categories of loss that are recoverable, arise as in relation to a claim for breach of contract, but the rules (which, again, are complex) are different in some important respects: for a detailed discussion, see *Clerk & Lindsell on Torts*, 18th edn, 2000, at 7-152 and *Chitty on Contracts*, 28th edn, 1999, at 1-059. The basic starting point is that the person is entitled to be placed in the position in which he would have been had the negligence not taken place.

6 The defence of contributory negligence under the Law Reform (Contributory Negligence) Act 1945 is particularly likely to be relevant.

7 See *Hedley Byrne & Co Ltd v Heller & Partners Ltd* [1964] AC 465.

Equitable claims

10.16 Certain relationships involve the imposition of more stringent obligations than arise in purely contractual relationships. The classic example is that of a trustee, including, say, of a pension fund or unit trust. But similar obligations arise in other situations where a firm acts in a 'fiduciary' capacity, for example as an agent or a company director. Also, a trust is, in some circumstances, imposed as a matter of law in situations which do not obviously involve one[1]. From the claimant's perspective, it may be advantageous to frame his claim on the basis of trust law, because, for example, it may confer some protection against insolvency and some of the legal hurdles may be lower. Therefore, whilst a discussion of trust law may seem somewhat archane, claims based on these principles do arise relatively often in practice[2]. A number of different bases of claim need to be outlined.

1 See, for example, the discussion of accessory liability and knowing receipt claims at, respectively, paras 10.19 and 10.20 below.

2 'In the modern world, the trust has become a valuable device in commercial and financial dealings': Lord Browne-Wilkinson in *Target Holdings Ltd. v Redferns* [1996] AC 421. Various examples appear in the footnotes that follow. By way of illustration, in the local authority swaps litigation, it was claimed that payments under the void swaps contracts were held on trust (a claim which the House of Lords rejected): *Westdeutsche Landesbank Girozentrale v Islington London Borough Council* [1996] AC 669. Other notable examples include *Guinness plc v Saunders* [1990] 2 AC 663; *Bishopsgate Investment Management Ltd v Maxwell (No 2)* [1994] 1 All ER 261; *Eagle Trust plc v SBC Securities Ltd* [1993] 1 WLR 484 and *United Pan-Europe Communications NV v Deutsche Bank AG* [2000] 2 BCLC 461.

Breach of trust

10.17 Where the firm acts as a trustee, it will owe a range of duties as trustee, the precise nature and extent of which will depend upon the situation, the nature of its role as trustee and the contents of any trust deed. In the present context, they could particularly encompass duties in respect of the holding and investment of fund assets and these duties may, in appropriate circumstances, require the trustee to take action to recover assets from third parties on behalf of the trust[1]. Where the trustee breaches such duties, its liability is, very broadly, to make good the loss caused to the trust[2]. Defences may be available, for example the lapse of time[3] or the acquiescence of or release by beneficiaries with full knowledge of the breach of trust[4]. In addition, the court has a discretion to relieve wholly or partly a trustee who acted honestly and reasonably and ought fairly to be excused[5].

1 The trustee may be able to protect his own personal position, and obtain an indemnity out of the trust assets for the costs of pursuing the claim, by means of a *Beddoe* order: see the discussion at *Snell's Equity*, 30th edn, 2000, at 11-97.
2 'Equitable compensation for breach of trust is designed to achieve exactly what the word compensation suggests: to make good a loss in fact suffered by the beneficiaries and which, using hindsight and common sense, can be seen to have been caused by the breach': Lord Browne-Wilkinson in *Target Holdings Ltd v Redferns* [1996] AC 421. The basic approach is thus to place the beneficiary in the position in which he would have been had there been no breach of trust; similar principles of causation and quantification of loss are applied as would apply to a common law claim. See also the discussion in *Snell's Equity*, 30th edn, 2000, at 13-14.
3 The Limitation Act 1980, s 21 and see the discussion in *Snell's Equity*, 30th edn, 2000, at 13-20.
4 See the discussion in *Snell's Equity*, 30th edn, 2000, at 13-20.
5 Trustee Act 1925, s 61.

Breach of fiduciary duty

10.18 Where the firm acts as a fiduciary, for example as an agent or company director, or as a trustee, various additional obligations characterised as fiduciary obligations are imposed on it. Primarily, these require the firm to subordinate its own interests to some extent to those of the beneficiary[1]: thus, the firm must act in good faith, it is precluded from making undisclosed profits or using for personal gain an opportunity that arises when it acts as trustee or in a fiduciary capacity[2] and it is required not to place itself in a position where its own interests and its duty may conflict[3], at least without informed consent[4]. If it profits improperly from its position, it must repay the profit to those to whom it owed its duties, irrespective whether they could have made the profit themselves[5].

1 A useful summary was provided by Millet LJ in *Bristol & West Building Society v Mothew* [1996] 4 All ER 698.
2 See *Keech v Sandford* (1726) Sel Cas Ch 61, Cas temp King 61; *Phipps v Boardman* [1967] 2 AC 46; *Guinness plc v Saunders* [1990] 2 AC 663 and see also *United Pan-Europe Communications NV v Deutsche Bank AG* [2000] 2 BCLC 461. For a further discussion, see *Clerk & Lindsell on Torts*, 18th edn, 2000 at 28-12 and *Snell's Equity*, 30th edn, 2000 at 11-68.
3 See *Bray v Ford* [1896] AC 44 and see the discussion in *Clerk & Lindsell on Torts*, 18th edn, 2000 at 28-15 and Snell's Equity, 30th edn, 2000 at 11-68.
4 See *Clark Boyce v Mouat* [1994] 1 AC 428 (Privy Council) and *Snell's Equity*, 30th edn, 2000, at 11-86.
5 See, for example, *Phipps v Boardman* [1967] 2 AC 46.

Accessory liability

10.19 A person who dishonestly assists in a breach of trust or fiduciary duty can also be made liable[1]. Dishonesty includes objective dishonesty, in other words that the defendant was dishonest by objective standards even if he believed he was doing nothing wrong. It also includes so-called blind eye dishonesty, in other words lending assistance after deliberately closing his eyes and ears and/or deliberately not asking questions for fear of learning something he would rather not know[2]. A firm could thus be liable for breach of trust, notwithstanding it was not otherwise a trustee, if it was involved in a breach of trust or fiduciary duty committed by another party.

1 See *Belmont Finance Corpn Ltd v Williams Furniture Ltd* [1979] 1 All ER 118, CA, *Royal Brunei Airlines v Tan* [1995] 3 All ER 97 (Privy Council), *Agip (Africa) Ltd v Jackson* [1992] 4 All ER 385 (Millet J) and *Grupo Torras SA v Al-Sabah* [2000] All ER (D) 1643, CA. In *Baden v Société Générale* [1992] 4 All ER 161, an attempt to make Société Générale liable on the basis of knowing assistance failed, but the case is an interesting illustration of when such a claim might arise.

2 See *Grupo Torras SA v Al-Sabah* [2000] All ER (D) 1643, CA.

Liability as a recipient of trust funds

10.20 A firm may be liable as a constructive trustee[1] if it receives trust funds from a third party that the third party transferred to it in breach of trust or fiduciary duty and either the firm had knowledge[2] that the funds were transferred in breach, or it afterwards acquired knowledge and dealt with the property in a manner inconsistent with the trust. Broadly, this may have the result that the firm is personally liable either to make restitution of the funds or other property, or to pay equitable damages[3]. In practice, this is often used, among other things, to obtain a remedy from third parties where a firm has been the subject of a fraud by one of its directors or other employees.

1 For a further discussion, see the *Law of Restitution*, Goff & Jones, 5th edn, 1998 from page 742 and *Snell's Equity*, 30th edn, 2000, at 9-43.

2 There has been much debate about the precise test for knowledge. The test seems to be that the recipient's state of knowledge was such as to make it unconscionable for him to retain the benefit of the receipt: *Bank of Credit & Commerce International (Overseas) Ltd v Akindele* [2000] 4 All ER 221, CA. See also the *Law of Restitution*, Goff & Jones, 5th edn, 1998 at page 744 and *Snell's Equity*, 30th edn, 2000 at 9-43.

3 For further discussion of the remedies that may be available, see the *Law of Restitution*, Goff & Jones, 5th edn, 1998 from page 745.

Tracing

10.21 Separately, in some situations, a firm could be required to return any identifiable trust assets that it still holds[1]. This could include the assets of a company misappropriated by its directors or employees.

1 For a discussion of tracing at common law and in equity, see *Snell's Equity*, 30th edn, 2000 at 13-29.

Misrepresentation

10.22 The law of misrepresentation may also be relevant, particularly in misselling or other similar cases[1]. In summary, it applies where a person is induced to enter into a contract with another person by a representation[2] that is false. Misrepresentations may be made fraudulently[3], negligently[4] or innocently. It may be possible, depending upon the circumstances, to obtain rescission of the contract[5] and/or a damages award[6].

1 The leading case of *Smith New Court Securities v Scrimgeour Vickers (Asset Management) Ltd* [1997] AC 254 , HL related to a purchase of shares as a result of a fraudulent misrepresentation.
2 Complex rules govern the types of statements that constitute representations for these purposes. In summary, this includes statements of fact but not, generally, of opinion. For a further discussion, see *Chitty on Contracts*, 28th edn, 1999 at 6-004.
3 A representation made without an honest belief in its truth: see *Derry v Peek* (1889) 14 App Cas 337 and the discussion in *Chitty on Contracts*, 28th edn, 1999 at 6-046.
4 A representation made carelessly or without reasonable grounds for believing it to be true: see *Chitty on Contracts*, 28th edn, 1999 at 6-067.
5 Rescission involves *restitutio in integrum* – in other words, both parties must return to the position that pertained before the contract was entered into. In many instances, this will be impossible, often because the contract has already been partly executed, in which case a court will not order rescission. For further discussion, see *Chitty on Contracts*, 28th edn, 1999 at 6-112. In addition, a party can lose the right to rescind a contract if he affirms it with knowledge of the facts and that he has a right to rescind it: see *Peyman v Lanjani* [1985] Ch 457.
6 In the case of a negligent or innocent misrepresentation, damages may be awarded in lieu of rescission if it would be equitable to do so having regard to the nature of the misrepresentation and the loss that would be caused by it if the contract were upheld, as well as to the loss that rescission would cause to the other party: Misrepresentation Act 1967, s 2(2).

Breach of statutory duty

10.23 The FSMA 2000 imposes a range of obligations on firms and, as we will see, in some instances allows certain types of persons to bring civil claims where those obligations are breached[1]. The question arises whether a breach can give rise to a civil claim in a situation where the FSMA 2000 does not specifically so provide[2].

1 This is discussed at para 10.27 ff below.
2 The most notable example is market abuse.

10.24 The law recognises a claim in tort, known as breach of statutory duty, based on a person's breach of an obligation imposed on him under statute. The key to such a claim is to show that, as a matter of construction, the duty was imposed for the protection of a limited class of the public and Parliament intended to confer on members of that class a private right of action for breach of the duty[1]. This causes a real difficulty in the context of the FSMA 2000 because, perhaps even more than the Financial Services Act 1986, it 'creates an elaborate scheme of duties backed by a mix of enforcement mechanisms but in each case the mechanism is earmarked to the duty in question'[2]. In other words, since the FSMA 2000 creates a series of obligations and makes specific provision as to how each obligation is to be enforced, involving administrative, criminal and civil consequences, there seems to be little room to imply that Parliament intended private rights of action to arise other than where the FSMA 2000 specifically so provides. This argument appears to have a great deal of force[3].

1 See *X (Minors) v Bedfordshire County Council* [1995] 2 AC 633, HL and see the discussion at *Clerk & Lindsell on Torts*, 18th edn, 2000 at 11-12. Whether or not such a right exists is a matter of construction of the statute concerned.

2 Per Lightman J in *Melton Medes Ltd v Securities and Investments Board* [1995] 3 All ER 880, in which it was held that the Financial Services Act 1986, s 179 did not give rise to a private right of action for breach of statutory duty.
3 'If the statute does provide some other means of enforcing the duty that will normally indicate that the statutory right was intended to be enforceable by those means and not by private right of action. . . . However, the mere existence of some other statutory remedy is not necessarily decisive. It is still possible to show that on the true construction of the statute the protected class was intended by Parliament to have a private remedy': Lord Browne-Wilkinson in *X (Minors) v Bedfordshire County Council* [1995] 2 AC 633, 731, HL

10.25 If it is possible to overcome this hurdle, and to show that the relevant provision is capable of giving rise to a claim for breach of statutory duty, then the person concerned must also show that[1]:

- the damage is of a type that the legislation was intended to protect against and that the claimant is within a class of persons the statute was intended to protect;
- the relevant statutory duty was breached[2]; and
- the breach of duty caused the loss[3];

and there may be defences available to the firm[4].

1 These other elements of the claim are discussed in more detail at para 10.27 ff below. See also *Clerk & Lindsell on Torts*, 18th edn, 2000 at 11-04.
2 This depends upon the construction of the relevant provision. For example, some duties imposed by statute require the person to take reasonable care while others are strict.
3 See the discussion at para 10.37 ff below.
4 These are briefly outlined at para 10.40 below.

Contribution claims

10.26 In some situations, several firms could potentially be liable for the same damage, for example because each owes duties to the same third party that has suffered the damage[1]. If one firm is liable to the third party[2], then it may be able to seek a contribution from the others[3]. Notably, there is no need for any particular connection between the firm seeking the contribution and that from which it is sought and, in particular, the latter need not owe any duties to the former. Liability to a contribution arises simply because two people are liable in respect of the same damage suffered by a third party. The amount of the contribution is within the discretion of the court[4].

1 An example would be a trustee of a unit trust, the manager of the scheme and its custodian, who may all owe duties to the holders of units.
2 Liability generally includes a compromise: Civil Liability (Contribution) Act 1978, s 1(4) and see the discussion in *Chitty on Contracts*, 28th edn, 1999, at 18-029.
3 Civil Liability (Contribution) Act 1978, s 1(1).
4 Civil Liability (Contribution) Act 1978, s 2(1).

BREACH OF STATUTORY DUTY AND OTHER CLAIMS UNDER THE FSMA 2000

10.27 The FSMA 2000 affects in a number of ways the civil claims that might arise from a matter which amounts to a regulatory breach. First, in some situations it gives certain people rights of action based on the regulatory breach, primarily on the grounds of breach of statutory duty. Second, it makes clear in other situations that no right of action arises from the breach. Third, it makes certain types of agreement unenforceable. Finally, it makes clear that certain types of agreements are not unenforceable. Each of these is considered in turn below.

Actions for breach of statutory duty

10.28 The FSMA 2000 contains one general right of action applicable in a range of situations, as well as certain specific rights applicable in specific situations. The formulation for each is similar but there are differences. We look first at the general right of action, and its various elements, before briefly reviewing the other rights of action available in specific cases.

The general right of action

10.29 Under the FSMA 2000[1]:

A a contravention by an authorised person of a rule;

B is actionable at the suit of a private person;

C who suffers loss as a result of the contravention;

D subject to the defences and other incidents applying to actions for breach of statutory duty; and

E in prescribed cases, is actionable on the same basis at the suit of a person who is not a private person.

1 FSMA 2000, s 150. A similar provision, although more limited in scope, existed in the Financial Services Act 1986, s 62 (among other provisions). There was, however, no previous, similar regime in respect of banks or insurance companies.

10.30 This is the provision likely to be applicable where the firm has committed some kind of regulatory breach which has caused loss to a customer or another party[1]. We briefly consider in turn each of the elements of this test.

1 Where there is no statutory right of action under these provisions, that does not preclude an action for breach of a common law duty: see *Gorham v British Telecommunications plc* [2000] 4 All ER 867, CA.

A A contravention by an authorised person of a rule

10.31 There must have been a contravention by an authorised person of a rule. 'Rule' means a rule made by the FSA under the FSMA 2000[1]. It does not however include[2]:

- rules that specify that contravention does not give rise to the right of action[3];
- listing rules made by the FSA in its capacity as UK Listing Authority[4]; and
- rules requiring an authorised person to have or maintain financial resources[5].

1 FSMA 2000, s 417(1).
2 FSMA 2000, s 150(2) and (4).
3 Most notably, this includes the Principles for Businesses: see para 2.51 ff above. It is an unusual feature of the regime that the regulator has some control over the extent to which civil claims may arise from rule breaches and this topic was the subject of considerable debate.
4 See Chapter 15 below.
5 See, for example, the Interim Prudential Sourcebook.

10.32 The same right of action applies where an authorised person:

- unlawfully promotes or approves the promotion of a collective investment scheme[1]; or
- contravenes a direction imposed by the FSA in relation to a unit trust scheme[2] or an OEIC[3].

1 FSMA 2000, s 241.
2 FSMA 2000, s 257(5) and see para 14.66 ff below.
3 The Open-Ended Investment Companies Regulations 2001, SI 2001/1228, reg 25(6) and see para 14.104 ff below.

10.33 A right of action under this provision could potentially arise in most cases where there has been a breach of one of the FSA's rules. The word 'rule' is more limited than the phrase 'requirement by or under the FSMA 2000', which is used in many of the enforcement provisions[1]. The latter would include requirements imposed directly by the FSMA 2000, including prohibitions which have criminal law consequences, as well as those imposed under subordinate legislation, such as HM Treasury regulations[2]. Breach of such requirements would not expose the firm to civil liability under this provision, although liability may arise under some other provision of the FSMA 2000 or under the general law.

1 For a brief discussion of the rule-making powers, see para 2.106 ff above. In particular, it should be noted that much of what is contained in the FSA Handbook does not constitute a 'rule', but rather is merely guidance.
2 This is discussed in detail at para 2.142 ff above.

10.34 The statutory right of action is only available in relation to a contravention by an authorised person. The FSA's rules do, in some circumstances, apply to other types of persons, for example there are rules relating to auditors and actuaries[1]. Contravention of the FSA rules by such persons does not give rise to liability under this provision.

1 These are made under FSMA 2000, s 340.

B At the suit of a private person

10.35 The contravention is actionable at the suit of a private person. Private person means[1]:

- any individual, unless he suffers the loss in question in the course of carrying on a regulated activity[2]; and
- any person who is not an individual, unless he suffers the loss in question in the course of carrying on business of any kind;

but does not include a government, local authority or international organisation.

1 The Financial Services and Markets Act 2000 (Rights of Action) Regulations 2001, SI 2001/2256 (the 'Rights of Action Regulations'), regs 3 and 6(1), made by HM Treasury under FSMA 2000, s 150(5). The FSMA 2000 does not prescribe the meaning of 'private persons', but leaves this to HM Treasury. The Regulations reflect the provisions under the former regime.
2 Or an activity which would be a regulated activity apart from any exclusion made by art 72 of the Financial Services and Markets Act 2000 (Regulated Activities) Order 2001, SI 2001/544. Under reg 3(2), an individual who suffers loss in the course of effecting or carrying out contracts of insurance written at Lloyd's is not to be taken to suffer loss in the course of carrying on a regulated activity.

10.36 In other words, individuals will normally be private persons, the main exception being where they are carrying on business which is regulated under the FSMA 2000. A sole trader who has a Part IV permission is not therefore a private person for these purposes to the extent he suffers a loss when he is carrying on his regulated business. Companies and other bodies will not normally be private persons[1], but they will be if they are not acting in the course of carrying on a business.

1 They may, though, nonetheless have other, non-statutory causes of action, such as those outlined at para 10.6 ff above. The fact that no action for breach of statutory duty can be brought does not mean that no action for breach of a duty of care will lie: see *Gorham v British Telecommunications plc* [2000] 4 All ER 867, CA.

C Who suffers loss as a result of the contravention

10.37 The contravention is only actionable at the suit of a private person who suffers loss as a result of the contravention. As has been seen[1], the purpose of an award of damages is to compensate a person for loss that they have suffered. The question of what losses are referable, in legal terms, to the firm's breaches is the subject of complex legal rules. Broadly, the damage must have been caused in legal and factual terms by the breach[2], not be too remote[3] and be of a type that a court will compensate with an award of damages[4].

1 See para 10.14 above.
2 The same principles apply as for a claim in negligence: see *Clerk & Lindsell on Torts*, 18th edn, 2000 at 11-53. The principles in relation to claims for negligence are briefly outlined at para 10.15 above.

3 The test is, broadly, whether the damage was of the type which the statute was intended to prevent. The point is well illustrated by the case of *Gorris v Scott* (1874) LR 9 Exch 125: on a sea voyage, sheep were washed overboard by reason of the defendant's failure to place them in pens as required by statutory rules, but since the object of the statute and rules was to prevent the spread of contagious disease, not to protect the sheep from the perils of the sea, the claimant could not recover his losses. Hence, it is quite possible, in some circumstances, that the consequences of a breach of FSA rules will not be compensated with an award of damages.

4 For a discussion of the rules in relation to damages, see *McGregor on Damages*, 16th edn, 1997.

10.38 This is often in practice the most significant hurdle for those who seek to bring claims against a firm arising from the firm's breaches. The mere fact that there was a regulatory breach, or a breach of a legal duty, does not entitle the person to compensation. The key question is what financial loss they can show they have suffered flowing from that breach. In some situations, the answer will be obvious because, for example, the firm's actions have directly impacted on the value of the person's investment. But, in many situations, the answer will not be that simple. The financial loss may have arisen less directly from the firm's breaches, for example because the person had to take some other action, as a result of the firm's actions, which involved him paying money to a third party. Or say, the investment that was affected was a long-term one and changes in its value in the short term may have made little difference to its value overall.

10.39 It can readily be seen that the question of what loss was suffered is an equally important point from the firm's perspective. Even if the firm has to concede that it committed a regulatory breach, for example to reach a settlement with the FSA on disciplinary or other enforcement issues, it does not necessarily follow that any loss is referable to that breach. Firms need to bear this in mind when considering the nature and scope of any admissions they make, as it may be possible to reach a settlement in a way that preserves the firm's ability to defend itself against civil law claims[1].

1 The impact of admissions made in the enforcement process upon subsequent civil claims is discussed at para 10.74 ff below.

D As a claim for breach of statutory duty

10.40 The claim is subject to the defences and other incidents applying to actions for breach of statutory duty. Whilst the contravention of the relevant rule is an important and necessary step towards rendering the firm liable for breach of statutory duty, it is not of itself sufficient. As discussed[1], the person must as a result have suffered loss and that loss must have been caused in legal terms by the breach, not be too remote and be of a type that a court will compensate with an award of damages. Additionally, the firm may have various defences to the claim, including that:

- the damage was caused by an intervening act[2];
- the claimant agreed to waive the claim[3];

- the customer was contributorily negligent[4]; and
- the defendant's breach of duty was co-existent with that of the claimant[5].

1 See para 10.37 above.
2 See *Clerk & Lindsell on Torts*, 18th edn, 2000 at 11-54.
3 The doctrine of volenti non fit injuria: see *Clerk & Lindsell on Torts*, 18th edn, 2000 at 11-55 and 3-72.
4 See *Clerk & Lindsell on Torts*, 18th edn, 2000 at 11-56.
5 See *Clerk & Lindsell on Torts*, 18th edn, 2000 at 11-58.

E Actionable by non-private persons in prescribed cases

10.41 In prescribed cases, a contravention of a rule which would be actionable at the suit of a private person is actionable at the suit of a person who is not a private person, subject to the defences and other incidents applying to actions for breach of statutory duty[1].

1 FSMA 2000, s 150(3).

10.42 A contravention is actionable by a person who is not a private person in cases where any of the following conditions apply[1]:

- the rule that has been contravened prohibits an authorised person from seeking to make provision excluding or restricting any duty or liability;
- the rule that has been contravened is directed at ensuring that transactions in any security or contractually based investment[2] are not effected with the benefit of unpublished information that, if made public, would be likely to affect the price of the investment; or
- the person would bring the action in a fiduciary or representative capacity on behalf of a private person and any remedy would be exclusively for the benefit of that person and could not be effected through action brought otherwise than at the suit of the fiduciary or representative.

1 Rights of Action Regulations, reg 6(2). This reflects the position under the former regime.
2 See the Financial Services and Markets Act 2000 (Regulated Activities) Order 2001, SI 2001/544.

Other rights of action

10.43 There are a number of additional rights of action to which the FSMA 2000 gives rise in the cases of certain specific types of contraventions.

10.44 First, a right of action arises in favour of a private person on the same basis as outlined above[1] where an authorised person fails to take reasonable care to ensure that, broadly:

- no person performs a controlled function who is not approved for that function[2]; or
- a prohibited person does not carry out a function from which he is prohibited[3].

1 FSMA 2000, s 71.
2 FSMA 2000, s 59(1) or (2).
3 FSMA 2000, s 56(6).

10.45 The elements of the claim are the same as those discussed at B to D above and 'private person' has, in this context, the same meaning as at para 10.35 above[1]. Further, a contravention is actionable by a person who is not a private person but only in one situation[2], namely where the action would be brought in a fiduciary or representative capacity on behalf of a private person and any remedy would be exclusively for the benefit of that private person and could not be effected through an action brought otherwise than at the suit of the fiduciary or representative.

1 Rights of Action Regulations, reg 5(1).
2 Rights of Action Regulations, reg 5(3).

10.46 Second, two connected types of contravention, namely:

- the carrying on by an authorised person of a regulated activity otherwise than in accordance with his permission[1]; and
- the breach of a requirement imposed on an incoming firm[2];

are actionable at the suit of a private person who suffers loss as a result of the contravention, subject to the defences and other incidents applying to actions for breach of statutory duty[3], except where the contravention is of a financial resources requirement[4]. The elements of the claim are the same as those discussed at C and D above. Most such contraventions are, therefore, actionable at the suit of a private person who suffers loss as a result.

1 FSMA 2000, s 20(3). An authorised person acting outside his permission does not breach the general prohibition but does commit a regulatory breach: see para 2.175 ff above. This would include breaching a restriction imposed on a variation of permission: see para 9.81 ff above.
2 FSMA 2000, s 202(2). This refers to breach of a requirement imposed on an incoming firm in the exercise of the FSA's powers of intervention: see para 9.83 above.
3 The FSMA 2000 provides that such breaches are not actionable save in prescribed cases, but HM Treasury has prescribed that breaches are actionable by private persons in most cases: see the Rights of Action Regulations, regs 4 and 7. In addition, they are actionable by a non-private person acting in a fiduciary or representative capacity: Rights of Action Regulations, regs 4 and 7.
4 A requirement on the firm to have or maintain financial resources, imposed under, as applicable, the FSMA 2000, Pt IV (for UK regulated firms) or Pt XIII (for incoming firms): Rights of Action Regulations, reg 1.

10.47 Third, in relation to the FSA's function as UK Listing Authority[1], a contravention of the rules requiring a prospectus to be published before securities are offered to the public[2] is actionable at the suit of a person who suffers loss as a result of the contravention, subject to the defences and other incidents applying to actions for breach of statutory duty. The elements of the claim are the same as those discussed at C and D above and the right of action is not limited to private persons.

1 See Chapter 15.
2 FSMA 2000, s 85(5).

10.48 Finally, a person responsible for listing particulars is in certain circumstances liable to pay compensation to a person who has acquired securities and suffered loss in respect of them[1]. This is not framed by the FSMA 2000 as a breach of statutory duty claim.

1 FSMA 2000, s 90.

Situations where there is expressly no right of action

10.49 In certain cases, the FSMA 2000 prescribes that the contravention of the rule or requirement does not give rise to any right of action for breach of statutory duty, namely:

- the carrying on by an authorised person of a regulated activity otherwise than in accordance with his permission[1], except in those cases where HM Treasury has prescribed that there is a right of action[2];
- the breach of a requirement imposed on an incoming firm, again except in those cases where HM Treasury has prescribed that there is a right of action[3]; and
- failure by an approved person to comply with a Statement of Principle[4].

1 FSMA 2000, s 20(2). An authorised person acting outside his permission does not breach the general prohibition but does commit a regulatory breach: see para 2.175 ff above. This would include breaching a restriction imposed on a variation of permission: see para 9.81 ff above.

2 FSMA 2000, s 20(3). As outlined at para 10.46 above, under current HM Treasury regulations, a private person will have a right of action, except where the requirement breached was a financial resources requirement.

3 FSMA 2000, s 202(2). As outlined at para 10.46 above, under current HM Treasury regulations, a private person will have a right of action, except where the requirement breached was a financial resources requirement.

4 FSMA 2000, s 64(8). The FSMA 2000 provides that this does not of itself give rise to any right of action by persons affected. For a discussion of the Statements of Principle for approved persons, see para 2.76 ff above.

10.50 It is important to understand the effect of these provisions. On their face, they do not preclude the relevant person from taking action against the firm based on some other cause of action which exists as a matter of law, for example if he has a claim in negligence or for breach of contract. They merely make clear that the contravention does not of itself give rise to any additional cause of action under the FSMA 2000.

10.51 In addition, the FSMA 2000 contains a more general exclusion for civil liability in respect of statements in or omissions from advertisements or other information issued in connection with an application for listing, provided the advertisement or other information has been properly approved or authorised[1]. In such circumstances, neither the person issuing it nor any person responsible for, or for any part of, the listing particulars incurs any civil liability by reason of such statements or omissions if the information and the listing particulars, taken together, would not be likely to mislead persons of the kind likely to consider acquiring the securities in question[2]. For present purposes, what is particularly notable about this provision is that, in contrast with those outlined at para 10.49 above, it appears to contain a general exclusion of civil liability. It is not limited to making clear that no statutory right of action arises.

1 FSMA 2000, s 98. Compare the Financial Services Act 1986, ss 150 and 151.
2 FSMA 2000, s 98(4). This appears to be an objective test; in other words, no liability would arise even though the particular person was in fact misled if the particulars were not, objectively, likely to mislead.

Unenforceable agreements

10.52 The FSMA 2000 also affects the civil rights of the firm and its customer by making agreements entered into unenforceable in certain circumstances. There are three main situations where the FSMA 2000 has this effect[1], namely where:

- an agreement is made by a person in the course of carrying on a regulated activity in breach of the general prohibition[2];
- an agreement made by an authorised person in the course of carrying on a regulated activity is made in consequence of something said or done by a third party acting in breach of the general prohibition[3]. An example would be a contract entered into as a result of investment advice given by an unauthorised third party[4]; and
- in consequence of an unlawful communication[5], certain types of agreements are entered into by a person as a customer or rights are exercised by a person in relation to certain types of investment[6].

There are various common elements to these provisions, which are considered below[7].

1 In addition, the court can, in certain circumstances, order the return of unlawful deposits: FSMA 2000, s 29.
2 FMSA 2000, s 26. The general prohibition is the prohibition against carrying on regulated activity without authorisation under the FSMA 2000: see para 2.175 above. Note that this does not encompass an agreement entered into by an authorised person acting outside the scope of its permission: FSMA 2000, s 20(2). Nor does it encompass the breach by an incoming firm of a restriction imposed on it: FSMA 2000, s 202(1).
3 FSMA 2000, s 27. The interaction between this provision and s 20(2)(b) is not clear. On the face of it, this provision would cover an agreement entered into by an authorised person outside the scope of its permission but within the scope of activities which are 'regulated activities' for the purposes of the FSMA 2000 (contrast the Financial Services Act 1986, s 5). However, s 20(2)(b) makes clear that if an authorised person acts outside the scope of his permission, that contravention does not make any transaction void or unenforceable. The more likely answer to this apparent contradiction is that, reading the two together, the agreement would be unenforceable, not because it had been entered into by the authorised person outside the scope of his permission, but because it had been entered into by it in consequence of something said or done by an unauthorised person.
4 See the Explanatory Notes to the FSMA 2000, para 72.
5 A communication in relation to which there has been a breach of the restrictions on financial promotions found at FSMA 2000, s 21(1): s 30(1).
6 FSMA 2000, s 30. An explanation of the rules on unlawful financial promotion is beyond the scope of this book.

7 The relevant provisions are almost identical to the Financial Services Act 1986, ss 5 and 132. When introduced into the 1986 Act, these provisions resolved an issue raised by *Bedford Insurance Co v Instituto de Resseguros do Brasil* [1985] QB 966, which had caused much concern within the insurance industry, and they provided 'a new code which could not have been achieved by any route explored or decided in any of the cases': *DR Insurance Co v Seguros America Banamex* [1993] 1 Lloyd's Rep 120, at 131.

The requirement for an 'agreement'

10.53 In the first two cases there must be an agreement and it must be one the making or performance of which constitutes, or is part of, the regulated activity in question[1]. In other words, not every agreement entered into by someone who is acting in breach of the general prohibition is unenforceable. The only agreements that are unenforceable are those referable to the breach. To take an example, an agreement by the person to buy stationery for use in his unauthorised business would not be unenforceable.

1 FSMA 2000, ss 26(3) and 27(3).

Achieving restitution

10.54 Where an agreement is rendered unenforceable the FSMA 2000 contains various provisions designed to achieve restitution[1]. As will be seen, restitution may not always be available and, notwithstanding one party is not 'innocent', the provisions aim to be even-handed between the parties.

1 For a discussion of the equivalent provisions of the Financial Services Act 1986, see *Securities and Investments Board v Pantell (No 2)* [1992] 1 All ER 134.

10.55 There are three relevant provisions[1]. First, the person with whom the agreement was made can recover any money or other property which he paid or transferred under the agreement, and can also obtain compensation for any loss sustained by him as a result of having parted with it[2].

1 The FSMA 2000 also provides that the contravention does not make the agreement concerned illegal or invalid to any greater extent than is provided by these provisions: FSMA 2000, s 28(9). This ensures that the contract is not illegal, but can be avoided only at the option of the customer: see *Group Josi Re v Walbrook Insurance Co Ltd* [1996] 1 WLR 1152.

2 FSMA 2000, ss 26(2), 27(2) and 30(2) and (3). The amount of compensation recoverable is such amount as the parties agree or is determined by the court on the application of either party: FSMA 2000, ss 28(2) and 30(10). It is not clear whether a court will apply any remoteness of damage rules: see the discussion in Lomnicka & Powell, *Encyclopaedia of Financial Services Law* at 2A-063.

10.56 Second, if the person elects not to perform the agreement or recovers money or other property which he paid or transferred under it, he must also repay any money and return any other property which he received under it[1].

1 FSMA 2000, ss 28(7) and 30(11) and (12). If property has been transferred to a third party, then the person must repay the value of the property at the time it was transferred: FSMA 2000, ss 28(8) and 30(13). The general rule is that he must return the property; he cannot retain the shares and claim back the purchase money less the financial value of the shares: see *Securities and Investments Board v Pantell (No 2)* [1992] 1 All ER 134.

10.57 Third, the court can nonetheless allow the agreement to be enforced or money and property paid or transferred under it to be retained, if satisfied that this is just and equitable in the circumstances of the case[1]. In considering whether to do so, the court must have regard to, as appropriate whether:

- the person who contravened the general prohibition reasonably believed that he was not doing so[2];
- the provider knew that the third party was contravening the general prohibition[3]; and/or
- the person, as the case may be, reasonably believed he was not making an unlawful communication or knew that the agreement was entered into in consequence of an unlawful communication[4].

1 FSMA 2000, ss 28(3) and 30(4).
2 FSMA 2000, s 28(4) and (5).
3 FSMA 2000, s 28(4) and (6).
4 FSMA 2000, s 30(5) to (7).

10.58 The test of whether it is just and equitable to enforce the agreement or allow the person to retain the money or other property thus appears to revolve primarily around the blameworthiness of the relevant person's conduct. A different test is applied dependent upon whether the firm itself committed the contravention or whether it entered into an agreement after a third party had committed a contravention. In the former case, the court looks at the existence and reasonableness of any belief that the firm was not committing a breach; in the latter case, it looks at whether the firm knew[1] about the third party's breach. In addition, whilst the FSMA 2000 prescribes that the court must have regard to these considerations, it is not clear that these are necessarily the only considerations; there may be other relevant matters which the court will take into account when deciding what it is just and equitable for it to do in the circumstances of the particular case.

1 Knowledge can include, in many contexts, not only actual knowledge but also circumstances where the person ought to have known. See, for example, paras 10.19 and 10.20 above.

10.59 One important point is not addressed in the restitution provisions, namely who takes the benefit of any profits that have accrued. Imagine, for example, that a customer has paid money to purchase units in an unauthorised fund. The fund has been invested and the units have increased significantly in value. The customer subsequently becomes aware that the fund was unauthorised and wants his money back (because, for example, he does not want to invest in an unauthorised fund or is concerned that the fund will now drop in value). He is clearly entitled to be repaid the money he originally paid for the units. He is also entitled to compensation for any loss he has sustained as a result of parting with his money, and this may allow him to obtain compensation on the basis that he would have invested that money elsewhere and made a particular return on it. But that compensation may be less than the amount that the units have increased in value, particularly if other comparable investments did not fare so well over the same period. So who takes the full benefit of the increase in value of the units?

This point does not seem to be covered in the restitution provisions. The profit made by the investment is neither 'money paid by the customer under the agreement', which would need to be returned to the customer, nor 'money or property received by the customer under the agreement', which the customer would have to pay to the firm. It may be that in practice such profits will be reflected in the amount of compensation that the firm is required to pay, whatever the difficulties of upholding that approach as a matter of principle[1]. In any event, it is likely that the firm could be required by a restitution order to pay the profit to the customer, as profits which have accrued to the firm as the result of a contravention of a requirement imposed by or under the FSMA 2000[2].

1 Among other things, it could be argued that the profit actually made is the best evidence of the compensation that the customer should receive based on the profit that the customer's funds could have made had he invested them elsewhere.
2 For a discussion of restitution orders, see para 7.43 ff above.

Agreements that are expressly not unenforceable

10.60 In four cases, the FSMA 2000 makes clear that the relevant regulatory breach does not render any transactions void or unenforceable, namely where:

- an authorised person carries on a regulated activity otherwise than in accordance with his permission[1];
- a penalty is imposed for market abuse[2];
- a person contravenes a rule made by the FSA[3]; and
- an incoming firm contravenes an intervention requirement imposed on it[4].

1 FSMA 2000, s 20(3). The authorised person does not thereby breach the general prohibition, but does commit a regulatory offence: see para 2.175 above.
2 FSMA 2000, s 131. For a discussion of market abuse, see Chapter 13 below.
3 FSMA 2000, s 151(2).
4 FSMA 2000, s 202(1).

10.61 It seems that the effect of this is not to preclude the person from bringing claims that at common law might render the transaction void or unenforceable or otherwise susceptible to challenge, for example that the agreement was induced by a misrepresentation or was entered into by a minor. The FSMA 2000 appears simply to make clear that the regulatory contravention does not of itself impeach the agreement.

PRACTICAL ISSUES ARISING FROM THE INVESTIGATION AND ENFORCEMENT PROCESS

10.62 The firm is unlikely to have the luxury of dealing in isolation with potential claims from customers and other parties. Its freedom of action is likely to be limited in a number of respects by its regulatory obligations[1] and, if a regulatory investigation and enforcement process is being or has been undergone, then this may have an impact upon the firm's potential exposure to damages claims.

1 This may affect how it deals with its customers and employees: see generally Chapter 3 above.

10.63 We discuss three issues here, namely:

- the overlap between civil claims and enforcement powers;
- whether material produced in the investigation and enforcement process can be used and may be discloseable in the civil proceedings; and
- the impact of admissions or findings in the enforcement process.

The overlap between civil claims and enforcement powers

10.64 As we have seen, the FSA has a wide range of enforcement powers available for a variety of purposes. One of the FSA's regulatory objectives under the FSMA 2000 is the protection of consumers[1] and this is reflected in the availability of various enforcement powers and other mechanisms designed to secure that consumers are compensated for their losses arising from regulatory breaches. Thus, for example:

- the FSA can impose or ask the court to impose a restitution order[2];
- the FSA can apply to the court for an injunction requiring the firm to remedy its breach[3];
- individual customers may seek compensation through the firm's complaints procedure and the ombudsman scheme[4]; and
- the firm will in any event need to consider compensating customers voluntarily as part of its own response to the regulatory issue[5].

But if the firm makes payments to compensate customers on any of these bases, to what extent does that prevent the customer from bringing further claims against it?

1 For a discussion of the regulatory objectives, see para 2.20 ff above.
2 See para 7.43 ff above.
3 See para 7.97 ff above.
4 See Chapter 12 below.
5 The importance of the firm dealing appropriately with its customers when a matter of regulatory concern arises is discussed at para 3.110 ff above.

10.65 There are two reasons why in practice this matters. First, the basis upon which, for example, restitution is ordered or on which the ombudsman awards compensation, is rather different from that on which a court awards damages. The most notable example is the cap of £100,000 on ombudsman awards, but there are other differences[1]. There may therefore be a difference between the customer's legal entitlement to damages and the amount that he receives under the FSMA 2000, or is paid voluntarily by the firm. If the customer receives significantly less compensation than he could obtain if he pursued his strict legal rights, then further legal claims may be in prospect. Second, the customer could try to argue that any payment he received was voluntary so far as he was concerned, and did not affect his strict legal rights. In other words, he might try to recover twice. The legal effect of any compensation paid is therefore important.

1 In imposing a restitution order, the FSA or, as appropriate, the court will require the firm to pay such amount as is considered 'just' having regard to, among other things, the amount of the losses: see para 7.86 ff above. The test for the ombudsman is to award 'fair compensation' for the loss or damage: see para 12.63 ff below. Not only do these tests not necessarily equate with each other, neither need equate with the complex common law rules on the assessment of damages which would apply to a civil claim.

10.66 As a general rule, a person is entitled to recover only his net loss, which means taking into account not only the amount he has lost but also any amount he has gained that he would not otherwise have received[1]. There is, in essence, a rule against double recovery. But this is only a general rule and in some circumstances gains are not taken into account. Unfortunately, it is difficult to articulate a general rule on when gains are and are not taken into account. The matter is said to be one of justice, reasonableness and public policy[2].

1 *Hussain v New Taplow Paper Mills Ltd* [1988] AC 514, 527 (Lord Bridge) and see also *Hunt v Severs* [1994] 2 All ER 385, HL.
2 Lord Reid in *Parry v Cleaver* [1970] AC 1, 13 and see *Hussain*, ibid, at 528.

10.67 Does the general rule apply in this context? There is no judicial authority directly on the point in the same context. Nonetheless, the authorities referred to above provide strong precedent that benefits voluntarily paid by a defendant are taken into account. If this is the case, then benefits paid under a legal obligation, such as a restitution order, should be taken into account. The basic position should therefore be that any amounts the firm pays over to the customer should be taken into account in assessing the damages that the customer can recover in a subsequent civil claim. This basic position does not appear to be changed by the relevant provisions of the FSMA 2000[1].

1 The analysis depends upon the following: (i) where the court grants a restitution order, whether or not for market abuse, the FSMA 2000 provides that 'nothing in this section affects the right of any person other than the FSA or the Secretary of State to bring proceedings in respect of the matters to which this section applies' (FSMA 2000, ss 382(7) and 383(9)); this appears to address only the question of whether proceedings can be brought, not what is recoverable in those proceedings, and not therefore to affect the general position outlined above; (ii) where the court grants an injunction, the FSA uses its administrative powers to make a restitution order, or the firm pays compensation voluntarily, the FSMA 2000 is silent on the effect as regards other potential claims; again, it is thought that there is nothing to dislodge the general principle; and (iii) if the ombudsman makes an award under the compulsory jurisdiction, which is accepted by the complainant, then the FSMA provides that the award is binding on both the firm and the complainant (FSMA 2000, s 228(5)); this would not seem to change the above general principle; indeed, although not entirely clear, it may be that the effect is to preclude the customer from bringing further claims in respect of the same matter.

10.68 The discussion above considers only the effect of compensation paid by the firm. But in some situations, the customer may also be entitled to or may receive compensation from another party relating to the same losses, for example another authorised firm that was involved and pays restitution. If the customer receives an indemnity for its losses from the third party, then that third party may be entitled to bring the customer's claim against the firm in the customer's name[1].

1 This arises from the doctrine of subrogation, typically, but by no means exclusively, in the context of insurance: see *Castellain v Preston* (1883) 11 QBD 380 and *Esso Petroleum v Hall Russell* [1989] AC 643, HL.

The disclosure and use of material produced in the enforcement process

10.69 As has already been highlighted[1], firms need to take care not to produce during the investigation and enforcement process additional documentary material which could be discloseable to third parties in any legal proceedings which might be brought against the firm, or indeed which the firm might need to bring, or which might be discloseable in the context of a complaint heard by the ombudsman in relation to the same matter. The concerns have been outlined in some detail already. To briefly summarise some of the main issues:

- any transcripts of interviews of the firm's staff conducted by the FSA are likely to be susceptible to disclosure; moreover, documents produced by the firm, including internal audit reports and interviews with staff, and drafts of documents, are also likely to be susceptible to disclosure unless protected by legal privilege;
- material that the firm produces in response to the regulatory process can often potentially be damaging, for example because it provides unhelpful evidence which may be of use to a third party or it highlights aspects of the matter that the third party may not otherwise have recognised;
- confidential information in the FSA's hands is, generally speaking, protected from disclosure[2]. Confidential information that the firm has received from the FSA may also, in the same way, be protected from disclosure;
- various steps that the firm could take to minimise the risks of creating discloseable material are outlined at para 4.218 above.

1 See para 3.155 ff above and the detailed discussion at para 4.189 ff above.
2 See the discussion at para 4.304 ff above.

10.70 A practical question for the firm is whether it can use, to defend itself against civil claims by third parties, information which it received from the FSA during the investigation and enforcement process. For example, the firm may have received from the FSA information to suggest that the firm did not breach any of the applicable regulatory requirements, or that the relevant breaches were substantially caused by another person, or that another person was the primary cause of any losses.

10.71 In many situations, the firm will not be able to use that information. This is because when the firm receives directly or indirectly from the FSA confidential information which relates to the business or affairs of a person, that information is, generally speaking, protected under the FSMA 2000[1] and, where it is protected, it will be a criminal offence to disclose it in breach.

1 FSMA 2000, s 348: see para 4.304 ff above.

10.72 The FSMA 2000 does not, however, prevent the firm from using or disclosing information obtained by the FSA from the firm itself and which relates only to the firm[1]. But firms must take care in relying upon this. If the information was obtained by the FSA from another party, even though the information itself relates only to the firm, or if the information relates to the affairs of another party[2], then disclosure would require the consent of the other parties concerned. Without such consent, the firm could potentially commit a criminal offence. In practice, it may be difficult for the firm to know whether material which it received from the FSA contains information which the FSA received from another party and it may be necessary for the firm to seek clarification from the FSA.

1 The firm is entitled to consent to the disclosure (FSMA 2000, s 348(1)), thereby effectively releasing itself.
2 The statutory provision is sufficiently wide to include the business or affairs of a person other than the person under investigation: see *BCCI v Price Waterhouse (Bank of England intervening)* [1997] 4 All ER 781, 791 (Laddie J).

10.73 Furthermore, once information that was confidential has been disclosed in public, for example in Tribunal proceedings[1], then it is no longer subject to the statutory restriction[2]. In some cases, it may be that the need to use information in pending civil proceedings could militate in favour of the firm exercising its right to refer enforcement proceedings to the Tribunal.

1 Tribunal proceedings are normally held in public. For a further discussion, see para 6.32 above.
2 'Information is not confidential information if … it has been made available to the public by virtue of being disclosed in any circumstances in which, or for any purposes for which, disclosure is not precluded by this section': FSMA 2000, s 348(4).

The impact of admissions or findings in the enforcement process

10.74 As we have seen, many enforcement issues, including the imposition of disciplinary sanctions, are in practice resolved by settlement between the FSA and the firm concerned. But in order to reach a settlement with the FSA, the firm will probably have to admit that it committed a regulatory breach. Or, if the FSA and the firm do not reach a settlement, then there may be a finding against the firm in the FSA's decision notice or second supervisory notice that it committed a regulatory breach[1]. Or there could be an adverse finding in the Tribunal. To what extent do these different outcomes increase the firm's exposure to civil liability?

1 The decision notice or second supervisory notice may well be discloseable documents in any civil proceedings, subject possibly to FSMA 2000, s 348: see the discussion at paras 4.189 ff and 4.304 ff above.

10.75 It is important to keep in mind that establishing that the firm committed a regulatory breach is only one element of the civil claim. This will not of itself make the firm liable to a civil claim, even where the claim is one for breach of statutory duty based on the regulatory breach[1]. Unless the FSA had applied for a restitution order, the other necessary elements of the civil claim, such as the amount and extent of any losses that were suffered by the particular third party and whether those losses were referable, in legal terms, to the firm's actions, are unlikely to have been in issue in the regulatory proceedings. Resolution of the regulatory enforcement issues should not affect the firm's ability to argue on those other issues to the extent they were not raised in the regulatory proceedings.

1 See the discussion at para 10.29 above.

10.76 The more difficult question is whether the firm is allowed to relitigate the particular issues resolved in the enforcement proceedings, for example whether or not it committed a breach of the relevant regulatory rule. A decision by the Tribunal on a particular matter of fact or law is binding as between the firm and the FSA, so as to prevent the same issue from being relitigated between them in any other forum[1]. But if the matter was not referred to the Tribunal, the decision having been made by the FSA and embodied in a decision notice or supervisory notice, then it is much less likely that the decision has any binding effect in any other forum. Moreover, even if the matter has been decided by the Tribunal and is therefore binding between the firm and the FSA, this should not prevent it from being reargued between the firm and any other party. There are, however, also practical considerations to take into account, like whether the firm would wish to be seen to be arguing that it did not commit a regulatory breach, having resolved that issue with the FSA, and whether admissions which it made in the regulatory context are likely to come back to haunt it at trial.

1 The particular point, having been decided by a Tribunal exercising judicial functions, is very likely to be res judicata: for further discussion, see *The Doctrine of Res Judicata*, Spencer, Bower, Turner & Handley, 3rd edn, 1996, at Chapter 2. See, for example, *Green v Hampshire County Council* [1979] ICR 861 and *Crown Estate Comrs v Dorset County Council* [1990] 1 All ER 19 (Millett J).

10.77 There are three scenarios. First, if the firm reached a settlement with the FSA, it will in practical terms be difficult for it to distance itself from the admissions it made and the ensuing finding by the FSA that it committed the relevant breach. Such admissions are likely to have been made public, they would provide fertile ground for cross-examination and, moreover, it may well be unpalatable for the firm to be seen to deny what it had agreed with the FSA and publicly admitted[1]. Indeed, the FSA may require, as a term of the settlement, that the firm agrees not to say anything which suggests it was not in breach.

1 An agreed settlement of enforcement issues is very likely to contain express admissions by the firm and to be made public by the FSA: for further discussion, see Chapter 5 above.

10.78 Second, if the firm did not reach any settlement with the FSA, but simply decided not to refer the enforcement case to the Tribunal, a finding by the FSA that it committed a breach is unlikely to preclude the firm from arguing in subsequent civil proceedings that it did not do so. If there were reasons for the firm not having sought to vindicate itself in the Tribunal, then there may be little practical bar to maintaining the same position.

10.79 Third, if the firm referred the matter to the Tribunal, and argued throughout that it did not commit a regulatory breach, but the Tribunal found against it, there is nothing to prevent the firm from maintaining the same position in subsequent civil proceedings against a third party[1]. In practice, it cannot be ruled out that the Tribunal's decision would be given some weight by a court considering the same matter.

1 As discussed at para 10.76 above, it could not, though, maintain that position as against the FSA.

10.80 Finally, it is important to note that if the earlier decision binds the firm only as against the FSA, then equally it is not binding on the third party. So if the firm managed to establish in the Tribunal that it did not commit any regulatory breach, there is, in theory, nothing to prevent a third party from seeking to prove in a civil court, perhaps with the benefit of a lower burden of proof in a civil case, that it did do so.

11 Criminal prosecutions

CONTENTS

Introduction	**465**
What offences can the FSA prosecute?	**466**
When will the FSA pursue a criminal prosecution?	**468**
Who can be prosecuted?	**472**
What other options does the FSA have?	**475**
Practical guidance for firms	**478**
Appendix: Criminal offences under the FSMA 2000	**481**

INTRODUCTION

11.1 The FSA has an important role under the FSMA 2000 as a criminal prosecutor in relation to offences under the FSMA 2000 and certain other offences[1]. The existence of a criminal aspect to the financial services regime is nothing new. Criminal investigations into, for example, unauthorised business, insider dealing, money laundering and fraud have been a regular feature for some time. But many regulated firms will have been used to the criminal aspects of regulation being handled by other organisations, particularly the Department of Trade and Industry and the Serious Fraud Office. The regulator is now directly involved in certain types of criminal prosecutions.

1 The FSA's powers of prosecution do not extend to Scotland: FSMA 2000, ss 401 and 402(1).

11.2 This, allied with the statutory nature of the FSA's powers under the FSMA 2000, requires an increased awareness of criminal prosecutions, or at least the risk of them. The FSA's statutory powers (for example its powers of investigation: see Chapter 4) are supported by criminal law provisions[1]. Additionally, where the FSA believes that a criminal offence which it can prosecute may have been committed, there is no additional practical hurdle of handing the matter over to some other prosecuting body. The FSA can itself consider whether there is any merit in pursuing the matter through the criminal justice system. Whether this leads to an increase in criminal prosecutions is perhaps questionable. But firms need to be conscious of the risks.

1 For example, it is a criminal offence knowingly or recklessly to provide the FSA with false or misleading information: FSMA 2000, ss 177(4) and 398. Whilst there were equivalent criminal offences in the previous regime, (see, for example, the Financial Services Act 1986, s 200) most investigations were rule-based (eg under the rules of the SROs) rather than statutory and, in addition, where there was a potential criminal offence the matter would have to have been referred to another body for prosecution.

11.3 The FSA is not the only body with responsibility for criminal prosecutions in this area. Other relevant prosecuting authorities include:

- the Secretary of State for Trade and Industry;
- the Serious Fraud Office;
- the Crown Prosecution Service[1]; and
- the Director General of Fair Trading (for consumer credit matters).

A key question for firms is whether they can be the subject of multiple investigations by different criminal prosecution organisations exercising the same or overlapping powers. This is discussed below.

1 Or, in Northern Ireland, the Director of Public Prosecutions in Northern Ireland.

11.4 In this chapter we review[1]:

- the FSA's role as a prosecuting body – what offences the FSA has the power to prosecute (para 11.5 ff);
- when the FSA will pursue a criminal prosecution (para 11.9 ff), including how issues of overlapping jurisdiction are resolved;
- who can be prosecuted (para 11.25 ff);
- what other options the FSA has instead of or as well as prosecuting (para 11.36 ff); and
- practical guidance for firms who, or whose employees, are prosecuted (para 11.47 ff).

1 A detailed discussion of criminal procedure is not undertaken here but can be found at *Archbold 2001*.

WHAT OFFENCES CAN THE FSA PROSECUTE?

11.5 The FSA has the power to prosecute any criminal offence under the FSMA 2000 or under subordinate legislation made under the FSMA 2000[1].

Those criminal offences most likely to be of relevance to a regulated firm in the context of a regulatory investigation include:

- knowingly or recklessly providing false or misleading information[2];
- destroying or falsifying documents[3];
- misleading statements and practices[4];
- the offences relating to listed securities[5];
- breach of a prohibition order[6]; and
- disclosing confidential information in breach of the statutory restrictions[7].

1 FSMA 2000, s 401. Note that this does not apply to Scotland. For a list of the relevant criminal offences, see the FSA Handbook at ENF 15.2.1.
2 FSMA 2000, ss 177(4), 346 and 398 and see para 4.287 above.
3 FSMA 2000, s 177(3) and see para 3.151 above.
4 FSMA 2000, s 397, encompassing what was formerly Financial Services Act 1986, s 47.
5 FSMA 2000, ss 83, 85 and 98 and see Chapter 15 below.
6 FSMA 2000, s 56 and see para 8.44 ff above.
7 FSMA 2000, ss 351 and 352 and see para 4.304 ff above.

11.6 The FSMA 2000[1] also gives the FSA the power to prosecute[2]:

- insider dealing[3]; and
- breaches of the money laundering regulations[4].

In various instances[5], the FSMA 2000 allows the FSA to use its regulatory powers against a person who has breached a requirement imposed by or under any other Act whose contravention constitutes an offence which the FSA has the power to prosecute under the FSMA 2000. This refers to these offences.

1 FSMA 2000, s 402. This does not apply in Scotland.
2 Subject to any conditions or restrictions imposed by HM Treasury: FSMA 2000, s 402(2).
3 Criminal Justice Act 1993, Pt V. This overlaps with the FSA's power to bring proceedings for a penalty for market abuse: see Chapter 13 below.
4 Money Laundering Regulations 1993, SI 1993/1933.
5 In particular, in relation to restitution orders (see paras 7.46 and 7.48 above) and civil injunctions (see paras 7.104, 7.110 and 7.116 above).

11.7 The FSMA 2000 specifically provides that certain regulatory contraventions do not constitute a criminal offence, namely:

- contravention of a rule made by the FSA[1];
- where a firm acts outside the scope of its permission[2]; and
- where an incoming firm contravenes an intervention requirement imposed on it by the FSA[3].

1 FSMA 2000, s 151(1).
2 FSMA 2000, s 20(2)(a).
3 FSMA 2000, s 202(1).

11.8 Finally, as discussed in Chapter 5 above, it is possible that the FSA's enforcement proceedings could, in a particular case, amount to the bringing of a 'criminal charge' for ECHR purposes, thus giving rise to the additional ECHR fair trial guarantees contained in art 6(2) and (3). This should not be confused with the classification of offences as criminal as a matter of domestic law under the FSMA 2000. Contraventions that are not classified as criminal by the FSMA 2000 are addressed purely within the regulatory arena and do not result in a prosecution, whatever their classification for ECHR purposes.

WHEN WILL THE FSA PURSUE A CRIMINAL PROSECUTION?

11.9 Not every potential criminal offence within the financial services arena will be investigated and prosecuted by the FSA. This is for two reasons. First, various other bodies have overlapping powers of investigation and prosecution and, second, not every potential criminal offence is suitable to be addressed through the criminal justice system. These two issues are considered in the following paragraphs.

Which body will investigate and prosecute?

11.10 The FSA's powers of investigation and prosecution overlap to a large extent with those of a number of other organisations. To some extent, this arises because the organisations have concurrent jurisdiction under the relevant legislation. For example, offences under the FSMA 2000 could be investigated and prosecuted either by the FSA or by the Department of Trade and Industry. But to a perhaps larger extent this arises because in some cases neither the FSA nor any of the other organisations has the power to deal with all of the different potential aspects of the same problem. For example, if a regulatory investigation uncovered fraud, the prosecution of the fraud would be a matter for the Serious Fraud Office, not the FSA, whereas the regulatory aspects of the matter would remain for the FSA. But a criminal prosecution for fraud may have a lower prospect of success than regulatory action by the FSA for breach of the relevant regulatory standards, perhaps with an associated restitution order to compensate the victims. It can readily be seen that the question of who should investigate and what action should be taken can be complex.

11.11 The difficulties that this could cause are mitigated by guidelines agreed between the FSA and the various other bodies involved[1] on investigating and prosecuting cases of mutual interest. The purpose of the guidelines is to help decide who should investigate, ensure co-operation between the different bodies, prevent the unnecessary duplication of effort and prevent the subject of investigations and proceedings from being treated unfairly. In very brief summary[2], the various bodies aim to liaise with each other:

- to consider whose functions are most appropriate to investigate;

- where there are concurrent investigations, to keep one another informed of significant developments, before taking significant steps and before deciding whether or not pursue proceedings; and
- to notify each other at the conclusion of the proceedings or, if no proceedings are taken, the conclusion of the investigation.

1 The Serious Fraud Office, the Department of Trade and Industry, the Crown Prosecution Service, the Association of Chief Police Officers in England, Wales and Northern Ireland, the Crown Office, the Department of the Director of Public Prosecutions for Northern Ireland and the Association of Chief Police Officers in Scotland.
2 The guidelines can be found in full in the FSA Handbook at ENF Chapter 2, Annex 1G.

11.12 This does not necessarily preclude concurrent investigations by several bodies. Indeed, given the different powers and responsibilities of each organisation, it may be necessary for more than one to be involved. The focus is therefore on co-ordination and co-operation.

What types of cases are suitable for the FSA?

11.13 As to which types of cases are likely to be suitable for prosecution by the FSA, the guidelines contain two lists of factors, one setting out those factors which tend towards action by the FSA, and the other showing those which tend towards action by one of the other agencies.

11.14 Factors which tend towards action by the FSA are[1]:

- where the conduct gives rise to concerns about market confidence or the protection of financial services consumers;
- where the conduct would best be dealt with by criminal prosecution under the FSMA 2000, the use of the FSA's other powers under the FSMA 2000 or proceedings for breaches of listing rules;
- where the likely defendants are authorised firms or approved persons (or listed companies, applicants for listing, directors or sponsors subject to the FSA in its role as UK Listing Authority);
- where there is likely to be a case for the use of the FSA's powers to take action as a matter of urgency;
- where it is likely the investigator will be seeking assistance from overseas regulatory authorities with functions equivalent to the FSA;
- where possible criminal offences are technical or in a grey area whereas the regulatory contraventions are clear;
- where the balance of public interest is in achieving reparation for victims and prosecution is likely to damage the prospects of that; and
- where there are distinct parts of the case that are best investigated with regulatory expertise.

1 See the FSA Handbook at ENF, Chapter 2, Annex 1G, para 9(a).

11.15 Factors which tend towards action by other bodies are[1]:

- where the main issues are best dealt with by other bodies, for example:
  - serious or complex fraud (Serious Fraud Office[2]);
  - criminal proceedings for which the FSA is not the prosecutor;
  - directors disqualification proceedings, winding-up proceedings or proceedings relating to the abuse of limited liability under the Companies Acts (Department of Trade and Industry); or
  - criminal proceedings in Scotland;
- where powers of arrest are likely to be necessary;
- where it is likely the investigator will rely on overseas law enforcement agencies with whom other bodies have regular liaison;
- where action by the FSA is likely to prejudice the public interest in the prosecution of offences for which the FSA is not the prosecutor; and
- where the case falls only partly within the regulated area and the prospects of splitting the investigation are not good.

1 See the FSA Handbook at ENF, Chapter 2, Annex 1G, para 9(b).
2 Historically, the FSA (or its predecessor bodies) has been a reasonably significant source of cases for the SFO: see the Serious Fraud Office 2000/2001 Annual Report, 19 July 2001.

11.16 The general approach seems relatively clear from this. There is a distinct regulatory arena within which it is likely to be the FSA that investigates and prosecutes, provided it has the necessary powers to do so. But the FSA will not always be the prosecuting body. Where there are wider issues, it may be that one of the other bodies would be better placed or that more than one organisation should be involved.

11.17 From the firm's point of view, the identity of the investigating and prosecuting body probably matters less than the general aim of co-ordination and liaison. Wherever possible, firms will want to avoid the uncertainty and additional time and cost of being subjected to multiple investigations.

In what circumstances will the FSA prosecute?

11.18 Not every case which the FSA has the power to prosecute and which it is appropriate for the FSA, rather than some other investigating or prosecuting body, to handle, will result in a criminal prosecution. In what circumstances will the FSA decide to pursue a criminal prosecution?

11.19 The FSA's general policy is to pursue through the criminal justice system all those cases where criminal prosecution is appropriate[1]. In deciding whether it is appropriate to prosecute, the FSA applies the two tests set out in the Code for Crown Prosecutors[2]:

- ***the evidential test:*** is there sufficient evidence to provide a realistic prospect of conviction against the defendant on each criminal charge? and
- ***the public interest test:*** having regard to the seriousness of the offence and all the circumstances, is criminal prosecution in the public interest?

We briefly consider each test in turn, and then consider what this means in practice.

1 See FSA Handbook at ENF 15.4.1.
2 See FSA Handbook at ENF 15.5. A copy of the Code appears at ENF Chapter 15, Annex 1G.

The evidential test

11.20 The evidential test[1] requires the FSA to consider whether the evidence is such that a jury or bench of magistrates, properly directed, is more likely than not to convict the defendant of each charge alleged. It involves considering what evidence can be used[2] and whether it is reliable. It also involves considering the likely defence.

1 For further discussion, see the FSA Handbook at ENF 15.5.3 and the Code for Crown Prosecutors, para 5.
2 Note that statements made under compulsion cannot generally be used in evidence in criminal proceedings against the maker: see para 4.242 ff above.

The public interest test

11.21 Only if the evidential test is passed will the FSA go on to consider the public interest test. As this indicates, not every case where there is sufficient evidence to obtain a conviction results in a criminal prosecution. The question is whether a prosecution is in the public interest.

11.22 In deciding whether or not prosecution is in the public interest, the FSA is required to balance carefully and fairly the factors for and against prosecution, relating usually to the seriousness of the offence and the circumstances of the suspect. Some factors commonly relevant can be found in the Code for Crown Prosecutors[1]. Among other things, this makes clear that a prosecution will normally take place in serious cases unless there are public interest factors militating against a prosecution which outweigh those in favour.

1 See the FSA Handbook at ENF Chapter 15, Annex 1G, para 6.

11.23 Some additional factors are relevant in cases of insider dealing or misleading statements or practices, which overlap with the market abuse regime, and these are considered at para 13.180 below. In cases of money laundering, the FSA will also have regard to whether the person concerned has complied with the Guidance Notes for the Financial Sector, produced by the Joint Money Laundering Steering Group[1].

1 See the FSA Handbook at ENF 15.4.1.

What does this mean in practice?

11.24 It is not clear quite what this means in practice. This is because the FSA Handbook is silent on one important point, namely whether the availability of the FSA's other enforcement powers affects its decision whether to prosecute. In other words, if a criminal prosecution would prejudice the FSA's chances of obtaining, say, a restitution order or would delay this[1], but the FSA regards the restitution order as more important, will this be a relevant factor in the public interest test? Whilst the FSA must, in accordance with the Code for Crown Prosecutors, act fairly, independently and objectively, it is not required to approach its prosecution function without regard to its enforcement function. It is thought that the need to take other enforcement action, such as imposing a restitution order, is a legitimate, and may be an important, factor in the public interest test. As a result, it may be that the decision whether or not to prosecute is in practice simply another aspect of the decision on what enforcement action it is appropriate to take in all the circumstances of the case.

1 Perhaps because of the higher burden of proof in the criminal case or because the proceedings for a restitution order may need to await the completion of the criminal proceedings.

WHO CAN BE PROSECUTED?

11.25 Those who could be prosecuted for criminal offences include:

- the firm;
- its employees; and
- its officers.

We outline briefly here how the criminal liability of each arises.

Criminal liability of the firm

11.26 Most of the criminal offences under the FSMA 2000 are, on their wording, committed by 'a person'. This includes not only natural persons but also corporate bodies and unincorporated bodies[1]. Hence, most of the criminal offences under the FSMA 2000 are capable of being committed by firms as well as individuals[2].

1 Interpretation Act 1978.
2 This is also recognised by FSMA 2000, ss 400 and 403.

11.27 But because firms have no physical existence, the commission of a crime by them produces complications which the law has developed to address[1]. Criminal offences generally involve two aspects, an act or omission and, for many offences, a mental element. In relation to both, it is necessary to identify the relevant individual or individuals whose acts or state of mind represent that of the firm. The acts of the firm's servants or agents may be sufficient to constitute the acts of the firm[2]. So, the actions of staff at any level could be relevant.

1 For a more detailed discussion, see Smith & Hogan, *Criminal Law*, 9th edn, 1999 from page 179.
2 See *HL Bolton (Engineering) Co Ltd v PJ Graham & Sons Ltd* [1957] 1 QB 159 (Denning LJ), *Tesco Supermarkets Ltd v Nattrass* [1972] AC 153, HL and *Meridian Global Funds Management Asia Ltd v Securities Commission* [1995] 2 AC 500, PC, and see the discussion in Smith & Hogan, *Criminal Law*, 9th edn, 1999, from page 176.

11.28 Where the offence includes a mental element, for example the need for false or misleading information to have been provided 'knowingly or recklessly' to the FSA[1], the attribution of the relevant state of mind to the firm causes more difficulty. The courts identify with the company the state of mind, not of its servants and agents generally, but of the controlling officers through whom it acts. This refers to the directors and managers who represent the directing mind and will of the company and control what it does[2]. In a small firm it may be relatively simple to identify those who are the directing will and mind of the company, and the question then is whether they were involved and whether they had the necessary state of mind for the offence. But this may be rather more difficult in a large, complex organisation and it may be rather less likely that those who control the company had the requisite knowledge or state of mind.

1 FSMA 2000, s 398.
2 Denning LJ in *HL Bolton (Engineering) Co Ltd v PJ Graham & Sons Ltd*. See also *Tesco Supermarket v Nattrass* [1972] AC 153, HL. For a more detailed discussion, see Smith & Hogan, *Criminal Law*, 9th edn, 1999 from page 179.

11.29 Many of the offences under the FSMA 2000, though, do not contain any mental element[1]. Examples include breach of the general prohibition[2], unlawful financial promotion[3] and offering securities before publishing a prospectus[4]. These offences of strict liability do not give rise to the same difficulties as there is no need to show that the firm had any particular state of mind. There may therefore be fewer obstacles to bringing a prosecution against the firm for a strict liability offence.

1 Although some do allow the firm a defence which involves a mental element: see for example FSMA 2000, s 25.
2 FSMA 2000, s 23.
3 FSMA 2000, s 25.
4 FSMA 2000, s 85.

Criminal liability of employees

11.30 Where the FSMA 2000 contains a prohibition the breach of which is a criminal offence, then if a particular person acting for the company breaches that prohibition he may be liable to prosecution. The FSA has not given any indication of when, in practice, it will bring criminal proceedings against the individual rather than, or in addition to, the firm. The answer in any particular case depends upon the application of the tests outlined at para 11.19 ff above and, in particular, whether it is in the public interest to prosecute the individual. In applying the public interest test, an important question will be where the blame lies – was it the individual that was at fault, or did the offence arise from a corporate failing? In many cases, the distinction may be difficult to draw or both may be true. The nature of the offence may also be relevant: compare, for example, the destruction of documents by a person, on the one hand, with the offering of securities before publishing a prospectus, on the other.

Criminal liability of officers

11.31 The FSMA 2000 also allows officers of the company to be prosecuted at the same time as the company. It provides[1] that if an offence under the FSMA 2000 committed by a body corporate is shown:

- to have been committed with the consent or connivance of an officer[2]; or
- to be attributable to any neglect on his part;

then the officer as well as the company is guilty of the offence and liable to be proceeded against and punished accordingly.

1 FSMA 2000, s 400. Similar provisions apply to: (i) the members of companies that are managed by their members; (ii) partners of partnerships and (iii) officers and members of the governing body of unincorporated associations: FSMA 2000, s 400(2), (3) and (6).

2 Officer means a director, member of the committee of management, chief executive, manager, secretary or other similar officer, or a person purporting to act in any such capacity, and also an individual who is a controller of the body: FSMA 2000, s 400(5). Note that 'manager' has a wide meaning which includes, broadly, employees who exercise managerial functions or are responsible for maintaining accounts or other records: FSMA 2000, s 423. Compare the more limited definition of 'manager' in *R v Boal* [1992] QB 591, CA.

11.32 This provision does not allow the individual officer to be prosecuted as an alternative to the company. Nor can the prosecution against him succeed if that against the company fails. It makes the individual liable 'as well as' the company and for the same offence. Thus, this is a form of secondary liability[1]. It is important to appreciate this because the provision, in particular the second limb, may otherwise appear to impose liability based on negligent actions, where the relevant criminal offence may contain a different standard (for example, that the act was committed knowingly or recklessly). But if the company has committed no offence because it has not acted, say, knowingly or recklessly, then no question should arise of an individual being liable on a secondary basis.

1 See Smith & Hogan, *Criminal Law*, 9th edn, 1999 at page 187 and Card, Cross and Jones, *Criminal Law*, 14th edn, 1998 at 21.61.

11.33 There are two key phrases which require further explanation. First, when will an offence have been committed with the consent or connivance of an individual? Second, when will it be attributable to his neglect?

Consent or connivance

11.34 A person consents to an offence if he is aware of what is going on and agrees to it. He connives in it if he is wilfully blind to it and, probably, acquiesces in it[1]. This equates broadly with liability as an accomplice. It requires some kind of involvement by the relevant officer, but the test is relatively low, particularly for connivance. The person need not necessarily be aware that what is happening amounts to an offence[2]; it is his knowledge of the facts that is relevant.

1 See *Huckerby v Elliott* [1970] 1 All ER 189 at 193.
2 Ignorance of the law is no defence. See, for example, *Grant v Borg* [1982] 2 All ER 257, HL.

Attributable to any neglect on his part

11.35 An offence is attributable to a person's neglect if he was under a duty to check the conduct of the person who committed the offence and that conduct resulted in the offence[1]. The courts have recognised that there is normally no duty to check on the conduct of an experienced member of staff whom the officer can expect to act in accordance with his instructions, unless there is something to prompt him into checking[2]. In the present context, the question of whether there was any duty to check could be examined against the relevant person's regulatory obligations of supervision and internal responsibilities within the firm.

1 See *Huckerby v Elliott* [1970] 1 All ER 189 at 193 (Lord Parker CJ) and 194 (Ashworth J).
2 See *Lewin v Bland* [1985] RTR 171, cited in Card, Cross and Jones, *Criminal Law*, 14th edn, 1998 at p. 697.

WHAT OTHER OPTIONS DOES THE FSA HAVE?

11.36 As ever, when considering the FSA's powers under the FSMA 2000, it is important not to focus purely on the particular power under consideration but to keep in mind the other options open to the FSA. We consider here two, separate issues. First, in some situations where a criminal offence has been committed, it may be appropriate for the FSA not to bring a prosecution, but instead to issue a caution to the person concerned. In what circumstances will it do so? And what is the effect of a caution? Second, we consider whether bringing a criminal prosecution precludes the FSA from exercising its other enforcement powers in relation to the same matter.

When will the FSA administer a caution?

11.37 The FSA has indicated[1] that it may, in some cases, decide to issue a formal caution, rather than pursuing a criminal prosecution. However, in accordance with Home Office guidance, it will not administer a caution unless satisfied that the following conditions are met:

- there is sufficient evidence of the person's guilt to give a realistic prospect of conviction;
- the person admits the offence; and

- the person understands the significance of a caution and gives informed consent to being cautioned.

1 See the FSA Handbook at ENF 15.6.

11.38 The FSA has not provided any indication of when in practice it is likely to consider issuing a caution. Note that unlike, for example, a private warning in a disciplinary case, a caution is only used where the relevant person admits the offence.

11.39 The primary effect of a caution, from the perspective of the person concerned, is that he is not subjected to a criminal prosecution. This will often be the main aim and the overriding factor. However, a caution may also have other less beneficial consequences which at least need to be recognised.

11.40 The FSA has indicated[1] that a record of the caution will be kept on file and may influence the decision whether or not to prosecute if the person ever offends again. But this is unlikely to be the only regulatory consequence. Since the caution is kept on file, it will form part of the person's general compliance history and in that case may be relevant to the enforcement decisions that the FSA makes about the person if some other incident arises involving him in the future: for example, whether or not to take formal disciplinary action in relation to that other matter[2]. The FSA has also confirmed that the caution may be a relevant factor when the FSA considers whether the person is a fit and proper person to be involved in regulated activities[3]. Because of this, it could be relevant to an application for the person to become an approved person or if the FSA has to consider the withdrawal of the person's approval[4] or the making of a prohibition order against him[5]. That is not to say that a caution would of itself give rise to these consequences: it ought not to do so. The point is that it may well reappear as an additional factor which is weighed into the balance when the FSA comes to make other decisions about the relevant person.

1 See the FSA Handbook at ENF 15.6.2.
2 The FSA has expressly recognised this: see the FSA Handbook at ENF 15.6.2 and 11.4.1(3)(d). What has not been made clear is whether the caution will also be relevant to the questions of what action the FSA should take and the amount of any fine that should be imposed. In principle, the person's compliance history is relevant to both of these questions: see the FSA Handbook at ENF 12.3.3(4) and 13.3.3(6). (Contrast the express statement in relation to private warnings, that a private warning will not be relied upon in determining the level of sanction for future breaches: see para 7.18 ff above and see the FSA Handbook at ENF 11.3.6).
3 See the FSA Handbook at ENF 15.6.2 and see also FIT 2.1.3(4).
4 See para 8.27 ff above.
5 See para 8.44 ff above.

Can the FSA use its other enforcement powers as well as prosecuting?

11.41 The criminal offence may not be the only regulatory misdemeanour that has occurred and the circumstances in which it occurred may give rise to other concerns about the firm or individual employees. For example, the FSA may be concerned as to how the offence was allowed to be committed given the firm's systems and controls and it may, as a result, be worried about whether consumers are adequately protected or whether the firm may cause further damage to the markets. Criminal proceedings may not therefore be sufficient to address all the regulatory implications of the situation. The FSA may therefore wish, for example, to:

- obtain an injunction to prevent further breaches, remedy breaches or secure assets[1];
- obtain compensation for customers[2];
- discipline the firm[3];
- discipline approved persons[4];
- vary or cancel the firm's permission or intervene in an incoming firm[5]; or
- withdraw the approval of approved persons or make prohibition orders against approved persons or other individuals[6].

1 See para 7.97 ff above.
2 See para 7.43 ff above.
3 See para 7.7 ff above.
4 See para 8.4 ff above.
5 See Chapter 9 above.
6 See, respectively, paras 8.27 ff and 8.44 ff above.

11.42 In some instances, the additional regulatory enforcement action may be linked to the criminal proceedings. For example, if it were found that a criminal offence had been committed under the FSMA 2000[1], then this would amount to the contravention of a requirement imposed by or under the FSMA 2000 and could lead to an injunction or restitution order being made or to disciplinary sanctions being imposed against the firm.

1 See the discussion at para 2.142 ff above.

11.43 Indeed, the FSA may prefer to take enforcement action rather than bringing a criminal prosecution and the question whether it can do so has been discussed at para 11.24 above. We consider here the other side of the same question: can the FSA bring enforcement action where a criminal prosecution is in prospect?

11.44 When the FSA decides whether to take civil or regulatory action where criminal proceedings are in contemplation, it has regard to the following factors[1]:

- whether, in the FSA's opinion, the taking of civil or regulatory action might unfairly prejudice the prosecution, or proposed prosecution, of criminal offences;

- whether, in the FSA's opinion, the taking of civil or regulatory action might unfairly prejudice the defendants in the criminal proceedings in the conduct of their defence; and
- whether it is appropriate to take civil or regulatory action having regard to the scope of the criminal proceedings and the powers available to the criminal courts.

1 See the FSA Handbook at ENF 15.4.4.

11.45 These factors reflect the legal position that a court may intervene to prevent injustice where the continuation of one set of proceedings may prejudice the fairness of the trial of other proceedings, but that it will only do so where there is a real risk of serious prejudice which may lead to injustice[1].

1 Per Neill LJ in *R v Panel on Takeovers and Mergers, ex p Fayed* [1992] BCC 524, at 531. See also *Jefferson Ltd v Bhetcha* [1979] 2 All ER 1108, *R v BBC, ex p Lavelle* [1983] 1 All ER 241, *R v Panel on Takeovers and Mergers, ex p Guinness plc* [1989] 1 All ER 509 and *R v Institute of Chartered Accountants of England and Wales, ex p Brindle* [1993] BCC 736.

11.46 As a general rule, the mere fact that there are criminal proceedings does not prevent civil or regulatory proceedings relating to the same matter from continuing. The trial of the civil or administrative proceedings may, though, be required to await the outcome of the criminal proceedings if there is otherwise a real risk of the criminal proceedings being prejudiced (for example, because both proceedings involved adjudication of the same issue). There is, however, no reason why the interlocutory processes should not continue in parallel, subject to any appropriate safeguards. It is also quite possible that the process of disclosure in civil proceedings could lead to evidence which would result in an additional criminal charge being brought.

PRACTICAL GUIDANCE FOR FIRMS

11.47 If the firm, or one of its employees, is the subject of a prosecution, or the firm can see that this is likely to be the case, then what practical steps should the firm be taking? Should it stand by its employee? How should it deal with its regulator, who may also be its prosecutor? We consider here some of the practical issues that arise and, in particular:

- what approach should the firm take as against its employee?
- should the firm continue to co-operate with the FSA? and
- are there any practical steps the firm can take to protect its position?

What approach should the firm take as against its employee?

11.48 One of the most difficult issues where an employee is charged with a criminal offence is what position the firm should take as against that employee.

At one end of the spectrum, the firm might publicly and privately support the individual. At the other end, it could take a hard line and implement its own steps to discipline him, without waiting for the criminal trial. There would also be a range of other options, perhaps involving a policy of awaiting the outcome before the firm committed itself and in the meantime providing financial and other assistance for him in relation to his defence to a greater or lesser extent as the firm considers appropriate.

11.49 What approach it is appropriate for the firm to take is impossible to say in the abstract. It depends very much upon factors such as the firm's view of the evidence against the individual, the relationship between the individual and the firm, whether the FSA is pressing the firm to take any particular line[1] and, often, internal pressures within the firm. In practice, it is unlikely the firm could simply await the outcome of the criminal process; it will probably need to take its own decision.

1 For example, the FSA may suggest that the firm should remove the individual from a particular area of responsibility. The firm may also be expected to consider taking disciplinary action: see para 3.135 ff above.

11.50 A particular point which ought to be addressed when a criminal charge against the individual seems to be in prospect is to ensure that the individual understands the need to take his own legal advice. It will often be inappropriate for the firm's lawyers, internal or external, to be representing the individual at that stage, given the clear potential conflict between his interests and those of the firm. The individual needs to understand this and, particularly, that the firm's in-house counsel are not acting for him personally. To illustrate the conflict, if the individual admitted the offence to the firm's lawyers, or even admitted sufficient facts or matters for the firm to conclude he may have committed the offence, the firm may be obliged to report that information to the FSA[1], and could expose itself to discipline or other regulatory action if it failed to do so. The firm would also need to consider taking disciplinary action against the individual, which may include questioning him about the same matters.

1 The firm's obligation to notify the FSA under Principle 11 and under certain specific FSA rules is considered at para 3.41 ff above.

Should the firm continue to co-operate with the FSA?

11.51 Assuming it is the firm, as well as or instead of the individual, against whom the criminal charge is laid by the FSA acting as criminal prosecutor, the question arises as to how that affects its relationship with the FSA in its capacity as regulator.

11.52 The firm's obligation of openness and co-operation with the FSA has already been discussed in detail[1]. The institution of a criminal charge against the firm does not relieve it of that obligation. There may still be an ongoing investigation or enforcement process and the firm will need to co-operate with the FSA for those purposes. It may wish to do so to avoid exacerbating the problem and causing the FSA to have other concerns about the firm that could lead to it seeking to exercise additional enforcement powers, for example to vary or cancel the firm's permission[2]. In addition, beyond the instant enforcement process, the firm has an ongoing supervisory relationship with the FSA to consider[3]. Where the FSA continues to investigate or take other enforcement action, notwithstanding a criminal charge has been instituted against the firm, there will be issues about self-incrimination privilege as discussed at para 4.242 ff above.

1 See paras 4.27 ff and 4.180 above.
2 The question whether the FSA can exercise its enforcement powers as well as bringing a criminal prosecution has been considered at para 11.41 ff above.
3 The FSA's approach to its supervisory role, and the impact of the enforcement process on that approach, are considered at para 2.29 ff above.

Are there any practical steps the firm can take to protect its position?

11.53 Where the firm is, or is likely to be, prosecuted, there are some basic steps that it can take to protect its position, namely:

- to preserve all relevant records[1];
- not unnecessarily to create further documents that might incriminate it[2];
- to take legal advice at all stages of the process; and
- in accordance with its legal advice, to obtain the best evidence available to explain its actions and defend itself.

1 The need to suspend any document destruction processes is considered in more detail at para 3.150 ff above.
2 For a further discussion, see para 3.155 ff above.

APPENDIX TO CHAPTER 11
CRIMINAL OFFENCES UNDER THE FSMA 2000

Offence	***Provision of the Act***	***Where is it discussed?***
Breach of the general prohibition	Section 23	Para 2.175 above
Falsely claiming to be an authorised or exempt person	Section 24	
Unlawful financial promotion	Section 25	
Breach of an assets requirement	Section 48(6)	Para 9.89 ff above
Breach of a prohibition order	Section 56	Para 8.44 ff above
Failure to register listing particulars	Section 83	Chapter 15 below
Offering securities before publishing a prospectus	Section 84	Chapter 15 below
Advertisements without FSA approval or authorisation	Section 98	Chapter 15 below
Breach of insurance business regulations re asset identification rules	Section 142	
Offences in connection with FSA investigations	Section 177	Para 3.151 and 4.287 above
Offences in connection with changes in control over authorised persons	Section 191	
Breach of a consumer credit prohibition on an incoming firm	Section 203	
Offences in connection with investigations into collective investment schemes	Section 284(6)	Chapter 14 below
Falsely claiming to be a person to whom the general prohibition does not apply	Section 333	
Providing false or misleading information to an auditor or actuary	Section 346	
Disclosing confidential information	Section 352	Para 4.304 ff above
Misleading statements and practices	Section 387	Chapter 13 below
Providing false or misleading information to the FSA	Section 398	Para 4.52 above

12 The ombudsman scheme

CONTENTS

Introduction	**483**
Practical issues for firms	**486**
Will the ombudsman investigate the complaint?	**491**
How does the ombudsman handle the complaint?	**497**
The ombudsman's decision	**503**

INTRODUCTION[1]

12.1 The ombudsman scheme is a scheme for the resolution of disputes between firms and, broadly, their customers. It provides for the first time 'a one-stop mechanism for dealing with consumer complaints across the financial services industry as a whole [and] . . . is . . . a major step forward in consumer protection'[2]. The scheme aims for disputes to be resolved in an expeditious, informal and cost-effective manner. In this chapter, we review the ombudsman scheme from the perspective of firms faced with proceedings and, in particular, we consider:

- various practical issues for firms faced with ombudsman proceedings (para 12.9 ff);
- the initial question of whether the complaint can, or should, be resolved by the ombudsman (para 12.23 ff);
- the handling of complaints by the ombudsman (para 12.41 ff); and
- the ombudsman's decision, including the remedies that can be granted (para 12.58 ff).

1 The discussion in this chapter of the detailed ombudsman scheme rules is based on the 'final' draft rules published by the FSA and the Financial Ombudsman Service Limited in December 2000 (Policy Statement: 'Complaints handling arrangements, response on CP49') and June 2001 (Consultation Paper 99, 'Complaints handling Rules: transitional arrangements and other amendments'). However, at the time of writing, certain aspects of the rules, principally relating to transitional provisions, were still the subject of consultation and the rules had not therefore yet been formally made. The discussion that follows of the framework for the ombudsman scheme under the FSMA 2000, the general policy, and the practical issues that arise should be unaffected by any further amendments to the rules.

2 Economic Secretary to HM Treasury in Standing Committee, 30 November 1999.

An overview of the ombudsman scheme

12.2 The ombudsman scheme[1] is a scheme for the resolution of customer complaints, operated by a company called the Financial Ombudsman Service Limited (referred to here as 'the scheme operator' or 'FOS')[2] and funded by the industry[3]. It replaces eight previous ombudsman schemes[4] operating on a variety of different bases[5].

1 The ombudsman scheme is headed by a chief ombudsman and is divided into three ombudsman divisions: insurance, investment, and banking and loans, each headed by a principal ombudsman: Annual Report of the scheme operator, 1999–2000.

2 FOS is governed by a chairman and board of directors. They are appointed by the FSA but on terms designed to secure their independence from the FSA in the operation of the scheme: FSMA 2000, Sch 17, para 3. It is the scheme operator, not the FSA, that appoints the ombudsmen. It appoints a panel of ombudsmen, and a chief ombudsman, and employs staff to assist in the consideration of complaints. The FOS is accountable to the FSA: it must make an annual report to the FSA and its budget must also be approved by the FSA: FSMA 2000, Sch 17.

3 The scheme is funded through fees levied on firms. Details are found in the FSA Handbook at DISP 5. There are proposed to be two components to the fee: (i) a general levy imposed on firms by reference to the proportion of the scheme's workload generated by the industry sector in which the firm operates and the proportion of that sector which the relevant firm represents and (ii) a charge levied per case referred to the ombudsman scheme. The purpose of levying charges by reference to cases is to try to encourage the early settlement of disputes and it is envisaged that the proportion of the overall fees levied in this way will be increased over time. For a detailed discussion, see Consultation Paper 74, 'Funding the Financial Ombudsman Scheme', November 2000.

4 The Banking Ombudsman, the Building Societies Ombudsman, the Investment Ombudsman, the Insurance Ombudsman, the Personal Investment Authority Ombudsman, the Personal Investment Arbitration Service, the Securities and Futures Authority Complaints Bureau and Arbitration Service and the FSA Complaints Unit and Independent Investigator.

5 Some voluntary, others compulsory; some statutory, others contractual; some involving ombudsmen, others arbitrators.

12.3 The ombudsman scheme is the second stage of a two-stage complaints handling process, operating where the matter cannot be resolved at the first stage, which is the firm's internal complaints handling procedures. The FSA's rules impose requirements on firms with regard to internal complaints handling procedures[1], ensuring, among other things, that they dovetail in certain respects with the ombudsman scheme. As will be seen, firms are encouraged to attempt to resolve complaints before they are referred to the ombudsman.

1 These are outlined at para 12.24 below.

12.4 The scheme is effectively two schemes. One, known as the compulsory jurisdiction, is compulsory for authorised firms in relation to complaints arising from certain types of business[1]. The other, known as the voluntary jurisdiction, is available for authorised firms outside the bounds of the compulsory jurisdiction and for other firms as well, in certain respects[2]. The voluntary scheme is voluntary in the sense that it applies only to firms who participate in it, but it is binding on those firms. Whilst the two schemes are different in scope and in their legal basis, they are almost identical in the way they operate.

1 These are outlined at para 12.33 below. The scope of the scheme can be altered from time to time within statutory limitations.
2 The scope of the voluntary scheme is outlined at para 12.34 below. The scope of the scheme can be altered from time to time, within statutory limitations.

12.5 The aim is to resolve cases in an informal and flexible way, at the earliest opportunity by whatever means appears most appropriate[1]. Although the procedure is informal, the ombudsman does have binding powers, for example to require firms to provide information[2], to make binding awards up to a limit of £100,000[3] (and recommendations beyond that limit) and to direct firms to take particular steps[4]. The ombudsman's determinations are enforceable by court order. Moreover, the FSA has imposed an obligation on firms to co-operate with the ombudsman[5]. In practice, most of the work of the ombudsman is carried out by staff employed by the scheme operator[6], although an ombudsman is appointed for the purpose of considering and reaching the final determination on each case[7].

1 FSMA 2000, s 225(1) and see the draft rules at DISP 3.2.10 and see para 12.42 below.
2 See para 12.50 below.
3 See para 12.63 below.
4 See para 12.65 below.
5 See the discussion at para 12.15 below.
6 This is permitted by the draft scheme rules: see DISP 3.7 and see FSMA 2000, Sch 17, para 14(2)(f). References in this chapter to the ombudsman therefore need to be read as referring also to the relevant members of staff.
7 And only an ombudsman can decide the circumstances in which information may be disclosed: see the draft rules at DISP 3.7.1(1).

12.6 In many cases, the ombudsman will be considering a relatively small claim arising from an isolated incident, which will barely register in a large institution. But firms need to appreciate the 'floodgates' potential, that large numbers of similar claims may be brought before the ombudsman arising from the same problem[1]. The cap of £100,000 on awards allows reasonably substantial claims to be brought in this forum and if a large number of similar claims are involved then the figures could potentially become very significant, even for large institutions. A single case may thus assume real significance for the firm as, effectively, setting a precedent for others[2].

1 As the FOS 1999/2000 Annual Report explains, in the year to March 2000 the SFA Complaints Bureau received over 260 complaints relating to a single new issue by one firm.
2 Some practical implications of this are outlined at paras 12.10 ff and 12.21 below.

12.7 In practice, a very significant number of customer complaints are resolved through these mechanisms[1] without the need for any formal court process. But, as we will see, the process is in various respects not entirely even-handed as between customers and firms. For example, the outcome of the process does not have to be binding on the customer, who can choose to reject the award and retain his right to take formal action[2].

1 The figures are staggering. In the year 2001/2, the FOS expected to handle 375,000 new initial customer contacts, leading to 38,000 cases (at an average direct cost of case handling of around £360 per case): see the FOS 2001/2 Plan and Budget.
2 This is discussed in more detail at para 12.70 below. In addition, the ombudsman has the ability to make a costs order against the firm, but cannot make a costs order against the complainant (see para 12.67 below). Furthermore, the right of access to the ombudsman scheme is one-sided, since it is only available to customers, not to firms.

12.8 The framework for the scheme is found in the FSMA 2000[1]. The detailed rules are found in the FSA Handbook at DISP. The rules relating to the compulsory jurisdiction are made by the FSA and the scheme operator, under powers granted under the FSMA 2000. The rules relating to the voluntary jurisdiction, known as the 'standard terms'[2], are made by the scheme operator and approved by the FSA, again under powers granted by the FSMA 2000.

1 FSMA 2000, Pt XVI and Sch 17.
2 The voluntary jurisdiction rules mostly incorporate by reference the relevant provisions of the compulsory jurisdiction rules, ensuring that the procedure for each of the two jurisdictions is for most practical purposes the same.

PRACTICAL ISSUES FOR FIRMS

12.9 Before turning to the procedural rules, we consider four practical issues for firms, namely:

- what approach will the firm take in relation to the process?
- how should the firm deal with the ombudsman?
- the risks of disclosing information to the ombudsman; and
- some practical guidance on dealing with ombudsman proceedings.

Each is considered in turn, below.

What approach will the firm take in relation to the process?

12.10 An important initial question for firms, particularly where it is thought that a particular complaint may be only the first of many similar complaints, is whether to resist or embrace the ombudsman process. In some instances, the process will be attractive to the firm as a cost-effective means for dealing with large numbers of disputes[1], often involving a lower risk of publicity than court proceedings would. On the other hand, as will be seen, the process is not entirely even-handed procedurally[2]. It is an informal process, it is not conducted adversarially[3], and it does not adopt any particular evidential rules[4], and for these reasons it may not necessarily be appropriate for the resolution of claims which involve the resolution of complex issues of law or fact, particularly where the claims are, overall, significant financially for the firm. Also the outcome may represent what is 'fair and reasonable', rather than what is legally correct[5], which may be acceptable in the interests of obtaining a cost-effective resolution where a small claim with a single customer is concerned but may be less attractive where significant sums are involved.

1 The aim of an expeditious and informal process is outlined at para 12.42 below.
2 The main issues are summarised at para 12.7 above.
3 See para 12.57 below.
4 See para 12.54 below.
5 This is discussed in more detail at para 12.60 below.

12.11 To what extent does the firm have any control over which complaints are heard by the ombudsman? As we have already seen, customers who have suffered loss arising from a problem can potentially obtain redress from the firm through a number of means, including bringing civil claims against the firm, or asking the FSA to make or apply for a restitution order, as well as bringing claims before the ombudsman. These processes overlap, in so far as they serve the same basic purpose of obtaining compensation for customers, but they involve very different procedures. Depending upon the circumstances, the firm may be able to influence which route is used.

12.12 First, the firm may be able to agree with the FSA to pay restitution to customers who have suffered loss on a basis agreed between the firm and the FSA. This may in practice largely eradicate the risk of complaints being made to the ombudsman[1] and there may be a prospect of the firm maintaining some element of control over the basis upon which restitution is paid[2].

1 Indeed, if large numbers of customers are affected then this may in itself militate in favour of a restitution order: see para 7.64 ff above. Note, though, that customers may be entitled to bring further claims against the firm to the extent that their losses remain uncompensated following payment of restitution: this is discussed in more detail at para 10.64 ff above.
2 This is discussed at para 7.94 ff above.

12.13 Second, the ombudsman has the power to decline to hear a complaint which is already the subject of some other dispute resolution process[1]. In some circumstances, it may be appropriate for the firm to take pre-emptive action by commencing legal proceedings in the same case[2], or perhaps in a similar case raising a particular issue likely to be common to a number of potential claims. The firm may then be in a position to object to the particular complaint being heard when it is referred to the ombudsman.

1 See the discussion at para 12.39 below.
2 It can in some circumstances be appropriate to commence an action for a negative declaration that the firm is not liable: see *Messier-Dowty Ltd v Sabena SA* [2000] 1 WLR 2040, CA.

12.14 Third, even if action has not been commenced in another forum, there may be a prospect of objecting to the complaint being heard by the ombudsman[1] on the ground that it would be more suitably dealt with by a court, for example because there is a conflict of evidence that would more fairly be resolved in a court[2], or that it would be more appropriately addressed by a restitution order which the firm is discussing with the FSA.

1 As to the ombudsman's discretion to terminate cases without considering the merits, see para 12.36 ff below.
2 See para 12.38 below.

How should the firm deal with the ombudsman?

12.15 The draft FSA rules on complaints handling procedures require firms to co-operate fully with the ombudsman in the handling of complaints[1]. This includes[2] producing documents the ombudsman requests, adhering to any time limits specified and attending hearings when requested to do so. Breach of this obligation, whether by an authorised firm or an unauthorised firm, may adversely affect the ombudsman's determination[3]. In addition, the rule is a requirement imposed by or under the FSMA 2000 and, so far as authorised firms are concerned, is therefore capable of giving rise to the same potential consequences as any other regulatory breach[4]. Even in relation to an unauthorised firm, the FSA could potentially apply to the court for an injunction requiring the person to remedy the breach[5], although this seems unlikely in practice.

1 See the draft rules at DISP 1.6.1. This obligation will apply both to authorised firms within the compulsory jurisdiction and to authorised and unauthorised firms within the voluntary jurisdiction: see the draft rules at DISP 1.1.
2 See the draft rules at DISP 1.6.2.
3 See paras 12.47 and 12.53 below.
4 For a discussion of this phrase and the potential consequences of breach, see para 2.142 ff above. Note also that the breach may be reported to the FSA by the ombudsman: see para 12.18 below.
5 FSMA 2000, s 380 and see para 7.97 ff above.

Risks of disclosing information to the ombudsman

12.16 As will be seen[1], the ombudsman may obtain information from the firm in the course of investigating a complaint, including information which is confidential. To what extent is that information protected from being misused? And to what uses can it properly be put? These issues are considered below.

1 See para 12.50 below.

Use of information by the ombudsman

12.17 The draft scheme rules require the ombudsman, in dealing with any information received by it in relation to the consideration and investigation of a complaint, to have regard to the parties' rights of privacy[1]. This does not prevent the ombudsman[2] disclosing information (either in full or in an edited version) to the extent he is required or authorised to do so by law, or to the parties, or in his determination, or at a hearing of the complaint. Nor does it prevent him from disclosing information to the FSA or other regulatory or statutory bodies for the purposes of the discharge of his or their functions, so long as he has regard to the parties' rights of privacy. This is plainly intended to reflect the right to respect for privacy under ECHR, art 8, discussed at para 3.29 ff above, and should also confer on such information, to the extent it is confidential, and subject to the limitations expressed in the rule, the normal protections which the civil law gives to confidential information, including allowing the firm to obtain, in an appropriate case, an injunction to restrain misuse[3]. The ombudsman is not, though, bound by any statutory restriction on the use of confidential information which he receives from the firm[4]. There is, therefore, no criminal sanction for the wrongful disclosure or use by an ombudsman of confidential information provided to him by the firm.

1 See the draft rules at DISP 3.10.1. As regards disclosures to the FSA, see para 12.18 below.

2 Decisions on the disclosure of information must be made by an ombudsman, not a staff member: see the draft rules at DISP 3.7.1(1).

3 See *Coco v AN Clark (Engineers) Ltd* [1969] RPC 41 and *A-G v Observer Ltd* [1990] 1 AC 109, HL, discussed at footnote 2 to para 12.19 below. A damages claim for breach of confidence would not generally be available against the ombudsman (unless he acts in bad faith or in breach of the Human Rights Act 1988), because of his statutory immunity from claims for damages: see para 12.76 below.

3 This refers to FSMA 2000, s 348, which does not apply because the ombudsman is not a 'primary recipient', although it would apply to the extent the ombudsman receives information directly or indirectly from the FSA or another primary recipient. For a further discussion of s 348, see para 4.304 ff above.

Disclosure of information to the FSA

12.18 Complaints to the ombudsman are regarded as an important source of regulatory information, providing a valuable early warning of problems with particular firms, products or rules. As a result, the ombudsman has agreed to provide the FSA with information regarding complaints, including general statistical information, information about major matters of principle arising from the ombudsman's functions, and specific information arising from specific complaints[1]. The specific information that the FSA and the scheme operator have agreed the scheme operator may pass to the FSA includes, broadly[2]:

- information which may be relevant to the FSA for its enforcement function; and
- information arising from an authorised firm's handling of a complaint, for example failure to comply with an ombudsman award, failure to comply with a requirement to provide information or documents to an ombudsman, or inadequate internal complaints handling mechanisms.

Whilst the scheme operator retains a discretion as to what information to pass to the FSA, and when to do so, if the firm discloses to the ombudsman information which suggests that regulatory breaches have been committed or that the firm or an individual employee may not be fit and proper[3], there is a risk of that information being disclosed to the FSA. Once disclosed to it, the FSA may use the information for, among other things, its own enforcement purposes.

1 Extracts from a Memorandum of Understanding between the FSA and the scheme operator with regard to the sharing of information ('the FSA/FOS MOU') can be found at Consultation Paper 49 ('Complaints handling arrangements: feedback statement on CP 33 and draft rules'), May 2000, Annex C.
2 For a full list, see the FSA/FOS MOU, para 16(d) and (e).
3 For a discussion of this phrase, see para 2.43 ff above (in relation to firms) and para 2.69 ff above (in relation to individuals).

Use of information by the complainant

12.19 The more serious risk in this context is of information being misused by complainants. Confidential information provided by the firm to the ombudsman and disclosed to the complainant is not specifically protected under the FSMA 2000[1]. There is also nothing in the scheme rules to require the customer to keep such information confidential. But the complainant may nonetheless be bound by a duty of confidence which a court would recognise[2], which would prevent him from disclosing or misusing[3] the information. If such a duty exists, the firm may be able to obtain an injunction to restrain a breach and/or damages for the breach. Whether a duty exists will, though, depend upon the precise circumstances. There is therefore a lack of clear protection for the firm. This is significant, particularly given the requirement on firms to co-operate with the ombudsman[4] and the statutory powers of the ombudsman to require firms to produce information and documents[5]. Among other things, there may be a risk of a complainant using the ombudsman scheme to obtain, effectively, pre-action disclosure from a firm before bringing a claim against it in the civil courts.

1 FSMA 2000, s 348 does not, generally speaking, apply to such information: see para 12.17 above.
2 The firm would have to show: (i) that the information was of a confidential nature; (ii) that it was communicated in circumstances importing an obligation of confidence and (iii) that there was an unauthorised use of it: *Coco v AN Clark (Engineers) Ltd* [1969] RPC 41 and *A-G v Observer Ltd* [1990] 1 AC 109, HL.
3 Misuse includes using confidential information as a springboard for activities detrimental to the person to whom it belongs: the so-called 'springboard' doctrine – see *Terrapin Ltd v Builders Supply Co (Hayes) Ltd* [1967] RPC 375.
4 See para 12.15 above.
5 See para 12.50 below.

12.20 There are some practical steps the firm can take to protect its position. First, as discussed below[1], the draft scheme rules allow the ombudsman to accept information in confidence, so that only an edited version or a summary or description is passed to the complainant. Firms may wish to rely upon this where sensitive information is to be disclosed. Second, in order to help ensure that a duty of confidence does arise, the firm may wish to ensure it is made clear to the complainant, when confidential material is disclosed, that the information is confidential. Whilst the draft scheme rules do not expressly address this issue, there appears to be nothing to prevent the firm from asking the ombudsman to produce documents to the complainant only on this basis.

1 See para 12.55 below.

Practical guidance for firms

12.21 If a firm faces or may face several complaints to the ombudsman in respect of the same matter, it is important that it takes a co-ordinated and consistent approach, bearing in mind not only the instant case but also the potential for further similar complaints. Whilst the ombudsman looks at each case on its own merits, and does not follow a doctrine of legal precedent, it is likely in practice to want to be consistent in dealing with one particular issue which arises in a whole series of cases. Where there are likely to be further, similar claims, firms need to approach the first cases with this in mind. Generally, the firm should be consistent in the arguments it uses and the evidence it deploys and should try to ensure that cases are not handled by the firm in isolation but that experience from one case is fed into others. This should help the firm to deal with cases in an efficient as well as effective way.

12.22 A number of practical issues arise when dealing with investigations and these are outlined at para 4.179 ff above. They may apply in the context of investigations by the ombudsman[1].

1 The requirement to be open and co-operative with the FSA, discussed at para 4.180 above, may not be relevant in this context.

WILL THE OMBUDSMAN INVESTIGATE THE COMPLAINT?

12.23 Only certain types of complaints are resolved through the ombudsman scheme. Some complaints may be ineligible for consideration by the ombudsman, others may be premature because they have not yet undergone the firm's own complaints handling process, while others may be too late and some may not, in the firm's view, be suitable for the ombudsman. Each of these may give the firm grounds to object to a complaint being handled through the ombudsman scheme. We outline here the initial stages, which may lead to a decision by the ombudsman whether to investigate the complaint and, in particular, we review:

- the FSA's proposed rules relating to complaints handling by firms, which is the first stage of the process before the complaint is considered by the ombudsman;
- when can a complaint be made to the ombudsman?
- what complaints can be referred to the ombudsman[1]? and
- is the ombudsman bound to investigate the complaint?

1 The draft rules contain transitional provisions relating to complaints partly completed before 'N2' and complaints relating to pre-N2 business. These provisions are not considered here.

Complaints handling by firms

12.24 As already outlined, the consideration of a complaint by the ombudsman is the second stage of a two-stage process. The first stage is for the customer to make a complaint to the firm itself and, as will be seen, the ombudsman may decline to hear a matter referred to him before the firm has been given a reasonable opportunity of considering it. The FSA's rules impose various requirements on firms with respect to complaints handling[1]. It is important to outline briefly some of these requirements as they impact on the procedure for the ombudsman scheme[2].

1 The draft complaints handling rules apply also to unauthorised firms that participate in the voluntary jurisdiction, but only in relation to (i) lending money secured by a charge over land, and (ii) a financial services activity covered by a former scheme (under the previous regime) in so far as the firm was a member of that scheme immediately before N2: see the draft scheme rules at DISP 1.1.5 and 2.6.9.

2 For the detailed draft rules, see DISP 1. The discussion that follows is confined to those rules that impact on the ombudsman process.

12.25 The basic requirement is that firms must have in place and operate appropriate and effective internal procedures for handling complaints[1]. So far as the timetable is concerned[2], the FSA requires that[3]:

- the firm sends a written acknowledgement within five business days of receipt;
- within four weeks of receiving the complaint, the firm must send the person making the complaint either[4]:
  - a final response, which means[5] a response accepting the complaint and, where appropriate, offering redress[6], offering redress without accepting the complaint or rejecting the complaint with reasons and information about the right to refer the complaint to the ombudsman, or
  - a holding response, explaining why the firm is not yet in a position to resolve the complaint and giving an indication of when it will make further contact, which must be within eight weeks of receipt of the complaint;
- by the end of eight weeks after receiving the complaint, the firm must send the complainant either a final response (as outlined above) or a response which explains that the firm is still not in a position to provide a final response, gives reasons for the further delay, and indicates when it will provide a final response[7], and informs the complainant of his right to refer the complaint to the ombudsman.

1 See the draft rules at DISP 1.2.1. 'Complaint' means any expression of dissatisfaction, whether oral or written, and whether justified or not, from a person who would be eligible to refer a complaint to the ombudsman (see para 12.30 below) about the firm's provision of, or failure to provide, a financial services activity. Note the firm's obligation to put in place appropriate management controls and take reasonable steps to ensure it identifies and remedies any recurring or systemic problems, as well as any specific problem identified by a complaint: see the draft rules at DISP 1.3.5(3). For a more detailed discussion of the practical steps firms might take to assess and deal with wider systemic issues revealed, see Chapter 3 above.

2 Save in the case of certain types of complaints: see the draft rules at DISP 1.3.1 and see also DISP 1.4.12.

3 For firms with two-tier complaints procedures, see the draft rules at DISP 1.4.10.

4 See the draft rules at DISP 1.4.4.

5 See the FSA Handbook, Glossary of Definitions.
6 Redress may not involve financial redress; it could involve an apology: see the draft rules at DISP 1.2.21. Whether to accept the complaint and whether to offer redress are matters for the firm. But the FSA's draft rules and guidance (see DISP 1.2.14 and 1.2.20) indicate that it expects firms to consider any guidance published by the FSA or the scheme operator when deciding whether to accept complaints and what would be appropriate redress and requires that where a firm decides that redress is appropriate, it should aim to provide the complainant with fair compensation for any acts or omissions for which the firm was responsible and comply with any offer of redress which the complainant accepts. There are various reasons why the firm might consider offering compensation in an appropriate case. First, this will save time and cost if the complainant is otherwise likely to take the matter to the ombudsman and it is likely the firm will lose there. Second, in some cases it will be important not to, effectively, set a precedent before the ombudsman and thereby open the floodgates to large numbers of similar complaints. Third, if the firm is an authorised firm, then if there were other regulatory breaches involved, whether the firm offered to pay compensation may be a factor taken into account by the FSA in deciding what enforcement action to take as a result of those breaches: see para 7.31 above. Finally, if the customer refers the complaint to the ombudsman, the ombudsman may decline to hear it if the firm has offered fair and reasonable compensation and that offer remains open: see para 12.38 below.
7 See the draft rules at DISP 1.4.5.

12.26 The rules thus allow an opportunity for the firm to investigate and for the complaint to be resolved without recourse to the ombudsman. The firm is not bound to provide its final response within eight weeks but, as will be seen, the complainant cannot refer the matter to the ombudsman within that period (unless the firm has already provided a final response).

When can a complaint be made to the ombudsman?

12.27 A complaint may not be made to the ombudsman until the firm has been given eight weeks to consider it[1]. Otherwise, the ombudsman will simply refer the matter back to the firm[2], unless the firm has already issued a final response.

1 This refers to the procedure outlined at para 12.25 above. If the firm should have been given more time, for example because there was a delay in obtaining information from third parties, or the complainant did not co-operate with the firm's investigation, the ombudsman may take this into account when considering at what stage to levy the case-related charge: see DISP 2.3.5.
2 See the draft rules at DISP 3.2.3.

12.28 Complaints must, generally speaking, be referred to the ombudsman not more than six months after the date when the person is advised by the firm in its final response of the right to refer the complaint to the ombudsman and not more than six years after the event complained of[1]. It seems that the complaint must fall within both time limits. The ombudsman can decide to hear a complaint outside the time limits, but only when in his view the failure to comply with the time limits was as a result of exceptional circumstances[2].

1 Or not more than three years from the date when he became aware, or ought reasonably to have become aware, that he had cause for complaint, if later: see the draft rules at DISP 2.3.1(b) and (c). This is intended, broadly, to mirror the normal limitation rules.
2 Examples given include where the complainant has been incapacitated or the firm has failed to inform him of his right to refer the matter to the ombudsman: see the draft rules at DISP 2.3.5.

What complaints can be referred to the scheme?

12.29 One of the first questions for a firm faced with a complaint made to the ombudsman will be whether the complaint is eligible to be considered under the scheme. There are a number of aspects to this. The primary questions are[1]: whether the complainant is eligible to use the scheme and whether the complaint is one that falls within the scope of the scheme. If, in the firm's view, either the complainant or the complaint are ineligible, it may raise this objection with the ombudsman for a decision on whether or not to hear the complaint[2].

1 Additional questions are whether, in relation to the compulsory jurisdiction, the act or omission occurred at a time when the scheme rules were in force in relation to the activity and whether the firm was at that time authorised by the FSA and, in relation to the voluntary jurisdiction, whether the person was a member of the scheme (or a former scheme) at the relevant time or had agreed to let the ombudsman consider such complaints and had not withdrawn from the scheme at the time when the matter was referred to the ombudsman: for a full list, see the draft rules at DISP 2.2.1.

2 The ombudsman must give the parties an opportunity to make representations before he reaches his decision and must give reasons for that decision: see the draft rules at DISP 3.2.7. The ombudsman must in any event himself consider these issues: see the draft rules at DISP 3.2.1 and, for the procedure, DISP 3.2.5 and 3.2.8. If the ombudsman decides that he does have jurisdiction, and the firm believes that decision is wrong, then the firm may be able to challenge the decision by way of judicial review: see, for example, *Legal & General Assurance Society Ltd v Pensions Ombudsman* [2000] 2 All ER 577, *Swansea City and County v Johnson* [1999] 1 All ER 863 and *Marsh & McLennan Companies UK Ltd v Pensions Ombudsman* [2001] IRLR 505. Alternatively, the firm may wish to wait until the complainant seeks to enforce any award and then argue that the ombudsman did not have jurisdiction to make the award. This latter option may, though, be difficult in practice given the firm's regulatory obligation to co-operate with the ombudsman and comply promptly with his award and could also give rise to arguments that the firm had waived the right to object. In addition, the short time limits for bringing judicial review proceedings (see Chapter 16 below) may preclude this.

Is the complainant entitled to use the scheme?

12.30 The draft rules on who is entitled to use the scheme are complicated and only a brief outline is given here[1]. The scheme is available to private individuals[2] and certain types of businesses[3]. It is not available to an intermediate customer or market counterparty of the firm[4]. In addition, firms cannot use the ombudsman scheme to complain about other firms, even if they apparently fall within the parameters of the scheme, if the complaint relates in any way to an activity which the firm itself is permitted to carry on[5].

1 For details, see the draft rules at DISP 2.4. The same rules apply equally to the voluntary jurisdiction: see the draft rules at DISP 4.2.4.

2 See the draft rules at DISP 2.4.3. But not, apparently, private individuals carrying on a business, because a sole trader is included within businesses: see DISP 2.4.4. It is irrelevant whether the complainant lives or is based in the UK: see the draft rules at DISP 2.7.4.

3 Broadly, those with a group annual turnover of less than £1 million at the time the complaint is referred to the scheme: see the draft rules at DISP 2.4.3. Also included are charities with an annual income of less than £1 million and trustees of a trust with a net asset value less than £1 million. Business includes a company, sole trader, unincorporated body and a partnership carrying out a trade or profession: see the draft rules at DISP 2.4.4.

4 See the draft rules at DISP 2.4.3(2).

5 See the draft rules at DISP 2.4.3(2). The same point applies to participants in the voluntary jurisdiction in relation to activities which they conduct.

12.31 Not all of those within the above categories may use the scheme against the firm. The scheme is available to such persons only if they are, broadly, a customer of the firm and the complaint arises out of matters relevant to their being or having been a customer of the firm. In certain circumstances, it is also available to potential customers. It is also available to a person making certain types of indirect complaints[1].

1 For the detailed draft rules, see DISP 2.4.7 to 2.4.14.

Does the complaint fall within the scope of the scheme?

12.32 The ombudsman can only consider those complaints which fall within the scope of the scheme. Again, the rules are complicated and only a brief outline is provided here[1].

1 For the detailed draft rules, see DISP 2.6.

12.33 The compulsory jurisdiction of the scheme is capable of encompassing any of the financial services activities of authorised firms, whether or not those activities are regulated[1]. Currently[2], it is proposed to cover complaints against authorised persons relating to an act or omission in the carrying on[3] of one or more regulated activities and a limited range of unregulated activities[4].

1 FSMA 2000, s 226(4). The FSA anticipates moving towards full coverage on this basis over time: see Consultation Paper 33, 'Consumer complaints and the new ombudsman scheme', from para 3.34 and Consultation Paper 49, 'Complaints handling arrangements: feedback statement on CP33 and draft rules', para 1.41.
2 See the draft rules at DISP 2.6.1.
3 Carrying on includes offering, providing or failing to provide and administering or failing to administer a service in relation to the relevant activities, and includes the manner in which a firm has administered its business provided that the business is an activity subject to the scheme: see the draft rules at DISP 2.6.4.
4 Namely, mortgage lending, lending money (other than restricted credit), lending or paying money by a plastic card (other than a store card), and the provision of ancillary banking services: see the draft rules at DISP 2.6.1.

12.34 The voluntary jurisdiction has the same potential scope, but in relation to unauthorised firms as well[1]. Currently, it is proposed to cover[2] complaints against a person that is a participant in the voluntary scheme, in relation to an act or omission in the carrying on of mortgage lending and other financial services activities in relation to which the particular person was formerly subject to one of the previous voluntary ombudsman schemes, but only if it is not covered by the compulsory jurisdiction[3].

1 FSMA 2000, s 227(4).
2 See the draft rules at DISP 2.6.9. This is likely to be expanded over time to encompass all the financial services activities of authorised firms not covered by the compulsory scheme and some other activities of unauthorised firms, such as mortgage intermediaries and general insurance intermediaries: for a further discussion, see Consultation Paper 33, 'Consumer complaints and the new ombudsman scheme', at para 3.49 and Consultation Paper 47, 'Complaints handling arrangements: feedback statement on CP33 and draft rules', at para 1.44.
3 Primarily, this covers a small number of general insurance intermediaries who had joined the Insurance Ombudsman Bureau, the aim being to ensure that their customers are not deprived of an existing means of redress: see Consultation Paper 47, 'Complaints handling arrangements: feedback statement on CP33 and draft rules', at para 1.44.

12.35 Territorially, the scheme covers complaints about the firm's activities conducted in or from an establishment maintained in the UK, whether or not the complainant lives or is based in the UK[1]. Firms are therefore within the scope of the scheme to the extent that they carry on the activity from a branch in the UK, but not if they carry on their business cross-border into the UK. Complaints concerning business conducted by overseas branches of firms are not subject to the scheme.

1 See the draft rules at DISP 2.7.

Is the ombudsman bound to investigate the complaint?

12.36 On receipt of the complaint, the first step is for the ombudsman to consider[1] whether or not the complaint is within the applicable time limits, and whether or not the complaint and the complainant are eligible[2]. These points have been considered above[3]. In addition, the ombudsman also considers whether or not the complaint is one which should be dismissed without consideration of its merits. In other words, even where the complaint and complainant are eligible, the ombudsman may choose not to investigate. We consider here this third issue.

1 See the draft rules at DISP 3.2.1.
2 Before reaching a decision to dismiss the complaint for lack of eligibility, either on his own initiative or on an objection raised by the firm, the ombudsman must give the complainant an opportunity to make representations and must give reasons for his decision: see the draft rules at DISP 3.2.5 and 3.2.7.
3 Respectively, paras 12.27 ff, 12.29 and 12.30 ff above.

12.37 The draft rules contain a lengthy list of grounds upon which the ombudsman may dismiss a complaint without considering its merits. A full list can be found at DISP 3.3.1.

12.38 In particular, these include cases where:

- the complainant has not suffered, or is unlikely to suffer, financial loss or material inconvenience or distress, the complaint has been referred outside the time limit and no exceptional circumstances apply, or the complaint is frivolous or vexatious or clearly has no reasonable prospect of success;
- the firm has made a fair and reasonable offer of compensation which remains open;
- the matter has been, is being, or is more suitable to be, dealt with in other proceedings, for example another comparable complaints scheme[1] or dispute resolution process, or court proceedings[2];
- the complaint is about the legitimate exercise of a firm's commercial judgement;
- the complaint relates to investment performance;
- the complaint relates to employment matters from an employee of a firm; or

- there are other compelling reasons why it is inappropriate for the complaint to be dealt with by the ombudsman.

1 The ombudsman may refer the matter to another, more suitable complaints body, if the complainant consents: see the draft rules at DISP 3.4.1. An example would be a hybrid complaint by a customer who was advised to pay into an unsuitable occupational pension scheme; this might fall within the remit of both the ombudsman and the Pensions Ombudsman: see Economic Secretary to HM Treasury in Standing Committee, 30 November 1999.
2 One question is whether, in view of a conflict of evidence, a fair resolution of the complaint could only be achieved through examination of the evidence by a court: see the draft rules at DISP 3.3.5.

12.39 One notable effect is to remove from the scope of the scheme many complaints that relate solely to the firm's judgement or to investment performance. But so far as the latter is concerned, the draft rules[1] allow the ombudsman to proceed with a complaint that would otherwise be dismissed if negligence or maladministration is alleged. It is not clear how in practice the line will be drawn, since many allegations could be framed as a failure to take reasonable care capable of giving rise to a claim in negligence.

1 See the draft rules at DISP 3.3.6.

12.40 Before making a decision to dismiss without consideration of the merits, the ombudsman must give the complainant an opportunity to make representations before he makes his decision and, if he decides to dismiss the complaint, must give reasons to the complainant and inform the firm[1]. Whether or not to dismiss a complaint is within the ombudsman's discretion. He is not bound to do so simply because the case falls within one of the above categories[2].

1 See the draft rules at DISP 3.2.8.
2 Although if he makes an irrational or wholly unreasonable decision then that may be capable of being challenged in court. An example might be if the ombudsman fails to dismiss a complaint which is clearly out of time and where no exceptional circumstances exist. For a brief discussion of judicial review in relation to ombudsman decisions, see para 12.73 below.

HOW DOES THE OMBUDSMAN HANDLE THE COMPLAINT?

12.41 We review here how the ombudsman handles a complaint. In particular, we consider[1]:

- the ombudsman's general approach;
- the settlement of complaints;
- the determination of complaints;
- what powers the ombudsman has to obtain information;
- what evidence the ombudsman considers; and
- whether there is an oral hearing.

1 The same rules apply to the voluntary jurisdiction as the compulsory jurisdiction, generally speaking: see the draft rules at DISP 4.2.6.

The ombudsman's general approach

12.42 Where the matter is suitable for consideration by the ombudsman[1], the complaint will not necessarily proceed to a contested hearing at which the rights and wrongs of the dispute will be determined in an adversarial context. In accordance with its statutory purpose[2], the ombudsman scheme aims to resolve disputes quickly[3] and with minimum formality[4]. As the draft scheme rules make clear[5], the ombudsman attempts to resolve complaints at the earliest possible stage, by whatever means appear to be most appropriate, including mediation or investigation. Whilst the scheme must incorporate the ECHR fair trial safeguards, it attempts to do so in such a way as not to undermine the essential informality and speed of the process[6]. The general approach is therefore one of informality, flexibility and expedition.

1 As to those cases where it is not, and the firm's right to object that a complaint should not be heard, see para 12.29 ff above.
2 FSMA 2000, s 225(1).
3 For example, the average number of hours worked on each complaint closed during 1999/2000 by the Investment Ombudsman was 4.1 hours and the average time taken to close complaints was 2.5 months: Investment Ombudsman 1999/2000 Annual Report. The FOS aims to close 70% of cases within six months: see FOS 2001/2 Plan and Budget.
4 'We should deal with consumers as far as possible using their preferred medium of communication – by phone, letter or e-mail as appropriate – only formalising matters when it is necessary to avoid confusion or for a final recorded decision': Chief Ombudsman's report, FOS 1999/2000 Annual Report.
5 See the draft rules at DISP 3.2.10.
6 Consultation Paper 33, 'Consumer complaints and the new ombudsman scheme', para 4.7. For a discussion of the fair process requirements of art 6, see para 6.26 above. The safeguards include that either party has the right to request an oral hearing: see para 12.56 below. Concern has been expressed as to how in practice the informal procedure will survive the implementation of an ECHR-compliant process: for a discussion, see the 1999/2000 Annual Report of the Personal Investment Authority Ombudsman. The FSA and scheme operator have said that the scheme will shape and adjust its processes in light of court decisions on the interpretation of the Human Rights Act 1998, whilst seeking to deploy minimum formality: see Policy Statement, 'Complaints handling arrangements, Response on CP49', December 2000, para 4.28 ff.

Settlement of complaints

12.43 The first step, at least in cases where the ombudsman considers there is a reasonable prospect of resolving the complaint by mediation[1], is to try to negotiate a settlement. The scheme staff[2] consider the information supplied by the parties and explore any reasonable prospect of resolving the complaint by conciliated settlement[3]. Historically, a large proportion of cases in the predecessor schemes have been resolved at this stage.

1 See the draft rules at DISP 3.2.9.
2 Most of the ombudsman's work, apart from reaching a final determination, is carried out by the scheme staff: see para 12.5 above.
3 Consultation Paper 33, 'Consumer complaints and the new ombudsman scheme', para 4.4.

12.44 In dealing with the scheme staff in relation to settlement, firms need to bear in mind the potential impact of any without prejudice admissions that they make for the purposes of reaching a settlement[1]. First, those admissions will be known to the scheme staff who are attempting to settle the complaint; it is not clear whether they will become known to the ombudsman if settlement fails and he is required to make a determination[2]. Second, if the firm's admissions could be relevant to the FSA for enforcement purposes, for example because the firm admitted having committed a regulatory breach, then it is possible that the scheme staff would pass that information on to the FSA[3]. Third, any document recording an admission could potentially be susceptible to disclosure to the FSA in the context of any ongoing investigation or enforcement proceedings[4].

1 These issues arise because the FSMA 2000 does not specifically protect without prejudice communications: FSMA 2000, s 413 and see the discussion at para 4.264 ff above. There is, however, a general public policy in favour of protecting without prejudice communications: *Rush & Tompkins v Greater London Council* [1989] AC 1280. The ombudsman should therefore be pressed to confer protection as a matter of practice and, for example, not to take without prejudice admissions into account when reaching his determination and not to use or disclose without prejudice material for any purpose.
2 For the reasons set out at footnote 1 above, in principle they ought not to be made known to him.
3 The circumstances in which information may be disclosed to the FSA are outlined at para 12.18 above.
4 Such a document would not be protected from disclosure under FSMA 2000, s 413: see the discussion at footnote 1 above. As a without prejudice document, it should not, though, be susceptible to disclosure to other third parties who bring civil claims against the firm.

Determination of complaints

12.45 If the ombudsman considers that an investigation is necessary, for example because there is no prospect of a mediated settlement, or this fails, the draft rules state merely that he will[1]:

- give both parties an opportunity of making representations;
- send the parties a provisional assessment, setting out his reasons and a time limit within which either party must respond; and
- if either party indicates disagreement with the provisional assessment, proceed to determination. The parties will be informed of their right to make representations before the ombudsman makes a determination[2].

1 See the draft rules at DISP 3.2.11.
2 See the draft rules at DISP 3.2.12.

12.46 In practice[1], therefore, the scheme staff investigate the complaint, calling for any information they need from either party, if need be using their statutory powers[2], and allowing both parties to make representations. They then issue an initial decision, setting out a recommended outcome and the reasons for it. If both parties accept it, that is the end of the matter. If one party does not accept it, the case is reviewed by one of the ombudsmen, leading, after any representations, to the issue of a final determination. As will be seen[3], either party or the ombudsman may call for an oral hearing.

1 See Consultation Paper 33, 'Consumer complaints and the new ombudsman scheme', paras 4.5 and 4.6
2 See para 12.50 below.
3 See para 12.56 below.

12.47 During the course of considering the complaint, the ombudsman can fix and extend time limits for any particular aspect[1] and has a variety of options if a party fails to comply with a time limit[2].

1 See the draft rules at DISP 3.6.1.
2 The ombudsman may proceed to the next stage or dismiss the complaint and in relation to a failure by the firm, he may make provision in his award for any material distress or inconvenience caused by the failure: see the draft rules at DISP 3.6.2/3.

12.48 What is notable about the scheme rules is the lack of detail. Thus, for example, it is left to the ombudsman to decide what evidence he wants to see and how that evidence should be provided to him[1], there is little mention of the ombudsman's powers to obtain information[2], there is no discussion of when or how documentary evidence produced by the firm will be disclosed to the complainant[3], and there is no explanation of how any oral hearing will be conducted[4]. The lack of formal procedural rules seems to reflect the desire to maintain a flexible process and to enable the ombudsman to reach a fair result in an informal, expeditious and cost-effective way in each case.

1 See para 12.54 below.
2 See para 12.50 below.
3 There is, however, provision allowing the ombudsman to accept evidence in confidence: see para 12.55 below.
4 See para 12.56 below.

12.49 The opportunity to make representations is, obviously, critical. It is an opportunity for the firm to set out all the reasons why the complaint is ill-founded and also to address any issues about the award or other remedy sought by the complainant. Firms must have in mind the need to be consistent with arguments raised, or likely to be raised, in similar cases[1], or in other contexts, for example in any related enforcement proceedings brought by the FSA. They should also bear in mind the risk of their written representations, and any evidence they provide, being used by the complainant for other purposes and being passed to the FSA by the ombudsman[2].

1 This is discussed in more detail at para 12.21 above.
2 This is discussed in more detail at paras 12.17 to 12.20 above.

The ombudsman's powers to obtain information

12.50 The ombudsman may[1] require a party to the complaint[2] to provide or produce before the end of such period as may be specified and, in the case of information, in such manner or form as may be specified:

- specified information or information of a specified description; or
- specified documents or documents of a specified description;

which the ombudsman considers necessary for the determination of the complaint. The requirement is imposed by written notice.

1 FSMA 2000, s 231.
2 In contrast with the FSA's investigation powers (see Chapter 4 above), the power cannot be exercised against a third party, even one connected with the firm. There is, though, nothing to prevent the ombudsman from asking a third party to provide information voluntarily and the firm may be asked to waive any duty of confidence owed to it by the third party to allow the information to be disclosed. It may be difficult for the firm to refuse given its obligation fully to co-operate with the ombudsman (see para 12.15 above). Indeed, in some cases, it may be in the firm's interests to ensure the ombudsman has all the information he requires, to ensure that a positive outcome deters further claims being made by the same complainant in another forum. Note that the ombudsman can require information to be provided not only by the firm but also by the complainant.

12.51 The test for the imposition of a requirement is fairly high. The ombudsman must consider the provision of the document or information to be 'necessary' for the determination of the complaint[1]. The ombudsman has not given any indication of when he is likely to use these formal powers. It ought to be relatively rare in practice that he will need to do so, given the firm's obligation to co-operate with him[2] and the complainant's own personal interest in doing so.

1 Precisely what 'necessary' means depends upon the circumstances. It lies somewhere between 'indispensable' on the one hand and 'useful' or 'expedient' on the other: Lord Griffiths in *Re an Inquiry under the Company Securities (Insider Dealing) Act 1985* [1988] 2 WLR 33, 65.
2 See para 12.15 above.

12.52 A requirement imposed under this provision does not have the benefit of all the ancillary provisions applicable to FSA investigations, discussed at para 4.111 ff above. Certain provisions do, however, apply. In particular:

- if a document is produced, the ombudsman can take copies or extracts or can require the person producing it to provide an explanation of it[1];
- if a person required to produce a document fails to do so, the ombudsman can require him to state to the best of his knowledge and belief where it is[2];
- the production of a document does not affect any lien on it[3]; and
- legally privileged material cannot, generally speaking, be required to be produced[4].

1 FSMA 2000, s 231(4).
2 FSMA 2000, s 231(5). Note that, in contrast with FSA investigations, the ombudsman has no power to obtain the document from any other person who has it. He is therefore reliant upon the relevant person voluntarily providing it or the firm concerned obtaining it for him.
3 FSMA 2000, s 231(6).
4 FSMA 2000, s 413. For a more detailed discussion of this provision, see para 4.264 ff above. Note that the FSMA 2000 effectively contains its own definition of legal privilege for these purposes.

12.53 Failure to comply with such a requirement could result in punishment for contempt of court[1]. There may also be other consequences. The failure may prejudice the person's case before the ombudsman[2]. For authorised firms, it could also amount to a breach of the duty to co-operate with the ombudsman[3], for which there may be regulatory enforcement consequences[4].

1 In the same way as a failure to comply with a requirement to provide information imposed by the FSA: FSMA 2000, s 232 and see para 4.284 ff above.
2 The ombudsman can determine the complaint on the basis of the information supplied, taking account of a failure to supply which he has requested or, if the complainant fails to supply information he has required, he can dismiss the complaint: see the draft rules at DISP 3.5.2(3) and (4).
3 See the draft rules at DISP 1.6.1 and see para 12.15 above. The ombudsman may report the failure to comply to the FSA: see para 12.18 above.
4 It would also amount to the contravention of a requirement imposed by or under the FSMA 2000: for a further discussion, see para 2.142 ff above.

What evidence will the ombudsman consider?

12.54 The ombudsman may, in relation to what evidence may be required or admitted in considering and determining a particular complaint, give directions as to the issues on which evidence is required, the extent to which the evidence required to decide those issues should be oral or written and the way in which the evidence should be presented[1].

1 See the draft rules at DISP 3.5.1.

12.55 The draft rules[1] provide some additional flexibility by allowing the ombudsman to exclude evidence that would be admissible in a court or include evidence that would not be admissible in a court or, where he considers it necessary or appropriate, to accept evidence in confidence so that only an edited version or (where this is not practicable) a summary or description is disclosed to the other party. The example given in relation to the latter is that this may include confidential evidence about third parties or security information[2]. This point may be of particular significance to firms who are concerned about the disclosure of confidential and sensitive information to individual customers[3]. However, if the eventual judgment is based on evidence which one party has not been allowed to see, and which he has not had an opportunity to comment upon or challenge, it is possible that the decision may be open to challenge on ECHR grounds[4]. Ultimately, while the firm can ask for particular material to be disclosed only in edited form, the question of what evidence should be disclosed is for the ombudsman, not for the firm.

1 See the draft rules at DISP 3.5.2.
2 See the draft rules at DISP 3.5.4.
3 The risks relating to disclosure are discussed in more detail at para 12.16 ff above.
4 See *Feldbrugge v Netherlands* (1986) 8 EHRR 425.

Is there an oral hearing?

12.56 Either party may request an oral hearing before the determination has been made[1], and the ombudsman must in any event (even when no request is made), consider whether the complaint can be fairly determined without an oral hearing[2]. If a request for an oral hearing is made, the ombudsman will consider whether the issues are material, whether a hearing should take place and, if so, whether it should be held in public or private. Thus, whether or not any request is made for a hearing, it is within the ombudsman's discretion not only how to hold any oral hearing but also whether to hold one at all. In practice, as the draft scheme rules recognise[3], the ombudsman's duty to comply with the ECHR fair trial safeguards will normally militate in favour of a hearing in public, where one is requested[4].

1 See the draft rules at DISP 3.2.13. Such a request must be in writing, setting out the issues the person wishes to raise and (if appropriate) any reasons why he considers the hearing should be in private.
2 See the draft rules at DISP 3.2.12.
3 See the draft rules at DISP 3.2.14.
4 This marks a significant change from the ombudsman schemes under the previous regime, where hearings were rarely held. ECHR, art 6(1) imposes a number of requirements on the process, if it is to fulfil the fair trial guarantees. The basic rights are outlined at para 6.26 above.

12.57 Where there is a hearing, it is conducted informally in the way the ombudsman considers best suited to the circumstances[1]. It does not have to be confrontational. Each party has the opportunity to hear and comment on the evidence of the other[2]. The ombudsman may ask questions of either party, set time limits and confine the hearing to material matters[3]. Parties have the right to be legally represented, although the ombudsman will conduct the hearing in such a way as to ensure that a person who is represented has no advantage over one who is not[4].

1 Consultation Paper 33, 'Consumer complaints and the new ombudsman scheme', para 4.7.
2 This is required by the ECHR, art 6(1): see para 12.55 above.
3 Consultation Paper 33, 'Consumer complaints and the new ombudsman scheme', para 4.8.
4 Consultation Paper 33, 'Consumer complaints and the new ombudsman scheme', para 4.8. In most cases, complainants will not need to have professional advisers: see the draft rules at DISP 3.9.11.

THE OMBUDSMAN'S DECISION

12.58 If the matter has not already been resolved, then the final stage is for the ombudsman to reach his determination. We consider here:

- how does the ombudsman reach his decision?
- what remedies can the ombudsman grant?
- can he award costs?
- what is the effect of the decision?
- can the decision be appealed or challenged?
- is the decision made public? and
- how is the decision enforced?

How is the decision reached?

12.59 The ombudsman[1] determines the complaint by reference to what is, in his opinion, fair and reasonable in all the circumstances of the case[2]. In doing so, the draft scheme rules require him to take into account the relevant law, regulations, regulators' rules and guidance and standards, relevant codes of practice and, where appropriate, what he considers to have been good industry practice at the relevant time.

1 The final determination is made by the ombudsman himself, not by a member of the scheme's staff: see the draft rules at DISP 3.7.1(1).

2 FSMA 2000, s 228(2) and see the draft rules at DISP 3.8.1.

12.60 Notably, the ombudsman does not determine the case simply on the basis of the legal rights and wrongs. His assessment is a broader one, the primary question being what is fair and reasonable in all the circumstances. What this means is unclear. It is plainly possible for a determination to be made against the firm in a situation where a court would not recognise that the customer had any cause of action and for that determination to be based on factors which the law would regard as irrelevant. The draft scheme rules reduce the risk to some extent by requiring the ombudsman to have regard to the factors listed above, the first of which is the relevant law[1]. However, the application of these factors in the context of a test of what is 'fair and reasonable in all the circumstances' will not necessarily lead to a predictable result. Moreover, these factors are not said to be exhaustive of the relevant factors, so the ombudsman may be entitled to decide to give little or no weight to them and to take other factors into account[2]. There is therefore a significant risk of decisions being taken by the ombudsman which might be criticised for being arbitrary and which could potentially be open to challenge[3]. Firms should, though, bear in mind that the broad test does not necessarily work only against them. It may act in the firm's favour if it can show that, for some reason, it is not fair and reasonable to make a determination in favour of the complainant even though in legal terms the firm was at fault[4].

1 Note the assurance by the Economic Secretary to HM Treasury that one rarely comes across a case in which it was not fair and reasonable to take into account all the rules and regulations and whether they had been complied with: Standing Committee, 30 November 1999.

2 See *Tesco Stores Ltd v Secretary of State for the Environment* [1995] 1 WLR 759, HL.

3 One major issue is whether the decision may amount to the arbitrary deprivation of property contrary to art 1 of the First Protocol to the ECHR, which guarantees the private right to property. It protects private property owners against deprivation of, or interference, with their possessions by the State. However, it also recognises the right of the State to control the use or ownership of property in the public interest. Therefore, an interference or deprivation will not infringe the ECHR so long as (in general terms) it pursues a legitimate aim, is proportionate to the aim pursued, strikes a fair balance between the general public interest and the interests of the private party concerned and is in accordance with law. Whilst an award of an independent ombudsman on 'fair and reasonable' grounds might meet the first three criteria, it could be argued to fail the 'in accordance with law' test, and might therefore be open to challenge.

4 For example, in the context of employment law, and awards of compensation of an amount 'just and equitable in all the circumstances', a tribunal may award nominal or no compensation in a situation where an employee is held to have been unfairly dismissed and did suffer loss as a result, but where there are other circumstances such that it is just and equitable not to award anything: see *W Devis & Sons Ltd v Atkins* [1977] 3 All ER 40, HL.

12.61 The ombudsman's determination is provided to the parties in a signed written statement, giving reasons[1]. The complainant must notify the ombudsman in writing before a specified date whether he accepts or rejects the determination[2].

1 FSMA 2000, s 228(3) and (4) and see the draft rules at DISP 3.8.3(1).
2 See further para 12.70 ff below.

What remedies can the ombudsman grant?

12.62 The ombudsman has significant powers in cases where he finds in favour of the complainant and, in particular, may:

- make a money award; and/or
- direct the firm to take particular steps.

These are considered in turn below.

Money awards

12.63 The ombudsman may make a money award against the firm of such amount as he considers fair compensation for loss or damage suffered by the complainant[1]. Loss or damage means financial loss (including consequential or prospective loss), pain and suffering, distress or inconvenience and damage to reputation[2]. The award is subject to a maximum of £100,000[3], but:

- the ombudsman may, if he considers that fair compensation requires the payment of a larger amount, make a non-binding recommendation to the firm that it pays the balance[4]; and
- the ombudsman may also award reasonable interest on the award, and determine the rate and period[5]. The interest award does not form part of the award for the purpose of calculating the maximum amount that can be awarded[6].

1 FSMA 2000, s 229 and see the draft rules at DISP 3.9.1.
2 FSMA 2000, s 229(2)(a) and (3) and see the draft rules at DISP 3.9.2/3.
3 See the draft rules at DISP 3.9.5. It may be possible for the ombudsman to make a direction which would have the effect of requiring the firm to pay more: see the discussion at para 12.66 below.
4 FSMA 2000, s 229(5) and see the draft rules at DISP 3.9.6.
5 FSMA 2000, s 229(8)(a) and see the draft rules at DISP 3.9.7.
6 See the draft rules at DISP 3.9.8.

12.64 The key phrase is 'fair compensation for the loss or damage'. This gives the ombudsman a significant discretion to assess the award of compensation[1]. Whilst the provision does require fair compensation to be linked to the loss or damage, it does not seem to require the ombudsman to have regard to the normal legal rules of causation, remoteness of loss, or mitigation of loss or, indeed, the categories of financial loss, pain and suffering, and so on, that are normally capable of being remedied with an award of damages. It is not, therefore, only the determination of liability that may be made irrespective of recognised legal principles, but the amount of the award itself may be arbitrary in legal terms. In practice, awards will be made very much on a case-by-case basis. If an award were made on a basis that did not reflect the law, then it may be capable of being challenged[2].

1 Although it is not as broad as the test for making a determination, namely what is 'fair and reasonable in all the circumstances'. In particular, the case of *W Devis & Sons Ltd v Atkins*, discussed at footnote 4 to para 12.60 above, would not seem to apply in relation to the amount of the award.

2 In *R v Investors Compensation Scheme Ltd, ex p Bowden* [1995] 3 All ER 605, the House of Lords held that a decision by the Investors Compensation Scheme on whether a claim was 'essential in order to provide fair compensation' could only be attacked on grounds of *Wednesbury* unreasonableness, in other words that it was a decision that no reasonable public authority could take, and that it was unnecessary to express any view on whether a court, applying ordinary rules as to the measure of damages, would have reached the same conclusion. However, it cannot be discounted that an award of compensation based on wholly non-legal considerations as to quantum, or which departs significantly from established legal criteria, might be exposed to challenge on the basis of art 1 of the First Protocol to the ECHR (see footnote 3 to para 12.60 above). This is particularly so where the arbitrary award cannot be challenged before a court by the firm, but can be challenged by the complainant, which might lead to further ECHR grounds for challenge under art 1 of the First Protocol in conjunction with the prohibition on discrimination under art 14.

Directing the firm to take steps

12.65 Alternatively, or in addition to making a money award[1], the ombudsman may direct the firm to take such steps in relation to the complainant as the ombudsman considers just and appropriate, whether or not a court could order those steps to be taken. The scheme rules do not give any indication of what directions the ombudsman might make and in what circumstances. There is no express limitation on the steps that the ombudsman can require the firm to take[2]. As with money awards, the need for directions will be assessed very much on a case-by-case basis.

1 FSMA 2000, s 229(2)(b) and see the draft rules at DISP 3.9.1(2).

2 Examples given in Standing Committee (30 November 1999) are taking steps to correct a situation or to apologise for an unacceptable error. In the context of the Pensions Ombudsman under the Pension Schemes Act 1993, it has been held to be implicit that the steps must be calculated to provide an appropriate remedy: see *Westminster City Council v Haywood* [1997] 2 All ER 84. For illustrations of the broad range of directions made by the Pensions Ombudsman, see the Pensions Ombudsman 1999–2000 Annual Report. The FSA and the scheme operator have given the example of requiring a firm to reconstruct the customer's account in order to put it in the state it would have been in if the mistake had not been made: see Policy Statement, 'Complaints handling arrangements, response on CP49', December 2000, para 4.51.

12.66 One issue is whether the ombudsman can use this power to direct the payment of a sum in excess of the £100,000 cap on money awards, either simply by directing the firm to make such a payment[1] or by directing it to take a step that would inevitably have the effect that it paid more than £100,000, for example requiring it to reconstitute a fund that had been negligently invested. Although the answer is not clear[2], it is likely that the power could not be used to direct compensation in excess of the statutory limit. It may be a moot point whether it could be used to achieve the same effect less directly.

1 In the context of the Pensions Ombudsman, the power to direct that steps are taken is used to award compensation, although, in contrast with the FSMA 2000 the relevant provisions of the Pension Schemes Act 1993 do not contain any express provisions dealing with awards of compensation.
2 The draft scheme rules contain the statement that the limit on the maximum money award has no bearing on any direction which an ombudsman may make (see DISP 3.9.9), but it is not clear what this is intended to mean.

Can the ombudsman award costs?

12.67 An ombudsman who finds in favour of a complainant may award an amount which covers some or all of the costs reasonably incurred by him in respect of the complaint[1]. The costs award can be interest bearing[2].

1 See the draft rules at DISP 3.11.
2 See the draft rules at DISP 3.9.13. It does not form part of the money award for the purposes of calculating the £100,000 cap: see the draft rules at DISP 3.9.14.

12.68 This cost provision is one sided[1], allowing costs to be awarded against the firm but not in its favour. The rationale[2] is that if complainants were at risk of costs this could discourage legitimate complaints.

1 This is notwithstanding the FSMA 2000 enables the scheme operator to make costs rules allowing the ombudsman to impose a costs order against a complainant whose conduct was improper or unreasonable or who was responsible for an unreasonable delay. The purpose of such costs is to provide a contribution towards the resources deployed in dealing with the complaint. An award of costs against a complainant in respect of the firm's costs is not permitted: see FSMA 2000, s 230.
2 Consultation Paper 49, 'Complaints handling arrangements, feedback statement on CP 33 and draft rules', May 2000, para 1.56.

12.69 The draft scheme rules indicate that costs awards are not anticipated to be common in practice, since in most cases complainants should not need to have professional advisers in order to bring complaints[1]. It is not clear whether a costs order remains effective notwithstanding the complainant rejects the substantive award, which he has the right to do as discussed below.

1 See the draft rules at DISP 3.9.11. It would seem wrong for costs to be awarded as a matter of course where the firm is unsuccessful, given that the firm has no equivalent right.

What is the effect of the ombudsman's decision?

12.70 The effect of the ombudsman's decision is entirely in the complainant's hands[1]. He is entitled either to accept or reject it. If he accepts it, then it is binding on both parties. If he rejects it, then neither party is bound by it.

1 FSMA 2000, s 228(5) and (6) and see the draft rules at DISP 3.8.3.

12.71 The complainant accepts the decision by notifying the ombudsman in writing within the time limit specified in the ombudsman's determination[1]. The decision is rejected if the complainant notifies the ombudsman that he rejects it or does not accept it by the date specified[2]. The ombudsman notifies the firm of the complainant's response or lack of response[3].

1 FSMA 2000, s 228(5) and see the draft rules at DISP 3.8.3(3).
2 FSMA 2000, s 228(6) and see the draft rules at DISP 3.8.3(4).
3 FSMA 2000, s 228(7) and see the draft rules at DISP 3.8.3(5).

12.72 It seems unfair that the complainant, but not the firm, should be able to decide whether or not to accept the ombudsman's decision[1] and it may be arguable that this contravenes the ECHR fair trial guarantees[2].

1 This was much debated in Standing Committee and was justified by the Economic Secretary to HM Treasury (30 November 1999) as being important for consumer confidence and to redress the inherent advantage to which a court-based process gives the better-resourced party, which is normally the firm.
2 In particular, it could be argued that, by allowing the complainant, but not the firm, a right to have the matter reheard in another forum, the complainant is put in a procedurally advantageous position in breach of the requirement of equality of arms under ECHR, art 6(1). It might also be argued that the availability to the complainant, but not to the firm, of a rehearing in court infringes the firm's right of access to a court under art 6(1), either on a free-standing basis or in conjunction with the prohibition on discrimination in art 14.

Can the decision be appealed or challenged?

12.73 The potential for significant cases or significant numbers of cases to be decided through the ombudsman scheme was highlighted at the outset. As a result, there is the potential for decisions to be made during or arising from the process that the firm may wish to challenge, for example the ombudsman's decision:

- on liability;
- on fair compensation or on the steps the firm is directed to take;
- not to dismiss a complaint the firm believes is ineligible or inappropriate to be resolved by the ombudsman;
- to hold or not to hold an oral hearing and, if so, whether to hold it in private;
- to exclude certain evidence or allow certain evidence to be included;
- to disclose particular, confidential information to the complainant; or
- to disclose particular information to the FSA or to use it for some other purpose.

12.74 To what extent can the firm challenge the ombudsman's decision? There is no right to appeal a decision of the ombudsman[1]. The firm will therefore need to establish a ground for judicial review, for example that the decision is unreasonable, irrational or unlawful, or that the process contravenes the ECHR fair trial guarantees or other of the firm's ECHR rights[2].

1 In effect, though, the complainant does have a right to appeal the ombudsman's substantive decision because he can reject the decision and try again in another forum: see para 12.70 above.
2 As the discussion above indicates, the process raises a number of potential ECHR compliance issues, including: (i) the potentially arbitrary nature of the tests applied in determining whether the firm is liable (see para 12.60 above) and, if so, the amount of compensation it must pay (see para 12.64 above) and (ii) the ability of the complainant, but not the firm, to choose whether or not the decision is binding (see para 12.70 above). If the ombudsman did act in a manner that was incompatible with the ECHR, the firm may have a right to bring a damages claim against him under the Human Rights Act 1988.

12.75 If the firm does have a particular objection, how might it go about making good that objection? There are several options:

- it could decline to comply with the ombudsman's order and then resist any proceedings brought to enforce it on the basis of the ground of challenge;
- it could commence a judicial review of the decision[1]; or
- it could commence a civil action based on ECHR non-compliance[2].

These issues are discussed in more detail in Chapter 16 below.

1 See para 16.16 ff below. Although not yet clear, it is likely that the ombudsman is capable of being judicially reviewed by a court. This appears to be the view of the Government ('The option of judicial review will be open to both firms and consumers once the ombudsman's decision has been taken': Economic Secretary to HM Treasury in Standing Committee, 30 November 1999). Contrast the position under the old regime, where many of the ombudsmen were not subject to judicial review, because the basis of their powers was contractual, not statutory: see *R v Insurance Ombudsman ex p Aegon Life Assurance Ltd* [1993] LRLR 100 and *R v Personal Investment Authority Ombudsman Bureau Ltd, ex p Johannes Mooyer* (5 April 2001, unreported) and see the analysis of Robert Walker J at first instance in *Westminster County Council v Haywood* [1996] 2 All ER 467 (overruled by the Court of Appeal on other grounds).
2 See para 16.25 ff below.

12.76 The scheme operator, the ombudsman and its staff are, generally speaking[1], immune from liability in damages for anything done in the discharge of the ombudsman's functions[2].

1 There is no immunity for acts or omissions in bad faith or for damages claims arising from the Human Rights Act 1998. The latter may in particular be significant: if the ombudsman acted in a manner that was incompatible with the ECHR, the firm may have a right to bring a damages claim against him under the Human Rights Act 1988.
2 For the detailed provisions, see FSMA 2000, Sch 17, para 10 and the draft rules at DISP 4.2.7. The similar provisions relating to the FSA are discussed at para 16.29 ff below.

Is the decision made public?

12.77 Decisions of the ombudsman will normally be published[1], although this may be done in such a way as to mask the identities of the parties. It is not clear whether a decision which is rejected by the complainant, and therefore not binding, will be published. There is no ECHR requirement to publish such a decision[2].

1 Consultation Paper 33, 'Consumer complaints and the new ombudsman scheme', para 4.9.
2 The main reason for publishing decisions is to ensure the process is ECHR compliant, since art 6(1), generally speaking, requires judgment to be publicly pronounced: see para 6.26 above. However, a decision which is rejected is not determinative of any rights and therefore the process does not fall to be measured against the ECHR.

How is the decision enforced?

12.78 Firms are required[1] to comply promptly with any money award and any directions made by the ombudsman and also with any settlement which it agrees at an earlier stage of the proceedings. In relation to authorised firms, compliance with this rule is enforceable in the same way as an FSA rule[2]. In relation to unauthorised firms, compliance may be enforceable by an injunction requiring the firm to remedy the breach on an application by the FSA[3].

1 See the draft rules at DISP 3.9.14.
2 It constitutes a requirement imposed by or under the FSMA 2000, breach of which may have the consequences outlined at para 2.142 ff above. The ombudsman may report a breach by an authorised firm to the FSA: see para 12.18 above.
3 FSMA 2000, s 380 and see para 7.97 ff above.

12.79 An ombudsman award made under the compulsory jurisdiction is enforceable directly by the court. A money award can be enforced by execution in the same way as an order of a county court[1] and a direction is enforceable by injunction[2]. An award made under the voluntary jurisdiction is also enforceable in court by the complainant[3].

1 FSMA 2000, Sch 17, para 16.
2 FSMA 2000, s 229(9).
3 See the draft rules at DISP 4.2.10.

13 Market misconduct

CONTENTS

Introduction 511

Recognising market abuse 516

Investigations into market misconduct 539

Sanctions for market misconduct 555

INTRODUCTION

13.1 In this chapter, we review the new regime for combating misconduct in the financial markets. The chapter is entitled 'market misconduct', rather than 'market abuse', because whilst the new regime of financial penalties for market abuse has attracted a great deal of attention it is only one of the range of tools which the FSA has to address market misconduct.

13.2 Within the rubric of market misconduct, therefore, we include not only financial penalties for market abuse, but also the other enforcement action which the FSA can take as a result of market abuse, the various relevant criminal offences, the regulatory action available to the FSA to address breaches of its rules where there is an overlap between market abuse and the FSA's rules, including the regulatory general principles, and the interaction of the FSA's regime with the rules of other relevant bodies such as recognised investment exchanges, the Takeover Panel and relevant overseas bodies.

13.3 We consider in this chapter the interaction between the various types of market misconduct and the different possible consequences. We outline the implications of being suspected of, or committing, misconduct in the markets, from the discovery of the misconduct, through its investigation by the FSA, to the options available to the FSA should market abuse be established or should some other criminal or regulatory offence have been committed.

13.4 This chapter therefore considers the following main issues:

- an overview of the new regime for combating market misconduct and of the policy and debates which have helped to shape it;
- recognising market abuse – in other words, what constitutes market abuse and what in practical terms should firms appreciate could involve market abuse? (para 13.17 ff below);
- if it is likely that market abuse or other market misconduct has taken place, what practical steps should firms or others involved take and what powers does the FSA have to investigate? (para 13.108 ff below); and
- the range of different sanctions or other enforcement action available to the FSA if market misconduct has occurred, including penalties for market abuse, the relevant criminal offences and the other possible regulatory consequences (including those involving other regulators) which might follow from the misconduct (para 13.173 ff below).

13.5 There are similarities between the market abuse regime and the general disciplinary regime described elsewhere in this book, in terms of the investigation process, the FSA's decision-making process, the firm's ability to challenge the imposition of sanctions and the measures that can be imposed. Where the regimes are the same or similar, we cross-refer to other sections of the book where the relevant issue is explained in detail, highlighting any particular issues arising in this context.

An overview of the regime for combating market misconduct

What is the regime designed to achieve?

13.6 The main objective behind the new regime is to secure that confidence in the UK financial markets is maintained. Whilst the Government recognised that the UK financial markets are perceived to be fair and clean, it wished to ensure that that reputation is kept and, where possible, improved[1].

1 'We are determined to ensure that the financial markets are open and clean places to do business. London's reputation depends on that. . . . The FSA's job is to sustain confidence in the market and to assist in the detection and prevention of financial crime. The FSA will have the powers it needs to do the job. . . . These proposals will further enhance the UK's position as one of the best regulated and attractive financial markets in the world. We are determined to maintain London's position as one of the foremost financial markets': Economic Secretary to HM Treasury in Standing Committee, 2 November 1999.

13.7 The new civil offence of market abuse was thus created as an additional part of the overall scheme to combat market misconduct, intended to complement rather than replace the previous criminal and regulatory regime. That regime was perceived to be flawed because there was no ability to address misconduct by those outside the regulated community save where they committed one of the criminal offences of insider dealing[1] and misleading statements and practices[2]. Those criminal offences applied only to two narrow types of conduct and even then were of use only where the conduct was sufficiently serious to be pursued through the criminal justice system. For market misconduct short of criminal conduct, although the regulators could take action against regulated firms or individuals, there was no regime enabling any action to be taken against anyone else.

1 Under the Criminal Justice Act 1993, Pt V.
2 Under the Financial Services Act 1986, s 47; now FSMA 2000, s 397.

13.8 In addition, so far as regulated firms and individuals are concerned, the regulatory regime was perceived to lack clarity in this area. It relied mainly on the enforcement of broad, general principles and, as a result, it was not clear precisely what conduct, short of criminal misconduct, was prohibited.

13.9 The new regime preserves the criminal and regulatory aspects of the previous regime but, through the market abuse regime, extends the coverage to all persons, whether authorised or approved under the FSMA 2000 or not. For authorised persons, it also gives greater transparency to the question of what does and does not amount to market abuse in most areas. It is an important tool available to the FSA to fulfil its regulatory objectives of maintaining confidence in the financial system, the protection of consumers and the reduction of financial crime[1].

1 For an explanation of the FSA's regulatory objectives, see 2.19 ff above.

How is the regime designed to achieve this?

13.10 Given the complexity of the regime, it may be instructive to have at the outset an overview as to how the FSA can go about dealing with suspected cases of market misconduct.

13.11 Where information comes to the FSA's attention to suggest that market misconduct may have taken place, it can use a variety of powers to investigate and has wide powers to obtain information from those who may have relevant information[1].

1 See para 13.130 ff below.

13.12 Armed with the results of the investigation, the FSA may consider using one or more of a number of enforcement powers available to it:

- if one of the criminal offences of insider dealing or misleading statements and practices may have been committed by any person (whether or not within the regulated community), then, in appropriate circumstances, the FSA will act as the prosecuting authority and bring a criminal prosecution for those offences[1];

- alternatively, if the civil offence of market abuse has been committed by any person (whether or not regulated) the FSA may:
  - impose a financial penalty against the person or publicly censure him[2],
  - make, or apply for, a restitution order against the person, requiring him to disgorge any profits he has made or make up any losses suffered by others as a result[3],
  - seek an injunction, among other things, prohibiting that person from undertaking further acts which would amount to market abuse[4],
- the FSA may, in some situations, become involved in, or take over, investigations by other UK regulators into misconduct in their own markets and/or may enforce the City Code at the request of the Takeover Panel and/or those other regulators may take their own enforcement action[5];
- the FSA may, in some situations, be able to address misconduct which occurred abroad, and in those situations will need to liaise with overseas regulators[6];
- if the misconduct was committed by a regulated firm, then the FSA may consider using its other enforcement powers, such as its disciplinary and/or own-initiative powers, particularly if it raises wider regulatory issues about the firm. In some circumstances the FSA may regard conduct, whether or not amounting to market abuse, as a breach of the FSA rules[7] deserving of disciplinary sanctions;
- if the conduct was committed by an approved person, then the FSA may consider using its other enforcement powers, such as to discipline him and/or withdraw his approval. In some circumstances, it may regard conduct, whether or not amounting to market abuse, as a breach of the Statements of Principle for approved persons[8], and take disciplinary action against the approved person for misconduct;
- if it was committed by an individual who was not an approved person, then the FSA may need to consider whether a prohibition order is appropriate[9].

1 See para 13.177 ff below.
2 See para 13.187 ff below.
3 See para 13.254 ff below.
4 See para 13.235 ff below.
5 See para 13.211 ff below.
6 See para 13.231 below.
7 In particular, Principle 5 of the Principles for Businesses ('a firm must observe proper standards of market conduct'): see the discussion at para 13.262 ff below.
8 In particular, Statement of Principle 3 ('an approved person must observe proper standards of market conduct in carrying out his controlled function'): see the discussion at para 13.272 ff below.
9 See para 13.263 below.

13.13 Dependent upon which course or courses of action it is appropriate for the FSA to take, specific procedures will need to be followed before the action is finally imposed.

13.14 For those familiar with the previous position, several principal differences from the old regime are notable. First, there is now a coherent system for addressing what is loosely described as market misconduct, involving a range of different actions appropriate to address different types of regulatory concerns. Second, since the FSA now has the authority to investigate all the relevant issues, and to prosecute any criminal offences, it can investigate suspected cases of market misconduct in their entirety and then decide afterwards what action is appropriate. Third, the concept of market abuse, as evidenced by the Code of Market Conduct, now includes a significant amount of information as to what behaviour is and is not prohibited, although clearly many issues still remain.

The implications of the Human Rights Act 1998

13.15 Human rights issues were much debated in the context of market abuse during the bill stages of the FSMA 2000. The main issue was whether the imposition of a penalty for market abuse could constitute a criminal charge for ECHR purposes, particularly given the potential severity of such penalties, the punitive nature of the market abuse regime, and the fact that it applies to the public at large, not only to those who have chosen to be part of the regulated community[1]. The Government did not agree that a market abuse penalty could constitute a criminal charge but nonetheless recognised the possibility[2] and, as a result, made various amendments to the bill. In particular:

- the definition of market abuse as originally proposed was considered too vague and the provision was amended and clarified and provisions were introduced providing a safe harbour for those who comply with the Code of Market Conduct[3];
- a scheme was introduced to provide legal assistance to those charged with market abuse who have insufficient means and where the interests of justice require[4];
- the statutory privilege against self-incrimination was extended to cover market abuse, so that statements made to the FSA under compulsion may not be used in proceedings for market abuse against the person who made the statement[5];
- the FSA can also be required to prove the allegation of market abuse before the Tribunal[6].

1 The latter in particular distinguishes market abuse penalties from disciplinary penalties imposed by the FSA on firms and approved persons. This issue is discussed in more detail at para 5.20 ff above.
2 Economic Secretary to HM Treasury in Standing Committee, 2 November 1999 and see the Second Report of the Joint Committee, para 3.
3 See para 13.22 below.
4 See para.13.207 below.
5 See para 13.162 ff below.
6 See para 13.208 ff below and Chapter 6 above.

13.16 Whilst this addresses the primary structural issues, the question of whether or not a person's human rights have been violated has to be judged on a case-by-case basis. It cannot therefore be ruled out that the FSA's actions in a particular case, for example the way in which it conducts its investigation, might give rise to arguments about non-compliance with the ECHR.

RECOGNISING MARKET ABUSE

Introduction

13.17 Anyone involved in a UK financial market, or in investments that are traded on one or are linked in some way to investments that are traded on one, will need to be familiar with the kinds of behaviour that could amount to market abuse. Whilst the focus of this book is on the enforcement consequences of committing market abuse, rather than a detailed analysis of what constitutes market abuse, we have provided a broad outline of market abuse because the consequences of committing it cannot be considered in a vacuum. As will be seen, the relevant provisions are complex and even an outline therefore requires some detail.

13.18 In the following paras, we look at:

- first, the main constituents of market abuse (para 13.19 ff);
- second, what in practical terms firms should be looking for in order to see whether a problem raises a market abuse issue (para 13.87 ff); and
- third, some common questions about market abuse (para 13.90 ff).

What is market abuse?

13.19 The starting point is the statutory definition of market abuse, which is found at FSMA 2000, s 118. This is cast in very broad terms. Guidance on what the FSA considers amounts, and does not amount, to market abuse is found in the Code of Market Conduct[1], which has been issued by the FSA in accordance with the requirements of the FSMA 2000. The two therefore need to be read together.

1 See the FSA Handbook at MAR 1.

The Code of Market Conduct

13.20 The FSMA 2000 recognises the breadth of the statutory definition and therefore requires the FSA to issue a code, known as the Code of Market Conduct, to give guidance to those determining whether or not behaviour amounts to market abuse. The Code may specify[1]:

- behaviour which, in the FSA's view, amounts to market abuse;
- behaviour which, in the FSA's view, does not amount to market abuse; and
- factors which, in the FSA's view, are to be taken into account in determining whether or not behaviour amounts to market abuse.

1 FSMA 2000, s 119.

13.21 The purpose of the Code is thus to provide greater clarity to the meaning of market abuse whilst at the same time allowing flexibility for the scope of the regime in what is always a dynamic market.

13.22 It is important to appreciate that the Code has, under the FSMA 2000, only limited effect in determining whether or not market abuse has occurred[1]:

- the only complete certainty it provides is that behaviour specified in the Code as, in the FSA's opinion, not amounting to market abuse is taken as not amounting to market abuse[2];
- beyond that, the Code is still an important factor evidentially because the FSMA 2000 provides that it may be relied upon in so far as it indicates whether or not behaviour should be taken to amount to market abuse[3].

Whilst the Code will inevitably form the centrepiece of any consideration by firms or individuals as to whether they can or cannot undertake a particular course of action, it remains subsidiary to the statutory definition. In other words, conduct which does not fall within the statutory definition cannot amount to market abuse, whatever the Code says. There may be tension between them, given the potential uncertainties in the statutory definition.

1 Note that the relevant Code is that in force at the time the behaviour occurred: FSMA 2000, s 122.
2 FSMA 2000, s 122(1).
3 FSMA 2000, s 122(3)

13.23 Beyond the statutory definition and the Code, other rules of the FSA or the rules of other bodies, for example, exchanges, the City Code or the UK Listing Rules, may cover the firm's conduct in the particular market and may also therefore be relevant.

The statutory definition of market abuse

13.24 The statutory definition sets the outer boundary of what constitutes market abuse. However, market abuse is a new concept, the definition is complex, and there will be difficulties in interpreting parts of it. The Code will therefore be particularly important in the early days of the regime until jurisprudence develops and provides greater certainty at the margin[1].

1 Economic Secretary to HM Treasury in Standing Committee, 2 November 1999.

13.25 The various elements of market abuse may be summarised as follows[1]:

A behaviour;

B which occurs in relation to qualifying investments traded on a prescribed market;

C the behaviour must involve one of:

— *Limb 1*: the misuse of information, or

— *Limb 2*: the giving of a false or misleading impression, or

— *Limb 3*: the distortion of the market,

D it must fall below the standard of behaviour which a regular user of the market in question would reasonably expect of a person in the position of the alleged abuser in relation to the market;

E but the behaviour will not amount to market abuse if:

— it conforms with a rule which expressly provides that behaviour which conforms will not amount to market abuse,

— it is specified in the Code as, in the FSA's view, not amounting to market abuse, or

— it conforms with the City Code and is specified in the Code of Market Conduct as not therefore amounting to market abuse,

F and even if it amounts to market abuse, it will not give rise to a penalty[2] if:

— the person believed on reasonable grounds that his behaviour did not amount to market abuse, or

— he took all reasonable precautions and exercised all due diligence to avoid committing market abuse, and

G finally, a penalty for market abuse[3] can be levied not only against the person who committed it but also (or alternatively) against a person who required or encouraged him to do it.

1 For the statutory definition of market abuse, see FSMA 2000, s 118. This list is derived from ss 118, 120, 122 and 123.
2 Or to a restitution order, but note that it may nonetheless give rise to an injunction: see para 13.249 ff below.
3 Or a restitution order: see para 13.255 below.

13.26 A brief summary of each of these elements, and its treatment in the Code, is given below, with a view to providing a basic understanding of the scope and nature of market abuse. It is not the intention to provide a detailed analysis of what constitutes market abuse. The Code should itself be consulted in specific cases.

A Behaviour

13.27 The question of what constitutes 'behaviour' is likely to be interpreted broadly. The FSMA 2000 states[1] only that behaviour includes action or inaction[2]. The Code[3] provides some additional clarification by giving examples of types of behaviour, which include the following:

- dealing;
- arranging deals;
- causing, procuring or advising others to deal;
- making statements or representations or otherwise disseminating information;
- providing corporate finance advice and conducting corporate finance activities; and
- managing investments belonging to others.

This is not an exhaustive list, but it serves to emphasise the wide range of activities which can amount to behaviour.

1 FSMA 2000, s 118(10).
2 The Code gives as an example of inaction a situation where a person is under a legal or regulatory obligation to make a particular disclosure and fails to do so: see the FSA Handbook at MAR 1.3.2.
3 See the FSA Handbook at MAR 1.3.

13.28 Behaviour can be by one person alone or by two or more persons jointly or in concert[1]. Persons can be individuals or organisations. If the FSMA 2000 refers to a person engaging in market abuse, it is referring to a person engaged in market abuse whether alone or with one or more other persons[2].

1 FSMA 2000, s 118(1).
2 FSMA 2000, s 118(9).

13.29 There are territorial limits to the types of behaviour that are caught. Behaviour is to be disregarded unless it occurs in the UK or in relation to qualifying investments traded on a prescribed market situated in the UK or accessible electronically from the UK. The question of what behaviour occurred in relation to qualifying investments traded on a prescribed market is discussed at para 13.33 below. It should become clear from that discussion that these territorial limits are in practice very wide.

B In relation to qualifying investments traded on a prescribed market

13.30 To understand the meaning of 'behaviour in relation to qualifying investments traded on a prescribed market' it is necessary to look at three separate questions:

- what are the prescribed markets?
- what investments are qualifying investments? and
- when does behaviour occur 'in relation to' qualifying investments traded on a prescribed market?

13.31 ***What are the prescribed markets?*** The market abuse provisions apply only to those markets that have been prescribed by HM Treasury[1]. The FSMA 2000 does not contain any limit on the markets that may be prescribed. Currently, HM Treasury has prescribed[2] all markets established under the rules of a UK recognised investment exchange. Currently, these are[3] the London Stock Exchange, LIFFE, the London Metal Exchange, the International Petroleum Exchange, OM London Exchange, COREDEAL, Jiway and virt-x. The description of prescribed markets can be amended by HM Treasury[4]. It could even be amended to include overseas markets accessible electronically from the UK if, for example, such a market had a major impact on the UK economy[5].

1 FSMA 2000, s 118(3).
2 See the Financial Services and Markets Act 2000 (Prescribed Markets and Qualifying Investments) Order 2001, SI 2001/996.
3 See the FSA Handbook at MAR 1.11.2.
4 The list is currently automatically amended (based on SI 2001/996) when the FSA recognises further RIEs or revokes the recognition of an RIE.
5 See the discussion at para 13.96 below.

13.32 ***What are qualifying investments?*** Again, the FSMA 2000 allows HM Treasury to prescribe what investments are qualifying in relation to the prescribed markets. HM Treasury has prescribed[1] that, in relation to each of the prescribed markets, qualifying investments means all investments of a kind specified for the purposes of the Regulated Activities Order[2]. In other words, all types of regulated investments traded on[3] the relevant markets are qualifying investments.

1 See the Financial Services and Markets Act 2000 (Prescribed Markets and Qualifying Investments) Order 2001, SI 2001/996.
2 See the Financial Services and Market Act 2000 (Regulated Activities) Order 2001, SI 2001/544, Pt III.
3 The FSA has also provided guidance as to when an investment is 'traded on' a prescribed market: see the FSA Handbook at MAR 1.11.3.

13.33 ***When does behaviour occur 'in relation to' qualifying investments traded on a prescribed market?*** This is the more difficult concept. In order to amount to market abuse, the behaviour must occur in relation to qualifying investments traded on a prescribed market[1]. This clearly includes behaviour which directly affects the investments themselves, but also anticipates that the regime may cover behaviour which is less directly connected to the investments on the relevant market.

1 FSMA 2000, s 118(1)(a). The rationale is that behaviour in relation to investments which are not themselves qualifying investments can have a damaging effect on confidence in prescribed markets and qualifying investments: see the FSA Handbook at MAR 1.11.8.

13.34 The FSMA 2000 does not contain any definition of what 'in relation to' means in this context, but does make clear that two types of behaviour are included[1], namely:

- behaviour which occurs in relation to anything which is the subject matter of a qualifying investment or whose price or value is expressed by reference to the price or value of a qualifying investment; and

- behaviour which occurs in relation to an investment (whether qualifying or not) whose subject matter is a qualifying investment.

1 FSMA 2000, s 118(6).

13.35 The FSA refers to these types of products, which are connected to qualifying investments, as 'relevant products'[1] and has given various examples of the application of these tests[2]. The FSA has said that something will be the subject matter of a qualifying investment where there is a clear relationship between the two, for example a contractual, documented relationship. Generally, it has given guidance that there must be a clear relationship between the behaviour and a qualifying investment for the behaviour to be regarded as occurring in relation to a qualifying investment[3]. Not every product which has some sort of correlation with a qualifying investment will therefore be a relevant product.

1 See the FSA Handbook at MAR 1.11.8.
2 See the FSA Handbook at MAR 1.11.9 to 1.11.11.
3 See the FSA Handbook at MAR 1.11.7.

13.36 Finally, the two types of behaviour listed above which the FSMA 2000 includes as behaviour which occurs 'in relation to' a qualifying investment are only examples and are not exhaustive of the implications of the test[1]. The full implications of that test are not therefore clear.

1 See the FSA Handbook at MAR 1.11.7.

C The three alternative conditions

13.37 Central to the definition of market abuse is the requirement for the behaviour to amount to one of:

- the misuse of information;
- giving a false or misleading impression; or
- distortion of the market.

Each of these is reviewed briefly below.

13.38 ***Limb 1: The misuse of information*** In order to be market abuse within this limb, the behaviour[1] must be[2]:

- based on information[3];
- which is not generally available to those using the market[4];
- the information, if available to a regular user of the market, must be likely to be regarded by him as relevant when deciding the terms on which transactions in investments of the kind in question should be effected[5].

The FSA has also given guidance[6] that the information must relate to matters which the regular user would reasonably expect to be disclosed to users of the particular market, whether at the time in question or in the future. This only includes information which has to be disclosed in accordance with a legal or regulatory requirement or which is routinely the subject of a public announcement although not subject to any formal disclosure requirement[7].

1 The FSA's guidance (see the FSA Handbook at MAR 1.4.4) refers in particular to dealing or arranging deals, although behaviour is not limited to this: see para 13. 27 above.
2 FSMA 2000, s 118(2)(a).
3 In other words, the person must be in possession of information and the information must have a material influence on the decision to engage in the behaviour: see the FSA Handbook at MAR 1.4.4(1).
4 Information is treated as generally available if it can be obtained by research or analysis conducted by or on behalf of users of a market: FSMA 2000, s 118(7) and see the FSA Handbook at MAR 1.4.5. The FSA, generally speaking, regards people as being free to use information that they have obtained through research, analysis or other legitimate means such as observation of a public event: see the FSA Handbook at MAR 1.4.6. For further guidance, see the FSA Handbook at MAR 1.4.5 to 1.4.8.
5 Examples of relevant information, and various factors to be taken into account in determining whether or not a particular piece of information would be, or would be likely to be, regarded as relevant by a regular user, are found in the FSA Handbook at MAR 1.4.9 to 1.4.11.
6 See the FSA Handbook at MAR 1.4.4(4).
7 See the FSA Handbook at MAR 1.4.12. For guidance, see the FSA Handbook at MAR 1.4.13 to 1.4.16.

13.39 For a more detailed discussion, reference should be made to the Code at MAR 1.4. The Code gives various examples of behaviour which in the FSA's view amounts to market abuse under this head[1] and provides for various safe harbours[2] of conduct which will not amount to market abuse.

1 See the FSA Handbook at MAR 1.4.17.
2 See the FSA Handbook at MAR 1.4.19 to 1.4.31.

13.40 It will be seen that the overall effect of this limb has many similarities with the insider dealing legislation[1]. However, the definition of market abuse is significantly wider for a number of reasons, including, first, that the concept of 'relevant information' is wider than 'inside information' and, second, that the requirement that it is 'not generally available' is somewhat wider than 'unpublished information'.

1 Criminal Justice Act 1993, Pt V.

13.41 ***Limb 2: Giving a false or misleading impression*** Behaviour will amount to market abuse within this limb if it is likely to give a regular user of the market a false or misleading impression as to the supply of, or demand for, or as to the price or value of, investments of the kind in question[1].

1 FSMA 2000, s 118(2)(b).

13.42 The Code provides[1] that the false or misleading impression must be material and there must be a real and not fanciful likelihood that the behaviour will have this effect, although the effect need not be more likely than not.

1 See the FSA Handbook at MAR 1.5.4.

13.43 The Code sets out various general factors to be taken into account in determining whether or not behaviour is likely to give the regular user a false or misleading impression[1]. The FSA also identifies four different types of conduct which it considers constitute market abuse under this head and these are worthwhile briefly outlining:

- artificial transactions[2], in other words entering into a transaction or series of transactions the principal effect of which the person knows, or could reasonably be expected to know, is or is likely to be to inflate, maintain or depress the apparent supply of or demand for, or price or value of, a qualifying investment or relevant product so that a false or misleading impression is likely to be given to a regular user, unless the regular user would regard the principal rationale for the transaction as a legitimate commercial rationale and the way in which the transaction is to be executed as proper;
- disseminating information which if true would be relevant information[3] in circumstances where the person knows, or could reasonably be expected to know, the information is false or misleading and disseminates the information in order to[4] create a false or misleading impression[5];
- dissemination of relevant information[6] through an accepted channel of communication, by the person responsible for doing so, where the information is likely to give a regular user a false or misleading impression and the person has not taken reasonable care to ensure the information is not false or misleading[7];
- a course of conduct the principal effect of which, the person knows, or could reasonably be expected to know, is or is likely to be to give the regular user a false or misleading impression, unless the regular user would regard the principal rationale as a legitimate commercial rationale and the way in which the conduct is engaged in as proper[8].

1 The experience and knowledge of market users, the structure of the market, the legal and regulatory requirements and accepted market practices, the identity and position of the person responsible for the behaviour and the extent and nature of the visibility or disclosure of the person's activity: see the FSA Handbook at MAR 1.5.5.

2 See the FSA Handbook at MAR 1.5.8 to 1.5.14.

3 In other words, likely to be regarded by a regular user as relevant when deciding the terms on which transactions in investments of the kind in question should be effected: see the FSA Handbook at MAR 1.4.4(3).

4 This need not be the sole purpose but must be a purpose which motivates or incites the person to act: an "actuating purpose" – see the FSA Handbook, Glossary of definitions.

5 An example would be posting false information on an internet bulletin board or chat room which contains false or misleading information about the takeover of a company whose shares are qualifying investments: see the FSA Handbook at MAR 1.5.17. Generally, see the FSA Handbook at MAR 1.5.15 to 1.5.17.

6 See footnote 3 above. Or information which, if true, would be relevant information.

7 The FSA recognises the importance of information disseminated through accepted channels and that users should be able to rely on the accuracy and integrity of such information: see the FSA Handbook at MAR 1.5.20. Generally, see the FSA Handbook at MAR 1.5.18 to 1.5.20. There is a clear overlap between this and the obligations of a listed company under the Listing Rules: see Chapter 15 below and see also the FSA Handbook at MAR 1.5.25.

8 See the FSA Handbook at MAR 1.5.21 to 1.5.22.

13.44 For a more detailed discussion of this limb, reference should be made to the Code at MAR 1.5. The Code provides three safe harbours of conduct which do not amount to market abuse under this limb[1].

1 See the FSA Handbook at MAR 1.5.23 to 1.5.29.

13.45 It will be seen that this and limb 3 have substantial similarities with the offence of misleading statements and practices under FSMA 2000, s 397 (formerly the Financial Services Act 1986, s 47). As in the case of limb 1, though, the market abuse test is significantly wider.

13.46 ***Limb 3: Distortion of the market*** The third limb is behaviour which a regular user of the market would, or would be likely to, regard as distorting, or being likely to distort, the market in investments of the kind in question[1].

1 FSMA 2000, s 118(2)(c).

13.47 Behaviour will amount to market abuse if it interferes with the proper operation of market forces with the purpose of positioning prices at a distorted level[1]. There must be a real and not fanciful likelihood that the behaviour will have such an effect, although the effect need not be more likely than not[2].

1 See the FSA Handbook at MAR 1.6.4. This need not be the sole purpose of the behaviour, but must be a purpose which motivates or incites the person to act: see footnote 3 to para 13.43 above.

2 See the FSA Handbook at MAR 1.6.4(2).

13.48 The Code provides two particular examples of behaviour that, in the FSA's view, amounts to market abuse in that it gives rise to market distortion[1], namely:

- price positioning, where a person enters into a transaction or series of transactions with the purpose of positioning the price at a distorted level[2]; and
- an abusive squeeze, which occurs where a person has a significant influence over the supply of or demand for or delivery mechanisms for a qualifying investment or relevant product and a position in an investment under which quantities of the investment or relevant product are deliverable, and engages in behaviour with the purpose of[3] positioning at a distorted level the price at which others have to deliver, take delivery or defer delivery to satisfy their obligations[4].

1 See the FSA Handbook at MAR 1.6.8 to 1.6.18.

2 See the FSA Handbook at MAR 1.6.9 to 1.6.12. Examples include simultaneously buying and selling the same investment to give the appearance of a legitimate transfer at a price outside the normal trading range, or buying a large volume of commodity futures just before the close of trading to position the price so as to make a profit from a derivatives position.

3 This need not be the sole purpose, but must be a purpose which motivates or incites the person to act: see footnote 3 to para 13.43 above.

4 See the FSA Handbook at MAR 1.6.13 and the detailed guidance at MAR 1.6.14 to 1.6.18.

13.49 For a more detailed discussion, see the Code at MAR 1.6. The Code specifies a safe harbour for behaviour which complies with LME rules relating to the behaviour expected of long position holders[1].

1 See the FSA Handbook at MAR 1.6.19.

D The test of the regular user

13.50 In order to constitute market abuse, the behaviour must be likely to be regarded by a regular user of that market who is aware of the behaviour as a failure on the part of the person or persons concerned to observe the standard of behaviour reasonably expected of a person in his or their position in relation to the market[1]. In other words, it must, broadly, fall below the standard of behaviour that a regular user would reasonably expect of a person in the position of the person concerned in relation to the market.

1 FSMA 2000, s 118(1)(c).

13.51 The test of the regular user is one of the key parts of the market abuse regime. There are two aspects. First, there is the question of the position of the person concerned in relation to the market. Second, there is the question of what constitutes the 'regular user' and what standards he would reasonably expect. The test is complicated and is only outlined here.

13.52 ***The position of the person concerned in relation to the market*** Given the breadth of the market abuse provisions, the lack of any significant territorial limits, and the ability for a person potentially to commit market abuse by behaving not in relation to investments traded on the market but purely in relation to other investments or products linked in some way to those investments (the provisions for so-called 'relevant products'), the market abuse provisions can apply to an extraordinarily wide range of people. The need to look at the position of the person concerned in relation to the market plays an important role in allowing the test of market abuse to be tailored to some extent to the position of the particular person. The example commonly cited is the question of whether striking African copper miners would commit market abuse because their actions would affect the price of copper, or financial products derived from it such as futures, on the UK exchanges. The standard required will differ according to the position of the person in relation to the market. Thus, a difficult question in each case will be how to define the particular person's position in relation to the market.

13.53 ***The standard of behaviour the regular user would reasonably expect*** Identifying the position of the person concerned in relation to the market is, however, only a small part of the picture. The question is then what is the standard that a regular user of the market in question would reasonably expect of a person in that position. This is an objective test. The knowledge or state of mind of the particular person is irrelevant, save in so far as it may be demonstrative of the standard to be expected of a person in the same position.

13.54 The meaning of 'regular user' requires explanation. A regular user means, in relation to a particular market, a reasonable person who regularly deals on that market in investments of the kind in question[1]. He is a hypothetical person, familiar with the market in question[2].

1 FSMA 2000, s 118(10).
2 See the FSA Handbook at MAR 1.2.2. 'The regular market user . . . has to be, effectively, the cousin of the court's reasonable man. He represents the distillation of the standards expected by those who regularly use the market. . . . he represents a single view. If people engage in behaviour that fails to meet the standards expected by the regular market user, that user's confidence in the market would be affected and he would be less likely to deal in it': see the Economic Secretary to HM Treasury in Standing Committee, 2 November 1999.

13.55 This does not, on the face of it, anticipate that there may be more than one, hypothetical, 'regular user' of a particular market, holding different views of what standard is acceptable[1]. This is likely to be an area of particular interest in practice. In a case where it becomes apparent that there is more than one view of a particular conduct, and that each view is held by a body of responsible market practitioners, it may be arguable that a regular user would not regard behaviour that complied with either one as falling below the standard expected. The FSA has given guidance that where there is a range of practices which are generally accepted by users of the market, each practice is to be judged objectively on its own merits[2]. As the FSA seems to recognise, just because the regular user is a hypothetical person does not mean that the test is insufficiently flexible to take account of different views held in the market. It may be reasonable to expect the regular user not to condemn as unacceptable a practice viewed as responsible by a responsible body of practitioners, even if he does not hold that view himself.

1 If this is correct, the regular user will need to represent a synthesis of the different types of users, whose view of market standards might be different – for example, brokers, fund managers, private investors. See also footnote 2 to para 13.54 above.
2 See the FSA Handbook at MAR 1.2.10.

13.56 The FSA has provided detailed guidance as to how it interprets the regular user test and the factors taken into account in determining whether a person's behaviour falls below the standards expected[1]. Whilst this is not reproduced here, it may be worth reinforcing some key points.

1 See the FSA Handbook at MAR 1.2.

13.57 First, a standard of behaviour which is accepted by some actual users of a market may not be consistent with the standard objectively acceptable to the regular user[1]. In other words, behaviour may conform with the standard of behaviour accepted or tolerated on the market and yet still amount to market abuse[2].

1 See the discussion in the FSA Handbook at MAR 1.2.10/11. Note that in cases where the FSA considers that a practice accepted in the market is likely to fall short of the standard expected by the regular user, the FSA will need to consider whether to make its views clear, or to revise the Code, as well as or instead of taking enforcement action. The FSA has said that it recognises that the former (ie signalling its views) will often be more appropriate, working with market participants and regulatory bodies.

2 The risk that this will be the view taken by the Tribunal is obviously greater where there are differing views among practitioners about what is acceptable. But that could be possible even where there is substantial unanimity among actual market users that a particular practice is acceptable.

13.58 Second, the rules and regulations of the particular market and the prevailing market mechanisms, practices and codes of conduct will clearly be relevant, although compliance with them may not be determinative (particularly if the rules are not specifically directed at market abuse)[1]. The FSA has confirmed it is satisfied that the RIE rulebooks do not permit or require behaviour which amounts to market abuse[2], nor do the City Code and the Takeover Panel's Rules Governing Substantial Acquisitions of Shares ('SARs')[3].

1 See the FSA Handbook at MAR 1.2.3 and 1.2.8.
2 See the FSA Handbook at MAR 1.2.12.
3 See the FSA Handbook at MAR 1.7.6. See also para 13.67 below.

13.59 Third, where a person's behaviour occurs on a non-UK market but has an impact on a prescribed market, an important (but not necessarily determinative) factor will be the local rules, practices and conventions prevailing in the relevant market and whether or not the person is in the UK[1].

1 See the FSA Handbook at MAR 1.2.9.

13.60 Finally, there is no requirement for a person to have intended to abuse the market, although what the person's purpose was may be relevant to whether his behaviour amounted to market abuse, as will be seen below. However, a mistake is unlikely to fall below the standards expected where the person has taken reasonable care to prevent and detect the occurrence of such mistakes[1].

1 See the FSA Handbook at MAR 1.2.6.

E Behaviour which does not amount to market abuse

13.61 The FSMA 2000 specifically provides that in three situations behaviour will not amount to market abuse. They are:

- behaviour which the Code says does not amount to market abuse;
- behaviour which an FSA rule says does not amount to market abuse; and
- behaviour which conforms with the City Code and is specified in the Code of Market Conduct as not therefore amounting to market abuse.

These are considered in turn below.

13.62 ***Behaviour which the Code says does not amount to market abuse*** If a person behaves in a way which is described in the Code in force at the time of the behaviour as behaviour that, in the FSA's opinion, does not amount to market abuse, that behaviour of his is to be taken, for the purposes of the FSMA 2000, as not amounting to market abuse[1].

1 FSMA 2000, s 122(1).

13.63 Various safe harbours are currently prescribed in the Code as highlighted above in the discussion of the three types of behaviour that constitute market abuse[1].

1 In addition, certain provisions of the Rules governing Substantial Acquisitions of Shares, issued by the Takeover Panel, are given safe-harbour status on the same basis: see para 13.67 below.

13.64 ***Behaviour which the FSA rules say does not amount to market abuse*** Where an FSA rule includes a provision to the effect that behaviour conforming with the rule does not amount to market abuse, then behaviour that conforms with the rule does not amount to market abuse[1].

1 FSMA 2000, s 118(8).

13.65 The FSA has indicated[1] that behaviour will be regarded as conforming with a rule only if it is required or expressly permitted by that rule. There must therefore be a specific rule that either requires or expressly permits the person to engage in the behaviour in question.

1 See the FSA Handbook at MAR 1.7.2.

13.66 The FSA rules which contain such provisions are[1]:

- the price stabilising rules[2];
- the rules on Chinese walls[3]; and
- certain UKLA listing rules, primarily relating to the disclosure of information[4].

1 See the list in the FSA Handbook at MAR 1.7.3.
2 See the FSA Handbook at MAR 2.
3 See the FSA Handbook at COB 2.4, MAR 1.4.21 and MAR 1.5.27.
4 A full list of the relevant disclosure rules can be found in the FSA Handbook at MAR 1, Annex 1G. Listing Rule 15.1(b) relating to share buy-backs is also specified.

13.67 ***Specified behaviour which conforms with the City Code*** The FSMA 2000 allows the FSA, with HM Treasury approval, to include in the Code of Market Conduct provision to the effect that in its opinion behaviour conforming with the City Code does not amount to market abuse[1]. Various provisions of the City Code are specified for this purpose[2], but only in relation to giving a false or misleading impression and/or distorting the market. The safe harbour only applies in so far as the behaviour is expressly required or permitted by the City Code rule[3] and provided it is not in breach of any relevant General Principle at Section B of the City Code. Certain provisions of the Rules governing Substantial Acquisitions of Shares ('SARs') also have safe harbour status[4]. None of the provisions of the City Code or SARs confer safe harbour status for the purposes of the misuse of information limb of market abuse[5].

1 FSMA 2000, s 120. The Code of Market Conduct may specify that the behaviour does not amount to market abuse in specified circumstances or if engaged in by a specified description of person.

2 In summary, this includes provisions relating to the disclosure of information which is not generally available, standards of care, timing of announcements, documentation and dealings, and content of announcements: see the FSA Handbook at MAR 1.7.7 and, for a full list of the relevant provisions, MAR Annex 2. A safe harbour is also provided for behaviour conforming with rule 4.2 (restrictions on dealings by the offeror and concert parties): see the FSA Handbook at MAR 1.7.8. As to the overlap between the City Code and the Code of Market Conduct more generally, see para 13.102 and 13.224 ff below.

3 The FSA has provided an example of how this works, namely that if a City Code rule deals with the timing of an announcement, the announcement falls within the safe harbour so far as its timing is concerned but this does not protect the method of dissemination, content and standard of care (each of which will need to accord with the relevant provisions): see the FSA Handbook at MAR 1.7.9.

4 These relate to the timing of disclosure: see the FSA Handbook at MAR 1, Annex 2G. The legal basis for this safe harbour is different from that applicable to the City Code, although the effect is the same: for an explanation, see the FSA Handbook at MAR 1.7.4

5 The reason for this is that insider dealing has for a number of years been investigated or prosecuted by other bodies such as the London Stock Exchange and the DTI without disrupting the takeover process: see Consultation Paper 76 ('Supplement to the draft Code of Market Conduct', November 2000, para 1.9).

F Behaviour which does not give rise to a penalty for market abuse

13.68 Behaviour which otherwise amounts to market abuse will in two situations not give rise to a penalty for market abuse. The two situations are where, having considered any representations made to it in response to a warning notice, there are reasonable grounds for the FSA to be satisfied that[1]:

- the person believed, on reasonable grounds, that his behaviour did not amount to market abuse[2]; or
- he took all reasonable precautions and exercised all due diligence to avoid engaging in market abuse[3].

These are considered in turn below, followed by the question of when the person concerned can rely on the defence.

1 FSMA 2000, s 123(2).

2 Or requiring or encouraging market abuse: see para 13.82 ff below.

3 See footnote 2 above.

13.69 It is worth first noting the limited effect of this provision. The effect is not to excuse the behaviour. It still amounts to market abuse and could, for example, still be prohibited by injunction on an application by the FSA[1]. The FSA is, however, prohibited from imposing a penalty or public censure in relation to it and, in addition, neither the FSA nor the court can impose a restitution order on the relevant person as a result of the behaviour[2]. There is, though, nothing to prevent the behaviour from giving rise to other regulatory consequences, for example if it highlights other issues of concern such as about the firm's systems and controls.

1 See para 13.235 ff below. Notably, an injunction could potentially be obtained to require the market abuse to be remedied – for example by the transfer or repurchase of shares – even in a situation where a restitution order or penalty was not available because of this provision.

2 FSMA 2000, ss 383(3) and 384(4).

13.70 ***A belief that the behaviour did not amount to market abuse*** The FSMA 2000 does not give any indication as to what might amount to reasonable grounds for believing that the behaviour did not amount to market abuse but it does require the FSA to provide in its policy an indication of the circumstances in which it is to be expected to regard a person as falling within this, or the second, defence[1].

1 FSMA 2000, s 124(3).

13.71 The FSA has provided[1] a list of the factors it may take into account when deciding whether a person reasonably believed that his behaviour did not amount to market abuse (including requiring or encouraging market abuse). These can be summarised as follows:

- the extent to which the person took reasonable precautions to avoid market abuse;
- the treatment of the relevant behaviour in the Code and any relevant FSA guidance;
- the rules of any relevant market or any other relevant regulatory requirements or codes of conduct or best practice;
- the level of knowledge, skill and experience to be expected of the person concerned; and
- whether the person can demonstrate a legitimate purpose for the behaviour.

1 See the FSA Handbook at ENF 14.5.1(1).

13.72 This guidance is expressly stated to be non exhaustive and there may be other relevant factors depending on the facts of each particular case. One notable point is that the question whether the person took legal advice is not said to be relevant to whether he reasonably believed that his behaviour did not amount to market abuse. It is, however, said to be relevant to the second defence, as outlined below.

13.73 The test which the FSA has to apply under the FSMA 2000 is also worth briefly reviewing, because it is complex and not entirely clear on the wording of the FSMA 2000. It appears that the test is as follows:

- there must be an actual belief by the firm or individual that the behaviour did not amount to market abuse;
- that belief must be based on reasonable grounds;
- once the FSA has considered the firm's representations, there must be reasonable grounds for it to be satisfied of the above two points.

13.74 This suggests that the relevant person does not have to satisfy the FSA that he did believe, on reasonable grounds, that his conduct was not market abuse. Rather, it seems to be sufficient for him to show reasonable grounds for the FSA to be satisfied of this. However, it seems unlikely the test was intended to be this low and unlikely in practice that the Tribunal or a court would uphold the defence in favour of a person who could not demonstrate that he did have that belief and that it was based on reasonable grounds.

13.75 ***Taking all reasonable precautions and exercising all due diligence*** Alternatively, the person must have taken all reasonable precautions and exercised all due diligence to avoid engaging in market abuse. Both reasonable precautions and due diligence are required and the word 'all' is used in relation to both.

13.76 As with the defence of reasonably believing the behaviour did not amount to market abuse, the FSA is required to provide in its policy an indication of the circumstances in which it is to be expected to regard a person as meeting this test[1]. The FSA has provided a list of factors which it may take into account in deciding whether the defence has been met[2] and these can be summarised as follows:

- the extent to which the person followed established internal consultation and escalation procedures;
- the extent to which he sought and followed legal or other expert professional advice;
- the extent to which he sought and followed advice from the relevant market authorities or, where relevant, the Takeover Panel;
- any relevant FSA guidance; and
- the rules of any relevant market or any other relevant regulatory requirements or codes of conduct or best practice.

1 FSMA 2000, s 124(3).
2 See the FSA Handbook at ENF 14.5.1(2).

13.77 The list is said expressly not to be exhaustive and there may be other factors that are relevant depending on the facts of each particular case[1].

1 See the FSA Handbook at ENF 14.5.2.

13.78 Again, it is not clear whether the person must show he actually took all reasonable precautions and exercised all due diligence, or whether it is sufficient to show reasonable grounds for the FSA to be satisfied of this[1].

1 See the discussion at para 13.74 above.

13.79 ***When do the defences apply?*** The FSMA 2000 provides that the FSA may not impose the penalty or restitution order if 'having considered any representations made to it in response to a warning notice', broadly, either of the defences is made out[1].

1 FSMA 2000, ss 123(2) and 384(4).

13.80 The procedure for the FSA to impose a fine or restitution order for market abuse, considered in detail below, involves the FSA issuing a warning notice when it proposes the action and then a decision notice when it decides that the action is appropriate. In the normal course, the first opportunity the firm will have to put forward its defence will be after the warning notice has been issued. Hence, the FSA will only be considering whether the defence is, in its view, made out when it considers whether to issue a decision notice.

13.81 But in some cases the FSA may already have sufficient information from its investigation, for example from interviews with the relevant individuals, to suggest that there is a good defence or, at least, that there are reasonable grounds for it to be satisfied that there is a defence[1]. In those cases, should it issue a warning notice and wait for the firm to try to substantiate its defence? Or should it consider the likely defence when deciding whether or not to issue a warning notice? The answer is unclear. The FSMA 2000 seems to suggest that it need not consider the defence until it decides whether or not to issue a decision notice. However, it is thought that if the FSA has information available to it to indicate that it would not be appropriate for it to take action for market abuse, then that information ought to be relevant to its decision whether or not to issue a warning notice. If that is correct, then the FSA should take the likely defence into account when considering issuing a warning notice[2].

1 This is the statutory test: see para 13.73 above.
2 The same point could be made in relation to the FSA's decision whether to apply to a court for a restitution order under FSMA 2000, s 383.

G Requiring or encouraging others to engage in market abuse

13.82 The market abuse regime does not apply only to the person who engaged in the market abuse. A penalty for market abuse may also be imposed against a person who the FSA is satisfied by taking or refraining from taking any action has required or encouraged another person or persons to engage in behaviour which, if engaged in by that person, would amount to market abuse[1]. The person requiring or encouraging can also be made the subject of a restitution order[2].

1 FSMA 2000, s 123(1)(b).
2 FSMA 2000, ss 383(1)(b) and 384(2)(b).

13.83 There are two limbs to this test. First, it must be shown that the behaviour would have amounted to market abuse if it had been carried out by the person who required or encouraged it and, second, that person must, by action or inaction, have required or encouraged another to engage in the behaviour in question.

13.84 It is to the first limb that the principles set out in the Code are applied. In other words, in testing what the regular user would expect of a person in the relevant person's position in relation to the market, this is judged by reference to the person who did the encouraging or requiring, not the person who was encouraged or required to carry out the market abuse[1]. This potentially means that the person who carried out the action may not have committed market abuse, while the person who required or encouraged him to do so did commit market abuse. The FSA has also made clear[2] that it is not necessary to show that the person who required or encouraged the conduct has benefited from it.

1 See the FSA Handbook at MAR 1.8.2.
2 See the FSA Handbook at MAR 1.8.2.

13.85 The FSA has provided detailed guidance on the application of this provision[1] and has given examples of conduct which might amount to requiring or encouraging, namely[2]:

- where a director of a company, while in possession of relevant, disclosable information which is not generally available, instructs an employee of the company to deal in the investments or relevant products in respect of which the information is relevant and disclosable;
- where one person recommends or advises another to engage in behaviour which, if engaged in by the first person, would amount to market abuse; and
- early, selective disclosure of information which a regular user would expect market users to have will generally be presumed to constitute requiring or encouraging unless, broadly, there is a legitimate purpose for making the disclosure and it is disclosed in confidence on terms that behaviour should not be based on it until after it is made generally available[3].

1 See the FSA Handbook at MAR 1.8.
2 See the FSA Handbook at MAR 1.8.3.
3 See the FSA Handbook at MAR 1.8.5. This overlaps with the obligations of a listed company under the Listing Rules: see para 13.220 ff below.

13.86 The Code also includes detailed guidance on behaviour which the FSA will not regard as amounting to requiring or encouraging[1], on the application of this provision in the context of a takeover bid[2], on transactions carried out through intermediaries, and on directors' dealings under the Model Code[3].

1 Examples include passing information, in certain circumstances, to employees for the proper performance of their functions, to professional advisers for the purpose of obtaining advice, or to a person with whom the person is negotiating for the purpose of facilitating the transactions: for the full list, see the FSA Handbook at MAR 1.8.6.
2 A person will not be regarded as requiring or encouraging another where (i) the first person is an adviser to the second and the second person is considering the acquisition or disposal of an equity or non-equity stake and (ii) the first person advises the second person to acquire or dispose of an equity or non-equity stake in the target company for the purposes and in the manner specified at MAR 1.4.28 C: see the FSA Handbook at MAR 1.8.7.
3 See the FSA Handbook at MAR 1.8.10.

Is there a market abuse problem?

13.87 A problem has arisen. The firm believes that there may be some sort of market misconduct implications. Does it have to be concerned that market abuse is a real issue?

13.88 The types of questions which the firm may ask itself should include the following:

- does the issue relate to investments traded on one of the recognised investment exchanges? If not, does it relate to some other product which is in some way related to such an investment (for example, priced by reference to a traded investment or the subject matter of which is a traded investment)?
- does it involve the use of information not generally available and not ascertainable from public sources?
- has it, or could it have, given a false or misleading impression to anyone as to the price or value of the investments?
- has it, or was it likely to have, distorted the market in that investment, in the sense of impeding the operation of market forces and interfering with supply and demand?
- is it behaviour which, objectively, could be thought to be below the standard reasonably expected of similar people in the market? It is not necessarily sufficient that it is an accepted practice on the market.

It should also be borne in mind that there need not have been any intention for the behaviour to have any of the above effects.

13.89 If the conduct falls within this territory, the next steps should be to:

- review the Code of Market Conduct[1], to identify whether the Code directly addresses the conduct in question or, if not, how the factors which the Code specifies as relevant in determining whether there has been market abuse apply to the particular conduct;
- review the statutory definition[2] to see whether the conduct falls within it; and
- consider whether one of the defences available under the FSMA 2000 applies[3].

1 See the FSA Handbook at MAR 1.
2 FSMA 2000, s 118. The statutory definition is plainly the basis for market abuse, but in practice it is likely the Code will be used as the starting point in considering whether particular behaviour is likely to constitute market abuse.
3 See para 13.68 above.

Answering some common questions about market abuse

13.90 We address here a number of common questions about the scope of the market abuse regime and, in particular:

- to whom does the regime apply?
- can behaviour outside the UK be market abuse?
- if a person complies with the FSA's rules, is he safe?

- if a person complies with the Code, is he safe?
- if a person fails to comply with the Code, has he committed market abuse?
- if a person complies with other regulatory rules, is he safe?
- if a person complies with normal market practice, is he safe? and
- is it sufficient that there is a commercial rationale for the action?

To whom does the regime apply?

13.91 The market abuse provisions apply to everyone, whether authorised or approved under the FSMA 2000 or not. The FSMA 2000 does not confine the market abuse regime to market participants.

13.92 However, the requirement for the person to have fallen below the standard a regular user would reasonably expect of someone in that person's position in relation to the market[1] distinguishes between different types of market user, reflecting different market experience and different levels of proximity to the market[2]. For example, people who are engaged in the market or who would be expected to be aware of market rules would have different positions in relation to the market than an ordinary member of the public. Someone abroad whose otherwise potentially abusive behaviour complies with local market rules would arguably be unlikely to have committed market abuse, on the basis that his behaviour would not be below the standard that would be expected of him in his position in relation to the market[3]. Generally, the more remote someone is from the market, the less likely it is that he will have committed market abuse.

1 See the discussion at para 13.50 ff above.
2 'Market' refers in this context to the prescribed market on which the qualifying investments concerned are traded: see para 13.30 above.
3 See the debate in Standing Committee, 2 November 1999.

13.93 The other point to have in mind in this context is that the market abuse regime affects not only the person whose behaviour is in question, but also any person who encouraged or required him to do that behaviour[1].

1 This is discussed in more detail at para 13.82 above.

Can behaviour outside the UK be market abuse?

13.94 Does market abuse only cover behaviour carried on in the UK or on a UK market? The short answer is no. First, activities on a non-UK market could constitute market abuse if those activities constituted behaviour which 'occurs in relation to' qualifying investments on a (UK) prescribed market. The meaning of 'occurs in relation to' is discussed at para 13.33 above. This would include, for example, where the price of the overseas investment or product was expressed by reference to the investment traded on a UK prescribed market.

13.95 Second, if the behaviour occurs somewhere other than in the UK, and not on a market, but has some effect on a qualifying investment traded on a prescribed market then the market abuse provisions could apply. The important questions will be first, whether it occurred 'in relation to' a qualifying investment and, particularly, what standard the regular user would expect from the relevant person given his position in relation to the market.

13.96 Third, as has been seen[1], whether investments on a particular market are covered depends on whether the market is prescribed by HM Treasury for this purpose. The FSMA 2000 does not provide any territorial limits on the markets that can be prescribed, although its effect is to limit market abuse to markets situated in or accessible electronically from the UK[2]. HM Treasury has at present only prescribed markets that are situated in the UK. However, the ability to include markets accessible electronically from the UK may become increasingly important, given the international nature of financial services. The Government has said that if a situation arose in which a major UK market, in the sense of a market which had a major impact on the UK economy, was not located in the UK but was accessible electronically from the UK, HM Treasury might wish to prescribe it[3]. It cannot therefore be ruled out that non-UK markets may in the future be included. This shows the wide potential jurisdictional reach of the market abuse regime.

1 See para 13.31 above.
2 FSMA 2000, s 118(5).
3 See the Economic Secretary to HM Treasury in Standing Committee, 2 November 1999.

13.97 Finally, if HM Treasury does prescribe markets situated outside the UK but accessible electronically from the UK then, in theory, anyone trading on that market, even locally, would fall within the market abuse regime. It is, however, to be hoped that in that situation the FSA would amend the Code to make clear when it will seek to use its powers extra-territorially.

If a person complies with the FSA's rules, is he safe?

13.98 To the extent the behaviour conforms with, and is required or expressly permitted by, those identified FSA rules[1] which specifically provide that compliance does not amount to market abuse then it will not amount to market abuse[2]. Beyond this, there is no safe harbour for compliance with FSA rules, although compliance with applicable rules will obviously be a factor in determining whether or not market abuse was committed[3].

1 These are listed at para 13.66 above.
2 See para 13.64 above.
3 See the FSA Handbook at MAR 1.2.3 and see para 13.58 above.

If a person complies with the Code, is he safe?

13.99 Compliance with the Code of Market Conduct only precludes market abuse from being committed where the behaviour in question is specified in the Code as not amounting to market abuse[1]. If, short of this, it appears from the Code (from the examples given of behaviour which does amount to market abuse, the examples given of behaviour that does not amount to market abuse, and the factors specified to be taken into account in determining whether or not behaviour amounts to market abuse) that the behaviour does not amount to market abuse, then the firm or individual can still not be certain that the conduct would not amount to market abuse. In practice, though, compliance with the Code should provide a reasonable amount of certainty, albeit not entirely without risk.

1 FSMA 2000, s 122(1) and see paras 13.22 and 13.62 above.

If a person fails to comply with the Code, has he committed market abuse?

13.100 Failure to comply with the Code of Market Conduct, in the sense of:

- carrying on behaviour which is not specified as not amounting to market abuse; or
- doing something which the Code says the FSA would regard as amounting to market abuse; or
- perhaps doing something which the factors outlined in the Code tend to suggest would amount to market abuse;

does not necessarily mean that the firm or individual has committed market abuse. Those rules are only of evidential value[1], in that they may be relied upon in so far as they indicate whether or not the behaviour should be taken to amount to market abuse. In practice, though, unless one of the defences applies[2], or the conduct falls outside the statutory definition of market abuse, or there is some other good reason why the conduct should not be taken as amounting to market abuse, then it is likely that market abuse will have been committed.

1 FSMA 2000, s 122(2) and see the discussion at para 13.22 above.
2 See para 13.68 above.

If a person complies with the other applicable regulatory rules, is he safe?

13.101 To the extent that firms or individuals are trading on organised markets, for example those of the recognised investment exchanges, they will need to comply with the rules of those markets as well as with the FSA's Code of Market Conduct. In some situations, the FSA's Listing Rules or the City Code on Takeovers and Mergers will also be relevant. There is, therefore, a clear overlap between the market abuse regime and other applicable regulatory requirements. An important question is whether conduct which is not prohibited under the rules of the relevant exchange or in the City Code is for that reason precluded from amounting to market abuse. The answer to this is two-fold.

13.102 First, behaviour which is required or expressly permitted under the rules of the relevant exchange, the City Code or the Listing Rules will not generally amount to market abuse. The FSA has confirmed both in relation to the rule books of the recognised investment exchanges and in relation to the City Code and the Takeover Panel's Rules governing Substantial Acquisitions of Shares ('SARs'), that they do not permit or require behaviour which constitutes market abuse[1]. In addition, certain conduct may fall within the safe harbour provisions of the Code of Market Conduct[2] and, beyond this, conduct permitted or required by a regulatory authority is unlikely to fall below the standard reasonably to be expected by the regular user of the relevant market.

1 See the FSA Handbook at, respectively, MAR 1.2.12 and MAR 1.7.6.
2 Specifically, certain provisions of the FSA's Listing Rules (see para 13.66 above), and of the City Code and SARs (see para 13.67 above).

13.103 Second, if the behaviour was not expressly permitted or required, the fact that it was not prohibited by the relevant rules will not of itself provide the person with much protection[1]. The key question will be whether the regular user of the market concerned would view the conduct as below the standard reasonably to be expected of a person in the same position in relation to the market as the relevant person. Conduct which is properly accepted by the market as legitimate should not be caught. Questionable practices, even if engaged in generally in the market, may well be caught.

1 This is illustrated, in the context of the City Code, by the FSA's express statement that where none of the safe harbours apply, the regular user may not necessarily consider that complying with the applicable requirements of the City Code and SARs will be sufficient in and of itself to demonstrate that behaviour does not amount to market abuse: see the FSA Handbook at MAR 1.7.13 (and the example given there).

13.104 In addition, it could be that the conduct is not prohibited under the rules of the relevant exchange not because it is regarded as appropriate conduct but because the exchange has no or only limited power to address the conduct or simply because the conduct in question is not covered by the exchange's rules. As will be seen[1], the question whether the exchange had the power to deal with the conduct in question is a relevant consideration for the FSA in deciding whether or not to exercise its powers to investigate and address the problem which has arisen. If the exchange has no power to deal with conduct which the FSA regards as market abuse, then it may make it more, rather than less, likely that the FSA will take action.

1 See para 13.137 ff below.

If a person complies with normal market practice, is he safe?

13.105 The FSA has made clear[1] that conduct may fall below the required standard even though market practice seems to accept that conduct. The key question will always be whether the regular user of the market in question would regard the conduct as below the standard of behaviour reasonably to be expected[2]. It is an objective test involving a hypothetical regular user.

1 See the discussion at para 13.57 above.
2 The regular user test is discussed at para 13.50 above.

Is it sufficient that there is a commercial rationale for the action?

13.106 The Code allows some flexibility for action taken with a legitimate commercial rationale. In particular:

- there is a safe harbour, in relation to the misuse of information limb[1], for dealing or arranging which was required in order to comply with a legal (including contractual) or regulatory obligation which existed before the relevant information was in the person's possession[2]; and
- behaviour that the regular user would regard as having a legitimate commercial rationale (and as having been properly executed) may, in some circumstances, be unlikely to amount to market abuse under the limbs of giving a false or misleading impression or distorting the market[3].

1 See the FSA Handbook at MAR 1.4.20.
2 There is also a general safe harbour allowing trading permitted by the FSA's rules on Chinese walls: see the FSA Handbook at MAR 1.7.3(2).
3 For details, see the FSA Handbook at MAR 1.5 and 1.6 (for example MAR 1.5.8, 1.5.21, 1.6.10).

13.107 Clearly, though, much will depend upon the precise circumstances.

INVESTIGATIONS INTO MARKET MISCONDUCT

Introduction

13.108 A problem comes to light which raises the spectre of market abuse or other market misconduct. What should the firm be doing, both internally and vis-à-vis its regulator? What powers does the FSA have to investigate the situation and use information which it obtains in its investigation? How should the firm deal with the FSA in that context? The answers to these and related questions are considered in the following paragraphs. Specifically, we address the following issues:

- practical steps to take when the problem arises (para 13.109 ff); and
- FSA investigations into market misconduct (para 13.130 ff).

Practical steps to take when the problem arises

13.109 A market abuse issue could come to light in any of a number of ways. For example, a problem could arise (perhaps after a complaint from a customer or competitor), the firm could identify a practice with market abuse connotations, a particular transaction may raise market abuse issues (for example because the firm is in possession of information which is not publicly available), or information suggesting market abuse could come to light via the FSA, whether from a supervisory visit or based on information it has received from some other source.

13.110 The issues which the firm will consider at the outset when the problem comes to light are the same as arise with any regulatory problem. Some of the main issues are:

- should the firm investigate?
- should it report the matter to the FSA?
- how should the firm deal with customers?
- what internal action should be taken?
- are criminal proceedings a possibility? and
- taking care over document creation and retention.

13.111 These matters are discussed in detail in Chapter 3 above. Highlighted here are some additional factors which arise specifically in the context of market abuse.

Should the firm investigate?

13.112 As discussed at para 3.9 ff above, almost invariably the firm should investigate internally since, until it has a proper understanding of the matter, it will not be in a position to assess properly what action it should take and the potential repercussions. In addition, the FSA will expect to see that the firm is taking appropriate steps to investigate.

13.113 An additional practical issue may arise in relation to market misconduct, namely that the issue may not be purely internal to the firm and the information that the firm needs in order to understand the problem properly may not be entirely within its control. For example, some of the information on which the FSA is basing its enquiries may have come from an exchange or from another financial institution.

13.114 Regulated firms and individuals should also keep in mind that a matter which arises as a suspected case of market misconduct may give rise to rather wider regulatory issues. For example, how did the employee obtain authorisation for the transaction? Did information cross Chinese walls? Are the firm's systems and controls operating properly? Are employees receiving proper training? If the firm is to fully understand and deal with the problem, then it will need to ask itself the wider questions and address the answers.

Should the matter be reported to the FSA?

13.115 Whether the matter should be reported to the FSA depends on whether the question is being considered by an authorised person, an approved person, or someone who is not part of the regulated community[1].

1 Market abuse and the related criminal offences of misleading statements and practices and insider dealing, can be committed by any person, whether or not within the regulated community.

The obligation of authorised firms to report to the FSA

13.116 Firms are under both general and specific obligations of reporting to the FSA. Among the specific reporting obligations is an obligation to notify the FSA immediately the firm becomes aware or has information which reasonably suggests that a significant breach of an FSA rule (or a Statement of Principle for approved persons) or a breach of a requirement imposed by the FSMA 2000 has or may have occurred or may in the foreseeable future occur[1]. This would cover cases of conduct suspected to amount to market abuse[2]. The firm also has a more general reporting obligation outlined at para 13.117 below.

1 See the FSA Handbook at SUP 15.3.11 and see para 3.50 above.
2 It is not entirely clear whether 'market abuse is a requirement imposed under the FSMA 2000', but in any event the FSA has made clear (see the FSA Handbook at ENF 14.8) that market abuse by an authorised person will also constitute a breach of Principle 5, Principles for Businesses (which is an FSA rule: see para 2.52 ff above).

13.117 The more difficult question is whether the firm has an obligation to report conduct which clearly does not amount to market abuse or a criminal offence, but which it believes the FSA may nonetheless regard as being wrong[1]. The firm has a general obligation to inform the FSA appropriately of anything relating to the firm of which the FSA would reasonably expect notice[2]. The FSA has given guidance that this includes reporting any significant failure in the firm's systems and controls[3]. In principle, the obligation to report could arise in cases of market misconduct not amounting to market abuse or a criminal offence. Whether a particular matter must be reported will depend upon the circumstances of the particular case.

1 For example, on the basis that it may constitute a breach of Principle 5 of the Principles for Business: see the discussion at para 13.265 ff below.
2 Principle 11, Principles for Businesses: see para 2.52 above and, particularly, para 3.66 ff above.
3 See the FSA Handbook at SUP 15.3.8 and see para 3.68 above.

13.118 Does the firm have to report known misconduct of others? The firm's specific reporting obligation is to notify the FSA of rule breaches not only committed by the firm, but also committed by any of its directors, officers, employees, approved persons or appointed representatives[1]. Beyond this, though, there is no clear, general whistleblowing obligation requiring the firm to notify the FSA of market misconduct by others, for example other firms[2].

1 See the FSA Handbook at SUP 13.5.11 and see para 3.50 above.
2 The wording of Principle 11 makes clear that the general obligation applies only to matters relating to the firm. The practice under the former regime was wider in some respects: see, for example, SFA Board Notice 141. For further discussion, see para 3.70 above.

13.119 The timing and extent of reporting to the FSA, and the consequences of not reporting, are discussed in more detail above[1]. The specific reporting obligation requires the report to be made immediately it becomes aware of or has information which reasonably suggests the breach. The firm cannot therefore wait until it has discovered all the details before reporting the matter to the FSA.

1 See, respectively, paras 3.74 ff and 3.101 ff above.

The obligation of an approved person to report to the FSA

13.120 An approved person is obliged to disclose appropriately any information of which the FSA would reasonably expect notice[1]. This is similar to the firm's obligation, although an approved person will normally need to report only within the firm (unless he is the person within the firm responsible for reporting to the FSA or the firm has no procedures for reporting internally). The extent of the approved person's obligation is discussed in more detail in para 3.85 ff above. Given the personal obligation on certain approved persons, particularly compliance officers, there is scope for tension between the position of the individual and that of the firm where the firm for some reason decides not to report.

1 Principle 4, Statements of Principle for approved persons: see para 3.85 ff above.

Obligations of unregulated firms and individuals to report to the FSA

13.121 Firms or individuals who are unregulated do not owe regulatory duties to the FSA and, accordingly, are under no obligation to report any matter to the FSA, including a suspected case of market abuse.

13.122 However, one of the factors which the FSA has said may be taken into account by it in deciding whether or not to take action for market abuse and, if so, the amount of any penalty that should be imposed, is the person's conduct following the contravention including his co-operation in any investigation and his conduct in bringing the contravention to the attention of the FSA or other regulatory authorities[1]. This does seem to place an onus on all those who are subject to the market abuse regime to report market abuse to the FSA and to co-operate with it. Nonetheless, it must be open to question whether a failure to report should be taken into account in considering the conduct of a person who was otherwise under no obligation to make a report. It may be that, in practice, it should be a factor in a person's favour if they do report the matter but not a negative factor if they do not.

1 See the FSA Handbook at ENF 14.4.2(2) and 14.7.4(5) and see paras 13.193 and 13.200 below.

How should the firm deal with its customers?

13.123 Although the market abuse regime is focused primarily on protecting the integrity of the markets, rather than on individual customer transactions, it is clearly possible for customers to suffer losses from market abuse. Indeed, one of the tools available to the FSA to redress market abuse is to make or apply for restitution orders requiring firms to compensate investors for their losses or to disgorge profits the firm has made[1]. The primary question arising in this context is whether the firm should be volunteering compensation to its customers. Again, the analysis depends upon whether or not the firm is authorised.

1 This is discussed in detail at para 13.254 ff below.

Authorised firms

13.124 Authorised firms owe an obligation to pay due regard to the interests of their customers[1] and may face regulatory disciplinary proceedings and other enforcement consequences if they fail to do so. The nature and extent of their obligations to their customers, and the various consequences of not complying with those obligations, are discussed in detail in para 3.110 ff above. The firm's actions following discovery of the market misconduct, including what steps it took to compensate investors, are relevant to the FSA's decisions whether to take action for market abuse and, if so, whether to impose a fine or public censure and the amount of any penalty[2].

1 Principle 6, Principles for Businesses: see para 2.52 above.
2 See the FSA Handbook at ENF 14.4.2(2), 14.6.2(3) and 14.7.4(5) and see paras 13.193, 13.198 and 13.200 below.

Unauthorised firms or individuals

13.125 Those who are unregulated do not owe the same regulatory obligation regarding their customers. Nonetheless, there are a number of factors militating in favour of treating customers fairly:

- it is a relevant consideration for the FSA in deciding whether to take action for the market abuse and, if so, whether to impose a fine or a public censure and, if a fine, the level of the penalty[1];
- the FSA may otherwise take action to secure redress for customers by, for example, applying for a restitution order[2]; and
- the firm may in any event owe legal obligations to its customers in the circumstances of the particular relationship which require it to make redress[3].

1 See the FSA Handbook at ENF 14.4.2(2), 14.6.2(3) and 14.7.4(5) and see paras 13.193, 13.198 and 13.200 below.
2 See para 13.254 ff below.
3 See the discussion in para 3.125 above.

13.126 It may therefore be prudent for unregulated firms or individuals who are subject to potential proceedings for market misconduct to consider offering compensation to any customers who suffered loss from their conduct.

What internal action should the firm take?

13.127 The discussion at para 3.128 ff above of the internal action which the firm might consider taking when a regulatory issue arises, is equally relevant in this context. The question of what steps the firm has taken to prevent recurrence of the behaviour is one of the factors taken into account by the FSA in determining whether to take action for the market abuse and, if so, the amount of any penalty[1]. It is therefore important that all firms, including those who are unauthorised, are seen to address this issue adequately.

1 See the FSA Handbook at ENF 14.4.2(2) and 14.7.4(5) and see paras 13.193 and 13.200 below.

Is there a risk of criminal proceedings?

13.128 There is a particular risk of criminal proceedings in the context of suspected market abuse, since the civil regime for market abuse overlaps with and complements the criminal regime for insider dealing and misleading statements and practices. When investigating a suspected case of market abuse, the FSA is unlikely to decide at the outset whether it will be pursuing criminal proceedings or taking civil action for market abuse, or some other action. Rather, unless there is a need for urgent regulatory action, it is likely to conduct the investigation first before deciding what action to take. If the conduct is serious enough to institute criminal proceedings, and the normal guidelines are fulfilled[1], then the FSA may do so. Thus, criminal proceedings may often be a potential risk, but the firm is unlikely to know through the investigation stage whether they will be pursued. Where this is the case, some particular issues arise and these are discussed in para 3.142 ff above.

1 See para 13.177 ff below.

Taking care over document creation and retention

13.129 Various concerns about creating and retaining documents once a regulatory issue arises are discussed at para 3.149 ff above. That discussion is equally relevant in this context.

FSA investigations into market misconduct

13.130 The FSA has a range of information gathering and investigation powers which it could use to obtain information about a suspected case of market misconduct, including one formal investigation power specifically aimed at market misconduct, and various other formal and informal powers applicable in different situations.

13.131 The various powers and obligations include the following:

- the regulated community owes a general obligation to co-operate and be open with the FSA[1];
- the FSA can require authorised persons, recognised investment exchanges and recognised clearing houses, among others, to provide information or documents reasonably required by the FSA in connection with the exercise by it of its functions under the FSMA 2000[2];
- the FSA may appoint an investigator to conduct an investigation into the business of an authorised person, or various connected persons, if it appears to it that there is good reason for doing so[3];

- the FSA may appoint an investigator to conduct an investigation if it appears to it that, among other things, there are circumstances suggesting breaches of the Principles for Businesses or Statements of Principle for approved persons[4]; or
- the FSA may appoint an investigator to conduct an investigation into suspected market abuse or the criminal offences of insider dealing or misleading statements and practices, if it appears to it that there are circumstances suggesting that one of these has been committed[5].

1 Principle 11, Principles for Businesses and Statement of Principle 4 for approved persons. For a detailed discussion of what this involves, see para 4.26 ff above.
2 FSMA 2000, s 165 and see para 4.59 ff above.
3 FSMA 2000, s 167 and see para 4.122 ff above.
4 FSMA 2000, s 168(4) and see para 4.134 ff above.
5 FSMA 2000, s 168(2) and see para 4.144 ff above.

13.132 It is the last of these, the market abuse investigation, which has tended to attract the most attention. However, it needs to be seen in context. As can be seen, so far as the regulated community is concerned, the FSA has a range of powers available for investigating cases of suspected market misconduct, of which that is only one. In contrast, where the suspected market misconduct relates to an unregulated firm or person, or if it relates to an authorised firm but information is required from third parties who are unauthorised and unconnected with the authorised firm, then it may be that a market abuse investigation is the only way forward[1].

1 Information could also be sought from unconnected third parties in connection with a ss 167 or 168(4) investigation, but the investigator's powers in connection with such investigations (particularly, s 167 investigations) are more limited than in an s 168(2) investigation.

13.133 The power to obtain information from recognised investment exchanges, and the ability to exchange information with them[1], is likely to be particularly relevant in this context. The focus of the market abuse provisions is on protecting the integrity of the markets[2]. The recognised investment exchanges will be a valuable source of information leading to market abuse investigations, particularly concerning market participants who are not authorised persons.

1 Under the so-called Gateway Regulations, which allow the provision of information without breaching the statutory criminal prohibition against disclosure: see para 4.304 ff above.
2 Currently, the markets that are prescribed for the purpose of market abuse are those of the recognised investment exchanges: see para 13.31 above.

13.134 Each of these powers has been considered in some detail in Chapter 4 above. We concentrate here on:

- the FSA's policy on when it will formally investigate market misconduct;
- formal investigations into market misconduct;
- what information the investigator can obtain;

- whether a person must comply with an investigator's requests for information; and
- the use that can be made of the information obtained.

When will the FSA investigate suspected market misconduct?

13.135 Not every case of suspected market misconduct will give rise to an investigation. The FSA has provided guidance as to its policy on the circumstances when it will conduct a formal investigation into market misconduct[1]. In particular, in deciding whether or not to investigate, it will take into account a number of factors, including:

- the seriousness of the FSA's concerns, including the effect on consumers or market confidence;
- the nature of the possible contravention, including the type of market involved and the duration and frequency of the possible contravention;
- the context of the possible contravention. An example given is where the conduct occurred in the context of a takeover bid, in which case if, in the FSA's views, any investigation may materially affect the timetable or outcome of the bid, the FSA will consult the Takeover Panel and give due weight to its views; and
- whether another regulatory authority is in a position to investigate and deal with the matters of concern[2].

1 See the FSA Handbook at ENF 2.6.
2 This is considered in more detail at para 13.137 below.

13.136 Interestingly, the question whether the FSA is able to obtain the information which it needs without resort to a formal market misconduct investigation is not included within this list. This is, though, likely to be an important factor in practice.

Whether another regulatory authority is investigating

13.137 One of the relevant factors is whether another regulatory authority is in a position to investigate and deal with the matter of concern. This arises because the particular exchange on which the suspected market misconduct took place may have its own powers of investigation and enforcement to address misconduct on its market. The FSA recognises this and will therefore consider the extent to which a recognised investment exchange or clearing house has adequate and appropriate powers to investigate and deal with the matters of concern[1]. Firms should be aware that the FSA is not saying that it will decline to investigate where some other regulator has concurrent powers. Rather, it will consider to what extent it still needs to investigate. Its own powers may be tougher, or may enable necessary information to be obtained from third parties, and the nature of the FSA's concerns may be different from those of the other regulator. There is therefore scope for multiple investigations[2].

1 See the FSA Handbook at ENF 2.6.2(4)(a).
2 Suspected market abuse may arise in the context of a takeover bid, in which case questions arise relating to the nature and timing of the FSA's investigation and the involvement of the Takeover Panel. This issue is considered at para 13.224 ff below.

13.138 The FSA has the power[1] to direct a recognised investment exchange or clearing house to terminate, suspend or limit the scope of any enquiry which it is conducting under its rules or not to conduct an enquiry which it proposes to conduct. This power is only exercisable where the FSA considers this desirable or expedient because of the exercise or possible exercise of its power to impose civil penalties for market abuse or to initiate a formal market abuse investigation.

1 FSMA 2000, s 128.

13.139 The FSA has not given any guidance on when it will seek to exercise this power, merely saying that it may do so where appropriate[1]. However, it made clear in the consultation process that one of the reasons for having this power is to ensure fairness to and reduce the resource burden upon persons under investigation and that the criteria for the use of the power are likely to reflect issues such as the seriousness of the suspected abuse, the involvement of persons outside the jurisdiction of the exchange or clearing house and whether novel or complex issues of application across the financial markets are involved[2]. The Government has said that it envisages the power being used only rarely[3].

1 See the FSA Handbook at ENF 2.6.2(4)(a).
2 See Consultation Paper 10 ('Market Abuse. Pt 1: Consultation on a draft Code of Market Conduct'), paras 145 and 146.
3 Economic Secretary to HM Treasury in Standing Committee, 2 November 1999.

13.140 Currently, market abuse can only occur in relation to the markets of one of the recognised investment exchanges, because it is only those markets that have been prescribed by HM Treasury for the purposes of the market abuse regime[1]. However, the FSMA 2000 allows the list of prescribed markets to be expanded, and to include exchanges which are not located in the UK but are accessible electronically from the UK. The market abuse regime will need to interact in a transparent and coherent way not only with the rules of the recognised investment exchanges, but also potentially with those of any non-UK exchanges which may be prescribed, if firms are not to be subject to inconsistent jurisdictions.

1 See para 13.31 above.

Formal market misconduct investigations

13.141 The FSA, or the Secretary of State, may appoint an investigator to conduct an investigation if it appears to it that there are circumstances suggesting that market abuse may have taken place or one of the criminal offences of insider dealing or misleading statements and practices may have been committed[1].

1 FSMA 2000, s 168(2).

The test for appointing an investigator

13.142 The test for appointing an investigator is fairly low. The FSA does not need to be satisfied or have reasonable grounds for believing that market misconduct has taken place. All that is required are circumstances suggesting this. Most notably, it is not necessary for the FSA to be able to identify, at the outset of the investigation, any person who may have engaged in the suspected market misconduct. This allows the FSA to commence an investigation based on, for example, information received from an exchange showing suspicious or inexplicable movements in the price of a particular investment.

13.143 The suspicion must be that market misconduct has already taken place; the FSA does not have power under this head to investigate market misconduct which it suspects may take place on some future date. The FSA does, however, have the ability to apply to the court for an injunction to prevent a person engaging in market abuse in the future, which the court may grant if satisfied that there is a reasonable likelihood that any person will engage in market abuse[1]. If the FSA has a suspicion that market abuse may occur, but insufficient evidence to obtain an injunction, then it will need to find another means of investigating. That should not be difficult where an authorised firm is involved but may be more difficult as against those who are not regulated.

1 See further at para 13.237 ff below.

What can be investigated?

13.144 The FSA can investigate suspected market abuse, or one of the criminal offences, or both, and will need to define the scope of the investigation accordingly. However, having commenced an investigation, there can be one investigation into all aspects of the suspected market misconduct: the decision in the more serious cases of whether to commence civil proceedings for market abuse or criminal proceedings for insider dealing or misleading statements and practices does not need to be taken at the outset.

13.145 In less serious cases involving regulated firms or approved persons, it may be that once the investigation starts it will become apparent that market abuse has not occurred and what is instead being investigated is a suspected breach of the Principles[1]. Provided it appeared to the FSA at the outset that there were circumstances suggesting market abuse, the investigation will have been commenced on the correct basis and there does not seem to be anything to prevent it proceeding on that statutory basis notwithstanding market abuse is no longer at issue[2].

1 In particular, Principle 5 of the Principles for Businesses or Statement of Principle 3 of the Statements of Principle for approved persons: see paras 13.265 and 13.272 below.

2 The advantage for the investigator is that a market abuse investigation confers wider powers than one into suspected breaches of FSA rules or the Principles. This is discussed further in para 4.177 above.

Investigations by the Secretary of State

13.146 The Secretary of State has concurrent power to appoint investigators for suspected cases of market abuse, insider dealing and/or misleading statements and practices. The reasons for this are discussed in para 4.144 above.

Will the person under investigation be notified of the investigation?

13.147 The FSA, or, as appropriate, the Secretary of State, is not required to give notice to the person under investigation of the appointment of the investigator[1]. This is an exception to the general rule and is in some respects mitigated by the FSA's stated policy[2].

1 FSMA 2000, s 170(3)(b).
2 See the discussion in para 4.160 ff above.

How does the FSA commence and control the investigation?

13.148 This is discussed in detail in para 4.157 ff above.

Will the FSA publicise the investigation?

13.149 The FSA will not, as a general policy, make public the fact that it is or is not investigating a particular matter or the outcome of the investigation. However, there are some exceptions, which are discussed at para 4.164 ff above.

What information can the investigator obtain?

13.150 If the investigator considers that any person is or may be able to give information which is or may be relevant to the investigation[1], he may require that person to:

- attend before him at a specified time and place and answer questions;
- otherwise provide such information as he may require for the purposes of the investigation;
- produce at a specified time and place any specified documents or documents of a specified description which appear to the investigator to relate to any matter relevant to the investigation; and
- otherwise give him all assistance in connection with the investigation which the person is reasonably able to give.

Each of these is considered in turn below. There are various ancillary provisions applicable to all the investigation powers, which are discussed at para 4.111 ff above. The question whether a person can refuse to provide material requested is considered at para 13.154 ff below.

1 FSMA 2000, s 173. This provision is similar to the former provision for insider dealing investigations, found in the Financial Services Act 1986, s 177.

Who can be required to provide information?

13.151 There is no limitation on the classes of person who can be called upon to provide information to the investigator. The person does not have to be an authorised firm, or an approved person. Nor does he have to be the person suspected of market abuse. He simply has to be a person who, in the view of the investigator, *may* have information which *may* be relevant to the investigation. This is consistent with the general theme that investigations into market misconduct may be, at least initially, investigations into particular situations, such as movements in share prices, rather than into particular persons. The investigator's power to require information to be provided is therefore framed not by reference to the person under investigation, but rather by reference to those who may have relevant information.

What information can they be asked to provide?

13.152 There is likely to be little that is not encompassed within answers to questions, production of documents, provision of other information (which probably means information not recorded in any form[1]) and any other assistance. The power is very widely drawn and a few examples may serve to highlight this:

- there is no requirement for the investigator to specify the questions that he intends to ask when imposing a requirement on a person to answer questions, nor is any limit prescribed upon the nature of the questions that can be asked (although they probably should relate to the information the person has which is believed to be relevant to the investigation)[2], nor is the investigator required to specify *in writing* the time and place for the person's attendance[3];
- there is no requirement for the investigator reasonably to consider the documents or information required to be provided to be relevant or to be satisfied that they are necessary or expedient for the purposes of the investigation[4] and, again, there is no requirement for the documents, or the time and place for them to be provided to be specified in writing; and
- the requirement to provide 'other assistance' is the most wide-ranging of all the investigation provisions. At its broadest, any person who the investigator believes 'may be able' to give information which 'may' be relevant can be required to provide 'all' assistance in connection with the investigation which he is reasonably able to give. The test is very low; the assistance simply has to be in connection with the investigation.

1 See para 4.113 above.
2 Compare an investigator appointed to investigate the business of an authorised person under FSMA 2000, s 167, who must reasonably consider the questions or information to be relevant to the purposes of the investigation: FSMA 2000, s 171(3) and see para 4.122 ff above. Similarly, an investigator appointed under s 168(1) or (4) can require people to attend before him and answer questions but only if he is satisfied that the requirement is necessary or expedient for the purposes of the investigation: FSMA 2000, s 172(3).
3 Again, contrast investigations under FSMA 2000, ss 167 and 168(1) or (4).
4 Contrast investigations under FSMA 2000, ss 167 and 168(1) or (4).

13.153 In reality, there are some limitations on the investigator's powers as a matter of law[1]. These are discussed further in para 4.273 ff above.

1 See, for example, *Re Mirror Group Newspapers plc* [1999] 3 WLR 583.

Is a person obliged to comply with an investigator's requests?

13.154 Unless there is some legitimate ground for objecting, a person requested by an investigator to provide information, documents, answers to questions or other assistance must comply with that request. Failure to comply without reasonable excuse could be punished by a court as though the person had committed contempt of court[1]. The failure could also lead to a warrant being obtained to enter the person's premises and seize the documents or information[2]. If the person concerned is an authorised firm or approved person then there could also be regulatory enforcement consequences[3].

1 FSMA 2000, s 177(1) and (2): see para 4.284 ff above.
2 FSMA 2000, s 176: see para 4.290 ff above.
3 See para 4.289 above.

13.155 The FSMA 2000 expressly provides only for two objections to providing documents or information, namely for information protected as being, broadly, legally privileged[1] and, in certain limited circumstances, for documents subject to a banker's duty of confidence. These are discussed at paras 4.264 ff and 4.267 ff above. Beyond this, the person may have legitimate objections on other grounds, depending upon the precise situation. Some of the more likely objections are outlined in para 4.260 ff above, followed by a discussion about how the person might go about making good the particular objection.

1 There is, though, no express statutory protection for without prejudice material: see footnote 1 to para 4.265 above.

13.156 One common objection that may be worth highlighting in the context of market abuse investigations is the so-called right of silence. The fact that a person may also be the subject of a criminal charge for insider dealing or misleading statements and practices, or indeed that market abuse may constitute a 'criminal charge' for ECHR purposes[1], does not give that person the right not to answer the investigator's questions. It does have an impact on the use that can be made of his evidence, as discussed at para 13.162 below. Also, it may prevent him from being questioned further once the FSA has sufficient evidence for a successful prosecution[2]. But it is not in general a legitimate objection to answering questions at a compulsory interview.

1 See para 13.15 above.
2 See para 4.248 ff above.

What use can be made of the information?

13.157 The FSA or, as appropriate, the investigator appointed by it may obtain a significant amount of information about the firm or particular individuals as a result of the investigation. One issue will be what use can be made of that information. This issue is discussed in more detail at para 4.300 ff above. For present purposes, several points may be made. First, to the extent that the information is confidential and relates to the business or affairs of any person, the FSA and the investigator are bound by a statutory duty of confidentiality, breach of which is a criminal offence[1].

1 FSMA 2000, s 348 and see para 4.304 ff above.

13.158 Second, this does not generally prevent the FSA from using the information for its own purposes. As we will see at para 13.173 ff below, the FSA can not only impose a penalty for market abuse or publicly censure the person concerned but also has an extensive range of enforcement powers which could be relevant depending upon the results of the investigation and the nature of its concerns. Where the investigation concerns an authorised firm or approved person, there is a greater range of possible regulatory action.

13.159 Third, the FSA may be entitled to pass information to other relevant bodies or regulators, for example the exchange concerned or any relevant overseas regulator[1].

1 To the extent permitted under the Gateway Regulations: see para 4.312 ff above.

13.160 Fourth, and often most importantly for a person accused of having committed market abuse or one of the criminal offences of insider dealing or misleading statements and practices, the FSMA 2000 provides a certain amount of protection against self-incrimination, by precluding statements made under compulsion from being used against the maker of the statement in certain circumstances. This is discussed in detail below.

13.161 Finally, if the market abuse could also potentially give rise to civil proceedings against the firm, there may be a risk of material being produced in the context of the investigation and enforcement process which may be prejudicial to the firm and may be required to be disclosed in those proceedings. This is considered in more detail in para 4.189 ff above.

The privilege against self-incrimination

13.162 In view of the ECHR issues arising in the market abuse context[1], the statutory protection for the privilege against self-incrimination extends to cover situations, not only where a criminal prosecution against a person or firm is in prospect, but also where the FSA is pursuing proceedings for market abuse. It therefore applies in this context both to the criminal offences of insider dealing and misleading statements and practices and also to (non-criminal) proceedings for market abuse.

1 See para 13.15 above.

13.163 The statutory provision[1] is discussed at para 4.242 ff above and that discussion applies equally here. Broadly, a statement made to an investigator by a person in compliance with a formal requirement may not be used in evidence against that person, and no questions may be asked relating to it, in:

- criminal proceedings in which that person is charged with an offence, but not proceedings for perjury or making false or misleading statements; or
- proceedings in relation to action to be taken against that person under FSMA 2000, s 123.

The first limb was discussed in para 4.243 above; it is on the second limb that we focus here, as well as on some specific points that arise in the context of market misconduct.

1 FSMA 2000, s 174.

13.164 ***What types of statements are covered?*** The statutory protection only applies to statements made to an investigator exercising his powers to compel the provision of a statement under certain provisions of the FSMA 2000[1]. It does not apply to statements made to the FSA using its powers under s 165[2]; nor would a statement provided in compliance with the Principles, or a voluntary statement, be protected, although in some circumstances, the law may imply the same protection[3].

1 FSMA 2000, ss 171, 172, 173 or 175: see FSMA 2000, s 174(5). A statement made in response to a formal requirement imposed in an investigation under FSMA 2000, ss 167, 168(1) or (4) or 168(2) would therefore be covered by the statutory protection.
2 See para 4.245 above.
3 This is discussed further in para 4.245 above. The person concerned may, therefore, in some circumstances wish to press for a formal investigation, to ensure that any statements receive the express statutory protection.

13.165 ***Does it matter why the statement was made?*** The prohibition applies to any statement made under an investigator's compulsory powers. It is not necessary that the investigator was appointed to investigate the market misconduct. He could have been appointed to investigate some other matter, following which market abuse could have become apparent. It should not matter that this was the case.

13.166 ***When can the statement not be used?*** The second limb of the prohibition prevents the use of the statement in 'proceedings in relation to action to be taken against a person under s 123'. It is not clear precisely what this phrase means and, in two particular respects, there are difficulties with its interpretation.

13.167 First, though, it is important to appreciate that there is no prohibition against using the statement to obtain other evidence which could be admissible and, indeed, the expectation is that the FSA will use its powers in that way[1].

1 See para 4.244 above.

13.168 As to the two difficulties with the meaning of this limb, the first difficulty is the question of what amounts to 'proceedings' for this purpose. Section 123 simply empowers the FSA to impose a penalty for market abuse, or publish a public statement. It does not refer to any particular proceedings. There are two different types of proceedings that could be involved:

- the internal decision-making process used by the FSA when it decides whether or not to impose a penalty or a public statement under s 123; and
- the subsequent Tribunal proceedings which may result if the person decides to oppose the imposition of the penalty or public statement.

13.169 Is the statement prohibited from being used in both? Or is it only when the matter is considered by the Tribunal that the privilege against self-incrimination applies? The view of HM Treasury[1] seems to be that it is limited to proceedings before the Tribunal. This approach may be justifiable, for reasons discussed at para 13.170 below. However, the FSMA 2000 clearly envisages elsewhere that the FSA's internal decision-making processes amount to 'proceedings'. For example, proceedings for misconduct are expressly commenced when a warning notice is issued[2], and the provisions relating to notices of discontinuance describe the FSA's internal processes as 'proceedings'[3]. The point is not therefore clear.

1 See the Explanatory Notes to the FSMA 2000, para 337.
2 FSMA 2000, s 66(5).
3 FSMA 2000, s 389(3).

13.170 The second difficulty is related. As will be seen, the imposition of a penalty or public statement for market abuse is only one of a range of actions the FSA can take. For example, it can apply to the court for an injunction or a restitution order, or it can make a restitution order or take wider enforcement action arising from the same matter. Are such other actions 'proceedings in relation to action to be taken against a person under s 123'? Whilst the answer is not entirely free from doubt, it seems likely they are not, in which case the statement could be used for those other purposes[1]. There could be some justification for this given the purpose of taking such other action. For example, an injunction can be used to prevent impending market abuse from taking place and it may be important that the FSA, in the interests of protecting consumers and safeguarding the market, is able to use all the information available to it in order to obtain such an injunction. For the same reason, the FSA may wish to take urgent action against an authorised firm, for example to vary its permission[2].

1 But if the other enforcement action which the FSA sought to take (particularly, disciplinary action based on breach of the regulatory general principles) constituted in the particular case a 'criminal charge' for ECHR purposes, then the FSA may be required to confer the same protection due to ECHR, art 6(2): see the discussion in para 5.20 ff above.
2 See para 9.194 ff above.

13.171 If that is indeed the scheme of the FSMA 2000, then the statement may need to be put before the FSA's decision-making body[1] when it is considering that other action, and it may be difficult then to isolate it from the decision whether to impose a sanction for market abuse in relation to the same matter. As indicated above, it may be that this is intended.

1 Normally the Regulatory Decisions Committee: see Chapters 5 and 9 above.

13.172 This could, of course, have the effect that information put before a court on an application for an injunction or a restitution order for market abuse could result in such an order where the Tribunal, based on the lesser evidence available to it, may find there was no market abuse in the same case. More difficult, the FSA may ask the court to impose a penalty for market abuse at the same time as hearing an application for a restitution order or injunction[1]. It may be attractive to the FSA to have the whole matter disposed of at the same time in this way. However, if statements that would be prohibited from use before the Tribunal can be put before the court on an application for an injunction or restitution order, how is that evidence to be excluded from consideration when the court goes on to consider the same matter as would be before the Tribunal, namely whether a penalty should be imposed? In that situation, it seems likely the entire court application would be regarded as 'proceedings in relation to action to be taken against a person under s 123' and that the evidence should not be admissible in those proceedings.

1 FSMA 2000, s 129.

SANCTIONS FOR MARKET MISCONDUCT

Introduction

13.173 Once the FSA has completed its investigation, it must decide which, if any, of the range of criminal and civil sanctions and disciplinary, preventative or restitutionary enforcement tools available should be invoked in the particular circumstances.

13.174 There are broadly three decisions to be made by the FSA at this stage:

- should any criminal prosecutions be brought?
- should the FSA exercise its powers to impose a penalty or make a public statement against any person for market abuse?
- should the FSA take some other, regulatory action against any person?

13.175 In practice, in light of the FSA's policy discussed below, criminal and civil proceedings in relation to market misconduct should generally speaking be mutually exclusive. There is, however, nothing in the FSMA 2000 to require this. The FSA's starting point is to consider whether it is appropriate to bring criminal proceedings. If it is, then it will normally do so[1]. Other regulatory action may need to be taken in any case, whether or not criminal or civil proceedings are also being taken, and indeed whether or not the conduct in question actually amounted to market abuse. Also, other regulators may also seek to take their own enforcement action.

1 See the FSA Handbook at ENF 15.4.1.

13.176 In the following paragraphs, we look at:

- when, and how, the FSA brings criminal proceedings (para 13.177 ff below);
- regulatory proceedings for market abuse, including when the FSA will take action, what action it will take and how it will take that action (para 13.187 ff below);
- the interaction between the FSA's role and that of other regulatory authorities, including the UK exchanges, the FSA in its capacity as UK Listing Authority, the Takeover Panel and overseas regulators (para 13.211 ff below);
- other enforcement action that the FSA may seek to take in relation to the matter (para 13.232 ff below); and
- the firm's potential liability to civil claims as a result of its market misconduct (para 13.276 ff).

Criminal proceedings for market misconduct

When will the FSA bring criminal proceedings?

13.177 The FSA's power to impose civil fines for market abuse complements rather than replaces the pre-existing criminal regime. It thus overlaps significantly with the criminal regime and there are likely to be cases where the same conduct may potentially involve a breach of the criminal law as well as a breach of the civil regime of market abuse. The FSA has power to institute criminal proceedings in England, Wales and Northern Ireland[1] in respect of the two relevant criminal offences of insider dealing[2] and misleading statements and practices[3]. It shares this power with the Secretary of State and the Crown Prosecution Service[4]. The question considered here is how the FSA decides which to pursue, criminal prosecution or the imposition of a civil penalty.

1 FSMA 2000, ss 401 and 402: but not Scotland.
2 Criminal Justice Act 1993, Pt V.
3 FSMA 2000, s 397, reflecting the previous offence in Financial Services Act 1986, s 47(2).
4 FSMA 2000, s 401 and Criminal Justice Act 1993, s 61.

The FSA's policy on bringing criminal proceedings

13.178 In deciding whether to bring criminal proceedings, the FSA considers whether a criminal prosecution is appropriate applying the two basic principles set out in the Code for Crown Prosecutors, namely:

- whether there is sufficient evidence to provide a realistic prospect of conviction against the defendant on each criminal charge; and
- whether, having regard to the seriousness of the offence and all the circumstances, criminal prosecution is in the public interest.

13.179 These two tests are applicable in any case where the FSA is considering whether to bring a prosecution, not only market misconduct cases, and their application is discussed in more detail in para 11.18 ff above.

Is it sufficient that there is a commercial rationale for the action?

13.106 The Code allows some flexibility for action taken with a legitimate commercial rationale. In particular:

- there is a safe harbour, in relation to the misuse of information limb[1], for dealing or arranging which was required in order to comply with a legal (including contractual) or regulatory obligation which existed before the relevant information was in the person's possession[2]; and
- behaviour that the regular user would regard as having a legitimate commercial rationale (and as having been properly executed) may, in some circumstances, be unlikely to amount to market abuse under the limbs of giving a false or misleading impression or distorting the market[3].

1 See the FSA Handbook at MAR 1.4.20.
2 There is also a general safe harbour allowing trading permitted by the FSA's rules on Chinese walls: see the FSA Handbook at MAR 1.7.3(2).
3 For details, see the FSA Handbook at MAR 1.5 and 1.6 (for example MAR 1.5.8, 1.5.21, 1.6.10).

13.107 Clearly, though, much will depend upon the precise circumstances.

INVESTIGATIONS INTO MARKET MISCONDUCT

Introduction

13.108 A problem comes to light which raises the spectre of market abuse or other market misconduct. What should the firm be doing, both internally and vis-à-vis its regulator? What powers does the FSA have to investigate the situation and use information which it obtains in its investigation? How should the firm deal with the FSA in that context? The answers to these and related questions are considered in the following paragraphs. Specifically, we address the following issues:

- practical steps to take when the problem arises (para 13.109 ff); and
- FSA investigations into market misconduct (para 13.130 ff).

Practical steps to take when the problem arises

13.109 A market abuse issue could come to light in any of a number of ways. For example, a problem could arise (perhaps after a complaint from a customer or competitor), the firm could identify a practice with market abuse connotations, a particular transaction may raise market abuse issues (for example because the firm is in possession of information which is not publicly available), or information suggesting market abuse could come to light via the FSA, whether from a supervisory visit or based on information it has received from some other source.

13.110 The issues which the firm will consider at the outset when the problem comes to light are the same as arise with any regulatory problem. Some of the main issues are:

- should the firm investigate?
- should it report the matter to the FSA?
- how should the firm deal with customers?
- what internal action should be taken?
- are criminal proceedings a possibility? and
- taking care over document creation and retention.

13.111 These matters are discussed in detail in Chapter 3 above. Highlighted here are some additional factors which arise specifically in the context of market abuse.

Should the firm investigate?

13.112 As discussed at para 3.9 ff above, almost invariably the firm should investigate internally since, until it has a proper understanding of the matter, it will not be in a position to assess properly what action it should take and the potential repercussions. In addition, the FSA will expect to see that the firm is taking appropriate steps to investigate.

13.113 An additional practical issue may arise in relation to market misconduct, namely that the issue may not be purely internal to the firm and the information that the firm needs in order to understand the problem properly may not be entirely within its control. For example, some of the information on which the FSA is basing its enquiries may have come from an exchange or from another financial institution.

13.114 Regulated firms and individuals should also keep in mind that a matter which arises as a suspected case of market misconduct may give rise to rather wider regulatory issues. For example, how did the employee obtain authorisation for the transaction? Did information cross Chinese walls? Are the firm's systems and controls operating properly? Are employees receiving proper training? If the firm is to fully understand and deal with the problem, then it will need to ask itself the wider questions and address the answers.

Should the matter be reported to the FSA?

13.115 Whether the matter should be reported to the FSA depends on whether the question is being considered by an authorised person, an approved person, or someone who is not part of the regulated community[1].

be whether the conduct amounted to market abuse within FSMA 2000, s 118 and, if so, whether the FSA should take enforcement action in relation to it. We look at:

- the grounds on which the FSA may impose a financial penalty or public censure for market abuse;
- the FSA's policy in determining whether to take such action;
- how the FSA decides what action to take;
- if the FSA is to impose a penalty, the factors relevant in determining the amount;
- the circumstances when the FSA is likely to take action against specific individuals rather than, or in addition to, the firm; and
- the procedure for taking action for market abuse and whether any publicity will result.

13.188 The focus in this section is on penalties and public censures. The other potential FSA enforcement consequences of market abuse (particularly, injunctions and restitution orders) are considered at para 13.232 ff below, together with other FSA enforcement measures that may arise from market misconduct more generally. It is notable that the imposition of a penalty for market abuse does not make any transaction void or unenforceable[1]. A counterparty or other person affected by the market abuse might, however, be able to pursue other remedies depending upon the nature of the abuse[2].

1 FSMA 2000, s 131.
2 Civil claims against firms are discussed in Chapter 10 and see also para 13.276 ff below.

What are the grounds for imposing a penalty or public censure?

13.189 The FSA may impose a penalty for market abuse if it is satisfied that a person[1]:

- is or has engaged in market abuse; or
- by taking or refraining from taking any action has required or encouraged another person or persons to engage in behaviour which, if engaged in by the first person, would amount to market abuse.

1 FSMA 2000, s 123.

13.190 The FSA may not, however, impose a penalty if there are reasonable grounds for it to be satisfied that either of the two defences outlined at para 13.68 above applies.

13.191 If the FSA is entitled to impose a penalty, it may instead publish a statement to the effect that the person has engaged in market abuse[1].

1 FSMA 2000, s 123(3).

13.192 The test for market abuse, the meaning of requiring or encouraging another to commit market abuse, and the two defences, have been considered at para 13.19 ff above.

When is the FSA likely to take action for market abuse?

13.193 The FSA will not take enforcement action in every case involving market abuse[1]. In deciding whether or not to take action in the particular case, and what action to take, the FSA will look at all the relevant circumstances of the case. Certain factors may in particular be relevant to the question of whether to take action, which can be summarised as follows[2]:

- the nature and seriousness of the behaviour in question[3];
- the conduct of the person concerned after the behaviour was identified[4];
- the sophistication of the users of the market, the size and liquidity of the market and its susceptibility to market abuse;
- the extent to which the market abuse can be adequately addressed by other authorities, including the nature and degree of sanction available[5];
- action taken by the FSA in previous similar cases;
- the impact that any penalty or public statement may have on the financial markets or on the interests of consumers[6];
- the likelihood that the same type of behaviour (whether by the same or another person) will happen again if no action is taken; and
- the previous disciplinary record and general compliance history of the person concerned[7].

1 See the FSA Handbook at ENF 14.4.1. The FSA is required to issue a statement of its policy with regard to the imposition and amount of penalties for market abuse and, in exercising, or deciding whether to exercise, its power under FSMA 2000, s 123, must have regard to the policy in force at the time when the behaviour concerned occurred: FSMA 2000, s 124(1) and (6). The policies outlined here constitute the FSA's policy for this purpose: see the FSA Handbook at ENF 14.2.1.

2 For a full list, see the FSA Handbook at ENF 14.4.2.

3 The FSA Handbook provides further details: see ENF 14.4.2(1).

4 This includes whether and how the person reported the matter to the FSA, co-operation during the regulatory investigation, steps taken to address the market abuse (including paying compensation, taking disciplinary action, remedying systems and controls issues and taking steps to correct misleading statements) and whether the person has complied with the requirements of any other applicable regulator relating to his behaviour: see the FSA Handbook at ENF 14.4.2(2).

5 In particular, the FSA compares its power to impose unlimited fines with the more limited powers of the recognised investment exchanges and refers also to cases where the Takeover Panel is involved (discussed at para 13.224 ff below): see the FSA Handbook at ENF 14.4.2(4).

6 The FSA suggests that a penalty may show that high standards of market conduct are being enforced and may bolster market confidence, and that a penalty protects the interests of consumers by deterring future market abuse and improving standards of conduct in the market; there may be additional considerations in cases involving a takeover bid: see the FSA Handbook at ENF 14.4.2(6).

7 This includes whether the FSA has previously taken action for market abuse (or requiring or encouraging it) which resulted in adverse findings, whether the person's conduct has caused concern to or been the subject of a warning or other action by another regulatory authority, whether the person has previously given the FSA any undertakings not to engage in particular behaviour, and the person's general compliance history (including any private warnings): see the FSA Handbook at ENF 14.4.2(8).

13.194 Where the issue arises in the context of a takeover bid, the FSA has given guidance on certain additional factors that it will consider. These are outlined at para 13.224 ff below.

How does the FSA decide what action to take?

13.195 If the FSA decides that action is appropriate, then what action should it take? There are three options:

- to give the firm or individual a private warning, rather than taking formal enforcement action;
- to impose a financial penalty; or
- to make a public statement that the person has engaged in market abuse.

Private warnings

13.196 In certain circumstances, the FSA may decide to issue a private warning rather than taking formal action. Whilst a private warning does not amount to formal enforcement action, it is not entirely free from regulatory consequences. For example, as indicated at para 13.193 above, one of the factors to which the FSA has regard when deciding whether or not to take action in relation to market abuse is the person's previous compliance history including any private warnings. The circumstances when the FSA is likely to issue a private warning, and the nature and consequences of private warnings, are discussed in more detail in para 7.18 ff above[1].

1 See also the FSA Handbook at ENF 11.3.3.

Fines and public statements

13.197 The FSA's policy[1] is to consider publishing a public statement that market abuse has occurred instead of imposing a financial penalty where it considers that such a statement may more appropriately address the particular behaviour in question. In determining whether this is the case, the FSA will take into account all the circumstances of the case, including similar factors to those that are relevant in deciding in any regulatory disciplinary case whether to fine or instead publicly censure a firm[2]. The FSA has acknowledged that, other things being equal, the more serious the behaviour, the more likely it will impose a penalty[3].

1 See the FSA Handbook at ENF 14.6.1.
2 These factors are outlined in para 7.31 ff above.
3 See the FSA Handbook at ENF 14.6.2(2).

13.198 Certain factors are identified as particularly likely to be relevant in a market abuse case, namely[1]:

- if a person has made a profit or avoided a loss, this may favour a fine on the basis that a person should not benefit from market abuse;
- the seriousness of the market abuse;
- the behaviour of the person concerned, particularly if he admitted the behaviour, provided full and immediate co-operation and paid full compensation;
- the FSA's approach in similar previous cases[2];
- the person's compliance history and, particularly, if he has a poor compliance history with previous adverse findings in relation to market abuse; and
- the impact of a financial penalty on the person concerned, particularly in exceptional cases where this would cause serious financial hardship.

1 For the full list, see the FSA Handbook at ENF 14.6.2.
2 The FSA seeks to achieve a consistent approach to its decisions: see the FSA Handbook at ENF 14.6.2(4).

How does the FSA determine the amount of the penalty?

13.199 Whilst it is for the FSA to determine, at least in the first instance[1], the amount of the penalty appropriate to be imposed, it is required to issue a statement of its policy with regard to, among other things[2], the amount of penalties and, when deciding upon the level of a penalty for a particular case of market abuse, must have regard to the policy in force at the time the behaviour occurred[3].

1 As will be seen, this can be challenged in the Tribunal.
2 See footnote 1 to para 13.193 above.
3 FSMA 2000, s 124.

13.200 The FSA has identified various factors which may be relevant when it determines the amount of a penalty for market abuse and these can be summarised as follows[1]:

- the adverse effect of the abuse on the market and the seriousness of the effect[2];
- the extent to which the behaviour was deliberate or reckless[3];
- whether the person on whom the penalty is to be imposed is an individual, including having regard to the financial resources and other circumstances of the individual[4];
- the amount of profits accrued or loss avoided[5];
- the conduct of the person concerned following the market abuse[6];

- the previous disciplinary record and general compliance history of the person, including any previous action taken for market abuse (although private warnings will not be taken into account);
- action taken by the FSA in relation to previous similar behaviour; and
- action by other regulatory authorities, including the degree to which the person has taken any steps they have required it to take.

1 For a full list, see the FSA Handbook at ENF 14.7.4.
2 The FSA recognises that a financial penalty must be in proportion to the nature and seriousness of the abuse in question. This may include considering the loss or risk of loss to consumers or other market users, the duration and frequency of the market abuse, and the impact on the orderliness of the markets and on market confidence: see the FSA Handbook at ENF 14.7.4(1).
3 Including, for example, whether the person intended or foresaw the consequences of their behaviour or gave any consideration to the consequences of their behaviour: see the FSA Handbook at ENF 14.7.4(2).
4 The FSA may take into account whether there is verifiable evidence of serious financial hardship or difficulties if the individual were to pay the level of the penalty that would otherwise be imposed: see the FSA Handbook at ENF 14.7.4(3).
5 The FSA seeks to ensure that people do not benefit from the market abuse and that the penalty acts as an incentive to comply with standards of market conduct: see the FSA Handbook at ENF 14.7.4(4).
6 Including bringing or failing to bring the behaviour quickly, effectively and completely to the FSA's attention, or to that of other regulatory authorities, the degree of co-operation shown during the investigation, any remedial steps taken since the breach was identified, and whether the person concerned has complied with any requirements or rulings of any other regulatory authority relating to the behaviour: see the FSA Handbook at ENF 14.7.4(5).

13.201 Again, the FSA has made clear that these factors are not exhaustive and that all the relevant circumstances of the case will be taken into consideration[1].

1 See the FSA Handbook at ENF 14.7.5.

Is there a tariff for financial penalties?

13.202 The FSA does not adopt a tariff of penalties for market abuse, given the wide range of conduct that may amount to market abuse[1]. However, consistency in comparable cases is clearly an important aspect of its fining policy, as well as its enforcement policy more generally[2], and it is therefore likely that some sort of predictable level will emerge.

1 See the FSA Handbook at ENF 14.7.2. The same is true of the FSA's disciplinary fines: see para 7.37 above.
2 Consistency is one of the principles underlying the FSA's exercise of its enforcement powers: see para 2.36 above.

When will the FSA punish an individual for market abuse?

13.203 The FSMA 2000 does not distinguish between individuals who commit market abuse and firms who do so. The same question therefore arises in this context as arises throughout the enforcement regime, namely in what circumstances the FSA will seek to punish individuals rather than, or in addition to, firms, for their behaviour whilst acting for the firm. The FSA's policy outlined above does in some respects differentiate the treatment of individuals, recognising that market abuse proceedings could be brought against either.

13.204 The FSA has not provided any guidance on when it will take action against individuals personally for market abuse. A difference between market abuse and other regulatory contraventions committed by individuals is that the question here is whether the individual has committed market abuse, whereas in many other cases the question will be about the level of involvement that the individual had in a breach committed by the firm for whom he works. The market abuse regime may thus apply to individuals rather more directly. One of the difficult issues, particularly where the individual is trading on behalf of the firm, is whether the FSA will take action for market abuse against the individual or the firm. In addition, there may not be a firm involved in a market abuse case. An isolated individual, not connected with any firm and not carrying on any regulated business, or even purporting to do so, could commit market abuse. But this does not answer the question of when individuals will be held personally responsible where they are acting within a firm.

13.205 The FSA's general approach on this question, considered at para 8.13 ff above, is that the primary responsibility for ensuring compliance with a firm's regulatory obligations rest with the firm itself[1] and the FSA's main focus in considering whether disciplinary action is appropriate is therefore normally on the firm rather than on those who work for it. There are, however, situations where the FSA will consider action against an approved person working for a firm, based primarily on the question of personal culpability, that is where the behaviour was deliberate or below the standard which it would be reasonable to have expected from the person in all the circumstances.

1 See the FSA Handbook at ENF 11.5.1.

13.206 In the absence of any specific guidance, it is not clear whether the same policy applies to market abuse. In many cases, a decision to undertake a particular trading strategy is likely to have been made by an identifiable individual. At one end of the spectrum, he may take that decision in a situation where he knows or should know of the risk of market abuse, perhaps without any regard for internal procedures or controls, and in that case it may be unobjectionable that the regulator seeks to hold him personally responsible. At the other end, he may act in good faith, having exercised due care and complied with the requisite controls and procedures, and if market abuse is nonetheless committed there may be much sympathy for the view that he should not incur personal liability. In the middle, there is, obviously, a substantial grey area[1]. It is not clear where the FSA will draw the line[2].

1 In some cases, the individual may have a defence, that he reasonably believed his behaviour did not amount to market abuse or took all reasonable precautions and exercised all due diligence to avoid committing market abuse: see para 13.68 above.

2 It is possible that one relevant factor in favour of taking proceedings against the firm in some cases will be that the FSA also wishes to obtain a restitution order against the firm in relation to market abuse.

13.207 Where the FSA does bring proceedings against an individual, the person may have the right to legal assistance if the matter is referred to the Tribunal[1]. Critically, though, he does not have the right to legal assistance in relation to the FSA investigation or in relation to the enforcement process before the matter is referred to the Tribunal, although in practice firms often provide such assistance to their employees and insurance cover may also be available[2].

1 FSMA 2000, ss 134 to 136. The legal assistance scheme rules have not been finally made by the Lord Chancellor's Department at the time of writing. In summary, the scheme proposed involved an application for assistance being made to the Tribunal at the same time as referring the matter to it. The Tribunal will grant assistance only where it is in the interests of justice to do so (the test follows that applied in criminal cases: see the Access to Justice Act 1999, Sch 3) and where the means of the person are such that they would be unable to meet the costs of legal representation themselves. Assistance is not available before the matter is referred to the Tribunal or for appeals from Tribunal decisions. The legal assistance scheme is funded by a levy imposed on authorised firms by the FSA.

2 This is discussed in more detail in footnote 2 to para 8.24 above.

Procedure and publicity

13.208 The procedure for the imposition of financial penalties or public statements for market abuse is the warning/decision notice procedure[1] considered in detail in Chapter 5 above. Among other things, this enables the firm or person to refer the matter to the Tribunal, for an independent determination[2]. The warning and decision notices are required to, as appropriate, state the amount of the penalty or the terms of the public statement. The mediation scheme may be available where the FSA and the person concerned are unable to resolve the market abuse proceedings by agreement[3].

1 FSMA 2000, ss 126 and 127.

2 The proceedings of the Tribunal are considered in Chapter 6 above.

3 See the FSA Handbook at DEC, Appendix 1, para 1.4.1.

13.209 In cases where the FSA applies to the court for an injunction or a restitution order, the procedure may be bypassed and instead the court may be asked at the same time to impose a financial penalty for the market abuse[1].

1 FSMA 2000, s 129. This is discussed at para 13.251 ff below.

13.210 In accordance with its general policy of publishing successful enforcement action, the FSA has indicated that it will ordinarily publicise a penalty or public statement for market abuse, by issuing a press release giving details of the behaviour and the sanction imposed[1]. It cannot publish details of a warning or decision notice[2]. Hence, publicity will normally arise only at the conclusion of the matter. If the matter is referred to the Tribunal, it is likely the proceedings will be in public and judgment will be pronounced publicly, and that publicity will therefore arise in that process[3].

1 See the FSA Handbook at ENF 14.12.2. For a more detailed discussion of the FSA's policy on publication more generally, see para 5.194 above.

2 FSMA 2000, s 391(1) and see para 5.76 ff above.

3 See para 6.32 above.

Action where other regulatory authorities are involved

13.211 In many situations, an issue which potentially amounts to market abuse will also raise enforcement questions for other regulators, whether one of the recognised investment exchanges or the Takeover Panel in the UK or a regulatory authority overseas. In that situation, the person concerned will wish to avoid being subject to multiple regulatory investigations relating to the same matter. The FSA has provided guidance on how it will act in those circumstances, which is considered below. As will be seen, this does not preclude action by more than one regulator and indeed this may well happen in appropriate cases.

13.212 We consider the overlap with investigation and enforcement by, first, the recognised investment exchanges, including particularly the London Stock Exchange, second, the UK Listing Authority, third, the Takeover Panel and, finally, overseas regulators.

The London Stock Exchange and other UK exchanges

13.213 Since the 'prescribed markets' for market abuse purposes[1] are currently limited to those markets established under the rules of the recognised investment exchanges, a trading issue on a market of a recognised investment exchange may well be both an enforcement issue for the exchange and a market abuse issue for the FSA. We briefly review the enforcement role of the recognised investment exchanges, and their powers of investigation and enforcement, before looking at how the overlap with market abuse is addressed.

1 See para 13.31 above.

The role of the exchanges

13.214 Whilst the admission of securities to the UK's official list is a matter for the FSA[1], the regulation of trading on the recognised investment exchanges, including the London Stock Exchange, is a matter for the exchanges themselves. Each has responsibility for admitting securities to trading on its own markets and for regulating trading on its markets. This includes, for example[2], deciding whether to permit trading in any listed security or any other security, and setting, monitoring and enforcing the procedures and standards which apply to that admission to trading on an ongoing basis.

1 The FSA's role as UK Listing Authority is considered in Chapter 15 below.
2 See Consultation Paper 37 ('The Transfer of the UK Listing Authority to the FSA'), December 1999, para 2.5.

13.215 The exchanges thus have regulatory powers over their members. The precise nature and scope of those powers depends upon the detailed rules of each exchange and differs as between the different exchanges. However, the basics are dictated by the recognition requirements which are required to be met as a condition of the FSA granting recognition to the exchange under the FSMA 2000[1]. In addition, the FSA has made specific rules with respect to exchanges. Thus, among other things, a recognised investment exchange must:

- have effective arrangements for monitoring and enforcing its rules[2];
- generally, be able and willing to promote and maintain high standards of integrity and fair dealing in the carrying on of regulated activities by persons in the course of using facilities provided by the exchange[3] and to co-operate by the sharing of information or otherwise with the FSA and other applicable bodies[4];
- notify the FSA immediately where it has evidence tending to suggest that any person has, among other things, been engaged in market abuse or has committed the criminal offences of insider dealing or misleading statements and practices[5]; and
- notify the FSA immediately where it has taken disciplinary action against a member or employee of a member in respect of a rule breach[6].

1 The recognised investment exchanges are thus in the position of both regulator and regulated, at the same time. As to the recognition requirements, see FSMA 2000, ss 286 and 290, the Financial Services and Markets Act 2000 (Recognition Requirements for Investment Exchanges and Clearing Houses) Regulations 2001, SI 2001/995 and the FSA Handbook at REC.
2 See the FSA Handbook at REC 2.15.
3 See the FSA Handbook at REC 2.13.1(1). One of the factors that may be taken into account is the extent to which the exchange seeks to promote and encourage conduct in regulated activities which is consistent with the Code of Market Conduct: see the FSA Handbook at REC 2.13.3.
4 See the FSA Handbook at REC 2.13(2). One of the factors that may be relevant is the extent to which the constitution and rules of the exchange and its agreements with its members enable it to obtain information from members and to disclose otherwise confidential information to the FSA and other appropriate bodies: see the FSA Handbook at REC 2.13.4.
5 See the FSA Handbook at REC 3.21.
6 See the FSA Handbook at REC 3.20.

13.216 As to the specific rules of the exchanges, the first point to note is that each recognised investment exchange has made rules requiring, broadly, proper standards of market conduct[1].

1 The detailed rules vary significantly as between the exchanges. They can be found as follows: London Stock Exchange – Rule 2.10; LIFFE – Rules 1.3, 2.2.4 and 2.2.5; London Metal Exchange – Pt 2, Sections 9.6 and 9.7; International Petroleum Exchange – Rule E 6; OM London Exchange – CMR.B.14; Coredeal – Rule 5.1; Jiway – Rule 2.3.8; Virt-x – Rule 2.10.

13.217 Second, each exchange has the power, under its own rules, to investigate and enforce standards on its markets, including in very broad terms, to[1]:

- investigate suspected rule breaches by members;
- take disciplinary action against members;
- take immediate action to suspend particular members or trading in particular securities in the interests of ensuring an orderly market; and
- provide information to other regulators including the FSA.

1 Again, the detailed rules vary significantly as between the exchanges. They can be found as follows: London Stock Exchange – Rule 14; LIFFE – Rules 2.4.1 and 5; London Metal Exchange – Pt 2, Rules 9, 11 and 14; International Petroleum Exchange – Chapter E and Rule D.10; OM London Exchange – CMR.A; Coredeal – Chapter 9 and Rules 1.6 and 6.7; Jiway – Chapter 13 and Rule 12.2.2; and Virt-x – Chapter 4 and Rules 1.10 and 2.20/21.

Overlap with FSA enforcement

13.218 The FSA recognises that market abuse cases may also involve potential action by other regulatory authorities. Where the behaviour occurred or is occurring on a market of one of the recognised investment exchanges, the FSA will refer to the exchange and give due weight to its views. Where both bodies wish to bring proceedings, the FSA will co-ordinate with the exchange to ensure that cases are dealt with in an effective and fair manner under agreed operating arrangements[1]. It will have regard to all the circumstances of the case, including whether the other regulatory authorities have adequate powers to address the behaviour in question. As has already been discussed[2], the FSA may in some circumstances, where the FSA wishes to investigate or take action for market abuse, require an exchange to suspend its investigations.

1 See the FSA Handbook at ENF 14.9.1.
2 See para 13.138 above.

13.219 What does this mean in practice? How the issue is dealt with will, in practice, depend largely upon the circumstances of the particular case. For example, in some cases the exchange concerned may have the necessary powers to address all the consequences of the conduct appropriately and, in those cases, the FSA may not need to take action itself. In others, the FSA will need to do so, particularly in serious cases, given the extensive powers that the FSA has against those who commit market abuse and also in cases where the FSA's wider responsibilities and powers in relation to the regulated community are relevant, for example because other regulatory action also needs to be taken. It is clearly possible for more than one body to have an interest in the same issue, but it is unclear whether, where the FSA does wish to exercise its powers, the exchange will defer to it at the expense of not taking its own enforcement action. From the firm's perspective, it is most important that concurrent proceedings by different bodies are minimised and, if they are required, are properly co-ordinated.

The UK Listing Authority

13.220 The powers of the UK Listing Authority to investigate and enforce breaches of the listing rules are considered in detail in Chapter 15 below. Issues which may both concern the UKLA and raise questions about market abuse include the misuse of unpublished price sensitive information[1] and breaches by directors and other employees of a company's code of dealings[2]. This gives rise to two issues.

1 For example, the Code of Market Conduct indicates that the practice of selectively briefing may constitute requiring or encouraging market abuse: see para 13.85 above. See also, generally, the UKLA's draft 'PSI Guide – The UKLA's guidance on the dissemination of price sensitive information', Appendix 2 to the draft Guidance Manual referred to in Chapter 15 below.
2 See the Listing Rules, Chapter 16.

13.221 First, as already noted[1], there is a safe harbour under the market abuse regime for compliance with certain requirements of the listing rules, which expressly require or permit behaviour which, in the absence of a safe harbour, might be interpreted as resulting in market abuse[2].

1 See para 13.64 ff above.
2 The listing rules concerned are set out in the FSA Handbook at MAR 1, Annex 1G.

13.222 Second, a question arises as to what action the UKLA or the FSA will take where a particular issue amounts to both a breach of the listing rules and market abuse. In that situation, and given that the UKLA is a part of the FSA, the FSA will obtain information about the behaviour, either voluntarily or using whatever statutory powers or powers under the listing rules are appropriate, and will then consider whether, in all the circumstances of the case[1], further action under the listing rules or under the market abuse regime appears appropriate[2]. It will thus consider both aspects of the behaviour in the round in the light of its investigation.

1 Including the factors which the UKLA considers in deciding whether or not take disciplinary action: see para 15.125 below.
2 See the discussion at para 15.103 ff below.

13.223 The UKLA has indicated that where more than one person is involved, action may be taken under the listing rules against one person and under the market abuse regime against a different person[1]. The example which it gives is that it may be appropriate to take action against an issuer under the listing rules and against a director under the market abuse regime. The UKLA does not address in its draft guidance the question of whether the FSA will take both types of action against one person. It may be that it will apply its general policy on taking both action for market abuse and disciplinary action against the same person, outlined below[2]. If this is the case, then it is possible that it would bring proceedings for both in an appropriate case.

1 See the draft Guidance Manual, para 12.5.4.
2 See para 13.265 ff below.

The Takeover Panel

13.224 Where the issue arises in the context of a takeover bid, there are two, quite separate issues to consider. First, the context gives rise to additional factors for consideration by the FSA when deciding whether to take action in relation to the market abuse. Second, in some circumstances the Takeover Panel may ask the FSA to exercise its statutory enforcement powers in order to enforce the City Code. Each of these is considered in turn, below. The FSA's approach to these issues arises after extensive consultations between it and the Takeover Panel and the overall aim is to establish robust and flexible operating arrangements which will involve the minimum disruption to the takeover timetable[1].

1 See Consultation Paper 76 ('Supplement to the draft Code of Market Conduct'), November 2000, para 5.14.

Additional factors in deciding whether to take action for market abuse

13.225 In relation to behaviour which may have occurred or may be occurring in the context of a takeover bid, or to which Substantial Acquisitions rules ('SARs') [1] are relevant, the FSA has provided the following guidance[2]:

- the FSA will refer to the Takeover Panel and give due weight to its views;
- where the City Code or the SARs provide procedures for complaint in respect of the behaviour, the FSA will not, save in exceptional circumstances, take action in respect of market abuse[3] before the conclusion of those procedures;
- the FSA will not take action against a person for behaviour which conforms with the City Code and which the Code of Market Conduct specifies does not amount to market abuse[4]. In determining whether behaviour complies with the City Code, the FSA will seek the views of the Takeover Panel and will attach considerable weight to its views[5];
- in any case where the FSA considers that the use of its market abuse powers[6] may be appropriate and may affect the timetable or outcome of a takeover bid or tender offer governed by the SARs, it will consult the Takeover Panel before using its powers[7];
- in relation to those who have responsibilities under the City Code[8], the FSA recognises that the informal powers of the Takeover Panel will often be sufficient to address the concerns. Where this is not the case, the FSA will need to consider whether it is appropriate to exercise any of its own powers in respect of market abuse. This is likely to be considered principally in circumstances where[9]:

  1. the Takeover Panel is unable to investigate properly due to lack of co-operation by the relevant person,
  2. the market abuse falls under the first limb (misuse of information)[10],
  3. a person has deliberately or recklessly failed to comply with a Takeover Panel ruling,
  4. the FSA's approach in previous similar cases (including those not involving a takeover bid) suggests that a financial penalty should be imposed,
  5. the Takeover Panel requests the FSA to consider exercising its power to impose a penalty for market abuse,
  6. the market abuse extends to securities outside the Takeover Panel's jurisdiction,
  7. the market abuse threatens or threatened the stability of the financial system, or
  8. the Takeover Panel asks the FSA to consider exercising any of its other powers in respect of the market abuse;
- even where the FSA considers that the exercise of its powers is appropriate, it will not take action[11] during the currency of an offer to which the City Code or SARs apply save in exceptional circumstances in situations 1, 3, 6, 7 and 8 above[12];
- so far as concerns publishing details of penalties for market abuse, where the FSA is of the opinion that publication of its action may affect the timetable

or outcome of the bid, it will consult the Takeover Panel over the timing of publication and give due weight to its views[13].

1 Rules made by the Takeover Panel governing Substantial Acquisitions of Shares: see the FSA Handbook, Glossary of Definitions.
2 See the FSA Handbook at ENF 14.9.2 to 14.9.9.
3 This includes not only the imposition of a penalty under FSMA 2000, ss 123 or 129 but also injunctions under s 381 and restitution orders under ss 383 and 384: see the FSA Handbook at ENF 14.9.2.
4 This mirrors FSMA 2000, s 120, and the relevant provisions are outlined at para 13.67 above.
5 See the FSA Handbook at ENF 14.9.3. Note, however, that the interpretation of the City Code for this purpose remains a matter for the FSA, not the Takeover Panel.
6 See footnote 3 above.
7 See the FSA Handbook at ENF 14.9.5.
8 See the FSA Handbook at ENF 14.9.8.
9 See the FSA Handbook at ENF 14.9.6.
10 See para 13.38 ff above.
11 See the FSA Handbook at ENF 14.9.8.
12 See the FSA Handbook at ENF 14.9.4 and 14.9.7.
13 See the FSA Handbook at ENF 14.9.9.

13.226 In summary, therefore, the position is that it is in some circumstances appropriate for the FSA to take action notwithstanding the market abuse arises in the context of a takeover bid. Where it is appropriate for the FSA to do so, it will not normally do so during the currency of the offer, but it may do so in exceptional circumstances where urgent action is required.

FSA enforcement of the City Code

13.227 The FSMA 2000 allows the FSA to endorse the City Code[1] and the SARs[2] and the FSA will do so[3]. As a result, at the request of the Takeover Panel, the FSA will be able to exercise its own enforcement powers[4] to enforce the City Code, including rulings made under it by the Takeover Panel[5].

1 This effectively replaces the endorsement under Financial Services Act 1986, s 47A in conjunction with the former SIB Principle 3. The purpose of endorsing the City Code is to give statutory support to a Code which does not have the force of law.
2 FSMA 2000, s 143.
3 At the time of writing, the FSA had not finally made its rules on the Endorsement of the City Code. When made, they will be found in the FSA Handbook at MAR 4. The discussion that follows is based on the draft rules published for consultation in Consultation Paper 87 ('Endorsement of the City Code on Takeovers and Mergers and the Rules Governing Substantial Acquisitions of Shares'), April 2001.
4 Specifically, its powers to (i) vary a firm's permission under FSMA 2000, Pt IV; (ii) discipline an approved person for misconduct under FSMA 2000, s 66; (iii) intervene in relation to an incoming firm under FSMA 2000, Pt XIII; (iv) discipline an authorised firm under FSMA 2000, Pt XIV and (v) make or apply for restitution orders or injunctions under FSMA 2000, Pt XXV: s 143(3) and (4) and see the draft rules at MAR 4.2.3.
5 FSMA 2000, s 143(5).

13.228 Quite apart from direct enforcement at the request of the Takeover Panel, the FSA has made clear that compliance with the City Code may be relevant to the FSA, for example by indicating whether a person is fit and proper[1] or by constituting a breach of the FSA's rules (for example, the Principles for Businesses) or a breach by an approved person of a Statement of Principle. The FSA may therefore wish to take enforcement action in relation to a breach of the City Code irrespective whether it has received a request to do so. In those circumstances it will nonetheless consult with the Takeover Panel and give due weight to its views[2].

1 See the FSA Handbook at ENF 14.10.3.
2 See the FSA Handbook at ENF 14.10.4.

13.229 The FSA has also indicated that it will make 'cold-shoulder' rules[1], requiring firms not to act or continue to act for any person in connection with a transaction to which the City Code or the SARs apply if the firm has reason to believe that the person in question, or his principal, is not complying or not likely to comply with the City Code or SARs[2].

1 Similar rules existed in certain parts of the previous regime.
2 See the draft rules at MAR 4.3.1.

13.230 In addition, the FSA proposes to provide further support for the Takeover Panel by making a rule requiring firms to provide information, documents and assistance to the Takeover Panel to enable it to perform its functions[1]. This gives the Takeover Panel additional, indirect powers to investigate breaches of the City Code, enabling it, among other things, to obtain information on which to decide whether to request the FSA to take enforcement action in relation to the City Code[2].

1 For details, see the draft rules at MAR 4.3.4.
2 See Consultation Paper 87, ('Endorsement of the City Code on Takeovers and Mergers and the Rules Governing Substantial Acquisitions of Shares'), April 2001, para 5.18/19.

Overseas regulatory authorities

13.231 The territorial scope of the market abuse provisions has been highlighted at para 13.94 ff above and, as has been seen, behaviour that takes place outside the UK may amount to market abuse in a variety of situations. Where this happens, the FSA will, in deciding whether to impose a penalty or public statement for market abuse, consider, in addition to the factors applicable in any case[2], the extent to which the behaviour is capable of being dealt with by the relevant overseas regulator or other enforcement agency[1]. It will consider in each case whether it is appropriate for the FSA or that other agency to take action. In some cases, both regulators may have an interest in pursuing enforcement action. In those circumstances, the FSA will work with the relevant overseas authority to co-ordinate effective enforcement action. As with other UK regulators, therefore, there could well be situations where the firm faces more than one investigation and enforcement process in relation to the same matter. Where this occurs, it may be important from the firm's perspective that the different bodies do not place unnecessary burdens on the firm but co-ordinate their action. Generally speaking, the FSA is likely to be able to pass information to the overseas regulator under the so-called Gateway Regulations[3].

1 See the FSA Handbook at ENF 14.11.
2 These are outlined at para 13.193 ff above.
3 These are outlined at para 4.312 above.

Other enforcement action available to the FSA

13.232 The FSMA 2000 gives the FSA various specific powers in cases of market abuse, in addition to the power to impose a financial penalty or make a public statement. In particular, the FSA has the power to apply to the court for an injunction, among other things to prevent the abuse, or for a restitution order to compensate victims. The FSA may also impose a restitution order itself, without applying to court.

13.233 However, the matter which constitutes market abuse may also give rise to more general regulatory concerns which might lead to the use of the FSA's other enforcement powers, primarily against those who are regulated. It could, for example, be appropriate for the FSA to use its own-initiative powers, its disciplinary powers against regulated firms or approved persons, or to withdraw the approval of an approved person or make a prohibition order against an individual. Such measures are most likely to be in prospect if the instance of market abuse is symptomatic of a wider problem within the firm, which casts doubt on its or its employees' fitness or propriety or gives rise to issues about the protection of consumers. Or they might be appropriate if the misconduct did not technically amount to market abuse but in the FSA's view nonetheless merits regulatory action. The market abuse regime cannot therefore be viewed in isolation but needs to be seen against the wider background of the FSA's regulatory objectives and powers.

13.234 In the following paragraphs, we consider:

- injunctions in relation to market abuse (para 13.235 ff below);
- restitution orders in relation to market abuse (para 13.254 ff below);
- disciplinary and other regulatory enforcement action (para 13.262 ff below); and
- civil liability arising from market abuse (para 13.276 ff below).

Injunctions

13.235 The court may grant an injunction, on the application of the FSA, broadly to prevent threatened or continuing market abuse, to address the consequences of the market abuse or to prevent the disposal of assets[1]. This power is very similar to the power to grant injunctions in respect of regulatory breaches, outlined in Chapter 7 above. Some general points about applications for injunctions are discussed at para 7.102 ff above. In market abuse cases, the FSA may apply to the court, at the same time as applying for an injunction, for an order imposing a penalty for the market abuse[2].

1 FSMA 2000, s 381.
2 FSMA 2000, s 129 and see para 13.251 ff below.

What orders can the court make?

13.236 The court may make three different types of orders, namely:

- restraining the market abuse;
- requiring the person engaging in market abuse to take specified steps to remedy the market abuse; or
- restraining the person concerned from disposing of or dealing with his assets.

Each is based upon the satisfaction of slightly different criteria.

13.237 ***Restraining the market abuse*** An order restraining market abuse may be made if the court is satisfied that[1]:

- there is a reasonable likelihood that any person will engage in market abuse; or
- any person is or has engaged in market abuse and there is a reasonable likelihood that the market abuse will continue or be repeated.

1 FSMA 2000, s 381(1).

13.238 An injunction may therefore be available pre-emptively where the FSA has information that action amounting to market abuse is going to be taken. Although the FSA only has to show a reasonable likelihood that market abuse will be undertaken[1], this may in practice be difficult because it will not often be aware of the proposed market abuse before it occurs. Indeed, part of the rationale behind the nature of the investigation regime for market abuse[2] is that the FSA will normally start with a situation which looks like market abuse, rather than with a suspected culprit.

1 It is likely that this power will be used in cases of urgency. Typically in court proceedings, injunctions at this stage (known as interim injunctions) are granted without needing to prove the claim on the balance of probabilities; a lower test of 'good arguable case' typically being applied. It is unclear how this will be applied in injunctions in market abuse situations given the statutory test. This is a particular issue as the interim injunction hearing is likely effectively to be the substantive hearing due to the timescale involved. See also the discussion at para 7.103 ff above.
2 See para 13.142 above.

13.239 This order is similar to that which a court can make to restrain regulatory breaches, as outlined in para 7.104 ff above.

13.240 ***Remedying the market abuse*** An order requiring a person to take such steps as the court may direct to remedy market abuse, or mitigate its effect, may be made if the court is satisfied that[1]:

- any person is or has engaged in market abuse; and
- there are steps which could be taken for remedying the market abuse (or mitigating its effect[2]).

1 FSMA 2000, s 381(2).
2 FSMA 2000, s 381(6).

13.241 Here, the market abuse must in fact have occurred or be in the process of occurring, reflecting the remedial nature of the order. In many situations, it will not be possible to remedy the market abuse, strictly speaking, because it has already occurred and cannot be undone. The inclusion of references to mitigating the effect of the market abuse helps ensure that that will not be a bar to the court requiring appropriate steps to be taken[1]. The remedial steps which the FSA might seek would depend upon the situation, but could, for example, include requiring a person to correct any misleading information disseminated to the market, or requiring them to release stocks of an investment or commodity that are being held in the course of a market distortion[2].

1 This is discussed in more detail in para 7.113 above.
2 See Consultation Paper 10 ('Market Abuse Part 1: Consultation on a draft Code of Market Conduct'), June 1998, para 130 ff.

13.242 This order is similar to that which can be made to remedy regulatory breaches, as outlined in para 7.110 ff above.

13.243 ***Restraining assets*** An order may be made by the court restraining a person from disposing of, or otherwise dealing with, any assets of his which the court is satisfied he is reasonably likely to dispose of, or otherwise deal with[1]. To make such an order, the court must be satisfied that the person[2]:

- may be engaged in market abuse; or
- may have been engaged in market abuse.

1 FSMA 2000, s 381(4).
2 FSMA 2000, s 381(3).

13.244 The FSMA 2000 does not expressly require any link between the market abuse and the assets that might be disposed of, so it will be entirely in the court's discretion in what circumstances it will be prepared to grant such an injunction. In practice, this provision may be used to obtain a freezing order in support of some other proceedings, to restrain a person from dissipating his assets so as to frustrate the enforcement of any judgment against him in those proceedings. Examples in this context of where a freezing order might be sought include where the person faces proceedings for a restitution order, or civil proceedings, arising from the market abuse or, possibly, proceedings for a civil penalty. A similar injunction may also be available under the court's inherent jurisdiction[1]. This order is similar to that which can be made in relation to regulatory breaches, as outlined at para 7.116 ff above.

1 See footnote 2 to para 7.116 above. Additionally, ancillary orders, such as requiring the disclosure of assets, might be sought on this basis.

The discretionary nature of the remedy

13.245 It is important to appreciate that each of these remedies is within the discretion of the court. The FSMA 2000 provides only that the court 'may' make the order if satisfied of the matters set out[1]. In other words, the court is not bound to make an injunction because the FSA establishes the grounds for making one. Whether an injunction will be available in a particular case will therefore depend upon the particular circumstances. The matters which the court takes into account in the exercise of its discretion to grant injunctive relief are briefly discussed in para 7.97 ff above. The court will often, initially, be considering an application for an interim injunction pending a full trial on whether an injunction should be granted and in many cases the interim injunction will effectively dispose of the matter. This gives rise to certain additional considerations, outlined in para 7.97 ff above.

1 The word 'may' appears to have accidentally been omitted from FSMA 2000, s 381(4).

In what circumstances will the FSA apply for an injunction?

13.246 Since the court will only grant an injunction on an application by the FSA, one of the key questions from the firm's perspective is when in practice the FSA will make such an application. When considering whether to apply for an injunction in relation to market abuse, the FSA takes into account the same factors as are relevant in deciding whether to make applications for an injunction in non-market abuse situations under FSMA 2000, s 380. These are discussed in para 7.122 above[1]. The basic criterion is whether an injunction would be the most effective means of dealing with the FSA's concerns[2].

1 They can be found in the FSA's Handbook at ENF 6.6.
2 See the FSA Handbook at ENF 6.6.2.

13.247 Particular factors highlighted as being potentially of relevance in the context of market abuse[1] are the nature and seriousness of the misconduct, or expected misconduct, in question, including its impact on the financial system and the extent to which it has or would result in disruption or distortion if it took place or continued, and the extent and nature of any losses or other costs imposed or likely to be imposed on other users as a result.

1 See the FSA Handbook at ENF 6.6.2(2).

13.248 As ever, this power needs to be viewed in context and in particular where the FSA is dealing with a regulated firm then it may be able more appropriately to achieve the same through varying the firm's permission[1].

1 Or imposing requirements on an incoming firm: see Chapter 9 above.

Are the defences to market abuse proceedings available?

13.249 It is a defence to the imposition of a penalty or public statement for market abuse that a person believed on reasonable grounds that his behaviour did not amount to market abuse or that he took all reasonable precautions and exercised all due diligence to avoid committing market abuse[1]. However, the availability of one of these defences in the particular case simply precludes the imposition of a penalty or public censure, or indeed a restitution order[2]. It does not prevent market abuse from having taken place and does not therefore preclude an injunction being granted in an appropriate case[3].

1 These defences are discussed in detail at para 13.68 above.
2 See para 13.255 below.
3 There is nothing on the face of the legislation to prevent an injunction being granted to remedy market abuse with substantially the same effect as a restitution order, in a situation where one of the defences applied and a restitution order would not therefore be available under the FSMA 2000.

13.250 Whether the court would be willing to grant an injunction in that situation may, however, be a different matter. At one end of the spectrum, there seems little reason why this should preclude an injunction to prevent further acts that would amount to market abuse. At the other end, it would seem wrong for the court to restrain a person from dealing with his own assets in a situation where he has done nothing culpable.

Applications for a penalty to be imposed

13.251 The FSMA 2000 allows the FSA, on an application for an injunction or restitution order, to request the court to consider whether the circumstances are such that a penalty should be imposed on the person to whom the application relates and the court may, if it considers it appropriate, make an order requiring the person concerned to pay the FSA a penalty of such amount as it considers appropriate[1].

1 FSMA 2000, s 129.

13.252 The FSA Handbook contains very little guidance on when the FSA will make use of this procedure, save[1] that in deciding whether to ask the court to impose a financial penalty the FSA will take into account the same factors as are relevant to the decisions whether to take action for market abuse and if so what action to take. Those factors are outlined at paras 13.193 and 13.198 above.

1 See the FSA Handbook at ENF 14.3.3.

13.253 The FSA has indicated in the past[1] that an application to the court to impose a penalty would not be appropriate in all cases where it applies for an injunction or restitution order. It has said that its primary concern would be to contain the overall costs of dealing with any case of market abuse. It will therefore depend upon, among other things, the extent to which the court would consider the same issues of fact and law in relation to the two applications. There may in practice be other relevant factors, such as the need to put an injunction in place on an expedited basis, as against the need for a full investigation and hearing on the imposition of a penalty.

1 Consultation Paper 17 ('Enforcing the new regime'), December 1998, para 165.

Restitution orders

13.254 The FSMA 2000 allows both the FSA and the court, separately, to make restitution orders to compensate the victims of market abuse. The provisions are similar to those in relation to restitution orders for other regulatory breaches, discussed in para 7.43 ff above. They represent an exception to the general position[1] that market abuse does not give rise to statutory claims by those who have suffered loss. The FSA may require a person, whether or not authorised[2], who has engaged in market abuse, or required or encouraged another to do so, to disgorge any profits made or pay compensation to the victims of the market abuse[3]. Alternatively, the FSA may apply to the court for a similar order[4]. If the FSA applies to the court for a restitution order, it may also apply to the court at the same time for an order imposing a penalty for the market abuse[5].

1 See para 13.276 below.
2 This marks a significant difference from the FSA's power to order restitution in relation to other regulatory breaches, which can only be exercised against authorised persons, as discussed in para 7.46 above.
3 FSMA 2000, s 384(2).
4 FSMA 2000, s 383.
5 See para 13.251 above.

When can the FSA make or seek a restitution order?

13.255 The circumstances in which the FSA may exercise its administrative power to make a restitution order, or where the court may make a restitution order on an application by the FSA, are the same. The FSA or the court, as appropriate, must be satisfied that a person[1]:

- has engaged in market abuse; or
- by taking or refraining from taking any action, has required or encouraged another person or persons to engage in behaviour which, if engaged in by the person concerned, would amount to market abuse[2]; and
- in either case, profits have accrued to the person concerned as a result or one or more persons have suffered loss or been otherwise adversely affected as a result[3].

But no restitution order may be made if, as applicable, the court is satisfied[4], or having considered any representations made to it in response to a warning notice there are reasonable grounds for the FSA to be satisfied[5], that the person concerned either believed on reasonable grounds that his behaviour did not amount to market abuse (or requiring or encouraging market abuse), or took all reasonable precautions and exercised all due diligence to avoid behaving in a way which was market abuse (or requiring or encouraging market abuse)[6].

1 FSMA 2000, ss 384(2) and 383.
2 This is considered in detail at para 13.82 above.
3 The meaning of adverse affect has been considered in para 7.58 above.
4 FSMA 2000, s 383(3).
5 FSMA 2000, s 384(4).
6 Note that the test for the court and that for the FSA are slightly different. The court has to be satisfied that one of these is the case. There only have to be reasonable grounds for the FSA to be satisfied. Hence, in theory, it is easier to prove the defence before the FSA. For a discussion of this test and the factors the FSA takes into account in determining whether the defences have been met, see para 13.82 ff.

The amount of a restitution order

13.256 If the above test is satisfied, the FSA or the court, as appropriate, may order the person concerned to pay such sum as appears to the FSA or the court to be just. In determining what figure is just, the FSA or the court must have regard to[1] the profits appearing to it to have accrued to the person concerned and/or, where one or more persons have suffered a loss or other adverse effect, the extent of that loss or adverse effect. The FSA's policy on the amount of restitution that is required to be paid and the requirements on how it should be distributed are discussed at para 7.85 ff above.

1 FSMA 2000, s 383(4) or 384(5).

When in practice will the FSA seek or make a restitution order?

13.257 The FSA has provided little indication, in the context of market abuse specifically, of its policy on when it will impose a restitution order and when it will apply for a restitution order from the court and, in any event when a restitution order is likely to be appropriate. The policy outlined in para 7.64 ff above in relation to restitution orders generally seems to apply equally in the case of market abuse.

13.258 There are, however, three points to note in this context. First, the circumstances when the FSA has indicated it may be appropriate to seek a restitution order from the court[1] include the following two which may be particularly relevant:

- where the FSA wishes to combine an application for an order for restitution with another court action, for example an application for an injunction; or
- where the FSA suspects that the person may not comply with an administrative requirement to give restitution, and wishes to ensure that the sanctions for breach of a court order are available.

1 See the FSA Handbook at ENF 9.7.3.

13.259 In the context of market abuse, the FSA can, as has been seen, apply for a financial penalty to be imposed in conjunction with an application for a restitution order or injunction. There may be an attraction in particular cases to having all of these regulatory issues addressed at one hearing before the court.

13.260 Second, an additional factor relevant in determining in any case whether to make or apply for a restitution order is whether the persons who have suffered losses are in a position to bring civil proceedings on their own behalf[1]. In most instances, this primarily involves considering the resources, sophistication and knowledge of those who have suffered the loss. However, in the context of market abuse, this factor may assume a wider significance because, as is discussed below[2], it may be unlikely that a civil claim is available in respect of market abuse. Thus, the persons who suffered the losses may be unable to bring civil proceedings, whatever their sophistication and resources.

1 See the FSA Handbook at ENF 9.3.1 and 9.6.8 and see para 7.64 ff above.
2 See para 13.276 ff below.

13.261 Third, the FSA recognised during the consultation process which preceded the FSA Handbook[1] that the nature of market manipulation and information misuse in financial markets is such that it is often difficult to identify 'victims' of the misconduct who should be compensated or who should benefit from any disgorgement of profits. The market abuse regime is directed at protecting the integrity of markets, rather than the interests of any particular group of market users. Since a restitution order may only be made where there are 'victims' who have suffered as a result of the market abuse, it was said that the FSA was likely to exercise its powers to require or seek restitution only where:

- there were identifiable persons whose interests were seriously prejudiced as a direct result of market abuse;
- the prejudice took the form of either:
  - — a quantifiable loss or other harm which could appropriately be addressed through the payment of compensation, or
  - — the abuse of a relationship of trust which was so serious that it was just and equitable in all the circumstances that the profits (or part of the profits) accruing from the abuse should be paid to them, and
- the maintenance of confidence in the UK financial markets and/or the protection of the interests of consumers require that the FSA take action.

This policy stated during the consultation process does not expressly feature in the FSA Handbook (save to the extent that these factors reflect elements of the FSA's more general policy on restitution orders). As a result, it is unclear whether the FSA will apply a similar policy in practice.

1 Consultation Paper 17 ('Enforcing the new regime'), December 1998, paras 153 to 155.

Disciplinary and other regulatory enforcement action

13.262 If an authorised firm or approved person is involved in the market abuse, it may be appropriate for the FSA also to consider the use of its disciplinary or other enforcement powers. This will particularly be the case where the circumstances of the market misconduct give rise to other concerns about the firm, such as supervision and controls or employee training, where the conduct amounts to a breach of the Principles[1], or where it gives rise to questions about whether particular individuals are fit and proper.

1 Principle 5 of the Principles for Businesses and Statement of Principle 3 for approved persons: see paras 13.265 and 13.272 below.

13.263 The various other courses of action available in relation to the regulated community include:

- in relation to an authorised person:

- disciplinary sanctions (public censure or fine)[1];
- the variation of the firm's permission, or equivalent intervention action for an incoming firm[2];
- the cancellation of permission[3];

- in the case of an approved person:
  - disciplinary sanctions for misconduct (public censure or fine)[4];
  - withdrawal of approval[5];
- in the case of any individual:
  - a prohibition order[6].

1 See para 7.7 ff above.
2 See Chapter 9 above.
3 See para 9.239 ff above.
4 See para 8.4 ff above.
5 See para 8.27 ff above.
6 See para 8.44 ff above.

13.264 These various regulatory enforcement actions are considered elsewhere in this book, as indicated above. One particular issue of concern is considered here, namely the overlap between market abuse proceedings and regulatory disciplinary proceedings and, particularly, in what circumstances the FSA will seek to impose disciplinary sanctions against either firms or approved persons in relation to market misconduct.

When will the FSA seek to discipline a firm?

13.265 There is an obvious overlap between market abuse, on the one hand, and Principle 5[1] on the other. To what extent will the FSA also seek to discipline a firm for breach of Principle 5 where it finds it guilty of market abuse? To what extent is a firm at risk of disciplinary action for breach of Principle 5 even where its actions do not amount to market abuse? These are difficult questions which are only partially answered by the FSA's policy guidance.

1 Principle 5, Principles for Businesses: a firm must observe proper standards of market conduct: see para 2.52 above.

13.266 The FSA has said that behaviour which constitutes market abuse, or requiring or encouraging market abuse, will also constitute a breach of Principle 5[1]. Where the principal mischief arising from the behaviour appears to be market abuse, or requiring or encouraging market abuse, then the FSA will take enforcement action under the market abuse regime, rather than as a breach of Principle 5. Where the firm has clearly committed market abuse, therefore, it ought not to face both proceedings for the same offence.

1 See the FSA Handbook at ENF 14.8.1.

13.267 However, the FSA acknowledges that Principle 5 and market abuse are not co-extensive in that behaviour which breaches Principle 5 may not necessarily be market abuse. Where the principal mischief appears to be a breach of Principle 5 and the FSA is satisfied that it would not be appropriate to deal with the case under the market abuse regime, it may take enforcement action for breach of the Principles[1]. In some situations, it may be unclear or arguable where the principal mischief lies and in those situations the FSA may take both forms of action as alternatives.

1 See the FSA Handbook at ENF 14.8.2.

13.268 The meaning of this rather broad statement is not entirely clear. Where a firm is involved in some form of market conduct to which the FSA objects but which does not constitute market abuse, it could find that it is charged with a breach of Principle 5. In some circumstances the conduct may concern an area of business which is wholly unaffected by the market abuse regime, for example because it plainly does not relate to investments traded on prescribed markets[1], and in those cases this approach is perhaps understandable. But the FSA seems to have left open the option of charging firms with breach of Principle 5 where their actions fall close to, but not quite within, market abuse. Indeed, in some situations where it is unclear whether the conduct constitutes market abuse, the FSA seems to envisage charging the firm with both market abuse and breach of Principle 5, so that if the firm successfully defends itself against market abuse it can still be disciplined. It will clearly be important to see how this is operated in practice.

1 For examples as to how the Principles are broader than the market abuse regime, see the FSA Handbook at MAR 1.9.3.

13.269 Among other things, this brings into sharp contrast the differentiation between the market abuse regime, which the Government has accepted there is a risk may be classed as a criminal charge for ECHR purposes, and the disciplinary regime, which it has not accepted there is any risk will be classed as criminal. As we have seen[1], there are protections available to firms and individuals charged with market abuse which are not ordinarily available in the context of regulatory disciplinary proceedings. For example, one potential outcome might be that where the FSA had insufficient evidence to bring proceedings for market abuse, because its evidence relied upon a statement which could not be used against the person who made it[2], it would instead bring disciplinary proceedings for breach of Principle 5 and use that statement in evidence in those disciplinary proceedings.

1 See the discussion at para 13.15 above.
2 The privilege against self-incrimination is discussed at para 13.162 ff above.

13.270 Furthermore, if the 'charges' related to an individual, the result of bringing regulatory disciplinary proceedings rather than market abuse proceedings might be to deny him the right to legal assistance (which he may have had in Tribunal proceedings for market abuse but would not have in Tribunal proceedings for a regulatory breach).

13.271 Finally, notwithstanding the Government's view, it is possible that in an appropriate case a breach of the regulatory general principles could constitute a criminal charge for ECHR purposes[1]. In that case, the ECHR criminal protections would need to be conferred and would give rise to a further issue of whether the offence was sufficiently clearly defined for ECHR purposes[2]. It is possible that a disciplinary charge that consisted purely of a breach of a regulatory general principle might not comply.

1 This is discussed further at para 5.22 above.
2 This is discussed further at para 2.161 above.

When will the FSA seek to discipline an approved person?

13.272 If the market abuse regime overlaps with the Principles for Business applicable to firms, it also overlaps with the Statements of Principle for approved persons and, in particular, Statement of Principle 3, which obliges approved persons to observe proper standards of market conduct in carrying out their controlled functions.

13.273 Unfortunately, neither the Enforcement Manual nor the Code of Market Conduct, nor indeed the Code of Conduct for approved persons, contains much indication as to how this overlap is to be addressed. The Code of Conduct for approved persons indicates that whether or not the person complied with the Code of Market Conduct will be a relevant factor in determining whether or not he complied with the Statement of Principle and that compliance with the Code of Market Conduct will tend to show compliance with Statement of Principle 3[1]. In addition, the accompanying guidance suggests that in many cases the required standard will be set out in the Code of Market Conduct. However, this gives rather a low level of comfort since it is not clear what 'compliance with the Code of Market Conduct' means.

1 See the FSA Handbook at APER 4.3 and see para 2.93 above.

13.274 For its part, the Code of Market Conduct[1] reinforces the implication that behaviour may fall short of proper standards of market conduct, and therefore breach Statement of Principle 3, but not fall within the scope of the market abuse regime.

1 See the FSA Handbook at MAR 1.9.3.

13.275 It cannot therefore be ruled out that the FSA would bring proceedings for misconduct against an individual for breach of Statement of Principle 3 in relation to actions which did not constitute market abuse. The FSA's general policy on when it will bring misconduct proceedings against individuals is discussed at para 8.14 ff above.

Civil liability arising from market abuse

13.276 Although it is possible to envisage market abuse resulting in significant losses across a large number of market users, or perhaps because of this, the

FSMA 2000 does not contain a coherent system of direct redress for those who suffer losses as a result of market abuse. In particular, there is no indication in the FSMA 2000 that market abuse would give rise to a breach of statutory duty claim for those who suffer loss (or, indeed, no prohibition against such claims), and given that the FSMA 2000 tends to provide expressly for claims for breach of statutory duty where they are intended to be available, it is unlikely that a court would find such a claim to exist as a matter of law[1]. This is reinforced by the fact that the FSA has disapplied breach of statutory duty claims in relation to the Principles for Businesses, which are the regulatory hook linking market abuse to regulation[2].

1 This issue is discussed in more detail in para 10.23 ff above.
2 If a specific FSA rule had been breached, then a breach of statutory duty claim under FSMA 2000, s 150 may arise: see para 10.27 ff above.

13.277 This does not, though, mean that the firm committing market abuse can avoid paying any compensation. As has been seen[1], the FSA can make or apply for a restitution order requiring the firm to pay compensation and/or to disgorge profits. This is likely to be used particularly where significant numbers of consumers are involved[2]. Individual consumers may also be able to bring claims for compensation before the ombudsman, even where there is no clear cause of action as a matter of law[3]. Indeed, whether the firm has paid compensation is one of the factors to be taken into account by the FSA in determining what action to take in relation to the market abuse. This seems to assume that a remedy would be available.

1 See para 13.254 ff above.
2 See para 7.64 ff above.
3 This is discussed in para 12.50 ff above.

13.278 Outside the regulatory arena, and the FSMA 2000, it may be possible that civil claims may be brought depending upon the circumstances and, particularly, the nature of the conduct constituting market abuse. For example, claims may be available based on negligent misstatement misrepresentation, even fraud, or perhaps for breach of an implied contractual term. This would depend very much on the circumstances. Various potential claims are discussed in more detail in Chapter 10.

14 Regulated collective investment schemes

CONTENTS

Introduction 585

Investigations into regulated collective investment schemes 587

Enforcement action in relation to regulated collective investment schemes 596

INTRODUCTION

An overview of Chapter 14

14.1 The FSMA 2000 contains separate provision for investigation and enforcement in relation to authorised unit trusts and other regulated collective investment schemes. The FSA's powers in relation to such schemes are considered in this chapter.

14.2 In particular, we consider:

- the FSA's powers to carry out investigations into regulated collective investment schemes (para 14.10 ff below); and
- the FSA's enforcement powers in relation to such schemes (para 14.41 ff below).

14.3 Before looking at the investigation and enforcement provisions, it is worth briefly setting them in context. The quantity of funds under management in the UK, not only in collective investment schemes but also in other types of funds, such as pensions, is enormous. Many unit trusts and other regulated schemes are sold to retail consumers and they involve the holding and management of very substantial sums. For an individual consumer, his investment in such a scheme is likely to be financially significant. Important consumer protection and consumer confidence issues plainly arise. Unsurprisingly, the FSMA 2000 gives the regulator extensive powers to investigate and address any issues that arise in relation to such schemes.

14.4 It is important to appreciate that the specific provisions outlined here are not the only ones which may be relevant to a problem relating to a regulated collective investment scheme. Authorised firms and approved persons that manage or are otherwise involved with such schemes are also subject to the FSA's more general investigation and enforcement powers outlined in this book[1]. It is not therefore sufficient to have in mind only the specific provisions outlined in this chapter.

1 This issue is discussed further at para 14.44 ff below.

14.5 As will be seen, the various provisions reflect in a number of respects some of the provisions already reviewed. Where that is the case reference is made in this Chapter to the relevant discussion elsewhere in the book.

Different types of collective investment scheme

14.6 In broad terms, collective investment schemes can be either regulated or unregulated. Unregulated schemes are, generally speaking, prohibited from being marketed to the public[1]. This chapter is concerned with enforcement in relation to regulated schemes only[2], although some of the investigation powers outlined are capable of applying also to unregulated schemes.

1 FSMA 2000, s 238.
2 Enforcement in relation to unregulated schemes will often be either perimeter enforcement (to the extent that such schemes are run by those who are not authorised to carry on regulated activities under the FSMA 2000: see para 2.175 ff above and, for examples, see FSA Press Releases 35 and 85 of 1998 and 84 of 2000) or enforcement against those who wrongly promote such schemes.

14.7 The statutory scheme is relatively complicated, in that different investigation and enforcement provisions apply to different types of regulated collective investment scheme[1]. It is therefore necessary to differentiate between the following types of regulated schemes:

- UK schemes which are either:
  - — authorised unit trust schemes ('unit trusts'), or
  - — authorised open-ended investment companies ('ICVCs')[2]; and
- overseas schemes (known as 'recognised schemes') which are either:
  - — constituted in other EEA countries and recognised in the UK under the UCITS Directive[3] and the FSMA 2000, s 264[4] ('UCITS schemes'),

— authorised in certain designated countries or territories[5] and recognised in the UK under the FSMA 2000, s 270 ('section 270 schemes'), or

— individually recognised in the UK under the FSMA 2000, s 272 ('section 272 schemes')[6].

1 For the definition of 'collective investment scheme', see FSMA 2000, s 235 and the Financial Services and Markets Act 2000 (Collective Investment Schemes) Order 2001, SI 2001/1062.
2 Defined in FSMA 2000, s 236. According to HM Treasury, prior to the FSMA 2000 coming into force, around 20% of funds under management in collective investment schemes were held in ICVCs. This figure is growing as unit trusts convert to ICVCs. In addition, the FSMA 2000 (together with the regulations and rules made under it) potentially allows a wider range of ICVCs and it is therefore anticipated that the proportion of funds held in ICVCs will rise further.
3 Council Directive of 20 December 1985 on the co-ordination of laws, regulations and administrative provisions relating to undertakings for collective investment in transferable securities (85/611/EEC). This is soon to be amended.
4 See also the Financial Services and Markets Act 2000 (Collective Investment Schemes constituted in other EEA States) Regulations 2001, SI 2001/2383. Authorisation for persons involved in such schemes is granted automatically under FSMA 2000, Sch 5: see para 2.6 ff above.
5 This is expected to encompass the Isle of Man, Bermuda, Guernsey and Jersey.
6 In practice, such schemes are very rare.

Sources of information

14.8 The provisions relating to unit trusts and other recognised schemes can be found in the FSMA 2000, Pt XVII (ss 235 to 284). The FSMA 2000 does not contain detailed provisions relating to ICVCs, but empowers HM Treasury to make detailed rules relating to them. HM Treasury has accordingly made the ICVC Regulations[1], which is where the detailed provisions are to be found.

1 The Open-Ended Investment Companies Regulations 2001, SI 2001/1228.

14.9 The FSA's policy on investigating regulated schemes is set out in Chapter 2 of the Enforcement Manual. Its policy on the use of its enforcement powers in relation to schemes can be found in Chapter 16 of the Enforcement Manual.

INVESTIGATIONS INTO REGULATED COLLECTIVE INVESTMENT SCHEMES

Introduction

14.10 We outline here the specific investigation powers relating to regulated collective investment schemes and, in particular:

- the circumstances in which an investigation can be commenced, including the statutory grounds for investigating and the FSA's policy on when it will do so (para 14.15 ff);
- the scope of the information that an investigator appointed under these provisions can obtain (para 14.33 ff); and

- how an investigation is commenced and controlled (para 14.39 ff).

Practical guidance for those facing a formal investigation can be found at para 4.179 ff above.

14.11 These investigation powers are not, however, the only means for the FSA to obtain information when an issue arises which relates to a collective investment scheme. These provisions overlap to a large extent with the FSA's more general investigation powers, particularly (but not exclusively) in relation to authorised firms, and approved persons working for them, who provide their services in connection with the collective investment scheme concerned – whether as manager, investment manager, trustee, distributor or otherwise. In addition, the operator, trustee or depositary of a non-UK UCITS scheme which has been recognised for marketing in the UK is automatically an authorised person[1], as is an ICVC[2].

1 FSMA 2000, Sch 5, para 1(1).
2 FSMA 2000, Sch 5, para 1(3).

14.12 As a result, additionally, or as an alternative, to using its specific powers of investigation into collective investment schemes, the FSA could obtain information by a variety of other means, including the following:

- requiring co-operation and assistance from an authorised person and/or an approved person[1];
- using the general information gathering power which enables the FSA to require information or documents to be provided by notice in writing[2]. This power can be exercised against an authorised person, various types of persons connected with authorised persons, and against an operator, trustee or depositary of a section 270 or section 272 scheme[3] who is not an authorised person[4];
- requiring an authorised person to commission a report from a skilled person (for example an actuary or accountant) into a particular matter[5];
- investigating the business of an authorised person on the ground there is good reason for doing so[6]; or
- investigating particular criminal or regulatory breaches[7]. By way of example, breaches that may be relevant in this context include:
  - breach of the Principles for Businesses[8] (particularly if the problem relating to the scheme gives rise to wider issues about a firm),
  - breach of specific FSA rules (including rules made specifically in relation to collective investment schemes[9]),
  - misconduct by approved persons[10], or
  - breach of the restriction on promoting unauthorised or unrecognised schemes[11].

1 Under, respectively, Principle 11 of the Principles for Businesses and Statement of Principle 4 of the Statements of Principle for approved persons: see para 4.27 ff above.

2 FSMA 2000, s 165 and see para 4.59 ff above.
3 Schemes authorised in designated territories and individually recognised schemes, respectively: see para 14.7 above.
4 FSMA 2000, s 165(7).
5 FSMA 2000, s 166 and see para 4.72 ff above.
6 FSMA 2000, s 167 and see para 4.122 ff above.
7 FSMA 2000, s 168 and see para 4.134 ff above. This power overlaps significantly with the specific power to investigate collective investment schemes discussed below, to the extent that there are specific rule breaches to investigate.
8 These are discussed at para 2.52 ff above.
9 For example, the FSA's trust scheme rules and scheme particulars rules, made under FSMA 2000, ss 247 and 248 and found in the FSA Handbook at CIS.
10 FSMA 2000, s 66 and see para 8.9 ff above.
11 FSMA 2000, s 168(2)(c).

14.13 In most instances, the FSA expects[1] those involved, such as managers of schemes, to provide information without the FSA having recourse to its formal powers. Indeed, in many cases those firms will be under an obligation to do so by virtue of Principle 11[2]. Nonetheless, there may be situations where the FSA will want to use its formal powers of investigation.

1 See the FSA Handbook at ENF 2.9.1.
2 Principle 11 of the Principles for Businesses: see para 2.52 above.

14.14 The FSA has not given any indication of how it will address the overlap between its general powers of investigation and its specific powers to investigate collective investment schemes. This is likely to depend on the nature of the problem and the scope of the investigation required. As will be seen, the specific powers relating to collective investment schemes are wide-ranging in scope, both in the categories of information that can be obtained and in the variety of people from whom information can be sought. In some cases, this may in itself be reason for the FSA to use those powers, rather than the more general investigation powers which, although capable of wider application, may often be more limited in scope.

In what circumstances can an investigation be commenced?

14.15 The FSA has separate investigation powers for:

- investigations into unit trusts, recognised schemes and other collective investment schemes (other than ICVCs)[1]; and
- investigations into ICVCs.

1 These powers would also allow the UKLA to investigate an unregulated collective investment scheme.

14.16 The distinction arises because the regulating provisions relating to ICVCs are contained in the ICVC Regulations, rather than in the FSMA 2000. As will be seen, though, the two sets of provisions are very similar.

Investigating unit trusts and recognised schemes

The power to investigate

14.17 The FSA may appoint an investigator to investigate on its behalf[1]:

- the affairs of, or of the manager or trustee of, any unit trust; or
- the affairs of, or of the operator, trustee or depositary of, any recognised scheme so far as relating to activities carried on in the UK; or
- the affairs of, or of the operator, trustee or depositary of, any other collective investment scheme except an ICVC[2].

The ground for commencing such an investigation is that it appears to the FSA that it is in the interests of the participants or potential participants to do so or that the matter is of public concern[3].

1 FSMA 2000, s 284(1). This replaces, and is very similar to, the former power under the Financial Services Act 1986, s 94.
2 This would include an unregulated collective investment scheme.
3 FSMA 2000, s 284(1).

14.18 Once such an investigator has been appointed, the investigator may, if he thinks it necessary for the purpose of the investigation, also investigate[1]:

- the affairs of, or of the manager, trustee, operator or depositary of, any other scheme with the same manager, trustee, operator or depositary; or
- the affairs of such other schemes and persons, including ICVCs and their depositaries, as may be prescribed.

1 FSMA 2000, s 284(2).

14.19 The Secretary of State has a parallel power to appoint an investigator[1].

1 FSMA 2000, s 284(11). For a discussion of the reason for this residual power, see footnote 8 to para 4.144 above.

14.20 A number of points may be made. First, this is a broad provision which overlaps to a large extent with the FSA's general investigation powers (which, in many instances, may be sufficient to enable appropriate investigations to take place). This may reflect the need to ensure that the statutory provisions are all-embracing, particularly given the consumer protection issues that arise in relation to collective investment schemes.

14.21 Second, in order to initiate an investigation, it has to appear to the FSA that it is in the interests of participants or potential participants for it to do so or that the matter is of public concern. This is a low test and leaves the question largely within the FSA's discretion.

14.22 'Participants' means those who take part in the scheme[1]. It thus refers, broadly, to those who hold an interest in it, not those who operate it. Neither the

FSMA 2000 nor the FSA Handbook provide any specific explanation or guidance on what the interests of participants and potential participants are for this purpose, or what is likely in this context to amount to a matter of public concern[2]. It is therefore a matter for the FSA's judgment in the particular case and, given the subjective nature of this test, it will be difficult for firms to challenge the commencement of a formal investigation on the ground that the statutory test was not met.

1 FSMA 2000, s 235(1) and (2).
2 The FSA has indicated that this might include issues about the nature and propriety of assets held by the scheme or the accuracy and propriety of valuation of units in the scheme: see the FSA Handbook at ENF 2.9.2.

14.23 Third, once appointed, the investigator may also review the wider matters set out at para 14.18 above but only if he thinks it necessary for the purpose of the investigation. The purpose of the investigation is to investigate the affairs of, as applicable, the scheme or its manager, trustee, operator or depositary. Thus, the investigator may be entitled to review, for example, suspected underlying systems and controls issues relating to the manager by looking at other schemes managed by the same firm. But the focus of the investigation, and its purpose, remains the affairs of the scheme or of its manager, trustee, operator or depositary. What he is unlikely therefore to be able to do, within the parameters of this statutory provision, is to investigate the other scheme for its own sake.

When will the FSA use the power to investigate?

14.24 The FSA has given limited guidance on the circumstances when it will use this formal investigation power[1]. It expects, in most instances, that those involved, such as managers of schemes, will provide information without the need for the use of formal powers. In addition, as indicated above, in some cases, the FSA will use its general investigation and information gathering powers.

1 See the FSA Handbook at ENF 2.9.1.

14.25 In some cases, however, the FSA will use its formal powers. The FSA has indicated that the types of concerns that may prompt it to do so cannot be listed exhaustively but would include any matters that could affect the interests of actual or potential participants or that could be of public concern, including questions about the nature and propriety of the scheme's assets or the accuracy or propriety of the valuation of units. The factors that the FSA will take into account in considering whether to use its formal powers include[1]:

- the seriousness, in the FSA's opinion, of the matter of concern;
- the degree to which the interests of consumers may be affected;
- whether the FSA considers that the persons concerned in the scheme are willing to co-operate in giving information; and
- whether confidentiality obligations may inhibit individuals from giving information without the FSA having to use its formal powers.

1 See the FSA Handbook at ENF 2.9.2.

14.26 An additional consideration may in practice be whether all of the information which the FSA needs to obtain can be obtained from those who fall within its jurisdiction. If third parties are involved, particularly unregulated entities, then there may be a need to use formal investigation powers.

Investigating ICVCs

The power to investigate

14.27 The FSA may appoint an investigator to investigate and report on the affairs of, or of any director or depositary of, an ICVC[1].

1 ICVC Regulations, reg 30(1).

14.28 The ground for doing so is that it appears to the FSA that it is in the interests of shareholders or potential shareholders of the ICVC to do so or that the matter is of public concern[1].

1 ICVC Regulations, reg 30(1).

14.29 Once such an investigator has been appointed, he may, if he thinks it necessary for the purposes of the investigation, also investigate the affairs of (or of the directors, depositary, trustee or operator of):

- another ICVC which has, broadly, any of the same directors or the same depositary as the ICVC being investigated, or, as appropriate, as the director or depositary which is being investigated[1]; or
- a collective investment scheme, broadly, whose manager, depositary or operator is being investigated or is a director of the ICVC being investigated or whose trustee is the depositary of the ICVC being investigated[2].

1 For the detailed rules, see the ICVC Regulations, reg 30(2)(a) to (d).
2 For the detailed rules, see the ICVC Regulations, reg 30(2)(e) to (g).

14.30 The Secretary of State has a parallel power to appoint an investigator[1].

1 See the ICVC Regulations, reg 30(1). For a discussion of the reasons for this residual power, see footnote 8 to para 4.144 above.

14.31 The investigation power in relation to ICVCs is in substance very similar to the FSA's power to investigate a collective investment scheme under FSMA 2000, s 284[1] and, to a large extent, uses the same tests[2]. It gives the FSA a broad discretion to commence an investigation, involving only a low threshold[3]. As a result, it will be difficult for firms to challenge the commencement of an investigation on the ground that the test was not met.

1 See para 14.17 ff above.
2 There are some minor differences in the wording which, broadly, reflect the differences between ICVCs and other forms of scheme. For example, the issue is whether the investigation is in the interests of 'shareholders', rather than 'participants'. Also, the investigator is appointed to 'investigate and report on' the affairs of the ICVC, and so on, rather than 'to investigate on [the FSA's] behalf'.

3 The power to investigate the affairs of a director is notable and, particularly, there is no express limitation on what aspects of the director's affairs can be investigated (eg his financial affairs).

When will the FSA use the power to investigate?

14.32 The FSA has not provided any guidance on the use of this power. Its policy on the investigation of other collective investment schemes is considered at para 14.24 ff above and it is likely that similar considerations will apply.

What information can the investigator obtain?

14.33 The investigator may require any person who he considers is, or may be, able to give information which is relevant to the investigation, to[1]:

- produce any documents in his possession or under his control which appear to the investigator to be relevant to the investigation;
- attend before him; and
- otherwise give him all assistance in connection with the investigation which he is reasonably able to give.

It is the duty of the person concerned to comply with the requirement[2].

1 FSMA 2000, s 284(3) (collective investment schemes) and ICVC Regulations, reg 30(3).
2 FSMA 2000, s 284(3) (collective investment schemes) and ICVC Regulations, reg 30(3).

14.34 This power is similar to that applicable to market abuse investigations under FSMA 2000, s 168(2)[1], in that the class of people who can be required to provide information is prescribed by reference not to the person under investigation but to those who may be able to provide relevant information[2]. On that basis, people can be required to produce documents and attend for interviews. Additionally, it contains the broad requirement that anybody who may be able to give relevant information can be required to provide all assistance which they are reasonably able to give. This provision is discussed at para 4.149 above[3].

1 See para 4.144 ff above. These powers are very similar to those of investigators appointed under the previous regime, under the Financial Services Act 1986, s 94 and the Companies Act 1985, s 434.
2 This provision is slightly (although probably imperceptibly in practice) narrower than an investigation under FSMA 2000, s 168(2), because the investigator here must consider that the person may have information which 'is relevant to the investigation' whereas under an s 168(2) investigation the relevant phrase is 'is or may be relevant to the investigation': see FSMA 2000, s 173(1).
3 See also the discussion at para 13.152 above.

14.35 Various ancillary provisions applicable to investigations generally are outlined at para 4.111 ff above. These apply equally to investigations under this provision, subject to the following points:

- an investigator appointed under s 284 or the ICVC Regulations has no ability to require a person failing to produce a document to state to the best of his knowledge and belief where the document is[1];

- there is no ability to exercise the power against a third person who has the document where the person the investigator has the power to require to produce the document does not do so[2].

1 FSMA 2000, s 175(3) is not applied to these provisions: see s 284(6) and ICVC Regulations, reg 30(6). The reason for this is not clear.
2 FSMA 2000, s 175(1) is not applied to these provisions: see s 284(6) and ICVC Regulations, reg 30(6). The reason for this is not clear.

14.36 Generally speaking, the three primary protections for those subject to investigations apply in this context, namely:

- the protection against self incrimination, where a person is charged with a criminal offence or proceedings are brought in relation to market abuse[1];
- the prohibition on being required to produce or disclose legally privileged information[2], although it is not entirely clear that this applies in the context of investigations under the ICVC Regulations[3]; and
- the limited protection for documents covered by a duty of banking confidentiality, with suitable modifications for the context[4].

There are certain restrictions on the use by the FSA of information which it obtains in an investigation, discussed at para 4.300 ff above.

1 FSMA 2000, s 284(5) (collective investment schemes) and ICVC Regulations, reg 30(5). For a more detailed discussion of the right of privilege against self-incrimination, see para 4.242 ff above.
2 FSMA 2000, s 413. Note that the FSMA 2000 effectively contains its own definition of legal privilege. Generally, see para 4.264 ff above.
3 FSMA 2000, s 413 says that a person may not be 'required under this Act to produce ...'. It is not clear that this encompasses a requirement imposed under the ICVC Regulations, which would be imposed not directly under the FSMA 2000 but under secondary legislation made under the FSMA 2000. Contrast s 413 with s 401, which refers to 'an offence under this Act or under subordinate legislation made under this Act'. Note also that HM Treasury felt it necessary specifically to provide in the ICVC Regulations (see regs 81 and 82) that certain general provisions of the FSMA 2000 relating to offences 'under this Act' apply to offences under the ICVC Regulations. There is no equivalent provision in the ICVC Regulations applying s 413 to those Regulations. In practice, it may be that the FSA would not require privileged material to be produced. Otherwise, it may be possible to argue against producing the material based not only on the construction of s 413 but also on ECHR rights to a fair trial (art 6(1)) and to respect for privacy (art 8).
4 FSMA 2000, s 284(8) to (10) (collective investment schemes) and ICVC Regulations, reg 30(8). For a more detailed discussion, see para 4.267 ff above.

Can the firm refuse to provide information?

14.37 In general, firms must comply with a requirement to provide information imposed by an investigator. The only clear exceptions are for legally privileged material[1] and, in some cases, information subject to a duty of banking confidentiality[2], although there may be other, specific objections to complying with a requirement in the particular case[3].

1 But, in relation to investigations under the ICVC Regulations, see para 14.36 above.

2 In practice, this protection is extremely limited and can be overridden: see the discussion at para 4.267 ff above.
3 Some of these are discussed at para 4.260 ff above.

14.38 Failure to comply with a requirement imposed in an investigation under s 284 or the ICVC Regulations has, broadly, the same consequences as a failure to comply in the context of an investigation under FSMA 2000, Pt XI, discussed in Chapter 4 above. Thus, for example[1]:

- a court may treat the person as if he were in contempt[2];
- the FSA may be able to obtain a warrant to search premises and seize the documents[3];
- the destruction or falsification of documents, or the provision of false or misleading information, may constitute a criminal offence[4]; and
- there may also be regulatory enforcement consequences, particularly if the person concerned is an authorised firm or approved person[5].

1 The consequences of failing to comply are discussed in more detail at para 4.283 ff above.
2 FSMA 2000, s 177(1) and (2), applied by s 284(6) (collective investment schemes) and ICVC Regulations, reg 30(6).
3 FSMA 2000, s 176, applied by s 284(7) (collective investment schemes) and ICVC Regulations, reg 30(7).
4 FSMA 2000, s 177(3) and (4), applied by s 284(6) (collective investment schemes) and ICVC Regulations, reg 30(6).
5 Note ICVC Regulations, reg 80 (a person who contravenes a provision of the Regulations is to be treated as having contravened FSA rules made under FSMA 2000, s 138).

How is an investigation commenced and controlled?

14.39 An investigation commenced under s 284 or the ICVC Regulations is, subject to one caveat, initiated and controlled by the FSA or, where appropriate, the Secretary of State, in the same way as any other investigation[1]. The provisions outlined at para 4.157 ff above regarding the appointment of investigators and control of the investigation therefore apply in this context. Practical guidance for firms dealing with investigations can be found at para 4.179 ff above.

1 The relevant provisions are found at FSMA 2000, s 170(5) to (9), applied in this context by FSMA 2000, s 284(4) (collective investment schemes) and ICVC Regulations, reg 30(4).

14.40 The one, notable difference is that there is no requirement in this context for written notice of the appointment of an investigator to be given to any of the persons under investigation or affected by the investigation[1]. It is not clear what the rationale is for disapplying the normal notice requirements. The reason for doing so in the context of market misconduct investigations is that in many situations there will not be a 'person under investigation', at least at the outset. However, it is difficult to see that the same issue arises here. In practice, those involved in the scheme are likely to be aware of the investigation because they will be asked to provide information to the investigator, and it is likely that the

FSA will provide an indication of the nature and subject matter of the investigation to those who are asked to assist[2]. In practice, the FSA may nonetheless consider notifying the person concerned, at least when it exercises its statutory powers to require information from that person[3]. However, this may not equate to the specific information as to the reasons for the appointment of an investigator, which the FSMA 2000 requires the FSA to provide where there is a statutory duty to notify[4].

1 Anomalously, the person subject to the investigation does have to be notified where there is a change in the scope or conduct of the investigation and, in the opinion of the FSA (or the Secretary of State), that person is likely to be significantly prejudiced by not being made aware of it. In that circumstance, the person must be given written notice of the change: FSMA 2000, s 170(9), applied by s 284(4) and ICVC Regulations, reg 30(4).
2 See the FSA Handbook at ENF 2.12.5 (although this guidance is not specifically said to apply in the current context).
3 See the FSA Handbook at ENF 2.12.4 to 2.12.6 and see the discussion at para 4.159 ff above.
4 FSMA 2000, s 170(4).

ENFORCEMENT ACTION IN RELATION TO REGULATED COLLECTIVE INVESTMENT SCHEMES

Introduction

14.41 Outlined in the following paragraphs are the FSA's specific enforcement powers in relation to regulated collective investment schemes. In summary, these are as follows:

- unit trusts:
  - to revoke the authorisation of a unit trust,
  - to intervene in a unit trust, by giving certain types of directions to the manager and/or trustee,
  - to apply to the court for an order removing and replacing the manager and/or trustee of a unit trust and in some circumstances to wind up the scheme;
- ICVCs:
  - to revoke the authorisation of the ICVC,
  - to intervene in an ICVC by giving certain types of directions,
  - to apply to the court for an order removing and replacing the depositary and/or any director of the ICVC and, in some circumstances, to wind up the scheme;
- other recognised schemes:
  - to suspend promotion of a UCITS scheme[1], and
  - to suspend or revoke the recognition of a section 270 scheme or a section 272 scheme[2].

1 A scheme constituted in another EEA State: see para 14.7 above.
2 See para 14.7 above.

14.42 As this indicates, which power is applicable depends upon the type of scheme. The powers are therefore outlined below separately in relation to each type of scheme. The procedure for exercising each power is also outlined.

14.43 Whilst the FSA has a range of statutory enforcement powers available to it in appropriate cases, experience under the previous regime suggests that it is rare in practice for it to need to exercise these powers. The FSA has given little indication of its policy on the exercise of its powers under the FSMA 2000 but, in practice, many issues relating to schemes may be capable of being resolved either by agreement outside the enforcement context (for example, by the manager or trustee agreeing to make particular changes to their procedures or controls) or by enforcement action against the manager or trustee, as distinct from the scheme itself.

14.44 As this indicates, these provisions need to be viewed in context. They are not exhaustive of the action the FSA may seek to take arising from activities in connection with a regulated collective investment scheme. Having investigated the situation, the FSA may wish to take action not only in relation to the scheme but also, or alternatively[1], against those involved in it, for example the manager, trustee, custodian and/or sales force[2]. It may therefore be appropriate for it to use its more general enforcement powers against such persons.

1 Indeed, one of the relevant factors for the FSA in deciding whether to take enforcement action in relation to a scheme is whether its concerns can be resolved by taking action against the manager and/or trustee instead: see para 14.90 below. For a list of the range of general enforcement powers, see para 4.320 above.
2 The position is significantly simpler than it was under the previous regime, where several regulators may typically have needed to be involved. The FSA had the power to take action in relation to the scheme itself, but the manager, trustee, custodian and sales force were likely to be regulated by different SROs.

14.45 Which power or combination of powers it is appropriate for the FSA to use will depend upon the particular situation. For example, if there has also been a breach of the FSA's Conduct of Business rules, then it may seek to exercise its disciplinary powers against a firm or an approved person involved[1], as well as or instead of taking action in relation to the scheme itself. Alternatively, the matter may raise more fundamental concerns about whether a particular firm should be involved in schemes at all, perhaps because its systems and controls were shown to be inadequate, in which case variation of the firm's permission could be under consideration. Firms thus need to consider the possible wider consequences, so that they can take appropriate action to address them and, where appropriate, to protect their position[2].

1 Numerous examples can be seen in IMRO's Press Releases under the previous regime.
2 Examples of issues relating to unit trusts which have led to wider regulatory action under the previous regime include: (i) the *Morgan Grenfell/Peter Young* affair in late 1996, which led to the suspension of the unit trusts, IMRO disciplinary action against the manager, the current and a former trustee and various individuals and to compensation being paid to investors (see IMRO

Press Releases of 20 December 1996, 37/96, 05/97, 03/98 and 04/98) and (ii) the problems relating to *Waverley Unit Trust Management* which led to various unit trusts being suspended in early 1998, to IMRO disciplinary action against the manager and to an individual's registration being terminated (see IMRO Press Releases 12/98 and 13/98 and FSA News Releases 7 and 8 of 1998). (Waverley's membership of the PIA was subsequently terminated when a resolution for its winding up was passed (see PIA/D0041/99)).

Enforcement in relation to unit trusts

14.46 The FSA has three separate powers in relation to unit trusts[1], namely:

- the power to revoke the scheme's authorisation;
- the power to direct the manager to cease issuing or redeeming units or to wind up the scheme[2]; and
- the power to apply to the court for an order removing and replacing the manager or trustee and in some circumstances appointing an authorised person to wind up the scheme.

Each is considered in turn below, followed by a review of the FSA's policy in deciding whether to exercise its powers and, if so, which power and, finally, an outline of the procedure for exercising each power.

1 This, broadly, repeats the statutory position under the previous regime, found in the Financial Services Act 1986, Pt I, Ch VIII. In practice, it was rare for these powers to be exercised.
2 It is notable that this power can be exercised as a matter of urgency, taking immediate effect: see para 14.74 below.

Revoking the scheme's authorisation

14.47 The authorisation of unit trusts, enabling them to be marketed to the public[1], is one of the FSA's responsibilities under the FSMA 2000[2]. A unit trust becomes authorised when the FSA makes an order declaring it to be an authorised unit trust scheme, which the FSA may do if the scheme fulfils certain requirements[3]. In certain circumstances, the FSMA 2000 allows the FSA to revoke an authorisation order. It is likely to be rare in practice that the FSA will do so, but the consequences are, plainly, extremely serious.

1 FSMA 2000, s 238 and see the Financial Services and Markets Act 2000 (Promotion of Collective Investment Schemes) (Exemptions) Order 2001, SI 2001/1060.
2 FSMA 2000, s 243.
3 FSMA 2000, s 243. The requirements are discussed briefly at para 14.52 below.

14.48 The FSA may revoke an authorisation order if it appears to it that[1]:

- one or more of the requirements for the making of the authorisation order are no longer satisfied;
- the manager or trustee of the scheme concerned has contravened a requirement imposed on him by or under the FSMA 2000;

- the manager or trustee of the scheme has knowingly or recklessly provided the FSA with false or misleading information;
- no regulated activity has been carried on in relation to the scheme for at least 12 months; or
- none of the above applies, but it is desirable to revoke the authorisation order to protect the interests of participants or potential participants.

Each of these grounds is considered in turn, at para 14.51 ff below.

1 FSMA 2000, s 254. The power, and the grounds for exercising it, are very similar to the former power under the Financial Services Act 1986, s 79.

14.49 In common with many other provisions of the FSMA 2000[1], the power is exercisable provided only that it 'appears to the FSA' that one of the criteria has been satisfied. This provides a fairly low hurdle for the FSA and leaves the matter to a large extent within its judgment, at least initially. This is particularly the case with criteria such as 'desirable in the interests of participants or potential participants', which are primarily a matter of judgment. Certain other criteria, for example whether or not any regulated activity has been carried on for 12 months, should be capable of ascertainment more objectively. Ultimately, though, whether the revocation of authorisation is an appropriate regulatory response may be tested in the Tribunal[2].

1 See, for example, the formal investigation powers discussed in Chapter 4 above.
2 See para 14.95 below and generally Chapter 6 above.

14.50 Before revoking a scheme's authorisation, the FSA will generally first require the manager or trustee to wind up the scheme (or seek a court order for the appointment of a firm to do so)[1], in recognition of the financial interest which participants have in the scheme property[2]. This is important, because it recognises that revoking a scheme's authorisation could potentially place the participants in a worse position.

1 See para 14.84 below.
2 See the FSA Handbook at ENF 16.2.14. As to the FSA's ability to order a scheme to be wound up, see para 14.66 below.

Requirements for authorisation order are no longer satisfied

14.51 An authorisation order may be revoked by an order made by the FSA if it appears to the FSA that one or more of the requirements for the making of the order are no longer satisfied[1].

1 FSMA 2000, s 254(1)(a).

14.52 The requirements which must be satisfied for a unit trust scheme to obtain authorisation are prescribed under FSMA 2000, s 243 and are of two basic types:

- the scheme must comply with certain, mostly formal, requirements set out in s 243[1]. Among other things, the manager and trustee must be independent of each other, each must be an authorised person and have the relevant permissions, and the purposes of the scheme must be reasonably capable of being successfully carried into effect; and

- the scheme must comply with the requirements of the trust scheme rules[2], that is the FSA's rules regulating unit trusts[3].

1 FSMA 2000, s 243(1)(a) and (c).
2 FSMA 2000, s 243(1)(b).
3 See the FSA Handbook at CIS. The rules are made under FSMA 2000, s 247. This provision is potentially wide enough to refer not only to the rules relating to the constitution of the scheme but also, for example, to those relating to its operation and the powers, duties etc of the manager and trustee. In theory, therefore, it seems that a breach of any of the trust scheme rules could give rise to the FSA exercising its power under this head. In practice, though, a breach of the rules other than those relating to the constitution of the scheme may be more likely to be dealt with under the second ground for revoking authorisation (see para 14.55 below).

14.53 In broad terms, the sorts of issues which could give rise to the criteria for revoking an authorisation order being fulfilled therefore include:

- a variation of permission of the manager or trustee, so that they no longer have permission to be a manager or trustee of the scheme, or the cancellation of their permission and authorisation[1];
- changes in circumstances such that the purposes of the scheme are no longer reasonably capable of being successfully carried into effect; and
- possibly, breaches of the trust scheme rules[2].

1 In practice, it may be more likely that the manager or trustee would be replaced, rather than the scheme's authorisation order being revoked.
2 See footnote 3 to para 14.52 above.

14.54 Whether the FSA would act in the particular case is a separate question. The FSA's general policy on enforcement action in relation to unit trusts is considered at para 14.88 below. In relation to this ground specifically, it has made clear[1] that it expects any non-compliance to be resolved as soon as possible. Important factors in considering whether to exercise its powers are likely to be whether participants have suffered loss due to the non-compliance and whether remedial steps will be taken to satisfy all the requirements of the order.

1 See the FSA Handbook at ENF 16.2.10(2).

Manager or trustee has contravened a requirement by or under the FSMA 2000

14.55 An authorisation order may be revoked by an order made by the FSA if it appears to the FSA that the manager or trustee of the scheme concerned has contravened a requirement imposed on him by or under the FSMA 2000[1].

1 FSMA 2000, s 254(1)(b).

14.56 The phrase 'contravene a requirement imposed by or under the FSMA 2000' recurs throughout the FSMA 2000[1]. It includes contraventions of the trust scheme rules, as well as breaches of the Principles for Businesses and other specific rules made by the FSA under the FSMA 2000. It also includes breaches of prohibitions imposed directly under the FSMA 2000, probably including those with criminal law consequences.

1 For a detailed discussion, see para 2.142 ff above.

14.57 In theory, any such contravention by a person who was a manager or trustee of a scheme, whether or not the contravention related to the scheme, would entitle the FSA to revoke the authorisation order[1]. Whether revoking authorisation is an appropriate regulatory response to a particular contravention is, however, a different matter and, ultimately, that issue could be referred to the Tribunal[2]. The FSA's general policy on using its enforcement powers is discussed at para 14.88 below. In relation to this ground specifically, the FSA will consider the seriousness of the contravention including[3]:

- the extent to which it was deliberate or reckless;
- the extent of loss or risk of loss caused to existing or potential participants in the scheme;
- whether it highlights serious or systemic weaknesses in the management or control of either the scheme itself or the scheme property;
- whether there are grounds for believing it is likely to be continued or repeated;
- the length of time over which it occurred; and
- whether participants in the scheme have been misled in a material way, for example, about the investment objectives or policy of the scheme or the level of investment risk.

1 This issue was debated in Standing Committee, with a proposal from the Opposition that only contraventions of rules made under Pt XVII should be relevant for this purpose. The Government's view (Economic Secretary to HM Treasury, 30 November 1999) was that it is vital the FSA can take action when any requirement imposed by or under the FSMA 2000 is breached. 'Obviously, the FSA must behave proportionately. If there is no danger to the scheme or cause for concern, the FSA could not revoke authorisation, but it could do so if the rule breach under another clause were relevant.'
2 See para 14.95 below and generally Chapter 6 above.
3 See the FSA Handbook at ENF 16.2.10(1).

14.58 Whether or not the contravention results in the authorisation order being revoked, it may give rise to other regulatory implications. For example, the firm may, as a result, be liable to FSA disciplinary proceedings[1], civil claims for damages[2], or other enforcement action such as a restitution order[3] or an injunction[4]. An incoming firm could be the subject of intervention action[5]. Any individual approved persons involved may also be personally liable to regulatory action[6].

1 See para 7.9 ff above.
2 See para 10.29 ff above.

3 See para 7.43 ff above.
4 See para 7.97 ff above.
5 See para 9.51 ff above.
6 See Chapter 8 above.

Provision of false or misleading information

14.59 An authorisation order may be revoked by an order made by the FSA if it appears to the FSA that the manager or trustee of the scheme has, in purported compliance with a requirement imposed on him by or under the FSMA 2000, knowingly or recklessly given the FSA information which is false or misleading in a material particular[1].

1 FSMA 2000, s 254(1)(c).

14.60 The provision of accurate information to the FSA is a central tenet of the regulatory regime. Not only do firms and approved persons owe general duties to the FSA in relation to the provision of information[1], but providing false or misleading information can, in many circumstances, amount to a criminal offence[2]. Thus, if the FSA believes that it has been provided with information which is false or misleading, there may be a serious potential problem[3], possibly with wider, perhaps criminal law, repercussions. In the present context specifically, the FSA has indicated that it would be very seriously concerned if the provision of false or misleading information indicated a risk of loss to scheme property or that participants' interests may have been, or may be, affected in some other way[4].

1 See, for example, Principle 11 of the Principles for Businesses (see para 2.52 above) and Statement of Principle 4 for approved persons (see para 2.95 above).
2 For example, FSMA 2000, ss 177(4) and 398 and see para 4.287 above.
3 This is reinforced in this context in the FSA Handbook at ENF 17.4.10(5).
4 See the FSA Handbook at ENF 16.2.10(6).

No regulated activity for at least 12 months

14.61 An authorisation order may be revoked by an order made by the FSA if it appears to the FSA that no regulated activity is being carried on in relation to the scheme and the period of inactivity began at least 12 months earlier[1].

1 FSMA 2000, s 254(1)(d). This ground for revoking authorisation did not exist under the previous regime.

14.62 This is, broadly, the equivalent of the provision which allows a firm's permission to be varied if it does not carry on a particular regulated activity for at least 12 months[1]. The rationale is, broadly, that it is inappropriate for people to have permissions or authorisations which they hold purely on a 'protective' basis, allowing them to carry on activities which they are not actually undertaking.

1 FSMA 2000, s 45(1)(b) and see para 9.21 ff above.

Desirable to protect the interests of participants or potential participants

14.63 An authorisation order may be revoked by an order made by the FSA if it appears to the FSA that none of the above grounds applies but it is desirable to revoke the authorisation order in order to protect the interests of participants or potential participants in the scheme[1].

1 FSMA 2000, s 254(1)(e).

14.64 In considering this, the FSA may take into account any matter relating to the scheme, the manager or trustee, any person employed by or associated with the manager or trustee in connection with the scheme, any director of, person exercising influence over, or body corporate in the same group as the manager or trustee or any director of or person exercising influence over any such body corporate[1].

1 FSMA 2000, s 254(2).

14.65 This is the broadest of the grounds for revoking a schreme's authorisation. It is similar to the provision allowing the FSA to vary a firm's permission where it appears to it that this is desirable in order to protect the interests of consumers or potential customers[1]. However, unlike that provision, neither the FSMA 2000 nor the FSA Handbook provides much assistance in interpreting this phrase[2]. Whether it is in the interests of participants or potential participants to act is therefore a matter of judgment for the FSA, subject ultimately to the views of the Tribunal, if the matter is referred to the Tribunal[3].

1 FSMA 2000, s 45(1)(c) and see para 9.25 ff above.
2 The FSMA 2000 does provide a definition of 'participants': see FSMA 2000, s 235(1) and (2). But it does not provide any indication of what 'the interests of participants' means. The same test is used in relation to the commencement of an investigation: see the discussion at para 14.22 above.
3 See para 14.95 below.

Giving directions

What directions can the FSA give?

14.66 The FSMA 2000 allows the FSA to give specific types of directions outlined below in relation to unit trust schemes[1]. Notwithstanding the title 'powers of intervention' in the FSMA 2000, this is not a general intervention power[2].

1 These provisions are broadly similar to those previously found in the Financial Services Act 1986, s 91.
2 If the FSA wishes to take more general action, it may be able to achieve this through informal means (see the discussion at para 14.88 ff below) or it may seek to vary the manager's or trustee's permission on its own-initiative; the variation of permission allows for rather more flexibility (see generally Chapter 9 above).

14.67 The FSA may make the following two types of direction[1]:

- requiring the manager of the scheme to cease the issue and/or redemption of units under the scheme; and/or
- requiring the manager and trustee of the scheme to wind it up.

1 FSMA 2000, s 257(2).

14.68 The ability to suspend the issue and redemption of units is particularly likely to be relevant in an enforcement situation[1]. As will be seen[2], these powers can be exercised as a matter of urgency.

1 See, for example, the suspension of certain *Waverley* and *Chartfield* unit trusts in March 1998 (FSA Press Releases 7 and 8 of 1998). Under the FSA's rules, the manager may (at the request or with the agreement of the trustee or depositary) suspend the issue, cancellation, sale and redemption of units for up to 28 days if, in their opinion, there is good and sufficient reason to do so in the interests of holders or potential holders: see the FSA Handbook at CIS 13.1. A similar provision applied previously and in practice it was sometimes possible for the suspension to be effected through this means without the FSA taking formal action to suspend: see, for example, the suspension of certain *Morgan Grenfell* unit trusts in September 1996 (IMRO Press Release 05/97).
2 See para 14.74 ff below.

In what circumstances can the FSA make a direction?

14.69 The FSA may give a direction if it appears to it that[1]:

- one or more of the requirements for the making of an authorisation order are no longer satisfied;
- the manager or trustee of an authorised unit trust scheme has contravened, or is likely to contravene, a requirement imposed on him by or under the FSMA 2000;
- the manager or trustee of such a scheme has, in purported compliance with a requirement imposed on him by or under the FSMA 2000, knowingly or recklessly given the FSA information which is false or misleading in a material particular; or
- none of the above applies, but it is desirable to give a direction in order to protect the interests of participants or potential participants in such a scheme.

1 FSMA 2000, s 257(1).

14.70 With two exceptions, these criteria are the same as those for the revocation of an authorisation order under FSMA 2000, s 254[1]. The two exceptions are as follows.

1 These are discussed at para 14.47 ff above.

14.71 First, it is not a ground for making such a direction that no regulated activity has been carried on for at least 12 months. The FSA cannot therefore require the scheme to be wound up on that basis, unless the situation also falls within one of the other criteria, for example, the FSA considers this desirable in order to protect the interests of participants or potential participants.

14.72 Second, a direction may be made not only in response to contraventions which have already taken place, but also to address prospective contraventions. Thus, if the FSA can foresee that the scheme is going to fail to meet one of the requirements, for example, because a particular event will result in it not fulfilling one of the criteria under the trust scheme rules, the FSA can act preemptively.

14.73 As to when it will be appropriate for the FSA to give a direction, the FSA's general policy on enforcement action is considered at para 14.88 ff below. Certain specific factors relevant to each particular ground for taking action are outlined above[1]. In addition, the FSA has indicated that, as an example, it may be necessary to suspend the issue and redemption of units to protect the interests of existing or potential participants if information suggests the current price of units may not accurately reflect the value of the scheme property or if the scheme property cannot be valued accurately[2].

1 See the discussion of revocation orders, from para 14.47 ff above.
2 See the FSA Handbook at ENF 16.2.10(3).

When does a direction take effect?

14.74 A direction may take effect either immediately, or on a specified date, or when the matter to which it relates is no longer open to review[1].

1 FSMA 2000, s 259(1).

14.75 If the direction is to take effect either immediately or on a specified date, then this must be specified in the first supervisory notice provided by the FSA to the manager and trustee when the direction is first formally proposed or imposed[1]. The FSA may only specify that the direction takes effect immediately, or specify a date when it takes effect, if it considers that this is necessary having regard to the ground upon which it is exercising its power[2]. If neither immediate action nor a particular date is specified in the first supervisory notice, then the direction takes effect when the matter is no longer open to review[3].

1 See para 14.96 ff below.
2 FSMA 2000, s 259(2).
3 FSMA 2000, s 259(1)(c). As to when the matter is no longer open to review, see para 9.174 above.

14.76 This provision is very similar to that applicable to the FSA's own-initiative powers[1]. It allows the FSA to take immediate, urgent action on a summary basis, with the firm having the opportunity to be involved in the decision, or to challenge it, only afterwards. It is for this reason that the FSA can take such action only if it considers it necessary[2]. It may be possible, in some circumstances, for the firm to seek to have the action suspended pending the matter being referred to the Tribunal for a full hearing[3]. The imposition of urgent action may also involve immediate publicity being given to the matter[4].

1 See paras 9.99 ff and 9.194 ff above.
2 For a further discussion of this test, see para 9.196 above. Note that this provision omits the word 'reasonably' where s 53(3) says 'reasonably considers it necessary'. For reasons discussed at para 9.196 above, it is not clear that this makes any real difference.
3 See para 6.104 ff above and the discussion of practical issues for firms facing urgent action, at para 9.211 ff above.
4 See para 9.183 ff above.

How long does a direction have effect?

14.77 A direction requiring the manager to cease the issue or redemption of units has effect until the date specified in the notice or, if none is specified, the notice will state that the direction has effect until a further direction is given[1]. This is subject to the provisions allowing directions to be revoked or varied[2].

1 FSMA 2000, s 259(5).
2 See para 14.79 below.

14.78 A direction requiring the manager and trustee to wind up the scheme will require it to be wound up by a date specified in the notice or if none is specified then it must be wound up as soon as practicable[1]. Again, this is subject to the provisions allowing directions to be revoked or varied[2].

1 FSMA 2000, s 259(6).
2 See para 14.79 below.

Can a direction be revoked or varied?

14.79 A direction may be revoked or varied by the FSA either on its own initiative or on the application of the manager or trustee[1]. The FSA may do so if it appears to it that it is no longer necessary for the direction to take effect or continue in force (in which case, it will be revoked) or that it should take effect or continue in force in a different form (in which case it will be varied).

1 FSMA 2000, s 257(6).

14.80 The procedure for varying or revoking a direction is considered below[1].

1 See para 14.99 below.

What are the consequences if a direction is not complied with?

14.81 A direction is a requirement imposed by the FSA by or under the FSMA 2000. Hence, contravention by the manager or trustee could lead to a range of regulatory consequences, including in appropriate circumstances:

- the revocation of the scheme's authorisation[1];
- an application by the FSA for an injunction to restrain the contravention or require the manager or trustee to remedy it[2];
- the imposition of disciplinary sanctions against the manager and/or trustee[3]; and
- proceedings for misconduct against any approved persons involved[4].

1 See para 14.48 above.
2 See para 7.97 ff above.
3 See para 7.9 ff above.
4 See para 8.4 ff above.

14.82 In addition, the contravention potentially exposes the firm to civil claims for breach of statutory duty by private persons who have suffered loss as a result[1].

1 FSMA 2000, s 257(5) and see para 10.32 above.

Removing and replacing the manager or trustee

14.83 If the FSA could give a direction under s 257, it may also apply to the court for an order[1]:

- removing the manager or trustee, or both, of the scheme; and
- replacing the person or persons removed with a suitable person or persons nominated by the FSA.

1 FSMA 2000, s 258. This is very similar to the former s 93 of the Financial Services Act 1986. As to the circumstances in which the FSA may make a direction, see para 14.69 ff above.

14.84 The FSMA 2000 prescribes certain criteria for those whom the FSA can nominate to replace the existing manager and/or trustee[1]. If it appears to the FSA that there is no person it can nominate then it may apply to the court for an order[2]:

- removing the manager or trustee or both; and
- appointing an authorised person to wind up the scheme.

1 The FSA may nominate a person only if satisfied that the requirements of FSMA 2000, ss 243(4) to (7) would be complied with: FSMA 2000, s 258(2).
2 FSMA 2000, s 258(3).

14.85 On an application under either limb the court may make such order as it thinks fit[1].

1 FSMA 2000, s 258(4).

14.86 Three particular points are notable. First, the FSMA 2000 distinguishes this enforcement power by allowing it to be exercised only by a court[1]. It is not, therefore, simply an administrative power. This may reflect the fact that the identity of the manager (whose name will often be closely associated with that of the scheme) and, perhaps less so, the trustee (who holds the scheme's assets on behalf of unit holders) may well be of some importance to the investors. The interests of investors therefore need to be carefully considered and some investors, particularly larger ones, may want to become involved in the application. Second, whilst the FSA has no clear administrative power to remove a manager or trustee, it may in practice seek to accomplish the same by varying the manager's or trustee's permission to prohibit them from undertaking such activities[2]. Such powers could in theory be used as a matter of urgency[3]. Third, it is unclear on the wording of the FSMA 2000 whether the FSA can apply to the court instead of making a direction under s 257, or whether it can only do so where it makes a direction[4]. It might seek to do both if, for example, it wished to appoint a new manager and trustee for the purposes of winding up the scheme or if it needed to suspend the scheme while a new manager or trustee was introduced.

1 The same approach was seen in the Financial Services Act 1986.
2 See generally Chapter 9 above. It may be arguable whether it would have the right to do so, given the lack of any express power.

3 See para 9.194 ff above; in practice, the FSA would have to consider how the scheme would in the meantime be operated.
4 The FSMA 2000 uses the phrase 'if the FSA *could give* a direction . . . it may *also* apply to the court for an order . . . .' (emphasis added). The word 'also' may suggest that the FSA can only apply where it takes both steps, but the phrase 'could give' (contrast 'has given') may indicate otherwise.

14.87 The FSA's general policy on using its powers is discussed at para 14.88 below. The FSA has given three examples of the circumstances when it may seek to remove the manager or trustee[1], namely where there are grounds for concern over their behaviour in respect of the management of the scheme or its assets or where they have committed a breach or knowingly or recklessly given the FSA false or misleading information. The latter two correspond with the grounds for exercising other enforcement action in respect of the scheme[2]. The FSA recognises the effect that an order to remove a manager or trustee may have upon the relevant person's reputation and has therefore made clear it will only exercise this power where that would be proportionate in all the circumstances of the case. In practice, the removal of managers and trustees is normally accomplished by agreement and it is likely to be only in very serious cases that these powers will need to be used.

1 See the FSA Handbook at ENF 16.2.13.
2 See paras 14.48 and 14.69 above.

The FSA's policy on exercising these powers

14.88 As the discussion above highlights, the statutory grounds for taking enforcement action are wide. It will not necessarily be appropriate for the FSA to take action simply because one of them has been met. For example, a single rule breach could in theory lead to a unit trust's authorisation being revoked, whereas in practice that will rarely be the appropriate regulatory response. A key question is therefore when in practice the FSA will seek to use the powers available to it. There are two elements to this, which are to some extent bound together. First, whether it is appropriate for the FSA to exercise its enforcement powers at all and, second, if so, which power it should exercise.

14.89 In deciding whether it is appropriate to take enforcement action, the FSA will consider all the relevant circumstances[1]. It has provided an indication of the factors it may take into account, both specific factors relevant to the different statutory grounds common to some of the powers outlined above[2] and general factors applicable overall.

1 See the FSA Handbook at 16.2.10.
2 The specific factors are outlined at, respectively, paras 14.54, 14.57, 14.60 and 14.73 above.

14.90 So far as general factors are concerned, the FSA has indicated that the following may be relevant considerations[1]:

- whether the FSA's concerns can be resolved by taking enforcement action against the manager and/or trustee, without using its powers in respect of the scheme itself[2];

- the conduct of the manager or trustee in relation to and following the identification of the issue, including whether they identified the issue and brought it promptly to the FSA's attention, the degree to which they were willing to co-operate with the FSA and take protective steps, for example by suspending the issue and redemption of units, and whether they have compensated participants who have suffered loss;
- the compliance history of the trustee or manager, including previous action in relation to any other collective investment scheme; and
- whether there is information to suggest that the scheme is being used for criminal purposes or that the manager or trustee is involved in financial crime.

1 See the FSA Handbook at ENF 16.2.10.

2 In some instances, the FSA may consider it appropriate only to take direct enforcement action against the manager or trustee; in others, it may combine such action with the use of its enforcement powers against the scheme. See also the discussion at para 14.43 above.

14.91 The stance taken by the manager and trustee is an important factor in practice. The formal courses of action available to the FSA of revoking the scheme's authorisation, directing it to be wound up or applying to the court to replace the manager or trustee, are all serious measures which may have a substantial impact on the participants. In practice, many issues relating to schemes, including performance issues, are resolved by agreement. The FSA may also be able to achieve its objectives by requiring the manager and trustee to co-operate with it pursuant to their general duties under Principle 11[1] and by closely monitoring the scheme. Some enforcement issues may be able to be addressed by taking action against the manager or trustee, without directly affecting the scheme itself. This is reflected in the FSA's policy on what enforcement action it should take.

1 Principle 11 of the Principles for Businesses: see para 2.52 above.

14.92 In considering which enforcement power to exercise in the particular situation, the starting point is that the various powers may be exercised individually, in combination with each other, and in addition to direct enforcement action against a trustee or manager in their capacity as authorised firms[1]. Thus, the FSA may exercise one or more of these powers and may take other forms of regulatory action in relation to the same matter.

1 See the FSA Handbook at ENF 16.2.11.

14.93 Where the FSA has a concern that must be dealt with urgently, it will generally use its power to give directions in the first instance[1]. This is because, as will be seen, that power can be exercised as a matter of urgency, whereas the other powers require a more lengthy process to be undergone before they take effect.

1 See the FSA Handbook at ENF 16.2.12.

The procedure for taking enforcement action

Revoking the scheme's authorisation

14.94 If the FSA proposes to revoke the authorisation of a unit trust, the warning/decision notice procedure applies[1]. For a detailed discussion of the warning/decision notice procedure, see Chapter 5 above.

1 FSMA 2000, s 255.

14.95 The FSA must give separate warning notices and decision notices to both the manager and the trustee of the scheme and each has the right to refer the matter to the Tribunal on issue of the decision notice[1]. A difficult issue in practice will be how the rights of the managers and trustees interact. There is certainly the potential for one to agree with the FSA's proposed action where the other does not. Alternatively, there is a risk of each seeking an amicable resolution with the FSA, but based on different arguments and on a different basis.

1 FSMA 2000, s 255.

Giving directions

14.96 Where the FSA seeks to give a direction in relation to a unit trust, the supervisory notice procedure applies[1]. The procedure is considered in detail in Chapter 9 above. Among other things, this means that the direction can be imposed as a matter of urgency, with the firm concerned having the ability to challenge it only subsequently[2].

1 FSMA 2000, ss 259 and 395(13)(d).
2 For a discussion of various practical issues that arise when action is taken as a matter of urgency, see para 9.194 ff above. Note that it may be possible to apply to the Tribunal for the FSA's action to be suspended pending the outcome of Tribunal proceedings: see para 6.104 ff above.

14.97 A first supervisory notice issued in this context must[1]:

- give details of the direction the FSA proposes to make;
- inform the person when the direction takes effect;
- give the FSA's reasons for giving the direction and for determining when it should take effect;
- inform the person of his right to make representations to the FSA within the period specified in the notice, irrespective of whether he refers the matter to the Tribunal; and
- inform him of his right to refer the matter to the Tribunal (and provide an indication of the procedure on such a reference)[2].

1 FSMA 2000, s 259(4).
2 FSMA 2000, s 259(12).

14.98 In some situations[1] the FSA may be able to inform the scheme management[2] of its concerns and the action it is considering before it exercises its statutory powers. Alternatively, the scheme management may ask the FSA to exercise one of its powers, for example to suspend the issue and redemption of units pending resolution of a temporary problem in valuing the scheme property. In such circumstances, if there is a common understanding between the FSA and all the members of the scheme management about the need for the exercise of the power, the FSA may use a modified decision-making procedure, considered in detail at para 9.232 ff above.

1 See the FSA Handbook at DEC 4.5.15.
2 This refers to, as applicable, the manager and trustee of a unit trust, directors and depositary of an ICVC, and the operator and any trustee or depositary of a recognised scheme: see the FSA Handbook at DEC 4.5.14.

14.99 Once a direction has been made, the firm may apply to the FSA to have it varied or revoked[1]. The FSA may also consider whether to vary or revoke a direction on its own initiative. In either case:

- if the FSA, on an application from the firm, declines to revoke or vary the direction or proposes to vary it in some other way, then the warning/ decision notice procedure applies[2];
- if the FSA decides on its own initiative to revoke a direction, it must give written notice to both the manager and the trustee[3]. If it decides to accede to an application to revoke or vary a direction, then it must give written notice to the applicant[4]. In both cases, the notice is simply a notification and neither the warning/decision notice procedure nor the supervisory notice procedure applies.

1 See para 14.79 above.
2 FSMA 2000, s 260. The warning/decision notice procedure is considered in detail in Chapter 5 above. Note that the warning and decision notice are required to be served only on the applicant (FSMA 2000, s 260), but see FSMA 2000, s 393 (rights of third parties; discussed at para 5.150 ff above).
3 FSMA 2000, s 261(1).
4 FSMA 2000, s 261(2).

Removing or replacing the manager or trustee

14.100 The power to remove and replace the manager or trustee is exercisable by the court, on an application by the FSA. There is no particular procedure for the FSA to reach a decision to make such an application, as the safeguards for the firm are provided in the court process, not in the FSA's internal decision-making process[1]. The application is made in accordance with the Civil Procedure Rules. Written notice of making the application must be given to both the manager and the trustee[2].

1 This notwithstanding, the FSA has provided a procedure to be followed in taking a decision to make most types of application to the civil courts under the FSMA 2000: see the FSA Handbook at DEC 4.6 and footnote 1 to para 7.126 above. However, that procedure is not said to apply in relation to an application under this provision: see the FSA Handbook at DEC 1.1.3.
2 FSMA 2000, s 258(6).

Enforcement in relation to ICVCs

14.101 The FSA has three powers in relation an ICVC, namely to:

- revoke its authorisation;
- intervene by making certain types of directions;
- apply to the court for an order removing and replacing the depositary and/or a director and in some circumstances to wind up the ICVC.

Each is considered in turn below. We then consider the FSA's policy on when it will exercise these powers and, finally, the procedure for doing so. These provisions mirror to a large extent those applicable to unit trusts and much of the discussion therefore refers to para 14.46 ff above.

Revoking the ICVC's authorisation

14.102 The FSA may revoke an authorisation order made in respect of an ICVC[1]. The grounds on which the power can be exercised are that it appears to the FSA that[2]:

- any requirement for the making of the authorisation order is no longer satisfied;
- the ICVC, any of its directors, or its depositary has contravened a requirement imposed by or under the FSMA 2000 or has, in purported compliance with any such requirement, knowingly or recklessly given the FSA information which is false or misleading in a material particular;
- no regulated activity has been carried on in relation to the company for the previous 12 months; or
- it is desirable to revoke the authorisation order in order to protect the interests of shareholders or potential shareholders in the company[3].

These grounds are very similar to those for the revocation of the authorisation of a unit trust scheme and are discussed in detail at para 14.48 ff above.

1 ICVC Regulations, reg 23.
2 ICVC Regulations, reg 23(1).
3 In considering whether to revoke the authorisation order on this basis, the FSA may take into account any matter relating to various categories of connected person: see ICVC Regulations, reg 23(2).

14.103 The authorisation order in respect of an ICVC is fundamental to the incorporation of the company[1]. Hence, the revocation of authorisation must be accompanied by its winding up. The ICVC Regulations therefore require that, before revoking any authorisation order that has come into effect, the FSA must ensure that such steps as are necessary and appropriate to secure the winding up of the company (whether by the court or otherwise) have been taken[2].

1 ICVC Regulations, reg 3.
2 ICVC Regulations, reg 23(3). In practice, this is similar to the position regarding unit trusts: see para 14.50 above.

Giving directions

14.104 The provisions relating to the giving of directions in relation to ICVCs are similar to those regarding directions in relation to unit trust schemes, discussed at para 14.66 ff above, but with modifications to take account of the corporate structure of an ICVC.

14.105 The ICVC Regulations prescribe the directions that may be given. Broadly, they may require[1]:

- the company to cease the issue and/or redemption of shares and/or certain types of transfers of shares in the company;
- the distribution and realisation of investments in umbrella companies[2]; or
- the winding up of the company.

1 For the details, see ICVC Regulations, reg 25(2).
2 Unlike a unit trust, an ICVC can operate as an umbrella fund, having a series of sub-funds (for example, Far Eastern Recovery, European Growth, etc).

14.106 The grounds on which a direction may be given[1] are that:

- one or more of the requirements for the making of the authorisation order are no longer satisfied;
- the ICVC, any of its directors, or its depositary has contravened or is likely to contravene any requirement imposed by or under the FSMA 2000 or has, in purported compliance with any such requirement, knowingly or recklessly given the FSA information which is false or misleading in a material particular; or
- it is desirable to revoke the authorisation order in order to protect the interests of shareholders or potential shareholders in the company[2].

These grounds are very similar to those applicable to directions in relation to unit trust schemes[3], save that they are concerned with the actions of the company, any of its directors or its depositary (rather than with the manager or trustee of the unit trust).

1 ICVC Regulations, reg 25(1).
2 In considering whether to revoke the authorisation order on this basis, the FSA may take into account any matter relating to various categories of connected person: see ICVC Regulations, reg 25(5).
3 See para 14.69 above.

14.107 In the same way as a direction relating to a unit trust scheme, a direction relating to an ICVC may take effect either immediately, or on a specified date, or when the matter to which it relates is no longer open to review[1]. This provision is discussed in more detail at para 14.74 ff above.

1 ICVC Regulations, reg 27(1).

14.108 Again, there are similar provisions in relation to the duration of a direction[1] and allowing the FSA to revoke or vary a direction either on its own initiative or on application by the ICVC or its depositary[2].

1 ICVC Regulations, reg 27(5) and (6) and see paras 14.77 and 14.78 above.
2 ICVC Regulations, reg 25(7) and see para 14.79 above.

14.109 Non-compliance with a direction carries broadly the same potential consequences as are outlined at para 14.81 above[1].

1 Note, in particular, reg 25(6) of the ICVC Regulations, which applies FSMA 2000, s 150 (actions for breach of statutory duty: see para 10.32 above) where a person contravenes a direction.

Removing and replacing the depositary or a director

14.110 If the FSA could give a direction under reg 25 then it may apply to the court for an order removing the depositary or any director of the ICVC and replacing the relevant person with a person nominated by the FSA[1]. On such an application, the court may make such order as it thinks fit[2].

1 ICVC Regulations, reg 26(1) and (2). Note the omission of the word 'also' which appears (in relation to unit trusts) in FSMA 2000, s 258(1): see the discussion at para 14.86 above and in particular footnote 4. This seems to suggest, in relation to ICVCs, that the FSA may make such an application to the court without also itself giving a direction.
2 ICVC Regulations, reg 26(5).

14.111 The ICVC Regulations prescribe certain criteria for those whom the FSA may nominate[1]. If it appears to the FSA that there is no person whom it may nominate, then it may apply to the court for an order removing the director or depositary and appointing an authorised person to wind up the company[2]. On such an application, the court may make such order as it thinks fit[3].

1 ICVC Regulations, reg 26(3).
2 ICVC Regulations, reg 26(4).
3 ICVC Regulations, reg 26(5).

14.112 These provisions are very similar to those relating to unit trusts.

The FSA's policy on exercising these powers

14.113 In deciding whether to exercise one or more of these powers, the FSA will take into account broadly similar factors as in relation to a unit trust[1] and, in deciding which power to use, will again adopt a broadly similar approach[2]. One notable difference is that the FSA's general disciplinary powers are also available against an ICVC[3].

1 See the FSA Handbook at ENF 16.3.4. As to those factors, see para 14.88 ff above.
2 As to the FSA's approach in relation to a unit trust, see para 14.92 above.
3 An ICVC is an authorised person: see para 14.11 above.

The procedure for taking enforcement action

Revoking the ICVC's authorisation

14.114 If the FSA proposes to revoke the authorisation of an ICVC[1], the warning/decision notice procedure applies[2]. For a detailed discussion, see Chapter 5 above.

1 ICVC Regulations, reg 23 and see para 14.102 above.

2 ICVC Regulations, reg 24. See also regulations 8 to 11, which apply the provisions of the FSMA 2000 relating to, respectively, notices (ss 387 to 390), publication (s 391), the FSA's procedures (s 395) and the Tribunal (s 133). FSMA 2000, ss 393 (third party rights) and 394 (right of access to the FSA's material) also apply in the normal way in relation to warning/decision notices under regulation 24: see reg 24(3). But compare reg 28 (See para 14.119 below).

14.115 The warning and decision notices must be given both to the company and to its depositary and, following issue of a decision notice, either may refer the matter to the Tribunal. Certain practical difficulties to which this may give rise have been outlined at para 14.95 above. Where there is a common understanding between the FSA and all of the scheme's management[1] about the need for the exercise of the power, the FSA may use a modified decision-making process[2].

1 See footnote 2 to para 14.98 above.

2 See the FSA Handbook at DEC 4.5.15 and see para 14.98 above. The decision is delegated by the RDC to FSA staff of an appropriate level of seniority and will be as outlined at para 9.232 ff above but adapted for a case involving warning/decision notices: see the FSA Handbook at DEC 4.5.15(2).

Giving directions

14.116 If the FSA proposes to give a direction in relation to an ICVC, then the supervisory notice procedure applies[1]. The procedure is considered in detail in Chapter 9 above.

1 ICVC Regulations, reg 27 and note in particular reg 27(15). However, it is not clear that FSMA 2000, s 391 (publication) applies to supervisory notices issued under this regulation. This does not seem to be achieved by either reg 9 (supervisory notices are not among those mentioned in reg 8) or reg 27(15).

14.117 A first supervisory notice issued in this context must[1]:

- give details of the direction;
- inform the person to whom it is given of when the direction takes effect;
- state the FSA's reasons for giving the direction and for its determination as to when it takes effect;
- inform the person that he may make representations to the FSA within a specified period (whether or not he has referred the matter to the Tribunal); and
- inform him of his right to refer the matter to the Tribunal (and give an indication of the procedure on such a reference[2]).

1 ICVC Regulations, reg 27(4).

2 ICVC Regulations, reg 27(12).

14.118 In cases where there is a common understanding between the FSA and all of the scheme management as to the need for the action, the FSA may use a modified decision-making process[1].

1 See the FSA Handbook at DEC 4.5.15 and the discussion at para 14.98 above.

14.119 Where the FSA considers whether to vary or revoke a direction already made, either on an application by the firm or on its own initiative:

- if the FSA, on an application from the firm, declines to revoke or vary the direction or proposes to vary it in some other way, then the warning/decision notice procedure applies[1];
- if the FSA decides, on its own initiative, to revoke a direction, it must give written notice to both the company and its depositary[2]. If it decides to accede to an application to revoke or vary a direction, it must give written notice to the applicant[3]. In either case, the notice is simply a notification and neither the warning/decision notice procedure nor the supervisory notice procedure applies.

1 ICVC Regulations, reg 28. The warning and decision notice is given only to the applicant. Note that FSMA 2000, ss 393 and 394 (third party rights and rights of access to FSA material: see respectively paras 5.150 and 5.81 above) do not appear to apply in relation to warning/decision notices under this regulation (compare reg 24(3)).
2 ICVC Regulations, reg 29(1).
3 ICVC Regulations, reg 29(2).

Removing and replacing the depositary or a director

14.120 This power is exercisable by the court on application by the FSA. The FSA's decision to make such an application does not require any particular procedure to be followed. The application to the court is made in accordance with the Civil Procedure Rules[1].

1 This notwithstanding, the FSA has provided a procedure to be followed in taking a decision to make most types of application to the civil courts under the FSMA 2000: see the FSA Handbook at DEC 4.6 and footnote 1 to para 7.126 above. However, that procedure is not said to apply in relation to an application under this provision: see the FSA Handbook at DEC 1.1.3.

14.121 The FSA is required to give written notice of the making of the application to the company and its depositary and, if the application seeks the removal of a director, the director concerned[1]. It must also take such steps as it considers appropriate to bring the making of the application to the attention of the shareholders of the company.

1 ICVC Regulations, reg 26(7).

Enforcement in relation to recognised schemes

14.122 The action which can be taken by the FSA depends on whether the scheme is:

- a UCITS scheme, recognised under FSMA 2000, s 264[1]; or
- a scheme from a designated territory or an individually recognised scheme, recognised under FSMA 2000, ss 270 or 272[2].

The provisions applicable to each, including the FSA's policy on exercising its powers and the procedure for doing so, are considered in turn below.

1 See para 14.7 above.
2 See para 14.7 above.

UCITS schemes

14.123 The FSA's enforcement power under the FSMA 2000 in relation to UCITS schemes is to suspend the promotion of the scheme[1]. The FSA suspends the promotion of the scheme by making, broadly, a direction to that effect[2], which it may do if it appears to it that the operator of a scheme has communicated an invitation or inducement in relation to the scheme in a manner contrary to the financial promotion rules[3].

1 It should, however, be borne in mind that the FSA would have the power to take other enforcement action, in appropriate circumstances, against any authorised persons or approved persons who are involved in the operation or promotion of the scheme: see para 14.130 below.
2 For the details, see FSMA 2000, s 267(2).
3 FSMA 2000, s 267(1). Note that a breach must already have occurred: it does not appear to be sufficient that the FSA believes the operator *will communicate* an invitation or inducement contrary to the financial promotion rules.

14.124 This is therefore a relatively limited power applicable only for breaches of the financial promotion rules.

When does the suspension take effect?

14.125 The suspension takes effect either immediately, or on such date as may be specified, or when the matter is no longer open to review[1]. This is a similar provision to that applicable to directions given by the FSA in relation to unit trusts[2].

1 FSMA 2000, s 268(1).
2 See the discussion at para 14.74 ff above.

How long does the suspension last?

14.126 The direction has effect for a specified period or until the occurrence of a specified event or until specified conditions are complied with[1]. The effect is slightly different, depending upon which formulation is used:

- if an event is specified, then the direction ceases to have effect on the occurrence of that event (unless it has been revoked earlier)[2];
- if conditions are specified, it is not clear whether the fulfilment of the conditions automatically discharges the suspension. This seems to be the implication[3], but the FSMA 2000 also allows the FSA to revoke a direction either on

its own initiative or on the application of the operator of the scheme if it appears to it that the conditions specified have been complied with[4];

- where a period is specified, it seems that the suspension is discharged automatically on the attainment of that period, but this is not clear[5].

Firms may therefore wish to confirm with the FSA at the relevant time that the suspension no longer applies.

1 FSMA 2000, s 267(3).
2 FSMA 2000, s 267(6).
3 See, in particular , FSMA 2000, s 267(3)(c): 'A direction under subsection (2) has effect … until the specified conditions are complied with'.
4 FSMA 2000, s 267(5)(a). Arguably, this provision would be otiose if the suspension had been automatically discharged on the fulfilment of the conditions.
5 The FSMA 2000 is entirely silent on this point. Whilst FSMA 2000, s 267(3) should have this effect, it is not clear given the provisions relating to directions for a specified period or until a specified event.

14.127 The direction need not necessarily remain in effect on the basis originally specified. The FSA may, either on its own initiative or on an application by the operator of the scheme, vary or revoke a direction[1]. It may do so if it appears to the FSA that it is no longer necessary for the direction to take effect or continue in force (in which case, it may be revoked) or that the direction should take effect or continue in force in a different form (in which case, it may be varied).

1 FSMA 2000, s 267(4) and (5).

When will the FSA consider suspending promotion of a scheme?

14.128 The FSA has given an indication of its policy on the use of this enforcement power[1]. In particular, in deciding whether a suspension order is appropriate, it will consider all the relevant circumstances, including:

- the seriousness of the breach[2]; and
- the conduct of the operator after the breach was identified, including whether it has compensated past and existing participants who have suffered loss.

1 See the FSA Handbook at ENF 16.4.3.
2 The factors listed at para 14.57 above may be relevant.

14.129 Whilst the FSA's powers in relation to UCITS schemes directly are limited, there are two additional options which may in practice provide a means for the FSA to achieve its objectives. First, the FSA may also request the UCITS scheme's home state regulator to take such action as will resolve the FSA's concerns[1], and in practice this may often be the best way for the FSA to achieve its objectives.

1 See the FSA Handbook at ENF 16.4.4.

14.130 Second, the operator, trustee or depositary of a UCITS scheme is an authorised person under FSMA 2000, Sch 5 and could therefore be subject to FSA enforcement action. The FSA may therefore consider using its more general enforcement powers, to the extent applicable to those authorised under Sch 5. For example, it could impose disciplinary sanctions for any rule breach that has been committed, apply for an injunction to prevent any further breaches or make a restitution order against the firm concerned[1].

1 See, more generally, Chapter 7 above.

Procedure for suspending the promotion of a UCITS scheme

14.131 Where the FSA proposes to give a direction suspending the promotion of a UCITS scheme[1], the supervisory notice procedure applies[2]. The procedure is considered in detail in Chapter 9 above.

1 See para 14.123 above.
2 FSMA 2000, ss 268 and 395(13)(e).

14.132 In this context, the first supervisory notice given to the scheme operator[1] must[2]:

- give details of the direction the FSA proposes to make;
- inform the operator of when the direction takes effect;
- give the FSA's reasons for giving the direction and for its determination as to when it takes effect;
- inform the operator of his right to make representations to the FSA within such period as may be specified in the notice, irrespective whether it refers the matter to the Tribunal; and
- inform the operator of its right to refer the matter to the Tribunal (and provide an indication of the procedure on such a reference[3]).

1 FSMA 2000, s 268(3)(a).
2 FSMA 2000, s 268(4).
3 FSMA 2000, s 268(12).

14.133 The FSA must also inform the competent authorities in the scheme's home state of its proposal or of the direction, as applicable[1]. It must again inform the competent authorities in the scheme's home state when issuing the second supervisory notice[2].

1 FSMA 2000, s 268(3)(b).
2 FSMA 2000, s 268(7)(b).

14.134 Where the FSA considers whether to vary or revoke a direction already made, either on an application or on its own initiative:

- if the operator applies for the direction to be varied or revoked and the FSA proposes to refuse that application or to vary the direction in some other way the warning/decision notice procedure applies[1];

- if the FSA decides to grant the application, or decides on its own initiative to revoke the direction it has already made, then it must give the operator a written notice[2]. That notice is simply a notification and neither the warning/decision notice procedure nor the supervisory notice procedure applies to it.

Also, in any of the above cases, the FSA must inform the competent authorities in the scheme's home state[3].

1 FSMA 2000, s 269(1) and (2). The warning/decision notice procedure is considered in detail in Chapter 5 above.
2 FSMA 2000, s 269(4) and (5).
3 FSMA 2000, s 269(6).

Section 270 and section 272 recognised schemes

14.135 The FSA has the power either to revoke or to suspend recognition of a scheme recognised under ss 270 or 272[1]. This is achieved in a slightly different way depending upon the type of scheme involved, but the criteria for taking such action are the same.

1 The FSA's powers in relation to schemes recognised under ss 270 or 272 are thus wider in scope than in relation to UCITS schemes and, particularly, the FSA is not limited to intervention powers relating to the promotion of the scheme.

In what circumstances can the FSA take action?

14.136 In relation to both types of schemes, the FSA may take action if it appears to it that[1]:

- the operator, trustee or depositary of the scheme has contravened (or, in relation to suspensions only, is likely to contravene) a requirement imposed on him by or under the FSMA 2000;
- the operator, trustee or depositary of the scheme has, in purported compliance with any such requirement, knowingly or recklessly given the FSA information which is false or misleading in a material particular;
- in relation to a scheme recognised under s 272 (only), one or more of the requirements for the recognition of the scheme are no longer satisfied[2];
- none of the above applies, but it is;
  - — either undesirable in the interests of the participants or potential participants that the scheme should continue to be recognised (for the revocation of the recognition); or
  - — desirable to act in order to protect the interests of participants or potential participants who are in the UK (for the suspension of the scheme).

1 FSMA 2000, ss 279 (revocation of recognition) and 281 (suspension of recognition).
2 These requirements are set out at FSMA 2000, s 272.

14.137 The first, second and fourth grounds are very similar to those applicable to the revocation of a unit trust's authorisation, and have already been considered[1]. Whether any of these tests has been satisfied is largely a matter for the FSA's judgment, at least unless or until the matter comes to be considered by the Tribunal[2].

1 See, respectively, paras 14.55, 14.59 and 14.63 above.
2 See para 14.143 ff below.

What action can the FSA take?

14.138 In the circumstances outlined above, the FSA may revoke or suspend the scheme's recognition. The revocation of recognition[1] is achieved by:

- directing that a scheme recognised under s 270 is to cease to be recognised; or
- in relation to a scheme recognised under s 272, revoking the order declaring the scheme to be a recognised scheme.

1 FSMA 2000, s 279.

14.139 The suspension of a scheme[1] is achieved by the FSA directing that that scheme is not to be a recognised scheme for a specified period or until the occurrence of a specified event or until specified conditions are complied with. The FSMA 2000 is silent on the mechanism by which a suspension is lifted once the period has elapsed, event has occurred or conditions have been complied with[2]. It therefore seems that the suspension lifts automatically in accordance with its terms, although this is not wholly clear. It may depend partly on precisely how the suspension is phrased in the particular case.

1 FSMA 2000, s 281.
2 Contrast the suspension of a UCITS Scheme: see para 14.126 above.

When does the direction take effect?

14.140 The direction takes effect either immediately, or on such date as may be specified, or when the matter to which it relates is no longer open to review[1].

1 For a further discussion, see para 14.74 ff above.

The FSA's policy on exercising these powers

14.141 The FSA has given little indication when in practice it will seek to exercise these powers, other than[1] that, in considering whether to do so, it will consider all the relevant circumstances of the case including the same factors as are relevant in deciding whether to exercise its enforcement powers in relation to unit trusts[2]. It will also take into account the conduct of the operator of the scheme and of the trustee or depositary.

1 See the FSA Handbook at ENF 16.4.7.
2 See further para 14.88 ff above.

14.142 The FSA may, as well as or instead of using these powers, ask the competent authorities of the country or territory in which the scheme is authorised to take such action as will resolve its concerns[1].

1 See the FSA Handbook at ENF 16.4.8.

The procedure for taking enforcement action

14.143 ***Revoking recognition*** If the FSA proposes to revoke the recognition of a section 270 or section 272 recognised scheme, the warning/decision notice procedure applies[1]. The procedure is considered in detail in Chapter 5 above. The relevant notices must be given to the operator and also, if there is any, the trustee or depositary of the scheme, each of whom has the right to refer the matter to the Tribunal on issue of the decision notice[2].

1 FSMA 2000, s 280.
2 Some potential practical difficulties to which this may give rise are outlined at para 14.95 above.

14.144 Where there is a common understanding between the FSA and all of the scheme's management about the need for the exercise of the power[1], the FSA may use a modified decision-making process.

1 See the FSA Handbook at DEC 4.5.15 and see the discussion at para 14.115 above (and in particular footnote 1).

14.145 There is no provision allowing the FSA to revoke a direction already given. Presumably, the operator must apply for a fresh recognition under, as appropriate, FSMA 2000, ss 270 or 272.

14.146 ***Suspending recognition*** Where the FSA proposes to make a direction suspending a section 270 or section 272 recognised scheme, the supervisory notice procedure applies[1]. The procedure is considered in detail in Chapter 9 above. Separate notices must be given to the operator of the scheme and any trustee or depositary, and each has the right to refer the matter to the Tribunal[2].

1 FSMA 2000, s 282 and 395(13)(f).
2 FSMA 2000, s 282(3), (6) and (8). Some potential practical difficulties arising from this are outlined at para 14.95 above. Note that FSMA 2000, s 282 does not specifically confer a right of reference to the Tribunal, although that is the clear implication.

14.147 In this context, the first supervisory notice must[1]:

- give details of the direction the FSA proposes to make;
- inform the person of when the direction takes effect;
- give the FSA's reasons for giving the direction and for its determination as to when it should take effect;
- inform the person of his right to make representations to the FSA within such period as may be specified in the notice, irrespective of whether he refers the matter to the Tribunal; and

- inform him of his right to refer the matter to the Tribunal (and provide an indication of the procedure on such a reference[2]).

1 FSMA 2000, s 282(4).
2 FSMA 2000, s 282(10).

14.148 Where there is a common understanding between the FSA and all of the scheme's management about the need for the exercise of the power[1], the FSA may decide to use a modified decision-making process.

1 See FSA Handbook at DEC 4.5.15 and see the discussion at para 14.98 above.

14.149 As to whether (and, if so, how) the FSA may vary a direction:

- before the second supervisory notice is issued, there is no separate procedure allowing the firm to apply for the direction, or proposed direction, to be varied. However, the firm could ask for the direction to be varied when it makes representations to the FSA, or refers the matter to the Tribunal, and as part of that process. If, in issuing the second supervisory notice, the FSA decides to give the direction in a way other than that proposed in the first supervisory notice, it must give a further first supervisory notice[1];
- once the second supervisory notice has been issued, there is no specific provision allowing the firm to apply for a variation, and none empowering the FSA to act on that application, or prescribing how it should do so;
- it may however be possible for the FSA to vary a direction on its own initiative[2], in which case it seems that the normal supervisory notice procedure applies.

1 FSMA 2000, ss 282(7)(b) and (9) and 395(13)(f) and see the discussion at para 9.169 above.
2 This is implicit in FSMA 2000, s 282(11), although the point is far from clear.

15 Listed companies

CONTENTS

Introduction 625

UKLA information gathering and investigations 630

Potential consequences of breaches of listing rules or Part VI 653

INTRODUCTION

15.1 A problem has arisen in relation to the shares of a listed company. The FSA believes that information may not have been disclosed to the market in breach of the listing rules, or that trading may have taken place by a director of the company in breach of the company's code of dealing. Who investigates? What powers do they have? Can they obtain information from the listed company? From one of the exchanges? From any authorised firms that were involved – for example, the company's brokers? From other third parties, such as the company's auditors? Following the investigation, what enforcement powers do they have, and against whom? If the exchange on which the company's shares were traded suspects that one of its own rules may have been breached, can it also take action?

15.2 As will be seen, the FSMA 2000 gives the FSA powers of investigating and enforcing the listing rules in its capacity as the UK Listing Authority. These powers overlap to some extent with the FSA's powers in relation to its more general regulatory functions, including its function of policing the market abuse regime, and with the powers of the recognised investment exchanges.

15.3 In this chapter, we review the regime under the FSMA 2000 for investigation and enforcement of the listing rules and, in particular:

- we outline briefly the FSA's function as UK Listing Authority and the overlap with its other regulatory functions and we answer the question of who may be affected by the enforcement powers of the UK Listing Authority (or 'UKLA') (para 15.6 ff);
- we consider the UKLA's powers of information gathering and investigation (para 15.18 ff); and
- we review the enforcement powers of the UKLA and the procedure for taking enforcement action (para 15.97 ff).

15.4 The FSMA 2000 contains, in Pt VI, a separate set of provisions relating to the UKLA (including separate rule-making powers[1]) and the UKLA makes its own rules and gives its own guidance as to its policy and procedures on the use of its investigation and enforcement powers[2]. These are contained in the Listing Rules and the UKLA Guidance Manual[3].

1 The UKLA also has the power to modify or dispense with the application of the listing rules in particular cases: FSMA 2000, s 101 and see the draft Listing Rules, rr 1.12 to 1.15 and draft Guidance Manual, Chapters 5 and 6. The UKLA will maintain a Helpdesk to provide assistance in interpreting the listing rules and has also proposed a procedure for the determination of issues relating to the interpretation of the listing rules outside of the statutory enforcement regime by a 'Listing Authority Review Committee': see the draft Guidance Manual, Chapter 5.

2 The discussion in this chapter of the detailed provisions of the Listing Rules and UKLA Guidance Manual is based on the draft Listing Rules and Guidance Manual published by the FSA in June 2001 (Consultation Paper 100, 'Proposed changes to the Listing Rules at N2', and Consultation Paper 100a, 'Proposed UKLA Guidance Manual'). At the time of writing, these remained in draft. However, the discussion that follows of the statutory framework for the UK Listing Authority's powers, much of the general policy, and the practical issues that arise should largely be unaffected by any amendments to the draft rules.

3 In particular, the draft Guidance Manual, Chapters 7 to 12 and Appendix 1. The draft Guidance Manual contains certain procedures and policies which the FSMA 2000 requires the UKLA to publish. Beyond this, it consists of guidance on particular rules or aspects of regulation, which is generally speaking non-binding (although if a person acts in accordance with guidance in the circumstances contemplated by that guidance, the UKLA will proceed on the footing that the person has complied with the aspects of the rules or other requirements to which the guidance relates). For a more detailed discussion of the status of guidance, see the draft Guidance Manual, paras 1.7.7 and 1.7.8, and para 2.122 ff above.

15.5 The UKLA's procedures and policy are, however, similar in many respects to those of the FSA in relation to its more general investigation and enforcement powers. Where this is the case, reference is made in this chapter to the more detailed discussion of the FSA's policy and procedures which can be found elsewhere in this book. In addition, many of the same practical issues arise when dealing with an UKLA investigation and enforcement process as arise in the context of investigation and enforcement by the FSA and, again, reference is therefore made in this chapter to the more detailed discussion that can be found elsewhere.

The FSA's function as UK Listing Authority

15.6 Since 1 May 2000, the FSA has been the UK's competent authority for listing (or 'UK Listing Authority' or 'UKLA'), a role which had historically been carried out by the London Stock Exchange. Until the FSMA 2000 came into force, the FSA carried on the functions of the UKLA under the previous legislative framework[1]. Those functions are now carried out under FSMA 2000, Pt VI.

1 Financial Services Act 1986, Pt IV.

15.7 The UKLA is a single management unit within the FSA, headed by a director who is part of the FSA's senior management team. It is funded separately from the rest of the FSA, by annual fees levied on listed companies[1].

1 Fines levied by the UKLA upon listed companies and directors for breaches of the Listing Rules are applied to reduce these fees: see para 15.129 below.

What is the UK Listing Authority?

15.8 The UKLA is a body referred to in various EU directives[1] as having functions in relation to the admission of securities to the UK's official list. Admission to the official list signifies that certain minimum standards of investor protection are in place and allows mutual recognition of listing particulars across the EU[2]. It is important to appreciate that the UKLA's functions relate only to the official list and, in particular, that the UKLA is not responsible for regulating the trading of listed securities on the recognised investment exchanges, or for admitting securities to trading on each exchange, which is a matter for each exchange itself[3].

1 The Admission to Listing Directive (79/279/EEC), Listing Particulars Directive (80/390/EEC), Interim Reports Directive (82/121/EEC) and Prospectus Directive (89/298/EEC).

2 The purpose of the official list is 'to protect investors and to improve the working of the single market by harmonising the arrangements for the listing of securities in member states. Whereas there is no obligation on issuers of securities to apply for listing, investors know that issuers of securities that are admitted to the official list of any member state are obliged to provide certain information and fulfil certain conditions if their securities are to remain on the official list. Investors can therefore have confidence that they will have access to information that is sufficient to enable them to make informed decisions. That is, of course, one of the main planks of investor protection': Economic Secretary to HM Treasury, 28 October 1999.

3 The role of the recognised investment exchanges, including their enforcement role, is briefly outlined at para 13.213 ff above. This distinction between the regulation of trading on the exchanges and the regulation of the official list was not, traditionally, easily drawn because the functions of the UKLA were (until May 2000) carried out by the London Stock Exchange. The LSE thus had the dual role of regulating trading activity on its own markets as well as being responsible for the official list. These roles have now been split and the LSE retains only the former.

15.9 The focus of the UKLA's role is therefore on the admission of securities to the official list and on the continuing obligations relevant to the continued admission of securities to the official list. This includes[1] admitting companies to be officially listed, and suspending or removing them from the official list, setting minimum standards for listing and for the continuing obligations of listed companies, enforcing those standards, including monitoring the dissemination of price sensitive information, and keeping the listing rules up to date. In particular, under the FSMA 2000 the UKLA has responsibility for the following functions[2]:

- applications for listing;
- cancellation and suspension of listing;
- approval of listing particulars, prospectuses and similar documents;
- the regulation of sponsors;
- investigation of breaches of the listing rules and certain offences under the FSMA 2000;
- disciplinary action against issuers, directors and sponsors;
- making the listing rules under FSMA 2000, Pt VI; and
- giving general guidance in relation to Pt VI.

1 See para 2.4, Consultation Paper 37, 'The Transfer of the UK Listing Authority to the FSA', December 1999.
2 See the draft Guidance Manual, para 1.3.8.

The application of the FSMA 2000 to the UKLA

15.10 The FSA's function as UKLA is treated separately in the FSMA 2000 from the FSA's wider regulatory functions. Thus:

- where the FSMA 2000 refers to the FSA in its capacity as UKLA, it refers to it specifically as 'the competent authority';
- the provisions governing the FSA in its capacity as UKLA are grouped together in the FSMA 2000, Pt VI;
- the more general provisions of the FSMA 2000 do apply to the FSA when it exercises its functions as UKLA[1], but this is subject to certain modifications set out in Sch 7. For example, the principles of good regulation[2] do not apply to the FSA's functions as UKLA under Pt VI[3]; rather, there is a separate set of principles applicable to the UKLA (although these are very similar to the principles of good regulation)[4].

1 FSMA 2000, Sch 7, para 1.
2 For the so-called principles for good regulation, see FSMA 2000, s 2(3) and see para 2.21 above.
3 FSMA 2000, Sch 7, para 2.
4 These apply to the UKLA when it exercises its general functions of: (i) making rules under Pt VI, (ii) giving general guidance in relation to Pt VI, and (iii) determining the general policy and principles by reference to which it performs particular functions under Part VI: FSMA 2000, s 73(2). The principles for good regulation applicable to such functions are, with one exception, the same as those applicable to the FSA more generally, the exception being that there is no requirement to have regard to the responsibilities of those who manage the affairs of authorised persons: FSMA 2000, s 73(1).

15.11 The UKLA has proposed guidance that it will consider the following five aims when carrying out its general functions, namely[1]:

- to provide issuers with ready access to the listed market for their securities without compromising investor protection;

- to promote investor confidence in standards of disclosure, in the conduct of issuers' affairs and in the market as a whole by the listing rules, and in particular the continuing obligations regime;
- to ensure that listed securities should be brought to the market in a way that is appropriate to their nature and number and which will facilitate an open and efficient market for trading in those listed securities;
- to ensure that an issuer makes full and timely disclosure about itself and its listed securities, at the time of listing and subsequently;
- to ensure that holders of listed equity securities should be given adequate opportunity to consider in advance and vote upon major changes in the company's business operations and matters of importance concerning the company's management and constitution.

1 See the draft Guidance Manual, para 1.3.7. These closely reflect the objectives and principles previously contained in the Introduction to the Listing Rules.

15.12 Whilst these aims are not enshrined in the legislation, they may help to explain the UKLA's approach to a particular problem and it may therefore be of assistance to have them in mind. The UKLA has also indicated that it will apply the Listing Rules flexibly in order to ensure an appropriate level of regulation[1].

1 See the draft Guidance Manual, para 1.3.10, reflecting the position under the former regime, as previously stated in the Introduction to the Listing Rules.

The overlap with the FSA's wider regulatory functions

15.13 Whilst the FSA's functions as UKLA are different from its wider role as financial services regulator[1], the two do overlap in various respects. First, although (as has already been noted) the regulation of trading on the regulated UK markets is a matter for the exchanges themselves, and not for the UKLA, the FSA does have a supervisory responsibility in relation to the recognised investment exchanges, in determining applications for recognition and monitoring their continued compliance with the recognition criteria[2].

1 'The competent authority function . . . is different from the FSA's general functions as a financial services regulator. . . . First, although there is some overlap, the constituencies covered are different. The competent authority deals with all companies with an official listing – from banks to chemical companies to telecommunication companies – and not just with financial services firms. Secondly, the duties of the competent authority are not as wide ranging. The competent authority is essentially concerned with ensuring that companies provide the necessary information for the market, with the bulk of the requirements laid down in the directives. It is not concerned with the conduct of an issuer's business in the way that the FSA is concerned with the conduct of authorised firms' dealings with their customers and each other': Economic Secretary to HM Treasury, 28 October 1999.
2 This is outlined at para 13.213 ff above.

15.14 Second, the FSA has an important role of policing market abuse and the criminal offences of insider dealing[1] and misleading statements and practices[2], including responsibility for setting the Code of Market Conduct and for bringing proceedings for market abuse and where relevant criminal proceedings[3]. The listing rules which the FSA makes in its capacity as UKLA, and the rules of the recognised investment exchanges (which, as indicated above, the FSA supervises), impact on the market abuse regime, both directly and indirectly. An important issue is how the Code of Market Conduct and these other various rules interact and this is considered at paras 13.101 ff and 13.211 ff above.

1 Under the Criminal Justice Act 1993, Pt V.
2 Under FSMA 2000, s 397.
3 These aspects of the FSA's functions are considered in Chapter 13 above.

15.15 Thirdly, the FSA has a more general role of regulating firms and approved persons who carry on regulated activities under the FSMA 2000. To the extent that a problem relating to a listed company involves a regulated firm (for example, the company's brokers or sponsor) or an approved person, there may potentially be wider regulatory consequences for that firm or person.

Who may be affected by the UKLA's enforcement powers?

15.16 As will become apparent, the UKLA's enforcement powers[1] can be exercised in relation to:

- issuers of listed securities and applicants for listing;
- directors and former directors of listed companies; and
- sponsors.

1 These are discussed in more detail at para 15.97 ff below.

15.17 Whilst these are the classes of people most directly affected by the UKLA's powers, others may also be affected, because:

- the UKLA has power to obtain information from a wide range of people[1], including unconnected third parties; and
- in addition, if a matter comes to its attention during its investigation which it considers may be of concern to another regulator, then the UKLA may be able to pass information on to that other regulator[2].

1 The UKLA's investigation powers are discussed at para 15.18 ff below.
2 The use of information by the UKLA is discussed at para 15.88 ff below.

UKLA INFORMATION GATHERING AND INVESTIGATIONS

An overview of the UKLA's investigation powers

15.18 In the following paragraphs, we review the statutory provisions and UKLA rules which allow the FSA, in its capacity as UKLA, to investigate suspected breaches of the listing rules and/or suspected criminal offences under FSMA 2000, Pt VI. As will be seen, the UKLA has both informal and formal powers of investigation and, in addition, there is an obligation on listed companies to report certain matters to the FSA without being asked specifically to do so. Thus, we review:

- the obligation on listed companies to report certain matters to the UKLA (and certain other issues to consider when a problem arises);
- the UKLA's 'informal' information gathering powers, to require listed companies and others to provide information to it (para 15.32 ff);
- formal investigations under FSMA 2000, Pt VI (para 15.46 ff); and
- the use that can be made of information obtained (para 15.88 ff).

In each case, we also outline the practical issues that arise.

15.19 Whilst the specific provisions and powers applicable to the UKLA are, as will be seen, wide-ranging in their scope and application, they nonetheless should not be viewed in isolation. The FSA also has a variety of other investigation powers which may be relevant, including:

- the power to obtain information from, require co-operation from or investigate a recognised investment exchange[1];
- if an authorised person is involved, for example because the issuer concerned happens to be an authorised person, the investigation relates to a sponsor, or information is required to be obtained from a broker, then the FSA has a range of powers, including:
  - to investigate the business of an authorised person if there is good reason for doing so[2],
  - to require information to be provided to it by notice in writing[3],
  - to require the authorised person to commission a report by a skilled person (for example an accountant) on any matter reasonably required by the FSA in connection with its functions under the FSMA 2000[4];
- the power to investigate regulatory or criminal offences, including market abuse and the criminal offences of insider dealing and misleading statements and practices[5].

1 The extent of these powers is not, on the whole, a matter for the regulated community and is therefore not considered in any detail here. Broadly, though, the FSA has formal statutory powers to obtain information from recognised investment exchanges (FSMA 2000, s 165) and, in addition, the standards which the FSA requires of recognised investment exchanges in order to secure and maintain their recognised status includes the ability and willingness to co-operate with the FSA and other regulators: see further para 13.213 ff above.
2 FSMA 2000, s 167 and see para 4.122 ff above.
3 FSMA 2000, s 165 and see para 4.59 ff above.
4 FSMA 2000, s 166 and see para 4.72 ff above.
5 FSMA 2000, s 168 and see paras 4.134 ff and 4.144 ff above.

15.20 In any situation, therefore, the FSA may have a number of options for investigating. Which it will use may depend upon the circumstances and, particularly, whether the primary matter of concern is the suspected breach of the listing rules or some other matter of regulatory concern to the FSA, such as possible market abuse or a matter relating to the conduct of an authorised person or recognised investment exchange. Where the matter may also concern another regulatory body, the UKLA will also need to consider whether it is more appropriate for that other body to investigate or whether both should investigate[1].

1 The UKLA recognises (see the draft Guidance Manual, para 7.7.4/5) that other organisations (eg the Serious Fraud Office, the Department of Trade and Industry or the Police) may have an interest in investigating and has agreed guidelines establishing a framework for liaison and co-operation among various criminal investigation and prosecution authorities: see para 11.10 ff above and the FSA Handbook at ENF Chapter 2, Annex 1G. Note that this does not eradicate the possibility of multiple investigations by different bodies.

15.21 It is important to recognise that the UKLA's powers of information gathering and investigation are fact-finding powers[1], allowing the UKLA to obtain the facts it needs before it decides what, if any, action it is appropriate to take in light of those facts[2].

1 See the draft Guidance Manual, para 7.8.1.
2 In certain circumstances, though, the UKLA may need to take urgent action before it has had the opportunity to investigate thoroughly, based on the facts then available to it: see para 15.171 below.

Obligations of self-reporting

15.22 Before any question of an investigation by the UKLA arises, the particular matter of concern must somehow come to the UKLA's attention. There is a variety of ways in which this could happen, for example, from media reporting on the market's reaction to a particular event, from information received from an exchange or another body, or from a complaint by an investor.

15.23 In addition, the draft listing rules propose to impose on companies and sponsors obligations to report breaches to it, although these proposals have been the subject of much criticism and debate. Specifically, it is proposed that:

- issuers must notify the UKLA without delay when they become aware that they have breached any provision of the listing rules[1];
- sponsors must notify the UKLA without delay when they become aware that they have breached any provision of the listing rules[2]; and
- a company must inform the UKLA as soon as practicable where it becomes aware that a director or relevant employee[3] has breached the company's code of dealing[4].

1 See the draft Listing Rules, r 1.2. This reflects the previous practice/guidance: see Consultation Paper 100 ('Proposed Changes to the Listing Rules at N2'), June 2001, para 8.5.
2 See the draft Listing Rules, r 2.2. Sponsors are also obliged to notify the UKLA in writing of certain specific matters, set out in the draft Listing Rules, r 12.29.
3 Broadly, an employee who, because of his office or employment, is likely to be in possession of

unpublished price sensitive information: see the definitions in para 1 of the Model Code, contained in the Appendix to the Listing Rules, Chapter 16.
4 See the draft Listing Rules, r 16.20.

15.24 These requirements are similar to the obligation of self-reporting imposed on authorised persons under Principle 11 of the Principles for Businesses, discussed (together with the practical implications) at para 3.41 ff above. The self-reporting obligations proposed under the listing rules are, however, not so stringent in their drafting or so wide-ranging in their scope as the self-reporting obligations imposed on authorised persons. For example, under the draft listing rules:

- the obligation to report does not arise until the relevant person becomes aware that they 'have breached' the listing rules. Suspicion that there may have been a breach, or awareness of circumstances which might arguably amount to a breach, would not appear to be sufficient to give rise to an obligation to report (although, in reality, it may be difficult to avoid hindsight being used to assess this);
- in practical terms, there may be more scope for investigating possible breaches before notifying the UKLA than there is for authorised persons under Principle 11 and the FSA's rules[1], and more scope for deciding not to report the matter to the UKLA based on reaching the view that no breach has occurred;
- the obligation to report only arises on breaches of listing rules. This is narrower than the obligation on authorised persons under Principle 11 to report, broadly, any matter relating to the firm of which the FSA would reasonably expect to be notified[2].

It is also notable that a sponsor is not obliged, under the draft listing rules, to report breaches by an issuer of which the sponsor becomes aware.

1 See the discussion at para 3.56 above.
2 See the discussion at para 3.66 ff above.

15.25 The company's or sponsor's obligation to report does not arise until it becomes aware that there has been a breach, but even then it may not wish to report to the UKLA until it has a proper command of the facts and has been able more fully to assess the risks in light of those facts. It may therefore want first to review the matter internally before making a report to the UKLA (and, indeed, in many circumstances it will be sensible to conduct a review at some stage[1]). To what extent is it open to it to do so?

1 Various legal and practical issues that arise in relation to such internal reviews are discussed at para 3.9 ff above.

15.26 Once the person concerned reaches the view that there has been a breach, it must report 'without delay' (or 'as soon as practicable', where a company becomes aware of a director's breach of the code of dealing). 'Without delay' requires something close to an immediate report. 'As soon as practicable' may allow some limited delay, if there are practical reasons for it in the circumstances[1].

1 This will allow the company sufficient opportunity to clarify the circumstances of the breach, without allowing the company to defer the investigation indefinitely': Consultation Paper 100, ('Proposed Changes to the Listing Rules at N2'), June 2001, para 5.6.

15.27 There may not, therefore, be much scope for the company or sponsor to carry out further investigations before reporting the matter to the UKLA, although the nature and extent of the report will obviously depend upon the nature and extent of the information then available[1]. This produces some difficult practical issues, discussed at para 3.81 ff above. As a general rule, once the company or sponsor becomes aware that there has been a breach, it will be preferable to provide some information promptly to the UKLA, together with an indication that further investigations are being carried out, than to await the results of a full internal enquiry and then present these to the UKLA without having given the UKLA any previous indication that the matter was under review.

1 The draft listing rules and the draft Guidance Manual do not contain any indication of the nature or extent of the report that the UKLA will expect to be made.

15.28 Once the issuer becomes aware that a breach has taken place, it may need to appoint a sponsor (if it does not already have one). The UKLA has the power, in the event of a breach of the listing rules, to notify the issuer that the appointment of a sponsor is required to give the issuer advice on the application of the listing rules[1]. The UKLA attaches great importance to the role and responsibilities of a sponsor and, where relevant, to the opinions and reports of the issuer's other professional advisers, in satisfying itself that all the relevant requirements of the Listing Rules have been complied with[2].

1 See the draft Listing Rules, r 2.8. In practice, an issuer will often be receiving advice from its brokers, even though they have not formally been appointed its sponsor; the UKLA is likely to need to require the issuer to appoint a sponsor in these circumstances only if, for example, it has a poor understanding of its obligations under the listing rules. Where a sponsor (whether or not formally appointed the issuer's sponsor for these purposes) provides guidance or advice to an issuer in relation to the application or interpretation of the listing rules, the sponsor is required to ensure that the issuer is properly guided and advised as to the application or interpretation of the relevant listing rules, and to provide that service with due care and skill: draft Listing Rules, r 2.11.

2 See the draft Guidance Manual, para 1.3.13. The UKLA will generally communicate with the sponsor, although it may communicate directly with the issuer: see para 15.38 below.

Other issues to consider when a problem arises

15.29 Certain practical steps that might be considered when a regulatory problem arises are reviewed in Chapter 3 above. Many of the issues discussed there arise equally in the context of potential breaches of the listing rules by issuers, particularly in the light of the UKLA's proposed policy on the factors that it will take into account when deciding whether to take enforcement action and, if so, what action it should take[1], although some of the detailed rules outlined in Chapter 3 above do not apply in this context.

1 See para 15.123 ff below.

15.30 In particular, in addition to the question of whether the breach must be reported to the UKLA, the person concerned may wish to consider:

- whether it should conduct an internal investigation and, if it does, how it should structure and conduct that investigation (see para 3.9 ff above);
- whether it should take steps to ensure that the problem does not reoccur (see para 3.131 ff above);
- what, if any, action it should take in respect of any employees who were involved (see para 3.135 ff above);
- whether it should report the matter to its insurers (see para 3.130 above);
- whether it should voluntarily compensate those who have suffered loss arising from its actions (see para 3.110 ff above);
- whether the matter potentially gives rise to any criminal proceedings (see para 3.146 ff above);
- whether the matter potentially gives rise to any civil claims (see Chapter 10 above);
- what steps it should take to safeguard documents (see para 3.150 ff above); and
- what steps it should take to ensure that further documents are not created (see para 3.155 ff above).

In addition, the issuer may want to consider whether to appoint, or at least take advice from, a sponsor (if it does not already have one)[1]. It may also be worth considering whether the matter falls within any guidance issued in the past by the UKLA, either generally or specifically.

1 See para 15.28 above.

15.31 The protection of legal privilege may cause particular difficulties in this context. For example, it may be difficult to ensure that communications with brokers and/or individual directors after the problem comes to light are legally privileged, because of the potential for conflict between the interests of the company and those of its brokers and/or individual directors. Issues may also arise as to whether the company should disclose to the UKLA legal advice that it received before carrying out the action which is now alleged to be a breach of the listing rules. It may wish to rely upon that advice in its defence. However, to disclose it may risk waiving privilege in the advice as well as potentially in a broader range of documents. This may have wider repercussions in the context of any civil claims that may be brought against the company. Various issues relating to the protection of legal privilege are discussed in more detail at para 4.189 ff above.

The UKLA's powers of information gathering

15.32 Once a potential breach of the listing rules comes to light, the UKLA may want to obtain further information in order to decide whether a breach has occurred and, if so, to consider what, if any, action it should take. There are, broadly, two options: it can exercise its powers under the listing rules to obtain information from listed companies and sponsors and/or it can initiate a formal investigation using its statutory powers. The former is considered here and the latter at para 15.46 ff below.

Powers to obtain information from listed companies and sponsors

15.33 The draft listing rules contain a number of provisions that allow the UKLA to obtain information from listed companies and sponsors for enforcement purposes, among others[1]. In particular:

- issuers must provide to the UKLA without delay[2]:
  - all the information that the UKLA considers appropriate in order to protect investors or ensure the smooth operation of the market, and
  - any other information or explanations that the UKLA may reasonably require for the purpose of verifying whether listing rules are being and have been complied with,
- a sponsor must provide to the UKLA:
  - any information or explanation known to it in such form and within such time limit as the UKLA may reasonably require for the purpose of verifying whether listing rules are being and have been complied with by it or an issuer[3], and
  - without delay any information or explanation in relation to the provision of services by the sponsor in response to any reasonable request by the UKLA in order for the UKLA to verify whether listing rules are being or have been complied with by the sponsor[4].

1 These provisions are similar to (and in some instances the same as) those in operation prior to the FSMA 2000 coming into force.
2 See the draft Listing Rules, r 1.4.
3 See the draft Listing Rules, r 2.10.
4 See the draft Listing Rules, r 2.30.

15.34 These are broad powers, containing no express limits on the range of information that the UKLA can request from the company and/or sponsor concerned. The range of people from whom the UKLA may request such information is, however, limited to listed companies and sponsors. Thus, it cannot, for example, require the company's brokers or auditors to provide information.

15.35 Plainly, the UKLA could approach the company, asking it to obtain information or an explanation from a third party and to provide that information or explanation to the UKLA (although it is not clear that it would in practice do so). If it did, it is arguable that the company could be required to approach the third party[1], particularly where it was within the power of the company to call for the information or explanation from the third party or where in practice it was likely the third party would provide it[2]. In practice, listed companies will usually want to be seen to be co-operating with the UKLA and may therefore be willing to obtain the information from the third party. The UKLA does not, though, have the power to go directly to the third party. The FSA may be able to obtain the information for the UKLA from third parties who are also authorised or approved persons (for example, the company's corporate brokers) by exercising its wider regulatory powers[3], including requiring the third party to provide information under Principle 11[4].

1 The wording of the draft Listing Rules, r 1.4 does not restrict the information or explanations to those known to the company: contrast r 2.10 (in relation to sponsors: see above). Against this, however, it could be argued that there is nothing in the wording of the rule expressly authorising this (and nothing in the draft Guidance Manual referring to the use of the power in this way).
2 In such a situation, it would be said that the UKLA could 'reasonably require' the company to provide the information within draft Listing Rules, r 1.4.
3 See para 4.59 ff above.
4 Principle 11, Principles for Businesses: see para 4.27 ff above. Third parties may owe confidentiality obligations which they may be concerned constrain them from complying with informal requests for information from the FSA: this is discussed further at para 4.54 above.

When in practice are these powers used?

15.36 These are essentially fact-finding powers and may therefore be used whenever the UKLA requires further information in order to fulfil its statutory functions. The UKLA has indicated[1] simply that these powers may be used in a broad range of circumstances (the draft Guidance Manual contains three specific examples).

1 See the draft Guidance Manual, para 7.4.4.

15.37 A separate question is when in practice the UKLA will proceed to investigate a potential rule breach by using its powers of information gathering under the listing rules, rather than by commencing a formal investigation using its statutory powers[1]. The UKLA has provided little guidance on this. Its proposed policy on when it will initiate a formal investigation, outlined below[2], provides some indication of the factors likely to be taken into account by it in deciding how to investigate in a particular case. Additional practical considerations may arise, such as whether the UKLA is likely to be able to obtain all of the information it needs by using its powers under the listing rules (given the limited scope of those powers, as discussed above) and whether the information that it requires is likely to be provided to it willingly[3].

1 There may in practice be limits on the extent to which an investigation should properly be conducted using the information gathering powers, given the statutory protections that apply to formal statutory investigations: see para 15.43 below.
2 See para 15.57 ff below.
3 In the context of a formal investigation, there are statutory powers to enforcement requirements to provide information: see para 15.73 ff below.

How are these powers exercised?

15.38 Little guidance has been given on how information will be asked to be provided in practice and the answer will depend upon the situation. The UKLA has indicated that[1] it will contact the issuer's agent or the issuer directly, usually by telephone in the first instance. Often, this will be a preliminary contact from the monitoring team, who will ascertain whether a breach may have been committed and whether the matter should be passed on for further investigation. In some circumstances, the UKLA may require information to be provided in writing. It will often be the sponsor's (or broker's) role to communicate with the UKLA on behalf of the issuer[2], although the UKLA is willing to communicate directly with an issuer or its advisers in appropriate circumstances, to discuss either matters of principle or the interpretation of the UKLA's requirements[3], but where the sponsor is not involved the issuer must ensure that the sponsor is informed in writing of the matters discussed as soon as practicable[4].

1 See the draft Guidance Manual, para 7.4.5.
2 See the draft Listing Rules, r 2.22(a).
3 See the draft Listing Rules, r 2.26.
4 See the draft Listing Rules, r 2.27. Caution needs to be exercised in communicating with the sponsor, to ensure that prejudicial material is not produced which might need to be disclosed in due course to the UKLA or to a third party in the context of any legal proceedings: see para 4.189 ff above.

15.39 The UKLA has explained that all telephone conversations are recorded[1]. This reinforces the need, when providing information over the telephone, to ensure that the information is accurate in the same way as would be done if information were provided in writing[2].

1 See the draft Guidance Manual, para 7.4.5.
2 Among other things, the provision of false or misleading information may amount to a criminal offence: see para 15.42 below.

Can the person concerned refuse to provide the information?

15.40 Generally speaking, listed companies and sponsors must comply when asked to provide information by the UKLA using its powers under the listing rules. Failure to comply could of itself amount to a breach of the listing rules, compounding the original breach and potentially leading to the disciplinary and/or enforcement consequences outlined below[1]. There is an exception for legally privileged material, which is, broadly speaking, protected from disclosure under the FSMA 2000[2]. There may also be other objections to providing particular information in a specific case[3].

1 See para 15.97 ff below.
2 FSMA 2000, s 413 and see the discussion at para 4.264 ff above. Note that legal privilege effectively has its own statutory definition for these purposes.
3 Some of the more common grounds for objecting are briefly reviewed at para 4.260 ff above. Note that there is no right to withhold documents or refuse to answer questions on the ground of any privilege against self-incrimination: for a further discussion, see para 4.242 ff above. Note also that there is no express provision applying in the context of requests under the listing rules the (limited) statutory protection for banking confidentiality (see para 15.71 below and, more generally, para 4.267 ff above).

15.41 If the person concerned believes that there is a legitimate objection to complying with a particular request, how does it make good that objection? The person may simply refuse to comply and then use the ground of objection as a defence to any enforcement proceedings brought in respect of that refusal. Alternatively, it may seek to challenge the decision which led to the UKLA imposing the requirement. These options are discussed in more detail at para 4.278 ff above[1].

1 Note that the certification procedure leading to contempt of court proceedings outlined at para 15.73 below does not apply in the context of requests for information made under the listing rules. Rather, the UKLA would bring disciplinary or other enforcement proceedings for breach of the listing rules based on the failure to provide information and the firm would defend those proceedings based on its objection to providing the information.

15.42 It seems that the UKLA cannot directly enforce a requirement to provide information or an explanation, in the sense of forcing the person concerned to provide the information or explanation[1]. It would, however, be a criminal offence:

- knowingly or recklessly to provide false or misleading information to the UKLA[2]; and/or
- to falsify, conceal, destroy or otherwise dispose of a document (or cause or permit another to do so) that the person knows or suspects is or would be relevant to an investigation which he knows or suspects is being or is likely to be conducted either by the FSA under Pt XI[3] or by the UKLA under Pt VI[4].

1 The UKLA's power to apply for a warrant to enter and search premises and seize documents appears to apply only to formal investigations under FSMA 2000, s 97 (discussed at para 15.46 ff below): see FSMA 2000, s 97(3). However, the draft Guidance Manual seems to indicate that such powers may apply also in the context of information gathering under the listing rules (see the draft Guidance Manual, para 7.14, which is headed 'The UKLA's powers to require persons to cooperate with information gathering and investigation'). The basis for this is unclear.
2 FSMA 2000, s 398, applied to the UKLA by Sch 7, para 1.
3 See para 3.151 above. An example would be a market abuse investigation.
4 See para 15.76 below. It is not entirely clear whether the offence applies where an investigation is not in fact commenced under Pt VI: see FSMA 2000, s 97(3) ('Pt XI applies to an investigation under subsection (2) . . .').

15.43 In practice, whilst an issuer or sponsor may be willing initially to provide information to the UKLA pursuant to its obligations under the listing rules, there may come a stage where it is preferable to be subject to a formal investigation, particularly where the questions arise in a situation which it is clear may lead to disciplinary or enforcement action being considered. A formal investigation will entail the person concerned being formally notified of the investigation and the reasons for appointment of the investigator, the investigator will be exercising statutory powers within clear limits and certain statutory safeguards will be available[1]. There may be a practical issue of whether the issuer or sponsor can decline to answer the UKLA's questions on the basis that it would prefer to be subject to a formal investigation, without risk of action being taken against it for breach of the listing rules for that refusal to answer questions. In practice, it ought to be possible to make that point to the UKLA, particularly if the person concerned has established a good working relationship with it and if the UKLA's information gathering under the listing rules is developing into something more akin to an investigation[2].

1 In particular, there is a statutory protection against self-incrimination in relation to statements made under compulsion: see para 15.69 below. The UKLA has made clear that statements made voluntarily are not covered by this statutory protection and can be used in evidence in any proceedings, subject to any requirements governing the admissibility of evidence in the circumstances in question: see the draft Guidance Manual, para 7.10.5.
2 This issue is also discussed at para 4.53 ff above.

Is there any risk of publicity?

15.44 The UKLA will not usually make public the fact that it is (or is not) exercising its information gathering powers[1]. No publicity will, therefore, normally attach to the information gathering process (and indeed the information which the UKLA obtains is, broadly speaking, protected by a statutory confidentiality obligation[2]). Publicity may, however, arise if, ultimately, the information gathering and any formal investigation lead to proceedings in the Tribunal and/or to the UKLA exercising its enforcement powers[3].

1 See the draft Guidance Manual, para 7.4.6.
2 This is discussed further at para 15.88 ff below.
3 This is discussed further at para 15.98 below.

15.45 However, there may be circumstances where the UKLA will make public the fact that it is using its information gathering powers. Whilst no further information has been given, the UKLA has explained its proposed policy on the same question in the context of formal investigations. This is discussed at para 15.84 ff below and it is thought that the same policy is likely to apply here.

Formal investigations under FSMA 2000, Pt VI

15.46 In addition to its powers of information gathering under the listing rules, the UKLA has the power to initiate a formal investigation using statutory powers under FSMA 2000, Pt VI. We review such investigations and, in particular:

- on what grounds can the UKLA initiate a formal investigation?
- when in practice will the UKLA commence a formal investigation?
- what powers does the investigator have to obtain information?
- practical issues in relation to investigations;
- how does the UKLA commence and control the investigation?
- will the person concerned be notified of the investigation? and
- will any publicity arise from the investigation?

Each is considered in turn below.

On what grounds can the UKLA initiate a formal investigation?

15.47 The UKLA may appoint an investigator to conduct an investigation on its behalf if it appears to it that there are circumstances suggesting that[1]:

- there may have been a breach of the listing rules;
- a director or former director of an issuer or applicant has been knowingly concerned in a breach of the listing rules by that issuer or applicant; or
- there may have been a contravention of ss 83, 85 or 98[2].

1 FSMA 2000, s 97 and the draft Listing Rules, r 1.8.
2 These are the three criminal offences under Pt VI, briefly outlined at para 15.55 below.

15.48 In common with many of the other statutory investigation powers[1], the hurdle which is required to be passed in order for the UKLA to initiate an investigation is a low one. It need only 'appear to [the UKLA]' that there are 'circumstances suggesting' one of the above (and, in two of the three, only circumstances suggesting that there 'may have been'). There do not need to be, for example, reasonable grounds for suspecting that a breach has occurred. This largely leaves within the discretion of the UKLA the question of whether an investigation should be commenced[2]. As a result, it would be difficult to challenge a decision to appoint an investigator on the ground that the statutory test had not been met.

1 See para 4.108 ff above.
2 It should be recognised that the UKLA may not have a great deal of information from which to conclude that the matter needs to be investigated.

15.49 Each of the circumstances when an investigation may be commenced is considered in turn below[1].

1 It is notable that there is no power to investigate breaches of requirements imposed directly by FSMA 2000, Pt VI (other than the criminal offences under ss 83, 85 and 98). Part VI primarily contains the framework for the listing rules, which is where the detailed provisions are found.

There may have been a breach of the listing rules

15.50 The UKLA may[1] appoint an investigator if it appears to it that there are circumstances suggesting that there may have been a breach of the listing rules[2].

1 FSMA 2000, s 97(1)(a).
2 Listing rules means the rules made by the FSA for the purposes of FSMA 2000, Pt VI: s 74(4).

15.51 This is the primary provision allowing the UKLA to investigate suspected breaches of its rules. In principle, such an investigation could be brought in relation to any person who has an obligation under the listing rules, including listed companies, applicants for listing and sponsors. The power is, though, expressed differently than that under s 168(4) (the primary investigation power in respect of rule breaches in the non-UKLA context[1]) because s 168(4) requires there to be circumstances suggesting that 'a person' has contravened a rule, the implication being that that person is the person under investigation. The reason for omitting those words here is unclear but the implication is that there need not be an identified person under investigation. Why does this matter? It may mean, at least in theory, that the UKLA can commence an investigation into a situation, rather than the behaviour of a particular person[2]. In addition, as will be seen[3], the powers of the investigator are framed by reference to 'the person under investigation' and the FSMA 2000 is therefore slightly inconsistent.

1 See para 4.134 ff above.
2 A similar formulation is used in s 168(2) for market abuse investigations and, in that context, the FSA has expressly indicated that it will, at least at the outset, often be investigating a situation, not a particular person: see para 13.142 above.
3 See para 15.59 ff below.

Directors of issuers or applicants

15.52 The UKLA may appoint an investigator if it appears to it that there are circumstances suggesting that a person who was at the material time a director of an issuer of listed securities, or of a person applying for the admission of securities to the official list, has been knowingly concerned in the breach of listing rules by that issuer or applicant[1].

1 FSMA 2000, s 97(1)(b) and (c).

15.53 The power to investigate directors reflects the potential personal liability of directors to regulatory sanctions under Pt VI[1]. 'Director' is defined to include shadow directors and de facto directors[2]. In addition, by referring to a person who was a director at the material time, the FSMA 2000 encompasses not only present but also former directors. The key part of the test is the phrase 'knowingly concerned', the meaning of which is considered at para 2.184 ff above.

1 See para 15.113 ff below.
2 FSMA 2000, s 417: 'director' includes a person occupying the position of a director, by whatever name that position is called, and a person in accordance with whose directions or instructions (not being advice given in a professional capacity) the directors are accustomed to act.

Contravention of sections 83, 85 or 98

15.54 The UKLA may appoint an investigator if it appears to it that there are circumstances suggesting that there may have been a contravention of ss 83, 85 or 98[1].

1 FSMA 2000, s 97(1)(c).

15.55 This covers the three criminal offences under FSMA 2000, Pt VI of:

- failing to deliver a copy of listing particulars to the registrar of companies[1];
- offering securities to the public before the prospectus is published, where publication is required by the listing rules[2]; and

- issuing in the UK, in connection with an application for listing, advertisements or other information specified in the listing rules which have not been approved or authorised by the FSA[3].

1 FSMA 2000, s 83(3).
2 FSMA 2000, s 85(2).
3 FSMA 2000, s 98(2).

15.56 As with investigations into suspected breaches of listing rules, the formulation 'there may have been a contravention' causes a slight mismatch between the drafting of the investigation power and that of the powers of investigation of the investigator thus appointed. The implications of this are discussed at para 15.63 below.

When in practice will the UKLA commence a formal investigation?

15.57 When a possible breach comes to its attention, the UKLA's primary aim is to confirm whether the listing rules (or the provisions of Pt VI) have been complied with and, if not, to determine the nature and extent of any breach[1]. It will therefore assess on a case-by-case basis whether to carry out a formal investigation after considering all available information, including considering the following factors[2]:

- the elements of the suspected breach;
- its views as to whether those concerned are willing to co-operate, including whether obligations of confidentiality would otherwise inhibit the provision of information[3];
- the evidence and information required, and its availability and accessibility; and
- any other factors, including the factors relevant when considering the amount of any penalty to be imposed[4].

1 See the draft Guidance Manual, para 7.7.2.
2 See the draft Guidance Manual, para 7.7.3.
3 These factors are discussed in more detail in the context of the UKLA's information gathering powers, at para 15.37 above.
4 These can be found in the draft Guidance Manual, para 8.8 and are discussed at para 15.127 below.

15.58 In practice, the overarching question for the UKLA is likely to be what represents the most effective and efficient means of obtaining the information it needs to confirm whether or not a breach has taken place. One factor not specifically mentioned above, but which is likely to be relevant in any decision, is the nature and seriousness of the suspected breach.

What powers does the investigator have to obtain information?

15.59 An investigator appointed under s 97 is treated as though he were appointed under s 167(1)[1]. The result is that he may, in so far as he reasonably considers the material to be relevant to the purposes of the investigation[2]:

- require the person under investigation to attend before him at a specified time and place and answer questions;
- require the person under investigation otherwise to provide such information as he may require;
- make the same requirements of any person connected with the person under investigation[3]; or
- require any person to produce at a specified time and place any specified documents or documents of a specified description.

1 FSMA 2000, s 97(3)(a).
2 FSMA 2000, s 171 and see the draft Guidance Manual, para 7.6.
3 The meaning of 'connected persons' in this context (see FSMA 2000, s 171(4)) is set out at para 4.130 above and see the draft Guidance Manual, para 7.6.4. Broadly, it includes not only affiliated companies, controllers and partnerships of which the person under investigation is a member, but also its employees, agents, appointed representatives, solicitors, bankers, auditors and/or actuaries (and those of other group members).

15.60 The scope of these obligations is discussed in detail at para 4.130 ff above, in the context of investigations under s 167(1). Various ancillary provisions, outlined at para 4.111 above, also apply, as though the investigator were appointed under s 167(1)[1].

1 FSMA 2000, s 97(3)(a).

15.61 Three points are notable regarding the scope of the investigation. First, only documents can be obtained from unconnected third parties, not information and not answers to questions (which would include an interview). Thus, the UKLA must rely upon such third parties voluntarily to provide information, or voluntarily to submit to interview, unless it can persuade another regulator, such as the FSA acting in its wider capacity, to investigate on some other basis, for example into market abuse, and then to pass information to it.

15.62 Second, the effect of this may in practice be limited by the very wide definition of 'connected persons', which includes, for example, employees, agents, auditors and actuaries[1]. It does not, though, seem that the company's brokers or sponsor would amount to a 'connected person' for this purpose, save perhaps to the extent that they acted as its agent[2].

1 See footnote 3 to para 15.59 above.
2 However, as an authorised person, sponsors and brokers must be open and co-operative with regulators under Principle 11: see para 2.52 above.

15.63 Third, as already mentioned, the list of matters that can be investigated under s 97 does not sit entirely easily with the way in which the investigation power has been framed. Two of the matters that can be investigated (namely, breaches of listing rules and contraventions of ss 83, 85 or 98) are expressed without reference to any 'person under investigation', allowing, at least in theory, an investigation to be commenced into a suspected breach by an unidentified person, based on circumstances suggesting that such a breach may have taken place. However, the powers that the investigator thus appointed would have to obtain information are expressed by reference to 'the person under investigation'. It is not clear how the investigator would act in that situation, but this is likely to occur rarely in practice.

Practical issues in relation to investigations

15.64 We consider here some of the practical issues that arise in relation to formal investigations and, in particular:

- when providing documents and information to investigators;
- in relation to the conduct of interviews by investigators;
- whether there is any information the person concerned can refuse to provide; and
- the consequences of not complying with a formal request for information.

Providing documents and information to investigators

15.65 Various practical issues that arise in relation to providing documents and information in response to formal requests are discussed at para 4.181 ff above.

15.66 In practice, much information is provided to the UKLA or its investigators without the need to use their formal statutory powers[1]. Where the UKLA does use its formal powers, it will make this clear to those to whom its enquiries are addressed and will inform them of the statutory requirements and the possible penalties for failure to comply[2].

1 See the draft Guidance Manual, para 7.8.1/2. There are practical benefits of maintaining a co-operative relationship with the FSA or an investigator. Therefore, whilst a listed company does not owe the same regulatory obligation of openness and co-operation as an authorised person, in practical terms it may be beneficial to be seen to be in an open and co-operative stance with the regulator.
2 See the draft Guidance Manual, para 7.8.2. The potential consequences of failing to comply are outlined at para 15.73 ff below.

Interviews by investigators

15.67 An investigator appointed under s 97 can compel the person under investigation, or any 'connected person' to attend an interview, but cannot compel an unconnected third party to do so[1].

1 See para 15.61 above.

15.68 As to the conduct of such interviews, the UKLA has provided its proposed guidance on its policy and procedure, as follows:

- it will, where appropriate, seek initially to conduct interviews on a voluntary, rather than compulsory basis[1];
- prior to any interview, it will write to the person concerned, notifying him that the interview will be recorded and explaining why[2];
- an interviewee may be accompanied by a legal or other advisor[3];
- a person interviewed voluntarily will be given a record of the interview and a transcript, if one is produced[4];
- a person interviewed compulsorily will be given 'an appropriate warning'[5] and an explanation of the limited privilege against self-incrimination[6] and will be given a record of the interview.

1 See the draft Guidance Manual, para 7.13.1. In relation to the privilege against self-incrimination, see footnote 3 to para 15.69 below.
2 See the draft Guidance Manual, para 7.13.2.
3 See the draft Guidance Manual, para 7.13.3 and 7.13.4(1).
4 See the draft Guidance Manual, para 7.13.3. Whilst not entirely clear, the draft Guidance Manual seems to indicate that the UKLA may decide not to produce a record of an interview with a person who is not the person under investigation.
5 It is presumed that this relates to the consequences of refusing to answer and/or not answering accurately: see para 15.73 ff below.
6 See para 15.69 below.

15.69 A person compelled to an interview cannot decline to answer questions on the ground that the answer might incriminate him. There is, however, some limited statutory protection in terms of the use to which information thus obtained can be put, if the person interviewed is later charged with a criminal offence or is subject to proceedings for market abuse. Broadly, in those circumstances, a statement compulsorily obtained cannot be used against the person who made it[1]. This may often be relevant in practice, particularly given the potential for insider dealing or market abuse proceedings to overlap with proceedings for breach of the listing rules[2], for example based on the misuse of unpublished price sensitive information, but also because of the three specific criminal offences under Pt VI, namely ss 83, 85 and 98. A more detailed discussion of the privilege against self-incrimination, and particularly the limits of this protection[3], can be found at para 4.242 ff above.

1 For a more detailed discussion, see para 4.242 ff above and, in the context of market abuse proceedings, para 13.162 ff above.
2 This overlap is discussed at para 13.220 ff above.
3 Note, particularly, that the statutory protection does not expressly apply to a person who gives a statement outside a formal investigation, although it is arguable that a criminal court (and probably the Tribunal or a court considering the imposition of a fine for market abuse) should confer a similar protection upon statements made under compulsion, as a matter of law: see the discussion at para 4.245 above. The UKLA's position (see the draft Guidance Manual, para 7.10.5) is that statements made voluntarily are not covered by FSMA 2000, s 174 and can be used in evidence in any proceedings subject to any requirements governing the admissibility of evidence in the circumstances in question.

15.70 Various practical issues in relation to interviews are considered at para 4.221 ff above.

Is there any information the person concerned can refuse to provide?

15.71 A person required to provide documents or information to an investigator, within the scope of his investigation powers, must, generally speaking, provide it. There are, however, limited exceptions, namely:

- the FSMA 2000 contains a general protection for legal privilege[1]. This applies equally here and is discussed in more detail at para 4.264 ff above;
- in addition, there is a limited protection for documents subject to a duty of banking confidentiality, which is discussed at para 4.267 ff above.

1 FSMA 2000, s 413. Note that the FSMA 2000 effectively contains its own definition of what is legally privileged.

15.72 Beyond this, unless there is, in the specific circumstances, some particular objection to complying with the requirement, those required to provide information or documents must comply. As to some of the types of objections that a person may have in a particular case, and how it might make good those objections, see para 4.260 ff above.

What are the consequences of not complying?

15.73 Non-compliance with a requirement imposed by an investigator may carry a number of consequences. First, a court may treat the person as though he were in contempt of court[1].

1 This applies as a result of FSMA 2000, s 97(3)(a). For a more detailed discussion of this sanction, see para 4.284 ff above.

15.74 Second, the FSA has the power to obtain a warrant to enter and search premises in support of an investigation. This allows the FSA to obtain a warrant in any of three situations, broadly[1]:

- where a person has failed to comply with a requirement to provide information or documents which are situated on the premises; or
- where the premises specified in the warrant are those of the person under investigation[2], there are on the premises documents or information in relation to which a requirement could be imposed and, if such a requirement were to be imposed, it would not be complied with or the documents or information would be removed, tampered with or destroyed; or
- one of the offences under ss 85 or 98[3] has been or is being committed by any person, there are on the premises documents or information in relation to which a requirement could be imposed and, if such a requirement were to be imposed, it would not be complied with or the documents or information would be removed, tampered with or destroyed.

1 For a more detailed explanation, see para 4.290 ff above.
2 This is the effect of FSMA 2000, s 97(3)(d). In the context of any other investigation, the question is whether they are premises of an authorised person or appointed representative.
3 This is the effect of FSMA 2000, s 97(3)(c). In the context of any other investigation, the question is whether an offence mentioned in s 168 for which the maximum sentence is two years or more has been or is being committed. Offences under s 83 are not included because the maximum sentence is not two years or more.

15.75 The UKLA has indicated that it will consider using these powers where it has concerns about whether requirements to provide information will be complied with and believes that the grounds for a search warrant are made out[1].

1 See the draft Guidance Manual, para 7.14.2. It will usually seek to ensure that its investigator is named on the warrant and entitled to accompany the police: See the draft Guidance Manual, para 7.14.4.

15.76 Third, there are criminal offences of:

- knowingly or recklessly providing false or misleading information in purported compliance with a requirement imposed during a statutory investigation[1]; and
- falsifying, concealing, destroying or otherwise disposing of a document (or causing or permitting another to do so) that the person knows or suspects is or would be relevant to an investigation which he knows or suspects is being or is likely to be conducted either by the FSA under Pt XI[2] or by the UKLA under Pt VI[3].

1 FSMA 2000, s 177(4), applied by FSMA 2000, s 97(3)(a). A simple failure to provide information ought not, without more, of itself to constitute a criminal offence: see the discussion at para 4.287 above.
2 See para 3.151 above. An example would be a market abuse investigation.
3 FSMA 2000, s 177(3), applied by FSMA 2000, s 97(3)(a).

15.77 Finally, if the person is also an authorised person then his failure may carry wider regulatory consequences, as outlined at para 4.289 above.

How does the FSA commence and control the investigation?

15.78 The investigation is commenced by the appointment of an investigator and controlled by the FSA by giving directions to the investigator in the same way as an investigation under s 167(1). A detailed discussion appears at para 4.157 ff above.

Will the person be notified of the investigation?

15.79 The person under investigation[1] must be given written notice of the appointment of the investigator, specifying the provisions under which the investigator was appointed and the reason for his appointment[2].

1 It is in theory possible to commence an investigation under s 97 without there being a 'person under investigation'. In that situation, it is unclear how the FSA would comply with the obligation to notify. See the discussion at para 15.51 above.
2 FSMA 2000, s 170(2) and (4), applied by s 97(3)(a) and (b).

15.80 The person under investigation will also be notified if there is a change in the scope or conduct of the investigation and in the opinion of the UKLA the person is likely to be significantly prejudiced by not being made aware of it[1]. The UKLA has given examples[2] that this may include a situation where a person may:

- otherwise incur unnecessary costs dealing with an aspect of the investigation which the UKLA no longer intends to pursue; or
- inadvertently incriminate himself by not knowing of the change in scope.

1 FSMA 2000, s 170(9), applied by FSMA 2000, s 97(3)(a) and (b).
2 See the draft Guidance Manual, para 7.9.3.

15.81 One potential difficulty is that the UKLA may initially be concerned with the company or its sponsor, rather than with the actions of a particular director, but may subsequently realise that it may wish to take enforcement action against a director. Clearly, the director will not have been formally notified, at the outset, of the commencement of the investigation, since he was not the person under investigation.

15.82 The issue is that a person may thus be required to provide information without realising that he is the target of the investigation. The UKLA addresses this in two ways. First, it will always provide an indication of the nature and subject matter of its enquiries to those who are required to provide information[1]. Second, once it becomes clear who the persons under investigation are, the UKLA will normally notify them when it proceeds to exercise its statutory powers to require information from them[2]. This ought in practice to mean that the director concerned, if asked to provide information before he was the target of the investigation, is at least aware of the nature of the investigation and, if asked to provide information after he has been identified as the person under investigation, is at that stage made aware of this. However, as discussed at para 4.161 above, it is not clear why he should not be notified immediately the UKLA identifies him as the person under investigation.

1 See the draft Guidance Manual, para 7.9.4.
2 See the draft Guidance Manual, para 7.9.5.

15.83 For a further discussion of notifications, see para 4.159 ff above.

Will any publicity arise from the investigation?

15.84 Generally speaking, the investigation process ought not of itself to give rise to any publicity. The expectation should be that no publicity will arise either in relation to the fact that the FSA is investigating or in relation to the outcome of the investigation, but there are exceptions.

15.85 The UKLA may, in exceptional circumstances, make a public announcement that it is or is not investigating a particular matter if it considers such an announcement desirable[1] to maintain public confidence in the market, maintain the smooth operation of the market, protect investors, prevent widespread malpractice, or help the investigation itself (for example, by bringing forward witnesses)[2]. The UKLA has identified particularly that this may arise where the matters under investigation are the subject of such public concern, speculation or rumour that it is desirable for it to do so to allay the concern, or contain the speculation or rumour[3]. In deciding whether to make an announcement, the UKLA will consider the potential prejudice that it believes may be caused to any persons who are, or who are likely to be, a subject of the investigation[4]. The UKLA will also need to consider to what extent it is able to disclose information given its obligations of confidentiality under FSMA 2000, s 348[5].

1 'Desirable' is a low test but, given the overall policy, it ought to be rare in practice that announcements are made.
2 See the draft Guidance Manual, paras 7.11.2 and 7.11.4. Where the matter arises in the context of a takeover bid, the UKLA will discuss any announcement beforehand with the Takeover Panel. In that situation, there may be additional considerations militating in favour of an announcement that the UKLA is not investigating: see the draft Guidance Manual, paras 7.11.3 and 7.11.5.
3 See the draft Guidance Manual, para 7.11.5.
4 See the draft Guidance Manual, para 7.11.4.
5 The statutory confidentiality obligation is discussed further at para 15.88 ff below. For a discussion of what it may mean in the context of public announcements about investigations, see para 4.164 ff above.

15.86 Similarly, the UKLA may, in exceptional circumstances, and where it is not prevented from doing so by FSMA 2000, s 348, publish details of the information found or conclusions reached in its investigations. In particular, it may do so where the fact that it was investigating was made public, and it subsequently concludes that the allegations were unfounded, particularly if the person concerned wants the UKLA to clarify this[1].

1 See the draft Guidance Manual, para 7.11.6.

15.87 In addition, it is important to recognise that publicity may arise[1]:

- unavoidably from the investigation itself, for example because the UKLA's enquiries attract publicity;
- from enforcement action taken by the UKLA whilst its enquiries are still continuing (for example, urgent action to suspend the listing of shares[2]) or by other regulatory authorities (for example, the FSA);
- ultimately, if the matter results in disciplinary or enforcement action being taken[3] or in the matter being referred to the Tribunal[4].

1 These issues are discussed in more detail at para 4.164 ff above.
2 See para 15.134 ff below.
3 In most cases, disciplinary or enforcement action will result in publicity: see para 15.98 below.
4 There is a presumption that Tribunal proceedings will be held in public: see para 6.32 above.

What use can be made of information obtained from the investigation?

15.88 Once the investigator completes his fact-finding investigation, he must report those findings to the UKLA, as the body that appointed him[1]. Clearly, the UKLA can use that information in order to consider whether to exercise any of its disciplinary or enforcement powers under FSMA 2000, Pt VI, as outlined below.

1 FSMA 2000, s 170(6), applied by s 7(3)(a) and (b).

15.89 But the UKLA is only one management unit within the FSA. Can it pass information internally within the FSA for use for other purposes, for example to consider whether to investigate or take action for market abuse or to exercise any of its wider regulatory powers? Can it pass the information on to other regulators, for example any recognised investment exchange that may have an interest in the matter concerned? Also, is there a risk of information being obtained by a third party who may seek to bring legal claims against the person concerned? These issues are considered below.

15.90 The starting point is that confidential information obtained by the UKLA or by an investigator appointed by it[1] is, generally speaking, protected against disclosure by the statutory prohibition found in FSMA 2000, s 348[2]. It is a criminal offence for a person to disclose information in breach[3]. The statutory prohibition is, though, subject to certain exceptions, most notably the ability to make disclosures permitted under the so-called Gateway Regulations made by HM Treasury[4].

1 Each of these is a 'primary recipient' for the purposes of s 348: FSMA 2000, s 348(5)(a), (b) & (f) and (6)(a).
2 This is discussed in more detail at para 4.304 ff above.
3 FSMA 2000, s 352.
4 The Financial Services and Markets Act 2000 (Disclosure of Confidential Information) Regulations 2001, SI 2001/2188 (the 'Gateway Regulations'): see para 4.312 above.

15.91 Against that background, we consider:

- whether the UKLA can pass to the FSA for its wider regulatory purposes information received by the UKLA or its investigator;
- whether the UKLA can pass such information on to other regulators; and
- whether there is any risk of third parties obtaining disclosure of such information.

Disclosure of information to the FSA

15.92 The UKLA may, in the course of its investigation, receive information that it considers may be relevant to the FSA's wider regulatory functions, for example because it raises possible concerns about the conduct of authorised persons or approved persons (for example, a broker or sponsor or their employees) or because it indicates that market abuse may have taken place. Under the Gateway Regulations, the UKLA and/or an investigator appointed by it may disclose confidential information to the FSA for the purpose of enabling or assisting it to discharge its wider regulatory functions[1]. It would therefore be prudent for those subjected to an investigation to assume that information provided to the UKLA or its investigator will, where relevant, be shared within the FSA.

1 Disclosure by any primary recipient to the FSA for the purpose of enabling or assisting the FSA to discharge any of its public functions is permitted under the Gateway Regulations, reg 3(2). Disclosure may also be permitted to be made to an investigator appointed by the FSA (for example, if the FSA is conducting a parallel investigation into, say, market abuse): see the Gateway Regulations, reg 12(1) and Sch 1.

Disclosure of information to other regulators or bodies

15.93 Moreover, the information provided to the UKLA or its investigator may highlight matters which potentially concern another regulator, in particular in this context, an exchange on whose market the securities in question are traded. Or it may indicate that there is an issue for some other body, such as a Companies Act issue for the Department of Trade and Industry or a criminal offence outside the FSMA 2000, for the Serious Fraud Office or the Police. Or the UKLA may receive a request from another regulator for the disclosure of the information.

15.94 The UKLA or the investigator will need to consider in each case whether disclosure to the particular regulator or body concerned is permitted under the Gateway Regulations. The Regulations are complex but, in very broad terms, they do permit a primary recipient to disclose information to, among others[1]:

- a UK recognised investment exchange, for the purpose of enabling or assisting it to discharge its functions as such;
- the Takeover Panel, for the purpose of enabling or assisting it to discharge any of its functions; and
- various types of overseas regulatory authorities.

They also permit the disclosure of information for the purposes of criminal investigations or proceedings[2].

1 See, in particular, the Gateway Regulations, reg 12 and schedules 1 and 2.
2 See the Gateway Regulations, reg 4.

15.95 The UKLA has indicated that it may pass on information where the circumstances indicate that this is appropriate[1]. Whether the UKLA will do so in the particular case will therefore depend largely upon the circumstances, including (where a request is not received) whether the UKLA identifies the matter as one that may concern the other body. It may also in practice depend upon the

UKLA's or the FSA's relationship with the body concerned. Again, it would be prudent to assume that information will be shared with any other relevant regulatory or prosecuting bodies.

1 See the draft Guidance Manual, para 7.15.1.

The risk of disclosure to third parties

15.96 The findings of the UKLA or its investigator may be of interest to third parties, particularly if they consider they have suffered loss from the matters alleged against the person concerned for which they may have a legal claim. An important question is therefore whether there is a risk of the third party obtaining a copy of any documents produced by the UKLA or its investigator, either from the UKLA or investigator direct or from the person under investigation, to the extent that such documents have been provided to that person. The answer is, broadly, that there are risks of a third party obtaining disclosure. These issues are considered in more detail at para 4.189 ff above.

POTENTIAL CONSEQUENCES OF BREACHES OF LISTING RULES OR PART VI

Introduction

15.97 The FSMA 2000 and the listing rules allow the UKLA to take a range of enforcement action for breaches of the listing rules or FSMA 2000, Pt VI. In addition, such breaches may carry civil and/or criminal law consequences. In the following paragraphs, we review the range of potential consequences and, in particular:

- disciplinary action[1] (against issuers, applicants for listing, directors (or former directors) and/or sponsors) (para 15.107 ff);
- other enforcement action by the UKLA or the FSA (para 15.133 ff);
- the procedure for taking enforcement action (para 15.156 ff); and
- the potential for civil liability to third parties to arise (para 15.179 ff[2]).

1 Including, for the first time, the power to impose fines on companies that breach the listing rules (and their directors).
2 The issue of paying compensation to those who have suffered loss arising from breaches of the listing rules also arises because, as is briefly outlined at para 15.153 below, the FSA has the power to make or apply to the court for a restitution order requiring the person concerned to compensate those who have suffered losses or to disgorge any gains that it has made.

15.98 It is important to appreciate that, in most cases, the UKLA, like the FSA, will publish successful enforcement action that it takes, usually by issuing a press release giving details of the breach and the fine imposed or other action taken[1]. Publicity will therefore usually arise from formal enforcement action[2].

1 See the draft Guidance Manual, paras 7.12 and 8.12. The FSA's policy in this regard is discussed in more detail at para 5.194 above, together with the statutory framework. In the UKLA context, it is also relevant that many types of enforcement action (for example, requiring a company to publish information about a director's breach of the code of dealings, suspending or cancelling the listing, or issuing a public censure) will inevitably involve publicity, irrespective of this policy.
2 Publicity should not, though, arise from a private warning: see para 15.124 below.

Resolving overlapping enforcement powers

15.99 Notwithstanding the range of potential disciplinary and enforcement action available to the UKLA and/or the FSA for breaches of the listing rules (and other breaches of FSMA 2000, Pt VI), as outlined here, these are not the only powers that may be relevant in relation to such breaches. First, the matter may also concern another regulator, such as an exchange or an overseas regulator, in which case there could be further regulatory consequences in that context[1]. Second, if the problem involves market misconduct then the FSA may need to consider taking action in relation to the market abuse or other market misconduct as well[2]. Finally, if the matter concerns an authorised firm or an approved person, then it may give rise to wider concerns which could have other regulatory consequences, for example leading to the exercise of the FSA's disciplinary powers or its power to vary a firm's permission or to withdraw an approved person's approval[3].

1 In the context of a listed company that goes into insolvency, there may be a question for the Department of Trade and Industry whether proceedings against any directors under the Company Directors (Disqualification) Act 1986 are appropriate, based on a failure properly to inform the market of the company's trading position.
2 See Chapter 13 above.
3 Each of the main regulatory consequences is considered elsewhere in this book. For an overview of the main potential FSA enforcement powers, see para 4.320 above.

15.100 Faced with not only the range of potential UKLA and FSA action applicable specifically to breaches of the listing rules, but also the possibility of other action by the FSA or other bodies, the question arises as to how the overlap between these various powers is addressed in practice. A number of propositions can be made.

15.101 First, if a criminal offence may have been committed, the FSA's general policy is to pursue, through the criminal justice system, all those cases where criminal prosecution is appropriate[1]. This involves the application of the two tests for crown prosecutors, namely the evidential test (whether there is sufficient evidence to provide a realistic prospect of conviction) and the public interest test (whether criminal prosecution is in the public interest, having regard to the seriousness of the offence and all the circumstances). The application of this policy is considered in more detail at para 11.18 ff above.

1 See the FSA Handbook at ENF 15.4.1 and see para 11.19 above.

15.102 If the FSA does contemplate a criminal prosecution, does this preclude it from taking other civil or regulatory action in relation to the same matter? The answer is that, broadly speaking, it does not, although the civil or regulatory proceedings may be required to await the outcome of the criminal proceedings if there is otherwise a real risk of prejudicing the criminal proceedings. This is discussed in more detail at para 11.41 ff above.

15.103 Second, it is quite possible to envisage circumstances where the action in question amounted both to market abuse and to a breach of the listing rules (for example, if the director dealt in the company's shares in breach of the company's code of dealings, thereby also committing market abuse, and the company failed to comply with its obligation under the listing rules to take all proper and reasonable steps to secure compliance with its code of dealings). The UKLA has indicated[1] that it may take both action under the listing rules against one person (ie, in this example, the company) and action under the market abuse regime against a different person (ie the director).

1 See the draft Guidance Manual, para 12.5.4 and see the discussion at para 13.220 ff above.

15.104 No guidance has, however, been given on whether the UKLA would take both types of action against one person – if, for example, the company repurchased its own shares during a closed period, thereby potentially committing both market abuse and a breach of the listing rules[1]. In practice, if the FSA wished to pursue the company for market abuse, then it is perhaps unlikely that the UKLA would also pursue it for a fine for breach of the listing rules, but it might want to publicly censure it for that breach or to take other action, such as suspending the company's shares or requiring it to publish information through the Company Announcements Office. Since market abuse and regulatory action for breach of the listing rules involve different procedures, it is difficult to see that the different proceedings could be run in tandem. Issues would therefore arise about which process should be pursued first and whether it might prejudice the other[2] and, from the company's perspective, it would be important to be aware of the potential effect of its actions in one context upon its potential liability in the other. For example, to settle the disciplinary case against it by admitting the breach might cause it great difficulty in defending the market abuse proceedings.

1 The FSA has provided guidance on the interaction of the market abuse regime with its own disciplinary and other enforcement powers (in the non-UKLA context), which may be instructive in this context. This is discussed at para 13.265 ff above.

2 For example, there is a privilege against self-incrimination in market abuse proceedings but not in proceedings in relation to breaches of the listing rules.

15.105 Third, the action in question may give rise both to UKLA enforcement issues and to FSA enforcement issues – for example, if it appeared that the issuer had breached the listing rules and that its sponsor or corporate brokers had failed to act with due skill, care and diligence. As has already been seen[1], the UKLA is generally speaking able to share with the FSA information which it receives in its investigation. The UKLA and the FSA have given no guidance on how they will act in that situation, but there is plainly nothing to prevent them from taking both types of action and indeed there may be good reason for them to do so[2].

1 See para 15.88 ff above.
2 There are some circumstances in which the issue may cause both the UKLA and the FSA to seek to exercise their powers against the same person – for example, a breach of the listing rules by a sponsor or by an issuer that was also an authorised person. No guidance has been given on how the UKLA and the FSA will act in that situation.

15.106 Finally, the matter may potentially give rise to action both by the UKLA and by another regulatory body, such as an exchange or an overseas regulator. In that situation, the UKLA will examine the circumstances of the case and consider, in the light of the relevant investigation and enforcement powers, which body should take action to address the breach, recognising that it may be appropriate for both to take action[1]. Moreover, the FSA is developing operating arrangements with other UK authorities concerning cases in which more than one regulatory authority may have an interest, with the aim of ensuring that cases are approached in a co-ordinated and efficient manner and that the person concerned is treated fairly[2]. Notably, there is no suggestion that there can never be multiple investigations by different regulators into the same matter and, in appropriate cases, this may be what occurs.

1 See the draft Guidance Manual, para 8.13.4.
2 See the draft Guidance Manual, para 8.13.3. See also the discussion at para 15.20 above and at para 7.15 ff above.

Disciplinary action

Discipline against issuers and applicants for listing

15.107 If the UKLA considers that an issuer of listed securities or an applicant for listing has contravened any provision of the listing rules, it may:

- impose on him a penalty of such amount as it considers appropriate[1]; or
- instead, publish a statement censuring him[2].

1 FSMA 2000, s 91(1) and draft Listing Rules, r 1.9. The ability to levy fines for breaches of the listing rules is a new aspect of the regulatory system which did not exist under the Financial Services Act 1986.
2 FSMA 2000, s 91(3) and draft Listing Rules, r 1.9.

15.108 Alternatively, the UKLA may decide to issue an informal private warning rather than taking any formal disciplinary action[1].

1 See the draft Guidance Manual, para 8.4 and see para 15.124 below.

15.109 This provision is relatively straightforward. There are three particular points to note. First, the imposition of disciplinary sanctions expressly does not preclude the UKLA from taking any other action available to it under Pt VI[1]. A disciplinary sanction may therefore be imposed in conjunction with other action, such as the suspension of listing of the issuer's securities.

1 FSMA 2000, s 91(4).

15.110 Second, fines and public censures are not truly alternatives, since the imposition of a fine, and the reasons for imposing it, will normally be made public[1]. Hence, the real question is whether or not the UKLA will impose a fine.

1 This is discussed at para 15.98 above.

15.111 Third, the FSMA 2000 prescribes a two-year limitation period for bringing disciplinary proceedings under this section[1]. Specifically, the UKLA may not take action against a person under this provision after the end of the period of two years beginning with the first day on which it knew of the contravention unless proceedings against that person in respect of the contravention were begun before the end of that period. As to what, precisely, this means:

- the two-year period begins with the first day on which the UKLA knew of the contravention. The UKLA is treated as knowing of a contravention if it has information from which the contravention can reasonably be inferred[2]. The answer to the question when time started to run therefore relies not upon when the FSA reached a conclusion that there was a contravention but upon when it had the information from which that conclusion could have been reached;
- it is not clear whether information known to the FSA, but not to the UKLA staff specifically, is taken into account for this purpose;
- to fall within the limitation period, proceedings must be begun before the end of the two-year period. Proceedings against a person in respect of a contravention are treated as begun when a warning notice is given[3]. The issue of a warning notice is the first formal step in the decision-making process[4].

1 FSMA 2000, s 91(6).
2 FSMA 2000, s 91(7)(a).
3 FSMA 2000, s 91(7)(b).
4 See para 15.160 below.

15.112 Where the UKLA considers that the listing rules have been contravened, it is not under any obligation to take disciplinary action, but has a discretion whether to do so. The key question in many cases is how it exercises that discretion, how it decides whether to impose a fine or a public censure, and how it determines the size of the penalty that it is appropriate to impose. These issues are considered at para 15.123 ff below.

Discipline against directors or former directors

15.113 Directors and, where relevant, former directors, may become amenable to UKLA enforcement action where they are involved in breaches of the listing rules by the company. In addition, the UKLA has certain powers where a director breaches the company's code of dealings[1]. The former is considered here and the latter at para 15.148 ff below.

1 Based upon the Model Code set out in the Appendix to the Listing Rules, Chapter 16. A breach of the code of the company's dealings does not, generally speaking, expose the director concerned

to a regulatory fine, although it may be possible for a situation to arise where the director's breach caused or evidenced a breach of the listing rules by the company (on the ground that it had failed to take all proper and reasonable steps to secure compliance with the code of dealings: see Listing Rules, r 16.18) and the director was liable to disciplinary action as a person knowingly concerned in that breach by the company.

15.114 If, in such a case[1], the UKLA considers that a person who was at the material time a director of the issuer or applicant was knowingly concerned in the contravention of the listing rules by the issuer or applicant, it may:

- impose a penalty on him of such amount as it considers appropriate[2]; or
- instead, publish a statement censuring him[3].

1 This seems to refer to a case where the UKLA considers that an issuer or applicant has contravened a provision of the listing rules.
2 FSMA 2000, s 91(2).
3 FSMA 2000, s 91(3).

15.115 Alternatively, the UKLA may decide to issue an informal private warning rather than, or instead of, taking any formal disciplinary action[1].

1 See the draft Guidance Manual, para 8.4 and see para 15.124 below.

15.116 A two-year limitation period applies in the same way as in relation to disciplinary action against issuers and applicants[1].

1 For a more detailed discussion, see para 15.111 above.

15.117 Directors[1] may therefore incur liability to personal disciplinary action in respect of breaches of listing rules by the company, where they were knowingly concerned in the company's breach. The meaning of 'knowingly concerned' is discussed at para 2.184 ff above. It should be apparent from that discussion that the test is not a particularly high one and that, in many situations, a director will potentially have been knowingly concerned in the company's breaches.

1 This term includes, broadly, shadow directors and de facto directors: FSMA 2000, s 417 and see footnote 2 to para 15.53 above.

15.118 The UKLA is not, though, under any obligation to take action against a director whom it considers was knowingly concerned in the company's breach. The same policy questions arise as in relation to disciplinary action against the issuer or applicant but, in addition, there is the question of when in practice the UKLA will take action against the individual in addition to the company. The FSA's policy is considered at para 15.123 ff below.

Discipline against sponsors

15.119 If the UKLA considers that a sponsor has breached any provision of the listing rules and considers it appropriate to impose a sanction, it will publish a statement censuring the sponsor[1].

1 Draft Listing Rules, r 2.28. The basis for this power is different for the power to discipline issuers, applicants and directors. The FSMA 2000 does not directly contain provision for disciplinary sanctions against sponsors but, rather (see FSMA 2000, s 89), empowers the UKLA to make provision in the listing rules for the public censure of sponsors.

15.120 Alternatively, the UKLA may decide to issue an informal private warning rather than taking any formal disciplinary action[1].

1 See the draft Guidance Manual, para 8.4 and see para 15.124 below.

15.121 The two-year limitation period applicable to disciplinary action against issuers, applicants and directors[1] does not apply in relation to action against sponsors.

1 See para 15.111 above.

15.122 The UKLA cannot, therefore, levy a fine against a sponsor. However, because a sponsor is an authorised person, it is amenable to the FSA's wider regulatory jurisdiction, including its powers to levy fines on authorised persons for regulatory breaches. Whilst not entirely clear, it seems that a breach of the listing rules by a sponsor could form the basis for a fine or public censure by the FSA under FSMA 2000, ss 205 or 206[1] and, where appropriate, also to other regulatory enforcement action by the FSA.

1 The FSA can impose such disciplinary action where an authorised person 'has contravened a requirement imposed on him by or under [the FSMA 2000]'. It seems likely that the listing rules fall within this, in so far as they impose requirements upon sponsors. This phrase is discussed in more detail at para 2.142 ff above. The FSA's powers to discipline authorised persons are considered in Chapter 7 above.

The UKLA's policy on the exercise of its disciplinary powers

In what circumstances will the FSA take disciplinary action?

15.123 As a matter of general policy, the UKLA recognises that disciplinary sanctions are only one of the regulatory tools available to it and that it may be possible to address many instances of non-compliance without resorting to formal disciplinary action[1]. Nonetheless, the effective and proportionate use of its powers plays an important role and, among other things, helps to deter others, demonstrate the benefits of compliance and increase public awareness of regulatory standards[2].

1 See the draft Guidance Manual, para 8.3.2. If the UKLA decides not take any formal action, either in the context of issuing a private warning or where there is insufficient evidence to substantiate a breach of the listing rules, it may issue a 'no further action' letter, indicating its view that based on the information and evidence available to it at the time, no further action is appropriate. Such a letter is not binding on the UKLA if further information comes to its attention: see the draft Guidance Manual, para 8.14.1.

2 See the draft Guidance Manual, paras 8.3.2 and 8.3.3. This is similar to the FSA's general policy on its enforcement role, outlined at para 2.34 above.

15.124 Where the UKLA has concerns about the behaviour of the person concerned but considers that it is not appropriate, in all the circumstances, to seek a formal disciplinary sanction, it may issue a private warning, rather than taking formal disciplinary action, where it considers that a private warning would be helpful to alert the person concerned that their conduct was such that the UKLA considered seeking a formal disciplinary sanction. The UKLA's proposed policy[1] on issuing private warnings, and the proposed nature and effect of a private warning, is very similar to the FSA's policy, considered in detail at para 7.18 ff above[2].

1 See the draft Guidance Manual, para 8.4.
2 For the FSA's policy, see the FSA Handbook at ENF 11.3.

15.125 In more serious cases, the UKLA will institute formal disciplinary action[1]. The UKLA's proposed policy is that, in determining whether to take disciplinary action, it will consider the full circumstances of the case and may, in particular, take account of a number of factors (the list of which is expressly non-exhaustive), namely[2]:

- whether the breach reveals serious or systemic weaknesses in compliance procedures[3];
- whether the person concerned has admitted the conduct and provided full and immediate co-operation[4];
- whether the person has previously given the UKLA any relevant undertakings about its behaviour, whether the UKLA has previously asked the person to take remedial action and the extent to which it was taken, and any applicable UKLA guidance[5]; and
- proposed action by other regulatory bodies: whether it would be adequate to address the UKLA's concerns and whether it is appropriate for the UKLA to take its own action[6].

1 See the draft Guidance Manual, para 8.11.2.
2 See the draft Guidance Manual, para 8.5.1.
3 Generally speaking, a one-off rule breach which has no systemic causes may be less likely to be treated as a serious breach (although clearly it is possible for an isolated rule breach to be extremely serious). For this reason, the UKLA will often focus not only on the specific rule breach in question but also on the potential systemic implications (for example, systems/controls) and issuers therefore need to consider the same question.
4 The conduct of the person concerned after the breach arose may thus be relevant to the UKLA in determining what action to take. This reinforces the need for issuers and others to co-operate with UKLA enquiries and investigations.
5 The UKLA will not take action against issuers, directors, former directors or sponsors for behaviour in line with current written guidance or binding oral guidance in the circumstances contemplated by the guidance: see the draft Guidance Manual, para 8.5.1(5). For a further discussion, see footnote 3 to para 15.4 above.
6 This is briefly discussed at para 15.106 above.

What action will the UKLA take?

15.126 If it is appropriate for the UKLA to take formal disciplinary action against an issuer, applicant or director[1], then the next question is what action it will take. The issue is whether it should issue a public censure, rather than a fine and, in deciding this question, the UKLA has indicated that it will consider all the relevant circumstances of the breach, including a non-exhaustive list of factors set out in the draft Guidance Manual[2]. The UKLA regards a public censure as a serious sanction, recognising the effect that it may have on the person's business or reputation[3].

1 This question does not arise in relation to sponsors, since the UKLA has no power to fine a sponsor.
2 See the draft Guidance Manual, para 8.11.3. These are very similar to the factors taken into account by the FSA when considering the same question: see para 7.31 above (and see the FSA Handbook at ENF 12.3), save that consistency (ie that the FSA will seek to achieve a consistent approach to its decisions on whether to impose a penalty or issues a public statement) is not listed as a factor in the UKLA context.
3 See the draft Guidance Manual, para 8.3.4.

How does the UKLA determine the amount of a fine?

15.127 Where the UKLA considers it is appropriate to impose a fine, the final question is the amount of the fine. There is no tariff for particular kinds of breaches (although it is likely, if the UKLA applies its policies consistently, that some kind of predictability will emerge over time). The UKLA has produced a list of factors that may be relevant when it determines the amount of the penalty[1]. These are, broadly, the same factors as are relevant when the FSA considers the same issue[2].

1 See the draft Guidance Manual, para 8.8.3.
2 See para 7.38 above and the FSA Handbook at ENF 13.3.3. An additional factor is listed as potentially relevant in this context, namely whether the person concerned obtained any professional advice before the breach occurred and whether they followed that advice: see the draft Guidance Manual, para 8.8.3(6). Note also that it is not the purpose of a fine to render an issuer or director insolvent or threaten their solvency and where this is a material consideration the UKLA will consider whether a lower penalty would be appropriate: see the draft Guidance Manual, para 8.8.3(4)(c). This highlights a further point, namely that a large fine against an issuer may effectively penalise the shareholders whose interests the UKLA is seeking to protect.

15.128 The FSMA 2000 prevents the UKLA from, broadly, seeking to recover through such penalties the cost of its investigation and enforcement process[1]. This is not, therefore, a factor that may be taken into account in determining the amount of the penalty.

1 This is the effect of FSMA 2000, s 100.

15.129 Fines are paid to the UKLA and go towards reducing the annual fees paid by issuers[1].

1 FSMA 2000, s 100 and see the draft Guidance Manual, para 13.6.

When will the UKLA take action against a director?

15.130 The basis for taking disciplinary action against a director personally, namely that he was knowingly concerned in a breach of the listing rules by the issuer concerned, is a broad one and, potentially, could apply in many situations where an issuer commits a breach. A key question is therefore when, in practice, the UKLA will pursue a director personally instead of, or in addition to, the company.

15.131 The UKLA has indicated that it regards the issuer as having primary responsibility for ensuring compliance with its own regulatory obligations and, therefore, any disciplinary action will normally be taken in the first instance against the issuer itself[1]. However, where a director was knowingly concerned in the issuer's breach, it may take action against the director. It may also do so where it does not consider it appropriate to seek a disciplinary sanction against the issuer[2].

1 See the draft Guidance Manual, para 8.6.1.
2 See the draft Guidance Manual, para 8.6.2.

15.132 Two points may be made about this policy statement. First, it does not expressly refer to action being taken against both the issuer and the director, although that is quite clearly possible. Second, and more importantly, it says little about when in practice the UKLA will pursue the director. A similar issue arises in the context of the FSA's wider regulatory functions, namely in what circumstances the FSA will take action personally against an approved person rather than, or in addition to, the firm for which the approved person works. The basic premise is the same – namely that primary responsibility for regulatory compliance rests with the firm, not the individual. The FSA's policy on taking action against an approved person, considered at para 8.13 ff above, is based on whether the approved person is personally culpable, which the FSA interprets as a partly objective test. In other words, a person could be regarded as personally culpable if he failed to act with the degree of care reasonably to be expected of him. It is unclear whether a similar policy will be applied by the UKLA.

Other regulatory action

15.133 Whilst the focus has thus far been on the UKLA's powers to impose fines and public censures, a range of potential enforcement action is available to the UKLA or the FSA to address the different implications of breaches of the listing rules or other regulatory issues that arise in the UKLA context, including:

- the suspension or cancellation of the listing of the relevant securities;
- the cancellation of a sponsor's approval;
- the publication of information through the Company Announcements Office;
- the FSA's powers to impose or apply for restitution orders and/or injunctions; and
- the FSA's powers to prosecute criminal offences.

Each is considered in turn below. Generally speaking, these powers can be exercised individually or in combination. Which power or combination of powers it is appropriate to exercise will depend upon the nature of the matter and of the concerns to which it gives rise and what the UKLA and/or the FSA seek to achieve in the particular circumstances.

Suspension or cancellation of listing

15.134 The UKLA has powers to suspend or cancel the listing of an issuer's securities. Each is considered below.

Suspension of listing

15.135 Where:

- the smooth operation of the market is, or may be, temporarily jeopardised; or
- the protection of investors so requires;

the UKLA may suspend, with effect from such time as it may determine, the listing of any securities at any time and in such circumstances as it thinks fit (whether or not at the request of the issuer or its agent on its behalf)[1]. The listing of securities can be suspended either unilaterally by the UKLA or at the request of the issuer concerned. We focus here on the former[2].

1 Draft Listing Rules, r 1.16. This rule is given statutory effect by FSMA 2000, s 77.
2 For guidance on the UKLA's approach to requests for suspension of listing, see the draft Guidance Manual, paras 9.8 and 9.9 and see para 9.12 for guidance on circumstances when the UKLA will not normally suspend listing at the request of the issuer.

15.136 The test for the suspension of securities from listing is a broad one and it leaves the UKLA a significant amount of discretion both to determine whether to act and to determine when to take action and for what period. The power to suspend listing can also be exercised as a matter of urgency[1].

1 See the draft Guidance Manual, para 9.3.2. The procedure for exercising this power is outlined at para 15.168 ff below. Various practical issues that arise in relation to the use of enforcement powers as a matter of urgency are discussed at para 9.211 ff above.

15.137 The UKLA has proposed a non-exhaustive list of examples of circumstances in which it will normally suspend listing[1], namely where:

- the issuer fails to publish financial information in accordance with the listing rules;
- the issuer fails to meet the continuing obligations of listing;
- the issuer is unable to assess accurately its financial position and inform the market accordingly;
- there is or may be a leak of price sensitive information and the issuer is unwilling or unable to issue an appropriate announcement within a reasonable amount of time;

- there is an announcement of a reverse takeover where this does not coincide with the publication of a class 1 circular and listing particulars;
- a secondary listed issuer is, or is going to be, suspended in its country of primary listing; or
- the issuer has appointed administrators or receivers, or is an investment trust and is winding up.

1 See the draft Guidance Manual, para 9.3.4.

15.138 The UKLA will also suspend a listing[1] of a security which it becomes aware has ceased to be admitted to trading on at least one recognised investment exchange[2].

1 See the draft Guidance Manual, para 9.5.1.
2 The UKLA has provided additional guidance in relation to securities which have a secondary listing in the UK, where it receives a request to suspend or cancel a listing from the overseas exchange or competent authority: see the draft Guidance Manual, para 9.7.

15.139 The UKLA has a broad discretion to determine when the suspension of listing becomes effective. The FSMA 2000 provides that the suspension takes effect either immediately, if the first supervisory notice[1] states that this is the case, or in any other case on such date as may be specified in the notice. There is no statutory hurdle which must be passed before the power can be exercised as a matter of urgency[2] nor is there any general fallback position that the suspension takes effect only when the enforcement process has been completed[3]. The UKLA's draft Guidance Manual gives no indication of its policy on when in practice it is likely to exercise its powers as a matter of urgency.

1 This is the first stage in the formal enforcement process: see para 15.168 below.
2 Contrast with this the similar provisions of the FSMA 2000 (see, for example, s 53 in relation to variations of permission (discussed at para 9.196 above) which allow the FSA to specify that action takes effect immediately only if it reasonably considers that this is necessary having regard to the ground upon which it is exercising its power.
3 Again, contrast the position in relation to the FSA's powers to vary a firm's permission: see para 9.99 above.

15.140 An issuer, the listing of whose securities is suspended, remains obliged to comply with the requirements of the listing rules unless the UKLA agrees otherwise[1], including the requirement to notify the UKLA of any breaches of listing rules of which it becomes aware.

1 Draft Listing Rules, r 1.17 and see the draft Guidance Manual, para 9.14.

15.141 Once the listing has been suspended, the question then arises of how to have the listing restored[1]. There are, broadly, two options and both may be pursued at different times. First, the issuer may seek to have the original decision to suspend the listing overturned through the enforcement process[2], ultimately in the Tribunal, in which case this will result in the listing being restored. Second, the issuer may apply to the UKLA to have its listing restored[3].

1 The draft listing rules allow the UKLA to impose on the procedure for listing the suspension such conditions as it considers appropriate: draft Listing Rules, r 1.19. No guidance on the use of this power is provided in the draft Guidance Manual.
2 The enforcement process is outlined at para 15.156 ff below.
3 This is the terminology used in the draft Listing Rules and Guidance Manual. The FSMA 2000 refers to the cancellation of the suspension of listing.

15.142 So far as the latter is concerned, the UKLA has given little indication of the circumstances when it is likely to grant such an application, save to make clear that it will not necessarily restore the listing on such an application if it is not satisfied that the circumstances prevailing at the time warrant a restoration[1]. It is thought that the issuer would have to satisfy the UKLA that the circumstances which gave rise to the suspension of listing have been resolved. It may also be relevant to the UKLA not to prejudice the shareholders or markets whose interests it seeks to protect by unnecessarily keeping the suspension in force.

1 See the draft Guidance Manual, para 9.17.8.

Cancellation of listing

15.143 The UKLA may cancel the listing of any securities if it is satisfied that:

- there are special circumstances which preclude normal regular dealings in them[1]; or
- the securities are no longer admitted to trading[2].

1 Draft Listing Rules, r 1.20. This rule is given statutory effect by FSMA 2000, s 77.
2 Draft Listing Rules, r 1.21.

15.144 The UKLA has a broad discretion to cancel[1] the listing of securities. This is clearly a serious power, not to be used lightly. The UKLA has given little indication in its draft Guidance Manual of the circumstances when it will exercise its power to cancel the listing of securities, stating simply that it will take into account all the relevant circumstances[2]. In addition, it will normally cancel listing if a security has its listing suspended for more than six months[3] or if the UKLA believes that there are insufficient shares held in public hands[4], or if it considers that the security has been suspended from trading for too long a period[5].

1 This is the terminology used in the draft Listing Rules and Guidance Manual. The FSMA 2000 refers to the 'discontinuance', rather than cancellation, of the listing.
2 See the draft Guidance Manual, para 9.4.2.
3 This reflects the former provisions of the Listing Rules.
4 See the draft Guidance Manual, para 9.4.3.
5 See the draft Guidance Manual, para 9.5.3. In such a case, the UKLA would normally expect to liaise with the issuer and the relevant recognised investment exchange.

15.145 As with a suspension of listing[1], the UKLA has a broad discretion to determine when the cancellation of listing becomes effective. The FSMA 2000 provides that the cancellation takes effect either immediately, if the first supervisory notice[2] states that this is the case, or in any other case on such date as may be specified in the notice. There is no statutory hurdle which must be passed before the power can be exercised as a matter of urgency[3] nor is there any general fallback position that the cancellation takes effect only when the enforcement process has been completed[4]. The UKLA has given no indication of its policy on when in practice it is likely to exercise its powers as a matter of urgency. In many cases, there will be no need to cancel the listing as a matter of urgency; the securities could be suspended in the first instance and cancellation may, if appropriate, follow in due course.

1 See para 15.139 above.
2 This is the first stage in the formal enforcement process: see para 15.168 ff below.
3 Contrast with this the similar provisions of the FSMA 2000 (see, for example, s 53 in relation to variations of permission (discussed at para 9.196 above), which allow the FSA to specify that action takes effect immediately only if it reasonably considers that this is necessary having regard to the ground upon which it is exercising its power.
4 Again, contrast the position in relation to the FSA's powers to vary a firm's permission: see para 9.99 above.

15.146 Once the listing has been cancelled, the cancellation can only be revoked through the enforcement process[1]. Beyond that, the issuer will need to make a new application for admission to listing[2].

1 This is outlined at para 15.168 below. 'Revoking the cancellation' of listing is the terminology listed in the draft Guidance Manual; the FSMA 2000 refers to 'cancelling the discontinuance'.
2 See the draft Guidance Manual, para 9.19.

Cancellation of a sponsor's approval

15.147 The UKLA has the power to cancel a person's approval to act as a sponsor[1]. It has indicated that it will do so only if it considers that the sponsor no longer meets the criteria for approval as a sponsor set out in Chapter 2 of the listing rules[2]. In deciding whether to cancel approval, the UKLA will take into account all relevant factors, including any matter which it could take into account if it were considering an application for approval as a sponsor, and the compliance record of the sponsor[3].

1 FSMA 2000, s 88 and the UKLA Guidance Manual, para 4.19.
2 See the draft Guidance Manual, paras 4.19.1 and 4.21.1. Examples would include if the sponsor's permission was cancelled or it no longer had four 'eligible employees' (as defined in para 4.6 of the draft Guidance Manual).
3 See the draft Guidance Manual, para 4.21.2.

Publication of information relating to breaches of the code of dealings

15.148 Where a director or any relevant employee breaches the company's code of dealing[1], the UKLA may, taking into account all relevant factors including the protection of investors, require the company to notify the Company Announcements Office of the circumstances of any such breach[2] (irrespective of whether the company has taken all proper and reasonable steps to secure compliance with the code of dealing[3]).

1 A code of dealing in terms no less exacting than the Model Code: see the draft Listing Rules, r 16.18 ff.
2 Draft Listing Rules, r 16.21.
3 This correlates with the situation where the company may itself be in breach of the listing rules in relation to a director's breach of its code of dealings: see draft Listing Rules, r 16.18.

15.149 The UKLA also has more general powers to require issuers to publish information[1], but these are not considered in detail here, since they are not on the whole an enforcement issue, although clearly the UKLA may both consider that information needs to be published to the market and that the issuer has breached the listing rules in not publishing that information.

1 The UKLA may, at any time, require an issuer to publish such information in such form and within such time limits as it considers appropriate for the purpose of protecting investors and maintaining the smooth operation of the market (and if the issuer fails to comply it may itself publish the information after having given the issuer an opportunity to make representations as to why the information should not be published): draft Listing Rules, rr 1.6 and 1.7.

15.150 The UKLA believes that information regarding significant breaches of a company's code of dealing is important to investors when making investment decisions and has therefore introduced this discretionary power to require the company to publish information about such breaches by directors or other employees[1]. This goes together with the requirement imposed on issuers to report such breaches to the UKLA[2].

1 See Consultation Paper 100 ('Proposed Changes to the Listing Rules at N2'), June 2001, para 5.4.
2 Draft Listing Rules, r 16.20 and see para 15.23 ff above.

15.151 Since the power is discretionary, an important question is when in practice the UKLA will exercise this power. In deciding whether to do so, or considering the timing of the announcement, the UKLA has indicated that it will take into account all relevant factors, including[1]:

- the protection of investors;
- the nature and seriousness of the breach;
- whether any regulatory investigation, enforcement action or prosecution is taking place in respect of the behaviour, which may be prejudiced;
- whether relevant information relating to the breach is in the public domain;
- whether the behaviour of the person concerned is the subject of proceedings between him and the company, which may be prejudiced; and
- whether the person concerned disputes that a breach has taken place.

1 See the draft Guidance Manual, para 11.4.2.

15.152 The UKLA has said that it will not require an announcement to be made unless it believes that a regulatory benefit would accrue to market participants[1]. For example, it will not do so in relation to an insignificant breach.

1 See the draft Guidance Manual, para 11.4.3.

Injunctions and restitution orders

15.153 The FSA, acting in its wider regulatory capacity, has the power in certain circumstances to:

- impose or apply to a court for a restitution order, requiring a person to compensate those who have suffered loss arising from its breach and/or to disgorge gains it has made; and/or
- to apply to a court for an injunction, restraining prospective breaches, requiring remedial steps to be taken and/or freezing assets[1].

These are discussed in more detail in Chapter 7 above.

1 As discussed in more detail at para 7.103 above, in many cases an injunction will be applied for initially on an interim basis without full consideration of the merits and this may in practice be dispositive of the matter.

15.154 The key test, for the imposition of an injunction or a restitution order, is a 'contravention of a requirement imposed by or under [the FSMA 2000]'. The meaning of this phrase is discussed at para 2.142 ff above. It probably includes breaches of the listing rules, as requirements imposed under the FSMA 2000, and certainly the UKLA's view is that an injunction or restitution order can be imposed in relation to a breach of the listing rules[1].

1 See the draft Guidance Manual, para 1.4.3(2).

Criminal law implications

15.155 In three situations, breaches of the FSMA 2000, Pt VI may have criminal law consequences[1]. In those situations, the FSA may well act as the prosecuting authority in relation to the offences. The question of when the FSA will act as prosecuting authority, and a discussion of some of the relevant issues, can be found in Chapter 11 above.

1 Sections 83, 85 and 98.

The procedure for taking enforcement action

15.156 In the following paragraphs we review the procedure involved where the UKLA seeks to exercise any of its enforcement powers, including the rights of the person against whom the relevant power is to be exercised. As will be seen, these procedures mark a significant change from the position under the previous regime.

15.157 We first provide a brief overview of the enforcement process, before outlining the process applicable to each type of enforcement action. The UKLA's enforcement procedures are, in most respects[1], the same as those of the FSA. To avoid repetition, we provide here only an outline of the procedure applicable to each type of enforcement action. The details, including a discussion of how each element of the process works in practice, can be found in, as appropriate, Chapter 5 (the general statutory framework and the warning/decision notice procedure) or Chapter 9 (the supervisory notice procedure).

1 One of the main differences is the involvement of the Listing Authority Committee: see para 15.164 below.

An overview of the UKLA enforcement process

15.158 There are, broadly speaking, three different types of enforcement process:

- the warning/decision notice procedure, for enforcement action in relation to which the FSMA 2000 requires the UKLA to issue warning and decision notices when it seeks to exercise its enforcement powers;
- the supervisory notice procedure, for enforcement action in relation to which the FSMA 2000 requires the UKLA to issue notices known as supervisory notices when it seeks to exercise its enforcement powers; and
- the procedure where the FSMA 2000 does not require any statutory notices to be served[1].

1 The procedure relating to each particular type of enforcement action for which there is no specified statutory process is outlined where the action concerned is discussed. This encompasses primarily: (i) requirements to publish information (see para 15.175 ff below) and (ii) decisions to commence civil or criminal proceedings (see respectively, paras 15.177 and 15.178 below).

15.159 The FSMA 2000 contains the framework for the UKLA's procedures[1], requiring it to issue notices in particular circumstances and making various provisions[2] with regard to such notices, including providing certain rights for the person on whom they are served and, in some circumstances, third parties. It also requires the UKLA[3] to determine and publish its detailed procedures and makes certain basic requirements of those procedures. Specifically, the procedures must be designed to secure, among other things, that the decision which gives rise to the obligation to issue such a notice is taken, normally, by a person who was not directly involved in establishing the evidence on which that decision is based[4]. In other words, there is a general requirement for a separation of the functions of investigating and decision making, subject to certain exceptions.

1 The same statutory framework applies to the FSA, in its wider regulatory capacity, and it is discussed in detail in Chapter 5 above.
2 FSMA 2000, ss 387 to 396 (applied to the UKLA by Sch 7, para 1). As well as warning/decision and supervisory notices, the FSMA 2000 makes provision for other statutory notices, known as final notices and notices of discontinuance.
3 FSMA 2000, s 395, as applied to the UKLA by Sch 7, para 1.
4 FSMA 2000, s 395(2). This is discussed in more detail at para 5.26 above. Note that there are certain exceptions to this requirement.

15.160 In broad terms[1], the warning/decision notice procedure operates as follows:

- the UKLA staff that investigate the firm decide whether or not to recommend that any action should be taken[2];
- that recommendation is placed before the decision-making body (either the Regulatory Decisions Committee ('RDC') or the Listing Authority Committee, depending upon the nature of the action recommended to be taken[3]), for a decision on whether to propose that enforcement action is taken[4];
- if the decision-making body decides to propose the enforcement action, the UKLA issues a warning notice to the person concerned (and in some circumstances to third parties)[5];
- there follows a process of negotiation to try to reach an agreed resolution of the matter and, in some cases, a mediation may occur[6]; the person concerned also has rights of access to certain documents of the UKLA[7];
- assuming that an agreed resolution cannot be reached, the person concerned has the opportunity to put written and/or oral representations to the decision-making body[8];
- the decision-making body considers what action it is appropriate to take in the light of those representations and, if it decides to take action, the UKLA issues a decision notice[9];
- the person concerned (and in some circumstances affected third parties) has the right to refer the matter to the Tribunal, for an independent determination[10];
- if the person does not do so, the action takes effect; otherwise it takes effect only once the reference to the Tribunal and any appeal (on points of law only) have been finally disposed of[11];
- a further notice, known as a final notice, is issued by the UKLA when taking the relevant action[12];
- publicity will, generally speaking, arise only at the end of the process, when the UKLA takes the action concerned, with the important exception that proceedings before the Tribunal will normally be in public[13].

1 For a detailed discussion of each stage of the process, and the statutory provisions underlying each of these points, see Chapter 5 above.
2 See the draft Guidance Manual, para 10.6.1.
3 See the draft Guidance Manual, paras 10.17, 10.18 and 10.23.
4 See the draft Guidance Manual, para 10.6.2.
5 See the draft Guidance Manual, para 10.6.3.
6 See the draft Guidance Manual, Appendix 1. The mediation scheme is available in cases involving disciplinary matters: see Appendix 1, para 4.1. This probably refers to cases where the UKLA seeks the imposition of a fine or public censure; it probably does not include cases where the UKLA seeks to suspend or cancel the listing, to cancel the approval of a sponsor, or to require the company to publish information regarding a director's breach.
7 See the draft Guidance Manual, para 10.12.
8 See the draft Guidance Manual, para 10.29.
9 See the draft Guidance Manual, para 10.7. Having issued a warning notice proposing a fine, the UKLA could, in its decision notice, decide to impose a different level of fine or a public censure: see the FSMA 2000, s 388(2) and the discussion at para 5.164 above.
10 See the draft Guidance Manual, para 10.36.
11 See the draft Guidance Manual, para 10.36.7.

12 See the draft Guidance Manual, para 10.10.
13 See para 6.32 above.

15.161 The supervisory notice procedure is similar[1], save that[2]:

- both notices are known as supervisory notices[3];
- the UKLA's enforcement action may, in an appropriate case, take effect immediately on service of the first supervisory notice, with the person concerned having the right to make representations, or refer the matter to the Tribunal, only afterwards. Action can therefore be taken as a matter of urgency[4];
- the person concerned has the right to refer the matter to the Tribunal immediately on receipt of the first supervisory notice;
- there is no right of access to the UKLA's documents and third parties do not have any right to become involved;
- the mediation scheme is not available and in practice there may be less focus on reaching an agreed settlement of the matter.

1 For a detailed discussion of each stage of the supervisory notice procedure, see para 9.105 ff above.
2 There are a number of more technical differences which are not outlined here. A list of the differences can be found in the draft Guidance Manual, para 10.14.4.
3 The relevant provisions of the FSMA 2000 do not use the term 'supervisory notice', but s 395(13) defines certain notices as supervisory notices.
4 Various practical issues to which this gives rise are discussed at para 9.211 ff above.

15.162 In practice, most enforcement matters have historically been resolved by agreement and the process aims to retain, and indeed to foster, this approach[1]. The nature and procedures of the decision-making body are clearly integral to this and will be of particular interest to those subjected to the process. There are two, alternative decision-making bodies, depending upon the nature of the enforcement action that is proposed[2], namely the RDC and the Listing Authority Committee. As will be seen, neither is independent from the FSA or the UKLA in the sense of being apart from the FSA's or the UKLA's regulatory agenda. The opportunity to have the matter heard before a wholly independent body will follow in the Tribunal. The key point, in accordance with the requirements of the FSMA 2000, is that the decision-making body is normally separate from those who conducted the investigation.

1 The policy issues which arose in designing the process are discussed at para 5.17 ff above.
2 Alternatively, where there is no statutory requirement to issue notices (particularly, when the UKLA decides to impose a requirement to publish information: see para 15.175 ff below), and therefore the procedure outlined above does not apply, the relevant decision will be taken at an appropriate level within the FSA.

The Regulatory Decisions Committee

15.163 Where the UKLA proposes or takes any of the following actions (in the enforcement context[1]):

- to cancel a listing;
- to cancel a person's approval as a sponsor; or
- to exercise the UKLA's powers to impose a financial penalty upon or issue a public censure about an issuer, director, former director or sponsor;

the decision-making body is the RDC. Very briefly, the RDC is a body that has been formed to take many decisions relating to warning/decision notices and supervisory notices[2]. It is answerable to the FSA Board, but its members are not members of the FSA's (or UKLA's) staff[3].

1 The RDC has additional functions, set out in the draft Guidance Manual, para 10.18.1.
2 In the context of the FSA's wider regulatory functions, most decisions involving such notices are taken by the RDC.
3 For a more detailed discussion of the RDC, its constitution and procedure, see para 5.26 ff above.

The Listing Authority Committee

15.164 That leaves decisions to suspend a listing[1], which are not taken by the RDC, but under so-called 'executive procedures' by a body called the Listing Authority Committee. The Listing Authority Committee is a committee of UKLA staff, accountable, ultimately, to the FSA Board. Certain details concerning the Listing Authority Committee have been provided[2]:

- it may operate through sub-committees to consider particular decisions or classes of decision;
- each meeting will include an individual with authority to act as chairman and at least one other member;
- it operates on the basis of a recommendation from a UKLA staff member of at least the level of associate[3]. It may take legal advice from an FSA staff member of at least the same level.

1 This refers to UKLA decisions unilaterally to suspend a listing. For the procedure where a suspension of listing is sought by the company concerned, see the draft Guidance Manual, para 10.25.
2 See the draft Guidance Manual, para 10.26.
3 This recommendation will not necessarily involve anyone of any particular seniority in the FSA.

15.165 However, in an exceptionally urgent case where in the UKLA staff's opinion, any delay would or might temporarily jeopardise the smooth operation of the market or where the protection of investors so requires, and two members of the Listing Authority Committee are not available, the UKLA staff's recommendation will be considered and the decisions made by a member of the FSA's executive of at least Director of Division level[1].

1 See the draft Guidance Manual, para 10.26.6. Generally, this will maintain the separation of functions required by FSMA 2000, s 395, but, in exceptional circumstances, it may be possible for the UKLA to take a decision without ensuring the separation of functions: see para 9.204 above.

Disciplinary action

15.166 Where the UKLA wishes to impose a financial penalty upon or publicly censure an issuer, applicant, director or former director under FSMA 2000, s 91, the warning/decision notice procedure applies[1]. The detailed procedure is discussed in Chapter 5 above. Among other things, the person concerned will have the right to refer the matter to the Tribunal[2]. The warning and decision notice are required to state, as appropriate, the amount of the penalty or the terms of the proposed censure[3].

1 FSMA 2000, s 92.
2 For details, see Chapter 6 above.
3 FSMA 2000, s 92.

15.167 Where the UKLA wishes to publish a statement in relation to a sponsor under FSMA 2000, s 89, the warning/decision notice procedure applies[1]. The detailed procedure is discussed in Chapter 5 above. Among other things, the sponsor will have the right to refer the matter to the Tribunal[2]. The warning and decision notice are required to state the terms of the proposed censure[3].

1 FSMA 2000, s 89.
2 For details, see Chapter 6 above.
3 FSMA 2000, s 89.

Other enforcement action

Suspension or cancellation of listing

15.168 Where the UKLA wishes to suspend or cancel a listing under FSMA 2000, s 77, the supervisory notice procedure applies[1]. The detailed procedure can be found at para 9.104 ff above. Among other things, the issuer concerned will have the right to refer the matter to the Tribunal[2].

1 FSMA 2000, ss 78 and 395(13)(b). Contrast the variation or cancellation of a firm's permission: whereas the former involves the supervisory notice procedure (and can therefore be achieved as a matter of urgency), the latter involves the warning/decision notice (and cannot therefore be achieved urgently): see Chapter 9 above.
2 For details, see Chapter 6 above.

15.169 There are several points to note. First, in such a case, the relevant decisions are taken:

- by the RDC, where the UKLA seeks to cancel the listing; but
- by the Listing Appeals Committee, where it seeks to suspend the listing[1].

1 This is outlined at para 15.164 above.

15.170 Second, if the UKLA's suspension or cancellation of the listing has already taken effect, for example because it was imposed with immediate effect on the issue of the first supervisory notice or with effect from a particular date which has then passed[1], then the UKLA will be considering whether to cancel the suspension or cancellation. If it refuses to do so, then the supervisory notice procedure applies. Otherwise, the UKLA must give the issuer written notice of its decision but no particular procedure is prescribed[2].

1 See para 15.139 above.
2 FSMA 2000, s 78(8)(b).

15.171 Third, the FSMA 2000 allows the UKLA to suspend or cancel the listing of securities as a matter of urgency where appropriate in the particular case[1]. The UKLA has indicated that where it does so, it will usually[2]:

- contact the issuer (or its sponsor) and explain the reasons why the UKLA considers it appropriate to act;
- allow the issuer (or an agent) to make representations in respect of the proposed action. The amount of time available will depend on the urgency;
- allow the issuer an opportunity to request the suspension or cancellation and to provide information in the same way as if it had requested the suspension or cancellation[3]; and
- the dealing notice will not state that the suspension or cancellation was at the issuer's request.

1 See the discussion at, respectively, paras 15.139 and 15.145 above.
2 See the draft Guidance Manual, para 9.11.6.
3 See the draft Guidance Manual, paras 9.8.2 and 9.9.1.

15.172 In addition, the UKLA will normally liaise with any recognised investment exchange on whose market the securities are traded, to enable so far as possible, suspension of listing and suspension of trading to take effect simultaneously[1].

1 See the draft Guidance Manual, para 9.5.2.

15.173 Finally, if an application is subsequently made to cancel a suspension already made[1], then if the UKLA proposes to refuse such an application, the warning/decision notice procedure applies[2]. If it accedes to the application, it must give the issuer written notice of its decision but no particular procedure is prescribed[3].

1 See para 15.141 above. As noted at para 15.146 above, such an application cannot be made in relation to a cancellation of listing. As to how to make such an application, see the draft Guidance Manual, para 9.17.
2 FSMA 2000, s 78(10) and (11).
3 FSMA 2000, S 78(11)(b).

Cancellation of a sponsor's approval

15.174 Where the UKLA wishes to cancel the approval of a sponsor under FSMA 2000, s 88, the warning/decision notice procedure applies. The detailed procedure is discussed in Chapter 5 above. Among other things, the sponsor will have the right to refer the matter to the Tribunal[1].

1 For details, see Chapter 6 above.

Publication of information about breaches of a code of dealings

15.175 There is no statutory procedure which the UKLA is required to follow when it seeks to require a company to publish information about breaches by a director of its code of dealing and little about the procedure has been made clear by the UKLA in its draft Guidance Manual.

15.176 The decision to require a company to publish information about a director's breach is taken by UKLA staff at an appropriate level of seniority[1]. Because the procedure is unclear, there seems to be limited opportunity for challenging such a decision:

- Where there is a dispute as to whether or not there has been a breach of the company's code of dealing, the company may refer the matter to the Listing Authority Review Committee[2], a body established by the UKLA to consider disputes relating to the interpretation of the listing rules[3]. Written or oral representations may be made to the Committee. The determination of the Committee is said to be final and determinative of the UKLA's opinion as to the interpretation or application of the listing rule in question[4].
- In many cases, particularly if the fact that a breach took place is admitted or is determined by the Listing Authority Review Committee, the key question will be whether the decision to require the publication of information relating to the breach is an appropriate regulatory response in the circumstances. It is not clear what, if any, rights the company or the director concerned has to make representations on that question and there is no provision for challenging the UKLA's decision. This is potentially quite significant, given the serious reputational impact that publishing the breach may have on the director concerned.
- So far as the terms of the announcement are concerned, the UKLA expects the company to discuss the contents of the announcement with it prior to release[5] but, again, neither the draft listing rules nor the draft Guidance Manual give the company or the director concerned any rights to challenge the UKLA's decision on what the announcement should say.

1 The appropriate level of seniority is determined having regard to the significance of the decision to those who would be affected by it, its novelty in light of stated policy and established practice, the complexity of the relevant considerations, the range of alternative options, and the extent to which the facts relating to the decision are or may be disputed: see the draft Guidance Manual, para 10.4.2.

2 See the draft Guidance Manual, para 11.3.3.

3 The Committee comprises a managing director of the FSA, who sits as chair, the Director of Listing, the General Counsel of the FSA (or a delegate) and two people drawn from a pool of practitioners with suitable listing experience. For further details, see the draft Guidance Manual, para 5.8.1.

4 See the draft Guidance Manual, para 5.8.1. It may nonetheless be open to challenge through the mechanism of judicial review, provided one of the grounds for judicial review can be made out: see further the discussion at Chapter 16 below.

5 See the draft Guidance Manual, para 11.4.4. Draft Listing Rules, r 9.3A (the requirement to take reasonable care to ensure that information is not misleading, false or deceptive and does not omit anything likely to affect its import) must be complied with.

Injunctions and restitution orders

15.177 The procedure for the FSA to impose or apply to the Court for an injunction or restitution order is outlined at, respectively, paras 7.125 ff and 7.76 ff above.

Criminal proceedings

15.178 The FSMA 2000 does not require the FSA to follow any particular procedure before initiating a criminal prosecution against a person, the rationale being that the safeguards for the person concerned are found in the criminal court process. However, the FSA recognises the potential serious effect of even commencing such proceedings and has therefore stated that the decision to commence such a prosecution will be taken by the RDC Chairman or, in an urgent case where he is not available, a Deputy Chairman and where possible, but subject to the need to act swiftly, one other RDC member[1].

1 See the FSA Handbook at DEC 4.6.1. In an exceptionally urgent case, the decision may be by the Director of Enforcement or, in his absence, another member of the FSA executive of at least director of division level.

Civil liability to third parties

15.179 If the matter which constitutes a contravention of the listing rules causes loss to a third party, then the issuer, sponsor or other person who contravened the rules may, depending upon the circumstances, incur a legal liability to compensate the third party for the losses which he was caused as a result. Whether the third party would have a claim, and precisely what claim he might have, would depend largely upon the particular circumstances. These issues are discussed in more detail in Chapter 10 above.

15.180 There are three specific points which need to be borne in mind in this context:

- with one exception, the provisions giving private persons civil claims for breach of statutory duty arising from a regulatory breach under the FSMA 2000 do not apply to breaches of Pt VI of the FSMA 2000;
- however, the FSMA 2000 does impose civil liability in certain circumstances arising from the contents of listing particulars;
- the FSMA 2000 also makes specific provision for advertisements published with the FSA's approval.

These are considered in more detail below.

Breach of statutory duty claims

15.181 The FSMA 2000[1] gives private persons a damages claim for breach of statutory duty where an authorised person contravenes a rule and they suffer loss as a result. This does not generally apply to breaches of the listing rules[2].

1 FSMA 2000, s 150. For a more detailed discussion, see para 10.28 ff above.
2 FSMA 2000, s 150(4)(a).

15.182 This is, however, subject to one exception. A breach of FSMA 2000, s 85, which prohibits securities from being offered to the public in the UK until the prospectus has been published, where a prospectus is required to be published, is actionable as a breach of statutory duty at the suit of a private person who suffers loss as a result[1]. The elements of this potential civil claim are discussed in more detail at para 10.47 above.

1 FSMA 2000, s 85(5).

Civil liability arising from the contents of listing particulars

15.183 The FSMA 2000 makes specific provision[1] for civil liability to arise in certain situations in relation to the content of listing particulars. The provision is complex and only a brief summary is provided here.

1 FSMA 2000, s 90.

15.184 Liability arises in two situations. First, any person responsible for listing particulars is liable to pay compensation to a person who has:

- acquired securities to which the listing particulars apply; and
- suffered loss in respect of them as a result of any untrue or misleading statement in the particulars or omission from the particulars of any matter required to be included by FSMA 2000, ss 80 or 81.

15.185 Second, any person who fails to comply with the requirements to issue Supplementary Listing Particulars under FSMA 2000, s 81 is liable to pay compensation to any person who acquired securities of the kind in question and suffered loss in respect of them as a result of the failure[1].

1 FSMA 2000, s 90(4).

15.186 Several points are worth noting. First, in contrast with s 150, the right of action is not limited to private persons, but applies to any person who suffers loss in the circumstances set out in the FSMA 2000. Second, it does not affect any other liability which may be incurred[1]. In other words, the existence of a cause of action under s 90 does not affect the person's ability to rely upon any alternative or additional causes of action which he might have as a matter of law. Third, whilst the provision makes clear that liability arises the person concerned would have to bring proceedings in the civil courts in order to obtain the damages to which he was entitled[2].

1 FSMA 2000, s 90(6).
2 Alternatively, he may be able to bring a claim before the ombudsman (see Chapter 12 above) and in some circumstances the FSA may consider making a restitution order (see para 7.43 ff above).

Civil liability arising from advertisements and information

15.187 FSMA 2000, s 98 precludes a person, in certain circumstances, from incurring civil liability for advertisements or other information published with the FSA's approval or authorisation, unless likely to be misleading[1].

1 FSMA 2000, s 98(4).

16 Challenges and complaints

CONTENTS

Introduction 679
Challenging the FSA 681
Complaining about the FSA 690

INTRODUCTION

An overview of Chapter 16

16.1 The Financial Services and Markets Tribunal, considered in Chapter 6 above, provides an important, impartial forum for firms and individuals aggrieved with the action which the FSA proposes to take in relation to them. Recourse to the Tribunal is not, though, generally available as of right. It is available only in those instances where the FSMA 2000 specifically prescribes that it is available; generally speaking, this is where the FSA decides to impose a particular regulatory sanction or action or takes a decision relating to a person's authorisation, permission, approval or recognition under the FSMA 2000[1].

1 A list of certain enforcement matters that can be referred to the Tribunal can be found at para 6.10 above.

16.2 There will therefore be many other situations where the FSA takes a decision which affects a firm or individual, which the person may wish to challenge and where there is no right of recourse to the Tribunal. A few examples may be given, among many others[1]:

- the FSA's decision to initiate a formal investigation[2].
- the FSA's decision on whether the appointment of an investigator should be notified to the person under investigation[3];

- the way that an investigator appointed to carry out a formal investigation exercises his investigation powers[4];
- the way that the FSA operates its internal decision-making procedure[5];
- the FSA's decision on the extent of the FSA material to which the person is entitled to have access during the enforcement process[6]; and
- the FSA's decision to publish information about urgent action that it wishes to take before the matter can be heard before the Tribunal[7].

1 Some further examples can be found at para 6.11 above.
2 See para 4.108 ff above.
3 See para 4.159 ff above.
4 See para 4.108 ff above.
5 See Chapter 5 above.
6 See para 5.81 ff above.
7 See para 9.217 above.

16.3 In such situations, how can the person affected challenge the action that the FSA has taken or proposes to take? In many cases, including all of the above examples, the issue will arise in the course of a process which ultimately may lead to Tribunal proceedings. For example, if the firm is aggrieved that an investigation has been commenced against it without, in its view, any good reason or is aggrieved by the way in which the investigation is being conducted, there may be some comfort to be drawn from the fact that, if any regulatory enforcement action follows based on the results of that investigation, the firm will, in most cases, have the option of referring the matter to the Tribunal[1]. Indeed, if the firm did so, the Tribunal would have the power to, among other things, make recommendations about the FSA's rules and procedures when determining the reference[2]. However, there may be a variety of reasons why the firm would not wish to refer the matter to the Tribunal, not least because whilst it may be aggrieved at aspects of the process, it may nonetheless not wish to dispute the substantive action which the FSA is taking against it.

1 It would not have that option if the FSA instituted civil proceedings for an injunction or restitution order or a criminal prosecution: see, respectively, Chapters 7 and 11 above (although in those cases the civil or criminal court would instead provide a forum for any relevant issues to be heard).
2 See para 6.140 above.

16.4 In some circumstances, therefore, the person concerned may wish to challenge aspects of the FSA's procedure or the decisions which the FSA has made in operating that procedure separately from the question of whether the result of the procedure was appropriate. Alternatively, the issue may arise in situations in which no right of recourse to the Tribunal arises. The question of how such challenges can be made is the focus of this chapter.

16.5 The firm has two options, either or both of which could be applicable depending upon the circumstances of the particular case. These are:

- to challenge the FSA's use of its powers through legal proceedings (considered at para 16.6 ff below); and

- to bring a complaint against the FSA before the independent complaints commissioner (considered at para 16.37 ff below).

CHALLENGING THE FSA

What options does the firm have?

16.6 There are two mechanisms for bringing legal proceedings against the FSA in relation to the misuse of its powers, depending upon what the firm is seeking to achieve and the circumstances of the case.

16.7 First, the acts and omissions of the FSA, as a public body, are, when it exercises public functions, almost certainly[1] amenable to the supervisory jurisdiction of the High Court, exercised by the procedure known as judicial review.

1 There seems little doubt that this is the case although, as at the date of writing, no judicial review proceedings have yet been brought against the FSA in relation to its functions under the FSMA 2000. As the authorities referred to in the footnotes to para 16.20 below indicate, the FSA's predecessor bodies were amenable to judicial review.

16.8 Second, where judicial review is inappropriate, or in some circumstances as an alternative to it, the person concerned may be able to bring civil proceedings against the FSA claiming damages or another remedy, such as an injunction or declaration. This is subject to the FSA's statutory immunity against liability in damages[1], discussed below.

1 FSMA 2000, Sch 1, para 19 and see para 16.29 ff below.

16.9 We review below the circumstances when each of these options is likely to be available, aiming to outline the framework for such challenges and to provide an indication of when in practice firms might consider bringing such proceedings[1].

1 For a more detailed discussion of judicial review, see *Judicial Review Handbook*, Michael Fordham, 2nd edn, 1997, *Judicial Review*, Supperstone and Goudie, 2nd edn, 1997, and the Civil Procedure Rules, Pt 54 and commentary.

Can the firm urgently prevent the FSA from taking action?

16.10 The most immediate question likely to face a person when the FSA takes or proposes to take action which the person believes is wrongful, is whether the FSA can be prevented from taking that action, as a matter of urgency, pending the outcome of the legal challenge. Or, if the action which the firm disputes is a requirement already imposed upon it to take a particular step (for example, to provide particular information to an investigator appointed by the FSA), the question will be whether the person can refuse to comply with that requirement pending the outcome of the legal proceedings.

16.11 In practice, the first step will often be to ask the FSA voluntarily to refrain from taking the relevant action pending the legal proceedings. If the FSA is unwilling to do so, the person may, in an appropriate case, be able to obtain an interim remedy from the court to protect it pending the determination of the substantive dispute. This might include, for example, an interim injunction restraining the FSA from taking a particular step or an interim declaration[1], or a stay of the administrative process which the person is seeking to challenge[2]. Whilst such interim measures are in theory available, they will rarely be of practical use in this context. Examples of where it might be appropriate to apply for an interim remedy include situations where the firm seeks to prevent the FSA from taking and publicising urgent action (where the Tribunal is unable or unwilling to suspend that action[3]) or where the firm seeks to prevent the FSA from publishing details of a warning notice contrary to s 391[4].

1 See the Civil Procedure Rules at CPR 54.3 (and in particular the commentary at 54.3.7) and CPR 25.1.

2 See the Civil Procedure Rules at CPR 54.10 and commentary. Stay of proceedings means, in this context, a stay of the process by which the decision challenged has been reached, including the decision itself: see *R v Secretary of State for Education and Science, ex p Avon County Council* [1991] 1 All ER 282, CA.

3 See paras 6.104 ff and 9.214 ff above.

4 See para 5.76 ff above.

16.12 Whether to grant such an interim remedy or stay is a matter within the court's discretion and the key question is therefore whether the court will exercise that discretion in the circumstances of the particular case.

16.13 In deciding whether to grant an interim injunction, the court considers whether the claim raises a serious issue to be tried and, if so, where the balance of convenience, including the wider public interest, lies[1]. It may also require the person applying for the interim remedy to give a cross-undertaking in damages. These tests, particularly the test of balance of convenience, can be difficult to apply in practice, given the different conflicting factors from the FSA's and the firm's respective points of view and where the balance falls will depend to a large extent upon the particular situation[2].

1 See the Civil Procedure Rules at CPR 54.3 (and in particular the commentary at 54.3.9) and *American Cyanamid Co v Ethicon Ltd* [1975] AC 396, HL.

2 The 'balance of convenience' approach has been described as 'the course which, in all the circumstances appears to offer the best prospect that eventual injustice will be avoided or minimised': see *R v Secretary of State for Transport, ex p Factortame (No 2)* [1991] 1 AC 603 at 659F (Lord Bridge).

16.14 Where the firm applies for a stay of the administrative process, rather than an interim injunction, it is not currently clear what test the court will apply, but it may be that a similar test will be applied as upon an application for an interim injunction[1].

1 See the Civil Procedure Rules at CPR 54.10 (and in particular the commentary at 54.10.4/5). If the stay affects a third party, then the court will apply the same principles as if the application was for an interim injunction as between the applicant and the third party: see *R v HM Inspectorate of Pollution, ex p Greenpeace Ltd* [1994] 1 WLR 570, CA.

16.15 Alternatively, in cases where a requirement has already been imposed upon the person, which it disputes, there may be an option of refusing to comply with the requirement and then using the contention that the requirement was unlawful as a defence to any proceedings which the FSA or, as appropriate, the investigator appointed by the FSA brings in relation to the person's failure to comply. For example, where the requirement is one to provide information to an investigator appointed by the FSA, then the primary sanction for non-compliance is that the court may punish the person as though he was in contempt of court if it finds that there was no reasonable excuse for the non-compliance[1]. In such a case, the person could argue that there was a reasonable excuse, based on its contentions about whether that requirement should have been imposed on it. This has been a relatively common strategy in the past[2] but involves risks, since the person may be punished by the court if the court does not agree that it had a reasonable excuse for non-compliance.

1 This is discussed in more detail at para 4.284 ff above.
2 Various examples are given in the footnote to para 4.286 above.

Bringing an application for judicial review

16.16 The question of bringing an application for judicial review, either against the FSA or against another body acting under the FSMA 2000, such as the ombudsman[1], may arise in an infinite variety of situations. Whether judicial review is available, and whether it is an appropriate means of seeking redress, will depend upon the circumstances of the particular case. Among the various factors that may be relevant, three are worth highlighting.

1 See Chapter 12 above.

16.17 First, where the court exercises its supervisory jurisdiction over a public body, it is, broadly, concerned with the lawfulness of the body's decision, not with the merits of that decision[1] (although the distinction between the two is not always easily drawn). Hence, the court can only intervene on certain, fairly limited grounds[2]. This is discussed further, below.

1 For a good example, see *R v Securities and Futures Authority, ex p Panton* (1995) CA LTL 6/3/95, CA. Mr Panton attempted to have judicially reviewed the SFA's decision not to continue investigating a firm in response to his complaints. The Court of Appeal upheld the refusal of leave to bring a judicial review, on the basis that 'the clear intention of the [Financial Services Act 1986] is that the bodies established under the Act should be the regulatory bodies and that it is not the function of the court in anything other than a clear case to second guess their decisions or, as it were, look over their shoulder. Thus the position I think we end up with is that these bodies are amenable to judicial review but are, in anything other than very clear circumstances, to be left to get on with it' (Bingham MR).
2 The limited scope of judicial review proceedings may have the result that such proceedings are incapable of 'curing' a process which is otherwise not ECHR, art 6(1) compliant. Whether or not the process in question is, as a whole, ECHR compliant will depend upon the nature of that process. Compare, for example, *Kingsley v United Kingdom* (2001) Times, 9 January, ECtHR with *R v Secretary of State for the Environment, Transport and the Regions, ex p Alconbury Developments Ltd* [2001] UKHL 23, [2001] 2 All ER 929, HL. For a more general discussion of judicial control, see *Human Rights*, Grosz, Beatson and Duffy, 2000, at 5-24. For an outline of the requirements of art 6(1), see para 6.26 above.

16.18 Second, not every decision made by the FSA or another body under the FSMA 2000 is necessarily capable of being judicially reviewed[1]. A decision for which there is otherwise no means of protection against abuse, such as a decision to initiate a particular investigation, is likely to be reviewable, whereas a decision for which there is an alternative remedy, such as a decision to take enforcement action which could be referred to the Tribunal, is unlikely to be reviewable until any remedies and recourse available under the rules have been exhausted. There may be a grey area in relation to a decision made in the course of the enforcement process (for example, a decision on the extent of secondary material which is disclosed to the firm[2]) which is not of itself capable of being referred to the Tribunal but which could ultimately be the subject of comment by the Tribunal, given the breadth of its powers[3], if the firm ultimately refers the enforcement action to the Tribunal.

1 For a further discussion, see *Judicial Review*, Supperstone & Goudie, 2nd edn, 1997, at 5.9 and *Judicial Review Handbook*, Fordham, at Chapters 35 and 36.
2 See para 5.86 ff above.
3 The Tribunal can, among other things, make recommendations about the FSA's procedures: see para 6.140 ff above.

16.19 Third, the person applying for judicial review must show that he has a sufficient interest to make the application[1]. This is unlikely to be an obstacle for a firm or approved person who wishes to challenge a decision taken by the FSA in relation to it. But on rare occasions others may seek to challenge the FSA, for example a customer or market counterparty of a firm who believes that a decision of the FSA in relation to the firm (for example, to publish particular information about a regulatory breach) affects them, or an industry body with a wider interest in the matter in dispute. Difficult questions may arise as to whether the person concerned has sufficient standing to make the application.

1 Supreme Court Act 1981, s 31(3) and see *Judicial Review Handbook*, Fordham, at Chapter 38 and the Civil Procedure Rules at CPR 54.1 (in particular the commentary at 54.1.22).

Grounds for judicial review

16.20 As has already been indicated, the grounds upon which a matter can be judicially reviewed are limited. By way of illustration, the grounds upon which a judicial review may be available might include that the FSA has:

- made an error of law, for example by misinterpreting the relevant provisions of the FSMA 2000 or attempting to exercise powers that it does not as a matter of law have[1];
- failed to comply with the procedural obligations imposed on it by the FSMA 2000[2] or, if the rules of natural justice apply[3], failed to comply with them;
- failed to adhere to its own stated policy[4] or procedure[5];
- made a decision that is irrational, or so unreasonable that no body properly directing itself could reasonably have reached it[6];
- acted for an improper purpose or in bad faith[7];

- had regard to irrelevant considerations or failed to have regard to relevant considerations[8]; or
- breached the firm's human rights[9], for example by breaching the firm's art 6 rights to a fair trial or investigating in an unnecessarily intrusive way in breach of its right of privacy.

1 See, for example, *R v Securities and Investments Board, ex p Sun Life Assurance Society plc* [1996] 2 BCLC 150, in which proceedings were brought (unsuccessfully) to challenge certain rules made by the SIB under powers in the Financial Services Act 1986, on the basis that the rules were contrary to the Act. See also *R v Securities and Investments Board, ex p Independent Financial Advisers Association* [1995] 2 BCLC 76. For further discussion of errors of law, see *Judicial Review Handbook*, Fordham, 2nd edn, 1997 at Chapter 48.

2 Note that, although the FSA is expressly obliged under the FSMA 2000 to follow its stated procedure for the giving of warning and decision notices (see Chapter 5 above), the FSMA 2000 also expressly states that failure in a particular case to follow that procedure does not affect the validity of the notice: s 395(9) and (11). Hence, judicial review is unlikely to be available in those circumstances. The failure may, though, be taken into account by the Tribunal: s 395(12).

3 In addition to procedural obligations imposed on it by the FSMA 2000, the FSA may be required to comply with general principles of natural justice or procedural fairness. A process may be amenable to judicial review on the basis of a person's legitimate expectations of fair procedure: see, for example, *Council of Civil Service Unions v Minister for Civil Service* [1985] AC 374, HL. See also *R v Life Assurance Unit Trust Regulatory Organisation Ltd., ex p Ross* [1993] QB 17, CA, where LAUTRO's intervention action against an appointed representative was challenged on the ground that it was contrary to natural justice. See further *R v Securities and Futures Authority, ex p Fleurose* [2001] All ER(D) 189. Note that the rules of natural justice probably do not apply to a body making a preliminary inquiry with a view to seeing whether there is charge to be made: see Denning MR in *Moran v Lloyd's* [1981] 1 Lloyd's Rep 423, CA and *Herring v Templeman* [1973] 3 All ER 569, CA.

4 Generally speaking, a public body can be held to its policy because of, among other things, its duty of consistency and because the policy may give rise to a legitimate expectation on the part of the person affected. It need not necessarily follow the policy; but if it is not going to do so, then it must give clear reasons why the decision is being made as an exception to the policy and the grounds upon which the decision is made. For further discussion, see *Judicial Review Handbook*, Fordham, 2nd, 1997 at 7.4.

5 See, for example, *R v Governor of Sheffield Hallam University, ex p R* [1995] ELR 267, 282B-284F, in which proceedings were successfully brought on grounds, among others, of failure by a university disciplinary committee to follow its own written procedure for the expulsion of students. For further discussion on failure to adhere to procedure, see *Judicial Review Handbook*, Fordham, 2nd edn, 1997 at 7.4.7.

6 *Associated Provincial Picture Houses Ltd v Wednesbury Corpn* [1948] 1 KB 223. See, for example, *R v Financial Intermediaries Managers and Brokers Regulatory Association, ex p Cochrane* [1991] BCLC 106, in which proceedings were brought (unsuccessfully) to challenge enforcement action taken by FIMBRA, and its appeal tribunal, on the ground (among others) that the action was so harsh as to be irrational. See also *R v Securities and Investments Board, ex p Independent Financial Advisers Association* [1995] 2 BCLC 76 (challenge to the SIB's decision to issue guidance) and *R v International Stock Exchange of the United Kingdom and the Republic of Ireland Ltd, ex p Else (1982) Ltd* [1993] QB 534 (challenge to a Stock Exchange decision to remove a company's shares from the official list).

7 For a further discussion of bad faith, see *Judicial Review Handbook*, Fordham, 2nd edn, 1997 at 51.1 and see also the discussion at para 16.32 ff below.

8 'It is for the courts, if the matter is brought before them, to decide what is a relevant consideration. If the decision maker wrongly takes the view that some consideration is not relevant, and therefore has no regard to it, the decision cannot stand and he must be required to think again. But it is entirely for the decision maker to attribute to the relevant considerations such weight as he thinks fit, and the courts will not interfere unless he has acted unreasonably in the *Wednesbury* sense': *Tesco Stores Ltd v Secretary of State for the Environment* [1995] 1 WLR 759 (Lord Keith). For a further discussion, see *Judicial Review Handbook*, Fordham, 2nd edn, 1997, at Chapter 56. It will, generally speaking, be difficult to challenge the FSA on this basis because its policies (outlined

throughout this book) on what factors it will take into account in taking particular decisions are normally extremely broad.

9 Under the Human Rights Act 1998, s 6(1) it is unlawful for a public authority to act in a manner that is incompatible with the ECHR. A person may bring a claim that a public authority has acted or proposes to act in a manner contrary to the ECHR in the appropriate court or tribunal, including on an application for judicial review: see s 7(1)(a) and 7(3).

How to bring a judicial review

16.21 Judicial review proceedings are brought in the Administrative Court under a procedure set out in the Civil Procedure Rules, Pt 54. There is a two-stage process, involving, first, an application for permission to proceed and, second, if that application is granted, the substantive judicial review itself. Permission is within the court's discretion, based on a basic test of whether there is an arguable case that a ground for seeking judicial review exists which merits full investigation[1]. Even then, the court retains a discretion to refuse permission, for example on grounds of delay, if it was not provided with full and frank information, or if alternative remedies are available. It is important that any application is made promptly and, in any event, within three months after the grounds to make it first arose[2].

1 See the Civil Procedure Rules at CPR 54.4 (and in particular the commentary of 54.4.7).

2 See the Civil Procedure Rules at CPR 54.5. The court has a discretion to grant an extension of time: see the commentary at CPR 54.5.4.

What remedies are available?

16.22 Ultimately, if the person obtains permission and is successful at the judicial review hearing itself, various remedies are available to the court. In very brief outline[1], they are:

- a quashing order[2], setting aside the decision of the public body and, in some cases, remitting it to the body for reconsideration;
- a mandatory order[3], requiring the public body to carry out its duty;
- a prohibiting order, restraining the body;
- a declaration[4] or injunction[5]; and/or
- damages[6].

1 For a more detailed discussion, see *Judicial Review Handbook*, Fordham, 2nd edn, 1997, Chapters 24 and 25 and *Judicial Review*, Supperstone and Goudie, Chapters 13 to 15.

2 This was formerly known as an order of certiorari.

3 This was formerly known as an order of mandamus.

4 Declarations are a particularly flexible type of relief and often used in practice: see the discussion in *Judicial Review Handbook*, Fordham, 2nd edn, 1997, at 24.2.

5 Judicial review proceedings will often be the appropriate means for seeking an injunction or declaration in this context: see the discussion at para 16.28 below.

6 Damages can only be sought in addition to one of the other remedies, and will only be awarded where there is some private law cause of action for damages. Maladministration does not of itself give rise to any claim: see the Civil Procedure Rules at CPR 54.3 (and in particular the commentary at 54.3.12) and *Judicial Review Handbook*, Fordham, at 25.3. In the case of the FSA, damages claims are probably only permissible where the FSA has acted in bad faith or for breaches of the Human Rights Act 1998: see para 16.29 ff below.

16.23 The granting of a remedy is at the discretion of the court. This means that the firm could successfully show that the FSA's actions were wrongful and yet find that the court refused to grant relief for some reason. The court's discretion is a wide one and may involve it taking into account many considerations[1].

1 *Judicial Review*, Supperstone and Goudie identifies (see Chapter 15) at least seven bases upon which the court may refuse relief, namely: (i) that the applicant lacks a sufficient interest; (ii) that the remedy would be of no practical benefit; (iii) having regard to the applicant's conduct, including delay; (iv) because of the effect of granting relief; (v) because of the availability of alternative remedies; (vi) where the issue is the criminality of future conduct; and (vii) where a procedural failure is purely technical.

Whether to bring a judicial review application

16.24 The answer to the question whether the person concerned should bring a judicial review application will obviously depend largely upon the particular circumstances. It should, though, be apparent from the above that judicial review will not always be an appropriate or attractive route. There is no right to bring an application for judicial review; this depends upon obtaining the court's permission to do so in each case. The grounds for making an application are limited and the remedies are discretionary. The presumption is that the proceedings will be in public. The person concerned will be at risk of being required to bear the FSA's costs if it is unsuccessful. However, in many situations there may be no other means of obtaining redress against what is perceived as an abuse by the FSA, at least beyond the complaints scheme outlined below. It is therefore an important means of obtaining effective redress in appropriate cases.

Bringing a civil action against the FSA

16.25 In some instances, the firm may wish to bring a civil claim against the FSA, rather than using the process of judicial review. For example, the time limit for bringing judicial review proceedings (see para 16.21 above) may have passed, the firm may primarily be seeking damages, the firm may wish to avoid having first to apply for permission to bring proceedings (which, as has been seen, is required for judicial review proceedings but is not required for normal civil claims), or the matter may be one which is not suitable for judicial review[1].

1 For example, the right under the Human Rights Act 1998 to bring proceedings against a public body for ECHR breaches is not necessarily co-extensive with the right to bring proceedings for judicial review. Cases may arise where judicial review is not available and civil proceedings are therefore the only option. For a discussion of this issue, see *Human Rights*, Grosz, Beatson and Duffy, 2000, at 4-05.

16.26 In considering bringing a civil claim against the FSA, three main obstacles arise. First, civil claims are, generally speaking, concerned with compensating claimants' quantifiable losses that they have suffered from wrongs committed by others.

16.27 Second, even where the person has suffered loss, they will in many instances be precluded from bringing a claim for damages because of the statutory immunity for liability in damages. This is considered in more detail below.

16.28 Third, civil proceedings can be used not only to obtain damages but also to obtain other remedies such as an injunction or declaration and this may appear an attractive alternative to bringing judicial review proceedings, particularly if the three-month limitation period for judicial review has expired. However, courts are wary of allowing civil proceedings to be used in this way precisely because this deprives the public body of the protections built into the judicial review process. In many situations, therefore, it will be regarded as an abuse of process to bring civil proceedings, rather than judicial review proceedings[1].

1 See Lord Diplock in *O'Reilly v Mackman* [1983] 2 AC 237, HL and, for a further discussion, *Judicial Review*, Supperstone and Goudie, from 3.21. There are, though, exceptions: one example is *Securities and Investments Board v Financial Intermediaries, Managers and Brokers Regulatory Association Ltd* [1992] Ch 268.

The statutory immunity for damages claims

16.29 The FSMA 2000 confers upon the FSA and others[1] a general immunity for liability in damages[2]. The need for such an immunity was much debated before the Joint Committee and during the bill stages of the legislation[3] and the strengthening of the FSA's accountability, particularly relating to the independent complaints commissioner, was seen as a necessary counterbalance[4].

1 See para 16.30 below.
2 Similar provisions were formerly found in the Banking Act 1987, s 1(4) and, particularly, the Financial Services Act 1986, s 187.
3 As regards the Government's view: 'without statutory immunity, the proper and efficient action of the regulator would be frustrated by lawsuits and red tape. Frivolous litigation could be an extremely easy ploy to distract or hinder the regulator. The absence or the weakening of the immunity could also have more dangerous effects on the industry. It could lead to a tendency to over-regulation with the FSA seeking to collect more information than it needed, setting tougher minimum standards than necessary, avoiding giving guidance or waivers or taking longer to reach decisions than it otherwise would': Economic Secretary to HM Treasury in Standing Committee, 13 July 1999.
4 'We consider that the proposals for immunity for the FSA are appropriate, provided that the complaints procedure is strengthened as we recommend below': First Report of the Joint Committee, paragraph 139. The complaints commissioner is considered in detail in para 16.37 ff below.

16.30 The FSMA 2000 thus confers an immunity from liability in damages which, in many instances, will preclude damages claims being brought[1]. The immunity covers:

- the FSA, and any person who is, or is acting as, a member of the FSA, an officer of the FSA or a member of the FSA's staff, in relation to anything done or omitted in the discharge, or purported discharge, of the FSA's functions[2];

- the FSA, when acting as UK Listing Authority, and any person who is, or is acting as, a member or officer of it or member of its staff, in relation to anything done or omitted in the discharge, or purported discharge, of its functions[3];
- the complaints commissioner and any person appointed to conduct an investigation on his behalf, in relation to anything done or omitted in the discharge, or purported discharge, of his functions in relation to the investigation of a complaint[4];
- a recognised investment exchange or recognised clearing house, and its officers and staff, in relation to anything done or omitted in the discharge of its regulatory functions[5]; and
- any person (referring, principally, to the ombudsman and his staff), in relation to anything done or omitted in the discharge, or purported discharge, of any functions under the FSMA 2000 in relation to the compulsory jurisdiction[6].

1 There may be room for argument on the validity of the statutory immunity under the ECHR, on the basis, broadly, that it is incompatible with the right of access to a court under art 6(1), although this is doubtful. See *Osman v UK* (1998) 29 EHRR 245, *Fayed v United Kingdom* (1994) 18 EHRR 393 and *Z v United Kingdom* Appl No 29392/95 [2001] 2 FCR 246. Such a challenge could probably only be made in the European Court of Human Rights because an English court would almost certainly be bound by the express statutory immunity, under the Human Rights Act 1998, s 3(2) and 4(6) even if it were incompatible with the ECHR.
2 FSMA 2000, Sch 1, para 19.
3 FSMA 2000, s 102 and see Chapter 15 above.
4 FSMA 2000, Sch 1, para 19(2) and see para 16.37 ff below.
5 FSMA 2000, s 291. Such bodies also carry on commercial activities and no immunity applies to them in relation to such activities (although there may be questions as to whether the line can be drawn effectively in practice): see the Economic Secretary to HM Treasury in Standing Committee, 13 July 1999.
6 FSMA 2000, Sch 17, para 10. The immunity also extends to the voluntary jurisdiction, by virtue of the scheme rules: see para 12.76 above.

16.31 The immunity does not apply to:

- acts or omissions shown to have been in bad faith; and
- awards of damages under the Human Rights Act 1998.

The meaning and scope of each of these exceptions is discussed briefly below.

Acts in bad faith

16.32 Bad faith has been held in the past in a similar context to connote either malice (in the sense of personal spite or a desire to injure for improper reasons) or knowledge of absence of power to make the decision in question[1]. The key point is that this involves a subjective analysis of the state of mind of the person concerned, as compared with an analysis of the person's behaviour against objective standards.

1 Per Lightman J in *Melton Medes Ltd v Securities and Investments Board* [1995] 3 All ER 880, considering the similar exception to the SIB's statutory immunity under the Financial Services Act 1986, s 187. For a discussion of bad faith in the public law context, see *Judicial Review Handbook*, Fordham, 2nd edn, 1997, at Chapter 51.

16.33 Bad faith thus clearly covers fraudulent or corrupt acts. It is also an element of the tort of misfeasance in public office[1]. Bad faith must not, though, be alleged unless there exists prima facie evidence justifying the allegation[2].

1 The ingredients of the tort were analysed in detail in *Three Rivers District Council v Governor and Company of the Bank of England* [2000] 3 All ER 1, HL.
2 *Melton Medes Ltd v Securities and Investments Board* [1995] 3 All ER 880.

Claims under the Human Rights Act 1998

16.34 The Human Rights Act 1998[1] allows a court to award a remedy, including damages, against a public body that acts in a way which is incompatible with the ECHR but it can only award damages if, taking into account all the circumstances of the case (including certain specific factors[2]), it is satisfied that the award is necessary to afford just satisfaction to the person affected.

1 Human Rights Act 1998, s 8.
2 Human Rights Act 1998, s 8(3).

16.35 The concept of 'just satisfaction' is found in ECHR, art 41 and has been developed by the European Court of Human Rights. The Human Rights Act 1998 requires the English courts to take into account the principles applied by the European Court of Human Rights in determining whether to award damages and the amount of any award[1].

1 Human Rights Act 1998, s 8(4).

16.36 The basic principle is, broadly, similar to an English law award of damages, in that it aims to put the victim, so far as possible, in the position in which he would have been had his rights not been violated[1]. This may be of particular use to those who suffer actual losses from FSA action in violation of their human rights.

1 An award based on 'just satisfaction' is within the discretion of the court. It is difficult to discern the principles upon which such awards are made, since the European Court of Human Rights has rarely given reasons for such awards, but some general propositions can be made. The basic principle is that the court will make an award on the basis of what is 'equitable'. An award may be made for actual pecuniary loss suffered which was caused by the ECHR violation. Awards may also be made for non-pecuniary loss and for costs/expenses. For a further discussion, see *Human Rights Practice*, June 2000, at 19.063.

COMPLAINING ABOUT THE FSA

An overview of the complaints scheme

16.37 Bringing a judicial review or other formal legal proceedings against the FSA may be an effective means for a person aggrieved with the FSA's actions to obtain redress in a suitable case, but it is also likely to be a time-consuming and expensive route. There is a cheaper, simpler alternative which may in some situations offer an adequate remedy. That is the complaints scheme.

16.38 The FSMA 2000[1] requires the FSA to put in place a complaints scheme and appoint an independent complaints commissioner to investigate, broadly, complaints about the FSA. This is an important aspect of the accountability mechanisms provided for in the FSMA 2000 and, as has already been noted[2], the establishment of a robust independent complaints body was seen as an important counterbalance to granting the FSA immunity from liability to claims for damages. There is therefore a strong political basis and support for the complaints scheme[3].

1 FSMA 2000, Sch 1, paras 7 and 8.
2 See para 16.29 above.
3 A similar scheme existed under the previous regime, although its use has been limited in practice. For example, in the year 1999/2000, the complaints commissioner investigated eight complaints against the FSA (and found one to be substantiated), rejected a further six complaints as outside its remit, and reviewed the FSA's handling of 11 complaints (47 the previous year) against other regulators (one of which it found to be substantiated): see the FSA's 1999/2000 Annual Report. In the year 2000/2001, the commissioner investigated 11 complaints against the FSA and found two to have given cause for concern: see the FSA's 2000/2001 Annual Report.

16.39 The FSA has acknowledged[1] that it needs to maintain high standards in its dealings with people and that, if it fails to meet such standards, those directly and adversely affected should be entitled to a thorough and impartial enquiry into what went wrong and to be told what the FSA will do to put things right. This is what, in the FSA's view, the complaints scheme is intended to achieve.

1 See Consultation Paper 73 ('Investigation of complaints against the FSA'), November 2000, at para 2.2.

16.40 As will be seen, though, the complaints scheme is limited in its scope and, particularly, is not suitable for challenging judgments made by the FSA within reasonable bounds, it will always be uncertain whether any remedy can be obtained, and, whilst it is intended to operate reasonably quickly, it is unlikely to provide a real-time solution to immediate issues regarding the FSA's exercise of its powers. Its use may therefore be limited in practice.

16.41 The complaints scheme comprises three phases, although not all may be required in any particular case. First, the FSA decides whether or not it regards the matter as falling within the ambit of the scheme and, if so, it carries out its own investigation and decides what, if any, action should be taken to give redress to the complainant. Second, if the individual is unhappy with the outcome of that process, or with the process itself, or if the FSA declines to investigate, the matter is referred to the independent complaints commissioner. Where it is referred to him, he decides whether to investigate and, if so, carries out an investigation and makes findings and, where appropriate, makes recommendations about what action should be taken by the FSA. Finally, the FSA decides what action to take in the light of those recommendations.

16.42 In the following paragraphs, we review the complaints scheme, including:

- the nature and role of the complaints commissioner (para 16.43 ff);
- when the complaints scheme is available and when firms might consider using it as a possible means for obtaining redress (para 16.50 ff);
- the remedies that can be obtained (para 16.66 ff);
- the procedure for making and handling complaints (para 16.75 ff); and
- the firm's options if it is unhappy with the outcome of the process (para 16.96 ff).

The complaints commissioner

Who is the complaints commissioner?

16.43 The complaints commissioner is an independent person which the FSMA 2000[1] requires the FSA to appoint to be responsible for the conduct of investigations in accordance with the complaints scheme which the FSMA 2000 requires the FSA to establish[2].

1 FMSA, Sch 1, para 7(1).
2 On 3 September 2001, the FSA announced that it had appointed Rosemary Radcliffe, former Chief Economist at PriceWaterhouseCoopers, as the commissioner.

How is the commissioner appointed?

16.44 The FSMA 2000 requires the commissioner to be appointed by the FSA[1]. However, it describes him as 'an independent person'[2] and requires that the terms and conditions upon which he is appointed are such as, in the FSA's opinion, are reasonably designed to secure that he will be free at all times to act independently of the FSA and that complaints will be investigated under the scheme without favouring the FSA[3].

1 FSMA 2000, Sch 1, para 7(1)(b).
2 FSMA 2000, Sch 1, para 7(1)(b).
3 FSMA 2000, Sch 1, para 7(4).

16.45 In taking the decision of who to appoint, the FSA is advised by an appointment panel, comprising[1] the Deputy Chairman of the FSA (who is a non-executive director), the Chairmen of the Practitioner Panel and the Consumer Panel, and a further, independent person (likely to be a former civil service commissioner acting in a personal capacity[2]). The appointment panel does not therefore involve any executive staff of the FSA or any executive members of the FSA Board.

1 See the FSA Handbook at COAF 1.3.1. The FSMA 2000 (Sch 1, para 7(1)(b)) requires the FSA to make the appointment.
2 See Consultation Paper 73, 'Investigation of complaints against the FSA, November 2000, at para 3.2.

Is the commissioner independent of the FSA?

16.46 The basic premise is that the commissioner is fully independent from the FSA and, indeed, there are a number of safeguards, both in the FSMA 2000 and in the rules of the complaints scheme, to ensure this. First, there is the manner of his appointment and, particularly, the involvement of an appointment panel[1].

1 See para 16.45 above.

16.47 Second, as has already been noted[1], the terms and conditions of appointment are required to be designed to secure his independence. For its part, the FSA has said that it attaches importance to protecting the independence and security of tenure of the commissioner through his terms of appointment[2]. The commissioner is therefore appointed for a period of three years and is subject to dismissal within that period only if he is incapacitated by physical or mental illness or otherwise unfit to discharge his functions and, in any case, subject to the approval of HM Treasury[3]. The FSA is not therefore able to dismiss him for misconduct or any other reason short of unfitness for office[4], and even then can only do so if HM Treasury agrees.

1 See para 16.44 above.
2 See Consultation Paper 93 ('Investigation of complaints against the FSA'), May 2001, at para 8.2.
3 See the FSA Handbook at COAF 1.3.2. The Commissioner will also be removed if he reaches 70 years of age.
4 The FSA believes that this would enable it to dismiss an incompetent commissioner: see Consultation Paper 93, ('Investigation of complaints against the FSA'), May 2001, at para 8.2.

16.48 Third, there is no express mechanism, either under the FSMA 2000 or under the scheme, for holding the commissioner accountable to the FSA. The commissioner is required to submit an annual report to the FSA Board[1], but there is no suggestion that the report is intended as a means of accountability to the Board. To the contrary, the FSA Handbook suggests that it will be an opportunity for the commissioner to draw to the attention of the Board any general lessons which he considers the FSA should learn.

1 See the FSA Handbook at COAF 1.6.2.

16.49 Finally, neither the commissioner nor any member of his staff may be an employee of or perform any duties for the FSA[1]. The FSA does pay the commissioner's remuneration and provide him with appropriate staff and offices[2], but it is for the commissioner to arrange the details of his own staff and secretariat[3] and the FSA does not propose that his offices should be on the FSA's premises.

1 FSMA 2000, Sch 1, para 8(9) and see the FSA Handbook at COAF 1.3.2(3) and 1.3.3.
2 See the FSA Handbook at COAF 1.3.1. The FSA is committed to providing the resources necessary to enable the commissioner to carry out his functions as he sees fit: see Consultation Paper 73, ('Investigation of complaints against the FSA'), November 2000, at para 3.12.
3 See Consultation Paper 73, ('Investigation of complaints against the FSA'), November 2000, at para 3.10.

When is the complaints scheme available?

Who can complain?

16.50 The complaints scheme is available, subject to the rules on the scope of the scheme[1], to anyone directly affected by the way in which the FSA has carried out its statutory functions[2]. This could include, not only regulated firms, approved persons and listed companies, but also a customer or prospective customer or a market counterparty, whether an individual or a body corporate. The sole criterion for eligibility is that the person must be seeking a remedy in respect of some inconvenience, distress or loss which they have suffered as a result of being directly affected by the FSA's actions or inaction[3]. This can include seeking simply an apology.

1 These are discussed at para 16.51 ff below.
2 See the FSA Handbook at COAF 1.2.1.
3 See the FSA handbook at COAF 1.4.1(3). The scheme will also accept complaints made on behalf of the person seeking the remedy, for example their close relatives, solicitors or accountants and in some cases MP's correspondence on behalf of constituents: see Consultation Paper 73, ('Investigation of complaints against the FSA'), November 2000, at para 2.16. As to the remedies that can be provided, see para 16.66 ff below.

What types of complaints are covered by the scheme?

The basic coverage of the scheme

16.51 The complaints scheme provides a procedure for enquiring into and, if necessary, addressing allegations of misconduct by the FSA arising from the way in which it has carried out or failed to carry out its functions[1]. This includes complaints alleging mistakes and lack of care, unreasonable delay, unprofessional behaviour, bias and lack of integrity[2].

1 See the FSA Handbook at COAF 1.4.1.
2 The FSA has deliberately avoided using terms such as 'negligence' or 'maladministration' which might (wrongly) imply that the Commissioner's report could amount to a determination of legal liability: see Consultation Paper 93, ('Investigation of complaints against the FSA'), May 2001, at para 5.4.

Matters excluded from the scheme

16.52 Certain types of complaints are specifically excluded under the FSMA 2000 and/or the rules of the scheme, in particular:

- complaints in relation to the performance of the FSA's legislative functions under the FSMA 2000, which includes, for example, making rules and issuing codes and general guidance[1]. This is discussed further below;
- complaints about the FSA's relationship with its employees or complaints connected with contractual or commercial disputes involving the FSA which are not connected to its functions under the FSMA 2000[2]; and
- complaints about the actions of the ombudsman[3] or the compensation scheme[4].

1 FSMA 2000, Sch 1, para 7(1)(a) and see the FSA Handbook at COAF 1.4.2(3).
2 See the FSA Handbook at COAF 1.4.2. The scheme does not therefore cover matters arising in the FSA's commercial or contractual relationships, as distinct from its actions as regulator, for example, employment contracts or commercial contracts.
3 See Chapter 12 above.
4 Deciding individual compensation and ombudsman cases is not a function of the FSA and therefore the scheme cannot, under the FSMA 2000, cover such cases: see Consultation Paper 93, ('Investigation of complaints against the FSA'), May 2001, at para 5.1.

16.53 As regards the exclusion of matters relating to the performance by the FSA of its legislative functions, the FSA's legislative functions are defined in the FSMA 2000[1] as making rules, issuing codes, issuing statements, giving directions and issuing general guidance (in each case, under the statutory provisions). The scope of this exclusion seems to be limited to the process by which the FSA makes, for example, rules or guidance, and decides on the content of those rules or that guidance.

1 FSMA 2000, Sch 1, para 1(2).

16.54 The question of how the rules or guidance are applied to a particular case is probably not the performance of the FSA's legislative function but of, for example, its enforcement function (depending upon the situation where the issue arises). In any event, as discussed further below[1], the FSA regards such matters, to which it refers as 'regulatory judgment', as unsuitable for the complaints scheme and will not therefore investigate them under the complaints scheme (although the commissioner may nonetheless decide to do so[2]).

1 See para 16.56 below.
2 See paras 16.60 and 16.61 below.

Matters that will not be investigated by the FSA

16.55 The FSA will not investigate a complaint which:

- it reasonably considers could have been, or would be, more appropriately dealt with in another way, for example by referring the matter to the Tribunal or by the institution of other legal proceedings[1]; or
- it reasonably considers amounts to no more than dissatisfaction with the FSA's general policies or with the exercise of discretion where no unreasonable, unprofessional or other misconduct is alleged[2]; or

- is connected with or arises from any form of continuing action by the FSA, until the complainant has exhausted the procedures and remedies under the FSMA 2000 which are relevant to that action (unless in the exceptional circumstances of the case, it would not be reasonable to expect the complainant to await the conclusion of the FSA's action)[3].

1 FSMA 2000, Sch 1, para 8(1) and see the FSA Handbook at COAF 1.4.3(1).
2 See the FSA Handbook at COAF 1.4.3(2).
3 See the FSA Handbook at COAF 1.4.4.

16.56 A number of points may be made. First, the FSA's approach[1] is that disagreements about matters of policy, regulatory judgment and legal interpretation are likely to be inappropriate for investigation under the complaints scheme. It regards the process of consultation on its policies before they are implemented as providing the main opportunity for those likely to be affected by the policy to take issue with the policy. It will not therefore investigate such matters under the complaints scheme (although the commissioner may nonetheless decide to do so[2]). The FSA does, though, recognise a need for arrangements allowing firms to question or challenge what it calls matters of 'regulatory judgment' for which there is otherwise no mechanism of challenge and has therefore put in place a procedure for dealing with such matters outside the formal complaints scheme[3], allowing the firm to complain, in the first instance, to the FSA staff member responsible and then, if necessary, to escalate the matter to more senior staff including, if required, the Director of the relevant FSA Division.

1 Consultation Paper 73, ('Investigation of complaints against the FSA'), November 2000, at para 2.14.
2 See paras 16.60 and 16.61 below.
3 See Consultation Paper 93, ('Investigation of complaints against the FSA'), May 2001, at paras 5.8 to 5.11.

16.57 A difficulty in practice is that the line which the FSA seeks to draw between matters of misconduct on the one hand, and dissatisfaction with the exercise of discretion on the other, is not easily drawn. If, to take an example, the FSA sought an interview at 6 a.m. on a Sunday morning when the matter could have waited until the Monday, would the complaint that followed be a complaint about unprofessional or unreasonable behaviour, falling within the scheme, or one about the exercise of regulatory judgment, falling outside it? The answer is unclear and may often be difficult for firms to predict.

16.58 Second, the FSA wishes to ensure the scheme does not duplicate or overlap with other arrangements, such as the FSA's internal decision-making processes or the procedures of the Tribunal, because of, among other things, the risk of confusion[1]. In general terms, the result of this policy is that the complaints scheme exists to fill the gap where there are no other applicable procedures, rather than as an additional, alternative procedure available in any case where it seems to the firm to be a more efficient or effective means of obtaining redress.

1 See Consultation Paper 93, ('Investigation of complaints against the FSA'), May 2001, at para 5.7. It is important that this is not interpreted too widely. In many instances, it will in theory be open to a firm to bring judicial review proceedings against the FSA. However, it would be

undesirable for this to preclude the matter being resolved through the simpler, more cost effective means of the complaints scheme, in appropriate cases.

16.59 Third, the provision precluding, save in exceptional circumstances, the investigation of the complaint whilst there is some form of continuing, connected regulatory action, seems to be[1] aimed to prevent the complaints scheme being used to frustrate legitimate regulatory action. It is difficult to see how the complaints scheme could result in the FSA's action being frustrated, particularly given that, as outlined at para 16.90 below, the FSA can continue taking action notwithstanding an investigation into a complaint on a connected matter. In many cases, the complainant may have a legitimate interest in having the matter resolved swiftly, particularly since it can take months, or even years, for the FSA to conclude all its enforcement processes. Nonetheless, the approach taken in the scheme rules is that it is for the complainant to show exceptional circumstances such that it would be unreasonable to expect him to wait.

1 See Consultation Paper 73, ('Investigation of complaints against the FSA'), November 2000, at para 2.29.

16.60 Finally, given the breadth of these exceptions, an important question is whether the complaints commissioner is able to take his own view and to investigate complaints falling within the above categories, whatever the FSA's views. The scheme provides[1] that the commissioner will not investigate any complaint which is outside the scope of the scheme, but that the final decision on whether a particular case is excluded rests with the commissioner. But not all of the categories of cases outlined above as being regarded as unsuitable for the complaints scheme are actually excluded from the scheme. Some are, rather, cases which the FSA regards as inappropriate to be considered by the scheme. The FSMA 2000 anticipates that the FSA may decide not to investigate a complaint and yet the commissioner may decide that it ought to be investigated[2].

1 See the FSA Handbook at COAF 1.5.9.
2 FSMA 2000, Sch 1, para 8(4).

16.61 In answering the question whether the commissioner can take his own view and decide to investigate notwithstanding the FSA regards the case as unsuitable for the scheme, therefore, it is necessary to differentiate between different types of objections to complaints being heard under the scheme:

- those matters listed at para 16.52 above are specified as excluded from the scheme. Hence, if he considers that a particular matter falls within one of those categories, the commissioner cannot investigate it;
- matters which are connected with or arise from continuing FSA action will not normally be investigated by either the FSA or the commissioner, unless there are exceptional circumstances[1]. In such cases, there may still be scope for the commissioner to investigate, because he may find that there are exceptional circumstances;
- so far as concerns the first two bullet points at para 16.55 above (matters which could be dealt with more appropriately in another way or which

involve dissatisfaction with the FSA's policies or the exercise of the FSA's discretion), the scheme rules specify that such matters will not be investigated by the FSA, but do not purport to prevent the commissioner from investigating such matters. It therefore seems to be open to the commissioner to decide whether or not to do so[2].

1 See para 16.55 above.
2 This is supported by FSMA 2000, Sch 1, para 8(4).

16.62 The FSA expects[1] the commissioner to appreciate the broader framework within which he operates – namely, the FSA's statutory objectives and duties and the procedures which the legislation puts in place for resolving certain kinds of disagreement between the FSA and regulated firms – and therefore to be guided by the same considerations as the FSA[2]. Within that framework, he may take a different view from the FSA on whether a particular complaint falls within the scope of the scheme or whether it should be investigated immediately or only following the conclusion of some other proceedings. However, the FSA envisages that he would not investigate a complaint which, for example, he reasonably considers would be dealt with more appropriately in another way. Ultimately, though, this remains entirely a matter for the commissioner.

1 See Consultation Paper 93, ('Investigation of complaints against the FSA'), May 2001, at para 9.1.
2 See Consultation Paper 73, ('Investigation of complaints against the FSA'), November 2000, at paras 3.7 to 3.9.

When might firms consider using the scheme?

16.63 The complaints scheme is certainly an option in any case which arguably falls within its scope. Whether or not, from the firm's perspective, it is appropriate for the firm to use the scheme, as opposed to seeking redress through some other means, is a different question.

16.64 From the firm's perspective, the scheme may be particularly useful:

- where the firm has suffered losses which cannot be redressed by any other means, particularly in the light of the FSA's statutory immunity from liability for damages[1]. In such a situation, the uncertainties about the amount of compensation that can be obtained under the scheme, as discussed at para 16.66 ff below, are likely to be outweighed by the inability to obtain any compensation by any other means and the simplicity and cost-effectiveness for the firm of using the complaints procedure;
- where the complaint is more minor in nature and did not significantly affect the outcome of the action that the FSA took or where the firm seeks an apology or some other remedy that a court could not grant. An example might be a complaint about the over-enthusiastic use by the FSA of its investigation powers where ultimately the result of the enforcement process either was not materially affected or was acceptable to the firm;

- in other cases where the firm does not want to incur the expense and resources that would be involved in legal proceedings or for other reasons does not want to bring legal proceedings against the FSA.

1 This is considered at para 16.29 ff above.

16.65 As should be apparent from the discussion above, the scheme is likely to be inappropriate:

- for those cases which are plainly excluded from its scope[1];
- for complaints which are particularly serious in nature or where substantial loss or damage has been suffered by the person concerned, at least where there is an alternative means of redress available[2]. This is because of the non-binding nature of the commissioner's recommendations[3], the likely limitations on compensation that will be paid by the FSA under the scheme[4] and the uncertainties as to the scope of the scheme;
- where the firm's primary aim is to undermine or change the FSA's policy in a particular area, for example because the firm regards that policy as unreasonable or in breach of its human rights, as opposed to seeking redress for the FSA's conduct in implementing the policy in the particular case. This is because the scheme is not intended to address, and cannot easily address, issues about the content of the FSA's policy;
- where the firm has the right to refer the matter of complaint to the Tribunal, for example where the complaint is the imposition of a disciplinary sanction, a variation of permission or some other regulatory action for which the Tribunal is available[5].

1 See para 16.52 above.
2 Examples would include serious breaches of the Human Rights Act 1998 and allegations of bad faith resulting in significant loss.
3 See para 16.66 ff below.
4 See para 16.73 ff below.
5 For a discussion of the Tribunal, see Chapter 6 above and, for a list of certain FSA decisions in the enforcement context which the person has the right to refer to the Tribunal, para 6.10 above.

What remedies are available?

The range of remedies

16.66 The outcome of a successful complaint will be either:

- an offer by the FSA, following its own investigation, of action to remedy the matters of complaint, for example to take steps to rectify an error, to apologise or to pay ex-gratia compensation[1]; or
- if the FSA's proposals were not acceptable, or the matter was referred to the commissioner before those proposals were made, a report by the commissioner to the FSA and the complainant on whether or not the complaint is well-founded and/or whether the FSA should be criticised, and:

- if he thinks it appropriate, he may make a recommendation that the FSA takes either or both of the following steps[2]:
  - — remedies the matters of complaint, or
  - — makes a compensatory payment to the complainant,
- he may publish his report or any part of it if he considers that it ought to be brought to the attention of the public[3];
- if he reports that a complaint is well-founded or criticises the FSA, the FSA must inform the commissioner and the complainant of the steps which it proposes to take by way of response[4];
- the commissioner may require the FSA to publish the whole or a specified part of its response[5].

1 See the FSA Handbook at COAF 1.5.4 and 1.5.5.
2 See the FSA Handbook at COAF 1.5.18.
3 See the FSA Handbook at COAF 1.5.21.
4 See the FSA Handbook at COAF 1.5.22.
5 See the FSA Handbook at COAF 1.5.23.

16.67 It is important to appreciate that the commissioner's recommendations are only recommendations; they are not binding. It is a matter for the FSA whether or not it chooses to follow those recommendations, although, if it does not, it runs the risk of adverse publicity and it also runs the risk of legal proceedings being brought against it (in those cases where the person who brought the complaint had such an option). The commissioner's recommendations do not therefore have any binding legal force. The FSA's policy on when it will pay compensation in accordance with the commissioner's recommendations is outlined below[1]. The commissioner's ability to publish his recommendations and the FSA's response to them should, in practice, be an important aspect of the accountability regime for the FSA.

1 See para 16.73 below.

Particular issues relating to awards of compensation

In what circumstances will the commissioner award compensation?

16.68 The scheme rules say little about the circumstances in which the commissioner will recommend that the FSA pays compensation and on what basis he will assess compensation awards. The rules provide simply that[1], in deciding whether a complaint is well-founded and, if so, in deciding what steps he should recommend the FSA to take, he will have regard to the FSA's statutory objectives and the 'principles for good regulation' set out at FSMA 2000, s 2(3)[2].

1 See the FSA Handbook at COAF 1.5.17.
2 And, in relation to the FSA's functions as UK Listing Authority, FSMA 2000, s 73(1). For a discussion of the regulatory objectives and principles of good regulation, see para 2.19 ff above. In relation to the UK Listing Authority, see para 15.10 above.

16.69 The award of compensation presents some particular difficulties. The cost of any compensation that the FSA pays is borne not by the public purse but by the regulated community, which funds the FSA through the payment of fees. If the FSA were faced with large numbers of recommendations for the payment of significant amounts of compensation, it would potentially be placed in a difficult position. On the one hand, there could be intense pressure to follow the recommendations of the commissioner and pay compensation due to those who had legitimate complaints about the FSA's conduct. On the other hand, it would be unpalatable for the FSA to pay away substantial resources at the expense of the regulated community.

16.70 The rules of the complaints scheme attempt to shift onto the complaints commissioner some of the onus of weighing up these counter-balancing factors, by imposing on the commissioner the duty to have regard to the FSA's regulatory objectives and the principles of good regulation. Although not stated, it is likely the FSA has particularly in mind the statutory requirement to have regard to the need to use its resources in the most efficient and economic way[1]. The FSA's rationale for imposing this duty[2] is that it is important to set the commissioner's recommendations in the broader context of the legislation and the FSA's wider responsibilities.

1 FSMA 2000, s 2(3) and see para 2.21 above. This is one of the principles of good regulation.
2 See Consultation Paper 93, ('Investigation of complaints against the FSA'), May 2001, at para 13.4.

16.71 For two main reasons, firms may wish to press the commissioner not to be overly influenced by such considerations[1]. First, and fundamentally, if the complaints mechanism is to operate effectively in holding the FSA accountable for its misconduct, the FSA should face the consequences of misconduct which causes loss. If the commissioner acts as a filter and only awards, effectively, such compensation as he feels the FSA can afford given all its other responsibilities, then the real cost of the FSA's misconduct will be obscured and some of the benefits of the complaints scheme will be lost. The alternative would be for the commissioner to recommend the payment of the compensation which he feels is appropriate given the loss suffered. If the FSA is unwilling or unable to comply with that recommendation, then that will be plain. This would enhance the FSA's accountability.

1 A requirement to 'have regard' to a particular matter may be capable of being satisfied by considering it and deciding to afford it little or no weight: see, for example, *Tesco Stores Ltd v Secretary of State for the Environment* [1995] 1 WLR 759, HL.

16.72 Second, it is in any event not clear that the regulatory objectives or principles of good regulation have any application to the complaints commissioner or to individual complaints. There are a number of reasons for this. Primarily, the commissioner is not part of the FSA, but an independent person whom the FSMA 2000 requires the FSA to appoint to a particular function. It is difficult to see that the objectives and principles apply to him. Further, as has already been noted[1], the regulatory objectives and principles of good regulation are not taken into account in deciding what action should be taken in individual cases. Rather, they apply at the policy level, when the FSA is considering its policy in relation to a particular aspect of its functions, or is considering issuing rules, codes or statements under the FSMA 2000. In the present context, though, the FSA is imposing a requirement on the commissioner to have regard to these objectives and principles at the level of individual cases. This is not what the FSMA 2000 requires, even of the FSA.

1 See para 2.22 ff above.

In what circumstances will the FSA pay compensation?

16.73 Since the commissioner's recommendations are non binding, an important question is how the FSA will in practice respond to them. The FSA will have regard to its regulatory objectives and the principles of good regulation and will also normally take into account the following[1]:

- the gravity of the misconduct which the commissioner has identified and its consequences for the complainant;
- the nature of the FSA's relationship with the complainant and the extent to which the complainant has been adversely affected in the course of direct dealings with the FSA;
- whether what has gone wrong is at the operational or administrative level, rather than in relation to matters of policy or where the FSA's actions have necessarily had to reflect a balancing of conflicting interests and complex issues; and
- the impact of the cost of compensatory payments on regulated firms, issuers of listed securities and, indirectly, consumers.

1 See the FSA Handbook at COAF 1.5.24.

16.74 The FSA thus reserves a discretion to consider in each case to what extent it should pay compensation in response to a recommendation from the commissioner. It has indicated[1] that it will give serious consideration to any such recommendation but, mindful of its statutory obligations to use its resources economically and efficiently, believes it should retain a wide discretion. Thus, it may be difficult to predict whether the FSA will pay compensation in any particular case and this will depend upon the circumstances of the case.

1 See Consultation Paper 93, ('Investigation of complaints against the FSA'), May 2001, at para 13.3.

How does the complaints scheme work?

16.75 The procedure for making a complaint under the scheme is fairly straightforward. It is reviewed in the following paragraphs and, in particular, we consider:

- how is a complaint made?
- when can a complaint be made?

- the first stage: the FSA's initial response to the complaint;
- the second stage: the commissioner's investigation;
- is the investigation confidential? and
- what will it cost?

16.76 The commissioner's powers to make recommendations as to the action the FSA should take as a result of the matter complained about are considered at para 16.66 above.

How is a complaint made?

16.77 Complaints may be made orally by a consumer. A complaint by a firm or an issuer of listed securities must be made in writing, which includes in electronic form, or must at least be confirmed in writing before the FSA will investigate[1]. It is not clear to whom the complaint must be addressed.

1 See the FSA Handbook at COAF 1.4.5.

When can a complaint be made?

16.78 A complaint should be made within 12 months of the date on which the complainant first became aware of the circumstances giving rise to the complaint[1]. However, complaints made later may be investigated if the complainant can show reasonable grounds for the delay[2].

1 See the FSA Handbook at COAF 1.4.6.

2 The purpose of the deadline is to encourage people to come forward promptly with their complaints. However, the FSA has given an assurance that complainants who have not been able to meet the deadline for good reason will still be able to have that complaint investigated under the scheme: see Consultation Paper 93, ('Investigation of complaints against the FSA'), May 2001, at para 6.2.

16.79 It is possible to make a complaint at too early a stage. If the matter is still the subject of continuing action by the FSA, the FSA or the commissioner may decline to investigate the complaint until the remedies or procedures under the FSMA 2000 have been exhausted. This is discussed at para 16.55 above.

The first stage: the FSA's response to the complaint

16.80 The investigation of the complaint is a two-stage process. The first stage is an investigation by the FSA. It is only where the FSA declines to investigate, or the matter is not resolved to the complainant's satisfaction by the FSA, or where the complainant is for some other reason dissatisfied with the FSA's progress in investigating, that it is referred to the commissioner[1]. We therefore consider, first, the FSA's investigation and response to the complaint, before turning to the commissioner's investigation.

1 See the FSA Handbook at COAF 1.5.6. This suggests that the person complaining who wishes to refer the matter straight to the commissioner should have a reason for not waiting for the

outcome of the FSA's investigation. This is consistent with the FSMA 2000 (see Sch 1, para 8(10)).

16.81 On receipt of the complaint, the FSA will:

- acknowledge the complaint within five working days of receipt[1]; and
- decide within 10 working days of receipt whether it will investigate it and, if it decides not to do so, inform the complaints commissioner and the complainant[2].

1 See the FSA Handbook at COAF 1.5.1.
2 See the FSA Handbook at COAF 1.5.7.

16.82 Where the FSA accepts that it should investigate, it will arrange for an initial investigation by a suitably senior member of staff who has not previously been involved in the matter complained of, with a view to resolving the matter as quickly as possible to the complainant's satisfaction[1]. The FSA will aim to ensure that investigations are completed within eight weeks and, if it has not completed it within four weeks, will notify the complainant of that[2].

1 See the FSA Handbook at COAF 1.5.2.
2 See the FSA Handbook at COAF 1.5.3.

16.83 As to the result of the investigation:

- if the FSA concludes that the complaint is well founded, it will tell the complainant what it proposes to do to remedy the matters of complaint[1];
- if the FSA decides to reject the complaint, it will give its reasons for doing so to the complainant[2];
- if the complainant is dissatisfied with the outcome, he may refer the matter to the complaints commissioner[3].

1 See the FSA Handbook at COAF 1.5.4 and 1.5.5 and see para 16.66 ff above.
2 See the FSA Handbook at COAF 1.5.5.
3 See the FSA Handbook at COAF 1.5.6.

The second stage: the commissioner's investigation

In what circumstances will the complaints commissioner investigate?

16.84 A matter may be referred to the complaints commissioner:

- by the FSA, if it decides not to investigate (in which case, it is required to notify the commissioner)[1];
- by the complainant, if dissatisfied with the outcome of the FSA's investigation or the FSA's progress in investigating[2]; or
- in some circumstances, by the complainant before the FSA has had the opportunity to conduct or complete its investigation[3].

1 See the FSA Handbook at COAF 1.5.7.
2 See the FSA Handbook at COAF 1.5.6.
3 See the FSA Handbook at COAF 1.5.8 and see footnote 1 to para 16.80 above.

16.85 Where a matter is referred to him, the commissioner decides whether or not to investigate. This is largely within his discretion, depending upon the situation:

- the commissioner will not investigate a complaint which he considers to be outside the scope of the complaints scheme[1];
- where the matter is referred to him after the FSA has decided not to investigate, the commissioner will hear representations from the complainant and the FSA before deciding whether the complaint falls within the scope of the scheme and, if so, whether to investigate[2];
- where the matter is referred to him before the FSA has had the opportunity to conduct or complete an investigation, the commissioner will consider whether it would be desirable to allow the FSA that opportunity before conducting his own investigation[3].

1 See the FSA Handbook at COAF 1.5.9. As to the scope of the complaints scheme, see para 16.52 ff above.
2 See the FSA Handbook at COAF 1.5.7.
3 See the FSA Handbook at COAF 1.5.8.

How does the commissioner conduct the investigation?

16.86 The FSA Handbook allows the commissioner to conduct an investigation in whatever manner he thinks appropriate[1]. It is therefore for the commissioner to determine his own procedure for each case. The scheme rules make various provisions for the conduct of investigations, as follows:

- in performing his functions, the commissioner must at all times act independently of the FSA[2];
- the commissioner may appoint a person to conduct the whole or any part of the investigation on his behalf but subject to his direction[3]. The extent to which he does so is entirely a matter for him[4]. If he does appoint a person, the person must not be an officer or employee of the FSA;
- the FSA will afford the commissioner all reasonable co-operation, including giving access to its staff and information. However, it may, in affording the commissioner access to information, have regard to the need to maintain confidentiality[5]. Examples given by the FSA of where this might be appropriate are to ensure the identity of an informant is not disclosed or to maintain the confidentiality of information given to the FSA under international arrangements[6];
- the commissioner may obtain reasonable external resources at the FSA's expense[7], including legal advice[8];

- the commissioner will ensure that, before he concludes an investigation and makes a report, any person who may be the subject of criticism in it is given notice of that criticism and an opportunity to respond to it[9];
- findings of fact and decisions by certain types of courts and tribunals, including the Tribunal, are conclusive evidence for the purposes of the investigation and findings of fact or decisions by other courts or tribunals carry such weight as the FSA or the commissioner, as applicable, considers appropriate in the circumstances[10].

1 See the FSA Handbook at COAF 1.5.10.
2 See the FSA Handbook at COAF 1.5.10, reflecting FSMA 2000, Sch 1, para 7(4).
3 See the FSA Handbook at COAF 1.5.11.
4 See Consultation Paper 73, ('Investigation of complaints against the FSA'), November 2000, at para 3.11.
5 The FSA refers to the fact that it has no ability to prevent the commissioner from including any particular information in his published report and has given an assurance that it will withhold information only in rare cases: see Consultation Paper 93, ('Investigation of complaints against the FSA'), May 2001, at para 11.2. Where the FSA does withhold information, it will inform the commissioner of the nature of the information and its reasons for withholding it: see the FSA Handbook at COAF 1.5.12.
6 See the FSA Handbook at COAF 1.5.12.
7 See the FSA Handbook at COAF 1.5.10.
8 See Consultation Paper 73, ('Investigation of complaints against the FSA'), November 2000, at para 3.12.
9 See the FSA Handbook at COAF 1.5.14.
10 See the FSA Handbook at COAF 1.5.15 and 1.5.16.

Reporting the results of the investigation

16.87 The commissioner is required to report to the FSA and the complainant on the results of his investigation, giving reasons for any determination he makes[1].

1 See the FSA Handbook at COAF 1.5.19.

16.88 The commissioner must ensure that his report does not mention the name of or contain particulars likely to identify any person other than the FSA unless in his opinion the omission of such particulars would be likely to impair the effectiveness of the report or he considers it necessary to do so after taking into account the public interest as well as the interests of the complainant and other persons[1]. This reflects the fact that the focus of the investigation and report is on the actions or inactions of the FSA, not the complainant (or anyone else), and therefore it will rarely be appropriate to identify anyone other than the FSA[2].

1 See the FSA Handbook at COAF 1.5.20.
2 See Consultation Paper 93, ('Investigation of complaints against the FSA'), May 2001, at para 12.2.

16.89 As far as the contents of the report are concerned, the conclusions or recommendations that it can contain, and the provisions as to publication, see para 16.66 ff above.

Can the FSA take other action in the meantime?

16.90 The investigation of the complaint does not prevent the FSA from continuing to take such action or such further action as it considers appropriate in relation to any related matter[1]. There is therefore nothing to prevent the FSA from, for example, continuing the enforcement action in the context of which the complaint arose or taking other enforcement action relating to the same matter or relating to another matter regarding the complainant[2].

1 See the FSA Handbook at COAF 1.5.13.
2 In many cases, the FSA or the commissioner may in any event decline to investigate the complaint until the other matters have been disposed of. See para 16.55 above.

Is the complaint confidential?

16.91 Whether the complaint and the work of the commissioner will be made public will largely be within the discretion of the commissioner. In order to explain this, a number of points need to be made.

16.92 Subject to any applicable statutory confidentiality restrictions, as outlined below, the commissioner can decide to publish all or part of his report, and all or part of the FSA's response to it[1]. It is therefore quite possible that matters relating to the complaint could become public knowledge, although, as has already been highlighted[2], the report will not normally enable anyone other than the FSA to be identified.

1 FSMA 2000, Sch 1, para 8(2)(b)(iii) and 8(7) and see the FSA Handbook at COAF 1.5.19 and 1.5.21. The FSA will, itself, publish in its annual report data about complaints that were resolved without the Commissioner being involved: see Consultation Paper 93, ('Investigation of complaints against the FSA'), May 2001, at para 12.5.
2 See para 16.88 above.

16.93 So far as the statutory confidentiality restrictions are concerned, the FSMA 2000[1] contains a prohibition on, broadly, the disclosure of confidential information relating to the business or affairs of any person obtained by a 'primary recipient' for the purposes of or in the discharge of any of the FSA's functions under the FSMA 2000, or by any person directly or indirectly from the primary recipient. The commissioner is not specified as a primary recipient for this purpose. Therefore:

- to the extent he receives information from the firm, or a third party who is involved (other than the FSA or another primary recipient), he is under no statutory obligation to keep that information confidential[2];
- but he would in principle be bound by the statutory prohibition to the extent that he receives information directly or indirectly from a primary recipient, such as the FSA.

1 FSMA 2000, s 348, discussed in more detail at para 4.304 ff above.
2 He may, though, be under a common law obligation of confidence, depending upon the circumstances: see further the discussion at para 12.19 above.

16.94 The application of any statutory restrictions is, though, subject to the exceptions in the so-called Gateway Regulations[1]. Very briefly, these generally speaking enable information to be disclosed both to and by the commissioner for the purpose of enabling or assisting him to discharge his functions. He can therefore receive and disclose information within the terms of the Gateway Regulations.

1 The Financial Services and Markets Act 2000 (Disclosure of Confidential Information) Regulations 2001, SI 2001/2188, particularly regs 9, 10 and 12 and Sch 1. For a further discussion, see para 4.312 above.

Costs

16.95 Use of the complaints process is free. The FSA does not levy any charge for making a complaint[1].

1 See the FSA Handbook at COAF 1.4.7.

Challenging the outcome of the complaints process

16.96 The outcome of the complaints process will not always be to the complainant's satisfaction. The commissioner may find that there were no grounds for complaint, or may decide that the matter is not one which he can or should investigate, or the amount of compensation that he recommends, or the amount that the FSA decides to pay, may be insufficient to recompense the complainant. If the complainant emerges unsatisfied from the process, what options are open to him?

16.97 There are two key points to note. First, the FSMA 2000 does not prescribe any appeal process for the complaints scheme and the matter is not one which of itself can be referred to the Tribunal. Hence, once the commissioner has made his decision, that is the end of the complaints process. Any further avenues of recourse that might exist[1] will have to be in a different forum.

1 The firm's options are, though, likely to be limited, because of the FSA's statutory immunity to damages claims (see para 16.29 ff above).

16.98 Second, the commissioner's decision is not binding in the sense of being determinative of any person's rights. In principle, therefore, any other options which the complainant had before he brought his complaint, for example the option of bringing a legal claim or judicial review proceedings, should in general terms remain unaffected. It is not however wholly without effect. For example:

- if the complainant does pursue further proceedings for damages[1] he will probably have to give credit for any compensation that he has received through the complaints process; and
- depending upon the extent of the commissioner's investigations and the nature of his findings, it may in practice be more difficult to persuade a court

to give permission for a judicial review[2]. Firms will also need to keep in mind the short timeframe for commencing a judicial review[3].

1 This would only apply if he falls within one of the exceptions to the statutory immunity to damages claims: see para 16.31 ff above.
2 The need to obtain permission is referred to briefly at para 16.21 above.
3 See para 16.21 above.

Index

Abuse *see* MARKET MISCONDUCT AND ABUSE
Access to FSA's materials 5.81–98
  action where additional material required 5.94–5
  decision on 5.92
  exceptions 5.83, 5.89–91
  primary material 5.82, 5.85
  request for 5.96–7
  secondary material 5.82, 5.86–8
  use made of materials 5.98
Accessory liability, equitable claims 10.19
Accountability, Financial Services Authority (FSA) 1.19–20
Accountants 1.10
Acquisition of control over UK regulated firm, variation of permission/intervention and 9.42–3
Actions
  against firms *see* SANCTIONS
  for breach of statutory duty 10.28–48
  civil action against FSA 16.8, 16.25–36
    statutory immunity for damages 16.29–36
  suspension of action by FSA 6.104–6
  see also DISCIPLINARY AND ENFORCEMENT REGIME
Actuaries
  assistance in compilation of reports 4.87–8
  requesting information from 4.234–5
Admissions 10.74–80
Advertisements 15.187
Agreement
  action with firm's agreement 9.232–5
  expressly not unenforceable agreements 10.60–1
  settlement by *see* SETTLEMENT BY AGREEMENT
  unenforceable agreements 10.52–9
Appeals
  from Ombudsman 12.73–6
  from Tribunal 6.161, 6.169–74
    applying for permission to appeal 6.172–4
    basis of 6.171
Appointed representatives 2.10
Assessment of firms
  classification of 2.31
Assessment of firms—*contd*
  Financial Services Authority (FSA) and 2.7, 2.43–5
  'fit and proper' 2.38, 2.43–5
    failure to be fit and proper 2.165–6
Assessment of risk 2.30
Assets
  freezing orders (injunctions securing assets) 7.116–21, 8.80, 13.243–4
  restrictions on firm's assets 9.89–94
Auditors
  assistance in compilation of reports 4.87–8
  requesting information from 4.234–5

Bad faith (dishonesty) 10.19, 16.32–3
Banks 1.10
  confidentiality and 4.184, 4.239, 4.267–70
  requesting information from 4.234–5
  restrictions on firm's assets and 9.90–3
Breach of contract 10.11–14
Breach of fiduciary duty 10.18
Breach of FSMA 2000
  conduct giving rise to enforcement 2.133–7, 2.189
  firm's obligation to report to FSA 3.50–8
  variation of permission/intervention and 9.51–5
Breach of general prohibition 2.175–7
Breach of Listing Rules 15.50–1, 15.97–187
Breach of perimeter 2.175–7
Breach of Principles for Businesses 2.156–64
Breach of statutory duty 10.23–5, 10.27, 10.28–51, 15.181–2
  actions for 10.28–48
    situations where no right of action 10.49–51
Breach of trust 10.17
Building societies 1.10

Cancellation of listing 15.134, 15.143–6, 15.168–73
Cancellation of permission 9.239–55
  challenge of decision 9.250
  choice not to cancel 9.246–9
  consequences of 9.253–5

Cancellation of permission—*contd*
procedure 9.251–2
when FSA will consider cancelling 9.243–50
Cancellation of sponsor's approval 15.147, 15.174
Cautions 11.37–40
Censure *see* PUBLIC CENSURE
Challenges to FSA 4.282, 16.1–5, 16.6–36
challenging outcome of complaints procedure 16.96–8
civil action against FSA 16.8, 16.25–36
statutory immunity for damages 16.29–36
judicial review 16.7, 16.16–24
grounds 16.20
how to bring 16.21
remedies available 16.22
whether to bring 16.24
options for firms 16.6–9
prevention of FSA from taking action 16.10–15
City Code 13.67, 13.101, 13.102, 13.227–30
Civil action against FSA 16.8, 16.25–36
statutory immunity for damages 16.29–36
Civil liability arising from market abuse 13.276–8
Civil liability to third parties 10.1–80
breach of contract 10.11–14
breach of statutory duty 10.23–5, 10.27, 10.28–51, 15.181–2
actions for 10.28–48
situations where no right of action 10.49–51
claims under FSMA 2000 10.27–60
claims under general law 10.6–26
contribution claims 10.26
equitable claims 10.16–21
accessory liability 10.19
breach of fiduciary duty 10.18
breach of trust 10.17
liability as recipient of trust funds 10.20
tracing 10.21
expressly not unenforceable agreements 10.60–1
listed companies 15.179–87
breach of statutory duty 15.181–2
contents of listing particulars 15.183–6
from advertisements and information 15.187
misrepresentation 10.22
negligence 10.15
practical guidance for firms 10.7–10
practical issues arising from investigation and enforcement process 10.62–80
unenforceable agreements 10.52–9
why firm might incur civil liability 10.2–5
Civil proceedings, firm's obligation to report to FSA 3.59–61
Classification of firms 2.31
Clearing houses 1.10, 2.10
Clients and customers
compensation *see* RESTITUTION ORDERS
complaints *see* FINANCIAL SERVICES OMBUDSMAN SCHEME
consumer protection of 2.20, 2.26, 3.110
collective investment schemes 14.3, 14.63–5
'own-initiative' powers and 9.4, 9.25–30, 9.60–2, 9.244
Clients and customers—*contd*
investigation of market misconduct and 13.123–6
obligations to 3.111–19
Principles for Businesses and 2.57–8
regulatory problems and dealing with 3.110–27
Code of Market Conduct 2.116, 2.118, 13.20–3, 13.62
compliance with 13.99, 13.100
Code of Practice for approved persons 2.67, 2.82–8, 2.116, 2.117
Statements of Principle and 2.83–8, 2.89, 2.101–5
Collective investment schemes 14.1–149
enforcement action 14.41–149
ICVCs 14.41, 14.101–21
overseas schemes 14.41, 14.122–49
unit trusts 14.41, 14.46–100
investigations 14.10–40
commencement 14.15–32, 14.39
control 14.39–40
ICVCs 14.11, 14.15, 14.16, 14.27–32
information obtainable 14.33–8
unit trusts 14.15, 14.17–26
types 14.6–7
Commercial rationale, market abuse and 13.106–7
Communications
between firm and FSA or investigator 4.211–14
between firm and its employees 4.207–9
compliance officers and 4.204–6
interception and monitoring of 3.25–7, 3.31
legal privilege and 4.197, 4.204–14, 4.264
without prejudice communications 4.210
Compensation
FSA complaints procedure and 16.68–74
see also RESTITUTION ORDERS
Complaints commissioner 16.43–9
appointment 16.44–5
compensation award 16.68–72
independence from FSA 16.46–9
investigation by 16.84–90
Complaints procedure
Financial Services Authority (FSA) 1.20, 4.281, 16.5, 16.37–98
challenging outcome 16.96–8
compensation awards 16.68–74
complaints commissioner 16.43–9, 16.68–72, 16.84–90
costs 16.95
exclusions 16.52–4
investigation by commissioner 16.84–90
overview 16.37–42
procedure 16.75–95
remedies available 16.66–74
response of FSA to complainant 16.80–3
types of complaints covered by scheme 16.51–62
when complaints scheme available 16.50–65
firms 12.3, 12.24–6
see also FINANCIAL SERVICES OMBUDSMAN SCHEME
Compliance officers, communications with/from 4.204–6

Confidence in financial system 2.20
Confidentiality 4.208
banks and 4.184, 4.239, 4.267–70
complaints investigation 16.91–4
in mediation 5.143–5
preliminary findings letter 5.51–4, 5.55
prohibition of disclosure of confidential information 4.304–14
Tribunal hearings and 6.125, 6.127–9
use of information by Ombudsman 12.17
warning notices 5.76–7
Connivance, criminal liability and 11.34
Consent, criminal liability and 11.34
Consolidation of Tribunal references 6.114–17
Consumer Panel of the FSA 1.20
Consumers
protection of 2.20, 2.26, 3.110
collective investment schemes 14.3, 14.63–5
'own-initiative' powers and 9.4, 9.25–30, 9.60–2, 9.244
Contempt of court 2.135, 4.284–6
Contract, breach of 10.11–14
Contribution claims 10.26
Co-operation with FSA
employees 4.42–9
approved persons 4.43–8
other employees 4.49
firms
criminal prosecutions and 11.51–2
investigations 4.180
as objection to exercise of formal power of investigation 4.271
obligation 4.27–56, 13.154–6
Costs
disciplinary and enforcement regime 5.196–9
FSA complaints scheme 16.95
Ombudsman scheme 12.67–9
Tribunal cases 6.153–60
Courts
challenging FSA in court 4.282
contempt of court 2.135, 4.284–6
restitution orders and
application by FSA 7.69–71
information gathering 7.73–5
orders made by court 7.48
see also INJUNCTIONS
Creation of documents 3.155–61, 13.129
Credit unions 1.10
Crime and criminal offences 2.20, 2.134, 5.21–2, 13.7
breach of general prohibition 2.175–7
compelling information from person suspected of criminal offence 4.242–54
consequences of not providing information to FSA 4.287–8
consequences of not reporting to FSA and 3.106
documents and 3.151–3
firm's obligation to report offences and breaches of FSMA 2000 to FSA 3.50–8
investigations 4.134–49
scope of power 4.139
what information can firm be required to provide 4.140–3, 4.147–9
Crime and criminal offences—*contd*
investigations—*contd*
when can investigation be commenced 4.134–7, 4.144–5
when will power be exercised 4.138, 4.146
listed companies 15.54–6, 15.76, 15.101–2, 15.155, 15.178
market misconduct and abuse 13.128
procedure for criminal proceedings 13.186
when FSA will bring criminal proceedings 13.177–85
regulatory problems and potential criminal proceedings 3.142–8
steps to take 3.146–8
types of offences 3.144–5
self-incrimination 4.275, 13.162–72
use of information criminal proceedings 4.317–18
see also PROSECUTIONS
Customers *see* CLIENTS AND CUSTOMERS

Damages 16.22
FSA's statutory immunity for damages 16.29–36
Dealings with regulators 2.95–6
Decision-making procedures 1.24–5
Financial Services and Markets Tribunal 6.142–3
FSA's executive procedures 9.224–31
on issue of warning notice 5.68–70, 5.87
on referral to RDC 5.57–60
on right of access to FSA materials 5.92
Decision notices 5.12, 5.103, 5.128, 5.162–87
acceptance of 5.183
consideration of representations 5.162–5
contents 5.172
effect of receipt 5.174–5
further decision notice 5.184–7
prohibition orders and 8.62–4
publicity 5.182
supervisory notices compared 9.113–14
third parties and 5.176–81
when received by firm 5.173
Decisions
Financial Services and Markets Tribunal 6.137–51
effect of 6.148–52
grounds for varying or setting aside 6.163–5
process of decision making 6.142–3
in public 6.144–7
what decisions Tribunal can make 6.137–41
Ombudsman 12.58–79
challenge and appeal 12.73–6
costs awards 12.67–9
effect of 12.70–2
enforcement 12.78–9
grant of remedies 12.62–6
how decision is reached 12.59–61
publication 12.77
Declaration 16.22
Department of Trade and Industry (DTI) 11.10
Destruction of documents 3.150–4
Directions from Tribunal 6.38–9

Directions from Tribunal—*contd*
application for 6.77–8
practical guidance for applicants 6.90–1
pre-hearing review 6.84–6
relating to disclosure 6.71–5
rules on 6.79–83
which directions Tribunal can make 6.87–9
Disciplinary actions against employees 3.140–1
Disciplinary and enforcement regime 1.7, 1.12–13, 1.26–7, 2.2, 5.1–199
admissions and 10.74–80
civil liability to third parties and 10.62–80
collective investment schemes 14.41–149
ICVCs 14.41, 14.101–21
overseas schemes 14.41, 14.122–49
unit trusts 14.41, 14.46–100
conduct giving rise to enforcement 2.131–89
breaches of FSMA 2000 2.133–7, 2.189
breaches of perimeter 2.175–7
breaches of Principles for Businesses 2.156–64
breaches of specific rules 2.138–55
failure to be fit and proper 2.165–6, 2.188
failure to comply with Statement of Principle 2.182–3
firms 2.131–77
individuals 2.178–89
issues arising abroad with implications in UK 2.167–73
issues arising in non-regulated business 2.174
knowingly concerned in contravention by authorised person 2.184–7
consequences of not providing information to FSA 4.289
consequences of not reporting to FSA 3.103, 3.105
costs 5.196–9
criminal prosecutions and 11.41–6
debates about 1.14–30
firm's obligation to report disciplinary proceedings to FSA 3.59–61
general approach to 2.34–6
general principles 1.28–9
listed companies 15.99, 15.107–32, 15.166–7
action against directors and former directors 15.113–18, 15.130–2
action against issuers and applicants for listing 15.107–12
action against sponsors 15.119–22
policy on use of 15.123–32
market misconduct and abuse and 13.262–75
nature of procedure 5.17–39
outline of procedure 5.8–16
own-initiative powers and 9.76–9
preliminary findings letter 5.41–55
suspension of action by FSA 6.104–6
threshold conditions and 2.41–2
treatment of customers and 3.120–4
what regime is designed to achieve 5.17–25
see also DECISION NOTICES; FINAL NOTICES; FINANCIAL SERVICES AND MARKETS TRIBUNAL; REGULATORY DECISIONS COMMITTEE (RDC); SANCTIONS; WARNING NOTICES
Disclosure
basic rules on 4.193–203
by FSA to others 4.300–16, 5.52
preliminary findings letter 5.52–4
public interest disclosure 4.48
reducing risk of disclosure 4.218–20
reports commissioned by FSA and 4.98–101
risks of information disclosure to Ombudsman 12.16–20
Tribunal cases 6.58–76
firm's obligation to provide disclosure 6.64
FSA's obligation to provide disclosure 6.60–3
FSA's obligation to provide secondary disclosure 6.65–6
legally privileged material 6.68–70
Tribunal's directions relating to disclosure 6.71–5
use made by applicant of disclosed documents 6.76
which documents need not be provided 6.67–70
use of information obtained from investigation of listed companies 15.88–96
see also PUBLIC DOMAIN AND PUBLICITY
Discontinuance, notice of 5.157, 5.166–9
publicity 5.167–9
Dishonesty 10.19, 16.32–3
Disproportionate request from FSA 4.272–4
Dispute resolution *see* FINANCIAL SERVICES OMBUDSMAN SCHEME; MEDIATION
Distortion of market 13.46–9
Documents 3.149–61, 4.112, 4.113
copies or explanations of 4.114
creation 3.155–61, 13.129
destruction 3.150–4
exceptions to requirements to produce 4.118
investigations 3.18–21, 4.184–8
listed companies 15.65–6
risks of producing material for or in investigations 4.189–220
liens on 4.117
location of documents not produced 4.115
in possession of third parties 4.116
retention 13.129
reviewing 4.182–6
see also DISCLOSURE; REPORTS
Duty *see* FIDUCIARY DUTY; STATUTORY DUTY

Employees
action required by firms 3.135–44
communication between firm and its employees 4.207–9
criminal liability 11.30
actions of firm 11.48–50
internal disciplinary actions against 3.140–1
investigations 3.22–38
interviewing 3.33–8
material recorded in course of business 3.25–7
misconduct 8.9
obligation to co-operate with FSA 4.42–9
approved persons 4.43–8

Employees—*contd*
obligation to co-operate with FSA—*contd*
other employees 4.49
reports commissioned by FSA and 4.97
restrictions on firm's employees 9.95–8
sanctions against 8.1–82
disciplinary action 8.4–43
fines 8.7, 8.24
injunctions 8.76, 8.77–80, 9.98
prohibition orders 2.68, 8.44–75
public censure 8.24
restitution orders 7.48, 8.76, 8.81–2
withdrawal of approval 8.27–43
Enforcement regime *see* DISCIPLINARY AND ENFORCEMENT REGIME
Equitable claims 10.16–21
accessory liability 10.19
breach of fiduciary duty 10.18
breach of trust 10.17
liability as recipient of trust funds 10.20
tracing 10.21
Errors, firm's obligation to report to FSA 3.62–5
European Bank for Reconstruction and Development 2.10
European Convention on Human Rights (ECHR)
decisions of Ombudsman and 12.72
disciplinary and enforcement regime and 1.26, 2.161, 5.17, 5.20–2
Financial Services and Markets Tribunal compatibility with 6.23–6
FSMA 2000, compatibility with 1.2
information gathering and investigation powers and 4.245, 4.246
market abuse regime and 1.22
market misconduct and abuse and 13.16
privacy rights 3.29, 4.274
remedies against public bodies and 16.34–6
European Investment Bank 2.10
European Union (EU)
FSA's own-initiative powers and 9.35–8
inward passport scheme 2.4, 2.8, 2.12
single market 2.8, 2.12
Treaty rights 2.8, 2.13
Evidence
Financial Services Ombudsman Scheme 12.54–5
Tribunal hearings 6.130–4
Evidential test, prosecutions 11.19, 11.20
Expert reports 5.91
Expert witnesses, Financial Services and Markets Tribunal 6.98–103
Expressly not unenforceable agreements 10.60–1

False or misleading impression 13.41–5
False or misleading information 9.56–9, 14.59–60
Fiduciary duty 10.16
breach of 10.18
Final notices 5.188–95
contents 5.192
publicity 5.194–5
when issued 5.189–91
Final notices—*contd*
to whom given 5.193
Financial penalties *see* FINES
Financial Services Authority (FSA) 1.3, 1.4–7, 1.9, 2.1–189
access to FSA's materials 5.81–98
accountability of 1.19–20
assessment of firms by 2.7, 2.43–5
challenges 4.282, 16.1–5, 16.6–36, 16.96–8
civil action against 16.8, 16.25–36
collective investment schemes and 14.1–149
commissioning of reports 4.72–107
complaints procedure 1.20, 4.281, 16.5, 16.37–98
Consumer Panel 1.20
criminal prosecutions 11.1–53
dealings with 2.95–6
debates about 1.14–30
decision-making procedures 1.24–5, 9.224–31
disciplinary and enforcement regime 1.7, 1.12–13, 1.26–7, 2.2, 5.1–199
executive procedures 9.224–31
exemptions from regulation 2.10
fundamental regulatory requirements applicable to firms 2.37–62
fundamental regulatory requirements applicable to individuals 2.63–105
handbook 1.4, 1.7, 2.2, 2.106–30
information gathering powers 4.1, 4.6, 4.10–259, 7.73–5, 13.150–3
investigation powers 4.1–299, 13.130–72
judicial review 16.7, 16.16–24
legal and policy framework 2.17–36, 2.125–30
investigation request contrary to policy 4.272–4
market misconduct and abuse regime 1.21–3, 2.118, 2.135, 13.1–278
'own-initiative' powers 9.1–255
permission system 2.4, 2.5, 2.6–10
Practitioner Panel 1.20
Principles for Businesses 2.51–62, 2.112
breaches of 2.156–64
principles of good regulation 2.19, 2.21, 2.22–4, 2.35
regulatory objectives 2.19, 2.20, 2.22–4
regulatory problems and 3.4–5
reporting to 3.39–109
as single statutory regulator 1.8–9
steps when regulatory problems arise 3.1–161
supervision 2.29–33, 2.128, 5.5, 9.72–5, 9.88, 9.105–93
suspension of action 6.104–6
terminology of regulatory regime 2.15
threshold conditions 2.38–45
toolkit 2.25–33
who is subject to regime 1.10–11, 2.3–16
see also LISTING AUTHORITY
Financial Services and Markets Tribunal 5.13, 5.14, 6.1–174
appeals from 6.161, 6.169–74
applying for permission to appeal 6.172–4
basis of 6.171
constitution of 6.4–6, 9.179
costs 6.153–60

Financial Services and Markets Tribunal—*contd*
decisions 6.137–51
effect of 6.148–52
grounds for varying or setting aside 6.163–5
process of decision making 6.142–3
in public 6.144–7
what decisions Tribunal can make 6.137–41
directions 6.38–9
application for 6.77–8
practical guidance for applicants 6.90–1
pre-hearing review 6.84–6
relating to disclosure 6.71–5
rules on 6.79–83
which directions Tribunal can make 6.87–9
disclosure of documents 6.58–76
firm's obligation to provide disclosure 6.64
FSA's obligation to provide disclosure 6.60–3
FSA's obligation to provide secondary disclosure 6.65–6
legally privileged material 6.68–70, 6.95
Tribunal's directions relating to disclosure 6.71–5
use made by applicant of disclosed documents 6.76
which documents need not be provided 6.67–70
European Convention on Human Rights compatibility 6.23–6
flexibility in process 6.20–2
functions 6.7–9, 9.180–1
hearings 6.118–35
conduct of 6.122–35
legal representation 6.135
preliminary 6.107–8
in public 6.124–9
submissions and evidence 6.130–4
when hearing takes place 6.119–21
witnesses 6.92–103
pre-hearing review 6.84–6
procedure 6.17–160
overview 6.17–55
publicity and 6.32
referrals to 6.33–117
consolidation of references 6.114–17
reference notice 6.33, 6.34–7, 6.40
supervisory notices 9.140–2, 9.176–82
what matters are referred 6.10–12
when firm should refer 6.13–16, 9.177–8, 9.182
review by 6.161, 6.162–8
grounds for varying or setting aside decision 6.163–5
outcome 6.168
procedure 6.166–7
statement of case 6.42–57
amendments 6.56–7
contents 6.43–6
filing 6.47–8
reply 6.49–53
supplementary 6.54–5
suspension of FSA action 6.104–6
withdrawal of cases 6.109, 6.110–13

Financial Services and Markets Tribunal—*contd*
withdrawal of cases—*contd*
by firms 6.110–11
by FSA 6.112–13
witnesses 6.92–103
compelling to attend 6.94–7
evidence 6.130–4
expert witnesses 6.98–103
Financial Services Ombudsman Scheme 12.1–79
compulsory jurisdiction 12.4, 12.8
decision of Ombudsman 12.58–79
challenge and appeal 12.73–6
costs awards 12.67–9
effect of 12.70–2
enforcement 12.78–9
grant of remedies 12.62–6
how decision is reached 12.59–61
publication 12.77
determination of complaint 12.45–9
dismissal of complaint 12.38–40
eligibility of complaint 12.29
entitlement to use scheme 12.30–1
evidence considered by 12.54–5
handling complaints 12.41–57
general approach 12.42
hearings 12.56–7
information
powers to obtain 12.50–3
risks of disclosure to Ombudsman 12.16–20
investigation by 12.23–40
when complaint can be made 12.27–35
whether Ombudsman bound to investigate 12.36–40
overview 12.2–8
practical issues for firms 12.9–22
approach taken by firm 12.10–14
dealing with Ombudsman 12.15
risks of disclosing information to Ombudsman 12.16–20
scope of scheme 12.32–5
settlement of complaint 12.43–4
voluntary jurisdiction 12.4, 12.8
Fines 7.8, 7.28, 7.31
against individuals 8.7, 8.24
amount of 7.36–42
determination of 7.37–40
practical guidance for firms 7.42
use of money paid as fines 7.41
listed companies 15.127–9
for market misconduct and abuse 13.187–231
application for injunction and 13.251–3
decision to impose 13.197–201
grounds for imposition 13.189–91
procedure 13.208–9
tariff 13.202
purpose of 7.30
Firms
action against *see* SANCTIONS
action with firm's agreement 9.232–5
assessment of 2.7, 2.31, 2.43–5
challenges to FSA 4.282, 16.1–5, 16.6–36, 16.96–8

Firms—*contd*
challenges to FSA—*contd*
civil action against FSA 16.8, 16.25–36
judicial review 16.7, 16.16–24
options 16.6–9
prevention of FSA from taking action 16.10–15
classification of 2.31
co-operation with FSA
criminal prosecutions and 11.51–2
investigations 4.180
as objection to exercise of formal power of investigation 4.271
obligation 4.27–56, 13.154–6
complaints procedure 12.3, 12.24–6
conduct giving rise to enforcement 2.131–77
breaches of FSMA 2000 2.133–7
breaches of perimeter 2.175–7
breaches of Principles for Businesses 2.156–64
breaches of specific rules 2.138–55
failure to be fit and proper 2.165–6
issues arising abroad with implications in UK 2.167–73
issues arising in non-regulated business 2.174
criminal liability 11.26–9
'fit and proper' 2.38, 2.43–5
failure to be fit and proper 2.165–6
foreign *see* FOREIGN FIRMS
FSA's 'own-initiative' powers in 9.1–255
actions which may be taken 9.80–103
alternative procedures in specific cases 9.219–38
cancellation of permission 9.239–55
exercise of 9.104–93
grounds for exercise 9.7–66
purpose of 9.4
urgent action 9.194–218
variation of permission/intervention 9.7–238
when used in practice 9.67–79
fundamental regulatory requirements 2.37–62
incrimination of 4.276
integrity and standards 2.46
internal actions
market misconduct 13.127
steps to take when regulatory problems arise 3.12, 3.128–44
investigation of *see* INVESTIGATIONS
listed companies 15.1–187
consequences of breach of Listing Rules 15.97–187
information gathering 15.32–45, 15.88–96
investigations 15.18–31, 15.46–96
management of 2.47
Statements of Principle for approved persons and 2.77, 2.97–100
market misconduct
dealing with customers 13.123–6
internal actions by firm 13.127
investigations carried out by firm 13.112–14
reporting to FSA 13.115–19, 13.121–2
obligation to report to other bodies 3.71, 3.107–9
obligation to report regulatory problems to FSA 3.41–84

Firms—*contd*
obligation to report regulatory problems to FSA—*contd*
civil, criminal or disciplinary proceedings 3.59–61
fraud, errors and other irregularities 3.62–5
matters having serious regulatory impact 3.44–9
notifications under Principle 11 3.66–73
offences and breaches of FSMA 2000 3.50–8
Ombudsman scheme and 12.9–22
approach in relation to process 12.10–14
dealing with Ombudsman 12.15–16
direction to firm to take steps 12.65–6
risks of information disclosure 12.16–20
practical guidance for, on investigation powers of FSA 4.25, 4.50–6, 4.94–107, 4.179–230, 4.299
Principles for Businesses 2.51–62, 2.112
breaches of 2.156–64
reports commissioned by FSA on 4.72–107
representations by *see* REPRESENTATIONS
requesting information from other member's of the firm's group 4.236–41
steps to take when regulatory problems arise 3.1–161
dealing with customers 3.110–27
internal action 3.12, 3.128–44
investigation 3.9–38
potential criminal proceedings and 3.142–8
reporting to FSA 3.39–106
reporting to other bodies 3.71, 3.107–9
taking care with documents 3.149–61
see also COLLECTIVE INVESTMENT SCHEMES
First supervisory notice 9.127–42
'Fit and proper'
firms 2.38, 2.43–5
failure to be fit and proper 2.165–6
individuals
failure to be a fit and proper person 2.188
test for 2.66, 2.69–75
Foreign firms
FSA's intervention powers 9.71, 9.236–8
actions that may be taken 9.83, 9.87
effects of action 9.103
when powers will be exercised 9.50–66
regulation of 2.8, 2.11–14
conduct giving rise to enforcement 2.172–3
EU Treaty rights 2.8, 2.13
inward passport scheme 2.4, 2.8, 2.12
Principles for Businesses and 2.62
Statements of Principle for approved persons and 2.81
top-up permissions 2.14
requesting information from 4.237–8, 4.239
Fraud, firm's obligation to report to FSA 3.62–5
Fraudulent misrepresentation 10.22
Freezing orders (injunctions securing assets) 7.116–21, 8.80, 13.243–4

Groups of firms, requesting information from other member's of the firm's group 4.236–41
Guidance from FSA 2.122–4

Handbook of the FSA 1.4, 1.7, 2.2, 2.106–30
codes of conduct 2.116–18
evidential or other non-binding provisions 2.119–21
general rules 2.111–13
guidance 2.122–4
policy and procedures 2.125–30
specific rules 2.114–15
Hearings
Financial Services and Markets Tribunal 6.118–35
conduct of 6.122–35
legal representation 6.135
preliminary 6.107–8
in public 6.124–9
submissions and evidence 6.130–4
when hearing takes place 6.119–21
witnesses 6.92–103
Financial Services Ombudsman Scheme 12.56–7

Impression, false or misleading 13.41–5
Incoming firms *see* FOREIGN FIRMS
Individuals 2.16
conduct giving rise to enforcement 2.178–89
breach of requirement imposed under FSMA 2000 2.189
failure to be a fit and proper person 2.188
failure to comply with Statement of Principle 2.182–3
knowingly concerned in contravention by authorised person 2.184–7
controlled functions 2.64, 2.65
criminal liability 11.31–5
'fit and proper'
failure to be a fit and proper person 2.188
test for 2.66, 2.69–75
fundamental requirements 2.63–105
investigations into business of authorised persons 4.122–33
scope of power 4.127–9
what information can firm be asked to provide 4.130–3
when can investigation be commenced 4.122–5
when will power be exercised 4.126
market misconduct and abuse
FSA's decision to punish 13.203–7
reporting to FSA 13.120, 13.121–2
obligation to report regulatory problems to FSA 3.85–100
on approved persons generally 3.87–93
disclosure to other regulators 3.99–100, 3.108
responsibility for reporting 3.94–8
sanctions against 8.1–82
disciplinary action 8.4–43
fines 8.7, 8.24
injunctions 8.76, 8.77–80, 9.98
prohibition orders 2.68, 8.44–75
public censure 8.24
restitution orders 7.48, 8.76, 8.81–2
withdrawal of approval 8.27–43
see also CODE OF PRACTICE FOR APPROVED PERSONS; STATEMENTS OF PRINCIPLE FOR APPROVED PERSONS

Informal private warnings 5.61, 7.18–26
challenge to 7.24
duration 7.26
effects 7.21–3
for market misconduct 13.196
Information 4.113
collective investment schemes investigations 14.33–8
refusal to provide information 14.37–8
exceptions to requirements to produce 4.118
false or misleading 9.56–9, 14.59–60
Financial Services Ombudsman Scheme
powers to obtain 12.50–3
risks of disclosure to Ombudsman 12.16–20
FSA's information gathering powers 4.1, 4.6, 4.10–259
compelling information from person suspected of criminal offence 4.242–54
formal requests for information 4.57–107
informal requests for information 4.26
investigations into business of authorised persons and 4.130–3
investigations into crime and criminal offences 4.140–3, 4.147–9
investigations requested by overseas regulator 4.156
market abuse investigations 13.150–3
obligation to co-operate with FSA 4.27–56, 13.154–6
range of powers available 4.10–11, 4.13
requesting information from particular types of person 4.231–41
for restitution orders 7.73–5
use of formal powers 4.16–25
use of information 4.300–22
on listed companies 15.32–45, 15.65–6
powers to obtain information from listed companies and sponsors 15.33–5
publication of information relating to breaches of dealing code 15.148–52, 15.175–6
publicity 15.44–5
refusal to provide information 15.40–3, 15.71–7
use of information obtained from investigation 15.88–96
use of powers 15.36–7, 15.38–9
misuse of information and market abuse 13.38–40
use in criminal proceedings 4.317–18
Injunctions 3.123, 7.59, 7.97–130, 16.22
against individuals 8.76, 8.77–80, 9.98
application to court 7.126, 13.246–8, 13.251–3
circumstances for FSA seeking injunction 7.122–4
discretionary nature 7.102, 13.245
interim 7.103, 7.107, 7.113, 7.129, 16.11–13
listed companies 15.153–4, 15.177
market misconduct and abuse and 13.235–53
procedure 7.125–30
publication 7.128–30
requiring breaches to be remedied 7.110–15, 8.79, 13.240–2
restraining contraventions 7.104–9, 8.78, 13.237–9

Injunctions—*contd*
securing assets 7.116–21, 8.80, 13.243–4
types of 7.100–21
Innocent misrepresentation 10.22
Insurance companies 1.10
Integrity
firms 2.46
individuals 2.91
Interception of communications 3.25–7, 3.31
Interim injunctions 7.103, 7.107, 7.113, 7.129, 16.11–13
Intervention *see* 'OWN-INITIATIVE' POWERS
Interviewing
compulsory 4.121
employees in investigations 3.33–8
investigations 4.221–30
conduct of interview 4.227–9
preparation for 4.222
record of interview 4.230
who attends interview 4.223–6
listed companies investigations 15.67–70
Investigations 3.9–38, 5.9–10
actions FSA may take as result of 4.319–22
business of authorised persons 4.122–33
scope of power 4.127–9
what information can firm be asked to provide 4.130–3
when can investigation be commenced 4.122–5
when will power be exercised 4.126
civil liability to third parties and 10.62
collective investment schemes 14.10–40
commencement 4.122–5, 4.134–7, 4.144–5, 4.150–3, 4.158
by complaints commissioner 16.84–90
conclusion of 4.178, 5.40
conduct of 3.15–38, 4.173–4
changes to 4.175–7
consequences of not reporting to FSA and 3.102
crime and criminal offences 4.134–49
scope of power 4.139
what information can firm be required to provide 4.140–3, 4.147–9
when can investigation be commenced 4.134–7, 4.144–5
when will power be exercised 4.138, 4.146
criminal prosecutions 11.10–12
documents 3.18–21, 4.184–8
listed companies 15.65–6
risks of producing material for or in investigations 4.189–220
employees 3.22–38
interviewing 3.33–8
material recorded in course of business 3.25–7
interviewing 4.221–30
conduct of interview 4.227–9
preparation for 4.222
record of interview 4.230
who attends interview 4.223–6
listed companies 15.18–31, 15.46–96
commencement 15.57–8, 15.78
Investigations—*contd*
listed companies—*contd*
formal investigations 15.46–87
grounds 15.47–56
notification 15.79–83
overview 15.18–31
practical issues 15.64–76
publicity 15.84–7
self-reporting obligation 15.22–8
use of information obtained from investigation 15.88–96
market misconduct 13.108–72
by firms 13.112–14
formal 13.141–9
by FSA 13.130–72
by other regulatory authority 13.137–40
practical steps when problem arises 13.109–29
notification of person under investigation 4.159–63, 13.147, 15.79–83
by Ombudsman 12.23–40
when complaint can be made 12.27–35
whether Ombudsman bound to investigate 12.36–40
powers of FSA 4.1–299
firm's obligation to co-operate with FSA 4.27–56, 13.154–6
formal investigations 4.108–78
market misconduct investigations 13.130–72
non-regulated business 4.252–9
objections to use of 4.260–99
practical guidance for firms 4.25, 4.50–6, 4.94–107, 4.179–230, 4.299
range of powers available 4.10–11, 4.12–14
when FSA will use its formal powers 4.16–25
preliminary findings letter 5.41–55
procedures 3.15–38, 4.157–74
publicity 4.164–75, 13.149, 15.84–7
reasons for 3.10–11
request contrary to policy 4.272–4
requested by overseas regulator 4.150–6
what information can firm be required to provide 4.156
when can investigation be commenced 4.150–3
when will power be exercised 4.154–5
risks of producing material for or in 4.189–220
scope of 3.17, 4.127–9, 4.139
changes to 4.175–7
who should investigate 3.12–14
Investment businesses 1.10, 5.18
see also COLLECTIVE INVESTMENT SCHEMES
Investment companies (ICVCs) 14.7, 14.8
enforcement action 14.41, 14.101–21
giving directions 14.104–9, 14.116–19
policy on exercise of 14.113
procedure 14.114–21
removal/replacing depository or director 14.110–12, 14.120–1
revoking authorisation 14.102–3, 14.114–15
investigations into 14.11, 14.15, 14.16, 14.27–32
power to investigate 14.27–31
use of power 14.32

Investment exchanges 1.10, 2.10
Inward passport scheme 2.4, 2.8, 2.12

Judicial review 16.7, 16.16–24
  grounds 16.20
  how to bring 16.21
  remedies available 16.22
  whether to bring 16.24

Legal privilege 4.183, 4.196–220, 4.235, 4.264–6, 5.90
  Financial Services and Markets Tribunal 6.68–70, 6.95
Legal representation
  at investigation interviews 4.223–6
  Tribunal hearings 6.135
  when interviewing employees in investigations 3.35, 3.36
Liens 4.117
Listed companies 15.1–187
  cancellation of listing 15.134, 15.143–6, 15.168–73
  cancellation of sponsor's approval 15.147, 15.174
  civil liability to third parties 15.179–87
    breach of statutory duty 15.181–2
    contents of listing particulars 15.183–6
    from advertisements and information 15.187
  consequences of breach of Listing Rules 15.97–187
  criminal offences 15.54–6, 15.76, 15.101–2, 15.155, 15.178
  disciplinary and enforcement regime 15.99, 15.107–32, 15.166–7
    action against directors and former directors 15.113–18, 15.130–2
    action against issuers and applicants for listing 15.107–12
    action against sponsors 15.119–22
    policy on use of 15.123–32
  information gathering 15.32–45, 15.65–6, 15.88–96
    powers to obtain information 15.33–5
    publication of information relating to breaches of dealing code 15.148–52, 15.175–6
    publicity 15.44–5
    refusal to provide information 15.40–3, 15.71–7
    use of information obtained from investigation 15.88–96
    use of powers 15.36–7, 15.38–9
  injunctions 15.153–4, 15.177
  investigations 15.18–31, 15.46–96
    commencement 15.57–8, 15.78
    formal investigations 15.46–87
    grounds 15.47–56
    notification 15.79–83
    overview 15.18–31
    practical issues 15.64–76
    publicity 15.84–7
    self-reporting obligation 15.22–8
    use of information obtained from investigation 15.88–96
Listed companies—*contd*
  other regulatory action 15.133–55
  procedure for taking regulatory action 15.156–78
  publication of information relating to breaches of dealing code 15.148–52, 15.175–6
  restitution orders 15.153–4, 15.177
  suspension of listing 15.134, 15.135–42, 15.168–73
Listing Authority 15.4–5
  application of FSMA 2000 15.10–12
  cancellation of listing 15.134, 15.143–6, 15.168–73
  cancellation of sponsor's approval 15.147, 15.174
  disciplinary and enforcement regime and 15.99, 15.107–32, 15.166–7
    action against directors and former directors 15.113–18, 15.130–2
    action against issuers and applicants for listing 15.107–12
    action against sponsors 15.119–22
    policy on use of 15.123–32
  FSA's function as 1.11, 1.13, 2.126, 5.6, 15.2, 15.3, 15.6–12
    overlap with FSA's wider functions 15.13–15
  functions 15.8–9
  information gathering 15.32–45, 15.65–6, 15.88–96
    powers to obtain information 15.33–5
    publication of information relating to breaches of dealing code 15.148–52, 15.175–6
    publicity 15.44–5
    refusal to provide information 15.40–3, 15.71–7
    use of information obtained from investigation 15.88–96
    use of powers 15.36–7, 15.38–9
  injunctions 15.153–4, 15.177
  investigation powers
    commencement 15.57–8, 15.78
    formal investigations 15.46–87
    grounds 15.47–56
    notification 15.79–83
    overview 15.18–31
    practical issues 15.64–76
    publicity 15.84–7
    use of information obtained from investigation 15.88–96
  market misconduct and abuse and 13.220–3
  other regulatory action 15.133–55
  procedure for taking regulatory action 15.156–78
  publication of information relating to breaches of dealing code 15.148–52, 15.175–6
  restitution orders 15.153–4, 15.177
  suspension of listing 15.134, 15.135–42, 15.168–73
  who is affected by enforcement powers 15.16–17
Listing Authority Committee 15.164–5
Listing Rules 13.101, 13.102
  consequences of breach of 15.50–1, 15.97–187

Lloyd's of London 1.10, 2.9, 2.10
London Stock Exchange 1.11, 13.213–19, 15.6
Lord Chancellor 6.4, 6.6
Lord Chancellor's Department 6.5

Management of firms 2.47
Statements of Principle for approved persons and 2.77, 2.97–100
Mandatory injunctions 7.113
Mandatory order 16.22
Market misconduct and abuse 1.21–3, 2.118, 2.135, 13.1–278
behaviour 13.27–9
occurring in relation to qualifying investments in prescribed markets 13.33–6
which does not amount to market abuse 13.61–7
which does not give rise to penalty for market abuse 13.68–81
Code of Market Conduct 2.116, 2.118, 13.20–3, 13.62
compliance with 13.99, 13.100
commercial rationale and 13.106–7
criminal proceedings and 13.128, 13.177–86
procedure for 13.186
when FSA will bring criminal proceedings 13.177–85
dealing with customers 13.123–6
defences 13.249–50
belief that behaviour did not amount to market abuse 13.70–4
due diligence 13.75–8
when defences apply 13.79–81
distortion of market 13.46–9
due diligence 13.75–8
FSA rules compliance 13.98
giving false or misleading impression 13.41–5
implications of Human Rights Act 1998 13.15–16
investigations into market misconduct 13.108–72
by firms 13.112–14
formal 13.141–9
by FSA 13.130–72
by other regulatory authority 13.137–40
practical steps when problem arises 13.109–29
misuse of information 13.38–40
normal market practice and 13.105
outside UK 13.94–7
overview of regime 13.6–14
practical guidance for firms 13.87–9
prescribed markets 13.30, 13.31, 13.33–6
qualifying investments 13.30, 13.32–6
recognition of market abuse 13.17–107
regular user test 13.50–60
regulatory rules compliance and 13.101–4
reporting to FSA 13.115–22
requiring or encouraging others to engage in market abuse 13.82–6
sanctions for market misconduct 13.173–278
criminal proceedings 13.177–86
FSA's decision on 13.195–202

Market misconduct and abuse—*contd*
sanctions for market misconduct—*contd*
other enforcement action 13.232–78
other regulatory authorities and 13.211–31
penalties and public censures 13.187–231
self-incrimination privilege 13.162–72
standards of market conduct 2.93–4
statutory definition of market abuse 13.19, 13.24–86
three alternative conditions 13.37–49
what regime is designed to achieve 13.6–9
to whom regime applies 13.91–3
Mediation
after issue of warning notices 5.128, 5.129–49
confidentiality in mediation 5.143–5
effect on timetable 5.140
exceptions 5.133
initiation of mediation 5.138–9
mediator 5.135–7
outcomes 5.142
procedure for mediation 5.141
when firm should consider mediation 5.148–9
when mediation takes place 5.130
who attends mediation 5.146–7
Minor breaches 5.61
Misconduct *see* MARKET MISCONDUCT AND ABUSE
Misleading impression 13.41–5
Misleading information 9.56–9, 14.59–60
Misrepresentation 10.22
Money awards
Ombudsman and 12.63–4
see also COMPENSATION
Monitoring of communications 3.25–7, 3.31
Mortgages 1.10

Neglect, criminal liability and 11.35
Negligence 10.15
Negligent misrepresentation 10.22
Non-regulated business
conduct giving rise to enforcement and 2.174
investigation powers of FSA 4.252–9
Notice
notification of person under investigation 4.159–63, 13.147, 15.79–83
obtaining information by notice in writing 4.59–71
firm's response to 4.71
scope of power 4.64–5
what information can be asked for 4.68–70
when power will be exercised 4.66–7
warning notices 5.101

Officers of companies, criminal liability 11.31–3
Ombudsman *see* FINANCIAL SERVICES OMBUDSMAN SCHEME
Oppression 4.272–4
Overseas collective investment schemes 2.8, 14.7
enforcement action 14.41, 14.122–49
other recognised schemes 14.135–49
UCITS schemes 14.123–34

Overseas firms *see* FOREIGN FIRMS
Overseas markets, market abuse and 13.94–7
Overseas regulators
cancellation of permission and 9.243
disclosure of information by FSA to 4.300, 5.52
investigations requested by 4.150–6
what information can firm be required to provide 4.156
when can investigation be commenced 4.150–3
when will power be exercised 4.154–5
market misconduct and abuse and 13.231
sanctions imposed by 7.15
variation of permission/intervention at request of 9.31–41, 9.63–6
'Own-initiative' powers 9.1–255
cancellation of permission 9.239–55
challenge of decision 9.250
choice not to cancel 9.246–9
consequences of 9.253–5
procedure 9.251–2
when FSA will consider cancelling 9.243–50
purpose of 9.4
variation of permission/intervention 9.7–238
actions which may be taken 9.80–103
alternative procedures in specific cases 9.219–38
exercise of powers 9.104–93
grounds for exercise 9.7–66
non-fundamental 9.209–10, 9.220–3
urgent action 9.194–218
when used in practice 9.67–79

Passport scheme 2.4, 2.8, 2.12
Penalties *see* FINES; SANCTIONS
Perimeter, breach of 2.175–7
Permission to appeal 6.172–4
Permission system 2.4, 2.5, 2.6–10
cancellation of permission 9.239–55
variation *see* VARIATION OF PERMISSION/INTERVENTION
Practitioner Panel of the FSA 1.20
Pre-hearing review, Financial Services and Markets Tribunal 6.84–6
Prejudice, reports commissioned by FSA and 4.98–101
Preliminary findings letter 5.41–55
confidentiality 5.51–4, 5.55
response to 5.48, 5.49, 5.50
what firm should do on receipt 5.44–8
Preliminary hearings, Financial Services and Markets Tribunal 6.107–8
Principles for Businesses 2.51–62, 2.112
application 2.53–6
businesses they apply to 2.59–62
breaches of 2.156–64
obligations to clients and customers 2.57–8
Private warnings 5.61, 7.18–26
challenge to 7.24
duration 7.26
effects 7.21–3
for market misconduct 13.196
Privilege
legal 4.183, 4.196–220, 4.235, 4.264–6, 5.90
Privilege—*contd*
legal—*contd*
Financial Services and Markets Tribunal 6.68–70, 6.95
self-incrimination privilege 13.162–72
Prohibition orders 2.68, 8.44–75, 16.22
against approved persons 8.56–8
against others 8.59–61
effect 8.65–8
grounds for 8.51–2
procedure 8.62–4
publicity 8.69–70
variation and revocation 8.71–5
when FSA will seek 8.53–61
Prosecutions 11.1–53, 13.12
circumstances in which FSA will prosecute 11.18–24
criminal liability
employees 11.30, 11.48–50
firms 11.26–9
officers 11.31–3
evidential test 11.19, 11.20
other options for FSA 11.36–46
caution 11.37–40
use of enforcement powers 11.41–6
practical guidance for firms 11.47–53
public interest test 11.19, 11.21–3
when FSA will pursue criminal prosecution 11.9–24
which body will investigate and prosecute 11.10–12
which offences FSA can prosecute 11.5–8
which types of cases are suitable for FSA 11.13–17
who can be prosecuted 11.25–35
Public censure 7.8, 7.28, 7.31
against individuals 8.24
contents of 7.32–5
effects 7.32
for market misconduct and abuse 13.187–231
decision to impose 13.197–8
grounds for imposition 13.189–91
procedure 13.208–9
purpose of 7.29
Public domain and publicity
complaints investigation 16.91–4
decision notices 5.182
decision of Ombudsman 12.77
final notices 5.194–5
injunctions 7.128–30
investigations 4.164–75, 13.149, 15.84–7
listed companies
information 15.44–5
investigations 15.84–7
market misconduct and abuse, sanctions 13.210
notice of discontinuance 5.167–9
preliminary findings letter 5.55
prohibition orders 8.69–70
public interest disclosure 4.48
on referral to RDC 5.63
restitution orders and 7.79–81
supervisory notices 9.126, 9.183–93
Tribunal procedure 6.32

Public domain and publicity—*contd*
Tribunal procedure—*contd*
decisions 6.144–7
hearings 6.124–9
Public interest test, prosecutions 11.19, 11.21–3
Public understanding of financial system 2.20

Quashing order 16.22

Recognised schemes *see* OVERSEAS COLLECTIVE INVESTMENT SCHEMES
Reference notice 6.33, 6.34–7
action on Tribunal's receipt of 6.40
filing 6.36–7
Regular user test for market abuse 13.50–60
Regulator *see* FINANCIAL SERVICES AUTHORITY (FSA); OVERSEAS REGULATORS
Regulatory Decisions Committee (RDC) 5.11, 5.26–39, 5.40
independence of 5.32
listed companies and 15.163
members 5.29, 5.30
procedure of 5.33–9
recommendations to
disciplinary and enforcement process 5.64–5, 5.67–70
supervisory notices 9.115–26
record of meeting 5.87
referral to 5.56–63
decision on 5.57–60
reporting to FSA 5.31
representations to *see* REPRESENTATIONS
supervisory notices and
decision on 9.163–9
recommendations to RDC 9.115–26
see also DECISION NOTICES; FINAL NOTICES
Regulatory problems 3.1–161
dealing with customers 3.110–27
discovery of 3.6–8
internal action by firms 3.12, 3.128–44
dealing with employees 3.135–44
taking steps to ensure problem will not recur 3.131–4
investigation *see* INVESTIGATIONS
potential criminal proceedings and 3.142–8
steps to take 3.146–8
types of offences 3.144–5
reporting to FSA 3.39–106
consequences of not reporting 3.101–5
firm's obligation to report 3.41–84
individual's obligation to report 3.85–100
reporting to other bodies 3.71, 3.99–100, 3.107–9
taking care with documents 3.149–61
Reporting to FSA 3.39–109
consequences of not reporting 3.101–5
firm's obligation to report 3.41–84
civil, criminal or disciplinary proceedings 3.59–61
fraud, errors and other irregularities 3.62–5
Reporting to FSA—*contd*
firm's obligation to report—*contd*
matters having serious regulatory impact 3.44–9
notifications under Principle 11 3.66–73
offences and breaches of FSMA 2000 3.50–8
individual's obligation to report 3.85–100
on approved persons generally 3.87–93
disclosure to other regulators 3.99–100
responsibility for reporting 3.94–8
methods 3.74–84
Reporting to other bodies 3.71, 3.99–100, 3.107–9
self-reporting obligation to UKLA 15.22–8
Reports
on conclusion of investigations 4.178
expert reports 5.91
FSA and commission of 4.72–107
assistance from auditor or actuary 4.87–8
dual reports 4.102–3
formal requests 4.107
person appointed to produce report 4.78–93, 4.104–6
practical guidance for firms 4.94–107
scope of power 4.74
terms of appointment of skilled person 4.81–6
when power will be exercised 4.75–7
Representations
on issue of warning notices 5.99–115
consideration before issue of decision notice 5.162–5
content of representations 5.109
failure to make representations 5.100–3
form of 5.104
process for 5.104–8
reasons for making representations 5.99
time period for 5.110–99
on supervisory notices 9.143–61
form of 9.151–7
no representations 9.150, 9.158–61
request for additional time 9.144–7
time period for 9.131–4
why firm should make representations 9.148–9
Restitution, unenforceable agreements 10.54–9
Restitution orders 3.124, 7.43–96
against individuals 7.48, 8.76, 8.81–2
application to court for 7.69–71, 7.78
calculation 7.85, 7.86–9
circumstances in which appropriate 7.66–8
discretionary nature 7.60
distribution of restitution 7.85, 7.90–1
effects 7.61–3
enforcement 7.82–4
guidance for firms 7.94–6
information required 7.73–5
listed companies 15.153–4, 15.177
made by court 7.48
made by FSA 7.46–7
market misconduct and abuse and 13.254–61
objections by person compensated 7.92–3
procedure 7.76–7
publicity and 7.79–81

Restitution orders—*contd*
test for making 7.49–60
disgorging gains 7.55–7
other adverse effects 7.58
persons knowingly concerned in breach 7.51–4
regulatory breach requirement 7.50
repayment of money only 7.59
when FSA will make or apply for 7.64–84, 13.255, 13.257–61
Retention of documents 13.129
Risks
assessment of 2.30
of information disclosure to Ombudsman 12.16–20
of producing material for or in investigations 4.189–220
reducing risk of disclosure 4.218–20

Sanctions 2.35, 5.3–4, 7.1–130
against individuals 8.1–82
disciplinary action 8.4–43
injunctions 8.76, 8.77–80, 9.98
prohibition orders 2.68, 8.44–75
restitution orders 7.48, 8.76, 8.81–2
consequences of not reporting to FSA and 3.104
disciplinary action 7.7–42
against individuals 8.4–43
fines 7.8, 7.28, 7.30–1, 7.36–42, 8.7, 8.24
formal 7.13–17, 8.7–26
informal private warnings 5.61, 7.18–26
powers of the FSA 7.8–11
public censure 7.8, 7.28, 7.29, 7.31, 7.32–5, 8.24
sanctions imposed 7.27–42, 8.24
when FSA will take action 7.12–26, 8.13–23
withdrawal of approval 8.27–43
for market misconduct 13.173–278
criminal proceedings 13.177–86
FSA's decision on 13.195–202
other enforcement action 13.232–78
other regulatory authorities and 13.211–31
penalties and public censures 13.187–231
see also INJUNCTIONS; RESTITUTION ORDERS
Second supervisory notice 9.162–75
Seizure, warrants for 4.290–9
Self-incrimination 4.275, 13.162–72
Serious Fraud Office 11.10
Settlement by agreement 5.18–19
right to enter into settlement discussions after issue of warning notices 5.18–19
candour in discussions 5.120–2
decline of settlement by RDC 5.124, 5.126
time for 5.117
when settlement not reached 5.128
when settlement reached 5.123–7
see also MEDIATION
Settlement of complaint by Ombudsman 12.43–4
Silence right 13.156
Single market 2.8, 2.12
Solicitors 1.10
requesting information from 4.234–5

Statement of case 6.42–57
amendments 6.56–7
contents 6.43–6
filing 6.47–8
reply 6.49–53
supplementary 6.54–5
Statements of Principle for approved persons 2.67, 2.76–7, 2.79, 2.90–100, 2.115
Code of Practice and 2.83–8, 2.89, 2.101–5
conduct subject to 2.79–81
failure to comply with 2.181, 2.182–3, 8.10
Statutory duty
breach of 10.23–5, 10.27, 10.28–51, 15.181–2
actions for 10.28–48
situations where no right of action 10.49–51
Statutory immunity for damages 16.29–36
Supervision 2.29–33, 2.128
own-initiative powers and 9.72–5, 9.88
supervisory notices 2.128, 5.5, 9.105–93
basic framework 9.106–12
comparison with warning/decision notice procedure 9.113–14
first supervisory notice 9.127–42
listed companies 15.161
publicity 9.126, 9.183–93
recommendation to RDC 9.115–26
referral to Tribunal 9.140–2, 9.176–82
representations from firm 9.131–4, 9.143–61
second supervisory notice 9.162–75
Suspension of action by FSA 6.104–6
Suspension of listing 15.134, 15.135–42, 15.168–73

Takeover Panel 4.171, 13.224–30
Third parties
civil liability to 10.1–80
breach of contract 10.11–14
breach of statutory duty 10.23–5, 10.27, 10.28–51
claims under FSMA 2000 10.27–60
claims under general law 10.6–26
contribution claims 10.26
equitable claims 10.16–21
expressly not unenforceable agreements 10.60–1
misrepresentation 10.22
negligence 10.15
practical guidance for firms 10.7–10
practical issues arising from investigation and enforcement process 10.62–80
unenforceable agreements 10.52–9
why firm might incur civil liability 10.2–5
decision notices and 5.176–81
disclosure of preliminary findings letter to 5.53
documents in possession of 4.116
injunctions and 7.109, 7.115
involvement in market abuse 13.82–6
obtaining material from FSA 4.215–17
requesting information from 4.232–3
restitution orders against 7.51–4
warning notices and 5.150–7
representations made on issue of warning notice 5.115, 5.157

Third parties—*contd*
warning notices and—*contd*
right to become involved in process 5.157
right to receive copy of warning notice 5.151–6
Threshold conditions 2.38–45
assessment of firms and 2.43–5
failing or being likely to fail to satisfy threshold conditions 9.14–20, 9.244
relevance to enforcement 2.41–2
to whom and what they apply 2.40
Time periods
for making representations
on issue of warning notices 5.99, 5.110–14
on supervisory notices 9.131–4
Top-up permissions 2.14
variation of 9.47
Tracing, equitable claims 10.21
Tribunal *see* FINANCIAL SERVICES AND MARKETS TRIBUNAL
Trusts 10.16
breach of trust 10.17
liability as recipient of trust funds 10.20
restrictions on firms assets and 9.94

UCITS schemes 2.8, 14.7, 14.123–34
UK Listing Authority *see* LISTING AUTHORITY
Unenforceable agreements 10.52–9
expressly not unenforceable agreements 10.60–1
Unit trusts 14.3, 14.7, 14.8
enforcement action 14.41, 14.46–100
FSA policy on exercise of powers 14.88–93
giving directions 14.66–82, 14.96–9
procedure 14.94–100
removing/replacing manager or trustee 14.83–7, 14.100
revoking authorisation 14.47–65, 14.94–5
investigations into 14.15, 14.17–26
power to investigate 14.17–23
use of power 14.24–6
Urgent action
variation of permission 9.194–218
practical guidance for firms 9.211–18
procedure 9.201–10
when urgent action will be taken 9.196–200
Urgent prevention of FSA from taking action 16.10–15

Variation of permission/intervention 9.7–238
actions which may be taken 9.80–103
effect of action 9.102–3
restrictions on firm's assets 9.89–94
restrictions on firm's employees 9.95–8
when action takes effect 9.99–101
alternative procedures in specific cases 9.219–38
exercise of powers 9.104–93
foreign (incoming) firms 9.50–66, 9.71, 9.83, 9.87, 9.103, 9.236–8
grounds for exercise of power 9.7–66
acquisition of control over UK regulated firm 9.42–3

Variation of permission/intervention—*contd*
grounds for exercise of power—*contd*
additional relevant circumstances 9.44–9
consumer protection 9.4, 9.25–30, 9.60–2
contravention of requirement of FSMA 2000 9.51–5
failing or being likely to fail to satisfy threshold conditions 9.14–20
failing to carry on regulated activity for 12 months 9.21–4
provision of false or misleading information 9.56–9
at request of overseas regulator 9.31–41, 9.63–6
non-fundamental 9.209–10, 9.220–3
supervisory notice procedure 9.105–93
basic framework 9.106–12
comparison with warning/decision notice procedure 9.113–14
first supervisory notice 9.127–42
publicity 9.126, 9.183–93
recommendation to RDC 9.115–26
referral to Tribunal 9.140–2, 9.176–82
representations from firm 9.131–4, 9.143–61
second supervisory notice 9.162–75
urgent action 9.194–218
practical guidance for firms 9.211–18
procedure 9.201–10
when urgent action will be taken 9.196–200
when used in practice 9.67–79
context of powers 9.69–70
enforcement and 9.76–9
foreign incoming firms 9.71
supervision and 9.72–5

Warning
private 5.61, 7.18–26
challenge to 7.24
duration 7.26
effects 7.21–3
for market misconduct 13.196
Warning notices 2.128, 5.11, 5.66–161
challenge to 5.75
confidentiality 5.76–7
consideration of FSA staff recommendation 5.67–70
contents 5.72–3
effect of receipt 5.78–9
further investigations or actions by FSA 5.158–60
issue of 5.71–80
length of procedure 5.161
listed companies 15.160
prohibition orders and 8.62–4
right of access to FSA's materials 5.81–98
action where additional material required 5.94–5
decision on 5.92
exceptions 5.83, 5.89–91
primary material 5.82, 5.85
request for 5.96–7
secondary material 5.82, 5.86–8
use made of materials 5.98

Warning notices—*contd*
right to enter into settlement discussions 5.116–28
candour in discussions 5.120–2
decline of settlement by RDC 5.124, 5.126
time for 5.117
when settlement not reached 5.128
when settlement reached 5.123–7
right to make representations 5.99–115
consideration before issue of decision notice 5.162–5
content of representations 5.109
failure to make representations 5.100–3
form of representations 5.104
process for 5.104–8
reasons for making representations 5.99
third parties and 5.115, 5.157
time period for 5.99, 5.110–14
right to mediation 5.128, 5.129–49
confidentiality in mediation 5.143–5
effect on timetable 5.140
exceptions 5.133
initiation of mediation 5.138–9
mediator 5.135–7
outcomes 5.142
procedure for mediation 5.141
when firm should consider mediation 5.148–9
when mediation takes place 5.130

Warning notices—*contd*
right to mediation—*contd*
who attends mediation 5.146–7
rights of third parties 5.150–7
representations made on issue of warning notice 5.115, 5.157
right to become involved in process 5.157
right to receive copy of warning notice 5.151–6
supervisory notices compared 9.113–14
Warrants 4.290–9
Whistleblowing 3.70, 3.109
Withdrawal of approval 8.27–43
effect of 8.34–7
grounds for 8.29–30
practical issues for firms 8.41–3
procedure 8.38–40
when FSA will seek to withdraw approval 8.31–3
Without prejudice
communications 4.210
settlement discussions 5.120–2
Witnesses
Financial Services and Markets Tribunal 6.92–103
compelling to attend 6.94–7
evidence 6.130–4
expert witnesses 6.98–103
World Bank 2.10